Microsoft®
Visual C++®
MFC Library Reference, Part 2

Microsoft Press

PUBLISHED BY
Microsoft Press
A Division of Microsoft Corporation
One Microsoft Way
Redmond, Washington 98052-6399

Copyright © 1997 by Microsoft Corporation

Library of Congress Cataloging-in-Publication Data
    Microsoft Visual C++ MFC Library Reference / Microsoft Corporation.
        p.   cm.
    Includes index.
    ISBN 1-57231-519-9
    1. C++ (Computer program language)   2. Microsoft Visual C++.
    3. Microsoft foundation class library.   I. Microsoft Corporation.
    QA76.73.C153M535   1997
    005.26'8--dc21   97-2421
                                                                  CIP

Printed and bound in the United States of America.

1 2 3 4 5 6 7 8 9   QMQM   2 1 0 9 8 7

Distributed to the book trade in Canada by Macmillan of Canada, a division of Canada Publishing Corporation.

A CIP catalogue record for this book is available from the British Library.

Microsoft Press books are available through booksellers and distributors worldwide. For further information about international editions, contact your local Microsoft Corporation office. Or contact Microsoft Press International directly at fax (206) 936-7329.

Macintosh and TrueType are registered trademarks of Apple Computer, Inc. FoxPro, Microsoft, Microsoft Press, MS, MS-DOS, Visual Basic, Visual C++, Win32, Windows, and Windows NT are registered trademarks of Microsoft Corporation. Other product and company names mentioned herein may be the trademarks of their respective owners.

Acquisitions Editor: Eric Stroo
Project Editor: Maureen Williams Zimmerman

Contents

Contents

Index

Part 2

MFC Macros and Globals   2279

COleDateTimeSpan

COleDateTimeSpan does not have a base class.

A **COleDateTimeSpan** object represents a relative time, a time span. A **COleDateTimeSpan** keeps time in days.

COleDateTimeSpan is used with its companion class **COleDateTime**. **COleDateTime** encapsulates the **DATE** data type of OLE automation. **COleDateTime** represents absolute time values. All **COleDateTime** calculations involve **COleDateTimeSpan** values. The relation between these classes is analogous to the one between **CTime** and **CTimeSpan**.

For more information on the **COleDateTime** and **COleDateTimeSpan** classes, see the article "Date and Time: Automation Support" in *Visual C++ Programmer's Guide* online.

#include <afxdisp.h>

COleDateTimeSpan Class Members

Constructor

COleDateTimeSpan	Constructs a **COleDateTimeSpan** object.

Attributes

GetStatus	Gets the status (validity) of this **COleDateTimeSpan** object.
SetStatus	Sets the status (validity) of this **COleDateTimeSpan** object.
GetDays	Returns the day portion of the span this **COleDateTimeSpan** object represents.
GetHours	Returns the hour portion of the span this **COleDateTimeSpan** object represents.
GetMinutes	Returns the minute portion of the span this **COleDateTimeSpan** object represents.
GetSeconds	Returns the second portion of the span this **COleDateTimeSpan** object represents.
GetTotalDays	Returns the number of days this **COleDateTimeSpan** object represents.
GetTotalHours	Returns the number of hours this **COleDateTimeSpan** object represents.
GetTotalMinutes	Returns the number of minutes this **COleDateTimeSpan** object represents.
GetTotalSeconds	Returns the number of seconds this **COleDateTimeSpan** object represents.

Operations

SetDateTimeSpan	Sets the value of this **COleDateTimeSpan** object.
Format	Generates a formatted string representation of a **COleDateTimeSpan** object.

Operators

operator double	Converts this **COleDateTimeSpan** value to a **double**.
operator =	Copies a **COleDateTimeSpan** value.
operator +, -	Add, subtract, and change sign for **COleDateTimeSpan** values.
operator +=, -=	Add and subtract a **COleDateTimeSpan** value from this **COleDateTimeSpan** value.
operator ==, <, <=	Compare two **COleDateTimeSpan** values.

Data Members

m_span	Contains the underlying **double** for this **COleDateTimeSpan** object.
m_status	Contains the status of this **COleDateTimeSpan** object.

Dump/Archive

operator <<	Outputs a **COleDateTimeSpan** value to **CArchive** or **CDumpContext**.
operator >>	Inputs a **COleDateTimeSpan** object from **CArchive**.

Member Functions
COleDateTimeSpan::COleDateTimeSpan

COleDateTimeSpan( );
COleDateTimeSpan(const COleDateTimeSpan& *dateSpanSrc* **);**
COleDateTimeSpan(double *dblSpanSrc* **);**
COleDateTimeSpan(long *lDays*, **int** *nHours*, **int** *nMins*, **int** *nSecs* **);**

Parameters

dateSpanSrc An existing **COleDateTimeSpan** object to be copied into the new **COleDateTimeSpan** object.

dblSpanSrc The number of days to be copied into the new **COleDateTimeSpan** object.

lDays, nHours, nMins, nSecs Indicate the day and time values to be copied into the new **COleDateTimeSpan** object.

Remarks

All of these constructors create new **COleDateTimeSpan** objects initialized to the specified value. A brief description of each of these constructors follows:

- **COleDateTimeSpan( )** Constructs a **COleDateTimeSpan** object initialized to 0.

- **COleDateTimeSpan(** *dateSpanSrc* **)** Constructs a **COleDateTimeSpan** object from an existing **COleDateTimeSpan** object.

- **COleDateTimeSpan(** *dblSpanSrc* **)** Constructs a **COleDateTimeSpan** object from a floating-point value.

- **COleDateTimeSpan(** *lDays*, *nHours*, *nMins*, *nSecs* **)** Constructs a **COleDateTimeSpan** object initialized to the specified numerical values.

The status of the new **COleDateTimeSpan** object is set to valid.

For more information about the bounds for **COleDateTimeSpan** values, see the article "Date and Time: Automation Support" in *Visual C++ Programmer's Guide* online.

Example

```
COleDateTimeSpan spanOne( 2.75 );          // 2 days and 18 hours
COleDateTimeSpan spanTwo( 2, 18, 0, 0 );   // 2 days and 18 hours
COleDateTimeSpan spanThree( 3, -6, 0, 0 ); // 2 days and 18 hours
```

See Also: **COleDateTimeSpan::operator =**, **COleDateTimeSpan::GetStatus**, **COleDateTimeSpan::m_span**, **COleDateTimeSpan::m_status**

COleDateTimeSpan::Format

CString Format(LPCTSTR *pFormat* **) const;**
CString Format(UINT *nID* **) const;**

Return Value

A **CString** that contains the formatted date/time-span value.

Parameters

pFormat A formatting string similar to the **printf** formatting string. Formatting codes, preceded by a percent (%) sign, are replaced by the corresponding **COleDateTimeSpan** component. Other characters in the formatting string are copied unchanged to the returned string. See the run-time function **strftime** for details. The value and meaning of the formatting codes for **Format** are listed below:

- **%D** Total days in this **COleDateTimeSpan**

- **%H** Hours in the current day

- **%M** Minutes in the current hour

- **%S** Seconds in the current minute

- **%%** Percent sign

nID The resource ID for the format-control string.

Remarks

Call these functions to create a formatted representation of the time-span value. If the status of this **COleDateTimeSpan** object is null, the return value is an empty string. If the status is invalid, the return string is specified by the string resource **IDS_INVALID_DATETIMESPAN**.

A brief description of the forms for this function follows:

Format(*pFormat* **)** This form formats the value using the format string which contains special formatting codes that are preceded by a percent sign (%), as in **printf**. The formatting string is passed as a parameter to the function.

Format(*nID* **)** This form formats the value using the format string which contains special formatting codes that are preceded by a percent sign (%), as in **printf**. The formatting string is a resource. The ID of this string resource is passed as the parameter.

For more information about the formatting codes used in this function, see **strftime, wcsftime** in the *Run-Time Library Reference*. For a listing of locale ID values, see the section "Supporting Multiple National Languages" in the *Win32 SDK OLE Programmer's Reference*.

See Also: COleDateTimeSpan::GetStatus

COleDateTimeSpan::GetDays

long GetDays( ) const;

Return Value

The day portion of this date/time-span value.

Remarks

Call this member function to retrieve the day portion of this date/time-span value.

The return values from this function range between approximately −3,615,000 and 3,615,000.

For other functions that query the value of a **COleDateTimeSpan** object, see the following member functions:

- **GetHours**
- **GetMinutes**
- **GetSeconds**
- **GetTotalDays**

- **GetTotalHours**
- **GetTotalMinutes**
- **GetTotalSeconds**

See Also: COleDateTimeSpan::SetDateTimeSpan

COleDateTimeSpan::GetHours

long GetHours( ) const;

Return Value

The hours portion of this date/time-span value.

Remarks

Call this member function to retrieve the hour portion of this date/time-span value.

The return values from this function range between −23 and 23.

For other functions that query the value of a **COleDateTimeSpan** object, see the following member functions:

- **GetDays**
- **GetMinutes**
- **GetSeconds**
- **GetTotalDays**
- **GetTotalHours**
- **GetTotalMinutes**
- **GetTotalSeconds**

See Also: COleDateTimeSpan::SetDateTimeSpan

COleDateTimeSpan::GetMinutes

long GetMinutes( ) const;

Return Value

The minutes portion of this date/time-span value.

Remarks

Call this member function to retrieve the minute portion of this date/time-span value.

The return values from this function range between −59 and 59.

For other functions that query the value of a **COleDateTimeSpan** object, see the following member functions:

- **GetDays**
- **GetHours**
- **GetSeconds**
- **GetTotalDays**
- **GetTotalHours**
- **GetTotalMinutes**
- **GetTotalSeconds**

See Also: **COleDateTimeSpan::SetDateTimeSpan**

COleDateTimeSpan::GetSeconds

long GetSeconds( ) const;

Return Value

The seconds portion of this date/time-span value.

Remarks

Call this member function to retrieve the second portion of this date/time-span value.

The return values from this function range between −59 and 59.

For other functions that query the value of a **COleDateTimeSpan** object, see the following member functions:

- **GetDays**
- **GetHours**
- **GetMinutes**
- **GetTotalDays**
- **GetTotalHours**
- **GetTotalMinutes**
- **GetTotalSeconds**

See Also: **COleDateTimeSpan::SetDateTimeSpan**

COleDateTimeSpan::GetStatus

DateTimeSpanStatus GetStatus( ) const;

Return Value

The status of this **COleDateTimeSpan** value.

Remarks

Call this member function to get the status (validity) of this **COleDateTimeSpan** object.

The return value is defined by the **DateTimeSpanStatus** enumerated type, which is defined within the **COleDateTimeSpan** class.

```
enum DateTimeSpanStatus{
    valid = 0,
    invalid = 1,
    null = 2,
};
```

For a brief description of these status values, see the following list:

- **COleDateTimeSpan::valid**   Indicates that this **COleDateTimeSpan** object is valid.

- **COleDateTimeSpan::invalid**   Indicates that this **COleDateTimeSpan** object is invalid; that is, its value may be incorrect.

- **COleDateTimeSpan::null**   Indicates that this **COleDateTimeSpan** object is null, that is, that no value has been supplied for this object. (This is "null" in the database sense of "having no value," as opposed to the C++ **NULL**.)

The status of a **COleDateTimeSpan** object is invalid in the following cases:

- If this object has experienced an overflow or underflow during an arithmetic assignment operation, namely, **+=** or **-=**.

- If an invalid value was assigned to this object.

- If the status of this object was explicitly set to invalid using **SetStatus**.

For more information about the operations that may set the status to invalid, see **COleDateTimeSpan::operator +, -** and **COleDateTimeSpan::operator +=, -=**.

For more information about the bounds for **COleDateTimeSpan** values, see the article "Date and Time: Automation Support" in *Visual C++ Programmer's Guide* online.

See Also: **COleDateTimeSpan::SetStatus, COleDateTimeSpan::m_status**

COleDateTimeSpan::GetTotalDays

double GetTotalDays( ) const;

Return Value

This date/time-span value expressed in days.

Remarks

Call this member function to retrieve this date/time-span value expressed in days.

The return values from this function range between approximately −3.65e6 and 3.65e6.

For other functions that query the value of a **COleDateTimeSpan** object, see the following member functions:

- **GetDays**
- **GetHours**
- **GetMinutes**
- **GetSeconds**
- **GetTotalHours**
- **GetTotalMinutes**
- **GetTotalSeconds**

See Also: **COleDateTimeSpan::SetDateTimeSpan,
COleDateTimeSpan::operator double**

COleDateTimeSpan::GetTotalHours

double GetTotalHours( ) const;

Return Value

This date/time-span value expressed in hours.

Remarks

Call this member function to retrieve this date/time-span value expressed in hours.

The return values from this function range between approximately −8.77e7 and 8.77e7.

For other functions that query the value of a **COleDateTimeSpan** object, see the following member functions:

- **GetDays**
- **GetHours**
- **GetMinutes**
- **GetSeconds**
- **GetTotalDays**
- **GetTotalMinutes**
- **GetTotalSeconds**

See Also: **COleDateTimeSpan::SetDateTimeSpan**

COleDateTimeSpan::GetTotalMinutes

double GetTotalMinutes( ) const;

Return Value

This date/time-span value expressed in minutes.

Remarks

Call this member function to retrieve this date/time-span value expressed in minutes.

The return values from this function range between approximately −5.26e9 and 5.26e9.

For other functions that query the value of a **COleDateTimeSpan** object, see the following member functions:

- **GetDays**
- **GetHours**
- **GetMinutes**
- **GetSeconds**
- **GetTotalDays**
- **GetTotalHours**
- **GetTotalSeconds**

See Also: **COleDateTimeSpan::SetDateTimeSpan**

COleDateTimeSpan::GetTotalSeconds

double GetTotalSeconds( ) const;

Return Value

This date/time-span value expressed in seconds.

Remarks

Call this member function to retrieve this date/time-span value expressed in seconds.

The return values from this function range between approximately −3.16e11 to 3.16e11.

For other functions that query the value of a **COleDateTimeSpan** object, see the following member functions:

- **GetDays**
- **GetHours**
- **GetMinutes**
- **GetSeconds**

- **GetTotalDays**
- **GetTotalHours**
- **GetTotalMinutes**

See Also: **COleDateTimeSpan::SetDateTimeSpan**

COleDateTimeSpan::SetDateTimeSpan

void SetDateTimeSpan(long *lDays*, **int** *nHours*, **int** *nMins*, **int** *nSecs* **);**

Parameters

lDays, nHours, nMins, nSecs   Indicate the date-span and time-span values to be copied into this **COleDateTimeSpan** object.

Remarks

Call this member function to set the value of this date/time-span value.

For functions that query the value of a **COleDateTimeSpan** object, see the following member functions:

- **GetDays**
- **GetHours**
- **GetMinutes**
- **GetSeconds**
- **GetTotalDays**
- **GetTotalHours**
- **GetTotalMinutes**
- **GetTotalSeconds**

Example

```
COleDateTimeSpan spanOne;
COleDateTimeSpan spanTwo;
spanOne.SetDateTimeSpan(0, 2, 45, 0);  // 2 hours and 45 seconds
spanTwo.SetDateTimeSpan(0, 3, -15, 0); // 2 hours and 45 seconds
```

See Also: **COleDateTimeSpan::GetStatus**, **COleDateTimeSpan::m_span**

COleDateTimeSpan::SetStatus

void SetStatus(DateTimeSpanStatus *nStatus* **);**

Parameters

nStatus   The new status value for this **COleDateTimeSpan** object.

Remarks

Call this member function to set the status (validity) of this **COleDateTimeSpan** object. The *nStatus* parameter value is defined by the **DateTimeSpanStatus** enumerated type, which is defined within the **COleDateTimeSpan** class.

```
enum DateTimeSpanStatus{
    valid = 0,
    invalid = 1,
    null = 2,
};
```

For a brief description of these status values, see the following list:

- **COleDateTimeSpan::valid**   Indicates that this **COleDateTimeSpan** object is valid.

- **COleDateTimeSpan::invalid**   Indicates that this **COleDateTimeSpan** object is invalid; that is, its value may be incorrect.

- **COleDateTimeSpan::null**   Indicates that this **COleDateTimeSpan** object is null, that is, that no value has been supplied for this object. (This is "null" in the database sense of "having no value," as opposed to the C++ **NULL**.)

Caution   This function is for advanced programming situations. This function does not alter the data in this object. It will most often be used to set the status to **null** or **invalid**. Note that the assignment operator (**operator =**) and **SetDateTimeSpan** do set the status of the object based on the source value(s).

See Also: **COleDateTimeSpan::GetStatus**, **COleDateTimeSpan::m_status**

Operators
COleDateTimeSpan::operator =

const COleDateTimeSpan& operator=(double *dblSpanSrc*);
const COleDateTimeSpan& operator=(const COleDateTimeSpan& *dateSpanSrc*);

Remarks

These overloaded assignment operators copy the source date/time-span value into this **COleDateTimeSpan** object.

See Also: **COleDateTimeSpan::COleDateTimeSpan**

COleDateTimeSpan::operator +, -

COleDateTimeSpan operator+(const COleDateTimeSpan& *dateSpan* **) const;**
COleDateTimeSpan operator-(const COleDateTimeSpan& *dateSpan* **) const;**
COleDateTimeSpan operator-( ) const;

Remarks

The first two operators let you add and subtract date/time-span values. The third lets you change the sign of a date/time-span value.

If either of the operands is null, the status of the resulting **COleDateTimeSpan** value is null.

If either of the operands is invalid and the other is not null, the status of the resulting **COleDateTimeSpan** value is invalid.

For more information on the valid, invalid, and null status values, see the **m_status** member variable.

See Also: **COleDateTimeSpan::operator +=, -=**

COleDateTimeSpan::operator +=, -=

const COleDateTimeSpan& operator+=(const COleDateTimeSpan *dateSpan* **);**
const COleDateTimeSpan& operator-=(const COleDateTimeSpan *dateSpan* **);**

Remarks

These operators let you add and subtract date/time-span values from this **COleDateTimeSpan** object.

If either of the operands is null, the status of the resulting **COleDateTimeSpan** value is null.

If either of the operands is invalid and the other is not null, the status of the resulting **COleDateTimeSpan** value is invalid.

For more information on the valid, invalid, and null status values, see the **m_status** member variable.

See Also: **COleDateTimeSpan::operator +, -**

COleDateTimeSpan::operator double

operator double( ) const;

Remarks

This operator returns the value of this **COleDateTimeSpan** value as a floating-point number of days.

See Also: **COleDateTimeSpan::GetTotalDays**,
COleDateTimeSpan::SetDateTimeSpan, **COleDateTimeSpan::m_span**

COleDateTimeSpan Relational Operators

BOOL operator==(const COleDateTimeSpan& *dateSpan* **) const;**
BOOL operator!=(const COleDateTimeSpan& *dateSpan* **) const;**
BOOL operator<(const COleDateTimeSpan& *dateSpan* **) const;**
BOOL operator>(const COleDateTimeSpan& *dateSpan* **) const;**
BOOL operator<=(const COleDateTimeSpan& *dateSpan* **) const;**
BOOL operator>=(const COleDateTimeSpan& *dateSpan* **) const;**

Remarks

These operators compare two date/time-span values and return nonzero if the
condition is true; otherwise 0.

Note The return value of the ordering operations (<, <=, >, >=) is undefined if the status of
either operand is null or invalid. The equality operators (==, !=) consider the status of the
operands.

Example

```
COleDateTimeSpan spanOne(3, 12, 0, 0); // 3 days and 12 hours
COleDateTimeSpan spanTwo(spanOne);     // 3 days and 12 hours
BOOL b;
b = spanOne == spanTwo;                // TRUE

spanTwo.SetStatus(COleDateTimeSpan::invalid);
b = spanOne == spanTwo;                // FALSE, different status
b = spanOne != spanTwo;                // TRUE, different status
b = spanOne < spanTwo;                 // FALSE, same value
b = spanOne > spanTwo;                 // FALSE, same value
b = spanOne <= spanTwo;                // TRUE, same value
b = spanOne >= spanTwo;                // TRUE, same value
```

Note The last four lines of the preceding example will **ASSERT** in debug mode.

COleDateTimeSpan::operator <<, >>

friend CDumpContext& AFXAPI operator<<(CDumpContext& *dc*,
↳ **COleDateTimeSpan** *dateSpan* **);**
friend CArchive& AFXAPI operator<<(CArchive& *ar*, **COleDateTimeSpan** *dateSpan* **);**
friend CArchive& AFXAPI operator>>(CArchive& *ar*, **COleDateTimeSpan&** *dateSpan* **);**

Remarks

The **COleDateTimeSpan** insertion (<<) operator supports diagnostic dumping and
storing to an archive. The extraction (>>) operator supports loading from an archive.

See Also: **CDumpContext**, **CArchive**

Data Members
COleDateTimeSpan::m_span

Remarks

The underlying **double** value for this **COleDateTime** object. This value expresses the date/time-span in days.

Caution Changing the value in the **double** data member will change the value of this **COleDateTimeSpan** object. It does not change the status of this **COleDateTimeSpan** object.

See Also: **COleDateTimeSpan::COleDateTimeSpan,
COleDateTimeSpan::SetDateTimeSpan, COleDateTimeSpan::operator double**

COleDateTimeSpan::m_status

Remarks

The type for this data member is the enumerated type **DateTimeSpanStatus**, which is defined within the **COleDateTimeSpan** class.

```
enum DateTimeSpanStatus{
    valid = 0,
    invalid = 1,
    null = 2,
};
```

For a brief description of these status values, see the following list:

- **COleDateTimeSpan::valid** Indicates that this **COleDateTimeSpan** object is valid.

- **COleDateTimeSpan::invalid** Indicates that this **COleDateTimeSpan** object is invalid; that is, its value may be incorrect.

- **COleDateTimeSpan::null** Indicates that this **COleDateTimeSpan** object is null, that is, that no value has been supplied for this object. (This is "null" in the database sense of "having no value," as opposed to the C++ **NULL**.)

The status of a **COleDateTimeSpan** object is invalid in the following cases:

- If this object has experienced an overflow or underflow during an arithmetic assignment operation, namely, += or -=.

- If an invalid value was assigned to this object.

- If the status of this object was explicitly set to invalid using **SetStatus**.

For more information about the operations that may set the status to invalid, see **COleDateTimeSpan::operator +, -** and **COleDateTimeSpan::operator +=, -=**.

Caution   This data member is for advanced programming situations. You should use the inline member functions **GetStatus** and **SetStatus**. See **SetStatus** for further cautions regarding explicitly setting this data member.

For more information about the bounds for **COleDateTimeSpan** values, see the article "Date and Time: Automation Support" in *Visual C++ Programmer's Guide* online.

See Also: **COleDateTimeSpan::GetStatus**, **COleDateTimeSpan::SetStatus**

COleDialog

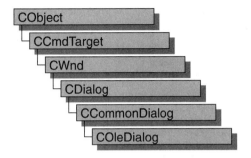

The **COleDialog** class provides functionality common to dialog boxes for OLE. The Microsoft Foundation Class Library provides several classes derived from **COleDialog**.

These are:

- **COleInsertDialog**
- **COleConvertDialog**
- **COleChangeIconDialog**
- **COleLinksDialog**
- **COleBusyDialog**
- **COleUpdateDialog**
- **COlePasteSpecialDialog**
- **COlePropertiesDialog**
- **COleChangeSourceDialog**

For more information about OLE-specific dialog boxes, see the article "Dialog Boxes in OLE" in *Visual C++ Programmer's Guide* online.

#include <afxodlgs.h>

COleDialog Class Members

Operations

GetLastError	Gets the error code returned by the dialog box.

Member Functions
COleDialog::GetLastError

UINT GetLastError( ) const;

Return Value

The error codes returned by **GetLastError** depend on the specific dialog box displayed.

Remarks

Call the **GetLastError** member function to get additional error information when **DoModal** returns **IDABORT**. See the **DoModal** member function in the derived classes for information about specific error messages.

See Also: **COleBusyDialog::DoModal, COleChangeIconDialog::DoModal, COleChangeSourceDialog::DoModal, COleConvertDialog::DoModal, COleInsertDialog::DoModal, COleLinksDialog::DoModal, COlePasteSpecialDialog::DoModal, COlePropertiesDialog::DoModal, COleUpdateDialog::DoModal**

COleDispatchDriver

COleDispatchDriver does not have a base class.

The **COleDispatchDriver** class implements the client side of OLE automation. OLE dispatch interfaces provide access to an object's methods and properties. Member functions of **COleDispatchDriver** attach, detach, create, and release a dispatch connection of type **IDispatch**. Other member functions use variable argument lists to simplify calling **IDispatch::Invoke**.

For more information, see **IDispatch** and **IDispatch::Invoke** in the *Win32 SDK OLE Programmer's Reference*.

This class can be used directly, but it is generally used only by classes created by ClassWizard. When you create new C++ classes by importing a type library, ClassWizard derives the new classes from **COleDispatchDriver**.

For more information on using **COleDispatchDriver**, see the following articles in *Visual C++ Programmer's Guide* online:

- **Automation Clients**
- **Automation Servers**
- **ClassWizard: Automation Support**

#include <afxdisp.h>

See Also: CCmdTarget

COleDispatchDriver Class Members

Data Members

m_bAutoRelease	Specifies whether to release the **IDispatch** during **ReleaseDispatch** or object destruction.
m_lpDispatch	Indicates the pointer to the **IDispatch** interface attached to this **COleDispatchDriver**.

Construction

COleDispatchDriver	Constructs a **COleDispatchDriver** object.

Operations

CreateDispatch	Creates an **IDispatch** connection and attaches it to the **COleDispatchDriver** object.
AttachDispatch	Attaches an **IDispatch** connection to the **COleDispatchDriver** object.
DetachDispatch	Detaches an **IDispatch** connection, without releasing it.

Operations *(continued)*

ReleaseDispatch	Releases an **IDispatch** connection.
InvokeHelper	Helper for calling automation methods.
SetProperty	Sets an automation property.
GetProperty	Gets an automation property.

Member Functions
COleDispatchDriver::AttachDispatch

void AttachDispatch(LPDISPATCH *lpDispatch***, BOOL** *bAutoRelease* **= TRUE);**

Parameters

lpDispatch   Pointer to an OLE **IDispatch** object to be attached to the **COleDispatchDriver** object.

bAutoRelease   Specifies whether the dispatch is to be released when this object goes out of scope.

Remarks

Call the **AttachDispatch** member function to attach an **IDispatch** pointer to the **COleDispatchDriver** object. This function releases any **IDispatch** pointer that is already attached to the **COleDispatchDriver** object.

**See Also: COleDispatchDriver::DetachDispatch,
COleDispatchDriver::ReleaseDispatch, COleDispatchDriver::CreateDispatch,
COleDispatchDriver::m_lpDispatch, COleDispatchDriver::m_bAutoRelease**

COleDispatchDriver::COleDispatchDriver

COleDispatchDriver( );
COleDispatchDriver(LPDISPATCH *lpDispatch***, BOOL** *bAutoRelease* **= TRUE);**
COleDispatchDriver(const COleDispatchDriver& *dispatchSrc* **);**

Parameters

lpDispatch   Pointer to an OLE **IDispatch** object to be attached to the **COleDispatchDriver** object.

bAutoRelease   Specifies whether the dispatch is to be released when this object goes out of scope.

dispatchSrc   Reference to an existing **COleDispatchDriver** object.

Remarks

Constructs a **COleDispatchDriver** object. The form
COleDispatchDriver(LPDISPATCH *lpDispatch*, **BOOL** *bAutoRelease* = **TRUE)**
connects the **IDispatch** interface.

The form **COleDispatchDriver(const COleDispatchDriver&** *dispatchSrc*) copies an
existing **COleDispatchDriver** object and increments the reference count.

The form **COleDispatchDriver( )** creates a **COleDispatchDriver** object but does not
connect the **IDispatch** interface. Before using **COleDispatchDriver( )** without
arguments, you should connect an **IDispatch** to it using either
COleDispatchDriver::CreateDispatch or **COleDispatchDriver::AttachDispatch**.

See Also: **COleDispatchDriver::AttachDispatch,**
COleDispatchDriver::CreateDispatch

COleDispatchDriver::CreateDispatch

BOOL CreateDispatch(REFCLSID *clsid*, **COleException*** *pError* = **NULL);**
BOOL CreateDispatch(LPCTSTR *lpszProgID*, **COleException*** *pError* = **NULL);**

Return Value

Nonzero on success; otherwise 0.

Parameters

clsid   Class ID of the **IDispatch** connection object to be created.

pError   Pointer to an OLE exception object, which will hold the status code resulting
from the creation.

lpszProgID   Pointer to the programmatic identifier, such as "Excel.Document.5", of
the automation object for which the dispatch object is to be created.

Remarks

Creates an **IDispatch** object and attaches it to the **COleDispatchDriver** object.

See Also: **COleDispatchDriver::DetachDispatch,**
COleDispatchDriver::ReleaseDispatch, COleDispatchDriver::AttachDispatch,
COleException, COleDispatchDriver::m_lpDispatch

COleDispatchDriver::DetachDispatch

LPDISPATCH DetachDispatch( );

Return Value

A pointer to the previously attached OLE **IDispatch** object.

Remarks

Detaches the current **IDispatch** connection from this object. The **IDispatch** is not released.

For more information about the **LPDISPATCH** type, see **IDispatch** in the *OLE Programmer's Reference*.

See Also: **COleDispatchDriver::ReleaseDispatch,
COleDispatchDriver::CreateDispatch, COleDispatchDriver::AttachDispatch,
COleDispatchDriver::m_lpDispatch**

COleDispatchDriver::GetProperty

void GetProperty(DISPID *dwDispID*, **VARTYPE** *vtProp*, **void*** *pvProp* **) const;**

Parameters

dwDispID   Identifies the property to be retrieved. This value is usually supplied by ClassWizard.

vtProp   Specifies the property to be retrieved. For possible values, see the Remarks section for **COleDispatchDriver::InvokeHelper**.

pvProp   Address of the variable that will receive the property value. It must match the type specified by *vtProp*.

Remarks

Gets the object property specified by *dwDispID*.

See Also: **COleDispatchDriver::InvokeHelper,
COleDispatchDriver::SetProperty**

COleDispatchDriver::InvokeHelper

void InvokeHelper(DISPID *dwDispID*, **WORD** *wFlags*, **VARTYPE** *vtRet*,
↪ **void*** *pvRet*, **const BYTE FAR*** *pbParamInfo*, ... **);**
throw(COleException);
throw(COleDispatchException);

Parameters

dwDispID   Identifies the method or property to be invoked. This value is usually supplied by ClassWizard.

wFlags   Flags describing the context of the call to **IDispatch::Invoke**. For possible values, see the *OLE Programmer's Reference*.

vtRet   Specifies the type of the return value. For possible values, see the Remarks section.

pvRet Address of the variable that will receive the property value or return value. It must match the type specified by *vtRet*.

pbParamInfo Pointer to a null-terminated string of bytes specifying the types of the parameters following *pbParamInfo*.

... Variable list of parameters, of types specified in *pbParamInfo*.

Remarks

Calls the object method or property specified by *dwDispID*, in the context specified by *wFlags*. The *pbParamInfo* parameter specifies the types of the parameters passed to the method or property. The variable list of arguments is represented by **...** in the syntax declaration.

Possible values for the *vtRet* argument are taken from the **VARENUM** enumeration. Possible values are as follows:

Symbol	Return Type
VT_EMPTY	void
VT_I2	short
VT_I4	long
VT_R4	float
VT_R8	double
VT_CY	CY
VT_DATE	DATE
VT_BSTR	BSTR
VT_DISPATCH	LPDISPATCH
VT_ERROR	SCODE
VT_BOOL	BOOL
VT_VARIANT	VARIANT
VT_UNKNOWN	LPUNKNOWN

The *pbParamInfo* argument is a space-separated list of **VTS_** constants. One or more of these values, separated by spaces (not commas), specifies the function's parameter list. Possible values are listed with the **EVENT_CUSTOM** macro.

This function converts the parameters to **VARIANTARG** values, then invokes the **IDispatch::Invoke** method. If the call to **Invoke** fails, this function will throw an exception. If the **SCODE** (status code) returned by **IDispatch::Invoke** is **DISP_E_EXCEPTION**, this function throws a **COleException** object; otherwise it throws a **COleDispatchException**.

For more information, see **VARIANTARG**, **IDispatch**, **IDispatch::Invoke**, and "Structure of OLE Error Codes" in the *Win32 SDK OLE Programmer's Reference*.

See Also: COleException, COleDispatchException

COleDispatchDriver::ReleaseDispatch

void ReleaseDispatch( );

Remarks

Releases the **IDispatch** connection. If auto release has been set for this connection, this function calls **IDispatch::Release** before releasing the interface.

See Also: **COleDispatchDriver::DetachDispatch, COleDispatchDriver::CreateDispatch, COleDispatchDriver::AttachDispatch, COleDispatchDriver::m_lpDispatch, COleDispatchDriver::m_bAutoRelease**

COleDispatchDriver::SetProperty

void SetProperty(DISPID *dwDispID***, VARTYPE** *vtProp***, ...);**

Parameters

dwDispID   Identifies the property to be set. This value is usually supplied by ClassWizard.

vtProp   Specifies the type of the property to be set. For possible values, see the Remarks section for **COleDispatchDriver::InvokeHelper**.

...   A single parameter of the type specified by *vtProp*.

Remarks

Sets the OLE object property specified by *dwDispID*.

See Also: **COleDispatchDriver::InvokeHelper, COleDispatchDriver::GetProperty**

Data Members
COleDispatchDriver::m_bAutoRelease

Remarks

If **TRUE**, the COM object accessed by **m_lpDispatch** will be automatically released when **ReleaseDispatch** is called or when this **COleDispatchDriver** object is destroyed.

By default, **m_bAutoRelease** is set to **TRUE** in the constructor.

For more information on releasing COM objects, see "Implementing Reference Counting" and **IUnknown::Release** in the *OLE 2 Programmer's Reference, Volume 1*.

See Also: **COleDispatchDriver::AttachDispatch, COleDispatchDriver::ReleaseDispatch, COleDispatchDriver::m_lpDispatch**

COleDispatchDriver::m_lpDispatch

Remarks

The pointer to the **IDispatch** interface attached to this **COleDispatchDriver**. The **m_lpDispatch** data member is a public variable of type **LPDISPATCH**.

For more information, see **IDispatch** in the *OLE Programmer's Reference*.

See Also: **COleDispatchDriver::AttachDispatch**, **COleDispatchDriver::ReleaseDispatch**, **COleDispatchDriver::CreateDispatch**, **COleDispatchDriver::DetachDispatch**

COleDispatchException

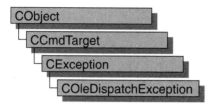

The **COleDispatchException** class handles exceptions specific to the OLE **IDispatch** interface, which is a key part of OLE automation.

Like the other exception classes derived from the **CException** base class, **COleDispatchException** can be used with the **THROW**, **THROW_LAST**, **TRY**, **CATCH**, **AND_CATCH**, and **END_CATCH** macros.

In general, you should call **AfxThrowOleDispatchException** to create and throw a **COleDispatchException** object.

For more information on exceptions, see the articles "Exceptions" and "Exceptions: OLE Exceptions" in *Visual C++ Programmer's Guide* online.

#include <afxdisp.h>

See Also: **COleDispatchDriver**, **COleException**

COleDispatchException Class Members

Data Members

m_wCode	**IDispatch**-specific error code.
m_strDescription	Verbal error description.
m_dwHelpContext	Help context for error.
m_strHelpFile	Help file to use with **m_dwHelpContext**.
m_strSource	Application that generated the exception.

Data Members
COleDispatchException::m_dwHelpContext

DWORD m_dwHelpContext;

Remarks

Identifies a help context in your application's help (.HLP) file. This member is set by the function **AfxThrowOleDispatchException** when an exception is thrown.

See Also: **COleDispatchException::m_strDescription,**
COleDispatchException::m_wCode, AfxThrowOleDispatchException

COleDispatchException::m_strDescription

CString m_strDescription;

Remarks

Contains a verbal error description, such as "Disk full." This member is set by the function **AfxThrowOleDispatchException** when an exception is thrown.

See Also: **COleDispatchException::m_dwHelpContext,**
COleDispatchException::m_wCode, AfxThrowOleDispatchException

COleDispatchException::m_strHelpFile

CString m_strHelpFile;

Remarks

The framework fills in this string with the name of the application's help file.

See Also: **AfxThrowOleDispatchException**

COleDispatchException::m_strSource

CString m_strSource;

Remarks

The framework fills in this string with the name of the application that generated the exception.

See Also: **AfxThrowOleDispatchException**

COleDispatchException::m_wCode

WORD m_wCode;

Remarks

Contains an error code specific to your application. This member is set by the function **AfxThrowOleDispatchException** when an exception is thrown.

See Also: **COleDispatchException::m_strDescription**, **COleDispatchException::m_dwHelpContext**, **AfxThrowOleDispatchException**

COleDocument

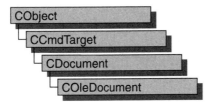

COleDocument is the base class for OLE documents that support visual editing. **COleDocument** is derived from **CDocument**, which allows your OLE applications to use the document/view architecture provided by the Microsoft Foundation Class Library.

COleDocument treats a document as a collection of **CDocItem** objects to handle OLE items. Both container and server applications require such an architecture because their documents must be able to contain OLE items. The **COleServerItem** and **COleClientItem** classes, both derived from **CDocItem**, manage the interactions between applications and OLE items.

If you are writing a simple container application, derive your document class from **COleDocument**. If you are writing a container application that supports linking to the embedded items contained by its documents, derive your document class from **COleLinkingDoc**. If you are writing a server application or combination container/server, derive your document class from **COleServerDoc**. **COleLinkingDoc** and **COleServerDoc** are derived from **COleDocument**, so these classes inherit all the services available in **COleDocument** and **CDocument**.

To use **COleDocument**, derive a class from it and add functionality to manage the application's non-OLE data as well as embedded or linked items. If you define **CDocItem**-derived classes to store the application's native data, you can use the default implementation defined by **COleDocument** to store both your OLE and non-OLE data. You can also design your own data structures for storing your non-OLE data separately from the OLE items. For more information, see the article "Containers: Compound Files" in *Visual C++ Programmer's Guide* online.

CDocument supports sending your document via mail if mail support (MAPI) is present. **COleDocument** has updated **OnFileSendMail** to handle compound documents correctly. For more information, see the articles "MAPI Topics" and "MAPI Support in MFC" in *Visual C++ Programmer's Guide* online.

#include <afxole.h>

COleDocument Class Members

Construction

COleDocument	Constructs a **COleDocument** object.

Operations

HasBlankItems	Checks for blank items in the document.
EnableCompoundFile	Causes documents to be stored using the OLE Structured Storage file format.
GetInPlaceActiveItem	Returns the OLE item that is currently in-place active.
GetStartPosition	Gets the initial position to begin iteration.
GetNextItem	Gets the next document item for iterating.
GetNextClientItem	Gets the next client item for iterating.
GetNextServerItem	Gets the next server item for iterating.
UpdateModifiedFlag	Marks the document as modified if any of the contained OLE items have been modified.
ApplyPrintDevice	Sets the print-target device for all client items in the document.
AddItem	Adds an item to the list of items maintained by the document.
RemoveItem	Removes an item from the list of items maintained by the document.

Overridables

GetPrimarySelectedItem	Returns the primary selected OLE item in the document.
OnShowViews	Called when the document becomes visible or invisible.

Mail Functions

OnFileSendMail	Sends a mail message with the document attached.

Message Handlers

OnEditChangeIcon	Handles events in the Change Icon menu command.
OnEditConvert	Handles the conversion of an embedded or linked object from one type to another.
OnEditLinks	Handles events in the Links command on the Edit menu.
OnUpdateEditChangeIcon	Called by the framework to update the command UI for the Edit/Change Icon menu option.
OnUpdateEditLinksMenu	Called by the framework to update the command UI for the Edit/Links menu option.

(continued)

Message Handlers *(continued)*	
OnUpdateObjectVerbMenu	Called by the framework to update the command UI for the Edit/*ObjectName* menu option and the Verb submenu accessed from Edit/*ObjectName*.
OnUpdatePasteLinkMenu	Called by the framework to update the command UI for the Paste Special menu option.
OnUpdatePasteMenu	Called by the framework to update the command UI for the Paste menu option.

Member Functions
COleDocument::AddItem

virtual void AddItem(CDocItem* *pItem* **);**

Parameters
pItem   Pointer to the document item being added.

Remarks
Call this function to add an item to the document. You do not need to call this function explicitly when it is called by the **COleClientItem** or **COleServerItem** constructor that accepts a pointer to a document.

See Also: **CDocItem, COleDocument::RemoveItem, COleServerItem::COleServerItem, COleClientItem::COleClientItem**

COleDocument::ApplyPrintDevice

BOOL ApplyPrintDevice(const DVTARGETDEVICE FAR* *ptd* **);**
BOOL ApplyPrintDevice(const PRINTDLG* *ppd* **);**

Return Value
Nonzero if the function was successful; otherwise 0.

Parameters
ptd   Pointer to a **DVTARGETDEVICE** data structure, which contains information about the new print-target device. Can be **NULL**.

ppd   Pointer to a **PRINTDLG** data structure, which contains information about the new print-target device. Can be **NULL**.

Remarks

Call this function to change the print-target device for all embedded **COleClientItem** items in your application's container document. This function updates the print-target device for all items but does not refresh the presentation cache for those items. To update the presentation cache for an item, call **COleClientItem::UpdateLink**.

The arguments to this function contain information that OLE uses to identify the target device. The **PRINTDLG** structure contains information that Windows uses to initialize the common Print dialog box. After the user closes the dialog box, Windows returns information about the user's selections in this structure. The **m_pd** member of a **CPrintDialog** object is a **PRINTDLG** structure.

For more information, see the **PRINTDLG** structure in the Win32 SDK documentation.

For more information, see the **DVTARGETDEVICE** structure in the *OLE 2 Programmer's Reference, Volume 1*.

See Also: **CPrintDialog**

COleDocument::COleDocument

COleDocument( );

Remarks

Constructs a **COleDocument** object.

COleDocument::EnableCompoundFile

void EnableCompoundFile(BOOL *bEnable* = **TRUE);**

Parameters

bEnable   Specifies whether compound file support is enabled or disabled.

Remarks

Call this function if you want to store the document using the compound-file format. This is also called structured storage. You typically call this function from the constructor of your **COleDocument**-derived class. For more information about compound documents, see the article "Containers: Compound Files" in *Visual C++ Programmer's Guide* online.

If you do not call this member function, documents will be stored in a nonstructured ("flat") file format.

After compound file support is enabled or disabled for a document, the setting should not be changed during the document's lifetime.

See Also: **COleClientItem**

COleDocument::GetInPlaceActiveItem

COleClientItem* GetInPlaceActiveItem(CWnd* *pWnd*);

Return Value

A pointer to the single, in-place active OLE item; **NULL** if there is no OLE item currently in the "in-place active" state.

Parameters

pWnd   Pointer to the window that displays the container document.

Remarks

Call this function to get the OLE item that is currently activated in place in the frame window containing the view identified by *pWnd*.

See Also: COleClientItem

COleDocument::GetNextClientItem

COleClientItem* GetNextClientItem(POSITION& *pos*) const;

Return Value

A pointer to the next client item in the document, or **NULL** if there are no more client items.

Parameters

pos   A reference to a **POSITION** value set by a previous call to **GetNextClientItem**; the initial value is returned by the **GetStartPosition** member function.

Remarks

Call this function repeatedly to access each of the client items in your document. After each call, the value of *pos* is set for the next item in the document, which might or might not be a client item.

Example

```
// Example for COleDocument::GetNextClientItem
// pDoc points to a COleDocument object
POSITION pos = pDoc->GetStartPosition();
COleClientItem *pItem;
while ( ( pItem = pDoc->GetNextClientItem( pos ) ) != NULL )
{
    // Use pItem
}
```

**See Also: COleClientItem, COleDocument::GetStartPosition,
COleDocument::GetNextServerItem, COleDocument::GetNextItem**

COleDocument::GetNextItem

virtual CDocItem* GetNextItem(POSITION& *pos* **) const;**

Return Value

A pointer to the document item at the specified position.

Parameters

pos   A reference to a **POSITION** value set by a previous call to **GetNextItem**; the initial value is returned by the **GetStartPosition** member function.

Remarks

Call this function repeatedly to access each of the items in your document. After each call, the value of *pos* is set to the **POSITION** value of the next item in the document. If the retrieved element is the last element in the document, the new value of *pos* is **NULL**.

Example

```
// Example for COleDocument::GetNextItem
// pDoc points to a COleDocument object
POSITION pos = pDoc->GetStartPosition();
CDocItem *pItem;
while( pos != NULL )
{
   pItem = pDoc->GetNextItem( pos );
   // Use pItem
}
```

**See Also: COleDocument::GetStartPosition,
COleDocument::GetNextClientItem, COleDocument::GetNextServerItem**

COleDocument::GetNextServerItem

COleServerItem* GetNextServerItem(POSITION& *pos* **) const;**

Return Value

A pointer to the next server item in the document, or **NULL** if there are no more server items.

Parameters

pos   A reference to a **POSITION** value set by a previous call to **GetNextServerItem**; the initial value is returned by the **GetStartPosition** member function.

Remarks

Call this function repeatedly to access each of the server items in your document. After each call, the value of *pos* is set for the next item in the document, which might or might not be a server item.

Example

```
// Example for COleDocument::GetNextServerItem
// pDoc points to a COleDocument object
POSITION pos = pDoc->GetStartPosition();
COleServerItem *pItem;
while ( ( pItem = pDoc->GetNextServerItem( pos ) ) != NULL )
{
    // Use pItem
}
```

See Also: **COleServerItem, COleDocument::GetStartPosition, COleDocument::GetNextClientItem, COleDocument::GetNextItem**

COleDocument::GetPrimarySelectedItem

virtual COleClientItem* GetPrimarySelectedItem(CView* *pView* **);**

Return Value

A pointer to the single, selected OLE item; **NULL** if no OLE items are selected or if more than one is selected.

Parameters

pView   Pointer to the active view object displaying the document.

Remarks

Called by the framework to retrieve the currently selected OLE item in the specified view. The default implementation searches the list of contained OLE items for a single selected item and returns a pointer to it. If there is no item selected, or if there is more than one item selected, the function returns **NULL**. You must override the **CView::IsSelected** member function in your view class for this function to work. Override this function if you have your own method of storing contained OLE items.

See Also: **CView::IsSelected**

COleDocument::GetStartPosition

virtual POSITION GetStartPosition( ) const;

Return Value

A **POSITION** value that can be used to begin iterating through the document's items; **NULL** if the document has no items.

Remarks

Call this function to get the position of the first item in the document. Pass the value returned to **GetNextItem**, **GetNextClientItem**, or **GetNextServerItem**.

See Also: **COleDocument::GetNextItem**, **COleDocument::GetNextClientItem**, **COleDocument::GetNextServerItem**

COleDocument::HasBlankItems

BOOL HasBlankItems( ) const;

Return Value

Nonzero if the document contains any blank items; otherwise 0.

Remarks

Call this function to determine whether the document contains any blank items. A blank item is one whose rectangle is empty.

See Also: **CDocItem::IsBlank**

COleDocument::OnEditChangeIcon

afx_msg void OnEditChangeIcon( );

Remarks

Displays the OLE Change Icon dialog box and changes the icon representing the currently selected OLE item to the icon the user selects in the dialog box. **OnEditChangeIcon** creates and launches a **COleChangeIconDialog** Change Icon dialog box.

See Also: **COleDocument::OnUpdateEditChangeIcon**, **COleChangeIconDialog**

COleDocument::OnEditConvert

afx_msg void OnEditConvert( );

Remarks

Displays the OLE Convert dialog box and converts or activates the currently selected OLE item according to user selections in the dialog box. **OnEditConvert** creates and launches a **COleConvertDialog** Convert dialog box.

An example of conversion is converting a Microsoft Word document into a WordPad document.

See Also: **COleDocument::OnUpdateObjectVerbMenu**, **COleConvertDialog**

COleDocument::OnEditLinks

afx_msg void OnEditLinks( );

Remarks

Displays the OLE Edit/Links dialog box. **OnEditLinks** creates and launches a **COleLinksDialog** Links dialog box that allows the user to change the linked objects.

See Also: COleDocument::OnUpdateEditLinksMenu, COleLinksDialog

COleDocument::OnFileSendMail

afx_msg void OnFileSendMail( );

Remarks

Sends a message via the resident mail host (if any) with the document as an attachment. **OnFileSendMail** calls **OnSaveDocument** to serialize (save) untitled and modified documents to a temporary file, which is then sent via electronic mail. If the document has not been modified, a temporary file is not needed; the original is sent. **OnFileSendMail** loads MAPI32.DLL if it has not already been loaded.

Unlike the implementation of **OnFileSendMail** for **CDocument**, this function handles compound files correctly.

For more information, see the "MAPI Topics" and "MAPI Support in MFC" articles in *Visual C++ Programmer's Guide* online.

See Also: CDocument::OnFileSendMail, CDocument::OnUpdateFileSendMail, CDocument::OnSaveDocument

COleDocument::OnShowViews

virtual void OnShowViews(BOOL *bVisible*);

Parameters

bVisible   Indicates whether the document has become visible or invisible.

Remarks

The framework calls this function after the document's visibility state changes.

The default version of this function does nothing. Override it if your application must perform any special processing when the document's visibility changes.

COleDocument::OnUpdateEditChangeIcon

afx_msg void OnUpdateEditChangeIcon(CCmdUI* *pCmdUI* **);**

Parameters

> *pCmdUI*   A pointer to a **CCmdUI** structure that represents the menu that generated the update command. The update handler calls the **Enable** member function of the **CCmdUI** structure through *pCmdUI* to update the user interface.

Remarks

> Called by the framework to update the Change Icon command on the Edit menu. **OnUpdateEditChangeIcon** updates the command's user interface depending on whether or not a valid icon exists in the document. Override this function to change the behavior.

> **See Also: COleDocument::OnEditChangeIcon, CCmdUI**

COleDocument::OnUpdateEditLinksMenu

afx_msg void OnUpdateEditLinksMenu(CCmdUI* *pCmdUI* **);**

Parameters

> *pCmdUI*   A pointer to a **CCmdUI** structure that represents the menu that generated the update command. The update handler calls the **Enable** member function of the **CCmdUI** structure through *pCmdUI* to update the user interface.

Remarks

> Called by the framework to update the Links command on the Edit menu. Starting with the first OLE item in the document, **OnUpdateEditLinksMenu** accesses each item, tests whether the item is a link, and, if it is a link, enables the Links command. Override this function to change the behavior.

> **See Also: COleDocument::OnEditLinks, COleDocument::GetStartPosition, COleDocument::GetNextClientItem, CCmdUI**

COleDocument::OnUpdateObjectVerbMenu

afx_msg void OnUpdateObjectVerbMenu(CCmdUI* *pCmdUI* **);**

Parameters

> *pCmdUI*   A pointer to a **CCmdUI** structure that represents the menu that generated the update command. The update handler calls the **Enable** member function of the **CCmdUI** structure through *pCmdUI* to update the user interface.

Remarks

> Called by the framework to update the *ObjectName* command on the Edit menu and the Verb submenu accessed from the *ObjectName* command, where *ObjectName* is the name of the OLE object embedded in the document. **OnUpdateObjectVerbMenu** updates the *ObjectName* command's user interface depending on whether or not a valid object exists in the document. If an object exists, the *ObjectName* command on the Edit menu is enabled. When this menu command is selected, the Verb submenu is displayed. The Verb submenu contains all the verb commands available for the object, such as Edit, Properties, and so on. Override this function to change the behavior.

> **See Also: COleDocument::OnEditConvert, CCmdUI**

COleDocument::OnUpdatePasteLinkMenu

afx_msg void OnUpdatePasteLinkMenu(CCmdUI* *pCmdUI* **);**

Parameters

> *pCmdUI* A pointer to a **CCmdUI** structure that represents the menu that generated the update command. The update handler calls the **Enable** member function of the **CCmdUI** structure through *pCmdUI* to update the user interface.

Remarks

> Called by the framework to determine whether a linked OLE item can be pasted from the Clipboard. The Paste Special menu command is enabled or disabled depending on whether the item can be pasted into the document or not.

> **See Also: COleDocument::OnUpdatePasteMenu, CCmdUI**

COleDocument::OnUpdatePasteMenu

afx_msg void OnUpdatePasteMenu(CCmdUI* *pCmdUI* **);**

Parameters

> *pCmdUI* A pointer to a **CCmdUI** structure that represents the menu that generated the update command. The update handler calls the **Enable** member function of the **CCmdUI** structure through *pCmdUI* to update the user interface.

Remarks

> Called by the framework to determine whether an embedded OLE item can be pasted from the Clipboard. The Paste menu command and button are enabled or disabled depending on whether the item can be pasted into the document or not.

> **See Also: COleDocument::OnUpdatePasteLinkMenu, CCmdUI**

COleDocument::RemoveItem

virtual void RemoveItem(CDocItem* *pItem* **);**

Parameters

pItem   Pointer to the document item to be removed.

Remarks

Call this function to remove an item from the document. You typically do not need to call this function explicitly; it is called by the destructors for **COleClientItem** and **COleServerItem**.

See Also: **COleServerItem**, **COleClientItem**, **COleDocument::AddItem**, **CDocItem**

COleDocument::UpdateModifiedFlag

void UpdateModifiedFlag( );

Remarks

Call this function to mark the document as modified if any of the contained OLE items have been modified. This allows the framework to prompt the user to save the document before closing, even if the native data in the document has not been modified.

See Also: **CDocument::SetModifiedFlag**, **COleClientItem::IsModified**

COleDropSource

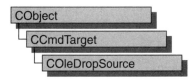

A **COleDropSource** object allows data to be dragged to a drop target. The **COleDropTarget** class handles the receiving portion of the drag-and-drop operation. The **COleDropSource** object is responsible for determining when a drag operation begins, providing feedback during the drag operation, and determining when the drag operation ends.

To use a **COleDropSource** object, just call the constructor. This simplifies the process of determining what events, such as a mouse click, begin a drag operation using **COleDataSource::DoDragDrop**, **COleClientItem::DoDragDrop**, or **COleServerItem::DoDragDrop** function. These functions will create a **COleDropSource** object for you. You might want to modify the default behavior of the **COleDropSource** overridable functions. These member functions will be called at the appropriate times by the framework.

For more information on drag-and-drop operations using OLE, see the article "Drag and Drop (OLE)" in *Visual C++ Programmer's Guide* online.

For more information, see **IDropSource** in the *OLE 2 Programmer's Reference*, *Volume 1*.

#include <afxole.h>

COleDropSource Class Members

Construction

COleDropSource	Constructs a **COleDropSource** object.

Overridables

GiveFeedback	Changes the cursor during a drag-and-drop operation.
OnBeginDrag	Handles mouse capture during a drag-and-drop operation.
QueryContinueDrag	Checks to see whether dragging should continue.

Member Functions
COleDropSource::COleDropSource

COleDropSource( );

Remarks

Constructs a **COleDropSource** object.

See Also: **COleDropTarget**

COleDropSource::GiveFeedback

virtual SCODE GiveFeedback(DROPEFFECT *dropEffect* **);**

Return Value

Returns **DRAGDROP_S_USEDEFAULTCURSORS** if dragging is in progress, **NOERROR** if it is not.

Parameters

dropEffect   The effect you would like to display to the user, usually indicating what would happen if a drop occurred at this point with the selected data. Typically, this is the value returned by the most recent call to **CView::OnDragEnter** or **CView::OnDragOver**. It can be one or more of the following:

- **DROPEFFECT_NONE**   A drop would not be allowed.

- **DROPEFFECT_COPY**   A copy operation would be performed.

- **DROPEFFECT_MOVE**   A move operation would be performed.

- **DROPEFFECT_LINK**   A link from the dropped data to the original data would be established.

- **DROPEFFECT_SCROLL**   A drag scroll operation is about to occur or is occurring in the target.

Remarks

Called by the framework after calling **COleDropTarget::OnDragOver** or **COleDropTarget::DragEnter**. Override this function to provide feedback to the user about what would happen if a drop occurred at this point. The default implementation uses the OLE default cursors. For more information on drag-and-drop operations using OLE, see the article "Drag and Drop (OLE)" in *Visual C++ Programmer's Guide* online.

For more information, see **IDropSource::GiveFeedback**, **IDropTarget::DragOver**, and **IDropTarget::DragEnter** in the *OLE 2 Programmer's Reference*, *Volume 1*.

See Also: **CView::OnDragEnter**, **CView::OnDragOver**

COleDropSource::OnBeginDrag

virtual BOOL OnBeginDrag(CWnd* *pWnd* **);**

Return Value

Nonzero if dragging is allowed, otherwise 0.

Parameters

pWnd   Points to the window that contains the selected data.

Remarks

Called by the framework when an event occurs that could begin a drag operation, such as pressing the left mouse button. Override this function if you want to modify the way the dragging process is started. The default implementation captures the mouse and stays in drag mode until the user clicks the left or right mouse button or hits ESC, at which time it releases the mouse.

See Also: COleDropSource::GiveFeedback

COleDropSource::QueryContinueDrag

virtual SCODE QueryContinueDrag(BOOL *bEscapePressed,* **DWORD** *dwKeyState* **);**

Return Value

DRAGDROP_S_CANCEL if the ESC key or right button is pressed, or left button is raised before dragging starts. **DRAGDROP_S_DROP** if a drop operation should occur. Otherwise **S_OK**.

Parameters

bEscapePressed   States whether the ESC key has been pressed since the last call to **COleDropSource::QueryContinueDrag**.

dwKeyState   Contains the state of the modifier keys on the keyboard. This is a combination of any number of the following: **MK_CONTROL, MK_SHIFT, MK_ALT, MK_LBUTTON, MK_MBUTTON,** and **MK_RBUTTON**.

Remarks

After dragging has begun, this function is called repeatedly by the framework until the drag operation is either canceled or completed. Override this function if you want to change the point at which dragging is canceled or a drop occurs.

The default implementation initiates the drop or cancels the drag as follows. It cancels a drag operation when the ESC key or the right mouse button is pressed. It initiates a drop operation when the left mouse button is raised after dragging has started. Otherwise, it returns **S_OK** and performs no further operations.

Because this function is called frequently, it should be optimized as much as possible.

See Also: COleDropSource::OnBeginDrag, COleDropTarget::OnDrop

COleDropTarget

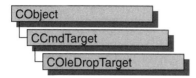

A **COleDropTarget** object provides the communication mechanism between a window and the OLE libraries. Creating an object of this class allows a window to accept data through the OLE drag-and-drop mechanism.

To get a window to accept drop commands, you should first create an object of the **COleDropTarget** class, and then call the **Register** function with a pointer to the desired **CWnd** object as the only parameter.

For more information on drag-and-drop operations using OLE, see the article "Drag and Drop (OLE)" in *Visual C++ Programmer's Guide* online.

#include <afxole.h>

See Also: **COleDropSource**

COleDropTarget Class Members

Construction

COleDropTarget	Constructs a **COleDropTarget** object.

Operations

Register	Registers the window as a valid drop target.
Revoke	Causes the window to cease being a valid drop target.

Overridables

OnDragEnter	Called when the cursor first enters the window.
OnDragLeave	Called when the cursor is dragged out of the window.
OnDragOver	Called repeatedly when the cursor is dragged over the window.
OnDragScroll	Called to determine whether the cursor is dragged into the scroll region of the window.
OnDrop	Called when data is dropped into the window, default handler.
OnDropEx	Called when data is dropped into the window, initial handler.

Member Functions
COleDropTarget::COleDropTarget

COleDropTarget( );

Remarks

Constructs an object of class **COleDropTarget**. Call **Register** to associate this object with a window.

See Also: **COleDropSource**, **COleDropTarget::Register**, **COleDropTarget::Revoke**

COleDropTarget::OnDragEnter

virtual DROPEFFECT OnDragEnter(CWnd* *pWnd*,
↪ **COleDataObject*** *pDataObject*, **DWORD** *dwKeyState*, **CPoint** *point* **);**

Return Value

The effect that would result if a drop were attempted at the location specified by *point*. It can be one or more of the following:

- **DROPEFFECT_NONE** A drop would not be allowed.
- **DROPEFFECT_COPY** A copy operation would be performed.
- **DROPEFFECT_MOVE** A move operation would be performed.
- **DROPEFFECT_LINK** A link from the dropped data to the original data would be established.
- **DROPEFFECT_SCROLL** A drag scroll operation is about to occur or is occurring in the target.

Parameters

pWnd Points to the window the cursor is entering.

pDataObject Points to the data object containing the data that can be dropped.

dwKeyState Contains the state of the modifier keys. This is a combination of any number of the following: **MK_CONTROL**, **MK_SHIFT**, **MK_ALT**, **MK_LBUTTON**, **MK_MBUTTON**, and **MK_RBUTTON**.

point Contains the current location of the cursor in client coordinates.

Remarks

Called by the framework when the cursor is first dragged into the window. Override this function to allow drop operations to occur in the window. The default implementation calls **CView::OnDragEnter**, which simply returns **DROPEFFECT_NONE** by default.

For more information, see **IDropTarget::DragEnter** in the *OLE 2 Programmer's Reference, Volume 1.*

See Also: **COleDropTarget::OnDragOver, COleDropTarget::OnDragLeave, COleDropTarget::OnDrop, COleDropTarget::OnDropEx, CView::OnDragEnter**

COleDropTarget::OnDragLeave

virtual void OnDragLeave(CWnd* *pWnd* **);**

Parameters

pWnd   Points to the window the cursor is leaving.

Remarks

Called by the framework when the cursor leaves the window while a dragging operation is in effect. Override this function if you want special behavior when the drag operation leaves the specified window. The default implementation of this function calls **CView::OnDragLeave**.

For more information, see **IDropTarget::DragLeave** in the *OLE 2 Programmer's Reference, Volume 1.*

See Also: **COleDropTarget::OnDragEnter, COleDropTarget::OnDragOver, COleDropTarget::OnDrop, COleDropTarget::OnDropEx**

COleDropTarget::OnDragOver

virtual DROPEFFECT OnDragOver(CWnd* *pWnd*,
↪ **COleDataObject*** *pDataObject*, **DWORD** *dwKeyState*, **CPoint** *point* **);**

Return Value

The effect that would result if a drop were attempted at the location specified by *point*. It can be one or more of the following:

- **DROPEFFECT_NONE**   A drop would not be allowed.
- **DROPEFFECT_COPY**   A copy operation would be performed.
- **DROPEFFECT_MOVE**   A move operation would be performed.
- **DROPEFFECT_LINK**   A link from the dropped data to the original data would be established.
- **DROPEFFECT_SCROLL**   Indicates that a drag scroll operation is about to occur or is occurring in the target.

Parameters

pWnd Points to the window that the cursor is over.

pDataObject Points to the data object that contains the data to be dropped.

dwKeyState Contains the state of the modifier keys. This is a combination of any number of the following: **MK_CONTROL**, **MK_SHIFT**, **MK_ALT**, **MK_LBUTTON**, **MK_MBUTTON**, and **MK_RBUTTON**.

point Contains the current location of the cursor in client coordinates.

Remarks

Called by the framework when the cursor is dragged over the window. This function should be overridden to allow drop operations to occur in the window. The default implementation of this function calls **CView::OnDragOver**, which returns **DROPEFFECT_NONE** by default. Because this function is called frequently during a drag-and-drop operation, it should be optimized as much as possible.

For more information, see **IDropTarget::DragOver** in the *OLE 2 Programmer's Reference, Volume 1*.

See Also: **COleDropTarget::OnDragEnter**, **COleDropTarget::OnDragLeave**, **COleDropTarget::OnDrop**, **COleDropTarget::OnDropEx**

COleDropTarget::OnDragScroll

virtual DROPEFFECT OnDragScroll(CWnd* *pWnd*,
  ↪ **DWORD** *dwKeyState*, **CPoint** *point*);

Return Value

The effect that would result if a drop were attempted at the location specified by *point*. It can be one or more of the following:

- **DROPEFFECT_NONE** A drop would not be allowed.
- **DROPEFFECT_COPY** A copy operation would be performed.
- **DROPEFFECT_MOVE** A move operation would be performed.
- **DROPEFFECT_LINK** A link from the dropped data to the original data would be established.
- **DROPEFFECT_SCROLL** Indicates that a drag scroll operation is about to occur or is occurring in the target.

Parameters

pWnd Points to the window the cursor is currently over.

dwKeyState Contains the state of the modifier keys. This is a combination of any number of the following: **MK_CONTROL**, **MK_SHIFT**, **MK_ALT**, **MK_LBUTTON**, **MK_MBUTTON**, and **MK_RBUTTON**.

point Contains the location of the cursor, in pixels, relative to the screen.

Remarks

Called by the framework before calling **OnDragEnter** or **OnDragOver** to determine whether *point* is in the scrolling region. Override this function when you want to provide special behavior for this event. The default implementation of this function calls **CView::OnDragScroll**, which returns **DROPEFFECT_NONE** and scrolls the window when the cursor is dragged into the default scroll region inside the border of the window.

COleDropTarget::OnDrop

virtual BOOL OnDrop(CWnd* *pWnd*, **COleDataObject*** *pDataObject*,
↪ **DROPEFFECT** *dropEffect*, **CPoint** *point* **);**

Return Value

Nonzero if the drop is successful; otherwise 0.

Parameters

pWnd   Points to the window the cursor is currently over.

pDataObject   Points to the data object that contains the data to be dropped.

dropEffect   The effect that the user chose for the drop operation. It can be one or more of the following:

- **DROPEFFECT_COPY**   A copy operation would be performed.

- **DROPEFFECT_MOVE**   A move operation would be performed.

- **DROPEFFECT_LINK**   A link from the dropped data to the original data would be established.

point   Contains the location of the cursor, in pixels, relative to the screen.

Remarks

Called by the framework when a drop operation is to occur. The framework first calls **OnDropEx**. If the **OnDropEx** function does not handle the drop, the framework then calls this member function, **OnDrop**. Typically, the application overrides **OnDropEx** in the view class to handle right mouse-button drag and drop. Typically, the view class **OnDrop** is used to handle simple drag and drop.

The default implementation of **COleDropTarget::OnDrop** calls **CView::OnDrop**, which simply returns **FALSE** by default.

For more information, see **IDropTarget::Drop** in the *OLE 2 Programmer's Reference, Volume 1*.

See Also: COleDropTarget::OnDragOver, COleDropTarget::OnDragEnter, COleDropTarget::OnDropEx

COleDropTarget::OnDropEx

virtual DROPEFFECT OnDropEx(CWnd* *pWnd***, COleDataObject*** *pDataObject***,**
↳ **DROPEFFECT** *dropDefault***, DROPEFFECT** *dropList***, CPoint** *point* **);**

Return Value

The drop effect that resulted from the drop attempt at the location specified by *point*. Drop effects are discussed in the Remarks section.

Parameters

pWnd   Points to the window the cursor is currently over.

pDataObject   Points to the data object that contains the data to be dropped.

dropDefault   The effect that the user chose for the default drop operation based on the current key state. It can be **DROPEFFECT_NONE**. Drop effects are discussed in the Remarks section.

dropList   A list of the drop effects that the drop source supports. Drop effect values can be combined using the bitwise OR (l) operation. Drop effects are discussed in the Remarks section.

point   Contains the location of the cursor, in pixels, relative to the screen.

Remarks

Called by the framework when a drop operation is to occur. The framework first calls this function. If it does not handle the drop, the framework then calls **OnDrop**. Typically, you will override **OnDropEx** in the view class to support right mouse-button drag and drop. Typically, the view class **OnDrop** is used to handle the case of support for simple drag and drop.

The default implementation of **COleDropTarget::OnDropEx** calls **CView::OnDropEx**. By default, **CView::OnDropEx** simply returns a dummy value to indicate the **OnDrop** member function should be called.

Drop effects describe the action associated with a drop operation. See the following list of drop effects:

- **DROPEFFECT_NONE**   A drop would not be allowed.
- **DROPEFFECT_COPY**   A copy operation would be performed.
- **DROPEFFECT_MOVE**   A move operation would be performed.
- **DROPEFFECT_LINK**   A link from the dropped data to the original data would be established.
- **DROPEFFECT_SCROLL**   Indicates that a drag scroll operation is about to occur or is occurring in the target.

For more information, see **IDropTarget::Drop** in the *OLE 2 Programmer's Reference, Volume 1*.

See Also: **COleDropTarget::OnDragOver**, **COleDropTarget::OnDragEnter**

COleDropTarget::Register

BOOL Register(CWnd* *pWnd* **);**

Return Value

Nonzero if registration is successful; otherwise 0.

Parameters

pWnd   Points to the window that is to be registered as a drop target.

Remarks

Call this function to register your window with the OLE DLLs as a valid drop target. This function must be called for drop operations to be accepted.

For more information, see **RegisterDragDrop** in the *OLE 2 Programmer's Reference, Volume 1*.

See Also: **COleDropTarget::Revoke**, **COleDropTarget::COleDropTarget**

COleDropTarget::Revoke

virtual void Revoke( );

Remarks

Call this function before destroying any window that has been registered as a drop target through a call to **Register** to remove it from the list of drop targets. This function is called automatically from the **OnDestroy** handler for the window that was registered, so it is usually not necessary to call this function explicitly.

For more information, see **RevokeDragDrop** in the *OLE 2 Programmer's Reference, Volume 1*.

COleException

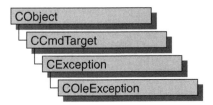

A **COleException** object represents an exception condition related to an OLE operation. The **COleException** class includes a public data member that holds the status code indicating the reason for the exception.

In general, you should not create a **COleException** object directly; instead, you should call **AfxThrowOleException**.

For more information on exceptions, see the articles "Exceptions" and "Exceptions: OLE Exceptions" in *Visual C++ Programmer's Guide* online.

#include <afxole.h>

COleException Class Members

Data Members

m_sc	Contains the status code that indicates the reason for the exception.

Operations

Process	Translates a caught exception into an OLE return code.

Member Functions

COleException::Process

static SCODE PASCAL Process(const CException* *pAnyException* **);**

Return Value

An OLE status code.

Parameters

pAnyException   Pointer to a caught exception.

Remarks

Call the **Process** member function to translate a caught exception into an OLE status code.

Note This function is **static**.

For more information on **SCODE**, see "Structure of OLE Error Codes" in the *OLE 2 Programmer's Reference*, *Volume 1*.

See Also: **CException**

Data Members

COleException::m_sc

SCODE m_sc;

Remarks

This data member holds the OLE status code that indicates the reason for the exception. This variable's value is set by **AfxThrowOleException**.

For more information on **SCODE**, see "Structure of OLE Error Codes" in the *OLE 2 Programmer's Reference*, *Volume 1*.

See Also: **AfxThrowOleException**

COleInsertDialog

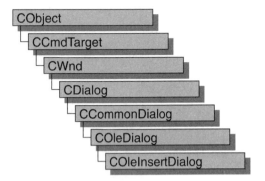

```
CObject
  CCmdTarget
    CWnd
      CDialog
        CCommonDialog
          COleDialog
            COleInsertDialog
```

The **COleInsertDialog** class is used for the OLE Insert Object dialog box. Create an object of class **COleInsertDialog** when you want to call this dialog box. After a **COleInsertDialog** object has been constructed, you can use the **m_io** structure to initialize the values or states of controls in the dialog box. The **m_io** structure is of type **OLEUIINSERTOBJECT**. For more information about using this dialog class, see the **DoModal** member function.

Note AppWizard-generated container code uses this class.

For more information, see the **OLEUIINSERTOBJECT** structure in the *OLE 2.01 User Interface Library*.

For more information regarding OLE-specific dialog boxes, see the article "Dialog Boxes in OLE" in *Visual C++ Programmer's Guide* online.

#include <afxodlgs.h>

See Also: COleDialog

COleInsertDialog Class Members

Data Members

m_io	A structure of type **OLEUIINSERTOBJECT** that controls the behavior of the dialog box.

Construction

COleInsertDialog	Constructs a **COleInsertDialog** object.

Operations and Attributes

DoModal	Displays the OLE Insert Object dialog box.
CreateItem	Creates the item selected in the dialog box.
GetSelectionType	Gets the type of object selected.
GetClassID	Gets the **CLSID** associated with the chosen item.
GetDrawAspect	Tells whether to draw the item as an icon.
GetIconicMetafile	Gets a handle to the metafile associated with the iconic form of this item.
GetPathName	Gets the full path to the file chosen in the dialog box.

Member Functions
COleInsertDialog::COleInsertDialog

COleInsertDialog (DWORD *dwFlags* = **IOF_SELECTCREATENEW**,
↳ **CWnd*** *pParentWnd* = **NULL**);

Parameters

dwFlags   Creation flag that contains any number of the following values to be combined using the bitwise-OR operator:

- **IOF_SHOWHELP**   Specifies that the Help button will be displayed when the dialog box is called.

- **IOF_SELECTCREATENEW**   Specifies that the Create New radio button will be selected initially when the dialog box is called. This is the default and cannot be used with **IOF_SELECTCREATEFROMFILE**.

- **IOF_SELECTCREATEFROMFILE**   Specifies that the Create From File radio button will be selected initially when the dialog box is called. Cannot be used with **IOF_SELECTCREATENEW**.

- **IOF_CHECKLINK**   Specifies that the Link check box will be checked initially when the dialog box is called.

- **IOF_DISABLELINK**   Specifies that the Link check box will be disabled when the dialog box is called.

- **IOF_CHECKDISPLAYASICON**   Specifies that the Display As Icon check box will be checked initially, the current icon will be displayed, and the Change Icon button will be enabled when the dialog box is called.

- **IOF_VERIFYSERVERSEXIST**   Specifies that the dialog box should validate the classes it adds to the list box by ensuring that the servers specified in the registration database exist before the dialog box is displayed. Setting this flag can significantly impair performance.

pParentWnd   Points to the parent or owner window object (of type **CWnd**) to which the dialog object belongs. If it is **NULL**, the parent window of the dialog object is set to the main application window.

Remarks

This function constructs only a **COleInsertDialog** object. To display the dialog box, call the **DoModal** function.

See Also: **COleInsertDialog::DoModal**

COleInsertDialog::CreateItem

BOOL CreateItem(COleClientItem* *pItem*);

Return Value

Nonzero if item was created; otherwise 0.

Parameters

pItem   Points to the item to be created.

Remarks

Call this function to create an object of type **COleClientItem** only if **DoModal** returns **IDOK**. You must allocate the **COleClientItem** object before you can call this function.

See Also: COleClientItem::CreateLinkFromFile, COleClientItem::CreateFromFile, COleClientItem::CreateNewItem, COleClientItem::SetDrawAspect, COleInsertDialog::GetSelectionType, COleInsertDialog::DoModal

---

COleInsertDialog::DoModal

virtual int DoModal( );

Return Value

Completion status for the dialog box. One of the following values:

- **IDOK** if the dialog box was successfully displayed.

- **IDCANCEL** if the user canceled the dialog box.

- **IDABORT** if an error occurred. If **IDABORT** is returned, call the **COleDialog::GetLastError** member function to get more information about the type of error that occurred. For a listing of possible errors, see the **OleUIInsertObject** function in the *OLE 2.01 User Interface Library*.

Remarks

Call this function to display the OLE Insert Object dialog box.

If you want to initialize the various dialog box controls by setting members of the **m_io** structure, you should do this before calling **DoModal**, but after the dialog object is constructed.

If **DoModal** returns **IDOK**, you can call other member functions to retrieve the settings or information input into the dialog box by the user.

See Also: **COleDialog::GetLastError, CDialog::DoModal, COleInsertDialog::GetSelectionType, COleInsertDialog::GetClassID, COleInsertDialog::GetDrawAspect, COleInsertDialog::GetIconicMetafile, COleInsertDialog::GetPathName, COleInsertDialog::m_io**

COleInsertDialog::GetClassID

const CLSID& GetClassID( ) const;

Return Value

Returns the **CLSID** associated with the selected item.

Remarks

Call this function to get the **CLSID** associated with the selected item only if **DoModal** returns **IDOK** and the selection type is **COleInsertDialog::createNewItem**.

For more information, see **CLSID Key** in the *OLE 2 Programmer's Reference, Volume 1*.

See Also: **COleInsertDialog::DoModal, COleInsertDialog::GetSelectionType**

COleInsertDialog::GetDrawAspect

DVASPECT GetDrawAspect( ) const;

Return Value

The method needed to render the object.

- **DVASPECT_CONTENT** Returned if the Display As Icon check box was not checked.

- **DVASPECT_ICON** Returned if the Display As Icon check box was checked.

Remarks

Call this function to determine if the user chose to display the selected item as an icon. Call this function only if **DoModal** returns **IDOK**.

For more information on drawing aspect, see **FORMATETC** data structure in the *OLE 2 Programmer's Reference, Volume 1*.

See Also: **COleInsertDialog::DoModal, COleInsertDialog::COleInsertDialog**

COleInsertDialog::GetIconicMetafile

HGLOBAL GetIconicMetafile( ) const;

Return Value

The handle to the metafile containing the iconic aspect of the selected item, if the Display As Icon check box was checked when the dialog was dismissed by choosing **OK**; otherwise **NULL**.

Remarks

Call this function to get a handle to the metafile that contains the iconic aspect of the selected item.

See Also: **COleInsertDialog::DoModal, COleInsertDialog::GetDrawAspect**

COleInsertDialog::GetPathName

CString GetPathName( ) const;

Return Value

The full path to the file selected in the dialog box. If the selection type is **createNewItem**, this function returns a meaningless **CString** in release mode or causes an assertion in debug mode.

Remarks

Call this function to get the full path of the selected file only if **DoModal** returns **IDOK** and the selection type is not **COleInsertDialog::createNewItem**.

See Also: **COleInsertDialog::GetSelectionType, COleInsertDialog::DoModal**

COleInsertDialog::GetSelectionType

UINT GetSelectionType( ) const;

Return Value

Type of selection made.

Remarks

Call this function to get the selection type chosen when the Insert Object dialog box was dismissed by choosing **OK**.

The return type values are specified by the **Selection** enumeration type declared in the **COleInsertDialog** class.

```
enum Selection
{
    createNewItem,
    insertFromFile,
    linkToFile
};
```

Brief descriptions of these values follow:

- **COleInsertDialog::createNewItem**   The Create New radio button was selected.
- **COleInsertDialog::insertFromFile**   The Create From File radio button was selected and the Link check box was not checked.
- **COleInsertDialog::linkToFile**   The Create From File radio button was selected and the Link check box was checked.

See Also: **COleInsertDialog::DoModal, COleInsertDialog::COleInsertDialog**

Data Members
COleInsertDialog::m_io

Remarks

Structure of type **OLEUIINSERTOBJECT** used to control the behavior of the Insert Object dialog box. Members of this structure can be modified either directly or through member functions.

For more information, see the **OLEUIINSERTOBJECT** structure in the *OLE 2.01 User Interface Library*.

See Also: **COleInsertDialog::COleInsertDialog, COleInsertDialog::DoModal**

COleIPFrameWnd

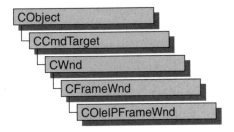

Use the **COleIPFrameWnd** class as the base for your application's in-place editing window. This class creates and positions control bars within the container application's document window. It also handles notifications generated by an embedded **COleResizeBar** object when the user resizes the in-place editing window.

For more information on using **COleIPFrameWnd**, see the article "Activation" in *Visual C++ Programmer's Guide* online.

#include <afxole.h>

See Also: CFrameWnd

COleIPFrameWnd Class Members

Construction

COleIPFrameWnd	Constructs a **COleIPFrameWnd** object.

Overridables

OnCreateControlBars	Called by the framework when an item is activated for in-place editing.
RepositionFrame	Called by the framework to reposition the in-place editing window.

Member Functions
COleIPFrameWnd::COleIPFrameWnd

COleIPFrameWnd( );

Remarks

Constructs a **COleIPFrameWnd** object and initializes its in-place state information, which is stored in a structure of type **OLEINPLACEFRAMEINFO**.

For more information, see **OLEINPLACEFRAMEINFO** in the *OLE 2 Programmer's Reference, Volume 1.*

See Also: **COleServerDoc::ActivateInPlace**

COleIPFrameWnd::OnCreateControlBars

virtual BOOL OnCreateControlBars(CWnd* *pWndFrame*, **CWnd*** *pWndDoc* **);**

Return Value

Nonzero on success; otherwise, 0.

Parameters

pWndFrame   Pointer to the container application's frame window.

pWndDoc   Pointer to the container's document-level window. Can be **NULL** if the container is an SDI application.

Remarks

The framework calls the **OnCreateControlBars** function when an item is activated for in-place editing.

The default implementation does nothing. Override this function to perform any special processing required when control bars are created.

See Also: **COleServerDoc::ActivateInPlace**

COleIPFrameWnd::RepositionFrame

virtual void RepositionFrame(LPCRECT *lpPosRect*, **LPCRECT** *lpClipRect* **);**

Parameters

lpPosRect   Pointer to a **RECT** structure or a **CRect** object containing the in-place frame window's current position coordinates, in pixels, relative to the client area.

lpClipRect   Pointer to a **RECT** structure or a **CRect** object containing the in-place frame window's current clipping-rectangle coordinates, in pixels, relative to the client area.

Remarks

The framework calls the **RepositionFrame** member function to lay out control bars and reposition the in-place editing window so all of it is visible.

Layout of control bars in the container window differs from that performed by a non-OLE frame window. The non-OLE frame window calculates the positions of control bars and other objects from a given frame-window size, as in a call to **CFrameWnd::RecalcLayout**. The client area is what remains after space for control bars and other objects is subtracted. A **COleIPFrameWnd** window, on the other hand, positions toolbars in accordance with a given client area. In other words, **CFrameWnd::RecalcLayout** works "from the outside in," whereas **COleIPFrameWnd::RepositionFrame** works "from the inside out."

See Also: **CFrameWnd::RecalcLayout**

COleLinkingDoc

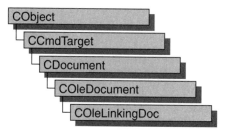

The **COleLinkingDoc** class is the base class for OLE container documents that support linking to the embedded items they contain. A container application that supports linking to embedded items is called a "link container." The OCLIENT sample application is an example of a link container.

When a linked item's source is an embedded item in another document, that containing document must be loaded in order for the embedded item to be edited. For this reason, a link container must be able to be launched by another container application when the user wants to edit the source of a linked item. Your application must also use the **COleTemplateServer** class so that it can create documents when launched programmatically.

To make your container a link container, derive your document class from **COleLinkingDoc** instead of **COleDocument**. As with any other OLE container, you must design your class for storing the application's native data as well as embedded or linked items. Also, you must design data structures for storing your native data. If you define a **CDocItem**-derived class for your application's native data, you can use the interface defined by **COleDocument** to store your native data as well as your OLE data.

To allow your application to be launched programmatically by another container, declare a **COleTemplateServer** object as a member of your application's **CWinApp**-derived class:

```
class COleClientApp : public CWinApp
{
// ...
protected:
   COleTemplateServer m_server;
// ...
};
```

In the **InitInstance** member function of your **CWinApp**-derived class, create a document template and specify your **COleLinkingDoc**-derived class as the document class:

```
// CMainDoc is derived from COleLinkingDoc
CMultiDocTemplate* pDocTemplate = new CMultiDocTemplate(IDR_OCLIENTTYPE,
    RUNTIME_CLASS(CMainDoc),
    RUNTIME_CLASS(CSplitFrame),
    RUNTIME_CLASS(CMainView));
pDocTemplate->SetContainerInfo(
    IDR_OCLIENTTYPE_CNTR_IP);
AddDocTemplate(pDocTemplate);
```

Connect your **COleTemplateServer** object to your document templates by calling the object's **ConnectTemplate** member function, and register all class objects with the OLE system by calling **COleTemplateServer::RegisterAll**:

```
m_server.ConnectTemplate(clsid, pDocTemplate, FALSE);
COleTemplateServer::RegisterAll();
```

For a sample **CWinApp**-derived class definition and **InitInstance** function, see OCLIENT.H and OCLIENT.CPP in the MFC sample OCLIENT.

For more information on using **COleLinkingDoc**, see the articles "Containers: Implementing a Container" and "Containers: Advanced Features" in *Visual C++ Programmer's Guide* online.

#include <afxole.h>

See Also: CDocTemplate, COleTemplateServer

COleLinkingDoc Class Members

Construction

COleLinkingDoc	Constructs a **COleLinkingDoc** object.

Operations

Register	Registers the document with the OLE system DLLs.
Revoke	Revokes the document's registration.

Overridables

OnFindEmbeddedItem	Finds the specified embedded item.
OnGetLinkedItem	Finds the specified linked item.

Member Functions
COleLinkingDoc::COleLinkingDoc

COleLinkingDoc( );

Remarks

Constructs a **COleLinkingDoc** object without beginning communications with the OLE system DLLs. You must call the **Register** member function to inform OLE that the document is open.

See Also: COleLinkingDoc::Register

COleLinkingDoc::OnFindEmbeddedItem

virtual COleClientItem* OnFindEmbeddedItem(LPCTSTR *lpszItemName* **);**

Return Value

A pointer to the specified item; **NULL** if the item is not found.

Parameters

lpszItemName   Pointer to the name of the embedded OLE item requested.

Remarks

Called by the framework to determine whether the document contains an embedded OLE item with the specified name. The default implementation searches the list of embedded items for an item with the specified name (the name comparison is case sensitive). Override this function if you have your own method of storing or naming embedded OLE items.

See Also: COleClientItem, COleLinkingDoc::OnGetLinkedItem

COleLinkingDoc::OnGetLinkedItem

virtual COleServerItem* OnGetLinkedItem(LPCTSTR *lpszItemName* **);**

Return Value

A pointer to the specified item; **NULL** if the item is not found.

Parameters

lpszItemName   Pointer to the name of the linked OLE item requested.

Remarks

Called by the framework to check whether the document contains a linked server item with the specified name. The default **COleLinkingDoc** implementation always returns **NULL**. This function is overriden in the derived class **COleServerDoc** to search the list of OLE server items for a linked item with the specified name (the name comparison is case sensitive). Override this function if you have implemented your own method of storing or retrieving linked server items.

See Also: **COleServerItem::GetItemName, COleServerItem::SetItemName, COleLinkingDoc::OnFindEmbeddedItem**

COleLinkingDoc::Register

BOOL Register(COleObjectFactory* *pFactory*, **LPCTSTR** *lpszPathName* **);**

Return Value

Nonzero if the document is successfully registered; otherwise 0.

Parameters

pFactory   Pointer to an OLE factory object (can be **NULL**).

lpszPathName   Pointer to the fully qualified path of the container document.

Remarks

Informs the OLE system DLLs that the document is open. Call this function when creating or opening a named file to register the document with the OLE system DLLs. There is no need to call this function if the document represents an embedded item.

If you are using **COleTemplateServer** in your application, **Register** is called for you by **COleLinkingDoc**'s implementation of **OnNewDocument**, **OnOpenDocument**, and **OnSaveDocument**.

See Also: **COleTemplateServer, COleObjectFactory, CDocument::OnNewDocument, CDocument::OnOpenDocument**

COleLinkingDoc::Revoke

void Revoke( );

Remarks

Informs the OLE system DLLs that the document is no longer open. Call this function to revoke the document's registration with the OLE system DLLs.

You should call this function when closing a named file, but you usually do not need to call it directly. **Revoke** is called for you by **COleLinkingDoc**'s implementation of **OnCloseDocument, OnNewDocument, OnOpenDocument**, and **OnSaveDocument**.

See Also: **COleTemplateServer, CDocument::OnCloseDocument, CDocument::OnNewDocument, CDocument::OnOpenDocument, CDocument::OnSaveDocument**

COleLinksDialog

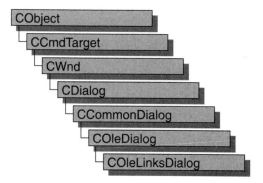

The **COleLinksDialog** object is used for the OLE Edit Links dialog box. Create an object of class **COleLinksDialog** when you want to call this dialog box. After a **COleLinksDialog** object has been constructed, you can use the **m_el** structure to initialize the values or states of controls in the dialog box. The **m_el** structure is of type **OLEUIEDITLINKS**. For more information about using this dialog class, see the **DoModal** member function.

Note AppWizard-generated container code uses this class.

For more information, see the **OLEUIEDITLINKS** structure in the *OLE 2.01 User Interface Library*.

For more information regarding OLE-specific dialog boxes, see the article "Dialog Boxes in OLE" in *Visual C++ Programmer's Guide* online.

#include <afxodlgs.h>

See Also: COleDialog

COleLinksDialog Class Members

Data Members

m_el	A structure of type **OLEUIEDITLINKS** that controls the behavior of the dialog box.

Construction

COleLinksDialog	Constructs a **COleLinksDialog** object.

Operations

DoModal	Displays the OLE Edit Links dialog box.

Member Functions
COleLinksDialog::COleLinksDialog

COleLinksDialog (**COleDocument*** *pDoc*, **CView*** *pView*, **DWORD** *dwFlags* = **0**,
↪ **CWnd*** *pParentWnd* = **NULL**);

Parameters

pDoc   Points to the OLE document that contains the links to be edited.

pView   Points to the current view on *pDoc*.

dwFlags   Creation flag, which contains either 0 or **ELF_SHOWHELP** to specify whether the Help button will be displayed when the dialog box is displayed.

pParentWnd   Points to the parent or owner window object (of type **CWnd**) to which the dialog object belongs. If it is **NULL**, the parent window of the dialog box is set to the main application window.

Remarks

This function constructs only a **COleLinksDialog** object. To display the dialog box, call the **DoModal** function.

See Also: **COleDocument**, **COleLinksDialog::DoModal**, **CView**, **CWnd**

COleLinksDialog::DoModal

virtual int DoModal( );

Return Value

Completion status for the dialog box. One of the following values:

- **IDOK** if the dialog box was successfully displayed.
- **IDCANCEL** if the user canceled the dialog box.
- **IDABORT** if an error occurred. If **IDABORT** is returned, call the **COleDialog::GetLastError** member function to get more information about the type of error that occurred. For a listing of possible errors, see the **OleUIEditLinks** function in the *OLE 2.01 User Interface Library*.

Remarks

Call this function to display the OLE Edit Links dialog box.

If you want to initialize the various dialog box controls by setting members of the **m_el** structure, you should do it before calling **DoModal**, but after the dialog object is constructed.

See Also: **COleDialog::GetLastError**, **CDialog::DoModal**, **COleLinksDialog::m_el**

Data Members
COleLinksDialog::m_el

Remarks

Structure of type **OLEUIEDITLINKS** used to control the behavior of the Edit Links dialog box. Members of this structure can be modified either directly or through member functions.

For more information, see the **OLEUIEDITLINKS** structure in the *OLE 2.01 User Interface Library*.

See Also: **COleLinksDialog::COleLinksDialog**, **COleLinksDialog::DoModal**

COleMessageFilter

The **COleMessageFilter** class manages the concurrency required by the interaction of OLE applications.

The **COleMessageFilter** class is useful in visual editing server and container applications, as well as OLE automation applications. For server applications that are being called, this class can be used to make the application "busy" so that incoming calls from other container applications are either canceled or retried later. This class can also be used to determine the action to be taken by a calling application when the called application is busy.

Common usage is for a server application to call **BeginBusyState** and **EndBusyState** when it would be dangerous for a document or other OLE accessible object to be destroyed. These calls are made in **CWinApp::OnIdle** during user-interface updates.

By default, a **COleMessageFilter** object is allocated when the application is initialized. It can be retrieved with **AfxOleGetMessageFilter**.

This is an advanced class; you seldom need to work with it directly.

For more information, see the article "Servers: Implementing a Server" in *Visual C++ Programmer's Guide* online.

#include <afxole.h>

See Also: **CCmdTarget, AfxOleGetMessageFilter, CWinApp::OnIdle**

COleMessageFilter Class Members

Construction

COleMessageFilter	Constructs a **COleMessageFilter** object.

Operations

Register	Registers the message filter with the OLE system DLLs.
Revoke	Revokes the message filter's registration with the OLE system DLLs.
BeginBusyState	Puts the application in the busy state.

Operations *(continued)*

EndBusyState	Terminates the application's busy state.
SetBusyReply	Determines the busy application's reply to an OLE call.
SetRetryReply	Determines the calling application's reply to a busy application.
SetMessagePendingDelay	Determines how long the application waits for a response to an OLE call.
EnableBusyDialog	Enables and disables the dialog box that appears when a called application is busy.
EnableNotRespondingDialog	Enables and disables the dialog box that appears when a called application is not responding.

Overridables

OnMessagePending	Called by the framework to process messages while an OLE call is in progress.

Member Functions

COleMessageFilter::BeginBusyState

virtual void BeginBusyState( );

Remarks

Call this function to begin a busy state. It works in conjunction with **EndBusyState** to control the application's busy state. The function **SetBusyReply** determines the application's reply to calling applications when it is busy.

The **BeginBusyState** and **EndBusyState** calls increment and decrement, respectively, a counter that determines whether the application is busy. For example, two calls to **BeginBusyState** and one call to **EndBusyState** still result in a busy state. To cancel a busy state it is necessary to call **EndBusyState** the same number of times **BeginBusyState** has been called.

By default, the framework enters the busy state during idle processing, which is performed by **CWinApp::OnIdle**. While the application is handling **ON_COMMANDUPDATEUI** notifications, incoming calls are handled later, after idle processing is complete.

See Also: **COleMessageFilter::EndBusyState**, **COleMessageFilter::SetBusyReply**, **CWinApp::OnIdle**

COleMessageFilter::COleMessageFilter

COleMessageFilter( );

Remarks

Creates a **COleMessageFilter** object.

See Also: COleMessageFilter::Register, COleMessageFilter::Revoke

---

COleMessageFilter::EnableBusyDialog

void EnableBusyDialog(BOOL *bEnableBusy* **= TRUE);**

Parameters

bEnableBusy   Specifies whether the "busy" dialog box is enabled or disabled.

Remarks

Enables and disables the busy dialog box, which is displayed when the message-pending delay expires (see **SetRetryReply**) during an OLE call.

See Also: COleMessageFilter::EnableNotRespondingDialog, COleMessageFilter::BeginBusyState, COleMessageFilter::SetBusyReply, COleMessageFilter::SetRetryReply, COleBusyDialog

---

COleMessageFilter::EnableNotRespondingDialog

void EnableNotRespondingDialog(BOOL *bEnableNotResponding* **= TRUE);**

Parameters

bEnableNotResponding   Specifies whether the "not responding" dialog box is enabled or disabled.

Remarks

Enables and disables the "not responding" dialog box, which is displayed if a keyboard or mouse message is pending during an OLE call and the call has timed out.

See Also: COleMessageFilter::EnableBusyDialog, COleMessageFilter::BeginBusyState, COleMessageFilter::SetBusyReply, COleBusyDialog

COleMessageFilter::EndBusyState

virtual void EndBusyState( );

Remarks

Call this function to end a busy state. It works in conjunction with **BeginBusyState** to control the application's busy state. The function **SetBusyReply** determines the application's reply to calling applications when it is busy.

The **BeginBusyState** and **EndBusyState** calls increment and decrement, respectively, a counter that determines whether the application is busy. For example, two calls to **BeginBusyState** and one call to **EndBusyState** still result in a busy state. To cancel a busy state it is necessary to call **EndBusyState** the same number of times **BeginBusyState** has been called.

By default, the framework enters the busy state during idle processing, which is performed by **CWinApp::OnIdle**. While the application is handling **ON_UPDATE_COMMAND_UI** notifications, incoming calls are handled after idle processing is complete.

See Also: **COleMessageFilter::BeginBusyState**, **COleMessageFilter::SetBusyReply**, **CWinApp::OnIdle**

COleMessageFilter::OnMessagePending

virtual BOOL OnMessagePending(const MSG* *pMsg* **);**

Return Value

Nonzero on success; otherwise 0.

Parameters

pMsg   Pointer to the pending message.

Remarks

Called by the framework to process messages while an OLE call is in progress.

When a calling application is waiting for a call to be completed, the framework calls **OnMessagePending** with a pointer to the pending message. By default, the framework dispatches **WM_PAINT** messages, so that window updates can occur during a call that is taking a long time.

You must register your message filter by means of a call to **Register** before it can become active.

See Also: **COleMessageFilter::Register**, **AfxOleInit**, **CWinApp::InitInstance**

COleMessageFilter::Register

BOOL Register( );

Return Value

Nonzero on success; otherwise 0.

Remarks

Registers the message filter with the OLE system DLLs. A message filter has no effect unless it is registered with the system DLLs. Usually your application's initialization code registers the application's message filter. Any other message filter registered by your application should be revoked before the program terminates by a call to **Revoke**.

The framework's default message filter is automatically registered during initialization and revoked at termination.

See Also: COleMessageFilter::Revoke

COleMessageFilter::Revoke

void Revoke( );

Remarks

Revokes a previous registration performed by a call to **Register**. A message filter should be revoked before the program terminates.

The default message filter, which is created and registered automatically by the framework, is also automatically revoked.

See Also: COleMessageFilter::Register

COleMessageFilter::SetBusyReply

void SetBusyReply(SERVERCALL *nBusyReply*);

Parameters

nBusyReply   A value from the **SERVERCALL** enumeration, which is defined in COMPOBJ.H. It can have any one of the following values:

- **SERVERCALL_ISHANDLED**   The application can accept calls but may fail in processing a particular call.

- **SERVERCALL_REJECTED**   The application probably will never be able to process a call.

- **SERVERCALL_RETRYLATER**   The application is temporarily in a state in which it cannot process a call.

Remarks

This function sets the application's "busy reply." The **BeginBusyState** and **EndBusyState** functions control the application's busy state.

When an application has been made busy with a call to **BeginBusyState**, it responds to calls from the OLE system DLLs with a value determined by the last setting of **SetBusyReply**. The calling application uses this busy reply to determine what action to take.

By default, the busy reply is **SERVERCALL_RETRYLATER**. This reply causes the calling application to retry the call as soon as possible.

See Also: **COleMessageFilter::BeginBusyState**, **COleMessageFilter::EndBusyState**

COleMessageFilter::SetMessagePendingDelay

void SetMessagePendingDelay(DWORD *nTimeout* **= 5000);**

Parameters

nTimeout   Number of milliseconds for the message-pending delay.

Remarks

Determines how long the calling application waits for a response from the called application before taking further action.

This function works in concert with **SetRetryReply**.

See Also: **COleMessageFilter::SetRetryReply**

COleMessageFilter::SetRetryReply

void SetRetryReply(DWORD *nRetryReply* **= 0);**

Parameters

nRetryReply   Number of milliseconds between retries.

Remarks

Determines the calling application's action when it receives a busy response from a called application.

When a called application indicates that it is busy, the calling application may decide to wait until the server is no longer busy, to retry right away, or to retry after a specified interval. It may also decide to cancel the call altogether.

The caller's response is controlled by the functions **SetRetryReply** and **SetMessagePendingDelay**. **SetRetryReply** determines how long the calling application should wait between retries for a given call. **SetMessagePendingDelay** determines how long the calling application waits for a response from the server before taking further action.

Usually the defaults are acceptable and do not need to be changed. The framework retries the call every *nRetryReply* milliseconds until the call goes through or the message-pending delay has expired. A value of 0 for *nRetryReply* specifies an immediate retry, and −1 specifies cancellation of the call.

When the message-pending delay has expired, the OLE "busy dialog box" (see **COleBusyDialog**) is displayed so that the user can choose to cancel or retry the call. Call **EnableBusyDialog** to enable or disable this dialog box.

When a keyboard or mouse message is pending during a call and the call has timed out (exceeded the message-pending delay), the "not responding" dialog box is displayed. Call **EnableNotRespondingDialog** to enable or disable this dialog box. Usually this state of affairs indicates that something has gone wrong and the user is getting impatient.

When the dialogs are disabled, the current "retry reply" is always used for calls to busy applications.

See Also: COleBusyDialog, COleMessageFilter::EnableNotRespondingDialog, COleMessageFilter::EnableBusyDialog, COleMessageFilter::SetMessagePendingDelay

COleObjectFactory

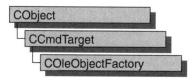

The **COleObjectFactory** class implements the OLE class factory, which creates OLE objects such as servers, automation objects, and documents.

The **COleObjectFactory** class has member functions for performing the following functions:

- Managing the registration of objects.

- Updating the OLE system register, as well as the run-time registration that informs OLE that objects are running and ready to receive messages.

- Enforcing licensing by limiting use of the control to licensed developers at design time and to licensed applications at run time.

- Registering control object factories with the OLE system registry.

For more information about object creation, see the articles "Data Objects and Data Sources (OLE)" and "Data Objects and Data Sources: Creation and Destruction". For more about registration, see the article "Registration". These articles are in *Visual C++ Programmer's Guide* online.

#include <afxdisp.h>

See Also: **COleTemplateServer**

COleObjectFactory Class Members

Construction

COleObjectFactory	Constructs a **COleObjectFactory** object.

Operations

Register	Registers this object factory with the OLE system DLLs.
RegisterAll	Registers all of the application's object factories with OLE system DLLs.
Revoke	Revokes this object factory's registration with the OLE system DLLs.

(continued)

Operations *(continued)*

RevokeAll	Revokes an application's object factories' registrations with the OLE system DLLs.
UpdateRegistryAll	Registers all of the application's object factories with the OLE system registry.

Attributes

IsRegistered	Indicates whether the object factory is registered with the OLE system DLLs.
GetClassID	Returns the OLE class ID of the objects this factory creates.

Overridables

OnCreateObject	Called by the framework to create a new object of this factory's type.
UpdateRegistry	Registers this object factory with the OLE system registry.
VerifyUserLicense	Verifies that the control is licensed for design-time use.
GetLicenseKey	Requests a unique key from the control's DLL.
VerifyLicenseKey	Verifies that the key embedded in the control matches the key embedded in the container.

Member Functions
COleObjectFactory::COleObjectFactory

COleObjectFactory(REFCLSID *clsid*, **CRuntimeClass*** *pRuntimeClass*,
↵ **BOOL** *bMultiInstance*, **LPCTSTR** *lpszProgID*);

Parameters

clsid Reference to the OLE class ID this object factory represents.

pRuntimeClass Pointer to the run-time class of the C++ objects this factory can create.

bMultiInstance Indicates whether a single instance of the application can support multiple instantiations. If **TRUE**, multiple instances of the application are launched for each request to create an object.

lpszProgID Pointer to a string containing a verbal program identifier, such as "Microsoft Excel."

Remarks

Constructs a **COleObjectFactory** object, initializes it as an unregistered object factory, and adds it to the list of factories. To use the object, however, you must register it.

For more information, see **CLSID Key** in the *OLE 2 Programmer's Reference,*
Volume 1.

See Also: **CRuntimeClass**

COleObjectFactory::GetClassID

REFCLSID GetClassID( ) const;

Return Value

Reference to the OLE class ID this factory represents.

Remarks

Returns a reference to the OLE class ID this factory represents.

For more information, see **CLSID Key** in the *OLE 2 Programmer's Reference,*
Volume 1.

See Also: **COleObjectFactory::COleObjectFactory**

COleObjectFactory::GetLicenseKey

virtual BOOL GetLicenseKey(DWORD *dwReserved***, BSTR** **pbstrKey* **);**

Return Value

Nonzero if the license-key string is not **NULL**; otherwise 0.

Parameters

dwReserved   Reserved for future use.

pbstrKey   Pointer to a **BSTR** that will store the license key.

Remarks

Requests a unique license key from the control's DLL and stores it in the **BSTR**
pointed to by *pbstrKey*.

The default implementation of this function returns 0 and stores nothing in the **BSTR**.
If you use MFC ActiveX ControlWizard to create your project, ControlWizard
supplies an override that retrieves the control's license key.

See Also: **COleObjectFactory::VerifyUserLicense,**
COleObjectFactory::VerifyLicenseKey

COleObjectFactory::IsRegistered

BOOL IsRegistered( ) const;

Return Value

Nonzero if the factory is registered; otherwise 0.

Remarks

Returns a nonzero value if the factory is registered with the OLE system DLLs.

See Also: COleObjectFactory::Register, COleObjectFactory::Revoke

---

COleObjectFactory::OnCreateObject

virtual CCmdTarget* OnCreateObject( );

Return Value

A pointer to the created object. It can throw a memory exception if it fails.

Remarks

Called by the framework to create a new object. Override this function to create the object from something other than the **CRuntimeClass** passed to the constructor.

See Also: COleObjectFactory::COleObjectFactory, CRuntimeClass

---

COleObjectFactory::Register

BOOL Register( );

Return Value

Nonzero if the factory is successfully registered; otherwise 0.

Remarks

Registers this object factory with the OLE system DLLs. This function is usually called by **CWinApp::InitInstance** when the application is launched.

See Also: COleObjectFactory::Revoke, COleObjectFactory::RegisterAll, CWinApp::InitInstance

---

COleObjectFactory::RegisterAll

static BOOL PASCAL RegisterAll( );

Return Value

Nonzero if the factories are successfully registered; otherwise 0.

Remarks

Registers all of the application's object factories with the OLE system DLLs. This function is usually called by **CWinApp::InitInstance** when the application is launched.

See Also: **COleObjectFactory::Revoke**, **COleObjectFactory::Register**, **CWinApp::InitInstance**

COleObjectFactory::Revoke

void Revoke( );

Remarks

Revokes this object factory's registration with the OLE system DLLs. The framework calls this function automatically before the application terminates. If necessary, call it from an override of **CWinApp::ExitInstance**.

See Also: **COleObjectFactory::RevokeAll**, **COleObjectFactory::Register**, **CWinApp::ExitInstance**

COleObjectFactory::RevokeAll

static void PASCAL RevokeAll( );

Remarks

Revokes all of the application's object factories' registrations with the OLE system DLLs. The framework calls this function automatically before the application terminates. If necessary, call it from an override of **CWinApp::ExitInstance**.

See Also: **COleObjectFactory::Revoke**, **COleObjectFactory::RegisterAll**, **CWinApp::ExitInstance**

COleObjectFactory::UpdateRegistry

void UpdateRegistry(LPCTSTR *lpszProgID* **= NULL);**
virtual void UpdateRegistry(BOOL *bRegister* **) = 0;**

Parameters

lpszProgID   Pointer to a string containing the human-readable program identifier, such as "Excel.Document.5."

bRegister   Determines whether the control class's object factory is to be registered.

Remarks

Brief discussions of the two forms for this function follow:

- **UpdateRegistry(** *lpszProgID* **)** Registers this object factory with the OLE system registry. This function is usually called by **CWinApp::InitInstance** when the application is launched.

- **UpdateRegistry(** *bRegister* **)** This form of the function is overridable. If *bRegister* is **TRUE**, this function registers the control class with the system registry. Otherwise, it unregisters the class.

  If you use MFC ActiveX ControlWizard to create your project, ControlWizard supplies an override to this pure virtual function.

See Also: **COleObjectFactory::Revoke, COleObjectFactory::Register, COleObjectFactory::UpdateRegistryAll, CWinApp::InitInstance**

COleObjectFactory::UpdateRegistryAll

static void PASCAL UpdateRegistryAll( );

Remarks

Registers all of the application's object factories with the OLE system registry. This function is usually called by **CWinApp::InitInstance** when the application is launched.

See Also: **COleObjectFactory::Revoke, COleObjectFactory::Register, COleObjectFactory::UpdateRegistry, CWinApp::InitInstance**

COleObjectFactory::VerifyLicenseKey

virtual BOOL VerifyLicenseKey(BSTR *bstrKey* **);**

Return Value

Nonzero if the run-time license is valid; otherwise 0.

Parameters

bstrKey A **BSTR** storing the container's version of the license string.

Remarks

This function verifies that the container is licensed to use the OLE control. The default version calls **GetLicenseKey** to get a copy of the control's license string and compares it with the string in *bstrKey*. If the two strings match, the function returns a nonzero value; otherwise it returns 0.

You can override this function to provide customized verification of the license.

The function **VerifyUserLicense** verifies the design-time license.

See Also: **COleObjectFactory::VerifyUserLicense**,
COleObjectFactory::GetLicenseKey

COleObjectFactory::VerifyUserLicense

virtual BOOL VerifyUserLicense( );

Return Value

Nonzero if the design-time license is valid; otherwise 0.

Remarks

Verifies the design-time license for the OLE control.

See Also: **COleObjectFactory::VerifyLicenseKey**,
COleObjectFactory::GetLicenseKey

COlePasteSpecialDialog

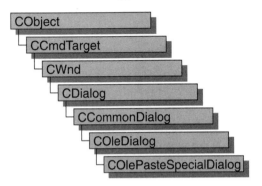

The **COlePasteSpecialDialog** class is used for the OLE Paste Special dialog box. Create an object of class **COlePasteSpecialDialog** when you want to call this dialog box. After a **COlePasteSpecialDialog** object has been constructed, you can use the **AddFormat** and **AddStandardFormats** member functions to add Clipboard formats to the dialog box. You can also use the **m_ps** structure to initialize the values or states of controls in the dialog box. The **m_ps** structure is of type **OLEUIPASTESPECIAL**.

For more information, see the **OLEUIPASTESPECIAL** structure in the *OLE 2.01 User Interface Library*.

For more information regarding OLE-specific dialog boxes, see the article "Dialog Boxes in OLE" in *Visual C++ Programmer's Guide* online.

#include <afxodlgs.h>

See Also: COleDialog

COlePasteSpecialDialog Class Members

Data Members

m_ps	A structure of type **OLEUIPASTESPECIAL** that controls the function of the dialog box.

Construction

COlePasteSpecialDialog	Constructs a **COlePasteSpecialDialog** object.

Operations and Attributes

DoModal	Displays the OLE Paste Special dialog box.
AddFormat	Adds custom formats to the list of formats your application can paste.
AddStandardFormats	Adds **CF_BITMAP**, **CF_DIB**, **CF_METAFILEPICT**, and optionally **CF_LINKSOURCE** to the list of formats your application can paste.
CreateItem	Creates the item in the container document using the specified format.
GetSelectionType	Gets the type of selection chosen.
GetDrawAspect	Tells whether to draw item as an icon or not.
GetIconicMetafile	Gets a handle to the metafile associated with the iconic form of this item.
GetPasteIndex	Gets the index of available paste options that was chosen by the user.

Member Functions
COlePasteSpecialDialog::AddFormat

> void **AddFormat**(const **FORMATETC&** *fmt*, **LPTSTR** *lpstrFormat*,
> ↪ **LPTSTR** *lpstrResult*, **DWORD** *flags*);
> void **AddFormat**(**UINT** *cf*, **DWORD** *tymed*, **UINT** *nFormatID*,
> ↪ **BOOL** *bEnableIcon*, **BOOL** *bLink*);

Parameters

fmt   Reference to the data type to add.

lpstrFormat   String that describes the format to the user.

lpstrResult   String that describes the result if this format is chosen in the dialog box.

flags   The different linking and embedding options available for this format. This flag is a bitwise combination of one or more of the different values in the **OLEUIPASTEFLAG** enumerated type.

cf   The clipboard format to add.

tymed   The types of media available in this format. This is a bitwise combination of one or more of the values in the **TYMED** enumerated type.

nFormatID   The ID of the string that identifies this format. The format of this string is two separate strings separated by a '\n' character. The first string is the same that would be passed in the *lpstrFormat* parameter, and the second is the same as the *lpstrResult* parameter.

bEnableIcon   Flag that determines whether the Display As Icon check box is enabled when this format is chosen in the list box.

bLink   Flag that determines whether the Paste Link radio button is enabled when this format is chosen in the list box.

Remarks

Call this function to add new formats to the list of formats your application can support in a Paste Special operation. This function can be called to add either standard formats such as **CF_TEXT** or **CF_TIFF** or custom formats that your application has registered with the system. For more information about pasting data objects into your application, see the article "Data Objects and Data Sources: Manipulation" in *Visual C++ Programmer's Guide* online.

For more information, see the **TYMED** enumeration type and the **FORMATETC** structure in the *OLE 2 Programmer's Reference, Volume 1*.

For more information, see the **OLEUIPASTEFLAG** enumerated type in the *OLE 2.01 User Interface Library*.

See Also: COlePasteSpecialDialog::AddStandardFormats

COlePasteSpecialDialog::AddStandardFormats

void AddStandardFormats(BOOL *bEnableLink* **= TRUE);**

Parameters

bEnableLink   Flag that determines whether to add **CF_LINKSOURCE** to the list of formats your application can paste.

Remarks

Call this function to add the following Clipboard formats to the list of formats your application can support in a Paste Special operation:

- **CF_BITMAP**
- **CF_DIB**
- **CF_METAFILEPICT**
- **"Embedded Object"**
- (optionally) **"Link Source"**

These formats are used to support embedding and linking.

See Also: COlePasteSpecialDialog::AddFormat

COlePasteSpecialDialog::COlePasteSpecialDialog

COlePasteSpecialDialog(DWORD *dwFlags* = **PSF_SELECTPASTE,**
↪ **COleDataObject*** *pDataObject* = **NULL, CWnd*** *pParentWnd* = **NULL);**

Parameters

dwFlags   Creation flag, contains any number of the following flags combined using the bitwise-OR operator:

- **PSF_SELECTPASTE**   Specifies that the Paste radio button will be checked initially when the dialog box is called. Cannot be used in combination with **PSF_SELECTPASTELINK**. This is the default.

- **PSF_SELECTPASTELINK**   Specifies that the Paste Link radio button will be checked initially when the dialog box is called. Cannot be used in combination with **PSF_SELECTPASTE**.

- **PSF_CHECKDISPLAYASICON**   Specifies that the Display As Icon check box will be checked initially when the dialog box is called.

- **PSF_SHOWHELP**   Specifies that the Help button will be displayed when the dialog box is called.

pDataObject   Points to the **COleDataObject** for pasting. If this value is **NULL**, it gets the **COleDataObject** from the Clipboard.

pParentWnd   Points to the parent or owner window object (of type **CWnd**) to which the dialog object belongs. If it is **NULL**, the parent window of the dialog box is set to the main application window.

Remarks

This function only constructs a **COlePasteSpecialDialog** object. To display the dialog box, call the **DoModal** function.

For more information, see the **OLEUIPASTEFLAG** enumerated type in the *OLE 2.01 User Interface Library*.

See Also: **COleDataObject, COlePasteSpecialDialog::DoModal**

COlePasteSpecialDialog::CreateItem

BOOL CreateItem(COleClientItem* *pNewItem* **);**

Return Value

Nonzero if the item was created successfully; otherwise 0.

Parameters

pNewItem   Points to a **COleClientItem** instance. Cannot be **NULL**.

Remarks

Call this function to create the new item that was chosen in the Paste Special dialog box. This function should only be called after **DoModal** returns **IDOK**.

See Also: **COleClientItem, COlePasteSpecialDialog::DoModal, COlePasteSpecialDialog::GetSelectionType, COlePasteSpecialDialog::COlePasteSpecialDialog**

COlePasteSpecialDialog::DoModal

virtual int DoModal( );

Return Value

Completion status for the dialog box. One of the following values:

- **IDOK** if the dialog box was successfully displayed.

- **IDCANCEL** if the user canceled the dialog box.

- **IDABORT** if an error occurred. If **IDABORT** is returned, call the **COleDialog::GetLastError** member function to get more information about the type of error that occurred. For a listing of possible errors, see the **OleUIPasteSpecial** function in the *OLE 2.01 User Interface Library*.

Remarks

Call this function to display the OLE Paste Special dialog box.

If you want to initialize the various dialog box controls by setting members of the **m_ps** structure, you should do this before calling **DoModal**, but after the dialog object is constructed.

If **DoModal** returns **IDOK**, you can call other member functions to retrieve the settings or information input by the user into the dialog box.

See Also: **COleDataObject, COleDialog::GetLastError, CDialog::DoModal, COlePasteSpecialDialog::COlePasteSpecialDialog, COlePasteSpecialDialog::GetDrawAspect, COlePasteSpecialDialog::GetIconicMetafile, COlePasteSpecialDialog::GetPasteIndex, COlePasteSpecialDialog::GetSelectionType**

COlePasteSpecialDialog::GetDrawAspect

DVASPECT GetDrawAspect( ) const;

Return Value

The method needed to render the object.

- **DVASPECT_CONTENT**   Returned if the Display As Icon check box was not checked when the dialog box was dismissed.

- **DVASPECT_ICON**   Returned if the Display As Icon check box was checked when the dialog box was dismissed.

Remarks

Call this function to determine if the user chose to display the selected item as an icon. Only call this function after **DoModal** returns **IDOK**.

For more information on drawing aspect, see the **FORMATETC** structure in the *OLE 2 Programmer's Reference, Volume 1.*

See Also: COlePasteSpecialDialog::DoModal

COlePasteSpecialDialog::GetIconicMetafile

HGLOBAL GetIconicMetafile( ) const;

Return Value

The handle to the metafile containing the iconic aspect of the selected item, if the Display As Icon check box was selected when the dialog box was dismissed by choosing **OK**; otherwise **NULL**.

Remarks

Gets the metafile associated with the item selected by the user.

**See Also: COlePasteSpecialDialog::GetDrawAspect,
COlePasteSpecialDialog::DoModal**

COlePasteSpecialDialog::GetPasteIndex

int GetPasteIndex( ) const;

Return Value

The index into the array of **OLEUIPASTEENTRY** structures that was selected by the user. The format that corresponds to the selected index should be used when performing the paste operation.

Remarks

Gets the index value associated with the entry the user selected.

For more information, see the **OLEUIPASTEENTRY** structure in the *OLE 2.01 User Interface Library.*

See Also: COlePasteSpecialDialog::DoModal

COlePasteSpecialDialog::GetSelectionType

UINT GetSelectionType( ) const;

Return Value

Returns type of selection made.

Remarks

Call this function to determine the type of selection the user made.

The return type values are specified by the **Selection** enumeration type declared in the **COlePasteSpecialDialog** class.

```
enum Selection
{
    pasteLink,
    pasteNormal,
    pasteOther,
    pasteStatic
};
```

Brief desccriptions of these values follow:

- **COlePasteSpecialDialog::pasteLink** The Paste Link radio button was checked and the chosen format was a standard OLE format.

- **COlePasteSpecialDialog::pasteNormal** The Paste radio button was checked and the chosen format was a standard OLE format.

- **COlePasteSpecialDialog::pasteOther** The selected format is not a standard OLE format.

- **COlePasteSpecialDialog::pasteStatic** The chosen format was a metafile.

See Also: **COlePasteSpecialDialog::DoModal**

Data Members

COlePasteSpecialDialog::m_ps

Remarks

Structure of type **OLEUIPASTESPECIAL** used to control the behavior of the Paste Special dialog box. Members of this structure can be modified directly or through member functions.

For more information, see the **OLEUIPASTESPECIAL** structure in the *OLE 2.01 User Interface Library*.

See Also: **COlePasteSpecialDialog::COlePasteSpecialDialog,**
COlePasteSpecialDialog::DoModal

COlePropertiesDialog

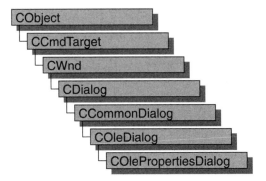

The **COlePropertiesDialog** class encapsulates the Windows common OLE Object Properties dialog box. Common OLE Object Properties dialog boxes provide an easy way to display and modify the properties of an OLE document item in a manner consistent with Windows standards. These properties include, among others, information on the file represented by the document item, options for displaying the icon and image scaling, and information on the item's link (if the item is linked).

To use a **COlePropertiesDialog** object, first create the object using the **COlePropertiesDialog** constructor. After the dialog box has been constructed, call the **DoModal** member function to display the dialog box and allow the user to modify any properties of the item. **DoModal** returns whether the user selected the OK (**IDOK**) or the Cancel (**IDCANCEL**) button. In addition to the OK and Cancel buttons, there is an Apply button. When the user selects Apply, any changes made to the properties of the document item are applied to the item and its image is automatically updated, but remains active.

The **m_psh** data member is a pointer to a **PROPSHEETHEADER** structure, and in most cases you will not need to access it explicitly. One exception is when you need additional property pages beyond the default General, View, and Link pages. In this case, you can modify the **m_psh** data member to include your custom pages before calling the **DoModal** member function.

For more information on OLE dialog boxes, see the article "Dialog Boxes in OLE" in *Visual C++ Programmer's Guide* online.

#include <afxodlgs.h>

See Also: COleDialog, CPropertyPage

COlePropertiesDialog Class Members

Construction

COlePropertiesDialog	Constructs a **COlePropertiesDialog** object.

Data Members

m_gp	A structure used to initialize the "General" page of a **COlePropertiesDialog** object.
m_lp	A structure used to initialize the "Link" page of a **COlePropertiesDialog** object.
m_op	A structure used to initialize the **COlePropertiesDialog** object.
m_psh	A structure used to add additional custom property pages.
m_vp	A structure used to customize the "View" page of a **COlePropertiesDialog** object.

Operations

DoModal	Displays the dialog box and allows the user to make a selection.

Overridables

OnApplyScale	Called by the framework when the scaling of the document item has changed.

Member Functions

COlePropertiesDialog::COlePropertiesDialog

COlePropertiesDialog(COleClientItem* *pItem***, UINT** *nScaleMin* **= 10,**
↪ **UINT** *nScaleMax* **= 500, CWnd*** *pParentWnd* **= NULL);**

Parameters

pItem   Pointer to the document item whose properties are being accessed.

nScaleMin   Minimum scaling percentage for the document item image.

nScaleMax   Maximum scaling percentage for the document item image.

pParentWnd   Pointer to the dialog box's parent or owner.

Remarks

Creates a **COlePropertiesDialog** object. Derive your common OLE Object Properties dialog class from **COlePropertiesDialog** in order to implement scaling for your document items. Any dialog boxes implemented by an instance of this class will not support scaling of the document item.

By default, the common OLE Object Properties dialog box has three default pages:

- General

  This page contains system information for the file represented by the selected document item. From this page, the user can convert the selected item to another type.

- View

  This page contains options for displaying the item, changing the icon, and changing the scaling of the image.

- Link

  This page contains options for changing the location of the linked item and updating the linked item. From this page, the user can break the link of the selected item.

To add pages beyond those provided by default, modify the **m_psh** member variable before exiting the constructor of your **COlePropertiesDialog**-derived class. This is an advanced implementation of the **COlePropertiesDialog** constructor.

See Also: COlePropertiesDialog::OnApplyScale

COlePropertiesDialog::DoModal

virtual int DoModal( );

Return Value

IDOK or **IDCANCEL** if successful; otherwise 0. **IDOK** and **IDCANCEL** are constants that indicate whether the user selected the OK or Cancel button.

If **IDCANCEL** is returned, you can call the Windows **CommDlgExtendedError** function to determine whether an error occurred.

Remarks

Call this member function to display the Windows common OLE Object Properties dialog box and allow the user to view and/or change the various properties of the document item.

See Also: COlePropertiesDialog::OnApplyScale, COlePropertiesDialog::m_psh

---

COlePropertiesDialog::OnApplyScale

virtual BOOL OnApplyScale(COleClientItem* *pItem,* **int** *nCurrentScale,*
↳ **BOOL** *bRelativeToOrig* **);**

Return Value

Nonzero if handled; otherwise 0.

Parameters

> *pItem* Pointer to the document item whose properties are being accessed.
>
> *nCurrentScale* Numerical value of the dialog scale.
>
> *bRelativeToOrig* Indicates whether scaling applies to the original size of the document item.

Remarks

> Called by the framework when the scaling value has changed and either OK or Apply was selected. The default implementation does nothing. You must override this function to enable the scaling controls.
>
> **Note** Before the common OLE Object Properties dialog box is displayed, the framework calls this function with a **NULL** for *pItem* and a−1 for *nCurrentScale*. This is done to determine if the scaling controls should be enabled.
>
> **See Also:** **COlePropertiesDialog::DoModal**

Data Members
COlePropertiesDialog::m_gp

Remarks

> A structure of type **OLEUIGNRLPROPS**, used to initialize the General page of the OLE Object Properties dialog box. This page shows the type and size of an embedding and allows the user access to the Convert dialog box. This page also shows the link destination if the object is a link.
>
> For more information on the **OLEUIGNRLPROPS** structure, see the OLE documentation.

COlePropertiesDialog::m_lp

Remarks

> A structure of type **OLEUILINKPROPS**, used to initialize the Link page of the OLE Object Properties dialog box. This page shows the location of the linked item and allows the user to update, or break, the link to the item.
>
> For more information on the **OLEUILINKPROPS** structure, see the OLE documentation.

COlePropertiesDialog::m_op

Remarks

A structure of type **OLEUIOBJECTPROPS**, used to initialize the common OLE Object Properties dialog box. This structure contains members used to initialize the General, Link, and View pages.

For more information, see the **OLEUIOBJECTPROPS** and **OLEUILINKPROPS** structures in the OLE documentation.

COlePropertiesDialog::m_psh

Remarks

A structure of type **PROPSHEETHEADER**, whose members store the characteristics of the dialog object. After constructing a **COlePropertiesDialog** object, you can use **m_psh** to set various aspects of the dialog box before calling the **DoModal** member function.

If you modify the **m_psh** data member directly, you will override any default behavior.

For more information on the **PROPSHEETHEADER** structure, see the Win32 SDK documentation.

See Also: **COlePropertiesDialog::DoModal**

COlePropertiesDialog::m_vp

Remarks

A structure of type **OLEUIVIEWPROPS**, used to initialize the View page of the OLE Object Properties dialog box. This page allows the user to toggle between "content" and "iconic" views of the object, and change its scaling within the container. It also allows the user access to the Change Icon dialog box when the object is being displayed as an icon.

For more information on the **OLEUIVIEWPROPS** structure, see the OLE documentation.

COlePropertyPage

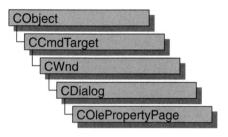

The **COlePropertyPage** class is used to display the properties of a custom control in a graphical interface, similar to a dialog box. For instance, a property page may include an edit control that allows the user to view and modify the control's caption property.

Each custom or stock control property can have a dialog control that allows the control's user to view the current property value and modify that value if needed.

For more information on using **COlePropertyPage**, see the article "ActiveX Controls: Property Pages" in *Visual C++ Programmer's Guide* online and "Modifying the Default Property Page" in *Visual C++ Tutorials* online.

#include <afxctl.h>

See Also: CDialog

COlePropertyPage Class Members

Construction

COlePropertyPage	Constructs a **COlePropertyPage** object.

Operations

GetObjectArray	Returns the array of objects being edited by the property page.
SetModifiedFlag	Sets a flag indicating whether the user has modified the property page.
IsModified	Indicates whether the user has modified the property page.
GetPageSite	Returns a pointer to the property page's **IPropertyPageSite** interface.
SetDialogResource	Sets the property page's dialog resource.
SetPageName	Sets the property page's name (caption).
SetHelpInfo	Sets the property page's brief help text, the name of its help file, and its help context.

Operations *(continued)*

GetControlStatus	Indicates whether the user has modified the value in the control.
SetControlStatus	Sets a flag indicating whether the user has modified the value in the control.
IgnoreApply	Determines which controls do not enable the Apply button.

Overridables

OnEditProperty	Called by the framework when the user edits a property.
OnHelp	Called by the framework when the user invokes help.
OnInitDialog	Called by the framework when the property page is initialized.
OnObjectsChanged	Called by the framework when another OLE control, with new properties, is chosen.
OnSetPageSite	Called by the framework when the property frame provides the page's site.

Member Functions
COlePropertyPage::COlePropertyPage

COlePropertyPage(UINT *idDlg***, UINT** *idCaption* **);**

Parameters
idDlg   Resource ID of the dialog template.

idCaption   Resource ID of the property page's caption.

Remarks
When you implement a subclass of **COlePropertyPage**, your subclass's constructor should use the **COlePropertyPage** constructor to identify the dialog-template resource on which the property page is based and the string resource containing its caption.

COlePropertyPage::GetControlStatus

BOOL GetControlStatus(UINT *nID* **);**

Return Value
TRUE if the control value has been modified; otherwise **FALSE**.

Parameters
nID   Resource ID of a property page control.

Remarks

Call this function to determine whether the user has modified the value of the property page control with the specified resource ID.

See Also: COlePropertyPage::SetControlStatus

COlePropertyPage::GetObjectArray

LPDISPATCH FAR* GetObjectArray(ULONG FAR* *pnObjects*);

Return Value

Pointer to an array of **IDispatch** pointers, which are used to access the properties of each control on the property page. The caller must not release these interface pointers.

Parameters

pnObjects   Pointer to an unsigned long integer that will receive the number of objects being edited by the page.

Remarks

Each property page object maintains an array of pointers to the **IDispatch** interfaces of the objects being edited by the page. This function sets its *pnObjects* argument to the number of elements in that array and returns a pointer to the first element of the array.

COlePropertyPage::GetPageSite

LPPROPERTYPAGESITE GetPageSite( );

Return Value

A pointer to the property page's **IPropertyPageSite** interface.

Remarks

Call this function to get a pointer to the property page's **IPropertyPageSite** interface.

Controls and containers cooperate so that users can browse and edit control properties. The control provides property pages, each of which is an OLE object that allows the user to edit a related set of properties. The container provides a property frame that displays the property pages. For each page, the property frame provides a page site, which supports the **IPropertyPageSite** interface.

See Also: COlePropertyPage::OnSetPageSite

COlePropertyPage::IgnoreApply

void IgnoreApply(UINT *nID* **);**

Parameters

nID   ID of the control to be ignored.

Remarks

The property page's Apply button is enabled only when values of property page controls have been changed. Use this function to specify controls that do not cause the Apply button to be enabled when their values change.

See Also: COlePropertyPage::GetControlStatus

COlePropertyPage::IsModified

BOOL IsModified( );

Return Value

TRUE if the property page has been modified.

Remarks

Call this function to determine whether the user has changed any values on the property page.

See Also: COlePropertyPage::SetModifiedFlag

COlePropertyPage::OnEditProperty

virtual BOOL OnEditProperty(DISPID *dispid* **);**

Return Value

The default implementation returns **FALSE**. Overrides of this function should return **TRUE**.

Parameters

dispid   Dispatch ID of the property being edited.

Remarks

The framework calls this function when a specific property is to be edited. You can override it to set the focus to the appropriate control on the page. The default implementation does nothing and returns **FALSE**.

COlePropertyPage::OnHelp

virtual BOOL OnHelp(LPCTSTR *lpszHelpDir* **);**

Return Value

The default implementation returns **FALSE**.

Parameters

lpszHelpDir   Directory containing the property page's help file.

Remarks

The framework calls this function when the user requests online help. Override it if your property page must perform any special action when the user accesses help. The default implementation does nothing and returns **FALSE**, which instructs the framework to call WinHelp.

COlePropertyPage::OnInitDialog

virtual BOOL OnInitDialog( );

Return Value

The default implementation returns **FALSE**.

Remarks

The framework calls this function when the property page's dialog is initialized. Override it if any special action is required when the dialog is initialized. The default implementation calls **CDialog::OnInitDialog** and returns **FALSE**.

See Also: CDialog::OnInitDialog

COlePropertyPage::OnObjectsChanged

virtual void OnObjectsChanged( );

Remarks

When viewing the properties of an OLE control in the developer environment, a modeless dialog box is used to display its property pages. If another control is selected, a different set of property pages must be displayed for the new set of properties. The framework calls this function to notify the property page of the change.

Override this function to receive notification of this action and perform any special actions.

COlePropertyPage::OnSetPageSite

virtual void OnSetPageSite( );

Remarks

The framework calls this function when the property frame provides the property page's page site. The default implementation loads the page's caption and attempts to determine the page's size from the dialog resource. Override this function if your property page requires any further action; your override should call the base-class implementation.

See Also: COlePropertyPage::GetPageSite

COlePropertyPage::SetControlStatus

BOOL SetControlStatus(UINT *nID*, BOOL *IsDirty*);

Return Value

TRUE, if the specified control was set; otherwise **FALSE**.

Parameters

nID   Contains the ID of a property page control.

IsDirty   Specifies if a field of the property page has been modified. Set to **TRUE** if the field has been modified, **FALSE** if it has not been modified.

Remarks

Call this function to change the status of a property page control.

If the status of a property page control is dirty when the property page is closed or the Apply button is chosen, the control's property will be updated with the appropriate value.

See Also: COlePropertyPage::GetControlStatus

COlePropertyPage::SetDialogResource

void SetDialogResource(HGLOBAL *hDialog*);

Parameters

hDialog   Handle to the property page's dialog resource.

Remarks

Call this function to set the property page's dialog resource.

COlePropertyPage::SetHelpInfo

void SetHelpInfo(LPCTSTR *lpszDocString***, LPCTSTR** *lpszHelpFile* **= NULL,**
↪ **DWORD** *dwHelpContext* **= 0);**

Parameters

lpszDocString   A string containing brief help information for display in a status bar or other location.

lpszHelpFile   Name of the property page's help file.

dwHelpContext   Help context for the property page.

Remarks

Use this function to specify "tool tip" information, the help filename, and the help context for your property page.

See Also: COlePropertyPage::OnHelp

COlePropertyPage::SetModifiedFlag

void SetModifiedFlag(BOOL *bModified* **= TRUE);**

Parameters

bModified   Specifies the new value for the property page's modified flag.

Remarks

Use this function to indicate whether the user has modified the property page.

See Also: COlePropertyPage::IsModified

COlePropertyPage::SetPageName

void SetPageName(LPCTSTR *lpszPageName* **);**

Parameters

lpszPageName   Pointer to a string containing the property page's name.

Remarks

Use this function to set the property page's name, which the property frame will typically display on the page's tab.

COleResizeBar

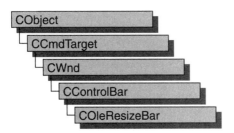

An object of the class **COleResizeBar** is a type of control bar that supports resizing of in-place OLE items. **COleResizeBar** objects appear as a **CRectTracker** with a hatched border and outer resize handles.

COleResizeBar objects are usually embedded members of frame-window objects derived from the **COleIPFrameWnd** class.

For more information, see the article Activation in *Visual C++ Programmer's Guide* online.

#include <afxole.h>

See Also: **COleServerDoc, CRectTracker, COleIPFrameWnd**

COleResizeBar Class Members

Construction

COleResizeBar	Constructs a **COleResizeBar** object.
Create	Creates and initializes a Windows child window and associates it to the **COleResizeBar** object.

Member Functions
COleResizeBar::Create

> **BOOL Create(CWnd*** *pParentWnd***, DWORD** *dwStyle* **= WS_CHILD | WS_VISIBLE,**
> ↪ **UINT** *nID* **= AFX_IDW_RESIZE_BAR);**

Return Value

Nonzero if the resize bar was created; otherwise 0.

Parameters

pParentWnd   Pointer to the parent window of the resize bar.

dwStyle   Specifies the window style attributes.

nID   The resize bar's child window ID.

Remarks

Creates a child window and associates it with the **COleResizeBar** object.

See Also: CWnd::Create, **CControlBar**

COleResizeBar::COleResizeBar

COleResizeBar( );

Remarks

Constructs a **COleResizeBar** object. Call **Create** to create the resize bar object.

See Also: COleResizeBar::Create

COleSafeArray

Class **COleSafeArray** is a class for working with arrays of arbitrary type and dimension. **COleSafeArray** derives from the OLE **VARIANT** structure. The OLE **SAFEARRAY** member functions are available through **COleSafeArray**, as well as a set of member functions specifically designed for one-dimensional arrays of bytes.

#include <afxdisp.h>

See Also: **COleVariant**, **CRecordSet**, **CDatabase**

COleSafeArray Class Members

Construction

COleSafeArray	Constructs a **COleSafeArray** object.

Operations

Attach	Gives control of the existing **VARIANT** array to the **COleSafeArray** object.
Clear	Frees all data in the underlying **VARIANT**.
Detach	Detaches the **VARIANT** array from the **COleSafeArray** object (so that the data will not be freed).

Win32 API Wrappers

AccessData	Retrieves a pointer to the array data.
AllocData	Allocates memory for the array.
AllocDescriptor	Allocates memory for the safe array descriptor.
Copy	Creates a copy of an existing array.
Create	Creates a safe array.
Destroy	Destroys an existing array.
DestroyData	Destroys data in a safe array.
DestroyDescriptor	Destroys a descriptor of a safe array.
GetDim	Returns the number of dimensions in the array.
GetElement	Retrieves a single element of the safe array.
GetElemSize	Returns the size, in bytes, of one element in a safe array.
GetLBound	Returns the lower bound for any dimension of a safe array.
GetUBound	Returns the upper bound for any dimension of a safe array.
Lock	Increments the lock count of an array and places a pointer to the array data in the array descriptor.

(continued)

Win32 API Wrappers *(continued)*

PtrOfIndex	Returns a pointer to the indexed element.
PutElement	Assigns a single element into the array.
Redim	Changes the least significant (rightmost) bound of a safe array.
UnaccessData	Decrements the lock count of an array and invalidates the pointer retrieved by **AccessData**.
Unlock	Decrements the lock count of an array so it can be freed or resized.

One-Dimensional Array Operations

CreateOneDim	Creates a one-dimensional **COleSafeArray** object.
GetOneDimSize	Returns the number of elements in the one-dimensional **COleSafeArray** object.
ResizeOneDim	Changes the number of elements in a one-dimensional **COleSafeArray** object.

Operators

operator =	Copies values into a **COleSafeArray** object (**SAFEARRAY**, **VARIANT**, **COleVariant**, or **COleSafeArray** array).
operator ==	Compares two variant arrays (**SAFEARRAY**, **VARIANT**, **COleVariant**, or **COleSafeArray** arrays).
operator LPVARIANT	Accesses the underlying **VARIANT** structure of the **COleSafeArray** object.
operator LPCVARIANT	Accesses the underlying **VARIANT** structure of the **COleSafeArray** object.

Member Functions

COleSafeArray::AccessData

void AccessData(void** *ppvData* **);**

Parameters

ppvData   A pointer to a pointer to the array data.

Remarks

Retrieves a pointer to the array data. On error, the function throws a **CMemoryException** or **COleException**.

See Also: **COleSafeArray::UnaccessData, SafeArrayAccessData**

COleSafeArray::AllocData

void AllocData( );

Remarks

Call this function to allocate memory for a safe array. On error, the function throws a **CMemoryException** or **COleException**.

See Also: **COleSafeArray::AllocDescriptor**, **SafeArrayAllocData**

COleSafeArray::AllocDescriptor

void AllocDescriptor(DWORD *dwDims* **);**

Parameters

dwDims   Number of dimensions in the safe array.

Remarks

Call this function to allocate memory for the descriptor of a safe array. On error, the function throws a **CMemoryException** or **COleException**.

See Also: **COleSafeArray::AllocData**, **SafeArrayAllocDescriptor**

COleSafeArray::Attach

void Attach(VARIANT& *varSrc* **);**

Parameters

varSrc   A **VARIANT** object. The *varSrc* parameter must have the **VARTYPE** **VT_ARRAY**.

Remarks

Call this function to give control of the data in an existing **VARIANT** array to the **COleSafeArray** object. The source **VARIANT**'s type is set to **VT_EMPTY**. This function clears the current array data, if any.

See Also: **COleSafeArray::Detach**

COleSafeArray::Clear

void Clear( );

Remarks

Call this function to clear the safe array. The function clears a safe array by setting the **VARTYPE** of the object to **VT_EMPTY**. The current contents are released and the array is freed.

See Also: **VariantClear**

COleSafeArray::COleSafeArray

COleSafeArray( );
COleSafeArray(const SAFEARRAY& *saSrc*, **VARTYPE** *vtSrc* **);**
COleSafeArray(LPCSAFEARRAY *psaSrc*, **VARTYPE** *vtSrc* **);**
COleSafeArray(const COleSafeArray& *saSrc* **);**
COleSafeArray(const VARIANT& *varSrc* **);**
COleSafeArray(LPCVARIANT *pSrc* **);**
COleSafeArray(const COleVariant& *varSrc* **);**

Parameters

saSrc An existing **COleSafeArray** object or **SAFEARRAY** to be copied into the new **COleSafeArray** object.

vtSrc The **VARTYPE** of the new **COleSafeArray** object.

psaSrc A pointer to a **SAFEARRAY** to be copied into the new **COleSafeArray** object.

varSrc An existing **VARIANT** or **COleVariant** object to be copied into the new **COleSafeArray** object.

pSrc A pointer to a **VARIANT** object to be copied into the new **COleSafeArray** object.

Remarks

All of these constructors create new **COleSafeArray** objects. If there is no parameter, an empty **COleSafeArray** object is created (**VT_EMPTY**). If the **COleSafeArray** is copied from another array whose **VARTYPE** is known implicitly (a **COleSafeArray**, **COleVariant**, or **VARIANT**), the **VARTYPE** of the source array is retained and need not be specified. If the **COleSafeArray** is copied from another array whose **VARTYPE** is not known (**SAFEARRAY**), the **VARTYPE** must be specified in the *vtSrc* parameter.

On error, the function throws a **CMemoryException** or **COleException**.

See Also: **VariantCopy**

COleSafeArray::Copy

void Copy(LPSAFEARRAY* *ppsa* **);**

Parameters

ppsa Pointer to a location in which to return the new array descriptor.

Remarks

Creates a copy of an existing safe array. On error, the function throws a **CMemoryException** or **COleException**.

See Also: **SafeArrayCopy**

COleSafeArray::Create

void Create(VARTYPE *vtSrc*, **DWORD** *dwDims*, **DWORD*** *rgElements*);
void Create(VARTYPE *vtSrc*, **DWORD** *dwDims*, **SAFEARRAYBOUND*** *rgsabounds*);

Parameters

vtSrc   The base type of the array (that is, the **VARTYPE** of each element of the array). The **VARTYPE** is restricted to a subset of the variant types. Neither the **VT_ARRAY** nor the **VT_BYREF** flag can be set. **VT_EMPTY** and **VT_NULL** are not valid base types for the array. All other types are legal.

dwDims   Number of dimensions in the array. This can be changed after the array is created with **Redim**.

rgElements   Pointer to an array of the number of elements for each dimension in the array.

rgsabounds   Pointer to a vector of bounds (one for each dimension) to allocate for the array.

Remarks

Call this function to allocate and initialize the data for the array. This function will clear the current array data if necessary. On error, the function throws a **CMemoryException**.

See Also: **SafeArrayCreate**

COleSafeArray::CreateOneDim

void CreateOneDim(VARTYPE *vtSrc*, **DWORD** *dwElements*,
↪ **void** *pvSrcData* = **NULL**, **long** *nLBound* = **0**);

Parameters

vtSrc   The base type of the array (that is, the **VARTYPE** of each element of the array).

dwElements   Number of elements in the array. This can be changed after the array is created with **ResizeOneDim**.

pvSrcData   Pointer to the data to copy into the array.

nLBound   The lower bound of the array.

Remarks

Call this function to create a new one-dimensional **COleSafeArray** object. The function allocates and initializes the data for the array, copying the specified data if the pointer *pvSrcData* is not **NULL**.

On error, the function throws a **CMemoryException**.

See Also: **COleSafeArray::GetOneDimSize**, **COleSafeArray::ResizeOneDim**, **COleSafeArray::Create**

COleSafeArray::Destroy

void Destroy( );

Remarks

Call this function to destroy an existing array descriptor and all the data in the array. If objects are stored in the array, each object is released. On error, the function throws a **CMemoryException** or **COleException**.

See Also: **COleSafeArray::DestroyData**, **COleSafeArray::DestroyDescriptor**, **SafeArrayDestroy**

COleSafeArray::DestroyData

void DestroyData( );

Remarks

Call this function to destroy all the data in a safe array. If objects are stored in the array, each object is released. On error, the function throws a **CMemoryException** or **COleException**.

See Also: **COleSafeArray::Destroy**, **COleSafeArray::DestroyDescriptor**, **SafeArrayDestroyData**

COleSafeArray::DestroyDescriptor

void DestroyDescriptor( );

Remarks

Call this function to destroy a descriptor of a safe array. On error, the function throws a **CMemoryException** or **COleException**.

See Also: **COleSafeArray::Destroy**, **COleSafeArray::DestroyData**, **SafeArrayDestroyDescriptor**

COleSafeArray::Detach

VARIANT Detach( );

Return Value

The underlying **VARIANT** value in the **COleSafeArray** object.

Remarks

Call this function to detach the **VARIANT** data from the **COleSafeArray** object. The function detaches the data in a safe array by setting the **VARTYPE** of the object to **VT_EMPTY**. It is the caller's responsibility to free the array by calling the Windows function **VariantClear**.

On error, the function throws a **COleException**.

See Also: COleSafeArray::Attach, VariantClear

COleSafeArray::GetDim

DWORD GetDim( );

Return Value

The number of dimensions in the safe array.

Remarks

Call this function to return the number of dimensions in the **COleSafeArray** object.

See Also: COleSafeArray::Create, COleSafeArray::Redim, SafeArrayGetDim

---

COleSafeArray::GetElement

void GetElement(long* *rgIndices***, void*** *pvData* **);**

Parameters

rgIndices   Pointer to an array of indexes for each dimension of the array.

pvData   Pointer to the location to place the element of the array.

Remarks

Call this function to retrieve a single element of the safe array. This function automatically calls the windows functions **SafeArrayLock** and **SafeArrayUnlock** before and after retrieving the element. If the data element is a string, object, or variant, the function copies the element in the correct way. The parameter *pvData* should point to a large enough buffer to contain the element.

On error, the function throws a **CMemoryException** or **COleException**.

See Also: COleSafeArray::PutElement, SafeArrayGetElement

COleSafeArray::GetElemSize

DWORD GetElemSize( );

Return Value

The size, in bytes, of the elements of a safe array.

Remarks

Call this function to retrieve the size of an element in a **COleSafeArray** object.

See Also: COleSafeArray::GetDim, SafeArrayGetElemSize

COleSafeArray::GetLBound

void GetLBound(DWORD *dwDim*, **long*** *pLBound* **);**

Parameters

dwDim   The array dimension for which to get the lower bound.

pLBound   Pointer to the location to return the lower bound.

Remarks

Call this function to return the lower bound for any dimension of a **COleSafeArray** object. On error, the function throws a **COleException**.

See Also: COleSafeArray::GetUBound, SafeArrayGetLBound

COleSafeArray::GetOneDimSize

DWORD GetOneDimSize( );

Return Value

The number of elements in the one-dimensional safe array.

Remarks

Call this function to return the number of elements in the one-dimensional **COleSafeArray** object.

See Also: COleSafeArray::CreateOneDimSize, COleSafeArray::ResizeOneDim, SafeArrayRedim

---

COleSafeArray::GetUBound

void GetUBound(DWORD *dwDim*, **long*** *pUBound* **);**

Parameters

dwDim   The array dimension for which to get the upper bound.

pUBound   Pointer to the location to return the upper bound.

Remarks

Call this function to return the upper bound for any dimension of a safe array. On error, the function throws a **COleException**.

See Also: **COleSafeArray::GetLBound**, **SafeArrayGetUBound**

COleSafeArray::Lock

void Lock( );

Remarks

Call this function to increment the lock count of an array and place a pointer to the array data in the array descriptor. On error, it throws a **COleException**.

The pointer in the array descriptor is valid until **Unlock** is called. Calls to **Lock** can be nested; an equal number of calls to **Unlock** are required.

An array cannot be deleted while it is locked.

See Also: **COleSafeArray::Unlock**, **SafeArrayLock**

COleSafeArray::PtrOfIndex

void PtrOfIndex(long* *rgIndices***, void**** *ppvData* **);**

Parameters

rgIndices An array of index values that identify an element of the array. All indexes for the element must be specified.

ppvData On return, pointer to the element identified by the values in *rgIndices*.

Remarks

Call this function to return a pointer to the element specified by the index values.

See Also: **SafeArrayPtrOfIndex**

COleSafeArray::PutElement

void PutElement(long* *rgIndices***, LPVOID** *pvData* **);**

Parameters

rgIndices Pointer to an array of indexes for each dimension of the array.

pvData Pointer to the data to assign to the array. **VT_DISPATCH**, **VT_UNKNOWN**, and **VT_BSTR** variant types are pointers and do not require another level of indirection.

Remarks

Call this function to assign a single element into the array. This function automatically calls the Windows functions **SafeArrayLock** and **SafeArrayUnlock** before and after assigning the element. If the data element is a string, object, or variant, the function copies it correctly, and if the existing element is a string, object, or variant, it is cleared correctly.

Note that you can have multiple locks on an array, so you can put elements into an array while the array is locked by other operations.

On error, the function throws a **CMemoryException** or **COleException**.

See Also: **COleSafeArray::GetElement, SafeArrayPutElement**

COleSafeArray::Redim

void Redim(SAFEARRAYBOUND* *psaboundNew* **);**

Parameters

psaboundNew Pointer to a new safe array bound structure containing the new array bound. Only the least significant dimension of an array may be changed.

Remarks

Call this function to change the least significant (rightmost) bound of a safe array. On error, the function throws a **COleException**.

See Also: **COleSafeArray::Create, COleSafeArray::GetDim, COleSafeArray::ResizeOneDim, SafeArrayRedim**

COleSafeArray::ResizeOneDim

void ResizeOneDim(DWORD *dwElements* **);**

Parameters

dwElements Number of elements in the one-dimensional safe array.

Remarks

Call this function to change the number of elements in a one-dimensional **COleSafeArray** object. On error, the function throws a **COleException**.

See Also: **COleSafeArray::Redim, COleSafeArray::GetOneDimSize, COleSafeArray::CreateOneDim, SafeArrayRedim**

COleSafeArray::UnaccessData

void UnaccessData( );

Remarks

Call this function to decrement the lock count of an array and invalidate the pointer retrieved by **AccessData**. On error, the function throws a **COleException**.

See Also: **COleSafeArray::AccessData**, **SafeArrayUnaccessData**

COleSafeArray::Unlock

void Unlock( );

Remarks

Call this function to decrement the lock count of an array so it can be freed or resized. This function is called after access to the data in an array is finished. On error, it throws a **COleException**.

See Also: **COleSafeArray::Lock**, **SafeArrayUnlock**

Operators
COleSafeArray::operator =

COleSafeArray& operator =(const COleSafeArray& *saSrc* **);**
COleSafeArray& operator =(const VARIANT& *varSrc* **);**
COleSafeArray& operator =(LPCVARIANT *pSrc* **);**
COleSafeArray& operator =(const COleVariant& *varSrc* **);**

Remarks

These overloaded assignment operators copy the source value into this **COleSafeArray** object. A brief description of each operator follows:

- **operator =(** *saSrc* **)** Copies an existing **COleSafeArray** object into this object.

- **operator =(** *varSrc* **)** Copies an existing **VARIANT** or **COleVariant** array into this object.

- **operator =(** *pSrc* **)** Copies the **VARIANT** array object accessed by *pSrc* into this object.

See Also: **VariantCopy**

COleSafeArray::operator ==

BOOL operator ==(const SAFEARRAY& *saSrc* **) const;**
BOOL operator ==(LPCSAFEARRAY *pSrc* **) const;**
BOOL operator ==(const COleSafeArray& *saSrc* **) const;**
BOOL operator ==(const VARIANT& *varSrc* **) const;**
BOOL operator ==(LPCVARIANT *pSrc* **) const;**
BOOL operator ==(const COleVariant& *varSrc* **) const;**

Remarks

This operator compares two arrays (**SAFEARRAY**, **VARIANT**, **COleVariant**, or **COleSafeArray** arrays) and returns nonzero if they are equal; otherwise 0. Two arrays are equal if they have an equal number of dimensions, equal size in each dimension, and equal element values.

COleSafeArray::operator LPCVARIANT

operator LPCVARIANT( ) const;

Remarks

Call this casting operator to access the underlying **VARIANT** structure for this **COleSafeArray** object.

COleSafeArray::operator LPVARIANT

operator LPVARIANT( );

Remarks

Call this casting operator to access the underlying **VARIANT** structure for this **COleSafeArray** object.

Note that changing the value in the **VARIANT** structure accessed by the pointer returned by this function will change the value of this **COleSafeArray** object.

COleServerDoc

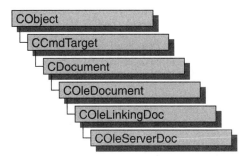

COleServerDoc is the base class for OLE server documents. A server document can contain **COleServerItem** objects, which represent the server interface to embedded or linked items. When a server application is launched by a container to edit an embedded item, the item is loaded as its own server document; the **COleServerDoc** object contains just one **COleServerItem** object, consisting of the entire document. When a server application is launched by a container to edit a linked item, an existing document is loaded from disk; a portion of the document's contents is highlighted to indicate the linked item.

COleServerDoc objects can also contain items of the **COleClientItem** class. This allows you to create container-server applications. The framework provides functions to properly store the **COleClientItem** items while servicing the **COleServerItem** objects.

If your server application does not support links, a server document will always contain only one server item, which represents the entire embedded object as a document. If your server application does support links, it must create a server item each time a selection is copied to the Clipboard.

To use **COleServerDoc**, derive a class from it and implement the **OnGetEmbeddedItem** member function, which allows your server to support embedded items. Derive a class from **COleServerItem** to implement the items in your documents, and return objects of that class from **OnGetEmbeddedItem**.

To support linked items, **COleServerDoc** provides the **OnGetLinkedItem** member function. You can use the default implementation or override it if you have your own way of managing document items.

You need one **COleServerDoc**-derived class for each type of server document your application supports. For example, if your server application supports worksheets and charts, you need two **COleServerDoc**-derived classes.

For more information on servers, see the article "Servers: Implementing a Server" in *Visual C++ Programmer's Guide* online.

#include <afxole.h>

See Also: **COleDocument**, **COleLinkingDoc**, **COleTemplateServer**, **COleServerItem**

COleServerDoc Class Members

Construction

COleServerDoc	Constructs a **COleServerDoc** object.

Attributes

IsEmbedded	Indicates whether the document is embedded in a container document or running stand-alone.
IsInPlaceActive	Returns **TRUE** if the item is currently activated in place.
GetEmbeddedItem	Returns a pointer to an item representing the entire document.
GetItemPosition	Returns the current position rectangle, relative to the container application's client area, for in-place editing.
GetItemClipRect	Returns the current clipping rectangle for in-place editing.
GetZoomFactor	Returns the zoom factor in pixels.

Operations

OnExecOleCmd	Executes a specified command or displays help for the command.
NotifyChanged	Notifies containers that the user has changed the document.
NotifyRename	Notifies containers that the user has renamed the document.
NotifySaved	Notifies containers that the user has saved the document.
NotifyClosed	Notifies containers that the user has closed the document.
SaveEmbedding	Tells the container application to save the document.
ActivateInPlace	Activates the document for in-place editing.
DeactivateAndUndo	Deactivates the server's user interface.
DiscardUndoState	Discards undo-state information.
RequestPositionChange	Changes the position of the in-place editing frame.
ScrollContainerBy	Scrolls the container document.
UpdateAllItems	Notifies containers that the user has changed the document.

Overridables

GetDocObjectServer	Override this function to create a new **CDocObjectServer** object and indicate that this document is a DocObject container.
OnUpdateDocument	Called by the framework when a server document that is an embedded item is saved, updating the container's copy of the item.

Overridables *(continued)*

OnGetEmbeddedItem	Called to get a **COleServerItem** that represents the entire document; used to get an embedded item. Implementation required.
OnClose	Called by the framework when a container requests to close the document.
OnSetHostNames	Called by the framework when a container sets the window title for an embedded object.
OnShowDocument	Called by the framework to show or hide the document.
OnDeactivate	Called by the framework when the user deactivates an item that was activated in place.
OnDeactivateUI	Called by the framework to destroy controls and other user-interface elements created for in-place activation.
OnSetItemRects	Called by the framework to position the in-place editing frame window within the container application's window.
OnReactivateAndUndo	Called by the framework to undo changes made during in-place editing.
OnFrameWindowActivate	Called by the framework when the container's frame window is activated or deactivated.
OnDocWindowActivate	Called by the framework when the container's document frame window is activated or deactivated.
OnShowControlBars	Called by the framework to show or hide control bars for in-place editing.
OnResizeBorder	Called by the framework when the container application's frame window or document window is resized.
CreateInPlaceFrame	Called by the framework to create a frame window for in-place editing.
DestroyInPlaceFrame	Called by the framework to destroy a frame window for in-place editing.

Member Functions

COleServerDoc::ActivateInPlace

BOOL ActivateInPlace( );

Return Value

Nonzero if successful; otherwise 0, which indicates that the item is fully open.

Remarks

Activates the item for in-place editing.

This function performs all operations necessary for in-place activation. It creates an in-place frame window, activates it and sizes it to the item, sets up shared menus and other controls, scrolls the item into view, and sets the focus to the in-place frame window.

This function is called by the default implementation of **COleServerItem::OnShow**. Call this function if your application supports another verb for in-place activation (such as Play).

See Also: **COleServerItem::OnShow**

COleServerDoc::COleServerDoc

COleServerDoc( );

Remarks

Constructs a **COleServerDoc** object without connecting with the OLE system DLLs. You must call **COleLinkingDoc::Register** to open communications with OLE. If you are using **COleTemplateServer** in your application, **COleLinkingDoc::Register** is called for you by **COleLinkingDoc**'s implementation of **OnNewDocument**, **OnOpenDocument**, and **OnSaveDocument**.

See Also: **COleLinkingDoc::Register**

COleServerDoc::DeactivateAndUndo

BOOL DeactivateAndUndo( );

Return Value

Nonzero on success; otherwise 0.

Remarks

Call this function if your application supports Undo and the user chooses Undo after activating an item but before editing it. If the container application is written using the Microsoft Foundation Class Library, calling this function causes **COleClientItem::OnDeactivateAndUndo** to be called, which deactivates the server's user interface.

See Also: **COleClientItem::OnDeactivateAndUndo**

COleServerDoc::CreateInPlaceFrame

virtual COleIPFrameWnd* CreateInPlaceFrame(CWnd* *pParentWnd* **);**

Return Value

A pointer to the in-place frame window, or **NULL** if unsuccessful.

Parameters

pParentWnd   Pointer to the container application's parent window.

Remarks

The framework calls this function to create a frame window for in-place editing. The default implementation uses information specified in the document template to create the frame. The view used is the first view created for the document. This view is temporarily detached from the original frame and attached to the newly created frame.

This is an advanced overridable.

See Also: COleServerDoc::DestroyInPlaceFrame

COleServerDoc::DestroyInPlaceFrame

virtual void DestroyInPlaceFrame(COleIPFrameWnd* *pFrame* **);**

Parameters

pFrame   Pointer to the in-place frame window to be destroyed.

Remarks

The framework calls this function to destroy an in-place frame window and return the server application's document window to its state before in-place activation.

This is an advanced overridable.

See Also: COleServerDoc::CreateInPlaceFrame

COleServerDoc::DiscardUndoState

BOOL DiscardUndoState( );

Return Value

Nonzero on success; otherwise 0.

Remarks

If the user performs an editing operation that cannot be undone, call this function to force the container application to discard its undo-state information.

This function is provided so that servers that support Undo can free resources that would otherwise be consumed by undo-state information that cannot be used.

See Also: **COleServerDoc::OnReactivateAndUndo**

COleServerDoc::GetDocObjectServer

virtual CDocObjectServer* GetDocObjectServer(LPOLEDOCUMENTSITE *pSite* **);**

Return Value

A pointer to a **CDocObjectServer**; **NULL** if the operation failed.

Parameters

pSite   Pointer to the **IOleDocumentSite** interface that will connect this document to the server.

Remarks

Override this function to create a new **CDocObjectServer** item and return a pointer to it. When a DocObject server is activated, the return of a non-**NULL** pointer shows that the client can support DocObjects. The default implementation returns **NULL**.

A typical implementation for a document that supports DocObjects will simply allocate a new **CDocObjectServer** object and return it to the caller. For example:

```
CDocObjectServer* COleServerDoc::GetDocObjectServer(LPOLEDOCUMENTSITE pSite)
{
    return new CDocObjectServer(this, pSite);
}
```

See Also: **CDocObjectServer::CDocObjectServer**

COleServerDoc::GetEmbeddedItem

COleServerItem* GetEmbeddedItem( );

Return Value

A pointer to an item representing the entire document; **NULL** if the operation failed.

Remarks

Call this function to get a pointer to an item representing the entire document. It calls **COleServerDoc::OnGetEmbeddedItem**, a virtual function with no default implementation.

See Also: **COleServerDoc::OnGetEmbeddedItem**

COleServerDoc::GetItemClipRect

void GetItemClipRect(LPRECT *lpClipRect* **) const;**

Parameters

lpClipRect   Pointer to a **RECT** structure or a **CRect** object to receive the clipping-rectangle coordinates of the item.

Remarks

Call the **GetItemClipRect** member function to get the clipping-rectangle coordinates of the item that is being edited in place. Coordinates are in pixels relative to the container application window's client area.

Drawing should not occur outside the clipping rectangle. Usually, drawing is automatically restricted. Use this function to determine whether the user has scrolled outside the visible portion of the document; if so, scroll the container document as needed by means of a call to **ScrollContainerBy**.

**See Also: COleServerDoc::GetItemPosition,
COleServerDoc::ScrollContainerBy**

COleServerDoc::GetItemPosition

void GetItemPosition(LPRECT *lpPosRect* **) const;**

Parameters

lpPosRect   Pointer to a **RECT** structure or a **CRect** object to receive the coordinates of the item.

Remarks

Call the **GetItemPosition** member function to get the coordinates of the item being edited in place. Coordinates are in pixels relative to the container application window's client area.

The item's position can be compared with the current clipping rectangle to determine the extent to which the item is visible (or not visible) on the screen.

See Also: COleServerDoc::GetItemClipRect

COleServerDoc::GetZoomFactor

BOOL GetZoomFactor(LPSIZE *lpSizeNum* = **NULL,
↪ LPSIZE** *lpSizeDenom* = **NULL, LPCRECT** *lpPosRect* = **NULL) const;**

Return Value

Nonzero if the item is activated for in-place editing and its zoom factor is other than 100% (1:1); otherwise 0.

Parameters

lpSizeNum   Pointer to an object of class **CSize** that will hold the zoom factor's numerator. Can be **NULL**.

lpSizeDenom   Pointer to an object of class **CSize** that will hold the zoom factor's denominator. Can be **NULL**.

lpPosRect   Pointer to an object of class **CRect** that describes the item's new position. If this argument is **NULL**, the function uses the item's current position.

Remarks

The **GetZoomFactor** member function determines the "zoom factor" of an item that has been activated for in-place editing. The zoom factor, in pixels, is the proportion of the item's size to its current extent. If the container application has not set the item's extent, its natural extent (as determined by **COleServerItem::OnGetExtent**) is used.

The function sets its first two arguments to the numerator and denominator of the item's "zoom factor." If the item is not being edited in place, the function sets these arguments to a default value of 100% (or 1:1) and returns zero. For further information, see Technical Note 40 online, MFC/OLE In-Place Resizing and Zooming.

See Also: COleServerDoc::GetItemPosition, COleServerDoc::GetItemClipRect, COleServerDoc::OnSetItemRects

---

COleServerDoc::IsEmbedded

BOOL IsEmbedded( ) const;

Return Value

Nonzero if the **COleServerDoc** object is a document that represents an object embedded in a container; otherwise 0.

Remarks

Call the **IsEmbedded** member function to determine whether the document represents an object embedded in a container. A document loaded from a file is not embedded although it may be manipulated by a container application as a link. A document which is an embedding in a container document is considered to be embedded.

COleServerDoc::IsInPlaceActive

BOOL IsInPlaceActive( ) const;

Return Value

Nonzero if the **COleServerDoc** object is active in place; otherwise 0.

Remarks

Call the **IsInPlaceActive** member function to determine whether the item is currently in the in-place active state.

See Also: **COleClientItem::OnActivate,
COleServerDoc::OnReactivateAndUndo**, **COleServerDoc::ActivateInPlace**

COleServerDoc::NotifyChanged

void NotifyChanged( );

Remarks

Call this function to notify all linked items connected to the document that the document has changed. Typically, you call this function after the user changes some global attribute such as the dimensions of the server document. If an OLE item is linked to the document with an automatic link, the item is updated to reflect the changes. In container applications written with the Microsoft Foundation Class Library, the **OnChange** member function of **COleClientItem** is called.

Note This function is included for compatibility with OLE 1. New applications should use **UpdateAllItems**.

See Also: **OleServerDoc::NotifyClosed, COleServerDoc::NotifySaved,
COleClientItem::OnChange**

COleServerDoc::NotifyClosed

void NotifyClosed( );

Remarks

Call this function to notify the container(s) that the document has been closed. When the user chooses the Close command from the File menu, **NotifyClosed** is called by **COleServerDoc**'s implementation of the **OnCloseDocument** member function. In container applications written with the Microsoft Foundation Class Library, the **OnChange** member function of **COleClientItem** is called.

See Also: **COleServerDoc::NotifyChanged, COleServerDoc::NotifySaved,
COleClientItem::OnChange, CDocument::OnCloseDocument**

COleServerDoc::NotifyRename

void NotifyRename(LPCTSTR *lpszNewName* **);**

Parameters

lpszNewName   Pointer to a string specifying the new name of the server document; this is typically a fully qualified path.

Remarks

Call this function after the user renames the server document. When the user chooses the Save As command from the File menu, **NotifyRename** is called by **COleServerDoc**'s implementation of the **OnSaveDocument** member function. This function notifies the OLE system DLLs, which in turn notify the containers. In container applications written with the Microsoft Foundation Class Library, the **OnChange** member function of **COleClientItem** is called.

See Also: **COleServerDoc::NotifySaved, CDocument::OnSaveDocument**

COleServerDoc::NotifySaved

void NotifySaved( );

Remarks

Call this function after the user saves the server document. When the user chooses the Save command from the File menu, **NotifySaved** is called for you by **COleServerDoc**'s implementation of **OnSaveDocument**. This function notifies the OLE system DLLs, which in turn notify the containers. In container applications written with the Microsoft Foundation Class Library, the **OnChange** member function of **COleClientItem** is called.

See Also: **COleServerDoc::NotifyChanged, COleServerDoc::NotifyClosed, COleClientItem::OnChange, CDocument::OnSaveDocument**

COleServerDoc::OnClose

virtual void OnClose(OLECLOSE *dwCloseOption* **);**

Parameters

dwCloseOption A value from the enumeration **OLECLOSE**. This parameter can have one of the following values:

- **OLECLOSE_SAVEIFDIRTY** The file is saved if it has been modified.
- **OLECLOSE_NOSAVE** The file is closed without being saved.
- **OLECLOSE_PROMPTSAVE** If the file has been modified, the user is prompted about saving it.

Remarks

Called by the framework when a container requests that the server document be closed. The default implementation calls **CDocument::OnCloseDocument**.

For more information and additional values, see **OLECLOSE** in the OLE documentation.

See Also: **COleException, CDocument::OnCloseDocument**

COleServerDoc::OnDeactivate

virtual void OnDeactivate( );

Remarks

Called by the framework when the user deactivates an embedded or linked item that is currently in-place active. This function restores the container application's user interface to its original state and destroys any menus and other controls that were created for in-place activation.

The undo state information should be unconditionally released at this point.

For more information, see the article "Activation" in *Visual C++ Programmer's Guide* online.

See Also: **COleServerDoc::ActivateInPlace**, **COleServerDoc::OnDeactivateUI**, **COleServerDoc::DestroyInPlaceFrame**

COleServerDoc::OnDeactivateUI

virtual void OnDeactivateUI(BOOL *bUndoable*);

Parameters

bUndoable   Specifies whether the editing changes can be undone.

Remarks

Called when the user deactivates an item that was activated in place. This function restores the container application's user interface to its original state, hiding any menus and other controls that were created for in-place activation.

The framework always sets *bUndoable* to **FALSE**. If the server supports undo and there is an operation that can be undone, call the base-class implementation with *bUndoable* set to **TRUE**.

See Also: **COleServerDoc::OnDeactivate**

COleServerDoc::OnDocWindowActivate

virtual void OnDocWindowActivate(BOOL *bActivate*);

Parameters

bActivate   Specifies whether the document window is to be activated or deactivated.

Remarks

The framework calls this function to activate or deactivate a document window for in-place editing. The default implementation removes or adds the frame-level user interface elements as appropriate. Override this function if you want to perform additional actions when the document containing your item is activated or deactivated.

For more information, see the article "Activation" in *Visual C++ Programmer's Guide* online.

See Also: **COleServerDoc::ActivateInPlace,**
COleServerDoc::OnReactivateAndUndo, COleServerDoc::OnShowControlBars,
COleServerDoc::OnDeactivateUI, COleServerDoc::OnFrameWindowActivate,
COleIPFrameWnd

COleServerDoc::OnExecOleCmd

HRESULT OnExecOleCmd(const GUID* *pGroup*, **DWORD** *nCmdID*,
↳ **DWORD** *nCmdExecOut*, **VARIANTARG*** *pvaIn*, **VARIANTARG*** *pvaOut*);

Return Value

Returns **S_OK** if successful; otherwise, one of the following error codes:

Value	Description
E_UNEXPECTED	Unexpected error occurred
E_FAIL	Error occurred
E_NOTIMPL	Indicates MFC itself should attempt to translate and dispatch the command
OLECMDERR_E_UNKNOWNGROUP	*pGroup* is non-**NULL** but does not specify a recognized command group
OLECMDERR_E_NOTSUPPORTED	*nCmdID* is not recognized as a valid command in the group *pGroup*
OLECMDERR_DISABLED	The command identified by *nCmdID* is disabled and cannot be executed
OLECMDERR_NOHELP	Caller asked for help on the command identified by *nCmdID* but no help is available
OLECMDERR_CANCELED	User canceled the execution

Parameters

pGroup   A pointer to a GUID that identifies a set of commands. Can be **NULL** to indicate the default command group.

nCmdID   The command to execute. Must be in the group identified by *pGroup*.

nCmdExecOut   The way the object should execute the command, one or more of the following values from the **OLECMDEXECOPT** enumeration:

- **OLECMDEXECOPT_DODEFAULT**
- **OLECMDEXECOPT_PROMPTUSER**
- **OLECMDEXECOPT_DONTPROMPTUSER**
- **OLECMDEXECOPT_SHOWHELP**

pvaIn   Pointer to a **VARIANTARG** containing input arguments for the command. Can be **NULL**.

pvaOut   Pointer to a **VARIANTARG** to receive the output return values from the command. Can be **NULL**.

Remarks

The framework calls this function to execute a specified command or display help for the command.

COleCmdUI can be used to enable, update, and set other properties of DocObject user interface commands. After the commands are initialized, you can execute them with **OnExecOleCmd**.

The framework calls the function before attempting to translate and dispatch an OLE document command. You don't need to override this function to handle standard OLE document commands, but you must supply an override to this function if you want to handle your own custom commands or handle commands that accept parameters or return results.

Most of the commands do not take arguments or return values. For a majority of commands the caller can pass **NULL**s for *pvaIn* and *pvaOut*. For commands that expect input values, the caller can declare and initialize a **VARIANTARG** variable and pass a pointer to the variable in *pvaIn*. For commands that require a single value, the argument can be stored directly in the **VARIANTARG** and passed to the function. Multiple arguments must be packaged within the **VARIANTARG** using one of the supported types (such as **IDispatch** and **SAFEARRAY**).

Similarly, if a command returns arguments the caller is expected to declare a **VARIANTARG**, initialize it to **VT_EMPTY**, and pass its address in *pvaOut*. If a command returns a single value, the object can store that value directly in *pvaOut*. Multiple output values must be packaged in some way appropriate for the **VARIANTARG**.

The base-class implementation of this function will walk the **OLE_COMMAND_MAP** structures associated with the command target and try to dispatch the command to an appropriate handler. The base-class implementation works only with commands that do not accept arguments or return values. If you need to handle commands that do accept arguments or return values, you must override this function and work with the *pvaIn* and *pvaOut* parameters yourself.

See Also: COleCmdUI

COleServerDoc::OnFrameWindowActivate

virtual void OnFrameWindowActivate(BOOL *bActivate* **);**

Parameters

bActivate   Specifies whether the frame window is to be activated or deactivated.

Remarks

The framework calls this function when the container application's frame window is activated or deactivated.

The default implementation cancels any help modes the frame window might be in. Override this function if you want to perform special processing when the frame window is activated or deactivated.

For more information, see the article "Activation" in *Visual C++ Programmer's Guide* online.

See Also: **COleServerDoc::OnDocWindowActivate**

COleServerDoc::OnGetEmbeddedItem

virtual COleServerItem* OnGetEmbeddedItem( ) = 0;

Return Value

A pointer to an item representing the entire document; **NULL** if the operation failed.

Remarks

Called by the framework when a container application calls the server application to create or edit an embedded item. There is no default implementation. You must override this function to return an item that represents the entire document. This return value should be an object of a **COleServerItem**-derived class.

See Also: **COleLinkingDoc::OnGetLinkedItem, COleServerItem**

COleServerDoc::OnReactivateAndUndo

virtual BOOL OnReactivateAndUndo( );

Return Value

Nonzero if successful; otherwise 0.

Remarks

The framework calls this function when the user chooses to undo changes made to an item that has been activated in place, changed, and subsequently deactivated. The default implementation does nothing except return **FALSE** to indicate failure.

Override this function if your application supports undo. Usually you would perform the undo operation, then activate the item by calling **ActivateInPlace**. If the container application is written with the Microsoft Foundation Class Library, calling **COleClientItem::ReactivateAndUndo** causes this function to be called.

See Also: **COleServerDoc::ActivateInPlace, COleServerDoc::IsInPlaceActive, COleClientItem::ReactivateAndUndo**

COleServerDoc::OnResizeBorder

virtual void OnResizeBorder(LPCRECT *lpRectBorder*,
↳ **LPOLEINPLACEUIWINDOW** *lpUIWindow*, **BOOL** *bFrame* **)**;

Parameters

lpRectBorder   Pointer to a **RECT** structure or a **CRect** object that specifies the coordinates of the border.

lpUIWindow   Pointer to an object of class **IOleInPlaceUIWindow** that owns the current in-place editing session.

bFrame   **TRUE** if *lpUIWindow* points to the container application's top-level frame window, or **FALSE** if *lpUIWindow* points to the container application's document-level frame window.

Remarks

The framework calls this function when the container application's frame windows change size. This function resizes and adjusts toolbars and other user-interface elements in accordance with the new window size.

For more information, see **IOleInPlaceUIWindow** in the OLE documentation.

This is an advanced overridable.

See Also: COleServerDoc::OnShowControlBars

COleServerDoc::OnSetHostNames

virtual void OnSetHostNames(LPCTSTR *lpszHost*, **LPCTSTR** *lpszHostObj* **)**;

Parameters

lpszHost   Pointer to a string that specifies the name of the container application.

lpszHostObj   Pointer to a string that specifies the container's name for the document.

Remarks

Called by the framework when the container sets or changes the host names for this document. The default implementation changes the document title for all views referring to this document.

Override this function if your application sets the titles through a different mechanism.

See Also: COleClientItem::SetHostNames

COleServerDoc::OnSetItemRects

virtual void OnSetItemRects(LPCRECT *lpPosRect***, LPCRECT** *lpClipRect* **);**

Parameters

lpPosRect   Pointer to a **RECT** structure or a **CRect** object that specifies the in-place frame window's position relative to the container application's client area.

lpClipRect   Pointer to a **RECT** structure or a **CRect** object that specifies the in-place frame window's clipping rectangle relative to the container application's client area.

Remarks

The framework calls this function to position the in-place editing frame window within the container application's frame window. Override this function to update the view's zoom factor, if necessary.

This function is usually called in response to a **RequestPositionChange** call, although it can be called at any time by the container to request a position change for the in-place item.

**See Also: COleServerDoc::RequestPositionChange,
COleIPFrameWnd::RepositionFrame, COleClientItem::SetItemRects,
COleServerDoc::GetZoomFactor**

COleServerDoc::OnShowControlBars

virtual void OnShowControlBars(CFrameWnd **pFrameWnd***, BOOL** *bShow* **);**

Parameters

pFrameWnd   Pointer to the frame window whose control bars should be hidden or shown.

bShow   Determines whether control bars are shown or hidden.

Remarks

The framework calls this function to show or hide the server application's control bars associated with the frame window identified by *pFrameWnd*. The default implementation enumerates all control bars owned by that frame window and hides or shows them.

**See Also: COleServerDoc::ActivateInPlace,
COleServerDoc::OnReactivateAndUndo,
COleServerDoc::OnFrameWindowActivate, COleServerDoc::IsInPlaceActive**

COleServerDoc::OnShowDocument

virtual void OnShowDocument(BOOL *bShow* **);**

Parameters

bShow   Specifies whether the user interface to the document is to be shown or hidden.

Remarks

The framework calls the **OnShowDocument** function when the server document must be hidden or shown. If *bShow* is **TRUE**, the default implementation activates the server application, if necessary, and causes the container application to scroll its window so that the item is visible. If *bShow* is **FALSE**, the default implementation deactivates the item through a call to **OnDeactivate**, then destroys or hides all frame windows that have been created for the document, except the first one. If no visible documents remain, the default implementation hides the server application.

See Also: **COleServerDoc::ActivateInPlace, COleServerItem::OnDoVerb, COleServerDoc::IsInPlaceActive, COleServerDoc::OnDeactivateUI**

COleServerDoc::OnUpdateDocument

virtual BOOL OnUpdateDocument( );

Return Value

Nonzero if the document was successfully updated; otherwise 0.

Remarks

Called by the framework when saving a document that is an embedded item in a compound document. The default implementation calls the **COleServerDoc::NotifySaved** and **COleServerDoc::SaveEmbedding** member functions and then marks the document as clean. Override this function if you want to perform special processing when updating an embedded item.

See Also: **COleServerDoc::NotifySaved, COleServerDoc::SaveEmbedding, CDocument::OnSaveDocument**

COleServerDoc::RequestPositionChange

void RequestPositionChange(LPCRECT *lpPosRect* **);**

Parameters

lpPosRect   Pointer to a **RECT** structure or a **CRect** object containing the item's new position.

Remarks

Call this member function to have the container application change the item's position. This function is usually called (in conjunction with **UpdateAllItems**) when the data in an in-place active item has changed. Following this call, the container might or might not perform the change by calling **OnSetItemRects**. The resulting position might be different from the one requested.

See Also: **COleServerDoc::ScrollContainerBy**

COleServerDoc::SaveEmbedding

void SaveEmbedding( );

Remarks

Call this function to tell the container application to save the embedded object. This function is called automatically from **OnUpdateDocument**. Note that this function causes the item to be updated on disk, so it is usually called only as a result of a specific user action.

See Also: **COleServerDoc::NotifyClosed**

COleServerDoc::ScrollContainerBy

BOOL ScrollContainerBy(CSize *sizeScroll* **);**

Return Value

Nonzero if successful; otherwise 0.

Parameters

sizeScroll   Indicates how far the container document is to scroll.

Remarks

Call the **ScrollContainerBy** member function to scroll the container document by the amount, in pixels, indicated by *sizeScroll*. Positive values indicate scrolling down and to the right; negative values indicate scrolling up and to the left.

See Also: **COleClientItem::OnScrollBy**

COleServerDoc::UpdateAllItems

void UpdateAllItems(COleServerItem* *pSender,* **LPARAM** *lHint* **= 0L,**
↳ CObject* *pHint* **= NULL, DVASPECT** *nDrawAspect* **= DVASPECT_CONTENT);**

Parameters

pSender   Pointer to the item that modified the document, or **NULL** if all items are to be updated.

lHint   Contains information about the modification.

pHint   Pointer to an object storing information about the modification.

nDrawAspect   Determines how the item is to be drawn. This is a value from the **DVASPECT** enumeration. This parameter can have one of the following values:

- **DVASPECT_CONTENT**   Item is represented in such a way that it can be displayed as an embedded object inside its container.

- **DVASPECT_THUMBNAIL**   Item is rendered in a "thumbnail" representation so that it can be displayed in a browsing tool.

- **DVASPECT_ICON**   Item is represented by an icon.

- **DVASPECT_DOCPRINT**   Item is represented as if it were printed using the Print command from the File menu.

Remarks

Call this function to notify all linked items connected to the document that the document has changed. You typically call this function after the user changes the server document. If an OLE item is linked to the document with an automatic link, the item is updated to reflect the changes. In container applications written with the Microsoft Foundation Class Library, the **OnChange** member function of **COleClientItem** is called.

This function calls the **OnUpdate** member function for each of the document's items except the sending item, passing *pHint*, *lHint*, and *nDrawAspect*. Use these parameters to pass information to the items about the modifications made to the document. You can encode information using *lHint* or you can define a **CObject**-derived class to store information about the modifications and pass an object of that class using *pHint*. Override the **OnUpdate** member function in your **COleServerItem**-derived class to optimize the updating of each item depending on whether its presentation has changed.

See Also: **COleServerDoc::NotifyChanged, COleServerItem::OnUpdate, COleServerDoc::NotifySaved, COleClientItem::OnChange**

COleServerItem

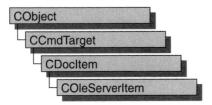

CObject
CCmdTarget
CDocItem
COleServerItem

The **COleServerItem** class provides the server interface to OLE items. A linked item can represent some or all of a server document. An embedded item always represents an entire server document.

The **COleServerItem** class defines several overridable member functions that are called by the OLE system dynamic-link libraries (DLLs), usually in response to requests from the container application. These member functions allow the container application to manipulate the item indirectly in various ways, such as by displaying it, executing its verbs, or retrieving its data in various formats.

To use **COleServerItem**, derive a class from it and implement the **OnDraw** and **Serialize** member functions. The **OnDraw** function provides the metafile representation of an item, allowing it to be displayed when a container application opens a compound document. The **Serialize** function of **CObject** provides the native representation of an item, allowing an embedded item to be transferred between the server and container applications. **OnGetExtent** provides the natural size of the item to the container, enabling the container to size the item.

For more information about servers and related topics, see the articles "Servers: Implementing a Server" and "Creating a Container/Server Application" in the article "Containers: Advanced Features." Both articles are in *Visual C++ Programmer's Guide* online.

#include <afxole.h>

See Also: **COleClientItem**, **COleServerDoc**, **COleTemplateServer**, **CObject::Serialize**

COleServerItem Class Members

Status

GetDocument	Returns the server document that contains the item.
GetItemName	Returns the name of the item. Used for linked items only.

Status *(continued)*

SetItemName	Sets the name of the item. Used for linked items only.
IsConnected	Indicates whether the item is currently attached to an active container.
IsLinkedItem	Indicates whether the item represents a linked OLE item.

Operations

CopyToClipboard	Copies the item to the Clipboard.
NotifyChanged	Updates all containers with automatic link update.
DoDragDrop	Performs a drag-and-drop operation.
GetClipboardData	Gets the data source for use in data transfer (drag and drop or Clipboard).
GetEmbedSourceData	Gets the **CF_EMBEDSOURCE** data for an OLE item.
AddOtherClipboardData	Places presentation and conversion formats in a **COleDataSource** object.
GetLinkSourceData	Gets the **CF_LINKSOURCE** data for an OLE item.
GetObjectDescriptorData	Gets the **CF_OBJECTDESCRIPTOR** data for an OLE item.

Construction

COleServerItem	Constructs a **COleServerItem** object.
GetDataSource	Gets the object used to store conversion formats.

Overridables

OnDraw	Called when the container requests to draw the item; implementation required.
OnDrawEx	Called for specialized item drawing.
OnUpdate	Called when some portion of the document the item belongs in is changed.
OnInitFromData	Called by the framework to initialize an OLE item using the contents of the data transfer object specified.
OnGetExtent	Called by the framework to retrieve the size of the OLE item.
OnSetExtent	Called by the framework to set the size of the OLE item.
OnGetClipboardData	Called by the framework to get the data that would be copied to the Clipboard.
OnSetColorScheme	Called to set the item's color scheme.
OnSetData	Called to set the item's data.
OnDoVerb	Called to execute a verb.
OnQueryUpdateItems	Called to determine whether any linked items require updating.
OnRenderData	Retrieves data as part of delayed rendering.
OnRenderFileData	Retrieves data into a **CFile** object as part of delayed rendering.

(continued)

Overridables *(continued)*	
OnRenderGlobalData	Retrieves data into an **HGLOBAL** as part of delayed rendering.
OnUpdateItems	Called to update the presentation cache of all items in the server document.
OnOpen	Called by the framework to display the OLE item in its own top-level window.
OnShow	Called when the container requests to show the item.
OnHide	Called by the framework to hide the OLE item.

Data Members	
m_sizeExtent	Informs the server about how much of the OLE item is visible.

Member Functions
COleServerItem::AddOtherClipboardData

void AddOtherClipboardData(COleDataSource* *pDataSource* **);**

Parameters

pDataSource Pointer to the **COleDataSource** object in which the data should be placed.

Remarks

Call this function to place the presentation and conversion formats for the OLE item in the specified **COleDataSource** object. You must have implemented the **OnDraw** member function to provide the presentation format (a metafile picture) for the item. To support other conversion formats, register them using the **COleDataSource** object returned by **GetDataSource** and override the **OnRenderData** member function to provide data in the formats you want to support.

See Also: **COleDataSource, COleServerItem::GetDataSource, COleServerItem::GetEmbedSourceData, COleServerItem::OnDraw**

COleServerItem::COleServerItem

COleServerItem(COleServerDoc* *pServerDoc***, BOOL** *bAutoDelete* **);**

Parameters

pServerDoc Pointer to the document that will contain the new item.

bAutoDelete Flag indicating whether the object can be deleted when a link to it is released. Set this to **FALSE** if the **COleServerItem** object is an integral part of your document's data which you must delete. Set this to **TRUE** if the object is a secondary structure used to identify a range in your document's data that can be deleted by the framework.

Remarks

Constructs a **COleServerItem** object and adds it to the server document's collection of document items.

See Also: **COleDocument::AddItem**

COleServerItem::CopyToClipboard

void CopyToClipboard(BOOL *bIncludeLink* **= FALSE);**

Parameters

bIncludeLink Set this to **TRUE** if link data should be copied to the Clipboard. Set this to **FALSE** if your server application does not support links.

Remarks

Call this function to copy the OLE item to the Clipboard. The function uses the **OnGetClipboardData** member function to create a **COleDataSource** object containing the OLE item's data in the formats supported. The function then places the **COleDataSource** object on the Clipboard by using the **COleDataSource::SetClipboard** function. The **COleDataSource** object includes the item's native data and its representation in **CF_METAFILEPICT** format, as well as data in any conversion formats you choose to support. You must have implemented **Serialize** and **OnDraw** for this member function to work.

See Also: **COleDataSource::SetClipboard, COleDataSource,**
COleServerItem::AddOtherClipboardData,
COleServerItem::GetClipboardData, COleServerItem::OnDraw,
CObject::Serialize

COleServerItem::DoDragDrop

DROPEFFECT DoDragDrop(LPCRECT *lpItemRect*, **CPoint** *ptOffset*,
  ↳ **BOOL** *bIncludeLink* **= FALSE, DWORD** *dwEffects* **= DROPEFFECT_COPY |**
  ↳ **DROPEFFECT_MOVE, LPCRECT** *lpRectStartDrag* **= NULL);**

Return Value

A value from the **DROPEFFECT** enumeration. If it is **DROPEFFECT_MOVE**, the original data should be removed.

Parameters

lpItemRect The item's rectangle on screen, in pixels, relative to the client area.

ptOffset The offset from *lpItemRect* where the mouse position was at the time of the drag.

bIncludeLink   Set this to **TRUE** if link data should be copied to the Clipboard. Set it to **FALSE** if your application does not support links.

dwEffects   Determines the effects that the drag source will allow in the drag operation (a combination of Copy, Move, and Link).

lpRectStartDrag   Pointer to the rectangle that defines where the drag actually starts. For more information, see the following Remarks section.

Remarks

Call the **DoDragDrop** member function to perform a drag-and-drop operation. The drag-and-drop operation does not start immediately. It waits until the mouse cursor leaves the rectangle specified by *lpRectStartDrag* or until a specified number of milliseconds have passed. If *lpRectStartDrag* is **NULL**, the size of the rectangle is one pixel. The delay time is specified by the **DragDelay** value in the [Windows] section of WIN.INI. If this value is not in WIN.INI, the default value of 200 milliseconds is used.

See Also: **COleDataSource::DoDragDrop, COleServerItem::CopyToClipboard**

COleServerItem::GetClipboardData

void GetClipboardData(COleDataSource* *pDataSource,*
↪ **BOOL** *bIncludeLink* = **FALSE, LPPOINT** *lpOffset* = **NULL,**
↪ **LPSIZE** *lpSize* = **NULL);**

Parameters

pDataSource   Pointer to the **COleDataSource** object that will receive the OLE item's data in all supported formats.

bIncludeLink   **TRUE** if link data should be copied to the Clipboard. **FALSE** if your server application does not support links.

lpOffset   The offset, in pixels, of the mouse cursor from the origin of the object.

lpSize   The size of the object in pixels.

Remarks

Call this function to fill the specified **COleDataSource** object with all the data that would be copied to the Clipboard if you called **CopyToClipboard** (the same data would also be transferred if you called **DoDragDrop**). This function calls the **GetEmbedSourceData** member function to get the native data for the OLE item and calls the **AddOtherClipboardData** member function to get the presentation format and any supported conversion formats. If *bIncludeLink* is **TRUE**, the function also calls **GetLinkSourceData** to get the link data for the item.

Override this function if you want to put formats in a **COleDataSource** object before or after those formats supplied by **CopyToClipboard**.

See Also: **COleDataSource**, **COleServerItem::AddOtherClipboardData**, **COleServerItem::CopyToClipboard**, **COleServerItem::DoDragDrop**, **COleServerItem::GetEmbedSourceData**, **COleServerItem::GetLinkSourceData**

COleServerItem::GetDataSource

COleDataSource* GetDataSource( );

Return Value

A pointer to the **COleDataSource** object used to store the conversion formats.

Remarks

Call this function to get the **COleDataSource** object used to store the conversion formats that the server application supports. If you want your server application to offer data in a variety of formats during data transfer operations, register those formats with the **COleDataSource** object returned by this function. For example, if you want to supply a **CF_TEXT** representation of the OLE item for Clipboard or drag-and-drop operations, you would register the format with the **COleDataSource** object this function returns, and then override the **OnRenderXxxData** member function to provide the data.

See Also: **COleDataSource**, **COleDataSource::DelayRenderData**, **COleServerItem::CopyToClipboard**, **COleServerItem::DoDragDrop**, **COleServerItem::OnRenderData**, **COleServerItem::OnRenderFileData**, **COleServerItem::OnRenderGlobalData**

COleServerItem::GetDocument

COleServerDoc* GetDocument( ) const;

Return Value

A pointer to the document that contains the item; **NULL** if the item is not part of a document.

Remarks

Call this function to get a pointer to the document that contains the item. This allows access to the server document that you passed as an argument to the **COleServerItem** constructor.

See Also: **COleServerItem::COleServerItem**, **COleServerDoc**

COleServerItem::GetEmbedSourceData

void GetEmbedSourceData(LPSTGMEDIUM *lpStgMedium* **);**

Parameters

lpStgMedium   Pointer to the **STGMEDIUM** structure that will receive the **CF_EMBEDSOURCE** data for the OLE item.

Remarks

Call this function to get the **CF_EMBEDSOURCE** data for an OLE item. This format includes the item's native data. You must have implemented the **Serialize** member function for this function to work properly.

The result can then be added to a data source by using **COleDataSource::CacheData**. This function is called automatically by **COleServerItem::OnGetClipboardData**.

For more information, see **STGMEDIUM** in the *OLE 2 Programmer's Reference, Volume 1*.

See Also: COleServerItem::GetLinkSourceData, COleServerItem::GetObjectDescriptorData, COleDataSource::CacheData, CObject::Serialize

---

COleServerItem::GetItemName

const CString& GetItemName( ) const;

Return Value

The name of the item.

Remarks

Call this function to get the name of the item. You typically call this function only for linked items.

See Also: COleServerItem::SetItemName, COleLinkingDoc::OnGetLinkedItem

---

COleServerItem::GetLinkSourceData

BOOL GetLinkSourceData(LPSTGMEDIUM *lpStgMedium* **);**

Return Value

Nonzero if successful; otherwise 0.

Parameters

lpStgMedium   Pointer to the **STGMEDIUM** structure that will receive the **CF_LINKSOURCE** data for the OLE item.

Remarks

Call this function to get the **CF_LINKSOURCE** data for an OLE item. This format includes the CLSID describing the type of the OLE item and the information needed to locate the document containing the OLE item.

The result can then be added to a data source with **COleDataSource::CacheData**. This function is called automatically by **OnGetClipboardData**.

For more information, see **STGMEDIUM** in the *OLE 2 Programmer's Reference, Volume 1*.

See Also: **COleServerItem::GetEmbedSourceData**, **COleServerItem::GetObjectDescriptorData**

COleServerItem::GetObjectDescriptorData

void GetObjectDescriptorData(LPPOINT* *lpOffset***, LPSIZE*** *lpSize***,**
↳ **LPSTGMEDIUM** *lpStgMedium* **);**

Parameters

lpOffset   Offset of the mouse click from the upper-left corner of the OLE item. Can be **NULL**.

lpSize   Size of the OLE item. Can be **NULL**.

lpStgMedium   Pointer to the **STGMEDIUM** structure that will receive the **CF_OBJECTDESCRIPTOR** data for the OLE item.

Remarks

Call this function to get the **CF_OBJECTDESCRIPTOR** data for an OLE item. The information is copied into the **STGMEDIUM** structure pointed to by *lpStgMedium*. This format includes the information needed for the Paste Special dialog.

For more information, see **STGMEDIUM** in the *OLE 2 Programmer's Reference, Volume 1*.

See Also: **COleServerItem::AddOtherClipboardData**, **COleServerItem::GetEmbedSourceData**, **COleServerItem::GetLinkSourceData**, **COlePasteSpecialDialog**

COleServerItem::IsConnected

BOOL IsConnected( ) const;

Return Value

Nonzero if the item is connected; otherwise 0.

Remarks

Call this function to see if the OLE item is connected. An OLE item is considered connected if one or more containers have references to the item. An item is connected if its reference count is greater than 0 or if it is an embedded item.

See Also: **COleServerItem::IsLinkedItem, COleLinkingDoc::OnGetLinkedItem**

COleServerItem::IsLinkedItem

BOOL IsLinkedItem( ) const;

Return Value

Nonzero if the item is a linked item; otherwise 0.

Remarks

Call this function to see if the OLE item is a linked item. An item is linked if the item is valid and is not returned in the document's list of embedded items. A linked item might or might not be connected to a container.

It is common to use the same class for both linked and embedded items. **IsLinkedItem** allows you to make linked items behave differently than embedded items, although many times the code is common.

See Also: **COleServerItem::IsConnected, COleLinkingDoc::OnGetLinkedItem**

COleServerItem::NotifyChanged

void NotifyChanged(DVASPECT *nDrawAspect* **= DVASPECT_CONTENT);**

Parameters

nDrawAspect A value from the **DVASPECT** enumeration that indicates which aspect of the OLE item has changed. This parameter can have any of the following values:

- **DVASPECT_CONTENT** Item is represented in such a way that it can be displayed as an embedded object inside its container.

- **DVASPECT_THUMBNAIL** Item is rendered in a "thumbnail" representation so that it can be displayed in a browsing tool.

- **DVASPECT_ICON** Item is represented by an icon.

- **DVASPECT_DOCPRINT** Item is represented as if it were printed using the Print command from the File menu.

Remarks

Call this function after the linked item has been changed. If a container item is linked to the document with an automatic link, the item is updated to reflect the changes. In container applications written using the Microsoft Foundation Class Library, **COleClientItem::OnChange** is called in response.

See Also: **COleClientItem::OnChange**, **COleServerItem::OnUpdate**, **COleServerDoc::NotifyChanged**

COleServerItem::OnDoVerb

virtual void OnDoVerb(LONG *iVerb* **);**

Parameters

iVerb Specifies the verb to execute. It can be any one of the following:

Value	Meaning	Symbol
0	Primary verb	**OLEIVERB_PRIMARY**
1	Secondary verb	(None)
−1	Display item for editing	**OLEIVERB_SHOW**
−2	Edit item in separate window	**OLEIVERB_OPEN**
−3	Hide item	**OLEIVERB_HIDE**

The −1 value is typically an alias for another verb. If open editing is not supported, −2 has the same effect as −1. For additional values, see **IOleObject::DoVerb** in the *OLE 2 Programmer's Reference, Volume 1*.

Remarks

Called by the framework to execute the specified verb. If the container application was written with the Microsoft Foundation Class Library, this function is called when the **COleClientItem::Activate** member function of the corresponding **COleClientItem** object is called. The default implementation calls the **OnShow** member function if the primary verb or **OLEIVERB_SHOW** is specified, **OnOpen** if the secondary verb or **OLEIVERB_OPEN** is specified, and **OnHide** if **OLEIVERB_HIDE** is specified. The default implementation calls **OnShow** if *iVerb* is not one of the verbs listed above.

Override this function if your primary verb does not show the item. For example, if the item is a sound recording and its primary verb is Play, you would not have to display the server application to play the item.

For more information, see **IOleObject::DoVerb** in the *OLE 2 Programmer's Reference, Volume 1*.

See Also: **COleClientItem::Activate**, **COleServerItem::OnShow**, **COleServerItem::OnOpen**, **COleServerItem::OnHide**

COleServerItem::OnDraw

virtual BOOL OnDraw(CDC* *pDC*, **CSize&** *rSize* **) = 0;**

Return Value

Nonzero if the item was successfully drawn; otherwise 0.

Parameters

pDC   A pointer to the **CDC** object on which to draw the item. The display context is automatically connected to the attribute display context so you can call attribute functions, although doing so would make the metafile device-specific.

rSize   Size, in **HIMETRIC** units, in which to draw the metafile.

Remarks

Called by the framework to render the OLE item into a metafile. The metafile representation of the OLE item is used to display the item in the container application. If the container application was written with the Microsoft Foundation Class Library, the metafile is used by the **Draw** member function of the corresponding **COleClientItem** object. There is no default implementation. You must override this function to draw the item into the device context specified.

See Also: COleClientItem::Draw

COleServerItem::OnDrawEx

virtual BOOL OnDrawEx(CDC* *pDC*, **DVASPECT** *nDrawAspect*, **CSize&** *rSize* **);**

Return Value

Nonzero if the item was successfully drawn; otherwise 0.

Parameters

pDC   A pointer to the **CDC** object on which to draw the item. The DC is automatically connected to the attribute DC so you can call attribute functions, although doing so would make the metafile device-specific.

nDrawAspect   A value from the **DVASPECT** enumeration. This parameter can have any of the following values:

- **DVASPECT_CONTENT**   Item is represented in such a way that it can be displayed as an embedded object inside its container.

- **DVASPECT_THUMBNAIL**   Item is rendered in a "thumbnail" representation so that it can be displayed in a browsing tool.

- **DVASPECT_ICON**   Item is represented by an icon.

- **DVASPECT_DOCPRINT**   Item is represented as if it were printed using the Print command from the File menu.

rSize   Size of the item in **HIMETRIC** units.

Remarks

Called by the framework for all drawing. The default implementation calls **OnDraw** when **DVASPECT** is equal to **DVASPECT_CONTENT**; otherwise it fails.

Override this function to provide presentation data for aspects other than **DVASPECT_CONTENT**, such as **DVASPECT_ICON** or **DVASPECT_THUMBNAIL**.

See Also: **COleServerItem::OnDraw**

COleServerItem::OnGetClipboardData

virtual COleDataSource* OnGetClipboardData(BOOL *bIncludeLink*,
↳ **LPPOINT** *lpOffset*, **LPSIZE** *lpSize* **);**

Return Value

A pointer to a **COleDataSource** object containing the Clipboard data.

Parameters

bIncludeLink   Set this to **TRUE** if link data should be copied to the Clipboard. Set this to **FALSE** if your server application does not support links.

lpOffset   The offset of the mouse cursor from the origin of the object in pixels.

lpSize   The size of the object in pixels.

Remarks

Called by the framework to get a **COleDataSource** object containing all the data that would be placed on the Clipboard by a call to the **CopyToClipboard** member function. The default implementation of this function calls **GetClipboardData**.

See Also: **COleDataSource, COleDataSource::SetClipboard, COleServerItem::CopyToClipboard, COleServerItem::GetClipboardData**

COleServerItem::OnGetExtent

virtual BOOL OnGetExtent(DVASPECT *nDrawAspect*, **CSize&** *rSize* **);**

Return Value

Nonzero if successful; otherwise 0.

Parameters

nDrawAspect   Specifies the aspect of the OLE item whose bounds are to be retrieved. This parameter can have any of the following values:

- **DVASPECT_CONTENT**   Item is represented in such a way that it can be displayed as an embedded object inside its container.

- **DVASPECT_THUMBNAIL**   Item is rendered in a "thumbnail" representation so that it can be displayed in a browsing tool.

- **DVASPECT_ICON**   Item is represented by an icon.

- **DVASPECT_DOCPRINT**   Item is represented as if it were printed using the Print command from the File menu.

rSize   Reference to a **CSize** object that will receive the size of the OLE item.

Remarks

Called by the framework to retrieve the size, in **HIMETRIC** units, of the OLE item.

If the container application was written with the Microsoft Foundation Class Library, this function is called when the **GetExtent** member function of the corresponding **COleClientItem** object is called. The default implementation does nothing. You must implement it yourself. Override this function if you want to perform special processing when handling a request for the size of the OLE item.

See Also: **COleClientItem::Draw**, **COleClientItem::GetExtent**

COleServerItem::OnHide

virtual void OnHide( );

Remarks

Called by the framework to hide the OLE item. The default calls **COleServerDoc::OnShowDocument(FALSE)**. The function also notifies the container that the OLE item has been hidden. Override this function if you want to perform special processing when hiding an OLE item.

See Also: **COleServerItem::OnOpen**, **COleServerItem::OnShow**, **COleServerDoc::OnShowDocument**

COleServerItem::OnInitFromData

virtual BOOL OnInitFromData(COleDataObject* *pDataObject***, BOOL** *bCreation* **);**

Return Value

Nonzero if successful; otherwise 0.

Parameters

pDataObject   Pointer to an OLE data object containing data in various formats for initializing the OLE item.

bCreation   **TRUE** if the function is called to initialize an OLE item being newly created by a container application. **FALSE** if the function is called to replace the contents of an already existing OLE item.

Remarks

Called by the framework to initialize an OLE item using the contents of *pDataObject*. If *bCreation* is **TRUE**, this function is called if a container implements Insert New

Object based on the current selection. The data selected is used when creating the new OLE item. For example, when selecting a range of cells in a spreadsheet program and then using the Insert New Object to create a chart based on the values in the selected range. The default implementation does nothing. Override this function to choose an acceptable format from those offered by *pDataObject* and initialize the OLE item based on the data provided. This is an advanced overridable.

For more information, see **IOleObject::InitFromData** in the *OLE 2 Programmer's Reference, Volume 1*.

COleServerItem::OnOpen

virtual void OnOpen( );

Remarks

Called by the framework to display the OLE item in a separate instance of the server application, rather than in place.

The default implementation activates the first frame window displaying the document that contains the OLE item; if the application is a mini-server, the default implementation shows the main window. The function also notifies the container that the OLE item has been opened.

Override this function if you want to perform special processing when opening an OLE item. This is especially common with linked items where you want to set the selection to the link when it is opened.

For more information, see **IOleClientSite::OnShowWindow** in the *OLE 2 Programmer's Reference, Volume 1*.

See Also: **COleServerItem::OnShow**

COleServerItem::OnQueryUpdateItems

virtual BOOL OnQueryUpdateItems( );

Return Value

Nonzero if the document has items needing updates; 0 if all items are up to date.

Remarks

Called by the framework to determine whether any linked items in the current server document are out of date. An item is out of date if its source document has been changed but the linked item has not been updated to reflect the changes in the document.

See Also: **COleServerItem::OnUpdate**, **COleServerItem::OnUpdateItems**

COleServerItem::OnRenderData

virtual BOOL OnRenderData(LPFORMATETC *lpFormatEtc,*
↪ **LPSTGMEDIUM** *lpStgMedium* **);**

Return Value

Nonzero if successful; otherwise 0.

Parameters

lpFormatEtc   Points to the **FORMATETC** structure specifying the format in which information is requested.

lpStgMedium   Points to a **STGMEDIUM** structure in which the data is to be returned.

Remarks

Called by the framework to retrieve data in the specified format. The specified format is one previously placed in the **COleDataSource** object using the **DelayRenderData** or **DelayRenderFileData** member function for delayed rendering. The default implementation of this function calls **OnRenderFileData** or **OnRenderGlobalData**, respectively, if the supplied storage medium is either a file or memory. If neither of these formats is supplied, the default implementation returns 0 and does nothing.

If *lpStgMedium->tymed* is **TYMED_NULL**, the **STGMEDIUM** should allocated and filled as specified by *lpFormatEtc->tymed*. If not **TYMED_NULL**, the **STGMEDIUM** should be filled in place with the data.

This is an advanced overridable. Override this function to provide your data in the requested format and medium. Depending on your data, you may want to override one of the other versions of this function instead. If your data is small and fixed in size, override **OnRenderGlobalData**. If your data is in a file, or is of variable size, override **OnRenderFileData**.

For more information, see **IDataObject::GetData**, **STGMEDIUM**, **FORMATETC**, and **TYMED** in the *OLE 2 Programmer's Reference, Volume 1*.

See Also: COleServerItem::OnRenderFileData

COleServerItem::OnRenderFileData

virtual BOOL OnRenderFileData(LPFORMATETC *lpFormatEtc,* **CFile*** *pFile* **);**

Return Value

Nonzero if successful; otherwise 0.

Parameters

lpFormatEtc   Points to the **FORMATETC** structure specifying the format in which information is requested.

pFile   Points to a **CFile** object in which the data is to be rendered.

Remarks

Called by the framework to retrieve data in the specified format when the storage medium is a file. The specified format is one previously placed in the **COleDataSource** object using the **DelayRenderData** member function for delayed rendering. The default implementation of this function simply returns **FALSE**.

This is an advanced overridable. Override this function to provide your data in the requested format and medium. Depending on your data, you might want to override one of the other versions of this function instead. If you want to handle multiple storage mediums, override **OnRenderData**. If your data is in a file, or is of variable size, override **OnRenderFileData**.

For more information, see **IDataObject::GetData** and **FORMATETC** in the *OLE 2 Programmer's Reference, Volume 1*.

See Also: **COleServerItem::OnRenderData**

COleServerItem::OnRenderGlobalData

virtual BOOL OnRenderGlobalData(LPFORMATETC *lpFormatEtc*,
↳ **HGLOBAL*** *phGlobal* **);**

Return Value

Nonzero if successful; otherwise 0.

Parameters

lpFormatEtc   Points to the **FORMATETC** structure specifying the format in which information is requested.

phGlobal   Points to a handle to global memory in which the data is to be returned. If no memory has been allocated, this parameter can be **NULL**.

Remarks

Called by the framework to retrieve data in the specified format when the specified storage medium is global memory. The specified format is one previously placed in the **COleDataSource** object using the **DelayRenderData** member function for delayed rendering. The default implementation of this function simply returns **FALSE**.

If *phGlobal* is **NULL**, then a new **HGLOBAL** should be allocated and returned in *phGlobal*. Otherwise, the **HGLOBAL** specified by *phGlobal* should be filled with the data. The amount of data placed in the **HGLOBAL** must not exceed the current size of the memory block. Also, the block cannot be reallocated to a larger size.

This is an advanced overridable. Override this function to provide your data in the requested format and medium. Depending on your data, you may want to override one of the other versions of this function instead. If you want to handle multiple storage mediums, override **OnRenderData**. If your data is in a file, or is of variable size, override **OnRenderFileData**.

For more information, see **IDataObject::GetData** and **FORMATETC** in the *OLE 2 Programmer's Reference, Volume 1*.

See Also: COleServerItem::OnRenderData

COleServerItem::OnSetColorScheme

virtual BOOL OnSetColorScheme(const LOGPALETTE FAR* *lpLogPalette* **);**

Return Value

Nonzero if the color palette is used; otherwise 0.

Parameters

lpLogPalette   Pointer to a Windows **LOGPALETTE** structure.

Remarks

Called by the framework to specify a color palette to be used when editing the OLE item. If the container application was written using the Microsoft Foundation Class Library, this function is called when the **IOleObject::SetColorScheme** function of the corresponding **COleClientItem** object is called. The default implementation returns **FALSE**. Override this function if you want to use the recommended palette. The server application is not required to use the suggested palette.

For more information, see **IOleObject::SetColorScheme** in the *OLE 2 Programmer's Reference, Volume 1*.

COleServerItem::OnSetData

virtual BOOL OnSetData(LPFORMATETC *pFormatEtc*,
↪ **LPSTGMEDIUM** *pStgMedium*, **BOOL** *bRelease* **);**

Return Value

Nonzero if successful; otherwise 0.

Parameters

pFormatEtc   Pointer to a **FORMATETC** structure specifying the format of the data.

pStgMedium   Pointer to a **STGMEDIUM** structure in which the data resides.

bRelease   Indicates who has ownership of the storage medium after completing the function call. The caller decides who is responsible for releasing the resources allocated on behalf of the storage medium. The caller does this by setting *bRelease*.

If *bRelease* is nonzero, the server item takes ownership, freeing the medium when it has finished using it. When *bRelease* is 0, the caller retains ownership and the server item can use the storage medium only for the duration of the call.

Remarks

Called by the framework to replace the OLE item's data with the specified data. The server item does not take ownership of the data until it has successfully obtained it. That is, it does not take ownership if it returns 0. If the data source takes ownership, it frees the storage medium by calling the **ReleaseStgMedium** function.

The default implementation does nothing. Override this function to replace the OLE item's data with the specified data. This is an advanced overridable.

For more information, see **STGMEDIUM**, **FORMATETC**, and **ReleaseStgMedium** in the *OLE 2 Programmer's Reference, Volume 1*.

See Also: **COleDataSource::OnSetData**

COleServerItem::OnSetExtent

> **virtual BOOL OnSetExtent(DVASPECT** n*DrawAspect*, **const CSize&** *size* **);**

Return Value

Nonzero if successful; otherwise 0.

Parameters

nDrawAspect   Specifies the aspect of the OLE item whose bounds are being specified. This parameter can have any of the following values:

- **DVASPECT_CONTENT**   Item is represented in such a way that it can be displayed as an embedded object inside its container.

- **DVASPECT_THUMBNAIL**   Item is rendered in a "thumbnail" representation so that it can be displayed in a browsing tool.

- **DVASPECT_ICON**   Item is represented by an icon.

- **DVASPECT_DOCPRINT**   Item is represented as if it were printed using the Print command from the File menu.

size   A **CSize** structure specifying the new size of the OLE item.

Remarks

Called by the framework to tell the OLE item how much space is available to it in the container document. If the container application was written with the Microsoft Foundation Class Library, this function is called when the **SetExtent** member function of the corresponding **COleClientItem** object is called. The default implementation sets the **m_sizeExtent** member to the specified size if *nDrawAspect* is **DVASPECT_CONTENT**; otherwise it returns 0. Override this function to perform special processing when you change the size of the item.

See Also: **COleClientItem::SetExtent**, **COleServerItem::OnGetExtent**, **COleServerItem::m_sizeExtent**

COleServerItem::OnShow

virtual void OnShow( );

Remarks

Called by the framework to instruct the server application to display the OLE item in place. This function is typically called when the user of the container application creates an item or executes a verb, such as Edit, that requires the item to be shown. The default implementation attempts in-place activation. If this fails, the function calls the **OnOpen** member function to display the OLE item in a separate window.

Override this function if you want to perform special processing when an OLE item is shown.

See Also: **COleServerItem::OnOpen, COleClientItem::Activate**

COleServerItem::OnUpdate

virtual void OnUpdate(COleServerItem* *pSender***, LPARAM** *lHint***,**
↳ **CObject*** *pHint***, DVASPECT** *nDrawAspect* **);**

Parameters

pSender   Pointer to the item that modified the document. Can be **NULL**.

lHint   Contains information about the modification.

pHint   Pointer to an object storing information about the modification.

nDrawAspect   A value from the **DVASPECT** enumeration. This parameter can have any one of the following values:

- **DVASPECT_CONTENT**   Item is represented in such a way that it can be displayed as an embedded object inside its container.

- **DVASPECT_THUMBNAIL**   Item is rendered in a "thumbnail" representation so that it can be displayed in a browsing tool.

- **DVASPECT_ICON**   Item is represented by an icon.

- **DVASPECT_DOCPRINT**   Item is represented as if it were printed using the Print command from the File menu.

Remarks

Called by the framework when an item has been modified. The default implementation calls **NotifyChanged**, regardless of the hint or sender.

See Also: **COleServerItem::NotifyChanged**

COleServerItem::OnUpdateItems

virtual void OnUpdateItems( );

Remarks

Called by the framework to update all items in the server document. The default implementation calls **UpdateLink** for all **COleClientItem** objects in the document.

See Also: **COleServerItem::OnUpdate**, **COleServerItem::OnQueryUpdateItems**

COleServerItem::SetItemName

void SetItemName(LPCTSTR *lpszItemName* **);**

Parameters

lpszItemName   Pointer to the new name of the item.

Remarks

Call this function when you create a linked item to set its name. The name must be unique within the document. When a server application is called to edit a linked item, the application uses this name to find the item. You do not need to call this function for embedded items.

See Also: **COleServerItem::GetItemName**, **COleLinkingDoc::OnGetLinkedItem**

Data Members
COleServerItem::m_sizeExtent

CSize m_sizeExtent;

Remarks

This member tells the server how much of the object is visible in the container document. The default implementation of **OnSetExtent** sets this member.

See Also: **COleServerItem::OnSetExtent**

COleStreamFile

A **COleStreamFile** object represents a stream of data (**IStream**) in a compound file as part of OLE Structured Storage. An **IStorage** object must exist before the stream can be opened or created unless it is a memory stream.

COleStreamFile objects are manipulated exactly like **CFile** objects.

For more information about manipulating streams and storages, see the article "Containers: Compound Files" in *Visual C++ Programmer's Guide* online.

For more information, see **IStream** and **IStorage** in the *OLE 2 Programmer's Reference, Volume 1*.

#include <afxole.h>

See Also: CFile

COleStreamFile Class Members

Construction

COleStreamFile	Constructs a **COleStreamFile** object.

Attributes and Operations

Attach	Associates a stream with the object.
CreateMemoryStream	Creates a stream from global memory and associates it with the object.
CreateStream	Creates a stream and associates it with the object.
Detach	Disassociates the stream from the object.
GetStream	Returns the current stream.
OpenStream	Safely opens a stream and associates it with the object.

Member Functions
COleStreamFile::Attach

void Attach(LPSTREAM *lpStream* **);**

Parameters

    lpStream   Points to the OLE stream (**IStream**) to be associated with the object. Cannot be **NULL**.

Remarks

    Associates the supplied OLE stream with the **COleStreamFile** object. The object must not already be associated with an OLE stream.

    For more information, see **IStream** in the *OLE 2 Programmer's Reference*, *Volume 1*.

    See Also: **COleStreamFile::Detach**

COleStreamFile::COleStreamFile

COleStreamFile(LPSTREAM *lpStream* **= NULL);**

Parameters

    lpStream   Pointer to the OLE stream to be associated with the object.

Remarks

    Creates a **COleStreamFile** object. If *lpStream* is **NULL**, the object is not associated with an OLE stream, otherwise, the object is associated with the supplied OLE stream.

    For more information, see **IStream** in the *OLE 2 Programmer's Reference*, *Volume 1*.

    See Also: **COleStreamFile::Attach**, **CFile**

COleStreamFile::CreateMemoryStream

BOOL CreateMemoryStream(CFileException* *pError* **= NULL);**

Return Value

    Nonzero if the stream is created successfully; otherwise 0.

Parameters

    pError   Points to a **CFileException** object or **NULL** that indicates the completion status of the create operation. Supply this parameter if you want to monitor possible exceptions generated by attempting to create the stream.

Remarks

Safely creates a new stream out of global, shared memory where a failure is a normal, expected condition. The memory is allocated by the OLE subsystem.

For more information, see **CreateStreamOnHGlobal** in the *OLE 2 Programmer's Reference, Volume 1*.

See Also: **COleStreamFile::OpenStream**, **COleStreamFile::CreateStream**, **CFileException**

COleStreamFile::CreateStream

BOOL CreateStream(LPSTORAGE *lpStorage*, **LPCTSTR** *lpszName*,
↳ **DWORD** *nOpenFlags* = **modeReadWrite|shareExclusive|modeCreate**,
↳ **CFileException*** *pError* = **NULL**);

Return Value

Nonzero if the stream is created successfully; otherwise 0.

Parameters

lpStorage   Points to the OLE storage object that contains the stream to be created. Cannot be **NULL**.

lpszStreamName   Name of the stream to be created. Cannot be **NULL**.

nOpenFlags   Access mode to use when opening the stream. Exclusive, read/write, and create modes are used by default. For a complete list of the available modes, see **CFile::CFile**.

pError   Points to a **CFileException** object or **NULL**. Supply this parameter if you want to monitor possible exceptions generated by attempting to create the stream.

Remarks

Safely creates a new stream in the supplied storage object where a failure is a normal, expected condition. A file exception will be thrown if the open fails and *pError* is not **NULL**.

For more information, see **IStorage::CreateStream** in the *OLE 2 Programmer's Reference, Volume 1*.

See Also: **COleStreamFile::OpenStream**, **COleStreamFile::CreateMemoryStream**, **CFileException**

COleStreamFile::Detach

LPSTREAM Detach( );

Return Value

A pointer to the stream (**IStream**) that was associated with the object.

Remarks

Disassociates the stream from the object without closing the stream. The stream must be closed in some other fashion before the program terminates.

For more information, see **IStream** in the *OLE 2 Programmer's Reference*, *Volume 1*.

See Also: COleStreamFile::Attach

COleStreamFile::GetStream

IStream* GetStream( ) const;

Return Value

A pointer to the current stream interface (**IStream**).

Remarks

Call this function to return a pointer to current stream.

COleStreamFile::OpenStream

BOOL OpenStream(LPSTORAGE *lpStorage*, **LPCTSTR** *lpszName*,
  ↪ **DWORD** *nOpenFlags* = **modeReadWrite|shareExclusive**,
  ↪ **CFileException*** *pError* = **NULL**);

Return Value

Nonzero if the stream is opened successfully; otherwise 0.

Parameters

lpStorage   Points to the OLE storage object that contains the stream to be opened. Cannot be **NULL**.

lpszName   Name of the stream to be opened. Cannot be **NULL**.

nOpenFlags   Access mode to use when opening the stream. Exclusive and read/write modes are used by default. For the complete list of the available modes, see **CFile::CFile**.

pError   Points to a **CFileException** object or **NULL**. Supply this parameter if you want to monitor possible exceptions generated by attempting to open the stream.

Remarks

Opens an existing stream. A file exception will be thrown if the open fails and *pError* is not **NULL**.

For more information, see **IStorage::OpenStream** in the *OLE 2 Programmer's Reference*, *Volume 1*.

See Also: COleStreamFile::CreateStream,
COleStreamFile::CreateMemoryStream, **CFileException**

COleTemplateServer

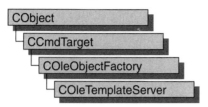

The **COleTemplateServer** class is used for OLE visual editing servers, automation servers, and link containers (applications that support links to embeddings). This class is derived from the class **COleObjectFactory**; usually, you can use **COleTemplateServer** directly rather than deriving your own class. **COleTemplateServer** uses a **CDocTemplate** object to manage the server documents. Use **COleTemplateServer** when implementing a full server, that is, a server that can be run as a standalone application. Full servers are typically multiple document interface (MDI) applications, although single document interface (SDI) applications are supported. One **COleTemplateServer** object is needed for each type of server document an application supports; that is, if your server application supports both worksheets and charts, you must have two **COleTemplateServer** objects.

COleTemplateServer overrides the **OnCreateInstance** member function defined by **COleObjectFactory**. This member function is called by the framework to create a C++ object of the proper type.

For more information about servers, see the article "Servers: Implementing a Server" in *Visual C++ Programmer's Guide* online.

#include <afxdisp.h>

See Also: **COleServerDoc**, **COleServerItem**

COleTemplateServer Class Members

Construction

COleTemplateServer	Constructs a **COleTemplateServer** object.

Operations

ConnectTemplate	Connects a document template to the underlying **COleObjectFactory** object.
UpdateRegistry	Registers the document type with the OLE system registry.

Member Functions

COleTemplateServer::COleTemplateServer

COleTemplateServer( );

Remarks

Constructs a **COleTemplateServer** object.

For a brief description of the use of the **COleTemplateServer** class, see the **COleLinkingDoc** class overview.

COleTemplateServer::ConnectTemplate

void ConnectTemplate(REFCLSID *clsid*, **CDocTemplate*** *pDocTemplate*,
↪ **BOOL** *bMultiInstance* **);**

Parameters

clsid   Reference to the OLE class ID that the template requests.

pDocTemplate   Pointer to the document template.

bMultiInstance   Indicates whether a single instance of the application can support multiple instantiations. If **TRUE**, multiple instances of the application are launched for each request to create an object.

Remarks

Connects the document template pointed to by *pDocTemplate* to the underlying **COleObjectFactory** object.

For more information, see **CLSID Key** in the *OLE 2 Programmer's Reference, Volume 1*.

See Also: CDocTemplate

COleTemplateServer::UpdateRegistry

void UpdateRegistry(OLE_APPTYPE *nAppType* = **OAT_INPLACE_SERVER,**
↪ **LPCSTR*** *rglpszRegister* = **NULL, LPCSTR FAR*** *rglpszOverwrite* = **NULL);**

Parameters

nAppType   A value from the **OLE_APPTYPE** enumeration, which is defined in AFXDISP.H. It can have any one of the following values:

- **OAT_INPLACE_SERVER**   Server has full server user-interface.

- **OAT_SERVER**   Server supports only embedding.

- **OAT_CONTAINER** Container supports links to embedded objects.

- **OAT_DISPATCH_OBJECT** Object is **IDispatch**-capable.

- **OAT_DOCOBJECT_SERVER** Server supports both embedding and the Document Object component model.

rglpszRegister A list of entries that is written into the registry only if no entries exist.

rglpszOverwrite A list of entries that is written into the registry regardless of whether any preceding entries exist.

Remarks

Loads file-type information from the document-template string and places that information in the OLE system registry.

The registration information is loaded by means of a call to **CDocTemplate::GetDocString**. The substrings retrieved are those identified by the indexes **regFileTypeId**, **regFileTypeName**, and **fileNewName**, as described in the **GetDocString** reference pages.

If the **regFileTypeId** substring is empty or if the call to **GetDocString** fails for any other reason, this function fails and the file information is not entered in the registry.

The information in the arguments *rglpszRegister* and *rglpszOverwrite* is written to the registry through a call to **AfxOleRegisterServerClass**. The default information, which is registered when the two arguments are **NULL**, is suitable for most applications. For information on the structure of the information in these arguments, see **AfxOleRegisterServerClass**.

For more information, see **IDispatch** in the *Win32 SDK OLE Programmer's Reference*.

See Also: **CDocTemplate::GetDocString, AfxOleRegisterServerClass**

COleUpdateDialog

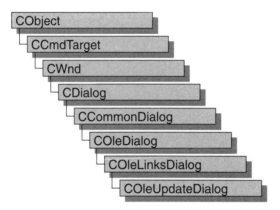

The **COleUpdateDialog** class is used for a special case of the OLE Edit Links dialog box, which should be used when you need to update only existing linked or embedded objects in a document.

For more information regarding OLE-specific dialog boxes, see the article "Dialog Boxes in OLE" in *Visual C++ Programmer's Guide* online.

#include <afxodlgs.h>

See Also: COleLinksDialog

COleUpdateDialog Class Members

Construction

COleUpdateDialog	Constructs a **COleUpdateDialog** object.

Operations

DoModal	Displays the Edit Links dialog box in an update mode.

Member Functions
COleUpdateDialog::COleUpdateDialog

COleUpdateDialog(COleDocument* *pDoc***, BOOL** *bUpdateLinks* **= TRUE,**
↳ **BOOL** *bUpdateEmbeddings* **= FALSE, CWnd*** *pParentWnd* **= NULL);**

Parameters

pDoc   Points to the document containing the links that may need updating.

bUpdateLinks   Flag that determines whether linked objects are to be updated.

bUpdateEmbeddings   Flag that determines whether embedded objects are to be updated.

pParentWnd   Points to the parent or owner window object (of type **CWnd**) to which the dialog object belongs. If it is **NULL**, the parent window of the dialog box will be set to the main application window.

Remarks

This function constructs only a **COleUpdateDialog** object. To display the dialog box, call **DoModal**. This class should be used instead of **COleLinksDialog** when you want to update only existing linked or embedded items.

See Also: **COleDialog, COleLinksDialog, COleDocument, CWnd, CDialog, COleUpdateDialog::DoModal**

COleUpdateDialog::DoModal

virtual int DoModal( );

Return Value

Completion status for the dialog box. One of the following values:

- **IDOK** if the dialog box returned successfully.

- **IDCANCEL** if none of the linked or embedded items in the current document need updating.

- **IDABORT** if an error occurred. If **IDABORT** is returned, call the **COleDialog::GetLastError** member function to get more information about the type of error that occurred. For a listing of possible errors, see the **OleUIEditLinks** function in the *OLE 2.01 User Interface Library*.

Remarks

Call this function to display the Edit Links dialog box in update mode. All links and/or embeddings are updated unless the user selects the Cancel button.

See Also: **COleDialog::GetLastError, COleLinksDialog::DoModal**

COleVariant

COleVariant does not have a base class.

A **COleVariant** object encapsulates the **VARIANT** data type. This data type is used in OLE automation. Specifically, the **DISPPARAMS** structure contains a pointer to an array of **VARIANT** structures. A **DISPPARAMS** structure is used to pass parameters to **IDispatch::Invoke**.

Note This class is derived from the **VARIANT** structure. This means you can pass a **COleVariant** in a parameter that calls for a **VARIANT** and that the data members of the **VARIANT** structure are accessible data members of **COleVariant**.

The two related MFC classes **COleCurrency** and **COleDateTime** encapsulate the variant data types **CURRENCY** (**VT_CY**) and **DATE** (**VT_DATE**). The **COleVariant** class is used extensively in the DAO classes; see these classes for typical usage of this class, for example **CDaoQueryDef** and **CDaoRecordset**.

For more information, see the **VARIANT**, **CURRENCY**, **DISPPARAMS**, and **IDispatch::Invoke** entries in the *Win32 SDK OLE Programmer's Reference*.

For more information on the **COleVariant** class and its use in OLE automation, see "Passing Parameters in OLE Automation" in the article "Automation" in *Visual C++ Programmer's Guide* online.

#include <afxdisp.h>

COleVariant Class Members

Construction

COleVariant	Constructs a **COleVariant** object.

Operations

Attach	Attaches a **VARIANT** to a **COleVariant**.
ChangeType	Changes the variant type of this **COleVariant** object.
Clear	Clears this **COleVariant** object.
Detach	Detaches a **VARIANT** from a **COleVariant** and returns the **VARIANT**.

Operators

operator LPCVARIANT	Converts a **COleVariant** value into an **LPCVARIANT**.
operator LPVARIANT	Converts a **COleVariant** object into an **LPVARIANT**.
operator =	Copies a **COleVariant** value.
operator ==	Compares two **COleVariant** values.

Archive/Dump	
operator <<	Outputs a **COleVariant** value to **CArchive** or **CDumpContext**.
operator >>	Inputs a **COleVariant** object from **CArchive**.

Member Functions

COleVariant::Attach

void Attach(VARIANT& *varSrc* **);**

Parameters

varSrc   An existing **VARIANT** object to be attached to the current **COleVariant** object.

Remarks

Call this function to attach the given **VARIANT** object to the current **COleVariant** object. This function sets the **VARTYPE** of *varSrc* to **VT_EMPTY**.

For more information, see the **VARIANT** and **VARTYPE** entries in the *Win32 SDK OLE Programmer's Reference*.

See Also: **COleVariant::operator LPCVARIANT**, **COleVariant::operator LPVARIANT**

COleVariant::COleVariant

COleVariant( );
COleVariant(const VARIANT& *varSrc* **);**
COleVariant(const COleVariant& *varSrc* **);**
COleVariant(LPCVARIANT *pSrc* **);**
COleVariant(LPCTSTR *lpszSrc* **);**
COleVariant(LPCTSTR *lpszSrc*, **VARTYPE** *vtSrc* **);**
COleVariant(CString& *strSrc* **);**
COleVariant(BYTE *nSrc* **);**
COleVariant(short *nSrc*, **VARTYPE** *vtSrc* = **VT_I2);**
COleVariant(long *lSrc*, **VARTYPE** *vtSrc* = **VT_I4);**
COleVariant(const COleCurrency& *curSrc* **);**
COleVariant(float *fltSrc* **);**
COleVariant(double *dblSrc* **);**
COleVariant(const COleDateTime& *dateSrc* **);**
COleVariant(const CByteArray& *arrSrc* **);**
COleVariant(const CLongBinary& *lbSrc* **);**

Parameters

varSrc   An existing **COleVariant** or **VARIANT** object to be copied into the new **COleVariant** object.

pSrc   A pointer to a **VARIANT** object that will be copied into the new **COleVariant** object.

lpszSrc   A null-terminated string to be copied into the new **COleVariant** object.

vtSrc   The **VARTYPE** for the new **COleVariant** object.

strSrc   A **CString** object to be copied into the new **COleVariant** object.

nSrc, *lSrc*   A numerical value to be copied into the new **COleVariant** object.

vtSrc   The **VARTYPE** for the new **COleVariant** object.

curSrc   A **COleCurrency** object to be copied into the new **COleVariant** object.

fltSrc, *dblSrc*   A numerical value to be copied into the new **COleVariant** object.

dateSrc   A **COleDateTime** object to be copied into the new **COleVariant** object.

arrSrc   A **CByteArray** object to be copied into the new **COleVariant** object.

lbSrc   A **CLongBinary** object to be copied into the new **COleVariant** object.

Remarks

All of these constructors create new **COleVariant** objects initialized to the specified value. A brief description of each of these constructors follows.

- **COleVariant( )**   Creates an empty **COleVariant** object, **VT_EMPTY**.

- **COleVariant(** *varSrc* **)**   Copies an existing **VARIANT** or **COleVariant** object. The variant type is retained.

- **COleVariant(** *pSrc* **)**   Copies an existing **VARIANT** or **COleVariant** object. The variant type is retained.

- **COleVariant(** *lpszSrc* **)**   Copies a string into the new object, **VT_BSTR** (UNICODE).

- **COleVariant(** *lpszSrc*, *vtSrc* **)**   Copies a string into the new object. The parameter *vtSrc* must be **VT_BSTR** (UNICODE) or **VT_BSTRT** (ANSI).

- **COleVariant(** *strSrc* **)**   Copies a string into the new object, **VT_BSTR** (UNICODE).

- **COleVariant(** *nSrc* **)**   Copies an 8-bit integer into the new object, **VT_UI1**.

- **COleVariant(** *nSrc*, *vtSrc* **)**   Copies a 16-bit integer (or Boolean value) into the new object. The parameter *vtSrc* must be **VT_I2** or **VT_BOOL**.

- **COleVariant(** *lSrc*, *vtSrc* **)**   Copies a 32-bit integer (or **SCODE** value) into the new object. The parameter *vtSrc* must be **VT_I4**, **VT_ERROR**, or **VT_BOOL**.

- **COleVariant(** *curSrc* **)**   Copies a **COleCurrency** value into the new object, **VT_CY**.

- **COleVariant(** *fltSrc* **)** Copies a 32-bit floating-point value into the new object, **VT_R4**.

- **COleVariant(** *dblSrc* **)** Copies a 64-bit floating-point value into the new object, **VT_R8**.

- **COleVariant(** *dateSrc* **)** Copies a **COleDateTime** value into the new object, **VT_DATE**.

- **COleVariant(** *arrSrc* **)** Copies a **CByteArray** object into the new object, **VT_EMPTY**.

- **COleVariant(** *lbSrc* **)** Copies a **CLongBinary** object into the new object, **VT_EMPTY**.

For more information, see the **VARIANT** and **VARTYPE** entries in the *Win32 SDK OLE Programmer's Reference*.

For more information on **SCODE**, see "Structure of OLE Error Codes" in the *Win32 SDK OLE Programmer's Reference*.

See Also: **COleVariant::operator =**, **CString**, **COleCurrency**, **COleDateTime**

COleVariant::ChangeType

void ChangeType(VARTYPE *vartype***, LPVARIANT** *pSrc* **= NULL);**

Parameters

vartype   The **VARTYPE** for this **COleVariant** object.

pSrc   A pointer to the **VARIANT** object to be converted. If this value is **NULL**, this **COleVariant** object is used as the source for the conversion.

Remarks

Call this function to convert the type of variant value in this **COleVariant** object.

For more information, see the **VARIANT**, **VARTYPE**, and **VariantChangeType** entries in the *Win32 SDK OLE Programmer's Reference*.

See Also: **COleVariant::operator =**

COleVariant::Clear

void Clear( );

Remarks

Call this function to clear the **VARIANT**. This sets the **VARTYPE** for this object to **VT_EMPTY**. The **COleVariant** destructor calls this function.

For more information, see the **VARIANT**, **VARTYPE**, and **VariantClear** entries in the *Win32 SDK OLE Programmer's Reference*.

COleVariant::Detach

VARIANT Detach( );

Return Type

The underlying **VARIANT** value of this **COleVariant** object.

Remarks

Call this function to detach the underlying **VARIANT** object from this **COleVariant** object. This function sets the **VARTYPE** for this **COleVariant** object to **VT_EMPTY**.

Note After calling **Detach**, it is the caller's responsibility to call **VariantClear** on the resulting **VARIANT** structure.

For more information, see the **VARIANT**, **VARTYPE**, and **VariantClear** entries in the *Win32 SDK OLE Programmer's Reference*.

See Also: **COleVariant::operator LPCVARIANT**, **COleVariant::operator LPVARIANT**

COleVariant::SetString

void SetString(LPCTSTR *lpszSrc***, VARTYPE** *vtSrc* **);**

Parameters

lpszSrc A null-terminated string to be copied into the new **COleVariant** object.

vtSrc The **VARTYPE** for the new **COleVariant** object.

Remarks

Call this function to set the string to a particular type. The parameter *vtSrc* must be **VT_BSTR** (UNICODE) or **VT_BSTRT** (ANSI). **SetString** is typically used to set strings to ANSI, since the default for the **COleVariant::COleVariant** constructor with a string or string pointer parameter and no **VARTYPE** is UNICODE.

A DAO recordset in a non-UNICODE build expects strings to be ANSI. Thus, for DAO functions that use **COleVariant** objects, if you are not creating a UNICODE recordset, you must use the **COleVariant::COleVariant(** *lpszSrc*, *vtSrc* **)** form of constructor with *vtSrc* set to **VT_BSTRT** (ANSI) or use **SetString** with *vtSrc* set to **VT_BSTRT** to make ANSI strings. For example, the **CDAORecordset** functions **CDAORecordset::Seek** and **CDAORecordset::SetFieldValue** use **COleVariant** objects as parameters. These objects must be ANSI if the DAO recordset is not UNICODE.

See Also: **COleVariant::COleVariant**, **CDAORecordset::Seek**, **CDAORecordset::SetFieldValue**

Operators
COleVariant::operator =

const COleVariant& operator =(const VARIANT& *varSrc* **);**
const COleVariant& operator =(LPCVARIANT *pSrc* **);**
const COleVariant& operator =(const COleVariant& *varSrc* **);**
const COleVariant& operator =(const LPCTSTR *lpszSrc* **);**
const COleVariant& operator =(const CString& *strSrc* **);**
const COleVariant& operator =(const BYTE *nSrc* **);**
const COleVariant& operator =(const short *nSrc* **);**
const COleVariant& operator =(const long *lSrc* **);**
const COleVariant& operator =(const COleCurrency& *curSrc* **);**
const COleVariant& operator =(const float *fltSrc* **);**
const COleVariant& operator =(const double *dblSrc* **);**
const COleVariant& operator =(const COleDateTime& *dateSrc* **);**
const COleVariant& operator =(const CByteArray& *arrSrc* **);**
const COleVariant& operator =(const CLongBinary& *lbSrc* **);**

Remarks

These overloaded assignment operators copy the source value into this **COleVariant** object. A brief description of each operator follows:

- **operator =(** *varSrc* **)** Copies an existing **VARIANT** or **COleVariant** object into this object.

- **operator =(** *pSrc* **)** Copies the **VARIANT** object accessed by *pSrc* into this object.

- **operator =(** *lpszSrc* **)** Copies a null-terminated string into this object and sets the **VARTYPE** to **VT_BSTR**.

- **operator =(** *strSrc* **)** Copies a **CString** object into this object and sets the **VARTYPE** to **VT_BSTR**.

- **operator =(** *nSrc* **)** Copies an 8- or 16-bit integer value into this object. If *nSrc* is an 8-bit value, the **VARTYPE** of this is set to **VT_UI1**. If *nSrc* is a 16-bit value and the **VARTYPE** of this is **VT_BOOL**, it is kept; otherwise, it is set to **VT_I2**.

- **operator =(** *lSrc* **)** Copies a 32-bit integer value into this object. If the **VARTYPE** of this is **VT_ERROR**, it is kept; otherwise, it is set to **VT_I4**.

- **operator =(** *curSrc* **)** Copies a **COleCurrency** object into this object and sets the **VARTYPE** to **VT_CY**.

- **operator =(** *fltSrc* **)** Copies a 32-bit floating-point value into this object and sets the **VARTYPE** to **VT_R4**.

- **operator =(** *dblSrc* **)** Copies a 64-bit floating-point value into this object and sets the **VARTYPE** to **VT_R8**.

- **operator =(** *dateSrc* **)** Copies a **COleDateTime** object into this object and sets the **VARTYPE** to **VT_DATE**.
- **operator =(** *arrSrc* **)** Copies a **CByteArray** object into this **COleVariant** object.
- **operator =(** *lbSrc* **)** Copies a **CLongBinary** object into this **COleVariant** object.

For more information, see the **VARIANT** and **VARTYPE** entries in the *Win32 SDK OLE Programmer's Reference*.

See Also: **COleVariant::COleVariant, COleCurrency, COleDateTime**

COleVariant::operator ==

BOOL operator ==(const VARIANT& *varSrc* **) const;**
BOOL operator ==(LPCVARIANT *pSrc* **) const;**

Remarks

This operator compares two variant values and returns nonzero if they are equal; otherwise 0.

See Also: **COleVariant::operator =**

COleVariant::operator LPCVARIANT

operator LPCVARIANT( ) const;

Remarks

This casting operator returns a **VARIANT** structure whose value is copied from this **COleVariant** object.

For more information, see the **VARIANT** entry in the *Win32 SDK OLE Programmer's Reference*.

See Also: **COleVariant::operator LPVARIANT**

COleVariant::operator LPVARIANT

operator LPVARIANT( );

Remarks

Call this casting operator to access the underlying **VARIANT** structure for this **COleVariant** object.

Caution Changing the value in the **VARIANT** structure accessed by the pointer returned by this function will change the value of this **COleVariant** object.

For more information, see the **VARIANT** entry in the *Win32 SDK OLE Programmer's Reference*.

See Also: **COleVariant::operator LPCVARIANT**

COleVariant::operator <<, >>

friend CDumpContext& AFXAPI operator <<(CDumpContext& *dc,*
↳ **OleVariant** *varSrc* **);**
friend CArchive& AFXAPI operator <<(CArchive& *ar,* **COleVariant** *varSrc* **);**
friend CArchive& AFXAPI operator >>(CArchive& *ar,* **COleVariant&** *varSrc* **);**

Remarks

The **COleVariant** insertion (<<) operator supports diagnostic dumping and storing to an archive. The extraction (>>) operator supports loading from an archive.

See Also: **CDumpContext**, **CArchive**

CPageSetupDialog

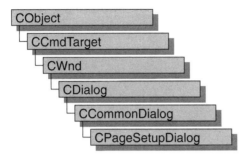

The **CPageSetupDialog** class encapsulates the services provided by the Windows common OLE Page Setup dialog box with additional support for setting and modifying print margins. This class is designed to take the place of the Print Setup dialog box.

To use a **CPageSetupDialog** object, first create the object using the **CPageSetupDialog** constructor. Once the dialog box has been constructed, you can set or modify any values in the **m_psd** data member to initialize the values of the dialog box's controls. The **m_psd** structure is of type **PAGESETUPDLG**. The topic "Setting Up the Printed Page" in the Win32 SDK documentation show an example of the initialization of this structure.

After initializing the dialog box controls, call the **DoModal** member function to display the dialog box and allow the user to select print options. **DoModal** returns whether the user selected the OK (**IDOK**) or Cancel (**IDCANCEL**) button.

If **DoModal** returns **IDOK**, you can use several of **CPageSetupDialog's** member functions, or access the **m_psd** data member, to retrieve information input by the user.

Note After the common OLE Page Setup dialog box is dismissed, any changes made by the user will not be saved by the framework. It is up to the application itself to save any values from this dialog box to a permanent location, such as member of the application's document or application class.

#include <afxdlgs.h>

CPageSetupDialog Class Members

Attributes

CreatePrinterDC	Creates a device context for printing.
GetDeviceName	Returns the device name of the printer.

(continued)

Attributes *(continued)*

GetDevMode	Returns the current **DEVMODE** of the printer.
GetDriverName	Returns the driver used by the printer.
GetMargins	Returns the current margin settings of the printer.
GetPortName	Returns the output port name.
GetPaperSize	Returns the paper size of the printer.

Construction

CPageSetupDialog	Constructs a **CPageSetupDialog** object.

Data Members

m_psd	A structure used to customize a **CPageSetupDialog** object.

Operations

DoModal	Displays the dialog box and allows the user make a selection.

Overridables

OnDrawPage	Called by the framework to render a screen image of a printed page.
PreDrawPage	Called by the framework before rendering a screen image of a printed page.

Member Functions

CPageSetupDialog::CPageSetupDialog

CPageSetupDialog(DWORD *dwFlags* **= PSD_MARGINS | PSD_INWININIINTLMEASURE,**
↪ **CWnd*** *pParentWnd* **= NULL);**

Parameters

dwFlags One or more flags you can use to customize the settings of the dialog box. The values can be combined using the bitwise-OR operator. These values have the following meanings:

- **PSD_DEFAULTMINMARGINS** Sets the minimum allowable widths for the page margins to be the same as the printer's minimums. This flag is ignored if the **PSD_MARGINS** and **PSD_MINMARGINS** flags are also specified.

- **PSD_INWININIINTLMEASURE** Not implemented.

- **PSD_MINMARGINS** Causes the system to use the values specified in the **rtMinMargin** member as the minimum allowable widths for the left, top, right, and bottom margins. The system prevents the user from entering a width that is less than the specified minimum. If **PSD_MINMARGINS** is not specified, the system sets the minimum allowable widths to those allowed by the printer.

- **PSD_MARGINS**   Activates the margin control area.

- **PSD_INTHOUSANDTHSOFINCHES**   Causes the units of the dialog box to be measured in 1/1000 of an inch.

- **PSD_INHUNDREDTHSOFMILLIMETERS**   Causes the units of the dialog box to be measured in 1/100 of a millimeter.

- **PSD_DISABLEMARGINS**   Disables the margin dialog box controls.

- **PSD_DISABLEPRINTER**   Disables the Printer button.

- **PSD_NOWARNING**   Prevents the warning message from being displayed when there is no default printer.

- **PSD_DISABLEORIENTATION**   Disables the page orientation dialog control.

- **PSD_RETURNDEFAULT**   Causes **CPageSetupDialog** to return **DEVMODE** and **DEVNAMES** structures that are initialized for the system default printer without displaying a dialog box. It is assumed that both **hDevNames** and **hDevMode** are **NULL**; otherwise, the function returns an error. If the system default printer is supported by an old printer driver (earlier than Windows version 3.0), only **hDevNames** is returned; **hDevMode** is **NULL**.

- **PSD_DISABLEPAPER**   Disables the paper selection control.

- **PSD_SHOWHELP**   Causes the dialog box to show the Help button. The **hwndOwner** member must not be **NULL** if this flag is specified.

- **PSD_ENABLEPAGESETUPHOOK**   Enables the hook function specified in **lpfnSetupHook**.

- **PSD_ENABLEPAGESETUPTEMPLATE**   Causes the operating system to create the dialog box by using the dialog template box identified by **hInstance** and **lpSetupTemplateName**.

- **PSD_ENABLEPAGESETUPTEMPLATEHANDLE**   Indicates that **hInstance** identifies a data block that contains a preloaded dialog box template. The system ignores **lpSetupTemplateName** if this flag is specified.

- **PSD_ENABLEPAGEPAINTHOOK**   Enables the hook function specified in **lpfnPagePaintHook**.

- **PSD_DISABLEPAGEPAINTING**   Disables the draw area of the dialog box.

pParentWnd   Pointer to the dialog box's parent or owner.

Remarks

Call this function to construct a **CPageSetupDialog** object. Use the **DoModal** function to display the dialog box.

See Also: CPrintDialog, CPageSetupDialog

CPageSetupDialog::CreatePrinterDC

HDC CreatePrinterDC( );

Return Value

Handle to the newly created printer device context (DC).

Remarks

Creates a printer device context from the **DEVMODE** and **DEVNAMES** structures.

**See Also: CPageSetupDialog::GetDevMode,
CPageSetupDialog::GetDeviceName, CPageSetupDialog::GetDriverName**

CPageSetupDialog::DoModal

virtual int DoModal( );

Return Value

IDOK or **IDCANCEL** if successful; otherwise 0. **IDOK** and **IDCANCEL** are constants that indicate whether the user selected the OK or Cancel button.

If **IDCANCEL** is returned, you can call the Windows **CommDlgExtendedError** function to determine whether an error occurred.

Remarks

Call this function to display the Windows common OLE Page Setup dialog box and allow the user to select various print setup options such as the printing margins, size and orientation of the paper, and destination printer. In addition, the user can access the printer setup options such as network location and properties specific to the selected printer.

If you want to initialize the various Page Setup dialog options by setting members of the **m_psd** structure, you should do so before calling **DoModal**, and after the dialog object is constructed. After calling **DoModal**, call other member functions to retrieve the settings or information input by the user into the dialog box.

If you want to propagate the current settings entered by the user, make a call to **CWinApp::SelectPrinter**. This function takes the information from the **CPageSetupDialog** object and initializes and selects a new printer DC with the proper attributes.

```
AfxGetApp()->SelectPrinter(dlg.m_psd.hDevNames, dlg.m_psd.hDevMode);
```

See Also: **CPageSetupDialog::m_psd**

CPageSetupDialog::GetDeviceName

CString GetDeviceName( ) const;

Return Value

The device name used by the **CPageSetupDialog** object.

Remarks

Call this function after **DoModal** to retrieve the name of the currently selected printer.

CPageSetupDialog::GetDevMode

LPDEVMODE GetDevMode( ) const;

Return Value

The **DEVMODE** data structure, which contains information about the device initialization and environment of a print driver.

Remarks

Call this function after calling **DoModal** to retrieve information about the printer device context of the **CPageSetupDialog** object.

CPageSetupDialog::GetDriverName

CString GetDriverName( ) const;

Return Value

The name of the currently selected printer device driver.

Remarks

Call this function after calling **DoModal** to retrieve the name of the currently selected printer device driver.

See Also: **CPageSetupDialog::GetDeviceName**, **CPageSetupDialog::GetDevMode**, **CPageSetupDialog::GetPortName**

CPageSetupDialog::GetMargins

void GetMargins(LPRECT *lpRectMargins*, **LPRECT** *lpRectMinMargins* **) const;**

Parameters

lpRectMargins   Pointer to a **RECT** structure or **CRect** object that describes (in 1/1000 inches or 1/100 mm) the print margins for the currently selected printer. Pass **NULL** for this parameter, if you are not interested in this rectangle.

lpRectMinMargins Pointer to a **RECT** structure or **CRect** object that describes (in 1/1000 inches or 1/100 mm) the minimum print margins for the currently selected printer. Pass **NULL** for this parameter, if you are not interested in this rectangle.

Remarks

Call this function after a call to **DoModal** to retrieve the margins of the printer device driver.

CPageSetupDialog::GetPaperSize

CSize GetPaperSize( ) const;

Return Value

A **CSize** object containing the size of the paper (in 1/1000 inches or 1/100 mm) selected for printing.

Remarks

Call this function to retrieve the size of the paper selected for printing.

CPageSetupDialog::GetPortName

CString GetPortName( ) const;

Return Value

The name of the currently selected printer port.

Remarks

Call this function after calling **DoModal** to retrieve the name of the currently selected printer port.

See Also: **CPageSetupDialog::GetDeviceName**, **CPageSetupDialog::GetDriverName**

CPageSetupDialog::OnDrawPage

virtual UINT OnDrawPage(CDC* *pDC*, **UINT** *nMessage*, **LPRECT** *lpRect* **);**

Return Value

Nonzero value if handled; otherwise 0.

Parameters

pDC Pointer to the printer device context.

nMessage Specifies a message, indicating the area of the page currently being drawn. Can be one of the following:

- **WM_PSD_FULLPAGERECT** The entire page area.

- **WM_PSD_MINMARGINRECT** Current minimum margins.

- **WM_PSD_MARGINRECT** Current margins.

- **WM_PSD_GREEKTEXTRECT** Contents of the page.

- **WM_PSD_ENVSTAMPRECT** Area reserved for a postage stamp representation.

- **WM_PSD_YAFULLPAGERECT** Area for a return address representation. This area extends to the edges of the sample page area.

lpRect Pointer to a **CRect** or **RECT** object containing the coordinates of the drawing area.

Remarks

Called by the framework to draw a screen image of a printed page. This image is then displayed as part of the common OLE Page Setup dialog box. The default implementation draws an image of a page of text.

Override this function to customize the drawing of a specific area of the image, or the entire image. You can do this by using a **switch** statement with **case** statements checking the value of *nMessage*. For example, to customize the rendering of the contents of the page image, you could use the following example code:

```
switch( nType )
{
   case WM_PSD_GREEKTEXTRECT:
      DrawMyImage(pDC, lpRect);      //draws my special graphic
      return 1;
   default:
      return ::Draw(CDC* pDC, UINT nDrawType, LPRECT lpRect);
};
```

Note that you do not need to handle every case of *nMessage*. You can choose to handle one component of the image, several components of the image, or the whole area.

See Also: **CPageSetupDialog::PreDrawPage**

CPageSetupDialog::PreDrawPage

virtual UINT PreDrawPage(WORD *wPaper*, **WORD** *wFlags*,
   ↪ LPPAGESETUPDLG *pPSD* **);**

Return Value

Nonzero value if handled; otherwise 0.

Parameters

wPaper Specifies a value that indicates the paper size. This value can be one of the **DMPAPER_** values listed in the description of the **DEVMODE** structure.

wFlags Indicates the orientation of the paper or envelope, and whether the printer is a dot-matrix or HPPCL (Hewlett Packard Printer Control Language) device. This parameter can have one of the following values:

- 0x001   Paper in landscape mode (dot matrix)
- 0x003   Paper in landscape mode (HPPCL)
- 0x005   Paper in portrait mode (dot matrix)
- 0x007   Paper in portrait mode (HPPCL)
- 0x00b   Envelope in landscape mode (HPPCL)
- 0x00d   Envelope in portrait mode (dot matrix)
- 0x019   Envelope in landscape mode (dot matrix)
- 0x01f   Envelope in portrait mode (dot matrix)

pPSD Pointer to a **PAGESETUPDLG** structure. For more information on this structure, see the Win32 documentation.

Remarks

Called by the framework before drawing the screen image of a printed page. Override this function to customize the drawing of the image. If you override this function and return **TRUE**, you must draw the entire image. If you override this function and return **FALSE**, the entire default image is drawn by the framework.

See Also: **CPageSetupDialog::OnDrawPage**

Data Members

CPageSetupDialog::m_psd

Remarks

A structure of type **PAGESETUPDLG**, whose members store the characteristics of the dialog object. After constructing a **CPageSetupDialog** object, you can use **m_psd** to set various aspects of the dialog box before calling the **DoModal** member function.

If you modify the **m_psd** data member directly, you will override any default behavior.

For more information on the **PAGESETUPDLG** structure, see the Win32 documentation.

CPaintDC

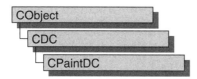

The **CPaintDC** class is a device-context class derived from **CDC**. It performs a **CWnd::BeginPaint** at construction time and **CWnd::EndPaint** at destruction time.

A **CPaintDC** object can only be used when responding to a **WM_PAINT** message, usually in your **OnPaint** message-handler member function.

For more information on using **CPaintDC**, see "Device Contexts" in *Visual C++ Programmer's Guide* online.

#include <afxwin.h>

CPaintDC Class Members

Data Members

m_ps	Contains the **PAINTSTRUCT** used to paint the client area.
m_hWnd	The **HWND** to which this **CPaintDC** object is attached.

Construction

CPaintDC	Constructs a **CPaintDC** connected to the specified **CWnd**.

Member Functions
CPaintDC::CPaintDC

CPaintDC(CWnd* *pWnd* **); throw(CResourceException);**

Parameters

    pWnd   Points to the **CWnd** object to which the **CPaintDC** object belongs.

Remarks

    Constructs a **CPaintDC** object, prepares the application window for painting, and stores the **PAINTSTRUCT** structure in the **m_ps** member variable.

An exception (of type **CResourceException**) is thrown if the Windows **GetDC** call fails. A device context may not be available if Windows has already allocated all of its available device contexts. Your application competes for the five common display contexts available at any given time under Windows.

Data Members
CPaintDC::m_hWnd

Remarks

The **HWND** to which this **CPaintDC** object is attached. **m_hWnd** is a protected variable of type **HWND**.

CPaintDC::m_ps

Remarks

m_ps is a public member variable of type **PAINTSTRUCT**. It is the **PAINTSTRUCT** that is passed to and filled out by **CWnd::BeginPaint**.

The **PAINTSTRUCT** contains information that the application uses to paint the client area of the window associated with a **CPaintDC** object.

Note that you can access the device-context handle through the **PAINTSTRUCT**. However, you can access the handle more directly through the **m_hDC** member variable that **CPaintDC** inherits from **CDC**.

CPalette

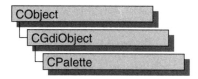

The **CPalette** class encapsulates a Windows color palette. A palette provides an interface between an application and a color output device (such as a display device). The interface allows the application to take full advantage of the color capabilities of the output device without severely interfering with the colors displayed by other applications. Windows uses the application's logical palette (a list of needed colors) and the system palette (which defines available colors) to determine the colors used.

A **CPalette** object provides member functions for manipulating the palette referred to by the object. Construct a **CPalette** object and use its member functions to create the actual palette, a graphics device interface (GDI) object, and to manipulate its entries and other properties.

For more information on using **CPalette**, see "Graphic Objects" in *Visual C++ Programmer's Guide* online.

#include <afxwin.h>

See Also: **CPalette::GetPaletteEntries**, **CPalette::SetPaletteEntries**

CPalette Class Members

Construction

CPalette	Constructs a **CPalette** object with no attached Windows palette. You must initialize the **CPalette** object with one of the initialization member functions before it can be used.

Initialization

CreatePalette	Creates a Windows color palette and attaches it to the **CPalette** object.
CreateHalftonePalette	Creates a halftone palette for the device context and attaches it to the **CPalette** object.

Operations

FromHandle	Returns a pointer to a **CPalette** object when given a handle to a Windows palette object.
AnimatePalette	Replaces entries in the logical palette identified by the **CPalette** object. The application does not have to update its client area, because Windows maps the new entries into the system palette immediately.
GetNearestPaletteIndex	Returns the index of the entry in the logical palette that most closely matches a color value.
ResizePalette	Changes the size of the logical palette specified by the **CPalette** object to the specified number of entries.

Attributes

GetEntryCount	Retrieves the number of palette entries in a logical palette.
GetPaletteEntries	Retrieves a range of palette entries in a logical palette.
SetPaletteEntries	Sets RGB color values and flags in a range of entries in a logical palette.
operator HPALETTE	Returns the **HPALETTE** attached to the **CPalette**.

Member Functions

CPalette::AnimatePalette

void AnimatePalette(UINT *nStartIndex***, UINT** *nNumEntries***,**
   → **LPPALETTEENTRY** *lpPaletteColors* **);**

Parameters

nStartIndex   Specifies the first entry in the palette to be animated.

nNumEntries   Specifies the number of entries in the palette to be animated.

lpPaletteColors   Points to the first member of an array of **PALETTEENTRY** structures to replace the palette entries identified by *nStartIndex* and *nNumEntries*.

Remarks

Replaces entries in the logical palette attached to the **CPalette** object. When an application calls **AnimatePalette**, it does not have to update its client area, because Windows maps the new entries into the system palette immediately.

The **AnimatePalette** function will only change entries with the **PC_RESERVED** flag set in the corresponding **palPaletteEntry** member of the **LOGPALETTE** structure that is attached to the **CPalette** object. See **LOGPALETTE** in the *Win32 SDK Programmer's Reference* for more information about this structure.

See Also: **CPalette::CreatePalette, ::AnimatePalette**

CPalette::CPalette

CPalette( );

Remarks

Constructs a **CPalette** object. The object has no attached palette until you call **CreatePalette** to attach one.

See Also: CPalette::CreatePalette

CPalette::CreateHalftonePalette

BOOL CreateHalftonePalette(CDC* *pDC* **);**

Return Value

Nonzero if the function is successful; otherwise 0.

Parameters

pDC   Identifies the device context.

Remarks

Creates a halftone palette for the device context. An application should create a halftone palette when the stretching mode of a device context is set to **HALFTONE**. The logical halftone palette returned by the **CreateHalftonePalette** member function should then be selected and realized into the device context before the **CDC::StretchBlt** or **::StretchDIBits** function is called.

See the *Win32 SDK Programmer's Reference* for more information about **CreateHalftonePalette** and **StretchDIBits**.

See Also: CDC::RealizePalette, CDC::SelectPalette, CDC::SetStretchBltMode, ::CreateHalftonePalette, ::StretchDIBits

---

CPalette::CreatePalette

BOOL CreatePalette(LPLOGPALETTE *lpLogPalette* **);**

Return Value

Nonzero if successful; otherwise 0.

Parameters

lpLogPalette   Points to a **LOGPALETTE** structure that contains information about the colors in the logical palette.

Remarks

Initializes a **CPalette** object by creating a Windows logical color palette and attaching it to the **CPalette** object.

See the *Win32 SDK Programmer's Reference* for more information about the **LOGPALETTE** structure.

See Also: **::CreatePalette**, **LOGPALETTE**

CPalette::FromHandle

static CPalette* PASCAL FromHandle(HPALETTE *hPalette* **);**

Return Value

A pointer to a **CPalette** object if successful; otherwise **NULL**.

Parameters

hPalette   A handle to a Windows GDI color palette.

Remarks

Returns a pointer to a **CPalette** object when given a handle to a Windows palette object. If a **CPalette** object is not already attached to the Windows palette, a temporary **CPalette** object is created and attached. This temporary **CPalette** object is valid only until the next time the application has idle time in its event loop, at which time all temporary graphic objects are deleted. In other words, the temporary object is valid only during the processing of one window message.

CPalette::GetEntryCount

int GetEntryCount( );

Return Value

Number of entries in a logical palette.

Remarks

Call this member function to retrieve the number of entries in a given logical palette.

See Also: **CPalette::GetPaletteEntries**, **CPalette::SetPaletteEntries**

CPalette::GetNearestPaletteIndex

UINT GetNearestPaletteIndex(COLORREF *crColor* **) const;**

Return Value

The index of an entry in a logical palette. The entry contains the color that most nearly matches the specified color.

Parameters

crColor   Specifies the color to be matched.

Remarks

Returns the index of the entry in the logical palette that most closely matches the specified color value.

See Also: **::GetNearestPaletteIndex**

CPalette::GetPaletteEntries

UINT GetPaletteEntries(UINT *nStartIndex*, **UINT** *nNumEntries*,
↳ **LPPALETTEENTRY** *lpPaletteColors*) **const;**

Return Value

The number of entries retrieved from the logical palette; 0 if the function failed.

Parameters

nStartIndex   Specifies the first entry in the logical palette to be retrieved.

nNumEntries   Specifies the number of entries in the logical palette to be retrieved.

lpPaletteColors   Points to an array of **PALETTEENTRY** data structures to receive the palette entries. The array must contain at least as many data structures as specified by *nNumEntries*.

Remarks

Retrieves a range of palette entries in a logical palette.

See Also: **::GetPaletteEntries**, **CPalette::SetPaletteEntries**

CPalette::operator HPALETTE

operator HPALETTE( ) const;

Return Value

If successful, a handle to the Windows GDI object represented by the **CPalette** object; otherwise **NULL**.

Remarks

Use this operator to get the attached Windows GDI handle of the **CPalette** object. This operator is a casting operator, which supports direct use of an **HPALETTE** object.

For more information about using graphic objects, see the article "Graphic Objects" in the *Win32 SDK Programmer's Reference*.

CPalette::ResizePalette

BOOL ResizePalette(UINT *nNumEntries* **);**

Return Value

Nonzero if the palette was successfully resized; otherwise 0.

Parameters

nNumEntries   Specifies the number of entries in the palette after it has been resized.

Remarks

Changes the size of the logical palette attached to the **CPalette** object to the number of entries specified by *nNumEntries*. If an application calls **ResizePalette** to reduce the size of the palette, the entries remaining in the resized palette are unchanged. If the application calls **ResizePalette** to enlarge the palette, the additional palette entries are set to black (the red, green, and blue values are all 0), and the flags for all additional entries are set to 0.

For more information on the Windows API **ResizePalette**, see **::ResizePalette** in the *Win32 SDK Programmer's Reference*.

See Also: ::ResizePalette

CPalette::SetPaletteEntries

UINT SetPaletteEntries(UINT *nStartIndex***, UINT** *nNumEntries***,**
↪ LPPALETTEENTRY *lpPaletteColors* **);**

Return Value

The number of entries set in the logical palette; 0 if the function failed.

Parameters

nStartIndex   Specifies the first entry in the logical palette to be set.

nNumEntries   Specifies the number of entries in the logical palette to be set.

lpPaletteColors   Points to an array of **PALETTEENTRY** data structures to receive the palette entries. The array must contain at least as many data structures as specified by *nNumEntries*.

Remarks

Sets RGB color values and flags in a range of entries in a logical palette.

If the logical palette is selected into a device context when the application calls **SetPaletteEntries**, the changes will not take effect until the application calls **CDC::RealizePalette**.

For more information on the Windows structure **PALETTEENTRY**, see **PALETTEENTRY** in the *Win32 SDK Programmer's Reference*.

See Also: CDC::RealizePalette, CPalette::GetPaletteEntries, ::SetPaletteEntries

CPen

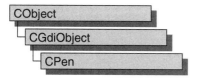

The **CPen** class encapsulates a Windows graphics device interface (GDI) pen.

For more information on using **CPen**, see "Graphic Objects" in *Visual C++ Programmer's Guide* online.

#include <afxwin.h>

See Also: **CBrush**

CPen Class Members

Construction

CPen	Constructs a **CPen** object.

Initialization

CreatePen	Creates a logical cosmetic or geometric pen with the specified style, width, and brush attributes, and attaches it to the **CPen** object.
CreatePenIndirect	Creates a pen with the style, width, and color given in a **LOGPEN** structure, and attaches it to the **CPen** object.

Operations

FromHandle	Returns a pointer to a **CPen** object when given a Windows **HPEN**.

Attributes

operator HPEN	Returns the Windows handle attached to the **CPen** object.
GetLogPen	Gets a **LOGPEN** underlying structure.
GetExtLogPen	Gets an **EXTLOGPEN** underlying structure.

Member Functions
CPen::CPen

CPen( );
CPen(int *nPenStyle*, **int** *nWidth*, **COLORREF** *crColor* **)**;
  throw(CResourceException);
CPen(int *nPenStyle*, **int** *nWidth*, **const LOGBRUSH*** *pLogBrush*,
  ↳ **int** *nStyleCount* **= 0, const DWORD*** *lpStyle* **= NULL)**;
  throw(CResourceException);

Parameters

nPenStyle Specifies the pen style. This parameter in the first version of the constructor can be one of the following values:

- **PS_SOLID** Creates a solid pen.

- **PS_DASH** Creates a dashed pen. Valid only when the pen width is 1 or less, in device units.

- **PS_DOT** Creates a dotted pen. Valid only when the pen width is 1 or less, in device units.

- **PS_DASHDOT** Creates a pen with alternating dashes and dots. Valid only when the pen width is 1 or less, in device units.

- **PS_DASHDOTDOT** Creates a pen with alternating dashes and double dots. Valid only when the pen width is 1 or less, in device units.

- **PS_NULL** Creates a null pen.

- **PS_INSIDEFRAME** Creates a pen that draws a line inside the frame of closed shapes produced by the Windows GDI output functions that specify a bounding rectangle (for example, the **Ellipse**, **Rectangle**, **RoundRect**, **Pie**, and **Chord** member functions). When this style is used with Windows GDI output functions that do not specify a bounding rectangle (for example, the **LineTo** member function), the drawing area of the pen is not limited by a frame.

The second version of the **CPen** constructor specifies a combination of type, style, end cap, and join attributes. The values from each category should be combined by using the bitwise OR operator (|). The pen type can be one of the following values:

- **PS_GEOMETRIC** Creates a geometric pen.

- **PS_COSMETIC** Creates a cosmetic pen.

The second version of the **CPen** constructor adds the following pen styles for *nPenStyle*:

- **PS_ALTERNATE** Creates a pen that sets every other pixel. (This style is applicable only for cosmetic pens.)

- **PS_USERSTYLE** Creates a pen that uses a styling array supplied by the user.

The end cap can be one of the following values:

- **PS_ENDCAP_ROUND** End caps are round.

- **PS_ENDCAP_SQUARE** End caps are square.

- **PS_ENDCAP_FLAT** End caps are flat.

The join can be one of the following values:

- **PS_JOIN_BEVEL** Joins are beveled.

- **PS_JOIN_MITER** Joins are mitered when they are within the current limit set by the **::SetMiterLimit** function. If the join exceeds this limit, it is beveled.

- **PS_JOIN_ROUND** Joins are round.

nWidth Specifies the width of the pen.

- For the first version of the constructor, if this value is 0, the width in device units is always 1 pixel, regardless of the mapping mode.

- For the second version of the constructor, if *nPenStyle* is **PS_GEOMETRIC**, the width is given in logical units. If *nPenStyle* is **PS_COSMETIC**, the width must be set to 1.

crColor Contains an RGB color for the pen.

pLogBrush Points to a **LOGBRUSH** structure. If *nPenStyle* is **PS_COSMETIC**, the *lbColor* member of the **LOGBRUSH** structure specifies the color of the pen and the *lbStyle* member of the **LOGBRUSH** structure must be set to **BS_SOLID**. If *nPenStyle* is **PS_GEOMETRIC**, all members must be used to specify the brush attributes of the pen.

nStyleCount Specifies the length, in doubleword units, of the *lpStyle* array. This value must be zero if *nPenStyle* is not **PS_USERSTYLE**.

lpStyle Points to an array of doubleword values. The first value specifies the length of the first dash in a user-defined style, the second value specifies the length of the first space, and so on. This pointer must be **NULL** if *nPenStyle* is not **PS_USERSTYLE**.

Remarks

If you use the constructor with no arguments, you must initialize the resulting **CPen** object with the **CreatePen**, **CreatePenIndirect**, or **CreateStockObject** member functions. If you use the constructor that takes arguments, then no further initialization is necessary. The constructor with arguments can throw an exception if errors are encountered, while the constructor with no arguments will always succeed.

See Also: **CPen::CreatePen, CPen::CreatePenIndirect,
CGdiObject::CreateStockObject**

CPen::CreatePen

BOOL CreatePen(int *nPenStyle*, **int** *nWidth*, **COLORREF** *crColor* **);**
BOOL CreatePen(int *nPenStyle*, **int** *nWidth*, **const LOGBRUSH*** *pLogBrush*,
→ **int** *nStyleCount* = **0, const DWORD*** *lpStyle* = **NULL);**

Return Value

Nonzero, or the handle of a logical pen, if successful; otherwise 0.

Parameters

nPenStyle   Specifies the style for the pen. For a list of possible values, see the
nPenStyle parameter in the **CPen** constructor.

nWidth   Specifies the width of the pen.

- For the first version of **CreatePen**, if this value is 0, the width in device units is
  always 1 pixel, regardless of the mapping mode.

- For the second version of **CreatePen**, if *nPenStyle* is **PS_GEOMETRIC**, the
  width is given in logical units. If *nPenStyle* is **PS_COSMETIC**, the width must
  be set to 1.

crColor   Contains an RGB color for the pen.

pLogBrush   Points to a **LOGBRUSH** structure. If *nPenStyle* is **PS_COSMETIC**, the
lbColor member of the **LOGBRUSH** structure specifies the color of the pen and
the **lbStyle** member of the **LOGBRUSH** structure must be set to **BS_SOLID**. If
nPenStyle is **PS_GEOMETRIC**, all members must be used to specify the brush
attributes of the pen.

nStyleCount   Specifies the length, in doubleword units, of the *lpStyle* array. This
value must be zero if *nPenStyle* is not **PS_USERSTYLE**.

lpStyle   Points to an array of doubleword values. The first value specifies the length of
the first dash in a user-defined style, the second value specifies the length of the first
space, and so on. This pointer must be **NULL** if *nPenStyle* is not **PS_USERSTYLE**.

Remarks

The first version of **CreatePen** initializes a pen with the specified style, width, and
color. The pen can be subsequently selected as the current pen for any device context.

Pens that have a width greater than 1 pixel should always have either the **PS_NULL**,
PS_SOLID, or **PS_INSIDEFRAME** style.

If a pen has the **PS_INSIDEFRAME** style and a color that does not match a color in
the logical color table, the pen is drawn with a dithered color. The **PS_SOLID** pen style
cannot be used to create a pen with a dithered color. The style **PS_INSIDEFRAME** is
identical to **PS_SOLID** if the pen width is less than or equal to 1.

The second version of **CreatePen** initializes a logical cosmetic or geometric pen that has the specified style, width, and brush attributes. The width of a cosmetic pen is always 1; the width of a geometric pen is always specified in world units. After an application creates a logical pen, it can select that pen into a device context by calling the **CDC::SelectObject** function. After a pen is selected into a device context, it can be used to draw lines and curves.

- If *nPenStyle* is **PS_COSMETIC** and **PS_USERSTYLE**, the entries in the *lpStyle* array specify lengths of dashes and spaces in style units. A style unit is defined by the device in which the pen is used to draw a line.

- If *nPenStyle* is **PS_GEOMETRIC** and **PS_USERSTYLE**, the entries in the *lpStyle* array specify lengths of dashes and spaces in logical units.

- If *nPenStyle* is **PS_ALTERNATE**, the style unit is ignored and every other pixel is set.

When an application no longer requires a given pen, it should call the **CGdiObject::DeleteObject** member function to delete the pen from the device context.

See Also: **CPen::CreatePenIndirect**, **CPen::CPen**, **CGdiObject::DeleteObject**, **LOGBRUSH**

CPen::CreatePenIndirect

BOOL CreatePenIndirect(LPLOGPEN *lpLogPen* **);**

Return Value
Nonzero if the function is successful; otherwise 0.

Parameters
lpLogPen   Points to the Windows **LOGPEN** structure that contains information about the pen.

Remarks
Initializes a pen that has the style, width, and color given in the structure pointed to by *lpLogPen*.

Pens that have a width greater than 1 pixel should always have either the **PS_NULL**, **PS_SOLID**, or **PS_INSIDEFRAME** style.

If a pen has the **PS_INSIDEFRAME** style and a color that does not match a color in the logical color table, the pen is drawn with a dithered color. The **PS_INSIDEFRAME** style is identical to **PS_SOLID** if the pen width is less than or equal to 1.

See Also: **CPen::CreatePen**, **CPen::CPen**

CPen::FromHandle

static CPen* PASCAL FromHandle(HPEN *hPen* **);**

Return Value

A pointer to a **CPen** object if successful; otherwise **NULL**.

Parameters

hPen   **HPEN** handle to Windows GDI pen.

Remarks

Returns a pointer to a **CPen** object given a handle to a Windows GDI pen object. If a **CPen** object is not attached to the handle, a temporary **CPen** object is created and attached. This temporary **CPen** object is valid only until the next time the application has idle time in its event loop, at which time all temporary graphic objects are deleted. In other words, the temporary object is only valid during the processing of one window message.

CPen::GetExtLogPen

int GetExtLogPen(EXTLOGPEN* *pLogPen* **);**

Return Value

Nonzero if successful; otherwise 0.

Parameters

pLogPen   Points to an **EXTLOGPEN** structure that contains information about the pen.

Remarks

Call this member function to get an **EXTLOGPEN** underlying structure. The **EXTLOGPEN** structure defines the style, width, and brush attributes of a pen. For example, call **GetExtLogPen** to match the particular style of a pen.

See the following topics in the *Win 32 SDK Programmer's Reference* for information about pen attributes:

- **GetObject**
- **EXTLOGPEN**
- **LOGPEN**
- **ExtCreatePen**

Example

The following code example demonstrates calling **GetExtLogPen** to retrieve a pen's attributes, and then create a new, cosmetic pen with the same color.

```
EXTLOGPEN extlogpen;
penExisting.GetExtLogPen( &extlogpen );
CPen penOther;
```

```
LOGBRUSH LogBrush={ extlogpen.elpBrushStyle, extlogpen.elpColor,
↪ extlogpen.elpHatch };
penOther.CreatePen( PS_COSMETIC, 1, &LogBrush );
```

See Also: CPen::GetLogPen, CPen::CreatePen

CPen::GetLogPen

int GetLogPen(LOGPEN* *pLogPen* **);**

Return Value

Nonzero if successful; otherwise 0.

Parameters

pLogPen   Points to a **LOGPEN** structure to contain information about the pen.

Remarks

Call this member function to get a **LOGPEN** underlying structure. The **LOGPEN** structure defines the style, color, and pattern of a pen.

For example, call **GetLogPen** to match the particular style of pen.

See the following topics in the *Win 32 SDK Programmer's Reference* for information about pen attributes:

- **GetObject**
- **LOGPEN**

Example

The following code example demonstrates calling **GetLogPen** to retrieve a pen character, and then create a new, solid pen with the same color.

```
LOGPEN logpen;
penExisting.GetLogPen( &logpen );
CPen penOther( PS_SOLID, 0, logpen.lopnColor);
```

See Also: CPen::GetExtLogPen

CPen::operator HPEN

operator HPEN( ) const;

Return Value

If successful, a handle to the Windows GDI object represented by the **CPen** object; otherwise **NULL**.

Remarks

Use this operator to get the attached Windows GDI handle of the **CPen** object. This operator is a casting operator, which supports direct use of an **HPEN** object.

For more information about using graphic objects, see the article "Graphic Objects" in *Win 32 SDK Programmer's Reference*.

CPictureHolder

CPictureHolder does not have a base class.

The purpose of the **CPictureHolder** class is implementation of a Picture property, which allows the user to display a picture in your control. With the stock Picture property, the developer can specify a bitmap, icon, or metafile for display.

For information on creating custom picture properties, see the article "ActiveX Controls: Using Pictures in an ActiveX Control" in *Visual C++ Programmer's Guide* online.

#include <afxctl.h>

See Also: **CFontHolder**

CPictureHolder Class Members

Data Members

m_pPict	A pointer to a picture object.

Construction

CPictureHolder	Constructs a **CPictureHolder** object.

Operations

GetDisplayString	Retrieves the string displayed in a control container's property browser.
CreateEmpty	Creates an empty **CPictureHolder** object.
CreateFromBitmap	Creates a **CPictureHolder** object from a bitmap.
CreateFromMetafile	Creates a **CPictureHolder** object from a metafile.
CreateFromIcon	Creates a **CPictureHolder** object from an icon.
GetPictureDispatch	Returns the **CPictureHolder** object's **IDispatch** interface.
SetPictureDispatch	Sets the **CPictureHolder** object's **IDispatch** interface.
GetType	Tells whether the **CPictureHolder** object is a bitmap, a metafile, or an icon.
Render	Renders the picture.

Member Functions

CPictureHolder::CPictureHolder

CPictureHolder( );

Remarks

Constructs a **CPictureHolder** object.

See Also: **CPictureHolder::CreateEmpty**

CPictureHolder::CreateEmpty

BOOL CreateEmpty( );

Return Value

Nonzero if the object is successfully created; otherwise 0.

Remarks

Creates an empty **CPictureHolder** object and connects it to an **IPicture** interface.

See Also: **CPictureHolder::CreateFromBitmap**, **CPictureHolder::CreateFromIcon**, **CPictureHolder::CreateFromMetafile**

CPictureHolder::CreateFromBitmap

BOOL CreateFromBitmap(UINT *idResource* **);**
BOOL CreateFromBitmap(CBitmap* *pBitmap*, **CPalette*** *pPal* **= NULL,**
   ➥ **BOOL** *bTransferOwnership* **= TRUE);**
BOOL CreateFromBitmap(HBITMAP *hbm*, **HPALETTE** *hpal* **= NULL);**

Return Value

Nonzero if the object is successfully created; otherwise 0.

Parameters

idResource   Resource ID of a bitmap resource.

pBitmap   Pointer to a **CBitmap** object.

pPal   Pointer to a **CPalette** object.

bTransferOwnership   Indicates whether the picture object will take ownership of the bitmap and palette objects.

hbm   Handle to the bitmap from which the **CPictureHolder** object is created.

hpal   Handle to the palette used for rendering the bitmap.

Remarks

Uses a bitmap to initialize the picture object in a **CPictureHolder**. If *bTransferOwnership* is **TRUE**, the caller should not use the bitmap or palette object in any way after this call returns. If *bTransferOwnership* is **FALSE**, the caller is responsible for ensuring that the bitmap and palette objects remain valid for the lifetime of the picture object.

See Also: **CPictureHolder::CreateEmpty**, **CPictureHolder::CreateFromIcon**, **CPictureHolder::CreateFromMetafile**

CPictureHolder::CreateFromIcon

BOOL CreateFromIcon(UINT *idResource* **);**
BOOL CreateFromIcon(HICON *hIcon*, **BOOL** *bTransferOwnership* = **FALSE);**

Return Value

Nonzero if the object is successfully created; otherwise 0.

Parameters

idResource   Resource ID of a bitmap resource.

hIcon   Handle to the icon from which the **CPictureHolder** object is created.

bTransferOwnership   Indicates whether the picture object will take ownership of the icon object.

Remarks

Uses an icon to initialize the picture object in a **CPictureHolder**. If *bTransferOwnership* is **TRUE**, the caller should not use the icon object in any way after this call returns. If *bTransferOwnership* is **FALSE**, the caller is responsible for ensuring that the icon object remains valid for the lifetime of the picture object.

See Also: **CPictureHolder::CreateEmpty**, **CPictureHolder::CreateFromBitmap**, **CPictureHolder::CreateFromMetafile**

CPictureHolder::CreateFromMetafile

BOOL CreateFromMetafile(HMETAFILE *hmf*, **int** *xExt*, **int** *yExt*,
↪ **BOOL** *bTransferOwnership* = **FALSE);**

Return Value

Nonzero if the object is successfully created; otherwise 0.

Parameters

hmf   Handle to the metafile used to create the **CPictureHolder** object.

xExt   X extent of the picture.

yExt   Y extent of the picture.

bTransferOwnership   Indicates whether the picture object will take ownership of the metafile object.

Remarks

Uses a metafile to initialize the picture object in a **CPictureHolder**. If *bTransferOwnership* is **TRUE**, the caller should not use the metafile object in any way after this call returns. If *bTransferOwnership* is **FALSE**, the caller is responsible for ensuring that the metafile object remains valid for the lifetime of the picture object.

See Also: **CPictureHolder::CreateEmpty**, **CPictureHolder::CreateFromBitmap**, **CPictureHolder::CreateFromIcon**

CPictureHolder::GetDisplayString

BOOL GetDisplayString(CString& *strValue* **);**

Return Value

Nonzero if the string is successfully retrieved; otherwise 0.

Parameters

strValue   Reference to the **CString** that is to hold the display string.

Remarks

Retrieves the string that is displayed in a container's property browser.

CPictureHolder::GetPictureDispatch

LPPICTUREDISP GetPictureDispatch( );

Return Value

A pointer to the **CPictureHolder** object's **IPictureDisp** interface.

Remarks

This function returns a pointer to the **CPictureHolder** object's **IPictureDisp** interface. The caller must call **Release** on this pointer when finished with it.

See Also: **CPictureHolder::SetPictureDispatch**

CPictureHolder::GetType

short GetType( );

Return Value

A value indicating the type of the picture. Possible values and their meanings are as follows:

Value	Meaning
PICTYPE_UNINITIALIZED	**CPictureHolder** object is unititialized.
PICTYPE_NONE	**CPictureHolder** object is empty.
PICTYPE_BITMAP	Picture is a bitmap.
PICTYPE_METAFILE	Picture is a metafile.
PICTYPE_ICON	Picture is an icon.

Remarks

Indicates whether the picture is a bitmap, metafile, or icon.

CPictureHolder::Render

> **void Render(CDC*** *pDC*, **const CRect&** *rcRender*, **const CRect&** *rcWBounds* **);**

Parameters

pDC   Pointer to the display context in which the picture is to be rendered.

rcRender   Rectangle in which the picture is to be rendered.

rcWBounds   A rectangle representing the bounding rectangle of the object rendering the picture. For a control, this rectangle is the *rcBounds* parameter passed to an override of **COleControl::OnDraw**.

Remarks

Renders the picture in the rectangle referenced by *rcRender*.

CPictureHolder::SetPictureDispatch

> **void SetPictureDispatch(LPPICTUREDISP** *pDisp* **);**

Parameters

pDisp   Pointer to the new **IPictureDisp** interface.

Remarks

Connects the **CPictureHolder** object to a **IPictureDisp** interface.

See Also: **CPictureHolder::GetPictureDispatch**

Data Members

CPictureHolder::m_pPict

Remarks

A pointer to the **CPictureHolder** object's **IPicture** interface.

CPoint

The **CPoint** class is similar to the Windows **POINT** structure. It also includes member functions to manipulate **CPoint** and **POINT** structures.

A **CPoint** object can be used wherever a **POINT** structure is used. The operators of this class that interact with a "size" accept either **CSize** objects or **SIZE** structures, since the two are interchangeable.

Note This class is derived from the **tagPOINT** structure. (The name **tagPOINT** is a less-commonly-used name for the **POINT** structure.) This means that the data members of the **POINT** structure, **x** and **y**, are accessible data members of **CPoint**.

#include <afxwin.h>

See Also: **CRect**, **CSize**

CPoint Class Members

Construction

CPoint	Constructs a **CPoint**.

Operations

Offset	Adds values to the **x** and **y** members of the **CPoint**.
operator ==	Checks for equality between two points.
operator !=	Checks for inequality between two points.

Operators Returning CPoint Values

operator +=	Offsets **CPoint** by adding a size or point.
operator −=	Offsets **CPoint** by subtracting a size or point.
operator +	Returns the sum of a **CPoint** and a size or point.
operator −	Returns the difference of a **CPoint** and a size, or the negation of a point.

Operators Returning CSize Values

operator −	Returns the size difference between two points.

Operators Returning CRect Values

operator +	Returns a **CRect** offset by a size.
operator −	Returns a **CRect** offset by a negative size.

Member Functions
CPoint::CPoint

> **CPoint( );**
> **CPoint(int** *initX*, **int** *initY* **);**
> **CPoint(POINT** *initPt* **);**
> **CPoint(SIZE** *initSize* **);**
> **CPoint(DWORD** *dwPoint* **);**

Parameters

initX Specifies the value of the **x** member of **CPoint**.

initY Specifies the value of the **y** member of **CPoint**.

initPt **POINT** structure or **CPoint** that specifies the values used to initialize **CPoint**.

initSize **SIZE** structure or **CSize** that specifies the values used to initialize **CPoint**.

dwPoint Sets the **x** member to the low-order word of *dwPoint* and the **y** member to the high-order word of *dwPoint*.

Remarks

Constructs a **CPoint** object. If no arguments are given, **x** and **y** members are not initialized.

CPoint::Offset

> **void Offset(int** *xOffset*, **int** *yOffset* **);**
> **void Offset(POINT** *point* **);**
> **void Offset(SIZE** *size* **);**

Parameters

xOffset Specifies the amount to offset the **x** member of the **CPoint**.

yOffset Specifies the amount to offset the **y** member of the **CPoint**.

point Specifies the amount (**POINT** or **CPoint**) to offset the **CPoint**.

size Specifies the amount (**SIZE** or **CSize**) to offset the **CPoint**.

Remarks

Adds values to the **x** and **y** members of the **CPoint**.

See Also: **CPoint::operator +=, CPoint::operator −=**

Operators
CPoint::operator ==

BOOL operator ==(POINT *point* **) const;**

Return Value

Nonzero if the points are equal; otherwise 0.

Parameters

point   Contains a **POINT** structure or **CPoint** object.

Remarks

Checks for equality between two points.

See Also: CPoint::Operator !=

CPoint::operator !=

BOOL operator !=(POINT *point* **) const;**

Return Value

Nonzero if the points are not equal; otherwise 0.

Parameters

point   Contains a **POINT** structure or **CPoint** object.

Remarks

Checks for inequality between two points.

See Also: CPoint::Operator ==

CPoint::operator +=

void operator +=(SIZE *size* **);**
void operator +=(POINT *point* **);**

Parameters

size   Contains a **SIZE** structure or **CSize** object.

point   Contains a **POINT** structure or **CPoint** object.

Remarks

The first overload adds a size to the **CPoint**.

The second overload adds a point to the **CPoint**.

In both cases, addition is done by adding the **x** (or **cx**) member of the right-hand operand to the **x** member of the **CPoint** and adding the **y** (or **cy**) member of the right-hand operand to the **y** member of the **CPoint**.

For example, adding CPoint(5, -7) to a variable which contains CPoint(30, 40) changes the variable to CPoint(35, 33).

See Also: **CPoint::operator –=**, **CPoint::operator +**, **CPoint::Offset**

CPoint::operator -=

void operator –=(SIZE *size* **);**
void operator–=(POINT *point* **);**

Parameters

size   Contains a **SIZE** structure or **CSize** object.

point   Contains a **POINT** structure or **CPoint** object.

Remarks

The first overload subtracts a size from the **CPoint**.

The second overload subtracts a point from the **CPoint**.

In both cases, subtraction is done by subtracting the **x** (or **cx**) member of the right-hand operand from the **x** member of the **CPoint** and subtracting the **y** (or **cy**) member of the right-hand operand from the **y** member of the **CPoint**.

For example, subtracting CPoint(5, -7) from a variable which contains CPoint(30, 40) changes the variable to CPoint(25, 47).

See Also: **CPoint::operator –**, **CPoint::operator +=**, **CPoint::Offset**

CPoint::operator +

CPoint operator +(SIZE *size* **) const;**
CPoint operator +(POINT *point* **) const;**
CRect operator +(const RECT* *lpRect* **) const;**

Return Value

A **CPoint** that is offset by a size, a **CPoint** that is offset by a point, or a **CRect** offset by a point.

Parameters

size   Contains a **SIZE** structure or **CSize** object.

point   Contains a **POINT** structure or **CPoint** object.

lpRect   Contains a pointer to a **RECT** structure or **CRect** object.

Remarks

Use this operator to offset **CPoint** by a **CPoint** or **CSize** object, or to offset a **CRect** by a **CPoint**.

For example, using one of the first two overloads to offset the point CPoint(25, -19) by a point CPoint(15, 5) or size CSize(15, 5) returns the value CPoint(40, -14).

Adding a rectangle to a point returns the rectangle after being offset by the the **x** and **y** values specified in the point. For example, using the last overload to offset a rectangle CRect(125, 219, 325, 419) by a point CPoint(25, -19) returns CRect(150, 200, 350, 400).

See Also: **CPoint::operator −=, CPoint::operator −, CPoint::operator +=, CSize::operator +, CRect::operator +, CPoint::Offset, CRect::OffsetRect**

CPoint::operator -

CSize operator −(POINT *point* **) const;**
CPoint operator −(SIZE *size* **) const;**
CRect operator −(const RECT* *lpRect* **) const;**
CPoint operator −( ) const;

Return Value

A **CSize** that is the difference between two points, a **CPoint** that is offset by the negation of a size, a **CRect** that is offset by the negation of a point, or a **CPoint** that is the negation of a point.

Parameters

point   A **POINT** structure or **CPoint** object.

size   A **SIZE** structure or **CSize** object.

lpRect   A pointer to a **RECT** structure or a **CRect** object.

Remarks

Use one of the first two overloads to subtract a **CPoint** or **CSize** object from **CPoint**. The third overload offsets a **CRect** by the negation of **CPoint**. Finally, use the unary operator to negate **CPoint**.

For example, using the first overload to find the difference between two points CPoint(25, -19) and CPoint(15, 5) returns CSize(10, -24).

Subtracting a **CSize** from **CPoint** does the same calculation as above but returns a **CPoint** object, not a **CSize** object. For example, using the second overload to find the difference between the point CPoint(25, -19) and the size CSize(15, 5) returns CPoint(10, -24).

Subtracting a rectangle from a point returns the rectangle offset by the negatives of the **x** and **y** values specified in the point. For example, using the last overload to offset the rectangle CRect(125, 200, 325, 400) by the point CPoint(25, -19) returns CRect(100, 219, 300, 419).

Use the unary operator to negate a point. For example, using the unary operator with the point CPoint(25, -19) returns CPoint(-25, 19).

See Also: **CPoint::operator –=**, **CPoint::operator +=**, **CPoint::operator +**, **CSize::operator -**, **CRect::operator -**, **CPoint::Offset**, **CRect::OffsetRect**

CPrintDialog

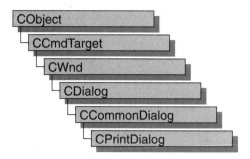

The **CPrintDialog** class encapsulates the services provided by the Windows common dialog box for printing. Common print dialog boxes provide an easy way to implement Print and Print Setup dialog boxes in a manner consistent with Windows standards.

If you wish, you can rely on the framework to handle many aspects of the printing process for your application. In this case, the framework automatically displays the Windows common dialog box for printing. You can also have the framework handle printing for your application but override the common Print dialog box with your own print dialog box. For more information on using the framework to handle printing tasks, see the article "Printing" in *Visual C++ Programmer's Guide* online.

If you want your application to handle printing without the framework's involvement, you can use the **CPrintDialog** class "as is" with the constructor provided, or you can derive your own dialog class from **CPrintDialog** and write a constructor to suit your needs. In either case, these dialog boxes will behave like standard MFC dialog boxes because they are derived from class **CCommonDialog**.

To use a **CPrintDialog** object, first create the object using the **CPrintDialog** constructor. Once the dialog box has been constructed, you can set or modify any values in the **m_pd** structure to initialize the values of the dialog box's controls. The **m_pd** structure is of type **PRINTDLG**. For more information on this structure, see the Win32 SDK documentation.

If you do not supply your own handles in **m_pd** for the **hDevMode** and **hDevNames** members, be sure to call the Windows function **GlobalFree** for these handles when you are done with the dialog box. When using the framework's Print Setup implementation provided by **CWinApp::OnFilePrintSetup**, you do not have to free these handles. The handles are maintained by **CWinApp** and are freed in **CWinApp**'s destructor. It is only necessary to free these handles when using **CPrintDialog** stand-alone.

After initializing the dialog box controls, call the **DoModal** member function to display the dialog box and allow the user to select print options. **DoModal** returns whether the user selected the OK (**IDOK**) or Cancel (**IDCANCEL**) button.

If **DoModal** returns **IDOK**, you can use one of **CPrintDialog**'s member functions to retrieve the information input by the user.

The **CPrintDialog::GetDefaults** member function is useful for retrieving the current printer defaults without displaying a dialog box. This member function requires no user interaction.

You can use the Windows **CommDlgExtendedError** function to determine whether an error occurred during initialization of the dialog box and to learn more about the error. For more information on this function, see the Win32 SDK documentation.

CPrintDialog relies on the COMMDLG.DLL file that ships with Windows versions 3.1 and later.

To customize the dialog box, derive a class from **CPrintDialog**, provide a custom dialog template, and add a message map to process the notification messages from the extended controls. Any unprocessed messages should be passed on to the base class. Customizing the hook function is not required.

To process the same message differently depending on whether the dialog box is Print or Print Setup, you must derive a class for each dialog box. You must also override the Windows **AttachOnSetup** function, which handles the creation of a new dialog box when the Print Setup button is selected within a Print dialog box.

For more information on using **CPrintDialog**, see "Common Dialog Classes" in *Visual C++ Programmer's Guide* online.

#include <afxdlgs.h>

See Also: CPrintInfo

CPrintDialog Class Members

Data Members

m_pd	A structure used to customize a **CPrintDialog** object.

Construction

CPrintDialog	Constructs a **CPrintDialog** object.

Operations

CreatePrinterDC	Creates a printer device context without displaying the Print dialog box.
DoModal	Displays the dialog box and allows the user to make a selection.
GetCopies	Retrieves the number of copies requested.

Operations *(continued)*

GetDefaults	Retrieves device defaults without displaying a dialog box.
GetDeviceName	Retrieves the name of the currently selected printer device.
GetDevMode	Retrieves the **DEVMODE** structure.
GetDriverName	Retrieves the name of the currently selected printer driver.
GetFromPage	Retrieves the starting page of the print range.
GetToPage	Retrieves the ending page of the print range.
GetPortName	Retrieves the name of the currently selected printer port.
GetPrinterDC	Retrieves a handle to the printer device context.
PrintAll	Determines whether to print all pages of the document.
PrintCollate	Determines whether collated copies are requested.
PrintRange	Determines whether to print only a specified range of pages.
PrintSelection	Determines whether to print only the currently selected items.

Member Functions

CPrintDialog::CPrintDialog

CPrintDialog(BOOL *bPrintSetupOnly*, **DWORD** *dwFlags* = **PD_ALLPAGES** |
   ↪ **PD_USEDEVMODECOPIES** | **PD_NOPAGENUMS** | **PD_HIDEPRINTTOFILE** |
   ↪ **PD_NOSELECTION, CWnd*** *pParentWnd* = **NULL**);

Parameters

bPrintSetupOnly Specifies whether the standard Windows Print dialog box or Print Setup dialog box is displayed. Set this parameter to **TRUE** to display the standard Windows Print Setup dialog box. Set it to **FALSE** to display the Windows Print dialog box. If *bPrintSetupOnly* is **FALSE**, a Print Setup option button is still displayed in the Print dialog box.

dwFlags One or more flags you can use to customize the settings of the dialog box, combined using the bitwise OR operator. For example, the **PD_ALLPAGES** flag sets the default print range to all pages of the document. See the **PRINTDLG** structure in the Win32 SDK documentation for more information on these flags.

pParentWnd A pointer to the dialog box's parent or owner window.

Remarks

Constructs either a Windows Print or Print Setup dialog object. This member function only constructs the object. Use the **DoModal** member function to display the dialog box.

Note that when you call the constructor with *bPrintSetupOnly* set to **FALSE**, the **PD_RETURNDC** flag is automatically used. After calling **DoModal**, **GetDefaults**, or **GetPrinterDC**, a printer DC will be returned in m_pd.hDC. This DC must be freed by the caller of **CPrintDialog**.

See Also: **CPrintDialog::DoModal, ::PrintDlg**

CPrintDialog::CreatePrinterDC

HDC CreatePrinterDC( );

Return Value

Handle to the newly created printer device context.

Remarks

Creates a printer device context (DC) from the **DEVMODE** and **DEVNAMES** structures. This DC is assumed to be the current printer DC, and any other previously obtained printer DCs must be deleted by the user. This function can be called, and the resulting DC used, without ever displaying the Print dialog box.

See Also: **CPrintDialog::GetDevMode**

CPrintDialog::DoModal

virtual int DoModal( );

Return Value

IDOK or **IDCANCEL** if the function is successful; otherwise 0. **IDOK** and **IDCANCEL** are constants that indicate whether the user selected the OK or Cancel button.

If **IDCANCEL** is returned, you can call the Windows **CommDlgExtendedError** function to determine whether an error occurred.

Remarks

Call this function to display the Windows common print dialog box and allow the user to select various printing options such as the number of copies, page range, and whether copies should be collated.

If you want to initialize the various print dialog options by setting members of the **m_pd** structure, you should do this before calling **DoModal**, but after the dialog object is constructed.

After calling **DoModal**, you can call other member functions to retrieve the settings or information input by the user into the dialog box.

See Also: **CPrintDialog::CPrintDialog, CDialog::DoModal**

CPrintDialog::GetCopies

int GetCopies( ) const;

Return Value

The number of copies requested.

Remarks

Call this function after calling **DoModal** to retrieve the number of copies requested.

See Also: CPrintDialog::PrintCollate

CPrintDialog::GetDefaults

BOOL GetDefaults( );

Return Value

Nonzero if the function was successful; otherwise 0.

Remarks

Call this function to retrieve the device defaults of the default printer without displaying a dialog box. The retrieved values are placed in the **m_pd** structure.

In some cases, a call to this function will call the constructor for **CPrintDialog** with *bPrintSetupOnly* set to **FALSE**. In these cases, a printer DC and **hDevNames** and **hDevMode** (two handles located in the **m_pd** data member) are automatically allocated.

If the constructor for **CPrintDialog** was called with *bPrintSetupOnly* set to **FALSE**, this function will not only return **hDevNames** and **hDevMode** (located in **m_pd.hDevNames** and **m_pd.hDevMode**) to the caller, but will also return a printer DC in m_**pd.hDC**. It is the responsibility of the caller to delete the printer DC and call the Windows **GlobalFree** function on the handles when you are finished with the **CPrintDialog** object.

See Also: CPrintDialog::m_pd

CPrintDialog::GetDeviceName

CString GetDeviceName( ) const;

Return Value

The name of the currently selected printer.

Remarks

Call this function after calling **DoModal** to retrieve the name of the currently selected printer.

See Also: **CPrintDialog::GetDriverName, CPrintDialog::GetDevMode, CPrintDialog::GetPortName**

CPrintDialog::GetDevMode

LPDEVMODE GetDevMode( ) const;

Return Value

The **DEVMODE** data structure, which contains information about the device initialization and environment of a print driver. You must free the memory taken by this structure with the Windows **GlobalFree** function. See **PRINTDLG** in the Win32 SDK documentation for more information about using **GlobalFree**.

Remarks

Call this function after calling **DoModal** to retrieve information about the printing device.

See Also: **CDC::GetDeviceCaps**

CPrintDialog::GetDriverName

CString GetDriverName( ) const;

Return Value

The name of the currently selected printer device driver.

Remarks

Call this function after calling **DoModal** to retrieve the name of the currently selected printer device driver.

See Also: **CPrintDialog::GetDeviceName, CPrintDialog::GetDevMode, CPrintDialog::GetPortName**

CPrintDialog::GetFromPage

int GetFromPage( ) const;

Return Value

The starting page number in the range of pages to be printed.

Remarks

Call this function after calling **DoModal** to retrieve the starting page number in the range of pages to be printed.

See Also: **CPrintDialog::GetToPage, CPrintDialog::PrintRange**

CPrintDialog::GetPortName

CString GetPortName( ) const;

Return Value

The name of the currently selected printer port.

Remarks

Call this function after calling **DoModal** to retrieve the name of the currently selected printer port.

See Also: **CPrintDialog::GetDriverName**, **CPrintDialog::GetDeviceName**

CPrintDialog::GetPrinterDC

HDC GetPrinterDC( ) const;

Return Value

A handle to the printer device context if successful; otherwise **NULL**.

Remarks

If the *bPrintSetupOnly* parameter of the **CPrintDialog** constructor was **FALSE** (indicating that the Print dialog box is displayed), then **GetPrinterDC** returns a handle to the printer device context. You must call the Windows **DeleteDC** function to delete the device context when you are done using it.

CPrintDialog::GetToPage

int GetToPage( ) const;

Return Value

The ending page number in the range of pages to be printed.

Remarks

Call this function after calling **DoModal** to retrieve the ending page number in the range of pages to be printed.

See Also: **CPrintDialog::GetFromPage**, **CPrintDialog::PrintRange**

CPrintDialog::PrintAll

BOOL PrintAll( ) const;

Return Value

Nonzero if all pages in the document are to be printed; otherwise 0.

Remarks

Call this function after calling **DoModal** to determine whether to print all pages in the document.

See Also: **CPrintDialog::PrintRange, CPrintDialog::PrintSelection**

CPrintDialog::PrintCollate

BOOL PrintCollate( ) const;

Return Value

Nonzero if the user selects the collate check box in the dialog box; otherwise 0.

Remarks

Call this function after calling **DoModal** to determine whether the printer should collate all printed copies of the document.

See Also: **CPrintDialog::GetCopies**

CPrintDialog::PrintRange

BOOL PrintRange( ) const;

Return Value

Nonzero if only a range of pages in the document are to be printed; otherwise 0.

Remarks

Call this function after calling **DoModal** to determine whether to print only a range of pages in the document.

See Also: **CPrintDialog::PrintAll, CPrintDialog::PrintSelection, CPrintDialog::GetFromPage, CPrintDialog::GetToPage**

CPrintDialog::PrintSelection

BOOL PrintSelection( ) const;

Return Value

Nonzero if only the selected items are to be printed; otherwise 0.

Remarks

Call this function after calling **DoModal** to determine whether to print only the currently selected items.

See Also: **CPrintDialog::PrintRange, CPrintDialog::PrintAll**

Data Members
CPrintDialog::m_pd

PRINTDLG& m_pd;

Remarks

A structure whose members store the characteristics of the dialog object. After constructing a **CPrintDialog** object, you can use **m_pd** to set various aspects of the dialog box before calling the **DoModal** member function. For more information on the **m_pd** structure, see **PRINTDLG** in the Win32 SDK documentation.

If you modify the **m_pd** data member directly, you will override any default behavior.

CPrintInfo

CPrintInfo does not have a base class.

CPrintInfo stores information about a print or print-preview job. The framework creates an object of **CPrintInfo** each time the Print or Print Preview command is chosen and destroys it when the command is completed.

CPrintInfo contains information about both the print job as a whole, such as the range of pages to be printed, and the current status of the print job, such as the page currently being printed. Some information is stored in an associated **CPrintDialog** object; this object contains the values entered by the user in the Print dialog box.

A **CPrintInfo** object is passed between the framework and your view class during the printing process and is used to exchange information between the two. For example, the framework informs the view class which page of the document to print by assigning a value to the **m_nCurPage** member of **CPrintInfo**; the view class retrieves the value and performs the actual printing of the specified page.

Another example is the case in which the length of the document is not known until it is printed. In this situation, the view class tests for the end of the document each time a page is printed. When the end is reached, the view class sets the **m_bContinuePrinting** member of **CPrintInfo** to **FALSE**; this informs the framework to stop the print loop.

CPrintInfo is used by the member functions of **CView** listed under "See Also." For more information about the printing architecture provided by the Microsoft Foundation Class Library, see "Frame Window Topics" and "Document/View Architecture Topics" and the articles "Printing" and "Printing: Multipage Documents" in *Visual C++ Programmer's Guide* online.

#include <afxext.h>

See Also: **CView::OnBeginPrinting, CView::OnEndPrinting, CView::OnEndPrintPreview, CView::OnPrepareDC, CView::OnPreparePrinting, CView::OnPrint**

CPrintInfo Class Members

Data Members

m_bDocObject	Contains a flag indicating whether the document being printed is a DocObject.
m_dwFlags	Specifies DocObject printing operations.
m_nOffsetPage	Specifies offset of a particular DocObject's first page in a combined DocObject print job.

Data Members *(continued)*

m_pPD	Contains a pointer to the **CPrintDialog** object used for the Print dialog box.
m_bDirect	Contains a flag indicating whether the document is being printed directly (without displaying the Print dialog box).
m_bPreview	Contains a flag indicating whether the document is being previewed.
m_bContinuePrinting	Contains a flag indicating whether the framework should continue the print loop.
m_nCurPage	Identifies the number of the page currently being printed.
m_nNumPreviewPages	Identifies the number of pages displayed in the preview window; either 1 or 2.
m_lpUserData	Contains a pointer to a user-created structure.
m_rectDraw	Specifies a rectangle defining the current usable page area.
m_strPageDesc	Contains a format string for page-number display.

Attributes

SetMinPage	Sets the number of the first page of the document.
SetMaxPage	Sets the number of the last page of the document.
GetMinPage	Returns the number of the first page of the document.
GetMaxPage	Returns the number of the last page of the document.
GetOffsetPage	Returns the number of the pages preceding the first page of a DocObject item being printed in a combined DocObject print job.
GetFromPage	Returns the number of the first page being printed.
GetToPage	Returns the number of the last page being printed.

Member Functions

CPrintInfo::GetFromPage

UINT GetFromPage( ) const;

Return Value

The number of the first page to be printed.

Remarks

Call this function to retrieve the number of the first page to be printed. This is the value specified by the user in the Print dialog box, and it is stored in the **CPrintDialog** object referenced by the **m_pPD** member. If the user has not specified a value, the default is the first page of the document.

See Also: **CPrintInfo::m_nCurPage**, **CPrintInfo::m_pPD**,
CPrintInfo::GetToPage

CPrintInfo::GetMaxPage

UINT GetMaxPage( ) const;

Return Value

The number of the last page of the document.

Remarks

Call this function to retrieve the number of the last page of the document. This value
is stored in the **CPrintDialog** object referenced by the **m_pPD** member.

See Also: **CPrintInfo::m_nCurPage**, **CPrintInfo::m_pPD**,
CPrintInfo::GetMinPage, **CPrintInfo::SetMaxPage**, **CPrintInfo::SetMinPage**

CPrintInfo::GetMinPage

UINT GetMinPage( ) const;

Return Value

The number of the first page of the document.

Remarks

Call this function to retrieve the number of the first page of the document. This value
is stored in the **CPrintDialog** object referenced by the **m_pPD** member.

See Also: **CPrintInfo::m_nCurPage**, **CPrintInfo::m_pPD**,
CPrintInfo::GetMaxPage, **CPrintInfo::SetMaxPage**, **CPrintInfo::SetMinPage**

CPrintInfo::GetOffsetPage

UINT GetOffsetPage( ) const;

Return Value

The number of pages preceding the first page of a DocObject item being printed in a
combined DocObject print job.

Remarks

Call this function to retrieve the offset when printing multiple DocObject items from a
DocObject client. This value is referenced by the **m_nOffsetPage** member. The first
page of your document will be numbered the **m_nOffsetPage** value + 1 when printed
as a DocObject with other active documents. The **m_nOffsetPage** member is valid
only if the **m_bDocObject** value is **TRUE**.

See Also: **CPrintInfo::m_nOffsetPage**, **CPrintInfo::m_bDocObject**

CPrintInfo::GetToPage

UINT GetToPage( ) const;

Return Value

The number of the last page to be printed.

Remarks

Call this function to retrieve the number of the last page to be printed. This is the value specified by the user in the Print dialog box, and it is stored in the **CPrintDialog** object referenced by the **m_pPD** member. If the user has not specified a value, the default is the last page of the document.

See Also: **CPrintInfo::m_nCurPage**, **CPrintInfo::m_pPD**, **CPrintInfo::GetFromPage**

CPrintInfo::SetMaxPage

void SetMaxPage(UINT *nMaxPage* **);**

Parameters

nMaxPage   Number of the last page of the document.

Remarks

Call this function to specify the number of the last page of the document. This value is stored in the **CPrintDialog** object referenced by the **m_pPD** member. If the length of the document is known before it is printed, call this function from your override of **CView::OnPreparePrinting**. If the length of the document depends on a setting specified by the user in the Print dialog box, call this function from your override of **CView::OnBeginPrinting**. If the length of the document is not known until it is printed, use the **m_bContinuePrinting** member to control the print loop.

See Also: **CPrintInfo::m_bContinuePrinting**, **CPrintInfo::m_nCurPage**, **CPrintInfo::m_pPD**, **CPrintInfo::GetMinPage**, **CPrintInfo::GetToPage**, **CPrintInfo::SetMinPage**, **CView::OnBeginPrinting**, **CView::OnPreparePrinting**

CPrintInfo::SetMinPage

void SetMinPage(UINT *nMinPage* **);**

Parameters

nMinPage   Number of the first page of the document.

Remarks

Call this function to specify the number of the first page of the document. Page numbers normally start at 1. This value is stored in the **CPrintDialog** object referenced by the **m_pPD** member.

See Also: **CPrintInfo::m_nCurPage**, **CPrintInfo::m_pPD**, **CPrintInfo::GetMaxPage**, **CPrintInfo::GetMinPage**, **CPrintInfo::SetMaxPage**

Data Members

CPrintInfo::m_bContinuePrinting

Remarks

Contains a flag indicating whether the framework should continue the print loop. If you are doing print-time pagination, you can set this member to **FALSE** in your override of **CView::OnPrepareDC** once the end of the document has been reached. You do not have to modify this variable if you have specified the length of the document at the beginning of the print job using the **SetMaxPage** member function. The **m_bContinuePrinting** member is a public variable of type **BOOL**.

See Also: **CPrintInfo::SetMaxPage**, **CView::OnPrepareDC**

CPrintInfo::m_bDirect

Remarks

The framework sets this member to **TRUE** if the Print dialog box will be bypassed for direct printing; **FALSE** otherwise. The Print dialog is normally bypassed when you print from the shell or when printing is done using the command ID **ID_FILE_PRINT_DIRECT**.

You normally don't change this member, but if you do change it, change it before you call **CView::DoPreparePrinting** in your override of **CView::OnPreparePrinting**.

See Also: **CView::DoPreparePrinting**, **CView::OnPreparePrinting**

CPrintInfo::m_bDocObject

Remarks

Contains a flag indicating whether the document being printed is a DocObject. Data members **m_dwFlags** and **m_nOffsetPage** are invalid unless this flag is **TRUE**.

See Also: **CPrintInfo::m_dwFlags**, **CPrintInfo::m_nOffsetPage**

CPrintInfo::m_bPreview

Remarks

Contains a flag indicating whether the document is being previewed. This is set by the framework depending on which command the user executed. The Print dialog box is not displayed for a print-preview job. The **m_bPreview** member is a public variable of type **BOOL**.

See Also: **CView::DoPreparePrinting**, **CView::OnPreparePrinting**

CPrintInfo::m_dwFlags

Remarks

Contains a combination of flags specifying DocObject printing operations. Valid only if data member **m_bDocObject** is **TRUE**.

The flags can be one or more of the following values:

PRINTFLAG_MAYBOTHERUSER
PRINTFLAG_PROMPTUSER
PRINTFLAG_USERMAYCHANGEPRINTER
PRINTFLAG_RECOMPOSETODEVICE
PRINTFLAG_DONTACTUALLYPRINT
PRINTFLAG_FORCEPROPERTIES
PRINTFLAG_PRINTTOFILE

See Also: **CPrintInfo::m_bDocObject**, **CPrintInfo::m_nOffsetPage**

CPrintInfo::m_lpUserData

Remarks

Contains a pointer to a user-created structure. You can use this to store printing-specific data that you do not want to store in your view class. The **m_lpUserData** member is a public variable of type **LPVOID**.

CPrintInfo::m_nCurPage

Remarks

Contains the number of the current page. The framework calls **CView::OnPrepareDC** and **CView::OnPrint** once for each page of the document, specifying a different value for this member each time; its values range from the value returned by **GetFromPage** to that returned by **GetToPage**. Use this member in your overrides of **CView::OnPrepareDC** and **CView::OnPrint** to print the specified page of the document.

When preview mode is first invoked, the framework reads the value of this member to determine which page of the document should be previewed initially. You can set the value of this member in your override of **CView::OnPreparePrinting** to maintain the user's current position in the document when entering preview mode. The **m_nCurPage** member is a public variable of type **UINT**.

See Also: **CPrintInfo::GetFromPage**, **CPrintInfo::GetToPage**, **CView::OnPrepareDC**, **CView::OnPreparePrinting**, **CView::OnPrint**

CPrintInfo::m_nNumPreviewPages

Remarks

Contains the number of pages displayed in preview mode; it can be either 1 or 2. The **m_nNumPreviewPages** member is a public variable of type **UINT**.

See Also: **CPrintInfo::m_strPageDesc**

CPrintInfo::m_nOffsetPage

Remarks

Contains the number of pages preceding the first page of a particular DocObject in a combined DocObject print job.

See Also: **CPrintInfo::m_bDocObject**, **CPrintInfo::m_dwFlags**

CPrintInfo::m_pPD

Remarks

Contains a pointer to the **CPrintDialog** object used to display the Print dialog box for the print job. The **m_pPD** member is a public variable declared as a pointer to **CPrintDialog**.

See Also: **CPrintDialog**

CPrintInfo::m_rectDraw

Remarks

Specifies the usable drawing area of the page in logical coordinates. You may want to refer to this in your override of **CView::OnPrint**. You can use this member to keep track of what area remains usable after you print headers, footers, and so on. The **m_rectDraw** member is a public variable of type **CRect**.

See Also: **CView::OnPrint**

CPrintInfo::m_strPageDesc

Remarks

Contains a format string used to display the page numbers during print preview; this string consists of two substrings, one for single-page display and one for double-page display, each terminated by a '\n' character. The framework uses "Page %u\nPages %u-%u\n" as the default value. If you want a different format for the page numbers, specify a format string in your override of **CView::OnPreparePrinting**. The **m_strPageDesc** member is a public variable of type **CString**.

See Also: **CView::OnPreparePrinting**

CProgressCtrl

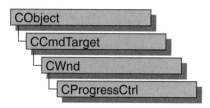

A "progress bar control" is a window that an application can use to indicate the progress of a lengthy operation. It consists of a rectangle that is gradually filled, from left to right, with the system highlight color as an operation progresses.

The **CProgressCtrl** class provides the functionality of the Windows common progress bar control. This control (and therefore the **CProgressCtrl** class) is available only to programs running under Windows 95 and Windows NT version 3.51 and later.

A progress bar control has a range and a current position. The range represents the entire duration of the operation, and the current position represents the progress the application has made toward completing the operation. The window procedure uses the range and the current position to determine the percentage of the progress bar to fill with the highlight color and to determine the text, if any, to display within the progress bar. Because the range and current position values are expressed as unsigned integers, the highest possible range or current position value is 65,535.

For more information on using **CProgressCtrl**, see Technical Note 60 online.

#include <afxcmn.h>

CProgressCtrl Class Members

Construction

CProgressCtrl	Constructs a **CProgressCtrl** object.
Create	Creates a progress bar control and attaches it to a **CProgressCtrl** object.

Attributes

SetRange	Sets the minimum and maximum ranges for a progress bar control and redraws the bar to reflect the new ranges.
SetPos	Sets the current position for a progress bar control and redraws the bar to reflect the new position.
OffsetPos	Advances the current position of a progress bar control by a specified increment and redraws the bar to reflect the new position.
SetStep	Specifies the step increment for a progress bar control.

Operations

StepIt	Advances the current position for a progress bar control by the step increment (see **SetStep**) and redraws the bar to reflect the new position.

Member Functions

CProgressCtrl::CProgressCtrl

CProgressCtrl( );

Remarks

Constructs a **CProgressCtrl** object.

After constructing the **CProgressCtrl** object, call **CProgressCtrl::Create** to create the progress bar control.

See Also: **CProgressCtrl::Create**

CProgressCtrl::Create

BOOL Create(DWORD *dwStyle*, **const RECT&** *rect*, **CWnd*** *pParentWnd*, **UINT** *nID* **);**

Return Value

TRUE if the **CProgressCtrl** object is successfully created; otherwise **FALSE**.

Parameters

dwStyle   Specifies the progress bar control's style. Apply any combination of window styles to the control.

rect   Specifies the progress bar control's size and position. It can be either a **CRect** object or a **RECT** structure

pParentWnd   Specifies the progress bar control's parent window, usually a **CDialog**. It must not be **NULL.**

nID   Specifies the progress bar control's ID.

Remarks

You construct a **CProgressCtrl** object in two steps. First call the constructor, which creates the **CProgressCtrl** object; then call **Create**, which creates the progress bar control.

See Also: **CProgressCtrl::CProgressCtrl**

CProgressCtrl::OffsetPos

int OffsetPos(int *nPos* **);**

Return Value

The previous position of the progress bar control.

Parameters

nPos   Amount to advance the position.

Remarks

Advances the progress bar control's current position by the increment specified by *nPos* and redraws the bar to reflect the new position.

See Also: CProgressCtrl::SetPos, CProgressCtrl::SetRange, CProgressCtrl::StepIt

---

CProgressCtrl::SetPos

int SetPos(int *nPos* **);**

Return Value

The previous position of the progress bar control.

Parameters

nPos   New position of the progress bar control.

Remarks

Sets the progress bar control's current position as specified by *nPos* and redraws the bar to reflect the new position.

See Also: CProgressCtrl::OffsetPos, CProgressCtrl::SetRange, CProgressCtrl::StepIt

---

CProgressCtrl::SetRange

void SetRange(int *nLower*, **int** *nUpper* **);**

Parameters

nLower   Specifies the lower limit of the range (default is zero).

nUpper   Specifies the upper limit of the range (default is 100).

Remarks

Sets the upper and lower limits of the progress bar control's range and redraws the bar to reflect the new ranges.

See Also: **CProgressCtrl::OffsetPos**, **CProgressCtrl::SetPos**, **CProgressCtrl::StepIt**

CProgressCtrl::SetStep

int SetStep(int *nStep* **);**

Return Value

The previous step increment.

Parameters

nStep　New step increment.

Remarks

Specifies the step increment for a progress bar control. The step increment is the amount by which a call to **CProgressCtrl::StepIt** increases the progress bar's current position.

The default step increment is 10.

See Also: **CProgressCtrl::OffsetPos**, **CProgressCtrl::SetPos**, **CProgressCtrl::StepIt**

CProgressCtrl::StepIt

int StepIt( );

Return Value

The previous position of the progress bar control.

Remarks

Advances the current position for a progress bar control by the step increment and redraws the bar to reflect the new position. The step increment is set by the **CProgressCtrl::SetStep** member function.

See Also: **CProgressCtrl::SetPos**, **CProgressCtrl::SetRange**, **CProgressCtrl::SetStep**

CPropertyPage

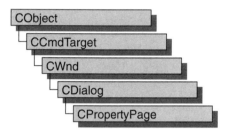

Objects of class **CPropertyPage** represent individual pages of a property sheet, otherwise known as a tab dialog box. As with standard dialog boxes, you derive a class from **CPropertyPage** for each page in your property sheet. To use **CPropertyPage**-derived objects, first create a **CPropertySheet** object, and then create an object for each page that goes in the property sheet. Call **CPropertySheet::AddPage** for each page in the sheet, and then display the property sheet by calling **CPropertySheet::DoModal** for a modal property sheet, or **CPropertySheet::Create** for a modeless property sheet.

You can create a type of tab dialog box called a wizard, which consists of a property sheet with a sequence of property pages that guide the user through the steps of an operation, such as setting up a device or creating a newsletter. In a wizard-type tab dialog box, the property pages do not have tabs, and only one property page is visible at a time. Also, instead of having OK and Apply Now buttons, a wizard-type tab dialog box has a Back button, a Next or Finish button, and a Cancel button.

For more information on establishing a property sheet as a wizard, see **CPropertySheet::SetWizardMode**. For more information on using **CPropertyPage** objects, see the article "Property Sheets" in *Visual C++ Programmer's Guide* online.

#include <afxdlgs.h>

See Also: CPropertySheet, CDialog, CPropertySheet::SetWizardMode

CPropertyPage Class Members

Data Members

m_psp	The Windows **PROPSHEETPAGE** structure. Provides access to basic property page parameters.

Construction

CPropertyPage	Constructs a **CPropertyPage** object.
Construct	Constructs a **CPropertyPage** object. Use **Construct** if you want to specify your parameters at run time, or if you are using arrays.

Operations

CancelToClose	Changes the OK button to read Close, and disables the Cancel button, after an unrecoverable change in the page of a modal property sheet.
SetModified	Call to activate or deactivate the Apply Now button.
QuerySiblings	Forwards the message to each page of the property sheet.

Overridables

OnCancel	Called by the framework when the Cancel button is clicked.
OnKillActive	Called by the framework when the current page is no longer the active page. Perform data validation here.
OnOK	Called by the framework when the OK, Apply Now, or Close button is clicked.
OnSetActive	Called by the framework when the page is made the active page.
OnApply	Called by the framework when the Apply Now button is clicked.
OnReset	Called by the framework when the Cancel button is clicked.
OnQueryCancel	Called by the framework when the Cancel button is clicked, and before the cancel has taken place.
OnWizardBack	Called by the framework when the Back button is clicked while using a wizard-type property sheet.
OnWizardNext	Called by the framework when the Next button is clicked while using a wizard-type property sheet.
OnWizardFinish	Called by the framework when the Finish button is clicked while using a wizard-type property sheet.

Member Functions
CPropertyPage::CancelToClose

void CancelToClose( );

Remarks

Call this function after an unrecoverable change has been made to the data in a page of a modal property sheet. This function will change the OK button to Close and disable the Cancel button. This change alerts the user that a change is permanent and the modifications cannot be cancelled.

The **CancelToClose** member function does nothing in a modeless property sheet, because a modeless property sheet does not have a Cancel button by default.

See Also: **CPropertyPage::OnKillActive**, **CPropertyPage::SetModified**

CPropertyPage::Construct

void Construct(UINT *nIDTemplate*, **UINT** *nIDCaption* **= 0);**
void Construct(LPCTSTR *lpszTemplateName*, **UINT** *nIDCaption* **= 0);**

Parameters

nIDTemplate   ID of the template used for this page.

nIDCaption   ID of the name to be placed in the tab for this page. If 0, the name will be taken from the dialog template for this page.

lpszTemplateName   Contains a null-terminated string that is the name of a template resource.

Remarks

Call this member function to construct a **CPropertyPage** object. The object is displayed after all of the following conditions are met:

- The page has been added to a property sheet using **CPropertySheet::AddPage**.
- The property sheet's **DoModal** or **Create** function has been called.
- The user has selected (tabbed to) this page.

Call **Construct** if one of the other class constructors has not been called. The **Construct** member function is flexible because you can leave the parameter statement blank and then specify multiple parameters and construction at any point in your code.

You must use **Construct** when you work with arrays, and you must call **Construct** for each member of the array so that the data members are assigned proper values.

See Also: **CPropertyPage::CPropertyPage**, **CPropertySheet::DoModal**, **CPropertySheet::AddPage**

CPropertyPage::CPropertyPage

CPropertyPage( );
CPropertyPage(UINT *nIDTemplate*, **UINT** *nIDCaption* **= 0);**
CPropertyPage(LPCTSTR *lpszTemplateName*, **UINT** *nIDCaption* **= 0);**

Parameters

nIDTemplate   ID of the template used for this page.

nIDCaption   ID of the name to be placed in the tab for this page. If 0, the name will be taken from the dialog template for this page.

lpszTemplateName   Points to a string containing the name of the template for this page. Cannot be **NULL**.

Remarks

Constructs a **CPropertyPage** object. The object is displayed after all of the following conditions are met:

- The page has been added to a property sheet using **CPropertySheet::AddPage**.
- The property sheet's **DoModal** or **Create** function has been called.
- The user has selected (tabbed to) this page.

If you have multiple parameters (for example, if you are using an array), use **CPropertySheet::Construct** instead of **CPropertyPage**.

See Also: **CPropertySheet::Create**, **CPropertySheet::DoModal**, **CPropertySheet::AddPage**, **CPropertyPage::Construct**

CPropertyPage::OnApply

virtual BOOL OnApply( );

Return Value

Nonzero if the changes are accepted; otherwise 0.

Remarks

This member function is called by the framework when the user chooses the OK or the Apply Now button. When the framework calls this function, changes made on all property pages in the property sheet are accepted, the property sheet retains focus, and **OnApply** returns **TRUE** (the value 1). Before **OnApply** can be called by the framework, you must have called **SetModified** and set its parameter to **TRUE**. This will activate the Apply Now button as soon as the user makes a change on the property page.

Override this member function to specify what action your program takes when the user clicks the Apply Now button. When overriding, the function should return **TRUE** to accept changes and **FALSE** to prevent changes from taking effect.

The default implementation of **OnApply** calls **OnOK**.

For more information about notification messages sent when the user presses the Apply Now or OK button in a property sheet, see "PSN_APPLY" in the Win32 documentation.

See Also: **CPropertyPage::SetModified**, **CPropertyPage::OnOK**

CPropertyPage::OnCancel

virtual void OnCancel( );

Remarks

This member function is called by the framework when the Cancel button is selected. Override this member function to perform Cancel button actions. The default negates any changes that have been made.

See Also: CPropertyPage::OnApply, CDialog::OnCancel, CPropertyPage::OnOK

CPropertyPage::OnKillActive

virtual BOOL OnKillActive( );

Return Value

Nonzero if data was updated successfully, otherwise 0.

Remarks

This member function is called by the framework when the page is no longer the active page. Override this member function to perform special data validation tasks.

The default implementation of this member function copies settings from the controls in the property page to the member variables of the property page. If the data was not updated successfully due to a dialog data validation (DDV) error, the page retains focus.

After this member function returns successfully, the framework will call the page's **OnOK** function.

See Also: CWnd::UpdateData, CPropertyPage::OnOK, CPropertyPage::OnSetActive

---

CPropertyPage::OnOK

virtual void OnOK( );

Remarks

This member function is called by the framework when the user chooses either the OK or Apply Now button, immediately after the framework calls **OnKillActive**. Override this member function to implement additional behavior specific to the currently active page when user dismisses the entire property sheet.

The default implementation of this member function marks the page as "clean" to reflect that the data was updated in the **OnKillActive** function.

See Also: CDialog::OnOK, CPropertyPage::OnKillActive

CPropertyPage::OnQueryCancel

virtual BOOL OnQueryCancel( );

Return Value

Returns **FALSE** to prevent the cancel operation or TRUE to allow it.

Remarks

This member function is called by the framework when the user clicks the Cancel button and before the cancel action has taken place.

Override this member function to specify an action the program takes when the user clicks the Cancel button.

The default implementation of **OnQueryCancel** returns **TRUE**.

CPropertyPage::OnReset

virtual void OnReset( );

Remarks

This member function is called by the framework when the user chooses the Cancel button. When the framework calls this function, changes to all property pages that were made by the user previously choosing the Apply Now button are discarded, and the property sheet retains focus.

Override this member function to specify what action the program takes when the user clicks the Cancel button.

The default implementation of **OnReset** does nothing.

See Also: **CPropertyPage::OnCancel**, **CPropertyPage::OnApply**

CPropertyPage::OnSetActive

virtual BOOL OnSetActive( );

Return Value

Nonzero if the page was successfully set active; otherwise 0.

Remarks

This member function is called by the framework when the page is chosen by the user and becomes the active page. Override this member function to perform tasks when a page is activated. Your override of this member function should call the default version before any other processing is done.

The default implementation creates the window for the page, if not previously created, and makes it the active page.

See Also: **CPropertyPage::OnKillActive**

CPropertyPage::OnWizardBack

virtual LRESULT OnWizardBack();

Return Value

0 to automatically advance to the next page; –1 to prevent the page from changing. To jump to a page other than the next one, return the identifier of the dialog to be displayed.

Remarks

This member function is called by the framework when the user clicks on the Back button in a wizard.

Override this member function to specify some action the user must take when the Back button is pressed.

For more information on how to make a wizard-type property sheet, see **CPropertySheet::SetWizardMode**.

See Also: **CPropertySheet::SetWizardMode**

CPropertyPage::OnWizardFinish

virtual BOOL OnWizardFinish( );

Return Value

Zero if the property sheet is not destroyed when the wizard finishes; otherwise nonzero.

Remarks

This member function is called by the framework when the user clicks on the Finish button in a wizard. When the framework calls this function, the property sheet is not destroyed when the wizard finishes and **OnWizardFinish** returns **FALSE** (the value 0).

Override this member function to specify some action the user must take when the Finish button is pressed. When overriding this function, return **FALSE** to prevent the property sheet from being destroyed.

For more information about notification messages sent when the user presses the Finish button in a wizard property sheet, see "PSN_WIZFINISH" in the Win32 documentation.

For more information on how to make a wizard-type property sheet, see **CPropertySheet::SetWizardMode**.

See Also: **CPropertySheet::SetWizardMode**

CPropertyPage::OnWizardNext

virtual LRESULT OnWizardNext();

Return Value

0 to automatically advance to the next page; –1 to prevent the page from changing. To jump to a page other than the next one, return the identifier of the dialog to be displayed.

Remarks

This member function is called by the framework when the user clicks on the Next button in a wizard.

Override this member function to specify some action the user must take when the Next button is pressed.

For more information on how to make a wizard-type property sheet, see **CPropertySheet::SetWizardMode**.

See Also: CPropertySheet::SetWizardMode

CPropertyPage::QuerySiblings

LRESULT QuerySiblings(WPARAM *wParam*, **LPARAM** *lParam* **);**

Return Value

The nonzero value from a page in the property sheet, or 0 if all pages return a value of 0.

Parameters

wParam   Specifies additional message-dependent information.

lParam   Specifies additional message-dependent information

Remarks

Call this member function to forward a message to each page in the property sheet. If a page returns a nonzero value, the property sheet does not send the message to subsequent pages.

CPropertyPage::SetModified

void SetModified(BOOL *bChanged* = **TRUE);**

Parameters

bChanged   **TRUE** to indicate that the property page settings have been modified since the last time they were applied; **FALSE** to indicate that the property page settings have been applied, or should be ignored.

Remarks

Call this member function to enable or disable the Apply Now button, based on whether the settings in the property page should be applied to the appropriate external object.

The framework keeps track of which pages are "dirty," that is, property pages for which you have called **SetModified(TRUE)**. The Apply Now button will always be enabled if you call **SetModified(TRUE)** for one of the pages. The Apply Now button will be disabled when you call **SetModified(FALSE)** for one of the pages, but only if none of the other pages is "dirty."

See Also: CPropertyPage::CancelToClose

Data Members
CPropertyPage::m_psp

Remarks

m_psp is a structure whose members store the characteristics of **PROPSHEETPAGE**. Use this structure to initialize the appearance of a property page after it is constructed.

For more information on this structure, including a listing of its members, see **PROPSHEETPAGE** in the *Windows SDK Programmer's Reference*.

See Also: CPropertySheet, PROPSHEETPAGE

CPropertySheet

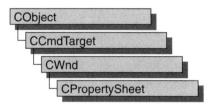

CObject

CCmdTarget

CWnd

CPropertySheet

Objects of class **CPropertySheet** represent property sheets, otherwise known as tab dialog boxes. A property sheet consists of a **CPropertySheet** object and one or more **CPropertyPage** objects. A property sheet is displayed by the framework as a window with a set of tab indices, with which the user selects the current page, and an area for the currently selected page.

Even though **CPropertySheet** is not derived from **CDialog**, managing a **CPropertySheet** object is similar to managing a **CDialog** object. For example, creation of a property sheet requires two-part construction: call the constructor, and then call **DoModal** for a modal property sheet or **Create** for a modeless property sheet. **CPropertySheet** has two types of constructors: **CPropertySheet::Construct** and **CPropertySheet::CPropertySheet**.

Exchanging data between a **CPropertySheet** object and some external object is similar to exchanging data with a **CDialog** object. The important difference is that the settings of a property sheet are normally member variables of the **CPropertyPage** objects rather than of the **CPropertySheet** object itself.

You can create a type of tab dialog box called a wizard, which consists of a property sheet with a sequence of property pages that guide the user through the steps of an operation, such as setting up a device or creating a newsletter. In a wizard-type tab dialog box, the property pages do not have tabs, and only one property page is visible at a time. Also, instead of having OK and Apply Now buttons, a wizard-type tab dialog box has a Back button, a Next or Finish button, a Cancel button, and a Help button.

To create a wizard-type dialog box, follow the same steps you would follow to create a standard property sheet, but call **SetWizardMode** before you call **DoModal**. To enable the wizard buttons, call **SetWizardButtons**, using flags to customize their function and appearance. To enable the Finish button, call **SetFinishText** after the user has taken action on the last page of the wizard.

For more information on how to use **CPropertySheet** objects, see the article "Property Sheets" in *Visual C++ Programmer's Guide* online.

#include <afxdlgs.h>

CPropertySheet Class Members

Data Members

m_psh	The Windows **PROPSHEETHEADER** structure. Provides access to basic property sheet parameters.

Construction

CPropertySheet	Constructs a **CPropertySheet** object.
Construct	Constructs a **CPropertySheet** object.

Attributes

GetActiveIndex	Retrieves the index of the active page of the property sheet.
GetPageIndex	Retrieves the index of the specified page of the property sheet.
GetPageCount	Retrieves the number of pages in the property sheet.
GetPage	Retrieves a pointer to the specified page.
GetActivePage	Returns the active page object.
SetActivePage	Programmatically sets the active page object.
SetTitle	Sets the caption of the property sheet.
GetTabControl	Retrieves a pointer to a tab control.
SetFinishText	Sets the text for the Finish button.
SetWizardButtons	Enables the wizard buttons.
SetWizardMode	Enables the wizard mode.

Operations

DoModal	Displays a modal property sheet.
Create	Displays a modeless property sheet.
AddPage	Adds a page to the property sheet.
RemovePage	Removes a page from the property sheet.
PressButton	Simulates the choice of the specified button in a property sheet.
EndDialog	Terminates the property sheet.

Member Functions

CPropertySheet::AddPage

void AddPage(CPropertyPage *_pPage_);

Parameters

    pPage Points to the page to be added to the property sheet. Cannot be **NULL**.

Remarks

This member function adds the supplied page with the rightmost tab in the property sheet. Add pages to the property sheet in the left-to-right order you want them to appear.

AddPage adds the **CPropertyPage** object to the **CPropertySheet** object's list of pages but does not actually create the window for the page. The framework postpones creation of the window for the page until the user selects that page.

It is not necessary to wait until creation of the property sheet window to call **AddPage**. Typically, you will call **AddPage** before calling **DoModal** or **Create**.

If you call **AddPage** after displaying the property page, the tab row will reflect the newly added page.

See Also: **CPropertySheet::RemovePage**

CPropertySheet::Construct

void Construct(UINT *nIDCaption*, **CWnd*** *pParentWnd* = **NULL,**
    ↳ **UINT** *iSelectPage* = **0**);
void Construct(LPCTSTR *pszCaption*, **CWnd*** *pParentWnd* = **NULL,**
    ↳ **UINT** *iSelectPage* = **0**);

Parameters

nIDCaption   ID of the caption to be used for the property sheet.

pParentWnd   Pointer to the parent window of the property sheet. If **NULL**, the parent window will be the main window of the application.

iSelectPage   The index of the page that will initially be on top. Default is the first page added to the sheet.

pszCaption   Pointer to a string containing the caption to be used for the property sheet. Cannot be **NULL**.

Remarks

Call this member function to construct a **CPropertySheet** object. Call this member function if one of the class constructors has not already been called. For example, call **Construct** when you declare or allocate arrays of **CPropertySheet** objects. In the case of arrays, you must call **Construct** for each member in the array.

To display the property sheet, call **DoModal** or **Create**. The string contained in the first parameter will be placed in the caption bar for the property sheet.

Example

The following example demonstrates under what circumstances you would call **Construct**.

```
int i;
CPropertySheet   grpropsheet[4];
```

```
CPropertySheet   someSheet;    // no need to call Construct for this one

UINT rgID[4] = {IDD_SHEET1, IDD_SHEET2, IDD_SHEET3, IDD_SHEET4};

for (i = 0; i < 4; i++)
   grpropsheet[i].Construct(rgID[i]);
```

See Also: **CPropertySheet::CPropertySheet, CPropertySheet::DoModal, CPropertySheet::Create**

CPropertySheet::CPropertySheet

CPropertySheet( );
CPropertySheet(UINT *nIDCaption*, **CWnd** **pParentWnd* **= NULL,**
   ↳ **UINT** *iSelectPage* **= 0);**
CPropertySheet(LPCTSTR *pszCaption*, **CWnd** **pParentWnd* **= NULL,**
   ↳ **UINT** *iSelectPage* **= 0);**

Parameters

nIDCaption   ID of the caption to be used for the property sheet.

pParentWnd   Points to the parent window of the property sheet. If **NULL**, the parent window will be the main window of the application.

iSelectPage   The index of the page that will initially be on top. Default is the first page added to the sheet.

pszCaption   Points to a string containing the caption to be used for the property sheet. Cannot be **NULL**.

Remarks

Use this member function to construct a **CPropertySheet** object. To display the property sheet, call **DoModal** or **Create**. The string contained in the first parameter will be placed in the caption bar for the property sheet.

If you have multiple parameters (for example, if you are using an array), use **Construct** instead of **CPropertySheet**.

See Also: **CPropertySheet::Construct, CPropertySheet::DoModal, CPropertySheet::Create, CPropertyPage**

CPropertySheet::Create

BOOL Create(CWnd* *pParentWnd* **= NULL, DWORD** *dwStyle* **= (DWORD)–1,**
   ↳ **DWORD** *dwExStyle* **= 0);**

Return Value

Nonzero if the property sheet is created successfully; otherwise 0.

Parameters

pParentWnd   Points to parent window. If **NULL**, parent is the desktop.

dwStyle   Window styles for property sheet. For a complete list of available styles, see "Window Styles" in the "Styles Used By MFC" section of this manual.

dwExStyle   Extended window styles for property sheet. For a complete list of available styles, see "Extended Window Styles" in the "Styles Used By MFC" section of this manual.

Remarks

Call this member function to display a modeless property sheet. The call to **Create** can be inside the constructor, or you can call it after the constructor is invoked.

The default style, expressed by passing –1 as *dwStyle*, is actually **WS_SYSMENU | WS_POPUP | WS_CAPTION | DS_MODALFRAME | DS_CONTEXT_HELP | WS_VISIBLE**. The default extended window style, expressed by passing 0 as *dwExStyle*, is actually **WS_EX_DLGMODALFRAME**.

The **Create** member function returns immediately after creating the property sheet. To destroy the property sheet, call **CWnd::DestroyWindow**.

Modeless property sheets displayed with a call to **Create** do not have OK, Cancel, Apply Now, and Help buttons as modal property sheets do. Desired buttons must be created by the user.

To display a modal property sheet, call **DoModal** instead.

See Also: **CDialog::Create**, **CPropertySheet::DoModal**

CPropertySheet::DoModal

virtual int DoModal( );

Return Value

IDOK or **IDCANCEL** if the function was successful; otherwise 0. If the property sheet has been established as a wizard (see **SetWizardMode**), **DoModal** returns either **ID_WIZFINISH** or **IDCANCEL**.

Remarks

Call this member function to display a modal property sheet. The return value corresponds to the ID of the control that closed the property sheet. After this function returns, the windows corresponding to the property sheet and all the pages will have been destroyed. The objects themselves will still exist. Typically, you will retrieve data from the **CPropertyPage** objects after **DoModal** returns **IDOK**.

To display a modeless property sheet, call **Create** instead.

Note The first time a property page is created from its corresponding dialog resource, it may cause a first-chance exception. This is a result of the property page changing the style of the dialog resource to the required style prior to creating the page. Because resources are generally read-only, this causes an exception. The exception is handled by the system, and a copy of the modified resource is made automatically by the system. The first-chance exception can thus be ignored.

Since this exception must be handled by the operating system, do not wrap calls to **CPropertySheet::DoModal** with a C++ **try/catch** block in which the catch handles all exceptions, for example, `catch (...)`. This will handle the exception intended for the operating system, causing unpredictable behavior. Using C++ exception handling with specific exception types or using structured exception handling where the Access Violation exception is passed through to the operating system is safe, however.

See Also: **CDialog::DoModal, CPropertySheet::Create**

CPropertySheet::EndDialog

void EndDialog(int *nEndID* **);**

Parameters

nEndID   Identifier to be used as return value of the property sheet.

Remarks

Use this member function to terminate the property sheet. This member function is called by the framework when the OK, Cancel, or Close button is pressed. Call this member function if an event occurs that should close the property sheet.

This member function is only used with a modal dialog box.

See Also: **CPropertyPage::OnOK, CPropertyPage::OnCancel, CWnd::DestroyWindow**

CPropertySheet::GetActiveIndex

int GetActiveIndex( ) const;

Return Value

The index number of the active page.

Remarks

Call this member function to get the index number of the property sheet window's active page, then use the returned index number as the parameter for **GetPage**.

See Also: **CPropertySheet::GetPage, CPropertySheet::GetActivePage**

CPropertySheet::GetActivePage

CPropertyPage* GetActivePage( ) const;

Return Value

The pointer to the active page.

Remarks

Call this member function to retrieve the property sheet window's active page.
Use this member function to perform some action on the active page.

See Also: **CPropertySheet::GetPage**

CPropertySheet::GetPage

CPropertyPage* GetPage(int *nPage*) const;

Return Value

The pointer to the page corresponding to the *nPage* parameter.

Parameters

nPage   Index of the desired page, starting at 0. Must be between 0 and one less than
the number of pages in the property sheet, inclusive.

Remarks

This member function returns a pointer to the specified page in this property sheet.

See Also: **CPropertySheet::AddPage**, **CPropertySheet::GetActivePage**,
CPropertySheet::GetPageCount, **CPropertySheet::RemovePage**,
CPropertySheet::SetTitle

CPropertySheet::GetPageIndex

int GetPageIndex(CPropertyPage* *pPage*) const;

Return Value

The index number of a page.

Parameters

pPage   Points to the page with the index to be found. Cannot be **NULL**.

Remarks

Use this member function to retreive the index number of the specified page in the
property sheet. For example, you would use **GetPageIndex** to get the page index in
order to use **SetActivePage** or **GetPage**.

See Also: **CPropertySheet::SetActivePage**, **CPropertySheet::GetPage**

CPropertySheet::GetPageCount

int GetPageCount( );

Return Value

The number of pages in the property sheet.

Remarks

Call this member function to determine the number of pages currently in the property sheet.

See Also: **CPropertySheet::GetPage, CPropertySheet::AddPage, CPropertySheet::RemovePage**

CPropertySheet::GetTabControl

CTabCtrl* GetTabControl( );

Return Value

A pointer to a tab control.

Remarks

Use this member function to retrieve a pointer to a tab control to do something specific to the tab control (that is, to use any of the APIs in **CTabCtrl**). For example, call this member function if you want to add bitmaps to each of the tabs during initialization.

See Also: **CTabCtrl::CTabCtrl**

CPropertySheet::PressButton

BOOL PressButton(int *nButton* **);**

Return Value

Nonzero if successful; otherwise zero.

Parameters

nButton   nButton : Identifies the button to be pressed. This parameter can be one of the following values:

- **PSBTN_BACK**   Chooses the Back button.
- **PSBTN_NEXT**   Chooses the Next button.
- **PSBTN_FINISH**   Chooses the Finish button.
- **PSBTN_OK**   Chooses the OK button.

- **PSBTN_APPLYNOW** Chooses the Apply Now button.
- **PSBTN_CANCEL** Chooses the Cancel button.
- **PSBTN_HELP** Chooses the Help button.

Remarks

Call this member function to simulate the choice of the specified button in a property sheet. See **PSM_PRESSBUTTON** for more information about the Windows SDK Pressbutton message.

CPropertySheet::RemovePage

void RemovePage(CPropertyPage **pPage* **);**
void RemovePage(int *nPage* **);**

Parameters

pPage   Points to the page to be removed from the property sheet. Cannot be **NULL**.

nPage   Index of the page to be removed. Must be between 0 and one less than the number of pages in the property sheet, inclusive.

Remarks

This member function removes a page from the property sheet and destroys the associated window. The **CPropertyPage** object itself is not destroyed until the owner of the **CPropertySheet** window is closed.

See Also: **CPropertySheet::AddPage**

CPropertySheet::SetActivePage

BOOL SetActivePage(int *nPage* **);**
BOOL SetActivePage(CPropertyPage* *pPage* **);**

Return Value

Nonzero if the property sheet is activated successfully; otherwise 0.

Parameters

nPage   Index of the page to set. It must be between 0 and one less than the number of pages in the property sheet, inclusive.

pPage   Points to the page to set in the property sheet. It cannot be **NULL**.

Remarks

Use this member function to change the active page. For example, use **SetActivePage** if a user's action on one page should cause another page to become the active page.

CPropertySheet::SetFinishText

void SetFinishText(LPCTSTR *lpszText* **);**

Parameters

lpszText   Points to the text to be displayed on the Finish command button.

Remarks

Call this member function to set the text in the Finish command button. Call **SetFinishText** to display the text on the Finish command button and hide the Next and Back buttons after the user completes action on the last page of the wizard.

CPropertySheet::SetTitle

void SetTitle(LPCTSTR *lpszText*, **UINT** *nStyle* = **0**);

Parameters

nStyle   Specifies the style of the property sheet title. The style must be specified at 0 or as **PSH_PROPTITLE**. If the style is set as **PSH_PROPTITLE**, the words "Properties for" appear before the text specified as the caption.

lpszText   Points to the text to be used as the caption in the title bar of the property sheet.

Remarks

Call this member function to specify the property sheet's caption (the text displayed in the title bar of a frame window).

By default, a property sheet uses the caption parameter in the property sheet constructor.

See Also: CPropertySheet::GetPage, CPropertySheet::GetActivePage

---

CPropertySheet::SetWizardButtons

void SetWizardButtons(DWORD *dwFlags* **);**

Parameters

dwFlags   A set of flags that customize the function and appearance of the wizard buttons. This parameter can be a combination of the following values:

- **PSWIZB_BACK**   Back button
- **PSWIZB_NEXT**   Next button
- **PSWIZB_FINISH**   Finish button
- **PSWIZB_DISABLEDFINISH**   Disabled Finish button

Remarks

Call this member function to enable or disable the Back, Next, or Finish button in a wizard property sheet. Call **SetWizardButtons** only after the dialog is open; you can't call **SetWizardButtons** before you call **DoModal**. Typically, you should call **SetWizardButtons** from **CPropertyPage::OnSetActive**.

If you want to change the text on the Finish button or hide the Next and Back buttons once the user has completed the wizard, call **SetFinishText**. Note that the same button is shared for Finish and Next. You can display a Finish or a Next button at one time, but not both.

CPropertySheet::SetWizardMode

void SetWizardMode( );

Remarks

Call this member function to establish a property page as a wizard. A key characteristic of a wizard property page is that the user navigates using Next or Finish, Back, and Cancel buttons instead of tabs.

Call **SetWizardMode** before calling **DoModal**. After you call **SetWizardMode**, **DoModal** will return either **ID_WIZFINISH** (if the user closes with the Finish button) or **IDCANCEL**.

SetWizardMode sets the PSF_WIZARD flag.

Example

```
CPropertySheet dlg;
CPropertyPage page1, page2;

dlg.AddPage(&page1);
dlg.AddPage(&page2);
dlg.SetWizardMode();
dlg.DoModal();
```

See Also: CPropertySheet::DoModal

Data Members
CPropertySheet::m_psh

Remarks

m_psh is a structure whose members store the characteristics of **PROPSHEETHEADER**. Use this structure to initialize the appearance of the property sheet after it is constructed but before it is displayed with the **DoModal** member function. For example, set the *dwSize* member of **m_psh** to the size you want the property sheet to have.

For more information on this structure, including a listing of its members, see **PROPSHEETHEADER** in the *Windows SDK Programmer's Reference*.

See Also: CPropertySheet::DoModal

CPropExchange

CPropExchange does not have a base class.

Establishes the context and direction of a property exchange.

The **CPropExchange** class supports the implementation of persistence for your OLE controls. Persistence is the exchange of the control's state information, usually represented by its properties, between the control itself and a medium.

The framework constructs an object derived from **CPropExchange** when it is notified that an OLE control's properties are to be loaded from or stored to persistent storage.

The framework passes a pointer to this **CPropExchange** object to your control's DoPropExchange function. If you used ClassWizard to create the starter files for your control, your control's DoPropExchange function calls **COleControl::DoPropExchange**. The base-class version exchanges the control's stock properties; you modify your derived class's version to exchange properties you have added to your control.

CPropExchange can be used to serialize a control's properties or initialize a control's properties upon the load or creation of a control. The **ExchangeProp** and **ExchangeFontProp** member functions of **CPropExchange** are able to store properties to and load them from different media.

For more information on using **CPropExchange**, see the article "ActiveX Controls: Property Pages" in *Visual C++ Programmer's Guide* online.

#include <afxctl.h>

See Also: **COleControl::DoPropExchange**

CPropExchange Class Members

Operations

ExchangeFontProp	Exchanges a font property.
ExchangeProp	Exchanges properties of any built-in type.
ExchangeBlobProp	Exchanges a binary large object (BLOB) property.
ExchangePersistentProp	Exchanges a property between a control and a file.
ExchangeVersion	Exchanges the version number of an OLE control.
IsLoading	Indicates whether properties are being loaded into the control or saved from it.
GetVersion	Retrieves the version number of an OLE control.

Member Functions

CPropExchange::ExchangeBlobProp

> **virtual BOOL ExchangeBlobProp(LPCTSTR** *pszPropName*, **void**** *ppvBlob*,
> ↪ **const void*** *pvBlobDefault* = **NULL**) = **0;**

Return Value

Nonzero if the exchange was successful; 0 if unsuccessful.

Parameters

pszPropName   The name of the property being exchanged.

ppvBlob   Pointer to a variable pointing to where the property is stored
(variable is typically a member of your class).

pvBlobDefault   Default value for the property.

Remarks

Serializes a property that stores binary large object (BLOB) data.

The property's value is read from or written to, as appropriate, the variable referenced
by *ppvBlob*. If *pvBlobDefault* is specified, it will be used as the property's default
value. This value is used if, for any reason, the control's serialization fails.

The functions **CArchivePropExchange::ExchangeBlobProp**,
CResetPropExchange::ExchangeBlobProp, and
CPropsetPropExchange::ExchangeBlobProp override this pure virtual function.

See Also: COleControl::DoPropExchange,
CPropExchange::ExchangeFontProp,
CPropExchange::ExchangePersistentProp, **CPropExchange::ExchangeProp**

CPropExchange::ExchangeFontProp

> **virtual BOOL ExchangeFontProp(LPCTSTR** *pszPropName*, **CFontHolder&** *font*,
> ↪ **const FONTDESC FAR*** *pFontDesc*, **LPFONTDISP** *pFontDispAmbient*) = **0;**

Return Value

Nonzero if the exchange was successful; 0 if unsuccessful.

Parameters

pszPropName   The name of the property being exchanged.

font   A reference to a **CFontHolder** object that contains the font property.

pFontDesc   A pointer to a **FONTDESC** structure containing values for initializing
the default state of the font property when *pFontDispAmbient* is **NULL**.

pFontDispAmbient A pointer to the **IFontDisp** interface of a font to be used for initializing the default state of the font property.

Remarks

Exchanges a font property between a storage medium and the control.

If the font property is being loaded from the medium to the control, the font's characteristics are retrieved from the medium and the **CFontHolder** object referenced by *font* is initialized with them. If the font property is being stored, the characteristics in the font object are written to the medium.

The functions **CArchivePropExchange::ExchangeFontProp**, **CResetPropExchange::ExchangeFontProp**, and **CPropsetPropExchange::ExchangeFontProp** override this pure virtual function.

See Also: **COleControl::DoPropExchange**, **CPropExchange::ExchangeBlobProp**, **CPropExchange::ExchangePersistentProp**, **CPropExchange::ExchangeProp**

CPropExchange::ExchangePersistentProp

virtual BOOL ExchangePersistentProp(LPCTSTR *pszPropName*, **↳ LPUNKNOWN FAR*** *ppUnk*, **REFIID** *iid*, **LPUNKNOWN** *pUnkDefault* **) = 0;**

Return Value

Nonzero if the exchange was successful; 0 if unsuccessful.

Parameters

pszPropName The name of the property being exchanged.

ppUnk A pointer to a variable containing a pointer to the property's **IUnknown** interface (this variable is typically a member of your class).

iid Interface ID of the interface on the property that the control will use.

pUnkDefault Default value for the property.

Remarks

Exchanges a property between the control and a file.

If the property is being loaded from the file to the control, the property is created and initialized from the file. If the property is being stored, its value is written to the file.

The functions **CArchivePropExchange::ExchangePersistentProp**, **CResetPropExchange::ExchangePersistentProp**, and **CPropsetPropExchange::ExchangePersistentProp** override this pure virtual function.

See Also: **COleControl::DoPropExchange**, **CPropExchange::ExchangeBlobProp**, **CPropExchange::ExchangeFontProp**, **CPropExchange::ExchangeProp**

CPropExchange::ExchangeProp

virtual BOOL ExchangeProp(LPCTSTR *pszPropName*, **VARTYPE** *vtProp*,
↳ **void*** *pvProp*, **const void*** *pvDefault* = **NULL**) = 0;

Return Value

Nonzero if the exchange was successful; 0 if unsuccessful.

Parameters

pszPropName   The name of the property being exchanged.

vtProp   A symbol specifying the type of the property being exchanged.
Possible values are:

Symbol	Property Type
VT_I2	**short**
VT_I4	**long**
VT_BOOL	**BOOL**
VT_BSTR	**CString**
VT_CY	**CY**
VT_R4	**float**
VT_R8	**double**

pvProp   A pointer to the property's value.

pvDefault   Pointer to a default value for the property.

Remarks

Exchanges a property between a storage medium and the control.

If the property is being loaded from the medium to the control, the property's value
is retrieved from the medium and stored in the object pointed to by *pvProp*. If the
property is being stored to the medium, the value of the object pointed to by *pvProp*
is written to the medium.

The functions **CArchivePropExchange::ExchangeProp**,
CResetPropExchange::ExchangeProp, and
CPropsetPropExchange::ExchangeProp override this pure virtual function.

See Also: **COleControl::DoPropExchange**,
**CPropExchange::ExchangeBlobProp, CPropExchange::ExchangeFontProp,
CPropExchange::ExchangePersistentProp**

CPropExchange::ExchangeVersion

BOOL ExchangeVersion(DWORD& *dwVersionLoaded,*
↳ **DWORD** *dwVersionDefault,* **BOOL** *bConvert* **);**

Return Value

Nonzero if the function succeeded; 0 otherwise.

Parameters

dwVersionLoaded   Reference to a variable where the version number of the persistent data being loaded will be stored.

dwVersionDefault   The current version number of the control.

bConvert   Indicates whether to convert persistent data to the current version or keep it at the same version that was loaded.

Remarks

Called by the framework to handle persistence of a version number.

See Also: COleControl::ExchangeVersion

CPropExchange::GetVersion

DWORD GetVersion( );

Return Value

The version number of the control.

Remarks

Call this function to retrieve the version number of the control.

CPropExchange::IsLoading

BOOL IsLoading( );

Return Value

Nonzero if properties are being loaded; otherwise 0.

Remarks

Call this function to determine whether properties are being loaded to the control or saved from it.

See Also: COleControl::DoPropExchange

CPtrArray

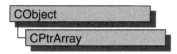

The **CPtrArray** class supports arrays of void pointers.

The member functions of **CPtrArray** are similar to the member functions of class **CObArray**. Because of this similarity, you can use the **CObArray** reference documentation for member function specifics. Wherever you see a **CObject** pointer as a function parameter or return value, substitute a pointer to **void**.

```
CObject* CObArray::GetAt( int <nIndex> ) const;
```

for example, translates to

```
void* CPtrArray::GetAt( int <nIndex> ) const;
```

CPtrArray incorporates the **IMPLEMENT_DYNAMIC** macro to support run-time type access and dumping to a **CDumpContext** object. If you need a dump of individual pointer array elements, you must set the depth of the dump context to 1 or greater.

Note   Before using an array, use **SetSize** to establish its size and allocate memory for it. If you do not use **SetSize**, adding elements to your array causes it to be frequently reallocated and copied. Frequent reallocation and copying are inefficient and can fragment memory.

Pointer arrays cannot be serialized.

When a pointer array is deleted, or when its elements are removed, only the pointers are removed, not the entities they reference.

For more information on using **CPtrArray**, see the article "Collections" in *Visual C++ Programmer's Guide* online.

#include <afxcoll.h>

See Also: CObArray

CPtrArray Class Members

Construction

CPtrArray	Constructs an empty array for void pointers.

Bounds

GetSize	Gets number of elements in this array.
GetUpperBound	Returns the largest valid index.
SetSize	Sets the number of elements to be contained in this array.

Operations

FreeExtra	Frees all unused memory above the current upper bound.
RemoveAll	Removes all the elements from this array.

Element Access

GetAt	Returns the value at a given index.
SetAt	Sets the value for a given index; array is not allowed to grow.
ElementAt	Returns a temporary reference to the element pointer within the array.
GetData	Allows access to elements in the array. Can be **NULL**.

Growing the Array

SetAtGrow	Sets the value for a given index; grows the array if necessary.
Add	Adds an element to the end of the array; grows the array if necessary.
Append	Appends another array to the array; grows the array if necessary.
Copy	Copies another array to the array; grows the array if necessary.

Insertion/Removal

InsertAt	Inserts an element (or all the elements in another array) at a specified index.
RemoveAt	Removes an element at a specific index.

Operators

operator []	Sets or gets the element at the specified index.

CPtrList

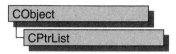

The **CPtrList** class supports lists of void pointers.

The member functions of **CPtrList** are similar to the member functions of class **CObList**. Because of this similarity, you can use the **CObList** reference documentation for member function specifics. Wherever you see a **CObject** pointer as a function parameter or return value, substitute a pointer to **void**.

```
CObject*& CObList::GetHead() const;
```

for example, translates to

```
void*& CPtrList::GetHead() const;
```

CPtrList incorporates the **IMPLEMENT_DYNAMIC** macro to support run-time type access and dumping to a **CDumpContext** object. If you need a dump of individual pointer list elements, you must set the depth of the dump context to 1 or greater.

Pointer lists cannot be serialized.

When a **CPtrList** object is deleted, or when its elements are removed, only the pointers are removed, not the entities they reference.

For more information on using **CPtrList**, see the article "Collections" in *Visual C++ Programmer's Guide* online.

#include <afxcoll.h>

See Also: **CObList**

CPtrList Class Members

Construction

CPtrList	Constructs an empty list for void pointers.

Head/Tail Access

GetHead	Returns the head element of the list (cannot be empty).
GetTail	Returns the tail element of the list (cannot be empty).

Operations

RemoveHead	Removes the element from the head of the list.
RemoveTail	Removes the element from the tail of the list.
AddHead	Adds an element (or all the elements in another list) to the head of the list (makes a new head).
AddTail	Adds an element (or all the elements in another list) to the tail of the list (makes a new tail).
RemoveAll	Removes all the elements from this list.

Iteration

GetHeadPosition	Returns the position of the head element of the list.
GetTailPosition	Returns the position of the tail element of the list.
GetNext	Gets the next element for iterating.
GetPrev	Gets the previous element for iterating.

Retrieval/Modification

GetAt	Gets the element at a given position.
SetAt	Sets the element at a given position.
RemoveAt	Removes an element from this list, specified by position.

Insertion

InsertBefore	Inserts a new element before a given position.
InsertAfter	Inserts a new element after a given position.

Searching

Find	Gets the position of an element specified by pointer value.
FindIndex	Gets the position of an element specified by a zero-based index.

Status

GetCount	Returns the number of elements in this list.
IsEmpty	Tests for the empty list condition (no elements).

CRecentFileList

CRecentFileList is a **CObject** class that supports control of the most recently used (MRU) file list. Files can be added to or deleted from the MRU file list, the file list can be read from or written to the registry or an .INI file, and the menu displaying the MRU file list can be updated.

#include <afxadv.h>

CRecentFileList Class Members

Construction

CRecentFileList	Constructs a **CRecentFileList** object.

Attributes

GetSize	Retrieves the number of files in the MRU file list.

Operations

Remove	Removes a file from the MRU file list.
Add	Adds a file to the MRU file list.
GetDisplayName	Provides a display name for menu display of an MRU filename.
UpdateMenu	Updates the menu display of the MRU file list.
ReadList	Reads the MRU file list from the registry or .INI file.
WriteList	Writes the MRU file list from the registry or .INI file.

Operators

operator[]	Returns a **CString** object at a given position.

Member Functions
CRecentFileList::Add

virtual void Add(LPCTSTR *lpszPathName* **);**

Parameters

lpszPathName   Pathname to be added to the list.

Remarks

Call this function to add the file whose path is given in *lpszPathName* to the most recently used (MRU) file list. The file name will be added to the top of the MRU list. If the file name already exists in the MRU list, it will be moved to the top.

See Also: **CRecentFileList::Remove CRecentFileList::UpdateMenu**

CRecentFileList::CRecentFileList

CRecentFileList(UINT *nStart***, LPCTSTR** *lpszSection***, LPCTSTR** *lpszEntryFormat***,**
↪ **int** *nSize***, int** *nMaxDispLen* **= AFX_ABBREV_FILENAME_LEN);**

Parameters

nStart Offset for the numbering in the menu display of the MRU (most recently used) file list.

lpszSection Points to the name of the section of the registry or the application's .INI file where the MRU file list is read and/or written.

lpszEntryFormat Points to a format string to be used for the names of the entries stored in the registry or the application's .INI file.

nSize Maximum number of files in the MRU file list.

nMaxDispLen Maximum length, in characters, available for the menu display of a filename in the MRU file list.

Remarks

Constructs a **CRecentFileList** object.

The format string pointed to by *lpszEntryFormat* should contain "%d", which will be used for substituting the index of each MRU item. For example, if the format string is "file%d" then the entries will be named file0, file1, and so on.

CRecentFileList::GetDisplayName

BOOL GetDisplayName(CString& *strName***, int** *nIndex***, LPCTSTR** *lpszCurDir***,**
↪ **int** *nCurDir***, BOOL** *bAtLeastName* **= TRUE) const;**

Return Value

FALSE if there is no filename at the specified index in the MRU (most recently used) file list.

Parameters

strName Full path of the file whose name is to be displayed in the menu list of MRU files.

nIndex Zero-based index of the file in the MRU file list.

lpszCurDir String holding the current directory.

nCurDir   Length of the current directory string.

bAtLeastName   If nonzero, indicates that the base name of the file should be returned, even if it exceeds the maximum display length (passed as the *nMaxDispLen* parameter to the **CRecentFileList** constructor).

Remarks

Call this function to obtain a display name for a file in the MRU file list, for use in the menu display of the MRU list. If the file is in the current directory, the function leaves the directory off the display. If the filename is too long, the directory and extension are stripped. If the filename is still too long, the display name is set to an empty string unless *bAtLeastName* is nonzero.

See Also: CRecentFileList::ReadList CRecentFileList::WriteList

CRecentFileList::GetSize

int GetSize( ) const;

Return Value

The number of files in the current MRU (most recently used) file list.

See Also: CRecentFileList::Add, CRecentFileList::Remove

CRecentFileList::ReadList

virtual void ReadList( );

Remarks

Call this function to read the most recently used (MRU) file list from the registry or the application's .INI file.

See Also: CRecentFileList::WriteList

CRecentFileList::Remove

virtual void Remove(int *nIndex*);

Parameters

nIndex   Zero-based index of the file to be removed from the MRU (most recently used) file list.

Remarks

Call this function to remove a file from the MRU file list.

See Also: CRecentFileList::Add, CRecentFileList::UpdateMenu

CRecentFileList::UpdateMenu

virtual void UpdateMenu(CCmdUI* *pCmdUI* **);**

Parameters

pCmdUI   A pointer to the MRU (most recently used) file list menu, which is a **CCmdUI** object.

Remarks

Updates the menu display of the MRU file list.

See Also: **CRecentFileList::Add**, **CRecentFileList::Remove**

CRecentFileList::WriteList

virtual void WriteList( );

Remarks

Call this function to write the most recently used (MRU) file list into the registry or the application's .INI file.

See Also: **CRecentFileList::ReadList**

Operators
CRecentFileList::operator [ ]

CString& operator[ ](int *nIndex* **);**

Parameters

nIndex   Zero-based index of a **CString** in a set of **CString**s.

Remarks

The overloaded subscript ([]) operator returns a single **CString** specified by the zero-based index in *nIndex*.

CRecordset

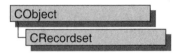

A **CRecordset** object represents a set of records selected from a data source. Known as "recordsets," **CRecordset** objects are typically used in two forms: dynasets and snapshots. A dynaset stays synchronized with data updates made by other users. A snapshot is a static view of the data. Each form represents a set of records fixed at the time the recordset is opened, but when you scroll to a record in a dynaset, it reflects changes subsequently made to the record, either by other users or by other recordsets in your application.

Note If you are working with the Data Access Objects (DAO) classes rather than the Open Database Connectivity (ODBC) classes, use class **CDaoRecordset** instead. For more information, see the article "Database Topics (General)" and the article "DAO and MFC." Both articles are in *Visual C++ Programmer's Guide* online.

To work with either kind of recordset, you typically derive an application-specific recordset class from **CRecordset**. Recordsets select records from a data source, and you can then:

- Scroll through the records.
- Update the records and specify a locking mode.
- Filter the recordset to constrain which records it selects from those available on the data source.
- Sort the recordset.
- Parameterize the recordset to customize its selection with information not known until run time.

To use your class, open a database and construct a recordset object, passing the constructor a pointer to your **CDatabase** object. Then call the recordset's **Open** member function, where you can specify whether the object is a dynaset or a snapshot. Calling **Open** selects data from the data source. After the recordset object is opened, use its member functions and data members to scroll through the records and operate on them. The operations available depend on whether the object is a dynaset or a snapshot, whether it is updatable or read-only (this depends on the capability of the Open Database Connectivity (ODBC) data source), and whether you have implemented bulk row fetching. To refresh records that may have been changed or added since the **Open** call, call the object's **Requery** member function. Call the object's **Close** member function and destroy the object when you finish with it.

In a derived **CRecordset** class, record field exchange (RFX) or bulk record field exchange (Bulk RFX) is used to support reading and updating of record fields.

For more information about recordsets and record field exchange, see the articles "Database Topics (General)," "Recordset (ODBC)," "Recordset: Fetching Records in Bulk (ODBC)," and "Record Field Exchange." For a focus on dynasets and snapshots, see the articles "Dynaset" and "Snapshot." All articles are in *Visual C++ Programmer's Guide* online.

#include <afxdb.h>

See Also: **CDatabase**, **CRecordView**

CRecordset Class Members

Data Members

m_hstmt	Contains the ODBC statement handle for the recordset. Type **HSTMT**.
m_nFields	Contains the number of field data members in the recordset. Type **UINT**.
m_nParams	Contains the number of parameter data members in the recordset. Type **UINT**.
m_pDatabase	Contains a pointer to the **CDatabase** object through which the recordset is connected to a data source.
m_strFilter	Contains a **CString** that specifies a Structured Query Language (SQL) **WHERE** clause. Used as a filter to select only those records that meet certain criteria.
m_strSort	Contains a **CString** that specifies an SQL **ORDER BY** clause. Used to control how the records are sorted.

Construction

CRecordset	Constructs a **CRecordset** object. Your derived class must provide a constructor that calls this one.
Open	Opens the recordset by retrieving the table or performing the query that the recordset represents.
Close	Closes the recordset and the ODBC **HSTMT** associated with it.

Recordset Attributes

CanAppend	Returns nonzero if new records can be added to the recordset via the **AddNew** member function.
CanBookmark	Returns nonzero if the recordset supports bookmarks.

(continued)

Recordset Attributes *(continued)*

CanRestart	Returns nonzero if **Requery** can be called to run the recordset's query again.
CanScroll	Returns nonzero if you can scroll through the records.
CanTransact	Returns nonzero if the data source supports transactions.
CanUpdate	Returns nonzero if the recordset can be updated (you can add, update, or delete records).
GetODBCFieldCount	Returns the number of fields in the recordset.
GetRecordCount	Returns the number of records in the recordset.
GetStatus	Gets the status of the recordset: the index of the current record and whether a final count of the records has been obtained.
GetTableName	Gets the name of the table on which the recordset is based.
GetSQL	Gets the SQL string used to select records for the recordset.
IsOpen	Returns nonzero if **Open** has been called previously.
IsBOF	Returns nonzero if the recordset has been positioned before the first record. There is no current record.
IsEOF	Returns nonzero if the recordset has been positioned after the last record. There is no current record.
IsDeleted	Returns nonzero if the recordset is positioned on a deleted record.

Recordset Update Operations

AddNew	Prepares for adding a new record. Call **Update** to complete the addition.
CancelUpdate	Cancels any pending updates due to an **AddNew** or **Edit** operation.
Delete	Deletes the current record from the recordset. You must explicitly scroll to another record after the deletion.
Edit	Prepares for changes to the current record. Call **Update** to complete the edit.
Update	Completes an **AddNew** or **Edit** operation by saving the new or edited data on the data source.

Recordset Navigation Operations

GetBookmark	Assigns the bookmark value of a record to the parameter object.
Move	Positions the recordset to a specified number of records from the current record in either direction.
MoveFirst	Positions the current record on the first record in the recordset. Test for **IsBOF** first.
MoveLast	Positions the current record on the last record or on the last rowset. Test for **IsEOF** first.

Recordset Navigation Operations *(continued)*

MoveNext	Positions the current record on the next record or on the next rowset. Test for **IsEOF** first.
MovePrev	Positions the current record on the previous record or on the previous rowset. Test for **IsBOF** first.
SetAbsolutePosition	Positions the recordset on the record corresponding to the specified record number.
SetBookmark	Positions the recordset on the record specified by the bookmark.

Other Recordset Operations

Cancel	Cancels an asynchronous operation or a process from a second thread.
FlushResultSet	Returns nonzero if there is another result set to be retrieved, when using a predefined query.
GetFieldValue	Returns the value of a field in a recordset.
GetODBCFieldInfo	Returns specific kinds of information about the fields in a recordset.
GetRowsetSize	Returns the number of records you wish to retrieve during a single fetch.
GetRowsFetched	Returns the actual number of rows retrieved during a fetch.
GetRowStatus	Returns the status of the row after a fetch.
IsFieldDirty	Returns nonzero if the specified field in the current record has been changed.
IsFieldNull	Returns nonzero if the specified field in the current record is Null (has no value).
IsFieldNullable	Returns nonzero if the specified field in the current record can be set to Null (having no value).
RefreshRowset	Refreshes the data and status of the specified row(s).
Requery	Runs the recordset's query again to refresh the selected records.
SetFieldDirty	Marks the specified field in the current record as changed.
SetFieldNull	Sets the value of the specified field in the current record to Null (having no value).
SetLockingMode	Sets the locking mode to "optimistic" locking (the default) or "pessimistic" locking. Determines how records are locked for updates.
SetParamNull	Sets the specified parameter to Null (having no value).
SetRowsetCursorPosition	Positions the cursor on the specified row within the rowset.

Recordset Overridables

Check	Called to examine the return code from an ODBC API function.
CheckRowsetError	Called to handle errors generated during record fetching.
DoBulkFieldExchange	Called to exchange bulk rows of data from the data source to the recordset. Implements bulk record field exchange (Bulk RFX).
DoFieldExchange	Called to exchange data (in both directions) between the field data members of the recordset and the corresponding record on the data source. Implements record field exchange (RFX).
GetDefaultConnect	Called to get the default connect string.
GetDefaultSQL	Called to get the default SQL string to execute.
OnSetOptions	Called to set options for the specified ODBC statement.
SetRowsetSize	Specifies the number of records you wish to retrieve during a fetch.

Member Functions

CRecordset::AddNew

> **virtual void AddNew( );**
> **throw(CDBException);**

Remarks

Call this member function to prepare for adding a new record to the table. You must call the **Requery** member function to see the newly added record. The record's fields are initially Null. (In database terminology, Null means "having no value" and is not the same as **NULL** in C++.) To complete the operation, you must call the **Update** member function. **Update** saves your changes to the data source.

Note If you have implemented bulk row fetching, you cannot call **AddNew**. This will result in a failed assertion. Although class **CRecordset** does not provide a mechanism for updating bulk rows of data, you can write your own functions by using the ODBC API function **SQLSetPos**. For an example of how to do this, see the sample "DBFETCH" online. For more information about bulk row fetching, see the article "Recordset: Fetching Records in Bulk (ODBC)" in *Visual C++ Programmer's Guide* online.

AddNew prepares a new, empty record using the recordset's field data members. After you call **AddNew**, set the values you want in the recordset's field data members. (You do not have to call the **Edit** member function for this purpose; use **Edit** only for existing records.) When you subsequently call **Update**, changed values in the field data members are saved on the data source.

Caution If you scroll to a new record before you call **Update**, the new record is lost, and no warning is given.

If the data source supports transactions, you can make your **AddNew** call part of a transaction. For more information about transactions, see class **CDatabase**. Note that you should call **CDatabase::BeginTrans** before calling **AddNew**.

Important For dynasets, new records are added to the recordset as the last record. Added records are not added to snapshots—you must call **Requery** to refresh the recordset.

It is illegal to call **AddNew** for a recordset whose **Open** member function has not been called. A **CDBException** is thrown if you call **AddNew** for a recordset that cannot be appended to. You can determine whether the recordset is updatable by calling **CanAppend**.

For more information, see the following articles in *Visual C++ Programmer's Guide* online: "Recordset: How Recordsets Update Records (ODBC)," "Recordset: Adding, Updating, and Deleting Records (ODBC),", and "Transaction (ODBC)."

Example

See the article "Transaction: Performing a Transaction in a Recordset (ODBC" in *Visual C++ Programmer's Guide* online.

See Also: **CRecordset::Edit, CRecordset::Delete, CRecordset::Update, CRecordset::Requery, CDatabase::BeginTrans, CDBException**

CRecordset::CanAppend

BOOL CanAppend( ) const;

Return Value

Nonzero if the recordset allows adding new records; otherwise 0. **CanAppend** will return 0 if you opened the recordset as read-only.

Remarks

Call this member function to determine whether the previously opened recordset allows you to add new records.

See Also: **CRecordset::AddNew, CRecordset::Requery**

CRecordset::CanBookmark

BOOL CanBookmark( ) const;

Return Value

Nonzero if the recordset supports bookmarks; otherwise 0.

Remarks

Call this member function to determine whether the recordset allows you to mark records using bookmarks. This function is independent of the **CRecordset::useBookmarks** option in the *dwOptions* parameter of the **Open** member function. **CanBookmark** indicates whether the given ODBC driver and cursor type support bookmarks. **CRecordset::useBookmarks** indicates whether bookmarks will be available, provided they are supported.

Note Bookmarks are not supported on forward-only recordsets.

For more information about bookmarks and recordset navigation, see the articles "Recordset: Bookmarks and Absolute Positions (ODBC)" and "Recordset: Scrolling (ODBC)" in *Visual C++ Programmer's Guide* online.

See Also: **CRecordset::GetBookmark, CRecordset::SetBookmark**

CRecordset::Cancel

void Cancel( );

Remarks

Call this member function to request that the data source cancel either an asynchronous operation in progress or a process from a second thread. Note that the MFC ODBC classes no longer use asynchronous processing; to perform an asychronous operation, you must directly call the ODBC API function **SQLSetConnectOption**. For more information, see the topic "Executing Functions Asynchronously" in the *ODBC SDK Programmer's Guide* online.

CRecordset::CancelUpdate

void CancelUpdate( );

Remarks

Call this member function to cancel any pending updates, due to an **Edit** or **AddNew** operation, before **Update** is called.

Note This member function is not applicable on recordsets that are using bulk row fetching, since such recordsets cannot call **Edit**, **AddNew**, or **Update**. For more information about bulk row fetching, see the article "Recordset: Fetching Records in Bulk (ODBC)" in *Visual C++ Programmer's Guide* online.

If automatic dirty field checking is enabled, **CancelUpdate** will restore the member variables to the values they had before **Edit** or **AddNew** was called; otherwise, any value changes will remain. By default, automatic field checking is enabled when the recordset is opened. To disable it, you must specify the

CRecordset::noDirtyFieldCheck in the *dwOptions* parameter of the **Open** member function.

For more information about updating data, see the article "Recordset: Adding, Updating, and Deleting Records (ODBC)" in *Visual C++ Programmer's Guide* online.

See Also: **CRecordset::AddNew**, **CRecordset::Edit**, **CRecordset::Update**

CRecordset::CanRestart

BOOL CanRestart( ) const;

Return Value

Nonzero if requery is allowed; otherwise 0.

Remarks

Call this member function to determine whether the recordset allows restarting its query (to refresh its records) by calling the **Requery** member function.

See Also: **CRecordset::Requery**

CRecordset::CanScroll

BOOL CanScroll( ) const;

Return Value

Nonzero if the recordset allows scrolling; otherwise 0.

Remarks

Call this member function to determine whether the recordset allows scrolling.

For more information about scrolling, see the article "Recordset: Scrolling (ODBC)" in *Visual C++ Programmer's Guide* online.

CRecordset::CanTransact

BOOL CanTransact( ) const;

Return Value

Nonzero if the recordset allows transactions; otherwise 0.

Remarks

Call this member function to determine whether the recordset allows transactions. For more information, see the article "Transaction (ODBC)" in *Visual C++ Programmer's Guide* online.

See Also: **CDatabase::BeginTrans, CDatabase::CommitTrans,
CDatabase::Rollback**

CRecordset::CanUpdate

BOOL CanUpdate( ) const;

Return Value

Nonzero if the recordset can be updated; otherwise 0.

Remarks

Call this member function to determine whether the recordset can be updated. A
recordset might be read-only if the underlying data source is read-only or if you
specified **CRecordset::readOnly** in the *dwOptions* parameter when you opened the
recordset.

See Also: **CRecordset::Open, CRecordset::AddNew, CRecordset::Edit,
CRecordset::Delete, CRecordset::Update**

CRecordset::Check

virtual BOOL Check(RETCODE *nRetCode* **) const;**

Return Value

Nonzero if the value of *nRetCode* is **SQL_SUCCESS,
SQL_SUCCESS_WITH_INFO, SQL_NO_DATA_FOUND** or
SQL_NEED_DATA; otherwise 0.

Parameters

nRetCode   An ODBC API function return code. For details, see Remarks.

Remarks

Call this member function to examine the return code from an ODBC API function.
The following table lists the possible values for *nRetCode*.

nRetCode	Description
SQL_SUCCESS	Function completed successfully; no additional information is available.
SQL_SUCCESS_WITH_INFO	Function completed successfully, possibly with a nonfatal error. Additional information can be obtained by calling **SQLError**.
SQL_NO_DATA_FOUND	All rows from the result set have been fetched.
SQL_ERROR	Function failed. Additional information can be obtained by calling **SQLError**.

(continued)

nRetCode	Description
SQL_INVALID_HANDLE	Function failed due to an invalid environment handle, connection handle, or statement handle. This indicates a programming error. No additional information is available from **SQLError**.
SQL_STILL_EXECUTING	A function that was started asynchronously is still executing. Note that by default, MFC will never pass this value to **Check** because MFC uses only synchronous processing.
SQL_NEED_DATA	While processing a statement, the driver determined that the application needs to send parameter data values.

For more information about **SQLError**, see the *ODBC SDK Programmer's Reference*.

Example

See the macro **AFX_ODBC_CALL**.

See Also: AFX_ODBC_CALL

CRecordset::CheckRowsetError

virtual void CheckRowsetError(RETCODE *nRetCode* **);**
  throw(CDBException);

Parameters

nRetCode   An ODBC API function return code. For details, see Remarks.

Remarks

This virtual member function handles errors that occur when records are fetched, and is useful during bulk row fetching. You may want to consider overriding **CheckRowsetError** in order to implement your own error handling.

CheckRowsetError is called automatically in a cursor navigation operation, such as **Open**, **Requery**, or any **Move** operation. It is passed the return value of the ODBC API function **SQLExtendedFetch**. The following table lists the possible values for the *nRetCode* parameter.

nRetCode	Description
SQL_SUCCESS	Function completed successfully; no additional information is available.
SQL_SUCCESS_WITH_INFO	Function completed successfully, possibly with a nonfatal error. Additional information can be obtained by calling **SQLError**.

(continued)

(continued)

nRetCode	Description
SQL_NO_DATA_FOUND	All rows from the result set have been fetched.
SQL_ERROR	Function failed. Additional information can be obtained by calling **SQLError**.
SQL_INVALID_HANDLE	Function failed due to an invalid environment handle, connection handle, or statement handle. This indicates a programming error. No additional information is available from **SQLError**.
SQL_STILL_EXECUTING	A function that was started asynchronously is still executing. Note that by default, MFC will never pass this value to **CheckRowsetError**; MFC will continue calling **SQLExtendedFetch** until it no longer returns **SQL_STILL_EXECUTING**.

For more information about **SQLError**, see the *ODBC SDK Programmer's Reference*. For more information about bulk row fetching, see the article "Recordset: Fetching Records in Bulk (ODBC)" in *Visual C++ Programmer's Guide* online.

See Also: **CRecordset::DoBulkFieldExchange**, **CRecordset::GetRowsetSize**, **CRecordset::SetRowsetSize**, **CRecordset::Move**

CRecordset::Close

virtual void Close( );

Remarks

Call this member function to close the recordset. The ODBC **HSTMT** and all memory the framework allocated for the recordset are deallocated. Usually after calling **Close**, you delete the C++ recordset object if it was allocated with **new**.

You can call **Open** again after calling **Close**. This lets you reuse the recordset object. The alternative is to call **Requery**.

Example

```
// Example for CRecordset::Close

// Construct a snapshot object
CCustSet rsCustSet( NULL );

if( !rsCustSet.Open( ) )
   return FALSE;

// Use the snapshot ...

// Close the snapshot
rsCustSet.Close( );

// Destructor is called when the function exits
```

See Also: **CRecordset::CRecordset**, **CRecordset::Open**, **CRecordset::Requery**

CRecordset::CRecordset

> **CRecordset**(**CDatabase*** *pDatabase* = **NULL**);

Parameters

> *pDatabase*   Contains a pointer to a **CDatabase** object or the value **NULL**. If not **NULL** and the **CDatabase** object's **Open** member function has not been called to connect it to the data source, the recordset attempts to open it for you during its own **Open** call. If you pass **NULL**, a **CDatabase** object is constructed and connected for you using the data source information you specified when you derived your recordset class with ClassWizard.

Remarks

> Constructs a **CRecordset** object. You can either use **CRecordset** directly or derive an application-specific class from **CRecordset**. You can use ClassWizard to derive your recordset classes.
>
> **Note** A derived class *must* supply its own constructor. In the constructor of your derived class, call the constructor **CRecordset::CRecordset**, passing the appropriate parameters along to it.
>
> Pass **NULL** to your recordset constructor to have a **CDatabase** object constructed and connected for you automatically. This is a useful shorthand that does not require you to construct and connect a **CDatabase** object prior to constructing your recordset.

Example

> For more information, see the article "Recordset: Declaring a Class for a Table (ODBC)" in *Visual C++ Programmer's Guide* online.
>
> See Also: **CRecordset::Open**, **CRecordset::Close**

CRecordset::Delete

> **virtual void Delete( );**
>   **throw(CDBException);**

Remarks

> Call this member function to delete the current record. After a successful deletion, the recordset's field data members are set to a Null value, and you must explicitly call one of the **Move** functions in order to move off the deleted record. Once you move off the deleted record, it is not possible to return to it. If the data source supports transactions, you can make the **Delete** call part of a transaction. For more information, see the article "Transaction (ODBC)" in *Visual C++ Programmer's Guide* online.

Note If you have implemented bulk row fetching, you cannot call **Delete**. This will result in a failed assertion. Although class **CRecordset** does not provide a mechanism for updating bulk rows of data, you can write your own functions by using the ODBC API function **SQLSetPos**. For an example of how to do this, see the sample "DBFETCH" online. For more information about bulk row fetching, see the article "Recordset: Fetching Records in Bulk (ODBC)" in *Visual C++ Programmer's Guide* online.

Caution The recordset must be updatable and there must be a valid record current in the recordset when you call **Delete**; otherwise, an error occurs. For example, if you delete a record but do not scroll to a new record before you call **Delete** again, **Delete** throws a **CDBException**.

Unlike **AddNew** and **Edit**, a call to **Delete** is not followed by a call to **Update**. If a **Delete** call fails, the field data members are left unchanged.

Example

This example shows a recordset created on the frame of a function. The example assumes the existence of m_dbCust, a member variable of type **CDatabase** already connected to the data source.

```
// Create a derived CRecordset object
CCustSet rsCustSet( &m_dbCust );
rsCustSet.Open( );

if( rsCustSet.IsEOF( ) || !rsCustSet.CanUpdate( ) ||
    !rsCustSet.CanTransact( ) )
    return;

if( !m_dbCust.BeginTrans( ) )
{
    // Do something to handle a failure
}
else
{
    // Perhaps scroll to a new record...
    // Delete the current record
    rsCustSet.Delete( );
    // ...

    // Finished commands for this transaction
    if( <the user confirms the transaction> )
        m_dbCust.CommitTrans( );
    else // User changed mind
        m_dbCust.Rollback( );
}
// ...
```

See Also: **Database::BeginTrans**, **CDatabase::CommitTrans**, **CDatabase::Rollback**, **CDBException**

CRecordset::DoBulkFieldExchange

virtual void DoBulkFieldExchange(CFieldExchange* *pFX* **);**
  throw(CDBException);

Parameters

pFX   A pointer to a **CFieldExchange** object. The framework will already have set up
this object to specify a context for the field exchange operation.

Remarks

When bulk row fetching is implemented, the framework calls this member function to
automatically transfer data from the data source to your recordset object.
DoBulkFieldExchange also binds your parameter data members, if any, to parameter
placeholders in the SQL statement string for the recordset's selection.

If bulk row fetching is not implemented, the framework calls **DoFieldExchange**. To
implement bulk row fetching, you must specify the **CRecordset::useMultiRowFetch**
option of the *dwOptions* parameter in the **Open** member function.

Note **DoBulkFieldExchange** is available only if you are using a class derived from
CRecordset. If you have created a recordset object directly from **CRecordset**, you must call
the **GetFieldValue** member function to retrieve data.

Bulk record field exchange (Bulk RFX) is similar to record field exchange (RFX).
Data is automatically transferred from the data source to the recordset object.
However, you cannot call **AddNew**, **Edit**, **Delete**, or **Update** to transfer changes back
to the data source. Class **CRecordset** currently does not provide a mechanism for
updating bulk rows of data; however, you can write your own functions by using the
ODBC API function **SQLSetPos**.

Note that ClassWizard does not support bulk record field exchange; therefore, you
must override **DoBulkFieldExchange** manually by writing calls to the Bulk RFX
functions. For more information about these functions, see the topic "Record Field
Exchange Functions" online.

For an example of how to implement bulk record field exchange, see the sample
"DBFETCH" online. For more information about bulk row fetching, see the article
"Recordset: Fetching Records in Bulk (ODBC)." For related information, see the
article "Record Field Exchange (RFX)." Both articles are in *Visual C++
Programmer's Guide* online.

See Also: **CRecordset::m_nFields**, **CRecordset::m_nParams**,
CRecordset::DoFieldExchange, **CRecordset::GetFieldValue**, **CFieldExchange**,
"Record Field Exchange Functions" online

CRecordset::DoFieldExchange

> **virtual void DoFieldExchange(CFieldExchange*** *pFX* **);**
> **throw(CDBException);**

Parameters

pFX   A pointer to a **CFieldExchange** object. The framework will already have set up this object to specify a context for the field exchange operation.

Remarks

When bulk row fetching is not implemented, the framework calls this member function to automatically exchange data between the field data members of your recordset object and the corresponding columns of the current record on the data source. **DoFieldExchange** also binds your parameter data members, if any, to parameter placeholders in the SQL statement string for the recordset's selection.

If bulk row fetching is implemented, the framework calls **DoBulkFieldExchange**. To implement bulk row fetching, you must specify the **CRecordset::useMultiRowFetch** option of the *dwOptions* parameter in the **Open** member function.

Note   **DoFieldExchange** is available only if you are using a class derived from **CRecordset**. If you have created a recordset object directly from **CRecordset**, you must call the **GetFieldValue** member function to retrieve data.

The exchange of field data, called record field exchange (RFX), works in both directions: from the recordset object's field data members to the fields of the record on the data source, and from the record on the data source to the recordset object.

The only action you must normally take to implement **DoFieldExchange** for your derived recordset class is to create the class with ClassWizard and specify the names and data types of the field data members. You might also add code to what ClassWizard writes to specify parameter data members or to deal with any columns you bind dynamically. For more information, see the article "Recordset: Dynamically Binding Data Columns (ODBC)" in *Visual C++ Programmer's Guide* online.

When you declare your derived recordset class with ClassWizard, the wizard writes an override of **DoFieldExchange** for you, which resembles the following example:

```
void CCustSet::DoFieldExchange(CFieldExchange* pFX)
{
    //{{AFX_FIELD_MAP(CCustSet)
    pFX->SetFieldType(CFieldExchange::outputColumn);
    RFX_Text(pFX, "Name", m_strName);
    RFX_Int(pFX, "Age", m_wAge);
    //}}AFX_FIELD_MAP
}
```

For more information about the RFX functions, see the topic "Record Field Exchange Functions" online.

For further examples and details about **DoFieldExchange**, see the article "Record Field Exchange: How RFX Works." For general information about RFX, see the article "Record Field Exchange." Both articles are in *Visual C++ Programmer's Guide* online.

See Also: **CRecordset::m_nFields**, **CRecordset::m_nParams**, **CRecordset::DoBulkFieldExchange**, **CRecordset::GetFieldValue**, **CFieldExchange**, "Record Field Exchange Functions" online

CRecordset::Edit

virtual void Edit( );
   throw(CDBException, CMemoryException);

Remarks

Call this member function to allow changes to the current record. After you call **Edit**, you can change the field data members by directly resetting their values. The operation is completed when you subsequently call the **Update** member function to save your changes on the data source.

Note If you have implemented bulk row fetching, you cannot call **Edit**. This will result in a failed assertion. Although class **CRecordset** does not provide a mechanism for updating bulk rows of data, you can write your own functions by using the ODBC API function **SQLSetPos**. For an example of how to do this, see the sample "DBFETCH." For more information about bulk row fetching, see the article "Recordset: Fetching Records in Bulk (ODBC)" in *Visual C++ Programmer's Guide* online.

Edit saves the values of the recordset's data members. If you call **Edit**, make changes, then call **Edit** again, the record's values are restored to what they were before the first **Edit** call.

In some cases, you may want to update a column by making it Null (containing no data). To do so, call **SetFieldNull** with a parameter of **TRUE** to mark the field Null; this also causes the column to be updated. If you want a field to be written to the data source even though its value has not changed, call **SetFieldDirty** with a parameter of **TRUE**. This works even if the field had the value Null.

If the data source supports transactions, you can make the **Edit** call part of a transaction. Note that you should call **CDatabase::BeginTrans** before calling **Edit** and after the recordset has been opened. Also note that calling **CDatabase::CommitTrans** is not a substitute for calling **Update** to complete the **Edit** operation. For more information about transactions, see class **CDatabase**.

Depending on the current locking mode, the record being updated may be locked by **Edit** until you call **Update** or scroll to another record, or it may be locked only during the **Edit** call. You can change the locking mode with **SetLockingMode**.

The previous value of the current record is restored if you scroll to a new record before calling **Update**. A **CDBException** is thrown if you call **Edit** for a recordset that cannot be updated or if there is no current record.

For more information, see the articles "Transaction (ODBC)" and "Recordset: Locking Records (ODBC)" in *Visual C++ Programmer's Guide* online.

Example

```
// Example for CRecordset::Edit
// To edit a record,
// First set up the edit buffer
rsCustSet.Edit( );

// Then edit field data members for the record
rsCustSet.m_dwCustID = 2795;
rsCustSet.m_strCustomer = "Jones Mfg";

// Finally, complete the operation
if( !rsCustSet.Update( ) )
    // Handle the failure to update
```

See Also: **CRecordset::Update**, **CRecordset::AddNew**, **CRecordset::Delete**, **CRecordset::SetFieldDirty**, **CRecordset::SetFieldNull**, **CRecordset::CanUpdate**, **CRecordset::CanTransact**, **CRecordset::SetLockingMode**

CRecordset::FlushResultSet

BOOL FlushResultSet( ) const;
    throw(CDBException);

Return Value

Nonzero if there are more result sets to be retrieved; otherwise 0.

Remarks

Call this member function to retrieve the next result set of a predefined query (stored procedure), if there are multiple result sets. You should call **FlushResultSet** only when you are completely finished with the cursor on the current result set. Note that when you retrieve the next result set by calling **FlushResultSet**, your cursor is not valid on that result set; you should call the **MoveNext** member function after calling **FlushResultSet**.

If a predefined query uses an output parameter or input/output parameters, you must call **FlushResultSet** until it returns **FALSE** (the value 0), in order to obtain these parameter values.

FlushResultSet calls the ODBC API function **SQLMoreResults**. If **SQLMoreResults** returns **SQL_ERROR** or **SQL_INVALID_HANDLE**, then **FlushResultSet** will throw an exception. For more information about **SQLMoreResults**, see the *ODBC SDK Programmer's Reference*.

Example

The following code assumes that COutParamRecordset is a **CRecordset**-derived object based on a predefined query with an input parameter and an output parameter, and having multiple result sets. Note the structure of the **DoFieldExchange** override.

```
// DoFieldExchange override
//
// Only necessary to handle parameter bindings.
// Don't use CRecordset-derived class with bound
// fields unless all result sets have same schema
// OR there is conditional binding code.

void COutParamRecordset::DoFieldExchange( CFieldExchange* pFX )
{
   pFX->SetFieldType( CFieldExchange::outputParam );
   RFX_Long( pFX, "Param1", m_nOutParamInstructorCount );
         // The "Param1" name here is a dummy name
         // that is never used

   pFX->SetFieldType( CFieldExchange::inputParam );
   RFX_Text( pFX, "Param2", m_strInParamName );
         // The "Param2" name here is a dummy name
         // that is never used

}


// Now implement COurParamRecordset.

// Assume db is an already open CDatabase object
COutParamRecordset rs( &db );
rs.m_strInParamName = _T("Some_Input_Param_Value");

// Get the first result set
// NOTE: SQL Server requires forwardOnly cursor
//       type for multiple rowset returning stored
//       procedures
rs.Open( CRecordset::forwardOnly,
         "{? = CALL GetCourses( ? )}",
         CRecordset::readOnly);

// Loop through all the data in the first result set
while ( !rs.IsEOF( ) )
{
   CString strFieldValue;
   for( int nIndex = 0;
        nIndex < rs.GetODBCFieldCount( );
        nIndex++ )
   {
      rs.GetFieldValue( nIndex, strFieldValue );

      // TO DO: Use field value string.
   }
   rs.MoveNext( );
}
```

```
        // Retrieve other result sets...
        while( rs.FlushResultSet( ) )
        {
            // must call MoveNext because cursor is invalid
            rs.MoveNext( );

            while ( !rs.IsEOF( ) )
            {
                CString strFieldValue;
                for( int nIndex = 0;
                     nIndex < rs.GetODBCFieldCount( );
                     nIndex++ )
                {
                    rs.GetFieldValue( nIndex, strFieldValue );

                    // TO DO: Use field value string.
                }
                rs.MoveNext( );
            }
        }


        // All result sets have been flushed. Cannot
        // use the cursor, but the output parameter,
        // m_nOutParamInstructorCount, has now been written.
        // Note that m_nOutParamInstructorCount not valid until
        // CRecordset::FlushResultSet has returned FALSE,
        // indicating no more result sets will be returned.

        // TO DO: Use m_nOutParamInstructorCount

        // Cleanup
        rs.Close( );
        db.Close( );
```

See Also: CFieldExchange::SetFieldType

CRecordset::GetBookmark

void GetBookmark(CDBVariant& *varBookmark* **);**
   throw(CDBException, CMemoryException);

Parameters

varBookmark   A reference to a **CDBVariant** object representing the bookmark
   on the current record.

Remarks

Call this member function to obtain the bookmark value for the current record.
To determine if bookmarks are supported on the recordset, call **CanBookmark**.
To make bookmarks available if they are supported, you must set the
CRecordset::useBookmarks option in the *dwOptions* parameter of the **Open**
member function.

Note If bookmarks are unsupported or unavailable, calling **GetBookmark** will result in an exception being thrown. Bookmarks are not supported on forward-only recordsets.

GetBookmark assigns the value of the bookmark for the current record to a **CDBVariant** object. To return to that record at any time after moving to a different record, call **SetBookmark** with the corresponding **CDBVariant** object.

Note After certain recordset operations, bookmarks may no longer be valid. For example, if you call **GetBookmark** followed by **Requery**, you may not be able to return to the record with **SetBookmark**. Call **CDatabase::GetBookmarkPersistence** to check whether you can safely call **SetBookmark**.

For more information about bookmarks and recordset navigation, see the articles "Recordset: Bookmarks and Absolute Positions (ODBC)" and "Recordset: Scrolling (ODBC)" in *Visual C++ Programmer's Guide* online.

See Also: **CRecordset::CanBookmark**, **CRecordset::SetBookmark**, **CDatabase::GetBookmarkPersistence**

CRecordset::GetDefaultConnect

virtual CString GetDefaultConnect( );

Return Value

A **CString** that contains the default connect string.

Remarks

The framework calls this member function to get the default connect string for the data source on which the recordset is based. ClassWizard implements this function for you by identifying the same data source you use in ClassWizard to get information about tables and columns. You will probably find it convenient to rely on this default connection while developing your application. But the default connection may not be appropriate for users of your application. If that is the case, you should reimplement this function, discarding ClassWizard's version. For more information about connect strings, see the article "Data Source (ODBC)" in *Visual C++ Programmer's Guide* online.

CRecordset::GetDefaultSQL

virtual CString GetDefaultSQL( );

Return Value

A **CString** that contains the default SQL statement.

Remarks

The framework calls this member function to get the default SQL statement on which the recordset is based. This might be a table name or an SQL **SELECT** statement.

You indirectly define the default SQL statement by declaring your recordset class with ClassWizard, and ClassWizard performs this task for you.

If you need the SQL statement string for your own use, call **GetSQL**, which returns the SQL statement used to select the recordset's records when it was opened. You can edit the default SQL string in your class's override of **GetDefaultSQL**. For example, you could specify a call to a predefined query using a **CALL** statement. For more information, see the article "Recordset: Declaring a Class for a Table (ODBC)" in *Visual C++ Programmer's Guide* online.

Caution The table name will be empty if the framework could not identify a table name, if multiple table names were supplied, or if a **CALL** statement could not be interpreted. Note that when using a **CALL** statement, you must not insert whitespace between the curly brace and the **CALL** keyword, nor should you insert whitespace before the curly brace or before the **SELECT** keyword in a **SELECT** statement.

See Also: **CRecordset::GetSQL**

CRecordset::GetFieldValue

void GetFieldValue(LPCTSTR *lpszName*, **CDBVariant&** *varValue*,
  ↪ **short** *nFieldType* = **DEFAULT_FIELD_TYPE**);
  throw(CDBException, CMemoryException);
void GetFieldValue(short *nIndex*, **CDBVariant&** *varValue*,
  ↪ **short** *nFieldType* = **DEFAULT_FIELD_TYPE**);
  throw(CDBException, CMemoryException);
void GetFieldValue(LPCTSTR *lpszName*, **CString&** *strValue*);
  throw(CDBException, CMemoryException);
void GetFieldValue(short *nIndex*, **CString&** *strValue*);
  throw(CDBException, CMemoryException);

Parameters

lpszName   The name of a field.

varValue   A reference to a **CDBVariant** object that will store the field's value.

nFieldType   The ODBC C data type of the field. Using the default value, **DEFAULT_FIELD_TYPE**, forces **GetFieldValue** to determine the C data type from the SQL data type, based on the following table. Otherwise, you can specify the data type directly or choose a compatible data type; for example, you can store any data type into **SQL_C_CHAR**.

C data type	SQL data type
SQL_C_BIT	**SQL_BIT**
SQL_C_UTINYINT	**SQL_TINYINT**
SQL_C_SSHORT	**SQL_SMALLINT**

(continued)

C data type	SQL data type
SQL_C_SLONG	SQL_INTEGER
SQL_C_FLOAT	SQL_REAL
SQL_C_DOUBLE	SQL_FLOAT
	SQL_DOUBLE
SQL_C_TIMESTAMP	SQL_DATE
	SQL_TIME
	SQL_TIMESTAMP
SQL_C_CHAR	SQL_NUMERIC
	SQL_DECIMAL
	SQL_BIGINT
	SQL_CHAR
	SQL_VARCHAR
	SQL_LONGVARCHAR
SQL_C_BINARY	SQL_BINARY
	SQL_VARBINARY
	SQL_LONGVARBINARY

For more information about ODBC data types, see the topics "SQL Data Types" and "C Data Types" in Appendix D of the *ODBC SDK Programmer's Reference*.

nIndex   The zero-based index of the field.

strValue   A reference to a **CString** object that will store the field's value converted to text, regardless of the field's data type.

Remarks

Call this member function to retrieve field data in the current record. You can look up a field either by name or by index. You can store the field value in either a **CDBVariant** object or a **CString** object.

If you have implemented bulk row fetching, the current record is always positioned on the first record in a rowset. To use **GetFieldValue** on a record within a given rowset, you must first call the **SetRowsetCursorPosition** member function to move the cursor to the desired row within that rowset. Then call **GetFieldValue** for that row. To implement bulk row fetching, you must specify the **CRecordset::useMultiRowFetch** option of the *dwOptions* parameter in the **Open** member function.

You can use **GetFieldValue** to dynamically fetch fields at run time rather than statically binding them at design time. For example, if you have declared a recordset object directly from **CRecordset**, you must use **GetFieldValue** to retrieve the field data; record field exchange (RFX), or bulk record field exchange (Bulk RFX), is not implemented.

Note   If you declare a recordset object without deriving from **CRecordset**, do not have the ODBC Cursor Library loaded. The cursor library requires that the recordset have at least one bound column; however, when you use **CRecordset** directly, none of the columns are bound.

The member functions **CDatabase::OpenEx** and **CDatabase::Open** control whether the cursor library will be loaded.

GetFieldValue calls the ODBC API function **SQLGetData**. If your driver outputs the value **SQL_NO_TOTAL** for the actual length of the field value, **GetFieldValue** throws an exception. For more information about **SQLGetData**, see the *ODBC SDK Programmer's Reference*.

Example

The following sample code illustrates calls to **GetFieldValue** for a recordset object declared directly from **CRecordset**.

```
// Create and open a database object;
// do not load the cursor library
CDatabase db;
db.OpenEx( NULL, CDatabase::forceOdbcDialog );

// Create and open a recordset object
// directly from CRecordset. Note that a
// table must exist in a connected database.
// Use forwardOnly type recordset for best
// performance, since only MoveNext is required
CRecordset rs( &db );
rs.Open( CRecordset::forwardOnly,
         _T( "SELECT * FROM SomeTable" ) );

// Create a CDBVariant object to
// store field data
CDBVariant varValue;

// Loop through the recordset,
// using GetFieldValue and
// GetODBCFieldCount to retrieve
// data in all columns
short nFields = rs.GetODBCFieldCount( );
while( !rs.IsEOF( ) )
{
    for( short index = 0; index < nFields; index++ )
    {
        rs.GetFieldValue( index, varValue );
        // do something with varValue
    }
    rs.MoveNext( );
}

rs.Close( );
db.Close( );
```

Note Unlike the DAO class **CDaoRecordset**, **CRecordset** does not have a **SetFieldValue** member function. If you create an object directly from **CRecordset**, it is effectively read-only.

For more information about bulk row fetching, see the article "Recordset: Fetching Records in Bulk (ODBC)" in *Visual C++ Programmer's Guide* online.

See Also: **CRecordset::DoFieldExchange**, **CRecordset::DoBulkFieldExchange**, **CRecordset::GetODBCFieldCount**, **CRecordset::GetODBCFieldInfo**, **CRecordset::SetRowsetCursorPosition**

CRecordset::GetODBCFieldCount

short GetODBCFieldCount( ) const;

Return Value

The number of fields in the recordset.

Remarks

Call this member function to retrieve the total number of fields in your recordset object.

For more information about creating recordsets, see the article "Recordset: Creating and Closing Recordsets (ODBC)" in *Visual C++ Programmer's Guide* online.

See Also: **CRecordset::GetFieldValue**

CRecordset::GetODBCFieldInfo

void GetODBCFieldInfo(LPCTSTR *lpszName*, **CODBCFieldInfo&** *fieldinfo* **);**
   throw(CDBException);
void GetODBCFieldInfo(short *nIndex*, **CODBCFieldInfo&** *fieldinfo* **);**
   throw(CDBException);

Parameters

lpszName   The name of a field.

fieldinfo   A reference to a **CODBCFieldInfo** structure.

nIndex   The zero-based index of the field.

Remarks

Call this member function to obtain information about the fields in the recordset. One version of the function lets you look up a field by name. The other version lets you look up a field by index.

For a description about the information returned, see the **CODBCFieldInfo** structure.

For more information about creating recordsets, see the article "Recordset: Creating and Closing Recordsets (ODBC)" in *Visual C++ Programmer's Guide* online.

See Also: **CRecordset::GetFieldValue**, **CODBCFieldInfo**

CRecordset::GetRecordCount

long GetRecordCount( ) const;

Return Value

The number of records in the recordset; 0 if the recordset contains no records; or −1 if the record count cannot be determined.

Remarks

Call this member function to determine the size of the recordset.

Caution The record count is maintained as a "high water mark"—the highest-numbered record yet seen as the user moves through the records. The total number of records is only known after the user has moved beyond the last record. For performance reasons, the count is not updated when you call **MoveLast**. To count the records yourself, call **MoveNext** repeatedly until **IsEOF** returns nonzero. Adding a record via **CRecordset:AddNew** and **Update** increases the count; deleting a record via **CRecordset::Delete** decreases the count.

See Also: **CRecordset::MoveLast, CRecordset::MoveNext, CRecordset::IsEOF, CRecordset::GetStatus**

CRecordset::GetRowsetSize

DWORD GetRowsetSize( ) const;

Return Value

The number of rows to retrieve during a given fetch.

Remarks

Call this member function to obtain the current setting for the number of rows you wish to retrieve during a given fetch. If you are using bulk row fetching, the default rowset size when the recordset is opened is 25; otherwise, it is 1.

To implement bulk row fetching, you must specify the **CRecordset::useMultiRowFetch** option in the *dwOptions* parameter of the **Open** member function. To change the setting for the rowset size, call **SetRowsetSize**.

For more information about bulk row fetching, see the article "Recordset: Fetching Records in Bulk (ODBC)" in *Visual C++ Programmer's Guide* online.

See Also: **CRecordset::Open, CRecordset::SetRowsetSize, CRecordset::CheckRowsetError, CRecordset::DoBulkFieldExchange**

CRecordset::GetRowsFetched

DWORD GetRowsFetched( ) const;

Return Value

The number of rows retrieved from the data source after a given fetch.

Remarks

Call this member function to determine how many records were actually retrieved after a fetch. This is useful when you have implemented bulk row fetching. The rowset size normally indicates how many rows will be retrieved from a fetch; however, the total number of rows in the recordset also affects how many rows will be retrieved in a rowset. For example, if your recordset has 10 records with a rowset size setting of 4, then looping through the recordset by calling **MoveNext** will result in the final rowset having only 2 records.

To implement bulk row fetching, you must specify the **CRecordset::useMultiRowFetch** option in the *dwOptions* parameter of the **Open** member function. To specify the rowset size, call **SetRowsetSize**.

For more information about bulk row fetching, see the article "Recordset: Fetching Records in Bulk (ODBC)" in *Visual C++ Programmer's Guide* online.

Example

```
MultiRowSet rs;

// Set the rowset size
rs.SetRowsetSize( 5 );

// Open the recordset
rs.Open( CRecordset::dynaset, NULL,
        CRecordset::useMultiRowFetch );

// loop through the recordset by rowsets
while( !rs.IsEOF( ) )
{
    for( int rowCount = 0;
        rowCount < (int)rs.GetRowsFetched( );
        rowCount++ )
    {
      // do something
    }

        rs.MoveNext( );
}

rs.Close( );
```

See Also: **CRecordset::SetRowsetSize**, **CRecordset::CheckRowsetError**

CRecordset::GetRowStatus

WORD GetRowStatus(WORD *wRow* **) const;**

Return Value

A status value for the row. For details, see Remarks.

Parameters

wRow   The one-based position of a row in the current rowset. This value can range from 1 to the size of the rowset.

Remarks

Call this member function to obtain the status for a row in the current rowset. **GetRowStatus** returns a value that indicates either any change in status to the row since it was last retrieved from the data source, or that no row corresponding to *wRow* was fetched. The following table lists the possible return values.

Status value	Description
SQL_ROW_SUCCESS	The row is unchanged.
SQL_ROW_UPDATED	The row has been updated.
SQL_ROW_DELETED	The row has been deleted.
SQL_ROW_ADDED	The row has been added.
SQL_ROW_ERROR	The row is unretrievable due to an error.
SQL_ROW_NOROW	There is no row that corresponds to *wRow*.

For more information, see the ODBC API function **SQLExtendedFetch** in the *ODBC SDK Programmer's Reference*.

See Also: **CRecordset::CheckRowsetError, CRecordset::GetRowsFetched, CRecordset::RefreshRowset**

CRecordset::GetStatus

void GetStatus(CRecordsetStatus& *rStatus* **) const;**

Parameters

rStatus   A reference to a **CRecordsetStatus** object. See the Remarks section for more information.

Remarks

Call this member function to determine the index of the current record in the recordset and/or whether the last record has been seen. **CRecordset** attempts to track the index, but under some circumstances this may not be possible. See **GetRecordCount** for an explanation.

The **CRecordsetStatus** structure has the following form:

```
struct CRecordsetStatus
{
    long m_lCurrentRecord;
    BOOL m_bRecordCountFinal;
};
```

The two members of **CRecordsetStatus** have the following meanings:

- **m_lCurrentRecord** Contains the zero-based index of the current record in the recordset, if known. If the index cannot be determined, this member contains **AFX_CURRENT_RECORD_UNDEFINED** (−2). If **IsBOF** is **TRUE** (empty recordset or attempt to scroll before first record), then **m_lCurrentRecord** is set to **AFX_CURRENT_RECORD_BOF** (−1). If on the first record, then it is set to 0, second record 1, and so on.

- **m_bRecordCountFinal** Nonzero if the total number of records in the recordset has been determined. Generally this must be accomplished by starting at the beginning of the recordset and calling **MoveNext** until **IsEOF** returns nonzero. If this member is zero, the record count as returned by **GetRecordCount**, if not −1, is only a "high water mark" count of the records.

See Also: **CRecordset::GetRecordCount**

CRecordset::GetSQL

const CString& GetSQL( ) const;

Return Value

A **const** reference to a **CString** that contains the SQL statement.

Remarks

Call this member function to get the SQL statement that was used to select the recordset's records when it was opened. This will generally be an SQL **SELECT** statement. The string returned by **GetSQL** is read-only.

The string returned by **GetSQL** is typically different from any string you may have passed to the recordset in the *lpszSQL* parameter to the **Open** member function. This is because the recordset constructs a full SQL statement based on what you passed to **Open**, what you specified with ClassWizard, what you may have specified in the **m_strFilter** and **m_strSort** data members, and any parameters you may have specified. For details about how the recordset constructs this SQL statement, see the article "Recordset: How Recordsets Select Records (ODBC)" in *Visual C++ Programmer's Guide* online.

Important Call this member function only after calling **Open**.

See Also: **CRecordset::GetDefaultSQL, CRecordset::Open, CRecordset::m_strFilter, CRecordset::m_strSort**

CRecordset::GetTableName

const CString& GetTableName( ) const;

Return Value

A **const** reference to a **CString** that contains the table name, if the recordset is based on a table; otherwise, an empty string.

Remarks

Call this member function to get the name of the SQL table on which the recordset's query is based. **GetTableName** is only valid if the recordset is based on a table, not a join of multiple tables or a predefined query (stored procedure). The name is read-only.

Important   Call this member function only after calling **Open**.

CRecordset::IsBOF

BOOL IsBOF( ) const;

Return Value

Nonzero if the recordset contains no records or if you have scrolled backward before the first record; otherwise 0.

Remarks

Call this member function before you scroll from record to record to learn whether you have gone before the first record of the recordset. You can also use **IsBOF** along with **IsEOF** to determine whether the recordset contains any records or is empty. Immediately after you call **Open**, if the recordset contains no records, **IsBOF** returns nonzero.When you open a recordset that has at least one record, the first record is the current record and **IsBOF** returns 0.

If the first record is the current record and you call **MovePrev**, **IsBOF** will subsequently return nonzero. If **IsBOF** returns nonzero and you call **MovePrev**, an error occurs. If **IsBOF** returns nonzero, the current record is undefined, and any action that requires a current record will result in an error.

Example

This example uses **IsBOF** and **IsEOF** to detect the limits of a recordset as the code scrolls through the recordset in both directions.

```
// Open a recordset; first record is current
CCustSet rsCustSet( NULL );
rsCustSet.Open( );

if( rsCustSet.IsBOF( ) )
   return;
   // The recordset is empty
```

```
// Scroll to the end of the recordset, past
// the last record, so no record is current
while ( !rsCustSet.IsEOF( ) )
   rsCustSet.MoveNext( );

// Move to the last record
rsCustSet.MoveLast( );

// Scroll to beginning of the recordset, before
// the first record, so no record is current
while( !rsCustSet.IsBOF( ) )
   rsCustSet.MovePrev( );

// First record is current again
rsCustSet.MoveFirst( );
```

See Also: **CRecordset::IsEOF**, **CRecordset::MoveFirst**, **CRecordset::MovePrev**

CRecordset::IsDeleted

BOOL IsDeleted( ) const;

Return Value

Nonzero if the recordset is positioned on a deleted record; otherwise 0.

Remarks

Call this member function to determine whether the current record has been deleted. If you scroll to a record and **IsDeleted** returns **TRUE** (nonzero), then you must scroll to another record before you can perform any other recordset operations.

Be aware that the result of **IsDeleted** depends on many factors, such as your recordset type, whether your recordset is updatable, whether you specified the **CRecordset::skipDeletedRecords** option when you opened the recordset, whether your driver packs deleted records, and whether there are multiple users.

For more information about **CRecordset::skipDeletedRecords** and driver packing, see the **Open** member function.

Note If you have implemented bulk row fetching, you should not call **IsDeleted**. Instead, call the **GetRowStatus** member function. For more information about bulk row fetching, see the article "Recordset: Fetching Records in Bulk (ODBC)" in *Visual C++ Programmer's Guide* online.

See Also: **CRecordset::Delete**, **CRecordset::IsBOF**, **CRecordset::IsEOF**

CRecordset::IsEOF

BOOL IsEOF( ) const;

Return Value

Nonzero if the recordset contains no records or if you have scrolled beyond the last record; otherwise 0.

Remarks

Call this member function as you scroll from record to record to learn whether you have gone beyond the last record of the recordset. You can also use **IsEOF** to determine whether the recordset contains any records or is empty. Immediately after you call **Open**, if the recordset contains no records, **IsEOF** returns nonzero. When you open a recordset that has at least one record, the first record is the current record and **IsEOF** returns 0.

If the last record is the current record when you call **MoveNext**, **IsEOF** will subsequently return nonzero. If **IsEOF** returns nonzero and you call **MoveNext**, an error occurs. If **IsEOF** returns nonzero, the current record is undefined, and any action that requires a current record will result in an error.

Example

See the example for **IsBOF**.

See Also: CRecordset::IsBOF, **CRecordset::MoveLast**, **CRecordset::MoveNext**

CRecordset::IsFieldDirty

BOOL IsFieldDirty(void* *pv* **);**
   throw(CMemoryException);

Return Value

Nonzero if the specified field data member has changed since calling **AddNew** or **Edit**; otherwise 0.

Parameters

pv   A pointer to the field data member whose status you want to check, or **NULL** to determine if any of the fields are dirty.

Remarks

Call this member function to determine whether the specified field data member has been changed since **Edit** or **AddNew** was called. The data in all dirty field data members will be transferred to the record on the data source when the current record is updated by a call to the **Update** member function of **CRecordset** (following a call to **Edit** or **AddNew**).

Note This member function is not applicable on recordsets that are using bulk row fetching. If you have implemented bulk row fetching, then **IsFieldDirty** will always return **FALSE** and will result in a failed assertion. For more information about bulk row fetching, see the article "Recordset: Fetching Records in Bulk (ODBC)" in *Visual C++ Programmer's Guide* online.

Calling **IsFieldDirty** will reset the effects of preceding calls to **SetFieldDirty** since the dirty status of the field is re-evaluated. In the **AddNew** case, if the current field value differs from the pseudo null value, the field status is set dirty. In the **Edit** case, if the field value differs from the cached value, then the field status is set dirty.

IsFieldDirty is implemented through **DoFieldExchange**.

For more information on the dirty flag, see the article "Recordset: How Recordsets Select Records (ODBC)" in *Visual C++ Programmer's Guide* online.

See Also: **CRecordset::SetFieldDirty**, **CRecordset::IsFieldNull**

CRecordset::IsFieldNull

BOOL IsFieldNull(void* *pv* **);**
   throw(CMemoryException);

Return Value

Nonzero if the specified field data member is flagged as Null; otherwise 0.

Parameters

pv A pointer to the field data member whose status you want to check, or **NULL** to determine if any of the fields are Null.

Remarks

Call this member function to determine whether the specified field data member of a recordset has been flagged as Null. (In database terminology, Null means "having no value" and is not the same as **NULL** in C++.) If a field data member is flagged as Null, it is interpreted as a column of the current record for which there is no value.

Note This member function is not applicable on recordsets that are using bulk row fetching. If you have implemented bulk row fetching, then **IsFieldNull** will always return **FALSE** and will result in a failed assertion. For more information about bulk row fetching, see the article "Recordset: Fetching Records in Bulk (ODBC)" in *Visual C++ Programmer's Guide* online.

IsFieldNull is implemented through **DoFieldExchange**.

See Also: **CRecordset::SetFieldNull**, **CRecordset::IsFieldDirty**

CRecordset::IsFieldNullable

BOOL IsFieldNullable(void* *pv* **);**
throw(CDBException)

Parameters

pv   A pointer to the field data member whose status you want to check, or **NULL** to determine if any of the fields can be set to a Null value.

Remarks

Call this member function to to determine whether the specified field data member is "nullable" (can be set to a Null value; C++ **NULL** is not the same as Null, which, in database terminology, means "having no value").

Note   If you have implemented bulk row fetching, you cannot call **IsFieldNullable**. Instead, call the **GetODBCFieldInfo** member function to determine whether a field can be set to a Null value. Note that you can always call **GetODBCFieldInfo**, regardless of whether you have implemented bulk row fetching. For more information about bulk row fetching, see the article "Recordset: Fetching Records in Bulk (ODBC)" in *Visual C++ Programmer's Guide* online.

A field that cannot be Null must have a value. If you attempt to set a such a field to Null when adding or updating a record, the data source rejects the addition or update, and **Update** will throw an exception. The exception occurs when you call **Update**, not when you call **SetFieldNull**.

Using **NULL** for the first argument of the function will apply the function only to **outputColumns**, not **params**. For instance, the call

```
SetFieldNull( NULL );
```

will set only **outputColumns** to **NULL**. **Params** will be unaffected.

To work on **params**, you must supply the actual address of the individual **param** you want to work on, such as:

```
SetFieldNull( &m_strParam );
```

This means you cannot set all **params NULL**, as you can with **outputColumns**.

IsFieldNullable is implemented through **DoFieldExchange**.

See Also: **CRecordset::IsFieldNull**, **CRecordset::SetFieldNull**

CRecordset::IsOpen

BOOL IsOpen( ) const;

Return Value

Nonzero if the recordset object's **Open** or **Requery** member function has previously been called and the recordset has not been closed; otherwise 0.

Remarks

Call this member function to determine if the recordset is already open.

CRecordset::Move

virtual void Move(long *nRows***, WORD** *wFetchType* **= SQL_FETCH_RELATIVE);**
throw(CDBException, CMemoryException);

Parameters

nRows   The number of rows to move forward or backward. Positive values move forward, toward the end of the recordset. Negative values move backward, toward the beginning.

wFetchType   Determines the rowset that **Move** will fetch. For details, see Remarks.

Remarks

Call this member function to move the current record pointer within the recordset, either forward or backward. If you pass a value of 0 for *nRows*, **Move** refreshes the current record; **Move** will end any current **AddNew** or **Edit** mode, and will restore the current record's value before **AddNew** or **Edit** was called.

Note   When moving through a recordset, deleted records may not be skipped. See the **IsDeleted** member function for details.

Move repositions the recordset by rowsets. Based on the values for *nRows* and *wFetchType*, **Move** fetches the appropriate rowset and then makes the first record in that rowset the current record. If you have not implemented bulk row fetching, then the rowset size is always 1. When fetching a rowset, **Move** directly calls the **CheckRowsetError** member function to handle any errors resulting from the fetch.

Depending on the values you pass, **Move** is equivalent to other **CRecordset** member functions. In particular, the value of *wFetchType* may indicate a member function that is more intuitive and often the preferred method for moving the current record.

The following table lists the possible values for *wFetchType*, the rowset that **Move** will fetch based on *wFetchType* and *nRows*, and any equivalent member function corresponding to *wFetchType*.

wFetchType	Fetched rowset	Equivalent member function
SQL_FETCH_RELATIVE (the default value)	The rowset starting *nRows* row(s) from the first row in the current rowset.	
SQL_FETCH_NEXT	The next rowset; *nRows* is ignored.	**MoveNext**

(continued)

(continued)

wFetchType	Fetched rowset	Equivalent member function
SQL_FETCH_PRIOR	The previous rowset; *nRows* is ignored.	**MovePrev**
SQL_FETCH_FIRST	The first rowset in the recordset; *nRows* is ignored.	**MoveFirst**
SQL_FETCH_LAST	The last complete rowset in the recordset; *nRows* is ignored.	**MoveLast**
SQL_FETCH_ABSOLUTE	If *nRows* > 0, the rowset starting *nRows* row(s) from the beginning of the recordset. If *nRows* < 0, the rowset starting *nRows* row(s) from the end of the recordset. If *nRows* = 0, then a beginning-of-file (BOF) condition is returned.	**SetAbsolutePosition**
SQL_FETCH_BOOKMARK	The rowset starting at the row whose bookmark value corresponds to *nRows*.	**SetBookmark**

Note For foward-only recordsets, **Move** is only valid with a value of **SQL_FETCH_NEXT** for *wFetchType*.

Caution Calling **Move** throws an exception if the recordset has no records. To determine whether the recordset has any records, call **IsBOF** and **IsEOF**.

If you have scrolled past the beginning or end of the recordset (**IsBOF** or **IsEOF** returns nonzero), calling a **Move** function will possibly throw a **CDBException**. For example, if **Is EOF** returns nonzero and **IsBOF** does not, then **MoveNext** will throw an exception, but **MovePrev** will not.

If you call **Move** while the current record is being updated or added, the updates are lost without warning.

For more information about recordset navigation, see the articles "Recordset: Scrolling (ODBC)" and "Recordset: Bookmarks and Absolute Positions (ODBC)" in *Visual C++ Programmer's Guide* online. For more information about bulk row fetching, see the article "Recordset: Fetching Records in Bulk (ODBC)" in *Visual C++ Programmer's Guide* online. For related information, see the ODBC API function **SQLExtendedFetch** in the *ODBC SDK Programmer's Reference*.

Example

```
// rs is a CRecordset or a
// CRecordset-derived object

// Change the rowset size to 5
rs.SetRowsetSize( 5 );

// Move to the first record
// in the recordset
rs.MoveFirst( );

// Move to the sixth record
rs.Move( 5 );
// Other equivalent ways to
// move to the sixth record:
// rs.Move( 6, SQL_FETCH_ABSOLUTE );
// rs.SetAbsolutePosition( 6 );
// In this case, the sixth record is
// the first record in the next rowset,
// so the following are also equivalent:
// rs.Move( 1, SQL_FETCH_NEXT );
// rs.MoveNext( );
```

See Also: **CRecordset::MoveNext, CRecordset::MovePrev, CRecordset::MoveFirst, CRecordset::MoveLast, CRecordset::SetAbsolutePosition, CRecordset::SetBookmark, CRecordset::IsBOF, CRecordset::IsEOF, CRecordset::CheckRowsetError**

CRecordset::MoveFirst

void MoveFirst( );
    throw(CDBException, CMemoryException);

Remarks

Call this member function to make the first record in the first rowset the current record. Regardless of whether bulk row fetching has been implemented, this will always be the first record in the recordset.

You do not have to call **MoveFirst** immediately after you open the recordset. At that time, the first record (if any) is automatically the current record.

Note This member function is not valid for forward-only recordsets.

Note When moving through a recordset, deleted records may not be skipped. See the **IsDeleted** member function for details.

> **Caution** Calling any of the **Move** functions throws an exception if the recordset has no records. To determine whether the recordset has any records, call **IsBOF** and **IsEOF**.
>
> If you call any of the **Move** functions while the current record is being updated or added, the updates are lost without warning.

For more information about recordset navigation, see the articles "Recordset: Scrolling (ODBC)" and "Recordset: Bookmarks and Absolute Positions (ODBC)" in *Visual C++ Programmer's Guide* online. For more information about bulk row fetching, see the article "Recordset: Fetching Records in Bulk (ODBC)" in *Visual C++ Programmer's Guide* online.

Example

See the example for **IsBOF**.

See Also: **CRecordset::Move, CRecordset::MoveLast, CRecordset::MoveNext, CRecordset::MovePrev, CRecordset::IsBOF, CRecordset::IsEOF**

CRecordset::MoveLast

void MoveLast( );
   throw(CDBException, CMemoryException);

Remarks

Call this member function to make the first record in the last complete rowset the current record. If you have not implemented bulk row fetching, your recordset has a rowset size of 1, so **MoveLast** simply moves to the last record in the recordset.

Note This member function is not valid for forward-only recordsets.

Note When moving through a recordset, deleted records may not be skipped. See the **IsDeleted** member function for details.

> **Caution** Calling any of the **Move** functions throws an exception if the recordset has no records. To determine whether the recordset has any records, call **IsBOF** and **IsEOF**.
>
> If you call any of the **Move** functions while the current record is being updated or added, the updates are lost without warning.

For more information about recordset navigation, see the articles "Recordset: Scrolling (ODBC)" and "Recordset: Bookmarks and Absolute Positions (ODBC)" in *Visual C++ Programmer's Guide* online. For more information about bulk row fetching, see the article "Recordset: Fetching Records in Bulk (ODBC)" in *Visual C++ Programmer's Guide* online.

Example

See the example for **IsBOF**.

See Also: CRecordset::Move, CRecordset::MoveFirst, CRecordset::MoveNext, CRecordset::MovePrev, CRecordset::IsBOF, CRecordset::IsEOF

CRecordset::MoveNext

void MoveNext( );
    throw(CDBException, CMemoryException);

Remarks

Call this member function to make the first record in the next rowset the current record. If you have not implemented bulk row fetching, your recordset has a rowset size of 1, so **MoveNext** simply moves to the next record.

Note When moving through a recordset, deleted records may not be skipped. See the **IsDeleted** member function for details.

Caution Calling any of the **Move** functions throws an exception if the recordset has no records. To determine whether the recordset has any records, call **IsBOF** and **IsEOF**.

It is also recommended that you call **IsEOF** before calling **MoveNext**. For example, if you have scrolled past the end of the recordset, **IsEOF** will return nonzero; a subsequent call to **MoveNext** would throw an exception.

If you call any of the **Move** functions while the current record is being updated or added, the updates are lost without warning.

For more information about recordset navigation, see the articles "Recordset: Scrolling (ODBC)" and "Recordset: Bookmarks and Absolute Positions (ODBC)" in *Visual C++ Programmer's Guide* online. For more information about bulk row fetching, see the article "Recordset: Fetching Records in Bulk (ODBC)" in *Visual C++ Programmer's Guide* online.

Example

See the example for **IsBOF**.

See Also: CRecordset::Move, CRecordset::MovePrev, CRecordset::MoveFirst, CRecordset::MoveLast, CRecordset::IsBOF, CRecordset::IsEOF

CRecordset::MovePrev

> **void MovePrev( );**
>   **throw(CDBException, CMemoryException);**

Remarks

Call this member function to make the first record in the previous rowset the current record. If you have not implemented bulk row fetching, your recordset has a rowset size of 1, so **MovePrev** simply moves to the previous record.

Note This member function is not valid for forward-only recordsets.

Note When moving through a recordset, deleted records may not be skipped. See the **IsDeleted** member function for details.

Caution Calling any of the **Move** functions throws an exception if the recordset has no records. To determine whether the recordset has any records, call **IsBOF** and **IsEOF**.

It is also recommended that you call **IsBOF** before calling **MovePrev**. For example, if you have scrolled ahead of the beginning of the recordset, **IsBOF** will return nonzero; a subsequent call to **MovePrev** would throw an exception.

If you call any of the **Move** functions while the current record is being updated or added, the updates are lost without warning.

For more information about recordset navigation, see the articles "Recordset: Scrolling (ODBC)" and "Recordset: Bookmarks and Absolute Positions (ODBC)" in *Visual C++ Programmer's Guide* online. For more information about bulk row fetching, see the article "Recordset: Fetching Records in Bulk (ODBC)" in *Visual C++ Programmer's Guide* online.

Example

See the example for **IsBOF**.

See Also: **CRecordset::Move, CRecordset::MoveNext, CRecordset::MoveFirst, CRecordset::MoveLast, CRecordset::IsBOF, CRecordset::IsEOF**

CRecordset::OnSetOptions

> **virtual void OnSetOptions(HSTMT** *hstmt* **);**

Parameters

hstmt The **HSTMT** of the ODBC statement whose options are to be set.

Remarks

The framework calls this member function to set initial options for the recordset. **OnSetOptions** determines the data source's support for scrollable cursors and for cursor concurrency and sets the recordset's options accordingly.

Override **OnSetOptions** to set additional options specific to the driver or the data source. For example, if your data source supports opening for exclusive access, you might override **OnSetOptions** to take advantage of that ability.

For more information about cursors, see the article "ODBC" in *Visual C++ Programmer's Guide* online.

See Also: **CDatabase::OnSetOptions**

CRecordset::Open

virtual BOOL Open(UINT *nOpenType* **= AFX_DB_USE_DEFAULT_TYPE,**
  ↪ **LPCTSTR** *lpszSQL* **= NULL, DWORD** *dwOptions* **= none);**
throw(CDBException, CMemoryException);

Return Value

Nonzero if the **CRecordset** object was successfully opened; otherwise 0 if **CDatabase::Open** (if called) returns 0.

Parameters

nOpenType   Accept the default value, **AFX_DB_USE_DEFAULT_TYPE**, or use one of the following values from the **enum OpenType**:

- **CRecordset::dynaset**   A recordset with bi-directional scrolling. The membership and ordering of the records are determined when the recordset is opened, but changes made by other users to the data values are visible following a fetch operation. Dynasets are also known as keyset-driven recordsets.

- **CRecordset::snapshot**   A static recordset with bi-directional scrolling. The membership and ordering of the records are determined when the recordset is opened; the data values are determined when the records are fetched. Changes made by other users are not visible until the recordset is closed and then reopened.

- **CRecordset::dynamic**   A recordset with bi-directional scrolling. Changes made by other users to the membership, ordering, and data values are visible following a fetch operation. Note that many ODBC drivers do not support this type of recordset.

- **CRecordset::forwardOnly**   A read-only recordset with only forward scrolling.

For **CRecordset**, the default value is **CRecordset::snapshot**. The default-value mechanism allows the Visual C++ wizards to interact with both ODBC **CRecordset** and DAO **CDaoRecordset**, which have different defaults.

For more information about these recordset types, see the article "Recordset (ODBC)" in *Visual C++ Programmer's Guide* online. For related information, see the article "Using Block and Scrollable Cursors" in the *ODBC SDK Programmer's Reference*.

Caution If the requested type is not supported, the framework throws an exception.

---

lpszSQL A string pointer containing one of the following:

- A **NULL** pointer.

- The name of a table.

- An SQL **SELECT** statement (optionally with an SQL **WHERE** or **ORDER BY** clause).

- A **CALL** statement specifying the name of a predefined query (stored procedure). Be careful that you do not insert whitespace between the curly brace and the **CALL** keyword.

For more information about this string, see the table and the discussion of ClassWizard's role under Remarks.

Note The order of the columns in your result set must match the order of the RFX or Bulk RFX function calls in your **DoFieldExchange** or **DoBulkFieldExchange** function override.

dwOptions A bitmask which can specify a combination of the values listed below. Some of these are mutually exclusive. The default value is **none**.

- **CRecordset::none** No options set. This parameter value is mutually exclusive with all other values. By default, the recordset can be updated with **Edit** or **Delete** and allows appending new records with **AddNew**. Updatability depends on the data source as well as on the *nOpenType* option you specify. Optimization for bulk additions is not available. Bulk row fetching will not be implemented. Deleted records will not be skipped during recordset navigation. Bookmarks are not available. Automatic dirty field checking is implemented.

- **CRecordset::appendOnly** Do not allow **Edit** or **Delete** on the recordset. Allow **AddNew** only. This option is mutually exclusive with **CRecordset::readOnly**.

- **CRecordset::readOnly** Open the recordset as read-only. This option is mutually exclusive with **CRecordset::appendOnly**.

- **CRecordset::optimizeBulkAdd** Use a prepared SQL statement to optimize adding many records at one time. Applies only if you are not using the ODBC API function **SQLSetPos** to update the recordset. The first update determines which fields are marked dirty. This option is mutually exclusive with **CRecordset::useMultiRowFetch**.

- **CRecordset::useMultiRowFetch** Implement bulk row fetching to allow multiple rows to be retrieved in a single fetch operation. This is an advanced feature designed to improve performance; however, bulk record field exchange is not supported by ClassWizard. This option is mutually exclusive with **CRecordset::optimizeBulkAdd**. Note that if you specify **CRecordset::useMultiRowFetch**, then the option **CRecordset::noDirtyFieldCheck** will be turned on automatically (double buffering will not be available); on forward-only recordsets, the option **CRecordset::useExtendedFetch** will be turned on automatically. For more information about bulk row fetching, see the article "Recordset: Fetching Records in Bulk (ODBC)" in *Visual C++ Programmer's Guide* online.

- **CRecordset::skipDeletedRecords** Skip all deleted records when navigating through the recordset. This will slow performance in certain relative fetches. This option is not valid on forward-only recordsets. Note that **CRecordset::skipDeletedRecords** is similar to *driver packing*, which means that deleted rows are removed from the recordset. However, if your driver packs records, then it will skip only those records that you delete; it will not skip records deleted by other users while the recordset is open. **CRecordset::skipDeletedRecords** will skip rows deleted by other users.

- **CRecordset::useBookmarks** May use bookmarks on the recordset, if supported. Bookmarks slow data retrieval but improve performance for data navigation. Not valid on forward-only recordsets. For more information, see the article "Recordset: Bookmarks and Absolute Positions (ODBC)" in *Visual C++ Programmer's Guide* online.

- **CRecordset::noDirtyFieldCheck** Turn off automatic dirty field checking (double buffering). This will improve performance; however, you must manually mark fields as dirty by calling the **SetFieldDirty** and **SetFieldNull** member functions.Note that double buffering in class **CRecordset** is similar to double buffering in class **CDaoRecordset**. However, in **CRecordset**, you cannot enable double buffering on individual fields; you either enable it for all fields or disable it for all fields. For more information about double buffering, see the DAO article "DAO Record Field Exchange: Double Buffering Records" in *Visual C++ Programmer's Guide* online. Note that if you specify the option **CRecordset::useMultiRowFetch**, then **CRecordset::noDirtyFieldCheck** will be turned on automatically; however, **SetFieldDirty** and **SetFieldNull** cannot be used on recordsets that implement bulk row fetching.

- **CRecordset::executeDirect** Do not use a prepared SQL statement. For improved performance, specify this option if the **Requery** member function will never be called.

- **CRecordset::useExtendedFetch** Implement **SQLExtendedFetch** instead of **SQLFetch**. This is designed for implementing bulk row fetching on forward-only recordsets. If you specify the option

CRecordset::useMultiRowFetch on a forward-only recordset, then
CRecordset::useExtendedFetch will be turned on automatically.

- **CRecordset::userAllocMultiRowBuffers**   The user will allocate
  storage buffers for the data. Use this option in conjunction with
  CRecordset::useMultiRowFetch if you want to allocate your own storage;
  otherwise, the framework will automatically allocate the necessary storage.
  For more information, see the article "Recordset: Fetching Records in Bulk
  (ODBC)" in *Visual C++ Programmer's Guide* online. Note that specifying
  CRecordset::userAllocMultiRowBuffers without specifying
  CRecordset::useMultiRowFetch will result in a failed assertion.

Remarks

You must call this member function to run the query defined by the recordset. Before
calling **Open**, you must construct the recordset object.

This recordset's connection to the data source depends on how you construct the
recordset before calling **Open**. If you pass a **CDatabase** object to the recordset
constructor that has not been connected to the data source, this member function uses
GetDefaultConnect to attempt to open the database object. If you pass **NULL** to the
recordset constructor, the constructor constructs a **CDatabase** object for you, and
Open attempts to connect the database object. For details on closing the recordset and
the connection under these varying circumstances, see **Close**.

Note   Access to a data source through a **CRecordset** object is always shared. Unlike the
CDaoRecordset class, you cannot use a **CRecordset** object to open a data source with
exclusive access.

When you call **Open**, a query, usually an SQL **SELECT** statement, selects records
based on criteria shown in the following table.

Value of the lpszSQL parameter	Records selected are determined by	Example
NULL	The string returned by **GetDefaultSQL**.	
SQL table name	All columns of the table-list in **DoFieldExchange** or **DoBulkFieldExchange**.	`"Customer"`
Predefined query (stored procedure) name	The columns the query is defined to return.	`"{call OverDueAccts}"`
SELECT column-list **FROM** table-list	The specified columns from the specified table(s).	`"SELECT CustId, CustName FROM Customer"`

Warning   Be careful that you do not insert extra whitespace in your SQL string. For example,
if you insert whitespace between the curly brace and the **CALL** keyword, MFC will misinterpret
the SQL string as a table name and incorporate it into a **SELECT** statement, which will result
in an exception being thrown. Similarly, if your predefined query uses an output parameter, do

not insert whitespace between the curly brace and the '?' symbol. Finally, you must not insert whitespace before the curly brace in a **CALL** statement or before the **SELECT** keyword in a **SELECT** statment.

The usual procedure is to pass **NULL** to **Open**; in this case, **Open** calls **GetDefaultSQL**. If you are using a derived **CRecordset** class, **GetDefualtSQL** gives the table name(s) you specified in ClassWizard. You can instead specify other information in the *lpszSQL* parameter.

Whatever you pass, **Open** constructs a final SQL string for the query (the string may have SQL **WHERE** and **ORDER BY** clauses appended to the *lpszSQL* string you passed) and then executes the query. You can examine the constructed string by calling **GetSQL** after calling **Open**. For additional details about how the recordset constructs an SQL statement and selects records, see the article "Recordset: How Recordsets Select Records (ODBC)" in *Visual C++ Programmer's Guide* online.

The field data members of your recordset class are bound to the columns of the data selected. If any records are returned, the first record becomes the current record.

If you want to set options for the recordset, such as a filter or sort, specify these after you construct the recordset object but before you call **Open**. If you want to refresh the records in the recordset after the recordset is already open, call **Requery**.

For more information, including additional examples, see the articles "Recordset (ODBC)," "Recordset: How Recordsets Select Records (ODBC)," and "Recordset: Creating and Closing Recordsets (ODBC)" in *Visual C++ Programmer's Guide* online.

Example

The following code examples show different forms of the **Open** call.

```
// rs is a CRecordset or
// CRecordset-derived object

// Open rs using the default SQL statement,
// implement bookmarks, and turn off
// automatic dirty field checking
rs.Open( CRecordset::snapshot, NULL,
        CRecordset::useBookmarks |
        CRecordset::noDirtyFieldCheck );

// Pass a complete SELECT statement
// and open as a dynaset
rs.Open( CRecordset::dynaset,
        _T( "Select L_Name from Customer" ) );

// Accept all defaults
rs.Open( );
```

See Also: CRecordset::CRecordset, CRecordset::Close, CRecordset::GetDefaultSQL, CRecordset::GetSQL, CRecordset::m_strFilter, CRecordset::m_strSort, CRecordset::Requery

---

CRecordset::RefreshRowset

void RefreshRowset(WORD *wRow***,**
　↳ WORD *wLockType* **= SQL_LOCK_NO_CHANGE);**

Parameters

wRow　The one-based position of a row in the current rowset. This value can range from zero to the size of the rowset.

wLockType　A value indicating how to lock the row after it has been refreshed. For details, see Remarks.

Remarks

Call this member function to update the data and the status for a row in the current rowset. If you pass a value of zero for *wRow*, then every row in the rowset will be refreshed.

To use **RefreshRowset**, you must have implemented bulk row fetching by specifying the **CRecordset::useMulitRowFetch** option in the **Open** member function.

RefreshRowset calls the ODBC API function **SQLSetPos**. The *wLockType* parameter specifies the lock state of the row after **SQLSetPos** has executed. The following table describes the possible values for *wLockTyp*e.

wLockType	Description
SQL_LOCK_NO_CHANGE (the default value)	The driver or data source ensures that the row is in the same locked or unlocked state as it was before **RefreshRowset** was called.
SQL_LOCK_EXCLUSIVE	The driver or data source locks the row exclusively. Not all data sources support this type of lock.
SQL_LOCK_UNLOCK	The driver or data source unlocks the row. Not all data sources support this type of lock.

For more information about **SQLSetPos**, see the *ODBC SDK Programmer's Reference*. For more information about bulk row fetching, see the article "Recordset: Fetching Records in Bulk (ODBC)" in *Visual C++ Programmer's Guide* online.

See Also: CRecordset::SetRowsetCursorPosition, CRecordset::SetRowsetSize

CRecordset::Requery

virtual BOOL Requery( );
    throw(CDBException, CMemoryException);

Return Value

Nonzero if the recordset was successfully rebuilt; otherwise 0.

Remarks

Call this member function to rebuild (refresh) a recordset. If any records are returned, the first record becomes the current record.

In order for the recordset to reflect the additions and deletions that you or other users are making to the data source, you must rebuild the recordset by calling **Requery**. If the recordset is a dynaset, it automatically reflects updates that you or other users make to its existing records (but not additions). If the recordset is a snapshot, you must call **Requery** to reflect edits by other users as well as additions and deletions.

For either a dynaset or a snapshot, call **Requery** any time you want to rebuild the recordset using a new filter or sort, or new parameter values. Set the new filter or sort property by assigning new values to **m_strFilter** and **m_strSort** before calling **Requery**. Set new parameters by assigning new values to parameter data members before calling **Requery**. If the filter and sort strings are unchanged, you can reuse the query, which improves performance.

If the attempt to rebuild the recordset fails, the recordset is closed. Before you call **Requery**, you can determine whether the recordset can be requeried by calling the **CanRestart** member function. **CanRestart** does not guarantee that **Requery** will succeed.

Caution   Call **Requery** only after you have called **Open**.

Example

This example rebuilds a recordset to apply a different sort order.

```
// Example for CRecordset::Requery

CCustSet rsCustSet( NULL );

// Open the recordset
rsCustSet.Open( );

// Use the recordset ...

// Set the sort order and Requery the recordset
rsCustSet.m_strSort = "District, Last_Name";
if( !rsCustSet.CanRestart( ) )
    return;    // Unable to requery

if( !rsCustSet.Requery( ) )
    // Requery failed, so take action
```

See Also: **CRecordset::CanRestart**, **CRecordset::m_strFilter**, **CRecordset::m_strSort**

CRecordset::SetAbsolutePosition

> **void SetAbsolutePosition(long** *nRows* **);**
> **throw(CDBException, CMemoryException);**

Parameters

nRows The one-based ordinal position for the current record in the recordset.

Remarks

Call this member function to position the recordset on the record corresponding to the specified record number. **SetAbsolutePosition** moves the current record pointer based on this ordinal position.

Note This member function is not valid on forward-only recordsets.

For ODBC recordsets, an absolute position setting of 1 refers to the first record in the recordset; a setting of 0 refers to the beginning-of-file (BOF) position.

You can also pass negative values to **SetAbsolutePosition**. In this case the recordset's position is evaluated from the end of the recordset. For example, `SetAbsolutePosition( -1 )` moves the current record pointer to the last record in the recordset.

Note Absolute position is not intended to be used as a surrogate record number. Bookmarks are still the recommended way of retaining and returning to a given position, since a record's position changes when preceding records are deleted. In addition, you cannot be assured that a given record will have the same absolute position if the recordset is re-created again because the order of individual records within a recordset is not guaranteed unless it is created with an SQL statement using an **ORDER BY** clause.

For more information about recordset navigation and bookmarks, see the articles "Recordset: Scrolling (ODBC)" and "Recordset: Bookmarks and Absolute Positions (ODBC)" in *Visual C++ Programmer's Guide* online.

See Also: **CRecordset::SetBookmark**

CRecordset::SetBookmark

> **void SetBookmark(const CDBVariant&** *varBookmark* **);**
> **throw(CDBException, CMemoryException);**

Parameters

varBookmark A reference to a **CDBVariant** object containing the bookmark value for a specific record.

Remarks

Call this member function to position the recordset on the record containing the specified bookmark. To determine if bookmarks are supported on the recordset, call **CanBookmark**. To make bookmarks available if they are supported, you must set the **CRecordset::useBookmarks** option in the *dwOptions* parameter of the **Open** member function.

Note If bookmarks are unsupported or unavailable, calling **SetBookmark** will result in an exception being thrown. Bookmarks are not supported on forward-only recordsets.

To first retrieve the bookmark for the current record, call **GetBookmark**, which saves the bookmark value to a **CDBVariant** object. Later, you can return to that record by calling **SetBookmark** using the saved bookmark value.

Note After certain recordset operations, you should check the bookmark persistence before calling **SetBookmark**. For example, if you retrieve a bookmark with **GetBookmark** and then call **Requery**, the bookmark may no longer be valid. Call **CDatabase::GetBookmarkPersistence** to check whether you can safely call **SetBookmark**.

For more information about bookmarks and recordset navigation, see the articles "Recordset: Bookmarks and Absolute Positions (ODBC)" and "Recordset: Scrolling (ODBC)" in *Visual C++ Programmer's Guide* online.

See Also: **CRecordset::CanBookmark, CRecordset::GetBookmark, CRecordset::SetAbsolutePosition, CDatabase::GetBookmarkPersistence**

CRecordset::SetFieldDirty

void SetFieldDirty(void* *pv*, **BOOL** *bDirty* = **TRUE**);

Parameters

pv Contains the address of a field data member in the recordset or **NULL**. If **NULL**, all field data members in the recordset are flagged. (C++ **NULL** is not the same as Null in database terminology, which means "having no value.")

bDirty **TRUE** if the field data member is to be flagged as "dirty" (changed). Otherwise **FALSE** if the field data member is to be flagged as "clean" (unchanged).

Remarks

Call this member function to flag a field data member of the recordset as changed or as unchanged. Marking fields as unchanged ensures the field is not updated and results in less SQL traffic.

Note This member function is not applicable on recordsets that are using bulk row fetching. If you have implemented bulk row fetching, then **SetFieldDirty** will result in a failed assertion. For more information about bulk row fetching, see the article "Recordset: Fetching Records in Bulk (ODBC)" in *Visual C++ Programmer's Guide* online.

The framework marks changed field data members to ensure they will be written to the record on the data source by the record field exchange (RFX) mechanism. Changing the value of a field generally sets the field dirty automatically, so you will seldom need to call **SetFieldDirty** yourself, but you might sometimes want to ensure that columns will be explicitly updated or inserted regardless of what value is in the field data member.

Important Call this member function only after you have called **Edit** or **AddNew**.

Using **NULL** for the first argument of the function will apply the function only to **outputColumns**, not **params**. For instance, the call

```
SetFieldNull( NULL );
```

will set only **outputColumns** to **NULL**. **Params** will be unaffected.

To work on **params**, you must supply the actual address of the individual **param** you want to work on, such as:

```
SetFieldNull( &m_strParam );
```

This means you cannot set all **params NULL**, as you can with **outputColumns**.

See Also: **CRecordset::IsFieldDirty**, **CRecordset::SetFieldNull**, **CRecordset::Edit**, **CRecordset::Update**

CRecordset::SetFieldNull

void SetFieldNull(void* *pv*, **BOOL** *bNull* = **TRUE**);

Parameters

pv Contains the address of a field data member in the recordset or **NULL**. If **NULL**, all field data members in the recordset are flagged. (C++ **NULL** is not the same as Null in database terminology, which means "having no value.")

bNull Nonzero if the field data member is to be flagged as having no value (Null). Otherwise 0 if the field data member is to be flagged as non-Null.

Remarks

Call this member function to flag a field data member of the recordset as Null (specifically having no value) or as non-Null. When you add a new record to a recordset, all field data members are initially set to a Null value and flagged as "dirty" (changed). When you retrieve a record from a data source, its columns either already have values or are Null.

Note Do not call this member function on recordsets that are using bulk row fetching. If you have implemented bulk row fetching, calling **SetFieldNull** results in a failed assertion. For more information about bulk row fetching, see the article "Recordset: Fetching Records in Bulk (ODBC)" in *Visual C++ Programmer's Guide* online.

If you specifically wish to designate a field of the current record as not having a value, call **SetFieldNull** with *bNull* set to **TRUE** to flag it as Null. If a field was previously marked Null and you now want to give it a value, simply set its new value. You do not have to remove the Null flag with **SetFieldNull**. To determine whether the field is allowed to be Null, call **IsFieldNullable**.

Important Call this member function only after you have called **Edit** or **AddNew**.

Using **NULL** for the first argument of the function will apply the function only to **outputColumns**, not **params**. For instance, the call

```
SetFieldNull( NULL );
```

will set only **outputColumns** to **NULL**. **Params** will be unaffected.

To work on **params**, you must supply the actual address of the individual **param** you want to work on, such as:

```
SetFieldNull( &m_strParam );
```

This means you cannot set all **params NULL**, as you can with **outputColumns**.

Note When setting parameters to Null, a call to **SetFieldNull** before the recordset is opened results in an assertion. In this case, call **SetParamNull**.

SetFieldNull is implemented through **DoFieldExchange**.

See Also: **CRecordset::IsFieldNull**, **CRecordset::SetFieldDirty**, **CRecordset::Edit**, **CRecordset::Update**, **CRecordset::IsFieldNullable**

CRecordset::SetLockingMode

void SetLockingMode(UINT *nMode* **);**

Parameters

nMode Contains one of the following values from the **enum LockMode**:

- **optimistic** Optimistic locking locks the record being updated only during the call to **Update**.

- **pessimistic** Pessimistic locking locks the record as soon as **Edit** is called and keeps it locked until the **Update** call completes or you move to a new record.

Remarks

Call this member function if you need to specify which of two record-locking strategies the recordset is using for updates. By default, the locking mode of a recordset is **optimistic**. You can change that to a more cautious **pessimistic** locking strategy. Call **SetLockingMode** after you construct and open the recordset object but before you call **Edit**.

See Also: **CRecordset::Edit**, **CRecordset::Update**

CRecordset::SetParamNull

void SetParamNull(int *nIndex***, BOOL** *bNull* **= TRUE);**

Parameters

nIndex   The zero-based index of the parameter.

bNull   If **TRUE** (the default value), the parameter is flagged as Null. Otherwise, the parameter is flagged as non-Null.

Remarks

Call this member function to flag a parameter as Null (specifically having no value) or as non-Null. Unlike **SetFieldNull**, you can call **SetParamNull** before you have opened the recordset.

SetParamNull is typically used with predefined queries (stored procedures).

See Also: CRecordset::FlushResultSet

CRecordset::SetRowsetCursorPosition

void SetRowsetCursorPosition(WORD *wRow*,
↳ **WORD** *wLockType* = **SQL_LOCK_NO_CHANGE);**

Parameters

wRow   The one-based position of a row in the current rowset. This value can range from 1 to the size of the rowset.

wLockType   Value indicating how to lock the row after it has been refreshed. For details, see Remarks.

Remarks

Call this member function to move the cursor to a row within the current rowset. When implementing bulk row fetching, records are retrieved by rowsets, where the first record in the fetched rowset is the current record. In order to make another record within the rowset the current record, call **SetRowsetCursorPosition**. For example, you can combine **SetRowsetCursorPosition** with the **GetFieldValue** member function to dynamically retrieve the data from any record of your recordset.

To use **SetRowsetCursorPosition**, you must have implemented bulk row fetching by specifying the **CRecordset::useMultiRowFetch** option of the *dwOptions* parameter in the **Open** member function.

SetRowsetCursorPosition calls the ODBC API function **SQLSetPos**. The *wLockType* parameter specifies the lock state of the row after **SQLSetPos** has executed. The following table describes the possible values for *wLockType*.

wLockType	Description
SQL_LOCK_NO_CHANGE (the default value)	The driver or data source ensures that the row is in the same locked or unlocked state as it was before **SetRowsetCursorPosition** was called.
SQL_LOCK_EXCLUSIVE	The driver or data source locks the row exclusively. Not all data sources support this type of lock.
SQL_LOCK_UNLOCK	The driver or data source unlocks the row. Not all data sources support this type of lock.

For more information about **SQLSetPos**, see the *ODBC SDK Programmer's Reference*. For more information about bulk row fetching, see the article "Recordset: Fetching Records in Bulk (ODBC)" in *Visual C++ Programmer's Guide* online.

See Also: **CRecordset::RefreshRowset**, **CRecordset::SetRowsetSize**

CRecordset::SetRowsetSize

virtual void SetRowsetSize(DWORD *dwNewRowsetSize* **);**

Parameters

dwNewRowsetSize The number of rows to retrieve during a given fetch.

Remarks

This virtual member function specifies how many rows you wish to retrieve during a single fetch when using bulk row fetching. To implement bulk row fetching, you must set the **CRecordset::useMultiRowFetch** option in the *dwOptions* parameter of the **Open** member function.

Note Calling **SetRowsetSize** without implementing bulk row fetching will result in a failed assertion.

Call **SetRowsetSize** before calling **Open** to initially set the rowset size for the recordset. The default rowset size when implementing bulk row fetching is 25.

Note Use caution when calling **SetRowsetSize**. If you are manually allocating storage for the data (as specified by the **CRecordset::userAllocMultiRowBuffers** option of the dwOptions parameter in **Open**), you should check whether you need to reallocate these storage buffers after you call **SetRowsetSize**, but before you perform any cursor navigation operation.

To obtain the current setting for the rowset size, call **GetRowsetSize**.

For more information about bulk row fetching, see the article "Recordset: Fetching Records in Bulk (ODBC)" in *Visual C++ Programmer's Guide* online.

See Also: **CRecordset::Open**, **CRecordset::GetRowsetSize**, **CRecordset::CheckRowsetError**, **CRecordset::DoBulkFieldExchange**

CRecordset::Update

virtual BOOL Update( );
throw(CDBException);

Return Value

Nonzero if one record was successfully updated; otherwise 0 if no columns have changed. If no records were updated, or if more than one record was updated, an exception is thrown. An exception is also thrown for any other failure on the data source.

Remarks

Call this member function after a call to the **AddNew** or **Edit** member function. This call is required to complete the **AddNew** or **Edit** operation.

Note If you have implemented bulk row fetching, you cannot call **Update**. This will result in a failed assertion. Although class **CRecordset** does not provide a mechanism for updating bulk rows of data, you can write your own functions by using the ODBC API function **SQLSetPos**. For an example of how to do this, see the sample "DBFETCH" online. For more information about bulk row fetching, see the article "Recordset: Fetching Records in Bulk (ODBC)" in *Visual C++ Programmer's Guide* online.

Both **AddNew** and **Edit** prepare an edit buffer in which the added or edited data is placed for saving to the data source. **Update** saves the data. Only those fields marked or detected as changed are updated.

If the data source supports transactions, you can make the **Update** call (and its corresponding **AddNew** or **Edit** call) part of a transaction. For more information about transactions, see the article "Transaction (ODBC)" in *Visual C++ Programmer's Guide* online.

Caution If you call **Update** without first calling either **AddNew** or **Edit**, **Update** throws a **CDBException**. If you call **AddNew** or **Edit**, you must call **Update** before you call a **Move** operation or before you close either the recordset or the data source connection. Otherwise, your changes are lost without notification.

For details on handling **Update** failures, see the article "Recordset: How Recordsets Update Records (ODBC)" in *Visual C++ Programmer's Guide* online.

Example

See the article "Transaction: Performing a Transaction in a Recordset (ODBC)" in *Visual C++ Programmer's Guide* online.

See Also: CRecordset::Edit, CRecordset::AddNew, CRecordset::SetFieldDirty, CDBException

Data Members
CRecordset::m_hstmt

Remarks

Contains a handle to the ODBC statement data structure, of type **HSTMT**, associated with the recordset. Each query to an ODBC data source is associated with an **HSTMT**.

Caution   Do not use **m_hstmt** before **Open** has been called.

Normally you do not need to access the **HSTMT** directly, but you might need it for direct execution of SQL statements. The **ExecuteSQL** member function of class **CDatabase** provides an example of using **m_hstmt**.

See Also: **CDatabase::ExecuteSQL**

CRecordset::m_nFields

Remarks

Contains the number of field data members in the recordset class — the number of columns selected by the recordset from the data source. The constructor for the recordset class must initialize **m_nFields** with the correct number. If you have not implemented bulk row fetching, ClassWizard writes this initialization for you when you use it to declare your recordset class. You can also write it manually.

The framework uses this number to manage interaction between the field data members and the corresponding columns of the current record on the data source.

Important   This number must correspond to the number of "output columns" registered in **DoFieldExchange** or **DoBulkFieldExchange** after a call to **SetFieldType** with the parameter **CFieldExchange::outputColumn**.

You can bind columns dynamically, as explained in the article "Recordset: Dynamically Binding Data Columns." If you do so, you must increase the count in **m_nFields** to reflect the number of RFX or Bulk RFX function calls in your **DoFieldExchange** or **DoBulkFieldExchange** member function for the dynamically bound columns.

For more information, see the articles "Recordset: Dynamically Binding Data Columns (ODBC)" and "Recordset: Fetching Records in Bulk (ODBC)" in *Visual C++ Programmer's Guide* online.

Example

See the article "Record Field Exchange: Using RFX" in *Visual C++ Programmer's Guide* online.

See Also: **CRecordset::DoFieldExchange, CRecordset::DoBulkFieldExchange, CRecordset::m_nParams, CFieldExchange::SetFieldType**

CRecordset::m_nParams

Remarks

Contains the number of parameter data members in the recordset class — the number of parameters passed with the recordset's query. If your recordset class has any parameter data members, the constructor for the class must initialize **m_nParams** with the correct number. The value of **m_nParams** defaults to 0. If you add parameter data members — which you must do manually — you must also manually add an initialization in the class constructor to reflect the number of parameters (which must be at least as large as the number of '?' placeholders in your **m_strFilter** or **m_strSort** string).

The framework uses this number when it parameterizes the recordset's query.

Important This number must correspond to the number of "params" registered in **DoFieldExchange** or **DoBulkFieldExchange** after a call to **SetFieldType** with a parameter value of **CFieldExchange::inputParam, CFieldExchange::param, CFieldExchange::outputParam**, or **CFieldExchange::inoutParam**.

Example

See the articles "Recordset: Parameterizing a Recordset (ODBC)" and "Record Field Exchange: Using RFX" in *Visual C++ Programmer's Guide* online.

See Also: **CRecordset::DoFieldExchange, CRecordset::DoBulkFieldExchange, CRecordset::m_nFields, CFieldExchange::SetFieldType**

CRecordset::m_pDatabase

Remarks

Contains a pointer to the **CDatabase** object through which the recordset is connected to a data source. This variable is set in two ways. Typically, you pass a pointer to an already connected **CDatabase** object when you construct the recordset object. If you pass **NULL** instead, **CRecordset** creates a **CDatabase** object for you and connects it. In either case, **CRecordset** stores the pointer in this variable.

Normally you will not directly need to use the pointer stored in **m_pDatabase**. If you write your own extensions to **CRecordset**, however, you might need to use the pointer. For example, you might need the pointer if you throw your own **CDBException**s. Or you might need it if you need to do something using the same **CDatabase** object, such as running transactions, setting timeouts, or calling the **ExecuteSQL** member function of class **CDatabase** to execute SQL statements directly.

CRecordset::m_strFilter

Remarks

After you construct the recordset object, but before you call its **Open** member function, use this data member to store a **CString** containing an SQL **WHERE** clause. The recordset uses this string to constrain — or filter — the records it selects during the **Open** or **Requery** call. This is useful for selecting a subset of records, such as "all salespersons based in California" ("state = CA"). The ODBC SQL syntax for a **WHERE** clause is

```
WHERE search-condition
```

Note that you do not include the **WHERE** keyword in your string. The framework supplies it.

You can also parameterize your filter string by placing '?' placeholders in it, declaring a parameter data member in your class for each placeholder, and passing parameters to the recordset at run time. This lets you construct the filter at run time. For more information, see the article "Recordset: Parameterizing a Recordset (ODBC)" in *Visual C++ Programmer's Guide* online.

For more information about SQL **WHERE** clauses, see the article "SQL." For more information about selecting and filtering records, see the article "Recordset: Filtering Records (ODBC)." Both articles are in *Visual C++ Programmer's Guide* online.

Example

```
// Example for CRecordset::m_strFilter

CCustSet rsCustSet( NULL );

// Set the filter
rsCustSet.m_strFilter = "state = 'CA'";

// Run the filtered query
rsCustSet.Open( CRecordset::snapshot, "Customers" );
```

See Also: **CRecordset::m_strSort**, **CRecordset::Requery**

CRecordset::m_strSort

Remarks

After you construct the recordset object, but before you call its **Open** member function, use this data member to store a **CString** containing an SQL **ORDER BY** clause. The recordset uses this string to sort the records it selects during the **Open** or **Requery** call. You can use this feature to sort a recordset on one or more columns. The ODBC SQL syntax for an **ORDER BY** clause is

```
ORDER BY sort-specification [, sort-specification]...
```

where a sort-specification is an integer or a column name. You can also specify ascending or descending order (the order is ascending by default) by appending "ASC" or "DESC" to the column list in the sort string. The selected records are sorted first by the first column listed, then by the second, and so on. For example, you might order a "Customers" recordset by last name, then first name. The number of columns you can list depends on the data source. For more information, see the *ODBC SDK Programmer's Reference.*

Note that you do not include the **ORDER BY** keyword in your string. The framework supplies it.

For more information about SQL clauses, see the article "SQL." For more information about sorting records, see the article "Recordset: Sorting Records (ODBC)." Both articles are in *Visual C++ Programmer's Guide* online.

Example

```
// Example for CRecordset::m_strSort

CCustSet rsCustSet( NULL );

// Set the sort string
rsCustSet.m_strSort = "District, Last_Name";

// Run the sorted query
rsCustSet.Open( CRecordset::snapshot, "Customers" );
```

See Also: CRecordset::m_strFilter, CRecordset::Requery

CRecordView

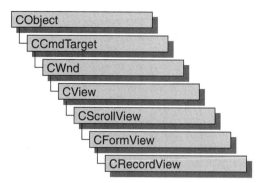

CObject
└ CCmdTarget
  └ CWnd
    └ CView
      └ CScrollView
        └ CFormView
          └ CRecordView

A **CRecordView** object is a view that displays database records in controls. The view is a form view directly connected to a **CRecordset** object. The view is created from a dialog template resource and displays the fields of the **CRecordset** object in the dialog template's controls. The **CRecordView** object uses dialog data exchange (DDX) and record field exchange (RFX) to automate the movement of data between the controls on the form and the fields of the recordset. **CRecordView** also supplies a default implementation for moving to the first, next, previous, or last record and an interface for updating the record currently on view.

Note If you are working with the Data Access Objects (DAO) classes rather than the Open Database Connectivity (ODBC) classes, use class **CDaoRecordView** instead. For more information, see the articles "Database Topics (General)" and "DAO and MFC" in *Visual C++ Programmer's Guide* online.

The most common way to create your record view is with AppWizard. AppWizard creates both the record view class and its associated recordset class as part of your skeleton starter application. If you don't create the record view class with AppWizard, you can create it later with ClassWizard. If you simply need a single form, the AppWizard approach is easier. ClassWizard lets you decide to use a record view later in the development process. Using ClassWizard to create a record view and a recordset separately and then connect them is the most flexible approach because it gives you more control in naming the recordset class and its .H/.CPP files. This approach also lets you have multiple record views on the same recordset class.

To make it easy for end-users to move from record to record in the record view, AppWizard creates menu (and optionally toolbar) resources for moving to the first, next, previous, or last record. If you create a record view class with ClassWizard, you need to create these resources yourself with the menu and bitmap editors. For more information about these resources, see "Overview: Creating a Program That Supports a Database" and "ClassWizard: Creating a Database Form."

For information about the default implementation for moving from record to record, see **IsOnFirstRecord** and **IsOnLastRecord** and the article "Record Views: Using a Record View."

CRecordView keeps track of the user's position in the recordset so that the record view can update the user interface. When the user moves to either end of the recordset, the record view disables user interface objects — such as menu items or toolbar buttons — for moving further in the same direction.

For more information about declaring and using your record view and recordset classes, see "Designing and Creating a Record View" in the article "Record Views." For more information about how record views work and how to use them, see the article "Record Views: Using a Record View." All the articles mentioned above are in *Visual C++ Programmer's Guide* online.

#include <afxdb.h>

See Also: CRecordset, CFormView

CRecordView Class Members

Construction

CRecordView	Constructs a **CRecordView** object.

Attributes

OnGetRecordset	Returns a pointer to an object of a class derived from **CRecordset**. ClassWizard overrides this function for you and creates the recordset if necessary.
IsOnFirstRecord	Returns nonzero if the current record is the first record in the associated recordset.
IsOnLastRecord	Returns nonzero if the current record is the last record in the associated recordset.

Operations

OnMove	If the current record has changed, updates it on the data source, then moves to the specified record (next, previous, first, or last).

Member Functions
CRecordView::CRecordView

CRecordView(LPCSTR *lpszTemplateName* **);**
CRecordView(UINT *nIDTemplate* **);**

Parameters

lpszTemplateName   Contains a null-terminated string that is the name of a dialog template resource.

nIDTemplate   Contains the ID number of a dialog template resource.

Remarks

When you create an object of a type derived from **CRecordView**, call either form of the constructor to initialize the view object and identify the dialog resource on which the view is based. You can either identify the resource by name (pass a string as the argument to the constructor) or by its ID (pass an unsigned integer as the argument). Using a resource ID is recommended.

Note   Your derived class *must* supply its own constructor. In the constructor of your derived class, call the constructor **CRecordView::CRecordView** with the resource name or ID as an argument, as shown in the example below.

CRecordView::OnInitialUpdate calls **UpdateData**, which calls **DoDataExchange**. This initial call to **DoDataExchange** connects **CRecordView** controls (indirectly) to **CRecordset** field data members created by ClassWizard. These data members cannot be used until after you call the base class **CFormView::OnInitialUpdate** member function.

Note   If you use ClassWizard, the wizard defines an **enum** value CRecordView::IDD and specifies it in the member initialization list for the constructor where you see IDD_MYFORM in the example. The example shows how you can specify the dialog template resource ID if you write the code yourself without the wizard.

Example

```
CMyRecordView::CMyRecordView()
    : CRecordView( IDD_MYFORM )
{
    //{{AFX_DATA_INIT( CMyRecordView )
        // NOTE: the ClassWizard will add member initialization here
    //}}AFX_DATA_INIT
    // Other construction code, such as data initialization
}
```

See Also: **CRecordset::DoFieldExchange, CView::OnInitialUpdate, CWnd::UpdateData**

CRecordView::IsOnFirstRecord

BOOL IsOnFirstRecord( );

Return Value

Nonzero if the current record is the first record in the recordset; otherwise 0.

Remarks

Call this member function to determine whether the current record is the first record in the recordset object associated with this record view. This function is useful for writing your own implementations of default command update handlers written by ClassWizard.

If the user moves to the first record, the framework disables any user interface objects you have for moving to the first or the previous record.

See Also: CRecordView::OnMove, CRecordView::IsOnLastRecord, CRecordset::IsBOF, CRecordset::GetRecordCount

CRecordView::IsOnLastRecord

BOOL IsOnLastRecord( );

Return Value

Nonzero if the current record is the last record in the recordset; otherwise 0.

Remarks

Call this member function to determine whether the current record is the last record in the recordset object associated with this record view. This function is useful for writing your own implementations of the default command update handlers that ClassWizard writes to support a user interface for moving from record to record.

Caution   The result of this function is reliable except that the view cannot detect the end of the recordset until the user has moved past it. The user must move beyond the last record before the record view can tell that it must disable any user interface objects for moving to the next or last record. If the user moves past the last record and then moves back to the last record (or before it), the record view can track the user's position in the recordset and disable user interface objects correctly. **IsOnLastRecord** is also unreliable after a call to the implementation function **OnRecordLast**, which handles the **ID_RECORD_LAST** command, or **CRecordset::MoveLast**.

See Also: CRecordView::OnMove, CRecordView::IsOnFirstRecord, CRecordset::IsEOF, CRecordset::GetRecordCount

CRecordView::OnGetRecordset

virtual CRecordset* OnGetRecordset( ) = 0;

Return Value

A pointer to a **CRecordset**-derived object if the object was successfully created; otherwise a **NULL** pointer.

Remarks

Returns a pointer to the **CRecordset**-derived object associated with the record view. You must override this member function to construct or obtain a recordset object and return a pointer to it. If you declare your record view class with ClassWizard, the wizard writes a default override for you. ClassWizard's default implementation returns the recordset pointer stored in the record view if one exists. If not, it constructs a recordset object of the type you specified with ClassWizard and calls its **Open** member function to open the table or run the query, and then returns a pointer to the object.

For more information and examples, see the article "Record Views: Using a Record View" in *Visual C++ Programmer's Guide* online.

See Also: CRecordset, CRecordset::Open

CRecordView::OnMove

virtual BOOL OnMove(UINT *nIDMoveCommand*);
   throw(CDBException);

Return Value

Nonzero if the move was successful; otherwise 0 if the move request was denied.

Parameters

nIDMoveCommand   One of the following standard command ID values:

- **ID_RECORD_FIRST** Move to the first record in the recordset.
- **ID_RECORD_LAST** Move to the last record in the recordset.
- **ID_RECORD_NEXT** Move to the next record in the recordset.
- **ID_RECORD_PREV** Move to the previous record in the recordset.

Remarks

Call this member function to move to a different record in the recordset and display its fields in the controls of the record view. The default implementation calls the appropriate **Move** member function of the **CRecordset** object associated with the record view.

By default, **OnMove** updates the current record on the data source if the user has changed it in the record view.

AppWizard creates a menu resource with First Record, Last Record, Next Record, and Previous Record menu items. If you select the Dockable Toolbar option, AppWizard also creates a toolbar with buttons corresponding to these commands.

If you move past the last record in the recordset, the record view continues to display the last record. If you move backward past the first record, the record view continues to display the first record.

Caution   Calling **OnMove** throws an exception if the recordset has no records. Call the appropriate user interface update handler function—**OnUpdateRecordFirst**, **OnUpdateRecordLast**, **OnUpdateRecordNext**, or **OnUpdateRecordPrev**—before the corresponding move operation to determine whether the recordset has any records. For information about the update handlers, see "Overview: Creating a Program That Supports a Database" in *Visual C++ Programmer's Guide* online.

See Also: CRecordset::Move

CRect

The **CRect** class is similar to a Windows **RECT** structure. **CRect** also includes member functions to manipulate **CRect** objects and Windows **RECT** structures.

A **CRect** object can be passed as a function parameter wherever a **RECT** structure, **LPCRECT**, or **LPRECT** can be passed.

Note This class is derived from the **tagRECT** structure. (The name **tagRECT** is a less-commonly-used name for the **RECT** structure.) This means that the data members (**left**, **top**, **right**, and **bottom**) of the **RECT** structure are accessible data members of **CRect**.

A **CRect** contains member variables that define the top-left and bottom-right points of a rectangle.

When specifying a **CRect**, you must be careful to construct it so that it is normalized—in other words, such that the value of the left coordinate is less than the right and the top is less than the bottom. For example, a top left of (10,10) and bottom right of (20,20) defines a normalized rectangle but a top left of (20,20) and bottom right of (10,10) defines a non-normalized rectangle. If the rectangle is not normalized, many **CRect** member functions may return incorrect results. (See **CRect::NormalizeRect** for a list of these functions.) Before you call a function that requires normalized rectangles, you can normalize non-normalized rectangles by calling the **NormalizeRect** function.

Use caution when manipulating a **CRect** with the **CDC::DPtoLP** and **CDC::LPtoDP** member functions. If the mapping mode of a display context is such that the y-extent is negative, as in **MM_LOENGLISH**, then **CDC::DPtoLP** will transform the **CRect** so that its top is greater than the bottom. Functions such as **Height** and **Size** will then return negative values for the height of the transformed **CRect**, and the rectangle will be non-normalized.

When using overloaded **CRect** operators, the first operand must be a **CRect**; the second can be either a **RECT** structure or a **CRect** object.

#include <afxwin.h>

See Also: **CPoint, CSize, RECT**

CRect Class Members

Construction

CRect	Constructs a **CRect** object.

Operations

Width	Calculates the width of **CRect**.
Height	Calculates the height of **CRect**.
Size	Calculates the size of **CRect**.
TopLeft	Returns the top-left point of **CRect**.
BottomRight	Returns the bottom-right point of **CRect**.
CenterPoint	Returns the centerpoint of **CRect**.
IsRectEmpty	Determines whether **CRect** is empty. **CRect** is empty if the width and/or height are 0.
IsRectNull	Determines whether the **top**, **bottom**, **left**, and **right** member variables are all equal to 0.
PtInRect	Determines whether the specified point lies within **CRect**.
SetRect	Sets the dimensions of **CRect**.
SetRectEmpty	Sets **CRect** to an empty rectangle (all coordinates equal to 0).
CopyRect	Copies the dimensions of a source rectangle to **CRect**.
EqualRect	Determines whether **CRect** is equal to the given rectangle.
InflateRect	Increases the width and height of **CRect**.
DeflateRect	Decreases the width and height of **CRect**.
NormalizeRect	Standardizes the height and width of **CRect**.
OffsetRect	Moves **CRect** by the specified offsets.
SubtractRect	Subtracts one rectangle from another.
IntersectRect	Sets **CRect** equal to the intersection of two rectangles.
UnionRect	Sets **CRect** equal to the union of two rectangles.

Operators

operator LPCRECT	Converts a **CRect** to an **LPCRECT**.
operator LPRECT	Converts a **CRect** to an **LPRECT**.
operator =	Copies the dimensions of a rectangle to **CRect**.
operator ==	Determines whether **CRect** is equal to a rectangle.
operator !=	Determines whether **CRect** is not equal to a rectangle.
operator +=	Adds the specified offsets to **CRect** or inflates **CRect**.
operator −=	Subtracts the specified offsets from **CRect** or deflates **CRect**.
operator &=	Sets **CRect** equal to the intersection of **CRect** and a rectangle.
operator |=	Sets **CRect** equal to the union of **CRect** and a rectangle.
operator +	Adds the given offsets to **CRect** or inflates **CRect** and returns the resulting **CRect**.
operator −	Subtracts the given offsets from **CRect** or deflates **CRect** and returns the resulting **CRect**.

Operators *(continued)*

operator &	Creates the intersection of **CRect** and a rectangle and returns the resulting **CRect**.
operator |	Creates the union of **CRect** and a rectangle and returns the resulting **CRect**.

Member Functions
CRect::BottomRight

CPoint& BottomRight( );
const CPoint& BottomRight( ) const;

Return Value

The coordinates of the bottom-right corner of the rectangle.

Remarks

The coordinates are returned as a reference to a **CPoint** object that is contained in **CRect**.

You can use this function to either get or set the bottom-right corner of the rectangle. Set the corner by using this function on the left side of the assignment operator.

See Also: CRect::TopLeft, CPoint, CRect::CenterPoint

CRect::CenterPoint

CPoint CenterPoint( ) const;

Return Value

A **CPoint** object that is the centerpoint of **CRect**.

Remarks

Calculates the centerpoint of **CRect** by adding the left and right values and dividing by two, and adding the top and bottom values and dividing by two.

See Also: CRect::Width, CRect::Height, CRect::Size, CRect::TopLeft, CRect::BottomRight, CRect::IsRectNull, Cpoint

CRect::CopyRect

void CopyRect(LPCRECT *lpSrcRect*);

Parameters

lpSrcRect   Points to the **RECT** structure or **CRect** object that is to be copied.

Remarks

Copies the *lpSrcRect* rectangle into **Crect**.

See Also: CRect::CRect, CRect::operator =, CRect::SetRect, CRect::SetRectEmpty

---

CRect::CRect

CRect( );
CRect(int *l*, **int** *t*, **int** *r*, **int** *b* **);**
CRect(const RECT& *srcRect* **);**
CRect(LPCRECT *lpSrcRect* **);**
CRect(POINT *point*, **SIZE** *size* **);**
CRect(POINT *topLeft*, **POINT** *bottomRight* **);**

Parameters

l   Specifies the left position of **CRect**.

t   Specifies the top of **CRect**.

r   Specifies the right position of **CRect**.

b   Specifies the bottom of **CRect**.

srcRect   Refers to the **RECT** structure with the coordinates for **CRect**.

lpSrcRect   Points to the **RECT** structure with the coordinates for **CRect**.

point   Specifies the origin point for the rectangle to be constructed. Corresponds to the top-left corner.

size   Specifies the displacement from the top-left corner to the bottom-right corner of the rectangle to be constructed.

topLeft   Specifies the top-left position of **CRect**.

bottomRight   Specifies the bottom-right position of **CRect**.

Remarks

Constructs a **CRect** object. If no arguments are given, **left**, **top**, **right**, and **bottom** members are not initialized.

The **CRect(const RECT&)** and **CRect(LPCRECT)** constructors perform a **CopyRect**. The other constructors initialize the member variables of the object directly.

See Also: **CRect::SetRect**, **CRect::CopyRect**, **CRect::operator =**, **CRect::SetRectEmpty**

CRect::DeflateRect

void DeflateRect(int *x*, **int** *y* **);**
void DeflateRect(SIZE *size* **);**
void DeflateRect(LPCRECT *lpRect* **);**
void DeflateRect(int *l*, **int** *t*, **int** *r*, **int** *b* **);**

Parameters

x   Specifies the number of units to deflate the left and right sides of **CRect**.

y   Specifies the number of units to deflate the top and bottom of **CRect**.

size   A **SIZE** or **CSize** that specifies the number of units to deflate **CRect**. The *cx* value specifies the number of units to deflate the left and right sides and the *cy* value specifies the number of units to deflate the top and bottom.

lpRect   Points to a **RECT** structure or **CRect** that specifies the number of units to deflate each side.

l   Specifies the number of units to deflate the left side of **CRect**.

t   Specifies the number of units to deflate the top of **CRect**.

r   Specifies the number of units to deflate the right side of **CRect**.

b   Specifies the number of units to deflate the bottom of **CRect**.

Remarks

DeflateRect deflates **CRect** by moving its sides toward its center. To do this, **DeflateRect** adds units to the left and top and subtracts units from the right and bottom. The parameters of **DeflateRect** are signed values; positive values deflate **CRect** and negative values inflate it.

The first two overloads deflate both pairs of opposite sides of **CRect** so that its total width is decreased by two times *x* (or *cx*) and its total height is decreased by two times *y* (or *cy*). The other two overloads deflate each side of **CRect** independently of the others.

See Also: **CRect::InflateRect**, **CRect::operator -**, **CRect::operator -=**, **::InflateRect**

CRect::EqualRect

BOOL EqualRect(LPCRECT *lpRect* **) const;**

Return Value

Nonzero if the two rectangles have the same top, left, bottom, and right values; otherwise 0.

Note Both of the rectangles must be normalized or this function may fail. You can call **NormalizeRect** to normalize the rectangles before calling this function.

Parameters

lpRect   Points to a **RECT** structure or **CRect** object that contains the upper-left and lower-right corner coordinates of a rectangle.

See Also: CRect::operator ==, CRect::operator !=, CRect::NormalizeRect, ::EqualRect

---

CRect::Height

int Height( ) const;

Return Value

The height of **CRect**.

Remarks

Calculates the height of **CRect** by subtracting the top value from the bottom value. The resulting value can be negative.

Note The rectangle must be normalized or this function may fail. You can call **NormalizeRect** to normalize the rectangle before calling this function.

See Also: CRect::Width, CRect::Size, CRect::CenterPoint, CRect::IsRectEmpty, CRect::IsRectNull, CRect::NormalizeRect

---

CRect::InflateRect

void InflateRect(int *x,* **int** *y* **);**
void InflateRect(SIZE *size* **);**
void InflateRect(LPCRECT *lpRect* **);**
void InflateRect(int *l,* **int** *t,* **int** *r,* **int** *b* **);**

Parameters

x   Specifies the number of units to inflate the left and right sides of **CRect**.

y   Specifies the number of units to inflate the top and bottom of **CRect**.

size A **SIZE** or **CSize** that specifies the number of units to inflate **CRect**. The *cx* value specifies the number of units to inflate the left and right sides and the *cy* value specifies the number of units to inflate the top and bottom.

lpRect Points to a **RECT** structure or **CRect** that specifies the number of units to inflate each side.

l Specifies the number of units to inflate the left side of **CRect**.

t Specifies the number of units to inflate the top of **CRect**.

r Specifies the number of units to inflate the right side of **CRect**.

b Specifies the number of units to inflate the bottom of **CRect**.

Remarks

InflateRect inflates **CRect** by moving its sides away from its center. To do this, **InflateRect** subtracts units from the left and top and adds units to the right and bottom. The parameters of **InflateRect** are signed values; positive values inflate **CRect** and negative values deflate it.

The first two overloads inflate both pairs of opposite sides of **CRect** so that its total width is increased by two times *x* (or *cx*) and its total height is increased by two times *y* (or *cy*). The other two overloads inflate each side of **CRect** independently of the others.

See Also: **CRect::DeflateRect**, **CRect::operator +**, **CRect::operator +=**, **::InflateRect**

CRect::IntersectRect

BOOL IntersectRect(LPCRECT *lpRect1*, **LPCRECT** *lpRect2* **);**

Return Value

Nonzero if the intersection is not empty; 0 if the intersection is empty.

Parameters

lpRect1 Points to a **RECT** structure or **CRect** object that contains a source rectangle.

lpRect2 Points to a **RECT** structure or **CRect** object that contains a source rectangle.

Remarks

Makes a **CRect** equal to the intersection of two existing rectangles. The intersection is the largest rectangle contained in both existing rectangles.

Note Both of the rectangles must be normalized or this function may fail. You can call **NormalizeRect** to normalize the rectangles before calling this function.

See Also: **CRect::operator &=**, **CRect::operator &**, **CRect::UnionRect**, **CRect::SubtractRect**, **CRect::NormalizeRect**, **::IntersectRect**

CRect::IsRectEmpty

BOOL IsRectEmpty( ) const;

Return Value

Nonzero if **CRect** is empty; 0 if **CRect** is not empty.

Remarks

Determines whether **CRect** is empty. A rectangle is empty if the width and/or height are 0 or negative. Differs from **IsRectNull**, which determines whether all coordinates of the rectangle are zero.

Note The rectangle must be normalized or this function may fail. You can call **NormalizeRect** to normalize the rectangle before calling this function.

See Also: **CRect::IsRectNull**, **CRect::SetRectEmpty**, **CRect::NormalizeRect**, **::IsRectEmpty**

CRect::IsRectNull

BOOL IsRectNull( ) const;

Return Value

Nonzero if **CRect**'s top, left, bottom, and right values are all equal to 0; otherwise 0.

Remarks

Determines whether the top, left, bottom, and right values of **CRect** are all equal to 0. Differs from **IsRectEmpty**, which determines whether the rectangle is empty.

See Also: **CRect::IsRectEmpty**, **CRect::SetRectEmpty**

CRect::NormalizeRect

void NormalizeRect( );

Remarks

Normalizes **CRect** so that both the height and width are positive. The rectangle is normalized for fourth-quadrant positioning, which Windows typically uses for coordinates. **NormalizeRect** compares the top and bottom values, and swaps them if the top is greater than the bottom. Similarly, it swaps the left and right values if the left is greater than the right. This function is useful when dealing with different mapping modes and inverted rectangles.

Note The following **CRect** member functions require normalized rectangles in order to work properly: **Height**, **Width**, **Size**, **IsRectEmpty**, **PtInRect**, **EqualRect**, **UnionRect**, **IntersectRect**, **SubtractRect**, **operator ==**, **operator !=**, **operator |**, **operator |=**, **operator &**, and **operator &=**.

CRect::OffsetRect

void OffsetRect(int *x*, **int** *y* **);**
void OffsetRect(POINT *point* **);**
void OffsetRect(SIZE *size* **);**

Parameters

x   Specifies the amount to move left or right. It must be negative to move left.

y   Specifies the amount to move up or down. It must be negative to move up.

point   Contains a **POINT** structure or **CPoint** object specifying both dimensions by which to move.

size   Contains a **SIZE** structure or **CSize** object specifying both dimensions by which to move.

Remarks

Moves **CRect** by the specified offsets. Moves **CRect** *x* units along the x-axis and *y* units along the y-axis. The *x* and *y* parameters are signed values, so **CRect** can be moved left or right and up or down.

See Also: **CRect::operator +**, **CRect::operator +=**, **CRect::operator -**, **CRect::operator -=**

CRect::PtInRect

BOOL PtInRect(POINT *point* **) const;**

Return Value

Nonzero if the point lies within **CRect**; otherwise 0.

Parameters

point   Contains a **POINT** structure or **CPoint** object.

Remarks

Determines whether the specified point lies within **CRect**. A point is within **CRect** if it lies on the left or top side or is within all four sides. A point on the right or bottom side is outside **CRect**.

Note   The rectangle must be normalized or this function may fail. You can call **NormalizeRect** to normalize the rectangle before calling this function.

See Also: **CRect::NormalizeRect**, **::PtInRect**

CRect::SetRect

void SetRect(int *x1***, int** *y1***, int** *x2***, int** *y2* **);**

Parameters

x1 Specifies the x-coordinate of the upper-left corner.

y1 Specifies the y-coordinate of the upper-left corner.

x2 Specifies the x-coordinate of the lower-right corner.

y2 Specifies the y-coordinate of the lower-right corner.

Remarks

Sets the dimensions of **CRect** to the specified coordinates.

See Also: **CRect::CRect**, **CRect::operator =**, **CRect::CopyRect**, **CRect::SetRectEmpty**, **::SetRect**

CRect::SetRectEmpty

void SetRectEmpty( );

Remarks

Makes **CRect** a null rectangle by setting all coordinates to zero.

See Also: **CRect::CRect**, **CRect::SetRect**, **CRect::CopyRect**, **CRect::operator =**, **CRect::IsRectEmpty**, **CRect::IsRectNull**, **::SetRectEmpty**

CRect::Size

CSize Size( ) const;

Return Value

A **CSize** object that contains the size of **CRect**.

Remarks

The *cx* and *cy* members of the return value contain the height and width of **CRect**. Either the height or width can be negative.

Note The rectangle must be normalized or this function may fail. You can call **NormalizeRect** to normalize the rectangle before calling this function.

See Also: **CRect::Height**, **CRect::Width**, **CRect::IsRectEmpty**, **CRect::IsRectNull**, **CRect::NormalizeRect**

CRect::SubtractRect

BOOL SubtractRect(LPCRECT *lpRectSrc1*, **LPCRECT** *lpRectSrc2* **);**

Return Value

Nonzero if the function is successful; otherwise 0.

Parameters

lpRectSrc1   Points to the **RECT** structure or **CRect** object from which a rectangle is to be subtracted.

lpRectSrc2   Points to the **RECT** structure or **CRect** object that is to be subtracted from the rectangle pointed to by the *lpRectSrc1* parameter.

Remarks

Makes the dimensions of the *lpRectSrc1* rectangle equal to the subtraction of *lpRectSrc2* from *lpRectSrc1*. The subtraction is the smallest rectangle that contains all of the points in *lpRectScr1* that are not in the intersection of *lpRectScr1* and *lpRectScr2*.

The rectangle specified by *lpRectSrc1* will be unchanged if the rectangle specified by *lpRectSrc2* doesn't completely overlap the rectangle specified by *lpRectSrc1* in at least one of the x- or y-directions.

For example, if *lpRectSrc1* were (10,10, 100,100) and *lpRectSrc2* were (50,50, 150,150), the rectangle pointed to by *lpRectSrc1* would be unchanged when the function returned. If *lpRectSrc1* were (10,10, 100,100) and *lpRectSrc2* were (50,10, 150,150), however, the rectangle pointed to by *lpRectSrc1* would contain the coordinates (10,10, 50,100) when the function returned.

SubtractRect is not the same as **operator -** nor **operator -=**. Neither of these operators ever calls **SubtractRect**.

Note   Both of the rectangles must be normalized or this function may fail. You can call **NormalizeRect** to normalize the rectangles before calling this function.

See Also: **CRect::operator -**, **CRect::operator -=**, **CRect::IntersectRect**, **CRect::UnionRect**, **CRect::NormalizeRect**, **::SubtractRect**

CRect::TopLeft

CPoint& TopLeft( );
const CPoint& TopLeft( ) const;

Return Value

The coordinates of the top-left corner of the rectangle.

Remarks

The coordinates are returned as a reference to a **CPoint** object that is contained in **CRect**.

You can use this function to either get or set the top-left corner of the rectangle. Set the corner by using this function on the left side of the assignment operator.

See Also: **CRect::BottomRight, CPoint, CRect::CenterPoint**

CRect::UnionRect

BOOL UnionRect(LPCRECT *lpRect1*, **LPCRECT** *lpRect2* **);**

Return Value

Nonzero if the union is not empty; 0 if the union is empty.

Parameters

lpRect1   Points to a **RECT** or **CRect** that contains a source rectangle.

lpRect2   Points to a **RECT** or **CRect** that contains a source rectangle.

Remarks

Makes the dimensions of **CRect** equal to the union of the two source rectangles. The union is the smallest rectangle that contains both source rectangles.

Windows ignores the dimensions of an empty rectangle; that is, a rectangle that has no height or has no width.

Note   Both of the rectangles must be normalized or this function may fail. You can call **NormalizeRect** to normalize the rectangles before calling this function.

See Also: **CRect::operator !=, CRect::operator |, CRect::IntersectRect, CRect::SubtractRect, CRect::NormalizeRect, ::UnionRect**

CRect::Width

int Width( ) const;

Return Value

The width of **CRect**.

Remarks

Calculates the width of **CRect** by subtracting the left value from the right value. The width can be negative.

Note   The rectangle must be normalized or this function may fail. You can call **NormalizeRect** to normalize the rectangle before calling this function.

See Also: **CRect::Height, CRect::Size, CRect::CenterPoint, CRect::IsRectEmpty, CRect::IsRectNull, CRect::NormalizeRect**

Operators
CRect::operator LPCRECT

operator LPCRECT( ) const;

Remarks

Converts a **CRect** to an **LPCRECT**. When you use this function, you don't need the address-of (**&**) operator. This operator will be automatically used when you pass a **CRect** object to a function that expects an **LPCRECT**.

See Also: CRect::operator LPRECT

CRect::operator LPRECT

operator LPRECT( );

Remarks

Converts a **CRect** to an **LPRECT**. When you use this function, you don't need the address-of (**&**) operator. This operator will be automatically used when you pass a **CRect** object to a function that expects an **LPRECT**.

See Also: CRect::operator LPCRECT

CRect::operator =

void operator =(const RECT& *srcRect* **);**

Parameters

srcRect   Refers to a source rectangle. Can be a **RECT** or **CRect**.

Remarks

Assigns *srcRect* to **CRect**.

See Also: CRect::CRect, CRect::SetRect, CRect::CopyRect, CRect::SetRectEmpty, ::CopyRect

CRect::operator ==

BOOL operator ==(const RECT& *rect* **) const;**

Return Value

Nonzero if equal; otherwise 0.

CRect::operator !=

Parameters

rect   Refers to a source rectangle. Can be a **RECT** or **CRect**.

Remarks

Determines whether *rect* is equal to **CRect** by comparing the coordinates of their upper-left and lower-right corners.

Note   Both of the rectangles must be normalized or this function may fail. You can call **NormalizeRect** to normalize the rectangles before calling this function.

See Also: **CRect::operator !=, CRect::NormalizeRect, ::EqualRect**

CRect::operator !=

BOOL operator !=(const RECT& *rect* **) const;**

Return Value

Nonzero if not equal; otherwise 0.

Parameters

rect   Refers to a source rectangle. Can be a **RECT** or **CRect**.

Remarks

Determines whether *rect* is not equal to **CRect** by comparing the coordinates of their upper-left and lower-right corners.

Note   Both of the rectangles must be normalized or this function may fail. You can call **NormalizeRect** to normalize the rectangles before calling this function.

See Also: **CRect::operator ==, CRect::NormalizeRect, ::EqualRect**

CRect::operator +=

void operator +=(POINT *point* **);**
void operator +=(SIZE *size* **);**
void operator +=(LPCRECT *lpRect* **);**

Parameters

point   A **POINT** structure or **CPoint** object that specifies the number of units to move the rectangle.

size   A **SIZE** structure or **CSize** object that specifies the number of units to move the rectangle.

lpRect   Points to a **RECT** structure or **CRect** object that contains the number of units to inflate each side of **CRect**.

Remarks

The first two overloads move **CRect** by the specified offsets. The parameter's *x* and *y* (or *cx* and *cy*) values are added to **CRect**.

The third overload inflates **CRect** by the number of units specifed in each member of the parameter.

See Also: **CRect::OffsetRect**, **CRect::InflateRect**, **CRect::operator +**, **CRect::operator -=**

CRect::operator -=

void operator –=(POINT *point* **);**
void operator –=(SIZE *size* **);**
void operator –=(LPCRECT *lpRect* **);**

Parameters

point   A **POINT** structure or **CPoint** object that specifies the number of units to move the rectangle.

size   A **SIZE** structure or **CSize** object that specifies the number of units to move the rectangle.

lpRect   Points to a **RECT** structure or **CRect** object that contains the number of units to deflate each side of **CRect**.

Remarks

The first two overloads move **CRect** by the specified offsets. The parameter's *x* and *y* (or *cx* and *cy*) values are subtracted from **CRect**.

The third overload deflates **CRect** by the number of units specifed in each member of the parameter. Note that this overload functions like **DeflateRect**.

See Also: **CRect::OffsetRect**, **CRect::DeflateRect**, **CRect::SubtractRect**, **CRect::operator -**, **CRect::operator +=**

CRect::operator &=

void operator &=(const RECT& *rect* **);**

Parameters

rect   Contains a **RECT** or **CRect**.

Remarks

Sets **CRect** equal to the intersection of **CRect** and *rect*. The intersection is the largest rectangle that is contained in both rectangles.

Note   Both of the rectangles must be normalized or this function may fail. You can call **NormalizeRect** to normalize the rectangles before calling this function.

See Also: **CRect::operator &, CRect::operator |=, CRect::IntersectRect,
CRect::NormalizeRect, ::IntersectRect**

CRect::operator |=

void operator |=(const RECT& *rect* **);**

Parameters

rect Contains a **CRect** or **RECT**.

Remarks

Sets **CRect** equal to the union of **CRect** and *rect*. The union is the smallest rectangle
that contains both source rectangles.

Note Both of the rectangles must be normalized or this function may fail. You can call
NormalizeRect to normalize the rectangles before calling this function.

See Also: **CRect::operator |, CRect::operator &=, CRect::UnionRect,
CRect::NormalizeRect, ::UnionRect**

CRect::operator +

CRect operator +(POINT *point* **) const;**
CRect operator +(LPCRECT *lpRect* **) const;**
CRect operator +(SIZE *size* **) const;**

Return Value

The **CRect** resulting from moving or inflating **CRect** by the number of units specified
in the parameter.

Parameters

point A **POINT** structure or **CPoint** object that specifies the number of units to
move the return value.

size A **SIZE** structure or **CSize** object that specifies the number of units to move the
return value.

lpRect Points to a **RECT** structure or **CRect** object that contains the number of units
to inflate each side of the return value.

Remarks

The first two overloads return a **CRect** object that is equal to **CRect** displaced by the
specified offsets. The parameter's *x* and *y* (or *cx* and *cy*) parameters are added to
CRect's position.

The third overload returns a new **CRect** that is equal to **CRect** inflated by the number
of units specifed in each member of the parameter.

See Also: **CRect::operator +=**, **CRect::operator -**, **CRect::OffsetRect**,
CRect::InflateRect

CRect::operator -

CRect operator –(POINT *point* **) const;**
CRect operator –(SIZE *size* **) const;**
CRect operator –(LPCRECT *lpRect* **) const;**

Return Value

The **CRect** resulting from moving or deflating **CRect** by the number of units specified
in the parameter.

Parameters

point   A **POINT** structure or **CPoint** object that specifies the number of units to
move the return value.

size   A **SIZE** structure or **CSize** object that specifies the number of units to move the
return value.

lpRect   Points to a **RECT** structure or **CRect** object that contains the number of units
to deflate each side of the return value.

Remarks

The first two overloads return a **CRect** object that is equal to **CRect** displaced by the
specified offsets. The parameter's *x* and *y* (or *cx* and *cy*) parameters are subtracted
from **CRect**'s position.

The third overload returns a new **CRect** that is equal to **CRect** deflated by the number
of units specifed in each member of the parameter. Note that this overload functions
like **DeflateRect**, not **SubtractRect**.

See Also: **CRect::operator -=**, **CRect::operator +**, **CRect::OffsetRect**,
CRect::DeflateRect, **CRect::SubtractRect**

CRect::operator &

CRect operator &(const RECT& *rect2* **) const;**

Return Value

A **CRect** that is the intersection of **CRect** and *rect2*.

Parameters

rect2   Contains a **RECT** or **CRect**.

Remarks

Returns a **CRect** that is the intersection of **CRect** and *rect2*. The intersection is the
largest rectangle that is contained in both rectangles.

Note Both of the rectangles must be normalized or this function may fail. You can call **NormalizeRect** to normalize the rectangles before calling this function.

See Also: **CRect::IntersectRect**, **CRect::operator &=**, **CRect::operator |**, **CRect::NormalizeRect**

CRect::operator |

CRect operator |(const RECT& *rect2* **) const;**

Return Value

A **CRect** that is the union of **CRect** and *rect2*.

Parameters

rect2 Contains a **RECT** or **CRect**.

Remarks

Returns a **CRect** that is the union of **CRect** and *rect2*. The union is the smallest rectangle that contains both rectangles.

Note Both of the rectangles must be normalized or this function may fail. You can call **NormalizeRect** to normalize the rectangles before calling this function.

See Also: **CRect::UnionRect**, **CRect::operator |=**, **CRect::operator &**, **CRect::NormalizeRect**

CRectTracker

CRectTracker does not have a base class.

The **CRectTracker** class allows an item to be displayed, moved, and resized in different fashions. Although the **CRectTracker** class is designed to allow the user to interact with OLE items by using a graphical interface, its use is not restricted to OLE-enabled applications. It can be used anywhere such a user interface is required.

CRectTracker borders can be solid or dotted lines. The item can be given a hatched border or overlaid with a hatched pattern to indicate different states of the item. You can place eight resize handles on either the outside or the inside border of the item. (For an explanation of the resize handles, see **GetHandleMask**.) Finally, a **CRectTracker** allows you to change the orientation of an item during resizing.

To use **CRectTracker**, construct a **CRectTracker** object and specify which display states are initialized. You can then use this interface to give the user visual feedback on the current status of the OLE item associated with the **CRectTracker** object.

For more information on using **CRectTracker**, see the article "Trackers" in *Visual C++ Programmer's Guide* online.

#include <afxext.h>

See Also: **COleResizeBar**, **CRect**, **CRectTracker::GetHandleMask**

CRectTracker Class Members

Data Members

m_nHandleSize	Determines size of resize handles.
m_rect	Current position (in pixels) of the rectangle.
m_sizeMin	Determines minimum rectangle width and height.
m_nStyle	Current style(s) of the tracker.

Construction

CRectTracker	Constructs a **CRectTracker** object.

Operations

Draw	Renders the rectangle.
GetTrueRect	Returns width and height of rectangle, including resize handles.
HitTest	Returns the current position of the cursor related to the **CRectTracker** object.

(continued)

Operations *(continued)*

NormalizeHit	Normalizes a hit-test code.
SetCursor	Sets the cursor, depending on its position over the rectangle.
Track	Allows the user to manipulate the rectangle.
TrackRubberBand	Allows the user to "rubber-band" the selection.

Overridables

AdjustRect	Called when the rectangle is resized.
DrawTrackerRect	Called when drawing the border of a **CRectTracker** object.
OnChangedRect	Called when the rectangle has been resized or moved.
GetHandleMask	Called to get the mask of a **CRectTracker** item's resize handles.

Member Functions

CRectTracker::AdjustRect

virtual void AdjustRect(int *nHandle***, LPRECT** *lpRect* **);**

Parameters

nHandle   Index of handle used.

lpRect   Pointer to the current size of the rectangle. (The size of a rectangle is given by its height and width.)

Remarks

Called by the framework when the tracking rectangle is resized by using a resize handle. The default behavior of this function allows the rectangle's orientation to change only when **Track** and **TrackRubberBand** are called with inverting allowed.

Override this function to control the adjustment of the tracking rectangle during a dragging operation. One method is to adjust the coordinates specified by *lpRect* before returning.

Special features that are not directly supported by **CRectTracker**, such as snap-to-grid or keep-aspect-ratio, can be implemented by overriding this function.

See Also: CRectTracker::Track, CRectTracker::TrackRubberBand, CRectTracker::OnChangedRect

CRectTracker::CRectTracker

CRectTracker( );
CRectTracker(LPCRECT *lpSrcRect*, **UINT** *nStyle* **);**

Parameters

lpSrcRect   The coordinates of the rectangle object.

nStyle   Specifies the style of the **CRectTracker** object. The following styles are supported:

- **CRectTracker::solidLine**   Use a solid line for the rectangle border.

- **CRectTracker::dottedLine**   Use a dotted line for the rectangle border.

- **CRectTracker::hatchedBorder**   Use a hatched pattern for the rectangle border.

- **CRectTracker::resizeInside**   Resize handles located inside the rectangle.

- **CRectTracker::resizeOutside**   Resize handles located outside the rectangle.

- **CRectTracker::hatchInside**   Hatched pattern covers the entire rectangle.

Remarks

Creates and initializes a **CRectTracker** object.

The default constructor initializes the **CRectTracker** object with the values from *lpSrcRect* and initializes other sizes to system defaults. If the object is created with no parameters, the **m_rect** and **m_nStyle** data members are uninitialized.

See Also: CRect::CRect

CRectTracker::Draw

void Draw(CDC* *pDC* **) const;**

Parameters

pDC   Pointer to the device context on which to draw.

Remarks

Call this function to draw the rectangle's outer lines and inner region. The style of the tracker determines how the drawing is done. See the constructor for **CRectTracker** for more information on the styles available.

See Also: CRectTracker::DrawTrackerRect, **CRectTracker::CRectTracker**, **CRect::NormalizeRect**

CRectTracker::DrawTrackerRect

virtual void DrawTrackerRect(LPCRECT *lpRect*, **CWnd*** *pWndClipTo*,
↪ **CDC*** *pDC*, **CWnd*** *pWnd*);

Parameters

lpRect   Pointer to the **RECT** that contains the rectangle to draw.

pWndClipTo   Pointer to the window to use in clipping the rectangle.

pDC   Pointer to the device context on which to draw.

pWnd   Pointer to the window on which the drawing will occur.

Remarks

Called by the framework whenever the position of the tracker has changed while inside the **Track** or **TrackRubberBand** member function. The default implementation makes a call to **CDC::DrawFocusRect**, which draws a dotted rectangle.

Override this function to provide different feedback during the tracking operation.

See Also: CRectTracker::Track, CRectTracker::TrackRubberBand, CDC::DrawFocusRect

---

CRectTracker::GetHandleMask

virtual UINT GetHandleMask( ) const;

Return Value

The mask of a **CRectTracker** item's resize handles.

Remarks

The framework calls this member function to retrieve the mask for a rectangle's resize handles.

The resize handles appear on the sides and corners of the rectangle and allow the user to control the shape and size of the rectangle.

A rectangle has 8 resize handles numbered 0–7. Each resize handle is represented by a bit in the mask; the value of that bit is 2^n, where n is the resize handle number. Bits 0–3 correspond to the corner resize handles, starting at the top left moving clockwise. Bits 4–7 correspond to the side resize handles starting at the top moving clockwise. The following illustration shows a rectangle's resize handles and their corresponding resize handle numbers and values:

Handle numbers

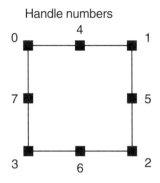

Bit values

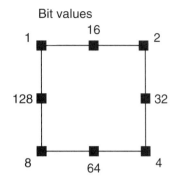

The default implementation of **GetHandleMask** returns the mask of the bits so that the resize handles appear. If the single bit is on, the corresponding resize handle will be drawn.

Override this member function to hide or show the indicated resize handles.

See Also: **CRectTracker::AdjustRect**

CRectTracker::GetTrueRect

void GetTrueRect(LPRECT *lpTrueRect* **) const;**

Parameters

lpTrueRect Pointer to the **RECT** structure that will contain the device coordinates of the **CRectTracker** object.

Remarks

Call this function to retrieve the coordinates of the rectangle. The dimensions of the rectangle include the height and width of any resize handles located on the outer border. Upon returning, **lpTrueRect* is always a normalized rectangle in device coordinates.

See Also: **CRect::NormalizeRect**

CRectTracker::HitTest

int HitTest(CPoint *point* **) const;**

Return Value

The value returned is based on the enumerated type **CRectTracker::TrackerHit** and can have one of the following values:

- **CRectTracker::hitNothing** −1

- **CRectTracker::hitTopLeft**   0
- **CRectTracker::hitTopRight**   1
- **CRectTracker::hitBottomRight**   2
- **CRectTracker:hitBottomLeft**   3
- **CRectTracker:hitTop**   4
- **CRectTracker:hitRight**   5
- **CRectTracker:hitBottom**   6
- **CRectTracker:hitLeft**   7
- **CRectTracker:hitMiddle**   8

Parameters

point   The point, in device coordinates, to test.

Remarks

Call this function to find out whether the user has grabbed a resize handle.

See Also: CRectTracker::NormalizeHit, CRectTracker::SetCursor

---

CRectTracker::NormalizeHit

int NormalizeHit(int *nHandle* **) const;**

Return Value

The index of the normalized handle.

Parameters

nHandle   Handle selected by the user.

Remarks

Call this function to convert a potentially inverted handle.

When **CRectTracker::Track** or **CRectTracker::TrackRubberBand** is called with inverting allowed, it is possible for the rectangle to be inverted on the x-axis, the y-axis, or both. When this happens, **HitTest** will return handles that are also inverted with respect to the rectangle. This is inappropriate for drawing cursor feedback because the feedback depends on the screen position of the rectangle, not the portion of the rectangle data structure that will be modified.

See Also: CRectTracker::HitTest, CRectTracker::Track, CRectTracker::TrackRubberBand

CRectTracker::OnChangedRect

virtual void OnChangedRect(const CRect& *rectOld* **);**

Parameters

rectOld   Contains the old device coordinates of the **CRectTracker** object.

Remarks

Called by the framework whenever the tracker rectangle has changed during a call to **Track**. At the time this function is called, all feedback drawn with **DrawTrackerRect** has been removed. The default implementation of this function does nothing.

Override this function when you want to perform any actions after the rectangle has been resized.

See Also: CRectTracker::AdjustRect, CRectTracker::Track, CRectTracker::TrackRubberBand

---

CRectTracker::SetCursor

BOOL SetCursor(CWnd* *pWnd***, UINT** *nHitTest* **) const;**

Return Value

Nonzero if the previous hit was over the tracker rectangle; otherwise 0.

Parameters

pWnd   Points to the window that currently contains the cursor.

nHitTest   Results of the previous hit test, from the **WM_SETCURSOR** message.

Remarks

Call this function to change the cursor shape while it is over the **CRectTracker** object's region.

Call this function from inside the function of your window that handles the **WM_SETCURSOR** message (typically **OnSetCursor**).

See Also: CRectTracker::NormalizeHit, CRectTracker::HitTest, CWinApp::LoadCursor, CWnd::OnSetCursor

---

CRectTracker::Track

BOOL Track(CWnd* *pWnd***, CPoint** *point***, BOOL** *bAllowInvert* **= FALSE,**
    ↳ **CWnd*** *pWndClipTo* **= NULL);**

Return Value

If the ESC key is pressed, the tracking process is halted, the rectangle stored in the tracker is not altered, and 0 is returned. If the change is committed, by moving the mouse and releasing the left mouse button, the new position and/or size is recorded in the tracker's rectangle and nonzero is returned.

Parameters

pWnd   The window object that contains the rectangle.

point   Device coordinates of the current mouse position relative to the client area.

bAllowInvert   If **TRUE**, the rectangle can be inverted along the x-axis or y-axis; otherwise **FALSE**.

pWndClipTo   The window that drawing operations will be clipped to. If **NULL**, *pWnd* is used as the clipping rectangle.

Remarks

Call this function to display the user interface for resizing the rectangle. This is usually called from inside the function of your application that handles the **WM_LBUTTONDOWN** message (typically **OnLButtonDown**).

This function will capture the mouse until the user releases the left mouse button, presses the ESC key, or presses the right mouse button. As the user moves the mouse cursor, the feedback is updated by calling **DrawTrackerRect** and **OnChangedRect**.

If *bAllowInvert* is **TRUE**, the tracking rectangle can be inverted on either the x-axis or y-axis.

See Also: CRectTracker::DrawTrackerRect, CRectTracker::OnChangedRect, CRectTracker::CRectTracker, CRectTracker::TrackRubberBand

---

CRectTracker::TrackRubberBand

BOOL TrackRubberBand(CWnd* *pWnd,* **CPoint** *point,*
↪ **BOOL** *bAllowInvert* = **TRUE);**

Return Value

Nonzero if the mouse has moved and the rectangle is not empty; otherwise 0.

Parameters

pWnd   The window object that contains the rectangle.

point   Device coordinates of the current mouse position relative to the client area.

bAllowInvert   If **TRUE,** the rectangle can be inverted along the x-axis or y-axis; otherwise **FALSE**.

Remarks

Call this function to do rubber-band selection. It is usually called from inside the function of your application that handles the **WM_LBUTTONDOWN** message (typically **OnLButtonDown**).

This function will capture the mouse until the user releases the left mouse button, presses the ESC key, or presses the right mouse button. As the user moves the mouse cursor, the feedback is updated by calling **DrawTrackerRect** and **OnChangedRect**.

Tracking is performed with a rubber-band-type selection from the lower-right handle. If inverting is allowed, the rectangle can be sized by dragging either up and to the left or down and to the right.

See Also: **CRectTracker::DrawTrackerRect, CRectTracker::OnChangedRect, CRectTracker::CRectTracker**

Data Members
CRectTracker::m_nHandleSize

Remarks

The size, in pixels, of the **CRectTracker** resize handles. Initialized with the default system value.

CRectTracker::m_rect

Remarks

The current position of the rectangle in client coordinates (pixels).

See Also: **CRectTracker::CRectTracker, CRectTracker::Track, CRectTracker::TrackRubberBand**

CRectTracker::m_sizeMin

Remarks

The minimum size of the rectangle. Both default values, **cx** and **cy**, are calculated from the default system value for the border width. This data member is used only by the **AdjustRect** member function.

See Also: **CRectTracker::Track, CRectTracker::TrackRubberBand, CRectTracker::AdjustRect**

CRectTracker::m_nStyle

Remarks

Current style of the rectangle. See **CRectTracker::CRectTracker** for a list of possible styles.

See Also: **CRectTracker::CRectTracker, CRectTracker::Draw**

CResourceException

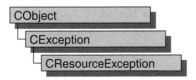

A **CResourceException** object is generated when Windows cannot find or allocate a requested resource. No further qualification is necessary or possible.

For more information on using **CResourceException**, see the article "Exceptions" in *Visual C++ Programmer's Guide* online.

#include <afxwin.h>

CResourceException Class Members

Construction

CResourceException	Constructs a **CResourceException** object.

Member Functions

CResourceException::CResourceException

CResourceException( );

Remarks

Constructs a **CResourceException** object.

Do not use this constructor directly, but rather call the global function **AfxThrowResourceException**. For more information about exceptions, see the article "Exceptions" in *Visual C++ Programmer's Guide* online.

See Also **AfxThrowResourceException**, Exception Processing

CRgn

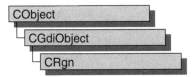

The **CRgn** class encapsulates a Windows graphics device interface (GDI) region. A region is an elliptical or polygonal area within a window. To use regions, you use the member functions of class **CRgn** with the clipping functions defined as members of class **CDC**.

The member functions of **CRgn** create, alter, and retrieve information about the region object for which they are called.

For more information on using **CRgn**, see "Graphic Objects" in *Visual C++ Programmer's Guide* online.

#include <afxwin.h>

CRgn Class Members

Construction

CRgn	Constructs a **CRgn** object.

Initialization

CreateRectRgn	Initializes a **CRgn** object with a rectangular region.
CreateRectRgnIndirect	Initializes a **CRgn** object with a rectangular region defined by a **RECT** structure.
CreateEllipticRgn	Initializes a **CRgn** object with an elliptical region.
CreateEllipticRgnIndirect	Initializes a **CRgn** object with an elliptical region defined by a **RECT** structure.
CreatePolygonRgn	Initializes a **CRgn** object with a polygonal region. The system closes the polygon automatically, if necessary, by drawing a line from the last vertex to the first.
CreatePolyPolygonRgn	Initializes a **CRgn** object with a region consisting of a series of closed polygons. The polygons may be disjoint, or they may overlap.
CreateRoundRectRgn	Initializes a **CRgn** object with a rectangular region with rounded corners.

(continued)

Member Functions

CRgn::CombineRgn

int **CombineRgn**(**CRgn*** *pRgn1*, **CRgn*** *pRgn2*, **int** *nCombineMode*);

Return Value

Specifies the type of the resulting region. It can be one of the following values:

- **COMPLEXREGION**   New region has overlapping borders.
- **ERROR**   No new region created.
- **NULLREGION**   New region is empty.
- **SIMPLEREGION**   New region has no overlapping borders.

Parameters

pRgn1   Identifies an existing region.

pRgn2   Identifies an existing region.

nCombineMode   Specifies the operation to be performed when combining the two source regions. It can be any one of the following values:

- **RGN_AND**   Uses overlapping areas of both regions (intersection).

- **RGN_COPY**   Creates a copy of region 1 (identified by *pRgn1*).

- **RGN_DIFF**   Creates a region consisting of the areas of region 1 (identified by *pRgn1*) that are not part of region 2 (identified by *pRgn2*).

- **RGN_OR**   Combines both regions in their entirety (union).

- **RGN_XOR**   Combines both regions but removes overlapping areas.

Remarks

Creates a new GDI region by combining two existing regions. The regions are combined as specified by *nCombineMode*.

The two specified regions are combined, and the resulting region handle is stored in the **CRgn** object. Thus, whatever region is stored in the **CRgn** object is replaced by the combined region.

The size of a region is limited to 32,767 by 32,767 logical units or 64K of memory, whichever is smaller.

Use **CopyRgn** to simply copy one region into another region.

See Also: CRgn::CopyRgn, **::CombineRgn**

CRgn::CopyRgn

int CopyRgn(CRgn* *pRgnSrc* **);**

Return Value

Specifies the type of the resulting region. It can be one of the following values:

- **COMPLEXREGION**   New region has overlapping borders.

- **ERROR**   No new region created.

- **NULLREGION**   New region is empty.

- **SIMPLEREGION**   New region has no overlapping borders.

Parameters

pRgnSrc   Identifies an existing region.

Remarks

Copies the region defined by *pRgnSrc* into the **CRgn** object. The new region replaces the region formerly stored in the **CRgn** object. This function is a special case of the **CombineRgn** member function.

See Also: **CRgn::CombineRgn, ::CombineRgn**

CRgn::CreateEllipticRgn

BOOL CreateEllipticRgn(int *x1***, int** *y1***, int** *x2***, int** *y2* **);**

Return Value

Nonzero if the operation succeeded; otherwise 0.

Parameters

x1 Specifies the logical x-coordinate of the upper-left corner of the bounding rectangle of the ellipse.

y1 Specifies the logical y-coordinate of the upper-left corner of the bounding rectangle of the ellipse.

x2 Specifies the logical x-coordinate of the lower-right corner of the bounding rectangle of the ellipse.

y2 Specifies the logical y-coordinate of the lower-right corner of the bounding rectangle of the ellipse.

Remarks

Creates an elliptical region. The region is defined by the bounding rectangle specified by *x1*, *y1*, *x2*, and *y2*. The region is stored in the **CRgn** object.

The size of a region is limited to 32,767 by 32,767 logical units or 64K of memory, whichever is smaller.

When it has finished using a region created with the **CreateEllipticRgn** function, an application should select the region out of the device context and use the **DeleteObject** function to remove it.

See Also: **CRgn::CreateEllipticRgnIndirect, ::CreateEllipticRgn**

CRgn::CreateEllipticRgnIndirect

BOOL CreateEllipticRgnIndirect(LPCRECT *lpRect* **);**

Return Value

Nonzero if the operation succeeded; otherwise 0.

Parameters

> *lpRect* Points to a **RECT** structure or a **CRect** object that contains the logical coordinates of the upper-left and lower-right corners of the bounding rectangle of the ellipse.

Remarks

> Creates an elliptical region. The region is defined by the structure or object pointed to by *lpRect* and is stored in the **CRgn** object.
>
> The size of a region is limited to 32,767 by 32,767 logical units or 64K of memory, whichever is smaller.
>
> When it has finished using a region created with the **CreateEllipticRgnIndirect** function, an application should select the region out of the device context and use the **DeleteObject** function to remove it.
>
> **See Also:** **CRgn::CreateEllipticRgn**, **::CreateEllipticRgnIndirect**

CRgn::CreateFromData

> **BOOL CreateFromData(const XFORM*** *lpXForm***, int** *nCount***,**
> ↳ **const RGNDATA*** *pRgnData* **);**

Return Value

> Nonzero if the function is successful; otherwise 0.

Parameters

> *lpXForm* Points to an **XFORM** data structure that defines the transformation to be performed on the region. If this pointer is **NULL**, the identity transformation is used.
>
> *nCount* Specifies the number of bytes pointed to by *pRgnData*.
>
> *pRgnData* Points to a **RGNDATA** data structure that contains the region data.

Remarks

> Creates a region from the given region and transformation data. An application can retrieve data for a region by calling the **CRgn::GetRegionData** function.
>
> **See Also:** **CRgn::GetRegionData**, **::ExtCreateRegion**

CRgn::CreateFromPath

> **BOOL CreateFromPath(CDC*** *pDC* **);**

Return Value

> Nonzero if the function is successful; otherwise 0.

Parameters

pDC   Identifies a device context that contains a closed path.

Remarks

Creates a region from the path that is selected into the given device context. The device context identified by the *pDC* parameter must contain a closed path. After **CreateFromPath** converts a path into a region, Windows discards the closed path from the device context.

See Also: CDC::BeginPath, CDC::EndPath, CDC::SetPolyFillMode

CRgn::CreatePolygonRgn

BOOL CreatePolygonRgn(LPPOINT *lpPoints***, int** *nCount***, int** *nMode* **);**

Return Value

Nonzero if the operation succeeded; otherwise 0.

Parameters

lpPoints   Points to an array of **POINT** structures or an array of **CPoint** objects. Each structure specifies the x-coordinate and y-coordinate of one vertex of the polygon. The **POINT** structure has the following form:

```
typedef struct tagPOINT {
   int x;
   int y;
} POINT;
```

nCount   Specifies the number of **POINT** structures or **CPoint** objects in the array pointed to by *lpPoints*.

nMode   Specifies the filling mode for the region. This parameter may be either **ALTERNATE** or **WINDING**.

Remarks

Creates a polygonal region. The system closes the polygon automatically, if necessary, by drawing a line from the last vertex to the first. The resulting region is stored in the **CRgn** object.

The size of a region is limited to 32,767 by 32,767 logical units or 64K of memory, whichever is smaller.

When the polygon-filling mode is **ALTERNATE**, the system fills the area between odd-numbered and even-numbered polygon sides on each scan line. That is, the system fills the area between the first and second side, between the third and fourth side, and so on.

When the polygon-filling mode is **WINDING**, the system uses the direction in which a figure was drawn to determine whether to fill an area. Each line segment in a polygon is drawn in either a clockwise or a counterclockwise direction. Whenever an imaginary line drawn from an enclosed area to the outside of a figure passes through a clockwise line segment, a count is incremented. When the line passes through a counterclockwise line segment, the count is decremented. The area is filled if the count is nonzero when the line reaches the outside of the figure.

When an application has finished using a region created with the **CreatePolygonRgn** function, it should select the region out of the device context and use the **DeleteObject** function to remove it.

See Also: **CRgn::CreatePolyPolygonRgn**, **::CreatePolygonRgn**

CRgn::CreatePolyPolygonRgn

BOOL CreatePolyPolygonRgn(LPPOINT *lpPoints*, **LPINT** *lpPolyCounts*,
↪ **int** *nCount*, **int** *nPolyFillMode* **);**

Return Value

Nonzero if the operation succeeded; otherwise 0.

Parameters

lpPoints   Points to an array of **POINT** structures or an array of **CPoint** objects that defines the vertices of the polygons. Each polygon must be explicitly closed because the system does not close them automatically. The polygons are specified consecutively. The **POINT** structure has the following form:

```
typedef struct tagPOINT {
    int x;
    int y;
} POINT;
```

lpPolyCounts   Points to an array of integers. The first integer specifies the number of vertices in the first polygon in the *lpPoints* array, the second integer specifies the number of vertices in the second polygon, and so on.

nCount   Specifies the total number of integers in the *lpPolyCounts* array.

nPolyFillMode   Specifies the polygon-filling mode. This value may be either **ALTERNATE** or **WINDING**.

Remarks

Creates a region consisting of a series of closed polygons. The resulting region is stored in the **CRgn** object.

The polygons may be disjoint, or they may overlap.

The size of a region is limited to 32,767 by 32,767 logical units or 64K of memory, whichever is smaller.

When the polygon-filling mode is **ALTERNATE**, the system fills the area between odd-numbered and even-numbered polygon sides on each scan line. That is, the system fills the area between the first and second side, between the third and fourth side, and so on.

When the polygon-filling mode is **WINDING**, the system uses the direction in which a figure was drawn to determine whether to fill an area. Each line segment in a polygon is drawn in either a clockwise or a counterclockwise direction. Whenever an imaginary line drawn from an enclosed area to the outside of a figure passes through a clockwise line segment, a count is incremented. When the line passes through a counterclockwise line segment, the count is decremented. The area is filled if the count is nonzero when the line reaches the outside of the figure.

When an application has finished using a region created with the **CreatePolyPolygonRgn** function, it should select the region out of the device context and use the **CGDIObject::DeleteObject** member function to remove it.

See Also: CRgn::CreatePolygonRgn, CDC::SetPolyFillMode, ::CreatePolyPolygonRgn

---

CRgn::CreateRectRgn

BOOL CreateRectRgn(int *x1*, int *y1*, int *x2*, int *y2*);

Return Value

Nonzero if the operation succeeded; otherwise 0.

Parameters

x1 Specifies the logical x-coordinate of the upper-left corner of the region.

y1 Specifies the logical y-coordinate of the upper-left corner of the region.

x2 Specifies the logical x-coordinate of the lower-right corner of the region.

y2 Specifies the logical y-coordinate of the lower-right corner of the region.

Remarks

Creates a rectangular region that is stored in the **CRgn** object.

The size of a region is limited to 32,767 by 32,767 logical units or 64K of memory, whichever is smaller.

When it has finished using a region created by **CreateRectRgn**, an application should use the **CGDIObject::DeleteObject** member function to remove the region.

See Also: CRgn::CreateRectRgnIndirect, CRgn::CreateRoundRectRgn, ::CreateRectRgn

CRgn::CreateRectRgnIndirect

BOOL CreateRectRgnIndirect(LPCRECT *lpRect* **);**

Return Value

Nonzero if the operation succeeded; otherwise 0.

Parameters

lpRect   Points to a **RECT** structure or **CRect** object that contains the logical coordinates of the upper-left and lower-right corners of the region. The **RECT** structure has the following form:

```
typedef struct tagRECT {
    int left;
    int top;
    int right;
    int bottom;
} RECT;
```

Remarks

Creates a rectangular region that is stored in the **CRgn** object.

The size of a region is limited to 32,767 by 32,767 logical units or 64K of memory, whichever is smaller.

When it has finished using a region created by **CreateRectRgnIndirect**, an application should use the **CGDIObject::DeleteObject** member function to remove the region.

**See Also: CRgn::CreateRectRgn, CRgn::CreateRoundRectRgn,
::CreateRectRgnIndirect**

CRgn::CreateRoundRectRgn

BOOL CreateRoundRectRgn(int *x1*, **int** *y1*, **int** *x2*, **int** *y2*, **int** *x3*, **int** *y3* **);**

Return Value

Nonzero if the operation succeeded; otherwise 0.

Parameters

x1   Specifies the logical x-coordinate of the upper-left corner of the region.

y1   Specifies the logical y-coordinate of the upper-left corner of the region.

x2   Specifies the logical x-coordinate of the lower-right corner of the region.

y2   Specifies the logical y-coordinate of the lower-right corner of the region.

x3   Specifies the width of the ellipse used to create the rounded corners.

y3   Specifies the height of the ellipse used to create the rounded corners.

Remarks

Creates a rectangular region with rounded corners that is stored in the **CRgn** object.

The size of a region is limited to 32,767 by 32,767 logical units or 64K of memory, whichever is smaller.

When an application has finished using a region created with the **CreateRoundRectRgn** function, it should select the region out of the device context and use the **CGDIObject::DeleteObject** member function to remove it.

See Also: CRgn::CreateRectRgn, CRgn::CreateRectRgnIndirect, ::CreateRoundRectRgn

CRgn::CRgn

CRgn( );

Remarks

Constructs a **CRgn** object. The **m_hObject** data member does not contain a valid Windows GDI region until the object is initialized with one or more of the other **CRgn** member functions.

CRgn::EqualRgn

BOOL EqualRgn(CRgn* *pRgn* **) const;**

Return Value

Nonzero if the two regions are equivalent; otherwise 0.

Parameters

pRgn   Identifies a region.

Remarks

Determines whether the given region is equivalent to the region stored in the **CRgn** object.

See Also: ::EqualRgn

CRgn::FromHandle

static CRgn* PASCAL FromHandle(HRGN *hRgn* **);**

Return Value

A pointer to a **CRgn** object. If the function was not successful, the return value is **NULL**.

Parameters

> *hRgn*   Specifies a handle to a Windows region.

Remarks

> Returns a pointer to a **CRgn** object when given a handle to a Windows region.
> If a **CRgn** object is not already attached to the handle, a temporary **CRgn** object is
> created and attached. This temporary **CRgn** object is valid only until the next time the
> application has idle time in its event loop, at which time all temporary graphic objects
> are deleted. Another way of saying this is that the temporary object is only valid
> during the processing of one window message.

CRgn::GetRegionData

> **Int GetRegionData(LPRGNDATA** *lpRgnData*, **int** *nCount*) **const;**

Return Value

> Specifies the type of the resulting region. It can be one of the following values:

> - **COMPLEXREGION**   New region has overlapping borders.
> - **ERROR**   No new region created.
> - **NULLREGION**   New region is empty.
> - **SIMPLEREGION**   New region has no overlapping borders.

Parameters

> *lpRgnData*   Points to a **RGNDATA** data structure that receives the information. If
> this parameter is **NULL**, the return value contains the number of bytes needed for
> the region data.

> *nCount*   Specifies the size, in bytes, of the *lpRgnData* buffer.

Remarks

> Fills the specified buffer with data describing the region. This data includes the
> dimensions of the rectangles that make up the region. This function is used in
> conjunction with the **CRgn::CreateFromData** function.

> **See Also: CRgn::CreateFromData**

CRgn::GetRgnBox

> **int GetRgnBox(LPRECT** *lpRect*) **const;**

Return Value

> Specifies the region's type. It can be any of the following values:

> - **COMPLEXREGION**   Region has overlapping borders.
> - **NULLREGION**   Region is empty.

- **ERROR** **CRgn** object does not specify a valid region.
- **SIMPLEREGION** Region has no overlapping borders.

Parameters

lpRect Points to a **RECT** structure or **CRect** object to receive the coordinates of the bounding rectangle. The **RECT** structure has the following form:

```
typedef struct tagRECT {
    int left;
    int top;
    int right;
    int bottom;
} RECT;
```

Remarks

Retrieves the coordinates of the bounding rectangle of the **CRgn** object.

See Also: ::GetRgnBox

CRgn::OffsetRgn

int OffsetRgn(int *x*, **int** *y* **);**
int OffsetRgn(POINT *point* **);**

Return Value

The new region's type. It can be any one of the following values:

- **COMPLEXREGION** Region has overlapping borders.
- **ERROR** Region handle is not valid.
- **NULLREGION** Region is empty.
- **SIMPLEREGION** Region has no overlapping borders.

Parameters

x Specifies the number of units to move left or right.

y Specifies the number of units to move up or down.

point The x-coordinate of *point* specifies the number of units to move left or right. The y-coordinate of *point* specifies the number of units to move up or down. The *point* parameter may be either a **POINT** structure or a **CPoint** object.

Remarks

Moves the region stored in the **CRgn** object by the specified offsets. The function moves the region *x* units along the x-axis and *y* units along the y-axis.

The coordinate values of a region must be less than or equal to 32,767 and greater than or equal to –32,768. The *x* and *y* parameters must be carefully chosen to prevent invalid region coordinates.

See Also: ::OffsetRgn

CRgn::PtInRegion

BOOL PtInRegion(int *x,* **int** *y* **) const;**
BOOL PtInRegion(POINT *point* **) const;**

Return Value

Nonzero if the point is in the region; otherwise 0.

Parameters

x   Specifies the logical x-coordinate of the point to test.

y   Specifies the logical y-coordinate of the point to test.

point   The x- and y-coordinates of *point* specify the x- and y-coordinates of the point
to test the value of. The *point* parameter can either be a **POINT** structure or a
CPoint object.

Remarks

Checks whether the point given by *x* and *y* is in the region stored in the **CRgn** object.

See Also: ::PtInRegion

CRgn::RectInRegion

BOOL RectInRegion(LPCRECT *lpRect* **) const;**

Return Value

Nonzero if any part of the specified rectangle lies within the boundaries of the region;
otherwise 0.

Parameters

lpRect   Points to a **RECT** structure or **CRect** object. The **RECT** structure has the
following form:

```
typedef struct tagRECT {
   int left;
   int top;
   int right;
   int bottom;
} RECT;
```

Remarks

Determines whether any part of the rectangle specified by *lpRect* is within the
boundaries of the region stored in the **CRgn** object.

See Also: ::RectInRegion

CRgn::SetRectRgn

void SetRectRgn(int *x1***, int** *y1***, int** *x2***, int** *y2* **);**
void SetRectRgn(LPCRECT *lpRect* **);**

Parameters

x1   Specifies the x-coordinate of the upper-left corner of the rectangular region.

y1   Specifies the y-coordinate of the upper-left corner of the rectangular region.

x2   Specifies the x-coordinate of the lower-right corner of the rectangular region.

y2   Specifies the y-coordinate of the lower-right corner of the rectangular region.

lpRect   Specifies the rectangular region. Can be either a pointer to a **RECT** structure or a **CRect** object.

Remarks

Creates a rectangular region. Unlike **CreateRectRgn**, however, it does not allocate any additional memory from the local Windows application heap. Instead, it uses the space allocated for the region stored in the **CRgn** object. This means that the **CRgn** object must already have been initialized with a valid Windows region before calling **SetRectRgn**. The points given by *x1*, *y1*, *x2*, and *y2* specify the minimum size of the allocated space.

Use this function instead of the **CreateRectRgn** member function to avoid calls to the local memory manager.

See Also: **CRgn::CreateRectRgn, ::SetRectRgn**

Operators

CRgn::operator HRGN

operator HRGN( ) const;

Return Value

If successful, a handle to the Windows GDI object represented by the **CRgn** object; otherwise **NULL**.

Remarks

Use this operator to get the attached Windows GDI handle of the **CRgn** object. This operator is a casting operator, which supports direct use of an **HRGN** object.

For more information about using graphic objects, see the article "Graphic Objects" in the *Win 32 SDK Programmer's Reference*.

CRichEditCntrItem

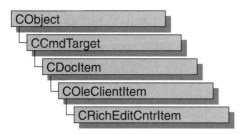

A "rich edit control" is a window in which the user can enter and edit text. The text can be assigned character and paragraph formatting, and can include embedded OLE objects. Rich edit controls provide a programming interface for formatting text. However, an application must implement any user interface components necessary to make formatting operations available to the user.

The **CRichEditCntrItem** class, with **CRichEditView** and **CRichEditDoc**, provides the functionality of the rich edit control within the context of MFC's document view architecture. **CRichEditView** maintains the text and formatting characteristic of text. **CRichEditDoc** maintains the list of OLE client items which are in the view. **CRichEditCntrItem** provides container-side access to the OLE client item.

This Windows Common control (and therefore the **CRichEditCtrl** and related classes) is available only to programs running under Windows 95 and Windows NT versions 3.51 and later.

For an example of using rich edit container items in an MFC application, see the WORDPAD sample application online.

#include <afxrich.h>

See Also: **CRichEditDoc, CRichEditView**

CRichEditCntrItem Class Members

Constructor

CRichEditCntrItem	Constructs a **CRichEditCntrItem** object.

Operations

SyncToRichEditObject	Activates the item as another type.

Member Functions
CRichEditCntrItem::CRichEditCntrItem

CRichEditCntrItem(REOBJECT* *preo* **= NULL,**
↪ **CRichEditDoc*** *pContainer* **= NULL);**

Parameters

preo Pointer to an **REOBJECT** structure which describes an OLE item. The new
CRichEditCntrItem object is constructed around this OLE item. If *preo* is **NULL**,
the client item is empty.

pContainer Pointer to the container document that will contain this item. If
pContainer is **NULL**, you must explicitly call **COleDocument::AddItem** to add
this client item to a document.

Remarks

Call this function to create a **CRichEditCntrItem** object and add it to the container
document. This function does not perform any OLE initialization.

For more information, see the **REOBJECT** structure in the Win32 documentation.

See Also: COleDocument::AddItem, CRichEditDoc

CRichEditCntrItem::SyncToRichEditObject

void SyncToRichEditObject(REOBJECT& *reo* **);**

Parameters

reo Reference to an **REOBJECT** structure which describes an OLE item.

Remarks

Call this function to synchronize the device aspect, **DVASPECT**, of this
CRichEditCntrItem to that specified by *reo*.

For more information, see **DVASPECT** in the OLE documentation.

CRichEditCtrl

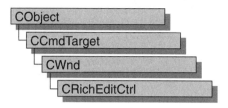

A "rich edit control" is a window in which the user can enter and edit text. The text can be assigned character and paragraph formatting, and can include embedded OLE objects. Rich edit controls provide a programming interface for formatting text. However, an application must implement any user interface components necessary to make formatting operations available to the user.

The **CRichEditCtrl** class provides the functionality of the rich edit control. This Windows Common control (and therefore the **CRichEditCtrl** class) is available only to programs running under Windows 95 and Windows NT versions 3.51 and later.

For more information on using **CRichEditCtrl**, see Technical Note 60 online.

For an example of using a rich edit control in an MFC application, see the WORDPAD sample application online.

#include <afxcmn.h>

See Also: **CEdit, CRichEditView**

CRichEditCtrl Class Members

Construction

CRichEditCtrl	Constructs a **CRichEditCtrl** object.
Create	Creates the Windows rich edit control and associates it with this **CRichEditCtrl** object.

Line Operations

GetLineCount	Retrieves the number of lines in this **CRichEditCtrl** object.
GetLine	Retrieves a line of text from this **CRichEditCtrl** object.
GetFirstVisibleLine	Determines the topmost visible line in this **CRichEditCtrl** object.
LineIndex	Retrieves the character index of a given line in this **CRichEditCtrl** object.

(continued)

Line Operations *(continued)*

LineFromChar	Determines which line contains the given character.
LineLength	Retrieves the length of a given line in this **CRichEditCtrl** object.
LineScroll	Scrolls the text in this **CRichEditCtrl** object.

Selection Operations

GetSel	Gets the starting and ending positions of the current selection in this **CRichEditCtrl** object.
GetSelText	Gets the text of the current selection in this **CRichEditCtrl** object
GetSelectionType	Retrieves the type of contents in the current selection in this **CRichEditCtrl** object.
Clear	Clears the current selection.
SetSel	Sets the selection in this **CRichEditCtrl** object.
ReplaceSel	Replaces the current selection in this **CRichEditCtrl** object with specified text.
HideSelection	Shows or hides the the current selection.

Formatting Operations

GetDefaultCharFormat	Retrieves the current default character formatting attributes in this **CRichEditCtrl** object.
GetSelectionCharFormat	Retrieves the character formatting attributes in the current selection in this **CRichEditCtrl** object.
GetParaFormat	Retrieves the paragraph formatting attributes in the current selection in this **CRichEditCtrl** object.
SetDefaultCharFormat	Sets the current default character formatting attributes in this **CRichEditCtrl** object.
SetSelectionCharFormat	Sets the character formatting attributes in the current selection in this **CRichEditCtrl** object.
SetWordCharFormat	Sets the character formatting attributes in the current word in this **CRichEditCtrl** object.
SetParaFormat	Sets the paragraph formatting attributes in the current selection in this **CRichEditCtrl** object.

Editing Operations

Undo	Reverses the last editing operation.
CanUndo	Determines if an editing operation can be undone.
EmptyUndoBuffer	Resets (clears) the undo flag of this **CRichEditCtrl** object.
StreamIn	Inserts text from an input stream into this **CRichEditCtrl** object.
StreamOut	Stores text from this **CRichEditCtrl** object into an output stream.

General Operations

GetModify	Determines if the contents of this **CRichEditCtrl** object have changed since the last save.
SetModify	Sets or clears the modification flag for this **CRichEditCtrl** object.
FindText	Locates text within this **CRichEditCtrl** object.
GetRect	Retrieves the formatting rectangle for this **CRichEditCtrl** object.
SetRect	Sets the formatting rectangle for this **CRichEditCtrl** object.
GetCharPos	Determines the location of a given character within this **CRichEditCtrl** object.
SetOptions	Sets the options for this **CRichEditCtrl** object.
SetReadOnly	Sets the read-only option for this **CRichEditCtrl** object.
GetTextLength	Retrieves the length of the text in this **CRichEditCtrl** object.
GetLimitText	Gets the limit on the amount of text a user can enter into this **CRichEditCtrl** object.
LimitText	Limits the amount of text a user can enter into the **CRichEditCtrl** object.
GetEventMask	Retrieves the event mask for this **CRichEditCtrl** object.
SetEventMask	Sets the event mask for this **CRichEditCtrl** object.
RequestResize	Forces this **CRichEditCtrl** object to send request resize notifications.
SetBackgroundColor	Sets the background color in this **CRichEditCtrl** object.
SetTargetDevice	Sets the target output device for this **CRichEditCtrl** object.
FormatRange	Formats a range of text for the target output device.
DisplayBand	Displays a portion of the contents of this **CRichEditCtrl** object.

Clipboard Operations

Copy	Copies the current selection to the Clipboard.
Cut	Cuts the current selection to the Clipboard.
Paste	Inserts the contents of the Clipboard into this rich edit control.
PasteSpecial	Inserts the contents of the Clipboard into this rich edit control in the specified data format.
CanPaste	Determines if the contents of the Clipboard can be pasted into this rich edit control.

OLE Operations

GetIRichEditOle	Retrieves a pointer to the **IRichEditOle** interface for this rich edit control.
SetOLECallback	Sets the **IRichEditOleCallback** COM object for this rich edit control.

Member Functions
CRichEditCtrl::CanPaste

BOOL CanPaste(UINT *nFormat* **= 0) const;**

Return Value

Nonzero if the Clipboard format can be pasted; otherwise 0.

Parameters

nFormat   The Clipboard data format to query. This parameter can be one of the predefined Clipboard formats or the value returned by **RegisterClipboardFormat**.

Remarks

Call this function to determine if the rich edit control can paste the specified Clipboard format. If *nFormat* is 0, **CanPaste** will try any format currently on the Clipboard.

For more information, see **EM_CANPASTE** message and **RegisterClipboardFormat** function in the Win32 documentation.

See Also: CRichEditCtrl::Paste, CRichEditCtrl::PasteSpecial

CRichEditCtrl::CanUndo

BOOL CanUndo( ) const;

Return Value

Nonzero if the last edit operation can be undone by a call to the **Undo** member function; 0 if it cannot be undone.

Remarks

Call this function to determine if the last editing operation can be undone.

For more information, see **EM_CANUNDO** in the Win32 documentation.

See Also: CRichEditCtrl::Undo, CRichEditCtrl::EmptyUndoBuffer

---

CRichEditCtrl::Clear

void Clear( );

Remarks

Call this function to delete (clear) the current selection (if any) in the rich edit control.

The deletion performed by **Clear** can be undone by calling the **Undo** member function.

To delete the current selection and place the deleted contents onto the Clipboard, call the **Cut** member function.

For more information, see **WM_CLEAR** in the Win32 documentation.

See Also: **CRichEditCtrl::Undo**, **CRichEditCtrl::Cut**, **CRichEditCtrl::Copy**, **CRichEditCtrl::Paste**

CRichEditCtrl::Copy

void Copy( );

Remarks

Call this function to copy the current selection (if any) in the rich edit control to the Clipboard.

For more information, see **WM_COPY** in the Win32 documentation.

See Also: **CRichEditCtrl::Paste**, **CRichEditCtrl::Cut**

CRichEditCtrl::Create

BOOL Create(DWORD *dwStyle***, const RECT&** *rect***, CWnd*** *pParentWnd***, UINT** *nID* **);**

Return Value

Nonzero if initialization is successful; otherwise, 0.

Parameters

dwStyle Specifies the edit control's style. Apply any combination of edit styles to the control.

rect Specifies the edit control's size and position. Can be a **CRect** object or **RECT** structure.

pParentWnd Specifies the edit control's parent window (often a **CDialog**). It must not be **NULL**.

nID Specifies the edit control's ID.

Remarks

You construct a **CRichEditCtrl** object in two steps. First, call the **CRichEditCtrl** constructor, then call **Create**, which creates the Windows edit control and attaches it to the **CRichEditCtrl** object.

When **Create** executes, Windows sends the **WM_NCCREATE**, **WM_NCCALCSIZE**, **WM_CREATE**, and **WM_GETMINMAXINFO** messages to the edit control.

These messages are handled by default by the **OnNcCreate**, **OnNcCalcSize**, **OnCreate**, and **OnGetMinMaxInfo** member functions in the **CWnd** base class.

To extend the default message handling, derive a class from **CRichEditCtrl**, add a message map to the new class, and override the above message-handler member functions. Override **OnCreate**, for example, to perform needed initialization for the new class.

Apply the following window styles to an edit control.

- **WS_CHILD** Always.
- **WS_VISIBLE** Usually.
- **WS_DISABLED** Rarely.
- **WS_GROUP** To group controls.
- **WS_TABSTOP** To include edit control in the tabbing order.

See Also: **CRichEditCtrl::CRichEditCtrl**

CRichEditCtrl::CRichEditCtrl

CRichEditCtrl( );

Remarks

Constructs a **CRichEditCtrl** object. Use **Create** to construct the Windows rich edit control.

See Also: **CRichEditCtrl::Create**

CRichEditCtrl::Cut

void Cut( );

Remarks

Call this function to delete (cut) the current selection (if any) in the rich edit control and copy the deleted text to the Clipboard.

The deletion performed by **Cut** can be undone by calling the **Undo** member function.

To delete the current selection without placing the deleted text into the Clipboard, call the **Clear** member function.

For more information, see **WM_CUT** in the Win32 documentation.

See Also: **CRichEditCtrl::Copy**, **CRichEditCtrl::Undo**, **CRichEditCtrl::Clear**

CRichEditCtrl::DisplayBand

BOOL DisplayBand(LPRECT *pDisplayRect* **);**

Return Value

Nonzero if the display of the formatted text succeeds, otherwise, 0.

Parameters

pDisplayRect Pointer to a **RECT** or **CRect** object specifying the area of the device to display the text.

Remarks

Call this function to display a portion of the contents of the rich edit control (text and OLE items), as previously formatted by **FormatRange**. The text and OLE items are clipped to the area specified by the pointer *pDisplayRect*.

For more information, see **EM_DISPLAYBAND** in the Win32 documentation.

See Also: CRichEditCtrl::FormatRange

CRichEditCtrl::EmptyUndoBuffer

void EmptyUndoBuffer( );

Remarks

Call this function to reset (clear) the undo flag of this rich edit control. The control will now be unable to undo the last editing operation. The undo flag is set whenever an operation within the rich edit control can be undone.

The undo flag is automatically cleared whenever you call the **CWnd** member function **SetWindowText**.

For more information, see **EM_EMPTYUNDOBUFFER** in the Win32 documentation.

See Also: CRichEditCtrl::CanUndo, CRichEditCtrl::Undo, CWnd::SetWindowText

---

CRichEditCtrl::FindText

long FindText(DWORD *dwFlags*, **FINDTEXTEX*** *pFindText* **) const;**

Return Value

Zero-based character position of the next match; −1 if there are no more matches.

Parameters

dwFlags Flags for the match criteria. Can be zero or more of the following values:

- **FR_MATCHCASE** Indicates that the search is case sensitive.

- **FR_WHOLEWORD**   Indicates that the word boundaries should be considered in the search.

pFindText   Pointer to the **FINDTEXTEX** structure giving the parameters for the search and returning the range where the match was found.

Remarks

Call this function to find text within the rich edit control. You can search either up or down by setting the proper range parameters in the **CHARRANGE** structure within the **FINDTEXTEX** structure.

For more information, see **EM_FINDTEXTEX** message and **FINDTEXTEX** structure in the Win32 documentation.

See Also: CRichEditCtrl::SetSel

CRichEditCtrl::FormatRange

long FormatRange(FORMATRANGE* *pfr*, **BOOL** *bDisplay* **= TRUE);**

Return Value

The index of the last character that fits in the region plus one.

Parameters

pfr   Pointer to the **FORMATRANGE** structure which contains information about the output device. **NULL** indicates that cached information within the rich edit control can be freed.

bDisplay   Indicates if the text should be rendered. If **FALSE**, the text is just measured.

Remarks

Call this function to format a range of text in a rich edit control for a specific device. Typically, this call is followed by a call to **DisplayBand**.

For more information, see **EM_FORMATRANGE** message and **FORMATRANGE** structure in the Win32 documentation.

See Also: CRichEditCtrl::DisplayBand

CRichEditCtrl::GetCharPos

CPoint GetCharPos(long *lChar* **) const;**

Return Value

The location of the top-left corner of the character specified by *lChar*.

Parameters

lChar   Zero-based index of the character.

Remarks

Call this function to get the position (top-left corner) of a given character within this **CRichEditCtrl** object. The character is specified by giving its zero-based index value. If *lChar* is greater than the index of the last character in this **CRichEditCtrl** object, the return value specifies the coordinates of the character position just past the last character in this **CRichEditCtrl** object.

For more information, see **EM_POSFROMCHAR** in the Win32 documentation.

See Also: **CRichEditCtrl::FindText**

CRichEditCtrl::GetDefaultCharFormat

DWORD GetDefaultCharFormat(CHARFORMAT& *cf* **) const;**

Return Value

The **dwMask** data member of *cf*. It specified the default character formatting attributes.

Parameters

cf Pointer to a **CHARFORMAT** structure which will hold the default character formatting attributes.

Remarks

Call this function to get the default character formatting attributes of this **CRichEditCtrl** object.

For more information, see **EM_GETCHARFORMAT** message and **CHARFORMAT** structure in the Win32 documentation.

See Also: **CRichEditCtrl::SetDefaultCharFormat**, **CRichEditCtrl::GetSelectionCharFormat**, **CRichEditCtrl::GetParaFormat**

CRichEditCtrl::GetEventMask

long GetEventMask( ) const;

Return Value

The event mask for this **CRichEditCtrl** object.

Remarks

Call this function to get the event mask for this **CRichEditCtrl** object. The event mask specifies which notification messages the **CRichEditCtrl** object sends to its parent window.

For more information, see **EM_GETEVENTMASK** in the Win32 documentation.

See Also: **CRichEditCtrl::SetEventMask**, **CRichEditCtrl::CRichEditCtrl**

CRichEditCtrl::GetFirstVisibleLine

int GetFirstVisibleLine( ) const;

Return Value

Zero-based index of the uppermost visible line in this **CRichEditCtrl** object.

Remarks

Call this function to determine the topmost visible line in this **CRichEditCtrl** object.

For more information, see **EM_GETFIRSTVISIBLELINE** in the Win32 documentation.

See Also: **CRichEditCtrl::GetLine, CRichEditCtrl::GetLineCount**

CRichEditCtrl::GetIRichEditOle

IRichEditOle* GetIRichEditOle( ) const;

Return Value

Pointer to the **IRichEditOle** interface that can be used to access this **CRichEditCtrl** object's OLE functionality; **NULL** if the interface is not accessible.

Remarks

Call this member function to access the **IRichEditOle** interface for this **CRichEditCtrl** object. Use this interface to access this **CRichEditCtrl** object's OLE functionality.

For more information, see **EM_GETOLEINTERFACE** message and **IRichEditOle** interface in the Win32 documentation.

See Also: **CRichEditCtrl::SetOLECallback**

CRichEditCtrl::GetLimitText

long GetLimitText( ) const;

Return Value

The current text limit, in bytes, for this **CRichEditCtrl** object.

Remarks

Call this member function to get the text limit for this **CRichEditCtrl** object. The text limit is the maximum amount of text, in bytes, the rich edit control can accept.

For more information, see **EM_GETLIMITTEXT** in the Win32 documentation.

See Also: **CRichEditCtrl::LimitText**

CRichEditCtrl::GetLine

int GetLine(int *nIndex*, **LPTSTR** *lpszBuffer* **) const;**
int GetLine(int *nIndex*, **LPTSTR** *lpszBuffer*, **int** *nMaxLength* **) const;**

Return Value

The number of characters copied into *lpszBuffer*.

Parameters

nIndex   Zero-based index of the line to retrieve.

lpszBuffer   Points to the buffer to receive the text. The first word of the buffer must specify the maximum number of bytes that can be copied into the buffer.

nMaxLength   Maximum number of characters that can be copied into *lpszBuffer*. The second form of **GetLine** places this value into the first word of the buffer specified by *lpszBuffer*.

Remarks

Call this function to retrieve a line of text from this **CRichEditCtrl** object. The copied line does not contain a terminating null character.

Note Because the first word of the buffer stores the number of characters to be copied, make sure that your buffer is at least 4 bytes long.

For more information, see **EM_GETLINE** in the Win32 documentation.

See Also: **CRichEditCtrl::LineLength**

CRichEditCtrl::GetLineCount

int GetLineCount( ) const;

Return Value

The number of lines in this **CRichEditCtrl** object.

Remarks

Call this function to retrieve the number of lines in the **CRichEditCtrl** object.

For more information, see **EM_GETLINECOUNT** in the Win32 documentation.

See Also: **CRichEditCtrl::GetLine**

CRichEditCtrl::GetModify

BOOL GetModify( ) const;

Return Value

Nonzero if the text in this **CRichEditCtrl** object has been modified; otherwise 0.

Remarks

Call this function to determine if the contents of this **CRichEditCtrl** object have been modified.

Windows maintains an internal flag indicating whether the contents of the rich edit control have been changed. This flag is cleared when the edit control is first created and can also be cleared by calling the **SetModify** member function.

For more information, see **EM_GETMODIFY** in the Win32 documentation.

See Also: **CRichEditCtrl::SetModify**

CRichEditCtrl::GetParaFormat

DWORD GetParaFormat(PARAFORMAT& *pf* **) const;**

Return Value

The **dwMask** data member of *pf*. It specifies the paragraph formatting attributes that are consistent throughout the current selection.

Parameters

pf   Pointer to a **PARAFORMAT** structure to hold the paragraph formatting attributes of the current selection.

Remarks

Call this function to get the paragraph formatting attributes of the current selection. If more than one paragraph is selected, *pf* receives the attributes of the first selected paragraph. The return value specifies which attributes are consistent throughout the selection.

For more information, see **EM_GETPARAFORMAT** message and **PARAFORMAT** structure in the Win32 documentation.

See Also: **CRichEditCtrl::SetParaFormat,
CRichEditCtrl::GetSelectionCharFormat**

CRichEditCtrl::GetRect

void GetRect(LPRECT *lpRect* **) const;**

Parameters

lpRect   **CRect** or pointer to a **RECT** to receive the formatting rectangle of this **CRichEditCtrl** object.

Remarks

Call this function to retrieve the formatting rectangle for this **CRichEditCtrl** object. The formatting rectangle is the bounding rectangle for the text. This value is independent of the size of the **CRichEditCtrl** object.

For more information, see **EM_GETRECT** in the Win32 documentation.

See Also: **CRichEditCtrl::SetRect**

CRichEditCtrl::GetSel

void GetSel(CHARRANGE& *cr* **) const;**
void GetSel(long& *nStartChar*, **long&** *nEndChar* **) const;**

Parameters

cr Reference to a **CHARRANGE** structure to receive the bounds of the current selection.

nStartChar Zero-based index of the first character in the current selection.

nEndChar Zero-based index of the last character in the current selection.

Remarks

Call this function to retrieve the bounds of the current selection in this **CRichEditCtrl** object.

The two forms of this function provide alternate ways to get the bounds for the selection. Brief descriptions of these forms follow:

- **GetSel(** *cr* **)** This form uses the **CHARRANGE** structure with its **cpMin** and **cpMax** members to return the bounds.

- **GetSel(** *nStartChar*, *nEndChar* **)** This form returns the bounds in the parameters *nStartChar* and *nEndChar*.

The selection includes everything if the beginning (**cpMin** or *nStartChar*) is 0 and the end (**cpMax** or *nEndChar*) is −1.

For more information, see **EM_EXGETSEL** message and **CHARRANGE** structure in the Win32 documentation.

See Also: **CRichEditCtrl::SetSel**, **CRichEditCtrl::GetSelText**, **CRichEditCtrl::GetParaFormat**, **CRichEditCtrl::GetSelectionCharFormat**

CRichEditCtrl::GetSelectionCharFormat

DWORD GetSelectionCharFormat(CHARFORMAT& *cf* **) const;**

Return Value

The **dwMask** data member of *cf*. It specifies the character formatting attributes that are consistent throughout the current selection.

Parameters

cf Pointer to a **CHARFORMAT** structure to receive the character formatting attributes of the current selection.

Remarks

Call this function to get the character formatting attributes of the current selection. The *cf* parameter receives the attributes of the first character in the current selection. The return value specifies which attributes are consistent throughout the selection.

For more information, see **EM_GETCHARFORMAT** message and **CHARFORMAT** structure in the Win32 documentation.

See Also: **CRichEditCtrl::GetDefaultCharFormat**, **CRichEditCtrl::GetParaFormat**, **CRichEditCtrl::SetSelectionCharFormat**, **CRichEditCtrl::GetSelText**

CRichEditCtrl::GetSelectionType

WORD GetSelectionType( ) const;

Return Value

Flags indicating the contents of the current selection. A combination of the following flags:

- **SEL_EMPTY**   Indicates that there is no current selection.
- **SEL_TEXT**   Indicates that the current selection contains text.
- **SEL_OBJECT**   Indicates that the current selection contains at least one OLE item.
- **SEL_MULTICHAR**   Indicates that the current selection contains more than one character of text.
- **SEL_MULTIOBJECT**   Indicates that the current selection contains more than one OLE object.

Remarks

Call this function to determine the selection type in this **CRichEditCtrl** object.

For more information, see **EM_SELECTIONTYPE** in the Win32 documentation.

See Also: **CRichEditCtrl::GetSel**, **CRichEditCtrl::GetSelText**

CRichEditCtrl::GetSelText

long GetSelText(LPTSTR *lpBuf* **) const;**
CString GetSelText( ) const;

Return Value

Depends on the form:

- **GetSelText(** *lpBuf* **)**   The number of characters copied into *lpBuf*, not including the null termination.

- **GetSelText( )** The string containing the current selection.

Parameters

lpBuf Pointer to the buffer to receive the text in the current selection.

Remarks

Call this function to retrieve the text from the current selection in this **CRichEditCtrl** object.

If you use the first form, **GetSelText(** *lpBuf* **)**, you must ensure that the buffer is large enough for the text it will receive. Call **GetSel** to determine the number of characters in the current selection.

For more information, see **EM_GETSELTEXT** in the Win32 documentation.

See Also: **CRichEditCtrl::GetSel**, **CRichEditCtrl::GetSelectionType**

CRichEditCtrl::GetTextLength

long GetTextLength( );

Return Value

The length of the text in this **CRichEditCtrl** object.

Remarks

Call this function to retrieve the length of the text in this **CRichEditCtrl** object.

For more information, see **WM_GETTEXTLENGTH** in the Win32 documentation.

See Also: **CRichEditCtrl::LimitText**, **CRichEditCtrl::GetLimitText**

CRichEditCtrl::HideSelection

void HideSelection(BOOL *bHide***, BOOL** *bPerm* **);**

Parameters

bHide Indicates if the selection should be shown or hidden, **TRUE** to hide the selection.

pPerm Indicates if this change in visibility for the selection should be permanent.

Remarks

Call the function to change the visibility of the selection.

When *pPerm* is **TRUE**, it changes the **ECO_NOHIDESEL** option for this **CRichEditCtrl** object. For a brief description of this option, see **SetOptions**. You can use this function to set all the options for this **CRichEditCtrl** object.

For more information, see **EM_HIDESELECTION** in the Win32 documentation.

See Also: CRichEditCtrl::SetSel, CRichEditCtrl::GetSelectionType

CRichEditCtrl::LimitText

void LimitText(long *nChars* **= 0);**

Parameters

nChars Specifies the length (in bytes) of the text that the user can enter. If this parameter is 0, the text length is set to **UINT_MAX** bytes. This is the default behavior.

Remarks

Call this function to limit the length of the text that the user can enter into an edit control.

Changing the text limit restricts only the text the user can enter. It has no effect on any text already in the edit control, nor does it affect the length of the text copied to the edit control by the **SetWindowText** member function in **CWnd**. If an application uses the **SetWindowText** function to place more text into an edit control than is specified in the call to **LimitText**, the user can delete any of the text within the edit control. However, the text limit will prevent the user from replacing the existing text with new text, unless deleting the current selection causes the text to fall below the text limit.

Note For the text limit, each OLE item counts as a single character.

For more information, see **EM_EXLIMITTEXT** in the Win32 documentation.

See Also: CRichEditCtrl::GetLimitText

CRichEditCtrl::LineFromChar

long LineFromChar(long *nIndex* **) const;**

Return Value

The zero-based line number of the line containing the character index specified by *nIndex*. If *nIndex* is −1, the number of the line that contains the first character of the selection is returned. If there is no selection, the current line number is returned.

Parameters

nIndex Contains the zero-based index value for the desired character in the text of the edit control, or contains −1. If *nIndex* is −1, it specifies the current line, that is, the line that contains the caret.

Remarks

Call this function to retrieve the line number of the line that contains the specified character index. A character index is the number of characters from the beginning of the rich edit control. For character counting, an OLE item is counted as a single character.

For more information, see **EM_EXLINEFROMCHAR** in the Win32 documentation.

See Also: CRichEditCtrl::GetLineCount, CRichEditCtrl::GetLine, CRichEditCtrl::LineIndex

CRichEditCtrl::LineIndex

int LineIndex(int *nLine* **= -1) const;**

Return Value

The character index of the line specified in *nLine* or –1 if the specified line number is greater then the number of lines in the edit control.

Parameters

nLine   Contains the index value for the desired line in the text of the edit control, or contains –1. If *nLine* is –1, it specifies the current line, that is, the line that contains the caret.

Remarks

Call this function to retrieve the character index of a line within this **CRichEditCtrl** object. The character index is the number of characters from the beginning of the rich edit control to the specified line.

For more information, see **EM_LINEINDEX** in the Win32 documentation.

See Also: CRichEditCtrl::LineFromChar, CRichEditCtrl::GetLineCount

CRichEditCtrl::LineLength

int LineLength(int *nLine* **= -1) const;**

Return Value

When **LineLength** is called for a multiple-line edit control, the return value is the length (in bytes) of the line specified by *nLine*. When **LineLength** is called for a single-line edit control, the return value is the length (in bytes) of the text in the edit control.

Parameters

nLine   Specifies the character index of a character in the line whose length is to be retrieved. If this parameter is –1, the length of the current line (the line that contains the caret) is returned, not including the length of any selected text within the line. When **LineLength** is called for a single-line edit control, this parameter is ignored.

Remarks

Call this function to retrieve the length of a line in a rich edit control.

Use the **LineIndex** member function to retrieve a character index for a given line number within this **CRichEditCtrl** object.

For more information, see **EM_LINELENGTH** in the Win32 documentation.

See Also: **CRichEditCtrl::LineIndex**

CRichEditCtrl::LineScroll

void LineScroll(int *nLines*, **int** *nChars* = 0);

Parameters

nLines Specifies the number of lines to scroll vertically.

nChars Specifies the number of character positions to scroll horizontally. This value is ignored if the rich edit control has either the **ES_RIGHT** or **ES_CENTER** style. Edit styles are specified in **Create**.

Remarks

Call this function to scroll the text of a multiple-line edit control.

The edit control does not scroll vertically past the last line of text in the edit control. If the current line plus the number of lines specified by *nLines* exceeds the total number of lines in the edit control, the value is adjusted so that the last line of the edit control is scrolled to the top of the edit-control window.

LineScroll can be used to scroll horizontally past the last character of any line.

For more information, see **EM_LINESCROLL** in the Win32 documentation.

See Also: **CRichEditCtrl::LineIndex**

CRichEditCtrl::Paste

void Paste( );

Remarks

Call this function to insert the data from the Clipboard into the **CRichEditCtrl** at the insertion point, the location of the caret. Data is inserted only if the Clipboard contains data in a recognized format.

For more information, see **WM_PASTE** in the Win32 documentation.

See Also: **CRichEditCtrl::Copy, CRichEditCtrl::Cut, CRichEditCtrl::PasteSpecial**

CRichEditCtrl::PasteSpecial

void PasteSpecial(UINT *nClipFormat*, **DWORD** *dvAspect* = **0,**
↳ **HMETAFILE** *hMF* = **0**);

Parameters

nClipFormat   Clipboard format to paste into this **CRichEditCtrl** object.

dvAspect   Device aspect for the data to be retrieved from the Clipboard.

hMF   Handle to the metafile containing the iconic view of the object to be pasted.

Remarks

Call this function to paste data in a specific Clipboard format into this **CRichEditCtrl** object. The new material is inserted at the insertion point, the location of the caret.

For more information, see **EM_PASTESPECIAL** in the Win32 documentation.

See Also: **CRichEditCtrl::Paste, CRichEditCtrl::Copy, CRichEditCtrl::Cut**

CRichEditCtrl::ReplaceSel

void ReplaceSel(LPCTSTR *lpszNewText*, **BOOL** *bCanUndo* = **FALSE**);

Parameters

lpszNewText   Pointer to a null-terminated string containing the replacement text.

bCanUndo   To specify that this function can be undone, set the value of this parameter to **TRUE**. The default value is **FALSE**.

Remarks

Call this function to replace the current selection in this **CRichEditCtrl** object with the specified text. To replace all the text in this **CRichEditCtrl** object, use **CWnd::SetWindowText**.

If there is no current selection, the replacement text is inserted at the insertion point, that is, the current caret location.

For more information, see **EM_REPLACESEL** in the Win32 documentation.

See Also: **CRichEditCtrl::CanUndo, CRichEditCtrl::Undo,
CWnd::SetWindowText**

CRichEditCtrl::RequestResize

void RequestResize( );

Remarks

Call this function to force this **CRichEditCtrl** object to send **EN_REQUESTRESIZE** notification messages to its parent window. This function is useful during **CWnd::OnSize** processing for a bottomless **CRichEditCtrl** object.

For more information, see the **EM_REQUESTRESIZE** message and the "Bottomless Rich Edit Controls" article in the Win32 documentation.

See Also: **CWnd::OnSize**, **CRichEditCtrl::Create**

CRichEditCtrl::SetBackgroundColor

COLORREF SetBackgroundColor(BOOL *bSysColor*, **COLORREF** *cr* **);**

Return Value

The previous background color for this **CRichEditCtrl** object.

Parameters

bSysColor   Indicates if the background color should be set to the system value. If this value is **TRUE**, *cr* is ignored.

cr   The requested background color. Used only if *bSysColor* is **FALSE**.

Remarks

Call this function to set the background color for this **CRichEditCtrl** object. The background color can be set to the system value or to a specified **COLORREF** value.

For more information, see **EM_SETBKGNDCOLOR** message and **COLORREF** structure in the Win32 documentation.

See Also: **CDC::SetBkColor**

CRichEditCtrl::SetDefaultCharFormat

BOOL SetDefaultCharFormat(CHARFORMAT& *cf* **);**

Return Value

Nonzero if successful; otherwise, 0.

Parameters

cf   **CHARFORMAT** structure containing the new default character formatting attributes.

Remarks

Call this function to set the character formatting attributes for new text in this **CRichEditCtrl** object. Only the attributes specified by the **dwMask** member of *cf* are changed by this function.

For more information, see **EM_SETCHARFORMAT** message and **CHARFORMAT** structure in the Win32 documentation.

See Also: **CRichEditCtrl::GetDefaultCharFormat**, **CRichEditCtrl::SetSelectionCharFormat**

CRichEditCtrl::SetEventMask

DWORD SetEventMask(DWORD *dwEventMask* **);**

Return Value

The previous event mask.

Parameters

dwEventMask   The new event mask for this **CRichEditCtrl** object.

Remarks

Call this function to set the event mask for this **CRichEditCtrl** object. The event mask specifies which notification messages the **CRichEditCtrl** object sends to its parent window.

For more information, see **EM_SETEVENTMASK** in the Win32 documentation.

See Also: **CRichEditCtrl::GetEventMask**

CRichEditCtrl::SetModify

void SetModify(BOOL *bModified* **= TRUE);**

Parameters

bModified   A value of **TRUE** indicates that the text has been modified, and a value of **FALSE** indicates it is unmodified. By default, the modified flag is set.

Remarks

Call this function to set or clear the modified flag for an edit control. The modified flag indicates whether or not the text within the edit control has been modified. It is automatically set whenever the user changes the text. Its value can be retrieved with the **GetModify** member function.

For more information, see **EM_SETMODIFY** in the Win32 documentation.

See Also: **CRichEditCtrl::GetModify**

CRichEditCtrl::SetOLECallback

BOOL SetOLECallback(IRichEditOleCallback* *pCallback* **);**

Parameters

pCallback   Pointer to an **IRichEditOleCallback** object that this **CRichEditCtrl** object will use to get OLE-related resources and information.

Return Value

Nonzero if successful; otherwise, 0.

Remarks

Call this function to give this **CRichEditCtrl** object an **IRichEditOleCallback** object to use to access OLE-related resources and information. This **CRichEditCtrl** object will call **IUnknown::AddRef** to increment the usage count for the COM object specified by *pCallback*.

For more information, see **EM_SETOLEINTERFACE** message and **IRichEditOleCallback** interface in the Win32 documentation.

See Also: CRichEditCtrl::GetIRichEditOle

CRichEditCtrl::SetOptions

void SetOptions(WORD *wOp*, **DWORD** *dwFlags* **);**

Parameters

wOp   Indicates the type of operation. One of the following values:

- **ECOOP_SET**   Set the options to those specified by *dwFlags*.

- **ECOOP_OR**   Combine the current options with those specified by *dwFlags*.

- **ECOOP_AND**   Retain only those current options that are also specified by *dwFlags*.

- **ECOOP_XOR**   Retain only those current options that are *not* specified by *dwFlags*.

dwFlags   Rich edit options. The flag values are listed in the Remarks section.

Remarks

Call this function to set the options for this **CRichEditCtrl** object.

The options can be a combination of the following values:

- **ECO_AUTOWORDSELECTION**   Automatic word selection on double-click.

- **ECO_AUTOVSCROLL**   Automatically scrolls text to the right by 10 characters when the user types a character at the end of the line. When the user presses the ENTER key, the control scrolls all text back to position zero.

- **ECO_AUTOHSCROLL**   Automatically scrolls text up one page when the user presses the ENTER key on the last line.

- **ECO_NOHIDESEL**   Negates the default behavior for an edit control. The default behavior hides the selection when the control loses the input focus and shows the selection when the control receives the input focus. If you specify **ECO_NOHIDESEL**, the selected text is inverted, even if the control does not have the focus.

- **ECO_READONLY**   Prevents the user from typing or editing text in the edit control.

- **ECO_WANTRETURN**   Specifies that a carriage return be inserted when the user presses the ENTER key while entering text into a multiple-line rich edit control in a dialog box. If you do not specify this style, pressing the ENTER key sends a command to the rich edit control's parent window, which mimics clicking the parent window's default button (for example, the OK button in a dialog box). This style has no effect on a single-line edit control.

- **ECO_SAVESEL**   Preserves the selection when the control loses the focus. By default, the entire contents of the control are selected when it regains the focus.

- **ECO_VERTICAL**   Draws text and objects in a vertical direction. Available for Asian languages only.

For more information, see **EM_SETOPTIONS** in the Win32 documentation.

See Also: **CRichEditCtrl::HideSelection, CRichEditCtrl::SetReadOnly**

CRichEditCtrl::SetParaFormat

BOOL SetParaFormat(PARAFORMAT& *pf* **);**

Return Value

Nonzero if successful; otherwise, 0.

Parameters

pf   **PARAFORMAT** structure containing the new default paragraph formatting attributes.

Remarks

Call this function to set the paragraph formatting attributes for the current selection in this **CRichEditCtrl** object. Only the attributes specified by the **dwMask** member of *pf* are changed by this function.

For more information, see **EM_SETPARAFORMAT** message and **PARAFORMAT** structure in the Win32 documentation.

See Also: **CRichEditCtrl::GetParaFormat, CRichEditCtrl::SetSelectionCharFormat**

CRichEditCtrl::SetReadOnly

BOOL SetReadOnly(BOOL *bReadOnly* **= TRUE);**

Return Value

Nonzero if successful; otherwise, 0.

Parameters

bReadOnly Indicates if this **CRichEditCtrl** object should be read only.

Remarks

Call this member function to change the **ECO_READONLY** option for this
CRichEditCtrl object. For a brief description of this option, see **SetOptions**. You can
use this function to set all the options for this **CRichEditCtrl** object.

For more information, see **EM_SETREADONLY** in the Win32 documentation.

See Also: CRichEditCtrl::Create, CRichEditCtrl::SetOptions

CRichEditCtrl::SetRect

void SetRect(LPCRECT *lpRect* **);**

Parameters

lpRect   **CRect** or pointer to a **RECT** that indicates the new bounds for the formatting
rectangle.

Remarks

Call this function to set the formatting rectangle for this **CRichEditCtrl** object. The
formatting rectangle is the limiting rectangle for the text. The limiting rectangle is
independent of the size of the rich edit control window. When this **CRichEditCtrl**
object is first created, the formatting rectangle is the same size as the client area of the
window. Use **SetRect** to make the formatting rectangle larger or smaller than the rich
edit window.

For more information, see **EM_SETRECT** in the Win32 documentation.

See Also: CRichEditCtrl::GetRect

CRichEditCtrl::SetSel

void SetSel(long *nStartChar*, **long** *nEndChar* **);**
void SetSel(CHARRANGE& *cr* **);**

Parameters

nStartChar Zero-based index of the first character for the selection.

nEndChar Zero-based index of the last character for the selection.

cr   **CHARRANGE** structure which holds the bounds of the current selection.

Remarks

Call this function to set the selection within this **CRichEditCtrl** object.

The two forms of this function provide alternate ways to set the bounds for the selection. Brief descriptions of these forms follow:

- **SetSel**(*cr*)   This form uses the **CHARRANGE** structure with its **cpMin** and **cpMax** members to set the bounds.
- **SetSel**(*nStartChar*, *nEndChar*)   This form use the parameters *nStartChar* and *nEndChar* to set the bounds.

The caret is placed at the end of the selection indicated by the greater of the start (**cpMin** or *nStartChar*) and end (**cpMax** or *nEndChar*) indices. This function does not scroll the contents of the **CRichEditCtrl** so that the caret is visible.

To select all the text in this **CRichEditCtrl** object, call **SetSel** with a start index of 0 and an end index of –1.

For more information, see **EM_EXSETSEL** message and **CHARRANGE** structure in the Win32 documentation.

See Also: **CRichEditCtrl::GetSel, CRichEditCtrl::GetSelectionType**

CRichEditCtrl::SetSelectionCharFormat

BOOL SetSelectionCharFormat(CHARFORMAT& *cf* **);**

Return Value

Nonzero if successful; otherwise, 0.

Parameters

cf   **CHARFORMAT** structure containing the new character formatting attributes for the current selection.

Remarks

Call this function to set the character formatting attributes for the text in the current selection in this **CRichEditCtrl** object. Only the attributes specified by the **dwMask** member of *cf* are changed by this function.

For more information, see **EM_SETCHARFORMAT** message and **CHARFORMAT** structure in the Win32 documentation.

See Also: **CRichEditCtrl::GetSelectionCharFormat,
CRichEditCtrl::SetDefaultCharFormat**

CRichEditCtrl::SetTargetDevice

BOOL SetTargetDevice(HDC *hDC***, long** *lLineWidth* **);**
BOOL SetTargetDevice(CDC& *dc***, long** *lLineWidth* **);**

Return Value

Nonzero if successful; otherwise, 0.

Parameters

hDC   Handle to the device context for the new target device.

lLineWidth   Line width to use for formatting.

dc   **CDC** for the new target device.

Remarks

Call this function to set the target device and line width used for WYSIWYG (what you see is what you get) formatting in this **CRichEditCtrl** object.

If this function is successful, the rich edit control owns the device context passed as a parameter. In that case, the calling function should not destroy the device context.

For more information, see **EM_SETTARGETDEVICE** in the Win32 documentation.

See Also: CRichEditCtrl::FormatRange, CRichEditCtrl::DisplayBand

---

CRichEditCtrl::SetWordCharFormat

BOOL SetWordCharFormat(CHARFORMAT& *cf* **);**

Return Value

Nonzero if successful; otherwise, 0.

Parameters

cf   **CHARFORMAT** structure containing the new character formatting attributes for the currently selected word.

Remarks

Call this function to set the character formatting attributes for the currently selected word in this **CRichEditCtrl** object. Only the attributes specified by the **dwMask** member of *cf* are changed by this function.

For more information, see **EM_SETCHARFORMAT** message and **CHARFORMAT** structure in the Win32 documentation.

See Also: CRichEditCtrl::SetSelectionCharFormat

CRichEditCtrl::StreamIn

long StreamIn(int *nFormat*, **EDITSTREAM&** *es* **);**

Return Value

Number of characters read from the input stream.

Parameters

nFormat   Flags specifying the input data formats. See the Remarks section for more information.

es   **EDITSTREAM** structure specifying the input stream. See the Remarks section for more information.

Remarks

Call this function to replace text in this **CRichEditCtrl** object with text from the specified input stream.

The value of *nFormat* must be one of the following:

- **SF_TEXT**   Indicates reading text only.
- **SF_RTF**   Indicates reading text and formatting.

Either of these values can be combined with **SFF_SELECTION**. If **SFF_SELECTION** is specified, **StreamIn** replaces the current selection with the contents of the input stream. If it is not specified, **StreamIn** replaces the entire contents of this **CRichEditCtrl** object.

In the **EDITSTREAM** parameter *es*, you specify a callback function which fills a buffer with text. This callback function is called repeatedly, until the input stream is exhausted.

For more information, see **EM_STREAMIN** message and **EDITSTREAM** structure in the Win32 documentation.

See Also: CRichEditCtrl::StreamOut

CRichEditCtrl::StreamOut

long StreamOut(int *nFormat*, **EDITSTREAM&** *es* **);**

Return Value

Number of characters written to the output stream.

Parameters

nFormat   Flags specifying the output data formats. See the Remarks section for more information.

es   **EDITSTREAM** structure specifying the output stream. See the Remarks section for more information.

Remarks

Call this function to write out the contents of this **CRichEditCtrl** object to the specified output stream.

The value of *nFormat* must be one of the following:

- **SF_TEXT**   Indicates writing text only.
- **SF_RTF**   Indicates writing text and formatting.
- **SF_RTFNOOBJS**   Indicates writing text and formatting, replacing OLE items with spaces.
- **SF_TEXTIZED**   Indicates writing text and formatting, with textual representations of OLE items.

Any of these values can be combined with **SFF_SELECTION**. If **SFF_SELECTION** is specified, **StreamOut** writes out the current selection into the output stream. If it is not specified, **StreamOut** writes out the the entire contents of this **CRichEditCtrl** object.

In the **EDITSTREAM** parameter *es*, you specify a callback function which fills a buffer with text. This callback function is called repeatedly, until the output stream is exhausted.

For more information, see **EM_STREAMOUT** message and **EDITSTREAM** structure in the Win32 documentation.

See Also: CRichEditCtrl::StreamIn

CRichEditCtrl::Undo

BOOL Undo( );

Return Value

Nonzero if the undo operation is successful; otherwise, 0.

Remarks

Call this function to undo the last operation in the rich edit control.

An undo operation can also be undone. For example, you can restore deleted text with the first call to **Undo**. As long as there is no intervening edit operation, you can remove the text again with a second call to **Undo**.

For more information, see **EM_UNDO** in the Win32 documentation.

See Also: CRichEditCtrl::CanUndo, CRichEditCtrl::EmptyUndoBuffer

CRichEditDoc

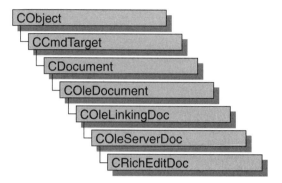

A "rich edit control" is a window in which the user can enter and edit text. The text can be assigned character and paragraph formatting, and can include embedded OLE objects. Rich edit controls provide a programming interface for formatting text. However, an application must implement any user interface components necessary to make formatting operations available to the user.

The **CRichEditDoc** class, with **CRichEditView** and **CRichEditCntrItem**, provides the functionality of the rich edit control within the context of MFC's document view architecture. **CRichEditView** maintains the text and formatting characteristic of text. **CRichEditDoc** maintains the list of client items which are in the view. **CRichEditCntrItem** provides container-side access to the OLE client items.

This Windows Common control (and therefore the **CRichEditCtrl** and related classes) is available only to programs running under Windows 95 and Windows NT versions 3.51 and later.

For an example of using a rich edit document in an MFC application, see the WORDPAD sample application online.

#include <afxrich.h>

See Also: **CRichEditView**, **CRichEditCntrItem**, **COleDocument**, **CRichEditCtrl**

CRichEditDoc Class Members

Attributes

GetStreamFormat	Indicates whether stream input and output should include formatting information.
GetView	Retrieves the asssociated **CRichEditView** object.

Data Members	
m_bRTF	Indicates whether stream I/O should include formatting.

Overridables	
CreateClientItem	Called to perform cleanup of the document.

Member Functions

CRichEditDoc::CreateClientItem

virtual CRichEditCntrItem* CreateClientItem(REOBJECT* *preo* **= NULL) const = 0;**

Return Value

Pointer to a new **CRichEditCntrItem** object which has been added to this document.

Parameters

preo Pointer to an **REOBJECT** structure which describes an OLE item. The new **CRichEditCntrItem** object is constructed around this OLE item. If *preo* is **NULL**, the new client item is empty.

Remarks

Call this function to create a **CRichEditCntrItem** object and add it to this document. This function does not perform any OLE initialization.

For more information, see the **REOBJECT** structure in the Win32 documentation.

See Also: CRichEditCntrItem::CRichEditCntrItem, COleDocument::AddItem

CRichEditDoc::GetStreamFormat

int GetStreamFormat( ) const;

Return Value

One of the following flags:

- **SF_TEXT**   Indicates that the rich edit control does not maintain formatting information.
- **SF_RTF**   Indicates that the rich edit control does maintain formatting information.

Remarks

Call this function to determine the text format for streaming the contents of the rich edit. The return value is based on the **m_bRTF** data member. This function returns **SF_RTF** if **m_bRTF** is **TRUE**; otherwise, **SF_TEXT**.

See Also: CRichEditDoc::m_bRTF, CRichEditCtrl::StreamIn, CRichEditCtrl::StreamOut

CRichEditDoc::GetView

CRichEditView* GetView( ) const;

Return Value

Pointer to the **CRichEditView** object associated with the document.

Remarks

Call this function to access the **CRichEditView** object associated with this **CRichEditDoc** object. The text and formatting information are contained within the **CRichEditView** object. The **CRichEditDoc** object maintains the OLE items for serialization. There should be only one **CRichEditView** for each **CRichEditDoc**.

See Also: **CRichEditView, CDocument::GetNextView**

Data Members
CRichEditDoc::m_bRTF

Remarks

When **TRUE**, indicates that **CRichEditCtrl::StreamIn** and **CRichEditCtrl::StreamOut** should store paragraph and character-formatting characteristics.

See Also: **CRichEditDoc::GetStreamFormat**

CRichEditView

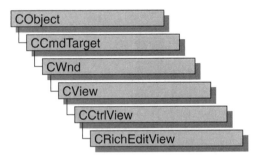

A "rich edit control" is a window in which the user can enter and edit text. The text can be assigned character and paragraph formatting, and can include embedded OLE objects. Rich edit controls provide a programming interface for formatting text. However, an application must implement any user interface components necessary to make formatting operations available to the user.

The **CRichEditView** class, with **CRichEditDoc** and **CRichEditCntrItem**, provides the functionality of the rich edit control within the context of MFC's document view architecture. **CRichEditView** maintains the text and formatting characteristic of text. **CRichEditDoc** maintains the list of OLE client items which are in the view. **CRichEditCntrItem** provides container-side access to the OLE client item.

This Windows Common control (and therefore the **CRichEditCtrl** and related classes) is available only to programs running under Windows 95 and Windows NT versions 3.51 and later.

For an example of using a rich edit view in an MFC application, see the WORDPAD sample application online.

#include <afxrich.h>

See Also: CRichEditDoc, CRichEditCntrItem

CRichEditView Class Members

Constructor

CRichEditView	Constructs a **CRichEditView** object.

Attributes

GetDocument	Retrieves a pointer to the related **CRichEditDoc**.
GetCharFormatSelection	Retrieves the character formatting attributes for the current selection.

Attributes *(continued)*

SetCharFormat	Sets the character formatting attributes for the current selection.
GetParaFormatSelection	Retrieves the paragraph formatting attributes for the current selection.
SetParaFormat	Sets the paragraph formatting attributes for the current selection.
GetTextLength	Retrieves the length of the text in the rich edit view.
GetPaperSize	Retrieves the paper size for this rich edit view.
SetPaperSize	Sets the paper size for this rich edit view.
GetMargins	Retrieves the margins for this rich edit view.
SetMargins	Sets the margins for this rich edit view.
GetPrintWidth	Retrieves the print width for this rich edit view.
GetPrintRect	Retrieves the print rectangle for this rich edit view.
GetPageRect	Retrieves the page rectangle for this rich edit view.
GetSelectedItem	Retrieves the selected item from the rich edit view.
GetInPlaceActiveItem	Retrieves the OLE item that is currently in-place active in the rich edit view.
GetRichEditCtrl	Retrieves the rich edit control.

Data Members

m_nBulletIndent	Indicates the amount of indent for bullet lists.
m_nWordWrap	Indicates the word wrap constraints.

Operations

FindText	Finds the specified text, invoking the wait cursor.
FindTextSimple	Finds the specified text.
IsRichEditFormat	Tells whether the Clipboard contains data in a rich edit or text format.
CanPaste	Tells whether the Clipboard contains data that can be pasted into the rich edit view.
DoPaste	Pastes an OLE item into this rich edit view.
InsertItem	Inserts a new item as an OLE item.
InsertFileAsObject	Inserts a file as an OLE item.
AdjustDialogPosition	Moves a dialog box so that it doesn't obscure the current selection.
OnCharEffect	Changes the character formatting for the current selection.
OnParaAlign	Changes the alignment of paragraphs.

(continued)

Operations *(continued)*

OnUpdateCharEffect	Updates the Command UI for character public member functions.
OnUpdateParaAlign	Updates the Command UI for paragraph public member functions.
PrintInsideRect	Formats the specified text within the given rectangle.
PrintPage	Formats the specified text within the given page.

Overridables

OnInitialUpdate	Refreshes a view when it is first attached to a document.
IsSelected	Indicates if the given OLE item is selected or not.
OnFindNext	Finds the next occurrence of a substring.
OnTextNotFound	Handles user notification that the requested text was not found.
OnReplaceAll	Replaces all occurrences of a given string with a new string.
OnReplaceSel	Replaces the current selection.
QueryAcceptData	Queries to see about the data on the **IDataObject**.
OnPasteNativeObject	Retrieves native data from an OLE item.
OnPrinterChanged	Sets the print characteristics to the given device.
WrapChanged	Adjusts the target output device for this rich edit view, based on the value of **m_nWordWrap**.
GetClipboardData	Retrieves a Clipboard object for a range in this rich edit view.
GetContextMenu	Retrieves a context menu to use on a right mouse-button down.

Member Functions

CRichEditView::AdjustDialogPosition

void AdjustDialogPosition(CDialog* *pDlg* **);**

Parameters

pDlg   Pointer to a **CDialog** object.

Remarks

Call this function to move the given dialog box so that it does not obscure the current selection.

See Also: CRichEditCtrl::GetSel

CRichEditView::CanPaste

BOOL CanPaste( ) const;

Return Value

Nonzero if the Clipboard contains data in a format which this rich edit view can accept; otherwise, 0.

Remarks

Call this function to determine if the Clipboard contains information that can be pasted into this rich edit view.

See Also: CRichEditCtrl::Paste, CRichEditView::DoPaste, CRichEditView::IsRichEditFormat

---

CRichEditView::CRichEditView

CRichEditView( );

Remarks

Call this function to create a **CRichEditView** object.

See Also: CRichEditDoc, CRichEditCtrl

CRichEditView::DoPaste

void DoPaste(COleDataObject& *dataobj*, **CLIPFORMAT** *cf*,
 ↪ **HMETAFILEPICT** *hMetaPict* **);**

Parameters

dataobj   The **COleDataObject** containing the data to paste.

cf   The desired Clipboard format.

hMetaPict   The metafile that represents the item to be pasted.

Remarks

Call this function to paste the OLE item in *dataobj* into this rich edit document/view. The framework calls this function as part of the default implementation of **QueryAcceptData**.

This function determines the type of paste based on the results of the handler for Paste Special. If *cf* is 0, the new item uses the current iconic representation. If *cf* is nonzero and *hMetaPict* is not **NULL**, the new item uses *hMetaPict* for its representation.

See Also: CRichEditCtrl::Paste, CRichEditView::IsRichEditFormat, CRichEditView::InsertItem

CRichEditView::FindText

BOOL FindText(LPCTSTR *lpszFind***, BOOL** *bCase* **= TRUE, BOOL** *bWord* **= TRUE);**

Return Value

Nonzero if the *lpszFind* text is found; otherwise 0.

Parameters

lpszFind   Contains the string to search for.

bCase   Indicates if the search is case sensitive.

bWord   Indicates if the search should match whole words only, not parts of words.

Remarks

Call this function to find the specified text and set it to be the current selection. This function displays the wait cursor during the find operation.

See Also: CRichEditCtrl::FindText, CRichEditCtrl::SetSel, CRichEditView::FindTextSimple, CWaitCursor

---

CRichEditView::FindTextSimple

BOOL FindTextSimple(LPCTSTR *lpszFind***, BOOL** *bCase* **= TRUE,**
↪ BOOL *bWord* **= TRUE);**

Return Value

Nonzero if the *lpszFind* text is found; otherwise 0.

Parameters

lpszFind   Contains the string to search for.

bCase   Indicates if the search is case sensitive.

bWord   Indicates if the search should match whole words only, not parts of words.

Remarks

Call this function to find the specified text and set it to be the current selection.

See Also: CRichEditCtrl::FindText, CRichEditCtrl::SetSel, CRichEditView::FindText

---

CRichEditView::GetCharFormatSelection

CHARFORMAT& GetCharFormatSelection( );

Return Value

A **CHARFORMAT** structure which contains the character formatting attributes of the current selection.

Remarks

Call this function to get the character formatting attributes of the current selection.

For more information, see the **EM_GETCHARFORMAT** message and the **CHARFORMAT** structure in the Win32 documentation.

See Also: **CRichEditView::SetCharFormat**, **CRichEditView::GetParaFormatSelection**, **CRichEditCtrl::GetSelectionCharFormat**

CRichEditView::GetClipboardData

virtual HRESULT GetClipboardData(CHARRANGE* *lpchrg*, **DWORD** *dwReco*,
⮑ **LPDATAOBJECT** *lpRichDataObj*, **LPDATAOBJECT*** *lplpdataobj* **);**

Return Value

An **HRESULT** value reporting the success of the operation. For more information on **HRESULT**, see "Structure of OLE Error Codes" in the OLE documentation.

Parameters

lpchrg   Pointer to the **CHARRANGE** structure specifying the range of characters (and OLE items) to copy to the data object specified by *lplpdataobj*.

dwReco   Clipboard operation flag. Can be one of these values.

- **RECO_COPY**   Copy to the Clipboard.

- **RECO_CUT**   Cut to the Clipboard.

- **RECO_DRAG**   Drag operation (drag and drop).

- **RECO_DROP**   Drop operation (drag and drop).

- **RECO_PASTE**   Paste from the Clipboard.

lpRichDataObj   Pointer to an **IDataObject** object containing the Clipboard data from the rich edit control (**IRichEditOle::GetClipboardData**).

lplpdataobj   Pointer to the pointer variable that receives the address of the **IDataObject** object representing the range specified in the *lpchrg* parameter. The value of *lplpdataobj* is ignored if an error is returned.

Remarks

The framework calls this function as part of the processing of **IRichEditOleCallback::GetClipboardData**. If the return value indicates success, **IRichEditOleCallback::GetClipboardData** returns the **IDataObject** accessed by *lplpdataobj*; otherwise, it returns the one accessed by *lpRichDataObj*. Override this function to supply your own Clipboard data. The default implementation of this function returns **E_NOTIMPL**.

This is an advanced overridable.

For more information, see **IRichEditOle::GetClipboardData**, **IRichEditOleCallback::GetClipboardData**, and **CHARRANGE** in the Win32 documentation and see **IDataObject** in the OLE documentation.

See Also: COleServerItem::GetClipboardData

CRichEditView::GetContextMenu

virtual HMENU GetContextMenu(WORD *seltyp***, LPOLEOBJECT** *lpoleobj***,**
↪ **CHARRANGE*** *lpchrg* **);**

Return Value

Handle to the context menu.

Parameters

seltyp   The selection type. The selection type values are described in the Remarks section.

lpoleobj   Pointer to a **OLEOBJECT** structure specifying the first selected OLE object if the selection contains one or more OLE items. If the selection contains no items, *lpoleobj* is **NULL**. The **OLEOBJECT** structure holds a pointer to an OLE object v-table.

lpchrg   Pointer to a **CHARRANGE** structure containing the current selection.

Remarks

The framework calls this function as part of the processing of **IRichEditOleCallback::GetContextMenu**. This function is a typical part of right mouse-button down processing.

The selection type can be any combination of the following flags:

- **SEL_EMPTY**   Indicates that there is no current selection.
- **SEL_TEXT**   Indicates that the current selection contains text.
- **SEL_OBJECT**   Indicates that the current selection contains at least one OLE item.
- **SEL_MULTICHAR**   Indicates that the current selection contains more than one character of text.
- **SEL_MULTIOBJECT**   Indicates that the current selection contains more than one OLE object.

The default implementation returns **NULL**. This is an advanced overridable.

For more information, see **IRichEditOleCallback::GetContextMenu** and **CHARRANGE** in the Win32 documentation.

For more information on the **OLEOBJECT** type, see the "OLE Data Structures and Structure Allocation" article in the *OLE Knowledge Base*.

See Also: **CRichEditCtrl::GetSelectionType**

CRichEditView::GetDocument

CRichEditDoc* GetDocument( ) const;

Return Value

Pointer to a **CRichEditDoc** object associated with your **CRichEditView** object.

Remarks

Call this function to get a pointer to the **CRichEditDoc** associated with this view.

See Also: **CRichEditDoc, CView::GetDocument, COleClientItem::GetDocument**

CRichEditView::GetInPlaceActiveItem

CRichEditCntrItem* GetInPlaceActiveItem( ) const;

Return Value

A pointer to the single, in-place active **CRichEditCntrItem** object in this rich edit view; **NULL** if there is no OLE item currently in the in-place active state.

Remarks

Call this function to get the OLE item that is currently activated in place in this **CRichEditView** object.

See Also: **COleDocument::GetInPlaceActiveItem, CRichEditCntrItem, CRichEditView::GetSelectedItem**

CRichEditView::GetMargins

CRect GetMargins( ) const;

Return Value

The margins used in printing, measured in **MM_TWIPS**.

Remarks

Call this function to retrieve the current margins used in printing.

See Also: **CRichEditView::SetMargins, CRichEditView::GetPrintWidth, CRichEditView::GetPrintRect, CRichEditView::GetPaperSize, CRichEditView::PrintPage, CRichEditView::WrapChanged**

CRichEditView::GetPageRect

CRect GetPageRect( ) const;

Return Value

The bounds of the page used in printing, measured in **MM_TWIPS**.

Remarks

Call this function to get the dimensions of the page used in printing. This value is based on the paper size.

See Also: **CRichEditView::GetMargins**, **CRichEditView::GetPrintWidth**, **CRichEditView::GetPrintRect**, **CRichEditView::GetPaperSize**, **CRichEditView::PrintPage**

CRichEditView::GetPaperSize

CSize GetPaperSize( ) const;

Return Value

The size of the paper used in printing, measured in **MM_TWIPS**.

Remarks

Call this function to retrieve the current paper size.

See Also: **CRichEditView::SetPaperSize**, **CRichEditView::GetMargins**, **CRichEditView::GetPrintWidth**, **CRichEditView::GetPrintRect**, **CRichEditView::GetPageRect**, **CRichEditView::PrintPage**

CRichEditView::GetParaFormatSelection

PARAFORMAT& GetParaFormatSelection( );

Return Value

A **PARAFORMAT** structure which contains the paragraph formatting attributes of the current selection.

Remarks

Call this function to get the paragraph formatting attributes of the current selection.

For more information, see **EM_GETPARAFORMAT** message and **PARAFORMAT** structure in the Win32 documentation.

See Also: **CRichEditView::GetCharFormatSelection**, **CRichEditView::SetParaFormat**, **CRichEditCtrl::GetParaFormat**

CRichEditView::GetPrintRect

CRect GetPrintRect( ) const;

Return Value

The bounds of the image area used in printing, measured in **MM_TWIPS**.

Remarks

Call this function to retrieve the bounds of the printing area within the page rectangle.

See Also: **CRichEditView::GetMargins**, **CRichEditView::GetPrintWidth**, **CRichEditView::GetPaperSize**, **CRichEditView::GetPageRect**, **CRichEditView::PrintPage**

CRichEditView::GetPrintWidth

int GetPrintWidth( ) const;

Return Value

The width of the printing area, measured in **MM_TWIPS**.

Remarks

Call this function to determine the width of the printing area.

See Also: **CRichEditView::GetMargins**, **CRichEditView::GetPrintRect**, **CRichEditView::GetPaperSize**, **CRichEditView::GetPageRect**, **CRichEditView::PrintPage**, **CRichEditView::WrapChanged**

CRichEditView::GetRichEditCtrl

CRichEditCtrl& GetRichEditCtrl( ) const;

Return Value

The **CRichEditCtrl** object for this view.

Remarks

Call this function to retrieve the **CRichEditCtrl** object associated with the **CRichEditView** object.

See Also: **CRichEditCtrl**, **CEditView::GetEditCtrl**, **CTreeView::GetTreeCtrl**, **CListView::GetListCtrl**

CRichEditView::GetSelectedItem

CRichEditCntrItem* GetSelectedItem( ) const;

Return Value

Pointer to a **CRichEditCntrItem** object selected in the **CRichEditView** object; **NULL** if no item is selected in this view.

Remarks

Call this function to retrieve the OLE item (a **CRichEditCntrItem** object) currently selected in this **CRichEditView** object.

See Also: **CRichEditCntrItem, CRichEditView::GetInPlaceActiveItem**

CRichEditView::GetTextLength

long GetTextLength( ) const;

Return Value

The length of the text in this **CRichEditView** object.

Remarks

Call this function to retrieve the length of the text in this **CRichEditView** object.

See Also: **CRichEditCtrl::GetTextLength**

CRichEditView::InsertFileAsObject

void InsertFileAsObject(LPCTSTR *lpszFileName* **);**

Parameters

lpszFileName String containing the name of the file to be inserted.

Remarks

Call this function to insert the specified file (as a **CRichEditCntrItem** object) into a rich edit view.

See Also: **CRichEditView::InsertItem, CRichEditCntrItem**

CRichEditView::InsertItem

HRESULT InsertItem(CRichEditCntrItem* *pItem* **);**

Return Value

An **HRESULT** value indicating the success of the insertion.

Parameters

pItem   Pointer to the item to be inserted.

Remarks

Call this function to insert a **CRichEditCntrItem** object into a rich edit view.

For more information on **HRESULT**, see "Structure of OLE Error Codes" in the OLE documentation.

See Also: **CRichEditView::InsertFileAsObject**, **CRichEditCntrItem**

CRichEditView::IsRichEditFormat

BOOL IsRichEditFormat(CLIPFORMAT *cf* **);**

Return Value

Nonzero if *cf* is a rich edit or text Clipboard format.

Parameters

cf   The Clipboard format of interest.

Remarks

Call this function to determine if *cf* is a Clipboard format which is text, rich text, or rich text with OLE items.

See Also: **CRichEditCtrl::CanPaste**, **CRichEditCtrl::Paste**, **CRichEditView::DoPaste**

CRichEditView::IsSelected

virtual BOOL IsSelected(const CObject* *pDocItem* **) const;**

Return Value

Nonzero if the object is selected; otherwise 0.

Parameters

pDocItem   Pointer to an object in the view.

Remarks

Call this function to determine if the specified OLE item is currently selected in this view.

Override this function if your derived view class has a different method for handling selection of OLE items.

See Also: **CRichEditView::GetSelectedItem**, **CRichEditView::GetInPlaceActiveItem**

CRichEditView::OnCharEffect

void OnCharEffect(DWORD *dwMask***, DWORD** *dwEffect* **);**

Parameters

dwMask 'The character formatting effects to modify in the current selection.

dwEffect The desired list of character formatting effects.

Remarks

Call this function to change the character formatting effects for the current selection.

For more information on the *dwMask* and *dwEffect* parameters and their potential values, see the corresponding data members of **CHARFORMAT** in the Win32 documentation.

See Also: **CRichEditView::SetCharFormat**

CRichEditView::OnFindNext

virtual void OnFindNext(LPCTSTR *lpszFind***, BOOL** *bNext***, BOOL** *bCase***,**
↪ BOOL *bWord* **);**

Parameters

lpszFind The string to find.

bNext The direction to search: **TRUE** indicates down; **FALSE**, up.

bCase Indicates whether the search is to be case sensitive.

bWord Indicates whether the search is to match whole words only or not.

Remarks

Called by the framework when processing commands from the Find/Replace dialog box. Call this function to find text within the **CRichEditView**. Override this function to alter search characterics for your derived view class.

See Also: **CRichEditView::FindText, CRichEditView::FindTextSimple**

CRichEditView::OnInitialUpdate

virtual void OnInitialUpdate( );

Remarks

Called by the framework after the view is first attached to the document, but before the view is initially displayed. The default implementation of this function calls the **CView::OnUpdate** member function with no hint information (that is, using the default values of 0 for the *lHint* parameter and **NULL** for the *pHint* parameter).

Override this function to perform any one-time initialization that requires information about the document. For example, if your application has fixed-sized documents, you can use this function to initialize a view's scrolling limits based on the document size. If your application supports variable-sized documents, use **OnUpdate** to update the scrolling limits every time the document changes.

See Also: **CView::OnUpdate**

CRichEditView::OnPasteNativeObject

> **virtual BOOL OnPasteNativeObject(LPSTORAGE** *lpStg* **);**

Return Value

Nonzero if successful; otherwise, 0;

Parameters

lpStg   Pointer to an **IStorage** object.

Remarks

Use this function to load native data from an embedded item. Typically, you would do this by creating a **COleStreamFile** around the **IStorage**. The **COleStreamFile** can be attached to an archive and **CObject::Serialize** called to load the data.

This is an advanced overridable.

For more information, see **IStorage** in the OLE documentation.

See Also: **COleStreamFile, CObject::Serialize, CArchive**

CRichEditView::OnParaAlign

> **void OnParaAlign(WORD** *wAlign* **);**

Parameters

wAlign   Desired paragraph alignment. One of the following values:

- **PFA_LEFT**   Align the paragraphs with the left margin.
- **PFA_RIGHT**   Align the paragraphs with the right margin.
- **PFA_CENTER**   Center the paragraphs between the margins.

Remarks

Call this function to change the paragraph alignment for the selected paragraphs.

See Also: **CRichEditView::OnUpdateParaAlign**

CRichEditView::OnPrinterChanged

virtual void OnPrinterChanged(const CDC& *dcPrinter* **);**

Parameters

dcPrinter   A **CDC** object for the new printer.

Remarks

Override this function to change characteristics for this rich edit view when the printer changes. The default implementation sets the paper size to the physical height and width for the output device (printer). If there is no device context associated wtih *dcPrinter*, the default implementation sets the paper size to 8.5 by 11 inches.

See Also: **CRichEditView::SetPaperSize, CRichEditView::WrapChanged**

CRichEditView::OnReplaceAll

virtual void OnReplaceAll(LPCTSTR *lpszFind*, **LPCTSTR** *lpszReplace*,
↪ **BOOL** *bCase*, **BOOL** *bWord* **);**

Parameters

lpszFind   The text to be replaced.

lpszReplace   The replacement text.

bCase   Indicates if the search is case sensitive.

bWord   Indicates if the search must select whole words or not.

Remarks

Called by the framework when processing **Replace All** commands from the **Replace** dialog box. Call this function to replace all occurrences of some given text with another string. Override this function to alter search characterics for this view.

See Also: **CRichEditView::OnReplaceSel, CRichEditView::OnFindNext**

CRichEditView::OnReplaceSel

virtual void OnReplaceSel(LPCTSTR *lpszFind*, **BOOL** *bNext*, **BOOL** *bCase*,
↪ **BOOL** *bWord*, **LPCTSTR** *lpszReplace* **);**

Parameters

lpszFind   The text to be replaced.

bNext   Indicates the direction of the search: **TRUE** is down; **FALSE**, up.

bCase   Indicates if the search is case sensitive.

bWord   Indicates if the search must select whole words or not.

lpszReplace   The replacement text.

Remarks

Called by the framework when processing **Replace** commands from the **Replace** dialog box. Call this function to replace one occurrence of some given text with another string. Override this function to alter search characterics for this view.

See Also: CRichEditView::OnReplaceAll

CRichEditView::OnTextNotFound

virtual void OnTextNotFound(LPCTSTR *lpszFind* **);**

Parameters

pszFind   The text which was not found.

Remarks

Called by the framework whenever a search fails. Override this function to change the output notification from a **MessageBeep**.

For more information, see **MessageBeep** in the Win32 documentation.

See Also: CRichEditView::FindText, **CRichEditView::FindTextSimple**, **CRichEditView::OnFindNext**

CRichEditView::OnUpdateCharEffect

void OnUpdateCharEffect(CCmdUI* *pCmdUI*, **DWORD** *dwMask*,
   ↪ DWORD *dwEffect* **);**

Parameters

pCmdUI   Pointer to a **CCmdUI** object.

dwMask   Indicates the character formatting mask.

dwEffect   Indicates the character formatting effect.

Remarks

The framework calls this function to update the command UI for character effect commands. The mask *dwMask* specifies which character formatting attributes to check. The flags *dwEffect* list the character formatting attributes to set/clear.

For more information on the *dwMask* and *dwEffect* parameters and their potential values, see the corresponding data members of **CHARFORMAT** in the Win32 documentation.

CRichEditView::OnUpdateParaAlign

void OnParaAlign(CCmdUI* *pCmdUI***, WORD** *wAlign* **);**

Parameters

pCmdUI   Pointer to a **CCmdUI** object.

wAlign   The paragraph alignment to check. One of the following values:

- **PFA_LEFT**   Align the paragraphs with the left margin.
- **PFA_RIGHT**   Align the paragraphs with the right margin.
- **PFA_CENTER**   Center the paragraphs between the margins.

Remarks

The framework calls this function to update the command UI for paragraph effect commands.

See Also: CRichEditView::GetParaFormatSelection, CRichEditView::OnParaAlign, CRichEditView::SetParaFormat

---

CRichEditView::PrintInsideRect

long PrintInsideRect(CDC* *pDC***, RECT&** *rectLayout***, long** *nIndexStart*,
↪ **long** *nIndexStop***, BOOL** *bOutput* **);**

Return Value

The index of the last character that fits in the output area plus one.

Parameters

pDC   Pointer to a device context for the output area.

rectLayout   **RECT** or **CRect** which defines the output area.

nIndexStart   Zero-based index of the first character to be formatted.

nIndexStop   Zero-based index of the last character to be formatted.

bOutput   Indicates if the text should be rendered. If **FALSE**, the text is just measured.

Remarks

Call this function to format a range of text in a rich edit control to fit within *rectLayout* for the device specified by *pDC*. Typically, this call is followed by a call to **CRichEditCtrl::DisplayBand** which generates the output.

CRichEditCtrl::FormatRange, CRichEditView::PrintPage, CRichEditCtrl::DisplayBand

CRichEditView::PrintPage

long PrintPage(CDC* *pDC***, long** *nIndexStart***, long** *nIndexStop* **);**

Return Value

The index of the last character that fits on the page plus one.

Parameters

pDC   Pointer to a device context for page output.

nIndexStart   Zero-based index of the first character to be formatted.

nIndexStop   Zero-based index of the last character to be formatted.

Remarks

Call this function to format a range of text in a rich edit control for the output device specified by *pDC*. The layout of each page is controlled by **GetPageRect** and **GetPrintRect**. Typically, this call is followed by a call to **CRichEditCtrl::DisplayBand** which generates the output.

Note that margins are relative to the physical page, not the logical page. Thus, margins of zero will often clip the text since many printers have unprintable areas on the page. To avoid clipping your text, you should call **SetMargins** and set reasonable margins before printing.

See Also: CRichEditView::PrintInsideRect, CRichEditView::GetPageRect, CRichEditView::GetPrintRect, CRichEditView::SetMargins

---

CRichEditView::QueryAcceptData

virtual HRESULT QueryAcceptData(LPDATAOBJECT *lpdataobj*,
→ **CLIPFORMAT FAR *** *lpcfFormat*, **DWORD** *dwReco*, **BOOL** *bReally*,
→ **HGLOBAL** *hMetaFile*);

Return Value

An **HRESULT** value reporting the success of the operation.

Parameters

lpdataobj   Pointer to the **IDataObject** to query.

lpcfFormat   Pointer to the acceptable data format.

dwReco   Not used.

bReally   Indicates if the paste operation should continue or not.

hMetaFile   A handle to the metafile used for drawing the item's icon.

Remarks

Called by the framework to paste an object into the rich edit. Override this function to handle different organization of OLE items in your derived document class. This is an advanced overridable.

For more information on **HRESULT** and **IDataObject**, see "Structure of OLE Error Codes" and **IDataObject**, respectively, in the OLE documentation.

CRichEditView::SetCharFormat

     void SetCharFormat(CHARFORMAT *cf* **);**

Parameters

    cf **CHARFORMAT** structure containing the new default character formatting attributes.

Remarks

Call this function to set the character formatting attributes for new text in this **CRichEditView** object. Only the attributes specified by the **dwMask** member of *cf* are changed by this function.

For more information, see **EM_SETCHARFORMAT** message and **CHARFORMAT** structure in the Win32 documentation.

    See Also: **CRichEditView::GetCharFormatSelection**, **CRichEditView::SetParaFormat**

CRichEditView::SetMargins

     void SetMargins(const CRect& *rectMargin* **);**

Parameters

    rectMargin The new margin values for printing, measured in **MM_TWIPS**.

Remarks

Call this function to set the printing margins for this rich edit view. If **m_nWordWrap** is **WrapToTargetDevice**, you should call **WrapChanged** after using this function to adjust printing characteristics.

Note that the margins used by **PrintPage** are relative to the physical page, not the logical page. Thus, margins of zero will often clip the text since many printers have unprintable areas on the page. To avoid clipping your text, you should call use **SetMargins** to set reasonable printer margins before printing.

See Also: **CRichEditView::GetMargins**, **CRichEditView::GetPrintWidth**, **CRichEditView::GetPrintRect**, **CRichEditView::GetPaperSize**, **CRichEditView::GetPageRect**, **CRichEditView::PrintPage**, **CRichEditView::WrapChanged**

CRichEditView::SetPaperSize

void SetPaperSize(CSize *sizePaper* **);**

Parameters

sizePaper   The new paper size values for printing, measured in **MM_TWIPS**.

Remarks

Call this function to set the paper size for printing this rich edit view. If **m_nWordWrap** is **WrapToTargetDevice**, you should call **WrapChanged** after using this function to adjust printing characteristics.

See Also: **CRichEditView::GetPaperSize**, **CRichEditView::GetMargins**, **CRichEditView::GetPrintWidth**, **CRichEditView::GetPrintRect**, **CRichEditView::GetPageRect**, **CRichEditView::PrintPage**, **CRichEditView::WrapChanged**

CRichEditView::SetParaFormat

void SetParaFormat(PARAFORMAT& *pf* **);**

Parameters

pf   **PARAFORMAT** structure containing the new default paragraph formatting attributes.

Remarks

Call this function to set the paragraph formatting attributes for the current selection in this **CRichEditView** object. Only the attributes specified by the **dwMask** member of *pf* are changed by this function.

For more information, see **EM_SETPARAFORMAT** message and **PARAFORMAT** structure in the Win32 documentation.

See Also: **CRichEditView::GetParaFormatSelection**, **CRichEditView::SetCharFormat**

CRichEditView::WrapChanged

virtual void WrapChanged( );

Remarks

Call this function when the printing characteristics have changed (**SetMargins** or **SetPaperSize**).

Override this function to modify the way the rich edit view responds to changes in **m_nWordWrap** or the printing characteristics (**OnPrinterChanged**).

See Also: **CRichEditView::m_nWordWrap**, **CRichEditView::OnPrinterChanged**, **CRichEditView::SetMargins**, **CRichEditView::SetPaperSize**

Data Members
CRichEditView::m_nBulletIndent

Remarks

The indentation for bullet items in a list; by default, 720 units, which is 1/2 inch.

CRichEditView::m_nWordWrap

Remarks

Indicates the type of word wrap for this rich edit view. One of the following values:

- **WrapNone**   Indicates no automatic word wrapping.
- **WrapToWindow**   Indicates word wrapping based on the width of the window.
- **WrapToTargetDevice**   Indicates word wrapping based on the characteristics of the target device.

See Also: **CRichEditView::WrapChanged**

CRuntimeClass

CRuntimeClass does not have a base class.

Each class derived from **CObject** is associated with a **CRuntimeClass** structure that you can use to obtain information about an object or its base class at run time. The ability to determine the class of an object at run time is useful when extra type checking of function arguments is needed, or when you must write special-purpose code based on the class of an object. Run-time class information is not supported directly by the C++ language.

The structure has the following members:

LPCSTR m_lpszClassName   A null-terminated string containing the ASCII class name.

int m_nObjectSize   The size of the object, in bytes. If the object has data members that point to allocated memory, the size of that memory is not included.

UINT m_wSchema   The schema number (–1 for nonserializable classes). See the **IMPLEMENT_SERIAL** macro for a description of the schema number.

CObject* (PASCAL* m_pfnCreateObject)( )   A function pointer to the default constructor that creates an object of your class (valid only if the class supports dynamic creation; otherwise, returns **NULL**).

CRuntimeClass* (PASCAL* m_pfn_GetBaseClass)( )   If your application is dynamically linked to the AFXDLL version of MFC, a pointer to a function that returns the **CRuntimeClass** structure of the base class.

CRuntimeClass* m_pBaseClass   If your application is statically linked to MFC, a pointer to the **CRuntimeClass** structure of the base class.

Feature Only in Professional and Enterprise Editions   Static linking to MFC is supported only in Visual C++ Professional and Enterprise Editions. For more information, see Visual C++ Editions online.

CObject* CreateObject( );   Classes derived from **CObject** can support dynamic creation, which is the ability to create an object of a specified class at run time. Document, view, and frame classes, for example, should support dynamic creation. The **CreateObject** member function can be used to implement this function and create objects for these classes during run time. For more information on dynamic creation and the **CreateObject** member, see "CObject Class Topics" and "CObject Class: Specifying Levels of Functionality" in *Visual C++ Programmer's Guide* online.

BOOL IsDerivedFrom(const CRuntimeClass* pBaseClass) const;   Returns **TRUE** if the class of the class member calling **IsDerivedFrom** is derived from the base class whose **CRuntimeClass** structure is given as a parameter. **IsDerivedFrom** walks from the member's class up the chain of derived classes all the way to the top and returns **FALSE** only if no match is found for the base class.

Note To use the **CRuntimeClass** structure, you must include the **IMPLEMENT_DYNAMIC**, **IMPLEMENT_DYNCREATE**, or **IMPLEMENT_SERIAL** macro in the implementation of the class for which you want to retrieve run-time object information.

For more information on using **CRuntimeClass**, see the article "CObject Class: Accessing Run-Time Class Information" in *Visual C++ Programmer's Guide* online.

See Also: **CObject::GetRuntimeClass, CObject::IsKindOf, RUNTIME_CLASS, IMPLEMENT_DYNAMIC, IMPLEMENT_DYNCREATE, IMPLEMENT_SERIAL**

CScrollBar

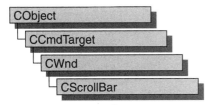

The **CScrollBar** class provides the functionality of a Windows scroll-bar control.

You create a scroll-bar control in two steps. First, call the constructor **CScrollBar** to construct the **CScrollBar** object, then call the **Create** member function to create the Windows scroll-bar control and attach it to the **CScrollBar** object.

If you create a **CScrollBar** object within a dialog box (through a dialog resource), the **CScrollBar** is automatically destroyed when the user closes the dialog box.

If you create a **CScrollBar** object within a window, you may also need to destroy it.

If you create the **CScrollBar** object on the stack, it is destroyed automatically. If you create the **CScrollBar** object on the heap by using the **new** function, you must call **delete** on the object to destroy it when the user terminates the Windows scroll bar.

If you allocate any memory in the **CScrollBar** object, override the **CScrollBar** destructor to dispose of the allocations.

For related information about using **CScrollBar**, see "Control Topics" in *Visual C++ Programmer's Guide* online.

#include <afxwin.h>

See Also: **CWnd, CButton, CComboBox, CEdit, CListBox, CStatic, CDialog**

CScrollBar Class Members

Construction

CScrollBar	Constructs a **CScrollBar** object.

Initialization

Create	Creates the Windows scroll bar and attaches it to the **CScrollBar** object.

Operations

GetScrollPos	Retrieves the current position of a scroll box.
SetScrollPos	Sets the current position of a scroll box.
GetScrollRange	Retrieves the current minimum and maximum scroll-bar positions for the given scroll bar.
SetScrollRange	Sets minimum and maximum position values for the given scroll bar.
ShowScrollBar	Shows or hides a scroll bar.
EnableScrollBar	Enables or disables one or both arrows of a scroll bar.
SetScrollInfo	Sets information about the scroll bar.
GetScrollInfo	Retrieves information about the scroll bar.
GetScrollLimit	Retrieves the limit of the scroll bar

Member Functions

CScrollBar::Create

BOOL Create(DWORD *dwStyle*, **const RECT&** *rect*, **CWnd*** *pParentWnd*, **UINT** *nID* **);**

Return Value

Nonzero if successful; otherwise 0.

Parameters

dwStyle   Specifies the scroll bar's style. Apply any combination of scroll-bar styles to the scroll bar.

rect   Specifies the scroll bar's size and position. Can be either a **RECT** structure or a **CRect** object.

pParentWnd   Specifies the scroll bar's parent window, usually a **CDialog** object. It must not be **NULL**.

nID   The scroll bar's control ID.

Remarks

You construct a **CScrollBar** object in two steps. First call the constructor, which constructs the **CScrollBar** object; then call **Create**, which creates and initializes the associated Windows scroll bar and attaches it to the **CScrollBar** object.

Apply the following window styles to a scroll bar:

- **WS_CHILD**   Always
- **WS_VISIBLE**   Usually
- **WS_DISABLED**   Rarely
- **WS_GROUP**   To group controls

See Also: **CScrollBar::CScrollBar**

CScrollBar::CScrollBar

CScrollBar( );

Remarks

Constructs a **CScrollBar** object. After constructing the object, call the **Create** member function to create and initialize the Windows scroll bar.

See Also: **CScrollBar::Create**

CScrollBar::EnableScrollBar

BOOL EnableScrollBar(UINT *nArrowFlags* **= ESB_ENABLE_BOTH);**

Return Value

Nonzero if the arrows are enabled or disabled as specified; otherwise 0, which indicates that the arrows are already in the requested state or that an error occurred.

Parameters

nArrowFlags   Specifies whether the scroll arrows are enabled or disabled and which arrows are enabled or disabled. This parameter can be one of the following values:

- **ESB_ENABLE_BOTH**   Enables both arrows of a scroll bar.

- **ESB_DISABLE_LTUP**   Disables the left arrow of a horizontal scroll bar or the up arrow of a vertical scroll bar.

- **ESB_DISABLE_RTDN**   Disables the right arrow of a horizontal scroll bar or the down arrow of a vertical scroll bar.

- **ESB_DISABLE_BOTH**   Disables both arrows of a scroll bar.

Remarks

Enables or disables one or both arrows of a scroll bar.

See Also: **CWnd::EnableScrollBar**, **::EnableScrollBar**

CScrollBar::GetScrollInfo

BOOL GetScrollInfo(LPSCROLLINFO *lpScrollInfo*, **UINT** *nMask* **);**

Return Value

If the message retrieved any values, the return is **TRUE**. Otherwise, it is **FALSE**.

Parameters

lpScrollInfo A pointer to a **SCROLLINFO** structure. See the *Win32 Programmer's Reference* for more information about this structure.

nMask Specifies the scroll bar parameters to retrieve. Typical usage, SIF_ALL, specifies a combination of SIF_PAGE, SIF_POS, SIF_TRACKPOS, and SIF_RANGE. See **SCROLLINFO** for more information on the nMask values.

Remarks

Call this member function to retrieve the information that the **SCROLLINFO** structure maintains about a scroll bar. **GetScrollInfo** enables applications to use 32-bit scroll positions.

The **SCROLLINFO** structure contains information about a scroll bar, including the minimum and maximum scrolling positions, the page size, and the position of the scroll box (the thumb). See the **SCROLLINFO** structure topic in the *Win32 SDK Programmer's Reference* for more information about changing the structure defaults.

The MFC Windows message handlers that indicate scroll bar position, **CWnd::OnHScroll** and **CWnd::OnVScroll**, provide only 16 bits of position data. **GetScrollInfo** and **SetScrollInfo** provide 32 bits of scroll bar position data. Thus, an application can call **GetScrollInfo** while processing either **CWnd::OnHScroll** or **CWnd::OnVScroll** to obtain 32-bit scroll bar position data.

See Also: **CScrollBar::SetScrollInfo, CWnd::SetScrollInfo, CWnd::SetScrollPos, CWnd::OnVScroll, CWnd::OnHScroll, SCROLLINFO**

CScrollBar::GetScrollLimit

int GetScrollLimit( );

Return Value

Specifies the maximum position of a scroll bar if successful; otherwise 0.

Remarks

Call this member function to retrieve the maximum scrolling position of the scroll bar.

See Also: **CWnd::GetScrollLimit**

CScrollBar::GetScrollPos

int GetScrollPos( ) const;

Return Value

Specifies the current position of the scroll box if successful; otherwise 0.

Remarks

Retrieves the current position of a scroll box. The current position is a relative value that depends on the current scrolling range. For example, if the scrolling range is 100 to 200 and the scroll box is in the middle of the bar, the current position is 150.

See Also: **CScrollBar::SetScrollPos, CScrollBar::GetScrollRange, CScrollBar::SetScrollRange, ::GetScrollPos**

CScrollBar::GetScrollRange

void GetScrollRange(LPINT *lpMinPos***, LPINT** *lpMaxPos* **) const;**

Parameters

lpMinPos   Points to the integer variable that is to receive the minimum position.

lpMaxPos   Points to the integer variable that is to receive the maximum position.

Remarks

Copies the current minimum and maximum scroll-bar positions for the given scroll bar to the locations specified by *lpMinPos* and *lpMaxPos*.

The default range for a scroll-bar control is empty (both values are 0).

See Also: **::GetScrollRange, CScrollBar::SetScrollRange, CScrollBar::GetScrollPos, CScrollBar::SetScrollPos**

CScrollBar::SetScrollInfo

BOOL SetScrollInfo(LPSCROLLINFO *lpScrollInfo***, BOOL** *bRedraw* **= TRUE);**

Return Value

If successful, the return is **TRUE**. Otherwise, it is **FALSE**.

Parameters

lpScrollInfo   A pointer to a **SCROLLINFO** structure.

bRedraw   Specifies whether the scroll bar should be redrawn to reflect the new information. If *bRedraw* is **TRUE**, the scroll bar is redrawn. If it is **FALSE**, it is not redrawn. The scroll bar is redrawn by default.

Remarks

Call this member function to set the information that the **SCROLLINFO** structure maintains about a scroll bar. You must provide the values required by the **SCROLLINFO** structure parameters, including the flag values.

The **SCROLLINFO** structure contains information about a scroll bar, including the minimum and maximum scrolling positions, the page size, and the position of the scroll box (the thumb). See the **SCROLLINFO** structure topic in the *Win32 SDK Programmer's Reference* for more information about changing the structure defaults.

See Also: **CScrollBar::GetScrollInfo, CWnd::SetScrollInfo,
CWnd::SetScrollPos, CWnd::OnVScroll, CWnd::OnHScroll,
CWnd::GetScrollInfo, SCROLLINFO**

CScrollBar::SetScrollPos

int SetScrollPos(int *nPos***, BOOL** *bRedraw* **= TRUE);**

Return Value

Specifies the previous position of the scroll box if successful; otherwise 0.

Parameters

nPos   Specifies the new position for the scroll box. It must be within the scrolling range.

bRedraw   Specifies whether the scroll bar should be redrawn to reflect the new position. If *bRedraw* is **TRUE**, the scroll bar is redrawn. If it is **FALSE**, it is not redrawn. The scroll bar is redrawn by default.

Remarks

Sets the current position of a scroll box to that specified by *nPos* and, if specified, redraws the scroll bar to reflect the new position.

Set *bRedraw* to **FALSE** whenever the scroll bar will be redrawn by a subsequent call to another function to avoid having the scroll bar redrawn twice within a short interval.

See Also: **CScrollBar::GetScrollPos, CScrollBar::GetScrollRange,
CScrollBar::SetScrollRange, ::SetScrollPos**

CScrollBar::SetScrollRange

void SetScrollRange(int *nMinPos***, int** *nMaxPos***, BOOL** *bRedraw* **= TRUE);**

Parameters

nMinPos   Specifies the minimum scrolling position.

nMaxPos   Specifies the maximum scrolling position.

bRedraw   Specifies whether the scroll bar should be redrawn to reflect the change. If *bRedraw* is **TRUE**, the scroll bar is redrawn; if **FALSE**, it is not redrawn. It is redrawn by default.

Remarks

Sets minimum and maximum position values for the given scroll bar. Set *nMinPos* and *nMaxPos* to 0 to hide standard scroll bars.

Do not call this function to hide a scroll bar while processing a scroll-bar notification message.

If a call to **SetScrollRange** immediately follows a call to the **SetScrollPos** member function, set *bRedraw* in **SetScrollPos** to 0 to prevent the scroll bar from being redrawn twice.

The difference between the values specified by *nMinPos* and *nMaxPos* must not be greater than 32,767. The default range for a scroll-bar control is empty (both *nMinPos* and *nMaxPos* are 0).

See Also: **CScrollBar::GetScrollPos, CScrollBar::SetScrollPos, CScrollBar::GetScrollRange, ::SetScrollRange**

CScrollBar::ShowScrollBar

void ShowScrollBar(BOOL *bShow* **= TRUE);**

Parameters

bShow   Specifies whether the scroll bar is shown or hidden. If this parameter is **TRUE**, the scroll bar is shown; otherwise it is hidden.

Remarks

Shows or hides a scroll bar.

An application should not call this function to hide a scroll bar while processing a scroll-bar notification message.

See Also: **CScrollBar::GetScrollPos, CScrollBar::GetScrollRange, CWnd::ScrollWindow, CScrollBar::SetScrollPos, CScrollBar::SetScrollRange**

CScrollView

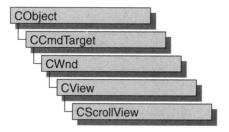

The **CScrollView** class is a **CView** with scrolling capabilities.

You can handle standard scrolling yourself in any class derived from **CView** by overriding the message-mapped **OnHScroll** and **OnVScroll** member functions. But **CScrollView** adds the following features to its **CView** capabilities:

- It manages window and viewport sizes and mapping modes.

- It scrolls automatically in response to scroll-bar messages.

- It scrolls automatically in response to messages from the keyboard, a non-scrolling mouse, or the IntelliMouse wheel.

You can handle mouse wheel scrolling yourself by overriding the message-mapped **OnMouseWheel** and **OnRegisteredMouseWheel** member functions. As they are for **CScrollView**, these member functions support the recommended behaviour for **WM_MOUSEWHEEL**, the wheel rotation message.

To take advantage of automatic scrolling, derive your view class from **CScrollView** instead of from **CView**. When the view is first created, if you want to calculate the size of the scrollable view based on the size of the document, call the **SetScrollSizes** member function from your override of either **CView::OnInitialUpdate** or **CView::OnUpdate**. (You must write your own code to query the size of the document. For an example, see "Enhancing Views" in *Visual C++ Tutorials* online.)

The call to the **SetScrollSizes** member function sets the view's mapping mode, the total dimensions of the scroll view, and the amounts to scroll horizontally and vertically. All sizes are in logical units. The logical size of the view is usually calculated from data stored in the document, but in some cases you may want to specify a fixed size. For examples of both approaches, see **CScrollView::SetScrollSizes**.

You specify the amounts to scroll horizontally and vertically in logical units. By default, if the user clicks a scroll bar shaft outside of the scroll box, **CScrollView** scrolls a "page." If the user clicks a scroll arrow at either end of a scroll bar, **CScrollView** scrolls a "line." By default, a page is 1/10 of the total size of the view; a line is 1/10 of the page size. Override these default values by passing custom sizes in the **SetScrollSizes** member function. For example, you might set the horizontal size to some fraction of the width of the total size and the vertical size to the height of a line in the current font.

Instead of scrolling, **CScrollView** can automatically scale the view to the current window size. In this mode, the view has no scroll bars and the logical view is stretched or shrunk to exactly fit the window's client area. To use this scale-to-fit capability, call **CScrollView::SetScaleToFitSize**. (Call either **SetScaleToFitSize** or **SetScrollSizes**, but not both.)

Before the OnDraw member function of your derived view class is called, **CScrollView** automatically adjusts the viewport origin for the **CPaintDC** device-context object that it passes to OnDraw.

To adjust the viewport origin for the scrolling window, **CScrollView** overrides **CView::OnPrepareDC**. This adjustment is automatic for the **CPaintDC** device context that **CScrollView** passes to OnDraw, but you must call **CScrollView::OnPrepareDC** yourself for any other device contexts you use, such as a **CClientDC**. You can override **CScrollView::OnPrepareDC** to set the pen, background color, and other drawing attributes, but call the base class to do scaling.

Scroll bars can appear in three places relative to a view, as shown in the following cases:

- Standard window-style scroll bars can be set for the view using the **WS_HSCROLL** and **WS_VSCROLL** styles.

- Scroll-bar controls can also be added to the frame containing the view, in which case the framework forwards **WM_HSCROLL** and **WM_VSCROLL** messages from the frame window to the currently active view.

- The framework also forwards scroll messages from a **CSplitterWnd** splitter control to the currently active splitter pane (a view). When placed in a **CSplitterWnd** with shared scroll bars, a **CScrollView** object will use the shared ones rather than creating its own.

For more information on using **CScrollView**, see "Document/View Architecture Topics" and "Derived View Classes" in *Visual C++ Programmer's Guide* online.

#include <afxwin.h>

See Also: **CView, CSplitterWnd**

CScrollView Class Members

Operations

FillOutsideRect	Fills the area of a view outside the scrolling area.
GetDeviceScrollPosition	Gets the current scroll position in device units.
GetDeviceScrollSizes	Gets the current mapping mode, the total size, and the line and page sizes of the scrollable view. Sizes are in device units.
GetScrollPosition	Gets the current scroll position in logical units.
GetTotalSize	Gets the total size of the scroll view in logical units.
ResizeParentToFit	Causes the size of the view to dictate the size of its frame.
ScrollToPosition	Scrolls the view to a given point, specified in logical units.
SetScaleToFitSize	Puts the scroll view into scale-to-fit mode.
SetScrollSizes	Sets the scroll view's mapping mode, total size, and horizontal and vertical scroll amounts.

Construction

CScrollView	Constructs a **CScrollView** object.

Member Functions

CScrollView::CScrollView

> **CScrollView( );**

Remarks

Constructs a **CScrollView** object. You must call either **SetScrollSizes** or **SetScaleToFitSize** before the scroll view is usable.

See Also: **CScrollView::SetScrollSizes, CScrollView::SetScaleToFitSize**

CScrollView::FillOutsideRect

> **void FillOutsideRect(CDC*** *pDC***, CBrush*** *pBrush* **);**

Parameters

pDC   Device context in which the filling is to be done.

pBrush   Brush with which the area is to be filled.

Remarks

Call **FillOutsideRect** to fill the area of the view that appears outside of the scrolling area. Use **FillOutsideRect** in your scroll view's **OnEraseBkgnd** handler function to prevent excessive background repainting.

Example

```
BOOL CScaleView::OnEraseBkgnd( CDC* pDC )
{
    CBrush br( GetSysColor( COLOR_WINDOW ) );
    FillOutsideRect( pDC, &br );
    return TRUE;                    // Erased
}
```

See Also: CWnd::OnEraseBkgnd

CScrollView::GetDeviceScrollPosition

CPoint GetDeviceScrollPosition( ) const;

Return Value

The horizontal and vertical positions (in device units) of the scroll boxes as a **CPoint** object.

Remarks

Call **GetDeviceScrollPosition** when you need the current horizontal and vertical positions of the scroll boxes in the scroll bars. This coordinate pair corresponds to the location in the document to which the upper-left corner of the view has been scrolled. This is useful for offsetting mouse-device positions to scroll-view device positions.

GetDeviceScrollPosition returns values in device units. If you want logical units, use **GetScrollPosition** instead.

See Also: CScrollView::GetScrollPosition

CScrollView::GetDeviceScrollSizes

void GetDeviceScrollSizes(int& *nMapMode***, SIZE&** *sizeTotal***, SIZE&** *sizePage***,**
↪ SIZE& *sizeLine* **) const;**

Parameters

nMapMode   Returns the current mapping mode for this view. For a list of possible values, see **SetScrollSizes**.

sizeTotal   Returns the current total size of the scroll view in device units.

sizePage   Returns the current horizontal and vertical amounts to scroll in each direction in response to a mouse click in a scroll-bar shaft. The **cx** member contains the horizontal amount. The **cy** member contains the vertical amount.

sizeLine   Returns the current horizontal and vertical amounts to scroll in each direction in response to a mouse click in a scroll arrow. The **cx** member contains the horizontal amount. The **cy** member contains the vertical amount.

Remarks

GetDeviceScrollSizes gets the current mapping mode, the total size, and the line and page sizes of the scrollable view. Sizes are in device units. This member function is rarely called.

See Also: **CScrollView::SetScrollSizes**, **CScrollView::GetTotalSize**

CScrollView::GetScrollPosition

CPoint GetScrollPosition( ) const;

Return Value

The horizontal and vertical positions (in logical units) of the scroll boxes as a **CPoint** object.

Remarks

Call **GetScrollPosition** when you need the current horizontal and vertical positions of the scroll boxes in the scroll bars. This coordinate pair corresponds to the location in the document to which the upper-left corner of the view has been scrolled.

GetScrollPosition returns values in logical units. If you want device units, use **GetDeviceScrollPosition** instead.

See Also: **CScrollView::GetDeviceScrollPosition**

CScrollView::GetTotalSize

CSize GetTotalSize( ) const;

Return Value

The total size of the scroll view in logical units. The horizontal size is in the **cx** member of the **CSize** return value. The vertical size is in the **cy** member.

Remarks

Call **GetTotalSize** to retrieve the current horizontal and vertical sizes of the scroll view.

See Also: **CScrollView::GetDeviceScrollSizes**, **CScrollView::SetScrollSizes**

CScrollView::ResizeParentToFit

void ResizeParentToFit(BOOL *bShrinkOnly* **= TRUE);**

Parameters

bShrinkOnly   The kind of resizing to perform. The default value, **TRUE**, shrinks the frame window if appropriate. Scroll bars will still appear for large views or small frame windows. A value of **FALSE** causes the view always to resize the frame window exactly. This can be somewhat dangerous since the frame window could get too big to fit inside the multiple document interface (MDI) frame window or the screen.

Remarks

Call **ResizeParentToFit** to let the size of your view dictate the size of its frame window. This is recommended only for views in MDI child frame windows. Use **ResizeParentToFit** in the **OnInitialUpdate** handler function of your derived **CScrollView** class. For an example of this member function, see **CScrollView::SetScrollSizes**.

ResizeParentToFit assumes that the size of the view window has been set. If the view window size has not been set when **ResizeParentToFit** is called, you will get an assertion. To ensure that this does not happen, make the following call before calling **ResizeParentToFit**:

```
GetParentFrame()->RecalcLayout();
```

See Also: **CView::OnInitialUpdate**, **CScrollView::SetScrollSizes**

CScrollView::ScrollToPosition

void ScrollToPosition(POINT *pt* **);**

Parameters

pt   The point to scroll to, in logical units. The **cx** member must be a positive value (greater than or equal to 0, up to the total size of the view). The same is true for the **cy** member when the mapping mode is **MM_TEXT**. The **cy** member is negative in mapping modes other than **MM_TEXT**.

Remarks

Call **ScrollToPosition** to scroll to a given point in the view. The view will be scrolled so that this point is at the upper-left corner of the window. This member function must not be called if the view is scaled to fit.

See Also: **CScrollView::GetDeviceScrollPosition**, **CScrollView::SetScaleToFitSize**, **CScrollView::SetScrollSizes**

CScrollView::SetScaleToFitSize

> **void SetScaleToFitSize(SIZE** *sizeTotal* **);**

Parameters

sizeTotal   The horizontal and vertical sizes to which the view is to be scaled. The scroll view's size is measured in logical units. The horizontal size is contained in the **cx** member. The vertical size is contained in the **cy** member. Both **cx** and **cy** must be greater than or equal to 0.

Remarks

Call **SetScaleToFitSize** when you want to scale the viewport size to the current window size automatically. With scroll bars, only a portion of the logical view may be visible at any time. But with the scale-to-fit capability, the view has no scroll bars and the logical view is stretched or shrunk to exactly fit the window's client area. When the window is resized, the view draws its data at a new scale based on the size of the window.

You'll typically place the call to **SetScaleToFitSize** in your override of the view's **OnInitialUpdate** member function. If you do not want automatic scaling, call the **SetScrollSizes** member function instead.

SetScaleToFitSize can be used to implement a "Zoom to Fit" operation. Use **SetScrollSizes** to reinitialize scrolling.

SetScaleToFitSize assumes that the size of the view window has been set. If the view window size has not been set when **SetScaleToFitSize** is called, you will get an assertion. To ensure that this does not happen, make the following call before calling **SetScaleToFitSize**:

```
GetParentFrame()->RecalcLayout();
```

See Also: **CScrollView::SetScrollSizes**, **CView::OnInitialUpdate**

CScrollView::SetScrollSizes

> **void SetScrollSizes(int** *nMapMode*, **SIZE** *sizeTotal*, **const SIZE&** *sizePage* = **sizeDefault**,
> ↳ **const SIZE&** *sizeLine* = **sizeDefault**);

Parameters

nMapMode   The mapping mode to set for this view. Possible values include:

Mapping Mode	Logical Unit	Positive y-axis Extends...
MM_TEXT	1 pixel	Downward
MM_HIMETRIC	0.01 mm	Upward
MM_TWIPS	1/1440 in	Upward
MM_HIENGLISH	0.001 in	Upward

(continued)

Mapping Mode	Logical Unit	Positive y-axis Extends...
MM_LOMETRIC	0.1 mm	Upward
MM_LOENGLISH	0.01 in	Upward

All of these modes are defined by Windows. Two standard mapping modes, **MM_ISOTROPIC** and **MM_ANISOTROPIC**, are not used for **CScrollView**. The class library provides the **SetScaleToFitSize** member function for scaling the view to window size. Column three in the table above describes the coordinate orientation.

sizeTotal   The total size of the scroll view. The **cx** member contains the horizontal extent. The **cy** member contains the vertical extent. Sizes are in logical units. Both **cx** and **cy** must be greater than or equal to 0.

sizePage   The horizontal and vertical amounts to scroll in each direction in response to a mouse click in a scroll-bar shaft. The **cx** member contains the horizontal amount. The **cy** member contains the vertical amount.

sizeLine   The horizontal and vertical amounts to scroll in each direction in response to a mouse click in a scroll arrow. The **cx** member contains the horizontal amount. The **cy** member contains the vertical amount.

Remarks

Call **SetScrollSizes** when the view is about to be updated. Call it in your override of the **OnUpdate** member function to adjust scrolling characteristics when, for example, the document is initially displayed or when it changes size.

You will typically obtain size information from the view's associated document by calling a document member function, perhaps called GetMyDocSize, that you supply with your derived document class. The following code shows this approach:

```
SetScrollSizes( nMapMode, GetDocument( )->GetMyDocSize( ) );
```

Alternatively, you might sometimes need to set a fixed size, as in the following code:

```
SetScrollSizes( nMapMode, CSize(100, 100) );
```

You must set the mapping mode to any of the Windows mapping modes except **MM_ISOTROPIC** or **MM_ANISOTROPIC**. If you want to use an unconstrained mapping mode, call the **SetScaleToFitSize** member function instead of **SetScrollSizes**.

Example

```
void CScaleView::OnUpdate( )
{
    // ...
    // Implement a GetDocSize( ) member function in
    // your document class; it returns a CSize.
    SetScrollSizes( MM_LOENGLISH, GetDocument( )->GetDocSize( ) );
    ResizeParentToFit( );   // Default bShrinkOnly argument
    // ...
}
```

See Also: **CScrollView::SetScaleToFitSize, CScrollView::GetDeviceScrollSizes, CScrollView::GetTotalSize**

CSemaphore

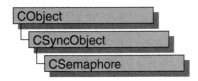

An object of class **CSemaphore** represents a "semaphore" — a synchronization object that allows a limited number of threads in one or more processes to access a resource. A **CSemaphore** object maintains a count of the number of threads currently accessing a specified resource.

Semaphores are useful in controlling access to a shared resource that can only support a limited number of users. The current count of the **CSemaphore** object is the number of additional users allowed. When the count reaches zero, all attempts to use the resource controlled by the **CSemaphore** object will be inserted into a system queue and wait until they either time out or the count rises above 0. The maximum number of users who can access the controlled resource at one time is specified during construction of the **CSemaphore** object.

To use a **CSemaphore** object, construct the **CSemaphore** object when it is needed. Specify the name of the semaphore you wish to wait on, and that your application should initially own it. You can then access the semaphore when the constructor returns. Call **CSyncObject::Unlock** when you are done accessing the controlled resource.

An alternative method for using **CSemaphore** objects is to add a variable of type **CSemaphore** as a data member to the class you wish to control. During construction of the controlled object, call the constructor of the **CSemaphore** data member specifying the initial access count, maximum access count, name of the semaphore (if it will be used across process boundaries), and desired security attributes.

To access resources contolled by **CSemaphore** objects in this manner, first create a variable of either type **CSingleLock** or type **CMultiLock** in your resource's access member function. Then call the lock object's **Lock** member function (for example, **CSingleLock::Lock**). At this point, your thread will either gain access to the resource, wait for the resource to be released and gain access, or wait for the resource to be released and time out, failing to gain access to the resource. In any case, your resource has been accessed in a thread-safe manner. To release the resource, use the lock object's **Unlock** member function (for example, **CSingleLock::Unlock**), or allow the lock object to fall out of scope.

Alternatively, you can create a **CSemaphore** object stand-alone, and access it explicitly before attempting to access the controlled resource. This method, while clearer to someone reading your source code, is more prone to error.

For more information on how to use **CSemaphore** objects, see the article "Multithreading: How to Use the Synchronization Classes" in *Visual C++ Programmer's Guide* online.

#include <afxmt.h>

CSemaphore Class Members

Construction

CSemaphore   Constructs a **CSemaphore** object.

Member Functions

CSemaphore::CSemaphore

CSemaphore(LONG *lInitialCount* = **1, LONG** *lMaxCount* = **1,**
 ↪ **LPCTSTR** *pstrName* = **NULL,**
 ↪ **LPSECURITY_ATTRIBUTES** *lpsaAttributes* = **NULL);**

Parameters

lInitialCount   The initial usage count for the semaphore. Must be greater than or equal to 0, and less than or equal to *lMaxCount*.

lMaxCount   The maximum usage count for the semaphore. Must be greater than 0.

pstrName   The name of the semaphore. Must be supplied if the semaphore will be accessed across process boundaries. If **NULL,** the object will be unnamed. If the name matches an existing semaphore, the constructor builds a new **CSemaphore** object which references the semaphore of that name. If the name matches an existing synchronization object that is not a semaphore, the construction will fail.

lpsaAttributes   Security attributes for the semaphore object. For a full description of this structure, see **SECURITY_ATTRIBUTES** in the *Win32 Programmer's Reference*.

Remarks

Constructs a named or unnamed **CSemaphore** object. To access or release a **CSemaphore** object, create a **CMultiLock** or **CSingleLock** object and call its **Lock** and **Unlock** member functions.

See Also: **CMutex, CEvent, CMultiLock, CSingleLock**

CSharedFile

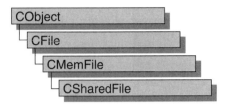

CSharedFile is the **CMemFile**-derived class that supports shared memory files. Memory files behave like disk files except that the file is stored in RAM rather than on disk. A memory file is useful for fast temporary storage or for transferring raw bytes or serialized objects between independent processes.

Shared memory files differ from other memory files in that memory for them is allocated with the **GlobalAlloc** Windows function. The **CSharedFile** class stores data in a globally allocated memory block (created using **GlobalAlloc**), and this memory block can be shared using DDE, the Clipboard, or other OLE/COM uniform data transfer operations, for example, using **IDataObject**.

GlobalAlloc returns an **HGLOBAL** handle rather than a pointer to memory, such as the pointer returned by **malloc**. The **HGLOBAL** handle is needed in certain applications. For example, to put data on the Clipboard you need an **HGLOBAL** handle.

Please note that **CSharedFile** does not use memory-mapped files, and the data cannot be directly shared between processes.

CSharedFile objects can automatically allocate their own memory or you can attach your own memory block to the **CSharedFile** object by calling **CSharedFile::SetHandle**. In either case, memory for growing the memory file automatically is allocated in *nGrowBytes*-sized increments if *nGrowBytes* is not zero.

For more information, see the article "Files in MFC" in the *Visual C++ Programmer's Guide* online and "File Handling" in the *Run-Time Library Reference*.

#include <afxadv.h>

See Also: **CMemFile**, **GlobalAlloc**, **GlobalFree**, **GlobalReallocss**

CSharedFile Class Members

Construction

CSharedFile	Constructs a **CSharedFile** object.

Operations

Detach	Closes the shared memory file and returns the handle of its memory block.
SetHandle	Attaches the shared memory file to a memory block.

Member Functions
CSharedFile::CSharedFile

CSharedFile(UINT *nAllocFlags* **= GMEM_DDESHARE | GMEM_MOVEABLE,**
↪ **UINT** *nGrowBytes* **= 4096);**

Parameters

nAllocFlags   Flags indicating how memory is to be allocated. See **GlobalAlloc** for a list of valid flag values.

nGrowBytes   The memory allocation increment in bytes.

Remarks

Constructs a **CSharedFile** object and allocates memory for it.

See Also: CSharedFile::Detach CSharedFile::SetHandle

CSharedFile::Detach

HGLOBAL Detach( );

Return Value

The handle of the memory block that contains the contents of the memory file.

Remarks

Call this function to close the memory file and detach it from the memory block. You can reopen it by calling **SetHandle**, using the handle returned by **Detach**.

See Also: CSharedFile::CSharedFile, CSharedFile::SetHandle

CSharedFile::SetHandle

void SetHandle(HGLOBAL *hGlobalMemory*, **BOOL** *bAllowGrow* **= TRUE);**

Parameters

hGlobalMemory   Handle to the global memory to be attached to the **CSharedFile**.

bAllowGrow   Specifies whether the memory block is allowed to grow.

Remarks

Call this function to attach a block of global memory to the **CSharedFile** object. If *bAllowGrow* is nonzero, the size of the memory block is increased as necessary, for example, if an attempt is made to write more bytes to the file than were allocated for the memory block.

See Also: **CSharedFile::CSharedFile**, **CSharedFile::Detach**

CSingleDocTemplate

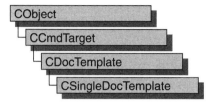

The **CSingleDocTemplate** class defines a document template that implements the single document interface (SDI). An SDI application uses the main frame window to display a document; only one document can be open at a time.

A document template defines the relationship between three types of classes:

- A document class, which you derive from **CDocument**.

- A view class, which displays data from the document class listed above. You can derive this class from **CView**, **CScrollView**, **CFormView**, or **CEditView**. (You can also use **CEditView** directly.)

- A frame window class, which contains the view. For an SDI document template, you can derive this class from **CFrameWnd**; if you do not need to customize the behavior of the main frame window, you can use **CFrameWnd** directly without deriving your own class.

An SDI application typically supports one type of document, so it has only one **CSingleDocTemplate** object. Only one document can be open at a time.

You don't need to call any member functions of **CSingleDocTemplate** except the constructor. The framework handles **CSingleDocTemplate** objects internally.

For more information on using **CSingleDocTemplate**, see "Document Templates and the Document/View Creation Process" in *Visual C++ Programmer's Guide* online.

See Also: **CDocTemplate**, **CDocument**, **CFrameWnd**, **CMultiDocTemplate**, **CView**, **CWinApp**

CSingleDocTemplate Class Members

Construction

CSingleDocTemplate	Constructs a **CSingleDocTemplate** object.

Member Functions
CSingleDocTemplate::CSingleDocTemplate

CSingleDocTemplate(UINT *nIDResource*, **CRuntimeClass*** *pDocClass*,
↳ **CRuntimeClass*** *pFrameClass*, **CRuntimeClass*** *pViewClass* **);**

Parameters

nIDResource   Specifies the ID of the resources used with the document type. This may include menu, icon, accelerator table, and string resources.

The string resource consists of up to seven substrings separated by the '\n' character (the '\n' character is needed as a placeholder if a substring is not included; however, trailing '\n' characters are not necessary); these substrings describe the document type. For information about the substrings, see **CDocTemplate::GetDocString**. This string resource is found in the application's resource file. For example:

```
// MYCALC.RC
STRINGTABLE PRELOAD DISCARDABLE
BEGIN
    IDR_MAINFRAME "MyCalc Windows Application\nSheet\nWorksheet\n
    ↳ Worksheets (*.myc)\n.myc\nMyCalcSheet\n MyCalc Worksheet"
END
```

You can edit this string using the string editor; the entire string appears as a single entry in the String Editor, not as seven separate entries.

For more information about these resource types, see the "String Editor" in the *Developer Studio User's Guide* online.

pDocClass   Points to the **CRuntimeClass** object of the document class. This class is a **CDocument**-derived class you define to represent your documents.

pFrameClass   Points to the **CRuntimeClass** object of the frame window class. This class can be a **CFrameWnd**-derived class, or it can be **CFrameWnd** itself if you want default behavior for your main frame window.

pViewClass   Points to the **CRuntimeClass** object of the view class. This class is a **CView**-derived class you define to display your documents.

Remarks

Constructs a **CSingleDocTemplate** object. Dynamically allocate a **CSingleDocTemplate** object and pass it to **CWinApp::AddDocTemplate** from the InitInstance member function of your application class.

Example

```
// example for CSingleDocTemplate::CSingleDocTemplate
BOOL CMyApp::InitInstance()
{
    // ...
```

```
        // Establish the document type
        // supported by the application

        AddDocTemplate( new CSingleDocTemplate( IDR_MAINFRAME,
                             RUNTIME_CLASS( CSheetDoc ),
                             RUNTIME_CLASS( CFrameWnd ),
                             RUNTIME_CLASS( CSheetView ) ) );

        // ...
}
```

**See Also: CDocTemplate::GetDocString, CWinApp::AddDocTemplate,
CWinApp::InitInstance, CRuntimeClass, RUNTIME_CLASS**

CSingleLock

CSingleLock does not have a base class.

An object of class **CSingleLock** represents the access-control mechanism used in controlling access to a resource in a multithreaded program. In order to use the synchronization classes **CSemaphore**, **CMutex**, **CCriticalSection**, and **CEvent**, you must create either a **CSingleLock** or **CMultiLock** object to wait on and release the synchronization object. Use **CSingleLock** when you only need to wait on one object at a time. Use **CMultiLock** when there are multiple objects that you could use at a particular time.

To use a **CSingleLock** object, call its constructor inside a member function in the controlled resource's class. Then call the **IsLocked** member function to determine if the resource is available. If it is, continue with the remainder of the member function. If the resource is unavailable, either wait for a specified amount of time for the resource to be released, or return failure. After use of the resource is complete, either call the **Unlock** function if the **CSingleLock** object is to be used again, or allow the **CSingleLock** object to be destroyed.

CSingleLock objects require the presence of an object derived from **CSyncObject**. This is usually a data member of the controlled resource's class. For more information on how to use **CSingleLock** objects, see the article "Multithreading: How to Use the Synchronization Classes" in *Visual C++ Programmer's Guide* online.

#include <afxmt.h>

See Also: CMultiLock

CSingleLock Class Members

Construction

CSingleLock	Constructs a **CSingleLock** object.

Methods

IsLocked	Determines if the object is locked.
Lock	Waits on a synchronization object.
Unlock	Releases a synchronization object.

Member Functions
CSingleLock::CSingleLock

CSingleLock(CSyncObject* *pObject*, **BOOL** *bInitialLock* = **FALSE**);

Parameters

pObject   Points to the synchronization object to be accessed. Cannot be **NULL**.

bInitialLock   Specifies whether to initially attempt to access the supplied object.

Remarks

Constructs a **CSingleLock** object. This function is generally called from within an access member function of the controlled resource.

CSingleLock::IsLocked

BOOL IsLocked( );

Return Value

Nonzero if the object is locked; otherwise 0.

Remarks

Determines if the object associated with the **CSingleLock** object is nonsignaled (unavailable).

CSingleLock::Lock

BOOL Lock(DWORD *dwTimeOut* = **INFINITE**);

Return Value

Nonzero if the function was successful; otherwise 0.

Parameters

dwTimeOut   Specifies the amount of time to wait for the synchronization object to be available (signaled). If **INFINITE**, **Lock** will wait until the object is signaled before returning.

Remarks

Call this function to gain access to the resource controlled by the synchronization object supplied to the **CSingleLock** constructor. If the synchronization object is signaled, **Lock** will return successfully and the thread now owns the object. If the synchronization object is nonsignaled (unavailable), **Lock** will wait for the synchronization object to become signaled up to the number of milliseconds specified in the *dwTimeOut* parameter. If the synchronization object did not become signaled in the specified amount of time, **Lock** returns failure.

CSingleLock::Unlock

BOOL Unlock( );
BOOL Unlock(LONG *lCount*, **LPLONG** *lPrevCount* = **NULL);**

Return Value

Nonzero if the function was successful; otherwise 0.

Parameters

lCount Number of accesses to release. Must be greater than 0. If the specified amount would cause the object's count to exceed its maximum, the count is not changed and the function returns **FALSE**.

lPrevCount Points to a variable to receive the previous count of the synchronization object. If **NULL**, the previous count is not returned.

Remarks

Releases the synchronization object owned by **CSingleLock**. This function is called by **CSingleLock**'s destructor.

If you need to release more than one access count of a semaphore, use the second form of **Unlock** and specify the number of accesses to release.

CSize

The **CSize** class is similar to the Windows **SIZE** structure, which implements a relative coordinate or position.

Note This class is derived from the **SIZE** structure. This means you can pass a **CSize** in a parameter that calls for a **SIZE** and that the data members of the **SIZE** structure are accessible data members of **CSize**.

The **cx** and **cy** members of **SIZE** (and **CSize**) are public. In addition, **CSize** implements member functions to manipulate the **SIZE** structure.

#include <afxwin.h>

Sample MFC Sample MDI

See Also **CRect**, **CPoint**

CSize Class Members

Construction

CSize	Constructs a **CSize** object.

Operators

operator ==	Checks for equality between **CSize** and a size.
operator !=	Checks for inequality between **CSize** and a size.
operator +=	Adds a size to **CSize**.
operator –=	Subtracts a size from **CSize**.

Operators Returning CSize Values

operator +	Adds two sizes.
operator –	Subtracts two sizes.

Member Functions
CSize::CSize

CSize( );
CSize(int *initCX,* **int** *initCY* **);**
CSize(SIZE *initSize* **);**
CSize(POINT *initPt* **);**
CSize(DWORD *dwSize* **);**

Parameters

initCX   Sets the **cx** member for the **CSize**.

initCY   Sets the **cy** member for the **CSize**.

initSize   **SIZE** structure or **CSize** object used to initialize **CSize**.

initPt   **POINT** structure or **CPoint** object used to initialize **CSize**.

dwSize   **DWORD** used to initialize **CSize**. The low-order word is the **cx** member and the high-order word is the **cy** member.

Remarks

Constructs a **CSize** object. If no arguments are given, **cx** and **cy** members are not initialized.

Operators
CSize::operator ==

BOOL operator ==(SIZE *size* **) const;**

Remarks

Checks for equality between two sizes. Returns nonzero if the sizes are equal, otherwize 0.

See Also   **CSize::operator !=**

CSize::operator !=

BOOL operator !=(SIZE *size* **) const;**

Remarks

Checks for inequality between two sizes. Returns nonzero if the sizes are not equal, otherwise 0.

See Also   **CSize::operator ==**

CSize::operator +=

void operator +=(SIZE *size* **);**

Remarks

Adds a size to this **Csize**.

See Also   **CSize::operator +**

CSize::operator –=

void operator –=(SIZE *size* **);**

Remarks

Subtracts a size from this **CSize**.

See Also   CSize::operator -

CSize::operator +

CSize operator +(SIZE *size* **) const;**
CPoint operator +(POINT *point* **) const;**
CRect operator +(const RECT* *lpRect* **) const;**

Remarks

These operators add this **CSize** value to the value of parameter. See the following descriptions of the individual operators:

- **operator +(** *size* **)**   This operation adds two **CSize** values.

- **operator +(** *point* **)**   This operation offsets (moves) a **POINT** (or **CPoint**) value by this **CSize** value. The **cx** and **cy** members of this **CSize** value are added to the **x** and **y** data members of the **POINT** value. It is analogous to the version of **CPoint::operator +** that takes a **SIZE** parameter.

- **operator +(** *lpRect* **)**   This operation offsets (moves) a **RECT** (or **CRect**) value by this **CSize** value. The **cx** and **cy** members of this **CSize** value are added to the **left**, **top**, **right**, and **bottom** data members of the **RECT** value. It is analogous to the version of **CRect::operator +** that takes a **SIZE** parameter.

See Also   CPoint::operator +, CRect::operator +

CSize::operator –

CSize operator –(SIZE *size* **) const;**
CPoint operator –(POINT *point* **) const;**
CRect operator –(const RECT* *lpRect* **) const;**
CSize operator –( ) const;

Remarks

The first three of these operators subtract this **CSize** value to the value of parameter. The fourth operator, the unary minus, changes the sign of the **CSize** value. See the following descriptions of the individual operators:

- **operator -(** *size* **)**   This operation subtracts two **CSize** values.

- **operator -(** *point* **)**   This operation offsets (moves) a **POINT** or **CPoint** value by the additive inverse of this **CSize** value. The **cx** and **cy** of this **CSize** value are subtracted from the **x** and **y** data members of the **POINT** value. It is analogous to the version of **CPoint::operator -** that takes a **SIZE** parameter.

- **operator -(** *lpRect* **)**   This operation offsets (moves) a **RECT** or **CRect** value by the additive inverse of this **CSize** value. The **cx** and **cy** members of this **CSize** value are subtracted from the **left**, **top**, **right**, and **bottom** data members of the **RECT** value. It is analogous to the version of **CRect::operator -** that takes a **SIZE** parameter.

- **operator -( )**   This operation returns the additive inverse of this **CSize** value.

See Also   **CPoint::operator -**, **CRect::operator -**

CSliderCtrl

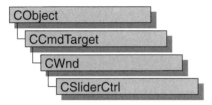

A "slider control" (also known as a trackbar) is a window containing a slider and optional tick marks. When the user moves the slider, using either the mouse or the direction keys, the control sends notification messages to indicate the change.

Slider controls are useful when you want the user to select a discrete value or a set of consecutive values in a range. For example, you might use a slider control to allow the user to set the repeat rate of the keyboard by moving the slider to a given tick mark.

The **CSliderCtrl** class provides the functionality of the Windows common slider control. This control (and therefore the **CSliderCtrl** class) is available only to programs running under Windows 95 and Windows NT version 3.51 and later.

The slider moves in increments that you specify when you create it. For example, if you specify that the slider should have a range of five, the slider can only occupy six positions: a position at the left side of the slider control and one position for each increment in the range. Typically, each of these positions is identified by a tick mark.

You create a slider by using the constructor and the **Create** member function of **CSliderCtrl**. Once you have created a slider control, you can use member functions in **CSliderCtrl** to change many of its properties. Changes that you can make include setting the minimum and maximum positions for the slider, drawing tick marks, setting a selection range, and repositioning the slider.

For more information on using **CSliderCtrl**, see Technical Note 60 online.

#include <afxcmn.h>

See Also: **CProgressCtrl**

CSliderCtrl Class Members

Construction

CSliderCtrl	Constructs a **CSliderCtrl** object.
Create	Creates a slider control and attaches it to a **CSliderCtrl** object.

Attributes

GetLineSize	Retrieves the line size of a slider control.
SetLineSize	Sets the line size of a slider control.
GetPageSize	Retrieves the page size of a slider control.
SetPageSize	Sets the page size of a slider control.
GetRangeMax	Retrieves the maximum position for a slider.
GetRangeMin	Retrieves the minimum position for a slider.
GetRange	Retrieves the minimum and maximum positions for a slider.
SetRangeMin	Sets the minimum position for a slider.
SetRangeMax	Sets the maximum position for a slider.
SetRange	Sets the minimum and maximum positions for a slider.
GetSelection	Retrieves the range of the current selection.
SetSelection	Sets the range of the current selection.
GetChannelRect	Retrieves the size of the slider control's channel.
GetThumbRect	Retrieves the size of the slider control's thumb.
GetPos	Retrieves the current position of the slider.
SetPos	Sets the current position of the slider.
GetNumTics	Retrieves the number of tick marks in a slider control.
GetTicArray	Retrieves the array of tick mark positions for a slider control.
GetTic	Retrieves the position of the specified tick mark.
GetTicPos	Retrieves the position of the specified tick mark, in client coordinates.
SetTic	Sets the position of the specified tick mark.
SetTicFreq	Sets the frequency of tick marks per slider control increment.

Operations

ClearSel	Clears the current selection in a slider control.
VerifyPos	Verifies that the position of a slider control is between the minimum and maximum values.
ClearTics	Removes the current tick marks from a slider control.

Member Functions
CSliderCtrl::ClearSel

void ClearSel(BOOL *bRedraw* **= FALSE);**

Parameters

> *bRedraw*   Redraw flag. If this parameter is **TRUE**, the slider is redrawn after the selection is cleared; otherwise the slider is not redrawn.

Remarks

Call this function to clear the current selection in a slider control.

See Also: **CSliderCtrl::GetSelection**, **CSliderCtrl::SetSelection**

CSliderCtrl::ClearTics

void ClearTics(BOOL *bRedraw* **= FALSE);**

Parameters

bRedraw   Redraw flag. If this parameter is **TRUE**, the slider is redrawn after the tick marks are cleared; otherwise the slider is not redrawn.

Remarks

Call this function to remove the current tick marks from a slider control.

See Also: **CSliderCtrl::GetTicArray**, **CSliderCtrl::GetTic**, **CSliderCtrl::GetNumTics**

CSliderCtrl::Create

BOOL Create(DWORD *dwStyle*, **const RECT&** *rect*, **CWnd*** *pParentWnd*, **UINT** *nID* **);**

Return Value

Nonzero if initialization was successful; otherwise 0.

Parameters

dwStyle   Specifies the slider control's style. Apply any combination of slider control styles to the control.

rect   Specifies the slider control's size and position. It can be either a **CRect** object or a **RECT** structure.

pParentWnd   Specifies the slider control's parent window, usually a **CDialog**. It must not be **NULL**.

nID   Specifies the slider control's ID.

Remarks

You construct a **CSliderCtrl** in two steps. First call the constructor, then call **Create**, which creates the slider control and attaches it to the **CSliderCtrl** object.

Slider controls can have either a vertical or horizontal orientation. They can have tick marks on either side, both sides, or neither. They can also be used to specify a range of consecutive values. These properties are controlled by using slider styles, which you specify when you create the slider control:

- **TBS_HORZ**   Orients the slider horizontally. This is the default orientation.

- **TBS_VERT**   Orients the slider vertically. If you do not specify an orientation, the slider is oriented horizontally.

- **TBS_AUTOTICKS**   Creates a slider that has a tick mark for each increment in its range of values. These tick marks are added automatically when an application calls the **SetRange** member function. You cannot use the **SetTic** and **SetTicFreq** member functions to specify the position of the tick marks if you use this style. Use the **ClearTics** member function instead.

- **TBS_NOTICKS**   Creates a slider that does not display tick marks.

- **TBS_BOTTOM**   Displays tick marks on the bottom of a horizontal slider. Can be used with the **TBS_TOP** style to display tick marks on both sides of the slider control.

- **TBS_TOP**   Displays tick marks on the top of a horizontal slider. Can be used with the **TBS_BOTTOM** style to display tick marks on both sides of the slider control.

- **TBS_RIGHT**   Displays tick marks on the right of a vertical slider. Can be used with the **TBS_LEFT** style to display tick marks on both sides of the slider control.

- **TBS_LEFT**   Displays tick marks on the left of a vertical slider. Can be used with the **TBS_RIGHT** style to display tick marks on both sides of the slider control.

- **TBS_BOTH**   Displays tick marks on both sides of the slider in any orientation.

- **TBS_ENABLESELRANGE**   Displays a selection range. When a slider control has this style, the tick marks at the starting and ending positions of a selection range are displayed as triangles (instead of vertical dashes) and the selection range is highlighted. For example, selection ranges might be useful in a simple scheduling application. The user could select a range of tick marks corresponding to hours in a day to identify a scheduled meeting time.

See Also: CSliderCtrl::CSliderCtrl

CSliderCtrl::CSliderCtrl

CSliderCtrl( );

Remarks

Constructs a **CSliderCtrl** object.

See Also: CSliderCtrl::Create

CSliderCtrl::GetChannelRect

void GetChannelRect(LPRECT *lprc* **) const;**

Parameters

lprc   A pointer to a **CRect** object that contains the size and position of the channel's bounding rectangle when the function returns.

Remarks

Call this function to retrieve the size and position of the bounding rectangle for a slider control's channel. The channel is the area over which the slider moves and which contains the highlight when a range is selected.

See Also: CSliderCtrl::GetThumbRect

CSliderCtrl::GetLineSize

int GetLineSize( ) const;

Return Value

The size of a line for the slider control.

Remarks

Call this function to retrieve the size of the line for a slider control. The line size affects how much the slider moves for the **TB_LINEUP** and **TB_LINEDOWN** notifications. The default setting for the line size is 1.

See Also: CSliderCtrl::SetLineSize, CSliderCtrl::GetPageSize

CSliderCtrl::GetNumTics

UINT GetNumTics( ) const;

Return Value

The number of tick marks in the slider control.

Remarks

Call this function to retrieve the number of tick marks in a slider control.

See Also: CSliderCtrl::GetTicArray, CSliderCtrl::GetTic, CSliderCtrl::GetTicPos, CSliderCtrl::SetTicFreq, CSliderCtrl::ClearTics

CSliderCtrl::GetPageSize

int GetPageSize( ) const;

Return Value

The size of a page for the slider control.

Remarks

Call this function to retrieve the size of the page for a slider control. The page size affects how much the slider moves for the **TB_PAGEUP** and **TB_PAGEDOWN** notifications.

See Also: CSliderCtrl::GetLineSize, CSliderCtrl::SetPageSize

CSliderCtrl::GetPos

int GetPos( ) const;

Return Value

The current position.

Remarks

Call this function to retrieve the current position of the slider in a slider control.

See Also: CSliderCtrl::SetPos, CSliderCtrl::GetTicPos

CSliderCtrl::GetRange

void GetRange(int& *nMin***, int&** *nMax* **) const;**

Parameters

nMin   Reference to an integer that receives the minimum position.

nMax   Reference to an integer that receives the maximum position.

Remarks

Call this function to retrieve the maximum and minimum positions for the slider in a slider control. This function copies the values into the integers referenced by *nMin* and *nMax*.

See Also: CSliderCtrl::GetRangeMin, CSliderCtrl::GetRangeMax, CSliderCtrl::SetRange

CSliderCtrl::GetRangeMax

int GetRangeMax( ) const;

Return Value

The control's maximum position.

Remarks

Call this function to retrieve the maximum position for the slider in a slider control.

See Also: **CSliderCtrl::GetRangeMin, CSliderCtrl::GetRange, CSliderCtrl::SetRange**

CSliderCtrl::GetRangeMin

int GetRangeMin( ) const;

Return Value

The control's minimum position.

Remarks

Call this function to retrieve the minimum position for the slider in a slider control.

See Also: **CSliderCtrl::GetRange, CSliderCtrl::GetRangeMax, CSliderCtrl::SetRange**

CSliderCtrl::GetSelection

void GetSelection(int& *nMin*, **int&** *nMax* **) const;**

Parameters

nMin   Reference to an integer that receives the starting position of the current selection.

nMax   Reference to an integer that receives the ending position of the current selection.

Remarks

Call this function to retrieve the starting and ending positions of the current selection in a slider control.

See Also: **CSliderCtrl::SetSelection, CSliderCtrl::ClearSel**

CSliderCtrl::GetThumbRect

void GetThumbRect(LPRECT *lprc* **) const;**

Parameters

lprc A pointer to a **CRect** object that contains the bounding rectangle for the slider when the function returns.

Remarks

Call this function to retrieve the size and position of the bounding rectangle for the slider (thumb) in a slider control.

See Also: CSliderCtrl::GetChannelRect

CSliderCtrl::GetTic

int GetTic(int *nTic* **) const;**

Return Value

The position of the specified tick mark or −1 if *nTic* does not specify a valid index.

Parameters

nTic Zero-based index identifying a tick mark.

Remarks

Call this function to retrieve the position of a tick mark in a slider control.

See Also: CSliderCtrl::SetTic, CSliderCtrl::GetTicArray, CSliderCtrl::GetTicPos, CSliderCtrl::SetTicFreq, CSliderCtrl::ClearTics

---

CSliderCtrl::GetTicArray

DWORD* GetTicArray( ) const;

Return Value

The address of the array containing tick mark positions for the slider control.

Remarks

Call this function to retrieve the address of the array containing the positions of tick marks for a slider control.

See Also: CSliderCtrl::SetTic, CSliderCtrl::GetTic, CSliderCtrl::GetTicPos, CSliderCtrl::SetTicFreq, CSliderCtrl::ClearTics

CSliderCtrl::GetTicPos

int GetTicPos(int *nTic* **) const;**

Return Value

The physical position, in client coordinates, of the specified tick mark or −1 if *nTic* does not specify a valid index.

Parameters

nTic   Zero-based index identifying a tick mark.

Remarks

Call this function to retrieve the current physical position of a tick mark in a slider control.

See Also: CSliderCtrl::SetTic, CSliderCtrl::GetTic, CSliderCtrl::SetTicFreq, CSliderCtrl::ClearTics

---

CSliderCtrl::SetLineSize

int SetLineSize(int *nSize* **);**

Return Value

The previous line size.

Parameters

nSize   The new line size of the slider control.

Remarks

Call this function to set the size of the line for a slider control. The line size affects how much the slider moves for the **TB_LINEUP** and **TB_LINEDOWN** notifications.

See Also: CSliderCtrl::GetLineSize, CSliderCtrl::SetPageSize

CSliderCtrl::SetPageSize

int SetPageSize(int *nSize* **);**

Return Value

The previous page size.

Parameters

nSize   The new page size of the slider control.

Remarks

Call this function to set the size of the page for a slider control. The page size affects how much the slider moves for the **TB_PAGEUP** and **TB_PAGEDOWN** notifications.

See Also: **CSliderCtrl::GetPageSize, CSliderCtrl::GetLineSize**

CSliderCtrl::SetPos

void SetPos(int *nPos* **);**

Parameters

nPos   Specifies the new slider position.

Remarks

Call this function to set the current position of the slider in a slider control.

See Also: **CSliderCtrl::GetPos, CSliderCtrl::SetTic, CSliderCtrl::VerifyPos**

CSliderCtrl::SetRange

void SetRange(int *nMin***, int** *nMax***, BOOL** *bRedraw* **= FALSE);**

Parameters

nMin   Minimum position for the slider.

nMax   Maximum position for the slider.

bRedraw   The redraw flag. If this parameter is **TRUE**, the slider is redrawn after the range is set; otherwise the slider is not redrawn.

Remarks

Call this function to set the range (minimum and maximum positions) for the slider in a slider control.

See Also: **CSliderCtrl::GetRange, CSliderCtrl::SetRangeMax, CSliderCtrl::SetRangeMin**

CSliderCtrl::SetRangeMax

void SetRangeMax(int *nMax***, BOOL** *bRedraw* **= FALSE);**

Parameters

nMax   Maximum position for the slider.

bRedraw   The redraw flag. If this parameter is **TRUE**, the slider is redrawn after the range is set; otherwise the slider is not redrawn.

Remarks

Call this function to set the maximum range for the slider in a slider control.

See Also: **CSliderCtrl::SetRange**, **CSliderCtrl::GetRangeMax**, **CSliderCtrl::SetRangeMin**

CSliderCtrl::SetRangeMin

void SetRangeMin(int *nMin***, BOOL** *bRedraw* **= FALSE);**

Parameters

nMin   Minimum position for the slider.

bRedraw   The redraw flag. If this parameter is **TRUE**, the slider is redrawn after the range is set; otherwise the slider is not redrawn.

Remarks

Call this function to set the minimum range for the slider in a slider control.

See Also: **CSliderCtrl::SetRange**, **CSliderCtrl::GetRangeMin**, **CSliderCtrl::SetRangeMax**

CSliderCtrl::SetSelection

void SetSelection(int *nMin***, int** *nMax* **);**

Parameters

nMin   Starting position for the slider.

nMax   Ending position for the slider.

Remarks

Call this function to set the starting and ending positions for the current selection in a slider control.

See Also: **CSliderCtrl::GetSelection**, **CSliderCtrl::ClearSel**

CSliderCtrl::SetTic

BOOL SetTic(int *nTic* **);**

Return Value

Nonzero if the tick mark is set; otherwise 0.

Parameters

nTic   Position of the tick mark. This parameter must specify a positive value.

Remarks

Call this function to set the position of a tick mark in a slider control.

See Also: **CSliderCtrl::GetTic, CSliderCtrl::GetTicArray,
CSliderCtrl::GetTicPos, CSliderCtrl::SetTicFreq, CSliderCtrl::ClearTics**

CSliderCtrl::SetTicFreq

void SetTicFreq(int *nFreq* **);**

Parameters

nFreq   Frequency of the tick marks.

Remarks

Call this function to set the frequency with which tick marks are displayed in a slider. For example, if the frequency is set to 2, a tick mark is displayed for every other increment in the slider's range. The default setting for the frequency is 1 (that is, every increment in the range is associated with a tick mark).

You must create the control with the **TBS_AUTOTICKS** style to use this function. For more information, see **CSliderCtrl::Create**.

See Also: **CSliderCtrl::Create, CSliderCtrl::SetTic, CSliderCtrl::GetTicArray**

CSliderCtrl::VerifyPos

void VerifyPos( );

Remarks

Call this function to verify that the current position of the slider in a slider control is between the minimum and maximum values.

See Also: **CSliderCtrl::GetRange, CSliderCtrl::SetPos, CSliderCtrl::GetTicPos**

CSocket

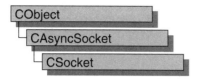

Class **CSocket** derives from **CAsyncSocket** and inherits its encapsulation of the Windows Sockets API. A **CSocket** object represents a higher level of abstraction of the Windows Sockets API than that of a **CAsyncSocket** object. **CSocket** works with classes **CSocketFile** and **CArchive** to manage the sending and receiving of data.

A **CSocket** object also provides blocking, which is essential to the synchronous operation of **CArchive**. Blocking functions, such as **Receive**, **Send**, **ReceiveFrom**, **SendTo**, and **Accept** (all inherited from **CAsyncSocket**), do not return a **WSAEWOULDBLOCK** error in **CSocket**. Instead, these functions wait until the operation completes. Additionally, the original call will terminate with the error **WSAEINTR** if **CancelBlockingCall** is called while one of these functions is blocking.

To use a **CSocket** object, call the constructor, then call **Create** to create the underlying **SOCKET** handle (type **SOCKET**). The default parameters of **Create** create a stream socket, but if you are not using the socket with a **CArchive** object, you can specify a parameter to create a datagram socket instead, or bind to a specific port to create a server socket. Connect to a client socket using **Connect** on the client side and **Accept** on the server side. Then create a **CSocketFile** object and associate it to the **CSocket** object in the **CSocketFile** constructor. Next, create a **CArchive** object for sending and one for receiving data (as needed), then associate them with the **CSocketFile** object in the **CArchive** constructor. When communications are complete, destroy the **CArchive**, **CSocketFile**, and **CSocket** objects. The **SOCKET** data type is described in the article "Windows Sockets: Background" in *Visual C++ Programmer's Guide* online.

For more information, see "Windows Sockets in MFC," "Windows Sockets: Using Sockets with Archives," "Windows Sockets: How Sockets with Archives Work," "Windows Sockets: Sequence of Operations," "Windows Sockets: Example of Sockets Using Archives," and related articles in *Visual C++ Programmer's Guide* online. Also see "Overview of Windows Sockets 2" and "Windows Sockets Programming Considerations" in the Win32 SDK documentation.

#include <afxsock.h>

See Also: **CAsyncSocket**, **CSocketFile**

CSocket Class Members

Construction

CSocket	Constructs a **CSocket** object.
Create	Creates a socket.

Attributes

IsBlocking	Determines whether a blocking call is in progress.
FromHandle	Returns a pointer to a **CSocket** object, given a **SOCKET** handle.
Attach	Attaches a **SOCKET** handle to a **CSocket** object.

Operations

CancelBlockingCall	Cancels a blocking call that is currently in progress.

Overridables

OnMessagePending	Called to process pending messages while waiting for a blocking call to complete.

Member Functions

CSocket::Attach

BOOL Attach(SOCKET *hSocket* **);**

Return Value

Nonzero if the function is successful.

Parameters

hSocket   Contains a handle to a socket.

Remarks

Call this member function to attach the *hSocket* handle to a **CSocket** object. The **SOCKET** handle is stored in the object's **m_hSocket** data member.

For more information, see "Windows Sockets: Using Sockets with Archives" and related articles in *Visual C++ Programmer's Guide* online. Also see "Windows Sockets Programming Considerations" in the Win32 SDK documentation.

See Also: CAsyncSocket::Attach

CSocket::CancelBlockingCall

void CancelBlockingCall( );

Remarks

Call this member function to cancel a blocking call currently in progress. This function cancels any outstanding blocking operation for this socket. The original blocking call will terminate as soon as possible with the error **WSAEINTR**.

In the case of a blocking **Connect** operation, the Windows Sockets implementation will terminate the blocking call as soon as possible, but it may not be possible for the socket resources to be released until the connection has completed (and then been reset) or timed out. This is likely to be noticeable only if the application immediately tries to open a new socket (if no sockets are available), or to connect to the same peer.

Canceling any operation other than **Accept** can leave the socket in an indeterminate state. If an application cancels a blocking operation on a socket, the only operation that the application can depend on being able to perform on the socket is a call to **Close**, although other operations may work on some Windows Sockets implementations. If you desire maximum portability for your application, you must be careful not to depend on performing operations after a cancel.

For more information, see "Windows Sockets: Using Sockets with Archives" and related articles in *Visual C++ Programmer's Guide* online. Also see "Windows Sockets Programming Considerations" in the Win32 SDK documentation.

See Also: CAsyncSocket::Accept, **CAsyncSocket::Close**, **CAsyncSocket::Connect**, **CSocket::IsBlocking**, **::WSASetBlockingHook**

CSocket::Create

BOOL Create(UINT *nSocketPort* **= 0, int** *nSocketType* **= SOCK_STREAM,**
➥ LPCTSTR *lpszSocketAddress* **= NULL);**

Return Value

Nonzero if the function is successful; otherwise 0, and a specific error code can be retrieved by calling **GetLastError**.

Parameters

nSocketPort   A particular port to be used with the socket, or 0 if you want MFC to select a port.

nSocketType   **SOCK_STREAM** or **SOCK_DGRAM**.

lpszSockAddress   A pointer to a string containing the network address of the connected socket, a dotted number such as "128.56.22.8".

Remarks

Call the **Create** member function after constructing a socket object to create the Windows socket and attach it. **Create** then calls **Bind** to bind the socket to the specified address. The following socket types are supported:

- **SOCK_STREAM** Provides sequenced, reliable, two-way, connection-based byte streams. Uses Transmission Control Protocol (TCP) for the Internet address family.

- **SOCK_DGRAM** Supports datagrams, which are connectionless, unreliable buffers of a fixed (typically small) maximum length. Uses User Datagram Protocol (UDP) for the Internet address family. To use this option, you must not use the socket with a **CArchive** object.

Note The **Accept** member function takes a reference to a new, empty **CSocket** object as its parameter. You must construct this object before you call **Accept**. Keep in mind that if this socket object goes out of scope, the connection closes. Do not call **Create** for this new socket object.

For more information about stream and datagram sockets, see the articles "Windows Sockets: Background," "Windows Sockets: Ports and Socket Addresses," and "Windows Sockets: Using Sockets with Archives" in *Visual C++ Programmer's Guide* online and "Windows Sockets Programming Considerations" in the Win32 SDK documentation.

See Also: CAsyncSocket::Create, CAsyncSocket::Bind

CSocket::CSocket

CSocket( );

Remarks

Constructs a **CSocket** object. After construction, you must call the **Create** member function.

For more information, see "Windows Sockets: Using Sockets with Archives" and related articles in *Visual C++ Programmer's Guide* online. Also see "Windows Sockets Programming Considerations" in the Win32 SDK documentation.

See Also: CAsyncSocket::Create

CSocket::FromHandle

static CSocket* PASCAL FromHandle(SOCKET *hSocket*);

Return Value

A pointer to a **CSocket** object, or **NULL** if there is no **CSocket** object attached to *hSocket*.

Parameters

hSocket   Contains a handle to a socket.

Remarks

Returns a pointer to a **CSocket** object. When given a **SOCKET** handle, if a **CSocket** object is not attached to the handle, the member function returns **NULL** and does not create a temporary object.

For more information, see "Windows Sockets: Using Sockets with Archives" and related articles in *Visual C++ Programmer's Guide* online. Also see "Windows Sockets Programming Considerations" in the Win32 SDK documentation.

See Also: CAsyncSocket::FromHandle

CSocket::IsBlocking

BOOL IsBlocking( );

Return Value

Nonzero if the socket is blocking; otherwise 0.

Remarks

Call this member function to determine if a blocking call is in progress.

For more information, see "Windows Sockets: Using Sockets with Archives" and related articles in *Visual C++ Programmer's Guide* online. Also see "Windows Sockets Programming Considerations" in the Win32 SDK documentation.

See Also: CSocket::CancelBlockingCall

CSocket::OnMessagePending

virtual BOOL OnMessagePending( );

Return Value

Nonzero if the message was handled; otherwise 0.

Remarks

Override this member function to look for particular messages from Windows and respond to them in your socket. This is an advanced overridable.

The framework calls **OnMessagePending** while the socket is pumping Windows messages to give you an opportunity to deal with messages of interest to your application. For examples of how you might use **OnMessagePending**, see the article "Windows Sockets: Deriving from Socket Classes" in *Visual C++ Programmer's Guide* online.

For more information, see "Windows Sockets: Using Sockets with Archives" and related articles in *Visual C++ Programmer's Guide* online. Also see "Windows Sockets Programming Considerations" in the Win32 SDK documentation.

See Also: CSocket::CancelBlockingCall, CSocket::IsBlocking

CSocketFile

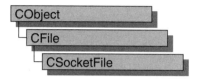

A **CSocketFile** object is a **CFile** object used for sending and receiving data across a network via Windows Sockets. You can attach the **CSocketFile** object to a **CSocket** object for this purpose. You also can — and usually do — attach the **CSocketFile** object to a **CArchive** object to simplify sending and receiving data using MFC serialization.

To serialize (send) data, you insert it into the archive, which calls **CSocketFile** member functions to write data to the **CSocket** object. To deserialize (receive) data, you extract from the archive. This causes the archive to call **CSocketFile** member functions to read data from the **CSocket** object.

Tip Besides using **CSocketFile** as described here, you can use it as a stand-alone file object, just as you can with **CFile**, its base class. You can also use **CSocketFile** with any archive-based MFC serialization functions. Because **CSocketFile** does not support all of **CFile**'s functionality, some default MFC serialize functions are not compatible with **CSocketFile**. This is particularly true of the **CEditView** class. You should not try to serialize **CEditView** data through a **CArchive** object attached to a **CSocketFile** object using **CEditView::SerializeRaw**; use **CEditView::Serialize** instead. The **SerializeRaw** function expects the file object to have functions, such as **Seek**, that **CSocketFile** does not have.

For more information, see "Windows Sockets in MFC," "Windows Sockets: Using Sockets with Archives," and related articles in *Visual C++ Programmer's Guide* online, as well as "Overview of Windows Sockets 2" and "Windows Sockets Programming Considerations" in the Win32 SDK documentation.

#include <afxsock.h>

See Also: **CAsyncSocket**, **CSocket**

CSocketFile Class Members

Construction

CSocketFile	Constructs a **CSocketFile** object.

Member Functions
CSocketFile::CSocketFile

CSocketFile(CSocket* *pSocket*, **BOOL** *bArchiveCompatible* = **TRUE**);

Parameters

pSocket   The socket to attach to the **CSocketFile** object.

bArchiveCompatible   Specifies whether the file object is for use with a **CArchive** object. Pass **FALSE** only if you want to use the **CSocketFile** object in a stand-alone manner as you would a stand-alone **CFile** object, with certain limitations. This flag changes how the **CArchive** object attached to the **CSocketFile** object manages its buffer for reading.

Remarks

Constructs a **CSocketFile** object. The object's destructor disassociates itself from the socket object when the object goes out of scope or is deleted.

Note A **CSocketFile** can also be used as a (limited) file without a **CArchive** object. By default, the **CSocketFile** constructor's *bArchiveCompatible* parameter is **TRUE**. This specifies that the file object is for use with an archive. To use the file object without an archive, pass **FALSE** in the *bArchiveCompatible* parameter.

In its "archive compatible" mode, a **CSocketFile** object provides better performance and reduces the danger of a "deadlock." A deadlock occurs when both the sending and receiving sockets are waiting on each other, or for a common resource. This situation might occur if the **CArchive** object worked with the **CSocketFile** the way it does with a **CFile** object. With **CFile**, the archive can assume that if it receives fewer bytes than it requested, the end of file has been reached.

With **CSocketFile**, however, data is message based; the buffer can contain multiple messages, so receiving fewer than the number of bytes requested does not imply end of file. The application does not block in this case as it might with **CFile**, and it can continue reading messages from the buffer until the buffer is empty. The **CArchive::IsBufferEmpty** function is useful for monitoring the state of the archive's buffer in such a case.

For more information on the use of **CSocketFile**, see the articles "Windows Sockets: Using Sockets with Archives" and "Windows Sockets: Example of Sockets Using Archives" in *Visual C++ Programmer's Guide* online.

See Also: **CFile::CFile, CFile::Read**

CSpinButtonCtrl

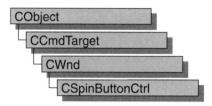

A "spin button control" (also known as an up-down control) is a pair of arrow buttons that the user can click to increment or decrement a value, such as a scroll position or a number displayed in a companion control. The value associated with a spin button control is called its current position. A spin button control is most often used with a companion control, called a "buddy window."

The **CSpinButtonCtrl** class provides the functionality of the Windows common spin button control. This control (and therefore the **CSpinButtonCtrl** class) is available only to programs running under Windows 95 and Windows NT version 3.51 and later.

To the user, a spin button control and its buddy window often look like a single control. You can specify that a spin button control automatically position itself next to its buddy window, and that it automatically set the caption of the buddy window to its current position. You can use a spin button control with an edit control to prompt the user for numeric input.

Clicking the up arrow moves the current position toward the maximum, and clicking the down arrow moves the current position toward the minimum. By default, the minimum is 100 and the maximum is 0. Any time the minimum setting is greater than the maximum setting (for example, when the default settings are used), clicking the up arrow decreases the position value and clicking the down arrow increases it.

A spin button control without a buddy window functions as a sort of simplified scroll bar. For example, a tab control sometimes displays a spin button control to enable the user to scroll additional tabs into view.

For more information on using **CSpinButtonCtrl**, see Technical Note 60 online.

#include <afxcmn.h>

See Also: CSliderCtrl

CSpinButtonCtrl Class Members

Construction

CSpinButtonCtrl	Constructs a **CSpinButtonCtrl** object.
Create	Creates a spin button control and attaches it to a **CSpinButtonCtrl** object.

Attributes

SetAccel	Sets the acceleration for a spin button control.
GetAccel	Retrieves acceleration information for a spin button control.
SetBase	Sets the base for a spin button control.
GetBase	Retrieves the current base for a spin button control.
SetBuddy	Sets the buddy window for a spin button control.
GetBuddy	Retrieves a pointer to the current buddy window.
SetPos	Sets the current position for the control.
GetPos	Retrieves the current position of a spin button control.
SetRange	Sets the upper and lower limits (range) for a spin button control.
GetRange	Retrieves the upper and lower limits (range) for a spin button control.

Member Functions

CSpinButtonCtrl::Create

> **BOOL Create(DWORD** *dwStyle***, const RECT&** *rect***,**
> ↳ **CWnd*** *pParentWnd***, UINT** *nID* **);**

Return Value

Nonzero if initialization was successful; otherwise 0.

Parameters

dwStyle Specifies the spin button control's style. Apply any combination of spin button control styles to the control.

rect Specifies the spin button control's size and position. It can be either a **CRect** object or a **RECT** structure

pParentWnd A pointer to the spin button control's parent window, usually a **CDialog**. It must not be **NULL.**

nID Specifies the spin button control's ID.

Remarks

You construct a **CSpinButtonCtrl** object in two steps. First call the constructor, then call **Create**, which creates the spin button control and attaches it to the **CSpinButtonCtrl** object.

The following styles are specific to spin button controls:

- **UDS_HORZ** Causes the control's arrows to point left and right instead of up and down.
- **UDS_WRAP** Causes the position to "wrap" if it is incremented or decremented beyond the ending or beginning of the range.
- **UDS_ARROWKEYS** Causes the control to increment and decrement the position when the UP ARROW and DOWN ARROW keys are pressed.
- **UDS_SETBUDDYINT** Causes the control to set the text of the buddy window (using the **WM_SETTEXT** message) when the position changes. The text consists of the position formatted as a decimal or hexadecimal string.
- **UDS_NOTHOUSANDS** Does not insert a thousands separator between every three decimal digits.
- **UDS_AUTOBUDDY** Automatically selects the previous window in the Z-order as the control's buddy window.
- **UDS_ALIGNRIGHT** Positions the spin button control next to the right edge of the buddy window. The width of the buddy window is decreased to accommodate the width of the control.
- **UDS_ALIGNLEFT** Positions the spin button control next to the left edge of the buddy window. The buddy window is moved to the right and its width decreased to accommodate the width of the control.

See Also: **CSpinButtonCtrl::CSpinButtonCtrl**

CSpinButtonCtrl::CSpinButtonCtrl

CSpinButtonCtrl( );

Remarks

Constructs a **CSpinButtonCtrl** object.

See Also: **CSpinButtonCtrl::Create**

CSpinButtonCtrl::GetAccel

UINT GetAccel(int *nAccel*, **UDACCEL*** *pAccel* **) const;**

Return Value

Number of accelerator structures retrieved.

Parameters

nAccel   Number of elements in the array specified by *pAccel*.

pAccel   Pointer to an array of **UDACCEL** structures that receives acceleration information. For more information on the definition of the **UDACCEL** structure, see **CSpinButtonCtrl::SetAccel**.

Remarks

Call this function to retrieve acceleration information for a spin button control.

See Also: CSpinButtonCtrl::SetAccel

CSpinButtonCtrl::GetBase

UINT GetBase( ) const;

Return Value

The current base value.

Remarks

Call this function to retrieve the current base for a spin button control.

See Also: CSpinButtonCtrl::SetBase

CSpinButtonCtrl::GetBuddy

CWnd* GetBuddy( ) const;

Return Value

A pointer to the current buddy window.

Remarks

Call this function to retrieve a pointer to the current buddy window.

See Also: CSpinButtonCtrl::SetBuddy

CSpinButtonCtrl::GetPos

int GetPos( ) const;

Return Value

The current position in the low-order word. The high-order word is nonzero if an error occurred.

Remarks

Call this function to retrieve the current position of a spin button control. When it processes the value returned, the control updates its current position based on the caption of the buddy window. The control returns an error if there is no buddy window or if the caption specifies an invalid or out-of-range value.

See Also: CSpinButtonCtrl::SetPos

CSpinButtonCtrl::GetRange

DWORD GetRange( ) const;
void GetRange(int &*lower***, int&** *upper* **) const;**

Return Value

The first version returns a 32-bit value containing the upper and lower limits. The low-order word is the upper limit for the control, and the high-order word is the lower limit.

Parameters

lower   Reference to an integer that receives the lower limit for the control.

upper   Reference to an integer that receives the upper limit for the control.

Remarks

Call this function to retrieve the upper and lower limits (range) for a spin button control.

See Also: CSpinButtonCtrl::SetRange

CSpinButtonCtrl::SetAccel

BOOL SetAccel(int *nAccel***, UDACCEL*** *pAccel* **);**

Return Value

Nonzero if successful; otherwise 0.

Parameters

nAccel   Number of **UDACCEL** structures specified by *pAccel*.

pAccel   Pointer to an array of **UDACCEL** structures, which contain acceleration information. Elements should be sorted in ascending order based on the **nSec** member.

Remarks

Call this function to set the acceleration for a spin button control. The **UDACCEL** structure is defined as follows:

```
typedef struct {
    int nSec;
    int nInc;
} UDACCEL;
```

nSec   Amount of elapsed time, in seconds, before the position-change increment specified by **nInc** is used.

nInc   Position-change increment to use after the time specified by **nSec** elapses.

See Also: CSpinButtonCtrl::GetAccel

CSpinButtonCtrl::SetBase

int SetBase(int *nBase* **);**

Return Value

The previous base value if successful, or zero if an invalid base is given.

Parameters

nBase   New base value for the control. It can be 10 for decimal or 16 for hexadecimal.

Remarks

Call this function to set the base for a spin button control. The base value determines whether the buddy window displays numbers in decimal or hexadecimal digits. Hexadecimal numbers are always unsigned; decimal numbers are signed.

See Also: CSpinButtonCtrl::GetBase

CSpinButtonCtrl::SetBuddy

CWnd* SetBuddy(CWnd* *pWndBuddy* **);**

Return Value

A pointer to the previous buddy window.

Parameters

pWndBuddy   Pointer to the new buddy window.

Remarks

Call this function to set the buddy window for a spin button control.

See Also: CSpinButtonCtrl::GetBuddy

CSpinButtonCtrl::SetPos

int SetPos(int *nPos* **);**

Return Value

The previous position.

Parameters

> *nPos*   New position for the control. This value must be in the range specified by the upper and lower limits for the control.

Remarks

> Call this function to set the current position for a spin button control.
>
> **See Also: CSpinButtonCtrl::SetRange**, **CSpinButtonCtrl::GetPos**

CSpinButtonCtrl::SetRange

> **void SetRange(int** *nLower*, **int** *nUpper* **);**

Parameters

> *nLower* and *nUpper*   Upper and lower limits for the control. Neither limit can be greater than **UD_MAXVAL** or less than **UD_MINVAL**. In addition, the difference between the two limits cannot exceed **UD_MAXVAL**.

Remarks

> Call this function to set the upper and lower limits (range) for a spin button control.
>
> **Note**   The default range for the spin button has the maximum set to zero (0) and the minimum set to 100. Since the maximum value is less than the minimum value, clicking the up arrow will decrease the position and clicking the down arrow will increase it. Use CSpinButtonCtrl::SetRange to adjust these values.
>
> **See Also: CSpinButtonCtrl::GetRange**, **CSpinButtonCtrl::GetPos**, "Using CSpinButtonCtrl" online

CSplitterWnd

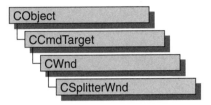

The **CSplitterWnd** class provides the functionality of a splitter window, which is a window that contains multiple panes. A pane is usually an application-specific object derived from **CView**, but it can be any **CWnd** object that has the appropriate child window ID.

A **CSplitterWnd** object is usually embedded in a parent **CFrameWnd** or **CMDIChildWnd** object. Create a **CSplitterWnd** object using the following steps:

1. Embed a **CSplitterWnd** member variable in the parent frame.

2. Override the parent frame's **CFrameWnd::OnCreateClient** member function.

3. From within the overridden **OnCreateClient**, call the **Create** or **CreateStatic** member function of **CSplitterWnd**.

Call the **Create** member function to create a dynamic splitter window. A dynamic splitter window typically is used to create and scroll a number of individual panes, or views, of the same document. The framework automatically creates an initial pane for the splitter; then the framework creates, resizes, and disposes of additional panes as the user operates the splitter window's controls.

When you call **Create**, you specify a minimum row height and column width that determine when the panes are too small to be fully displayed. After you call **Create**, you can adjust these minimums by calling the **SetColumnInfo** and **SetRowInfo** member functions.

Also use the **SetColumnInfo** and **SetRowInfo** member functions to set an "ideal" width for a column and "ideal" height for a row. When the framework displays a splitter window, it first displays the parent frame, then the splitter window. The framework then lays out the panes in columns and rows according to their ideal dimensions, working from the upper-left to the lower-right corner of the splitter window's client area.

All panes in a dynamic splitter window must be of the same class. Familiar applications that support dynamic splitter windows include Microsoft Word and Microsoft Excel.

Use the **CreateStatic** member function to create a static splitter window. The user can change only the size of the panes in a static splitter window, not their number or order.

You must specifically create all the static splitter's panes when you create the static splitter. Make sure you create all the panes before the parent frame's **OnCreateClient** member function returns, or the framework will not display the window correctly.

The **CreateStatic** member function automatically initializes a static splitter with a minimum row height and column width of 0. After you call **Create**, adjust these minimums by calling the **SetColumnInfo** and **SetRowInfo** member functions. Also use **SetColumnInfo** and **SetRowInfo** after you call **CreateStatic** to indicate desired ideal pane dimensions.

The individual panes of a static splitter often belong to different classes. For examples of static splitter windows, see the graphics editor and the Windows File Manager.

A splitter window supports special scroll bars (apart from the scroll bars that panes may have). These scroll bars are children of the **CSplitterWnd** object and are shared with the panes.

You create these special scroll bars when you create the splitter window. For example, a **CSplitterWnd** that has one row, two columns, and the **WS_VSCROLL** style will display a vertical scroll bar that is shared by the two panes. When the user moves the scroll bar, **WM_VSCROLL** messages are sent to both panes. When the panes set the scroll-bar position, the shared scroll bar is set.

For further information on splitter windows, see Technical Note 29 online. For more information on how to create dynamic splitter windows, see "Adding Splitter Windows to Scribble" in "Enhancing Views" in *Visual C++ Tutorials* online, and the MFC General sample "VIEWEX."

#include <afxext.h>

See Also: **CView**, **CWnd**

CSplitterWnd Class Members

Construction

CSplitterWnd	Call to construct a **CSplitterWnd** object.
Create	Call to create a dynamic splitter window and attach it to the **CSplitterWnd** object.
CreateStatic	Call to create a static splitter window and attach it to the **CSplitterWnd** object.
CreateView	Call to create a pane in a splitter window.

Operations

GetRowCount	Returns the current pane row count.
GetColumnCount	Returns the current pane column count.
GetRowInfo	Returns information on the specified row.
SetRowInfo	Call to set the specified row information.
GetColumnInfo	Returns information on the specified column.
SetColumnInfo	Call to set the specified column information.
GetPane	Returns the pane at the specified row and column.
IsChildPane	Call to determine whether the window is currently a child pane of this splitter window.
IdFromRowCol	Returns the child window ID of the pane at the specified row and column.
RecalcLayout	Call to redisplay the splitter window after adjusting row or column size.
GetScrollStyle	Returns the shared scroll-bar style.
SetScrollStyle	Specifies the new scroll-bar style for the splitter window's shared scroll-bar support.

Overridables

OnDrawSplitter	Renders an image of a split window.
OnInvertTracker	Renders the image of a split window to be the same size and shape as the frame window.
CreateScrollBarCtrl	Creates a shared scroll bar control.
DeleteView	Deletes a view from the splitter window.
SplitRow	Indicates where a frame window splits horizontally.
SplitColumn	Indicates where a frame window splits vertically.
DeleteRow	Deletes a row from the splitter window.
DeleteColumn	Deletes a column from the splitter window.
GetActivePane	Determines the active pane from the focus or active view in the frame.
SetActivePane	Sets a pane to be the active one in the frame.
CanActivateNext	Checks to see if the Next Pane or Previous Pane command is currently possible.
ActivateNext	Performs the Next Pane or Previous Pane command.
DoKeyboardSplit	Performs the keyboard split command, usually "Window Split."
DoScroll	Performs synchronized scrolling of split windows.
DoScrollBy	Scrolls split windows by a given number of pixels.

Member Functions
CSplitterWnd::ActivateNext

virtual void ActivateNext(BOOL *bPrev* **= FALSE);**

Parameters

bPrev   Indicates which window to activate. **TRUE** for previous; **FALSE** for next.

Remarks

This member function is called by the framework to perform the Next Pane or Previous Pane command.

This member function is a high level command that is used by the **CView** class to delegate to the **CSplitterWnd** implementation.

See Also: CView, CSplitterWnd::CanActivateNext, CSplitterWnd::SetActivePane

---

CSplitterWnd::CanActivateNext

virtual BOOL CanActivateNext(BOOL *bPrev* **= FALSE);**

Return Value

Nonzero if successful; otherwise 0.

Parameters

bPrev   Indicates which window to activate. **TRUE** for previous; **FALSE** for next.

Remarks

This member function is called by the framework to check to see if the Next Pane or Previous Pane command is currently possible.

This member function is a high level command that is used by the **CView** class to delegate to the **CSplitterWnd** implementation.

See Also: CSplitterWnd::ActivateNext, CSplitterWnd::SetActivePane

CSplitterWnd::Create

BOOL Create(CWnd* *pParentWnd*, **int** *nMaxRows*, **int** *nMaxCols*, **SIZE** *sizeMin*,
↪ **CCreateContext*** *pContext*, **DWORD** *dwStyle* = **WS_CHILD I WS_VISIBLE I**
↪ **WS_HSCROLL I WS_VSCROLL I SPLS_DYNAMIC_SPLIT, UINT** *nID* =
↪ **AFX_IDW_PANE_FIRST**);

Return Value

Nonzero if successful; otherwise 0.

Parameters

pParentWnd   The parent frame window of the splitter window.

nMaxRows   The maximum number of rows in the splitter window. This value must
not exceed 2.

nMaxCols   The maximum number of columns in the splitter window. This value must
not exceed 2.

sizeMin   Specifies the minimum size at which a pane may be displayed.

pContext   A pointer to a **CCreateContext** structure. In most cases, this can be the
pContext passed to the parent frame window.

dwStyle   Specifies the window style.

nID   The child window ID of the window. The ID can be **AFX_IDW_PANE_FIRST**
unless the splitter window is nested inside another splitter window.

Remarks

To create a dynamic splitter window, call the **Create** member function.

You can embed a **CSplitterWnd** in a parent **CFrameWnd** or **CMDIChildWnd**
object by taking the following steps:

1. Embed a **CSplitterWnd** member variable in the parent frame.

2. Override the parent frame's **CFrameWnd::OnCreateClient** member function.

3. Call the **Create** member function from within the overridden **OnCreateClient**.

When you create a splitter window from within a parent frame, pass the parent frame's
pContext parameter to the splitter window. Otherwise, this parameter can be **NULL**.

The initial minimum row height and column width of a dynamic splitter window are
set by the *sizeMin* parameter. These minimums, which determine whether a pane is too
small to be shown in its entirety, can be changed with the **SetRowInfo** and
SetColumnInfo member functions.

For more on dynamic splitter windows, see "Splitter Windows" in the article
"Multiple Document Types, Views, and Frame Windows" in *Visual C++
Programmer's Guide* online, Technical Note 29 online, and the **CSplitterWnd** class
overview.

See Also: **CSplitterWnd::CreateStatic**, **CFrameWnd::OnCreateClient**, **CSplitterWnd::SetRowInfo**, **CSplitterWnd::SetColumnInfo**, **CSplitterWnd::CreateView**

CSplitterWnd::CreateScrollBarCtrl

virtual BOOL CreateScrollBarCtrl(DWORD *dwStyle*, **UINT** *nID* **);**

Return Value

Nonzero if successful; otherwise 0.

Parameters

dwStyle   Specifies the window style.

nID   The child window ID of the window. The ID can be **AFX_IDW_PANE_FIRST** unless the splitter window is nested inside another splitter window.

Remarks

This member function is called by the framework to create a shared scroll bar control. Override **CreateScrollBarCtrl** to include extra controls next to a scroll bar. The default behavior is to create normal Windows scroll bar controls.

See Also: **AfxGetInstanceHandle**

CSplitterWnd::CreateStatic

BOOL CreateStatic(CWnd* *pParentWnd*, **int** *nRows*, **int** *nCols*, **DWORD**
↪ *dwStyle* = **WS_CHILD | WS_VISIBLE, UINT** *nID* = **AFX_IDW_PANE_FIRST);**

Return Value

Nonzero if successful; otherwise 0.

Parameters

pParentWnd   The parent frame window of the splitter window.

nRows   The number of rows. This value must not exceed 16.

nCols   The number of columns. This value must not exceed 16.

dwStyle   Specifies the window style.

nID   The child window ID of the window. The ID can be **AFX_IDW_PANE_FIRST** unless the splitter window is nested inside another splitter window.

Remarks

To create a static splitter window, call the **CreateStatic** member function.

A **CSplitterWnd** is usually embedded in a parent **CFrameWnd** or **CMDIChildWnd** object by taking the following steps:

1. Embed a **CSplitterWnd** member variable in the parent frame.

2. Override the parent frame's **OnCreateClient** member function.

3. Call the **CreateStatic** member function from within the overridden **CFrameWnd::OnCreateClient**.

A static splitter window contains a fixed number of panes, often from different classes.

When you create a static splitter window, you must at the same time create all its panes. The **CreateView** member function is usually used for this purpose, but you can create other nonview classes as well.

The initial minimum row height and column width for a static splitter window is 0. These minimums, which determine when a pane is too small to be shown in its entirety, can be changed with the **SetRowInfo** and **SetColumnInfo** member functions.

To add scroll bars to a static splitter window, add the **WS_HSCROLL** and **WS_VSCROLL** styles to *dwStyle*.

See "Splitter Windows" in the article "Multiple Document Types, Views, and Frame Windows" in *Visual C++ Programmer's Guide* online, Technical Note 29 online, and the **CSplitterWnd** class overview for more on static splitter windows.

See Also: **CSplitterWnd::Create**, **CFrameWnd::OnCreateClient**, **CSplitterWnd::SetRowInfo**, **CSplitterWnd::SetColumnInfo**, **CSplitterWnd::CreateView**

CSplitterWnd::CreateView

virtual BOOL CreateView(int *row*, **int** *col*, **CRuntimeClass*** *pViewClass*, ↪ **SIZE** *sizeInit*, **CCreateContext*** *pContext* **);**

Return Value

Nonzero if successful; otherwise 0.

Parameters

row   Specifies the splitter window row in which to place the new view.

col   Specifies the splitter window column in which to place the new view.

pViewClass   Specifies the **CRuntimeClass** of the new view.

sizeInit   Specifies the initial size of the new view.

pContext   A pointer to a creation context used to create the view (usually the *pContext* passed into the parent frame's overridden **CFrameWnd::OnCreateClient** member function in which the splitter window is being created).

Remarks

Call this member function to create the panes for a static splitter window. All panes of a static splitter window must be created before the framework displays the splitter.

The framework also calls this member function to create new panes when the user of a dynamic splitter window splits a pane, row, or column.

See Also: CSplitterWnd::Create

CSplitterWnd::CSplitterWnd

CSplitterWnd( );

Remarks

Construct a **CSplitterWnd** object in two steps. First call the constructor, which creates the **CSplitterWnd** object, then call the **Create** member function, which creates the splitter window and attaches it to the **CSplitterWnd** object.

See Also: CSplitterWnd::Create

CSplitterWnd::DeleteColumn

virtual void DeleteColumn(int *colDelete* **);**

Parameters

colDelete   Specifies the column to be deleted.

Remarks

This member function is called when a column is to be deleted.

This member function is called by the framework to implement the logic of the dynamic splitter window (that is, if the splitter window has the **SPLS_DYNAMIC_SPLIT** style). It can be customized, along with the virtual function **CreateView**, to implement more advanced dynamic splitters.

See Also: CSplitterWnd::DeleteRow, CSplitterWnd::CreateView, CSplitterWnd::DeleteView

CSplitterWnd::DeleteRow

virtual void DeleteRow(int *rowDelete* **);**

Parameters

rowDelete   Specifies the row to be deleted.

Remarks

DeleteRow is called when a row is to be deleted.

This member function is called by the framework to implement the logic of the dynamic splitter window (that is, if the splitter window has the **SPLS_DYNAMIC_SPLIT** style). It can be customized, along with the virtual function **CreateView**, to implement more advanced dynamic splitters.

See Also: **CSplitterWnd::DeleteColumn**, **CSplitterWnd::CreateView**, **CSplitterWnd::DeleteView**

CSplitterWnd::DeleteView

virtual void DeleteView(int *row*, **int** *col* **);**

Parameters

row   Specifies the splitter window row at which to delete the view.

col   Specifies the splitter window column at which to delete the view.

Remarks

DeleteView is called when a view is to be deleted. If the active view is being deleted, the next view will become active. The default implementation assumes the view will auto delete in **PostNcDestroy**.

This member function is called by the framework to implement the logic of the dynamic splitter window (that is, if the splitter window has the **SPLS_DYNAMIC_SPLIT** style). It can be customized, along with the virtual function **CreateView**, to implement more advanced dynamic splitters.

See Also: **CWnd::PostNcDestroy**, **CSplitterWnd::CreateView**, **CSplitterWnd::DeleteColumn**, **CSplitterWnd::DeleteRow**

CSplitterWnd::DoKeyboardSplit

virtual BOOL DoKeyboardSplit( );

Return Value

Nonzero if successful; otherwise 0.

Remarks

This member function is called by the framework to perform a keyboard split command, usually Window Split.

This member function is a high level command that is used by the **CView** class to delegate to the **CSplitterWnd** implementation.

See Also: **CView**

CSplitterWnd::DoScroll

virtual BOOL DoScroll(CView* *pViewFrom***, UINT** *nScrollCode***,**
↳ **BOOL** *bDoScroll* = **TRUE**);

Return Value

Nonzero if synchronized scrolling occurs; otherwise 0.

Parameters

pViewFrom   A pointer to the view from which the scrolling message originates.

nScrollCode   A scroll-bar code that indicates the user's scrolling request. This parameter is composed of two parts: a low-order byte, which determines the type of scrolling occurring horizontally, and a high-order byte, which determines the type of scrolling occurring vertically:

- **SB_BOTTOM**   Scrolls to bottom.

- **SB_LINEDOWN**   Scrolls one line down.

- **SB_LINEUP**   Scrolls one line up.

- **SB_PAGEDOWN**   Scrolls one page down.

- **SB_PAGEUP**   Scrolls one page up.

- **SB_TOP**   Scrolls to top.

bDoScroll   Determines whether the specified scrolling action occurs. If *bDoScroll* is **TRUE** (that is, if a child window exists, and if the split windows have a scroll range), then the specified scrolling action can take place; if *bDoScroll* is **FALSE** (that is, if no child window exists, or the split views have no scroll range), then scrolling does not occur.

Remarks

This member function is called by the framework to perform synchronized scrolling of split windows when the view receives a scroll message.

Override to require an action by the user before synchronized scrolling is allowed.

See Also: CSplitterWnd::DoScrollBy, CView::OnScroll

CSplitterWnd::DoScrollBy

virtual BOOL DoScrollBy(CView* *pViewFrom***, CSize** *sizeScroll***,**
↳ **BOOL** *bDoScroll* = **TRUE**);

Return Value

Nonzero if synchronized scrolling occurs; otherwise 0.

Parameters

pViewFrom   A pointer to the view from which the scrolling message originates.

sizeScroll   Number of pixels to be scrolled horizontally and vertically.

bDoScroll   Determines whether the specified scrolling action occurs. If *bDoScroll* is **TRUE** (that is, if a child window exists, and if the split windows have a scroll range), then the specified scrolling action can take place; if *bDoScroll* is **FALSE** (that is, if no child window exists, or the split views have no scroll range), then scrolling does not occur.

Remarks

This member function is called by the framework in response to a scroll message, to perform synchronized scrolling of the split windows by the amount, in pixels, indicated by *sizeScroll*. Positive values indicate scrolling down and to the right; negative values indicate scrolling up and to the left.

Override to require an action by the user before allowing scroll.

See Also: CSplitterWnd::DoScroll, CView::OnScroll

CSplitterWnd::GetActivePane

virtual CWnd* GetActivePane(int* *pRow* **= NULL, int*** *pCol* **= NULL);**

Return Value

Pointer to the active pane. **NULL** if no active pane exists.

Parameters

pRow   A pointer to an **int** to retrieve the row number of the active pane.

pCol   A pointer to an **int** to retrieve the column number of the active pane.

Remarks

This member function is called by the framework to determine the active pane in a splitter window.

Override to require an action by the user before getting the active pane.

**See Also: CSplitterWnd::SetActivePane,
CFrameWnd::GetActiveView, CWnd::GetParentFrame, CWnd::GetFocus**

CSplitterWnd::GetColumnCount

int GetColumnCount( );

Return Value

Returns the current number of columns in the splitter. For a static splitter, this will also be the maximum number of columns.

See Also: **CSplitterWnd::GetRowCount**

CSplitterWnd::GetColumnInfo

void GetColumnInfo(int *col*, **int&** *cxCur*, **int&** *cxMin* **);**

Parameters

col   Specifies a column.

cxCur   A reference to an **int** to be set to the current width of the column.

cxMin   A reference to an **int** to be set to the current minimum width of the column.

Remarks

Call this member function to obtain information about the specified column.

See Also: **CSplitterWnd::SetColumnInfo**, **CSplitterWnd::GetRowInfo**

CSplitterWnd::GetPane

CWnd* GetPane(int *row*, **int** *col* **);**

Return Value

Returns the pane at the specified row and column. The returned pane is usually a **CView**-derived class.

Parameters

row   Specifies a row.

col   Specifies a column.

See Also: **CSplitterWnd::GetActivePane**, **CSplitterWnd::IdFromRowCol**, **CSplitterWnd::IsChildPane**

CSplitterWnd::GetRowCount

int GetRowCount( );

Return Value

Returns the current number of rows in the splitter window. For a static splitter window, this will also be the maximum number of rows.

See Also: **CSplitterWnd::GetColumnCount**

CSplitterWnd::GetRowInfo

void GetRowInfo(int *row*, **int&** *cyCur*, **int&** *cyMin* **);**

Parameters

row   Specifies a row.

cyCur   Reference to **int** to be set to the current height of the row in pixels.

cyMin   Reference to **int** to be set to the current minimum height of the row in pixels.

Remarks

Call this member function to obtain information about the specified row. The *cyCur* parameter is filled with the current height of the specified row, and *cyMin* is filled with the minimum height of the row.

See Also: CSplitterWnd::SetRowInfo, CSplitterWnd::GetColumnInfo

CSplitterWnd::GetScrollStyle

DWORD GetScrollStyle( ) const;

Return Value

One or more of the following windows style flags, if successful:

- **WS_HSCROLL**   If the splitter currently manages shared horizontal scroll bars.
- **WS_VSCROLL**   If the splitter currently manages shared vertical scroll bars.

If zero, the splitter window does not currently manage any shared scroll bars.

Remarks

Returns the shared scroll-bar style for the splitter window.

See Also: CSplitterWnd::SetScrollStyle

CSplitterWnd::IdFromRowCol

int IdFromRowCol(int *row*, int *col*);

Return Value

The child window ID for the pane.

Parameters

row   Specifies the splitter window row.

col   Specifies the splitter window column.

Remarks

Call this member function to obtain the child window ID for the pane at the specified row and column. This member function is used for creating nonviews as panes and may be called before the pane exists.

See Also: CSplitterWnd::GetPane, CSplitterWnd::IsChildPane

CSplitterWnd::IsChildPane

BOOL IsChildPane(CWnd* *pWnd*, **int&** *row*, **int&** *col* **);**

Return Value

If nonzero, *pWnd* is currently a child pane of this splitter window, and *row* and *col* are filled in with the position of the pane in the splitter window. If *pWnd* is not a child pane of this splitter window, 0 is returned.

Parameters

pWnd   A pointer to a **CWnd** object to be tested.

row   Reference to an **int** in which to store row number.

col   Reference to an **int** in which to store a column number.

Remarks

Call this member function to determine whether *pWnd* is currently a child pane of this splitter window.

See Also: CSplitterWnd::GetPane

CSplitterWnd::OnDrawSplitter

virtual void OnDrawSplitter(CDC* *pDC*, **ESplitType** *nType*, **const CRect&** *rect* **);**

Parameters

pDC   A pointer to the device context in which to draw. If *pDC* is **NULL**, then **CWnd::RedrawWindow** is called by the framework and no split window is drawn.

nType   A value of the **enum ESplitType**, which can be one of the following:

- **splitBox**   The splitter drag box.

- **splitBar**   The bar that appears between the two split windows.

- **splitIntersection**   The intersection of the split windows. This element will not be called when running on Windows 95.

- **splitBorder**   The split window borders.

rect   A reference to a **CRect** object specifying the size and shape of the split windows.

Remarks

This member function is called by the framework to draw and specify the exact characteristics of a splitter window.

Override **OnDrawSplitter** for advanced customization of the imagery for the various graphical components of a splitter window. The default imagery is similar to the splitter in Microsoft Works for Windows or Microsoft Windows 95, in that the intersections of the splitter bars are blended together.

For more on dynamic splitter windows, see "Splitter Windows" in the article "Multiple Document Types, Views, and Frame Windows" in *Visual C++ Programmer's Guide* online, Technical Note 29 online, and the **CSplitterWnd** class overview.

See Also: **CSplitterWnd::OnInvertTracker**

CSplitterWnd::OnInvertTracker

virtual void OnInvertTracker(const CRect& *rect* **);**

Parameters

rect   Reference to a **CRect** object specifying the tracking rectangle.

Remarks

This member function is called by the framework during resizing of splitters.

Override **OnInvertTracker** for advanced customization of the imagery of the splitter window. The default imagery is similar to the splitter in Microsoft Works for Windows or Microsoft Windows 95, in that the intersections of the splitter bars are blended together.

For more on dynamic splitter windows, see "Splitter Windows" in the article "Multiple Document Types, Views, and Frame Windows" in *Visual C++ Programmer's Guide* online, Technical Note 29 online, and the **CSplitterWnd** class overview.

See Also: **CSplitterWnd::OnDrawSplitter**

CSplitterWnd::RecalcLayout

void RecalcLayout( );

Remarks

Call this member function to correctly redisplay the splitter window after you have adjusted row and column sizes with the **SetRowInfo** and **SetColumnInfo** member functions. If you change row and column sizes as part of the creation process before the splitter window is visible, it is not necessary to call this member function.

The framework calls this member function whenever the user resizes the splitter window or moves a split.

See Also: **CSplitterWnd::SetRowInfo**, **CSplitterWnd::SetColumnInfo**

CSplitterWnd::SetActivePane

virtual void SetActivePane(int *row***, int** *col***, CWnd*** *pWnd* **= NULL);**

Parameters

row   If *pWnd* is **NULL**, specifies the row in the pane that will be active.

col   If *pWnd* is **NULL**, specifies the column in the pane that will be active.

pWnd   A pointer to a **CWnd** object. If **NULL**, the pane specified by *row* and *col* is set active. If not **NULL**, specifies the pane that is set active.

Remarks

This member function is called by the framework to set a pane as active when the user changes the focus to a pane within the frame window. You may explicitly call **SetActivePane** to change the focus to the specified view.

Specify pane by providing either row and column, **or** by providing *pWnd*.

See Also: CSplitterWnd::GetActivePane, CSplitterWnd::GetPane, CFrameWnd::SetActiveView

---

CSplitterWnd::SetColumnInfo

void SetColumnInfo(int *col***, int** *cxIdeal***, int** *cxMin* **);**

Parameters

col   Specifies a splitter window column.

cxIdeal   Specifies an ideal width for the splitter window column in pixels.

cxMin   Specifies a minimum width for the splitter window column in pixels.

Remarks

Call this member function to set a new minimum width and ideal width for a column. The column minimum value determines when the column will be too small to be fully displayed.

When the framework displays the splitter window, it lays out the panes in columns and rows according to their ideal dimensions, working from the upper-left to the lower-right corner of the splitter window's client area.

See Also: CSplitterWnd::GetRowInfo, CSplitterWnd::RecalcLayout

---

CSplitterWnd::SetRowInfo

void SetRowInfo(int *row***, int** *cyIdeal***, int** *cyMin* **);**

Parameters

row   Specifies a splitter window row.

cyIdeal   Specifies an ideal height for the splitter window row in pixels.

cyMin   Specifies a minimum height for the splitter window row in pixels.

Remarks

Call this member function to set a new minimum height and ideal height for a row. The row minimum value determines when the row will be too small to be fully displayed.

When the framework displays the splitter window, it lays out the panes in columns and rows according to their ideal dimensions, working from the upper-left to the lower-right corner of the splitter window's client area.

See Also: CSplitterWnd::GetRowInfo, CSplitterWnd::SetColumnInfo, CSplitterWnd::RecalcLayout

CSplitterWnd::SetScrollStyle

void SetScrollStyle(DWORD *dwStyle* **);**

Parameters

dwStyle   The new scroll style for the splitter window's shared scroll-bar support, which can be one of the following values:

- **WS_HSCROLL**   Create/show horizontal shared scroll bars.
- **WS_VSCROLL**   Create/show vertical shared scroll bars.

Remarks

Specifies the new scroll style for the splitter window's shared scroll-bar support. Once a scroll bar is created it will not be destroyed even if **SetScrollStyle** is called without that style; instead those scroll bars are hidden. This allows the scroll bars to retain their state even though they are hidden. After calling **SetScrollStyle** it is necessary to call **RecalcLayout** for all the changes to take effect.

See Also: CSplitterWnd::GetScrollStyle

CSplitterWnd::SplitColumn

virtual BOOL SplitColumn(int *cxBefore* **);**

Return Value

Nonzero if successful; otherwise 0.

Parameters

cxBefore   The position, in pixels, before which the split occurs.

Remarks

This member function is called when a vertical splitter window is created. **SplitColumn** indicates the default location where the split occurs.

SplitColumn is called by the framework to implement the logic of the dynamic splitter window (that is, if the splitter window has the **SPLS_DYNAMIC_SPLIT** style). It can be customized, along with the virtual function **CreateView**, to implement more advanced dynamic splitters.

See Also: CSplitterWnd::CreateView, CSplitterWnd::SplitRow, CSplitterWnd::RecalcLayout

---

CSplitterWnd::SplitRow

virtual BOOL SplitRow(int *cyBefore* **);**

Return Value

Nonzero if successful; otherwise 0.

Parameters

cyBefore   The position, in pixels, before which the split occurs.

Remarks

This member function is called when a horizontal splitter window is created. **SplitRow** indicates the default location where the split occurs.

SplitRow is called by the framework to implement the logic of the dynamic splitter window (that is, if the splitter window has the **SPLS_DYNAMIC_SPLIT** style). It can be customized, along with the virtual function **CreateView**, to implement more advanced dynamic splitters.

See Also: CSplitterWnd::SplitColumn, CSplitterWnd::CreateView, CSplitterWnd::RecalcLayout

CStatic

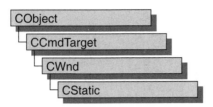

CObject
CCmdTarget
CWnd
CStatic

The **CStatic** class provides the functionality of a Windows static control. A static control displays a text string, box, rectangle, icon, cursor, bitmap, or enhanced metafile. It can be used to label, box, or separate other controls. A static control normally takes no input and provides no output; however, it can notify its parent of mouse clicks if it's created with **SS_NOTIFY** style.

Create a static control in two steps. First, call the constructor to construct the **CStatic** object, then call the **Create** member function to create the static control and attach it to the **CStatic** object.

If you create a **CStatic** object within a dialog box (through a dialog resource), the **CStatic** object is automatically destroyed when the user closes the dialog box.

If you create a **CStatic** object within a window, you may also need to destroy it. A **CStatic** object created on the stack within a window is automatically destroyed. If you create the **CStatic** object on the heap by using the **new** function, you must call **delete** on the object to destroy it when the you are done with it.

#include <afxwin.h>

See Also: **CWnd, CButton, CComboBox, CEdit, CListBox, CScrollBar, CDialog**

CStatic Class Members

Construction

CStatic	Constructs a **CStatic** object.

Initialization

Create	Creates the Windows static control and attaches it to the **CStatic** object.

Operations

SetBitmap	Specifies a bitmap to be displayed in the static control.
GetBitmap	Retrieves the handle of the bitmap previously set with **SetBitmap**.
SetIcon	Specifies an icon to be displayed in the static control.

GetIcon	Retrieves the handle of the icon previously set with **SetIcon**.
SetCursor	Specifies a cursor image to be displayed in the static control.
GetCursor	Retrieves the handle of the cursor image previously set with **SetCursor**.
SetEnhMetaFile	Specifies an enhanced metafile to be displayed in the static control.
GetEnhMetaFile	Retrieves the handle of the enhanced metafile previously set with **SetEnhMetaFile**.

Member Functions

CStatic::Create

BOOL Create(LPCTSTR *lpszText*, **DWORD** *dwStyle*, **const RECT&** *rect*,
  ↳ **CWnd*** *pParentWnd*, **UINT** *nID* **= 0xffff);**

Return Value
Nonzero if successful; otherwise 0.

Parameters
lpszText Specifies the text to place in the control. If **NULL**, no text will be visible.

dwStyle Specifies the static control's window style. Apply any combination of static control styles to the control.

rect Specifies the position and size of the static control. It can be either a **RECT** structure or a **CRect** object.

pParentWnd Specifies the **CStatic** parent window, usually a **CDialog** object. It must not be **NULL**.

nID Specifies the static control's control ID.

Remarks
Construct a **CStatic** object in two steps. First call the constructor **CStatic**, then call **Create**, which creates the Windows static control and attaches it to the **CStatic** object.

Apply the following window styles to a static control:

- **WS_CHILD** Always
- **WS_VISIBLE** Usually
- **WS_DISABLED** Rarely

If you're going to display a bitmap, cursor, icon, or metafile in the static control, you'll need to apply one of the following styles:

- **SS_BITMAP** Use this style for bitmaps.

- **SS_ICON**   Use this style for cursors and icons.
- **SS_ENHMETAFILE**   Use this style for enhanced metafiles.

For cursors, bitmaps, or icons, you may also want to use the following style:

- **SS_CENTERIMAGE**   Use to center the image in the static control.

See Also: **CStatic::Cstatic**

CStatic::CStatic

CStatic( );

Remarks

Constructs a **CStatic** object.

See Also: **CStatic::Create**

CStatic::GetBitmap

HBITMAP GetBitmap( ) const;

Return Value

A handle to the current bitmap, or **NULL** if no bitmap has been set.

Remarks

Call this member function to get the handle of the bitmap, previously set with **SetBitmap**, that is associated with **CStatic**.

See Also: **CStatic::SetBitmap**, **STM_GETIMAGE**, "Bitmaps" online

---

CStatic::GetCursor

HCURSOR GetCursor( );

Return Value

A handle to the current cursor, or **NULL** if no cursor has been set.

Remarks

Call this member function to get the handle of the cursor, previously set with **SetCursor**, that is associated with **CStatic**.

See Also: **CStatic::SetCursor**, **STM_GETIMAGE**, "Cursors" online

CStatic::GetEnhMetaFile

HENHMETAFILE GetEnhMetaFile( ) const;

Return Value

A handle to the current enhanced metafile, or **NULL** if no enhanced metafile has been set.

Remarks

Call this member function to get the handle of the enhanced metafile, previously set with **SetEnhMetafile**, that is associated with **Cstatic**.

See Also: **CStatic::SetEnhMetafile**, **STM_GETIMAGE**

CStatic::GetIcon

HICON GetIcon( ) const;

Return Value

A handle to the current icon, or **NULL** if no icon has been set.

Remarks

Call this member function to get the handle of the icon, previously set with **SetIcon**, that is associated with **CStatic**.

See Also: **CStatic::SetIcon**, **STM_GETICON**, "Icons" online

---

CStatic::SetBitmap

HBITMAP SetBitmap(HBITMAP *hBitmap* **);**

Return Value

The handle of the bitmap previously associated with the static control, or **NULL** if no bitmap was associated with the static control.

Parameters

hBitmap   Handle of the bitmap to be drawn in the static control.

Remarks

Call this member function to associate a new bitmap with the static control.

The bitmap will be automatically drawn in the static control. By default, it will be drawn in the upper-left corner and the static control will be resized to the size of the bitmap.

You can use various window and static control styles, including the following:

- **SS_BITMAP**   Use this style always for bitmaps.

- **SS_CENTERIMAGE**   Use to center in the static control. If the image is larger than the static control, it will be clipped. If it is smaller than the static control, the empty space around the image will be filled by the color of the pixel in the upper left corner of the bitmap.

See Also: **CStatic::GetBitmap**, **STM_SETIMAGE**, "Bitmaps" online

---

CStatic::SetCursor

HCURSOR SetCursor(HCURSOR *hCursor* **);**

Return Value

The handle of the cursor previously associated with the static control, or **NULL** if no cursor was associated with the static control.

Parameters

hCursor   Handle of the cursor to be drawn in the static control.

Remarks

Call this member function to associate a new cursor image with the static control.

The cursor will be automatically drawn in the static control. By default, it will be drawn in the upper-left corner and the static control will be resized to the size of the cursor.

You can use various window and static control styles, including the following:

- **SS_ICON**   Use this style always for cursors and icons.
- **SS_CENTERIMAGE**   Use to center in the static control. If the image is larger than the static control, it will be clipped. If it is smaller than the static control, the empty space around the image will be filled with the background color of the static control.

See Also: **CStatic::GetCursor**, **STM_SETIMAGE**, "Cursors" online

---

CStatic::SetEnhMetaFile

HENHMETAFILE SetEnhMetaFile(HENHMETAFILE *hMetaFile* **);**

Return Value

The handle of the enhanced metafile previously associated with the static control, or **NULL** if no enhanced metafile was associated with the static control.

Parameters

hMetaFile   Handle of the enhanced metafile to be drawn in the static control.

Remarks

Call this member function to associate a new enhanced metafile image with the static control.

The enhanced metafile will be automatically drawn in the static control. The enhanced metafile is scaled to fit the size of the static control.

You can use various window and static control styles, including the following:

- **SS_ENHMETAFILE**   Use this style always for enhanced metafiles.

See Also: **CStatic::GetEnhMetafile**, **STM_SETIMAGE**

CStatic::SetIcon

HICON SetIcon(HICON *hIcon* **);**

Return Value

The handle of the icon previously associated with the static control, or **NULL** if no icon was associated with the static control.

Parameters

hIcon   Handle of the icon to be drawn in the static control.

Remarks

Call this member function to associate a new icon image with the static control.

The icon will be automatically drawn in the static control. By default, it will be drawn in the upper-left corner and the static control will be resized to the size of the icon.

You can use various window and static control styles, including the following:

- **SS_ICON**   Use this style always for cursors and icons.
- **SS_CENTERIMAGE**   Use to center in the static control. If the image is larger than the static control, it will be clipped. If it is smaller than the static control, the empty space around the image will be filled with the background color of the static control.

See Also: **CStatic::GetIcon**, **STM_SETICON**, "Icons" online

CStatusBar

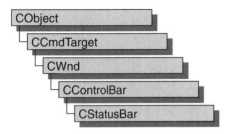

A **CStatusBar** object is a control bar with a row of text output panes, or "indicators." The output panes commonly are used as message lines and as status indicators. Examples include the menu help-message lines that briefly explain the selected menu command and the indicators that show the status of the SCROLL LOCK, NUM LOCK, and other keys.

CStatusBar::GetStatusBarCtrl, a member function new to MFC 4.0, allows you to take advantage of the Windows common control's support for status bar customization and additional functionality. **CStatusBar** member functions give you most of the functionality of the Windows common controls; however, when you call **GetStatusBarCtrl**, you can give your status bars even more of the characteristics of a Windows 95 status bar. When you call **GetStatusBarCtrl**, it will return a reference to a **CStatusBarCtrl** object. See **CStatusBarCtrl** for more information about designing toolbars using Windows common controls. For more general information about common controls, see "Common Controls" in the *Windows 95 SDK Programmer's Reference*.

The framework stores indicator information in an array with the leftmost indicator at position 0. When you create a status bar, you use an array of string IDs that the framework associates with the corresponding indicators. You can then use either a string ID or an index to access an indicator.

By default, the first indicator is "elastic": it takes up the status-bar length not used by the other indicator panes, so that the other panes are right-aligned.

To create a status bar, follow these steps:

1. Construct the **CStatusBar** object.
2. Call the **Create** function to create the status-bar window and attach it to the **CStatusBar** object.
3. Call **SetIndicators** to associate a string ID with each indicator.

There are three ways to update the text in a status-bar pane:

1. Call **CWnd::SetWindowText** to update the text in pane 0 only.

2. Call **CCmdUI::SetText** in the status bar's **ON_UPDATE_COMMAND_UI** handler.

3. Call **SetPaneText** to update the text for any pane.

Call **SetPaneStyle** to update the style of a status-bar pane.

For more information on using **CStatusBar**, see the article "Status Bars" in *Visual C++ Programmer's Guide* online and Technical Note 31 online, Control Bars.

#include <afxext.h>

See Also: **CStatusBarCtrl**, **CControlBar**, **CWnd::SetWindowText**, **CStatusBar::SetIndicators**

CStatusBar Class Members

Construction

CStatusBar	Constructs a **CStatusBar** object.
Create	Creates the status bar, attaches it to the **CStatusBar** object, and sets the initial font and bar height.
SetIndicators	Sets indicator IDs.

Attributes

CommandToIndex	Gets index for a given indicator ID.
GetItemID	Gets indicator ID for a given index.
GetItemRect	Gets display rectangle for a given index.
GetPaneInfo	Gets indicator ID, style, and width for a given index.
GetPaneStyle	Gets indicator style for a given index.
GetPaneText	Gets indicator text for a given index.
GetStatusBarCtrl	Allows direct access to the underlying common control.
SetPaneStyle	Sets indicator style for a given index.
SetPaneText	Sets indicator text for a given index.
SetPaneInfo	Sets indicator ID, style, and width for a given index.

Member Functions

CStatusBar::CommandToIndex

int CommandToIndex(UINT *nIDFind* **) const;**

Return Value

The index of the indicator if successful; −1 if not successful.

Parameters

nIDFind   String ID of the indicator whose index is to be retrieved.

Remarks

Gets the indicator index for a given ID. The index of the first indicator is 0.

See Also: CStatusBar::GetItemID

CStatusBar::Create

BOOL Create(CWnd* *pParentWnd***,**
↪ **DWORD** *dwStyle* **= WS_CHILD | WS_VISIBLE | CBRS_BOTTOM,**
↪ **UINT** *nID* **= AFX_IDW_STATUS_BAR);**

Return Value

Nonzero if successful; otherwise 0.

Parameters

pParentWnd   Pointer to the **CWnd** object whose Windows window is the parent of the status bar.

dwStyle   The status-bar style. In addition to the standard Windows styles, these styles are supported.

- **CBRS_TOP**   Control bar is at top of frame window.

- **CBRS_BOTTOM**   Control bar is at bottom of frame window.

- **CBRS_NOALIGN**   Control bar is not repositioned when the parent is resized.

nID   The toolbar's child-window ID.

Remarks

Creates a status bar (a child window) and associates it with the **CStatusBar** object. Also sets the initial font and sets the status bar's height to a default value.

See Also: CStatusBar::SetIndicators

CStatusBar::CStatusBar

CStatusBar( );

Remarks

Constructs a **CStatusBar** object, creates a default status-bar font if necessary, and sets the font characteristics to default values.

See Also: CStatusBar::Create

CStatusBar::GetItemID

UINT GetItemID(int *nIndex*) const;

Return Value

The ID of the indicator specified by *nIndex*.

Parameters

nIndex   Index of the indicator whose ID is to be retrieved.

Remarks

Returns the ID of the indicator specified by *nIndex*.

See Also: CStatusBar::CommandToIndex

CStatusBar::GetItemRect

void GetItemRect(int *nIndex*, LPRECT *lpRect*) const;

Parameters

nIndex   Index of the indicator whose rectangle coordinates are to be retrieved.

lpRect   Points to a **RECT** structure or a **CRect** object that will receive the coordinates of the indicator specified by *nIndex*.

Remarks

Copies the coordinates of the indicator specified by *nIndex* into the structure pointed to by *lpRect*. Coordinates are in pixels relative to the upper-left corner of the status bar.

See Also: CStatusBar::CommandToIndex, CStatusBar::GetPaneInfo

---

CStatusBar::GetPaneInfo

void GetPaneInfo(int *nIndex*, UINT& *nID*, UINT& *nStyle*, int& *cxWidth*) const;

Parameters

nIndex   Index of the pane whose information is to be retrieved.

nID   Reference to a **UINT** that is set to the ID of the pane.

nStyle   Reference to a **UINT** that is set to the style of the pane.

cxWidth   Reference to an integer that is set to the width of the pane.

Remarks

Sets *nID*, *nStyle*, and *cxWidth* to the ID, style, and width of the indicator pane at the location specified by *nIndex*.

See Also: **CStatusBar::SetPaneInfo, CStatusBar::GetItemID, CStatusBar::GetItemRect**

CStatusBar::GetPaneStyle

UINT GetPaneStyle(int *nIndex* **) const;**

Return Value

The style of the status-bar pane specified by *nIndex*.

Parameters

nIndex Index of the pane whose style is to be retrieved.

Remarks

Call this member function to retrieve the style of a status bar's pane. A pane's style determines how the pane appears.

For a list of styles available for status bars, see **Create**.

See Also: **CStatusBar::Create, CStatusBar::SetPaneStyle**

CStatusBar::GetPaneText

CString GetPaneText(int *nIndex* **) const;**
void GetPaneText(int *nIndex***, CString&** *rString* **) const;**

Return Value

A **CString** object containing the pane's text.

Parameters

nIndex Index of the pane whose text is to be retrieved.

rString A reference to a **CString** object that contains the text to be retrieved.

Remarks

Call this member function to retrieve the text that appears in a status-bar pane. The second form of this member function fills a **CString** object with the string text.

See Also: **CStatusBar::SetPaneText**

CStatusBar::GetStatusBarCtrl

CStatusBarCtrl& GetStatusBarCtrl( ) const;

Return Value

Contains a reference to a **CStatusBarCtrl** object.

Remarks

This member function allows direct access to the underlying common control.

Use **GetStatusBarCtrl** to take advantage of the functionality of the Windows status-bar common control, and to take advantage of the support **CStatusBarCtrl** provides for status-bar customization. For example, by using the common control, you can specify a style that includes a sizing grip on the status bar, or you can specify a style to have the status bar appear at the top of the parent window's client area.

For more general information about common controls, See "Common Controls" in the *Windows 95 SDK Programmer's Reference*.

CStatusBar::SetIndicators

> **BOOL SetIndicators(const UINT*** *lpIDArray***, int** *nIDCount* **);**

Return Value

Nonzero if successful; otherwise 0.

Parameters

lpIDArray   Pointer to an array of IDs.

nIDCount   Number of elements in the array pointed to by *lpIDArray*.

Remarks

Sets each indicator's ID to the value specified by the corresponding element of the array *lpIDArray*, loads the string resource specified by each ID, and sets the indicator's text to the string.

See Also: CStatusBar::CStatusBar, CStatusBar::Create, CStatusBar::SetPaneInfo, CStatusBar::SetPaneText

CStatusBar::SetPaneInfo

> **void SetPaneInfo(int** *nIndex***, UINT** *nID***, UINT** *nStyle***, int** *cxWidth* **);**

Parameters

nIndex   Index of the indicator pane whose style is to be set.

nID   New ID for the indicator pane.

nStyle   New style for the indicator pane.

cxWidth   New width for the indicator pane.

Remarks

Sets the specified indicator pane to a new ID, style, and width.

The following indicator styles are supported:

- **SBPS_NOBORDERS** No 3-D border around the pane.
- **SBPS_POPOUT** Reverse border so that text "pops out."
- **SBPS_DISABLED** Do not draw text.
- **SBPS_STRETCH** Stretch pane to fill unused space. Only one pane per status bar can have this style.
- **SBPS_NORMAL** No stretch, borders, or pop-out.

See Also: CStatusBar::GetPaneInfo

CStatusBar::SetPaneStyle

void SetPaneStyle(int *nIndex,* **UINT** *nStyle* **);**

Parameters

nIndex Index of the pane whose style is to be set.

nStyle Style of the pane whose style is to be set.

Remarks

Call this member function to set the style of a status bar's pane. A pane's style determines how the pane appears.

For a list of styles available for status bars, see **SetPaneInfo**.

See Also: CStatusBar::Create, CStatusBar::GetPaneStyle

CStatusBar::SetPaneText

BOOL SetPaneText(int *nIndex,* **LPCTSTR** *lpszNewText,* **BOOL** *bUpdate* **= TRUE);**

Return Value

Nonzero if successful; otherwise 0.

Parameters

nIndex Index of the pane whose text is to be set.

lpszNewText Pointer to the new pane text.

bUpdate If **TRUE**, the pane is invalidated after the text is set.

Remarks

Sets the pane text to the string pointed to by *lpszNewText*.

See Also: CStatusBar::GetPaneText

CStatusBarCtrl

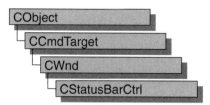

A "status bar control" is a horizontal window, usually displayed at the bottom of a parent window, in which an application can display various kinds of status information. The status bar control can be divided into parts to display more than one type of information.

The **CStatusBarCtrl** class provides the functionality of the Windows common status bar control. This control (and therefore the **CStatusBarCtrl** class) is available only to programs running under Windows 95 and Windows NT version 3.51 and later.

For more information on using **CStatusBarCtrl**, see Technical Note 60 online.

#include <afxcmn.h>

See Also: CToolBarCtrl

CStatusBarCtrl Class Members

Construction

CStatusBarCtrl	Constructs a **CStatusBarCtrl** object.
Create	Creates a status bar control and attaches it to a **CStatusBarCtrl** object.

Attributes

SetText	Sets the text in the given part of a status bar control.
GetText	Retrieves the text from the given part of a status bar control.
GetTextLength	Retrieve the length, in characters, of the text from the given part of a status bar control.
SetParts	Sets the number of parts in a status bar control and the coordinate of the right edge of each part.
GetParts	Retrieves a count of the parts in a status bar control.

(continued)

Attributes *(continued)*

GetBorders	Retrieves the current widths of the horizontal and vertical borders of a status bar control.
SetMinHeight	Sets the minimum height of a status bar control's drawing area.
SetSimple	Specifies whether a status bar control displays simple text or displays all control parts set by a previous call to **SetParts**.
GetRect	Retrieves the bounding rectangle of a part in a status bar control.

Overridables

DrawItem	Called when a visual aspect of an owner-draw status bar control changes.

Member Functions

CStatusBarCtrl::Create

BOOL Create(DWORD *dwStyle*, **const RECT&** *rect*, **CWnd*** *pParentWnd*, **UINT** *nID* **);**

Return Value

Nonzero if successful; otherwise zero.

Parameters

dwStyle   Specifies the status bar control's style. Apply any combination of status bar control styles to the control. This parameter must include the **WS_CHILD** style. It should also include the **WS_VISIBLE** style. See the Remarks section for more information.

rect   Specifies the status bar control's size and position. It can be either a **CRect** object or a **RECT** structure.

pParentWnd   Specifies the status bar control's parent window, usually a **CDialog**. It must not be **NULL.**

nID   Specifies the status bar control's ID.

Remarks

You construct a **CStatusBarCtrl** in two steps. First call the constructor, then call **Create**, which creates the status bar control and attaches it to the **CStatusBarCtrl** object.

The *dwStyle* parameter can have any combination of the following values:

- **CCS_BOTTOM**   Causes the control to position itself at the bottom of the parent window's client area and sets the width to be the same as the parent window's width. Status bar controls have this style by default.

- **CCS_NODIVIDER**   Prevents a two-pixel highlight from being drawn at the top of the control.

- **CCS_NOHILITE**   Prevents a one-pixel highlight from being drawn at the top of the control.

- **CCS_NOMOVEY**   Causes the control to resize and move itself horizontally, but not vertically, in response to a **WM_SIZE** message. If the **CCS_NORESIZE** style is used, this style does not apply.

- **CCS_NOPARENTALIGN**   Prevents the control from automatically moving to the top or bottom of the parent window. Instead, the control keeps its position within the parent window despite changes to the size of the parent window. If the **CCS_TOP** or **CCS_BOTTOM** style is also used, the height is adjusted to the default, but the position and width remain unchanged.

- **CCS_NORESIZE**   Prevents the control from using the default width and height when setting its initial size or a new size. Instead, the control uses the width and height specified in the request for creation or sizing.

- **CCS_TOP**   Causes the control to position itself at the top of the parent window's client area and sets the width to be the same as the parent window's width.

The default position of a status window is along the bottom of the parent window, but you can specify the **CCS_TOP** style to have it appear at the top of the parent window's client area. You can specify the **SBARS_SIZEGRIP** style to include a sizing grip at the right end of the status window. Combining the **CCS_TOP** and **SBARS_SIZEGRIP** styles is not recommended, because the resulting sizing grip is not functional even though the system draws it in the status window.

See Also: CStatusBarCtrl::CStatusBarCtrl

CStatusBarCtrl::CStatusBarCtrl

CStatusBarCtrl( );

Remarks

Constructs a **CStatusBarCtrl** object.

See Also: CStatusBarCtrl::Create

CStatusBarCtrl::DrawItem

virtual void DrawItem(LPDRAWITEMSTRUCT *lpDrawItemStruct* **);**

Parameters

lpDrawItemStruct   A long pointer to a **DRAWITEMSTRUCT** structure that contains information about the type of drawing required.

Remarks

Called by the framework when a visual aspect of an owner-draw status bar control changes. The **itemAction** member of the **DRAWITEMSTRUCT** structure defines the drawing action that is to be performed.

By default, this member function does nothing. Override this member function to implement drawing for an owner-draw **CStatusBarCtrl** object.

The application should restore all graphics device interface (GDI) objects selected for the display context supplied in *lpDrawItemStruct* before this member function terminates.

See Also: **CWnd::OnDrawItem**

CStatusBarCtrl::GetBorders

BOOL GetBorders(int* *pBorders* **) const;**
BOOL GetBorders(int& *nHorz***, int&** *nVert***, int&** *nSpacing* **) const;**

Return Value

Nonzero if successful; otherwise zero.

Parameters

pBorders   Address of an integer array having three elements. The first element receives the width of the horizontal border, the second receives the width of the vertical border, and the third receives the width of the border between rectangles.

nHorz   Reference to an integer that receives the width of the horizontal border.

nVert   Reference to an integer that receives the width of the vertical border.

nSpacing   Reference to an integer that receives the width of the border between rectangles.

Remarks

Call this function to retrieve the status bar control's current widths of the horizontal and vertical borders and of the space between rectangles. These borders determine the spacing between the outside edge of the control and the rectangles within the control that contain text.

See Also: **CStatusBarCtrl::GetParts, CStatusBarCtrl::SetParts**

CStatusBarCtrl::GetParts

int GetParts(int *nParts***, int*** *pParts* **) const;**

Return Value

The number of parts in the control if successful, or zero otherwise.

Parameters

nParts   Number of parts for which to retrieve coordinates. If this parameter is greater than the number of parts in the control, the message retrieves coordinates for existing parts only.

pParts   Address of an integer array having the same number of elements as the number of parts specified by *nParts*. Each element in the array receives the client coordinate of the right edge of the corresponding part. If an element is set to −1, the position of the right edge for that part extends to the right edge of the status bar.

Remarks

Call this function to retrieve a count of the parts in a status bar control. This member function also retrieves the coordinate of the right edge of the given number of parts.

See Also: **CStatusBarCtrl::GetBorders**, **CStatusBarCtrl::SetParts**

CStatusBarCtrl::GetRect

BOOL GetRect(int *nPane***, LPRECT** *lpRect* **) const;**

Return Value

Nonzero if successful; otherwise zero.

Parameters

nPane   Zero-based index of the part whose bounding rectangle is to be retrieved.

lpRect   Address of a **RECT** structure that receives the bounding rectangle.

Remarks

Retrieves the bounding rectangle of a part in a status bar control.

See Also: **CStatusBarCtrl::GetParts**

CStatusBarCtrl::GetText

int GetText(LPCTSTR *lpszText***, int** *nPane***, int*** *pType* **) const;**

Return Value

The length, in characters, of the text.

Parameters

lpszText   Address of the buffer that receives the text. This parameter is a null-terminated string.

nPane   Zero-based index of the part from which to retrieve text.

pType   Pointer to an integer that receives the type information. The type can be one of these values:

- **0**   The text is drawn with a border to appear lower than the plane of the status bar.

- **SBT_NOBORDERS**   The text is drawn without borders.

- **SBT_POPOUT**   The text is drawn with a border to appear higher than the plane of the status bar.

Remarks

Call this function to retrieve the text from the given part of a status bar control.

See Also: CStatusBarCtrl::SetText, CStatusBarCtrl::GetTextLength

---

CStatusBarCtrl::GetTextLength

int GetTextLength(int *nPane*, int* *pType*) const;

Return Value

The length, in characters, of the text.

Parameters

nPane   Zero-based index of the part from which to retrieve text.

pType   Pointer to an integer that receives the type information. The type can be one of these values:

- **0**   The text is drawn with a border to appear lower than the plane of the status bar.

- **SBT_NOBORDERS**   The text is drawn without borders.

- **SBT_OWNERDRAW**   The text is drawn by the parent window.

- **SBT_POPOUT**   The text is drawn with a border to appear higher than the plane of the status bar.

Remarks

Call this function to retrieve the length, in characters, of the text from the given part of a status bar control.

See Also: CStatusBarCtrl::GetText, CStatusBarCtrl::SetText

CStatusBarCtrl::SetMinHeight

void SetMinHeight(int *nMin*);

Parameters

nMin   Minimum height, in pixels, of the control.

Remarks

Call this function to set the minimum height of a status bar control's drawing area. The minimum height is the sum of *nMin* and twice the width, in pixels, of the vertical border of the status bar control.

See Also: CStatusBarCtrl::GetRect, CStatusBarCtrl::GetBorders

CStatusBarCtrl::SetParts

BOOL SetParts(int *nParts***, int*** *pWidths* **);**

Return Value

Nonzero if successful; otherwise zero.

Parameters

nParts Number of parts to set. The number of parts cannot be greater than 255.

pWidths Address of an integer array having the same number of elements as parts specified by *nParts*. Each element in the array specifies the position, in client coordinates, of the right edge of the corresponding part. If an element is –1, the position of the right edge for that part extends to the right edge of the control.

Remarks

Call this function to set the number of parts in a status bar control and the coordinate of the right edge of each part.

See Also: CStatusBarCtrl::GetBorders, CStatusBarCtrl::GetParts

CStatusBarCtrl::SetSimple

BOOL SetSimple(BOOL *bSimple* **= TRUE);**

Return Value

Zero if an error occurs.

Parameters

bSimple Display-type flag. If this parameter is **TRUE**, the control displays simple text; if it is **FALSE**, it displays multiple parts.

Remarks

Call this function to specify whether a status bar control displays simple text or displays all control parts set by a previous call to **SetParts**.

If the status bar control is being changed from nonsimple to simple, or vice versa, the control is immediately redrawn.

See Also: CStatusBarCtrl::SetParts

CStatusBarCtrl::SetText

BOOL SetText(LPCTSTR *lpszText***, int** *nPane***, int** *nType* **);**

Return Value

Nonzero if successful; otherwise zero.

Parameters

lpszText   Address of a null-terminated string specifying the text to set. If *nType* is **SBT_OWNERDRAW**, *lpszText* represents 32 bits of data.

nPane   Zero-based index of the part to set. If this value is 255, the status bar control is assumed to be a simple control having only one part.

nType   Type of drawing operation. It can be one of these values:

- **0**   The text is drawn with a border to appear lower than the plane of the status bar.

- **SBT_NOBORDERS**   The text is drawn without borders.

- **SBT_OWNERDRAW**   The text is drawn by the parent window.

- **SBT_POPOUT**   The text is drawn with a border to appear higher than the plane of the status bar.

Remarks

Call this function to set the text in the given part of a status bar control. The message invalidates the portion of the control that has changed, causing it to display the new text when the control next receives the **WM_PAINT** message.

See Also: CStatusBarCtrl::GetText, CStatusBarCtrl::GetTextLength

CStdioFile

A **CStdioFile** object represents a C run-time stream file as opened by the run-time function **fopen**. Stream files are buffered and can be opened in either text mode (the default) or binary mode.

Text mode provides special processing for carriage return–linefeed pairs. When you write a newline character (0x0A) to a text-mode **CStdioFile** object, the byte pair (0x0A, 0x0D) is sent to the file. When you read, the byte pair (0x0A, 0x0D) is translated to a single 0x0A byte.

The **CFile** functions **Duplicate**, **LockRange**, and **UnlockRange** are not supported for **CStdioFile**.

If you call these functions on a **CStdioFile**, you will get a **CNotSupportedException**.

For more information on using **CStdioFile**, see the article "Files in MFC" in *Visual C++ Programmer's Guide* online and "File Handling" in the *Run-Time Library Reference*.

#include <afx.h>

See Also: **CFile**, **CFile::Duplicate**, **CFile::LockRange**, **CFile::UnlockRange**, **CNotSupportedException**

CStdioFile Class Members

Data Members

m_pStream	Contains a pointer to an open file.

Construction

CStdioFile	Constructs a **CStdioFile** object from a path or file pointer.

Text Read/Write

ReadString	Reads a single line of text.
WriteString	Writes a single line of text.

Member Functions
CStdioFile::CStdioFile

CStdioFile( );
CStdioFile(FILE* *pOpenStream* **);**
CStdioFile(LPCTSTR *lpszFileName*, **UINT** *nOpenFlags* **);**
 throw(CFileException);

Parameters

pOpenStream   Specifies the file pointer returned by a call to the C run-time function **fopen**.

lpszFileName   Specifies a string that is the path to the desired file. The path can be relative or absolute.

nOpenFlags   Sharing and access mode. Specifies the action to take when the file is opened. You can combine options by using the bitwise OR (|) operator. One access permission and a text-binary specifier are required; the **create** and **noInherit** modes are optional. See **CFile::CFile** for a list of mode options and other flags. In MFC version 3.0 and later, share flags are allowed.

Remarks

The default version of the constructor works in conjunction with the **CFile::Open** member function to test errors.

The one-parameter version constructs a **CStdioFile** object from a pointer to a file that is already open. Allowed pointer values include the predefined input/output file pointers **stdin**, **stdout**, or **stderr**.

The two-parameter version constructs a **CStdioFile** object and opens the corresponding operating-system file with the given path.

CFileException is thrown if the file cannot be opened or created.

Example

```
// example for CStdioFile::CStdioFile
char* pFileName = "test.dat";
CStdioFile f1;
if( !f1.Open( pFileName, CFile::modeCreate
      | CFile::modeWrite | CFile::typeText ) ) {
      #ifdef _DEBUG
      afxDump << "Unable to open file" << "\n";
   #endif
   exit( 1 );
}
CStdioFile f2( stdout );
TRY
```

```
{
   CStdioFile f3( pFileName,
      CFile::modeCreate | CFile::modeWrite | CFile::typeText );
}
CATCH( CFileException, e )
{
   #ifdef _DEBUG
      afxDump << "File could not be opened "
              << e->m_cause << "\n";
   #endif
}
END_CATCH
```

CStdioFile::ReadString

virtual LPTSTR ReadString(LPTSTR *lpsz*, **UINT** *nMax* **);**
  throw(CFileException);
BOOL ReadString(CString& *rString***);**
  throw(CFileException);

Return Value

A pointer to the buffer containing the text data. **NULL** if end-of-file was reached without reading any data; or if boolean, **FALSE** if end-of-file was reached without reading any data.

Parameters

lpsz   Specifies a pointer to a user-supplied buffer that will receive a null-terminated text string.

nMax   Specifies the maximum number of characters to read. Should be one less than the size of the *lpsz* buffer.

rString   A reference to a **CString** object that will contain the string when the function returns.

Remarks

Reads text data into a buffer, up to a limit of *nMax*–1 characters, from the file associated with the **CStdioFile** object. Reading is stopped by a carriage return–linefeed pair. If, in that case, fewer than *nMax*–1 characters have been read, a newline character is stored in the buffer. A null character ('\0') is appended in either case.

CFile::Read is also available for text-mode input, but it does not terminate on a carriage return–linefeed pair.

Note The **CString** version of this function removes the ' /n ' if present; the **LPTSTR** version does not.

Example

```
// example for CStdioFile::ReadString
extern CStdioFile f;
char buf[100];

f.ReadString( buf, 99 );
```

See Also: CStdioFile::WriteString, CFile::Read

CStdioFile::WriteString

virtual void WriteString(LPCTSTR *lpsz*);
    throw(CFileException);

Parameters

    lpsz Specifies a pointer to a buffer containing a null-terminated text string.

Remarks

Writes data from a buffer to the file associated with the **CStdioFile** object. The terminating null character ('\0') is not written to the file. Any newline character in *lpsz* is written to the file as a carriage return–linefeed pair.

WriteString throws an exception in response to several conditions, including the disk-full condition.

This is a text-oriented write function available to **CStdioFile** and its descendents, and to **CArchive**. **CFile::Write** is also available, but rather than terminating on a null character, it writes the requested number of bytes to the file.

Example

```
// example for CStdioFile::WriteString
extern CStdioFile f;
char buf[] = "test string";

f.WriteString( buf );
```

See Also: CArchive::ReadString, CFile::Write

Data Members

CStdioFile::m_pStream

Remarks

The **m_pStream** data member is the pointer to an open file as returned by the C run-time function **fopen**. It is **NULL** if the file has never been opened or has been closed.

CString

CString does not have a base class.

A **CString** object consists of a variable-length sequence of characters. **CString** provides functions and operators using a syntax similar to that of Basic. Concatenation and comparison operators, together with simplified memory management, make **CString** objects easier to use than ordinary character arrays.

CString is based on the **TCHAR** data type. If the symbol **_UNICODE** is defined for your program, **TCHAR** is defined as type **wchar_t**, a 16-bit character type; otherwise, it is defined as **char**, the normal 8-bit character type. Under Unicode, then, **CString** objects are composed of 16-bit characters. Without Unicode, they are composed of 8-bit **char** type.

When not using **_UNICODE**, **CString** is enabled for multibyte character sets (MBCS, also known as double-byte character sets, DBCS). Note that for MBCS strings, **CString** still counts, returns, and manipulates strings based on 8-bit characters, and your application must interpret MBCS lead and trail bytes itself.

CString objects also have the following characteristics:

- **CString** objects can grow as a result of concatenation operations.

- **CString** objects follow "value semantics." Think of a **CString** object as an actual string, not as a pointer to a string.

- You can freely substitute **CString** objects for **const char*** and **LPCTSTR** function arguments.

- A conversion operator gives direct access to the string's characters as a read-only array of characters (a C-style string).

Tip Where possible, allocate **CString** objects on the frame rather than on the heap. This saves memory and simplifies parameter passing.

CString assists you in conserving memory space by allowing two strings sharing the same value also to share the same buffer space. However, if you attempt to change the contents of the buffer directly (not using MFC), you can alter both strings unintentionally. **CString** provides two member functions, **CString::LockBuffer** and **CString::UnlockBuffer**, to help you protect your data. When you call **LockBuffer**, you create a copy of a string, then set the reference count to -1, which "locks" the buffer. While the buffer is locked, no other string can reference the data in that string, and the locked string will not reference another string. By locking the string in the buffer, you ensure that the string's exclusive hold on the data will remain intact. When you have finished with the data, call **UnlockBuffer** to reset the reference count to 1.

For more information, see the "Strings in MFC" and "Strings: Unicode and Multibyte Character Set (MBCS) Support" articles in *Visual C++ Programmer's Guide* online and "String Manipulation Routines" in the *Run-Time Library Reference*.

#include <afx.h>

See Also: In *Visual C++ Programmer's Guide* online: "Strings: Basic CString Operations," "Strings: CString Semantics," "Strings: CString Operations Relating to C-Style Strings," "Strings: CString Exception Cleanup," "Strings: CString Argument Passing"

CString Class Members

Construction

CString	Constructs **CString** objects in various ways.

The String as an Array

GetLength	Returns the number of characters in a **CString** object. For multibyte characters, counts each 8-bit character; that is, a lead and trail byte in one multibyte character are counted as two characters.
IsEmpty	Tests whether a **CString** object contains no characters.
Empty	Forces a string to have 0 length.
GetAt	Returns the character at a given position.
operator []	Returns the character at a given position — operator substitution for **GetAt**.
SetAt	Sets a character at a given position.
operator LPCTSTR	Directly accesses characters stored in a **CString** object as a C-style string.

Assignment/Concatenation

operator =	Assigns a new value to a **CString** object.
operator +	Concatenates two strings and returns a new string.
operator +=	Concatenates a new string to the end of an existing string.

Comparison

operator == <, etc.	Comparison operators (case sensitive).
Compare	Compares two strings (case sensitive).
CompareNoCase	Compares two strings (case insensitive).
Collate	Compares two strings (case sensitive, uses locale-specific information).

Extraction

Mid	Extracts the middle part of a string (like the Basic MID$ function).
Left	Extracts the left part of a string (like the Basic LEFT$ function).
Right	Extracts the right part of a string (like the Basic RIGHT$ function).
SpanIncluding	Extracts a substring that contains only the characters in a set.
SpanExcluding	Extracts a substring that contains only the characters not in a set.

Other Conversions

MakeUpper	Converts all the characters in this string to uppercase characters.
MakeLower	Converts all the characters in this string to lowercase characters.
MakeReverse	Reverses the characters in this string.
Format	Format the string as **sprintf** does.
TrimLeft	Trim leading whitespace characters from the string.
TrimRight	Trim trailing whitespace characters from the string.
FormatMessage	Formats a message string.

Searching

Find	Finds a character or substring inside a larger string.
ReverseFind	Finds a character inside a larger string; starts from the end.
FindOneOf	Finds the first matching character from a set.

Archive/Dump

operator <<	Inserts a **CString** object to an archive or dump context.
operator >>	Extracts a **CString** object from an archive.

Buffer Access

GetBuffer	Returns a pointer to the characters in the **CString**.
GetBufferSetLength	Returns a pointer to the characters in the **CString**, truncating to the specified length.
ReleaseBuffer	Releases control of the buffer returned by **GetBuffer**.
FreeExtra	Removes any overhead of this string object by freeing any extra memory previously allocated to the string.
LockBuffer	Disables reference counting and protects the string in the buffer.
UnlockBuffer	Enables reference counting and releases the string in the buffer.

Windows-Specific	
AllocSysString	Allocates a **BSTR** from **CString** data.
SetSysString	Sets an existing **BSTR** object with data from a **CString** object.
LoadString	Loads an existing **CString** object from a Windows resource.
AnsiToOem	Makes an in-place conversion from the ANSI character set to the OEM character set.
OemToAnsi	Makes an in-place conversion from the OEM character set to the ANSI character set.

Member Functions
CString::AllocSysString

> **BSTR AllocSysString ( ) const;**
>   **throw(CMemoryException);**

Return Value

Points to the newly allocated string.

Remarks

Allocates a new OLE Automation–compatible string of the type **BSTR** and copies the contents of the **CString** object into it, including the terminating null character. A **CMemoryException** is thrown if insufficient memory exists. This function is normally used to return strings for OLE Automation.

Use **::SysFreeString** in the rare case that you need to deallocate the returned string.

For more information about OLE allocation functions in Windows, see **::SysAllocString** and **::SysFreeString** in the *Win32 SDK OLE Programmer's Reference*.

See Also: **::SysAllocString, ::SysFreeString, CMemoryException**

CString::AnsiToOem

> **void AnsiToOem( );**

Remarks

Converts all the characters in this **CString** object from the ANSI character set to the OEM character set. See the "ANSI Character Codes Chart" in the *C++ Language Reference*.

The function is not available if **_UNICODE** is defined.

See Also: **CString::OemToAnsi**

CString::Collate

int Collate(LPCTSTR *lpsz* **) const;**

Return Value

Zero if the strings are identical, –1 if this **CString** object is less than *lpsz*, or 1 if this **CString** object is greater than *lpsz*.

Parameters

lpsz The other string used for comparison.

Remarks

Compares this **CString** object with another string using the generic-text function **_tcscoll**. The generic-text function **_tcscoll**, which is defined in TCHAR.H, maps to either **strcoll**, **wcscoll**, or **_mbscoll** depending on the character set that is defined at compile time. Each of these functions performs a case-sensitive comparison of the strings according to the code page currently in use. For more information, see **strcat**, **wcscat**, **_mbscat** in the *Run-Time Library Reference*.

See Also: CString::Compare, CString::CompareNoCase

CString::Compare

int Compare(LPCTSTR *lpsz* **) const;**

Return Value

Zero if the strings are identical, < 0 if this **CString** object is less than *lpsz*, or > 0 if this **CString** object is greater than *lpsz*.

Parameters

lpsz The other string used for comparison.

Remarks

Compares this **CString** object with another string using the generic-text function **_tcscmp**. The generic-text function **_tcscmp**, which is defined in TCHAR.H, maps to either **strcmp**, **wcscmp**, or **_mbscmp** depending on the character set that is defined at compile time. Each of these functions performs a case-sensitive comparison of the strings, and is not affected by locale. For more information, see **strcmp**, **wcscmp**, **_mbscmp** in the *Run-Time Library Reference*.

Example

The following example demonstrates the use of **CString::Compare**.

```
// example for CString::Compare
CString s1( "abc" );
CString s2( "abd" );
ASSERT( s1.Compare( s2 ) == -1 ); // Compare with another CString.
ASSERT( s1.Compare( "abe" ) == -1 ); // Compare with LPTSTR string.
```

See Also: CString::CompareNoCase

CString::CompareNoCase

int CompareNoCase(LPCTSTR *lpsz* **) const;**

Return Value

Zero if the strings are identical (ignoring case), –1 if this **CString** object is less than *lpsz* (ignoring case), or 1 if this **CString** object is greater than *lpsz* (ignoring case).

Remarks

Compares this **CString** object with another string using the generic-text function **_tcsicmp**. The generic-text function **_tcsicmp**, which is defined in TCHAR.H, maps to either **_stricmp, _wcsicmp, _mbsicmp** depending on the character set that is defined at compile time. Each of these functions performs a case-insensitive comparison of the strings, and is not affected by locale. For more information, see **_stricmp, _wcsicmp, _mbsicmp** in the *Run-Time Library Reference*.

Example

The following example demonstrates the use of **CString::CompareNoCase**.

```
// example for CString::CompareNoCase
CString s1( "abc" );
CString s2( "ABD" );
ASSERT( s1.CompareNoCase( s2 ) == -1 ); // Compare with a CString.
ASSERT( s1.Compare( "ABE" ) == -1 ); // Compare with LPTSTR string.
```

See Also: CString::Compare, CString::Collate

CString::CString

CString( );
CString(const CString& *stringSrc* **);**
   throw(CMemoryException);
CString(TCHAR *ch*, **int** *nRepeat* = **1);**
   throw(CMemoryException);
CString(LPCTSTR *lpch*, **int** *nLength* **);**
   throw(CMemoryException);
CString(const unsigned char* *psz* **);**
   throw(CMemoryException);
CString(LPCWSTR *lpsz* **);**
   throw(CMemoryException);
CString(LPCSTR *lpsz* **);**
   throw(CMemoryException);

Parameters

stringSrc   An existing **CString** object to be copied into this **CString** object.

ch   A single character to be repeated *nRepeat* times.

nRepeat   The repeat count for *ch*.

lpch   A pointer to an array of characters of length *nLength*, not null-terminated.

nLength   A count of the number of characters in *pch*.

psz   A null-terminated string to be copied into this **CString** object.

lpsz   A null-terminated string to be copied into this **CString** object.

Remarks

Each of these constructors initializes a new **CString** object with the specified data.

Because the constructors copy the input data into new allocated storage, you should be aware that memory exceptions may result. Note that some of these constructors act as conversion functions. This allows you to substitute, for example, an **LPTSTR** where a **CString** object is expected.

Several forms of the constructor have special purposes:

- **CString(LPCSTR** *lpsz*)   Constructs a Unicode **CString** from an ANSI string. You can also use this constructor to load a string resource as shown in the example below.

- **CString(LPCWSTR** *lpsz*)   Constructs a **CString** from a Unicode string.

- **CString(const unsigned char*** *psz*)   Allows you to construct a **CString** from a pointer to **unsigned char**.

For more information, see "Strings: CString Exception Cleanup" in *Visual C++ Programmer's Guide* online.

Example

The following example demonstrates the use of **CString::CString**.

```
// example for CString::CString
CString s1;                         // Empty string
CString s2( "cat" );                // From a C string literal
CString s3 = s2;                    // Copy constructor
CString s4( s2 + " " + s3 );        // From a string expression

CString s5( 'x' );                  // s5 = "x"
CString s6( 'x', 6 );               // s6 = "xxxxxx"

CString s7((LPCSTR)ID_FILE_NEW);    // s7 = "Create a new document"

CString city = "Philadelphia";      // NOT the assignment operator
```

See Also: **CString::operator =**

CString::Empty

void Empty( );

Remarks

Makes this **CString** object an empty string and frees memory as appropriate.

For more information, see "Strings: CString Exception Cleanup" in *Visual C++ Programmer's Guide* online.

Example

The following example demonstrates the use of **CString::Empty**.

```
// example for CString::Empty
CString s( "abc" );
s.Empty();
ASSERT( s.GetLength( ) == 0 );
```

See Also: CString::IsEmpty

CString::Find

int Find(TCHAR *ch* **) const;**
int Find(LPCTSTR *lpszSub* **) const;**

Return Value

The zero-based index of the first character in this **CString** object that matches the requested substring or characters; –1 if the substring or character is not found.

Parameters

ch   A single character to search for.

lpszSub   A substring to search for.

Remarks

Searches this string for the first match of a substring. The function is overloaded to accept both single characters (similar to the run-time function **strchr**) and strings (similar to **strstr**).

Example

The following example demonstrates the use of **CString::Find**.

```
// example for CString::Find
CString s( "abcdef" );
ASSERT( s.Find( 'c' ) == 2 );
ASSERT( s.Find( "de" ) == 3 );
```

See Also: CString::ReverseFind, CString::FindOneOf

CString::FindOneOf

int FindOneOf(LPCTSTR *lpszCharSet* **) const;**

Return Value

The zero-based index of the first character in this string that is also in *lpszCharSet*; –1 if there is no match.

Parameters

lpszCharSet   String containing characters for matching.

Remarks

Searches this string for the first character that matches any character contained in *lpszCharSet*.

Example

The following example demonstrates the use of **CString::FindOneOf**.

```
// example for CString::FindOneOf
CString s( "abcdef" );
ASSERT( s.FindOneOf( "xd" ) == 3 ); // 'd' is first match
```

See Also: CString::Find

CString::Format

void Format(LPCTSTR *lpszFormat*, **...**);
void Format(UINT *nFormatID*, **...**);

Parameters

lpszFormat   A format-control string.

nFormatID   The string resource identifier that contains the format-control string.

Remarks

Call this member function to write formatted data to a **CString** in the same way that **sprintf** formats data into a C-style character array. This function formats and stores a series of characters and values in the **CString**. Each optional argument (if any) is converted and output according to the corresponding format specification in *lpszFormat* or from the string resource identified by *nFormatID*.

When you pass a character string as an optional argument, you **must** cast it explicitly as **LPCTSTR**. The format has the same form and function as the format argument for the **printf** function. (For a description of the format and arguments, see **printf** in the *Run-Time Library Reference*.) A null character is appended to the end of the characters written.

For more information, see **sprintf** in the *Run-Time Library Reference*.

See Also: CString::GetBuffer

CString::FormatMessage

void FormatMessage(LPCTSTR *lpszFormat*, **...**);
void FormatMessage(UINT *nFormatID*, **...**);

Parameters

lpszFormat   Points to the format-control string. It will be scanned for inserts and
   formatted accordingly. The format string is similar to run-time function **printf**-style

format strings, except it allows for the parameters to be inserted in an arbitrary order.

nFormatID   The string resource identifier that contains the unformatted message text.

Remarks

Call this member function to format a message string. The function requires a message definition as input. The message definition is determined by *lpszFormat* or from the string resource identified by *nFormatID*. The function copies the formatted message text to the **CString**, processing any embedded insert sequences if requested.

Each insert must have a corresponding parameter following the *lpszFormat* or *nFormatID* parameter. Within the message text, several escape sequences are supported for dynamically formatting the message. For a description of these escape sequences and their meanings, see the Windows **::FormatMessage** function in the *Win32 SDK Programmer's Reference*.

See Also: **::FormatMessage, CString::LoadString, CString::Format**

CString::FreeExtra

void FreeExtra( );

Remarks

Call this member function to free any extra memory previously allocated by the string but no longer needed. This should reduce the memory overhead consumed by the string object. The function reallocates the buffer to the exact length returned by **GetLength**.

CString::GetAt

TCHAR GetAt(int *nIndex*) const;

Return Value

A **TCHAR** containing the character at the specified position in the string.

Parameters

nIndex   Zero-based index of the character in the **CString** object. The *nIndex* parameter must be greater than or equal to 0 and less than the value returned by **GetLength**. The Debug version of the Microsoft Foundation Class Library validates the bounds of *nIndex*; the Release version does not.

Remarks

You can think of a **CString** object as an array of characters. The **GetAt** member function returns a single character specified by an index number. The overloaded subscript ([]) operator is a convenient alias for **GetAt**.

Example

The following example demonstrates the use of **CString::GetAt**.

```
// example for CString::GetAt
CString s( "abcdef" );
ASSERT( s.GetAt(2) == 'c' );
```

See Also: **CString::GetAt**, **CString::GetLength**, **CString::operator []**

CString::GetBuffer

LPTSTR GetBuffer(int *nMinBufLength* **); throw(CMemoryException);**

Return Value

An **LPTSTR** pointer to the object's (null-terminated) character buffer.

Parameters

nMinBufLength   The minimum size of the character buffer in characters. This value
does not include space for a null terminator.

Remarks

Returns a pointer to the internal character buffer for the **CString** object. The returned
LPTSTR is not **const** and thus allows direct modification of **CString** contents.

If you use the pointer returned by **GetBuffer** to change the string contents, you must
call **ReleaseBuffer** before using any other **CString** member functions.

The address returned by **GetBuffer** may not be valid after the call to **ReleaseBuffer**
since additional **CString** operations may cause the **CString** buffer to be reallocated.
The buffer will not be reallocated if you do not change the length of the **CString**.

The buffer memory will be freed automatically when the **CString** object is destroyed.

Note that if you keep track of the string length yourself, you should not append the
terminating null character. You must, however, specify the final string length when
you release the buffer with **ReleaseBuffer**. If you do append a terminating null
character, you should pass –1 for the length to **ReleaseBuffer** and **ReleaseBuffer**
will perform a **strlen** on the buffer to determine its length.

Example

The following example demonstrates the use of **CString::GetBuffer**.

```
// example for CString::GetBuffer
CString s( "abcd" );
#ifdef _DEBUG
afxDump << "CString s " << s << "\n";
#endif
LPTSTR p = s.GetBuffer( 10 );
strcpy( p, "Hello" );// directly access CString buffer
s.ReleaseBuffer( );
#ifdef _DEBUG
afxDump << "CString s " << s << "\n";
#endif
```

See Also: **CString::GetBufferSetLength, CString::ReleaseBuffer**

CString::GetBufferSetLength

LPTSTR GetBufferSetLength(int *nNewLength* **);**
  throw(CMemoryException);

Return Value

An **LPTSTR** pointer to the object's (null-terminated) character buffer.

Parameters

nNewLength   The exact size of the **CString** character buffer in characters.

Remarks

Returns a pointer to the internal character buffer for the **CString** object, truncating or growing its length if necessary to exactly match the length specified in *nNewLength*. The returned **LPTSTR** pointer is not **const** and thus allows direct modification of **CString** contents.

If you use the pointer returned by **GetBuffer** to change the string contents, you must call **ReleaseBuffer** before using any other **CString** member functions.

The address returned by **GetBufferSetLength** may not be valid after the call to **ReleaseBuffer** since additional **CString** operations may cause the **CString** buffer to be reallocated. The buffer will not be reassigned if you do not change the length of the **CString**.

The buffer memory will be freed automatically when the **CString** object is destroyed.

Note that if you keep track of the string length yourself, you should not append the terminating null character. You must, however, specify the final string length when you release the buffer with **ReleaseBuffer**. If you do append a terminating null character when you call **ReleaseBuffer**, you should pass –1 (the default) for the length. **ReleaseBuffer** will perform a **strlen** on the buffer to determine its length.

For more information about reference counting, see the following articles:

- "Managing Object Lifetimes through Reference Counting" in the *Win32 SDK Programmer's Reference*

- "Implementing Reference Counting" in the *Win32 SDK Programmer's Reference*

- "Rules for Managing Reference Counts" in the *Win32 SDK Programmer's Reference*

See Also: **CString::GetBuffer, CString::ReleaseBuffer**

CString::GetLength

int GetLength( ) const;

Return Value

A count of the bytes in the string.

Remarks

Call this member function to get a count of the bytes in this **CString** object. The count does not include a null terminator.

For multibyte character sets (MBCS), **GetLength** counts each 8-bit character; that is, a lead and trail byte in one multibyte character are counted as two bytes.

Example

The following example demonstrates the use of **CString::GetLength**.

```
// example for CString::GetLength
CString s( "abcdef" );
ASSERT( s.GetLength() == 6 );
```

See Also: CString::IsEmpty

CString::IsEmpty

BOOL IsEmpty( ) const;

Return Value

Nonzero if the **CString** object has 0 length; otherwise 0.

Remarks

Tests a **CString** object for the empty condition.

Example

The following example demonstrates the use of **CString::IsEmpty**.

```
// example for CString::IsEmpty
CString s;
ASSERT( s.IsEmpty() );
```

See Also: CString::GetLength

CString::Left

CString Left(int *nCount*) const;
    throw(CMemoryException);

Return Value

A **CString** object containing a copy of the specified range of characters. Note that the returned **CString** object may be empty.

Parameters

nCount   The number of characters to extract from this **CString** object.

Remarks

Extracts the first (that is, leftmost) *nCount* characters from this **CString** object and returns a copy of the extracted substring. If *nCount* exceeds the string length, then the entire string is extracted. **Left** is similar to the Basic LEFT$ function (except that indexes are zero-based).

For multibyte character sets (MBCS), *nCount* refers to each 8-bit character; that is, a lead and trail byte in one multibyte character are counted as two characters.

Example

The following example demonstrates the use of **CString::Left**.

```
// example for CString::Left
CString s( _T("abcdef") );
ASSERT( s.Left(2) == _T("ab") );
```

See Also: **CString::Mid**, **CString::Right**

CString::LoadString

BOOL LoadString(UINT *nID*);
   throw(CMemoryException);

Return Value

Nonzero if resource load was successful; otherwise 0.

Parameters

nID   A Windows string resource ID.

Remarks

Reads a Windows string resource, identified by *nID*, into an existing **CString** object.

Example

The following example demonstrates the use of **CString::LoadString**.

```
// example for CString::LoadString
#define IDS_FILENOTFOUND 1
CString s;
if (! s.LoadString( IDS_FILENOTFOUND ))
{
    AfxMessageBox("Error Loading String: IDS_FILENOTFOUND");
    ...
}
```

CString::LockBuffer

LPTSTR LockBuffer( );

Return Value

A pointer to a **CString** object or a **NULL**-terminated string.

Remarks

Call this member function to lock a string in the buffer.

By calling **LockBuffer**, you create a copy of the string, and then set the reference count to -1. When the reference count is set to -1, the string in the buffer is considered to be in a "locked" state. While in a locked state, the string is protected in two ways:

- No other string can get a reference to the data in the locked string, even if that string is assigned to the locked string.

- The locked string will never reference another string, even if that other string is copied to the locked string.

By locking the string in the buffer, you ensure that the string's exclusive hold on the buffer will remain intact.

After you have finished with **LockBuffer**, call **UnlockBuffer** to reset the reference count to 1.

For more information about reference counting, see the following articles:

- "Managing Object Lifetimes through Reference Counting" in the *Win32 SDK Programmer's Reference*

- "Implementing Reference Counting" in the *Win32 SDK Programmer's Reference*

- "Rules for Managing Reference Counts" in the *Win32 SDK Programmer's Reference*

See Also: **CString::UnlockBuffer, CString::GetBuffer, CString::ReleaseBuffer**

CString::MakeLower

void MakeLower( );

Remarks

Converts this **CString** object to a lowercase string.

Example

The following example demonstrates the use of **CString::MakeLower**.

```
// example for CString::MakeLower
CString s( "ABC" );
s.MakeLower();
ASSERT( s == "abc" );
```

See Also: **CString::MakeUpper**

CString::MakeReverse

void MakeReverse( );

Remarks

Reverses the order of the characters in this **CString** object.

Example

The following example demonstrates the use of **CString::MakeReverse**.

```
// example for CString::MakeReverse
CString s( "abc" );
s.MakeReverse();
ASSERT( s == "cba" );
```

CString::MakeUpper

void MakeUpper( );

Remarks

Converts this **CString** object to an uppercase string.

Example

The following example demonstrates the use of **CString::MakeUpper**.

```
// example for CString::MakeUpper
CString s( "abc" );
s.MakeUpper();
ASSERT( s == "ABC" );
```

See Also: CString::MakeLower

CString::Mid

CString Mid(int *nFirst*) const;
   throw(CMemoryException);
CString Mid(int *nFirst*, int *nCount*) const;
   throw(CMemoryException);

Return Value

A **CString** object that contains a copy of the specified range of characters. Note that the returned **CString** object may be empty.

Parameters

nFirst   The zero-based index of the first character in this **CString** object that is to be included in the extracted substring.

nCount   The number of characters to extract from this **CString** object. If this parameter is not supplied, then the remainder of the string is extracted.

Remarks

Extracts a substring of length *nCount* characters from this **CString** object, starting at position *nFirst* (zero-based). The function returns a copy of the extracted substring. **Mid** is similar to the Basic MID$ function (except that indexes are zero-based).

For multibyte character sets (MBCS), *nCount* refers to each 8-bit character; that is, a lead and trail byte in one multibyte character are counted as two characters.

Example

The following example demonstrates the use of **CString::Mid**.

```
// example for CString::Mid
CString s( _T("abcdef") );
ASSERT( s.Mid( 2, 3 ) == _T("cde") );
```

See Also: **CString::Left**, **CString::Right**

CString::OemToAnsi

void OemToAnsi( );

Remarks

Converts all the characters in this **CString** object from the OEM character set to the ANSI character set. See the "ANSI Character Codes Chart" in the *C++ Language Reference*.

This function is not available if **_UNICODE** is defined.

See Also: **CString::AnsiToOem**

CString::ReleaseBuffer

void ReleaseBuffer(int *nNewLength* = –1);

Parameters

nNewLength   The new length of the string in characters, not counting a null terminator. If the string is null-terminated, the –1 default value sets the **CString** size to the current length of the string.

Remarks

Use **ReleaseBuffer** to end use of a buffer allocated by **GetBuffer**. If you know that the string in the buffer is null-terminated, you can omit the *nNewLength* argument. If your string is not null-terminated, then use *nNewLength* to specify its length. The address returned by **GetBuffer** is invalid after the call to **ReleaseBuffer** or any other **CString** operation.

Example

The following example demonstrates the use of **CString::ReleaseBuffer**.

```
// example for CString::ReleaseBuffer
CString s;
s = "abc";
LPTSTR p = s.GetBuffer( 1024 );
strcpy(p, "abc"); // use the buffer directly
ASSERT( s.GetLength() == 3 ); // String length = 3
s.ReleaseBuffer();  // Surplus memory released, p is now invalid.
ASSERT( s.GetLength() == 3 ); // Length still 3
```

See Also: **CString::GetBuffer**

CString::ReverseFind

int ReverseFind(TCHAR *ch* **) const;**

Return Value

The index of the last character in this **CString** object that matches the requested character; –1 if the character is not found.

Parameters

ch   The character to search for.

Remarks

Searches this **CString** object for the last match of a substring. The function is similar to the run-time function **strrchr**.

Example

The following example demonstrates the use of **CString::ReverseFind**.

```
// example for CString::ReverseFind
CString s( "abcabc" );
ASSERT( s.ReverseFind( 'b' ) == 4 );
```

See Also: **CString::Find, CString::FindOneOf**

CString::Right

CString Right(int *nCount* **) const;**
   throw(CMemoryException);

Return Value

A **CString** object that contains a copy of the specified range of characters. Note that the returned **CString** object may be empty.

Parameters

nCount   The number of characters to extract from this **CString** object.

Remarks

Extracts the last (that is, rightmost) *nCount* characters from this **CString** object and returns a copy of the extracted substring. If *nCount* exceeds the string length, then the entire string is extracted. **Right** is similar to the Basic RIGHT$ function (except that indexes are zero-based).

For multibyte character sets (MBCS), *nCount* refers to each 8-bit character; that is, a lead and trail byte in one multibyte character are counted as two characters.

Example

The following example demonstrates the use of **CString::Right**.

```
// example for CString::Right
CString s( _T("abcdef") );
ASSERT( s.Right(2) == _T("ef") );
```

See Also: **CString::Mid**, **CString::Left**

CString::SetAt

void SetAt(int *nIndex*, **TCHAR** *ch* **);**

Parameters

nIndex   Zero-based index of the character in the **CString** object. The *nIndex* parameter must be greater than or equal to 0 and less than the value returned by **GetLength**. The Debug version of the Microsoft Foundation Class Library will validate the bounds of *nIndex*; the Release version will not.

ch   The character to insert. Must not be '\0'.

Remarks

You can think of a **CString** object as an array of characters. The **SetAt** member function overwrites a single character specified by an index number. **SetAt** will not enlarge the string if the index exceeds the bounds of the existing string.

See Also: **CString::GetAt**, **CString::operator [ ]**

CString::SetSysString

BSTR SetSysString(BSTR* *pbstr* **) const;**

Return Value

The new string.

Parameters

pbstr   A pointer to a character string.

Remarks

Reallocates the **BSTR** pointed to by *pbstr* and copies the contents of the **CString** object into it, including the **NULL** character. The value of the **BSTR** referenced by *pbstr* may change. The function throws a **CMemoryException** if insufficient memory exists.

This function is normally used to change the value of strings passed by reference for OLE Automation.

For more information about OLE reallocation functions in Windows, see **::SysReallocStringLen** and **::SysFreeString** in the *Win32 SDK OLE Programmer's Reference*.

CString::SpanExcluding

CString SpanExcluding(LPCTSTR *lpszCharSet* **) const;**
   throw(CMemoryException);

Return Value

A substring that contains characters in the string that are not in *lpszCharSet*, beginning with the first character in the string and ending with the first character found in the string that is also in *lpszCharSet* (that is, starting with the first character in the string and up to but **excluding** the first character in the string that is found *lpszCharSet*). It returns the entire string if no character in *lpszCharSet* is found in the string.

Parameters

lpszCharSet   A string interpreted as a set of characters.

Remarks

Use this function to search the string for the first occurrence of any character in the specified set *lpszCharSet*. **SpanExcluding** extracts and returns all characters preceding the first occurrence of a character from *lpszCharSet* (in other words, the character from *lpszCharSet* and all characters following it in the string, are **not** returned). If no character from *lpszCharSet* is found in the string, then **SpanExcluding** returns the entire string.

Example

The following function returns the first portion of the *src* param.

```
// Portions are delimited by a semi-colon( ; ),
//   a comma( , ), a period( . ), a dash( - ),
// or a colon( : ).

CString GetFirstPart( CString src)
{
    return src.SpanExcluding( ";,.- :");
}
```

See Also: CString::SpanIncluding

CString::SpanIncluding

CString SpanIncluding(LPCTSTR *lpszCharSet* **) const;**
throw(CMemoryException);

Return Value

A substring that contains characters in the string that are in *lpszCharSet*, beginning with the first character in the string and ending when a character is found in the string that is not in *lpszCharSet*. **SpanIncluding** returns an empty substring if the first character in the string is **not** in the specified set.

Parameters

lpszCharSet   A string interpreted as a set of characters.

Remarks

Call this member function to extract characters from the string, starting with the first character, that are in the set of characters identified by *lpszCharSet*. If the first character of the string is **not** in the character set, then **SpanIncluding** returns an empty string. Otherwise, it returns a sequence of consecutive characters which **are** in the set.

Example

The following example demonstrates the use of **CString::SpanIncluding**.

```
// example for CString::SpanIncluding
CString str( "cabbage" );
CString res = str.SpanIncluding( "abc" );
ASSERT( res == "cabba" );
res = str.SpanIncluding( "xyz" );
ASSERT( res.IsEmpty( ) );
```

See Also: CString::SpanExcluding

CString::TrimLeft

void TrimLeft( );

Remarks

Call this member function to trim leading whitespace characters from the string. Removes newline, space, and tab characters.

For more information, see "Strings Topics" in *Visual C++ Programmer's Guide* online.

See Also: CString::TrimRight, CString::Mid, CString::Left, CString::Right, CString::MakeUpper, CString::MakeLower, CString::MakeReverse, CString::Format

CString::TrimRight

> **void TrimRight( );**

Remarks

Call this member function to trim trailing whitespace characters from the string.
Removes trailing newline, space, and tab characters from the string.

For more information, see "Strings Topics" in *Visual C++ Programmer's Guide*
online.

See Also: **CString::TrimLeft**, **CString::Mid**, **CString::Left**, **CString::Right**,
CString::MakeUpper, **CString::MakeLower**, **CString::MakeReverse**,
CString::Format

CString::UnlockBuffer

> **void UnlockBuffer( );**

Remarks

Call this member function to unlock the buffer that was previously secured by calling
LockBuffer. **UnlockBuffer** resets the reference count to 1.

The **CString** destructor implies **UnlockBuffer** to ensure that you do not leave the
buffer locked when the destructor is called.

See Also: **CString::LockBuffer**, **CString::GetBuffer**, **CString::ReleaseBuffer**

Operators
CString::operator =

> **const CString& operator =(const CString&** *stringSrc* **);**
>   **throw(CMemoryException);**
> **const CString& operator =(TCHAR** *ch* **);**
>   **throw(CMemoryException);**
> **const CString& operator =(const unsigned char*** *psz* **);**
>   **throw(CMemoryException);**
> **const CString& operator =(LPCWSTR** *lpsz* **);**
>   **throw(CMemoryException);**
> **const CString& operator =(LPCSTR** *lpsz* **);**
>   **throw(CMemoryException);**

Remarks

The **CString** assignment (=) operator reinitializes an existing **CString** object with
new data. If the destination string (that is, the left side) is already large enough to store
the new data, no new memory allocation is performed. You should be aware that

memory exceptions may occur whenever you use the assignment operator because new storage is often allocated to hold the resulting **CString** object.

Example

The following example demonstrates the use of **CString::operator =**.

```
// example for CString::operator =
CString s1, s2;          // Empty CString objects

s1 = "cat";              // s1 = "cat"
s2 = s1;                 // s1 and s2 each = "cat"
s1 = "the " + s1;        // Or expressions
s1 = 'x';                // Or just individual characters
```

See Also: CString::CString

CString::operator LPCTSTR

operator LPCTSTR ( ) const;

Return Value

A character pointer to the string's data.

Remarks

This useful casting operator provides an efficient method to access the null-terminated C string contained in a **CString** object. No characters are copied; only a pointer is returned. Be careful with this operator. If you change a **CString** object after you have obtained the character pointer, you may cause a reallocation of memory that invalidates the pointer.

CString::operator <<, >>

friend CArchive& operator <<(CArchive& *ar*, const CString& *string*);
   throw(CArchiveException);
friend CArchive& operator >>(CArchive& *ar*, CString& *string*);
   throw(CArchiveException);
friend CDumpContext& operator <<(CDumpContext& *dc*, const CString& *string*);

Remarks

The **CString** insertion (<<) operator supports diagnostic dumping and storing to an archive. The extraction (>>) operator supports loading from an archive.

The **CDumpContext** operators are valid only in the Debug version of the Microsoft Foundation Class Library.

Example

The following example demonstrates the use of **CString::operator <<, >>**.

```
// example for CString::operator <<, >>
    extern CArchive ar;
    CString s( "abc" );
```

```
#ifdef _DEBUG
   afxDump << s;  // Prints the value (abc)
   afxDump << &s;  // Prints the address
#endif

   if( ar.IsLoading() )
      ar >> s;
   else
      ar << s;
```

See Also: CDumpContext

CString::operator +

friend CString operator +(const CString& *string1*, **const CString&** *string2* **);**
   throw(CMemoryException);
friend CString operator +(const CString& *string*, **TCHAR** *ch* **);**
   throw(CMemoryException);
friend CString operator +(TCHAR *ch*, **const CString&** *string* **);**
   throw(CMemoryException);
friend CString operator +(const CString& *string*, **LPCTSTR** *lpsz* **);**
   throw(CMemoryException);
friend CString operator +(LPCTSTR *lpsz*, **const CString&** *string* **);**
   throw(CMemoryException);

Return Value

A **CString** object that is the temporary result of the concatenation. This return value makes it possible to combine several concatenations in the same expression.

Parameters

string, *string1*, *string2*   **CString** objects to concatenate.

ch A character to concatenate to a string or to concatenate a string to.

lpsz A pointer to a null-terminated character string.

Remarks

The + concatenation operator joins two strings and returns a **CString** object. One of the two argument strings must be a **CString** object. The other can be a character pointer or a character. You should be aware that memory exceptions may occur whenever you use the concatenation operator since new storage may be allocated to hold temporary data.

Example

The following example demonstrates the use of **CString::operator +**.

```
// example for CString::operator +
CString s1( "abc" );
CString s2( "def" );
ASSERT( (s1 + s2 ) == "abcdef" );
CString s3;
s3 = CString( "abc" ) + "def" ; // Correct
```

```
s3 = "abc" + "def";
// Wrong! The first argument must be a CString.
```

See Also: **CString::operator +=**

CString::operator +=

const CString& operator +=(const CString& *string* **);**
   throw(CMemoryException);
const CString& operator +=(TCHAR *ch* **);**
   throw(CMemoryException);
const CString& operator +=(LPCTSTR *lpsz* **);**
   throw(CMemoryException);

Parameters

string   A **CString** to concatenate to this string.

ch   A character to concatenate to this string.

lpsz   A pointer to a null-terminated string to concatenate to this string.

Remarks

The += concatenation operator joins characters to the end of this string. The operator accepts another **CString** object, a character pointer, or a single character. You should be aware that memory exceptions may occur whenever you use this concatenation operator because new storage may be allocated for characters added to this **CString** object.

Example

The following example demonstrates the use of **CString::operator +=**.

```
// example for CString::operator +=
CString s( "abc" );
ASSERT( ( s += "def" ) == "abcdef" );
```

See Also: **CString::operator +**

CString Comparison Operators

BOOL operator ==(const CString& *s1*, **const CString&** *s2* **);**
BOOL operator ==(const CString& *s1*, **LPCTSTR** *s2* **);**
BOOL operator ==(LPCTSTR *s1*, **const CString&** *s2* **);**
BOOL operator !=(const CString& *s1*, **const CString&** *s2* **);**
BOOL operator !=(const CString& *s1*, **LPCTSTR** *s2* **);**
BOOL operator !=(LPCTSTR *s1*, **const CString&** *s2* **);**
BOOL operator <(const CString& *s1*, **const CString&** *s2* **);**
BOOL operator <(const CString& *s1*, **LPCTSTR** *s2* **);**
BOOL operator <(LPCTSTR *s1*, **const CString&** *s2* **);**
BOOL operator >(const CString& *s1*, **const CString&** *s2* **);**
BOOL operator >(const CString& *s1*, **LPCTSTR** *s2* **);**

BOOL operator >(LPCTSTR *s1,* **const CString&** *s2* **);**
BOOL operator <=(const CString& *s1,* **const CString&** *s2* **);**
BOOL operator <=(const CString& *s1,* **LPCTSTR** *s2* **);**
BOOL operator <=(LPCTSTR *s1,* **const CString&** *s2* **);**
BOOL operator >=(const CString& *s1,* **const CString&** *s2* **);**
BOOL operator >=(const CString& *s1,* **LPCTSTR** *s2* **);**
BOOL operator >=(LPCTSTR *s1,* **const CString&** *s2* **);**

Return Value

Nonzero if the strings meet the comparison condition; otherwise 0.

Parameters

s1, s2 **CString** objects to compare.

Remarks

These comparison operators compare two strings. The operators are a convenient substitute for the case-sensitive **Compare** member function.

Example

The following example demonstrates the use of **CString Comparison Operators**.

```
// example for CString Comparison Operators
CString s1( "abc" );
CString s2( "abd" );
ASSERT( s1 < s2 ); // Operator is overloaded for both.
ASSERT( "ABC" < s1 ); // CString and char*
ASSERT( s2 > "abe" );
```

CString::operator [ ]

TCHAR operator [](int *nIndex* **) const;**

Parameters

nIndex Zero-based index of a character in the string.

Remarks

You can think of a **CString** object as an array of characters. The overloaded subscript ([]) operator returns a single character specified by the zero-based index in *nIndex*. This operator is a convenient substitute for the **GetAt** member function.

Important You can use the subscript ([]) operator to get the value of a character in a **CString**, but you cannot use it to change the value of a character in a **CString**.

Example

The following example demonstrates the use of **CString::operator [ ]**.

```
// example for CString::operator [ ]
CString s( "abc" );
ASSERT( s[1] == 'b' );
```

See Also: **CString::GetAt, CString::SetAt**

CStringArray

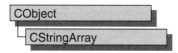

The **CStringArray** class supports arrays of **CString** objects.

The member functions of **CStringArray** are similar to the member functions of class **CObArray**. Because of this similarity, you can use the **CObArray** reference documentation for member function specifics. Wherever you see a **CObject** pointer as a return value, substitute a **CString** (not a **CString** pointer). Wherever you see a **CObject** pointer as a function parameter, substitute a **LPCTSTR**.

```
CObject* CObArray::GetAt( int <nIndex> ) const;
```

for example, translates to

```
CString CStringArray::GetAt( int <nIndex> ) const;
```

and

```
void SetAt( int <nIndex>, CObject* <newElement> )
```

translates to

```
void SetAt( int <nIndex>, LPCTSTR <newElement> )
```

CStringArray incorporates the **IMPLEMENT_SERIAL** macro to support serialization and dumping of its elements. If an array of **CString** objects is stored to an archive, either with an overloaded insertion operator or with the **Serialize** member function, each element is serialized in turn.

Note Before using an array, use **SetSize** to establish its size and allocate memory for it. If you do not use **SetSize**, adding elements to your array causes it to be frequently reallocated and copied. Frequent reallocation and copying are inefficient and can fragment memory.

If you need a dump of individual string elements in the array, you must set the depth of the dump context to 1 or greater.

When a **CString** array is deleted, or when its elements are removed, string memory is freed as appropriate.

For more information on using **CStringArray**, see the article "Collections" in *Visual C++ Programmer's Guide* online.

#include <afxcoll.h>

CStringArray Class Members

Construction

CStringArray	Constructs an empty array for **CString** objects.

Bounds

GetSize	Gets number of elements in this array.
GetUpperBound	Returns the largest valid index.
SetSize	Sets the number of elements to be contained in this array.

Operations

FreeExtra	Frees all unused memory above the current upper bound.
RemoveAll	Removes all the elements from this array.

Element Access

GetAt	Returns the value at a given index.
SetAt	Sets the value for a given index; array not allowed to grow.
ElementAt	Returns a temporary reference to the element pointer within the array.
GetData	Allows access to elements in the array. Can be **NULL**.

Growing the Array

SetAtGrow	Sets the value for a given index; grows the array if necessary.
Add	Adds an element to the end of the array; grows the array if necessary.
Append	Appends another array to the array; grows the array if necessary.
Copy	Copies anolther array to the array; grows the array if necessary.

Insertion/Removal

InsertAt	Inserts an element (or all the elements in another array) at a specified index.
RemoveAt	Removes an element at a specific index.

Operators

operator []	Sets or gets the element at the specified index.

CStringList

The **CStringList** class supports lists of **CString** objects. All comparisons are done by value, meaning that the characters in the string are compared instead of the addresses of the strings.

The member functions of **CStringList** are similar to the member functions of class **CObList**. Because of this similarity, you can use the **CObList** reference documentation for member function specifics. Wherever you see a **CObject** pointer as a return value, substitute a **CString** (not a **CString** pointer). Wherever you see a **CObject** pointer as a function parameter, substitute an **LPCTSTR**.

```
CObject*& CObList::GetHead() const;
```

for example, translates to

```
CString& CStringList::GetHead() const;
```

and

```
POSITION AddHead( CObject* <newElement> );
```

translates to

```
POSITION AddHead( LPCTSTR <newElement> );
```

CStringList incorporates the **IMPLEMENT_SERIAL** macro to support serialization and dumping of its elements. If a list of **CString** objects is stored to an archive, either with an overloaded insertion operator or with the **Serialize** member function, each **CString** element is serialized in turn.

If you need a dump of individual **CString** elements, you must set the depth of the dump context to 1 or greater.

When a **CStringList** object is deleted, or when its elements are removed, the **CString** objects are deleted as appropriate.

For more information on using **CStringList**, see the article "Collections" in *Visual C++ Programmer's Guide* online.

#include <afxcoll.h>

CStringList Class Members

Construction

CStringList	Constructs an empty list for **CString** objects.

Head/Tail Access

GetHead	Returns the head element of the list (cannot be empty).
GetTail	Returns the tail element of the list (cannot be empty).

Operations

RemoveHead	Removes the element from the head of the list.
RemoveTail	Removes the element from the tail of the list.
AddHead	Adds an element (or all the elements in another list) to the head of the list (makes a new head).
AddTail	Adds an element (or all the elements in another list) to the tail of the list (makes a new tail).
RemoveAll	Removes all the elements from this list.

Iteration

GetHeadPosition	Returns the position of the head element of the list.
GetTailPosition	Returns the position of the tail element of the list.
GetNext	Gets the next element for iterating.
GetPrev	Gets the previous element for iterating.

Retrieval/Modification

GetAt	Gets the element at a given position.
SetAt	Sets the element at a given position.
RemoveAt	Removes an element from this list as specified by position.

Insertion

InsertBefore	Inserts a new element before a given position.
InsertAfter	Inserts a new element after a given position.

Searching

Find	Gets the position of an element specified by string value.
FindIndex	Gets the position of an element specified by a zero-based index.

Status

GetCount	Returns the number of elements in this list.
IsEmpty	Tests for the empty list condition (no elements).

CSyncObject

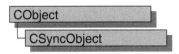

The **CSyncObject** class is a pure virtual class that provides functionality common to the synchronization objects in Win32. The Microsoft Foundation Class Library provides several classes derived from **CSyncObject**. These are **CEvent**, **CMutex**, **CCriticalSection**, and **CSemaphore**.

For information on how to use the synchronization objects, see the article "Multithreading: How to Use the Synchronization Classes" in *Visual C++ Programmer's Guide* online.

#include <afxmt.h>

CSyncObject Class Members

Construction

CSyncObject	Constructs a **CSyncObject** object.

Methods

Lock	Gains access to the synchronization object.
Unlock	Releases access to the synchronization object.

Attributes

operator HANDLE	Gains access to the synchronization object.

Member Functions

CSyncObject::CSyncObject

CSyncObject(LPCTSTR *pstrName* **);**
virtual ~CSyncObject( );

Parameters

    pstrName   The name of the object. If **NULL**, *pstrName* will be null.

Remarks

Constructs a synchronization object with the supplied name.

CSyncObject::Lock

virtual BOOL Lock(DWORD *dwTimeout* **= INFINITE);**

Return Value

Nonzero if the function was successful; otherwise 0.

Parameters

dwTimeout   Specifies the amount of time to wait for the synchronization object to be available (signaled). If **INFINITE, Lock** will wait until the object is signaled before returning.

Remarks

Call this function to gain access to the resource controlled by the synchronization object. If the synchronization object is signaled, **Lock** will return successfully and the thread now owns the object. If the synchronization object is nonsignaled (unavailable), **Lock** will wait for the synchronization object to become signaled up to the number of milliseconds specified in the *dwTimeOut* parameter. If the synchronization object did not become signaled in the specified amount of time, **Lock** returns failure.

CSyncObject::operator HANDLE

operator HANDLE( ) const;

Return Value

If successful, the handle of the synchronization object; otherwise, **NULL**.

Remarks

Use this operator to get the handle of the **CSyncObject** object. You can use the handle to call Windows APIs directly.

CSyncObject::Unlock

virtual BOOL Unlock( ) = 0;
virtual BOOL Unlock(LONG *lCount***, LPLONG** *lpPrevCount* **= NULL);**

Return Value

Default implementation always returns **TRUE**.

Parameters

lCount   Not used by default implementation.

lpPrevCount   Not used by default implementation.

Remarks

The declaration of **Unlock** with no parameters is a pure virtual function, and must be overridden by all classes deriving from **CSyncObject**. The default implementation of the declaration with two parameters always returns **TRUE**. This function is called to release access to the synchronization object owned by the calling thread. The second declaration is provided for synchronization objects such as semaphores that allow more than one access of a controlled resource.

CTabCtrl

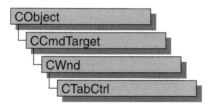

A "tab control" is analogous to the dividers in a notebook or the labels in a file cabinet. By using a tab control, an application can define multiple pages for the same area of a window or dialog box. Each page consists of a set of information or a group of controls that the application displays when the user selects the corresponding tab. A special type of tab control displays tabs that look like buttons. Clicking a button should immediately perform a command instead of displaying a page.

The **CTabCtrl** class provides the functionality of the Windows common tab control. This control (and therefore the **CTabCtrl** class) is available only to programs running under Windows 95 and Windows NT version 3.51 and later.

For more information on using **CTabCtrl**, see Technical Note 60 online.

#include <afxcmn.h>

See Also: CHeaderCtrl, **CListCtrl**

CTabCtrl Class Members

Construction

CTabCtrl	Constructs a **CTabCtrl** object.
Create	Creates a tab control and attaches it to an instance of a **CTabCtrl** object.

Attributes

GetImageList	Retrieves the image list associated with a tab control.
SetImageList	Assigns an image list to a tab control.
GetItemCount	Retrieves the number of tabs in the tab control.
GetItem	Retrieves information about a tab in a tab control.
SetItem	Sets some or all of a tab's attributes.

Attributes *(continued)*

GetItemRect	Retrieves the bounding rectangle for a tab in a tab control.
GetCurSel	Determines the currently selected tab in a tab control.
SetCurSel	Selects a tab in a tab control.
SetItemSize	Sets the width and height of an item.
SetPadding	Sets the amount of space (padding) around each tab's icon and label in a tab control.
GetRowCount	Retrieves the current number of rows of tabs in a tab control.
GetTooltips	Retrieves the handle of the tool tip control associated with a tab control.
SetTooltips	Assigns a tool tip control to a tab control.
GetCurFocus	Retrieves the tab with the current focus of a tab control.

Operations

InsertItem	Inserts a new tab in a tab control.
DeleteItem	Removes an item from a tab control.
DeleteAllItems	Removes all items from a tab control.
AdjustRect	Calculates a tab control's display area given a window rectangle, or calculates the window rectangle that would correspond to a given display area.
RemoveImage	Removes an image from a tab control's image list.
HitTest	Determines which tab, if any, is at a specified screen position.

Overridables

DrawItem	Draws a specified item of a tab control.

Member Functions

CTabCtrl::AdjustRect

void AdjustRect(BOOL *bLarger***, LPRECT** *lpRect* **);**

Parameters

bLarger Indicates which operation to perform. If this parameter is **TRUE**, *lpRect* specifies a display rectangle and receives the corresponding window rectangle. If this parameter is **FALSE**, *lpRect* specifies a window rectangle and receives the corresponding display rectangle.

lpRect Pointer to a **RECT** structure that specifies the given rectangle and receives the calculated rectangle.

Remarks

Call this function to calculate a tab control's display area given a window rectangle, or calculate the window rectangle that would correspond to a given display area.

See Also: **CTabCtrl::SetItemSize**, **CTabCtrl::GetItemRect**, **CTabCtrl::AdjustRect**

CTabCtrl::Create

BOOL Create(DWORD *dwStyle***, const RECT&** *rect***, CWnd*** *pParentWnd***, UINT** *nID* **);**

Return Value

TRUE if initialization of the object was successful; otherwise **FALSE**.

Parameters

dwStyle   Specifies the tab control's style. Apply any combination of tab control styles to the control.

rect   Specifies the tab control's size and position. It can be either a **CRect** object or a **RECT** structure.

pParentWnd   Specifies the tab control's parent window, usually a **CDialog**. It must not be **NULL**.

nID   Specifies the tab control's ID.

Remarks

You construct a **CTabCtrl** object in two steps. First call the constructor, then call **Create**, which creates the tab control and attaches it to the **CTabCtrl** object.

The following styles can be applied to a tab control:

- **TCS_BUTTONS**   Modifies the appearance of the tabs to look like buttons.
- **TCS_FIXEDWIDTH**   Makes all tabs the same width. (By default, the tab control automatically sizes each tab to fit its icon.) You cannot use this style with the **TCS_RIGHTJUSTIFY** style.
- **TCS_FOCUSNEVER**   Specifies that a tab never receives the input focus.
- **TCS_FOCUSONBUTTONDOWN**   Specifies that a tab receives the input focus when clicked. This style is typically used only with the **TCS_BUTTONS** style.
- **TCS_FORCEICONLEFT**   Forces the icon to the left, but leaves the tab label centered. (By default, the control centers the icon and label with the icon to the left of the label.)
- **TCS_FORCELABELLEFT**   Left-aligns both the icon and label.
- **TCS_MULTILINE**   Causes a tab control to display multiple rows of tabs. Thus all tabs can be displayed at once. (By default, a tab control displays a single row of tabs.)

- **TCS_OWNERDRAWFIXED**   Specifies that the parent window draws the tabs in the control.

- **TCS_RIGHTJUSTIFY**   Right justifies tabs. (By default, tabs are left-justified within each row.)

- **TCS_SHAREIMAGELISTS**   Specifies that a tab control's image lists are not destroyed when the control is destroyed.

- **TCS_TOOLTIPS**   Specifies that the tab control has a tool tip control associated with it.

- **TCS_TABS**   Tabs appear as tabs, and a border is drawn around the display area. This style is the default.

- **TCS_SINGLELINE**   Displays only one row of tabs. The user can scroll to see more tabs, if necessary. This style is the default.

- **TCS_RAGGEDRIGHT**   Does not stretch each row of tabs to fill the entire width of the control. This style is the default.

In addition, you can apply the following window styles to a tab control:

- **WS_CHILD**   Creates a child window that represents the tab control. Cannot be used with the **WS_POPUP** style.

- **WS_VISIBLE**   Creates a tab control that is initially visible.

- **WS_DISABLED**   Creates a window that is initially disabled.

- **WS_GROUP**   Specifies the first control of a group of controls in which the user can move from one control to the next with the arrow keys. All controls defined with the **WS_GROUP** style after the first control belong to the same group. The next control with the **WS_GROUP** style ends the style group and starts the next group (that is, one group ends where the next begins).

- **WS_TABSTOP**   Specifies one of any number of controls through which the user can move by using the TAB key. The TAB key moves the user to the next control specified by the **WS_TABSTOP** style.

See Also: **CTabCtrl::CTabCtrl**

CTabCtrl::CTabCtrl

CTabCtrl( );

Remarks

Call this function to construct a **CTabCtrl** object.

See Also: **CTabCtrl::Create**

CTabCtrl::DeleteAllItems

BOOL DeleteAllItems( );

Return Value

Nonzero if successful; otherwise 0.

Remarks

Call this function to remove all items from a tab control.

See Also: CTabCtrl::DeleteItem

CTabCtrl::DeleteItem

BOOL DeleteItem(int *nItem*);

Return Value

Nonzero if successful; otherwise 0.

Parameters

nItem   Zero-based value of the item to delete.

Remarks

Call this function to remove the specified item from a tab control.

See Also: CTabCtrl::DeleteAllItems

CTabCtrl::DrawItem

void DrawItem(LPDRAWITEMSTRUCT *lpDrawItemStruct*);

Parameters

lpDrawItemStruct   A pointer to a **DRAWITEMSTRUCT** structure describing the item to be painted.

Remarks

Called by the framework when a visual aspect of an owner-draw tab control changes. The **itemAction** member of the **DRAWITEMSTRUCT** structure defines the drawing action that is to be performed.

By default, this member function does nothing. Override this member function to implement drawing for an owner-draw **CTabCtrl** object.

The application should restore all graphics device interface (GDI) objects selected for the display context supplied in *lpDrawItemStruct* before this member function terminates.

See Also: CWnd::OnDrawItem

CTabCtrl::GetCurFocus

int GetCurFocus( ) const;

Return Value

The zero-based index of the tab with the current focus.

Remarks

Call this function to retrieve the index of the tab with the current focus.

See Also: **CTabCtrl::GetCurSel**

CTabCtrl::GetCurSel

int GetCurSel( ) const;

Return Value

Zero-based index of the selected tab if successful or −1 if no tab is selected.

Remarks

Call this function to retrieve the currently selected tab in a tab control.

See Also: **CTabCtrl::SetCurSel, CTabCtrl::GetCurFocus**

CTabCtrl::GetImageList

HIMAGELIST GetImageList( ) const;

Return Value

The handle of the image list of the tab control if successful; otherwise **NULL**.

Remarks

Call this function to retrieve the image list associated with a tab control.

See Also: **CTabCtrl::SetImageList, CImageList**

CTabCtrl::GetItem

BOOL GetItem(int *nItem*, **TC_ITEM*** *pTabCtrlItem* **) const;**

Return Value

Returns **TRUE** if successful; **FALSE** otherwise.

Parameters

nItem   Zero-based index of the tab.

pTabCtrlItem   Pointer to a **TC_ITEM** structure, used to specify the information to retrieve. Also used to receive information about the tab. This structure is used with the **InsertItem**, **GetItem**, and **SetItem** member functions.

Remarks

Call this function to retrieve information about a tab in a tab control.

When the message is sent, the **mask** member specifies which attributes to return. If the **mask** member specifies the **TCIF_TEXT** value, the **pszText** member must contain the address of the buffer that receives the item text and the **cchTextMax** member must specify the size of the buffer.

The **TC_ITEM** structure is defined as follows:

```
typedef struct _TC_ITEM {
    UINT mask;
    UINT lpReserved1;   // reserved; do not use
    UINT lpReserved2;   // reserved; do not use
    LPSTR pszText;
    int cchTextMax;
    int iImage;
    LPARAM lParam;
} TC_ITEM;
```

mask   Value specifying which members to retrieve or set. This member can be **TCIF_ALL** (meaning all members), zero, or a combination of the following values:

- **TCIF_TEXT**   The **pszText** member is valid.

- **TCIF_IMAGE**   The **iImage** member is valid.

- **TCIF_PARAM**   The **lParam** member is valid.

pszText   Pointer to a null-terminated string containing the tab text if the structure contains information about a tab. If the structure is receiving information, this member specifies the address of the buffer that receives the tab text.

cchTextMax   Size of the buffer pointed to by **pszText**. This member is ignored if the structure is not receiving information.

iImage   Index into the tab control's image list, or −1 if there is no image for the tab.

lParam   Application-defined data associated with the tab. If there are more than four bytes of application-defined data per tab, an application must define a structure and use it instead of the **TC_ITEM** structure. The first member of the application-defined structure must be a **TC_ITEMHEADER** structure. The **TC_ITEMHEADER** structure is identical to the **TC_ITEM** structure, but without the **lParam** member. The difference between the size of your structure and the size of the **TC_ITEMHEADER** structure should equal the number of extra bytes per tab.

See Also: **CTabCtrl::InsertItem**, **CTabCtrl::SetItem**

CTabCtrl::GetItemCount

int GetItemCount( ) const;

Return Value

Number of items in the tab control.

Remarks

Call this function to retrieve the number of tabs in the tab control.

See Also: **CTabCtrl::GetItem**, **CTabCtrl::SetItem**

CTabCtrl::GetItemRect

BOOL GetItemRect(int *nItem***, LPRECT** *lpRect* **) const;**

Return Value

Nonzero if successful; otherwise 0.

Parameters

nItem   Zero-based index of the tab item.

lpRect   Pointer to a **RECT** structure that receives the bounding rectangle of the tab.
These coordinates use the viewport's current mapping mode.

Remarks

Retrieves the bounding rectangle for the specified tab in a tab control.

See Also: **CTabCtrl::SetItemSize**, **CTabCtrl::AdjustRect**

CTabCtrl::GetRowCount

int GetRowCount( ) const;

Return Value

The number of rows of tabs in the tab control.

Remarks

Retrieves the current number of rows in a tab control. Only tab controls that have the
TCS_MULTILINE style can have multiple rows of tabs.

See Also: **CTabCtrl::Create**

CTabCtrl::GetTooltips

CWnd* GetTooltips( ) const;

Return Value

Handle of the tool tip control if successful; otherwise **NULL**.

Remarks

Retrieves the handle of the tool tip control associated with a tab control. A tab control creates a tool tip control if it has the **TCS_TOOLTIPS** style. You can also assign a tool tip control to a tab control by using the **SetTooltips** member function.

See Also: **CTabCtrl::SetTooltips, CTabCtrl::Create**

CTabCtrl::HitTest

int HitTest(TC_HITTESTINFO* *pHitTestInfo* **) const;**

Return Value

Returns the zero-based index of the tab or −1 if no tab is at the specified position.

Parameters

pHitTestInfo   Pointer to a **TC_HITTESTINFO** structure, which specifies the screen position to test.

Remarks

Call this function to determine which tab, if any, is at the specified screen position.

The **TC_HITTESTINFO** structure is defined as follows:

```
typedef struct _TC_HITTESTINFO {
    POINT pt;      // position to hit test, in client coordinates
    UINT  flags;   // receives results of hit test
} TC_HITTESTINFO;
```

flags   Variable that receives the results of a hit test. The tab control sets this member to one of the following values:

- **TCHT_NOWHERE**   The position is not over a tab.

- **TCHT_ONITEM**   The position is over a tab, but not over its icon or its text. For owner-drawn tab controls, this value is specified if the position is anywhere over a tab. **TCHT_ONITEM** is a bitwise-OR operation on the **TCHT_ONITEMICON** and **TCHT_ONITEMLABEL** values.

- **TCHT_ONITEMICON**   The position is over a tab's icon.

- **TCHT_ONITEMLABEL**   The position is over a tab's text.

CTabCtrl::InsertItem

BOOL InsertItem(int *nItem*, **TC_ITEM*** *pTabCtrlItem* **);**

Return Value

Zero-based index of the new tab if successful; otherwise −1.

Parameters

nItem   Zero-based index of the new tab.

pTabCtrlItem   Pointer to a **TC_ITEM** structure that specifies the attributes of the tab.
For a description of this structure, see the **CTabCtrl::GetItem** member function.

Remarks

Call this function to insert a new tab in an existing tab control.

See Also: CTabCtrl::GetItem, **CTabCtrl::SetItem**

CTabCtrl::RemoveImage

void RemoveImage(int *nImage* **);**

Parameters

nImage   Zero-based index of the image to remove.

Remarks

Call this function to remove the specified image from a tab control's image list. The
tab control updates each tab's image index so that each tab remains associated with the
same image.

See Also: CTabCtrl::GetImageList, **CTabCtrl::SetImageList**

CTabCtrl::SetCurSel

int SetCurSel(int *nItem* **);**

Return Value

Zero-based index of the previously selected tab if successful, otherwise −1.

Parameters

nItem   The zero-based index of the item to be selected.

Remarks

Selects a tab in a tab control. A tab control does not send a **TCN_SELCHANGING**
or **TCN_SELCHANGE** notification message when a tab is selected using this
function. These notifications are sent, using **WM_NOTIFY**, when the user clicks or
uses the keyboard to change tabs.

See Also: CTabCtrl::GetCurSel, **CTabCtrl::GetCurFocus**

CTabCtrl::SetImageList

CImageList * SetImageList(CImageList * *pImageList* **);**

Return Value

Returns the handle of the previous image list or **NULL** if there is no previous image list.

Parameters

pImageList   Pointer to the image list to be assigned to the tab control.

Remarks

Call this function to assign an image list to a tab control.

See Also: CTabCtrl::GetImageList, CImageList

CTabCtrl::SetItem

BOOL SetItem(int *nItem*, **TC_ITEM*** *pTabCtrlItem* **);**

Return Value

Nonzero if successful; otherwise 0.

Parameters

nItem   Zero-based index of the item.

pTabCtrlItem   Pointer to a **TC_ITEM** structure that contains the new item attributes. The **mask** member specifies which attributes to set. If the **mask** member specifies the **TCIF_TEXT** value, the **pszText** member is the address of a null-terminated string and the **cchTextMax** member is ignored. For a description of this structure, see the **CTabCtrl::GetItem** member function.

Remarks

Call this function to set some or all of a tab's attributes.

See Also: CTabCtrl::InsertItem, CTabCtrl::GetItem

CTabCtrl::SetItemSize

CSize SetItemSize(CSize *size* **);**

Return Value

Returns the old width and height of the tab control items.

Parameters

size   The new width and height, in pixels, of the tab control items.

Remarks

Call this function to set the width and height of the tab control items.

See Also: **CTabCtrl::AdjustRect**, **CTabCtrl::GetItemRect**, **CTabCtrl::SetItemSize**

CTabCtrl::SetPadding

void SetPadding(CSize *size* **);**

Parameters

size   Sets the amount of space (padding) around each tab's icon and label in a tab control.

Remarks

Call this function to set the amount of space (padding) around each tab's icon and label in a tab control.

CTabCtrl::SetTooltips

void SetTooltips(CTooltipCtrl* *pWndTip* **);**

Parameters

pWndTip   Handle of the tool tip control.

Remarks

Call this function to assign a tool tip control to a tab control. You can get the tool tip control associated with a tab control by making a call to **GetTooltips**.

See Also: **CTabCtrl::GetTooltips**

CTime

CTime does not have a base class.

A **CTime** object represents an absolute time and date. The **CTime** class incorporates the ANSI **time_t** data type and its associated run-time functions, including the ability to convert to and from a Gregorian date and 24-hour time.

CTime values are based on coordinated universal time (UTC), which is equivalent to Greenwich mean time (GMT). The local time zone is controlled by the **TZ** environment variable.

When creating a **CTime**, field to 0 to indicate that standard time is in effect, or to a value greater than 0 to indicate that daylight savings time is in effect, or to a value less than zero to have the C run-time library code compute whether standard time or daylight savings time is in effect. **tm_isdst** is a required field. If not set, its value is undefined and the return value from **mktime** is unpredictable. If *timeptr* points to a tm structure returned by a previous call to **asctime**, **gmtime**, or **localtime**, the **tm_isdst** field contains the correct value.

See the *Run-Time Library Reference* for more information on the **time_t** data type and the run-time functions that are used by **CTime**. Note that **CTime** uses the **strftime** function, which is not supported for Windows dynamic-link libraries (DLL). Therefore, **CTime** cannot be used in Windows DLLs.

A companion class, **CTimeSpan**, represents a time interval—the difference between two **CTime** objects.

The **CTime** and **CTimeSpan** classes are not designed for derivation. Because there are no virtual functions, the size of **CTime** and **CTimeSpan** objects is exactly 4 bytes. Most member functions are inline.

For more information on using **CTime**, see the article "Date and Time" in *Visual C++ Programmer's Guide* online and "Time Management" in the *Run-Time Library Reference*.

#include <afx.h>

See Also: Run-time functions: **asctime**, **_ftime**, **gmtime**, **localtime**, **strftime**, **time**

CTime Class Members

Construction

CTime	Constructs **CTime** objects in various ways.
GetCurrentTime	Creates a **CTime** object that represents the current time (static member function).

Extraction

GetTime	Returns a **time_t** that corresponds to this **CTime** object.
GetYear	Returns the year that this **CTime** object represents.
GetMonth	Returns the month that this **CTime** object represents (1 through 12).
GetDay	Returns the day that this **CTime** object represents (1 through 31).
GetHour	Returns the hour that this **CTime** object represents (0 through 23).
GetMinute	Returns the minute that this **CTime** object represents (0 through 59).
GetSecond	Returns the second that this **CTime** object represents (0 through 61).
GetDayOfWeek	Returns the day of the week (1 for Sunday, 2 for Monday, and so forth).

Conversion

GetGmtTm	Breaks down a **CTime** object into components—based on UTC.
GetLocalTm	Breaks down a **CTime** object into components—based on the local time zone.
Format	Converts a **CTime** object into a formatted string—based on the local time zone.
FormatGmt	Converts a **CTime** object into a formatted string—based on UTC.

Operators

operator =	Assigns new time values.
operator + –	Add and subtract **CTimeSpan** and **CTime** objects.
operator +=, –=	Add and subtract a **CTimeSpan** object to and from this **CTime** object.
operator ==, < , etc.	Compare two absolute times.

Archive/Dump

operator <<	Outputs a **CTime** object to **CArchive** or **CDumpContext**.
operator >>	Inputs a **CTime** object from **CArchive**.

Member Functions

CTime::CTime

CTime( );
CTime(const CTime& *timeSrc* **);**
CTime(time_t *time* **);**
CTime(int *nYear*, **int** *nMonth*, **int** *nDay*, **int** *nHour*, **int** *nMin*, **int** *nSec*, **int** *nDST* **= -1);**
CTime(WORD *wDosDate*, **WORD** *wDosTime*, **int** *nDST* **= -1);**
CTime(const SYSTEMTIME& *sysTime*, **int** *nDST* **= -1);**
CTime(const FILETIME& *fileTime*, **int** *nDST* **= -1);**

Parameters

timeSrc   Indicates a **CTime** object that already exists.

time   Indicates a time value.

nYear, nMonth, nDay, nHour, nMin, nSec   Indicates the date and time values to be copied into the new **CTime** object.

nDST   Indicates whether daylight savings time is in effect. Can have one of three values, as follows:

- *nDST* set to 0   Standard time is in effect.

- *nDST* set to a value greater than 0   Daylight savings time is in effect.

- *nDST* set to a value less than 0   The default. Automatically computes whether standard time or daylight savings time is in effect.

wDosDate, wDosTime   MS-DOS date and time values to be converted to a date/time value and copied into the new **CTime** object.

sysTime   A **SYSTEMTIME** structure to be converted to a date/time value and copied into the new **CTime** object.

fileTime   A **FILETIME** structure to be converted to a date/time value and copied into the new **CTime** object.

Remarks

All these constructors create a new **CTime** object initialized with the specified absolute time, based on the current time zone.

Each constructor is described below:

- **CTime( );**   Constructs an unitialized **CTime** object. This constructor allows you to define **CTime** object arrays. You should initialize such arrays with valid times prior to use.

- **CTime(const CTime&);**   Constructs a **CTime** object from another **CTime** value.

- **CTime(time_t);**   Constructs a **CTime** object from a **time_t** type.

- **CTime(int, int,** etc.**);** Constructs a **CTime** object from local time components with each component constrained to the following ranges:

Component	Range
nYear	1970–2038*
nMonth	1–12
nDay	1–31
nHour	no constraint
nMin	no constraint
nSec	no constraint

*   The upper date limit is 1/18/2038. For a wider range of dates, see **COleDateTime**.

This constructor makes the appropriate conversion to UTC. The Debug version of the Microsoft Foundation Class Library asserts if one or more of the year, month, or day components is out of range. It is your responsibility to validate the arguments prior to calling.

- **CTime(WORD, WORD);** Constructs a **CTime** object from the specified MS-DOS date and time values.

- **CTime(const SYSTEMTIME&);** Constructs a **CTime** object from a **SYSTEMTIME** structure.

- **CTime(const FILETIME&);** Constructs a **CTime** object from a **FILETIME** structure. You most likely will not use **CTime FILETIME** initialization directly. If you use a **CFile** object to manipulate a file, **CFile::GetStatus** retrieves the file time stamp for you via a **CTime** object initialized with a **FILETIME** structure.

For more information on the **time_t** data type, see the **time** function in the *Run-Time Library Reference*.

For more information, see the **SYSTEMTIME** and **FILETIME** structure in the *Win32 SDK Programmer's Reference*.

For more information, see the "MS-DOS Date and Time" entry in the Win32 SDK documentation.

Example

```
// example for CTime::CTime
time_t osBinaryTime;  // C run-time time (defined in <time.h>)
time( &osBinaryTime ) ;  // Get the current time from the
                         // operating system.
CTime time1; // Empty CTime. (0 is illegal time value.)
CTime time2 = time1; // Copy constructor.
CTime time3( osBinaryTime );  // CTime from C run-time time
CTime time4( 1999, 3, 19, 22, 15, 0 ); // 10:15PM March 19, 1999
```

See Also: CTime::GetTime, GetCurrentTime, operator =

CTime::Format

CString Format(LPCTSTR *pFormat* **) const;**
CString Format(UINT *nFormatID* **) const;**

Return Value

A **CString** that contains the formatted time.

Parameters

pFormat   A formatting string similar to the **printf** formatting string. Formatting
codes, preceded by a percent (%) sign, are replaced by the corresponding **CTime**
component. Other characters in the formatting string are copied unchanged to the
returned string. See the run-time function **strftime** for details. The value and
meaning of the formatting codes for **Format** are listed below:

- **%D**   Total days in this **CTime**

- **%H**   Hours in the current day

- **%M**   Minutes in the current hour

- **%S**   Seconds in the current minute

- **%%**   Percent sign

nFormatID   The ID of the string that identifies this format.

Remarks

Call this member function to create a formatted representation of the date/time value.
If the status of this **CTime** object is null, the return value is an empty string. If the
status of **CTime** is invalid, the return value is an empty string.

Example

```
// example for CTime::Format and CTime::FormatGmt
CTime t( 1999, 3, 19, 22, 15, 0 );
// 10:15PM March 19, 1999
CString s = t.Format( "%A, %B %d, %Y" );
ASSERT( s == "Friday, March 19, 1999" );
```

See Also: CTime::FormatGmt

CTime::FormatGmt

CString FormatGmt(LPCTSTR *pFormat* **) const;**
CString FormatGmt(UINT *nFormatID* **) const;**

Return Value

A **CString** that contains the formatted time.

Parameters

pFormat   Specifies a formatting string similar to the **printf** formatting string. See the run-time function **strftime** for details.

nFormatID   The ID of the string that identifies this format.

Remarks

Generates a formatted string that corresponds to this **CTime** object. The time value is not converted and thus reflects UTC.

See Also: CTime::Format

CTime::GetCurrentTime

static CTime PASCAL GetCurrentTime( );

Remarks

Returns a **CTime** object that represents the current time.

Example

```
// example for CTime::GetCurrentTime
CTime t = CTime::GetCurrentTime();
```

CTime::GetDay

int GetDay( ) const;

Remarks

Returns the day of the month, based on local time, in the range 1 through 31. This function calls **GetLocalTm**, which uses an internal, statically allocated buffer. The data in this buffer is overwritten as a result of calls to other **CTime** member functions.

Example

```
// example for CTime::GetDay, CTime::GetMonth, and CTime::GetYear
CTime t( 1999, 3, 19, 22, 15, 0 ); // 10:15PM March 19, 1999
ASSERT( t.GetDay() == 19 );
ASSERT( t.GetMonth() == 3 );
ASSERT( t.GetYear() == 1999 );
```

See Also: CTime::GetDayOfWeek

CTime::GetDayOfWeek

int GetDayOfWeek( ) const;

Remarks

Returns the day of the week based on local time; 1 = Sunday, 2 = Monday, ..., 7 = Saturday. This function calls **GetLocalTm**, which uses an internal, statically allocated buffer. The data in this buffer is overwritten as a result of calls to other **CTime** member functions.

CTime::GetGmtTm

struct tm* GetGmtTm(struct tm* *ptm* **= NULL) const;**

Return Value

A pointer to a filled-in **struct tm** as defined in the include file TIME.H. The members and the values they store are as follows:

- **tm_sec** Seconds
- **tm_min** Minutes
- **tm_hour** Hours (0–23)
- **tm_mday** Day of month (1–31)
- **tm_mon** Month (0–11; January = 0)
- **tm_year** Year (actual year minus 1900)
- **tm_wday** Day of week (1–7; Sunday = 1)
- **tm_yday** Day of year (0–365; January 1 = 0)
- **tm_isdst** Always 0

Note The year in **struct tm** is in the range 70 to 138; the year in the **CTime** interface is in the range January 1, 1970 to January 18, 2038 (inclusive).

Parameters

ptm Points to a buffer that will receive the time data. If this pointer is **NULL**, an internal, statically allocated buffer is used. The data in this default buffer is overwritten as a result of calls to other **CTime** member functions.

Remarks

Gets a **struct tm** that contains a decomposition of the time contained in this **CTime** object. **GetGmtTm** returns UTC.

This function calls **GetLocalTm**, which uses an internal, statically allocated buffer. The data in this buffer is overwritten as a result of calls to other **CTime** member functions.

Example

See the example for **GetLocalTm**.

CTime::GetHour

int GetHour( ) const;

Remarks

Returns the hour, based on local time, in the range 0 through 23. This function calls
GetLocalTm, which uses an internal, statically allocated buffer. The data in this
buffer is overwritten as a result of calls to other **CTime** member functions.

Example

```
// example for CTime::GetHour, CTime::GetMinute, and CTime::GetSecond.
CTime t( 1999, 3, 19, 22, 15, 0 ); // 10:15PM March 19, 1999
ASSERT( t.GetSecond() == 0 );
ASSERT( t.GetMinute() == 15 );
ASSERT( t.GetHour() == 22 );
```

CTime::GetLocalTm

struct tm* GetLocalTm(struct tm* *ptm* **= NULL) const;**

Return Value

A pointer to a filled-in **struct tm** as defined in the include file TIME.H. See
GetGmtTm for the structure layout.

Parameters

ptm   Points to a buffer that will receive the time data. If this pointer is **NULL**, an
internal, statically allocated buffer is used. The data in this default buffer is
overwritten as a result of calls to other **CTime** member functions.

Remarks

Gets a **struct tm** containing a decomposition of the time contained in this **CTime**
object. **GetLocalTm** returns local time.

Example

```
// example for CTime::GetLocalTm
CTime t( 1999, 3, 19, 22, 15, 0 ); // 10:15PM March 19, 1999
struct tm* osTime;  // A pointer to a structure containing time
                // elements.
osTime = t.GetLocalTm( NULL );
ASSERT( osTime->tm_mon == 2 ); // Note zero-based month!
```

CTime::GetMinute

int GetMinute( ) const;

Remarks

Returns the minute, based on local time, in the range 0 through 59. This function calls **GetLocalTm**, which uses an internal, statically allocated buffer. The data in this buffer is overwritten as a result of calls to other **CTime** member functions.

CTime::GetMonth

int GetMonth( ) const;

Remarks

Returns the month, based on local time, in the range 1 through 12 (1 = January). This function calls **GetLocalTm**, which uses an internal, statically allocated buffer. The data in this buffer is overwritten as a result of calls to other **CTime** member functions.

Example

See the example for **GetDay**.

CTime::GetSecond

int GetSecond( ) const;

Remarks

Returns the second, based on local time, in the range 0 through 59. This function calls **GetLocalTm**, which uses an internal, statically allocated buffer. The data in this buffer is overwritten as a result of calls to other **CTime** member functions.

CTime::GetTime

time_t GetTime( ) const;

Remarks

Returns a **time_t** value for the given **CTime** object.

Example

```
// example for CTime::GetTime
CTime t( 1999, 3, 19, 22, 15, 0 ); // 10:15PM March 19, 1999
time_t osBinaryTime = t.GetTime(); // time_t defined in <time.h>
printf( "time_t = %ld\n", osBinaryTime );
```

See Also: CTime::CTime

CTime::GetYear

int GetYear( ) const;

Remarks

Returns the year, based on local time, in the range January 1,1970 to January 18, 2038 (inclusive). This function calls **GetLocalTm**, which uses an internal, statically allocated buffer. The data in this buffer is overwritten as a result of calls to other **CTime** member functions.

Example

See the example for **GetDay**.

See Also: CTime::CTime

Operators

CTime::operator =

const CTime& operator =(const CTime& *timeSrc* **);**
const CTime& operator =(time_t *t* **);**

Remarks

These overloaded assignment operators copy the source time into this **CTime** object.

The internal time storage in a **CTime** object is independent of time zone. Time-zone conversion is not necessary during assignment.

Example

```
// example for CTime::operator =
time_t osBinaryTime;  // C run-time time (defined in <time.h>)
CTime t1 = osBinaryTime; // Assignment from time_t
CTime t2 = t1; // Assignment from CTime
```
See Also: CTime::CTime

CTime::operator +, -

CTime operator +(CTimeSpan *timeSpan* **) const;**
CTime operator –(CTimeSpan *timeSpan* **) const;**
CTimeSpan operator –(CTime *time* **) const;**

Remarks

CTime objects represent absolute time. **CTimeSpan** objects represent relative time. The first two operators allow you to add and subtract **CTimeSpan** objects to and from **CTime** objects. The third allows you to subtract one **CTime** object from another to yield a **CTimeSpan** object.

Example

```
// example for CTime::operator  +, -
CTime t1( 1999, 3, 19, 22, 15, 0 ); // 10:15PM March 19, 1999
CTime t2( 1999, 3, 20, 22, 15, 0 ); // 10:15PM March 20, 1999
CTimeSpan ts = t2 - t1;  // Subtract 2 CTimes
ASSERT( ts.GetTotalSeconds() == 86400L );
ASSERT( ( t1 + ts ) == t2 );  // Add a CTimeSpan to a CTime.
ASSERT( ( t2 - ts ) == t1 );  // Subtract a CTimeSpan from a Ctime.
```

CTime::operator +=, -=

const CTime& operator +=(CTimeSpan *timeSpan* **);**
const CTime& operator –=(CTimeSpan *timeSpan* **);**

Remarks

These operators allow you to add and subtract a **CTimeSpan** object to and from this **CTime** object.

Example

```
// example for CTime::operator -=
CTime t( 1999, 3, 19, 22, 15, 0 ); // 10:15PM March 19, 1999
t += CTimeSpan( 0, 1, 0, 0 ); // 1 hour exactly
ASSERT( t.GetHour() == 23 );
```

CTime Comparison Operators

BOOL operator ==(CTime *time* **) const;**
BOOL operator !=(CTime *time* **) const;**
BOOL operator <(CTime *time* **) const;**
BOOL operator >(CTime *time* **) const;**
BOOL operator <=(CTime *time* **) const;**
BOOL operator >=(CTime *time* **) const;**

Remarks

These operators compare two absolute times and return nonzero if the condition is true; otherwise 0.

Example

```
// example for CTime comparison operators
CTime t1 = CTime::GetCurrentTime();
CTime t2 = t1 + CTimeSpan( 0, 1, 0, 0 );    // 1 hour later
ASSERT( t1 != t2 );
ASSERT( t1 < t2 );
ASSERT( t1 <= t2 );
```

CTime::operators <<, >>

friend CDumpContext& AFXAPI operator<<(CDumpContext& *dc,* **CTime** *time* **);**
friend CArchive& AFXAPI operator<<(CArchive& *ar,* **CTime** *time* **);**
friend CArchive& AFXAPI operator>>(CArchive& *ar,* **CTime&** *rtime* **);**

Remarks

The **CTime** insertion (<<) operator supports diagnostic dumping and storing to an archive. The extraction (>>) operator supports loading from an archive.

When you send a **CTime** object to the dump context, the local time is displayed in readable date-time format.

Example

```
// example for CTime::operators <<, >>
CTime t( 1999, 3, 19, 22, 15, 0 ); // 10:15PM March 19, 1999
afxDump << t << "\n"; // Prints 'CTime("Fri Mar 19 22:15:00 1999")'.

extern CArchive ar;
if( ar.IsLoading() )
    ar >> t;
else
    ar << t;
```

See Also: CArchive, CDumpContext

CTimeSpan

CTimeSpan does not have a base class.

A **CTimeSpan** object represents a relative time span. The **CTimeSpan** class incorporates the ANSI **time_t** data type and its associated run-time functions. These functions convert seconds to various combinations of days, hours, minutes, and seconds.

A **CTimeSpan** object keeps time in seconds. Because the **CTimeSpan** object is stored as a signed number in 4 bytes, the maximum allowed span is approximately ± 68 years.

A companion class, **CTime**, represents an absolute time. A **CTimeSpan** is the difference between two **CTime** values.

The **CTime** and **CTimeSpan** classes are not designed for derivation. Because there are no virtual functions, the size of both **CTime** and **CTimeSpan** objects is exactly 4 bytes. Most member functions are inline.

For more information on using **CTimeSpan**, see the article "Date and Time" in *Visual C++ Programmer's Guide* online and "Time Management" in the *Run-Time Library Reference*.

#include <afx.h>

See Also: Run-time functions: **asctime**, **_ftime**, **gmtime**, **localtime**, **strftime**, **time**

CTimeSpan Class Members

Construction

CTimeSpan	Constructs **CTimeSpan** objects in various ways.

Extraction

GetDays	Returns the number of complete days in this **CTimeSpan**.
GetHours	Returns the number of hours in the current day (–23 through 23).
GetTotalHours	Returns the total number of complete hours in this **CTimeSpan**.
GetMinutes	Returns the number of minutes in the current hour (–59 through 59).
GetTotalMinutes	Returns the total number of complete minutes in this **CTimeSpan**.
GetSeconds	Returns the number of seconds in the current minute (–59 through 59).
GetTotalSeconds	Returns the total number of complete seconds in this **CTimeSpan**.

Conversion

Format	Converts a **CTimeSpan** into a formatted string.

Operators

operator =	Assigns new time-span values.
operator + –	Adds and subtracts **CTimeSpan** objects.
operator += –=	Adds and subtracts a **CTimeSpan** object to and from this **CTimeSpan**.
operator == < etc.	Compares two relative time values.

Archive/Dump

operator <<	Outputs a **CTimeSpan** object to **CArchive** or **CDumpContext**.
operator >>	Inputs a **CTimeSpan** object from **CArchive**.

Member Functions
CTimeSpan::CTimeSpan

CTimeSpan( );
CTimeSpan(const CTimeSpan& *timeSpanSrc* **);**
CTimeSpan(time_t *time* **);**
CTimeSpan(LONG *lDays*, **int** *nHours*, **int** *nMins*, **int** *nSecs* **);**

Parameters

timeSpanSrc   A **CTimeSpan** object that already exists.

time   A **time_t** time value.

lDays, *nHours*, *nMins*, *nSecs*   Days, hours, minutes, and seconds, respectively.

Remarks

All these constructors create a new **CTimeSpan** object initialized with the specified relative time. Each constructor is described below:

- **CTimeSpan( );**   Constructs an uninitialized **CTimeSpan** object.

- **CTimeSpan(const CTimeSpan&);**   Constructs a **CTimeSpan** object from another **CTimeSpan** value.

- **CTimeSpan(time_t);**   Constructs a **CTimeSpan** object from a **time_t** type. This value should be the difference between two absolute **time_t** values.

- **CTimeSpan(LONG, int, int, int);**   Constructs a **CTimeSpan** object from components with each component constrained to the following ranges:

Component	Range
lDays	0–25,000 (approximately)
nHours	0–23
nMins	0–59
nSecs	0–59

Note that the Debug version of the Microsoft Foundation Class Library asserts if one or more of the time-day components is out of range. It is your responsibility to validate the arguments prior to calling.

Example

```
// example for CTimeSpan::CTimeSpan
CTimeSpan ts1;  // Uninitialized time value
CTimeSpan ts2a( ts1 ); // Copy constructor
CTimeSpan ts2b = ts1; // Copy constructor again
CTimeSpan ts3( 100 ); // 100 seconds
CTimeSpan ts4( 0, 1, 5, 12 );    // 1 hour, 5 minutes, and 12 seconds
```

CTimeSpan::Format

CString Format(LPCSTR *pFormat* **) const;**
CString Format(LPCTSTR *pFormat* **) const;**
CString Format(UINT *nID* **) const;**

Return Value

A **CString** object that contains the formatted time.

Parameters

pFormat   A formatting string similar to the **printf** formatting string. Formatting codes, preceded by a percent (%) sign, are replaced by the corresponding **CTimeSpan** component. Other characters in the formatting string are copied unchanged to the returned string. The value and meaning of the formatting codes for **Format** are listed below:

- **%D**   Total days in this **CTimeSpan**

- **%H**   Hours in the current day

- **%M**   Minutes in the current hour

- **%S**   Seconds in the current minute

- **%%**   Percent sign

nID   The ID of the string that identifies this format.

Remarks

Generates a formatted string that corresponds to this **CTimeSpan**.

The Debug version of the library checks the formatting codes and asserts if the code is not in the list above.

Example

```
// example for CTimeSpan::Format
CTimeSpan ts( 3, 1, 5, 12 ); // 3 days, 1 hour, 5 min, and 12 sec
CString s = ts.Format( "Total days: %D, hours: %H, mins: %M, secs: %S" );
ASSERT( s == "Total days: 3, hours: 01, mins: 05, secs: 12" );
```

CTimeSpan::GetDays

LONG GetDays( ) const;

Remarks

Returns the number of complete days. This value may be negative if the time span is negative.

Example

```
// example for CTimeSpan::GetDays
CTimeSpan ts( 3, 1, 5, 12 ); // 3 days, 1 hour, 5 min, and 12 sec
ASSERT( ts.GetDays() == 3 );
```

CTimeSpan::GetHours

int GetHours( ) const;

Remarks

Returns the number of hours in the current day. The range is –23 through 23.

Example

```
// example for CTimeSpan::GetHours
CTimeSpan ts( 3, 1, 5, 12 ); // 3 days, 1 hour, 5 min, and 12 sec
ASSERT( ts.GetHours() == 1 );
ASSERT( ts.GetMinutes() == 5 );
ASSERT( ts.GetSeconds() == 12 );
```

CTimeSpan::GetMinutes

int GetMinutes( ) const;

Remarks

Returns the number of minutes in the current hour. The range is –59 through 59.

Example

See the example for **GetHours**.

CTimeSpan::GetSeconds

int GetSeconds( ) const;

Remarks

Returns the number of seconds in the current minute. The range is –59 through 59.

Example

See the example for **GetHours**.

CTimeSpan::GetTotalHours

LONG GetTotalHours( ) const;

Remarks

Returns the total number of complete hours in this **CTimeSpan**.

Example

```
// example for CTimeSpan::GetTotalHours
CTimeSpan ts( 3, 1, 5, 12 ); // 3 days, 1 hour, 5 min, and 12 sec
ASSERT( ts.GetTotalHours() == 73 );
ASSERT( ts.GetTotalMinutes() == 4385 );
ASSERT( ts.GetTotalSeconds() == 263112 );
```

CTimeSpan::GetTotalMinutes

LONG GetTotalMinutes( ) const;

Remarks

Returns the total number of complete minutes in this **CTimeSpan**.

Example

See the example for **GetTotalHours**.

CTimeSpan::GetTotalSeconds

LONG GetTotalSeconds( ) const;

Remarks

Returns the total number of complete seconds in this **CTimeSpan**.

Example

See the example for **GetTotalHours**.

Operators
CTimeSpan::operator =

const CTimeSpan& operator =(const CTimeSpan& *timeSpanSrc* **);**

Remarks

The overloaded assignment operator copies the source **CTimeSpan** *timeSpanSrc*
object into this **CTimeSpan** object.

Example

```
// example for CTimeSpan::operator =
CTimeSpan ts1;
CTimeSpan ts2( 3, 1, 5, 12 ); // 3 days, 1 hour, 5 min, and 12 sec
ts1 = ts2;
ASSERT( ts1 == ts2 );
```

See Also: **CTimeSpan::CTimeSpan**

CTimeSpan::operator +, -

CTimeSpan operator +(CTimeSpan *timeSpan* **) const;**
CTimeSpan operator –(CTimeSpan *timeSpan* **) const;**

Remarks

These two operators allow you to add and subtract **CTimeSpan** objects to and from each other.

Example

```
// example for CTimeSpan::operator +, -
CTimeSpan ts1( 3, 1, 5, 12 ); // 3 days, 1 hour, 5 min, and 12 sec
CTimeSpan ts2( 100 ); // 100 seconds
CTimeSpan ts3 = ts1 + ts2;
ASSERT( ts3.GetSeconds() == 52 ); // 6 mins, 52 secs
```

CTimeSpan::operator +=, -=

const CTimeSpan& operator +=(CTimeSpan *timeSpan* **);**
const CTimeSpan& operator –=(CTimeSpan *timeSpan* **);**

Remarks

These operators allow you to add and subtract a **CTimeSpan** object to and from this **CTimeSpan**.

Example

```
// example for CTimeSpan::operator +=, -=
CTimeSpan ts1( 10 ); // 10 seconds
CTimeSpan ts2( 100 ); // 100 seconds
ts2 -= ts1;
ASSERT( ts2.GetTotalSeconds() == 90 );
```

CTimeSpan Comparison Operators

BOOL operator ==(CTimeSpan *timeSpan* **) const;**
BOOL operator !=(CTimeSpan *timeSpan* **) const;**
BOOL operator <(CTimeSpan *timeSpan* **) const;**
BOOL operator >(CTimeSpan *timeSpan* **) const;**
BOOL operator <=(CTimeSpan *timeSpan* **) const;**
BOOL operator >=(CTimeSpan *timeSpan* **) const;**

Remarks

These operators compare two relative time values. They return nonzero if the condition is true; otherwise 0.

Example

```
// example for CTimeSpan comparison operators
CTimeSpan ts1( 100 );
CTimeSpan ts2( 110 );
ASSERT( ( ts1 != ts2 ) && ( ts1 < ts2 ) && ( ts1 <= ts2 ) );
```

CTimeSpan::operators <<, >>

friend CDumpContext& AFXAPI operator<<(CDumpContext& *dc*,
➥ **CTimeSpan** *timeSpan* **);**
friend CArchive& AFXAPI operator<<(CArchive& *ar*, **CTimeSpan** *timeSpan* **);**
friend CArchive& AFXAPI operator>>(CArchive& *ar*, **CTimeSpan&** *rtimeSpan* **);**

Remarks

The **CTimeSpan** insertion (<<) operator supports diagnostic dumping and storing to an archive. The extraction (>>) operator supports loading from an archive.

When you send a **CTimeSpan** object to the dump context, the value is displayed in an alphanumeric format that shows days, hours, minutes, and seconds.

Example

```
// example for CTimeSpan::operators <<, >>
CTimeSpan ts( 3, 1, 5, 12 ); // 3 days, 1 hour, 5 min, and 12 sec
#ifdef _DEBUG
afxDump << ts << "\n";
#endif
// Prints 'CTimeSpan(3 days, 1 hours, 5 minutes and 12 seconds)'

extern CArchive ar;
if( ar.IsLoading( ))
   ar >> ts;
else
   ar << ts;
```

CToolBar

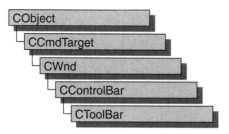

Objects of the class **CToolBar** are control bars that have a row of bitmapped buttons and optional separators. The buttons can act like pushbuttons, check-box buttons, or radio buttons. **CToolBar** objects are usually embedded members of frame-window objects derived from the class **CFrameWnd** or **CMDIFrameWnd**.

CToolBar::GetToolBarCtrl, a member function new to MFC 4.0, allows you to take advantage of the Windows common control's support for toolbar customization and additional functionality. **CToolBar** member functions give you most of the functionality of the Windows common controls; however, when you call **GetToolBarCtrl**, you can give your toolbars even more of the characteristics of Windows 95 toolbars. When you call **GetToolBarCtrl**, it will return a reference to a **CToolBarCtrl** object. See **CToolBarCtrl** for more information about designing toolbars using Windows common controls. For more general information about common controls, see "Common Controls" in the *Windows 95 SDK Programmer's Reference*.

Visual C++ provides you with two methods to create a toolbar. To create a toolbar resource using the Resource Editor, follow these steps:

1. Create a toolbar resource.
2. Construct the **CToolBar** object.
3. Call the **Create** function to create the Windows toolbar and attach it to the **CToolBar** object.
4. Call **LoadToolBar** to load the toolbar resource.

Otherwise, follow these steps:

1. Construct the **CToolBar** object.
2. Call the **Create** function to create the Windows toolbar and attach it to the **CToolBar** object.
3. Call **LoadBitmap** to load the bitmap that contains the toolbar button images.
4. Call **SetButtons** to set the button style and associate each button with an image in the bitmap.

All the button images in the toolbar are taken from one bitmap, which must contain one image for each button. All images must be the same size; the default is 16 pixels wide and 15 pixels high. Images must be side by side in the bitmap.

The **SetButtons** function takes a pointer to an array of control IDs and an integer that specifies the number of elements in the array. The function sets each button's ID to the value of the corresponding element of the array and assigns each button an image index, which specifies the position of the button's image in the bitmap. If an array element has the value **ID_SEPARATOR**, no image index is assigned.

The order of the images in the bitmap is typically the order in which they are drawn on the screen, but you can use the **SetButtonInfo** function to change the relationship between image order and drawing order.

All buttons in a toolbar are the same size. The default is 24 x 22 pixels, in accordance with *Windows Interface Guidelines for Software Design*. Any additional space between the image and button dimensions is used to form a border around the image.

Each button has one image. The various button states and styles (pressed, up, down, disabled, disabled down, and indeterminate) are generated from that one image. Although bitmaps can be any color, you can achieve the best results with images in black and shades of gray.

Toolbar buttons imitate pushbuttons by default. However, toolbar buttons can also imitate check-box buttons or radio buttons. Check-box buttons have three states: checked, cleared, and indeterminate. Radio buttons have only two states: checked and cleared.

To set an individual button or separator style without pointing to an array, call **GetButtonStyle** to retrieve the style, and then call **SetButtonStyle** instead of **SetButtons**. **SetButtonStyle** is most useful when you want to change a button's style at run time.

To assign text to appear on a button, call **GetButtonText** to retrieve the text to appear on the button, and then call **SetButtonText** to set the text.

To create a check-box button, assign it the style **TBBS_CHECKBOX** or use a **CCmdUI** object's **SetCheck** member function in an **ON_UPDATE_COMMAND_UI** handler. Calling **SetCheck** turns a pushbutton into a check-box button. Pass **SetCheck** an argument of 0 for unchecked, 1 for checked, or 2 for indeterminate.

To create a radio button, call a **CCmdUI** object's **SetRadio** member function from an **ON_UPDATE_COMMAND_UI** handler. Pass **SetRadio** an argument of 0 for unchecked or nonzero for checked. In order to provide a radio group's mutually exclusive behavior, you must have **ON_UPDATE_COMMAND_UI** handlers for all of the buttons in the group.

For more information on using **CToolBar**, see the article "Toolbars" in *Visual C++ Programmer's Guide* online and Technical Note 31 online, "Control Bars."

#include <afxext.h>

See Also: **CToolBarCtrl**, **CControlBar**, **CToolBar::Create**, **CToolBar::LoadBitmap**, **CToolBar::SetButtons**, **CCmdUI::SetCheck**, **CCmdUI::SetRadio**

CToolBar Class Members

Construction

CToolBar	Constructs a **CToolBar** object.
Create	Creates the Windows toolbar and attaches it to the **CToolBar** object.
SetSizes	Sets the sizes of buttons and their bitmaps.
SetHeight	Sets the height of the toolbar.
LoadToolBar	Loads a toolbar resource created with the resource editor.
LoadBitmap	Loads the bitmap containing bitmap-button images.
SetBitmap	Sets a bitmapped image.
SetButtons	Sets button styles and an index of button images within the bitmap.

Attributes

CommandToIndex	Returns the index of a button with the given command ID.
GetItemID	Returns the command ID of a button or separator at the given index.
GetItemRect	Retrieves the display rectangle for the item at the given index.
GetButtonStyle	Retrieves the style for a button.
SetButtonStyle	Sets the style for a button.
GetButtonInfo	Retrieves the ID, style, and image number of a button.
SetButtonInfo	Sets the ID, style, and image number of a button.
GetButtonText	Retrieves the text that will appear on a button.
SetButtonText	Sets the text that will appear on a button.
GetToolBarCtrl	Allows direct access to the underlying common control.

Member Functions
CToolBar::CommandToIndex

> int **CommandToIndex**(UINT *nIDFind*);

Return Value

> The index of the button, or −1 if no button has the given command ID.

Parameters

> *nIDFind*   Command ID of a toolbar button.

Remarks

> This member function returns the index of the first toolbar button, starting at position 0, whose command ID matches *nIDFind*.

> **See Also: CToolBar::GetItemId**

CToolBar::Create

> **BOOL Create(CWnd*** *pParentWnd***,**
> ↪ **DWORD** *dwStyle* = **WS_CHILD | WS_VISIBLE | CBRS_TOP,**
> ↪ **UINT** *nID* = **AFX_IDW_TOOLBAR);**

Return Value

> Nonzero if successful; otherwise 0.

Parameters

> *pParentWnd*   Pointer to the window that is the toolbar's parent.

> *dwStyle*   The toolbar style. Additional toolbar styles supported are:

> - **CBRS_TOP**   Control bar is at top of the frame window.
> - **CBRS_BOTTOM**   Control bar is at bottom of the frame window.
> - **CBRS_NOALIGN**   Control bar is not repositioned when the parent is resized.
> - **CBRS_TOOLTIPS**   Control bar displays tool tips.
> - **CBRS_SIZE_DYNAMIC**   Control bar is dynamic.
> - **CBRS_SIZE_FIXED**   Control bar is fixed.
> - **CBRS_FLOATING**   Control bar is floating.
> - **CBRS_FLYBY**   Status bar displays information about the button.
> - **CBRS_HIDE_INPLACE**   Control bar is not displayed to the user.

> *nID*   The toolbar's child-window ID.

Remarks

This member function creates a Windows toolbar (a child window) and associates it with the **CToolBar** object. It also sets the toolbar height to a default value.

See Also: **CToolBar::CToolBar**, **CToolBar::LoadBitmap**, **CToolBar::SetButtons**, **CToolBar::LoadToolBar**, **CControlBar::CalcDynamicLayout**, **CControlBar::CalcFixedLayout**

CToolBar::CToolBar

CToolBar( );

Remarks

This member function constructs a **CToolBar** object and sets the default sizes.

Call the **Create** member function to create the toolbar window.

See Also: **CToolBar::Create**

CToolBar::GetButtonInfo

void GetButtonInfo(int *nIndex*, **UINT&** *nID*, **UINT&** *nStyle*, **int&** *iImage* **) const;**

Parameters

nIndex   Index of the toolbar button or separator whose information is to be retrieved.

nID   Reference to a **UINT** that is set to the command ID of the button.

nStyle   Reference to a **UINT** that is set to the style of the button.

iImage   Reference to an integer that is set to the index of the button's image within the bitmap.

Remarks

This member function retrieves the control ID, style, and image index of the toolbar button or separator at the location specified by *nIndex*. Those values are assigned to the variables referenced by *nID*, *nStyle*, and *iImage*. The image index is the position of the image within the bitmap that contains images for all the toolbar buttons. The first image is at position 0.

If *nIndex* specifies a separator, *iImage* is set to the separator width in pixels.

See Also: **CToolBar::SetButtonInfo**, **CToolBar::GetItemID**

CToolBar::GetButtonStyle

UINT GetButtonStyle(int *nIndex* **) const;**

Return Value

The style of the button or separator specified by *nIndex*.

Parameters

nIndex   The index of the toolbar button or separator style to be retrieved.

Remarks

Call this member function to retrieve the style of a button or separator on the toolbar. A button's style determines how the button appears and how it responds to user input. See **SetButtonStyle** for examples of button styles.

See Also: CToolBar::SetButtonStyle

CToolBar::GetButtonText

CString GetButtonText(int *nIndex* **) const;**
void GetButtonText(int *nIndex***, CString&** *rString* **) const;**

Return Value

A **CString** object containing the button text.

Parameters

nIndex   Index of the text to be retrieved.

rString   A reference to a **CString** object that will contain the text to be retrieved.

Remarks

Call this member function to retrieve the text that appears on a button. The second form of this member function fills a **CString** object with the string text.

See Also: CToolBar::SetButtonText, Cstring

CToolBar::GetItemID

UINT GetItemID(int *nIndex* **) const;**

Return Value

The command ID of the button or separator specified by *nIndex*.

Parameters

nIndex   Index of the item whose ID is to be retrieved.

Remarks

This member function returns the command ID of the button or separator specified by *nIndex*. Separators return **ID_SEPARATOR**.

See Also: **CToolBar::CommandToIndex**, **CControlBar::GetCount**

CToolBar::GetItemRect

virtual void GetItemRect(int *nIndex***, LPRECT** *lpRect* **);**

Parameters

nIndex   Index of the item (button or separator) whose rectangle coordinates are to be retrieved.

lpRect   Address of the **RECT** structure that will contain the item's coordinates.

Remarks

This member function fills the **RECT** structure whose address is contained in *lpRect* with the coordinates of the button or separator specified by *nIndex*. Coordinates are in pixels relative to the upper-left corner of the toolbar.

Use **GetItemRect** to get the coordinates of a separator you want to replace with a combo box or other control.

See Also: **CToolBar::CommandToIndex**

CToolBar::GetToolBarCtrl

CToolBarCtrl& GetToolBarCtrl( ) const;

Return Value

A reference to a **CToolBarCtrl** object.

Remarks

This member function allows direct access to the underlying common control.

Use **GetToolBarCtrl** to take advantage of the functionality of the Windows toolbar common control, and to take advantage of the support **CToolBarCtrl** provides for toolbar customization.

For more information about using common controls, see the article "Control Topics" in *Visual C++ Programmer's Guide* online and "Common Controls" in the *Windows 95 SDK Programmer's Reference*.

See Also: **CToolBarCtrl**

CToolBar::LoadBitmap

BOOL LoadBitmap(LPCTSTR *lpszResourceName* **);**
BOOL LoadBitmap(UINT *nIDResource* **);**

Return Value

Nonzero if successful; otherwise 0.

Parameters

lpszResourceName   Pointer to the resource name of the bitmap to be loaded.

nIDResource   Resource ID of the bitmap to be loaded.

Remarks

Call this member function to load the bitmap specified by *lpszResourceName* or *nIDResource*. The bitmap should contain one image for each toolbar button. If the images are not of the standard size (16 pixels wide and 15 pixels high), call **SetSizes** to set the button sizes and their images.

See Also: CToolBar::Create, CToolBar::SetButtons, CToolBar::SetSizes, CToolBar::LoadToolBar

---

CToolbar::LoadToolBar

BOOL LoadToolBar(LPCTSTR *lpszResourceName* **);**
BOOL LoadToolBar(UINT *nIDResource* **);**

Return Value

Nonzero if successful; otherwise 0.

Parameters

lpszResourceName   Pointer to the resource name of the toolbar to be loaded.

nIDResource   Resource ID of the toolbar to be loaded.

Remarks

Call this member function to load the toolbar specified by *lpszResourceName* or *nIDResource*.

See toolbar editor in the *Developer Studio User's Guide* online for more information about creating a toolbar resource.

See Also: CToolBar::Create, CToolbar::LoadBitmap, CToolBar::SetButtons

CToolBar::SetBitmap

BOOL SetBitmap(HBITMAP *hbmImageWell* **);**

Return Value

Nonzero if successful; otherwise 0.

Parameters

hbmImageWell   Handle of a bitmap image that is associated with a toolbar.

Remarks

Call this member function to set the bitmap image for the toolbar. For example, call **SetBitmap** to change the bitmapped image after the user takes an action on a document that changes the action of a button.

CToolBar::SetButtonInfo

void SetButtonInfo(int *nIndex*, **UINT** *nID*, **UINT** *nStyle*, **int** *iImage* **);**

Parameters

nIndex   Index of the button or separator whose information is to be set.

nID   The value to which the button's command ID is set.

nStyle   The new button style. The following button styles are supported:

- **TBBS_BUTTON**   Standard pushbutton (default)

- **TBBS_SEPARATOR**   Separator

- **TBBS_CHECKBOX**   Auto check-box button

- **TBBS_GROUP**   Marks the start of a group of buttons

- **TBBS_CHECKGROUP**   Marks the start of a group of check-box buttons

iImage   New index for the button's image within the bitmap.

Remarks

Call this member function to set the button's command ID, style, and image number. For separators, which have the style **TBBS_SEPARATOR**, this function sets the separator's width in pixels to the value stored in *iImage*.

For information on bitmap images and buttons, see the **CToolBar** Overview and **CToolBar::LoadBitmap**.

See Also: **CToolBar::GetButtonInfo**

CToolBar::SetButtons

BOOL SetButtons(const UINT* *lpIDArray***, int** *nIDCount* **);**

Return Value

Nonzero if successful; otherwise 0.

Parameters

lpIDArray   Pointer to an array of command Ids. It can be **NULL** to allocate empty buttons.

nIDCount   Number of elements in the array pointed to by *lpIDArray*.

Remarks

This member function sets each toolbar button's command ID to the value specified by the corresponding element of the array *lpIDArray*. If an element of the array has the value **ID_SEPARATOR**, a separator is created in the corresponding position of the toolbar. This function also sets each button's style to **TBBS_BUTTON** and each separator's style to **TBBS_SEPARATOR**, and assigns an image index to each button. The image index specifies the position of the button's image within the bitmap.

You do not need to account for separators in the bitmap because this function does not assign image indexes for separators. If your toolbar has buttons at positions 0, 1, and 3 and a separator at position 2, the images at positions 0, 1, and 2 in your bitmap are assigned to the buttons at positions 0, 1, and 3, respectively.

If *lpIDArray* is **NULL**, this function allocates space for the number of items specified by *nIDCount*. Use **SetButtonInfo** to set each item's attributes.

See Also: CToolBar::Create, CToolBar::SetButtonInfo, CToolBar::SetButtonStyle, CToolBar::LoadToolBar

---

CToolBar::SetButtonStyle

void SetButtonStyle(int *nIndex***, UINT** *nStyle* **);**

Parameters

nIndex   Index of the button or separator whose information is to be set.

nStyle   The button style. The following button styles are supported:

- **TBBS_BUTTON**   Standard pushbutton (default)
- **TBBS_SEPARATOR**   Separator
- **TBBS_CHECKBOX**   Auto check-box button
- **TBBS_GROUP**   Marks the start of a group of buttons
- **TBBS_CHECKGROUP**   Marks the start of a group of check-box buttons

Remarks

Call this member function to set the style of a button or separator, or to group buttons. A button's style determines how the button appears and how it responds to user input.

Before calling **SetButtonStyle**, call the **GetButtonStyle** member function to retrieve the button or separator style.

See Also: **CToolBar::GetButtonStyle**

CToolBar::SetButtonText

BOOL SetButtonText(int *nIndex*, **LPCTSTR** *lpszText* **);**

Return Value

Nonzero if successful; otherwise 0.

Parameters

nIndex   Index of the button whose text is to be set.

lpszText   Points to the text to be set on a button.

Remarks

Call this function to set the text on a button.

See Also: **CToolBar::GetButtonText**

CToolBar::SetHeight

void SetHeight(int *cyHeight* **);**

Parameters

cyHeight   The height in pixels of the toolbar.

Remarks

This member function sets the toolbar's height to the value, in pixels, specified in *cyHeight*.

After calling **SetSizes**, use this member function to override the standard toolbar height. If the height is too small, the buttons will be clipped at the bottom.

If this function is not called, the framework uses the size of the button to determine the toolbar height.

See Also: **CToolBar::SetSizes**, **CToolBar::SetButtonInfo**, **CToolBar::SetButtons**

CToolBar::SetSizes

void SetSizes(SIZE *sizeButton***, SIZE** *sizeImage* **);**

Parameters

sizeButton   The size in pixels of each button.

sizeImage   The size in pixels of each image.

Remarks

Call this member function to set the toolbar's buttons to the size, in pixels, specified in *sizeButton*. The *sizeImage* parameter must contain the size, in pixels, of the images in the toolbar's bitmap. The dimensions in *sizeButton* must be sufficient to hold the image plus 7 pixels extra in width and 6 pixels extra in height. This function also sets the toolbar height to fit the buttons.

Call this member function only for toolbars that do not follow *Windows Interface Guidelines for Software Design* recommendations for button and image sizes.

See Also: CToolBar::LoadBitmap, CToolBar::SetButtonInfo, CToolBar::SetButtons,

CToolBarCtrl

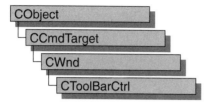

The **CToolBarCtrl** class provides the functionality of the Windows toolbar common control. This control (and therefore the **CToolBarCtrl** class) is available only to programs running under Windows 95 and Windows NT version 3.51 and later.

A Windows toolbar common control is a rectangular child window that contains one or more buttons. These buttons can display a bitmap image, a string, or both. When the user chooses a button, it sends a command message to the toolbar's owner window. Typically, the buttons in a toolbar correspond to items in the application's menu; they provide a more direct way for the user to access an application's commands.

CToolBarCtrl objects contain several important internal data structures: a list of button image bitmaps, a list of button label stings, and a list of **TBBUTTON** structures which associate an image and/or string with the position, style, state, and command ID of the button. Each of the elements of these data structures is referred to by a zero-based index. Before you can use a **CToolBarCtrl** object, you must set up these data structures. The list of strings can only be used for button labels; you cannot retrieve strings from the toolbar.

To use a **CToolBarCtrl** object, you will typically follow these steps:

1. Construct the **CToolBarCtrl** object.

2. Call **Create** to create the Windows toolbar common control and attach it to the **CToolBarCtrl** object.

3. If you want bitmap images for buttons, add the button bitmaps to the toolbar by calling **AddBitmap**. If you want string labels for buttons, add the strings to the toolbar by calling **AddString** and/or **AddStrings**.

4. Add button structures to the toolbar by calling **AddButtons**.

5. If you want tool tips for a toolbar button in an owner window that is not a **CFrameWnd**, you need to handle the **TTN_NEEDTEXT** messages in the toolbar's owner window as described in "CToolBarCtrl: Handling Tool Tip Notifications." If the parent window of the toolbar is derived from **CFrameWnd**, tool tips are displayed without any extra effort from you because **CFrameWnd** provides a default handler.

6. If you want your user to be able to customize the toolbar, handle customization notification messages in the owner window as described in "CToolBarCtrl: Handling Customization Notifications."

You can use **SaveState** to save the current state of a toolbar control in the registry and **RestoreState** to restore the state based on information previously stored in the registry. In addition to saving the toolbar state between uses of the application, applications typically store the state before the user begins customizing the toolbar in case the user later wants to restore the toolbar to its original state.

For more information on using **CToolBarCtrl**, see Technical Note 60 online.

#include <afxcmn.h>

See Also: CToolBar

CToolBarCtrl Class Members

Construction

CToolBarCtrl	Constructs a **CToolBarCtrl** object.
Create	Creates a toolbar control and attaches it to a **CToolBarCtrl** object.

Attributes

IsButtonEnabled	Tells whether the specified button in a toolbar control is enabled.
IsButtonChecked	Tells whether the specified button in a toolbar control is checked.
IsButtonPressed	Tells whether the specified button in a toolbar control is pressed.
IsButtonHidden	Tells whether the specified button in a toolbar control is hidden.
IsButtonIndeterminate	Tells whether the state of the specified button in a toolbar control is indeterminate (gray).
SetState	Sets the state for the specified button in a toolbar control.
GetState	Retrieves information about the state of the specified button in a toolbar control, such as whether it is enabled, pressed, or checked.
GetButton	Retrieves information about the specified button in a toolbar control.
GetButtonCount	Retrieves a count of the buttons currently in the toolbar control.
GetItemRect	Retrieves the bounding rectangle of a button in a toolbar control.

Attributes *(continued)*

SetButtonStructSize	Specifies the size of the **TBBUTTON** structure.
SetButtonSize	Sets the size of the buttons to be added to a toolbar control.
SetBitmapSize	Sets the size of the bitmapped images to be added to a toolbar control.
GetToolTips	Retrieves the handle of the tool tip control, if any, associated with the toolbar control.
SetToolTips	Associates a tool tip control with the toolbar control.
SetOwner	Sets the window to receive notification messages from the toolbar control.
SetRows	Sets the number of rows of buttons displayed in the toolbar.
GetRows	Retrieves the number of rows of buttons currently displayed in the toolbar.
SetCmdID	Sets the command identifier to be sent to the owner window when the specified button is pressed.
GetBitmapFlags	Gets flags associated with the toolbar's bitmap.

Operations

EnableButton	Enables or disables the specified button in a toolbar control.
CheckButton	Checks or clears a given button in a toolbar control.
PressButton	Presses or releases the specified button in a toolbar control.
HideButton	Hides or shows the specified button in a toolbar control.
Indeterminate	Sets or clears the indeterminate (gray) state of the specified button in a toolbar control.
AddBitmap	Adds one or more bitmap button images to the list of button images available for a toolbar control.
AddButtons	Adds one or more buttons to a toolbar control.
InsertButton	Inserts a button in a toolbar control.
DeleteButton	Deletes a button from the toolbar control.
CommandToIndex	Retrieves the zero-based index for the button associated with the specified command identifier.
RestoreState	Restores the state of the toolbar control.
SaveState	Saves the state of the toolbar control.
Customize	Displays the Customize Toolbar dialog box.
AddString	Adds a new string, passed as a resource ID, to the toolbar's internal list of strings.
AddStrings	Adds a new string or strings, passed as a pointer to a buffer of null-separated strings, to the toolbar's internal list of strings.
AutoSize	Resizes a toolbar control.

CToolBarCtrl: Handling Tool Tip Notifications

When you specify the **TBSTYLE_TOOLTIPS** style, the toolbar creates and manages a tool tip control. A tool tip is a small pop-up window that contains a line of text describing a toolbar button. The tool tip is hidden, appearing only when the user puts the cursor on a toolbar button and leaves it there for approximately one-half second. The tool tip is displayed near the cursor.

Before the tool tip is displayed, the **TTN_NEEDTEXT** notification message is sent to the toolbar's owner window to retrieve the descriptive text for the button. If the toolbar's owner window is a **CFrameWnd** window, tool tips are displayed wihout any extra effort, because **CFrameWnd** has a default handler for the **TTN_NEEDTEXT** notification. If the toolbar's owner window is not derived from **CFrameWnd**, such as a dialog box or form view, you must add an entry to your owner window's message map and provide a notification handler in the message map. The entry to your owner window's message map is as follows:

ON_NOTIFY_EX(TTN_NEEDTEXT, 0, *memberFxn*)

memberFxn   The member function to be called when text is needed for this button.

Note that the id of a tool tip is always 0.

In addition to the **TTN_NEEDTEXT** notification, a tool tip control can send the following notifications to a toolbar control:

Notification	Meaning
TTN_NEEDTEXTA	Tool tip control requires ASCII text (Win95 only)
TTN_NEEDTEXTW	Tool tip control requires UNICODE text (Windows NT only)

For an example handler function and more information about enabling tool tips, see "Tool Tips" in *Visual C++ Programmer's Guide* online.

CToolBarCtrl: Handling Customization Notifications

A Windows toolbar common control has built-in customization features, including a system-defined customization dialog box, which allow the user to insert, delete, or rearrange toolbar buttons. The application determines whether the customization features are available and controls the extent to which the user can customize the toolbar.

You can make these customization features available to the user by giving the toolbar the **CCS_ADJUSTABLE** style. The customization features allow the user to drag a button to a new position or to remove a button by dragging it off the toolbar. In addition, the user can double-click the toolbar to display the Customize Toolbar dialog box, which allows the user to add, delete, and rearrange toolbar buttons. The application can display the dialog box by using the **Customize** member function.

The toolbar control sends notification messages to the parent window at each step in the customization process. If the user holds the SHIFT key down and begins dragging a button, the toolbar automatically handles the drag operation. The toolbar sends the **TBN_QUERYDELETE** notification message to the parent window to determine whether the button may be deleted. The drag operation ends if the parent window returns **FALSE**. Otherwise, the toolbar captures mouse input and waits for the user to release the mouse button.

When the user releases the mouse button, the toolbar control determines the location of the mouse cursor. If the cursor is outside the toolbar, the button is deleted. If the cursor is on another toolbar button, the toolbar sends the **TBN_QUERYINSERT** notification message to the parent window to determine if a button may be inserted to the left of the given button. The button is inserted if the parent window returns **TRUE**; otherwise, it is not. The toolbar sends the **TBN_TOOLBARCHANGE** notification message to signal the end of the drag operation.

If the user begins a drag operation without holding down the SHIFT key, the toolbar control sends the **TBN_BEGINDRAG** notification message to the owner window. An application that implements its own button-dragging code can use this message as a signal to begin a drag operation. The toolbar sends the **TBN_ENDDRAG** notification message to signal the end of the drag operation.

A toolbar control sends notification messages when the user customizes a toolbar by using the Customize Toolbar dialog box. The toolbar sends the **TBN_BEGINADJUST** notification message after the user double-clicks the toolbar, but before the dialog box is created. Next, the toolbar begins sending a series of **TBN_QUERYINSERT** notification messages to determine whether the toolbar allows buttons to be inserted. When the parent window returns **TRUE**, the toolbar stops sending **TBN_QUERYINSERT** notification messages. If the parent window does not return **TRUE** for any button, the toolbar destroys the dialog box.

Next, the toolbar control determines if any buttons may be deleted from the toolbar by sending one **TBN_QUERYDELETE** notification message for each button in the toolbar. The parent window returns **TRUE** to indicate that a button may be deleted; otherwise, it returns **FALSE**. The toolbar adds all toolbar buttons to the dialog box, but grays those that may not be deleted.

Whenever the toolbar control needs information about a button in the Customize Toolbar dialog box, it sends the **TBN_GETBUTTONINFO** notification message, specifying the index of the button for which it needs information and the address of a

TBNOTIFY structure. The parent window must fill the structure with the relevant information.

The Customize Toolbar dialog box includes a Help button and a Reset button. When the user chooses the Help button, the toolbar control sends the **TBN_CUSTHELP** notification message. The parent window should respond by displaying help information. The dialog box sends the **TBN_RESET** notification message when the user selects the Reset button. This message signals that the toolbar is about to reinitialize the dialog box.

These messages are all **WM_NOTIFY** messages, and they can be handled in your owner window by adding message-map entries of the following form to your owner window's message map:

ON_NOTIFY(*wNotifyCode*, *idControl*, *memberFxn*)

wNotifyCode   Notification message identifier code, such as **TBN_BEGINADJUST**.

idControl   The identifier of the control sending the notification.

memberFxn   The member function to be called when this notification is received.

Your member function would be declared with the following prototype:

afx_msg void *memberFxn*(**NMHDR** * *pNotifyStruct*, **LRESULT** * *result*);

If the notification message handler returns a value, it should put it in the **LRESULT** pointed to by *result*.

For each message, *pNotifyStruct* points to either an **NMHDR** structure or a **TBNOTIFY** structure. These structures are described below:

The **NMHDR** structure contains the following members:

```
typedef struct tagNMHDR {
    HWND hwndFrom;    // handle of control sending message
    UINT idFrom;      // identifier of control sending message
    UINT code;        // notification code; see below
} NMHDR;
```

hwndFrom   Window handle of the control that is sending the notification. To convert this handle to a **CWnd** pointer, use **CWnd::FromHandle**.

idFrom   Identifier of the control sending the notification.

code   Notification code. This member can be a value specific to a control type, such as **TBN_BEGINADJUST** or **TTN_NEEDTEXT**, or it can be one of the common notification values listed below:

- **NM_CLICK**   The user has clicked the left mouse button within the control.

- **NM_DBLCLK**   The user has double-clicked the left mouse button within the control.

- **NM_KILLFOCUS**   The control has lost the input focus.

- **NM_OUTOFMEMORY** The control could not complete an operation because there is not enough memory available.

- **NM_RCLICK** The user has clicked the right mouse button within the control.

- **NM_RDBLCLK** The user has double-clicked the right mouse button within the control.

- **NM_RETURN** The control has the input focus, and the user has pressed the ENTER key.

- **NM_SETFOCUS** The control has received the input focus.

The **TBNOTIFY** structure contains the following members:

```
typedef struct {
    NMHDR hdr;          // information common to all WM_NOTIFY messages
    int iItem;          // index of button associated with notification
    TBBUTTON tbButton;  // info about button associated with notification
    int cchText;        // count of characters in button text
    LPSTR lpszText;     // address of button text
} TBNOTIFY, FAR* LPTBNOTIFY;
```

hdr Information common to all **WM_NOTIFY** messages.

iItem Index of button associated with notification.

tbButton **TBBUTTON** structure that contains information about the toolbar button associated with the notification.

cchText Count of characters in button text.

lpszText Pointer to button text.

The notifications the toolbar sends are as follows:

- **TBN_BEGINADJUST** Sent when the user begins customizing a toolbar control. The pointer points to an **NMHDR** structure that contains information about the notification. The handler doesn't need to return any specific value.

- **TBN_BEGINDRAG** Sent when the user begins dragging a button in a toolbar control. The pointer points to a **TBNOTIFY** structure. The **iItem** member contains the zero-based index of the button being dragged. The handler doesn't need to return any specific value.

- **TBN_CUSTHELP** Sent when the user chooses the Help button in the Customize Toolbar dialog box. No return value. The pointer points to an **NMHDR** structure that contains information about the notification message. The handler doesn't need to return any specific value.

- **TBN_ENDADJUST** Sent when the user stops customizing a toolbar control. The pointer points to an **NMHDR** structure that contains information about the notification message. The handler doesn't need to return any specific value.

- **TBN_ENDDRAG**   Sent when the user stops dragging a button in a toolbar control. The pointer points to a **TBNOTIFY** structure. The **iItem** member contains the zero-based index of the button being dragged. The handler doesn't need to return any specific value.

- **TBN_GETBUTTONINFO**   Sent when the user is customizing a toolbar control. The toolbar uses this notification message to retrieve information needed by the Customize Toolbar dialog box. The pointer points to a **TBNOTIFY** structure. The **iItem** member specifies the zero-based index of a button. The **pszText** and **cchText** members specify the address and length, in characters, of the current button text. An application should fill the structure with information about the button. Return **TRUE** if button information was copied to the structure, or **FALSE** otherwise.

- **TBN_QUERYDELETE**   Sent while the user is customizing a toolbar to determine whether a button may be deleted from a toolbar control. The pointer points to a **TBNOTIFY** structure. The **iItem** member contains the zero-based index of the button to be deleted. Return **TRUE** to allow the button to be deleted or **FALSE** to prevent the button from being deleted.

- **TBN_QUERYINSERT**   Sent while the user is customizing a toolbar control to determine whether a button may be inserted to the left of the given button. The pointer points to a **TBNOTIFY** structure. The **iItem** member contains the zero-based index of the button to be inserted. Return **TRUE** to allow a button to be inserted in front of the given button or **FALSE** to prevent the button from being inserted.

- **TBN_RESET**   Sent when the user resets the content of the Customize Toolbar dialog box. The pointer points to an **NMHDR** structure that contains information about the notification message. The handler doesn't need to return any specific value.

- **TBN_TOOLBARCHANGE**   Sent after the user has customized a toolbar control. The pointer points to an **NMHDR** structure that contains information about the notification message. The handler doesn't need to return any specific value.

Member Functions

CToolBarCtrl::AddBitmap

int AddBitmap(int *nNumButtons*, **UINT** *nBitmapID* **);**
int AddBitmap(int *nNumButtons*, **CBitmap*** *pBitmap* **);**

Return Value
Zero-based index of the first new image if successful; otherwise −1.

Parameters
nNumButtons   Number of button images in the bitmap.

nBitmapID   Resource identifier of the bitmap that contains the button image or images to add.

pBitmap   Pointer to the **CBitmap** object that contains the button image or images to add.

Remarks

Call this function to add one or more button images to the list of button images stored in the toolbar control. You can use the Windows API **CreateMappedBitmap** to map colors before adding the bitmap to the toolbar.

If you pass a pointer to a **CBitMap** object, you must ensure that the bitmap is not destroyed until after the toolbar is destroyed.

See Also: CToolBarCtrl::AddButtons, CToolBarCtrl::InsertButton, CToolBarCtrl::AddString, CToolBarCtrl::AddStrings

---

CToolBarCtrl::AddButtons

BOOL AddButtons(int *nNumButtons***, LPTBBUTTON** *lpButtons* **);**

Return Value

Nonzero if successful; otherwise zero.

Parameters

nNumButtons   Number of buttons to add.

lpButtons   Address of an array of **TBBUTTON** structures that contains information about the buttons to add. There must be the same number of elements in the array as buttons specified by *nNumButtons*.

Remarks

Call this function to add one or more buttons to a toolbar control.

The *lpButtons* pointer points to an array of **TBBUTTON** structures. Each **TBBUTTON** structure associates the button being added with the button's style, image and/or string, command ID, state, and user-defined data:

```
typedef struct _TBBUTTON {
    int iBitmap;      // zero-based index of button image
    int idCommand;    // command to be sent when button pressed
    BYTE fsState;     // button state--see below
    BYTE fsStyle;     // button style--see below
    DWORD dwData;     // application-defined value
    int iString;      // zero-based index of button label string
} TBBUTTON;
```

The members are as follows:

iBitmap   Zero-based index of button image. **NULL** if no image for this button.

idCommand Command identifier associated with the button. This identifier is sent in a **WM_COMMAND** message when the button is chosen. If the **fsStyle** member has the **TBSTYLE_SEP** value, this member must be zero.

fsState Button state flags. It can be a combination of the values listed below:

- **TBSTATE_CHECKED** The button has the **TBSTYLE_CHECKED** style and is being pressed.

- **TBSTATE_ENABLED** The button accepts user input. A button that does not have this state does not accept user input and is grayed.

- **TBSTATE_HIDDEN** The button is not visible and cannot receive user input.

- **TBSTATE_INDETERMINATE** The button is grayed.

- **TBSTATE_PRESSED** The button is being pressed.

- **TBSTATE_WRAP** A line break follows the button. The button must also have the **TBSTATE_ENABLED** state.

fsStyle Button style. It can be a combination of the values listed below:

- **TBSTYLE_BUTTON** Creates a standard push button.

- **TBSTYLE_CHECK** Creates a button that toggles between the pressed and unpressed states each time the user clicks it. The button has a different background color when it is in the pressed state.

- **TBSTYLE_CHECKGROUP** Creates a check button that stays pressed until another button in the group is pressed.

- **TBSTYLE_GROUP** Creates a button that stays pressed until another button in the group is pressed.

- **TBSTYLE_SEP** Creates a separator, providing a small gap between button groups. A button that has this style does not receive user input.

dwData User-defined data.

iString Zero-based index of the string to use as the button's label. **NULL** if there is no string for this button.

The image and/or string whose index you provide must have previously been added to the toolbar control's list using **AddBitmap**, **AddString**, and/or **AddStrings**.

See Also: **CToolBarCtrl::InsertButton, CToolBarCtrl::DeleteButton, CToolBarCtrl::AddBitmap, CToolBarCtrl::AddString, CToolBarCtrl::AddStrings**

CToolBarCtrl::AddString

int AddString(UINT *nStringID* **);**

Return Value

The zero-based index of the first new string added if successful; otherwise –1.

Parameters

nStringID   Resource identifier of the string resource to add to the toolbar control's string list.

Remarks

Call this function to add a new string, passed as a resource ID, to the toolbar's internal list of strings.

See Also: CToolBarCtrl::AddStrings, CToolBarCtrl::AddButtons, CToolBarCtrl::InsertButton, CToolBarCtrl::AddBitmap

---

CToolBarCtrl::AddStrings

int AddStrings(LPCTSTR *lpszStrings* **);**

Return Value

The zero-based index of the first new string added if successful; otherwise –1.

Parameters

lpszStrings   Address of a buffer that contains one or more null-terminated strings to add to the toolbar's string list. The last string must be terminated with two null characters.

Remarks

Call this function to add a new string or strings to the list of strings available for a toolbar control. Strings in the buffer must be separated by a null character.

You must ensure that the last string has two null terminators. To properly format a constant string, you might write it as:

```
// one null added automatically
lpszStrings = "Only one string to add\0";
```

or:

```
// adds three strings with one call
lpszStrings = "String 1\0String 2\0String 3\0";
```

You should not pass a **CString** object to this function since it is not possible to have more than one null character in a **CString**.

See Also: CToolBarCtrl::AddString, CToolBarCtrl::AddButtons, CToolBarCtrl::InsertButton, CToolBarCtrl::AddBitmap

CToolBarCtrl::AutoSize

void AutoSize( );

Remarks

Call this function to resize the entire toolbar control. You should call this function when the size of the parent window changes or when the size of the toolbar changes (such as when you set the button or bitmap size, or add strings).

See Also: CToolBarCtrl::SetBitmapSize, CToolBarCtrl::SetButtonSize, CToolBarCtrl::AddString, CToolBarCtrl::AddStrings

---

CToolBarCtrl::CheckButton

BOOL CheckButton(int *nID*, BOOL *bCheck* = TRUE);

Return Value

Nonzero if successful; otherwise zero.

Parameters

nID   Command identifier of the button to check or clear.

bCheck   **TRUE** to check the button, **FALSE** to clear it.

Remarks

Call this function to check or clear a given button in a toolbar control. When a button has been checked, it appears to have been pressed. If you want to change more than one button state, consider calling **SetState** instead.

See Also: CToolBarCtrl::IsButtonChecked, CToolBarCtrl::EnableButton, CToolBarCtrl::PressButton, CToolBarCtrl::HideButton, CToolBarCtrl::Indeterminate, CToolBarCtrl::GetState, CToolBarCtrl::SetState

---

CToolBarCtrl::CommandToIndex

UINT CommandToIndex(UINT *nID*) const;

Return Value

The zero-based index for the button associated with the command ID.

Parameters

nID   Command ID whose button index you want to find.

Remarks

Call this function to retrieve the zero-based index for the button associated with the specified command identifier.

See Also: **CToolBarCtrl::SetCmdID**, **CToolBarCtrl::GetButton**, **CToolBarCtrl::AddButtons**, **CToolBarCtrl::InsertButton**

CToolBarCtrl::Create

BOOL Create(DWORD *dwStyle***, const RECT&** *rect***, CWnd*** *pParentWnd***, UINT** *nID* **);**

Return Value

Nonzero if successful; otherwise zero.

Parameters

dwStyle   Specifies the toolbar control's style. Toolbars must always have the **WS_CHILD** style. In addition, you can specify any combination of toolbar styles and window styles as described under Remarks.

rect   Optionally specifies the toolbar control's size and position. It can be either a **CRect** object or a **RECT** structure.

pParentWnd   Specifies the toolbar control's parent window. It must not be **NULL**.

nID   Specifies the toolbar control's ID.

Remarks

You construct a **CToolBarCtrl** in two steps. First call the constructor, then call **Create**, which creates the toolbar control and attaches it to the **CToolBarCtrl** object.

The toolbar control automatically sets the size and position of the toolbar window. The height is based on the height of the buttons in the toolbar. The width is the same as the width of the parent window's client area. The **CCS_TOP** and **CCS_BOTTOM** styles determine whether the toolbar is positioned along the top or bottom of the client area. By default, a toolbar has the **CCS_TOP** style.

Apply the following window styles to a toolbar control.

- **WS_CHILD**   Always
- **WS_VISIBLE**   Usually
- **WS_DISABLED**   Rarely

Next, you may want to apply one or more of the common control styles:

- **CCS_ADJUSTABLE**   Allows toolbars to be customized by the user. If this style is used, the toolbar's owner window must handle the customization notification messages sent by the toolbar, as described in "CToolBarCtrl: Handling Customization Notifications."

- **CCS_BOTTOM**   Causes the control to position itself at the bottom of the parent window's client area and sets the width to be the same as the parent window's width.

- **CCS_NODIVIDER**   Prevents a two-pixel highlight from being drawn at the top of the control.

- **CCS_NOHILITE**   Prevents a one-pixel highlight from being drawn at the top of the control.

- **CCS_NOMOVEY**   Causes the control to resize and move itself horizontally, but not vertically, in response to a **WM_SIZE** message. If the **CCS_NORESIZE** style is used, this style does not apply.

- **CCS_NOPARENTALIGN**   Prevents the control from automatically moving to the top or bottom of the parent window. Instead, the control keeps its position within the parent window despite changes to the size of the parent window. If the **CCS_TOP** or **CCS_BOTTOM** style is also used, the height is adjusted to the default, but the position and width remain unchanged.

- **CCS_NORESIZE**   Prevents the control from using the default width and height when setting its initial size or a new size. Instead, the control uses the width and height specified in the request for creation or sizing.

- **CCS_TOP**   Causes the control to position itself at the top of the parent window's client area and sets the width to be the same as the parent window's width. Toolbars have this style by default.

Finally, you may want to apply one or both of the following toolbar control styles to a toolbar control:

- **TBSTYLE_TOOLTIPS**   Causes the toolbar to create and manage a tool tip control. A tool tip is a small pop-up window that contains a line of text describing a toolbar button. It appears only when the user puts the cursor on a toolbar button and leaves it there for approximately one-half second. The tool tip is displayed near the cursor. If you use this style, you must handle tool tip notifications as described in "CToolBarCtrl: Handling Tool Tip Notifications."

- **TBSTYLE_WRAPABLE**   Creates a toolbar control that can have multiple lines of buttons. Toolbar buttons can "wrap" to the next line when the toolbar becomes too narrow to include all buttons on the same line.

See Also: **CToolBarCtrl::CToolBarCtrl**, **CToolBarCtrl::SetButtonStructSize**

CToolBarCtrl::CToolBarCtrl

CToolBarCtrl( );

Remarks

Constructs a **CToolBarCtrl** object. You must call **Create** to make the toolbar usable.

See Also: **CToolBarCtrl::Create**

CToolBarCtrl::Customize

void Customize( );

Remarks

Call this function to display the Customize Toolbar dialog box. This dialog box allows the user to customize the toolbar by adding and deleting buttons.

To support customization, your toolbar's parent window must handle the customization notification messages as described in "CToolBarCtrl: Handling Customization Notifications." Your toolbar must also have been created with the **CCS_ADJUSTABLE** style, as described in **CToolBarCtrl::Create**.

See Also: "CToolBarCtrl: Handling Customization Notifications"

CToolBarCtrl::DeleteButton

BOOL DeleteButton(int *nIndex* **);**

Return Value

Nonzero if successful; otherwise zero.

Parameters

nIndex   Zero-based index of the button to delete.

Remarks

Call this function to delete a button from the toolbar control.

See Also: CToolBarCtrl::AddButtons, **CToolBarCtrl::AutoSize**, **CToolBarCtrl::InsertButton**

CToolBarCtrl::EnableButton

BOOL EnableButton(int *nID*, **BOOL** *bEnable* = **TRUE** **);**

Return Value

Nonzero if successful; otherwise zero.

Parameters

nID   Command identifier of the button to enable or disable.

bEnable   **TRUE** to enable the button; **FALSE** to disable the button.

Remarks

Call this function to enable or disable the specified button in a toolbar control. When a button has been enabled, it can be pressed and checked. If you want to change more than one button state, consider calling **SetState** instead.

See Also: **CToolBarCtrl::IsButtonEnabled, CToolBarCtrl::CheckButton, CToolBarCtrl::PressButton, CToolBarCtrl::HideButton, CToolBarCtrl::Indeterminate, CToolBarCtrl::GetState, CToolBarCtrl::SetState**

CToolBarCtrl::GetBitmapFlags

UINT GetBitmapFlags( ) const;

Return Value

A **UINT** that has the **TBBF_LARGE** flag set if the display can support large toolbar bitmaps, clear otherwise.

Remarks

Call this function to retrieve the bitmap flags from the toolbar. You should call it after creating the toolbar but before adding bitmaps to the toolbar.

The return value indicates whether the display supports large bitmaps or not. If the display supports large bitmaps and if you choose to use them, call **SetBitmapSize** and **SetButtonSize** before adding your large bitmap using **AddBitmap**.

See Also: **CToolBarCtrl::AddBitmap, CToolBarCtrl::SetBitmapSize, CToolBarCtrl::SetButtonSize**

CToolBarCtrl::GetButton

BOOL GetButton(int *nIndex***, LPTBBUTTON** *lpButton* **) const;**

Return Value

Nonzero if successful; otherwise zero.

Parameters

nIndex   Zero-based index of the button for which to retrieve information.

lpButton   Address of the **TBBUTTON** structure that is to receive a copy of the button information. See **CToolBarCtrl::AddButtons** for information about the **TBBUTTON** structure.

Remarks

Call this function to retrieve information about the specified button in a toolbar control.

See Also: **CToolBarCtrl::GetState, CToolBarCtrl::SetState, CToolBarCtrl::GetButtonCount, CToolBarCtrl::GetItemRect, CToolBarCtrl::CommandToIndex, CToolBarCtrl::AddButtons, CToolBarCtrl::InsertButton**

CToolBarCtrl::GetButtonCount

int GetButtonCount( ) const;

Return Value

The count of the buttons.

Remarks

Call this function to retrieve a count of the buttons currently in the toolbar control.

See Also: **CToolBarCtrl::GetButton**, **CToolBarCtrl::GetState**, **CToolBarCtrl::GetItemRect**, **CToolBarCtrl::AddButtons**, **CToolBarCtrl::InsertButton**, **CToolBarCtrl::DeleteButton**

CToolBarCtrl::GetItemRect

BOOL GetItemRect(int *nIndex*, LPRECT *lpRect*) const;

Return Value

Nonzero if successful; otherwise zero.

Parameters

nIndex   Zero-based index of the button for which to retrieve information.

lpRect   Address of a **RECT** structure or a **CRect** object that receives the coordinates of the bounding rectangle.

Remarks

Call this function to retrieve the bounding rectangle of a button in a toolbar control. This function does not retrieve the bounding rectangle for buttons whose state is set to **TBSTATE_HIDDEN**.

See Also: **CToolBarCtrl::GetButton**, **CToolBarCtrl::GetButtonCount**, **CToolBarCtrl::GetState**, **CToolBarCtrl::SetButtonSize**, **CToolBarCtrl::SetBitmapSize**

CToolBarCtrl::GetRows

int GetRows( ) const;

Return Value

Number of rows of buttons currently displayed on the toolbar.

Remarks

Call this function to retrieve the number of rows of buttons currently displayed by the toolbar control. Note that the number of rows will always be one unless the toolbar was created with the **TBSTYLE_WRAPABLE** style.

See Also: TBSTYLE_WRAPABLE in CToolBarCtrl::Create,
CToolBarCtrl::SetRows

CToolBarCtrl::GetState

int GetState(int *nID*) const;

Return Value

The button state information if successful or −1 otherwise. The button state
information can be a combination of the values listed in **CToolBarCtrl::AddButtons**.

Parameters

nID   Command identifier of the button for which to retrieve information.

Remarks

Call this function to retrieve information about the state of the specified button in a
toolbar control, such as whether it is enabled, pressed, or checked.

This function is especially handy if you want to retrieve more than one of the button
states. To just retrieve one state, use one of the following member functions:
IsButtonEnabled, IsButtonChecked, IsButtonPressed, IsButtonHidden, or
IsButtonIndeterminate. However, the **GetState** member function is the only way to
detect the **TBSTATE_WRAP** button state.

**See Also: CToolBarCtrl::SetState, CToolBarCtrl::GetItemRect,
CToolBarCtrl::IsButtonEnabled, CToolBarCtrl::IsButtonChecked,
CToolBarCtrl::IsButtonPressed, CToolBarCtrl::IsButtonHidden,
CToolBarCtrl::IsButtonIndeterminate**

CToolBarCtrl::GetToolTips

CToolTipCtrl* GetToolTips( ) const;

Return Value

A pointer to the **CToolTipCtrl** object associated with this toolbar or **NULL** if the
toolbar has no associated tool tip control.

Remarks

Call this function to retrieve the handle of the tool tip control, if any, associated with
the toolbar control. Since the toolbar control normally creates and maintains its own
tool tip control, most programs don't need to call this function.

See Also: CToolBarCtrl::SetToolTips, "CToolBarCtrl: Handling Tool Tip
Notifications," **CToolTipCtrl**

CToolBarCtrl::HideButton

BOOL HideButton(int *nID,* **BOOL** *bHide* **= TRUE);**

Return Value

Nonzero if successful; otherwise zero.

Parameters

nID   Command identifier of the button to hide or show.

bHide   **TRUE** to hide the button, **FALSE** to show it.

Remarks

Call this function to hide or show the specified button in a toolbar control. If you want to change more than one button state, consider calling **SetState** instead.

See Also: **CToolBarCtrl::IsButtonHidden, CToolBarCtrl::EnableButton, CToolBarCtrl::CheckButton, CToolBarCtrl::PressButton, CToolBarCtrl::Indeterminate, CToolBarCtrl::GetState, CToolBarCtrl::SetState**

CToolBarCtrl::Indeterminate

BOOL Indeterminate(int *nID,* **BOOL** *bIndeterminate* **= TRUE);**

Return Value

Nonzero if successful; otherwise zero.

Parameters

nID   Command identifier of the button whose indeterminate state is to be set or cleared.

bIndeterminate   **TRUE** to set the indeterminate state for the specified button, **FALSE** to clear it.

Remarks

Call this function to set or clear the indeterminate state of the specified button in a toolbar control. Indeterminate buttons are displayed grayed, such as the way the bold button on the toolbar of a word processor would look when the text selected contains both bold and regular characters.

If you want to change more than one button state, consider calling **SetState** instead.

See Also: Button styles in **CToolBarCtrl::AddButtons, CToolBarCtrl::IsButtonIndeterminate, CToolBarCtrl::EnableButton, CToolBarCtrl::CheckButton, CToolBarCtrl::PressButton, CToolBarCtrl::HideButton, CToolBarCtrl::GetState, CToolBarCtrl::SetState**

CToolBarCtrl::InsertButton

BOOL InsertButton(int *nIndex*, **LPTBBUTTON** *lpButton* **);**

Return Value

Nonzero if successful; otherwise zero.

Parameters

nIndex   Zero-based index of a button. This function inserts the new button to the left of this button.

lpButton   Address of a **TBBUTTON** structure containing information about the button to insert. See **CToolBarCtrl::AddButtons** for a description of the **TBBUTTON** structure.

Remarks

Call this function to insert a button in a toolbar control.

The image and/or string whose index you provide must have previously been added to the toolbar control's list using **AddBitmap**, **AddString**, and/or **AddStrings**.

See Also: **CToolBarCtrl::AddButtons, CToolBarCtrl::DeleteButton, CToolBarCtrl::AddBitmap, CToolBarCtrl::AddString, CToolBarCtrl::AddStrings**

CToolBarCtrl::IsButtonChecked

BOOL IsButtonChecked(int *nID* **) const;**

Return Value

Nonzero if the button is checked; otherwise zero.

Parameters

nID   Command identifier of the button in the toolbar.

Remarks

Call this function to determine whether the specified button in a toolbar control is checked. Consider calling **GetState** if you want to retrieve more than one button state.

See Also: **CToolBarCtrl::CheckButton, CToolBarCtrl::GetState, CToolBarCtrl::SetState, CToolBarCtrl::IsButtonEnabled, CToolBarCtrl::IsButtonPressed, CToolBarCtrl::IsButtonHidden, CToolBarCtrl::IsButtonIndeterminate**

CToolBarCtrl::IsButtonEnabled

BOOL IsButtonEnabled(int *nID* **) const;**

Return Value

Nonzero if the button is enabled; otherwise zero.

Parameters

nID   Command identifier of the button in the toolbar.

Remarks

Call this function to determine whether the specified button in a toolbar control is enabled. Consider calling **GetState** if you want to retrieve more than one button state.

See Also: **CToolBarCtrl::EnableButton, CToolBarCtrl::GetState, CToolBarCtrl::SetState, CToolBarCtrl::IsButtonChecked, CToolBarCtrl::IsButtonPressed, CToolBarCtrl::IsButtonHidden, CToolBarCtrl::IsButtonIndeterminate**

CToolBarCtrl::IsButtonHidden

BOOL IsButtonHidden(int *nID* **) const;**

Return Value

Nonzero if the button is hidden; otherwise zero.

Parameters

nID   Command identifier of the button in the toolbar.

Remarks

Call this function to determine whether the specified button in a toolbar control is hidden. Consider calling **GetState** if you want to retrieve more than one button state.

See Also: **CToolBarCtrl::HideButton, CToolBarCtrl::GetState, CToolBarCtrl::SetState, CToolBarCtrl::IsButtonEnabled, CToolBarCtrl::IsButtonChecked, CToolBarCtrl::IsButtonPressed, CToolBarCtrl::IsButtonIndeterminate**

CToolBarCtrl::IsButtonIndeterminate

BOOL IsButtonIndeterminate(int *nID* **) const;**

Return Value

Nonzero if the button is indeterminate; otherwise zero.

Parameters

nID   Command identifier of the button in the toolbar.

Remarks

Call this function to determine whether the specified button in a toolbar control is indeterminate. Indeterminate buttons are displayed grayed, such as the way the bold button on the toolbar of a word processor would look when the text selected contains both bold and regular characters.

Consider calling **GetState** if you want to retrieve more than one button state.

See Also: **CToolBarCtrl::Indeterminate, CToolBarCtrl::GetState, CToolBarCtrl::SetState, CToolBarCtrl::IsButtonEnabled, CToolBarCtrl::IsButtonChecked, CToolBarCtrl::IsButtonPressed, CToolBarCtrl::IsButtonHidden**

CToolBarCtrl::IsButtonPressed

BOOL IsButtonPressed(int *nID*) const;

Return Value

Nonzero if the button is pressed, otherwise zero.

Parameters

nID   Command identifier of the button in the toolbar.

Remarks

Call this function to determine whether the specified button in a toolbar control is pressed. Consider calling **GetState** if you want to retrieve more than one button state.

See Also: **CToolBarCtrl::PressButton, CToolBarCtrl::GetState, CToolBarCtrl::SetState, CToolBarCtrl::IsButtonEnabled, CToolBarCtrl::IsButtonChecked, CToolBarCtrl::IsButtonHidden, CToolBarCtrl::IsButtonIndeterminate**

CToolBarCtrl::PressButton

BOOL PressButton(int *nID*, BOOL *bPress* = TRUE);

Return Value

Nonzero if successful; otherwise zero.

Parameters

nID   Command identifier of the button to press or release.

bPress   **TRUE** to press the specified button; **FALSE** to release the specified button.

Remarks

Call this function to press or release the specified button in a toolbar control. If you want to change more than one button state, consider calling **SetState** instead.

See Also: **CToolBarCtrl::IsButtonPressed, CToolBarCtrl::EnableButton,
CToolBarCtrl::CheckButton, CToolBarCtrl::HideButton,
CToolBarCtrl::Indeterminate, CToolBarCtrl::GetState, CToolBarCtrl::SetState**

CToolBarCtrl::RestoreState

void RestoreState(HKEY *hKeyRoot*, **LPCTSTR** *lpszSubKey*, **LPCTSTR** *lpszValueName*);

Parameters

   hKeyRoot   Identifies a currently open key in the registry or any of the following
predefined reserved handle values:

- **HKEY_CLASSES_ROOT**
- **HKEY_CURRENT_USER**
- **HKEY_LOCAL_MACHINE**
- **HKEY_USERS**

   lpszSubKey   Points to a null-terminated string containing the name of the subkey with
which a value is associated. This parameter can be null or a pointer to an empty
string. If the parameter is **NULL**, the value will be added to the key identified by
the *hKeyRoot* parameter.

   lpszValueName   Points to a string containing the name of the value to retrieve. If a
value with this name is not already present in the key, the function adds it to the
key.

Remarks

Call this function to restore the state of the toolbar control from the location in the
registry specified by the parameters.

See Also: **CToolBarCtrl::SaveState**

CToolBarCtrl::SaveState

void SaveState(HKEY *hKeyRoot*, **LPCTSTR** *lpszSubKey*, **LPCTSTR** *lpszValueName*);

Parameters

   hKeyRoot   Identifies a currently open key in the registry or any of the following
predefined reserved handle values:

- **HKEY_CLASSES_ROOT**
- **HKEY_CURRENT_USER**
- **HKEY_LOCAL_MACHINE**
- **HKEY_USERS**

lpszSubKey   Points to a null-terminated string containing the name of the subkey with which a value is associated. This parameter can be null or a pointer to an empty string. If the parameter is **NULL**, the value will be added to the key identified by the *hKeyRoot* parameter.

lpszValueName   Points to a string containing the name of the value to set. If a value with this name is not already present in the key, the function adds it to the key.

Remarks

Call this function to save the state of the toolbar control in the location in the registry specified by the parameters.

See Also: CToolBarCtrl::RestoreState

CToolBarCtrl::SetBitmapSize

BOOL SetBitmapSize(CSize *size* **);**

Return Value

Nonzero if successful; otherwise zero.

Parameters

size   Width and height, in pixels, of the bitmapped images.

Remarks

Call this function to set the size of the actual bitmapped images to be added to a toolbar control.

This function must be called only before adding any bitmaps to the toolbar. If the application does not explicitly set the bitmap size, it defaults to 16 by 15 pixels.

See Also: CToolBarCtrl::SetButtonSize, CToolBarCtrl::GetItemRect

CToolBarCtrl::SetButtonSize

BOOL SetButtonSize(CSize *size* **);**

Return Value

Nonzero if successful; otherwise zero.

Parameters

size   Width and height, in pixels, of the buttons.

Remarks

Call this function to set the size of the buttons in the toolbar control. The button size must always be at least as large as the bitmap size it encloses.

This function must be called only before adding any bitmaps to the toolbar. If the application does not explicitly set the button size, it defaults to 24 by 22 pixels.

See Also: **CToolBarCtrl::SetBitmapSize**, **CToolBarCtrl::GetItemRect**

CToolBarCtrl::SetButtonStructSize

void SetButtonStructSize(int *nSize* **);**

Parameters

nSize   Size, in bytes, of the **TBBUTTON** structure.

Remarks

Call this function to specify the size of the **TBBUTTON** structure. If you wanted to store extra data in the **TBBUTTON** structure, you could either derive a new structure from **TBBUTTON**, adding the members you needed, or create a new structure that contains a **TBBUTTON** structure as its first member. You would then call this function to tell the toolbar control the size of the new structure.

See **CToolBarCtrl::AddButtons** for more information on the **TBBUTTON** structure.

See Also: **CToolBarCtrl::Create**, **CToolBarCtrl::AddButtons**, **CToolBarCtrl::InsertButton**, **CToolBarCtrl::GetButton**

CToolBarCtrl::SetCmdID

BOOL SetCmdID(int *nIndex*, **UINT** *nID* **);**

Return Value

Returns nonzero if successful; otherwise zero.

Parameters

nIndex   The zero-based index of the button whose command ID is to be set.

nID   The command ID to set the selected button to.

Remarks

Call this function to set the command identifier which will be sent to the owner window when the specified button is pressed.

See Also: **CToolBarCtrl::CommandToIndex**, **CToolBarCtrl::GetButton**, **CToolBarCtrl::AddButtons**, **CToolBarCtrl::InsertButton**

CToolBarCtrl::SetOwner

void SetOwner(CWnd* *pWnd* **);**

Parameters

pWnd   Pointer to the **CWnd** or **CWnd**-derived object that will be the new owner window for the toolbar control.

Remarks

Call this function to set the owner window for the toolbar control. The owner window is the window that receives notifications from the toolbar.

See Also: CToolBarCtrl::Create

CToolBarCtrl::SetRows

void SetRows(int *nRows***, BOOL** *bLarger***, LPRECT** *lpRect* **);**

Parameters

nRows   Requested number of rows.

bLarger   Tells whether to use more rows or fewer rows if the toolbar cannot be resized to the requested number of rows.

lpRect   Points to the **CRect** object or **RECT** structure that will receive the new bounding rectangle of the toolbar.

Remarks

Call this function to ask the toolbar control to resize itself to the requested number of rows.

If the toolbar cannot resize itself to the requested number or rows, it will resize itself to either the next larger or next smaller valid size, depending on the value of *bLarger*. If *bLarger* is **TRUE**, the new number of rows will be larger than the number requested. If *bLarger* is **FALSE**, the new number of rows will be smaller than the number requested.

A given number of rows is valid for the toolbar if the buttons can be arranged such that all of the rows have the same number of buttons (except perhaps the last row). For example, a toolbar that contains four buttons could not be sized to three rows because the last two rows would have to be shorter. If you attempted to size it to three rows, you would get four rows if *bLarger* was **TRUE** and two rows if *bLarger* was **FALSE**.

If there are separators in the toolbar, the rules for when a given number of rows is valid are more complicated. The layout is computed such that button groups (buttons with a separator before the first and the last button in the group) are never broken up on several rows unless the group cannot fit on one row.

If a group does not fit on one row, the next group will start on the next row even if it would fit on the row where the large group ended. The purpose of this rule is to make the separation between large groups more noticeable. The resulting vertical separators are counted as rows.

Note also that the **SetRows** member function will always chose the layout that results in the smallest toolbar size. Creating a toolbar with the **TBSTYLE_WRAPABLE** style and then resizing the control will simply apply the method outlined above given the width of the control.

This function can only be called for toolbars that were created with the **TBSTYLE_WRAPABLE** style.

See Also: Toolbar styles in **CToolBarCtrl::Create**, **CToolBarCtrl::GetRows**

CToolBarCtrl::SetState

BOOL SetState(int *nID*, **UINT** *nState* **);**

Return Value
Nonzero if successful; otherwise zero.

Parameters
nID   Command identifier of the button.

nState   State flags. It can be a combination of the values listed for button states in **CToolBarCtrl::AddButtons**.

Remarks
Call this function to set the state for the specified button in a toolbar control.

This function is especially handy if you want to set more than one of the button states. To just set one state, use one of the following member functions: **EnableButton**, **CheckButton**, **HideButton**, **Indeterminate**, or **PressButton**.

See Also: **CToolBarCtrl::GetState**, **CToolBarCtrl::AddButtons**, **CToolBarCtrl::EnableButton**, **CToolBarCtrl::CheckButton**, **CToolBarCtrl::HideButton**, **CToolBarCtrl::Indeterminate**, **CToolBarCtrl::PressButton**

CToolBarCtrl::SetToolTips

void SetToolTips(CToolTipCtrl* *pTip* **);**

Parameters
pTip   Pointer to the **CToolTipCtrl** object.

Remarks
Call this function to associate a tool tip control with a toolbar control.

See Also: **CToolBarCtrl::GetToolTips**, "CToolBarCtrl: Handling Tool Tip Notifications," **CToolTipCtrl**

CToolTipCtrl

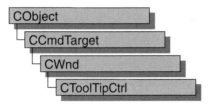

The **CToolTipCtrl** class encapsulates the functionality of a "tool tip control," a small pop-up window that displays a single line of text describing the purpose of a tool in an application. A "tool" is either a window, such as a child window or control, or an application-defined rectangular area within a window's client area. A tool tip is hidden most of the time, appearing only when the user puts the cursor on a tool and leaves it there for approximately one-half second. The tool tip appears near the cursor and disappears when the user clicks a mouse button or moves the cursor off of the tool.

A single tool tip control can provide information for more than one tool.

The **CToolTipCtrl** class provides the functionality of the Windows common tool tip control. This control (and therefore the **CToolTipCtrl** class) is available only to programs running under Windows 95 and Windows NT versions 3.51 and later.

For more information about enabling tool tips, see "Tool Tips" in *Visual C++ Programmer's Guide* online.

For more information on using **CToolTipCtrl**, see Technical Note 60 online.

#include <afxcmn.h>

See Also: CToolBar

CToolTipCtrl Class Members

Construction

CToolTipCtrl	Constructs a **CToolTipCtrl** object.
Create	Creates a tool tip control and attaches it to a **CToolTipCtrl** object.

Attributes

GetText	Retrieves the text that a tool tip control maintains for a tool.
GetToolInfo	Retrieves the information that a tool tip control maintains about a tool.
SetToolInfo	Sets the information that a tool tip maintains for a tool.
GetToolCount	Retrieves a count of the tools maintained by a tool tip control.

Operations

Activate	Activates and deactivates the tool tip control.
AddTool	Registers a tool with the tool tip control.
DelTool	Removes a tool from the tool tip control.
HitTest	Tests a point to determine whether it is within the bounding rectangle of the given tool and, if so, retrieves information about the tool.
RelayEvent	Passes a mouse message to a tool tip control for processing.
SetToolRect	Sets a new bounding rectangle for a tool.
SetDelayTime	Sets the delay time for a tool tip control.
UpdateTipText	Sets the tool tip text for a tool.

Member Functions

CToolTipCtrl::Activate

void Activate(BOOL *bActivate* **);**

Parameters

bActivate   Specifies whether the tool tip control is to be activated or deactivated.

Remarks

Call this function to activate or deactivate a tool tip control. If *bActivate* is **TRUE**, the control is activated; if **FALSE**, it is deactivated.

When a tool tip control is active, the tool tip information appears when the cursor is on a tool that is registered with the control; when it is inactive, the tool tip information does not appear, even when the cursor is on a tool.

See Also: CToolTipCtrl::UpdateTipText, CToolTipCtrl::SetDelayTime

CToolTipCtrl::AddTool

BOOL AddTool(CWnd* *pWnd*, **UINT** *nIDText*, **LPCRECT** *lpRectTool* **= NULL,**
↪ UINT *nIDTool* **= 0);**
BOOL AddTool(CWnd* *pWnd*, **LPCTSTR** *lpszText* **= LPSTR_TEXTCALLBACK,**
↪ LPCRECT *lpRectTool* **= NULL, UINT** *nIDTool* **= 0);**

Return Value

Nonzero if successful; otherwise 0.

Parameters

pWnd   Pointer to the window that contains the tool.

nIDText   ID of the string resource that contains the text for the tool.

lpRectTool   Pointer to a **RECT** structure containing coordinates of the tool's bounding rectangle. The coordinates are relative to the upper-left corner of the client area of the window identified by *pWnd*.

nIDTool   ID of the tool.

lpszText   Pointer to the text for the tool. If this parameter contains the value **LPSTR_TEXTCALLBACK**, **TTN_NEEDTEXT** notification messages go to the parent of the window that *pWnd* points to.

Remarks

A tool tip control can be associated with more than one tool. Call this function to register a tool with the tool tip control, so that the information stored in the tool tip is displayed when the cursor is on the tool.

See Also: CToolTipCtrl::DelTool

CToolTipCtrl::Create

BOOL Create(CWnd* *pParentWnd*, **DWORD** *dwStyle* = **0**);

Return Value

Nonzero if the **CToolTipCtrl** object is successfully created; otherwise 0.

Parameters

pParentWnd   Specifies the tool tip control's parent window, usually a **CDialog**. It must not be **NULL**.

dwStyle   Specifies the tool tip control's style. Apply any combination of control styles needed to the control.

Remarks

You construct a **CToolTipCtrl** in two steps. First call the constructor to construct the **CToolTipCtrl** object; then call **Create** to create the tool tip control and attach it to the **CToolTipCtrl** object.

The *dwStyle* parameter can be any combination of Window Styles. In addition, a tool tip control has two class-specific styles: **TTS_ALWAYSTIP** and **TTS_NOPREFIX**.

Style	Meaning
TTS_ALWAYSTIP	Specifies that the tool tip will appear when the cursor is on a tool, regardless of whether the tool tip control's owner window is active or inactive. Without this style, the tool tip control appears when the tool's owner window is active, but not when it is inactive.
TTS_NOPREFIX	This style prevents the system from stripping the ampersand (&) character from a string. If a tool tip control does not have the **TTS_NOPREFIX** style, the system automatically strips ampersand characters, allowing an application to use the same string as both a menu item and as text in a tool tip control.

A tool tip control has the **WS_POPUP** and **WS_EX_TOOLWINDOW** window styles, regardless of whether you specify them when creating the control.

See Also: **CToolTipCtrl::CToolTipCtrl**

CToolTipCtrl::CToolTipCtrl

CToolTipCtrl( );

Remarks

Constructs a **CToolTipCtrl** object. You must call **Create** after constructing the object.

See Also: **CToolTipCtrl::Create**

CToolTipCtrl::DelTool

void DelTool(CWnd* *pWnd*, **UINT** *nIDTool* = **0**);

Parameters

pWnd   Pointer to the window that contains the tool.

nIDTool   ID of the tool.

Remarks

Call this function to remove the tool specified by *pWnd* and *nIDTool* from the collection of tools supported by a tool tip control.

See Also: **CToolTipCtrl::AddTool**

CToolTipCtrl::GetText

void GetText(CString& *str*, **CWnd*** *pWnd*, **UINT** *nIDTool* = **0**) **const;**

Parameters

str   Reference to a **CString** object that receives the tool's text.

pWnd   Pointer to the window that contains the tool.

nIDTool   ID of the tool.

Remarks

Call this function to retrieve the text that a tool tip control maintains for a tool. The *pWnd* and *nIDTool* parameters identify the tool. If that tool has been previously registered with the tool tip control through a previous call to **CToolTip::AddTool**, the object referenced by the *str* parameter is assigned the tool's text.

See Also: **CToolTipCtrl::AddTool**, **CToolTipCtrl::DelTool**

CToolTipCtrl::GetToolCount

int GetToolCount( ) const;

Return Value

A count of tools registered with the tool tip control.

Remarks

Call this function to retrieve a count of the tools registered with the tool tip control.

See Also: CToolTipCtrl::AddTool, CToolTipCtrl::DelTool

CToolTipCtrl::GetToolInfo

BOOL GetToolInfo(CToolInfo& *CToolInfo*, **CWnd*** *pWnd*, **UINT** *nIDTool* = 0) **const;**

Return Value

Nonzero if successful; otherwise 0.

Parameters

CToolInfo   Reference to a **TOOLINFO** object that receives the tool's text.

pWnd   Pointer to the window that contains the tool.

nIDTool   ID of the tool.

Remarks

Call this function to retrieve the information that a tool tip control maintains about a tool. The **hwnd** and **uId** members of the **TOOLINFO** structure referenced by *CToolInfo* identify the tool. If that tool has been registered with the tool tip control through a previous call to **AddTool**, the **TOOLINFO** structure is filled with information about the tool.

The **TOOLINFO** structure is defined as follows:

```
typedef struct {
    UINT      cbSize;
    UINT      uFlags;
    HWND      hwnd;
    UINT      uId;
    RECT      rect;
    HINSTANCE hinst;
    LPSTR     lpszText;
} TOOLINFO, NEAR *PTOOLINFO, FAR *LPTOOLINFO;
```

cbSize   Size, in bytes, of this structure.

uFlags   Flag that determines how the **uId** member is interpreted. If **uFlags** is equal to **TTF_IDISHWND, uId** is the handle of the tool. Otherwise, **uId** is the identifier of the tool.

hwnd   Handle of the window that contains the tool. If **lpszText** includes the **LPSTR_TEXTCALLBACK** value, **hwnd** identifies the window that receives **TTN_NEEDTEXT** notification messages.

uId   Application-defined identifier of the tool, if **uFlags** is not equal to **TTF_WIDISHWND**. If **uFlags** is equal to **TTF_WIDISHWND**, **uId** specifies the window handle of the tool.

rect   Coordinates of the tool's bounding rectangle. The coordinates are relative to the upper-left corner of the client area of the window identified by **hwnd**. If **uFlags** is equal to **TTF_WIDISHWND**, this member is ignored.

hinst   Handle of the instance that contains the string resource for the tool. If **lpszText** specifies the identifier of a string resource, this member is used.

lpszText   Address of the buffer that contains the text for the tool, or identifier of the string resource that contains the text. If this member is set to the **LPSTR_TEXTCALLBACK** value, the control sends the **TTN_NEEDTEXT** notification message to the parent window to retrieve the text.

See Also: CToolTipCtrl::AddTool

CToolTipCtrl::HitTest

BOOL HitTest(CWnd* *pWnd***, CPoint** *pt***, LPTOOLINFO** *lpToolInfo* **) const;**

Return Value

Nonzero if the point specified by the hit-test information is within the tool's bounding rectangle; otherwise 0.

Parameters

pWnd   Pointer to the window that contains the tool.

pt   Pointer to a **CPoint** structure containing the coordinates of the point to be tested.

lpToolInfo   Pointer to **TOOLINFO** structure that contains information about the tool. For information on this structure, see **CToolTipCtrl::GetToolInfo**.

Remarks

Call this function to test a point to determine whether it is within the bounding rectangle of the given tool and, if so, retrieve information about the tool.

If this function returns a nonzero value, the structure pointed to by *lpToolInfo* is filled with information on the tool within whose rectangle the point lies.

The **TTHITTESTINFO** structure is defined as follows:

```
typedef struct _TT_HITTESTINFO { // tthti
   HWND hwnd;   // handle of tool or window with tool
   POINT pt;    // client coordinates of point to test
   TOOLINFO ti; // receives information about the tool
} TTHITTESTINFO, FAR * LPHITTESTINFO;
```

hwnd   Specifies the tool's handle.

pt   Specifies the coordinates of a point if the point is in the tool's bounding rectangle.

ti   Information about the tool. For more information about the **TOOLINFO** structure, see **CToolTipCtrl::GetToolInfo**.

See Also: **CToolTipCtrl::GetToolInfo**

CToolTipCtrl::RelayEvent

void RelayEvent(LPMSG *lpMsg* **);**

Parameters

lpMsg   Pointer to a **MSG** structure that contains the message to relay.

Remarks

Call this function to pass a mouse message to a tool tip control for processing. A tool tip control processes only the following messages, which are sent to it by **RelayEvent**:

WM_LBUTTONDOWN	**WM_MOUSEMOVE**
WM_LBUTTONUP	**WM_RBUTTONDOWN**
WM_MBUTTONDOWN	**WM_RBUTTONUP**
WM_MBUTTONUP	

See Also: **CWnd::PreTranslateMessage**, **CWinApp::PreTranslateMessage**

CToolTipCtrl::SetDelayTime

void SetDelayTime(UINT *nDelay* **);**

Parameters

nDelay   Specifies the new delay time, in milliseconds.

Remarks

Call this function to set the delay time for a tool tip control. The delay time is the length of time the cursor must remain on a tool before the tool tip window appears. The default delay time is 500 milliseconds.

See Also: **CToolTipCtrl::Activate**, **CToolTipCtrl::HitTest**

CToolTipCtrl::SetToolInfo

void SetToolInfo(LPTOOLINFO *lpToolInfo* **);**

Parameters

lpToolInfo   A pointer to a **TOOLINFO** structure that specifies the information to set. For more information about the **TOOLINFO** structure, see **CToolTipCtrl::GetToolInfo**.

Remarks

Call this function to set the information that a tool tip maintains for a tool.

See Also: **CToolTipCtrl::GetToolInfo**

CToolTipCtrl::SetToolRect

void SetToolRect(CWnd* *pWnd*, **UINT** *nIDTool*, **LPCRECT** *lpRect* **);**

Parameters

pWnd   Pointer to the window that contains the tool.

nIDTool   ID of the tool.

lpRect   Pointer to a **RECT** structure specifying the new bounding rectangle.

Remarks

Call this function to set a new bounding rectangle for a tool.

See Also: **CToolTipCtrl::GetToolInfo**

CToolTipCtrl::UpdateTipText

void UpdateTipText(LPCTSTR *lpszText*, **CWnd*** *pWnd*, **UINT** *nIDTool* = **0** **);**
void UpdateTipText(UINT *nIDText*, **CWnd*** *pWnd*, **UINT** *nIDTool* = **0** **);**

Parameters

lpszText   Pointer to the text for the tool.

pWnd   Pointer to the window that contains the tool.

nIDTool   ID of the tool.

nIDText   ID of the string resource that contains the text for the tool.

Remarks

Call this function to update the tool tip text for this control's tools.

See Also: **CToolTipCtrl::GetToolInfo**

CTreeCtrl

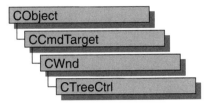

A "tree view control" is a window that displays a hierarchical list of items, such as the headings in a document, the entries in an index, or the files and directories on a disk. Each item consists of a label and an optional bitmapped image, and each item can have a list of subitems associated with it. By clicking an item, the user can expand and collapse the associated list of subitems.

The **CTreeCtrl** class provides the functionality of the Windows common tree view control. This control (and therefore the **CTreeCtrl** class) is available only to programs running under Windows 95 and Windows NT versions 3.51 and later.

For more information on using **CTreeCtrl**, see Technical Note 60 online.

#include <afxcmn.h>

See Also: CImageList

CTreeCtrl Class Members

Construction

CTreeCtrl	Constructs a **CTreeCtrl** object.
Create	Creates a tree view control and attaches it to a **CTreeCtrl** object.

Attributes

GetCount	Retrieves the number of tree items associated with a tree view control.
GetIndent	Retrieves the offset (in pixels) of a tree view item from its parent.
SetIndent	Sets the offset (in pixels) of a tree view item from its parent.
GetImageList	Retrieves the handle of the image list associated with a tree view control.
SetImageList	Sets the handle of the image list associated with a tree view control.

Attributes *(continued)*

GetNextItem	Retrieves the next tree view item that matches a specified relationship.
ItemHasChildren	Returns nonzero if the specified item has child items.
GetChildItem	Retrieves the child of a specified tree view item.
GetNextSiblingItem	Retrieves the next sibling of the specified tree view item.
GetPrevSiblingItem	Retrieves the previous sibling of the specified tree view item.
GetParentItem	Retrieves the parent of the specified tree view item.
GetFirstVisibleItem	Retrieves the first visible item of the specified tree view item.
GetNextVisibleItem	Retrieves the next visible item of the specified tree view item.
GetPrevVisibleItem	Retrieves the previous visible item of the specified tree view item.
GetSelectedItem	Retrieves the currently selected tree view item.
GetDropHilightItem	Retrieves the target of a drag-and-drop operation.
GetRootItem	Retrieves the root of the specified tree view item.
GetItem	Retrieves the attributes of a specified tree view item.
SetItem	Sets the attributes of a specified tree view item.
GetItemState	Returns the state of an item.
SetItemState	Sets the state of an item.
GetItemImage	Retrieves the images associated with an item.
SetItemImage	Associates images with an item.
GetItemText	Returns the text of an item.
SetItemText	Sets the text of an item.
GetItemData	Returns the 32-bit application-specific value associated with an item.
SetItemData	Sets the 32-bit application-specific value associated with an item.
GetItemRect	Retrieves the bounding rectangle of a tree view item.
GetEditControl	Retrieves the handle of the edit control used to edit the specified tree view item.
GetVisibleCount	Retrieves the number of visible tree items associated with a tree view control.

Operations

InsertItem	Inserts a new item in a tree view control.
DeleteItem	Deletes a new item in a tree view control.
DeleteAllItems	Deletes all items in a tree view control.

(continued)

Operations *(continued)*

Expand	Expands, or collapses, the child items of the specified tree view item.
Select	Selects, scrolls into view, or redraws a specified tree view item.
SelectItem	Selects a specified tree view item.
SelectDropTarget	Redraws the tree item as the target of a drag-and-drop operation.
SelectSetFirstVisible	Selects a specified tree view item as the first visible item.
EditLabel	Edits a specified tree view item in-place.
HitTest	Returns the current position of the cursor related to the **CTreeCtrl** object.
CreateDragImage	Creates a dragging bitmap for the specified tree view item.
SortChildren	Sorts the children of a given parent item.
EnsureVisible	Ensures that a tree view item is visible in its tree view control.
SortChildrenCB	Sorts the children of a given parent item using an application-defined sort function.

Member Functions

CTreeCtrl::Create

BOOL Create(DWORD *dwStyle***, const RECT&** *rect***, CWnd*** *pParentWnd***,**
➥ **UINT** *nID* **);**

Return Value

Nonzero if initialization was successful; otherwise 0.

Parameters

dwStyle Specifies the tree view control's style. Apply any combination of tree view control styles to the control.

rect Specifies the tree view control's size and position. It can be either a **CRect** object or a **RECT** structure.

pParentWnd Specifies the tree view control's parent window, usually a **CDialog**. It must not be **NULL**.

nID Specifies the tree view control's ID.

Remarks

You construct a **CTreeCtrl** in two steps. First call the constructor, then call **Create**, which creates the tree view control and attaches it to the **CTreeCtrl** object.

The following styles can be applied to a tree view control:

- **TVS_HASLINES**   The tree view control has lines linking child items to their corresponding parent items.

- **TVS_LINESATROOT**   The tree view control has lines linking child items to the root of the hierarchy.

- **TVS_HASBUTTONS**   The tree view control adds a button to the left of each parent item.

- **TVS_EDITLABELS**   The tree view control allows the user to edit the labels of tree view items.

- **TVS_SHOWSELALWAYS**   Causes a selected item to remain selected when the tree-view control loses focus.

- **TVS_DISABLEDRAGDROP**   The tree-view control is prevented from sending **TVN_BEGINDRAG** notification messages.

See Also: CTreeCtrl::CTreeCtrl

CTreeCtrl::CreateDragImage

CImageList* CreateDragImage(HTREEITEM *hItem* **);**

Return Value

Pointer to the image list to which the dragging bitmap was added, if successful; otherwise **NULL**.

Parameters

hItem   Handle of the tree item to be dragged.

Remarks

Call this function to create a dragging bitmap for the given item in a tree view control, create an image list for the bitmap, and add the bitmap to the image list. An application uses the image-list functions to display the image when the item is being dragged.

The **CImageList** object is permanent, and you must delete it when finished. For example:

```
CImageList* pImageList = MyTreeCtrl.CreateDragImage(nItem, &point);
   ...
   ...
   delete pImageList;
```

See Also: CTreeCtrl::SelectDropTarget, CTreeCtrl::GetDropHilightItem, CTreeCtrl::SetImageList

CTreeCtrl::CTreeCtrl

CTreeCtrl( );

Remarks

Constructs a **CTreeCtrl** object.

See Also: **CTreeCtrl::Create**

CTreeCtrl::DeleteAllItems

BOOL DeleteAllItems( );

Return Value

Nonzero if successful; otherwise 0.

Remarks

Call this function to delete all items from the tree view control.

See Also: **CTreeCtrl::DeleteItem, CTreeCtrl::InsertItem**

CTreeCtrl::DeleteItem

BOOL DeleteItem(HTREEITEM *hItem* **);**

Return Value

Nonzero if successful; otherwise 0.

Parameters

hItem Handle of the tree item to be deleted. If *hitem* has the **TVI_ROOT** value, all items are deleted from the tree view control.

Remarks

Call this function to delete an item from the tree view control.

See Also: **CTreeCtrl::DeleteAllItems, CTreeCtrl::InsertItem**

CTreeCtrl::EditLabel

CEdit* EditLabel(HTREEITEM *hItem* **);**

Return Value

If successful, a pointer to the **CEdit** object that is used to edit the item text; otherwise **NULL**.

Parameters

hItem Handle of the tree item to be edited.

Remarks

Call this function to begin in-place editing of the specified item's text. The editing is accomplished by replacing the text of the item with a single-line edit control containing the text.

See Also: **CTreeCtrl::GetEditControl**

CTreeCtrl::EnsureVisible

BOOL EnsureVisible(HTREEITEM *hItem* **);**

Return Value

Nonzero if successful; otherwise 0.

Parameters

hItem   Handle of the tree item being made visible.

Remarks

Call this function to ensure that a tree view item is visible. If necessary, the function expands the parent item or scrolls the tree view control so that the item is visible.

See Also: **CTreeCtrl::GetFirstVisibleItem, CTreeCtrl::GetVisibleCount**

CTreeCtrl::Expand

BOOL Expand(HTREEITEM *hItem*, **UINT** *nCode* **);**

Return Value

Nonzero if successful; otherwise 0.

Parameters

hItem   Handle of the tree item being expanded.

nCode   A flag indicating the type of action to be taken. This flag can have one of the following values:

- **TVE_COLLAPSE**   Collapses the list.
- **TVE_COLLAPSERESET**   Collapses the list and removes the child items.
- **TVE_EXPAND**   Expands the list.
- **TVE_TOGGLE**   Collapses the list if it is currently expanded or expands it if it is currently collapsed.

Remarks

Call this function to expand or collapse the list of child items, if any, associated with the given parent item.

See Also: **CTreeCtrl::EnsureVisible**

CTreeCtrl::GetChildItem

HTREEITEM GetChildItem(HTREEITEM *hItem* **);**

Return Value

The handle of the child item if successful; otherwise **NULL**.

Parameters

hItem   Handle of a tree item.

Remarks

Call this function to retrieve the tree view item that is the child of the item specified by *hItem*.

**See Also: CTreeCtrl::GetItem, CTreeCtrl::GetParentItem,
CTreeCtrl::SortChildren**

CTreeCtrl::GetCount

UINT GetCount( );

Return Value

The number of items in the tree view control; otherwise -1.

Remarks

Call this function to retrieve a count of the items in a tree view control.

See Also: CTreeCtrl::GetVisibleCount

CTreeCtrl::GetDropHilightItem

HTREEITEM GetDropHilightItem( );

Return Value

The handle of the item dropped if successful; otherwise **NULL**.

Remarks

Call this function to retrieve the item that is the target of a drag-and-drop operation.

See Also: CTreeCtrl::SelectDropTarget

CTreeCtrl::GetEditControl

CEdit* GetEditControl( );

Return Value

A pointer to the edit control used to edit the item text, if successful; otherwise **NULL**.

Remarks

Call this function to retrieve the handle of the edit control being used to edit a tree view item's text.

See Also: **CTreeCtrl::EditLabel**

CTreeCtrl::GetFirstVisibleItem

HTREEITEM GetFirstVisibleItem( );

Return Value

The handle of the first visible item; otherwise **NULL**.

Remarks

Call this function to retrieve the first visible item of the tree view control.

See Also: **CTreeCtrl::GetNextVisibleItem**, **CTreeCtrl::GetPrevVisibleItem**, **CTreeCtrl::EnsureVisible**, **CTreeCtrl::GetVisibleCount**

CTreeCtrl::GetImageList

CImageList* GetImageList(UINT *nImage* **);**

Return Value

Pointer to the control's image list if successful; otherwise **NULL**.

Parameters

nImage   Type of image list to retrieve. The image list can be one of the following values:

- **TVSIL_NORMAL**   Retrieves the normal image list, which contains the selected and nonselected images for the tree view item.

- **TVSIL_STATE**   Retrieves the state image list, which contains the images for tree view items that are in a user-defined state.

Remarks

Call this function to retrieve the handle of the normal or state image list associated with the tree view control. Each item in a tree view control can have a pair of bitmapped images associated with it. One image is displayed when the item is selected, and the other is displayed when the item is not selected. For example, an item might display an open folder when it is selected and a closed folder when it is not selected.

For more information on image lists, see the **CImageList** class.

See Also: **CImageList**, **CTreeCtrl::SetImageList**

CTreeCtrl::GetIndent

UINT GetIndent( );

Return Value

The amount of indentation measured in pixels.

Remarks

Call this function to retrieve the amount, in pixels, that child items are indented relative to their parent items.

See Also: CTreeCtrl::SetIndent

CTreeCtrl::GetItem

BOOL GetItem(TV_ITEM* *pItem*);

Return Value

Nonzero if successful; otherwise 0.

Parameters

pItem   A pointer to a **TV_ITEM** structure.

Remarks

Call this function to retrieve the attributes of the specified tree view item.

The **TV_ITEM** structure is defined as follows:

```
typedef struct _TV_ITEM {   tvi
    UINT        mask;
    HTREEITEM   hItem;              // item this structure refers to
    UINT        state;
    UINT        stateMask;
    LPSTR       pszText;
    int         cchTextMax;
    int         iImage;
    int         iSelectedImage;
    int         cChildren;
    LPARAM      lParam;            // 32-bit value to associate with item
} TV_ITEM;
```

mask   Array of flags that indicate which of the other structure members contain valid data or which are to be filled in. It can be a combination of these values:

- **TVIF_CHILDREN**   The **cChildren** member is valid.

- **TVIF_HANDLE**   The **hItem** member is valid.

- **TVIF_IMAGE**   The **iImage** member is valid.

- **TVIF_PARAM**   The **lParam** member is valid.

- **TVIF_SELECTEDIMAGE**   The **iSelectedImage** member is valid.

- **TVIF_STATE**   The **state** and **stateMask** members are valid.

- **TVIF_TEXT**   The **pszText** and **cchTextMax** members are valid.

state and **stateMask**   Variables specifying the current state of the item and the valid tates of the item. They can be any valid combination of state values. Valid states are:

- **TVIS_BOLD**   The item is bold.

- **TVIS_CUT**   The item is selected as part of a cut and paste operation.

- **TVIS_DROPHILITED**   The item is selected as a drag-and-drop target.

- **TVIS_EXPANDED**   The item's list of child items is currently expanded; that is, the child items are visible. This value applies only to parent items.

- **TVIS_EXPANDEDONCE**   The item's list of child items has been expanded at least once. The **TVN_ITEMEXPANDING** and **TVN_ITEMEXPANDED** notification messages are not sent for parent items that have specified this value. This value applies only to parent items.

- **TVIS_OVERLAYMASK**   The item's overlay image is included when the item is drawn. The index of the overlay image must be specified in the **state** member of the **TV_ITEM** structure by using the Win32 **INDEXTOOVERLAYMASK** macro. The overlay image must be added to the tree view's image list by using the **CImageList::SetOverlayImage** function. This value should not be combined with any other value.

- **TVIS_SELECTED**   The item is selected. The appearance of a selected item depends on whether it has the focus and on whether the system colors are used for selection.

- **TVIS_STATEIMAGEMASK**   The item's state image is included when the item is drawn. The index of the state image must be specified in the **state** member of the **TV_ITEM** structure by using the Win32 **INDEXTOSTATEIMAGEMASK** macro. This value should not be combined with any other value.

- **TVIS_USERMASK**   Same as **TVIS_STATEIMAGEMASK**.

pszText   Address of a null-terminated string containing the item text if the structure specifies item attributes. If this member is the **LPSTR_TEXTCALLBACK** value, the parent window is responsible for storing the name. In this case, the tree view control sends the parent window a **TVN_GETDISPINFO** notification message when it needs the item text for displaying, sorting, or editing, and the tree view sends a **TVN_SETDISPINFO** notification when the item text changes. If the structure is receiving item attributes, this member is the address of the buffer that receives the item text.

cchTextMax Size of the buffer pointed to by the **pszText** member if the structure is receiving item attributes. This member is ignored if the structure specifies item attributes.

iImage and **iSelectedImage** Indexes of the icon image and selected icon image within the image list. If either member is the **I_IMAGECALLBACK** value, the parent window is responsible for storing the corresponding images. In this case, the tree view control sends the parent a **TVN_GETDISPINFO** notification message when it needs to display the images and a **TVN_SETDISPINFO** notification message when the images change.

cChildren Flag indicating whether the item has assoicated child items. Can be one of the following values:

- **0** The item has no child items.

- **1** The item has one or more child items.

- **I_CHILDRENCALLBACK** The parent window keeps track of whether the item has child items. In this case, the tree view control sends the parent a **TVN_GETDISPINFO** notification message when it needs to display the child items and a **TVN_SETDISPINFO** notification message when the attributes of a child item change.

See Also: **CTreeCtrl::SetItem, CTreeCtrl::GetChildItem, CTreeCtrl::GetNextItem, CTreeCtrl::SelectItem**

CTreeCtrl::GetItemData

DWORD GetItemData(HTREEITEM *hItem* **) const;**

Return Value

A 32-bit application-specific value associated with the item specified by *hItem*.

Parameters

hItem Handle of the item whose data is to be retrieved.

Remarks

Call this function to retrieve the 32-bit application-specific value associated with the specified item.

See Also: **CTreeCtrl::SetItemData**

CTreeCtrl::GetItemImage

BOOL GetItemImage(HTREEITEM *hItem*, **int&** *nImage*, **int&** *nSelectedImage* **) const;**

Return Value

Nonzero if successful; otherwise 0.

Parameters

hItem   The handle of the item whose image is to be retrieved.

nImage   An integer that receives the index of the item's image within the tree view control's image list.

nSelectedImage   An integer that receives the index of the item's selected image within the tree view control's image list.

Remarks

Each item in a tree view control can have a pair of bitmapped images associated with it. The images appear on the left side of an item's label. One image is displayed when the item is selected, and the other is displayed when the item is not selected. For example, an item might display an open folder when it is selected and a closed folder when it is not selected.

Call this function to retrieve the index of the item's image and its selected image within the tree view control's image list.

See Also: **CTreeCtrl::SetItemImage**, **CImageList**

CTreeCtrl::GetItemRect

> **BOOL GetItemRect(HTREEITEM** *hItem*, **LPRECT** *lpRect*, **BOOL** *bTextOnly*);

Return Value

Nonzero if the item is visible, with the bounding rectangle contained in *lpRect*. Otherwise, 0 with *lpRect* uninitialized.

Parameters

hItem   The handle of a tree view control item.

lpRect   Pointer to a **RECT** structure that receives the bounding rectangle. The coordinates are relative to the upper-left corner of the tree view control.

bTextOnly   If this parameter is nonzero, the bounding rectangle includes only the text of the item. Otherwise it includes the entire line that the item occupies in the tree view control.

Remarks

Call this function to retrieve the bounding rectangle for *hItem* and determine whether it is visible or not.

See Also: **CTreeCtrl::GetVisibleCount**, **CTreeCtrl::GetNextVisibleItem**, **CTreeCtrl::GetPrevVisibleItem**, **CTreeCtrl::EnsureVisible**

CTreeCtrl::GetItemState

> **UINT GetItemState(HTREEITEM** *hItem*, **UINT** *nStateMask*) **const**;

Return Value

A **UINT** specifying the item's state. For information on possible values, see **CTreeCtrl::GetItem**.

Parameters

hItem   Handle of the item whose state is to be retrieved.

nStateMask   Mask indicating which states are to be retrieved. For more information on possible values for *nStateMask*, see the discussion of the **state** and **stateMask** members of the **TV_ITEM** structure in **CTreeCtrl::GetItem**.

Remarks

Returns the state of the item specified by *hItem*.

See Also: CTreeCtrl::GetItem

CTreeCtrl::GetItemText

CString GetItemText(HTREEITEM *hItem*) const;

Return Value

A **CString** object containing the item's text.

Parameters

hItem   Handle of the item whose text is to be retrieved.

Remarks

Returns the text of the item specified by *hItem*.

See Also: CTreeCtrl::SetItemText

CTreeCtrl::GetNextItem

HTREEITEM GetNextItem(HTREEITEM *hItem*, UINT *nCode*);

Return Value

The handle of the next item if successful; otherwise **NULL**.

Parameters

hItem   Handle of a tree item.

nCode   A flag indicating the type of relation to *hItem*. This flag can be one of the following values:

- **TVGN_CARET**   Retrieves the currently selected item.

- **TVGN_CHILD**   Retrieves the first child item. The *hItem* parameter must be **NULL**.

- **TVGN_DROPHILITE**   Retrieves the item that is the target of a drag-and-drop operation.

- **TVGN_FIRSTVISIBLE**   Retrieves the first visible item.

- **TVGN_NEXT**   Retrieves the next sibling item.

- **TVGN_NEXTVISIBLE**   Retrieves the next visible item that follows the specified item.

- **TVGN_PARENT**   Retrieves the parent of the specified item.

- **TVGN_PREVIOUS**   Retrieves the previous sibling item.

- **TVGN_PREVIOUSVISIBLE**   Retrieves the first visible item that precedes the specified item.

- **TVGN_ROOT**   Retrieves the first child item of the root item of which the specified item is a part.

Remarks

Call this function to retrieve the tree view item that has the specified relationship, indicated by the *nCode* parameter, to *hItem*.

See Also: CTreeCtrl::SetItem, CTreeCtrl::GetChildItem, CTreeCtrl::GetItem, CTreeCtrl::SelectItem, CTreeCtrl::GetPrevSiblingItem

CTreeCtrl::GetNextSiblingItem

HTREEITEM GetNextSiblingItem(HTREEITEM *hItem*);

Return Value

The handle of the next sibling item; otherwise **NULL**.

Parameters

hItem   Handle of a tree item.

Remarks

Call this function to retrieve the next sibling of *hItem*.

See Also: CTreeCtrl::GetPrevSiblingItem, CTreeCtrl::GetChildItem, CTreeCtrl::GetItem, CTreeCtrl::SelectItem, CTreeCtrl::GetParentItem

CTreeCtrl::GetNextVisibleItem

HTREEITEM GetNextVisibleItem(HTREEITEM *hItem*);

Return Value

The handle of the next visible item; otherwise **NULL**.

Parameters

    hItem   Handle of a tree item.

Remarks

    Call this function to retrieve the next visible item of *hItem*.

    See Also: **CTreeCtrl::GetPrevVisibleItem, CTreeCtrl::GetFirstVisibleItem, CTreeCtrl::EnsureVisible, CTreeCtrl::GetParentItem**

CTreeCtrl::GetParentItem

    HTREEITEM GetParentItem(HTREEITEM *hItem* **);**

Return Value

    The handle of the parent item; otherwise **NULL**.

Parameters

    hItem   Handle of a tree item.

Remarks

    Call this function to retrieve the parent of *hItem*.

    See Also: **CTreeCtrl::GetChildItem, CTreeCtrl::GetRootItem, CTreeCtrl::GetItem, CTreeCtrl::GetPrevSiblingItem**

CTreeCtrl::GetPrevSiblingItem

    HTREEITEM GetPrevSiblingItem(HTREEITEM *hItem* **);**

Return Value

    The handle of the previous sibling; otherwise **NULL**.

Parameters

    hItem   Handle of a tree item.

Remarks

    Call this function to retrieve the previous sibling of *hItem*.

    See Also: **CTreeCtrl::GetNextSiblingItem, CTreeCtrl::GetParentItem, CTreeCtrl::GetChildItem**

CTreeCtrl::GetPrevVisibleItem

    HTREEITEM GetPrevVisibleItem(HTREEITEM *hItem* **);**

Return Value

    The handle of the previous visible item; otherwise **NULL**.

Parameters

hItem   Handle of a tree item.

Remarks

Call this function to retrieve the previous visible item of *hItem*.

See Also: CTreeCtrl::GetNextVisibleItem, CTreeCtrl::GetFirstVisibleItem, CTreeCtrl::EnsureVisible, CTreeCtrl::GetVisibleCount

---

CTreeCtrl::GetRootItem

HTREEITEM GetRootItem( );

Return Value

The handle of the root item; otherwise **NULL**.

Remarks

Call this function to retrieve the root item of the tree view control.

See Also: CTreeCtrl::GetItem, CTreeCtrl::GetChildItem, CTreeCtrl::GetParentItem

---

CTreeCtrl::GetSelectedItem

HTREEITEM GetSelectedItem( );

Return Value

The handle of the selected item; otherwise **NULL**.

Remarks

Call this function to retrieve the currently selected item of the tree view control.

See Also: CTreeCtrl::Select, CTreeCtrl::SelectDropTarget, CTreeCtrl::GetDropHilightItem

---

CTreeCtrl::GetVisibleCount

UINT GetVisibleCount( );

Return Value

The number of visible items in the tree view control; otherwise −1.

Remarks

Call this function to retrieve a count of the visible items in a tree view control.

See Also: CTreeCtrl::GetCount, CTreeCtrl::EnsureVisible

CTreeCtrl::HitTest

HTREEITEM HitTest(CPoint *pt*, **UINT*** *pFlags* **);**
HTREEITEM HitTest(TV_HITTESTINFO* *pHitTestInfo* **);**

Return Value

The handle of the tree view item that occupies the specified point or **NULL** if no item occupies the point.

Parameters

pt   Client coordinates of the point to test.

pFlags   Pointer to an integer that receives information about the results of the hit test. It can be one or more of the values listed under the **flags** member in the Remarks section.

pHitTestInfo   Address of a **TV_HITTESTINFO** structure that contains the position to hit test and that receives information about the results of the hit test.

Remarks

Call this function to determine the location of the specified point relative to the client area of a tree view control.

When this function is called, the *pt* parameter specifies the coordinates of the point to test. The function returns the handle of the item at the specified point or **NULL** if no item occupies the point. In addition, the *pFlags* parameter contains a value that indicates the location of the specified point.

The **TV_HITTESTINFO** structure is defined as follows:

```
typedef struct _TVHITTESTINFO {
    POINT     pt;     // client coordinates of point to test
    UINT      flags;  // see below
    HTREEITEM hItem;  // handle of item that occupies point
} TV_HITTESTINFO, FAR *LPTV_HITTESTINFO;
```

flags   Variable that receives information about the results of a hit test. It can be one or more of these values:

- **TVHT_ABOVE**   Above the client area.

- **TVHT_BELOW**   Below the client area.

- **TVHT_NOWHERE**   In the client area but below the last item.

- **TVHT_ONITEM**   On the bitmap or label associated with an item.

- **TVHT_ONITEMBUTTON**   On the button associated with an item.

- **TVHT_ONITEMICON**   On the bitmap associated with an item.

- **TVHT_ONITEMINDENT**   In the indentation associated with an item.

- **TVHT_ONITEMLABEL**   On the label (string) associated with an item.

- **TVHT_ONITEMRIGHT**   In the area to the right of an item.

- **TVHT_ONITEMSTATEICON**   On the state icon for a tree view item that is in a user-defined state.

- **TVHT_TOLEFT**   To the right of the client area.

- **TVHT_TORIGHT**   To the left of the client area.

See Also: **CTreeCtrl::GetItemRect**

CTreeCtrl::InsertItem

HTREEITEM InsertItem(LPTV_INSERTSTRUCT *lpInsertStruct* **);**

HTREEITEM InsertItem(UINT *nMask*, **LPCTSTR** *lpszItem*, **int** *nImage*,
↪ **int** *nSelectedImage*, **UINT** *nState*, **UINT** *nStateMask*, **LPARAM** *lParam*,
↪ **HTREEITEM** *hParent*, **HTREEITEM** *hInsertAfter* **);**

HTREEITEM InsertItem(LPCTSTR *lpszItem*, **HTREEITEM** *hParent* = **TVI_ROOT**,
↪ **HTREEITEM** *hInsertAfter* = **TVI_LAST** **);**

HTREEITEM InsertItem(LPCTSTR *lpszItem*, **int** *nImage*, **int** *nSelectedImage*,
↪ **HTREEITEM** *hParent* = **TVI_ROOT**, **HTREEITEM** *hInsertAfter* = **TVI_LAST**);

Return Value

Handle of the new item if successful; otherwise **NULL**.

Parameters

lpInsertStruct   A pointer to a **TV_INSERTSTRUCT** that specifies the attributes of the tree view item to be inserted.

nMask   Integer specifying which attributes to set.

lpszItem   Address of a string containing the item's text.

nImage   Index of the item's image in the tree view control's image list.

nSelectedImage   Index of the item's selected image in the tree view control's image list.

nState   Specifies values for the item's states.

nStateMask   Specifies which states are to be set.

lParam   A 32-bit application-specific value associated with the item.

hParent   Handle of the inserted item's parent.

hInsertAfter   Handle of the item after which the new item is to be inserted.

Remarks

Call this function to insert a new item in a tree view control.

The **TV_INSERTSTRUCT** structure is defined as follows:

```
typedef struct _TV_INSERTSTRUCT {
    HTREEITEM hParent;
    HTREEITEM hInsertAfter;
    TV_ITEM   item;
} TV_INSERTSTRUCT;
```

hParent Handle of the parent item. If this parameter is the **TVI_ROOT** value or **NULL**, the item is inserted at the root of the tree view control.

hInsertAfter Handle of the item after which the new item is to be inserted or one of the following values:

- **TVI_FIRST** Inserts the item at the beginning of the list.

- **TVI_LAST** Inserts the item at the end of the list.

- **TVI_SORT** Inserts the item into the list in alphabetical order.

item A **TV_ITEM** structure, which contains information about the item to be added to the tree view control. For more information on this structure, see **CTreeCtrl::GetItem**.

See Also: **CTreeCtrl::DeleteItem**, **CTreeCtrl::HitTest**, **CTreeCtrl::SelectDropTarget**, **CTreeCtrl::GetItem**

CTreeCtrl::ItemHasChildren

BOOL ItemHasChildren(HTREEITEM *hItem* **);**

Return Value

Nonzero if the tree item specified by *hItem* has child items; 0 if it does not.

Parameters

hItem Handle of a tree item.

Remarks

Use this function to determine whether the tree item specified by *hItem* has child items. If so, you can then use **CTreeCtrl::GetChildItem** to retrieve those child items.

See Also: **CTreeCtrl::GetChildItem**

CTreeCtrl::Select

BOOL Select(HTREEITEM *hItem*, **UINT** *nCode* **);**

Return Value

Nonzero if successful; otherwise 0.

Parameters

hItem Handle of a tree item.

nCode   The type of action to take. This parameter can be one of the following values:

- **TVGN_CARET**   Sets the selection to the given item.
- **TVGN_DROPHILITE**   Redraws the given item in the style used to indicate the target of a drag-and-drop operation.
- **TVGN_FIRSTVISIBLE**   Scrolls the tree view vertically so that the given item is the first visible item.

Remarks

Call this function to select the given tree view item, scroll the item into view, or redraw the item in the style used to indicate the target of a drag-and-drop operation.

If *nCode* contains the value **TVGN_CARET**, the parent window receives the **TVN_SELCHANGING** and **TVN_SELCHANGED** notification messages. In addition, if the specified item is the child of a collapsed parent item, the parent's list of child items is expanded to reveal the specified item. In this case, the parent window receives the **TVN_ITEMEXPANDING** and **TVN_ITEMEXPANDED** notification messages.

See Also: **CTreeCtrl::SelectItem, CTreeCtrl::GetSelectedItem, CTreeCtrl::SelectDropTarget**

CTreeCtrl::SelectDropTarget

BOOL SelectDropTarget(HTREEITEM *hItem* **);**

Return Value

Nonzero if successful; otherwise 0.

Parameters

hItem   Handle of a tree item.

Remarks

Call this function to redraw the item in the style used to indicate the target of a drag-and-drop operation.

See Also: **CTreeCtrl::SelectItem, CTreeCtrl::GetDropHilightItem, CTreeCtrl::CreateDragImage**

CTreeCtrl::SelectItem

BOOL SelectItem(HTREEITEM *hItem* **);**

Return Value

Nonzero if successful; otherwise 0.

Parameters

hItem   Handle of a tree item.

Remarks

Call this function to select the given tree view item.

See Also: CTreeCtrl::Select, CTreeCtrl::GetSelectedItem, CTreeCtrl::SelectDropTarget

---

CTreeCtrl::SelectSetFirstVisible

BOOL SelectSetFirstVisible(HTREEITEM *hItem*);

Return Value

Nonzero if successful; otherwise 0.

Parameters

hItem   Handle of the tree item to be set as the first visible item.

Remarks

Call this function to scroll the tree view vertically so that the given item is the first visible item. The function sends a message to the window with the **TVM_SELECTITEM** and **TVGN_FIRSTVISIBLE** message parameters.

See Also: CTreeCtrl::Select, CTreeCtrl::SelectItem, CTreeCtrl::SelectDropTarget

---

CTreeCtrl::SetImageList

CImageList* SetImageList(CImageList * *pImageList*, int *nImageListType*);

Return Value

Pointer to the previous image list, if any; otherwise **NULL**.

Parameters

pImageList   Pointer to the image list to assign. If *pImageList* is **NULL**, all images are removed from the tree view control.

nImageListType   Type of image list to set. The image list can be one of the following values:

- **TVSIL_NORMAL**   Sets the normal image list, which contains the selected and nonselected images for the tree view item.

- **TVSIL_STATE**   Sets the state image list, which contains the images for tree view items that are in a user-defined state.

Remarks

Call this function to set the normal or state image list for a tree view control and redraw the control using the new images.

See Also: **CImageList**, **CTreeCtrl::GetImageList**

CTreeCtrl::SetIndent

void SetIndent(UINT *nIndent* **);**

Parameters

nIndent   Width, in pixels, of the indentation. If *nIndent* is less than the system-defined minimum width, the new width is set to the system-defined minimum.

Remarks

Call this function to set the width of indentation for a tree view control and redraw the control to reflect the new width.

See Also: **CTreeCtrl::GetIndent**, **CTreeCtrl::GetItemRect**

CTreeCtrl::SetItem

BOOL SetItem(TV_ITEM* *pItem* **);**
BOOL SetItem(HTREEITEM *hItem*, **UINT** *nMask*, **LPCTSTR** *lpszItem*,
  ↳ **int** *nImage*, **int** *nSelectedImage*, **UINT** *nState*, **UINT** *nStateMask*, **LPARAM** *lParam* **);**

Return Value

Nonzero if successful; otherwise 0.

Parameters

pItem   A pointer to a **TV_ITEM** structure that contains the new item attributes. For more information on the **TV_ITEM** structure, see **CTreeCtrl::GetItem**.

hItem   Handle of the item whose attributes are to be set.

nMask   Integer specifying which attributes to set.

lpszItem   Address of a string containing the item's text.

nImage   Index of the item's image in the tree view control's image list.

nSelectedImage   Index of the item's selected image in the tree view control's image list.

nState   Specifies values for the item's states.

nStateMask   Specifies which states are to be set.

lParam   A 32-bit application-specific value associated with the item.

Remarks

Call this function to set the attributes of the specified tree view item.

In the **TV_ITEM** structure, the **hItem** member identifies the item, and the **mask** member specifies which attributes to set.

If the **mask** member or the *nMask* parameter specifies the **TVIF_TEXT** value, the **pszText** member or the *lpszItem* is the address of a null-terminated string and the **cchTextMax** member is ignored. If **mask** (or *nMask*) specifies the **TVIF_STATE** value, the **stateMask** member or the *nStateMask* parameter specifies which item states to change and the **state** member or *nState* parameter contains the values for those states.

See Also: CTreeCtrl::GetItem

CTreeCtrl::SetItemData

BOOL SetItemData(HTREEITEM *hItem*, **DWORD** *dwData* **);**

Return Value

Nonzero if successful; otherwise 0.

Parameters

hItem   Handle of the item whose data is to be retrieved.

dwData   A 32-bit application-specific value associated with the item specified by *hItem*.

Remarks

Call this function to set the 32-bit application-specific value associated with the specified item.

See Also: CTreeCtrl::GetItemData

CTreeCtrl::SetItemImage

BOOL SetItemImage(HTREEITEM *hItem*, **int** *nImage*, **int** *nSelectedImage* **);**

Return Value

Nonzero if successful; otherwise 0.

Parameters

hItem   Handle of the item whose image is to be set.

nImage   Index of the item's image in the tree view control's image list.

nSelectedImage   Index of the item's selected image in the tree view control's image list.

Remarks

Each item in a tree view control can have a pair of bitmapped images associated with it. The images appear on the left side of an item's label. One image is displayed when the item is selected, and the other is displayed when the item is not selected. For example, an item might display an open folder when it is selected and a closed folder when it is not selected.

Call this function to set the index of the item's image and its selected image within the tree view control's image list.

For more information on images, see **CImageList**.

See Also: CTreeCtrl::GetItemImage, CImageList

CTreeCtrl::SetItemState

BOOL SetItemState(HTREEITEM *hItem*, **UINT** *nState*, **UINT** *nStateMask* **);**

Return Value

Nonzero if successful; otherwise 0.

Parameters

hItem   Handle of the item whose state is to be set.

nState   Specifies new states for the item.

nStateMask   Specifies which states are to be changed.

Remarks

Sets the state of the item specified by *hItem*. For information on states, see **CTreeCtrl::GetItem**.

See Also: CTreeCtrl::GetItem, CTreeCtrl::GetItemState

CTreeCtrl::SetItemText

BOOL SetItemText(HTREEITEM *hItem*, **LPCTSTR** *lpszItem* **);**

Return Value

Nonzero if successful; otherwise 0.

Parameters

hItem   Handle of the item whose text is to be set.

lpszItem   Address of a string containing the new text for the item

Remarks

Sets the text of the item specified by *hItem*.

See Also: CTreeCtrl::GetItemText

CTreeCtrl::SortChildren

BOOL SortChildren(HTREEITEM *hItem* **);**

Return Value

Nonzero if successful; otherwise 0.

Parameters

hItem   Handle of the parent item whose child items are to be sorted.

Remarks

Call this function to sort the child items of the given parent item in a tree view control. If *hItem* is **NULL**, the entire tree control is sorted.

See Also: CTreeCtrl::SortChildrenCB

CTreeCtrl::SortChildrenCB

BOOL SortChildrenCB(LPTV_SORTCB *pSort* **);**

Return Value

Nonzero if successful; otherwise 0.

Parameters

pSort   Pointer to a **TV_SORTCB** structure.

Remarks

Call this function to sort tree view items using an application-defined callback function that compares the items.

The **TV_SORTCB** structure is defined as follows:

```
typedef struct _TV_SORTCB { tvscb
    HTREEITEM    hParent;        // handle of parent item
    PFNTVCOMPARE lpfnCompare;
    LPARAM       lParam;         // application-defined 32-bit value
} TV_SORTCB;
```

lpfnCompare   Pointer to an application-defined comparison function. It is called during a sort operation each time the relative order of two list items needs to be compared. The comparison function has the following form:

```
int CALLBACK CompareFunc(LPARAM lParam1, LPARAM lParam2, LPARAM
            lParamSort);
```

The comparison function must return a negative value if the first item should precede the second, a positive value if the first item should follow the second, or zero if the two items are equivalent.

The *lParam1* and *lParam2* parameters correspond to the **lParam** member of the **TV_ITEM** structure for the two items being compared. For more information on the **TV_ITEM** structure, see **CTreeCtrl::GetItem**. The *lParamSort* parameter corresponds to the **lParam** member of the **TV_SORTCB** structure.

See Also: **CTreeCtrl::SortChildren**

CTreeView

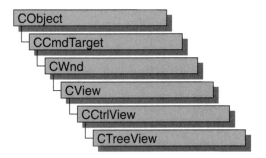

The **CTreeView** class simplifies use of the tree control and of **CTreeCtrl**, the class that encapsulates tree-control functionality, with MFC's document-view architecture. For more information on this architecture, see the overview for the **CView** class and the cross-references cited there.

#include <afxcview.h>

See Also: **CView, CCtrlView, CTreeCtrl**

CTreeView Class Members

Construction

CTreeView	Constructs a **CTreeView** object.

Attributes

GetTreeCtrl	Returns the tree control associated with the view.

Member Functions
CTreeView::CTreeView

CTreeView( );

Remarks

Constructs a **CTreeView** object.

See Also: **CTreeCtrl**

CTreeView::GetTreeCtrl

CTreeCtrl& GetTreeCtrl( ) const;

Remarks

Returns a reference to the tree control associated with the view.

See Also: **CTreeCtrl**

CTypedPtrArray

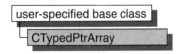

template< class *BASE_CLASS*, **class** *TYPE* >
  ↳ **class CTypedPtrArray : public BASE_CLASS**

Parameters

BASE_CLASS   Base class of the typed pointer array class; must be an array class (**CObArray** or **CPtrArray**).

TYPE   Type of the elements stored in the base-class array.

Remarks

The **CTypedPtrArray** class provides a type-safe "wrapper" for objects of class **CPtrArray** or **CObArray**. When you use **CTypedPtrArray** rather than **CPtrArray** or **CObArray**, the C++ type-checking facility helps eliminate errors caused by mismatched pointer types.

In addition, the **CTypedPtrArray** wrapper performs much of the casting that would be required if you used **CObArray** or **CPtrArray**.

Because all **CTypedPtrArray** functions are inline, use of this template does not significantly affect the size or speed of your code.

For more information on using **CTypedPtrArray**, see the articles "Collections" and "Collections: Template-Based Classes" in *Visual C++ Programmer's Guide* online.

#include <afxtempl.h>

See Also: **CPtrArray, CObArray**

CTypedPtrArray Class Members

Element Access

GetAt	Returns the value at a given index.
ElementAt	Returns a temporary reference to the element pointer within the array.
SetAt	Sets the value for a given index; array not allowed to grow.
SetAtGrow	Sets the value for a given index; grows the array if necessary.
Add	Adds a new element to the end of an array. Grows the array if necessary

Element Access *(continued)*

Append	Adds the contents of one array to the end of another. Grows the array if necessary
Copy	Copies another array to the array; grows the array if necessary.
InsertAt	Inserts an element (or all the elements in another array) at a specified index.

Operators

operator[]	Sets or gets the element at the specified index.

Member Functions
CTypedPtrArray::Add

> **int Add(** *TYPE newElement* **);**

Return Value

The index of the added element.

Parameters

TYPE   Template parameter specifying the type of element to be added to the array.

newElement   The element to be added to this array.

Remarks

This member function calls *BASE_CLASS***::Add**. For more detailed remarks, see **CObArray::Add**.

CTypedPtrArray::Append

> **int Append(const CTypedPtrArray<***BASE_CLASS, TYPE***>&** *src* **);**

Return Value

The index of the first appended element.

Parameters

BASE_CLASS   Base class of the typed pointer array class; must be an array class (**CObArray** or **CPtrArray**).

TYPE   Type of the elements stored in the base-class array.

src   Source of the elements to be appended to an array.

Remarks

This member function calls *BASE_CLASS*::**Append**. For more detailed remarks, see **CObArray::Append**.

CTypedPtrArray::Copy

void Copy(const CTypedPtrArray<*BASE_CLASS, TYPE***>&** *src* **);**

Parameters

BASE_CLASS   Base class of the typed pointer array class; must be an array class (**CObArray** or **CPtrArray**).

TYPE   Type of the elements stored in the base-class array.

src   Source of the elements to be copied to an array.

Remarks

This member function calls *BASE_CLASS*::**Copy**. For more detailed remarks, see **CObArray::Copy**.

CTypedPtrArray::ElementAt

*TYPE***& ElementAt(int** *nIndex* **);**

Return Value

A temporary reference to the element at the location specified by *nIndex*. This element is of the type specified by the template parameter *TYPE*.

Parameters

TYPE   Template parameter specifying the type of elements stored in this array.

nIndex   An integer index that is greater than or equal to 0 and less than or equal to the value returned by *BASE_CLASS*::**GetUpperBound**.

Remarks

This inline function calls *BASE_CLASS*::**ElementAt**. For more detailed remarks, see **CObArray::ElementAt**.

See Also: CObArray::ElementAt, CObArray::GetUpperBound

CTypedPtrArray::GetAt

TYPE **GetAt(int** *nIndex* **) const;**

Return Value

A copy of the element at the location specified by *nIndex*. This element is of the type specified by the template parameter *TYPE*.

Parameters

TYPE   Template parameter specifying the type of elements stored in the array.

nIndex   An integer index that is greater than or equal to 0 and less than or equal to the value returned by *BASE_CLASS*::**GetUpperBound**.

Remarks

This inline function calls *BASE_CLASS*::**GetAt**. For more detailed remarks, see **CObArray::GetAt**.

See Also: **CObArray::GetAt**, **CObArray::GetUpperBound**

CTypedPtrArray::InsertAt

> **void InsertAt(int** *nIndex*, *TYPE newElement*, **int** *nCount* = **1**);
> **void InsertAt(int** *nStartIndex*, **CTypedPtrArray**<*BASE_CLASS*, *TYPE*>* *pNewArray*);

Parameters

nIndex   An integer index that may be greater than the value returned by **CObArray::GetUpperBound**.

TYPE   Type of the elements stored in the base-class array.

newElement   The object pointer to be placed in this array. A *newElement* of value **NULL** is allowed.

nCount   The number of times this element should be inserted (defaults to 1).

nStartIndex   An integer index that may be greater than the value returned by **CObArray::GetUpperBound**.

BASE_CLASS   Base class of the typed pointer array class; must be an array class (**CObArray** or **CPtrArray**).

pNewArray   Another array that contains elements to be added to this array.

Remarks

This member function calls *BASE_CLASS*::**InsertAt**. For more detailed remarks, see **CObArray::InsertAt**.

CTypedPtrArray::SetAt

> **void SetAt(int** *nIndex*, *TYPE ptr*);

Parameters

nIndex   An integer index that is greater than or equal to 0 and less than or equal to the value returned by **CObArray::GetUpperBound**.

TYPE   Type of the elements stored in the base-class array.

ptr   A pointer to the element to be inserted in the array at the nIndex. A NULL value is allowed.

Remarks

This member function calls *BASE_CLASS*::**SetAt**. For more detailed remarks, see **CObArray::SetAt**.

CTypedPtrArray::SetAtGrow

void SetAtGrow(int *nIndex*, *TYPE newElement* **);**

Parameters

nIndex   An integer index that is greater than or equal to 0.

TYPE   Type of the elements stored in the base-class array.

newElement   The object pointer to be added to this array. A **NULL** value is allowed.

Remarks

This member function calls *BASE_CLASS*::**SetAtGrow**. For more detailed remarks, see **CObArray::SetAtGrow**.

Operators
CTypedPtrArray::operator [ ]

*TYPE***& operator[ ](** **int** *nIndex* **);**
TYPE **operator[ ](** **int** *nIndex* **) const;**

Parameters

TYPE   Template parameter specifying the type of elements stored in the array.

nIndex   An integer index that is greater than or equal to 0 and less than or equal to the value returned by *BASE_CLASS*::**GetUpperBound**.

Remarks

These inline operators call *BASE_CLASS*::**operator [ ]**.

The first operator, called for arrays that are not **const**, can be used on either the right (r-value) or the left (l-value) of an assignment statement. The second, invoked for **const** arrays, can be used only on the right.

The Debug version of the library asserts if the subscript (either on the left or right side of an assignment statement) is out of bounds.

See Also: CObArray::operator []

CTypedPtrList

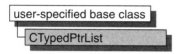

template< class *BASE_CLASS*, class *TYPE* > class **CTypedPtrList : public** *BASE_CLASS*

Parameters

BASE_CLASS   Base class of the typed pointer list class; must be a pointer list class (**CObList** or **CPtrList**).

TYPE   Type of the elements stored in the base-class list.

Remarks

The **CTypedPtrList** class provides a type-safe "wrapper" for objects of class **CPtrList**. When you use **CTypedPtrList** rather than **CObList** or **CPtrList**, the C++ type-checking facility helps eliminate errors caused by mismatched pointer types.

In addition, the **CTypedPtrList** wrapper performs much of the casting that would be required if you used **CObList** or **CPtrList**.

Because all **CTypedPtrList** functions are inline, use of this template does not significantly affect the size or speed of your code.

Lists derived from **CObList** can be serialized, but those derived from **CPtrList** cannot.

When a **CTypedPtrList** object is deleted, or when its elements are removed, only the pointers are removed, not the entities they reference.

For more information on using **CTypedPtrList**, see the articles "Collections" and "Collections: Template-Based Classes" in *Visual C++ Programmer's Guide* online.

#include <afxtempl.h>

See Also: **CPtrList**, **CObList**

CTypedPtrList Class Members

Head/Tail Access

GetHead	Returns the head element of the list (cannot be empty).
GetTail	Returns the tail element of the list (cannot be empty).

Operations	
RemoveHead	Removes the element from the head of the list.
RemoveTail	Removes the element from the tail of the list.
AddHead	Adds an element (or all the elements in another list) to the head of the list (makes a new head).
AddTail	Adds an element (or all the elements in another list) to the tail of the list (makes a new tail).

Iteration	
GetNext	Gets the next element for iterating.
GetPrev	Gets the previous element for iterating.

Retrieval/Modification	
GetAt	Gets the element at a given position.
SetAt	Sets the element at a given position.

Member Functions

CTypedPtrList::AddHead

POSITION AddHead(*TYPE newElement* **);**
void AddHead(CTypedPtrList<<i>BASE_CLASS</i>, *TYPE>* **pNewList* **);**

Return Value

The first version returns the **POSITION** value of the newly inserted element.

Parameters

TYPE   Type of the elements stored in the base-class list.

newElement   The object pointer to be added to this list. A **NULL** value is allowed.

BASE_CLASS   Base class of the typed pointer list class; must be a pointer list class (**CObList** or **CPtrList**).

pNewList   A pointer to another **CTypedPtrList** object. The elements in *pNewList* will be added to this list.

Remarks

This member function calls *BASE_CLASS*::**AddHead**. The first version adds a new element before the head of the list. The second version adds another list of elements before the head.

CTypedPtrList::AddTail

POSITION AddTail(*TYPE newElement* **);**
void AddTail(CTypedPtrList<*BASE_CLASS, TYPE***> *****pNewList* **);**

Return Value

The first version returns the **POSITION** value of the newly inserted element.

Parameters

TYPE   Type of the elements stored in the base-class list.

newElement   The object pointer to be added to this list. A **NULL** value is allowed.

BASE_CLASS   Base class of the typed pointer list class; must be a pointer list class (**CObList** or **CPtrList**).

pNewList   A pointer to another **CTypedPtrList** object. The elements in *pNewList* will be added to this list.

Remarks

This member function calls *BASE_CLASS***::AddTail**. The first version adds a new element after the tail of the list. The second version adds another list of elements after the tail of the list.

CTypedPtrList::GetAt

*TYPE***& GetAt(POSITION** *position* **);**
TYPE **GetAt(POSITION** *position* **) const;**

Return Value

If the list is accessed through a pointer to a **const CTypedPtrList**, then **GetAt** returns a pointer of the type specified by the template parameter *TYPE*. This allows the function to be used only on the right side of an assignment statement and thus protects the list from modification.

If the list is accessed directly or through a pointer to a **CTypedPtrList**, then **GetAt** returns a reference to a pointer of the type specified by the template parameter *TYPE*. This allows the function to be used on either side of an assignment statement and thus allows the list entries to be modified.

Parameters

TYPE   Template parameter specifying the type of elements stored in the list.

position   A **POSITION** value returned by a previous **GetHeadPosition** or **Find** member function call.

Remarks

A variable of type **POSITION** is a key for the list. It is not the same as an index, and you cannot operate on a **POSITION** value yourself. **GetAt** retrieves the **CObject** pointer associated with a given position.

You must ensure that your **POSITION** value represents a valid position in the list. If it is invalid, then the Debug version of the Microsoft Foundation Class Library asserts.

This inline function calls *BASE_CLASS***::GetAt**.

See Also: CObList::GetAt

CTypedPtrList::GetHead

*TYPE***& GetHead( );**
TYPE **GetHead( ) const;**

Return Value

If the list is accessed through a pointer to a **const CTypedPtrList**, then **GetHead** returns a pointer of the type specified by the template parameter *TYPE*. This allows the function to be used only on the right side of an assignment statement and thus protects the list from modification.

If the list is accessed directly or through a pointer to a **CTypedPtrList**, then **GetHead** returns a reference to a pointer of the type specified by the template parameter *TYPE*. This allows the function to be used on either side of an assignment statement and thus allows the list entries to be modified.

Parameters

TYPE   Template parameter specifying the type of elements stored in the list.

Remarks

Gets the pointer that represents the head element of this list.

You must ensure that the list is not empty before calling **GetHead**. If the list is empty, then the Debug version of the Microsoft Foundation Class Library asserts. Use **IsEmpty** to verify that the list contains elements.

See Also: CPtrList::IsEmpty, CTypedPtrList::GetTail, CTypedPtrList::GetNext, CTypedPtrList::GetPrev

CTypedPtrList::GetNext

TYPE& **GetNext(POSITION&** *rPosition*);
TYPE **GetNext(POSITION&** *rPosition*) **const;**

Return Value

If the list is accessed through a pointer to a **const CTypedPtrList**, then **GetNext** returns a pointer of the type specified by the template parameter *TYPE*. This allows the function to be used only on the right side of an assignment statement and thus protects the list from modification.

If the list is accessed directly or through a pointer to a **CTypedPtrList**, then **GetNext** returns a reference to a pointer of the type specified by the template parameter *TYPE*. This allows the function to be used on either side of an assignment statement and thus allows the list entries to be modified.

Parameters

TYPE   Template parameter specifying the type of elements contained in this list.

rPosition   A reference to a **POSITION** value returned by a previous **GetNext**, **GetHeadPosition**, or other member function call.

Remarks

Gets the list element identified by *rPosition*, then sets *rPosition* to the **POSITION** value of the next entry in the list. You can use **GetNext** in a forward iteration loop if you establish the initial position with a call to **GetHeadPosition** or **CPtrList::Find**.

You must ensure that your **POSITION** value represents a valid position in the list. If it is invalid, then the Debug version of the Microsoft Foundation Class Library asserts.

If the retrieved element is the last in the list, then the new value of *rPosition* is set to **NULL**.

It is possible to remove an element during an iteration. See the example for **CObList::RemoveAt**.

See Also: **CObList::Find, CObList::GetHeadPosition, CObList::GetTailPosition, CTypedPtrList::GetPrev, CTypedPtrList::GetHead, CTypedPtrList::GetTail**

CTypedPtrList::GetPrev

TYPE& **GetPrev(POSITION&** *rPosition*);
TYPE **GetPrev(POSITION&** *rPosition*) **const;**

Return Value

If the list is accessed through a pointer to a **const CTypedPtrList**, then **GetPrev** returns a pointer of the type specified by the template parameter *TYPE*. This allows the function to be used only on the right side of an assignment statement and thus protects the list from modification.

If the list is accessed directly or through a pointer to a **CTypedPtrList**, then **GetPrev** returns a reference to a pointer of the type specified by the template parameter *TYPE*. This allows the function to be used on either side of an assignment statement and thus allows the list entries to be modified.

Parameters

TYPE   Template parameter specifying the type of elements contained in this list.

rPosition   A reference to a **POSITION** value returned by a previous **GetPrev** or other member function call.

Remarks

Gets the list element identified by *rPosition*, then sets *rPosition* to the **POSITION** value of the previous entry in the list. You can use **GetPrev** in a reverse iteration loop if you establish the initial position with a call to **GetTailPosition** or **Find**.

You must ensure that your **POSITION** value represents a valid position in the list. If it is invalid, then the Debug version of the Microsoft Foundation Class Library asserts.

If the retrieved element is the first in the list, then the new value of *rPosition* is set to **NULL**.

See Also: **CPtrList::Find, CPtrList::GetTailPosition, CPtrList::GetHeadPosition, CTypedPtrList::GetNext, CTypedPtrList::GetHead, CTypedPtrList::GetTail**

CTypedPtrList::GetTail

TYPE& **GetTail( );**
TYPE **GetTail( ) const;**

Return Value

If the list is accessed through a pointer to a **const CTypedPtrList**, then **GetTail** returns a pointer of the type specified by the template parameter *TYPE*. This allows the function to be used only on the right side of an assignment statement and thus protects the list from modification.

If the list is accessed directly or through a pointer to a **CTypedPtrList**, then **GetTail** returns a reference to a pointer of the type specified by the template parameter *TYPE*. This allows the function to be used on either side of an assignment statement and thus allows the list entries to be modified.

Parameters

TYPE   Template parameter specifying the type of elements stored in the list.

Remarks

Gets the pointer that represents the head element of this list.

You must ensure that the list is not empty before calling **GetTail**. If the list is empty, then the Debug version of the Microsoft Foundation Class Library asserts. Use **IsEmpty** to verify that the list contains elements.

See Also: **CPtrList::IsEmpty**, **CPtrList::Find**, **CPtrList::GetTailPosition**, **CPtrList::GetHeadPosition**, **CTypedPtrList::GetPrev**, **CTypedPtrList::GetNext**, **CTypedPtrList::GetHead**

CTypedPtrList::RemoveHead

TYPE **RemoveHead( );**

Return Value

The pointer previously at the head of the list. This pointer is of the type specified by the template parameter *TYPE*.

Parameters

TYPE　Template parameter specifying the type of elements stored in the list.

Remarks

Removes the element from the head of the list and returns it.

You must ensure that the list is not empty before calling **RemoveHead**. If the list is empty, then the Debug version of the Microsoft Foundation Class Library asserts. Use **IsEmpty** to verify that the list contains elements.

See Also: **CTypedPtrList::RemoveTail**, **CPtrList::IsEmpty**, **CPtrList::GetHead**, **CPtrList::AddHead**

CTypedPtrList::RemoveTail

TYPE **RemoveTail( );**

Return Value

The pointer previously at the tail of the list. This pointer is of the type specified by the template parameter *TYPE*.

Parameters

TYPE　Template parameter specifying the type of elements stored in the list.

Remarks

Removes the element from the tail of the list and returns it.

You must ensure that the list is not empty before calling **RemoveTail**. If the list is empty, then the Debug version of the Microsoft Foundation Class Library asserts. Use **IsEmpty** to verify that the list contains elements.

See Also: **CTypedPtrList::RemoveHead, CPtrList::IsEmpty, CPtrList::GetTail, CPtrList::AddTail**

CTypedPtrList::SetAt

void SetAt(POSITION *pos***,** *TYPE newElement* **);**

Parameters

pos   The **POSITION** of the element to be set.

TYPE   Type of the elements stored in the base-class list.

newElement   The object pointer to be written to the list.

Remarks

This member function calls *BASE_CLASS*::**SetAt**.

A variable of type **POSITION** is a key for the list. It is not the same as an index, and you cannot operate on a **POSITION** value yourself. **SetAt** writes the object pointer to the specified position in the list.

You must ensure that your **POSITION** value represents a valid position in the list. If it is invalid, then the Debug version of the Microsoft Foundation Class Library asserts.

For more detailed remarks, see **CObList::SetAt**.

CTypedPtrMap

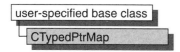

template< class *BASE_CLASS*, **class** *KEY*, **class** *VALUE* >
  ↪ **class CTypedPtrMap : public BASE_CLASS**

Parameters

BASE_CLASS Base class of the typed pointer map class; must be a pointer map class
  (**CMapPtrToPtr**, **CMapPtrToWord**, **CMapWordToPtr**, or **CMapStringToPtr**).

KEY Class of the object used as the key to the map.

VALUE Class of the object stored in the map.

Remarks

The **CTypedPtrMap** class provides a type-safe "wrapper" for objects of the
pointer-map classes **CMapPtrToPtr**, **CMapPtrToWord**, **CMapWordToPtr**, and
CMapStringToPtr. When you use **CTypedPtrMap**, the C++ type-checking facility
helps eliminate errors caused by mismatched pointer types.

Because all **CTypedPtrMap** functions are inline, use of this template does not
significantly affect the size or speed of your code.

For more information on using **CTypedPtrMap**, see the articles "Collections" and
"Collections: Template-Based Classes" in *Visual C++ Programmer's Guide* online.

#include <afxtempl.h>

See Also: **CMapPtrToPtr**, **CMapPtrToWord**, **CMapWordToPtr**,
CMapStringToPtr

CTypedPtrMap Class Members

Element Access

Lookup	Returns a *KEY* based on a *VALUE*.
GetNextAssoc	Gets the next element for iterating.
RemoveKey	Removes an element specified by a key.
SetAt	Inserts an element into the map; replaces an existing element if a matching key is found.

Operators

operator[]	Inserts an element into the map.

Member Functions
CTypedPtrMap::GetNextAssoc

void GetNextAssoc(POSITION& *rPosition*, *KEY&* *rKey*, *VALUE&* *rValue*) **const;**

Parameters

rPosition   Specifies a reference to a **POSITION** value returned by a previous **GetNextAssoc** or *BASE_CLASS*::**GetStartPosition** call.

KEY   Template parameter specifying the type of the map's keys.

rKey   Specifies the returned key of the retrieved element.

VALUE   Template parameter specifying the type of the map's values.

rValue   Specifies the returned value of the retrieved element.

Remarks

Retrieves the map element at *rNextPosition*, then updates *rNextPosition* to refer to the next element in the map. This function is most useful for iterating through all the elements in the map. Note that the position sequence is not necessarily the same as the key value sequence.

If the retrieved element is the last in the map, then the new value of *rNextPosition* is set to **NULL**.

This inline function calls *BASE_CLASS*::**GetNextAssoc**.

See Also: CMapStringToOb::GetNextAssoc,
CMapStringToOb::GetStartPosition

CTypedPtrMap::Lookup

BOOL Lookup(*BASE_CLASS*::**BASE_ARG_KEY** *key*, *VALUE&* *rValue*) **const;**

Return Value

Nonzero if the element was found; otherwise 0.

Parameters

BASE_CLASS   Template parameter specifying the base class of this map's class.

key   The key of the element to be looked up.

VALUE   Template parameter specifying the type of values stored in this map.

rValue   Specifies the returned value of the retrieved element.

Remarks

Lookup uses a hashing algorithm to quickly find the map element with a key that matches exactly.

This inline function calls *BASE_CLASS*::**Lookup**.

See Also: **CMapStringToOb::Lookup**

CTypedPtrMap::RemoveKey

BOOL RemoveKey(*KEY key* **);**

Return Value

Nonzero if the entry was found and successfully removed; otherwise 0.

Parameters

KEY   Template parameter specifying the type of the map's keys.

key   Key for the element to be removed.

Remarks

This member function calls *BASE_CLASS*::**RemoveKey**. For more detailed remarks, see **CMapStringToOb::RemoveKey**.

CTypedPtrMap::SetAt

void SetAt(*KEY key*, *VALUE newValue* **);**

Parameters

KEY   Template parameter specifying the type of the map's keys.

key   Specifies the key value of the newValue.

newValue   Specifies the object pointer that is the value of the new element.

Remarks

This member function calls *BASE_CLASS*::**SetAt**. For more detailed remarks, see **CMapStringToOb::SetAt**.

Operators
CTypedPtrMap::operator [ ]

*VALUE***& operator [ ](** *BASE_CLASS*::**BASE_ARG_KEY** *key* **);**

Parameters

VALUE   Template parameter specifying the type of values stored in this map.

BASE_CLASS   Template parameter specifying the base class of this map's class.

key   The key of the element to be looked up or created in the map.

Remarks

This operator can be used only on the left side of an assignment statement (an l-value). If there is no map element with the specified key, then a new element is created. There is no "right side" (r-value) equivalent to this operator because there is a possibility that a key may not be found in the map. Use the **Lookup** member function for element retrieval.

See Also: CTypedPtrMap::Lookup

CUIntArray

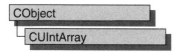

The **CUIntArray** class supports arrays of unsigned integers. An unsigned integer, or **UINT**, differs from words and doublewords in that the physical size of a **UINT** can change depending on the target operating environment. Under Windows version 3.1, a **UINT** is the same size as a **WORD**. Under Windows NT and Windows 95, a **UINT** is the same size as a doubleword.

The member functions of **CUIntArray** are similar to the member functions of class **CObArray**. Because of this similarity, you can use the **CObArray** reference documentation for member function specifics. Wherever you see a **CObject** pointer as a function parameter or return value, substitute a **UINT**.

```
CObject* CObArray::GetAt( int <nIndex> ) const;
```

for example, translates to

```
UINT CUIntArray::GetAt( int <nIndex> ) const;
```

CUIntArray incorporates the **IMPLEMENT_DYNAMIC** macro to support run-time type access and dumping to a **CDumpContext** object. If you need a dump of individual unsigned integer elements, you must set the depth of the dump context to 1 or greater. Unsigned integer arrays cannot be serialized.

Note Before using an array, use **SetSize** to establish its size and allocate memory for it. If you do not use **SetSize**, adding elements to your array causes it to be frequently reallocated and copied. Frequent reallocation and copying are inefficient and can fragment memory.

For more information on using **CUIntArray**, see the article "Collections" in *Visual C++ Programmer's Guide* online.

#include <afxcoll.h>

CUIntArray Class Members

Construction

CUIntArray	Constructs an empty array for unsigned integers.

Bounds

GetSize	Gets the number of elements in this array.
GetUpperBound	Returns the largest valid index.
SetSize	Sets the number of elements to be contained in this array.

Operations

FreeExtra	Frees all unused memory above the current upper bound.
RemoveAll	Removes all the elements from this array.

Element Access

GetAt	Returns the value at a given index.
SetAt	Sets the value for a given index; the array is not allowed to grow.
ElementAt	Returns a temporary reference to the element pointer within the array.
GetData	Allows access to elements in the array. Can be **NULL**.

Growing the Array

SetAtGrow	Sets the value for a given index; grows the array if necessary.
Add	Adds an element to the end of the array; grows the array if necessary.
Append	Appends another array to the array; grows the array if necessary.
Copy	Copies another array to the array; grows the array if necessary.

Insertion/Removal

InsertAt	Inserts an element (or all the elements in another array) at a specified index.
RemoveAt	Removes an element at a specific index.

Operators

operator [ ]	Sets or gets the element at the specified index.

CUserException

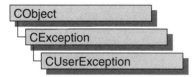

```
CObject
  CException
    CUserException
```

A **CUserException** is thrown to stop an end-user operation. Use **CUserException** when you want to use the throw/catch exception mechanism for application-specific exceptions. "User" in the class name can be interpreted as "my user did something exceptional that I need to handle."

A **CUserException** is usually thrown after calling the global function **AfxMessageBox** to notify the user that an operation has failed. When you write an exception handler, handle the exception specially since the user usually has already been notified of the failure. The framework throws this exception in some cases. To throw a **CUserException** yourself, alert the user and then call the global function **AfxThrowUserException**.

In the example below, a function containing operations that may fail alerts the user and throws a **CUserException**. The calling function catches the exception and handles it specially:

```
void DoSomeOperation( )
{
   // Processing
   // If something goes wrong...
   AfxMessageBox( "The x operation failed" );
   AfxThrowUserException( );
}

BOOL TrySomething( )
{
   TRY
   {
      // Could throw a CUserException or other exception.
      DoSomeOperation( );
   }
   CATCH( CUserException, e )
   {
      return FALSE;    // User already notified.
   }
   AND_CATCH( CException, e )
   {
      // For other exception types, notify user here.
      AfxMessageBox( "Some operation failed" );
      return FALSE;
   }
```

```
    END_CATCH
    return TRUE;    // No exception thrown.
}
```

For more information on using **CUserException**, see the article "Exceptions" in *Visual C++ Programmer's Guide* online.

#include <afxwin.h>

See Also: CException, AfxMessageBox, AfxThrowUserException

CView

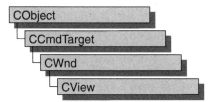

The **CView** class provides the basic functionality for user-defined view classes. A view is attached to a document and acts as an intermediary between the document and the user: the view renders an image of the document on the screen or printer and interprets user input as operations upon the document.

A view is a child of a frame window. More than one view can share a frame window, as in the case of a splitter window. The relationship between a view class, a frame window class, and a document class is established by a **CDocTemplate** object. When the user opens a new window or splits an existing one, the framework constructs a new view and attaches it to the document.

A view can be attached to only one document, but a document can have multiple views attached to it at once—for example, if the document is displayed in a splitter window or in multiple child windows in a multiple document interface (MDI) application. Your application can support different types of views for a given document type; for example, a word-processing program might provide both a complete text view of a document and an outline view that shows only the section headings. These different types of views can be placed in separate frame windows or in separate panes of a single frame window if you use a splitter window.

A view may be responsible for handling several different types of input, such as keyboard input, mouse input or input via drag-and-drop, as well as commands from menus, toolbars, or scroll bars. A view receives commands forwarded by its frame window. If the view does not handle a given command, it forwards the command to its associated document. Like all command targets, a view handles messages via a message map.

The view is responsible for displaying and modifying the document's data but not for storing it. The document provides the view with the necessary details about its data. You can let the view access the document's data members directly, or you can provide member functions in the document class for the view class to call.

When a document's data changes, the view responsible for the changes typically calls the **CDocument::UpdateAllViews** function for the document, which notifies all the other views by calling the **OnUpdate** member function for each. The default implementation of **OnUpdate** invalidates the view's entire client area. You can override it to invalidate only those regions of the client area that map to the modified portions of the document.

To use **CView**, derive a class from it and implement the **OnDraw** member function to perform screen display. You can also use **OnDraw** to perform printing and print preview. The framework handles the print loop for printing and previewing your document.

A view handles scroll-bar messages with the **CWnd::OnHScroll** and **CWnd::OnVScroll** member functions. You can implement scroll-bar message handling in these functions, or you can use the **CView** derived class **CScrollView** to handle scrolling for you.

Besides **CScollView**, the Microsoft Foundation Class Library provides nine other classes derived from **CView**:

- **CCtrlView**, a view that allows usage of document-view architecture with tree, list, and rich edit controls.

- **CDaoRecordView**, a view that displays database records in dialog-box controls.

- **CEditView**, a view that provides a simple multiline text editor. You can use a **CEditView** object as a control in a dialog box as well as a view on a document.

- **CFormView**, a scrollable view that contains dialog-box controls and is based on a dialog template resource.

- **CListView**, a view that allows usage of document-view architecture with list controls.

- **CRecordView**, a view that displays database records in dialog-box controls.

- **CRichEditView**, a view that allows usage of document-view architecture with rich edit controls.

- **CScrollView**, a view that automatically provides scrolling support.

- **CTreeView**, a view that allows usage of document-view architecture with tree controls.

The **CView** class also has a derived implementation class named **CPreviewView**, which is used by the framework to perform print previewing. This class provides support for the features unique to the print-preview window, such as a toolbar, single- or double-page preview, and zooming, that is, enlarging the previewed image. You don't need to call or override any of **CPreviewView**'s member functions unless you want to implement your own interface for print preview (for example, if you want to support editing in print preview mode). For more information on using **CView**, see "Document/View Architecture Topics" and "Printing" in *Visual C++ Programmer's Guide* online. In addition, see Technical Note 30 online for more details on customizing print preview.

#include <afxwin.h>

See Also: **CWnd, CFrameWnd, CSplitterWnd, CDC, CDocTemplate, CDocument**

CView Class Members

Operations

DoPreparePrinting	Displays Print dialog box and creates printer device context; call when overriding the **OnPreparePrinting** member function.
GetDocument	Returns the document associated with the view.

OLE Overridables

OnDragEnter	Called when an item is first dragged into the drag-and-drop region of a view.
OnDragLeave	Called when a dragged item leaves the drag-and-drop region of a view.
OnDragOver	Called when an item is dragged over the drag-and-drop region of a view.
OnDrop	Called when an item has been dropped into the drag-and-drop region of a view, default handler.
OnDropEx	Called when an item has been dropped into the drag-and-drop region of a view, primary handler.
OnDragScroll	Called to determine whether the cursor is dragged into the scroll region of the window.
OnInitialUpdate	Called after a view is first attached to a document.
OnScrollBy	Called when a view containing active in-place OLE items is scrolled.
OnScroll	Called when OLE items are dragged beyond the borders of the view.

Overridables

IsSelected	Tests whether a document item is selected. Required for OLE support.
OnActivateView	Called when a view is activated.
OnActivateFrame	Called when the frame window containing the view is activated or deactivated.
OnBeginPrinting	Called when a print job begins; override to allocate graphics device interface (GDI) resources.
OnDraw	Called to render an image of the document for screen display, printing, or print preview. Implementation required.
OnEndPrinting	Called when a print job ends; override to deallocate GDI resources.

(continued)

Overridables *(continued)*	
OnEndPrintPreview	Called when preview mode is exited.
OnPrepareDC	Called before the **OnDraw** member function is called for screen display or the **OnPrint** member function is called for printing or print preview.
OnPreparePrinting	Called before a document is printed or previewed; override to initialize Print dialog box.
OnPrint	Called to print or preview a page of the document.
OnUpdate	Called to notify a view that its document has been modified.
Constructors	
CView	Constructs a **CView** object.

Member Functions

CView::CView

CView( );

Remarks

Constructs a **CView** object. The framework calls the constructor when a new frame window is created or a window is split. Override the **OnInitialUpdate** member function to initialize the view after the document is attached.

See Also: CView::OnInitialUpdate

CView::DoPreparePrinting

BOOL DoPreparePrinting(CPrintInfo* *pInfo* **);**

Return Value

Nonzero if printing or print preview can begin; 0 if the operation has been canceled.

Parameters

pInfo Points to a **CPrintInfo** structure that describes the current print job.

Remarks

Call this function from your override of **OnPreparePrinting** to invoke the Print dialog box and create a printer device context.

This function's behavior depends on whether it is being called for printing or print preview (specified by the **m_bPreview** member of the *pInfo* parameter). If a file is being printed, this function invokes the Print dialog box, using the values in the

CPrintInfo structure that *pInfo* points to; after the user has closed the dialog box, the function creates a printer device context based on settings the user specified in the dialog box and returns this device context through the *pInfo* parameter. This device context is used to print the document.

If a file is being previewed, this function creates a printer device context using the current printer settings; this device context is used for simulating the printer during preview.

See Also: **CPrintInfo**, **CView::OnPreparePrinting**

CView::GetDocument

CDocument* GetDocument( ) const;

Return Value

A pointer to the **CDocument** object associated with the view. **NULL** if the view is not attached to a document.

Remarks

Call this function to get a pointer to the view's document. This allows you to call the document's member functions.

See Also: **CDocument**

CView::IsSelected

virtual BOOL IsSelected(const CObject* *pDocItem* **) const;**

Return Value

Nonzero if the specified document item is selected; otherwise 0.

Parameters

pDocItem   Points to the document item being tested.

Remarks

Called by the framework to check whether the specified document item is selected. The default implementation of this function returns **FALSE**. Override this function if you are implementing selection using **CDocItem** objects. You must override this function if your view contains OLE items.

See Also: **CDocItem**, **COleClientItem**

CView::OnActivateFrame

virtual void OnActivateFrame(UINT *nState*, **CFrameWnd*** *pFrameWnd* **);**

Parameters

nState   Specifies whether the frame window is being activated or deactivated. It can be one of the following values:

- **WA_INACTIVE**   The frame window is being deactivated.

- **WA_ACTIVE**   The frame window is being activated through some method other than a mouse click (for example, by use of the keyboard interface to select the window).

- **WA_CLICKACTIVE**   The frame window is being activated by a mouse click

pFrameWnd   Pointer to the frame window that is to be activated.

Remarks

Called by the framework when the frame window containing the view is activated or deactivated. Override this member function if you want to perform special processing when the frame window associated with the view is activated or deactivated. For example, **CFormView** performs this override when it saves and restores the control that has focus.

See Also: CWnd::OnActivate, CFormView

CView::OnActivateView

virtual void OnActivateView(BOOL *bActivate*, **CView*** *pActivateView*,
↳ **CView*** *pDeactiveView* **);**

Parameters

bActivate   Indicates whether the view is being activated or deactivated.

pActivateView   Points to the view object that is being activated.

pDeactiveView   Points to the view object that is being deactivated.

Remarks

Called by the framework when a view is activated or deactivated. The default implementation of this function sets the focus to the view being activated. Override this function if you want to perform special processing when a view is activated or deactivated. For example, if you want to provide special visual cues that distinguish the active view from the inactive views, you would examine the *bActivate* parameter and update the view's appearance accordingly.

The *pActivateView* and *pDeactiveView* parameters point to the same view if the application's main frame window is activated with no change in the active view¾for example, if the focus is being transferred from another application to this one, rather than from one view to another within the application or when switching amongst MDI child windows. This allows a view to re-realize its palette, if needed.

These parameters differ when **CFrameWnd::SetActiveView** is called with a view that is different from what **CFrameWnd::GetActiveView** would return. This happens most often with splitter windows.

See Also: **CWnd::OnActivate**, **CFrameWnd::SetActiveView**, **CFrameWnd::GetActiveView**

CView::OnBeginPrinting

virtual void OnBeginPrinting(CDC* *pDC***, CPrintInfo*** *pInfo* **);**

Parameters

pDC   Points to the printer device context.

pInfo   Points to a **CPrintInfo** structure that describes the current print job.

Remarks

Called by the framework at the beginning of a print or print preview job, after **OnPreparePrinting** has been called. The default implementation of this function does nothing. Override this function to allocate any GDI resources, such as pens or fonts, needed specifically for printing. Select the GDI objects into the device context from within the **OnPrint** member function for each page that uses them. If you are using the same view object to perform both screen display and printing, use separate variables for the GDI resources needed for each display; this allows you to update the screen during printing.

You can also use this function to perform initializations that depend on properties of the printer device context. For example, the number of pages needed to print the document may depend on settings that the user specified from the Print dialog box (such as page length). In such a situation, you cannot specify the document length in the **OnPreparePrinting** member function, where you would normally do so; you must wait until the printer device context has been created based on the dialog box settings. **OnBeginPrinting** is the first overridable function that gives you access to the **CDC** object representing the printer device context, so you can set the document length from this function. Note that if the document length is not specified by this time, a scroll bar is not displayed during print preview.

See Also: **CView::OnEndPrinting**, **CView::OnPreparePrinting**, **CView::OnPrint**

CView::OnDragEnter

virtual DROPEFFECT OnDragEnter(COleDataObject* *pDataObject*,
➟ **DWORD** *dwKeyState*, **CPoint** *point*);

Return Value

A value from the **DROPEFFECT** enumerated type, which indicates the type of drop that would occur if the user dropped the object at this position. The type of drop usually depends on the current key state indicated by *dwKeyState*. A standard mapping of keystates to **DROPEFFECT** values is:

- **DROPEFFECT_NONE**   The data object cannot be dropped in this window.
- **DROPEFFECT_LINK** for **MK_CONTROL I MK_SHIFT**   Creates a linkage between the object and its server.
- **DROPEFFECT_COPY** for **MK_CONTROL**   Creates a copy of the dropped object.
- **DROPEFFECT_MOVE** for **MK_ALT**   Creates a copy of the dropped object and delete the original object. This is typically the default drop effect, when the view can accept this data object.

For more information, see the MFC Advanced Concepts sample OCLIENT.

Parameters

pDataObject   Points to the **COleDataObject** being dragged into the drop area of the view.

dwKeyState   Contains the state of the modifier keys. This is a combination of any number of the following: **MK_CONTROL**, **MK_SHIFT**, **MK_ALT**, **MK_LBUTTON**, **MK_MBUTTON**, and **MK_RBUTTON**.

point   The current mouse position relative to the client area of the view.

Remarks

Called by the framework when the mouse first enters the non-scrolling region of the drop target window. Default implementation is to do nothing and return **DROPEFFECT_NONE**.

Override this function to prepare for future calls to the **OnDragOver** member function. Any data required from the data object should be retrieved at this time for later use in the **OnDragOver** member function. The view should also be updated at this time to give the user visual feedback. For more information, see the article "Drag and Drop: Implementing a Drop Target" in *Visual C++ Programmer's Guide* online.

See Also: **CView::OnDragOver, CView::OnDrop, CView::OnDropEx, CView::OnDragLeave, COleDropTarget::OnDragEnter**

CView::OnDragLeave

virtual void OnDragLeave( );

Remarks

Called by the framework during a drag operation when the mouse is moved out of the valid drop area for that window.

Override this function if the current view needs to clean up any actions taken during **OnDragEnter** or **OnDragOver** calls, such as removing any visual user feedback while the object was dragged and dropped.

See Also: **CView::OnDragEnter**, **CView::OnDragOver**, **CView::OnScroll**, **COleDropTarget::OnDragLeave**

CView::OnDragOver

virtual DROPEFFECT OnDragOver(COleDataObject* *pDataObject*,
↳ **DWORD** *dwKeyState*, **CPoint** *point* **);**

Return Value

A value from the **DROPEFFECT** enumerated type, which indicates the type of drop that would occur if the user dropped the object at this position. The type of drop often depends on the current key state as indicated by *dwKeyState*. A standard mapping of keystates to **DROPEFFECT** values is:

- **DROPEFFECT_NONE** The data object cannot be dropped in this window.
- **DROPEFFECT_LINK** for **MK_CONTROL | MK_SHIFT** Creates a linkage between the object and its server.
- **DROPEFFECT_COPY** for **MK_CONTROL** Creates a copy of the dropped object.
- **DROPEFFECT_MOVE** for **MK_ALT** Creates a copy of the dropped object and delete the original object. This is typically the default drop effect, when the view can accept the data object.

For more information, see the MFC Advanced Concepts sample OCLIENT online.

Parameters

pDataObject Points to the **COleDataObject** being dragged over the drop target.

dwKeyState Contains the state of the modifier keys. This is a combination of any number of the following: **MK_CONTROL**, **MK_SHIFT**, **MK_ALT**, **MK_LBUTTON**, **MK_MBUTTON**, and **MK_RBUTTON**.

point The current mouse position relative to the view client area.

Remarks

Called by the framework during a drag operation when the mouse is moved over the drop target window. The default implementation is to do nothing and return **DROPEFFECT_NONE**.

Override this function to give the user visual feedback during the drag operation. Since this function is called continuously, any code contained within it should be optimized as much as possible. For more information, see the article "Drag and Drop: Implementing a Drop Target" in *Visual C++ Programmer's Guide* online.

See Also: **CView::OnDragEnter**, **CView::OnDrop**, **CView::OnDropEx**, **CView::OnDragLeave**, **COleDropTarget::OnDragOver**

CView::OnDragScroll

virtual DROPEFFECT OnDragScroll(DWORD *dwKeyState*, **CPoint** *point* **);**

Return Value

A value from the **DROPEFFECT** enumerated type, which indicates the type of drop that would occur if the user dropped the object at this position. The type of drop usually depends on the current key state indicated by *dwKeyState*. A standard mapping of keystates to **DROPEFFECT** values is:

- **DROPEFFECT_NONE**   The data object cannot be dropped in this window.
- **DROPEFFECT_LINK** for **MK_CONTROL | MK_SHIFT**   Creates a linkage between the object and its server.
- **DROPEFFECT_COPY** for **MK_CONTROL**   Creates a copy of the dropped object.
- **DROPEFFECT_MOVE** for **MK_ALT**   Creates a copy of the dropped object and delete the original object.
- **DROPEFFECT_SCROLL**   Indicates that a drag scroll operation is about to occur or is occurring in the target view.

For more information, see the MFC Advanced Concepts sample OCLIENT online.

Parameters

dwKeyState   Contains the state of the modifier keys. This is a combination of any number of the following: **MK_CONTROL**, **MK_SHIFT**, **MK_ALT**, **MK_LBUTTON**, **MK_MBUTTON**, and **MK_RBUTTON**.

point   Contains the location of the cursor, in pixels, relative to the screen.

Remarks

Called by the framework before calling **OnDragEnter** or **OnDragOver** to determine whether the point is in the scrolling region. Override this function when you want to provide special behavior for this event. The default implementation automatically scrolls windows when the cursor is dragged into the default scroll region inside the border of each window.For more information, see the article "Drag and Drop: Implementing a Drop Target" in *Visual C++ Programmer's Guide* online.

See Also: **CView::OnDragEnter**, **CView::OnDragOver**, **CView::OnDrop**, **CView::OnDragLeave**, **COleDropTarget::OnDragScroll**

CView::OnDraw

virtual void OnDraw(CDC* *pDC* **) = 0;**

Parameters

pDC   Points to the device context to be used for rendering an image of the document.

Remarks

Called by the framework to render an image of the document. The framework calls this function to perform screen display, printing, and print preview, and it passes a different device context in each case. There is no default implementation.

You must override this function to display your view of the document. You can make graphic device interface (GDI) calls using the **CDC** object pointed to by the *pDC* parameter. You can select GDI resources, such as pens or fonts, into the device context before drawing and then deselect them afterwards. Often your drawing code can be device-independent; that is, it doesn't require information about what type of device is displaying the image.

To optimize drawing, call the **RectVisible** member function of the device context to find out whether a given rectangle will be drawn. If you need to distinguish between normal screen display and printing, call the **IsPrinting** member function of the device context.

See Also: **CDC::IsPrinting**, **CDC::RectVisible**, **CView::OnPrint**, **CWnd::OnCreate**, **CWnd::OnDestroy**, **CWnd::PostNcDestroy**

CView::OnDrop

virtual BOOL OnDrop(COleDataObject* *pDataObject*,
  ↪ **DROPEFFECT** *dropEffect*, **CPoint** *point* **);**

Return Value

Nonzero if the drop was successful; otherwise 0.

Parameters

pDataObject   Points to the **COleDataObject** that is dropped into the drop target.

dropEffect   The drop effect that the user has requested.

- **DROPEFFECT_COPY**   Creates a copy of the data object being dropped.

- **DROPEFFECT_MOVE**   Moves the data object to the current mouse location.

- **DROPEFFECT_LINK** Creates a link between a data object and its server.

point The current mouse position relative to the view client area.

Remarks

Called by the framework when the user releases a data object over a valid drop target. The default implementation does nothing and returns **FALSE**.

Override this function to implement the effect of an OLE drop into the client area of the view. The data object can be examined via *pDataObject* for Clipboard data formats and data dropped at the specified point.

Note The framework does not call this function if there is an override to **OnDropEx** in this view class.

See Also: **CView::OnDragEnter, CView::OnDragOver, CView::OnDropEx, CView::OnDragLeave, COleDropTarget::OnDrop**

CView::OnDropEx

virtual DROPEFFECT OnDropEx(COleDataObject* *pDataObject,*
↳ **DROPEFFECT** *dropDefault,* **DROPEFFECT** *dropList,* **CPoint** *point* **);**

Return Value

The drop effect that resulted from the drop attempt at the location specified by *point*. This must be one of the values indicated by *dropEffectList*. Drop effects are discussed in the Remarks section.

Parameters

pDataObject Points to the **COleDataObject** that is dropped into the drop target.

dropDefault The effect that the user chose for the default drop operation based on the current key state. It may be **DROPEFFECT_NONE**. Drop effects are discussed in the Remarks section.

dropList A list of the drop effects that the drop source supports. Drop effect values can be combined using the bitwise OR (l) operation. Drop effects are discussed in the Remarks section.

point The current mouse position relative to the view client area.

Remarks

Called by the framework when the user releases a data object over a valid drop target. The default implementation is to do nothing and return a dummy value (−1) to indicate that the framework should call the **OnDrop** handler.

Override this function to implement the effect of an right mouse-button drag and drop. Right mouse-button drag and drop typically displays a menu of choices when the right mouse-button is released.

Your override of **OnDropEx** should query for the right mouse-button. You can call **GetKeyState** or store the right mouse-button state from your **OnDragEnter** handler.

- If the right mouse-button is down, your override should display a popup menu which offers the drop effects support by the drop source.

    - Examine *dropList* to determine the drop effects supported by the drop source. Enable only these actions on the popup menu.

    - Use **SetMenuDefaultItem** to set the default action based on *dropDefault*.

    - Finally, take the action indicated by the user selection from the popup menu.

- If the right mouse-button is not down, your override should process this as a standard drop request. Use the drop effect specified in *dropDefault*. Alternately, your override can return the dummy value (−1) to indicate that **OnDrop** will handle this drop operation.

Use *pDataObject* to examine the **COleDataObject** for Clipboard data format and data dropped at the specified point.

Drop effects describe the action associated with a drop operation. See the following list of drop effects:

- **DROPEFFECT_NONE**   A drop would not be allowed.
- **DROPEFFECT_COPY**   A copy operation would be performed.
- **DROPEFFECT_MOVE**   A move operation would be performed.
- **DROPEFFECT_LINK**   A link from the dropped data to the original data would be established.
- **DROPEFFECT_SCROLL**   Indicates that a drag scroll operation is about to occur or is occurring in the target.

For more information on setting the default menu command, see **SetMenuDefaultItem** in the Win32 documentation and **CMenu::GetSafeHmenu** in this volume.

See Also: **CView::OnDragEnter**, **CView::OnDragOver**, **CView::OnDrop**, **CView::OnDragLeave**, **COleDropTarget::OnDropEx**

CView::OnEndPrinting

virtual void OnEndPrinting(CDC* *pDC*, **CPrintInfo*** *pInfo* **);**

Parameters

pDC   Points to the printer device context.

pInfo   Points to a **CPrintInfo** structure that describes the current print job.

Remarks

Called by the framework after a document has been printed or previewed. The default implementation of this function does nothing. Override this function to free any GDI resources you allocated in the **OnBeginPrinting** member function.

See Also: **CView::OnBeginPrinting**

CView::OnEndPrintPreview

virtual void OnEndPrintPreview(CDC* *pDC*, **CPrintInfo*** *pInfo*,
↪ **POINT** *point*, **CPreviewView*** *pView* **);**

Parameters

pDC   Points to the printer device context.

pInfo   Points to a **CPrintInfo** structure that describes the current print job.

point   Specifies the point on the page that was last displayed in preview mode.

pView   Points to the view object used for previewing.

Remarks

Called by the framework when the user exits print preview mode. The default implementation of this function calls the **OnEndPrinting** member function and restores the main frame window to the state it was in before print preview began. Override this function to perform special processing when preview mode is terminated. For example, if you want to maintain the user's position in the document when switching from preview mode to normal display mode, you can scroll to the position described by the *point* parameter and the **m_nCurPage** member of the **CPrintInfo** structure that the *pInfo* parameter points to.

Always call the base class version of **OnEndPrintPreview** from your override, typically at the end of the function.

See Also: **CPrintInfo, CView::OnEndPrinting**

CView::OnInitialUpdate

virtual void OnInitialUpdate( );

Remarks

Called by the framework after the view is first attached to the document, but before the view is initially displayed. The default implementation of this function calls the **OnUpdate** member function with no hint information (that is, using the default values of 0 for the *lHint* parameter and **NULL** for the *pHint* parameter). Override this function to perform any one-time initialization that requires information about the document. For example, if your application has fixed-sized documents, you can use this function to initialize a view's scrolling limits based on the document size. If your application supports variable-sized documents, use **OnUpdate** to update the scrolling limits every time the document changes.

See Also: **CView::OnUpdate**

CView::OnPrepareDC

virtual void OnPrepareDC(CDC* *pDC***, CPrintInfo*** *pInfo* **= NULL);**

Parameters

pDC   Points to the device context to be used for rendering an image of the document.

pInfo   Points to a **CPrintInfo** structure that describes the current print job if **OnPrepareDC** is being called for printing or print preview; the **m_nCurPage** member specifies the page about to be printed. This parameter is **NULL** if **OnPrepareDC** is being called for screen display.

Remarks

Called by the framework before the **OnDraw** member function is called for screen display and before the **OnPrint** member function is called for each page during printing or print preview. The default implementation of this function does nothing if the function is called for screen display. However, this function is overridden in derived classes, such as **CScrollView**, to adjust attributes of the device context; consequently, you should always call the base class implementation at the beginning of your override.

If the function is called for printing, the default implementation examines the page information stored in the *pInfo* parameter. If the length of the document has not been specified, **OnPrepareDC** assumes the document to be one page long and stops the print loop after one page has been printed. The function stops the print loop by setting the **m_bContinuePrinting** member of the structure to **FALSE**.

Override **OnPrepareDC** for any of the following reasons:

- To adjust attributes of the device context as needed for the specified page. For example, if you need to set the mapping mode or other characteristics of the device context, do so in this function.

- To perform print-time pagination. Normally you specify the length of the document when printing begins, using the **OnPreparePrinting** member function. However, if you don't know in advance how long the document is (for example, when printing an undetermined number of records from a database), override **OnPrepareDC** to test for the end of the document while it is being printed. When there is no more of the document to be printed, set the **m_bContinuePrinting** member of the **CPrintInfo** structure to **FALSE**.

- To send escape codes to the printer on a page-by-page basis. To send escape codes from **OnPrepareDC**, call the **Escape** member function of the *pDC* parameter.

Call the base class version of **OnPrepareDC** at the beginning of your override.

See Also: **CDC::Escape, CPrintInfo, CView::OnBeginPrinting,
CView::OnDraw, CView::OnPreparePrinting, CView::OnPrint**

CView::OnPreparePrinting

virtual BOOL OnPreparePrinting(CPrintInfo* *pInfo* **);**

Return Value

Nonzero to begin printing; 0 if the print job has been canceled.

Parameters

pInfo   Points to a **CPrintInfo** structure that describes the current print job.

Remarks

Called by the framework before a document is printed or previewed. The default implementation does nothing.

You must override this function to enable printing and print preview. Call the **DoPreparePrinting** member function, passing it the *pInfo* parameter, and then return its return value; **DoPreparePrinting** displays the Print dialog box and creates a printer device context. If you want to initialize the Print dialog box with values other than the defaults, assign values to the members of *pInfo*. For example, if you know the length of the document, pass the value to the **SetMaxPage** member function of *pInfo* before calling **DoPreparePrinting**. This value is displayed in the To: box in the Range portion of the Print dialog box.

DoPreparePrinting does not display the Print dialog box for a preview job. If you want to bypass the Print dialog box for a print job, check that the **m_bPreview** member of *pInfo* is **FALSE** and then set it to **TRUE** before passing it to **DoPreparePrinting**; reset it to **FALSE** afterwards.

If you need to perform initializations that require access to the **CDC** object representing the printer device context (for example, if you need to know the page size before specifying the length of the document), override the **OnBeginPrinting** member function.

If you want to set the value of the **m_nNumPreviewPages** or **m_strPageDesc** members of the *pInfo* parameter, do so after calling **DoPreparePrinting**. The **DoPreparePrinting** member function sets **m_nNumPreviewPages** to the value found in the application's .INI file and sets **m_strPageDesc** to its default value.

Example

The following is an override of **OnPreparePrinting** provided by AppWizard if you select the printing option when you create a set of starter files. This override is sufficient unless you want to initialize the Print dialog box.

```
BOOL CMyView::OnPreparePrinting( CPrintInfo *pInfo )
{
    return DoPreparePrinting( pInfo );
}
```

See Also: **CPrintInfo**, **CView::DoPreparePrinting**, **CView::OnBeginPrinting**, **CView::OnPrepareDC**, **CView::OnPrint**

CView::OnPrint

virtual void OnPrint(CDC* *pDC*, CPrintInfo* *pInfo*);

Parameters

pDC   Points to the printer device context.

pInfo   Points to a **CPrintInfo** structure that describes the current print job.

Remarks

Called by the framework to print or preview a page of the document. For each page being printed, the framework calls this function immediately after calling the **OnPrepareDC** member function. The page being printed is specified by the **m_nCurPage** member of the **CPrintInfo** structure that *pInfo* points to. The default implementation calls the **OnDraw** member function and passes it the printer device context.

Override this function for any of the following reasons:

- To allow printing of multipage documents. Render only the portion of the document that corresponds to the page currently being printed. If you're using **OnDraw** to perform the rendering, you can adjust the viewport origin so that only the appropriate portion of the document is printed.

- To make the printed image look different from the screen image (that is, if your application is not WYSIWYG). Instead of passing the printer device context to **OnDraw**, use the device context to render an image using attributes not shown on the screen.

  If you need GDI resources for printing that you don't use for screen display, select them into the device context before drawing and deselect them afterwards. These GDI resources should be allocated in **OnBeginPrinting** and released in **OnEndPrinting**.

- To implement headers or footers. You can still use **OnDraw** to do the rendering by restricting the area that it can print on.

Note that the **m_rectDraw** member of the *pInfo* parameter describes the printable area of the page in logical units.

Do not call **OnPrepareDC** in your override of **OnPrint**; the framework calls **OnPrepareDC** automatically before calling **OnPrint**.

Example

The following is a skeleton for an overridden **OnPrint** function:

```
void CMyView::OnPrint( CDC *pDC, CPrintInfo *pInfo )
{
    // Print headers and/or footers, if desired.
    // Find portion of document corresponding to pInfo->m_nCurPage.
    OnDraw( pDC );
}
```

See Also: **CView::OnBeginPrinting, CView::OnEndPrinting, CView::OnPrepareDC, CView::OnDraw**

CView::OnScroll

virtual BOOL CView::OnScroll(UINT *nScrollCode*, **UINT** *nPos*,
→ **BOOL** *bDoScroll* = **TRUE**);

Return Value

If *bDoScroll* is **TRUE** and the view was actually scrolled, then return nonzero; otherwise 0. If *bDoScroll* is **FALSE**, then return the value that you would have returned if *bDoScroll* were **TRUE**, even though you don't actually do the scrolling.

Parameters

nScrollCode   A scroll-bar code that indicates the user's scrolling request. This parameter is composed of two parts: a low-order byte, which determines the type of scrolling occurring horizontally, and a high-order byte, which determines the type of scrolling occurring vertically:

- **SB_BOTTOM**   Scrolls to bottom.

- **SB_LINEDOWN**   Scrolls one line down.

- **SB_LINEUP**   Scrolls one line up.

- **SB_PAGEDOWN**   Scrolls one page down.

- **SB_PAGEUP**   Scrolls one page up.

- **SB_THUMBTRACK**   Drags scroll box to specified position. The current position is specified in *nPos*.

- **SB_TOP**   Scrolls to top.

nPos   Contains the current scroll-box position if the scroll-bar code is **SB_THUMBTRACK**; otherwise it is not used. Depending on the initial scroll range, *nPos* may be negative and should be cast to an **int** if necessary.

bDoScroll   Determines whether you should actually do the specified scrolling action. If **TRUE,** then scrolling should take place; if **FALSE,** then scrolling should not occur.

Remarks

Called by the framework to determine whether scrolling is possible.

In one case this function is called by the framework with *bDoScroll* set to **TRUE** when the view receives a scrollbar message. In this case, you should actually scroll the view. In the other case this function is called with *bDoScroll* set to **FALSE** when an OLE item is initially dragged into the auto-scrolling region of a drop target before scrolling actually takes place. In this case, you should not actually scroll the view.

See Also: **CView::OnScrollBy**, **COleClientItem**

CView::OnScrollBy

> **BOOL CView::OnScrollBy(CSize** *sizeScroll*, **BOOL** *bDoScroll* = **TRUE**);

Return Value

Nonzero if the view was able to be scrolled; otherwise 0.

Parameters

sizeScroll   Number of pixels scrolled horizontally and vertically.

bDoScroll   Determines whether scrolling of the view occurs. If **TRUE,** then scrolling takes place; if **FALSE**, then scrolling does not occur.

Remarks

Called by the framework when the user views an area beyond the present view of the document, either by dragging an OLE item against the view's current borders or by manipulating the vertical or horizontal scrollbars. The default implementation does nothing. In derived classes the function checks to see whether the view is scrollable in the direction the user requested and then updates the new region if necessary. This function is automatically called by **CWnd::OnHScroll** and **CWnd::OnVScroll** to perform the actual scrolling request.

CView::OnUpdate

> **virtual void OnUpdate(CView*** *pSender*, **LPARAM** *lHint*, **CObject*** *pHint*);

Parameters

pSender   Points to the view that modified the document, or **NULL** if all views are to be updated.

lHint   Contains information about the modifications.

pHint   Points to an object storing information about the modifications.

Remarks

Called by the framework after the view's document has been modified; this function is called by **CDocument::UpdateAllViews** and allows the view to update its display to reflect those modifications. It is also called by the default implementation of **OnInitialUpdate**. The default implementation invalidates the entire client area, marking it for painting when the next **WM_PAINT** message is received. Override this function if you want to update only those regions that map to the modified portions of the document. To do this you must pass information about the modifications using the hint parameters.

To use *lHint*, define special hint values, typically a bitmask or an enumerated type, and have the document pass one of these values. To use *pHint*, derive a hint class from **CObject** and have the document pass a pointer to a hint object; when overriding **OnUpdate**, use the **CObject::IsKindOf** member function to determine the run-time type of the hint object.

Typically you should not perform any drawing directly from **OnUpdate**. Instead, determine the rectangle describing, in device coordinates, the area that requires updating; pass this rectangle to **CWnd::InvalidateRect**. This causes painting to occur the next time a **WM_PAINT** message is received.

If *lHint* is 0 and *pHint* is **NULL**, the document has sent a generic update notification. If a view receives a generic update notification, or if it cannot decode the hints, it should invalidate its entire client area.

See Also: CDocument::UpdateAllViews, CView::OnInitialUpdate, CWnd::Invalidate, CWnd::InvalidateRect

CWaitCursor

CWaitCursor does not have a base class.

The **CWaitCursor** class provides a one-line way to show a wait cursor, which is usually displayed as an hourglass, while you're doing a lengthy operation. Good Windows programming practices require that you display a wait cursor whenever you're performing an operation that takes a noticeable amount of time.

To display a wait cursor, just define a **CWaitCursor** variable before the code that performs the lengthy operation. The object's constructor automatically causes the wait cursor to be displayed.

When the object goes out of scope (at the end of the block in which the **CWaitCursor** object is declared), its destructor sets the cursor to the previous cursor. In other words, the object performs the necessary clean-up automatically.

Note Because of how their constructors and destructors work, **CWaitCursor** objects are always declared as local variables—they're never declared as global variables nor are they allocated with **new**.

If you perform an operation which might cause the cursor to be changed, such as displaying a message box or dialog box, call the **Restore** member function to restore the wait cursor. It is okay to call **Restore** even when a wait cursor is currently displayed.

Another way to display a wait cursor is to use the combination of **CCmdTarget::BeginWaitCursor**, **CCmdTarget::EndWaitCursor**, and perhaps **CCmdTarget::RestoreWaitCursor**. However, **CWaitCursor** is easier to use because you don't need to set the cursor to the previous cursor when you're done with the lengthy operation.

Note MFC sets and restores the cursor using the **CWinApp::DoWaitCursor** virtual function. You can override this function to provide custom behavior.

#include <afxwin.h>

See Also: **CCmdTarget::BeginWaitCursor**, **CCmdTarget::EndWaitCursor**, **CCmdTarget::RestoreWaitCursor**, **CWinApp::DoWaitCursor**

CWaitCursor Class Members

Construction/Destruction

CWaitCursor   Constructs a **CWaitCursor** object and displays the wait cursor.

Operations

Restore   Restores the wait cursor after it's been changed.

Member Functions
CWaitCursor::CWaitCursor

CWaitCursor( );

Remarks

To display a wait cursor, just declare a **CWaitCursor** object before the code that performs the lengthy operation. The constructor automatically causes the wait cursor to be displayed.

When the object goes out of scope (at the end of the block in which the **CWaitCursor** object is declared), its destructor sets the cursor to the previous cursor. In other words, the object performs the necessary clean-up automatically.

You can take advantage of the fact that the destructor is called at the end of the block (which might be before the end of the function) to make the wait cursor active in only part of your function. This technique is shown in the second example below.

Note Because of how their constructors and destructors work, **CWaitCursor** objects are always declared as local variables—they're never declared as global variables, nor are they allocated with **new**.

Example

```
// The following example illustrates the most common case
// of displaying the wait cursor during some lengthy
// processing.

void LengthyFunction( )
{
    // perhaps you display a dialog box before displaying a
    // wait cursor

    CWaitCursor wait; // display wait cursor

    // do some lengthy processing

}  // destructor automatically removes the wait cursor
```

```
// This example shows using a CWaitCursor object inside a block
// so the wait cursor is displayed only while the program is
// performing a lengthy operation.

void ConditionalFunction( )
{
    if ( SomeCondition )
    {
        CWaitCursor wait; // display wait cursor in this block only

        // do some lengthy processing

    }  // at this point, the destructor removes the wait cursor
    else
    {
        // no wait cursor--only quick processing
    }
}
```

See Also: **CWaitCursor::Restore**, **CCmdTarget::BeginWaitCursor**,
CCmdTarget::EndWaitCursor

CWaitCursor::Restore

void Restore( );

Remarks

To restore the wait cursor, call this function after performing an operation, such as displaying a message box or dialog box, which might change the wait cursor to another cursor.

It is OK to call **Restore** even when the wait cursor is currently displayed.

If you need to restore the wait cursor while in a function other than the one in which the **CWaitCursor** object is declared, you can call **CCmdTarget::RestoreWaitCursor**.

Examples

```
// This example illustrates performing an operation
// which changes the wait cursor. You should call
// CWaitCursor::Restore to restore the wait
// cursor after an operation which changes the cursor.

void AnotherLengthyFunction( )
{
    CWaitCursor wait; // display wait cursor

    // do some lengthy processing

    // The dialog box will normally change the cursor to
    // the standard arrow cursor.
    CSomeDialog dlg;
    dlg.DoModal( );
```

```
    // It is necessary to call Restore here in order
    // to change the cursor back to the wait cursor.
    wait.Restore( );

    // do some more lengthy processing

    // destructor automatically removes the wait cursor
}

// If the wait cursor is changed by a function called by
// the function which created the wait cursor, you
// can call CCmdTarget::RestoreWaitCursor to restore
// the wait cursor.
void CalledFunction()
{
    CSomeDialog dlg;
    dlg.DoModal();

    // Since CWinApp is derived from CCmdTarget, we can use a
    // pointer to our application object to make the call to
    // CCmdTarget::RestoreWaitCursor.
    AfxGetApp()->RestoreWaitCursor( );

    // Yet more lengthy processing...
}
```

See Also: CCmdTarget::RestoreWaitCursor

CWinApp

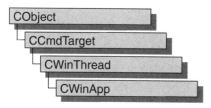

The **CWinApp** class is the base class from which you derive a Windows application object. An application object provides member functions for initializing your application (and each instance of it) and for running the application.

Each application that uses the Microsoft Foundation classes can only contain one object derived from **CWinApp**. This object is constructed when other C++ global objects are constructed and is already available when Windows calls the **WinMain** function, which is supplied by the Microsoft Foundation Class Library. Declare your derived **CWinApp** object at the global level.

When you derive an application class from **CWinApp**, override the **InitInstance** member function to create your application's main window object.

In addition to the **CWinApp** member functions, the Microsoft Foundation Class Library provides the following global functions to access your **CWinApp** object and other global information:

- **AfxGetApp**   Obtains a pointer to the **CWinApp** object.
- **AfxGetInstanceHandle**   Obtains a handle to the current application instance.
- **AfxGetResourceHandle**   Obtains a handle to the application's resources.
- **AfxGetAppName**   Obtains a pointer to a string containing the application's name. Alternately, if you have a pointer to the **CWinApp** object, use **m_pszExeName** to get the application's name.

See "CWinApp: The Application Class" in *Visual C++ Programmer's Guide* online for more on the **CWinApp** class, including an overview of the following:

- **CWinApp**-derived code written by AppWizard.
- **CWinApp**'s role in the execution sequence of your application.
- **CWinApp**'s default member function implementations.
- **CWinApp**'s key overridables.

#include <afxwin.h>

CWinApp Class Members

Data Members

m_pszAppName	Specifies the name of the application.
m_hInstance	Identifies the current instance of the application.
m_hPrevInstance	Set to **NULL** in a 32-bit application.
m_lpCmdLine	Points to a null-terminated string that specifies the command line for the application.
m_nCmdShow	Specifies how the window is to be shown initially.
m_bHelpMode	Indicates if the user is in Help context mode (typically invoked with SHIFT+F1).
m_pActiveWnd	Pointer to the main window of the container application when an OLE server is in-place active.
m_pszExeName	The module name of the application.
m_pszHelpFilePath	The path to the application's Help file.
m_pszProfileName	The application's .INI filename.
m_pszRegistryKey	Used to determine the full registry key for storing application profile settings.

Construction

CWinApp	Constructs a **CWinApp** object.

Operations

LoadCursor	Loads a cursor resource.
LoadStandardCursor	Loads a Windows predefined cursor that the **IDC_** constants specify in WINDOWS.H.
LoadOEMCursor	Loads a Windows OEM predefined cursor that the **OCR_** constants specify in WINDOWS.H.
LoadIcon	Loads an icon resource.
LoadStandardIcon	Loads a Windows predefined icon that the **IDI_** constants specify in WINDOWS.H.
LoadOEMIcon	Loads a Windows OEM predefined icon that the **OIC_** constants specify in WINDOWS.H.
RunAutomated	Tests the application's command line for the **/Automation** option. Obsolete. Use the value in **CCommandLineInfo::m_bRunEmbedded** after calling **ParseCommandLine**. instead.
RunEmbedded	Tests the application's command line for the **/Embedding** option. Obsolete. Use the value in **CCommandLineInfo::m_bRunEmbedded** after calling **ParseCommandLine**. instead.

Operations *(continued)*

ParseCommandLine	Parses individual parameters and flags in the command line.
ProcessShellCommand	Handles command-line arguments and flags.
GetProfileInt	Retrieves an integer from an entry in the application's .INI file.
WriteProfileInt	Writes an integer to an entry in the application's .INI file.
GetProfileString	Retrieves a string from an entry in the application's .INI file.
WriteProfileString	Writes a string to an entry in the application's .INI file.
AddDocTemplate	Adds a document template to the application's list of available document templates.
GetFirstDocTemplatePosition	Retrieves the position of the first document template.
GetNextDocTemplate	Retrieves the position of a document template. Can be used recursively.
OpenDocumentFile	Called by the framework to open a document from a file.
AddToRecentFileList	Adds a filename to the most recently used (MRU) file list.
SelectPrinter	Selects a printer previously indicated by a user through a print dialog box.
CreatePrinterDC	Creates a printer device context.
GetPrinterDeviceDefaults	Retrieves the printer device defaults.

Overridables

InitInstance	Override to perform Windows instance initialization, such as creating your window objects.
Run	Runs the default message loop. Override to customize the message loop.
OnIdle	Override to perform application-specific idle-time processing.
ExitInstance	Override to clean up when your application terminates.
HideApplication	Hides the application before closing all documents.
CloseAllDocuments	Closes all open documents.
PreTranslateMessage	Filters messages before they are dispatched to the Windows functions **::TranslateMessage** and **::DispatchMessage**.

(continued)

Overridables *(continued)*

SaveAllModified	Prompts the user to save all modified documents.
DoMessageBox	Implements **AfxMessageBox** for the application.
ProcessMessageFilter	Intercepts certain messages before they reach the application.
ProcessWndProcException	Intercepts all unhandled exceptions thrown by the application's message and command handlers.
DoWaitCursor	Turns the wait cursor on and off.
OnDDECommand	Called by the framework in response to a dynamic data exchange (DDE) execute command.
WinHelp	Calls the **WinHelp** Windows function.

Initialization

LoadStdProfileSettings	Loads standard .INI file settings and enables the MRU file list feature.
SetDialogBkColor	Sets the default background color for dialog boxes and message boxes.
SetRegistryKey	Causes application settings to be stored in the registry instead of .INI files.
EnableShellOpen	Allows the user to open data files from the Windows File Manager.
RegisterShellFileTypes	Registers all the application's document types with the Windows File Manager.
Enable3dControls	Enables controls with three-dimensional appearance.
Enable3dControlsStatic	Enables controls with a three-dimensional appearance.

Command Handlers

OnFileNew	Implements the **ID_FILE_NEW** command.
OnFileOpen	Implements the **ID_FILE_OPEN** command.
OnFilePrintSetup	Implements the **ID_FILE_PRINT_SETUP** command.
OnContextHelp	Handles SHIFT+F1 Help within the application.
OnHelp	Handles F1 Help within the application (using the current context).
OnHelpIndex	Handles the **ID_HELP_INDEX** command and provides a default Help topic.
OnHelpFinder	Handles the **ID_HELP_FINDER** and **ID_DEFAULT_HELP** commands.
OnHelpUsing	Handles the **ID_HELP_USING** command.

Member Functions
CWinApp::AddDocTemplate

void AddDocTemplate(CDocTemplate* *pTemplate* **);**

Parameters

pTemplate   A pointer to the **CDocTemplate** to be added.

Remarks

Call this member function to add a document template to the list of available document templates that the application maintains. You should add all document templates to an application before you call **RegisterShellFileTypes**.

Example

```
BOOL CMyApp::InitInstance()
{
    // ...
    // The following code is produced by AppWizard when you
    // choose the MDI (multiple document interface) option.
    CMultiDocTemplate* pDocTemplate;
    pDocTemplate = new CMultiDocTemplate(
        IDR_MYTYPE,
        RUNTIME_CLASS(CMyDoc),
        RUNTIME_CLASS(CMDIChildWnd),        // standard MDI child frame
        RUNTIME_CLASS(CMyView));
    AddDocTemplate(pDocTemplate);
    // ...
}
```

See Also: CWinApp::RegisterShellFileTypes, CMultiDocTemplate, CSingleDocTemplate

---

CWinApp::AddToRecentFileList

virtual void AddToRecentFileList(LPCTSTR *lpszPathName* **);**

Parameters

lpszPathName   The path of the file.

Remarks

Call this member function to add *lpszPathName* to the MRU file list. You should call the **LoadStdProfileSettings** member function to load the current MRU file list before you use this member function.

The framework calls this member function when it opens a file or executes the Save As command to save a file with a new name.

Example

```
// This adds the pathname c:\temp\test.doc to the top of
// the most recently used (MRU) list in the File menu.
 AfxGetApp()->AddToRecentFileList("c:\\temp\\test.doc");
```

See Also: **CWinApp::LoadStdProfileSettings**

CWinApp::CloseAllDocuments

void CloseAllDocuments(BOOL *bEndSession* **);**

Parameters

bEndSession   Specifies whether or not the Windows session is being ended. It is
TRUE if the session is being ended; otherwise **FALSE**.

Remarks

Call this member function to close all open documents before exiting. Call
HideApplication before calling **CloseAllDocuments**.

See Also: **CWinApp::SaveAllModified, CWinApp::HideApplication**

CWinApp::CreatePrinterDC

BOOL CreatePrinterDC(CDC& *dc* **);**

Return Value

Nonzero if the printer device context is created successfully; otherwise 0.

Parameters

dc   A reference to a printer device context.

Remarks

Call this member function to create a printer device context (DC) from the selected
printer.

See Also: **CWinApp::SelectPrinter**

CWinApp::CWinApp

CWinApp(LPCTSTR *lpszAppName* = **NULL);**

Parameters

lpszAppName   A null-terminated string that contains the application name that
Windows uses. If this argument is not supplied or is **NULL**, **CWinApp** uses the
resource string **AFX_IDS_APP_TITLE** or the filename of the executable file.

Remarks

Constructs a **CWinApp** object and passes *lpszAppName* to be stored as the application name. You should construct one global object of your **CWinApp**-derived class. You can have only one **CWinApp** object in your application. The constructor stores a pointer to the **CWinApp** object so that **WinMain** can call the object's member functions to initialize and run the application.

CWinApp::DoMessageBox

virtual int DoMessageBox(LPCTSTR *lpszPrompt*, **UINT** *nType*, **UINT** *nIDPrompt* **);**

Return Value

Returns the same values as **AfxMessageBox**.

Parameters

lpszPrompt   Address of text in the message box.

nType   The message box style.

nIDPrompt   An index to a Help context string.

Remarks

The framework calls this member function to implement a message box for the global function **AfxMessageBox**.

Do not call this member function to open a message box; use **AfxMessageBox** instead.

Override this member function to customize your application-wide processing of **AfxMessageBox** calls.

See Also: **AfxMessageBox**, **::MessageBox**

CWinApp::DoWaitCursor

virtual void DoWaitCursor(int *nCode* **);**

Parameters

nCode   If this parameter is 1, a wait cursor appears. If 0, the wait cursor is restored without incrementing the reference count. If –1, the wait cursor ends.

Remarks

This member function is called by the framework to implement **CWaitCursor**, **CCmdTarget::BeginWaitCursor**, **CCmdTarget::EndWaitCursor**, and **CCmdTarget::RestoreWaitCursor**. The default implements an hourglass cursor. **DoWaitCursor** maintains a reference count. When positive, the hourglass cursor is displayed.

While you would not normally call **DoWaitCursor** directly, you could override this member function to change the wait cursor or to do additional processing while the wait cursor is displayed.

For an easier, more streamlined way to implement a wait cursor, use **CWaitCursor**.

See Also: CCmdTarget::BeginWaitCursor, CCmdTarget::EndWaitCursor, CCmdTarget::RestoreWaitCursor, CWaitCursor

CWinApp::Enable3dControls

BOOL Enable3dControls( );
BOOL Enable3dControlsStatic( );

Note   Both **Enable3dControls** and **Enable3dControlsStatic** are described in this topic.

Return Value

TRUE if the CTL3D32.DLL is loaded successfully; otherwise **FALSE**.

This function will return **FALSE** if the operating system supports the three-dimensional look for controls.

Remarks

Call either of these member functions from your override of the **InitInstance** member function to enable dialog boxes and windows whose controls have a three-dimensional appearance. These member functions load the CTL3D32.DLL and registers the application with the DLL. If you call **Enable3dControls** or **Enable3dControlsStatic**, you do not need to call the **SetDialogBkColor** member function.

Enable3dControls should be used when linking to the MFC DLLs. **Enable3dControlsStatic** should be used when statically linking to the MFC libraries.

Feature Only in Professional and Enterprise Editions   Static linking to MFC is supported only in Visual C++ Professional and Enterprise Editions. For more information, see *Visual C++ Editions* online.

MFC automatically provides 3D control effects for the following classes of windows:

- **CDialog**
- **CDialogBar**
- **CFormView**
- **CPropertyPage**
- **CPropertySheet**
- **CControlBar**
- **CToolBar**

If the controls for which you want a 3D effect are in a window of any of these types, all you need is the enabling call to **Enable3dControls** or **Enable3dControlsStatic**. If you want to give a 3D effect to controls in windows based on other classes, you must call the CTL3D32 API functions directly.

Example

```
#ifdef _AFXDLL
    Enable3dControls( );    //Call Enable3dControls
#else
    Enable3dControlsStatic( );
//Call Enable3dControlsStatic
#endif
```

See Also: CWinApp::InitInstance, CWinApp::SetDialogBkColor

CWinApp::EnableShellOpen

void EnableShellOpen( );

Remarks

Call this function, typically from your **InitInstance** override, to enable your application's users to open data files when they double-click the files from within the Windows File Manager. Call the **RegisterShellFileTypes** member function in conjunction with this function, or provide a .REG file with your application for manual registration of document types.

Example

```
BOOL CMyApp::InitInstance()
{
    // ...

    CMultiDocTemplate* pDocTemplate;
    pDocTemplate = new CMultiDocTemplate(
        IDR_MYTYPE,
        RUNTIME_CLASS(CMyDoc),
        RUNTIME_CLASS(CMDIChildWnd),        // standard MDI child frame
        RUNTIME_CLASS(CMyView));
    AddDocTemplate(pDocTemplate);

    // Create main MDI Frame window.
    CMainFrame* pMainFrame = new CMainFrame;
    if (!pMainFrame->LoadFrame(IDR_MAINFRAME))
        return FALSE;
    // Save the pointer to the main frame window.  This is the
    // only way the framework will have knowledge of what the
    // main frame window is.
    m_pMainWnd = pMainFrame;

    // enable file manager drag/drop and DDE Execute open
    EnableShellOpen();
    RegisterShellFileTypes();
    // ...
```

```
// Show the   main window using the nCmdShow parameter
// passed to the application when it was first launched.
pMainFrame->ShowWindow(m_nCmdShow);
pMainFrame->UpdateWindow();

// ...
}
```

See Also: **CWinApp::OnDDECommand**, **CWinApp::RegisterShellFileTypes**

CWinApp::ExitInstance

virtual int ExitInstance( );

Return Value

The application's exit code; 0 indicates no errors, and values greater than 0 indicate an error. This value is used as the return value from **WinMain**.

Remarks

Called by the framework from within the **Run** member function to exit this instance of the application.

Do not call this member function from anywhere but within the **Run** member function.

The default implementation of this function writes framework options to the application's .INI file. Override this function to clean up when your application terminates.

See Also: **CWinApp::Run**, **CWinApp::InitInstance**

CWinApp::GetFirstDocTemplatePosition

POSITION GetFirstDocTemplatePosition( ) const;

Return Value

A **POSITION** value that can be used for iteration or object pointer retrieval; **NULL** if the list is empty.

Remarks

Gets the position of the first document template in the application. Use the **POSITION** value returned in a call to **GetNextDocTemplate** to get the first **CDocTemplate** object.

See Also: **CWinApp::AddDocTemplate**, **CWinApp::GetNextDocTemplate**

CWinApp::GetNextDocTemplate

CDocTemplate* GetNextDocTemplate(POSITION& *pos* **) const;**

Return Value

A pointer to a **CDocTemplate** object.

Parameters

pos   A reference to a **POSITION** value returned by a previous call to
GetNextDocTemplate or **GetFirstDocTemplatePosition**. The value is updated to
the next position by this call.

Remarks

Gets the document template identified by *pos*, then sets *pos* to the **POSITION** value.
You can use **GetNextDocTemplate** in a forward iteration loop if you establish the
initial position with a call to **GetFirstDocTemplatePosition**.

You must ensure that your **POSITION** value is valid. If it is invalid, then the Debug
version of the Microsoft Foundation Class Library asserts.

If the retrieved document template is the last available, then the new value of *pos* is
set to **NULL**.

See Also: CWinApp::AddDocTemplate,
CWinApp::GetFirstDocTemplatePosition

CWinApp::GetPrinterDeviceDefaults

BOOL GetPrinterDeviceDefaults(PRINTDLG* *pPrintDlg* **);**

Return Value

Nonzero if successful; otherwise 0.

Parameters

pPrintDlg   A pointer to a **PRINTDLG** structure.

Remarks

Call this member function to prepare a printer device context for printing. Retrieves
the current printer defaults from the Windows .INI file as necessary, or uses the last
printer configuration set by the user in Print Setup.

See Also: CPrintDialog

CWinApp::GetProfileInt

UINT GetProfileInt(LPCTSTR *lpszSection*, **LPCTSTR** *lpszEntry*, **int** *nDefault* **);**

Return Value

The integer value of the string that follows the specified entry if the function is successful. The return value is the value of the *nDefault* parameter if the function does not find the entry. The return value is 0 if the value that corresponds to the specified entry is not an integer.

This member function supports hexadecimal notation for the value in the .INI file. When you retrieve a signed integer, you should cast the value into an **int**.

Parameters

lpszSection   Points to a null-terminated string that specifies the section containing the entry.

lpszEntry   Points to a null-terminated string that contains the entry whose value is to be retrieved.

nDefault   Specifies the default value to return if the framework cannot find the entry. This value can be an unsigned value in the range 0 through 65,535 or a signed value in the range –32,768 through 32,767.

Remarks

Call this member function to retrieve the value of an integer from an entry within a specified section of the application's .INI file.

This member function is not case sensitive, so the strings in the *lpszSection* and *lpszEntry* parameters may differ in case.

See Also: CWinApp::GetProfileString, CWinApp::WriteProfileInt, ::GetPrivateProfileInt

---

CWinApp::GetProfileString

CString GetProfileString(LPCTSTR *lpszSection*, **LPCTSTR** *lpszEntry*,
   ↪ **LPCTSTR** *lpszDefault* = **NULL** **);**

Return Value

The return value is the string from the application's .INI file or *lpszDefault* if the string cannot be found. The maximum string length supported by the framework is **_MAX_PATH**. If *lpszDefault* is **NULL**, the return value is an empty string.

Parameters

lpszSection   Points to a null-terminated string that specifies the section containing the entry.

lpszEntry　Points to a null-terminated string that contains the entry whose string is to be retrieved. This value must not be **NULL**.

lpszDefault　Points to the default string value for the given entry if the entry cannot be found in the initialization file.

Remarks

Call this member function to retrieve the string associated with an entry within the specified section in the application's .INI file.

Example

```
CString strSection       = "My Section";
CString strStringItem    = "My String Item";
CString strIntItem       = "My Int Item";

CWinApp* pApp = AfxGetApp();

pApp->WriteProfileString(strSection, strStringItem, "test");

CString strValue;
strValue = pApp->GetProfileString(strSection, strStringItem);
ASSERT(strValue == "test");

pApp->WriteProfileInt(strSection, strIntItem, 1234);
int nValue;
nValue = pApp->GetProfileInt(strSection, strIntItem, 0);
ASSERT(nValue == 1234);
```

See Also:　**CWinApp::GetProfileInt**, **CWinApp::WriteProfileString**, **::GetPrivateProfileString**

CWinApp::HideApplication

void HideApplication( );

Remarks

Call this member function to hide an application before closing the open documents.

See Also:　**CWinApp::CloseAllDocuments**

CWinApp::InitInstance

virtual BOOL InitInstance( );

Return Value

Nonzero if initialization is successful; otherwise 0.

Remarks

Windows allows several copies of the same program to run at the same time. Application initialization is conceptually divided into two sections: one-time application initialization that is done the first time the program runs, and instance initialization that runs each time a copy of the program runs, including the first time. The framework's implementation of **WinMain** calls this function.

Override **InitInstance** to initialize each new instance of your application running under Windows. Typically, you override **InitInstance** to construct your main window object and set the **CWinThread::m_pMainWnd** data member to point to that window. For more information on overriding this member function, see "CWinApp: The Application Class" in *Visual C++ Programmer's Guide* online.

Example

```
// AppWizard implements the InitInstance overridable function
// according to options you select.  For example, the single document
// interface (SDI) option was chosen for the AppWizard code created
// below. You can add other per-instance initializations to the code
// created by AppWizard.

BOOL CMyApp::InitInstance()
{
    // Standard initialization
    // If you are not using these features and wish to reduce the size
    //  of your final executable, you should remove from the following
    //  the specific initialization routines you do not need.

    SetDialogBkColor();          // Set dialog background color to gray
    LoadStdProfileSettings();  // Load standard INI file options (including MRU)

    // Register the application's document templates.  Document templates
    //  serve as the connection between documents, frame windows and views.

    CSingleDocTemplate* pDocTemplate;
    pDocTemplate = new CSingleDocTemplate(
        IDR_MAINFRAME,
        RUNTIME_CLASS(CMyDoc),
        RUNTIME_CLASS(CMainFrame),       // main SDI frame window
        RUNTIME_CLASS(CMyView));
    AddDocTemplate(pDocTemplate);

    // create a new (empty) document
    OnFileNew();

    if (m_lpCmdLine[0] != '\0')
    {
        // TODO: add command line processing here
    }

    return TRUE;
}
```

CWinApp::LoadCursor

HCURSOR LoadCursor(LPCTSTR *lpszResourceName*) **const;**
HCURSOR LoadCursor(UINT *nIDResource*) **const;**

Return Value

A handle to a cursor if successful; otherwise **NULL**.

Parameters

lpszResourceName   Points to a null-terminated string that contains the name of the cursor resource. You can use a **CString** for this argument.

nIDResource   ID number of the cursor resource.

Remarks

Loads the cursor resource named by *lpszResourceName* or specified by *nIDResource* from the current executable file. **LoadCursor** loads the cursor into memory only if it has not been previously loaded; otherwise, it retrieves a handle of the existing resource.

Use the **LoadStandardCursor** or **LoadOEMCursor** member function to access the predefined Windows cursors.

Example

```
HCURSOR hCursor;

    // Load a cursor resource that was originally created using
    // the Graphics Editor and assigned the i.d. IDC_MYCURSOR.
    hCursor = AfxGetApp()->LoadCursor(IDC_MYCURSOR);
```

**See Also: CWinApp::LoadStandardCursor, CWinApp::LoadOEMCursor,
::LoadCursor**

CWinApp::LoadIcon

HICON LoadIcon(LPCTSTR *lpszResourceName*) **const;**
HICON LoadIcon(UINT *nIDResource*) **const;**

Return Value

A handle to an icon if successful; otherwise **NULL**.

Parameters

lpszResourceName   Points to a null-terminated string that contains the name of the icon resource. You can also use a **CString** for this argument.

nIDResource   ID number of the icon resource.

Remarks

Loads the icon resource named by *lpszResourceName* or specified by *nIDResource* from the executable file. **LoadIcon** loads the icon only if it has not been previously loaded; otherwise, it retrieves a handle of the existing resource.

You can use the **LoadStandardIcon** or **LoadOEMIcon** member function to access the predefined Windows icons.

Note This member function calls the Win32 API function **LoadIcon**, which can only load an icon whose size conforms to the **SM_CXICON** and **SM_CYICON** system metric values.

See Also: **CWinApp::LoadStandardIcon**, **CWinApp::LoadOEMIcon**, **::LoadIcon**

CWinApp::LoadOEMCursor

HCURSOR LoadOEMCursor(UINT *nIDCursor* **) const;**

Return Value

A handle to a cursor if successful; otherwise **NULL**.

Parameters

nIDCursor An **OCR_** manifest constant identifier that specifies a predefined Windows cursor. You must have **#define OEMRESOURCE** before **#include <afxwin.h>** to gain access to the **OCR_** constants in WINDOWS.H.

Remarks

Loads the Windows predefined cursor resource specified by *nIDCursor*.

Use the **LoadOEMCursor** or **LoadStandardCursor** member function to access the predefined Windows cursors.

Example

```
// In the stdafx.h file, add #define OEMRESOURCE to
// include the windows.h definitions of OCR_ values.
#define OEMRESOURCE
#include <afxwin.h>          // MFC core and standard components
#include <afxext.h>          // MFC extensions (including VB)

   HCURSOR hCursor;
   // Load the predefined WIndows "size all" cursor.
   hCursor = AfxGetApp()->LoadOEMCursor(OCR_SIZEALL);
```

See Also: **CWinApp::LoadCursor**, **CWinApp::LoadStandardCursor**, **::LoadCursor**

CWinApp::LoadOEMIcon

HICON LoadOEMIcon(UINT *nIDIcon* **) const;**

Return Value

A handle to an icon if successful; otherwise **NULL**.

Parameters

nIDIcon   An **OIC_** manifest constant identifier that specifies a predefined Windows icon. You must have **#define OEMRESOURCE** before **#include <afxwin.h>** to access the **OIC_** constants in WINDOWS.H.

Remarks

Loads the Windows predefined icon resource specified by *nIDIcon*.

Use the **LoadOEMIcon** or **LoadStandardIcon** member function to access the predefined Windows icons.

See Also: **CWinApp::LoadStandardIcon, CWinApp::LoadIcon, ::LoadIcon**

CWinApp::LoadStandardCursor

HCURSOR LoadStandardCursor(LPCTSTR *lpszCursorName* **) const;**

Return Value

A handle to a cursor if successful; otherwise **NULL**.

Parameters

lpszCursorName   An **IDC_** manifest constant identifier that specifies a predefined Windows cursor. These identifiers are defined in WINDOWS.H. The following list shows the possible predefined values and meanings for *lpszCursorName*:

- **IDC_ARROW**   Standard arrow cursor

- **IDC_IBEAM**   Standard text-insertion cursor

- **IDC_WAIT**   Hourglass cursor used when Windows performs a time-consuming task

- **IDC_CROSS**   Cross-hair cursor for selection

- **IDC_UPARROW**   Arrow that points straight up

- **IDC_SIZE**   Obsolete and unsupported; use **IDC_SIZEALL**

- **IDC_SIZEALL**   A four-pointed arrow. The cursor to use to resize a window.

- **IDC_ICON**   Obsolete and unsupported. Use **IDC_ARROW**.

- **IDC_SIZENWSE**   Two-headed arrow with ends at upper left and lower right

- **IDC_SIZENESW**   Two-headed arrow with ends at upper right and lower left

- **IDC_SIZEWE** Horizontal two-headed arrow

- **IDC_SIZENS** Vertical two-headed arrow

Remarks

Loads the Windows predefined cursor resource that *lpszCursorName* specifies.

Use the **LoadStandardCursor** or **LoadOEMCursor** member function to access the predefined Windows cursors.

Example

```
HCURSOR hCursor;

// Load the predefined Windows "up arrow" cursor.
hCursor = AfxGetApp()->LoadStandardCursor(IDC_UPARROW);
```

See Also: **CWinApp::LoadOEMCursor, CWinApp::LoadCursor, ::LoadCursor**

CWinApp::LoadStandardIcon

HICON LoadStandardIcon(LPCTSTR *lpszIconName* **) const;**

Return Value

A handle to an icon if successful; otherwise **NULL**.

Parameters

lpszIconName A manifest constant identifier that specifies a predefined Windows icon. These identifiers are defined in WINDOWS.H. The following list shows the possible predefined values and meanings for *lpszIconName*:

- **IDI_APPLICATION** Default application icon

- **IDI_HAND** Hand-shaped icon used in serious warning messages

- **IDI_QUESTION** Question-mark shape used in prompting messages

- **IDI_EXCLAMATION** Exclamation point shape used in warning messages

- **IDI_ASTERISK** Asterisk shape used in informative messages

Remarks

Loads the Windows predefined icon resource that *lpszIconName* specifies.

Use the **LoadStandardIcon** or **LoadOEMIcon** member function to access the predefined Windows icons.

See Also: **CWinApp::LoadOEMIcon, CWinApp::LoadIcon, ::LoadIcon**

CWinApp::LoadStdProfileSettings

void LoadStdProfileSettings(UINT *nMaxMRU* **= _AFX_MRU_COUNT);**

Parameters

nMaxMRU   The number of recently used files to track.

Remarks

Call this member function from within the **InitInstance** member function to enable
and load the list of most recently used (MRU) files and last preview state. If
nMaxMRU is 0, no MRU list will be maintained.

See Also: CWinApp::OnFileOpen, CWinApp::AddToRecentFileList

CWinApp::OnContextHelp

afx_msg void OnContextHelp( );

Remarks

You must add an

```
ON_COMMAND( ID_CONTEXT_HELP, OnContextHelp )
```

statement to your **CWinApp** class message map and also add an accelerator table
entry, typically SHIFT+F1, to enable this member function.

OnContextHelp puts the application into Help mode. The cursor changes to an arrow
and a question mark, and the user can then move the mouse pointer and press the left
mouse button to select a dialog box, window, menu, or command button. This member
function retrieves the Help context of the object under the cursor and calls the
Windows function **WinHelp** with that Help context.

See Also: CWinApp::OnHelp, CWinApp::WinHelp

CWinApp::OnDDECommand

virtual BOOL OnDDECommand(LPTSTR *lpszCommand* **);**

Return Value

Nonzero if the command is handled; otherwise 0.

Parameters

lpszCommand   Points to a DDE command string received by the application.

Remarks

Called by the framework when the main frame window receives a DDE execute
message. The default implementation checks whether the command is a request to
open a document and, if so, opens the specified document. The Windows File

Manager usually sends such DDE command strings when the user double-clicks a data file. Override this function to handle other DDE execute commands, such as the command to print.

Example

```
BOOL CMyApp::OnDDECommand(LPTSTR lpszCommand)
{
    if (CWinApp::OnDDECommand(lpszCommand))
        return TRUE;

    // Handle any DDE commands recognized by your application
    // and return TRUE.  See implementation of CWinApp::OnDDEComand
    // for example of parsing the DDE command string.

    // Return FALSE for any DDE commands you do not handle.
    return FALSE;
}
```

See Also: CWinApp::EnableShellOpen

CWinApp::OnFileNew

afx_msg void OnFileNew( );

Remarks

You must add an

```
ON_COMMAND( ID_FILE_NEW, OnFileNew )
```

statement to your **CWinApp** class message map to enable this member function.

If enabled, this function handles execution of the File New command.

See Technical Note 22 online for information on default behavior and guidance on how to override this member function.

Example

```
// The following message map, produced by AppWizard, binds the
// File New, Open, and Print Setup menu commands to default
// framework implementations of these commands.
BEGIN_MESSAGE_MAP(CMyApp, CWinApp)
    //{{AFX_MSG_MAP(CMyApp)
    ON_COMMAND(ID_APP_ABOUT, OnAppAbout)
        // NOTE - the ClassWizard will add and remove mapping macros here.
        //    DO NOT EDIT what you see in these blocks of generated code!
    //}}AFX_MSG_MAP
    // Standard file based document commands
    ON_COMMAND(ID_FILE_NEW, CWinApp::OnFileNew)
    ON_COMMAND(ID_FILE_OPEN, CWinApp::OnFileOpen)
    // Standard print setup command
    ON_COMMAND(ID_FILE_PRINT_SETUP, CWinApp::OnFilePrintSetup)
END_MESSAGE_MAP()
```

```
// The following message map illustrates how to rebind the
// File New, Open and Print Setup menu commands to handlers that
// you implement in your CWinApp-derived class.  You can use
// ClassWizard to bind the commands, as illustrated below, since
// the message map entries are bracketed by //{{AFX_MSG_MAP
// and //}}AFX_MSG_MAP.  Note, you can name the handler
// CMyApp::OnFileNew instead of CMyApp::OnMyFileNew, and likewise
// for the other handlers, if desired.
BEGIN_MESSAGE_MAP(CMyApp, CWinApp)
    //{{AFX_MSG_MAP(CMyApp)
    ON_COMMAND(ID_APP_ABOUT, OnAppAbout)
    ON_COMMAND(ID_FILE_NEW, OnMyFileNew)
    ON_COMMAND(ID_FILE_OPEN, OnMyFileOpen)
    ON_COMMAND(ID_FILE_PRINT_SETUP, OnMyFilePrintSetup)
    //}}AFX_MSG_MAP
END_MESSAGE_MAP()
```

See Also: **CWinApp::OnFileOpen**

CWinApp::OnFileOpen

afx_msg void OnFileOpen( );

Remarks

You must add an

```
ON_COMMAND( ID_FILE_OPEN, OnFileOpen )
```

statement to your **CWinApp** class message map to enable this member function.

If enabled, this function handles execution of the File Open command.

For information on default behavior and guidance on how to override this member function, see Technical Note 22 online.

Example

```
// The following message map, produced by AppWizard, binds the
// File New, Open, and Print Setup menu commands to default
// framework implementations of these commands.
BEGIN_MESSAGE_MAP(CMyApp, CWinApp)
    //{{AFX_MSG_MAP(CMyApp)
    ON_COMMAND(ID_APP_ABOUT, OnAppAbout)
        // NOTE - the ClassWizard will add and remove mapping macros here.
        //    DO NOT EDIT what you see in these blocks of generated code!
    //}}AFX_MSG_MAP
    // Standard file based document commands
    ON_COMMAND(ID_FILE_NEW, CWinApp::OnFileNew)
    ON_COMMAND(ID_FILE_OPEN, CWinApp::OnFileOpen)
    // Standard print setup command
    ON_COMMAND(ID_FILE_PRINT_SETUP, CWinApp::OnFilePrintSetup)
END_MESSAGE_MAP()
```

```
// The following message map illustrates how to rebind the
// File New, Open and Print Setup menu commands to handlers that
// you implement in your CWinApp-derived class.  You can use
// ClassWizard to bind the commands, as illustrated below, since
// the message map entries are bracketed by //{{AFX_MSG_MAP
// and //}}AFX_MSG_MAP.  Note, you can name the handler
// CMyApp::OnFileNew instead of CMyApp::OnMyFileNew, and likewise
// for the other handlers, if desired.
BEGIN_MESSAGE_MAP(CMyApp, CWinApp)
    //{{AFX_MSG_MAP(CMyApp)
    ON_COMMAND(ID_APP_ABOUT, OnAppAbout)
    ON_COMMAND(ID_FILE_NEW, OnMyFileNew)
    ON_COMMAND(ID_FILE_OPEN, OnMyFileOpen)
    ON_COMMAND(ID_FILE_PRINT_SETUP, OnMyFilePrintSetup)
    //}}AFX_MSG_MAP
END_MESSAGE_MAP()
```

See Also: **CWinApp::OnFileNew**

CWinApp::OnFilePrintSetup

afx_msg void OnFilePrintSetup( );

Remarks

You must add an

```
ON_COMMAND( ID_FILE_PRINT_SETUP, OnFilePrintSetup )
```

statement to your **CWinApp** class message map to enable this member function.

If enabled, this function handles execution of the File Print command.

For information on default behavior and guidance on how to override this member function, see Technical Note 22 online.

Example

```
// The following message map, produced by AppWizard, binds the
// File New, Open, and Print Setup menu commands to default
// framework implementations of these commands.
BEGIN_MESSAGE_MAP(CMyApp, CWinApp)
    //{{AFX_MSG_MAP(CMyApp)
    ON_COMMAND(ID_APP_ABOUT, OnAppAbout)
        // NOTE - the ClassWizard will add and remove mapping macros here.
        //    DO NOT EDIT what you see in these blocks of generated code!
    //}}AFX_MSG_MAP
    // Standard file based document commands
    ON_COMMAND(ID_FILE_NEW, CWinApp::OnFileNew)
    ON_COMMAND(ID_FILE_OPEN, CWinApp::OnFileOpen)
    // Standard print setup command
    ON_COMMAND(ID_FILE_PRINT_SETUP, CWinApp::OnFilePrintSetup)
END_MESSAGE_MAP()
```

```
// The following message map illustrates how to rebind the
// File New, Open and Print Setup menu commands to handlers that
// you implement in your CWinApp-derived class.  You can use
// ClassWizard to bind the commands, as illustrated below, since
// the message map entries are bracketed by //{{AFX_MSG_MAP
// and //}}AFX_MSG_MAP.  Note, you can name the handler
// CMyApp::OnFileNew instead of CMyApp::OnMyFileNew, and likewise
// for the other handlers, if desired.
BEGIN_MESSAGE_MAP(CMyApp, CWinApp)
    //{{AFX_MSG_MAP(CMyApp)
    ON_COMMAND(ID_APP_ABOUT, OnAppAbout)
    ON_COMMAND(ID_FILE_NEW, OnMyFileNew)
    ON_COMMAND(ID_FILE_OPEN, OnMyFileOpen)
    ON_COMMAND(ID_FILE_PRINT_SETUP, OnMyFilePrintSetup)
    //}}AFX_MSG_MAP
END_MESSAGE_MAP()
```

See Also: CWinApp::OnFileNew

CWinApp::OnHelp

afx_msg void OnHelp( );

Remarks

You must add an

```
ON_COMMAND( ID_HELP, OnHelp )
```

statement to your **CWinApp** class message map to enable this member function. Usually you will also add an accelerator-key entry for the F1 key. Enabling the F1 key is only a convention, not a requirement.

If enabled, called by the framework when the user presses the F1 key.

The default implementation of this message-handler function determines the Help context that corresponds to the current window, dialog box, or menu item and then calls WINHELP.EXE. If no context is currently available, the function uses the default context.

Override this member function to set the Help context to something other than the window, dialog box, menu item, or toolbar button that currently has the focus. Call **WinHelp** with the desired Help context ID.

See Also: CWinApp::OnContextHelp, CWinApp::OnHelpUsing, CWinApp::OnHelpIndex, CWinApp::WinHelp

CWinApp::OnHelpFinder

afx_msg void OnHelpFinder( );

Remarks

You must add an

```
ON_COMMAND( ID_HELP_FINDER, OnHelpFinder )
```

statement to your **CWinApp** class message map to enable this member function.

If enabled, the framework calls this message-handler function when the user of your application selects the Help Finder command to invoke **WinHelp** with the standard **HELP_FINDER** topic.

See Also: **CWinApp::OnHelp, CWinApp::OnHelpUsing, CWinApp::WinHelp, CWinApp::OnHelpIndex**

CWinApp::OnHelpIndex

afx_msg void OnHelpIndex( );

Remarks

You must add an

```
ON_COMMAND( ID_HELP_INDEX, OnHelpIndex )
```

statement to your **CWinApp** class message map to enable this member function.

If enabled, the framework calls this message-handler function when the user of your application selects the Help Index command to invoke **WinHelp** with the standard **HELP_INDEX** topic.

See Also: **CWinApp::OnHelp, CWinApp::OnHelpUsing, CWinApp::WinHelp**

CWinApp::OnHelpUsing

afx_msg void OnHelpUsing( );

Remarks

You must add an

```
ON_COMMAND( ID_HELP_USING, OnHelpUsing )
```

statement to your **CWinApp** class message map to enable this member function.

The framework calls this message-handler function when the user of your application selects the Help Using command to invoke the **WinHelp** application with the standard **HELP_HELPONHELP** topic.

See Also: **CWinApp::OnHelp, CWinApp::OnHelpIndex, CWinApp::WinHelp**

CWinApp::OnIdle

virtual BOOL OnIdle(LONG *lCount* **);**

Return Value

Nonzero to receive more idle processing time; 0 if no more idle time is needed.

Parameters

lCount   A counter incremented each time **OnIdle** is called when the application's message queue is empty. This count is reset to 0 each time a new message is processed. You can use the *lCount* parameter to determine the relative length of time the application has been idle without processing a message.

Remarks

Override this member function to perform idle-time processing. **OnIdle** is called in the default message loop when the application's message queue is empty. Use your override to call your own background idle-handler tasks.

OnIdle should return 0 to indicate that no idle processing time is required. The *lCount* parameter is incremented each time **OnIdle** is called when the message queue is empty and resets to 0 each time a new message is processed. You can call your different idle routines based on this count.

The following summarizes idle loop processing:

1. If the message loop in the Microsoft Foundation Class Library checks the message queue and finds no pending messages, it calls OnIdle for the application object and supplies 0 as the *lCount* argument.

2. OnIdle performs some processing and returns a nonzero value to indicate it should be called again to do further processing.

3. The message loop checks the message queue again. If no messages are pending, it calls OnIdle again, incrementing the *lCount* argument.

4. Eventually, OnIdle finishes processing all its idle tasks and returns 0. This tells the message loop to stop calling OnIdle until the next message is received from the message queue, at which point the idle cycle restarts with the argument set to 0.

Do not perform lengthy tasks during **OnIdle** because your application cannot process user input until **OnIdle** returns.

Note   The default implementation of **OnIdle** updates command user-interface objects such as menu items and toolbar buttons, and it performs internal data structure cleanup. Therefore, if you override **OnIdle**, you must call **CWinApp::OnIdle** with the *lCount* in your overridden version. First call all base-class idle processing (that is, until the base class **OnIdle** returns 0). If you need to perform work before the base-class processing completes, review the base-class implementation to select the proper *lCount* during which to do your work.

Example

The following two examples show how to use **OnIdle**. The first example processes two idle tasks using the *lCount* argument to prioritize the tasks. The first task is high priority, and you should do it whenever possible. The second task is less important and should be done only when there is a long pause in user input. Note the call to the base-class version of **OnIdle**. The second example manages a group of idle tasks with different priorities.

```
BOOL CMyApp::OnIdle(LONG lCount)
{
    BOOL bMore = CWinApp::OnIdle(lCount);

    if (lCount == 0)
    {
    TRACE("App idle for short period of time\n");
    bMore = TRUE;
    }
    else if (lCount == 10)
    {
    TRACE("App idle for longer amount of time\n");
       bMore = TRUE;
    }
    else if (lCount == 100)
    {
       TRACE("App idle for even longer amount of time\n");
       bMore = TRUE;
    }
    else if (lCount == 1000)
    {
       TRACE("App idle for quite a long period of time\n");
     // bMore is not set to TRUE, no longer need idle
     // IMPORTANT: bMore is not set to FALSE since CWinApp::OnIdle may
     // have more idle tasks to complete.
    }

    return bMore;
    // return TRUE as long as there is any more idle tasks
}
```

Second Example

```
// In this example, four idle loop tasks are given various
// opportunities to run:
// Task1 is always given a chance to run during idle time, provided
//    that no message has queued up while the framework was processing
//    its own idle loop tasks (at lCount levels 0 and 1).
// Task2 is given a chance to run only if Task1 has already run,
//    provided that no message has queued up while Task1 was running.
// Task3 and Task4 are given a chance to run only if both Task1 and
//    Task2 have already run, and no message has queued up in the mean
//    time.  If Task3 gets its chance to run, then Task4 always gets
//    a chance to run immediately after Task3.
```

```
BOOL CMyApp::OnIdle(LONG lCount)
{
    // In this example, as in most applications, you should let the
    // base class CWinApp::OnIdle complete its processing before you
    // attempt any additional idle loop processing.
    if (CWinApp::OnIdle(lCount))
        return TRUE;

    // The base class CWinApp::OnIdle reserves the lCount values 0
    // and 1 for the framework's own idle processing.  If you wish to
    // share idle processing time at a peer level with the framework,
    // then replace the above if-statement with a straight call to
    // CWinApp::OnIdle; and then add a case statement for lCount value
    // 0 and/or 1. Study the base class implementation first to
    // understand how your idle loop tasks will compete with the
    // framework's idle loop processing.

    switch (lCount)
    {
        case 2:
            Task1();
            return TRUE; // next time give Task2 a chance
        case 3:
            Task2();
            return TRUE; // next time give Task3 and Task4 a chance
        case 4:
            Task3();
            Task4();
            return FALSE; // cycle through the idle loop tasks again
    }
    return FALSE;
}
```

CWinApp::OpenDocumentFile

virtual CDocument* OpenDocumentFile(LPCTSTR *lpszFileName* **);**

Return Value

A pointer to a **CDocument** if successful; otherwise **NULL**.

Parameters

lpszFileName   The name of the file to be opened.

Remarks

The framework calls this member function to open the named **CDocument** file for the application. If a document with that name is already open, the first frame window that contains that document will be activated. If an application supports multiple document templates, the framework uses file extension to find the appropriate document template to attempt to load the document. If successful, the document template then creates a frame window and view for the document.

Example

```
BOOL CMyApp::InitInstance()
{
    // ...
    if (m_lpCmdLine[0] == '\0')
    {
        // Create a new (empty) document.
        OnFileNew();
    }
    else
    {
        // Open a file passed as the first command line parameter.
        OpenDocumentFile(m_lpCmdLine);
    }

    // ...
}
```

CWinApp::ParseCommandLine

void ParseCommandLine(CCommandLineInfo& *rCmdInfo* **);**

Parameters

rCmdInfo   A reference to a **CCommandLineInfo** object.

Remarks

Call this member function to parse the command line and send the parameters, one at a time, to **CCommandLineInfo::ParseParam**.

When you start a new MFC project using AppWizard, AppWizard will create a local instance of **CCommandLineInfo**, and then call **ProcessShellCommand** and **ParseCommandLine** in the **InitInstance** member function. A command line follows the route described below:

1. After being created in **InitInstance**, the **CCommandLineInfo** object is passed to **ParseCommandLine**.

2. **ParseCommandLine** then calls **CCommandLineInfo::ParseParam** repeatedly, once for each parameter.

3. **ParseParam** fills the **CCommandLineInfo** object, which is then passed to **ProcessShellCommand**.

4. **ProcessShellCommand** handles the command-line arguments and flags.

Note that you can call **ParseCommandLine** directly as needed.

For a description of the command-line flags, see **CCommandLineInfo::m_nShellCommand**.

See Also: **CCommandLineInfo**, **CWinApp::InitInstance**,
CCommandLineInfo::ParseParam, **CWinApp::ProcessShellCommand**,
CCommandLineInfo::m_nShellCommand

CWinApp::PreTranslateMessage

virtual BOOL PreTranslateMessage(MSG* *pMsg* **);**

Return Value

Nonzero if the message was fully processed in **PreTranslateMessage** and should not
be processed further. Zero if the message should be processed in the normal way.

Parameters

pMsg   A pointer to a **MSG** structure that contains the message to process.

Remarks

Override this function to filter window messages before they are dispatched to the
Windows functions **TranslateMessage** and **DispatchMessage** The default
implementation performs accelerator-key translation, so you must call the
CWinApp::PreTranslateMessage member function in your overridden version.

See Also: **::DispatchMessage**, **::TranslateMessage**

CWinApp::ProcessMessageFilter

virtual BOOL ProcessMessageFilter(int *code*, **LPMSG** *lpMsg* **);**

Return Value

Nonzero if the message is processed; otherwise 0.

Parameters

code   Specifies a hook code. This member function uses the code to determine how to
process *lpMsg*.

lpMsg   A pointer to a Windows **MSG** structure.

Remarks

The framework's hook function calls this member function to filter and respond to
certain Windows messages. A hook function processes events before they are sent to
the application's normal message processing.

If you override this advanced feature, be sure to call the base-class version to maintain
the framework's hook processing.

See Also: **MessageProc**, **WH_MSGFILTER**

CWinApp::ProcessShellCommand

BOOL ProcessShellCommand(CCommandLineInfo& *rCmdInfo* **);**

Return Value

Nonzero if the shell command is processed successfully. If 0, return **FALSE** from **InitInstance**.

Parameters

rCmdInfo   A reference to a **CCommandLineInfo** object.

Remarks

This member function is called by **InitInstance** to accept the parameters passed from the **CCommandLineInfo** object identified by *rCmdInfo*, and perform the indicated action.

When you start a new MFC project using AppWizard, AppWizard will create a local instance of **CCommandLineInfo**, and then call **ProcessShellCommand** and **ParseCommandLine** in the **InitInstance** member function. A command line follows the route described below:

1. After being created in **InitInstance**, the **CCommandLineInfo** object is passed to **ParseCommandLine**.
2. **ParseCommandLine** then calls **CCommandLineInfo::ParseParam** repeatedly, once for each parameter.
3. **ParseParam** fills the **CCommandLineInfo** object, which is then passed to **ProcessShellCommand**.
4. **ProcessShellCommand** handles the command-line arguments and flags.

The data members of the **CCommandLineInfo** object, identified by **CCommandLineInfo::m_nShellCommand**, are of the following enumerated type, which is defined within the **CCommandLineInfo** class.

```
enum{
    FileNew,
    FileOpen,
    FilePrint,
    FilePrintTo,
    FileDDE,
};
```

For a brief description of each of these values, see **CCommandLineInfo::m_nShellCommand**.

See Also: **CWinApp::ParseCommandLine, CCommandLineInfo, CCommandLineInfo::ParseParam, CCommandLineInfo::m_nShellCommand**

CWinApp::ProcessWndProcException

virtual LRESULT ProcessWndProcException(CException* *e*, const MSG* *pMsg*);

Return Value

The value that should be returned to Windows. Normally this is 0L for windows messages, 1L (**TRUE**) for command messages.

Parameters

e A pointer to an uncaught exception.

pMsg A **MSG** structure that contains information about the windows message that caused the framework to throw an exception.

Remarks

The framework calls this member function whenever the handler does not catch an exception thrown in one of your application's message or command handlers.

Do not call this member function directly.

The default implementation of this member function creates a message box. If the uncaught exception originates with a menu, toolbar, or accelerator command failure, the message box displays a "Command failed" message; otherwise, it displays an "Internal application error" message.

Override this member function to provide global handling of your exceptions. Only call the base functionality if you wish the message box to be displayed.

See Also: CWnd::WindowProc, **CException**

CWinApp::RegisterShellFileTypes

void RegisterShellFileTypes(BOOL bCompat = FALSE);

Parameters

bCompat **TRUE** adds registration entries for shell commands Print and Print To, allowing a user to print files directly from the shell, or by dragging the file to a printer object. It also adds a DefaultIcon key. By default, this parameter is **FALSE** for backward compatibility.

Remarks

Call this member function to register all of your application's document types with the Windows File Manager. This allows the user to open a data file created by your application by double-clicking it from within File Manager. Call **RegisterShellFileTypes** after you call **AddDocTemplate** for each of the document templates in your application. Also call the **EnableShellOpen** member function when you call **RegisterShellFileTypes**.

RegisterShellFileTypes iterates through the list of **CDocTemplate** objects that the application maintains and, for each document template, adds entries to the registration database that Windows maintains for file associations. File Manager uses these entries to open a data file when the user double-clicks it. This eliminates the need to ship a .REG file with your application.

If the registration database already associates a given filename extension with another file type, no new association is created. See the **CDocTemplate** class for the format of strings necessary to register this information.

See Also: **CDocTemplate**, **CWinApp::EnableShellOpen**, **CWinApp::AddDocTemplate**

CWinApp::Run

virtual int Run( );

Return Value

An **int** value that is returned by **WinMain**.

Remarks

Provides a default message loop. **Run** acquires and dispatches Windows messages until the application receives a **WM_QUIT** message. If the application's message queue currently contains no messages, **Run** calls **OnIdle** to perform idle-time processing. Incoming messages go to the **PreTranslateMessage** member function for special processing and then to the Windows function **TranslateMessage** for standard keyboard translation; finally, the **DispatchMessage** Windows function is called.

Run is rarely overridden, but you can override it to provide special behavior.

See Also: **CWinApp::PreTranslateMessage**, **WM_QUIT**, **::DispatchMessage**, **::TranslateMessage**

CWinApp::RunAutomated

BOOL RunAutomated( );

Return Value

Nonzero if the option was found; otherwise 0.

Remarks

Call this function to determine whether the "**/Automation**" or "**-Automation**" option is present, which indicates whether the server application was launched by a client application. If present, the option is removed from the command line. For more information on OLE Automation, see the article "Automation Servers" in *Visual C++ Programmer's Guide* online.

See Also: **CWinApp::RunEmbedded**

CWinApp::RunEmbedded

BOOL RunEmbedded( );

Return Value

Nonzero if the option was found; otherwise 0.

Remarks

Call this function to determine whether the "**/Embedding**" or "**-Embedding**" option is present, which indicates whether the server application was launched by a client application. If present, the option is removed from the command line. For more information on embedding, see the article "Servers: Implementing a Server" in *Visual C++ Programmer's Guide* online.

See Also: CWinApp::RunAutomated

CWinApp::SaveAllModified

virtual BOOL SaveAllModified( );

Return Value

Nonzero if safe to terminate the application; 0 if not safe to terminate the application.

Remarks

Called by the framework to save all documents when the application's main frame window is to be closed, or through a **WM_QUERYENDSESSION** message.

The default implementation of this member function calls the **CDocument::SaveModified** member function in turn for all modified documents within the application.

CWinApp::SelectPrinter

void SelectPrinter(HANDLE *hDevNames*, **HANDLE** *hDevMode*,
↳ **BOOL** *bFreeOld* = **TRUE**);

Parameters

hDevNames   A handle to a **DEVNAMES** structure that identifies the driver, device, and output port names of a specific printer.

hDevMode   A handle to a **DEVMODE** structure that specifies information about the device initialization and environment of a printer.

bFreeOld   Frees the previously-selected printer.

Remarks

Call this member function to select a specific printer, and release the printer that was previously selected in the Print Dialog box.

If both *hDevMode* and *hDevNames* are **NULL**, **SelectPrinter** uses the current default printer.

See Also: **CPrintDialog, DEVMODE, DEVNAMES**

CWinApp::SetDialogBkColor

void SetDialogBkColor(COLORREF *clrCtlBk* **= RGB(192, 192, 192),**
↳ **COLORREF** *clrCtlText* **= RGB(0, 0, 0));**

Parameters

clrCtlBk   The dialog background color for the application.

clrCtlText   The dialog control color for the application.

Remarks

Call this member function from within the **InitInstance** member function to set the default background and text color for dialog boxes and message boxes within your application.

Example

```
BOOL CMyApp::InitInstance()
{
    // Standard initialization

    SetDialogBkColor();        // Set dialog background color to gray
    LoadStdProfileSettings();  // Load standard INI file options (including MRU)

    // ...
}
```

CWinApp::SetRegistryKey

void SetRegistryKey(LPCTSTR *lpszRegistryKey* **);**
void SetRegistryKey(UINT *nIDRegistryKey* **);**

Parameters

lpszRegistryKey   Pointer to a string containing the name of the key.

nIDRegistryKey   ID/index of a key in the registry.

Remarks

Causes application settings to be stored in the registry instead of INI files. This function sets *m_pszRegistryKey*, which is then used by the **GetProfileInt**, **GetProfileString**, **WriteProfileInt**, and **WriteProfileString** member functions of **CWinApp**. If this function has been called, the list of most recently-used (MRU) files is also stored in the registry. The registry key is usually the name of a company. It is stored in a key of the following form: HKEY_CURRENT_USER\Software\<company name>\<application name>\<section name>\<value name>.

See Also: **CWinApp::InitInstance**, **CWinApp::GetProfileInt**, **CWinApp::GetProfileString**, **CWinApp::WriteProfileInt**, **CWinApp::WriteProfileString**

CWinApp::WinHelp

virtual void WinHelp(DWORD *dwData*, **UINT** *nCmd* = **HELP_CONTEXT**);

Parameters

dwData   Specifies additional data. The value used depends on the value of the *nCmd* parameter.

nCmd   Specifies the type of help requested. For a list of possible values and how they affect the *dwData* parameter, see the **WinHelp** Windows function.

Remarks

Call this member function to invoke the WinHelp application. The framework also calls this function to invoke the WinHelp application.

The framework will automatically close the WinHelp application when your application terminates.

Example

```
// Header File: HELPIDS.H
//
// This example header file is #include'd twice:
// (1) It is #include'd by the .CPP file that passes the DWORD
//     context i.d. to CWinApp::WinHelp.
// (2) It is #include'd in the [MAP] section of the .HPJ file,
//     to associate the help context string "HID_MYTOPIC" with
//     the help context numeric i.d., 101.
// The help context string "HID_MYTOPIC" is what identifies the
// help topic in the help .RTF source file, in the "#" footnote:
//     # HID_MYTOPIC
//
// Note, it is not necessary to manage help context id's this way
// for help topics associated with command id's and user interface
// id's defined in your RESOURCE.H file; you should use the MAKEHM
// tool, or the MAKEHELP.BAT file produced by AppWizard's Context
// Help option, to produce a help map (.HM) file for these id's.
// It is necessary to manage help context id's as illustrated here
// only for help topics not associated with command id's or user
// interface id's.

#define HID_MYTOPIC 101


    // Show the custom help topic that has the context string
    // "HID_MYTOPIC" in the help .RTF file, and which is mapped
    // to the DWORD i.d. HID_MYTOPIC in the above HELPIDS.H file.
    AfxGetApp()->WinHelp(HID_MYTOPIC);
```

```
// The following is one line of code in the help map (.HM)
// file produced by the MAKEHM tool, which in turn is called
// by the MAKEHELP.BAT file produced by the AppWizard Context
// Help option.  The MAKEHM tool reads the following #define
// in the application's RESOURCE.H file:
//    #define ID_MYCOMMAND 0x08004
// and adds a help id offset value of 0x10000 to create the
// help context DWORD value 0x18004.  See MFC Tech Note 28
// for more information on help id offset values.

HID_MYCOMMAND                          0x18004


// Rarely will you need to directly call WinHelp yourself
// with the help context i.d. for a command or user interface
// object. The framework will call WinHelp automatically when
// the user, for example, hits F1 when the focus is on a
// My Command menu item. However, if you do want to directly
// call WinHelp for the help topic associated with the command,
// here is how you would do it:

AfxGetApp()->WinHelp(0x10000 + ID_MYCOMMAND);
```

**See Also: CWinApp::OnContextHelp, CWinApp::OnHelpUsing,
CWinApp::OnHelp, CWinApp::OnHelpIndex, ::WinHelp**

CWinApp::WriteProfileInt

BOOL WriteProfileInt(LPCTSTR *lpszSection*, **LPCTSTR** *lpszEntry*, **int** *nValue* **);**

Return Value

Nonzero if successful; otherwise 0.

Parameters

lpszSection Points to a null-terminated string that specifies the section containing the entry. If the section does not exist, it is created. The name of the section is case independent; the string may be any combination of uppercase and lowercase letters.

lpszEntry Points to a null-terminated string that contains the entry into which the value is to be written. If the entry does not exist in the specified section, it is created.

nValue Contains the value to be written.

Remarks

Call this member function to write the specified value into the specified section of the application's .INI file.

Example

```
CString strSection      = "My Section";
CString strStringItem   = "My String Item";
CString strIntItem      = "My Int Item";

CWinApp* pApp = AfxGetApp();

pApp->WriteProfileString(strSection, strStringItem, "test");

CString strValue;
strValue = pApp->GetProfileString(strSection, strStringItem);
ASSERT(strValue == "test");

pApp->WriteProfileInt(strSection, strIntItem, 1234);
int nValue;
nValue = pApp->GetProfileInt(strSection, strIntItem, 0);
ASSERT(nValue == 1234);
```

See Also: **CWinApp::GetProfileInt**, **CWinApp::WriteProfileString**

CWinApp::WriteProfileString

BOOL WriteProfileString(LPCTSTR *lpszSection*, **LPCTSTR** *lpszEntry*,
→ **LPCTSTR** *lpszValue* **);**

Return Value

Nonzero if successful; otherwise 0.

Parameters

lpszSection   Points to a null-terminated string that specifies the section containing the entry. If the section does not exist, it is created. The name of the section is case independent; the string may be any combination of uppercase and lowercase letters.

lpszEntry   Points to a null-terminated string that contains the entry into which the value is to be written. If the entry does not exist in the specified section, it is created.

lpszValue   Points to the string to be written. If this parameter is **NULL**, the entry specified by the *lpszEntry* parameter is deleted.

Remarks

Call this member function to write the specified string into the specified section of the application's .INI file.

Example

```
CString strSection      = "My Section";
CString strStringItem   = "My String Item";
CString strIntItem      = "My Int Item";

CWinApp* pApp = AfxGetApp();

pApp->WriteProfileString(strSection, strStringItem, "test");
```

```
CString strValue;
strValue = pApp->GetProfileString(strSection, strStringItem);
ASSERT(strValue == "test");

pApp->WriteProfileInt(strSection, strIntItem, 1234);
int nValue;
nValue = pApp->GetProfileInt(strSection, strIntItem, 0);
ASSERT(nValue == 1234);
```

See Also: **CWinApp::GetProfileString, CWinApp::WriteProfileInt, ::WritePrivateProfileString**

Data Members
CWinApp::m_bHelpMode

Remarks

TRUE if the application is in Help context mode (conventionally invoked with SHIFT + F1); otherwise **FALSE**. In Help context mode, the cursor becomes a question mark and the user can move it about the screen. Examine this flag if you want to implement special handling when in the Help mode. **m_bHelpMode** is a public variable of type **BOOL**.

CWinApp::m_hInstance

Remarks

Corresponds to the *hInstance* parameter passed by Windows to **WinMain**. The **m_hInstance** data member is a handle to the current instance of the application running under Windows. This is returned by the global function **AfxGetInstanceHandle**. **m_hInstance** is a public variable of type **HINSTANCE**.

Example

```
// Typically you do not need to pass the application's hInstance
// to Windows APIs directly because there are equivalent MFC
// member functions that pass the hInstance for you.  The following
// example is not typical:

HCURSOR hCursor;
hCursor = ::LoadCursor(AfxGetApp()->m_hInstance,
   MAKEINTRESOURCE(IDC_MYCURSOR));

// A more direct way to get the application's hInstance is to
// call AfxGetInstanceHandle:
hCursor = ::LoadCursor(AfxGetInstanceHandle(),
   MAKEINTRESOURCE(IDC_MYCURSOR));
```

```
// If you need the hInstance to load a resource, it is better
// to call AfxGetResourceHandle instead of AfxGetInstanceHandle:
hCursor = ::LoadCursor(AfxGetResourceHandle(),
    MAKEINTRESOURCE(IDC_MYCURSOR));

// A better way to load the cursor resource is to call
// CWinApp::LoadCursor
hCursor = AfxGetApp()->LoadCursor(IDC_MYCURSOR);
```

CWinApp::m_hPrevInstance

Remarks

Corresponds to the *hPrevInstance* parameter passed by Windows to **WinMain**.

The **m_hPrevInstance** data member is always set to **NULL** in a Win32 application. To find previous instances of an application, use **CWnd::FindWindow**.

CWinApp::m_lpCmdLine

Remarks

Corresponds to the *lpCmdLine* parameter passed by Windows to **WinMain**. Points to a null-terminated string that specifies the command line for the application. Use **m_lpCmdLine** to access any command-line arguments the user entered when the application was started. **m_lpCmdLine** is a public variable of type **LPSTR**.

Example

```
BOOL CMyApp::InitInstance()
{
    // ...

    if (m_lpCmdLine[0] == '\0')
    {
        // Create a new (empty) document.
        OnFileNew();
    }
    else
    {
        // Open a file passed as the first command line parameter.
        OpenDocumentFile(m_lpCmdLine);
    }

    // ...
}
```

CWinApp::m_nCmdShow

Remarks

Corresponds to the *nCmdShow* parameter passed by Windows to **WinMain**. You should pass **m_nCmdShow** as an argument when you call **CWnd::ShowWindow** for your application's main window. **m_nCmdShow** is a public variable of type **int**.

Example

```
BOOL CMyApp::InitInstance()
{
    // ...

    // Create main MDI Frame window.
    CMainFrame* pMainFrame = new CMainFrame;
    if (!pMainFrame->LoadFrame(IDR_MAINFRAME))
        return FALSE;
    // Save the pointer to the main frame window.  This is the
    // only way the framework will have knowledge of what the
    // main frame window is.
    m_pMainWnd = pMainFrame;

    // Show the   main window using the nCmdShow parameter
    // passed to the application when it was first launched.
    pMainFrame->ShowWindow(m_nCmdShow);
    pMainFrame->UpdateWindow();

    // ...
}
```

CWinApp::m_pActiveWnd

Remarks

Use this data member to store a pointer to the main window of the OLE container application that has your OLE server application in-place activated. If this data member is **NULL**, the application is not in-place active.

The framework sets this member variable when the frame window is in-place activated by an OLE container application.

See Also: AfxGetMainWnd, **CWinThread::m_pMainWnd**

CWinApp::m_pszAppName

Remarks

Specifies the name of the application. The application name can come from the parameter passed to the **CWinApp** constructor, or, if not specified, to the resource string with the ID of **AFX_IDS_APP_TITLE**. If the application name is not found in the resource, it comes from the program's .EXE filename.

Returned by the global function **AfxGetAppName**. **m_pszAppName** is a public variable of type **const char***.

Note If you assign a value to **m_pszAppName**, it must be dynamically allocated on the heap. The **CWinApp** destructor calls **free**( ) with this pointer. You many want to use the **_tcsdup**( ) run-time library function to do the allocating. Also, free the memory associated with the current pointer before assigning a new value. For example:

```
//First free the string allocated by MFC at CWinApp startup.
//The string is allocated before InitInstance is called.
free((void*)m_pszAppName);
//Change the name of the application file.
//The CWinApp destructor will free the memory.
m_pszAppName=_tcsdup(_T("d:\\somedir\\myapp.exe"));
```

Example

```
CWnd* pWnd;
    // Set pWnd to some CWnd object whose window has already
    // been created.

    // The following call to CWnd::MessageBox uses the application
    // title as the message box caption.
    pWnd->MessageBox("Some message", AfxGetApp()->m_pszAppName);

    // A more direct way to get the application title is to
    // call AfxGetAppName:
    pWnd->MessageBox("Some message", AfxGetAppName());

    // An easier way to display a message box using the application
    // title as the message box caption is to call AfxMessageBox:
    AfxMessageBox("Some message");
```

CWinApp::m_pszExeName

Remarks

Contains the name of the application's executable file without an extension. Unlike **m_pszAppName**, this name cannot contain blanks. **m_pszExeName** is a public variable of type **const char***.

Note If you assign a value to **m_pszExeName**, it must be dynamically allocated on the heap. The **CWinApp** destructor calls **free**( ) with this pointer. You many want to use the **_tcsdup**( ) run-time library function to do the allocating. Also, free the memory associated with the current pointer before assigning a new value. For example:

```
//First free the string allocated by MFC at CWinApp startup.
//The string is allocated before InitInstance is called.
free((void*)m_pszExeName);
//Change the name of the .EXE file.
//The CWinApp destructor will free the memory.
m_pszExeName=_tcsdup(_T("d:\\somedir\\myapp"));
```

CWinApp::m_pszHelpFilePath

Remarks

Contains the path to the application's Help file. By default, the framework initializes **m_pszHelpFilePath** to the name of the application with ".HLP" appended. To change the name of the help file, set **m_pszHelpFilePath** to point to a string that contains the complete name of the desired help file. A convenient place to do this is in the application's **InitInstance** function. **m_pszHelpFilePath** is a public variable of type **const char***.

Note If you assign a value to **m_pszHelpFilePath**, it must be dynamically allocated on the heap. The **CWinApp** destructor calls **free( )** with this pointer. You many want to use the **_tcsdup( )** run-time library function to do the allocating. Also, free the memory associated with the current pointer before assigning a new value. For example:

```
//First free the string allocated by MFC at CWinApp startup.
//The string is allocated before InitInstance is called.
free((void*)m_pszHelpFilePath);
//Change the name of the .HLP file.
//The CWinApp destructor will free the memory.
m_pszHelpFilePath=_tcsdup(_T("d:\\somedir\\myhelp.hlp"));
```

CWinApp::m_pszProfileName

Remarks

Contains the name of the application's .INI file. **m_pszProfileName** is a public variable of type **const char***.

Note If you assign a value to **m_pszProfileName**, it must be dynamically allocated on the heap. The **CWinApp** destructor calls **free( )** with this pointer. You many want to use the **_tcsdup( )** run-time library function to do the allocating. Also, free the memory associated with the current pointer before assigning a new value. For example:

```
//First free the string allocated by MFC at CWinApp startup.
//The string is allocated before InitInstance is called.
free((void*)m_pszProfileName);
//Change the name of the .INI file.
//The CWinApp destructor will free the memory.
m_pszProfileName=_tcsdup(_T("d:\\somedir\\myini.ini"));
```

See Also: **CWinApp::GetProfileString, CWinApp::GetProfileInt, CWinApp::WriteProfileInt, CWinApp::WriteProfileString**

CWinApp::m_pszRegistryKey

LPCTSTR m_pszRegistryKey;

Remarks

Used to determine the full registry key for storing application profile settings. Normally, this data member is treated as read-only.

Note If you assign a value to **m_pszRegistryKey**, it must be dynamically allocated on the heap. The **CWinApp** destructor calls **free**( ) with this pointer. You many want to use the **_tcsdup**( ) run-time library function to do the allocating. Also, free the memory associated with the current pointer before assigning a new value. For example:

```
//First free the string allocated by MFC at CWinApp startup.
//The string is allocated before InitInstance is called.
free((void*)m_pszRegistryKey);
//Change the name of the registry key.
//The CWinApp destructor will free the memory.
m_pszRegistryKey=_tcsdup(_T("HKEY_CURRENT_USER\\Software
↪ \\mycompany\\myapp\\thissection\\thisvalue"));
```

See Also: CWinApp::SetRegistryKey

CWindowDC

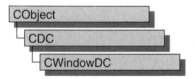

The **CWindowDC** class is derived from **CDC**. It calls the Windows functions **GetWindowDC** at construction time and **ReleaseDC** at destruction time. This means that a **CWindowDC** object accesses the entire screen area of a **CWnd** (both client and nonclient areas).

For more information on using **CWindowDC**, see "Device Contexts" in *Visual C++ Programmer's Guide* online.

#include <afxwin.h>

See Also: CDC

CWindowDC Class Members

Construction

CWindowDC	Constructs a **CWindowDC** object.

Data Members

m_hWnd	The **HWND** to which this **CWindowDC** is attached.

Member Functions

CWindowDC::CWindowDC

CWindowDC(CWnd* *pWnd*); throw(CResourceException);

Parameters

pWnd   The window whose client area the device-context object will access.

Remarks

Constructs a **CWindowDC** object that accesses the entire screen area (both client and nonclient) of the **CWnd** object pointed to by *pWnd*. The constructor calls the Windows function **GetWindowDC**.

An exception (of type **CResourceException**) is thrown if the Windows **GetWindowDC** call fails. A device context may not be available if Windows has already allocated all of its available device contexts. Your application competes for the five common display contexts available at any given time under Windows.

See Also: **CDC**, **CClientDC**, **CWnd**

Data Members
CWindowDC::m_hWnd

Remarks

The **HWND** of the **CWnd** pointer is used to construct the **CWindowDC** object. **m_hWnd** is a protected variable of type **HWND**.

CWinThread

A **CWinThread** object represents a thread of execution within an application. The main thread of execution is usually provided by an object derived from **CWinApp**; **CWinApp** is derived from **CWinThread**. Additional **CWinThread** objects allow multiple threads within a given application.

There are two general types of threads that **CWinThread** supports: worker threads and user-interface threads. Worker threads have no message pump: for example, a thread that performs background calculations in a spreadsheet application. User-interface threads have a message pump and process messages received from the system. **CWinApp** and classes derived from it are examples of user-interface threads. Other user-interface threads can also be derived directly from **CWinThread**.

Objects of class **CWinThread** typically exist for the duration of the thread. If you wish to modify this behavior, set **m_bAutoDelete** to **FALSE**.

The **CWinThread** class is necessary to make your code and MFC fully thread-safe. Thread-local data used by the framework to maintain thread-specific information is managed by **CWinThread** objects. Because of this dependence on **CWinThread** to handle thread-local data, any thread that uses MFC must be created by MFC. For example, a thread created by the run-time function **_beginthreadex** cannot use any MFC APIs.

To create a thread, call **AfxBeginThread**. There are two forms, depending on whether you want a worker or user-interface thread. If you want a user-interface thread, pass to **AfxBeginThread** a pointer to the **CRuntimeClass** of your **CWinThread**-derived class. If you want to create a worker thread, pass to **AfxBeginThread** a pointer to the controlling function and the parameter to the controlling function. For both worker threads and user-interface threads, you can specify optional parameters that modify priority, stack size, creation flags, and security attributes. **AfxBeginThread** will return a pointer to your new **CWinThread** object.

Instead of calling **AfxBeginThread**, you can construct a **CWinThread**-derived object and then call **CreateThread**. This two-stage construction method is useful if you want to reuse the **CWinThread** object between successive creation and terminations of thread executions.

For more information on **CWinThread**, see the articles "Multithreading with C++ and MFC," "Multithreading: Creating User-Interface Threads," "Multithreading: Creating

Worker Threads," and "Multithreading: How to Use the Synchronization Classes" in *Visual C++ Programmer's Guide* online.

See Also: **CWinApp**, **CCmdTarget**

CWinThread Class Members

Data Members

m_bAutoDelete	Specifies whether to destroy the object at thread termination.
m_hThread	Handle to the current thread.
m_nThreadID	ID of the current thread.
m_pMainWnd	Holds a pointer to the application's main window.
m_pActiveWnd	Pointer to the main window of the container application when an OLE server is in-place active.

Construction

CWinThread	Constructs a **CWinThread** object.
CreateThread	Starts execution of a **CWinThread** object.

Operations

GetMainWnd	Retrieves a pointer to the main window for the thread.
GetThreadPriority	Gets the priority of the current thread.
PostThreadMessage	Posts a message to another **CWinThread** object.
ResumeThread	Decrements a thread's suspend count.
SetThreadPriority	Sets the priority of the current thread.
SuspendThread	Increments a thread's suspend count.

Overridables

ExitInstance	Override to clean up when your thread terminates.
InitInstance	Override to perform thread instance initialization.
OnIdle	Override to perform thread-specific idle-time processing.
PreTranslateMessage	Filters messages before they are dispatched to the Windows functions **TranslateMessage** and **DispatchMessage**.
IsIdleMessage	Checks for special messages.
ProcessWndProcException	Intercepts all unhandled exceptions thrown by the thread's message and command handlers.
ProcessMessageFilter	Intercepts certain messages before they reach the application.
Run	Controlling function for threads with a message pump. Override to customize the default message loop.

Member Functions
CWinThread::CreateThread

BOOL CreateThread(DWORD *dwCreateFlags* **= 0, UINT** *nStackSize* **= 0,**
↳ **LPSECURITY_ATTRIBUTES** *lpSecurityAttrs* **= NULL);**

Return Value

Nonzero if the thread is created successfully; otherwise 0.

Parameters

dwCreateFlags Specifies an additional flag that controls the creation of the thread. This flag can contain one of two values:

- **CREATE_SUSPENDED** Start the thread with a suspend count of one. The thread will not execute until **ResumeThread** is called.

- **0** Start the thread immediately after creation.

nStackSize Specifies the size in bytes of the stack for the new thread. If **0**, the stack size defaults to the same size as that of the process's primary thread.

lpSecurityAttrs Points to a **SECURITY_ATTRIBUTES** structure that specifies the security attributes for the thread.

Remarks

Creates a thread to execute within the address space of the calling process. Use **AfxBeginThread** to create a thread object and execute it in one step. Use **CreateThread** if you want to reuse the thread object between successive creation and termination of thread executions.

See Also: **AfxBeginThread, CWinThread::CWinThread, ::CreateThread**

CWinThread::CWinThread

CWinThread( );

Remarks

Constructs a **CWinThread** object. To begin the thread's execution, call the **CreateThread** member function. You will usually create threads by calling **AfxBeginThread**, which will call this constructor and **CreateThread**.

See Also: **CWinThread::CreateThread**

CWinThread::ExitInstance

virtual int ExitInstance( );

Return Value

The thread's exit code; 0 indicates no errors, and values greater than 0 indicate an error. This value can be retrieved by calling **::GetExitCodeThread**.

Remarks

Called by the framework from within a rarely overridden **Run** member function to exit this instance of the thread, or if a call to **InitInstance** fails.

Do not call this member function from anywhere but within the **Run** member function. This member function is used only in user-interface threads.

The default implementation of this function deletes the **CWinThread** object if **m_bAutoDelete** is **TRUE**. Override this function if you wish to perform additional clean-up when your thread terminates. Your implementation of **ExitInstance** should call the base class's version after your code is executed.

See Also: CWinApp::ExitInstance

CWinThread::GetMainWnd

virtual CWnd * GetMainWnd( );

Return Value

This function returns a pointer to one of two types of windows. If your thread is part of an OLE server and has an object that is in-place active inside an active container, this function returns the **CWinApp::m_pActiveWnd** data member of the **CWinThread** object.

If there is no object that is in-place active within a container or your application is not an OLE server, this function returns the **m_pMainWnd** data member of your thread object.

Remarks

If your application is an OLE server, call this function to retrieve a pointer to the active main window of the application instead of directly referring to the **m_pMainWnd** member of the application object. For user-interface threads, this is equivalent to directly referring to the **m_pActiveWnd** member of your application object.

If your application is not an OLE server, then calling this function is equivalent to directly referring to the **m_pMainWnd** member of your application object.

Override this function to modify the default behavior.

See Also: AfxGetMainWnd

CWinThread::GetThreadPriority

int GetThreadPriority( );

Return Value

The current thread priority level within its priority class. The value returned will be one of the following, listed from highest priority to lowest:

- **THREAD_PRIORITY_TIME_CRITICAL**
- **THREAD_PRIORITY_HIGHEST**
- **THREAD_PRIORITY_ABOVE_NORMAL**
- **THREAD_PRIORITY_NORMAL**
- **THREAD_PRIORITY_BELOW_NORMAL**
- **THREAD_PRIORITY_LOWEST**
- **THREAD_PRIORITY_IDLE**

For more information on these priorities, see **::SetThreadPriority** in the *Win32 SDK Programmer's Reference, Volume 4.*

Remarks

Gets the current thread priority level of this thread.

See Also: **CWinThread::SetThreadPriority, ::GetThreadPriority**

CWinThread::InitInstance

virtual BOOL InitInstance( );

Return Value

Nonzero if initialization is successful; otherwise 0.

Remarks

InitInstance must be overridden to initialize each new instance of a user-interface thread. Typically, you override **InitInstance** to perform tasks that must be completed when a thread is first created.

This member function is used only in user-interface threads. Perform initialization of worker threads in the controlling function passed to **AfxBeginThread**.

See Also: **CWinApp::InitInstance**

CWinThread::IsIdleMessage

virtual BOOL IsIdleMessage(MSG* *pMsg* **);**

Return Value

Nonzero if **OnIdle** should be called after processing message; otherwise 0.

Parameters

pMsg   Points to the current message being processed.

Remarks

Override this function to keep **OnIdle** from being called after specific messages are generated. The default implementation does not call **OnIdle** after redundant mouse messages and messages generated by blinking carets.

If an application has created a short timer, **OnIdle** will be called frequently, causing performance problems. To improve such an application's performance, override **IsIdleMessage** in the application's **CWinApp**-derived class to check for **WM_TIMER** messages as follows:

```
BOOL CMyApp::IsIdleMessage( MSG* pMsg )
{
   if (!CWinApp::IsIdleMessage( pMsg ) ||
      pMsg->message == WM_TIMER)
      return FALSE;
   else
      return TRUE;
}
```

Handling **WM_TIMER** in this fashion will improve performance of applications that use short timers.

CWinThread::OnIdle

virtual BOOL OnIdle(LONG *lCount* **);**

Return Value

Nonzero to receive more idle processing time; 0 if no more idle processing time is needed.

Parameters

lCount   A counter incremented each time **OnIdle** is called when the thread's message queue is empty. This count is reset to 0 each time a new message is processed. You can use the *lCount* parameter to determine the relative length of time the thread has been idle without processing a message.

Remarks

Override this member function to perform idle-time processing. **OnIdle** is called in the default message loop when the thread's message queue is empty. Use your override to call your own background idle-handler tasks.

OnIdle should return 0 to indicate that no additional idle processing time is required. The *lCount* parameter is incremented each time **OnIdle** is called when the message queue is empty and is reset to 0 each time a new message is processed. You can call your different idle routines based on this count.

The default implementation of this member function frees temporary objects and unused dynamic link libraries from memory.

This member function is used only in user-interface threads.

Because the application cannot process messages until **OnIdle** returns, do not perform lengthy tasks in this function.

See Also: **CWinApp::OnIdle**

CWinThread::PostThreadMessage

BOOL PostThreadMessage(UINT *message* **, WPARAM** *wParam***, LPARAM** *lParam* **);**

Return Value

Nonzero if successful; otherwise 0.

Parameters

message   ID of the user-defined message.

wParam   First message parameter.

lParam   Second message parameter.

Remarks

Called to post a user-defined message to another **CWinThread** object. The posted message is mapped to the proper message handler by the message map macro **ON_THREAD_MESSAGE**.

See Also: **ON_THREAD_MESSAGE**

CWinThread::PreTranslateMessage

virtual BOOL PreTranslateMessage(MSG **pMsg* **);**

Return Value

Nonzero if the message was fully processed in **PreTranslateMessage** and should not be processed further. Zero if the message should be processed in the normal way.

Parameters

pMsg   Points to a **MSG** structure containing the message to process.

Remarks

Override this function to filter window messages before they are dispatched to the Windows functions **::TranslateMessage** and **::DispatchMessage**.

This member function is used only in user-interface threads.

See Also: **CWinApp::PreTranslateMessage**

CWinThread::ProcessMessageFilter

virtual BOOL ProcessMessageFilter(int *code*, **LPMSG** *lpMsg* **);**

Return Value

Nonzero if the message is processed; otherwise 0.

Parameters

code   Specifies a hook code. This member function uses the code to determine how to process *lpMsg*.

lpMsg   A pointer to a Windows **MSG** structure.

Remarks

The framework's hook function calls this member function to filter and respond to certain Windows messages. A hook function processes events before they are sent to the application's normal message processing.

If you override this advanced feature, be sure to call the base-class version to maintain the framework's hook processing.

See Also: **MessageProc**, **WH_MSGFILTER**

CWinThread::ProcessWndProcException

virtual LRESULT ProcessWndProcException(CException **e*, **const MSG** **pMsg* **);**

Return Value

−1 if a **WM_CREATE** exception is generated; otherwise 0.

Parameters

e   Points to an unhandled exception.

pMsg   Points to a **MSG** structure containing information about the windows message that caused the framework to throw an exception.

Remarks

The framework calls this member function whenever the handler does not catch an exception thrown in one of your thread's message or command handlers.

Do not call this member function directly.

The default implementation of this member function handles only exceptions generated from the following messages:

Command	Action
WM_CREATE	Fail.
WM_PAINT	Validate the affected window, thus preventing another **WM_PAINT** message from being generated.

Override this member function to provide global handling of your exceptions. Call the base functionality only if you wish to display the default behavior.

This member function is used only in threads that have a message pump.

See Also: **CWinApp::ProcessWndProcException**

CWinThread::ResumeThread

DWORD ResumeThread( );

Return Value

The thread's previous suspend count if successful; 0xFFFFFFFF otherwise. If the return value is zero, the current thread was not suspended. If the return value is one, the thread was suspended, but is now restarted. Any return value greater than one means the thread remains suspended.

Remarks

Called to resume execution of a thread that was suspended by the **SuspendThread** member function, or a thread created with the **CREATE_SUSPENDED** flag. The suspend count of the current thread is reduced by one. If the suspend count is reduced to zero, the thread resumes execution; otherwise the thread remains suspended.

See Also: **CWinThread::SuspendThread, ::ResumeThread**

CWinThread::Run

virtual int Run( );

Return Value

An **int** value that is returned by the thread. This value can be retrieved by calling **::GetExitCodeThread**.

Remarks

Provides a default message loop for user-interface threads. **Run** acquires and dispatches Windows messages until the application receives a **WM_QUIT** message. If the thread's message queue currently contains no messages, **Run** calls **OnIdle** to perform idle-time processing. Incoming messages go to the **PreTranslateMessage** member function for special processing and then to the Windows function **::TranslateMessage** for standard keyboard translation. Finally, the **::DispatchMessage** Windows function is called.

Run is rarely overridden, but you can override it to implement special behavior.

This member function is used only in user-interface threads.

See Also: **CWinApp::Run**

CWinThread::SetThreadPriority

BOOL SetThreadPriority(int *nPriority* **);**

Return Value

Nonzero if function was successful; otherwise 0.

Parameters

nPriority Specifies the new thread priority level within its priority class. This parameter must be one of the following values, listed from highest priority to lowest:

- **THREAD_PRIORITY_TIME_CRITICAL**

- **THREAD_PRIORITY_HIGHEST**

- **THREAD_PRIORITY_ABOVE_NORMAL**

- **THREAD_PRIORITY_NORMAL**

- **THREAD_PRIORITY_BELOW_NORMAL**

- **THREAD_PRIORITY_LOWEST**

- **THREAD_PRIORITY_IDLE**

For more information on these priorities, see **::SetThreadPriority** in the *Win32 SDK Programmer's Reference, Volume 4*.

Remarks

This function sets the priority level of the current thread within its priority class. It can only be called after **CreateThread** successfully returns.

See Also: **CWinThread::GetThreadPriority**, **::SetThreadPriority**

CWinThread::SuspendThread

DWORD SuspendThread( );

Return Value

The thread's previous suspend count if successful; 0xFFFFFFFF otherwise.

Remarks

Increments the current thread's suspend count. If any thread has a suspend count above zero, that thread does not execute. The thread can be resumed by calling the **ResumeThread** member function.

See Also: **CWinThread::ResumeThread, ::SuspendThread**

Data Members
CWinThread::m_bAutoDelete

Remarks

Specifies whether the **CWinThread** object should be automatically deleted at thread termination. The **m_bAutoDelete** data member is a public variable of type **BOOL**.

CWinThread::m_hThread

Remarks

Handle to the thread attached to this **CWinThread**. The **m_hThread** data member is a public variable of type **HANDLE**. It is only valid if underlying thread currently exists.

CWinThread::m_nThreadID

Remarks

ID of the thread attached to this **CWinThread**. The **m_nThreadID** data member is a public variable of type **DWORD**. It is only valid if underlying thread currently exists.

CWinThread::m_pActiveWnd

Remarks

Use this data member to store a pointer to your thread's active window object. The Microsoft Foundation Class Library will automatically terminate your thread when the window referred to by **m_pActiveWnd** is closed. If this thread is the primary thread for an application, the application will also be terminated. If this data member is **NULL**, the active window for the application's **CWinApp** object will be inherited. **m_pActiveWnd** is a public variable of type **CWnd***.

Typically, you set this member variable when you override **InitInstance**. In a worker thread, the value of this data member is inherited from its parent thread.

See Also: **CWinThread::InitInstance, CWinThread::m_pMainWnd**

CWinThread::m_pMainWnd

Remarks

Use this data member to store a pointer to your thread's main window object. The Microsoft Foundation Class Library will automatically terminate your thread when the window referred to by **m_pMainWnd** is closed. If this thread is the primary thread for an application, the application will also be terminated. If this data member is **NULL**, the main window for the application's **CWinApp** object will be used to determine when to terminate the thread. **m_pMainWnd** is a public variable of type **CWnd***.

Typically, you set this member variable when you override **InitInstance**. In a worker thread, the value of this data member is inherited from its parent thread.

See Also: **CWinThread::InitInstance**

CWnd

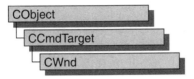

The **CWnd** class provides the base functionality of all window classes in the Microsoft Foundation Class Library.

A **CWnd** object is distinct from a Windows window, but the two are tightly linked. A **CWnd** object is created or destroyed by the **CWnd** constructor and destructor. The Windows window, on the other hand, is a data structure internal to Windows that is created by a **Create** member function and destroyed by the **CWnd** virtual destructor. The **DestroyWindow** function destroys the Windows window without destroying the object.

The **CWnd** class and the message-map mechanism hide the **WndProc** function. Incoming Windows notification messages are automatically routed through the message map to the proper **On***Message* **CWnd** member functions. You override an **On***Message* member function to handle a member's particular message in your derived classes.

The **CWnd** class also lets you create a Windows child window for your application. Derive a class from **CWnd**, then add member variables to the derived class to store data specific to your application. Implement message-handler member functions and a message map in the derived class to specify what happens when messages are directed to the window.

You create a child window in two steps. First, call the constructor **CWnd** to construct the **CWnd** object, then call the **Create** member function to create the child window and attach it to the **CWnd** object.

When the user terminates your child window, destroy the **CWnd** object, or call the **DestroyWindow** member function to remove the window and destroy its data structures.

Within the Microsoft Foundation Class Library, further classes are derived from **CWnd** to provide specific window types. Many of these classes, including **CFrameWnd**, **CMDIFrameWnd**, **CMDIChildWnd**, **CView**, and **CDialog**, are designed for further derivation. The control classes derived from **CWnd**, such as **CButton**, can be used directly or can be used for further derivation of classes.

For more information on using **CWnd**, see "Frame Window Topics" and "Window Object Topics" in *Visual C++ Programmer's Guide* online.

#include <afxwin.h>

See Also: CFrameWnd, CView

CWnd Class Members

Data Members

m_hWnd	Indicates the **HWND** attached to this **CWnd**.

Construction/Destruction

CWnd	Constructs a **CWnd** object.
DestroyWindow	Destroys the attached Windows window.

Initialization

Create	Creates and initializes the child window associated with the **CWnd** object.
PreCreateWindow	Called before the creation of the Windows window attached to this **CWnd** object.
CalcWindowRect	Called to calculate the window rectangle from the client rectangle.
GetStyle	Returns the current window style.
GetExStyle	Returns the window's extended style.
Attach	Attaches a Windows handle to a **CWnd** object.
Detach	Detaches a Windows handle from a **CWnd** object and returns the handle.
PreSubclassWindow	Allows other necessary subclassing to occur before **SubclassWindow** is called.
SubclassWindow	Attaches a window to a **CWnd** object and makes it route messages through the **CWnd**'s message map.
UnsubclassWindow	Detaches a window from a **CWnd** object
FromHandle	Returns a pointer to a **CWnd** object when given a handle to a window. If a **CWnd** object is not attached to the handle, a temporary **CWnd** object is created and attached.
FromHandlePermanent	Returns a pointer to a **CWnd** object when given a handle to a window. If a **CWnd** object is not attached to the handle, **NULL** is returned.
DeleteTempMap	Called automatically by the **CWinApp** idle-time handler and deletes any temporary **CWnd** objects created by **FromHandle**.
GetSafeHwnd	Returns **m_hWnd**, or **NULL** if the **this** pointer is **NULL**.
CreateEx	Creates a Windows overlapped, pop-up, or child window and attaches it to a **CWnd** object.
CreateControl	Create an OLE control that will be represented in an MFC program by a **CWnd** object.

Window State Functions

IsWindowEnabled	Determines whether the window is enabled for mouse and keyboard input.
EnableWindow	Enables or disables mouse and keyboard input.
GetActiveWindow	Retrieves the active window.
SetActiveWindow	Activates the window.
GetCapture	Retrieves the **CWnd** that has the mouse capture.
SetCapture	Causes all subsequent mouse input to be sent to the **CWnd**.
GetFocus	Retrieves the **CWnd** that currently has the input focus.
SetFocus	Claims the input focus.
GetDesktopWindow	Retrieves the Windows desktop window.
GetForegroundWindow	Returns a pointer to the foreground window (the top-level window with which the user is currently working).
SetForegroundWindow	Puts the thread that created the window into the foreground and activates the window.
GetIcon	Retrieves the handle to an icon.
SetIcon	Sets the handle to a specific icon.
GetWindowContextHelpId	Retrieves the help context identifier.
SetWindowContextHelpId	Sets the help context identifier.
ModifyStyle	Modifies the current window style.
ModifyStyleEx	Modifies the window's extended style.

Window Size and Position

GetWindowPlacement	Retrieves the show state and the normal (restored), minimized, and maximized positions of a window.
SetWindowPlacement	Sets the show state and the normal (restored), minimized, and maximized positions for a window.
GetWindowRgn	Retrieves a copy of the window region of a window.
SetWindowRgn	Sets the region of a window.
IsIconic	Determines whether **CWnd** is minimized (iconic).
IsZoomed	Determines whether **CWnd** is maximized.
MoveWindow	Changes the position and dimensions of **CWnd**.
SetWindowPos	Changes the size, position, and ordering of child, pop-up, and top-level windows.
ArrangeIconicWindows	Arranges all the minimized (iconic) child windows.
BringWindowToTop	Brings **CWnd** to the top of a stack of overlapping windows.
GetWindowRect	Gets the screen coordinates of **CWnd**.
GetClientRect	Gets the dimensions of the **CWnd** client area.

Window Access Functions

ChildWindowFromPoint	Determines which, if any, of the child windows contains the specified point.
FindWindow	Returns the handle of the window, which is identified by its window name and window class.
GetNextWindow	Returns the next (or previous) window in the window manager's list.
GetOwner	Retrieves a pointer to the owner of a **CWnd**.
SetOwner	Changes the owner of a **CWnd**.
GetTopWindow	Returns the first child window that belongs to the **CWnd**.
GetWindow	Returns the window with the specified relationship to this window.
GetLastActivePopup	Determines which pop-up window owned by **CWnd** was most recently active.
IsChild	Indicates whether **CWnd** is a child window or other direct descendant of the specified window.
GetParent	Retrieves the parent window of **CWnd** (if any).
GetSafeOwner	Retrieves the safe owner for the given window.
SetParent	Changes the parent window.
WindowFromPoint	Identifies the window that contains the given point.
GetDlgItem	Retrieves the control with the specified ID from the specified dialog box.
GetDlgCtrlID	If the **CWnd** is a child window, calling this function returns its ID value.
SetDlgCtrlID	Sets the window or control ID for the window (which can be any child window, not only a control in a dialog box).
GetDescendantWindow	Searches all descendant windows and returns the window with the specified ID.
GetParentFrame	Retrieves the **CWnd** object's parent frame window.
SendMessageToDescendants	Sends a message to all descendant windows of the window.
GetTopLevelParent	Retrieves the window's top-level parent.
GetTopLevelOwner	Retrieves the top-level window.
GetParentOwner	Returns a pointer to a child window's parent window.
GetTopLevelFrame	Retrieves the window's top-level frame window.
UpdateDialogControls	Call to update the state of dialog buttons and other controls.
UpdateData	Initializes or retrieves data from a dialog box.
CenterWindow	Centers a window relative to its parent.

Update/Painting Functions

BeginPaint	Prepares **CWnd** for painting.
EndPaint	Marks the end of painting.
Print	Draws the current window in the specified device context.
PrintClient	Draws any window in the specified device context (usually a printer device context).
LockWindowUpdate	Disables or reenables drawing in the given window.
UnlockWindowUpdate	Unlocks a window that was locked with **CWnd::LockWindowUpdate**.
GetDC	Retrieves a display context for the client area.
GetDCEx	Retrieves a display context for the client area, and enables clipping while drawing.
RedrawWindow	Updates the specified rectangle or region in the client area.
GetWindowDC	Retrieves the display context for the whole window, including the caption bar, menus, and scroll bars.
ReleaseDC	Releases client and window device contexts, freeing them for use by other applications.
UpdateWindow	Updates the client area.
SetRedraw	Allows changes in **CWnd** to be redrawn or prevents changes from being redrawn.
GetUpdateRect	Retrieves the coordinates of the smallest rectangle that completely encloses the **CWnd** update region.
GetUpdateRgn	Retrieves the **CWnd** update region.
Invalidate	Invalidates the entire client area.
InvalidateRect	Invalidates the client area within the given rectangle by adding that rectangle to the current update region.
InvalidateRgn	Invalidates the client area within the given region by adding that region to the current update region.
ValidateRect	Validates the client area within the given rectangle by removing the rectangle from the current update region.
ValidateRgn	Validates the client area within the given region by removing the region from the current update region.
ShowWindow	Shows or hides the window.
IsWindowVisible	Determines whether the window is visible.
ShowOwnedPopups	Shows or hides all pop-up windows owned by the window.
EnableScrollBar	Enables or disables one or both arrows of a scroll bar.

Coordinate Mapping Functions

MapWindowPoints	Converts (maps) a set of points from the coordinate space of the **CWnd** to the coordinate space of another window.
ClientToScreen	Converts the client coordinates of a given point or rectangle on the display to screen coordinates.
ScreenToClient	Converts the screen coordinates of a given point or rectangle on the display to client coordinates.

Window Text Functions

SetWindowText	Sets the window text or caption title (if it has one) to the specified text.
GetWindowText	Returns the window text or caption title (if it has one).
GetWindowTextLength	Returns the length of the window's text or caption title.
SetFont	Sets the current font.
GetFont	Retrieves the current font.

Scrolling Functions

GetScrollPos	Retrieves the current position of a scroll box.
GetScrollRange	Copies the current minimum and maximum scroll-bar positions for the given scroll bar.
ScrollWindow	Scrolls the contents of the client area.
ScrollWindowEx	Scrolls the contents of the client area. Similar to **ScrollWindow**, with additional features.
GetScrollInfo	Retrieves the information that the **SCROLLINFO** structure maintains about a scroll bar.
GetScrollLimit	Retrieves the limit of the scroll bar.
SetScrollInfo	Sets information about the scroll bar.
SetScrollPos	Sets the current position of a scroll box and, if specified, redraws the scroll bar to reflect the new position.
SetScrollRange	Sets minimum and maximum position values for the given scroll bar.
ShowScrollBar	Displays or hides a scroll bar.
EnableScrollBarCtrl	Enables or disables a sibling scroll-bar control.
GetScrollBarCtrl	Returns a sibling scroll-bar control.
RepositionBars	Repositions control bars in the client area.

Drag-Drop Functions

DragAcceptFiles	Indicates the window will accept dragged files.

Caret Functions

CreateCaret	Creates a new shape for the system caret and gets ownership of the caret.
CreateSolidCaret	Creates a solid block for the system caret and gets ownership of the caret.
CreateGrayCaret	Creates a gray block for the system caret and gets ownership of the caret.
GetCaretPos	Retrieves the client coordinates of the caret's current position.
SetCaretPos	Moves the caret to a specified position.
HideCaret	Hides the caret by removing it from the display screen.
ShowCaret	Shows the caret on the display at the caret's current position. Once shown, the caret begins flashing automatically.

Dialog-Box Item Functions

CheckDlgButton	Places a check mark next to or removes a check mark from a button control.
CheckRadioButton	Checks the specified radio button and removes the check mark from all other radio buttons in the specified group of buttons.
GetCheckedRadioButton	Returns the ID of the currently checked radio button in a group of buttons.
DlgDirList	Fills a list box with a file or directory listing.
DlgDirListComboBox	Fills the list box of a combo box with a file or directory listing.
DlgDirSelect	Retrieves the current selection from a list box.
DlgDirSelectComboBox	Retrieves the current selection from the list box of a combo box.
GetDlgItemInt	Translates the text of a control in the given dialog box to an integer value.
GetDlgItemText	Retrieves the caption or text associated with a control.
GetNextDlgGroupItem	Searches for the next (or previous) control within a group of controls.
GetNextDlgTabItem	Retrieves the first control with the **WS_TABSTOP** style that follows (or precedes) the specified control.
IsDlgButtonChecked	Determines whether a button control is checked.
IsDialogMessage	Determines whether the given message is intended for the modeless dialog box and, if so, processes it.
SendDlgItemMessage	Sends a message to the specified control.

Dialog-Box Item Functions *(continued)*

SetDlgItemInt	Sets the text of a control to the string that represents an integer value.
SetDlgItemText	Sets the caption or text of a control in the specified dialog box.
SubclassDlgItem	Attaches a Windows control to a **CWnd** object and makes it route messages through the **CWnd**'s message map.
ExecuteDlgInit	Initiates a dialog resource.
RunModalLoop	Retrieves, translates, or dispatches messages for a window that is in modal status.
ContinueModal	Continues a window's modal status.
EndModalLoop	Ends a window's modal status.

Data-Binding Functions

BindDefaultProperty	Binds the calling object's default simple bound property, as marked in the type library, to a cursor associated with a data-source control.
BindProperty	Binds a cursour-bound property on a data-bound control to a data-source control and registers that relationship with the MFC binding manager.
GetDSCCursor	Retrieves a pointer to the underlying cursor that is defined by the DataSource, UserName, Password, and SQL properties of a data-source control.

Menu Functions

GetMenu	Retrieves a pointer to the specified menu.
SetMenu	Sets the menu to the specified menu.
DrawMenuBar	Redraws the menu bar.
GetSystemMenu	Allows the application to access the Control menu for copying and modification.
HiliteMenuItem	Highlights or removes the highlighting from a top-level (menu-bar) menu item.

ToolTip Functions

EnableToolTips	Enables the tooltip control.
CancelToolTips	Disables the tooltip control.
FilterToolTipMessage	Retrieves the title or text associated with a control in a dialog box.
OnToolHitTest	Detemines whether a point is in the bounding rectangle of the specified tool and retrieves information about the tool.

Timer Functions

SetTimer	Installs a system timer that sends a **WM_TIMER** message when triggered.
KillTimer	Kills a system timer.

Alert Functions

FlashWindow	Flashes the window once.
MessageBox	Creates and displays a window that contains an application-supplied message and caption.

Window Message Functions

GetCurrentMessage	Returns a pointer to the message this window is currently processing. Should only be called when in an **On***Message* message-handler member function.
Default	Calls the default window procedure, which provides default processing for any window messages that an application does not process.
PreTranslateMessage	Used by **CWinApp** to filter window messages before they are dispatched to the **TranslateMessage** and **DispatchMessage** Windows functions.
SendMessage	Sends a message to the **CWnd** object and does not return until it has processed the message.
PostMessage	Places a message in the application queue, then returns without waiting for the window to process the message.
SendNotifyMessage	Sends the specified message to the window and returns as soon as possible, depending on whether the calling thread created the window.

Clipboard Functions

ChangeClipboardChain	Removes **CWnd** from the chain of Clipboard viewers.
SetClipboardViewer	Adds **CWnd** to the chain of windows that are notified whenever the contents of the Clipboard are changed.
OpenClipboard	Opens the Clipboard. Other applications will not be able to modify the Clipboard until the Windows **CloseClipboard** function is called.
GetClipboardOwner	Retrieves a pointer to the current owner of the Clipboard.
GetOpenClipboardWindow	Retrieves a pointer to the window that currently has the Clipboard open.
GetClipboardViewer	Retrieves a pointer to the first window in the chain of Clipboard viewers.

OLE Controls

SetProperty	Sets an OLE control property.
OnAmbientProperty	Implement ambient property values.
GetControlUnknown	Retrieves a pointer to an unknown OLE control.
GetProperty	Retrieves an OLE control property.
InvokeHelper	Invokes an OLE control method or property.

Overridables

WindowProc	Provides a window procedure for a **CWnd**. The default dispatches messages through the message map.
DefWindowProc	Calls the default window procedure, which provides default processing for any window messages that an application does not process.
PostNcDestroy	This virtual function is called by the default **OnNcDestroy** function after the window has been destroyed.
OnNotify	Called by the framework to inform a parent window an event has occurred in one of its controls or that the control needs information.
OnChildNotify	Called by a parent window to give a notifying control a chance to respond to a control notification.
DoDataExchange	For dialog data exchange and validation. Called by **UpdateData**.

Initialization Message Handlers

OnInitMenu	Called when a menu is about to become active.
OnInitMenuPopup	Called when a pop-up menu is about to become active.

System Message Handlers

OnSysChar	Called when a keystroke translates to a system character.
OnSysCommand	Called when the user selects a command from the Control menu, or when the user selects the Maximize or Minimize button.
OnSysDeadChar	Called when a keystroke translates to a system dead character (such as accent characters).
OnSysKeyDown	Called when the user holds down the ALT key and then presses another key.
OnSysKeyUp	Called when the user releases a key that was pressed while the ALT key was held down.
OnCompacting	Called when Windows detects that system memory is low.

(continued)

System Message Handlers *(continued)*

OnDevModeChange	Called for all top-level windows when the user changes device-mode settings.
OnFontChange	Called when the pool of font resources changes.
OnPaletteIsChanging	Informs other applications when an application is going to realize its logical palette.
OnPaletteChanged	Called to allow windows that use a color palette to realize their logical palettes and update their client areas.
OnSysColorChange	Called for all top-level windows when a change is made in the system color setting.
OnWindowPosChanging	Called when the size, position, or Z-order is about to change as a result of a call to **SetWindowPos** or another window-management function.
OnWindowPosChanged	Called when the size, position, or Z-order has changed as a result of a call to **SetWindowPos** or another window-management function.
OnDropFiles	Called when the user releases the left mouse button over a window that has registered itself as the recipient of dropped files.
OnSpoolerStatus	Called from Print Manager whenever a job is added to or removed from the Print Manager queue.
OnTimeChange	Called for all top-level windows after the system time changes.
OnWinIniChange	Called for all top-level windows after the Windows initialization file, WIN.INI, is changed.

General Message Handlers

OnCommand	Called when the user selects a command.
OnActivate	Called when **CWnd** is being activated or deactivated.
OnActivateApp	Called when the application is about to be activated or deactivated.
OnCancelMode	Called to allow **CWnd** to cancel any internal modes, such as mouse capture.
OnChildActivate	Called for multiple document interface (MDI) child windows whenever the size or position of **CWnd** changes or **CWnd** is activated.
OnClose	Called as a signal that **CWnd** should be closed.
OnCreate	Called as a part of window creation.
OnCtlColor	Called if **CWnd** is the parent of a control when the control is about to be drawn.
OnDestroy	Called when **CWnd** is being destroyed.

General Message Handlers *(continued)*

OnEnable	Called when **CWnd** is enabled or disabled.
OnEndSession	Called when the session is ending.
OnEnterIdle	Called to inform an application's main window procedure that a modal dialog box or a menu is entering an idle state.
OnEraseBkgnd	Called when the window background needs erasing.
OnGetMinMaxInfo	Called whenever Windows needs to know the maximized position or dimensions, or the minimum or maximum tracking size.
OnIconEraseBkgnd	Called when **CWnd** is minimized (iconic) and the background of the icon must be filled before painting the icon.
OnKillFocus	Called immediately before **CWnd** loses the input focus.
OnMenuChar	Called when the user presses a menu mnemonic character that doesn't match any of the predefined mnemonics in the current menu.
OnMenuSelect	Called when the user selects a menu item.
OnMove	Called after the position of the **CWnd** has been changed.
OnMoving	Indicates that a user is moving a **CWnd** object.
OnDeviceChange	Notifies an application or device driver of a change to the hardware configuration of a device or the computer.
OnStyleChanged	Indicates that the **::SetWindowLong** Windows function has changed one or more of the window's styles.
OnStyleChanging	Indicates that the **::SetWindowLong** Windows function is about to change one or more of the window's styles.
OnPaint	Called to repaint a portion of the window.
OnParentNotify	Called when a child window is created or destroyed, or when the user clicks a mouse button while the cursor is over the child window.
OnQueryDragIcon	Called when a minimized (iconic) **CWnd** is about to be dragged by the user.
OnQueryEndSession	Called when the user chooses to end the Windows session.
OnQueryNewPalette	Informs **CWnd** that it is about to receive the input focus.
OnQueryOpen	Called when **CWnd** is an icon and the user requests that the icon be opened.
OnSetFocus	Called after **CWnd** gains the input focus.
OnShowWindow	Called when **CWnd** is to be hidden or shown.
OnSize	Called after the size of **CWnd** has changed.
OnSizing	Indicates that the user is resizing the rectangle.

(continued)

General Message Handlers *(continued)*

OnStyleChanged	Indicates that one or more of the window's styles has changed.
OnStyleChanging	Indicates that one or more of the window's styles is about to change.

Control Message Handlers

OnCharToItem	Called by a child list box with the **LBS_WANTKEYBOARDINPUT** style in response to a **WM_CHAR** message.
OnCompareItem	Called to determine the relative position of a new item in a child sorted owner-draw combo box or list box.
OnDeleteItem	Called when an owner-draw child list box or combo box is destroyed or when items are removed from the control.
OnDrawItem	Called when a visual aspect of an owner-draw child button control, combo-box control, list-box control, or menu needs to be drawn.
OnDSCNotify	Called in response to an event that a data-source control fires when a control to which the data-source control is bound modifies or attempts to modify the underlying cursor.
OnGetDlgCode	Called for a control so the control can process arrow-key and TAB-key input itself.
OnMeasureItem	Called for an owner-draw child combo box, list box, or menu item when the control is created. **CWnd** informs Windows of the dimensions of the control.
SendChildNotifyLastMsg	Provides a notification message to a child window, from the parent window, so the child window can handle a task.
ReflectChildNotify	Helper function which reflects a message to its source.
OnWndMsg	Indicates if a windows message was handled.
ReflectLastMsg	Reflects the last message to the child window.
OnVKeyToItem	Called by a list box owned by **CWnd** in response to a **WM_KEYDOWN** message.

Input Message Handlers

OnChar	Called when a keystroke translates to a nonsystem character.
OnDeadChar	Called when a keystroke translates to a nonsystem dead character (such as accent characters).
OnHScroll	Called when the user clicks the horizontal scroll bar of **CWnd**.
OnKeyDown	Called when a nonsystem key is pressed.
OnKeyUp	Called when a nonsystem key is released.

Input Message Handlers *(continued)*

OnLButtonDblClk	Called when the user double-clicks the left mouse button.
OnLButtonDown	Called when the user presses the left mouse button.
OnLButtonUp	Called when the user releases the left mouse button.
OnMButtonDblClk	Called when the user double-clicks the middle mouse button.
OnMButtonDown	Called when the user presses the middle mouse button.
OnMButtonUp	Called when the user releases the middle mouse button.
OnMouseActivate	Called when the cursor is in an inactive window and the user presses a mouse button.
OnMouseMove	Called when the mouse cursor moves.
OnMouseWheel	Called when a user rotates the mouse wheel. Uses Windows NT 4.0 message handling.
OnRegisteredMouseWheel	Called when a user rotates the mouse wheel. Uses Windows 95 and Windows NT 3.51 message-handling.
OnRButtonDblClk	Called when the user double-clicks the right mouse button.
OnRButtonDown	Called when the user presses the right mouse button.
OnRButtonUp	Called when the user releases the right mouse button.
OnSetCursor	Called if mouse input is not captured and the mouse causes cursor movement within a window.
OnTimer	Called after each interval specified in **SetTimer**.
OnVScroll	Called when the user clicks the window's vertical scroll bar.
OnCaptureChanged	Sends a message to the window that is losing the mouse capture.

Nonclient-Area Message Handlers

OnNcActivate	Called when the nonclient area needs to be changed to indicate an active or inactive state.
OnNcCalcSize	Called when the size and position of the client area need to be calculated.
OnNcCreate	Called prior to **OnCreate** when the nonclient area is being created.
OnNcDestroy	Called when the nonclient area is being destroyed.
OnNcHitTest	Called by Windows every time the mouse is moved if **CWnd** contains the cursor or has captured mouse input with **SetCapture**.
OnNcLButtonDblClk	Called when the user double-clicks the left mouse button while the cursor is within a nonclient area of **CWnd**.
OnNcLButtonDown	Called when the user presses the left mouse button while the cursor is within a nonclient area of **CWnd**.

(continued)

Nonclient-Area Message Handlers *(continued)*

OnNcLButtonUp	Called when the user releases the left mouse button while the cursor is within a nonclient area of **CWnd**.
OnNcMButtonDblClk	Called when the user double-clicks the middle mouse button while the cursor is within a nonclient area of **CWnd**.
OnNcMButtonDown	Called when the user presses the middle mouse button while the cursor is within a nonclient area of **CWnd**.
OnNcMButtonUp	Called when the user releases the middle mouse button while the cursor is within a nonclient area of **CWnd**.
OnNcMouseMove	Called when the cursor is moved within a nonclient area of **CWnd**.
OnNcPaint	Called when the nonclient area needs painting.
OnNcRButtonDblClk	Called when the user double-clicks the right mouse button while the cursor is within a nonclient area of **CWnd**.
OnNcRButtonDown	Called when the user presses the right mouse button while the cursor is within a nonclient area of **CWnd**.
OnNcRButtonUp	Called when the user releases the right mouse button while the cursor is within a nonclient area of **CWnd**.

MDI Message Handlers

OnMDIActivate	Called when an MDI child window is activated or deactivated.

Clipboard Message Handlers

OnAskCbFormatName	Called by a Clipboard viewer application when a Clipboard owner will display the Clipboard contents.
OnChangeCbChain	Notifies that a specified window is being removed from the chain.
OnDestroyClipboard	Called when the Clipboard is emptied through a call to the Windows **EmptyClipboard** function.
OnDrawClipboard	Called when the contents of the change.
OnHScrollClipboard	Called when a Clipboard owner should scroll the Clipboard image, invalidate the appropriate section, and update the scroll-bar values.
OnPaintClipboard	Called when the client area of the Clipboard viewer needs repainting.
OnRenderAllFormats	Called when the owner application is being destroyed and needs to render all its formats.
OnRenderFormat	Called for the Clipboard owner when a particular format with delayed rendering needs to be rendered.

Clipboard Message Handlers *(continued)*	
OnSizeClipboard	Called when the size of the client area of the Clipboard-viewer window has changed.
OnVScrollClipboard	Called when the owner should scroll the Clipboard image, invalidate the appropriate section, and update the scroll-bar values.

Menu Loop Notification	
OnEnterMenuLoop	Called when a menu modal loop has been entered.
OnExitMenuLoop	Called when a menu modal loop has been exited.

Member Functions

CWnd::ArrangeIconicWindows

UINT ArrangeIconicWindows( );

Return Value

The height of one row of icons if the function is successful; otherwise 0.

Remarks

Arranges all the minimized (iconic) child windows.

This member function also arranges icons on the desktop window, which covers the entire screen. The **GetDesktopWindow** member function retrieves a pointer to the desktop window object.

To arrange iconic MDI child windows in an MDI client window, call **CMDIFrameWnd::MDIIconArrange**.

See Also: CWnd::GetDesktopWindow, CMDIFrameWnd::MDIIconArrange, ::ArrangeIconicWindows

CWnd::Attach

BOOL Attach(HWND *hWndNew* **);**

Return Value

Nonzero if successful; otherwise 0.

Parameters

hWndNew   Specifies a handle to a Windows window.

Remarks

Attaches a Windows window to a **CWnd** object.

See Also: CWnd::Detach, CWnd::m_hWnd, CWnd::SubclassWindow

CWnd::BeginPaint

CDC* BeginPaint(LPPAINTSTRUCT *lpPaint* **);**

Return Value

Identifies the device context for **CWnd**. The pointer may be temporary and should not be stored beyond the scope of **EndPaint**.

Parameters

lpPaint   Points to the **PAINTSTRUCT** structure that is to receive painting information.

Remarks

Prepares **CWnd** for painting and fills a **PAINTSTRUCT** data structure with information about the painting.

The paint structure contains a **RECT** data structure that has the smallest rectangle that completely encloses the update region and a flag that specifies whether the background has been erased.

The update region is set by the **Invalidate**, **InvalidateRect**, or **InvalidateRgn** member functions and by the system after it sizes, moves, creates, scrolls, or performs any other operation that affects the client area. If the update region is marked for erasing, **BeginPaint** sends an **WM_ONERASEBKGND** message.

Do not call the **BeginPaint** member function except in response to a **WM_PAINT** message. Each call to the **BeginPaint** member function must have a matching call to the **EndPaint** member function. If the caret is in the area to be painted, the **BeginPaint** member function automatically hides the caret to prevent it from being erased.

See Also: CWnd::EndPaint, CWnd::Invalidate, CWnd::InvalidateRgn, ::BeginPaint, CPaintDC

CWnd::BindDefaultProperty

void BindDefaultProperty(DISPID *dwDispID***, VARTYPE** *vtProp***,**
↪ **LPCTSTR** *szFieldName***, CWnd *** *pDSCWnd* **);**

Parameters

dwDispID   Specifies the DISPID of a property on a data-bound control that is to be bound to a data-source control.

vtProp   Specifies the type of the property to be bound¾for example, **VT_BSTR**, **VT_VARIANT**, and so on.

szFieldName   Specifies the name of the column, in the cursor provided by the data-source control, to which the property will be bound.

pDSCWnd   Points to the window that hosts the data-source control to which the property will be bound. Call **GetDlgItem** with the resource ID of the DCS's host window to retrieve this pointer.

Remarks

Binds the calling object's default simple bound property (such as an edit control), as marked in the type library, to the underlying cursor that is defined by the DataSource, UserName, Password, and SQL properties of the data-source control. The **CWnd** object on which you call this function must be a data-bound control.
BindDefaultProperty might be used in the following context:

```
BOOL CMyDlg::OnInitDialog()
{
   ...
   CWnd* pDSC = GetDlgItem(IDC_REMOTEDATACONTROL);
   CWnd* pList = GetDlgItem(IDC_DBLISTBOX);
   pList->BindDefaultProperty(0x2,
      VT_BSTR, _T("CourseID"), pDSC);
   CWnd* pEdit = GetDlgItem(IDC_MASKEDBOX);
   pEdit->BindDefaultProperty(0x16,
      VT_BSTR, _T("InstuctorID"), pDSC);
   ...
   return TRUE;
}
```

See Also: CWnd::GetDSCCursor, CWnd::BindProperty

CWnd::BindProperty

void BindProperty(DISPID *dwDispID*, **CWnd** * *pWndDSC* **);**

Parameters

dwDispID   Specifies the DISPID of a property on a data-bound control that is to be bound to a data-source control.

pWndDSC   Points to the window that hosts the data-source control to which the property will be bound. Call **GetDlgItem** with the resource ID of the DCS's host window to retrieve this pointer.

Remarks

Binds a cursor-bound property on a data-bound control (such as a grid control) to a data-source control and registers that relationship with the MFC binding manager. The **CWnd** object on which you call this function must be a data-bound control.
BindProperty might be used in the following context:

```
BOOL CMyDlg::OnInitDialog()
{
   ...
   CWnd* pDSC = GetDlgItem(IDC_REMOTEDATACONTROL);
   CWnd* pList= GetDlgItem(IDC_DBLISTBOX);
   pList.BindProperty(0x9, pDSC);
```

```
    ...
    return TRUE;
}
```

See Also: **CWnd::GetDSCCursor, CWnd::BindDefaultProperty**

CWnd::BringWindowToTop

void BringWindowToTop( );

Remarks

Brings **CWnd** to the top of a stack of overlapping windows. In addition,
BringWindowToTop activates pop-up, top-level, and MDI child windows. The
BringWindowToTop member function should be used to uncover any window that
is partially or completely obscured by any overlapping windows.

Calling this function is similar to calling the **SetWindowPos** function to change
a window's position in the Z-order. The **BringWindowToTop** function does not
change the window style to make it a top-level window of the desktop.

See Also: **::BringWindowToTop**

CWnd::CalcWindowRect

virtual void CalcWindowRect(LPRECT *lpClientRect*,
↪ UINT *nAdjustType* = **adjustBorder**);

Parameters

lpClientRect Points to a **RECT** structure or **CRect** object that contains the resultant
value of the window rectangle.

nAdjustType An enumerated type used for in-place editing. It can have the following
values: **CWnd::adjustBorder** = 0, which means that scroll-bar sizes are ignored in
calculation; and **CWnd::adjustOutside** = 1, which means that they are added into
the final measurements of the rectangle.

Remarks

Call this member function to compute the required size of the window rectangle based
on the desired client-rectangle size. The resulting window rectangle (contained in
lpClientRect) can then be passed to the **Create** member function to create a window
whose client area is the desired size.

Called by the framework to size windows prior to creation.

A client rectangle is the smallest rectangle that completely encloses a client area. A
window rectangle is the smallest rectangle that completely encloses the window.

See Also: **::AdjustWindowRectEx**

CWnd::CancelToolTips

static void PASCAL CancelToolTips(BOOL *bKeys* **= FALSE);**

Parameters

bKeys   **TRUE** to cancel tooltips when a key is pressed and set the status bar text to the default; otherwise **FALSE**.

Remarks

Call this member function to remove a tooltip from the screen if a tooltip is currently displayed.

Note   Using this member function has no effect on tooltips managed by your code. It only affects the tooltip control managed by **CWnd::EnableToolTips**.

See Also: **EnableToolTips**, **TTM_ACTIVATE**

CWnd::CenterWindow

void CenterWindow(CWnd* *pAlternateOwner* **= NULL);**

Parameters

pAlternateOwner   Pointer to an alternate window relative to which it will be centered (other than the parent window).

Remarks

Centers a window relative to its parent. Usually called from **CDialog::OnInitDialog** to center dialog boxes relative to the main window of the application. By default, the function centers child windows relative to their parent window, and pop-up windows relative to their owner. If the pop-up window is not owned, it is centered relative to the screen. To center a window relative to a specific window which is not the owner or parent, the *pAlternateOwner* parameter may be set to a valid window. To force centering relative to the screen, pass the value returned by **CWnd::GetDesktopWindow** as *pAlternateOwner*.

See Also: **CWnd::GetDesktopWindow**, **CDialog::OnInitDialog**

CWnd::ChangeClipboardChain

BOOL ChangeClipboardChain(HWND *hWndNext* **);**

Return Value

Nonzero if successful; otherwise 0.

Parameters

hWndNext   Identifies the window that follows **CWnd** in the Clipboard-viewer chain.

Remarks

Removes **CWnd** from the chain of Clipboard viewers and makes the window specified by *hWndNext* the descendant of the **CWnd** ancestor in the chain.

See Also: **CWnd::SetClipboardViewer, ::ChangeClipboardChain**

CWnd::CheckDlgButton

> **void CheckDlgButton(int** *nIDButton***, UINT** *nCheck* **);**

Parameters

nIDButton   Specifies the button to be modified.

nCheck   Specifies the action to take. If *nCheck* is nonzero, the **CheckDlgButton** member function places a check mark next to the button; if 0, the check mark is removed. For three-state buttons, if *nCheck* is 2, the button state is indeterminate.

Remarks

Selects (places a check mark next to) or clears (removes a check mark from) a button, or it changes the state of a three-state button.

The **CheckDlgButton** function sends a **BM_SETCHECK** message to the specified button.

See Also: **CWnd::IsDlgButtonChecked, CButton::SetCheck, ::CheckDlgButton**

CWnd::CheckRadioButton

> **void CheckRadioButton(int** *nIDFirstButton***, int** *nIDLastButton***, int** *nIDCheckButton* **);**

Parameters

nIDFirstButton   Specifies the integer identifier of the first radio button in the group.

nIDLastButton   Specifies the integer identifier of the last radio button in the group.

nIDCheckButton   Specifies the integer identifier of the radio button to be checked.

Remarks

Selects (adds a check mark to) a given radio button in a group and clears (removes a check mark from) all other radio buttons in the group.

The **CheckRadioButton** function sends a **BM_SETCHECK** message to the specified radio button.

See Also: **CWnd::GetCheckedRadioButton, CButton::SetCheck, ::CheckRadioButton**

CWnd::ChildWindowFromPoint

CWnd* ChildWindowFromPoint(POINT *point* **) const;**
CWnd* ChildWindowFromPoint(POINT *point*, **UINT** *nFlags* **) const;**

Return Value

Identifies the child window that contains the point. It is **NULL** if the given point lies outside of the client area. If the point is within the client area but is not contained within any child window, **CWnd** is returned.

This member function will return a hidden or disabled child window that contains the specified point.

More than one window may contain the given point. However, this function returns only the **CWnd*** of the first window encountered that contains the point.

The **CWnd*** that is returned may be temporary and should not be stored for later use.

Parameters

point   Specifies the client coordinates of the point to be tested.

nflags   Specifies which child windows to skip. This parameter can be a combination of the following values:

Value	Meaning
CWP_ALL	Do not skip any child windows
CWP_SKIPINVISIBLE	Skip invisible child windows
CWP_SKIPDISABLED	Skip disabled child windows
CWP_SKIPTRANSPARENT	Skip transparent child windows

Remarks

Determines which, if any, of the child windows belonging to **CWnd** contains the specified point.

See Also: CWnd::WindowFromPoint, ::ChildWindowFromPoint

CWnd::ClientToScreen

void ClientToScreen(LPPOINT *lpPoint* **) const;**
void ClientToScreen(LPRECT *lpRect* **) const;**

Parameters

lpPoint   Points to a **POINT** structure or **CPoint** object that contains the client coordinates to be converted.

lpRect   Points to a **RECT** structure or **CRect** object that contains the client coordinates to be converted.

Remarks

Converts the client coordinates of a given point or rectangle on the display to screen coordinates. The **ClientToScreen** member function uses the client coordinates in the **POINT** or **RECT** structure or the **CPoint** or **CRect** object pointed to by *lpPoint* or *lpRect* to compute new screen coordinates; it then replaces the coordinates in the structure with the new coordinates. The new screen coordinates are relative to the upper-left corner of the system display.

The **ClientToScreen** member function assumes that the given point or rectangle is in client coordinates.

See Also: **CWnd::ScreenToClient, ::ClientToScreen**

CWnd::ContinueModal

> **BOOL ContinueModal( );**

Return Value

Nonzero if modal loop is to be continued; 0 when **EndModalLoop** is called.

Remarks

This member function is called by **RunModalLoop** to determine when the modal state should be exited. By default, it returns non-zero until **EndModalLoop** is called.

See Also: **RunModalLoop, EndModalLoop**

CWnd::Create

> **virtual BOOL Create(LPCTSTR** *lpszClassName*, **LPCTSTR** *lpszWindowName*,
> ↪ **DWORD** *dwStyle*, **const RECT&** *rect*, **CWnd*** *pParentWnd*, **UINT** *nID*,
> ↪ **CCreateContext*** *pContext* = **NULL);**

Return Value

Nonzero if successful; otherwise 0.

Parameters

lpszClassName   Points to a null-terminated character string that names the Windows class (a **WNDCLASS** structure). The class name can be any name registered with the global **AfxRegisterWndClass** function or any of the predefined control-class names. If **NULL**, uses the default **CWnd** attributes.

lpszWindowName   Points to a null-terminated character string that contains the window name.

dwStyle   Specifies the window style attributes. **WS_POPUP** cannot be used. If you wish to create a pop-up window, use **CWnd::CreateEx** instead.

rect   The size and position of the window, in client coordinates of *pParentWnd*.

pParentWnd   The parent window.

nID   The ID of the child window.

pContext   The create context of the window.

Remarks

Creates a Windows child window and attaches it to the **CWnd** object.

You construct a child window in two steps. First, call the constructor, which constructs the **CWnd** object. Then call **Create**, which creates the Windows child window and attaches it to **CWnd**. **Create** initializes the window's class name and window name and registers values for its style, parent, and ID.

See Also: **CWnd::CWnd**, **CWnd::CreateEx**

CWnd::CreateCaret

void CreateCaret(CBitmap* *pBitmap* **);**

Parameters

pBitmap   Identifies the bitmap that defines the caret shape.

Remarks

Creates a new shape for the system caret and claims ownership of the caret.

The bitmap must have previously been created by the **CBitmap::CreateBitmap** member function, the **CreateDIBitmap** Windows function, or the **CBitmap::LoadBitmap** member function.

CreateCaret automatically destroys the previous caret shape, if any, regardless of which window owns the caret. Once created, the caret is initially hidden. To show the caret, the **ShowCaret** member function must be called.

The system caret is a shared resource. **CWnd** should create a caret only when it has the input focus or is active. It should destroy the caret before it loses the input focus or becomes inactive.

See Also: **CBitmap::CreateBitmap**, **::CreateDIBitmap**, **::DestroyCaret**, **CBitmap::LoadBitmap**, **CWnd::ShowCaret**, **::CreateCaret**

CWnd::CreateControl

BOOL CWnd::CreateControl(LPCTSTR *lpszClass*, **LPCTSTR** *lpszWindowName*,
   ↪ **DWORD** *dwStyle*, **const RECT&** *rect*, **CWnd*** *pParentWnd*, **UINT** *nID*,
   ↪ **CFile*** *pPersist* = **NULL, BOOL** *bStorage* = **FALSE, BSTR** *bstrLicKey* = **NULL);**
BOOL CWnd::CreateControl(REFCLSID *clsid*, **LPCTSTR** *lpszWindowName*,
   ↪ **DWORD** *dwStyle*, **const RECT&** *rect*, **CWnd*** *pParentWnd*, **UINT** *nID*,
   ↪ **CFile*** *pPersist* = **NULL, BOOL** *bStorage* = **FALSE, BSTR** *bstrLicKey* = **NULL);**

Return Value

Nonzero if successful; otherwise 0.

Parameters

lpszClass   This string may contain the OLE "short name" (ProgID) for the class, e.g., "CIRC3.Circ3Ctrl.1". The name needs to match the same name registered by the control. Alternatively, the string may contain the string form of a **CLSID**, contained in braces, e.g., "{9DBAFCCF-592F-101B-85CE-00608CEC297B}". In either case, **CreateControl** converts the string to the corresponding class ID.

lpszWindowName   A pointer to the text to be displayed in the control. Sets the value of the control's Caption or Text property (if any). If **NULL**, the control's Caption or Text property is not changed.

dwStyle   Windows styles. The available styles are listed under Remarks.

rect   Specifies the control's size and position. It can be either a **CRect** object or a **RECT** structure.

pParentWnd   Specifies the control's parent window. It must not be **NULL**.

nID   Specifies the control's ID.

pPersist   A pointer to a **CFile** containing the persistent state for the control. The default value is **NULL**, indicating that the control initializes itself without restoring its state from any persistent storage. If not **NULL**, it should be a pointer to a **CFile**-derived object which contains the control's persistent data, in the form of either a stream or a storage. This data could have been saved in a previous activation of the client. The **CFile** can contain other data, but must have its read-write pointer set to the first byte of persistent data at the time of the call to **CreateControl**.

bStorage   Indicates whether the data in *pPersist* should be interpreted as IStorage or IStream data. If the data in *pPersist* is a storage, *bStorage* should be **TRUE**. If the data in *pPersist* is a stream, *bStorage* should be **FALSE**. The default value is **FALSE**.

bstrLicKey   Optional license key data. This data is needed only for creating controls that require a run-time license key. If the control supports licensing, you must provide a license key for the creation of the control to succeed. The default value is **NULL**.

clsid   The unique class ID of the control.

Remarks

Use this member function to create an OLE control that will be represented in the MFC program by a **CWnd** object. **CreateControl** is a direct analog of the **CWnd::Create** function, which creates the window for a **CWnd**. **CreateControl** creates an OLE control instead of an ordinary window.

Only a subset of the Windows *dwStyle* flags are supported for **CreateControl**:

- **WS_VISIBLE** Creates a window that is initially visible. Required if you want the control to be visible immediately, like ordinary windows.

- **WS_DISABLED** Creates a window that is initially disabled. A disabled window cannot receive input from the user. Can be set if the control has an Enabled property.

- **WS_BORDER** Creates a window with a thin-line border. Can be set if control has a BorderStyle property.

- **WS_GROUP** Specifies the first control of a group of controls. The user can change the keyboard focus from one control in the group to the next by using the direction keys. All controls defined with the **WS_GROUP** style after the first control belong to the same group. The next control with the **WS_GROUP** style ends the group and starts the next group.

- **WS_TABSTOP** Specifies a control that can receive the keyboard focus when the user presses the TAB key. Pressing the TAB key changes the keyboard focus to the next control of the **WS_TABSTOP** style.

See Also: In *Visual C++ Programmer's Guide* online: "ActiveX Control Topics"

CWnd::CreateEx

BOOL CreateEx(DWORD *dwExStyle*, **LPCTSTR** *lpszClassName*,
 ↪ **LPCTSTR** *lpszWindowName*, **DWORD** *dwStyle*, **int** *x*, **int** *y*,
 ↪ **int** *nWidth*, **int** *nHeight*, **HWND** *hwndParent*, **HMENU** *nIDorHMenu*,
 ↪ **LPVOID** *lpParam* = **NULL**);
BOOL CreateEx(DWORD *dwExStyle*, **LPCTSTR** *lpszClassName*,
 ↪ **LPCTSTR** *lpszWindowName*, **DWORD** *dwStyle*, **const RECT&** *rect*,
 ↪ **CWnd*** *pParentWnd*, **UINT** *nID*, **LPVOID** *lpParam* = **NULL**);

Return Value

Nonzero if successful; otherwise 0.

Parameters

dwExStyle Specifies the extended style of the **CWnd** being created. Apply any of the extended window styles to the window.

lpszClassName Points to a null-terminated character string that names the Windows class (a **WNDCLASS** structure). The class name can be any name registered with the global **AfxRegisterWndClass** function or any of the predefined control-class names. It must not be **NULL**.

lpszWindowName Points to a null-terminated character string that contains the window name.

dwStyle Specifies the window style attributes. See "Window Styles" and **CWnd::Create** for a description of the possible values.

x Specifies the initial x-position of the **CWnd** window.

y Specifies the initial top position of the **CWnd** window.

nWidth Specifies the width (in device units) of the **CWnd** window.

nHeight Specifies the height (in device units) of the **CWnd** window.

hwndParent Identifies the parent or owner window of the **CWnd** window being created. Use **NULL** for top-level windows.

nIDorHMenu Identifies a menu or a child-window identifier. The meaning depends on the style of the window.

lpParam Points to the data referenced by the **lpCreateParams** field of the **CREATESTRUCT** structure.

rect The size and position of the window, in client coordinates of *pParentWnd*.

pParentWnd The parent window.

nID The ID of the child window.

Remarks

Creates an overlapped, pop-up, or child window with the extended style specified in *dwExStyle*.

The **CreateEx** parameters specify the **WNDCLASS**, window title, window style, and (optionally) initial position and size of the window. **CreateEx** also specifies the window's parent (if any) and ID.

When **CreateEx** executes, Windows sends the **WM_GETMINMAXINFO**, **WM_NCCREATE**, **WM_NCCALCSIZE**, and **WM_CREATE** messages to the window.

To extend the default message handling, derive a class from **CWnd**, add a message map to the new class, and provide member functions for the above messages. Override **OnCreate**, for example, to perform needed initialization for a new class.

Override further **On***Message* message handlers to add further functionality to your derived class.

If the **WS_VISIBLE** style is given, Windows sends the window all the messages required to activate and show the window. If the window style specifies a title bar, the window title pointed to by the *lpszWindowName* parameter is displayed in the title bar.

The *dwStyle* parameter can be any combination of window styles.

See Also: **CWnd::Create, ::CreateWindowEx**

CWnd::CreateGrayCaret

void CreateGrayCaret(int *nWidth***, int** *nHeight* **);**

Parameters

nWidth   Specifies the width of the caret (in logical units). If this parameter is 0, the width is set to the system-defined window-border width.

nHeight   Specifies the height of the caret (in logical units). If this parameter is 0, the height is set to the system-defined window-border height.

Remarks

Creates a gray rectangle for the system caret and claims ownership of the caret. The caret shape can be a line or a block.

The parameters *nWidth* and *nHeight* specify the caret's width and height (in logical units); the exact width and height (in pixels) depend on the mapping mode.

The system's window-border width or height can be retrieved by the **GetSystemMetrics** Windows function with the **SM_CXBORDER** and **SM_CYBORDER** indexes. Using the window-border width or height ensures that the caret will be visible on a high-resolution display.

The **CreateGrayCaret** member function automatically destroys the previous caret shape, if any, regardless of which window owns the caret. Once created, the caret is initially hidden. To show the caret, the **ShowCaret** member function must be called.

The system caret is a shared resource. **CWnd** should create a caret only when it has the input focus or is active. It should destroy the caret before it loses the input focus or becomes inactive.

See Also: **::DestroyCaret**, **::GetSystemMetrics**, **CWnd::ShowCaret**, **::CreateCaret**

CWnd::CreateSolidCaret

void CreateSolidCaret(int *nWidth***, int** *nHeight* **);**

Parameters

nWidth   Specifies the width of the caret (in logical units). If this parameter is 0, the width is set to the system-defined window-border width.

nHeight   Specifies the height of the caret (in logical units). If this parameter is 0, the height is set to the system-defined window-border height.

Remarks

Creates a solid rectangle for the system caret and claims ownership of the caret. The caret shape can be a line or block.

The parameters *nWidth* and *nHeight* specify the caret's width and height (in logical units); the exact width and height (in pixels) depend on the mapping mode.

The system's window-border width or height can be retrieved by the **GetSystemMetrics** Windows function with the **SM_CXBORDER** and **SM_CYBORDER** indexes. Using the window-border width or height ensures that the caret will be visible on a high-resolution display.

The **CreateSolidCaret** member function automatically destroys the previous caret shape, if any, regardless of which window owns the caret. Once created, the caret is initially hidden. To show the caret, the **ShowCaret** member function must be called.

The system caret is a shared resource. **CWnd** should create a caret only when it has the input focus or is active. It should destroy the caret before it loses the input focus or becomes inactive.

See Also: **::DestroyCaret, ::GetSystemMetrics, CWnd::ShowCaret, ::CreateCaret**

CWnd::CWnd

CWnd( );

Remarks

Constructs a **CWnd** object. The Windows window is not created and attached until the **CreateEx** or **Create** member function is called.

See Also: **CWnd::CreateEx, CWnd::Create**

CWnd::Default

LRESULT Default( );

Return Value

Depends on the message sent.

Remarks

Calls the default window procedure. The default window procedure provides default processing for any window message that an application does not process. This member function ensures that every message is processed.

See Also: **CWnd::DefWindowProc, ::DefWindowProc**

CWnd::DefWindowProc

virtual LRESULT DefWindowProc(UINT *message***, WPARAM** *wParam***,**
➥ **LPARAM** *lParam* **);**

Return Value

Depends on the message sent.

Parameters

message   Specifies the Windows message to be processed.

wParam   Specifies additional message-dependent information.

lParam   Specifies additional message-dependent information.

Remarks

Calls the default window procedure, which provides default processing for any
window message that an application does not process. This member function ensures
that every message is processed. It should be called with the same parameters as those
received by the window procedure.

See Also: CWnd::Default, ::DefWindowProc

CWnd::DeleteTempMap

static void PASCAL DeleteTempMap( );

Remarks

Called automatically by the idle time handler of the **CWinApp** object. Deletes any
temporary **CWnd** objects created by the **FromHandle** member function.

See Also: CWnd::FromHandle

CWnd::DestroyWindow

virtual BOOL DestroyWindow( );

Return Value

Nonzero if the window is destroyed; otherwise 0.

Remarks

Destroys the Windows window attached to the **CWnd** object. The **DestroyWindow**
member function sends appropriate messages to the window to deactivate it and
remove the input focus. It also destroys the window's menu, flushes the application
queue, destroys outstanding timers, removes Clipboard ownership, and breaks the
Clipboard-viewer chain if **CWnd** is at the top of the viewer chain. It sends
WM_DESTROY and **WM_NCDESTROY** messages to the window. It does
not destroy the **CWnd** object.

DestroyWindow is a place holder for performing cleanup. Because **DestroyWindow** is a virtual function, it is shown in any **CWnd**-derived class in ClassWizard. But even though you override this function in your **CWnd**-derived class, **DestroyWindow** is not necessarily called. If **DestroyWindow** is not called in the MFC code, then you have to explicitly call it in your own code if you want it to be called.

Assume, for example, you have overridden **DestroyWindow** in a **CView**-derived class. Since MFC source code does not call **DestroyWindow** in any of its **CFrameWnd**-derived classes, your overridden **DestroyWindow** will not be called unless you call it explicitly.

If the window is the parent of any windows, these child windows are automatically destroyed when the parent window is destroyed. The **DestroyWindow** member function destroys child windows first and then the window itself.

The **DestroyWindow** member function also destroys modeless dialog boxes created by **CDialog::Create**.

If the **CWnd** being destroyed is a child window and does not have the **WS_EX_NOPARENTNOTIFY** style set, then the **WM_PARENTNOTIFY** message is sent to the parent.

See Also: **CWnd::OnDestroy**, **CWnd::Detach**, **::DestroyWindow**

CWnd::Detach

HWND Detach( );

Return Value

A **HWND** to the Windows object.

Remarks

Detaches a Windows handle from a **CWnd** object and returns the handle.

See Also: **CWnd::Attach**

CWnd::DlgDirList

int DlgDirList(LPTSTR *lpPathSpec***, int** *nIDListBox***, int** *nIDStaticPath***,**
↪ **UINT** *nFileType* **);**

Return Value

Nonzero if the function is successful; otherwise 0.

Parameters

lpPathSpec   Points to a null-terminated string that contains the path or filename. **DlgDirList** modifies this string, which should be long enough to contain the modifications. For more information, see the following Remarks section.

nIDListBox   Specifies the identifier of a list box. If *nIDListBox* is 0, **DlgDirList** assumes that no list box exists and does not attempt to fill one.

nIDStaticPath   Specifies the identifier of the static-text control used to display the current drive and directory. If *nIDStaticPath* is 0, **DlgDirList** assumes that no such text control is present.

nFileType   Specifies the attributes of the files to be displayed. It can be any combination of the following values:

- **DDL_READWRITE**   Read-write data files with no additional attributes.

- **DDL_READONLY**   Read-only files.

- **DDL_HIDDEN**   Hidden files.

- **DDL_SYSTEM**   System files.

- **DDL_DIRECTORY**   Directories.

- **DDL_ARCHIVE**   Archives.

- **DDL_POSTMSGS   LB_DIR** flag. If the **LB_DIR** flag is set, Windows places the messages generated by **DlgDirList** in the application's queue; otherwise, they are sent directly to the dialog-box procedure.

- **DDL_DRIVES**   Drives. If the **DDL_DRIVES** flag is set, the **DDL_EXCLUSIVE** flag is set automatically. Therefore, to create a directory listing that includes drives and files, you must call **DlgDirList** twice: once with the **DDL_DRIVES** flag set and once with the flags for the rest of the list.

- **DDL_EXCLUSIVE**   Exclusive bit. If the exclusive bit is set, only files of the specified type are listed; otherwise normal files and files of the specified type are listed.

Remarks

Fills a list box with a file or directory listing. **DlgDirList** sends **LB_RESETCONTENT** and **LB_DIR** messages to the list box. It fills the list box specified by *nIDListBox* with the names of all files that match the path given by *lpPathSpec*.

The *lpPathSpec* parameter has the following form:

[*drive:*] [[\u]*directory*[\i*directory*]...\u] [*filename*]

In this example, *drive* is a drive letter, *directory* is a valid directory name, and *filename* is a valid filename that must contain at least one wildcard. The wildcards are a question mark (**?**), which means match any character, and an asterisk (*****), meaning match any number of characters.

If you specify a 0-length string for *lpPathSpec*, or if you specify only a directory name but do not include any file specification, the string will be changed to "*.*".

If *lpPathSpec* includes a drive and/or directory name, the current drive and directory are changed to the designated drive and directory before the list box is filled. The text control identified by *nIDStaticPath* is also updated with the new drive and/or directory name.

After the list box is filled, *lpPathSpec* is updated by removing the drive and/or directory portion of the path.

See Also: CWnd::DlgDirListComboBox, ::DlgDirList

CWnd::DlgDirListComboBox

int DlgDirListComboBox(LPTSTR *lpPathSpec***, int** *nIDComboBox***,**
↪ int *nIDStaticPath***, UINT** *nFileType* **);**

Return Value

Specifies the outcome of the function. It is nonzero if a listing was made, even an empty listing. A 0 return value implies that the input string did not contain a valid search path.

Parameters

lpPathSpec   Points to a null-terminated string that contains the path or filename. **DlgDirListComboBox** modifies this string, which should be long enough to contain the modifications. For more information, see the following Remarks section.

nIDComboBox   Specifies the identifier of a combo box in a dialog box. If *nIDComboBox* is 0, **DlgDirListComboBox** assumes that no combo box exists and does not attempt to fill one.

nIDStaticPath   Specifies the identifier of the static-text control used to display the current drive and directory. If *nIDStaticPath* is 0, **DlgDirListComboBox** assumes that no such text control is present.

nFileType   Specifies DOS file attributes of the files to be displayed. It can be any combination of the following values:

- **DDL_READWRITE**   Read-write data files with no additional attributes.

- **DDL_READONLY**   Read-only files.

- **DDL_HIDDEN**   Hidden files.

- **DDL_SYSTEM**   System files.

- **DDL_DIRECTORY**   Directories.

- **DDL_ARCHIVE**   Archives.

- **DDL_POSTMSGS   CB_DIR** flag. If the **CB_DIR** flag is set, Windows places the messages generated by **DlgDirListComboBox** in the application's queue; otherwise, they are sent directly to the dialog-box procedure.

- **DDL_DRIVES** Drives. If the **DDL_DRIVES** flag is set, the **DDL_EXCLUSIVE** flag is set automatically. Therefore, to create a directory listing that includes drives and files, you must call **DlgDirListComboBox** twice: once with the **DDL_DRIVES** flag set and once with the flags for the rest of the list.

- **DDL_EXCLUSIVE** Exclusive bit. If the exclusive bit is set, only files of the specified type are listed; otherwise normal files and files of the specified type are listed.

Remarks

Fills the list box of a combo box with a file or directory listing. **DlgDirListComboBox** sends **CB_RESETCONTENT** and **CB_DIR** messages to the combo box. It fills the list box of the combo box specified by *nIDComboBox* with the names of all files that match the path given by *lpPathSpec*.

The *lpPathSpec* parameter has the following form:

[*drive*:] [[\u]*directory*[\i*directory*]...\u] [*filename*]

In this example, *drive* is a drive letter, *directory* is a valid directory name, and *filename* is a valid filename that must contain at least one wildcard. The wildcards are a question mark (**?**), which means match any character, and an asterisk (*****), which means match any number of characters.

If you specify a zero-length string for *lpPathSpec*, or if you specify only a directory name but do not include any file specification, the string will be changed to "*.*".

If *lpPathSpec* includes a drive and/or directory name, the current drive and directory are changed to the designated drive and directory before the list box is filled. The text control identified by *nIDStaticPath* is also updated with the new drive and/or directory name.

After the combo-box list box is filled, *lpPathSpec* is updated by removing the drive and/or directory portion of the path.

See Also: **CWnd::DlgDirList**, **CWnd::DlgDirSelect**, **::DlgDirListComboBox**

CWnd::DlgDirSelect

BOOL DlgDirSelect(LPTSTR *lpString***, int** *nIDListBox* **);**

Return Value

Nonzero if successful; otherwise 0.

Parameters

lpString Points to a buffer that is to receive the current selection in the list box.

nIDListBox Specifies the integer ID of a list box in the dialog box.

Remarks

Retrieves the current selection from a list box. It assumes that the list box has been filled by the **DlgDirList** member function and that the selection is a drive letter, a file, or a directory name.

The **DlgDirSelect** member function copies the selection to the buffer given by *lpString*. If there is no selection, *lpString* does not change.

DlgDirSelect sends **LB_GETCURSEL** and **LB_GETTEXT** messages to the list box.

It does not allow more than one filename to be returned from a list box. The list box must not be a multiple-selection list box.

See Also: **CWnd::DlgDirList**, **CWnd::DlgDirListComboBox**, **CWnd::DlgDirSelectComboBox**, **::DlgDirSelectEx**

CWnd::DlgDirSelectComboBox

BOOL DlgDirSelectComboBox(LPTSTR *lpString***, int** *nIDComboBox* **);**

Return Value

Nonzero if successful; otherwise 0.

Parameters

lpString   Points to a buffer that is to receive the selected path.

nIDComboBox   Specifies the integer ID of the combo box in the dialog box.

Remarks

Retrieves the current selection from the list box of a combo box. It assumes that the list box has been filled by the **DlgDirListComboBox** member function and that the selection is a drive letter, a file, or a directory name.

The **DlgDirSelectComboBox** member function copies the selection to the specified buffer. If there is no selection, the contents of the buffer are not changed.

DlgDirSelectComboBox sends **CB_GETCURSEL** and **CB_GETLBTEXT** messages to the combo box.

It does not allow more than one filename to be returned from a combo box.

See Also: **CWnd::DlgDirListComboBox**, **::DlgDirSelectComboBoxEx**

CWnd::DoDataExchange

virtual void DoDataExchange(CDataExchange* *pDX* **);**

Parameters

pDX   A pointer to a **CDataExchange** object.

Remarks

Called by the framework to exchange and validate dialog data.

Never call this function directly. It is called by the **UpdateData** member function. Call **UpdateData** to initialize a dialog box's controls or retrieve data from a dialog box.

When you derive an application-specific dialog class from **CDialog**, you need to override this member function if you wish to utilize the framework's automatic data exchange and validation. ClassWizard will write an overridden version of this member function for you containing the desired "data map" of dialog data exchange (DDX) and validation (DDV) global function calls.

To automatically generate an overridden version of this member function, first create a dialog resource with the dialog editor, then derive an application-specific dialog class. Then call ClassWizard and use it to associate variables, data, and validation ranges with various controls in the new dialog box. ClassWizard then writes the overridden **DoDataExchange**, which contains a data map. The following is an example DDX/DDV code block generated by ClassWizard:

```
void CPenWidthsDlg::DoDataExchange(CDataExchange* pDX)
{
    CDialog::DoDataExchange(pDX);
    //{{AFX_DATA_MAP(CPenWidthsDlg)

        DDX_Text(pDX, IDC_THIN_PEN_WIDTH, m_nThinWidth);

        DDV_MinMaxInt(pDX, m_nThinWidth, 1, 20);

        DDX_Text(pDX, IDC_THICK_PEN_WIDTH, m_nThickWidth);

        DDV_MinMaxInt(pDX, m_nThickWidth, 1, 20);
    //}}AFX_DATA_MAP
}
```

ClassWizard will maintain the code within the \\{{ and \\}} delimiters. You should not modify this code.

The **DoDataExchange** overridden member function must precede the macro statements in your source file.

For more information on dialog data exchange and validation, see "Displaying and Manipulating Data in a Form" in the article ODBC and MFC, "Dialog Data Exchange and Validation," and "Using ClassWizard" in the *Visual C++ Programmer's Guide* online. For a description of the DDX_ and DDV_ macros generated by ClassWizard, see Technical Note 26 online.

See Also: CWnd::UpdateData

CWnd::DragAcceptFiles

void DragAcceptFiles(BOOL *bAccept* **= TRUE);**

Parameters

bAccept   Flag that indicates whether dragged files are accepted.

Remarks

Call this member function from within the main window in your application's
CWinApp::InitInstance function to indicate that your main window and all child
windows accept dropped files from the Windows File Manager.

To discontinue receiving dragged files, call the member function with *bAccept* equal
to **FALSE**.

See Also: ::DragAcceptFiles, WM_DROPFILES

CWnd::DrawMenuBar

void DrawMenuBar( );

Remarks

Redraws the menu bar. If a menu bar is changed after Windows has created the
window, call this function to draw the changed menu bar.

See Also: ::DrawMenuBar

CWnd::EnableScrollBar

BOOL EnableScrollBar(int *nSBFlags***, UINT** *nArrowFlags* **= ESB_ENABLE_BOTH);**

Return Value

Nonzero if the arrows are enabled or disabled as specified. Otherwise it is 0, which
indicates that the arrows are already in the requested state or that an error occurred.

Parameters

nSBFlags   Specifies the scroll-bar type. Can have one of the following values:

- **SB_BOTH**   Enables or disables the arrows of the horizontal and vertical scroll
  bars associated with the window.

- **SB_HORZ**   Enables or disables the arrows of the horizontal scroll bar
  associated with the window.

- **SB_VERT**   Enables or disables the arrows of the vertical scroll bar associated
  with the window.

nArrowFlags   Specifies whether the scroll-bar arrows are enabled or disabled and
which arrows are enabled or disabled. Can have one of the following values:

- **ESB_ENABLE_BOTH** Enables both arrows of a scroll bar (default).

- **ESB_DISABLE_LTUP** Disables the left arrow of a horizontal scroll bar or the up arrow of a vertical scroll bar.

- **ESB_DISABLE_RTDN** Disables the right arrow of a horizontal scroll bar or the down arrow of a vertical scroll bar.

- **ESB_DISABLE_BOTH** Disables both arrows of a scroll bar.

Remarks

Enables or disables one or both arrows of a scroll bar.

See Also: **CWnd::ShowScrollBar**, **CScrollBar::EnableScrollBar**

CWnd::EnableScrollBarCtrl

void EnableScrollBarCtrl(int *nBar***, BOOL** *bEnable* **= TRUE);**

Parameters

nBar The scroll-bar identifier.

bEnable Specifies whether the scroll bar is to be enabled or disabled.

Remarks

Call this member function to enable or disable the scroll bar for this window. If the window has a sibling scroll-bar control, that scroll bar is used; otherwise the window's own scroll bar is used.

See Also: **CWnd::GetScrollBarCtrl**

CWnd::EnableToolTips

BOOL EnableToolTips(BOOL *bEnable* **);**

Return Value

TRUE if tooltips are enabled; otherwise **FALSE**.

Parameters

bEnable Specifies whether the tooltip control is enabled or disabled. **TRUE** enables the control; **FALSE** disables the control.

Remarks

Call this member function to enable tooltips for the given window. Override **OnToolHitTest** to provide the **TOOLINFO** struct(s) for the window.

Note Some windows, such as **CToolBar**, provide a built-in implementation of **OnToolHitTest**.

See **TOOLINFO** in the *Win32 SDK Programmer's Reference* for more information on this structure.

Simply calling **EnableToolTips** is not enough to display tool tips for your child controls unless the parent window is derived from **CFrameWnd**. This is because **CFrameWnd** provides a default handler for the **TTN_NEEDTEXT** notification. If your parent window is not derived from **CFrameWnd**, that is, if it is a dialog box or a form view, tool tips for your child controls will not display correctly unless you provide a handler for the **TTN_NEEDTEXT** tool tip notification. See "Tool Tips" in *Visual C++ Programmer's Guide* online for a sample handler.

The default tool tips provided for your windows by **EnableToolTips** do not have text associated with them. In order to retrieve text for the tool tip to display, the **TTN_NEEDTEXT** notification is sent to the tool tip control's parent window just before the tool tip window is displayed. If there is no handler for this message to assign some value to the *pszText* member of the **TOOLTIPTEXT** structure, there will be no text displayed for the tool tip.

See Also: **CWnd::CancelToolTips, CWnd::OnToolHitTest, CToolBar, TOOLINFO**

CWnd::EnableWindow

BOOL EnableWindow(BOOL *bEnable* **= TRUE);**

Return Value

Indicates the state before the **EnableWindow** member function was called. The return value is nonzero if the window was previously disabled. The return value is 0 if the window was previously enabled or an error occurred.

Parameters

bEnable   Specifies whether the given window is to be enabled or disabled. If this parameter is **TRUE**, the window will be enabled. If this parameter is **FALSE**, the window will be disabled.

Remarks

Enables or disables mouse and keyboard input. When input is disabled, input such as mouse clicks and keystrokes is ignored. When input is enabled, the window processes all input.

If the enabled state is changing, the **WM_ENABLE** message is sent before this function returns.

If disabled, all child windows are implicitly disabled, although they are not sent **WM_ENABLE** messages.

A window must be enabled before it can be activated. For example, if an application is displaying a modeless dialog box and has disabled its main window, the main window must be enabled before the dialog box is destroyed. Otherwise, another window will get the input focus and be activated. If a child window is disabled, it is ignored when Windows tries to determine which window should get mouse messages.

By default, a window is enabled when it is created. An application can specify the **WS_DISABLED** style in the **Create** or **CreateEx** member function to create a window that is initially disabled. After a window has been created, an application can also use the **EnableWindow** member function to enable or disable the window.

An application can use this function to enable or disable a control in a dialog box. A disabled control cannot receive the input focus, nor can a user access it.

See Also: **::EnableWindow**, **CWnd::OnEnable**

CWnd::EndModalLoop

void EndModalLoop(int *nResult* **);**

Parameters

nResult   Contains the value to be returned to the caller of **RunModalLoop**.

Remarks

Call this member function to terminate a call to **RunModalLoop**. The *nResult* parameter is propagated to the return value from **RunModalLoop**.

See Also: **CWnd::RunModalLoop**, **CWnd::ContinueModal**

CWnd::EndPaint

void EndPaint(LPPAINTSTRUCT *lpPaint* **);**

Parameters

lpPaint   Points to a **PAINTSTRUCT** structure that contains the painting information retrieved by the **BeginPaint** member function.

Remarks

Marks the end of painting in the given window. The **EndPaint** member function is required for each call to the **BeginPaint** member function, but only after painting is complete.

If the caret was hidden by the **BeginPaint** member function, **EndPaint** restores the caret to the screen.

See Also: **CWnd::BeginPaint**, **::EndPaint**, **CPaintDC**

CWnd::ExecuteDlgInit

BOOL ExecuteDlgInit(LPCTSTR *lpszResourceName* **);**
BOOL ExecuteDlgInit(LPVOID *lpResource* **);**

Return Value

TRUE if a dialog resource is executed; otherwise **FALSE**.

Parameters

lpszResourceName   A pointer to a null-terminated string specifying the name of the resource.

lpResource   A pointer to a resource.

Remarks

Call this member function to initiate a dialog resource.

ExecuteDlgInit will use resources bound to the executing module, or resources from other sources. To accomplish this, **ExecuteDlgInit** finds a resource handle by calling **AfxFindResourceHandle**. If your MFC application does not use the shared DLL (MFCx0[U][D].DLL), **AfxFindResourceHandle** calls **AfxGetResourceHandle**, which returns the current resource handle for the executable. If your MFC application that uses MFCx0[U][D].DLL, **AfxFindResourceHandle** traverses the **CDynLinkLibrary** object list of shared and extension DLLs looking for the correct resource handle.

See Also: CDialog::OnInitDialog, ::WM_INITDIALOG

CWnd::FilterToolTipMessage

void FilterToolTipMessage(MSG* *pMsg* **);**

Parameters

pMsg   A pointer to the tooltip message.

Remarks

This member function is called by the framework to to display the tooltip message associated with a button on the toolbar. It is normally called from **PreTranslateMessage**.

Call it when the framework does not call it for you.

See Also: CWnd::OnToolHitTest

CWnd::FindWindow

static CWnd* PASCAL FindWindow(LPCTSTR *lpszClassName*,
↳ **LPCTSTR** *lpszWindowName* **);**

Return Value

Identifies the window that has the specified class name and window name. It is **NULL** if no such window is found.

The **CWnd*** may be temporary and should not be stored for later use.

Parameters

lpszClassName   Points to a null-terminated string that specifies the window's class name (a **WNDCLASS** structure). If *lpClassName* is **NULL**, all class names match.

lpszWindowName   Points to a null-terminated string that specifies the window name (the window's title). If *lpWindowName* is **NULL**, all window names match.

Remarks

Returns the top-level **CWnd** whose window class is given by *lpszClassName* and whose window name, or title, is given by *lpszWindowName*. This function does not search child windows.

See Also: ::FindWindow

CWnd::FlashWindow

BOOL FlashWindow(BOOL *bInvert* **);**

Return Value

Nonzero if the window was active before the call to the **FlashWindow** member function; otherwise 0.

Parameters

bInvert   Specifies whether the **CWnd** is to be flashed or returned to its original state. The **CWnd** is flashed from one state to the other if *bInvert* is **TRUE**. If *bInvert* is **FALSE**, the window is returned to its original state (either active or inactive).

Remarks

Flashes the given window once. For successive flashing, create a system timer and repeatedly call **FlashWindow**. Flashing the **CWnd** means changing the appearance of its title bar as if the **CWnd** were changing from inactive to active status, or vice versa.

(An inactive title bar changes to an active title bar; an active title bar changes to an inactive title bar.)

Typically, a window is flashed to inform the user that it requires attention but that it does not currently have the input focus.

The *bInvert* parameter should be **FALSE** only when the window is getting the input focus and will no longer be flashing; it should be **TRUE** on successive calls while waiting to get the input focus.

This function always returns nonzero for minimized windows. If the window is minimized, **FlashWindow** will simply flash the window's icon; *bInvert* is ignored for minimized windows.

See Also: ::FlashWindow

CWnd::FromHandle

static CWnd* PASCAL FromHandle(HWND *hWnd*);

Return Value

Returns a pointer to a **CWnd** object when given a handle to a window. If a **CWnd** object is not attached to the handle, a temporary **CWnd** object is created and attached.

The pointer may be temporary and should not be stored for later use.

Parameters

hWnd   An **HWND** of a Windows window.

See Also: CWnd::DeleteTempMap

CWnd::FromHandlePermanent

static CWnd* PASCAL FromHandlePermanent(HWND *hWnd*);

Return Value

A pointer to a **CWnd** object.

Parameters

hWnd   An **HWND** of a Windows window.

Remarks

Returns a pointer to a **CWnd** object when given a handle to a window. If a **CWnd** object is not attached to the handle, **NULL** is returned.

This function, unlike **FromHandle**, does not create temporary objects.

See Also: CWnd::FromHandle

CWnd::GetActiveWindow

static CWnd* PASCAL GetActiveWindow( );

Return Value

The active window or **NULL** if no window was active at the time of the call. The pointer may be temporary and should not be stored for later use.

Remarks

Retrieves a pointer to the active window. The active window is either the window that has the current input focus or the window explicitly made active by the **SetActiveWindow** member function.

See Also: **CWnd::SetActiveWindow**, **::GetActiveWindow**

CWnd::GetCapture

static CWnd* PASCAL GetCapture( );

Return Value

Identifies the window that has the mouse capture. It is **NULL** if no window has the mouse capture.

The return value may be temporary and should not be stored for later use.

Remarks

Retrieves the window that has the mouse capture. Only one window has the mouse capture at any given time. A window receives the mouse capture when the **SetCapture** member function is called. This window receives mouse input whether or not the cursor is within its borders.

See Also: **CWnd::SetCapture**, **::GetCapture**

CWnd::GetCaretPos

static CPoint PASCAL GetCaretPos( );

Return Value

CPoint object containing the coordinates of the caret's position.

Remarks

Retrieves the client coordinates of the caret's current position and returns them as a **CPoint**.

The caret position is given in the client coordinates of the **CWnd** window.

See Also: **::GetCaretPos**

CWnd::GetCheckedRadioButton

int GetCheckedRadioButton(int *nIDFirstButton***, int** *nIDLastButton* **);**

Return Value

ID of the checked radio button, or 0 if none is selected.

Parameters

nIDFirstButton   Specifies the integer identifier of the first radio button in the group.

nIDLastButton   Specifies the integer identifier of the last radio button in the group.

Remarks

Retrieves the ID of the currently checked radio button in the specified group.

See Also: CWnd::CheckRadioButton

CWnd::GetClientRect

void GetClientRect(LPRECT *lpRect* **) const;**

Parameters

lpRect   Points to a **RECT** structure or a **CRect** object to receive the client
coordinates. The **left** and **top** members will be 0. The **right** and **bottom** members
will contain the width and height of the window.

Remarks

Copies the client coordinates of the **CWnd** client area into the structure pointed to by
lpRect. The client coordinates specify the upper-left and lower-right corners of the
client area. Since client coordinates are relative to the upper-left corners of the **CWnd**
client area, the coordinates of the upper-left corner are (0,0).

See Also: CWnd::GetWindowRect, ::GetClientRect

CWnd::GetClipboardOwner

static CWnd* PASCAL GetClipboardOwner( );

Return Value

Identifies the window that owns the Clipboard if the function is successful. Otherwise,
it is **NULL**.

The returned pointer may be temporary and should not be stored for later use.

Remarks

Retrieves the current owner of the Clipboard.

The Clipboard can still contain data even if it is not currently owned.

See Also: **CWnd::GetClipboardViewer, ::GetClipboardOwner**

CWnd::GetClipboardViewer

static CWnd* PASCAL GetClipboardViewer( );

Return Value

Identifies the window currently responsible for displaying the Clipboard if successful; otherwise **NULL** (for example, if there is no viewer).

The returned pointer may be temporary and should not be stored for later use.

Remarks

Retrieves the first window in the Clipboard-viewer chain.

See Also: **CWnd::GetClipboardOwner, ::GetClipboardViewer**

CWnd::GetControlUnknown

LPUNKNOWN GetControlUnknown( );

Return Value

A pointer to the **IUnknown** interface of the OLE control represented by this **CWnd** object. If this object does not represent an OLE control, the return value is **NULL**.

Remarks

Call this member function to retrieve a pointer to an unknown OLE control. You should not release this **IUnknown** pointer. Typically, you would use to obtain a specific interface of the control.

The interface pointer returned by **GetControlUnknown** is not reference-counted. Do not call **IUnknown::Release** on the pointer unless you have previously called **IUnknown::AddRef** on it.

See Also: **IUnknown::Release, IUnknown::QueryInterface**

CWnd::GetCurrentMessage

static const MSG* PASCAL GetCurrentMessage( );

Return Value

Returns a pointer to the **MSG** structure that contains the message the window is currently processing. Should only be called when in an **On***Message* handler.

CWnd::GetDC

CDC* GetDC( );

Return Value

Identifies the device context for the **CWnd** client area if successful; otherwise, the return value is **NULL**. The pointer may be temporary and should not be stored for later use.

Remarks

Retrieves a pointer to a common, class, or private device context for the client area depending on the class style specified for the **CWnd**. For common device contexts, **GetDC** assigns default attributes to the context each time it is retrieved. For class and private contexts, **GetDC** leaves the previously assigned attributes unchanged. The device context can be used in subsequent graphics device interface (GDI) functions to draw in the client area.

Unless the device context belongs to a window class, the **ReleaseDC** member function must be called to release the context after painting. Since only five common device contexts are available at any given time, failure to release a device context can prevent other applications from accessing a device context.

A device context belonging to the **CWnd** class is returned by the **GetDC** member function if **CS_CLASSDC**, **CS_OWNDC**, or **CS_PARENTDC** was specified as a style in the **WNDCLASS** structure when the class was registered.

See Also: **CWnd::GetDCEx**, **CWnd::ReleaseDC**, **CWnd::GetWindowDC**, **::GetDC**, **CClientDC**

CWnd::GetDCEx

CDC* GetDCEx(CRgn* *prgnClip*, **DWORD** *flags* **);**

Return Value

The device context for the specified window if the function is successful; otherwise **NULL**.

Parameters

prgnClip   Identifies a clipping region that may be combined with the visible region of the client window.

flags   Can have one of the following preset values:

- **DCX_CACHE**   Returns a device context from the cache rather than the **OWNDC** or **CLASSDC** window. Overrides **CS_OWNDC** and **CS_CLASSDC**.

- **DCX_CLIPCHILDREN**   Excludes the visible regions of all child windows below the **CWnd** window.

- **DCX_CLIPSIBLINGS** Excludes the visible regions of all sibling windows above the **CWnd** window.

- **DCX_EXCLUDERGN** Excludes the clipping region identified by *prgnClip* from the visible region of the returned device context.

- **DCX_INTERSECTRGN** Intersects the clipping region identified by *prgnClip* within the visible region of the returned device context.

- **DCX_LOCKWINDOWUPDATE** Allows drawing even if there is a **LockWindowUpdate** call in effect that would otherwise exclude this window. This value is used for drawing during tracking.

- **DCX_PARENTCLIP** Uses the visible region of the parent window and ignores the parent window's **WS_CLIPCHILDREN** and **WS_PARENTDC** style bits. This value sets the device context's origin to the upper-left corner of the **CWnd** window.

- **DCX_WINDOW** Returns a device context that corresponds to the window rectangle rather than the client rectangle.

Remarks

Retrieves the handle of a device context for the **CWnd** window. The device context can be used in subsequent GDI functions to draw in the client area.

This function, which is an extension to the **GetDC** function, gives an application more control over how and whether a device context for a window is clipped.

Unless the device context belongs to a window class, the **ReleaseDC** function must be called to release the context after drawing. Since only five common device contexts are available at any given time, failure to release a device context can prevent other applications from gaining access to a device context.

In order to obtain a cached device context, an application must specify **DCX_CACHE**. If **DCX_CACHE** is not specified and the window is neither **CS_OWNDC** nor **CS_CLASSDC**, this function returns **NULL**.

A device context with special characteristics is returned by the **GetDCEx** function if the **CS_CLASSDC**, **CS_OWNDC**, or **CS_PARENTDC** style was specified in the **WNDCLASS** structure when the class was registered.

For more information about these characteristics, see the description of the **WNDCLASS** structure in the Win32 SDK documentation.

See Also: **CWnd::BeginPaint**, **CWnd::GetDC**, **CWnd::GetWindowDC**, **CWnd::ReleaseDC**, **::GetDCEx**

CWnd::GetDescendantWindow

CWnd* GetDescendantWindow(int *nID*, **BOOL** *bOnlyPerm* = **FALSE) const;**

Return Value

A pointer to a **CWnd** object, or **NULL** if no child window is found.

Parameters

nID   Specifies the identifier of the control or child window to be retrieved.

bOnlyPerm   Specifies whether the window to be returned can be temporary. If **TRUE**, only a permanent window can be returned; if **FALSE,** the function can return a temporary window. For more information on temporary windows see Technical Note 3 online.

Remarks

Call this member function to find the descendant window specified by the given ID. This member function searches the entire tree of child windows, not only the windows that are immediate children.

See Also: CWnd::GetParentFrame, CWnd::IsChild, CWnd::GetDlgItem

CWnd::GetDesktopWindow

static CWnd* PASCAL GetDesktopWindow( );

Return Value

Identifies the Windows desktop window. This pointer may be temporary and should not be stored for later use.

Remarks

Returns the Windows desktop window. The desktop window covers the entire screen and is the area on top of which all icons and other windows are painted.

See Also: ::GetDesktopWindow

CWnd::GetDlgCtrlID

int GetDlgCtrlID( ) const;

Return Value

The numeric identifier of the **CWnd** child window if the function is successful; otherwise 0.

Remarks

Returns the window or control ID value for any child window, not only that of a control in a dialog box. Since top-level windows do not have an ID value, the return value of this function is invalid if the **CWnd** is a top-level window.

See Also: ::GetDlgCtrlID

CWnd::GetDlgItem

CWnd* GetDlgItem(int *nID* **) const;**
void CWnd::GetDlgItem(int *nID***, HWND*** *phWnd* **) const;**

Return Value

A pointer to the given control or child window. If no control with the integer ID given by the *nID* parameter exists, the value is **NULL**.

The returned pointer may be temporary and should not be stored for later use.

Parameters

nID   Specifies the identifier of the control or child window to be retrieved.

phWnd   A pointer to a child window.

Remarks

Retrieves a pointer to the specified control or child window in a dialog box or other window. The pointer returned is usually cast to the type of control identified by *nID*.

See Also: CWnd::GetWindow, CWnd::GetDescendantWindow,
CWnd::GetWindow, ::GetDlgItem

CWnd::GetDlgItemInt

UINT GetDlgItemInt(int *nID***, BOOL*** *lpTrans* **= NULL,**
   ↪ **BOOL** *bSigned* **= TRUE) const;**

Return Value

Specifies the translated value of the dialog-box item text. Since 0 is a valid return value, *lpTrans* must be used to detect errors. If a signed return value is desired, cast it as an **int** type.

The function returns 0 if the translated number is greater than 32,767 (for signed numbers) or 65,535 (for unsigned).

When errors occur, such as encountering nonnumeric characters and exceeding the above maximum, **GetDlgItemInt** copies 0 to the location pointed to by *lpTrans*. If there are no errors, *lpTrans* receives a nonzero value. If *lpTrans* is **NULL**, **GetDlgItemInt** does not warn about errors.

Parameters

nID   Specifies the integer identifier of the dialog-box control to be translated.

lpTrans   Points to the Boolean variable that is to receive the translated flag.

bSigned   Specifies whether the value to be retrieved is signed.

Remarks

Retrieves the text of the control identified by *nID*. It translates the text of the specified control in the given dialog box into an integer value by stripping any extra spaces at the beginning of the text and converting decimal digits. It stops the translation when it reaches the end of the text or encounters any nonnumeric character.

If *bSigned* is **TRUE**, **GetDlgItemInt** checks for a minus sign (–) at the beginning of the text and translates the text into a signed number. Otherwise, it creates an unsigned value.

It sends a **WM_GETTEXT** message to the control.

See Also: **CWnd::GetDlgItemText, ::GetDlgItemInt**

CWnd::GetDlgItemText

int GetDlgItemText(int *nID***, LPTSTR** *lpStr***, int** *nMaxCount* **) const;**
int GetDlgItemText(int *nID***, CString&** *rString* **) const;**

Return Value

Specifies the actual number of bytes copied to the buffer, not including the terminating null character. The value is 0 if no text is copied.

Parameters

nID   Specifies the integer identifier of the control whose title is to be retrieved.

lpStr   Points to the buffer to receive the control's title or text.

nMaxCount   Specifies the maximum length (in bytes) of the string to be copied to *lpStr*. If the string is longer than *nMaxCount*, it is truncated.

rString   A reference to a **CString**.

Remarks

Call this member function to retrieve the title or text associated with a control in a dialog box. The **GetDlgItemText** member function copies the text to the location pointed to by *lpStr* and returns a count of the number of bytes it copies.

See Also: **CWnd::GetDlgItem, CWnd::GetDlgItemInt, ::GetDlgItemText, WM_GETTEXT**

CWnd::GetDSCCursor

IUnknown * GetDSCCursor( );

Return Value

A pointer to a cursor that is defined by a data-source control. MFC takes care of calling **AddRef** for the pointer.

Remarks

Call this member function to retrieve a pointer to the underlying cursor that is defined by the DataSource, UserName, Password, and SQL properties of the data-source control. Use the returned pointer to set the ICursor property of a complex data-bound control, such as the data-bound grid control. A data-source control will not become active until the first bound control requests its cursor. This can happen either explicitly by a call to **GetDSCCursor** or implicitly by the MFC binding manager. In either case, you can force a data-source control to become active by calling **GetDSCCursor** and then calling **Release** on the returned pointer to **IUnknown**. Activation will cause the data-source control to attempt to connect to the underlying data source. The returned pointer might be used in the following context:

```
BOOL CMyDlg::OnInitDialog()
{
    // Find the child controls on the dialog
    CWnd* pDSC = GetDlgItem(IDC_REMOTEDATACONTROL);
    CDBListBox* pList = (CDBListBox*)
    GetDlgItem(IDC_DBLISTBOX);

    // Tell the MFC binding manager that we are
    // binding DISPID 3 to the data-source control.
    pList->BindProperty(0x3, pDSC);

    // Tell the listbox which field to expose as its
    // bound column
    pList->SetBoundColumn(_T("CourseID"));

    // Tell the listbox which cursor and column
    // to populate its list from
    pList->SetListField(_T("CourseID"));
    IPUNKNOWN *pcursor = pDSC->GetDSCCursor();
    ...
    if (!pcursor)
    {
    // The pointer was not successfully assigned.
        return FALSE;
    }
    // The pointer was successfully assigned,
    pList->SetRowSource(pcursor);
    ...
    pcursor->Release();
    return TRUE;
}
```

See Also: **CWnd::BindDefaultProperty**, **CWnd::BindProperty**

CWnd::GetExStyle

DWORD GetExStyle( ) const;

Return Value

The window's extended style.

See Also: **CWnd::GetStyle**, **::GetWindowLong**

CWnd::GetFocus

static CWnd* PASCAL GetFocus( );

Return Value

A pointer to the window that has the current focus, or **NULL** if there is no focus window.

The pointer may be temporary and should not be stored for later use.

Remarks

Retrieves a pointer to the **CWnd** that currently has the input focus.

See Also: **CWnd::GetActiveWindow**, **CWnd::GetCapture**, **CWnd::SetFocus**, **::GetFocus**

CWnd::GetFont

CFont* GetFont( ) const;

Return Value

A pointer to a **CFont** that contains the current font.

The pointer may be temporary and should not be stored for later use.

Remarks

Gets the current font for this window.

See Also: **CWnd::SetFont**, **WM_GETFONT**, **CFont**

CWnd::GetForegroundWindow

static CWnd* PASCAL GetForegroundWindow( );

Return Value

A pointer to the foreground window. This may be a temporary **CWnd** object.

Remarks

Returns a pointer to the foreground window (the window with which the user is currently working). The foreground window applies only to top-level windows (frame windows or dialog boxes).

See Also: **CWnd::SetForegroundWindow**

CWnd::GetIcon

HICON GetIcon(BOOL *bBigIcon* **) const;**

Return Value

A handle to an icon. If unsuccessful, returns **NULL**.

Parameters

bBigIcon　Specifies a 32 pixel by 32 pixel icon if **TRUE**; specifies a 16 pixel by 16 pixel icon if **FALSE**.

Remarks

Call this member function to get the handle to either a big (32x32) or the handle to a small (16x16) icon, as indicated by *bBigIcon*.

See Also:　SetIcon

CWnd::GetLastActivePopup

CWnd* GetLastActivePopup( ) const;

Return Value

Identifies the most recently active pop-up window. The return value will be the window itself if any of the following conditions are met:

- The window itself was most recently active.
- The window does not own any pop-up windows.
- The window is not a top-level window or is owned by another window.

The pointer may be temporary and should not be stored for later use.

Remarks

Determines which pop-up window owned by **CWnd** was most recently active.

See Also:　::GetLastActivePopup

CWnd::GetMenu

CMenu* GetMenu( ) const;

Return Value

Identifies the menu. The value is **NULL** if **CWnd** has no menu. The return value is undefined if **CWnd** is a child window.

The returned pointer may be temporary and should not be stored for later use.

Remarks

Retrieves a pointer to the menu for this window. This function should not be used for child windows because they do not have a menu.

See Also: ::GetMenu

CWnd::GetNextDlgGroupItem

CWnd* GetNextDlgGroupItem(CWnd* *pWndCtl***, BOOL** *bPrevious* **= FALSE) const;**

Return Value

Pointer to the previous (or next) control in the group if the member function is successful.

The returned pointer may be temporary and should not be stored for later use.

Parameters

pWndCtl   Identifies the control to be used as the starting point for the search.

bPrevious   Specifies how the function is to search the group of controls in the dialog box. If **TRUE**, the function searches for the previous control in the group; if **FALSE**, it searches for the next control in the group.

Remarks

Searches for the previous (or next) control within a group of controls in a dialog box. A group of controls begins with a control that was created with the **WS_GROUP** style and ends with the last control that was not created with the **WS_GROUP** style.

By default, the **GetNextDlgGroupItem** member function returns a pointer to the next control in the group. If *pWndCtl* identifies the first control in the group and *bPrevious* is **TRUE**, **GetNextDlgGroupItem** returns a pointer to the last control in the group.

See Also: CWnd::GetNextDlgTabItem, ::GetNextDlgGroupItem

CWnd::GetNextDlgTabItem

CWnd* GetNextDlgTabItem(CWnd* *pWndCtl***, BOOL** *bPrevious* **= FALSE) const;**

Return Value

Pointer to the previous (or next) control that has the **WS_TABSTOP** style, if the member function is successful.

The returned pointer may be temporary and should not be stored for later use.

Parameters

pWndCtl   Identifies the control to be used as the starting point for the search.

bPrevious   Specifies how the function is to search the dialog box. If **TRUE**, the function searches for the previous control in the dialog box; if **FALSE**, it searches for the next control.

Remarks

Retrieves a pointer to the first control that was created with the **WS_TABSTOP** style and that precedes (or follows) the specified control.

See Also: CWnd::GetNextDlgGroupItem, **::GetNextDlgTabItem**

CWnd::GetNextWindow

CWnd* GetNextWindow(UINT *nFlag* **= GW_HWNDNEXT) const;**

Return Value

Identifies the next (or the previous) window in the window manager's list if the member function is successful.

The returned pointer may be temporary and should not be stored for later use.

Parameters

nFlag   Specifies whether the function returns a pointer to the next window or the previous window. It can be either **GW_HWNDNEXT**, which returns the window that follows the **CWnd** object on the window manager's list, or **GW_HWNDPREV**, which returns the previous window on the window manager's list.

Remarks

Searches for the next (or previous) window in the window manager's list. The window manager's list contains entries for all top-level windows, their associated child windows, and the child windows of any child windows.

If **CWnd** is a top-level window, the function searches for the next (or previous) top-level window; if **CWnd** is a child window, the function searches for the next (or previous) child window.

See Also: ::GetNextWindow

CWnd::GetOpenClipboardWindow

static CWnd* PASCAL GetOpenClipboardWindow( );

Return Value

The handle of the window that currently has the Clipboard open if the function is successful; otherwise **NULL**.

Remarks

Retrieves the handle of the window that currently has the Clipboard open.

See Also: **CWnd::GetClipboardOwner**, **CWnd::GetClipboardViewer**, **CWnd::OpenClipboard**, **::GetOpenClipboardWindow**

CWnd::GetOwner

CWnd* GetOwner( ) const;

Return Value

A pointer to a **CWnd** object.

Remarks

Retrieves a pointer to the owner of the window. If the window has no owner, then a pointer to the parent window object is returned by default. Note that the relationship between the owner and the owned differs from the parent-child aspect in several important aspects. For example, a window with a parent is confined to its parent window's client area. Owned windows can be drawn at any location on the desktop.

The ownership concept of this function is different from the ownership concept of **GetWindow**.

See Also: **CWnd::GetParent**, **CWnd::SetOwner**

CWnd::GetParent

CWnd* GetParent( ) const;

Return Value

Identifies the parent window if the member function is successful. Otherwise, the value is **NULL**, which indicates an error or no parent window.

The returned pointer may be temporary and should not be stored for later use.

Remarks

Call this function to get a pointer to a child window's parent window (if any). The **GetParent** function returns a pointer the immediate parent. In contrast, the **GetParentOwner** function returns a pointer to the most immediate parent or owner window that is not a child window (does not have the **WS_CHILD** style). If you have a child window within a child window **GetParent** and **GetParentOwner** return different results.

See Also: **CWnd::GetParentOwner**, **CWnd::GetOwner**, **CWnd::SetOwner**, **CWnd::SetParent**, **::GetParent**

CWnd::GetParentFrame

CFrameWnd* GetParentFrame( ) const;

Return Value

A pointer to a frame window if successful; otherwise **NULL**.

Remarks

Call this member function to retrieve the parent frame window. The member function searches up the parent chain until a **CFrameWnd** (or derived class) object is found.

See Also: **CWnd::GetDescendantWindow**, **CWnd::GetParent**, **CFrameWnd::GetActiveView**

CWnd::GetParentOwner

CWnd* GetParentOwner( ) const;

Return Value

A pointer to a **CWnd** object. If a **CWnd** object is not attached to the handle, a temporary **CWnd** object is created and attached. The pointer may be temporary and should not be stored for later use.

Remarks

Call this member function to get a pointer to a child window's parent window or owner window. **GetParentOwner** returns a pointer to the most immediate parent or owner window that is not a child window (does not have the **WS_CHILD** style). The current owner window can be set with **SetOwner**. By default, the parent of a window is its owner.

In contrast, the **GetParent** function returns a pointer to the immediate parent, whether it is a child window or not. If you have a child window within a child window **GetParent** and **GetParentOwner** return different results.

See Also: **CWnd::GetParent**, **CWnd::GetOwner**, **CWnd::SetOwner**, **CWnd::SetParent**, **::GetParent**

CWnd::GetProperty

void GetProperty(DISPID *dwDispID*, **VARTYPE** *vtProp*, **void*** *pvProp* **)const;**

Parameters

dwDispID   Identifies the property to be retrieved. This value is usually supplied by Component Gallery.

vtProp   Specifies the type of the property to be retrieved. For possible values, see the Remarks section for **COleDispatchDriver::InvokeHelper**.

pvProp   Address of the variable that will that will receive the property value. It must match the type specified by *vtProp*.

Remarks

Call this member function to get the OLE control property specified by *dwDispID*. **GetProperty** then returns the value through *pvProp*.

Note This function should be called only on a **CWnd** object that represents an OLE control.

For more information about using this member function with OLE Control Containers, see the article "ActiveX Control Containers: Programming ActiveX Controls in an ActiveX Control Container," in *Visual C++ Programmer's Guide* online.

See Also: **CWnd::InvokeHelper**, **COleDispatchDriver**, **CWnd::CreateControl**

CWnd::GetSafeHwnd

HWND GetSafeHwnd( ) const;

Return Value

Returns the window handle for a window. Returns **NULL** if the **CWnd** is not attached to a window or if it is used with a **NULL CWnd** pointer.

CWnd::GetSafeOwner

CWnd* PASCAL GetSafeOwner(CWnd* *pParent*, **HWND*** *pWndTop* **);**

Return Value

A pointer to the safe owner for the given window.

Parameters

pParent A pointer to a parent **CWnd** window.

pWndTop A pointer to the window that is currently on top. May be **NULL**.

Remarks

Call this member function to retrieve the owner window that should be used for dialog boxes or other modal windows. The safe owner is the first non-child parent window of *pParentWnd*. If *pParentWnd* is **NULL**, the thread's main window (retrieved via **AfxGetMainWnd**) is used to find an owner.

Note The framework itself uses this function to determine the correct owner window for dialog boxes and property sheets where the owner is not specified.

See Also: **AfxGetMainWnd**

CWnd::GetScrollBarCtrl

virtual CScrollBar* GetScrollBarCtrl(int *nBar* **) const;**

Return Value

A sibling scroll-bar control, or **NULL** if none.

Parameters

nBar   Specifies the type of scroll bar. The parameter can take one of the following values:

- **SB_HORZ**   Retrieves the position of the horizontal scroll bar.

- **SB_VERT**   Retrieves the position of the vertical scroll bar.

Remarks

Call this member function to obtain a pointer to the specified sibling scroll bar or splitter window.

This member function does not operate on scroll bars created when the **WS_HSCROLL** or **WS_VSCROLL** bits are set during the creation of a window. The **CWnd** implementation of this function simply returns **NULL**. Derived classes, such as **CView**, implement the described functionality.

See Also: CWnd::EnableScrollBarCtrl

CWnd::GetScrollInfo

BOOL GetScrollInfo(int *nBar***, LPSCROLLINFO** *lpScrollInfo***,**
↪ UINT *nMask* **= SIF_ALL);**

Return Value

If the message retrieved any values, the return is **TRUE**. Otherwise, it is **FALSE**.

Parameters

nBar   Specifies whether the scroll bar is a control or part of a window's nonclient area. If it is part of the nonclient area, *nBar* also indicates whether the scroll bar is positioned horizontally, vertically, or both. It must be one of the following:

- **SB_BOTH**   Specifies the horizontal and vertical scroll bars of the window.

- **SB_HORZ**   Specifies that the window is a horizontal scroll bar.

- **SB_VERT**   Specifies that the window is a vertical scroll bar.

lpScrollInfo   A pointer to a **SCROLLINFO** structure. See the *Win32 SDK Programmer's Reference* for more information about this structure.

nMask   Specifies the scroll bar parameters to retrieve. The default specifies a combination of **SIF_PAGE**, **SIF_POS**, **SIF_TRACKPOS**, and **SIF_RANGE**. See **SCROLLINFO** for more information on the *nMask* values.

Remarks

Call this member function to retrieve the information that the **SCROLLINFO** structure maintains about a scroll bar. **GetScrollInfo** enables applications to use 32-bit scroll positions.

The **SCROLLINFO** structure contains information about a scroll bar, including the minimum and maximum scrolling positions, the page size, and the position of the scroll box (the thumb). See the **SCROLLINFO** structure topic in the *Win32 SDK Programmer's Reference* for more information about changing the structure defaults.

The MFC Windows message handlers that indicate scroll-bar position, **CWnd::OnHScroll** and **CWnd::OnVScroll**, provide only 16 bits of position data. **GetScrollInfo** and **SetScrollInfo** provide 32 bits of scroll-bar position data. Thus, an application can call **GetScrollInfo** while processing either **CWnd::OnHScroll** or **CWnd::OnVScroll** to obtain 32-bit scroll-bar position data.

See Also: **CScrollBar::GetScrollInfo, CWnd::SetScrollInfo, CWnd::SetScrollPos, CWnd::OnVScroll, CWnd::OnHScroll, SCROLLINFO**

CWnd::GetScrollLimit

int GetScrollLimit(int *nBar* **);**

Return Value

Specifies the maximum position of a scroll bar if successful; otherwise 0.

Parameters

nBar   Specifies the type of scroll bar. The parameter can take one of the following values:

- **SB_HORZ**   Retrieves the scroll limit of the horizontal scroll bar.
- **SB_VERT**   Retrieves the scroll limit of the vertical scroll bar.

Remarks

Call this member function to retrieve the maximum scrolling position of the scroll bar.

See Also: **CScrollBar::GetScrollLimit**

CWnd::GetScrollPos

int GetScrollPos(int *nBar* **) const;**

Return Value

Specifies the current position of the scroll box in the scroll bar if successful; otherwise 0.

Parameters

> *nBar*   Specifies the scroll bar to examine. The parameter can take one of the following values:
>
> - **SB_HORZ**   Retrieves the position of the horizontal scroll bar.
> - **SB_VERT**   Retrieves the position of the vertical scroll bar.

Remarks

> Retrieves the current position of the scroll box of a scroll bar. The current position is a relative value that depends on the current scrolling range. For example, if the scrolling range is 50 to 100 and the scroll box is in the middle of the bar, the current position is 75.
>
> **See Also: ::GetScrollPos, CScrollBar::GetScrollPos**

CWnd::GetScrollRange

> **void GetScrollRange(int** *nBar***, LPINT** *lpMinPos***, LPINT** *lpMaxPos* **) const;**

Parameters

> *nBar*   Specifies the scroll bar to examine. The parameter can take one of the following values:
>
> - **SB_HORZ**   Retrieves the position of the horizontal scroll bar.
> - **SB_VERT**   Retrieves the position of the vertical scroll bar.
>
> *lpMinPos*   Points to the integer variable that is to receive the minimum position.
>
> *lpMaxPos*   Points to the integer variable that is to receive the maximum position.

Remarks

> Copies the current minimum and maximum scroll-bar positions for the given scroll bar to the locations specified by *lpMinPos* and *lpMaxPos*. If **CWnd** does not have a scroll bar, then the **GetScrollRange** member function copies 0 to *lpMinPos* and *lpMaxPos*.
>
> The default range for a standard scroll bar is 0 to 100. The default range for a scroll-bar control is empty (both values are 0).
>
> **See Also: ::GetScrollRange**

CWnd::GetStyle

> **DWORD GetStyle( ) const;**

Return Value

> The window's style.
>
> **See Also: ::GetWindowLong**

CWnd::GetSystemMenu

CMenu* GetSystemMenu(BOOL *bRevert* **) const;**

Return Value

Identifies a copy of the Control menu if *bRevert* is **FALSE**. If *bRevert* is **TRUE**, the return value is undefined.

The returned pointer may be temporary and should not be stored for later use.

Parameters

bRevert   Specifies the action to be taken. If *bRevert* is **FALSE**, **GetSystemMenu** returns a handle to a copy of the Control menu currently in use. This copy is initially identical to the Control menu but can be modified. If *bRevert* is **TRUE**, **GetSystemMenu** resets the Control menu back to the default state. The previous, possibly modified, Control menu, if any, is destroyed. The return value is undefined in this case.

Remarks

Allows the application to access the Control menu for copying and modification.

Any window that does not use **GetSystemMenu** to make its own copy of the Control menu receives the standard Control menu.

The pointer returned by the **GetSystemMenu** member function can be used with the **CMenu::AppendMenu**, **CMenu::InsertMenu**, or **CMenu::ModifyMenu** functions to change the Control menu.

The Control menu initially contains items identified with various ID values such as **SC_CLOSE**, **SC_MOVE**, and **SC_SIZE**. Items on the Control menu generate **WM_SYSCOMMAND** messages. All predefined Control-menu items have ID numbers greater than 0xF000. If an application adds items to the Control menu, it should use ID numbers less than F000.

Windows may automatically dim items on the standard Control menu. **CWnd** can carry out its own checking or dimming by responding to the **WM_INITMENU** messages, which are sent before any menu is displayed.

See Also: **CMenu::AppendMenu, CMenu::InsertMenu, CMenu::ModifyMenu, ::GetSystemMenu**

CWnd::GetTopLevelFrame

CFrameWnd* GetTopLevelFrame( ) const;

Return Value

Identifies the top-level frame window of the window.

The returned pointer may be temporary and should not be stored for later use.

Remarks

Call this member function to retrieve the window's top level frame window, if any. If **CWnd** has no attached window, or its top-level parent is not a **CFrameWnd**-derived object, this function returns **NULL**.

See Also: **CWnd::GetTopLevelOwner**, **CWnd::GetTopLevelParent**

CWnd::GetTopLevelOwner

CWnd* GetTopLevelOwner( ) const;

Return Value

Identifies the top-level window. The returned pointer may be temporary and should not be stored for later use.

Remarks

Call this member function to retrieve the top-level window. The top-level window is the window that is a child of the desktop. If **CWnd** has no attached window, this function returns **NULL**.

See Also: **CWnd::GetTopLevelFrame**, **CWnd::GetTopLevelParent**

CWnd::GetTopLevelParent

CWnd* GetTopLevelParent( ) const;

Return Value

Identifies the top-level parent window of the window.

The returned pointer may be temporary and should not be stored for later use.

Remarks

Call this member function to retrieve the window's top-level parent. **GetTopLevelParent** is similar to **GetTopLevelFrame** and **GetTopLevelOwner**; however, it ignores the value set as the current owner window.

See Also: **CWnd::GetTopLevelOwner**, **CWnd::GetTopLevelFrame**, **CWnd::GetOwner**, **CWnd::SetOwner**

CWnd::GetTopWindow

CWnd* GetTopWindow( ) const;

Return Value

Identifies the top-level child window in a **CWnd** linked list of child windows. If no child windows exist, the value is **NULL**.

The returned pointer may be temporary and should not be stored for later use.

Remarks

Searches for the top-level child window that belongs to **CWnd**. If **CWnd** has no children, this function returns **NULL**.

See Also: ::GetTopWindow

CWnd::GetUpdateRect

BOOL GetUpdateRect(LPRECT *lpRect*, **BOOL** *bErase* = **FALSE**);

Return Value

Specifies the status of the update region. The value is nonzero if the update region is not empty; otherwise 0.

If the *lpRect* parameter is set to **NULL**, the return value is nonzero if an update region exists; otherwise 0.

Parameters

lpRect   Points to a **CRect** object or **RECT** structure that is to receive the client coordinates of the update that encloses the update region.

Set this parameter to **NULL** to determine whether an update region exists within the **CWnd**. If *lpRect* is **NULL**, the **GetUpdateRect** member function returns nonzero if an update region exists and 0 if one does not. This provides a way to determine whether a **WM_PAINT** message resulted from an invalid area. Do not set this parameter to **NULL** in Windows version 3.0 and earlier.

bErase   Specifies whether the background in the update region is to be erased.

Remarks

Retrieves the coordinates of the smallest rectangle that completely encloses the update region. If **CWnd** was created with the **CS_OWNDC** style and the mapping mode is not **MM_TEXT**, the **GetUpdateRect** member function gives the rectangle in logical coordinates. Otherwise, **GetUpdateRect** gives the rectangle in client coordinates. If there is no update region, **GetUpdateRect** sets the rectangle to be empty (sets all coordinates to 0).

The *bErase* parameter specifies whether **GetUpdateRect** should erase the background of the update region. If *bErase* is **TRUE** and the update region is not empty, the background is erased. To erase the background, **GetUpdateRect** sends the **WM_ERASEBKGND** message.

The update rectangle retrieved by the **BeginPaint** member function is identical to that retrieved by the **GetUpdateRect** member function.

The **BeginPaint** member function automatically validates the update region, so any call to **GetUpdateRect** made immediately after a call to **BeginPaint** retrieves an empty update region.

See Also: **CWnd::BeginPaint**, **::GetUpdateRect**, **CWnd::OnPaint**, **CWnd::RedrawWindow**

CWnd::GetUpdateRgn

int GetUpdateRgn(CRgn* *pRgn*, **BOOL** *bErase* **= FALSE);**

Return Value

Specifies a short-integer flag that indicates the type of resulting region. The value can take any one of the following:

- **SIMPLEREGION**   The region has no overlapping borders.
- **COMPLEXREGION**   The region has overlapping borders.
- **NULLREGION**   The region is empty.
- **ERROR**   No region was created.

Parameters

pRgn   Identifies the update region.

bErase   Specifies whether the background will be erased and nonclient areas of child windows will be drawn. If the value is **FALSE**, no drawing is done.

Remarks

Retrieves the update region into a region identified by *pRgn*. The coordinates of this region are relative to the upper-left corner (client coordinates).

The **BeginPaint** member function automatically validates the update region, so any call to **GetUpdateRgn** made immediately after a call to **BeginPaint** retrieves an empty update region.

See Also: **CWnd::BeginPaint**, **::GetUpdateRgn**

CWnd::GetWindow

CWnd* GetWindow(UINT *nCmd* **) const;**

Return Value

Returns a pointer to the window requested, or **NULL** if none.

The returned pointer may be temporary and should not be stored for later use.

Parameters

nCmd   Specifies the relationship between **CWnd** and the returned window. It can take one of the following values:

- **GW_CHILD**   Identifies the **CWnd** first child window.

- **GW_HWNDFIRST** If **CWnd** is a child window, returns the first sibling window. Otherwise, it returns the first top-level window in the list.

- **GW_HWNDLAST** If **CWnd** is a child window, returns the last sibling window. Otherwise, it returns the last top-level window in the list.

- **GW_HWNDNEXT** Returns the next window on the window manager's list.

- **GW_HWNDPREV** Returns the previous window on the window manager's list.

- **GW_OWNER** Identifies the **CWnd** owner.

See Also: **CWnd::GetParent**, **CWnd::GetNextWindow**, **::GetWindow**

CWnd::GetWindowContextHelpId

DWORD GetWindowContextHelpId( ) const;

Return Value

The help context identifier. Returns 0 if the window has none.

Remarks

Call this member function to retrieve the help context identifier, if any, associated with the window.

CWnd::GetWindowDC

CDC* GetWindowDC( );

Return Value

Identifies the display context for the given window if the function is successful; otherwise **NULL**.

The returned pointer may be temporary and should not be stored for later use. **ReleaseDC** should be called once for each successful call to **GetWindowDC**.

Remarks

Retrieves the display context for the entire window, including caption bar, menus, and scroll bars. A window display context permits painting anywhere in **CWnd**, since the origin of the context is the upper-left corner of **CWnd** instead of the client area.

Default attributes are assigned to the display context each time it retrieves the context. Previous attributes are lost.

GetWindowDC is intended to be used for special painting effects within the **CWnd** nonclient area. Painting in nonclient areas of any window is not recommended.

The **GetSystemMetrics** Windows function can be used to retrieve the dimensions of various parts of the nonclient area, such as the caption bar, menu, and scroll bars.

After painting is complete, the **ReleaseDC** member function must be called to release the display context. Failure to release the display context will seriously affect painting requested by applications due to limitations on the number of device contexts that can be open at the same time.

See Also: **::GetSystemMetrics**, **CWnd::ReleaseDC**, **::GetWindowDC**, **CWnd::GetDC**, **CWindowDC**

CWnd::GetWindowPlacement

BOOL GetWindowPlacement(WINDOWPLACEMENT* *lpwndpl* **) const;**

Return Value

Nonzero if the function is successful; otherwise 0.

Parameters

lpwndpl   Points to the **WINDOWPLACEMENT** structure that receives the show state and position information.

Remarks

Retrieves the show state and the normal (restored), minimized, and maximized positions of a window.

The **flags** member of the **WINDOWPLACEMENT** structure retrieved by this function is always 0. If **CWnd** is maximized, the **showCmd** member of **WINDOWPLACEMENT** is **SW_SHOWMAXIMIZED**. If the window is minimized, it is **SW_SHOWMINIMIZED.** It is **SW_SHOWNORMAL** otherwise.

See Also: **CWnd::SetWindowPlacement**, **::GetWindowPlacement**

CWnd::GetWindowRect

void GetWindowRect(LPRECT *lpRect* **) const;**

Parameters

lpRect   Points to a **CRect** object or a **RECT** structure that will receive the screen coordinates of the upper-left and lower-right corners.

Remarks

Copies the dimensions of the bounding rectangle of the **CWnd** object to the structure pointed to by *lpRect*. The dimensions are given in screen coordinates relative to the upper-left corner of the display screen. The dimensions of the caption, border, and scroll bars, if present, are included.

See Also: **CWnd::GetClientRect**, **CWnd::MoveWindow**,
CWnd::SetWindowPos, **::GetWindowRect**

CWnd::GetWindowRgn

int GetWindowRgn(HRGN *hRgn* **)const;**

Return Value

The return value specifies the type of the region that the function obtains. It can be
one of the following values:

- **NULLREGION** The region is empty.

- **SIMPLEREGION** The region is a single rectangle.

- **COMPLEXREGION** The region is more than one rectangle.

- **ERROR** An error occurred; the region is unaffected.

Parameters

hRgn A handle to a window region.

Remarks

Call this member function to get the window region of a window. The window region
determines the area within the window where the operating system permits drawing.
The operating system does not display any portion of a window that lies outside of
the window region.

The coordinates of a window's window region are relative to the upper-left corner
of the window, not the client area of the window.

To set the window region of a window, call **CWnd::SetWindowRgn**.

See Also: **CWnd::SetWindowRgn**

CWnd::GetWindowText

int GetWindowText(LPTSTR *lpszStringBuf*, **int** *nMaxCount* **) const;**
void GetWindowText(CString& *rString* **) const;**

Return Value

Specifies the length, in bytes, of the copied string, not including the terminating
null character. It is 0 if **CWnd** has no caption or if the caption is empty.

Parameters

lpszStringBuf Points to the buffer that is to receive the copied string of the
window's title.

nMaxCount   Specifies the maximum number of characters to be copied to the buffer. If the string is longer than the number of characters specified in *nMaxCount*, it is truncated.

rString   A **CString** object that is to receive the copied string of the window's title.

Remarks

Copies the **CWnd** caption title (if it has one) into the buffer pointed to by *lpszStringBuf* or into the destination string *rString*. If the **CWnd** object is a control, the **GetWindowText** member function copies the text within the control instead of copying the caption.

This member function causes the **WM_GETTEXT** message to be sent to the **CWnd** object.

See Also: **CWnd::SetWindowText, WM_GETTEXT, CWnd::GetWindowTextLength**

CWnd::GetWindowTextLength

int GetWindowTextLength( ) const;

Return Value

Specifies the text length, not including any null-termination character. The value is 0 if no such text exists.

Remarks

Returns the length of the **CWnd** object caption title. If **CWnd** is a control, the **GetWindowTextLength** member function returns the length of the text within the control instead of the caption.

This member function causes the **WM_GETTEXTLENGTH** message to be sent to the **CWnd** object.

See Also: **::GetWindowTextLength, WM_GETTEXTLENGTH, CWnd::GetWindowText**

CWnd::HideCaret

void HideCaret( );

Remarks

Hides the caret by removing it from the display screen. Although the caret is no longer visible, it can be displayed again by using the **ShowCaret** member function. Hiding the caret does not destroy its current shape.

Hiding is cumulative. If **HideCaret** has been called five times in a row, the **ShowCaret** member function must be called five times before the caret will be shown.

See Also: **CWnd::ShowCaret**, **::HideCaret**

CWnd::HiliteMenuItem

BOOL HiliteMenuItem(CMenu* *pMenu*, **UINT** *nIDHiliteItem*, **UINT** *nHilite* **);**

Return Value

Specifies whether the menu item was highlighted. Nonzero if the item was highlighted; otherwise 0.

Parameters

pMenu   Identifies the top-level menu that contains the item to be highlighted.

nIDHiliteItem   Specifies the menu item to be highlighted, depending on the value of the *nHilite* parameter.

nHilite   Specifies whether the menu item is highlighted or the highlight is removed. It can be a combination of **MF_HILITE** or **MF_UNHILITE** with **MF_BYCOMMAND** or **MF_BYPOSITION**. The values can be combined using the bitwise OR operator. These values have the following meanings:

- **MF_BYCOMMAND**   Interprets *nIDHiliteItem* as the menu-item ID (the default interpretation).

- **MF_BYPOSITION**   Interprets *nIDHiliteItem* as the zero-based offset of the menu item.

- **MF_HILITE**   Highlights the item. If this value is not given, the highlight is removed from the item.

- **MF_UNHILITE**   Removes the highlight from the item.

Remarks

Highlights or removes the highlight from a top-level (menu-bar) menu item.

The **MF_HILITE** and **MF_UNHILITE** flags can be used only with this member function; they cannot be used with the **CMenu::ModifyMenu** member function.

See Also: **CMenu::ModifyMenu**, **::HiliteMenuItem**

CWnd::Invalidate

void Invalidate(BOOL *bErase* = **TRUE);**

Parameters

bErase   Specifies whether the background within the update region is to be erased.

Remarks

Invalidates the entire client area of **CWnd**. The client area is marked for painting when the next **WM_PAINT** message occurs. The region can also be validated before a **WM_PAINT** message occurs by the **ValidateRect** or **ValidateRgn** member function.

The *bErase* parameter specifies whether the background within the update area is to be erased when the update region is processed. If *bErase* is **TRUE**, the background is erased when the **BeginPaint** member function is called; if *bErase* is **FALSE**, the background remains unchanged. If *bErase* is **TRUE** for any part of the update region, the background in the entire region, not just in the given part, is erased.

Windows sends a **WM_PAINT** message whenever the **CWnd** update region is not empty and there are no other messages in the application queue for that window.

See Also: **CWnd::BeginPaint**, **CWnd::ValidateRect**, **CWnd::ValidateRgn**, **::InvalidateRect**

CWnd::InvalidateRect

void InvalidateRect(LPCRECT *lpRect*, **BOOL** *bErase* = TRUE **);**

Parameters

lpRect   Points to a **CRect** object or a **RECT** structure that contains the rectangle (in client coordinates) to be added to the update region. If *lpRect* is **NULL**, the entire client area is added to the region.

bErase   Specifies whether the background within the update region is to be erased.

Remarks

Invalidates the client area within the given rectangle by adding that rectangle to the **CWnd** update region. The invalidated rectangle, along with all other areas in the update region, is marked for painting when the next **WM_PAINT** message is sent. The invalidated areas accumulate in the update region until the region is processed when the next **WM_PAINT** call occurs, or until the region is validated by the **ValidateRect** or **ValidateRgn** member function.

The *bErase* parameter specifies whether the background within the update area is to be erased when the update region is processed. If *bErase* is **TRUE**, the background is erased when the **BeginPaint** member function is called; if *bErase* is **FALSE**, the background remains unchanged. If *bErase* is **TRUE** for any part of the update region, the background in the entire region is erased, not just in the given part.

Windows sends a **WM_PAINT** message whenever the **CWnd** update region is not empty and there are no other messages in the application queue for that window.

See Also: **CWnd::BeginPaint**, **CWnd::ValidateRect**, **CWnd::ValidateRgn**, **::InvalidateRect**

CWnd::InvalidateRgn

void InvalidateRgn(CRgn* *pRgn*, **BOOL** *bErase* = **TRUE**);

Parameters

pRgn   A pointer to a **CRgn** object that identifies the region to be added to the update region. The region is assumed to have client coordinates. If this parameter is **NULL**, the entire client area is added to the update region.

bErase   Specifies whether the background within the update region is to be erased.

Remarks

Invalidates the client area within the given region by adding it to the current update region of **CWnd**. The invalidated region, along with all other areas in the update region, is marked for painting when the **WM_PAINT** message is next sent. The invalidated areas accumulate in the update region until the region is processed when a **WM_PAINT** message is next sent, or until the region is validated by the **ValidateRect** or **ValidateRgn** member function.

The *bErase* parameter specifies whether the background within the update area is to be erased when the update region is processed. If *bErase* is **TRUE**, the background is erased when the **BeginPaint** member function is called; if *bErase* is **FALSE**, the background remains unchanged. If *bErase* is **TRUE** for any part of the update region, the background in the entire region, not just in the given part, is erased.

Windows sends a **WM_PAINT** message whenever the **CWnd** update region is not empty and there are no other messages in the application queue for that window.

The given region must have been previously created by one of the region functions.

See Also: **CWnd::BeginPaint, CWnd::ValidateRect, CWnd::ValidateRgn, ::InvalidateRgn**

CWnd::InvokeHelper

void InvokeHelper(DISPID *dwDispID*, **WORD** *wFlags*, **VARTYPE** *vtRet*,
↪ **void*** *pvRet*, **const BYTE*** *pbParamInfo*, ... **);**
throw(COleException);
throw(COleDispatchException);

Parameters

dwDispID   Identifies the method or property to be invoked. This value is usually supplied by Component Gallery.

wFlags   Flags describing the context of the call to **IDispatch::Invoke**. For possible *wFlags* values, see **IDispatch::Invoke** in the *Win32 SDK OLE Programmer's Reference*.

vtRet   Specifies the type of the return value. For possible values, see the Remarks section for **COleDispatchDriver::InvokeHelper**.

pvRet   Address of the variable that will that will receive the property value or return value. It must match the type specified by *vtRet*.

pbParamInfo   Pointer to a null-terminated string of bytes specifying the types of the parameters following *pbParamInfo*. For possible values, see the Remarks section for **COleDispatchDriver::InvokeHelper**.

...   Variable List of parameters, of types specified in *pbParamInfo*.

Remarks

Call this member function to invoke the OLE control method or property specified by *dwDispID*, in the context specified by *wFlags*. The *pbParamInfo* parameter specifies the types of the parameters passed to the method or property. The variable list of arguments is represented by ... in the syntax declaration.

This function converts the parameters to **VARIANTARG** values, then invokes the **IDispatch::Invoke** method on the OLE control. If the call to **IDispatch::Invoke** fails, this function will throw an exception. If the **SCODE** (status code) returned by **IDispatch::Invoke** is **DISP_E_EXCEPTION**, this function throws a **COleException** object, otherwise it throws a **COleDispatchException**.

Note   This function should be called only on a **CWnd** object that represents an OLE control.

For more information about using this member function with OLE Control Containers, see the article "ActiveX Control Containers: Programming ActiveX Controls in an ActiveX Control Container," in *Visual C++ Programmer's Guide* online.

See Also: **CWnd::GetProperty**, **CWnd::SetProperty**, **COleDispatchDriver**, **CWnd::CreateControl**

CWnd::IsChild

BOOL IsChild(const CWnd* *pWnd* **) const;**

Return Value

Specifies the outcome of the function. The value is nonzero if the window identified by *pWnd* is a child window of **CWnd**; otherwise 0.

Parameters

pWnd   Identifies the window to be tested.

Remarks

Indicates whether the window specified by *pWnd* is a child window or other direct descendant of **CWnd**. A child window is the direct descendant of **CWnd** if the **CWnd** object is in the chain of parent windows that leads from the original pop-up window to the child window.

See Also: **::IsChild**

CWnd::IsDialogMessage

BOOL IsDialogMessage(LPMSG *lpMsg* **);**

Return Value

Specifies whether the member function has processed the given message. It is nonzero if the message has been processed; otherwise 0. If the return is 0, call the **CWnd::PreTranslateMessage** member function of the base class to process the message. In an override of the **CWnd::PreTranslateMessage** member function the code looks like this :

```
BOOL CMyDlg::PreTranslateMessage( msg )
{
    if( IsDialogMessage( msg ) )
        return TRUE;
    else
        return CWnd::PreTranslateMessage( msg );
}
```

Parameters

lpMsg   Points to an **MSG** structure that contains the message to be checked.

Remarks

Call this member function to determine whether the given message is intended for a modeless dialog box; if it is, this function processes the message. When the **IsDialogMessage** function processes a message, it checks for keyboard messages and converts them to selection commands for the corresponding dialog box. For example, the TAB key selects the next control or group of controls, and the DOWN ARROW key selects the next control in a group.

You must not pass a message processed by **IsDialogMessage** to the **::TranslateMessage** or **::DispatchMessage** Windows functions, because it has already been processed.

See Also: **::DispatchMessage**, **::TranslateMessage**, **::GetMessage**, **CWnd::PreTranslateMessage**, **::IsDialogMessage**

CWnd::IsDlgButtonChecked

UINT IsDlgButtonChecked(int *nIDButton* **) const;**

Return Value

Nonzero if the given control is checked, and 0 if it is not checked. Only radio buttons and check boxes can be checked. For three-state buttons, the return value can be 2 if the button is indeterminate. This member function returns 0 for a pushbutton.

Parameters

nIDButton   Specifies the integer identifier of the button control.

Remarks

Determines whether a button control has a check mark next to it. If the button is a three-state control, the member function determines whether it is dimmed, checked, or neither.

See Also: **::IsDlgButtonChecked**, **CButton::GetCheck**

CWnd::IsIconic

BOOL IsIconic( ) const;

Return Value

Nonzero if **CWnd** is minimized; otherwise 0.

Remarks

Specifies whether **CWnd** is minimized (iconic).

See Also: **::IsIconic**

CWnd::IsWindowEnabled

BOOL IsWindowEnabled( ) const;

Return Value

Nonzero if **CWnd** is enabled; otherwise 0.

Remarks

Specifies whether **CWnd** is enabled for mouse and keyboard input.

See Also: **::IsWindowEnabled**

CWnd::IsWindowVisible

BOOL IsWindowVisible( ) const;

Return Value

Nonzero if **CWnd** is visible (has the **WS_VISIBLE** style bit set, and parent window is visible). Because the return value reflects the state of the **WS_VISIBLE** style bit, the return value may be nonzero even though **CWnd** is totally obscured by other windows.

Remarks

Determines the visibility state of the given window.

A window possesses a visibility state indicated by the **WS_VISIBLE** style bit. When this style bit is set with a call to the **ShowWindow** member function, the window is displayed and subsequent drawing to the window is displayed as long as the window has the style bit set.

Any drawing to a window that has the **WS_VISIBLE** style will not be displayed if the window is covered by other windows or is clipped by its parent window.

See Also: **CWnd::ShowWindow**, **::IsWindowVisible**

CWnd::IsZoomed

> **BOOL IsZoomed( ) const;**

Return Value

> Nonzero if **CWnd** is maximized; otherwise 0.

Remarks

> Determines whether **CWnd** has been maximized.

> **See Also:** **::IsZoomed**

CWnd::KillTimer

> **BOOL KillTimer(int** *nIDEvent* **);**

Return Value

> Specifies the outcome of the function. The value is nonzero if the event was killed. It is 0 if the **KillTimer** member function could not find the specified timer event.

Parameters

> *nIDEvent*   The value of the timer event passed to **SetTimer**.

Remarks

> Kills the timer event identified by *nIDEvent* from the earlier call to **SetTimer**. Any pending **WM_TIMER** messages associated with the timer are removed from the message queue.

> **See Also:** **CWnd::SetTimer**, **::KillTimer**

CWnd::LockWindowUpdate

> **BOOL LockWindowUpdate( );**

Return Value

> Nonzero if the function is successful. It is 0 if a failure occurs or if the **LockWindowUpdate** function has been used to lock another window.

Remarks

Disables drawing in the given window. A locked window cannot be moved. Only one window can be locked at a time. To unlock a window locked with **LockWindowUpdate**, call **UnlockWindowUpdate**.

If an application with a locked window (or any locked child windows) calls the **GetDC, GetDCEx,** or **BeginPaint** Windows function, the called function returns a device context whose visible region is empty. This will occur until the application unlocks the window by calling the **LockWindowUpdate** member function.

While window updates are locked, the system keeps track of the bounding rectangle of any drawing operations to device contexts associated with a locked window. When drawing is reenabled, this bounding rectangle is invalidated in the locked window and its child windows to force an eventual **WM_PAINT** message to update the screen. If no drawing has occurred while the window updates were locked, no area is invalidated.

The **LockWindowUpdate** member function does not make the given window invisible and does not clear the **WS_VISIBLE** style bit.

See Also: **CWnd::GetDCEx**, **::LockWindowUpdate**

CWnd::MapWindowPoints

void MapWindowPoints(CWnd* *pwndTo*, **LPRECT** *lpRect* **) const;**
void MapWindowPoints(CWnd* *pwndTo*, **LPPOINT** *lpPoint*, **UINT** *nCount* **) const;**

Parameters

pwndTo   Identifies the window to which points are converted. If this parameter is **NULL**, the points are converted to screen coordinates.

lpRect   Specifies the rectangle whose points are to be converted. The first version of this function is available only for Windows 3.1 and later.

lpPoint   A pointer to an array of **POINT** structures that contain the set of points to be converted.

nCount   Specifies the number of **POINT** structures in the array pointed to by *lpPoint*.

Remarks

Converts (maps) a set of points from the coordinate space of the **CWnd** to the coordinate space of another window.

See Also: **CWnd::ClientToScreen**, **CWnd::ScreenToClient**, **::MapWindowPoints**

CWnd::MessageBox

int MessageBox(LPCTSTR *lpszText*, **LPCTSTR** *lpszCaption* = **NULL,**
⮑ **UINT** *nType* = **MB_OK**);

Return Value

Specifies the outcome of the function. It is 0 if there is not enough memory to create
the message box.

Parameters

lpszText Points to a **CString** object or null-terminated string containing the message
to be displayed.

lpszCaption Points to a **CString** object or null-terminated string to be used for the
message-box caption. If *lpszCaption* is **NULL**, the default caption "Error" is used.

nType Specifies the contents and behavior of the message box.

Remarks

Creates and displays a window that contains an application-supplied message and
caption, plus a combination of the predefined icons and pushbuttons described in the
Message-Box Styles list. Use the global function **AfxMessageBox** instead of this
member function to implement a message box in your application.

The following shows the various system icons that can be used in a message box:

  MB_ICONHAND, MB_ICONSTOP, and **MB_ICONERROR**

  MB_ICONQUESTION

  MB_ICONEXCLAMATION and **MB_ICONWARNING**

  MB_ICONASTERISK and **MB_ICONINFORMATION**

See Also: **::MessageBox, AfxMessageBox**

CWnd::ModifyStyle

BOOL ModifyStyle(DWORD *dwRemove*, **DWORD** *dwAdd*, **UINT** *nFlags* = 0);

Return Value

Nonzero if style was successfully modified; otherwise, 0.

Parameters

dwRemove Specifies window styles to be removed during style modification.

dwAdd Specifies window styles to be added during style modification.

nFlags Flags to be passed to **SetWindowPos**, or zero if **SetWindowPos** should not
be called. The default is zero. See the Remarks section for a list of preset flags.

Remarks

Call this member function to modify a window's style. Styles to be added or removed can be combined by using the bitwise OR (|) operator. See the topics "General Window Styles" and **::CreateWindow** in the *Win32 SDK Programmer's Reference* for information about the available window styles.

If *nFlags* is nonzero, **ModifyStyle** calls the Windows API function **::SetWindowPos** and redraws the window by combining *nFlags* with the following four preset flags:

- **SWP_NOSIZE**   Retains the current size.
- **SWP_NOMOVE**   Retains the current position.
- **SWP_NOZORDER**   Retains the current Z order.
- **SWP_NOACTIVATE**   Does not activate the window.

To modify a window's extended styles, see **ModifyStyleEx**.

See Also: SetWindowPos, **CWnd::ModifyStyleEx**, "General Window Styles," **::SetWindowPos**

CWnd::ModifyStyleEx

BOOL ModifyStyleEx(DWORD *dwRemove*, **DWORD** *dwAdd*, **UINT** *nFlags* = 0);

Return Value

Nonzero if style was successfully modified; otherwise, 0.

Parameters

dwRemove   Specifies extended styles to be removed during style modification.

dwAdd   Specifies extended styles to be added during style modification.

nFlags   lags to be passed to **SetWindowPos**, or zero if **SetWindowPos** should not be called. The default is zero. See the Remarks section for a list of preset flags.

Remarks

Call this member function to modify a window's extended style. Styles to be added or removed can be combined by using the bitwise OR (|) operator. See the topics "Extended Window Styles" in this book and **::CreateWindowEx** in the *Win32 SDK Programmer's Reference* for information about the available extended styles

If *nFlags* is nonzero, **ModifyStyleEx** calls the Windows API function **::SetWindowPos** and redraws the window by combining *nFlags* with the following four preset flags:

- **SWP_NOSIZE**   Retains the current size.
- **SWP_NOMOVE**   Retains the current position.
- **SWP_NOZORDER**   Retains the current Z order.
- **SWP_NOACTIVATE**   Does not activate the window.

To modify windows using regular window styles, see **ModifyStyle**.

See Also: **CWnd::ModifyStyle, CreateWindowEx**

CWnd::MoveWindow

void MoveWindow(int *x*, **int** *y*, **int** *nWidth*, **int** *nHeight*, **BOOL** *bRepaint* = **TRUE**);
void MoveWindow(LPCRECT *lpRect*, **BOOL** *bRepaint* = **TRUE**);

Parameters

x   Specifies the new position of the left side of the **CWnd**.

y   Specifies the new position of the top of the **CWnd**.

nWidth   Specifies the new width of the **CWnd**.

nHeight   Specifies the new height of the **CWnd**.

bRepaint   Specifies whether **CWnd** is to be repainted. If **TRUE**, **CWnd** receives a
WM_PAINT message in its **OnPaint** message handler as usual. If this parameter
is **FALSE**, no repainting of any kind occurs. This applies to the client area, to the
nonclient area (including the title and scroll bars), and to any part of the parent
window uncovered as a result of **Cwnd**'s move. When this parameter is **FALSE**,
the application must explicitly invalidate or redraw any parts of **CWnd** and parent
window that must be redrawn.

lpRect   The **CRect** object or **RECT** structure that specifies the new size and position.

Remarks

Changes the position and dimensions.

For a top-level **CWnd** object, the *x* and *y* parameters are relative to the upper-left
corner of the screen. For a child **CWnd** object, they are relative to the upper-left
corner of the parent window's client area.

The **MoveWindow** function sends the **WM_GETMINMAXINFO** message.
Handling this message gives **CWnd** the opportunity to modify the default values for
the largest and smallest possible windows. If the parameters to the **MoveWindow**
member function exceed these values, the values can be replaced by the minimum or
maximum values in the **WM_GETMINMAXINFO** handler.

See Also: **CWnd::SetWindowPos, WM_GETMINMAXINFO, ::MoveWindow**

CWnd::OnActivate

afx_msg void OnActivate(UINT *nState*, **CWnd*** *pWndOther*, **BOOL** *bMinimized*);

Parameters

nState   Specifies whether the **CWnd** is being activated or deactivated. It can be one
of the following values:

- **WA_INACTIVE**   The window is being deactivated.

- **WA_ACTIVE**   The window is being activated through some method other than a mouse click (for example, by use of the keyboard interface to select the window).

- **WA_CLICKACTIVE**   The window is being activated by a mouse click.

pWndOther   Pointer to the **CWnd** being activated or deactivated. The pointer can be **NULL**, and it may be temporary.

bMinimized   Specifies the minimized state of the **CWnd** being activated or deactivated. A value of **TRUE** indicates the window is minimized.

   If **TRUE**, the **CWnd** is being activated; otherwise deactivated.

Remarks

The framework calls this member function when a **CWnd** object is being activated or deactivated. First, the main window being deactivated has **OnActivate** called, and then the main window being activated has **OnActivate** called.

If the **CWnd** object is activated with a mouse click, it will also receive an **OnMouseActivate** member function call.

Note   This member function is called by the framework to allow your application to handle a Windows message. The parameters passed to your function reflect the parameters received by the framework when the message was received. If you call the base-class implementation of this function, that implementation will use the parameters originally passed with the message and not the parameters you supply to the function.

See Also: WM_MOUSEACTIVATE, WM_NCACTIVATE, WM_ACTIVATE

CWnd::OnActivateApp

afx_msg void OnActivateApp(BOOL *bActive*, **HTASK** *hTask* **);**

Parameters

bActive   Specifies whether the **CWnd** is being activated or deactivated. **TRUE** means the **CWnd** is being activated. **FALSE** means the **CWnd** is being deactivated.

hTask   Specifies a task handle. If *bActive* is **TRUE**, the handle identifies the task that owns the **CWnd** being deactivated. If *bActive* is **FALSE**, the handle identifies the task that owns the **CWnd** being activated.

Remarks

The framework calls this member function to all top-level windows of the task being activated and for all top-level windows of the task being deactivated.

Note   This member function is called by the framework to allow your application to handle a Windows message. The parameters passed to your function reflect the parameters received by

the framework when the message was received. If you call the base-class implementation of this function, that implementation will use the parameters originally passed with the message and not the parameters you supply to the function.

See Also: WM_ACTIVATEAPP

CWnd::OnAmbientProperty

BOOL OnAmbientProperty(COleControlSite* *pSite***, DISPID** *dispid***, VARIANT*** *pvar* **)**

Return Value

TRUE if the ambient property is supported; **FALSE** if not.

Parameters

pSite   Pointer to the site of the control that requested the ambient property.

dispid   The dispatch ID of the requested ambient property.

pvar   Pointer to a caller-allocated **VARIANT** structure, through which the ambient property's value will be returned.

Remarks

The framework calls this member function to obtain ambient property values from a window that contains OLE controls. Override this function to alter the default ambient property values returned by an OLE control container to its controls. Any ambient property requests not handled by an overriding function should be forwarded to the base class implementation.

CWnd::OnAskCbFormatName

afx_msg void OnAskCbFormatName(UINT *nMaxCount***, LPTSTR** *lpszString* **);**

Parameters

nMaxCount   Specifies the maximum number of bytes to copy.

lpszString   Points to the buffer where the copy of the format name is to be stored.

Remarks

The framework calls this member function when the Clipboard contains a data handle for the **CF_OWNERDISPLAY** format (that is, when the Clipboard owner will display the Clipboard contents). The Clipboard owner should provide a name for its format.

Override this member function and copy the name of the **CF_OWNERDISPLAY** format into the specified buffer, not exceeding the maximum number of bytes specified.

Note   This member function is called by the framework to allow your application to handle a Windows message. The parameters passed to your function reflect the parameters received by

the framework when the message was received. If you call the base-class implementation of this function, that implementation will use the parameters originally passed with the message and not the parameters you supply to the function.

See Also: WM_ASKCBFORMATNAME

CWnd::OnCancelMode

afx_msg void OnCancelMode( );

Remarks

The framework calls this member function to inform **CWnd** to cancel any internal mode. If the **CWnd** object has the focus, its **OnCancelMode** member function is called when a dialog box or message box is displayed. This gives the **CWnd** the opportunity to cancel modes such as mouse capture.

The default implementation responds by calling the **ReleaseCapture** Windows function. Override this member function in your derived class to handle other modes.

See Also: CWnd::Default, ::ReleaseCapture, WM_CANCELMODE

CWnd::OnCaptureChanged

afx_msg void OnCaptureChanged(CWnd* *pWnd* **);**

Parameters

pWnd A pointer to the window to gain mouse capture

Remarks

The framework calls this member function to notify the window that is losing the mouse capture.

A window receives this message even if it calls **::ReleaseCapture** itself. An application should not attempt to set the mouse capture in response to this message. When it receives this message, a window should redraw itself, if necessary, to reflect the new mouse-capture state.

See the *Win32 SDK Programmer's Reference* for information on the **ReleaseCapture** Windows function.

Note This member function is called by the framework to allow your application to handle a Windows message. The parameters passed to your function reflect the parameters received by the framework when the message was received. If you call the base-class implementation of this function, that implementation will use the parameters originally passed with the message and not the parameters you supply to the function.

See Also: WM_CAPTURECHANGED

CWnd::OnChangeCbChain

afx_msg void OnChangeCbChain(HWND *hWndRemove***, HWND** *hWndAfter* **);**

Parameters

> *hWndRemove*   Specifies the window handle that is being removed from the Clipboard-viewer chain.
>
> *hWndAfter*   Specifies the window handle that follows the window being removed from the Clipboard-viewer chain.

Remarks

> The framework calls this member function for each window in the Clipboard-viewer chain to notify it that a window is being removed from the chain.
>
> Each **CWnd** object that receives an **OnChangeCbChain** call should use the **SendMessage** Windows function to send the **WM_CHANGECBCHAIN** message to the next window in the Clipboard-viewer chain (the handle returned by **SetClipboardViewer**). If *hWndRemove* is the next window in the chain, the window specified by *hWndAfter* becomes the next window, and Clipboard messages are passed on to it.
>
> **Note** This member function is called by the framework to allow your application to handle a Windows message. The parameters passed to your function reflect the parameters received by the framework when the message was received. If you call the base-class implementation of this function, that implementation will use the parameters originally passed with the message and not the parameters you supply to the function.
>
> **See Also:** **CWnd::ChangeClipboardChain**, **::SendMessage**

CWnd::OnChar

afx_msg void OnChar(UINT *nChar***, UINT** *nRepCnt***, UINT** *nFlags* **);**

Parameters

> *nChar*   Contains the character code value of the key.
>
> *nRepCnt*   Contains the repeat count, the number of times the keystroke is repeated when user holds down the key.
>
> *nFlags*   Contains the scan code, key-transition code, previous key state, and context code, as shown in the following list:

Value	Description of nFlags
0–7	Scan code (OEM-dependent value).
8	Extended key, such as a function key or a key on the numeric keypad (1 if it is an extended key; otherwise 0).
9-10	Not used.

(continued)

Value	Description of nFlags
11–12	Used internally by Windows.
13	Context code (1 if the ALT key is held down while the key is pressed; otherwise 0).
14	Previous key state (1 if the key is down before the call; 0 if the key is up).
15	Transition state (1 if the key is being released; 0 if the key is being pressed).

Remarks

The framework calls this member function when a keystroke translates to a nonsystem character. This function is called before the **OnKeyUp** member function and after the **OnKeyDown** member function are called. **OnChar** contains the value of the keyboard key being pressed or released.

Because there is not necessarily a one-to-one correspondence between keys pressed and **OnChar** calls generated, the information in *nFlags* is generally not useful to applications. The information in *nFlags* applies only to the most recent call to the **OnKeyUp** member function or the **OnKeyDown** member function that precedes the call to **OnChar**.

For IBM Enhanced 101- and 102-key keyboards, enhanced keys are the right ALT and the right CTRL keys on the main section of the keyboard; the INS, DEL, HOME, END, PAGE UP, PAGE DOWN, and arrow keys in the clusters to the left of the numeric keypad; and the slash (/) and ENTER keys in the numeric keypad. Some other keyboards may support the extended-key bit in *nFlags*.

Note This member function is called by the framework to allow your application to handle a Windows message. The parameters passed to your function reflect the parameters received by the framework when the message was received. If you call the base-class implementation of this function, that implementation will use the parameters originally passed with the message and not the parameters you supply to the function.

See Also: WM_CHAR, WM_KEYDOWN, WM_KEYUP

CWnd::OnCharToItem

afx_msg int OnCharToItem(UINT *nChar*, **CListBox*** *pListBox*, **UINT** *nIndex* **);**

Return Value

The framework calls this member function to specify the action that the application performed in response to the call. A return value of –2 indicates that the application handled all aspects of selecting the item and wants no further action by the list box. A return value of –1 indicates that the list box should perform the default action in response to the keystroke. A return value of 0 or greater specifies the zero-based index of an item in the list box and indicates that the list box should perform the default action for the keystroke on the given item.

Parameters

nChar   Specifies the value of the key pressed by the user.

pListBox   Specifies a pointer to the list box. It may be temporary.

nIndex   Specifies the current caret position.

Remarks

Called when a list box with the **LBS_WANTKEYBOARDINPUT** style sends its owner a **WM_CHARTOITEM** message in response to a **WM_CHAR** message.

Note This member function is called by the framework to allow your application to handle a Windows message. The parameters passed to your function reflect the parameters received by the framework when the message was received. If you call the base-class implementation of this function, that implementation will use the parameters originally passed with the message and not the parameters you supply to the function.

See Also: WM_CHAR, WM_CHARTOITEM

CWnd::OnChildActivate

afx_msg void OnChildActivate( );

Remarks

If the **CWnd** object is a multiple document interface (MDI) child window, **OnChildActivate** is called by the framework when the user clicks the window's title bar or when the window is activated, moved, or sized.

See Also: CWnd::SetWindowPos, WM_CHILDACTIVATE

CWnd::OnChildNotify

virtual BOOL OnChildNotify(UINT *message***, WPARAM** *wParam***,**
↳ LPARAM *lParam***, LRESULT*** *pLResult* **);**

Return Value

Nonzero if this window is responsible for handling the message sent to its parent; otherwise 0.

Parameters

message   A Windows message number sent to a parent window.

wParam   The **wparam** associated with the message.

lParam   The **lparam** associated with the message.

pLResult   A pointer to a value to be returned from the parent's window procedure. This pointer will be **NULL** if no return value is expected.

Remarks

This member function is called by this window's parent window when it receives a notification message that applies to this window.

Never call this member function directly.

The default implementation of this member function returns 0, which means that the parent should handle the message.

Override this member function to extend the manner in which a control responds to notification messages.

CWnd::OnClose

afx_msg void OnClose( );

Remarks

The framework calls this member function as a signal that the **CWnd** or an application is to terminate. The default implementation calls **DestroyWindow**.

See Also: CWnd::DestroyWindow, WM_CLOSE

CWnd::OnCommand

virtual BOOL OnCommand(WPARAM *wParam***, LPARAM** *lParam* **);**

Return Value

An application returns nonzero if it processes this message; otherwise 0.

Parameters

wParam   The low-order word of *wParam* identifies the command ID of the menu item or control. The high-order word of *wParam* specifies the notification message if the message is from a control. If the message is from an accelerator, the high-order word is 1. If the message is from a menu, the high-order word is 0.

lParam   Identifies the control that sends the message if the message is from a control. Otherwise, *lParam* is 0.

Remarks

The framework calls this member function when the user selects an item from a menu, when a child control sends a notification message, or when an accelerator keystroke is translated.

OnCommand processes the message map for control notification and **ON_COMMAND** entries, and calls the appropriate member function.

Override this member function in your derived class to handle the **WM_COMMAND** message. An override will not process the message map unless the base class **OnCommand** is called.

Note This member function is called by the framework to allow your application to handle a Windows message. The parameters passed to your function reflect the parameters received by the framework when the message was received. If you call the base-class implementation of this function, that implementation will use the parameters originally passed with the message and not the parameters you supply to the function.

See Also: **WM_COMMAND**, **CCmdTarget::OnCmdMsg**

CWnd::OnCompacting

afx_msg void OnCompacting(UINT *nCpuTime* **);**

Parameters

nCpuTime Specifies the ratio of CPU time currently spent by Windows compacting memory to CPU time spent performing other operations. For example, 8000h represents 50 percent of CPU time spent compacting memory.

Remarks

The framework calls this member function for all top-level windows when Windows detects that more than 12.5 percent of system time over a 30- to 60-second interval is being spent compacting memory. This indicates that system memory is low.

When a **CWnd** object receives this call, it should free as much memory as possible, taking into account the current level of activity of the application and the total number of applications running in Windows. The application can call the Windows function to determine how many applications are running.

Note This member function is called by the framework to allow your application to handle a Windows message. The parameters passed to your function reflect the parameters received by the framework when the message was received. If you call the base-class implementation of this function, that implementation will use the parameters originally passed with the message and not the parameters you supply to the function.

See Also: **WM_COMPACTING**

CWnd::OnCompareItem

afx_msg int OnCompareItem(int *nIDCtl*,
　↪ **LPCOMPAREITEMSTRUCT** *lpCompareItemStruct* **);**

Return Value

Indicates the relative position of the two items. It may be any of the following values:

Value	Meaning
−1	Item 1 sorts before item 2.
0	Item 1 and item 2 sort the same.
1	Item 1 sorts after item 2.

Parameters

nIDCtl   The identifier of the control that sent the **WM_COMPAREITEM** message.

lpCompareItemStruct   Contains a long pointer to a **COMPAREITEMSTRUCT** data structure that contains the identifiers and application-supplied data for two items in the combo or list box.

Remarks

The framework calls this member function to specify the relative position of a new item in a child sorted owner-draw combo or list box.

If a combo or list box is created with the **CBS_SORT** or **LBS_SORT** style, Windows sends the combo-box or list-box owner a **WM_COMPAREITEM** message whenever the application adds a new item.

Two items in the combo or list box are reformed in a **COMPAREITEMSTRUCT** structure pointed to by *lpCompareItemStruct*. **OnCompareItem** should return a value that indicates which of the items should appear before the other. Typically, Windows makes this call several times until it determines the exact position for the new item.

If the **hwndItem** member of the **COMPAREITEMSTRUCT** structure belongs to a **CListBox** or **CComboBox** object, then the **CompareItem** virtual function of the appropriate class is called. Override **CComboBox::CompareItem** or **CListBox::CompareItem** in your derived **CListBox** or **CComboBox** class to do the item comparison.

Note   This member function is called by the framework to allow your application to handle a Windows message. The parameters passed to your function reflect the parameters received by the framework when the message was received. If you call the base-class implementation of this function, that implementation will use the parameters originally passed with the message and not the parameters you supply to the function.

See Also: COMPAREITEMSTRUCT, WM_COMPAREITEM, **CListBox::CompareItem, CComboBox::CompareItem**

CWnd::OnContextMenu

afx_msg void OnContextMenu(CWnd* *pWnd***, CPoint** *pos* **);**

Parameters

pWnd   Handle to the window in which the user right clicked the mouse. This can be a child window of the window receiving the message. For more information about processing this message, see the Remarks section.

pos   Position of the cursor, in screen coordinates, at the time of the mouse click.

Remarks

Called by the framework when the user has clicked the right mouse button (right clicked) in the window. You can process this message by displaying a context menu using the **TrackPopupMenu**.

If you do not display a context menu you should pass this message onto the **DefWindowProc** function. If your window is a child window, **DefWindowProc** sends the message to the parent. Otherwise, **DefWindowProc** displays a default context menu if the specified position is in the window's caption.

CWnd::OnCreate

afx_msg int OnCreate(LPCREATESTRUCT *lpCreateStruct* **);**

Return Value

OnCreate must return 0 to continue the creation of the **CWnd** object. If the application returns –1, the window will be destroyed.

Parameters

lpCreateStruct   Points to a **CREATESTRUCT** structure that contains information about the **CWnd** object being created.

Remarks

The framework calls this member function when an application requests that the Windows window be created by calling the **Create** or **CreateEx** member function. The **CWnd** object receives this call after the window is created but before it becomes visible. **OnCreate** is called before the **Create** or **CreateEx** member function returns.

Override this member function to perform any needed initialization of a derived class.

The **CREATESTRUCT** structure contains copies of the parameters used to create the window.

Note This member function is called by the framework to allow your application to handle a Windows message. The parameters passed to your function reflect the parameters received by the framework when the message was received. If you call the base-class implementation of this function, that implementation will use the parameters originally passed with the message and not the parameters you supply to the function.

See Also: **CWnd::CreateEx**, **CWnd::OnNcCreate**, **WM_CREATE**, **CWnd::Default**, **CWnd::FromHandle**

CWnd::OnCtlColor

afx_msg HBRUSH OnCtlColor(CDC* *pDC***, CWnd*** *pWnd***, UINT** *nCtlColor* **);**

Return Value

OnCtlColor must return a handle to the brush that is to be used for painting the control background.

Parameters

pDC   Contains a pointer to the display context for the child window. May be temporary.

pWnd   Contains a pointer to the control asking for the color. May be temporary.

nCtlColor   Contains one of the following values, specifying the type of control:

- **CTLCOLOR_BTN**   Button control
- **CTLCOLOR_DLG**   Dialog box
- **CTLCOLOR_EDIT**   Edit control
- **CTLCOLOR_LISTBOX**   List-box control
- **CTLCOLOR_MSGBOX**   Message box
- **CTLCOLOR_SCROLLBAR**   Scroll-bar control
- **CTLCOLOR_STATIC**   Static control

Remarks

The framework calls this member function when a child control is about to be drawn. Most controls send this message to their parent (usually a dialog box) to prepare the *pDC* for drawing the control using the correct colors.

To change the text color, call the **SetTextColor** member function with the desired red, green, and blue (RGB) values.

To change the background color of a single-line edit control, set the brush handle in both the **CTLCOLOR_EDIT** and **CTLCOLOR_MSGBOX** message codes, and call the **CDC::SetBkColor** function in response to the **CTLCOLOR_EDIT** code.

OnCtlColor will not be called for the list box of a drop-down combo box because the drop-down list box is actually a child of the combo box and not a child of the window. To change the color of the drop-down list box, create a **CComboBox** with an override of **OnCtlColor** that checks for **CTLCOLOR_LISTBOX** in the *nCtlColor* parameter. In this handler, the **SetBkColor** member function must be used to set the background color for the text.

Note   This member function is called by the framework to allow your application to handle a Windows message. The parameters passed to your function reflect the parameters received by

the framework when the message was received. If you call the base-class implementation of this function, that implementation will use the parameters originally passed with the message and not the parameters you supply to the function.

See Also: **CDC::SetBkColor**

CWnd::OnDeadChar

afx_msg void OnDeadChar(UINT *nChar***, UINT** *nRepCnt***, UINT** *nFlags* **);**

Parameters

nChar   Specifies the dead-key character value.

nRepCnt   Specifies the repeat count.

nFlags   Specifies the scan code, key-transition code, previous key state, and context code, as shown in the following list:

Value	Description
0–7	Scan code (OEM-dependent value). Low byte of high-order word.
8	Extended key, such as a function key or a key on the numeric keypad (1 if it is an extended key; otherwise 0).
9–10	Not used.
11–12	Used internally by Windows.
13	Context code (1 if the ALT key is held down while the key is pressed; otherwise 0).
14	Previous key state (1 if the key is down before the call, 0 if the key is up).
15	Transition state (1 if the key is being released, 0 if the key is being pressed).

Remarks

The framework calls this member function when the **OnKeyUp** member function and the **OnKeyDown** member functions are called. This member function can be used to specify the character value of a dead key. A dead key is a key, such as the umlaut (double-dot) character, that is combined with other characters to form a composite character. For example, the umlaut-O character consists of the dead key, umlaut, and the O key.

An application typically uses **OnDeadChar** to give the user feedback about each key pressed. For example, an application can display the accent in the current character position without moving the caret.

Since there is not necessarily a one-to-one correspondence between keys pressed and **OnDeadChar** calls, the information in *nFlags* is generally not useful to applications. The information in *nFlags* applies only to the most recent call to the **OnKeyUp** member function or the **OnKeyDown** member function that precedes the **OnDeadChar** call.

For IBM Enhanced 101- and 102-key keyboards, enhanced keys are the right ALT and the right CTRL keys on the main section of the keyboard; the INS, DEL, HOME, END, PAGE UP, PAGE DOWN, and arrow keys in the clusters to the left of the numeric keypad; and the slash (/) and ENTER keys in the numeric keypad. Some other keyboards may support the extended-key bit in *nFlags*.

Note This member function is called by the framework to allow your application to handle a Windows message. The parameters passed to your function reflect the parameters received by the framework when the message was received. If you call the base-class implementation of this function, that implementation will use the parameters originally passed with the message and not the parameters you supply to the function.

See Also: WM_DEADCHAR

CWnd::OnDeleteItem

afx_msg void OnDeleteItem(int *nIDCtl*,
↳ **LPDELETEITEMSTRUCT** *lpDeleteItemStruct* **);**

Parameters

nIDCtl   The identifier of the control that sent the **WM_DELETEITEM** message.

lpDeleteItemStruct   Specifies a long pointer to a **DELETEITEMSTRUCT** data structure that contains information about the deleted list box item.

Remarks

The framework calls this member function to inform the owner of an owner-draw list box or combo box that the list box or combo box is destroyed or that items have been removed by **CComboBox::DeleteString**, **CListBox::DeleteString**, **CComboBox::ResetContent**, or **CListBox::ResetContent**.

If the **hwndItem** member of the **DELETEITEMSTRUCT** structure belongs to a combo box or list box, then the **DeleteItem** virtual function of the appropriate class is called. Override the **DeleteItem** member function of the appropriate control's class to delete item-specific data.

Note This member function is called by the framework to allow your application to handle a Windows message. The parameters passed to your function reflect the parameters received by the framework when the message was received. If you call the base-class implementation of this function, that implementation will use the parameters originally passed with the message and not the parameters you supply to the function.

See Also: CComboBox::DeleteString, CListBox::DeleteString, CComboBox::ResetContent, CListBox::ResetContent, WM_DELETEITEM, CListBox::DeleteItem, CComboBox::DeleteItem

CWnd::OnDestroy

afx_msg void OnDestroy( );

Remarks

The framework calls this member function to inform the **CWnd** object that it is being destroyed. **OnDestroy** is called after the **CWnd** object is removed from the screen.

OnDestroy is called first for the **CWnd** being destroyed, then for the child windows of **CWnd** as they are destroyed. It can be assumed that all child windows still exist while **OnDestroy** runs.

If the **CWnd** object being destroyed is part of the Clipboard-viewer chain (set by calling the **SetClipboardViewer** member function), the **CWnd** must remove itself from the Clipboard-viewer chain by calling the **ChangeClipboardChain** member function before returning from the **OnDestroy** function.

See Also: **CWnd::ChangeClipboardChain, CWnd::DestroyWindow, CWnd::SetClipboardViewer**

CWnd::OnDestroyClipboard

afx_msg void OnDestroyClipboard( );

Remarks

The framework calls this member function for the Clipboard owner when the Clipboard is emptied through a call to the **EmptyClipboard** Windows function.

See Also: **::EmptyClipboard, WM_DESTROYCLIPBOARD**

CWnd::OnDeviceChange

afx_msg BOOL OnDeviceChange(UINT *nEventType***, DWORD** *dwData* **);**

Parameters

nEventType   An event type. See the Remarks section for a description of the available values

dwData   The address of a structure that contains event-specific data. Its meaning depends on the given event.

Remarks

The framework calls this member function to notify an application or device driver of a change to the hardware configuration of a device or the computer.

For devices that offer software-controllable features, such as ejection and locking, the operating system typically sends a **DBT_DEVICEREMOVEPENDING** message to let applications and device drivers end their use of the device gracefully.

If the operating system forcefully removes of a device, it may not send a **DBT_DEVICEQUERYREMOVE** message before doing so.

The *nEvent* parameter can be one of these values:

- **DBT_DEVICEARRIVAL**   A device has been inserted and is now available.
- **DBT_DEVICEQUERYREMOVE**   Permission to remove a device is requested. Any application can deny this request and cancel the removal.
- **DBT_DEVICEQUERYREMOVEFAILED**   Request to remove a device has been canceled.
- **DBT_DEVICEREMOVEPENDING**   Device is about to be removed. Cannot be denied.
- **DBT_DEVICEREMOVECOMPLETE**   Device has been removed.
- **DBT_DEVICETYPESPECIFIC**   Device-specific event.
- **DBT_CONFIGCHANGED**   Current configuration has changed.
- **DBT_DEVNODES_CHANGED**   Device node has changed.

Note   This member function is called by the framework to allow your application to handle a Windows message. The parameters passed to your function reflect the parameters received by the framework when the message was received. If you call the base-class implementation of this function, that implementation will use the parameters originally passed with the message and not the parameters you supply to the function.

See Also: WM_DEVICECHANGE

CWnd::OnDevModeChange

afx_msg void OnDevModeChange(LPTSTR *lpDeviceName* **);**

Parameters

lpDeviceName   Points to the device name specified in the Windows initialization file, WIN.INI.

Remarks

The framework calls this member function for all top-level **CWnd** objects when the user changes device-mode settings.

Applications that handle the **WM_DEVMODECHANGE** message may reinitialize their device-mode settings. Applications that use the Windows **ExtDeviceMode** function to save and restore device settings typically do not process this function.

This function is not called when the user changes the default printer from Control Panel. In this case, the **OnWinIniChange** function is called.

Note This member function is called by the framework to allow your application to handle a Windows message. The parameters passed to your function reflect the parameters received by the framework when the message was received. If you call the base-class implementation of this function, that implementation will use the parameters originally passed with the message and not the parameters you supply to the function.

See Also: WM_DEVMODECHANGE

CWnd::OnDrawClipboard

afx_msg void OnDrawClipboard( );

Remarks

The framework calls this member function for each window in the Clipboard-viewer chain when the contents of the Clipboard change. Only applications that have joined the Clipboard-viewer chain by calling the **SetClipboardViewer** member function need to respond to this call.

Each window that receives an **OnDrawClipboard** call should call the **SendMessage** Windows function to pass a **WM_DRAWCLIPBOARD** message on to the next window in the Clipboard-viewer chain. The handle of the next window is returned by the **SetClipboardViewer** member function; it may be modified in response to an **OnChangeCbChain** member function call.

See Also: ::SendMessage, CWnd::SetClipboardViewer, WM_CHANGECBCHAIN, WM_DRAWCLIPBOARD

CWnd::OnDrawItem

afx_msg void OnDrawItem(int *nIDCtl*, LPDRAWITEMSTRUCT *lpDrawItemStruct*);

Parameters

nIDCtl Contains the identifier of the control that sent the **WM_DRAWITEM** message. If a menu sent the message, *nIDCtl* contains 0.

lpDrawItemStruct Specifies a long pointer to a **DRAWITEMSTRUCT** data structure that contains information about the item to be drawn and the type of drawing required.

Remarks

The framework calls this member function for the owner of an owner-draw button control, combo-box control, list-box control, or menu when a visual aspect of the control or menu has changed.

The **itemAction** member of the **DRAWITEMSTRUCT** structure defines the drawing operation that is to be performed. The data in this member allows the owner of the control to determine what drawing action is required.

Before returning from processing this message, an application should ensure that the device context identified by the **hDC** member of the **DRAWITEMSTRUCT** structure is restored to the default state.

If the **hwndItem** member belongs to a **CButton**, **CMenu**, **CListBox**, or **CComboBox** object, then the **DrawItem** virtual function of the appropriate class is called. Override the **DrawItem** member function of the appropriate control's class to draw the item.

Note This member function is called by the framework to allow your application to handle a Windows message. The parameters passed to your function reflect the parameters received by the framework when the message was received. If you call the base-class implementation of this function, that implementation will use the parameters originally passed with the message and not the parameters you supply to the function.

See Also: **DRAWITEMSTRUCT, WM_DRAWITEM, CButton::DrawItem, CMenu::DrawItem, CListBox::DrawItem, CComboBox::DrawItem**

CWnd::OnDropFiles

afx_msg void OnDropFiles(HDROP *hDropInfo* **);**

Parameters

hDropInfo A pointer to an internal data structure that describes the dropped files. This handle is used by the **DragFinish**, **DragQueryFile**, and **DragQueryPoint** Windows functions to retrieve information about the dropped files.

Remarks

The framework calls this member function when the user releases the left mouse button over a window that has registered itself as the recipient of dropped files.

Typically, a derived class will be designed to support dropped files and it will register itself during window construction.

Note This member function is called by the framework to allow your application to handle a Windows message. The parameters passed to your function reflect the parameters received by the framework when the message was received. If you call the base-class implementation of this function, that implementation will use the parameters originally passed with the message and not the parameters you supply to the function.

See Also: **CWnd::DragAcceptFiles, WM_DROPFILES, ::DragAcceptFiles, ::DragFinish, ::DragQueryFile, ::DragQueryPoint**

CWnd::OnDSCNotify

afx_msg BOOL OnDSCNotify(DSCSTATE *nState***, DSCREASON** *nReason***, BOOL** *pBool* **);**

Return Value

Returns **TRUE** if the operation represented by *nReason* and *nState* was handled. Otherwise, returns **FALSE**.

Parameters

nState One of the named constants found in the **DSCSTATE** enumerator, which are listed under Remarks.

nReason One of the named constants found in the **DSCREASON** enumerator, which are listed under Remarks.

pBool A Boolean answer indicating whether the operation represented by *nState* and *nReason* should continue.

Remarks

This sink notification is called in response to an event that a data-source control fires when a control to which the data-source control is bound modifies or attempts to modify the underlying cursor. Use it to trap reasons (*nReason*) and states (*nState*) generated by a data-source control. All combinations of states and reasons are allowed by default. Write your code to test the states and reasons that are important to your application and return **TRUE** or **FALSE** as appropriate.

To use **OnDSCNotify**, declare a sink map and a handler for the sink notification in the header of the class that wishes to receive the sink notification as follows:

```
class CMyDlg : public CDialog
{
    ...
    DECLARE_EVENTSINK_MAP()
    BOOL OnDSCNotify(DSCSTATE nState,
            DSCREASON nReason, BOOL* pBool);
    ...
};
```

Then, in the implementation of your class, define the sink map and specify the function to receive the events as follows:

```
BEGIN_EVENTSINK_MAP(CMyDlg, CDialog)
   ON_DSCNOTIFY(CMyDlg, IDC_RDCCTRL1, OnDSCNotify)
END_EVENTSINK_MAP()
```

The notification callback function, your implementation of **OnDSCNotify**, will be called when the following events occur inside the data-source control:

```
enum DSCREASON
{
   dscNoReason = 0,
   dscClose, dscCommit, dscDelete,
   dscEdit, dscInsert, dscModify, dscMove
};
```

It will also be called multiple times for each of the following states:

```
enum DSCSTATE
{
    dscNoState = 0,
    dscOKToDo,
    dscCancelled,
    dscSyncBefore,
    dscAboutToDo,
    dscFailedToDo,
    dscSyncAfter,
    dscDidEvent
};
```

The multiple calls allow you to trap an event at different times. For example, since events are usually generated in response to modification of the cursor state by a control, the first thing that the data-source control will do is to fire events asking if it is okay to actually perform that action; hence the reason for the **dscOKToDo** state. If all clients that monitor the event (the data control, your application, and so on) accept the event, the data-source control will then move into the **dscSyncBefore** state, at which time all outstanding data will be flushed, if necessary. For example, if the content of an edit field has changed, the change will be committed to the cursor. Following this event, the data-source control moves into the **dscAboutToDo** and **dscSyncAfter** states and finally into the **dscDidEvent** state. These provide you with further opportunities to catch notifications from the data-source control.

See Also: CWnd::GetDSCCursor, CWnd::BindDefaultProperty, CWnd::BindProperty

CWnd::OnEnable

afx_msg void OnEnable(BOOL *bEnable* **);**

Parameters

bEnable   Specifies whether the **CWnd** object has been enabled or disabled. This parameter is **TRUE** if the **CWnd** has been enabled; it is **FALSE** if the **CWnd** has been disabled.

Remarks

The framework calls this member function when an application changes the enabled state of the **CWnd** object. **OnEnable** is called before the **EnableWindow** member function returns, but after the window enabled state (**WS_DISABLED** style bit) has changed.

Note   This member function is called by the framework to allow your application to handle a Windows message. The parameters passed to your function reflect the parameters received by the framework when the message was received. If you call the base-class implementation of this function, that implementation will use the parameters originally passed with the message and not the parameters you supply to the function.

See Also: **CWnd::EnableWindow**, **WM_ENABLE**

CWnd::OnEndSession

afx_msg void OnEndSession(BOOL *bEnding* **);**

Parameters

bEnding   Specifies whether or not the session is being ended. It is **TRUE** if the session is being ended; otherwise **FALSE**.

Remarks

The framework calls this member function after the **CWnd** object has returned a nonzero value from a **OnQueryEndSession** member function call. The **OnEndSession** call informs the **CWnd** object whether the session is actually ending.

If *bEnding* is **TRUE**, Windows can terminate any time after all applications have returned from processing this call. Consequently, have an application perform all tasks required for termination within **OnEndSession**.

You do not need to call the **DestroyWindow** member function or **PostQuitMessage** Windows function when the session is ending.

Note   This member function is called by the framework to allow your application to handle a Windows message. The parameters passed to your function reflect the parameters received by the framework when the message was received. If you call the base-class implementation of this function, that implementation will use the parameters originally passed with the message and not the parameters you supply to the function.

See Also: **CWnd::DestroyWindow**, **CWnd::OnQueryEndSession**, **::ExitWindows**, **::PostQuitMessage**, **WM_QUERYENDSESSION**, **CWnd::Default**, **WM_ENDSESSION**

CWnd::OnEnterIdle

afx_msg void OnEnterIdle(UINT *nWhy*, **CWnd*** *pWho* **);**

Parameters

nWhy   Specifies whether the message is the result of a dialog box or a menu being displayed. This parameter can be one of the following values:

- **MSGF_DIALOGBOX**   The system is idle because a dialog box is being displayed.

- **MSGF_MENU**   The system is idle because a menu is being displayed.

pWho   Specifies a pointer to the dialog box (if *nWhy* is **MSGF_DIALOGBOX**), or the window that contains the displayed menu (if *nWhy* is **MSGF_MENU**). This pointer may be temporary and should not be stored for later use.

Remarks

The framework calls this member function to inform an application's main window procedure that a modal dialog box or a menu is entering an idle state. A modal dialog box or menu enters an idle state when no messages are waiting in its queue after it has processed one or more previous messages.

Note This member function is called by the framework to allow your application to handle a Windows message. The parameters passed to your function reflect the parameters received by the framework when the message was received. If you call the base-class implementation of this function, that implementation will use the parameters originally passed with the message and not the parameters you supply to the function.

See Also: **WM_ENTERIDLE**

CWnd::OnEnterMenuLoop

afx_msg void OnEnterMenuLoop(BOOL *bIsTrackPopupMenu* **);**

Parameters

bIsTrackPopupMenu Specifies whether the menu involved is a popup menu. Has a nonzero value if the function is successful; otherwise 0.

Remarks

The framework calls this member function when a menu modal loop has been entered.

Note This member function is called by the framework to allow your application to handle a Windows message. The parameters passed to your function reflect the parameters received by the framework when the message was received. If you call the base-class implementation of this function, that implementation will use the parameters originally passed with the message and not the parameters you supply to the function.

See Also: **CWnd::OnExitMenuLoop, WM_ENTERMENULOOP**

CWnd::OnEraseBkgnd

afx_msg BOOL OnEraseBkgnd(CDC* *pDC* **);**

Return Value

Nonzero if it erases the background; otherwise 0.

Parameters

pDC Specifies the device-context object.

Remarks

The framework calls this member function when the **CWnd** object background needs erasing (for example, when resized). It is called to prepare an invalidated region for painting.

The default implementation erases the background using the window class background brush specified by the **hbrBackground** member of the window class structure.

If the **hbrBackground** member is **NULL**, your overridden version of **OnEraseBkgnd** should erase the background color. Your version should also align the origin of the intended brush with the **CWnd** coordinates by first calling **UnrealizeObject** for the brush, and then selecting the brush.

An overridden **OnEraseBkgnd** should return nonzero in response to **WM_ERASEBKGND** if it processes the message and erases the background; this indicates that no further erasing is required. If it returns 0, the window will remain marked as needing to be erased. (Typically, this means that the **fErase** member of the **PAINTSTRUCT** structure will be **TRUE**.)

Windows assumes the background is computed with the **MM_TEXT** mapping mode. If the device context is using any other mapping mode, the area erased may not be within the visible part of the client area.

Note This member function is called by the framework to allow your application to handle a Windows message. The parameters passed to your function reflect the parameters received by the framework when the message was received. If you call the base-class implementation of this function, that implementation will use the parameters originally passed with the message and not the parameters you supply to the function.

See Also: **WM_ICONERASEBKGND**, **CGdiObject::UnrealizeObject**, **WM_ERASEBKGND**

CWnd::OnExitMenuLoop

afx_msg void OnExitMenuLoop(BOOL *bIsTrackPopupMenu* **);**

Parameters

bIsTrackPopupMenu   Specifies whether the menu involved is a pop-up menu. Has a nonzero value if the function is successful; otherwise 0.

Remarks

The framework calls this member function when a menu modal loop has been exited.

Note This member function is called by the framework to allow your application to handle a Windows message. The parameters passed to your function reflect the parameters received by the framework when the message was received. If you call the base-class implementation of this function, that implementation will use the parameters originally passed with the message and not the parameters you supply to the function.

See Also: **CWnd::OnEnterMenuLoop**; **WM_EXITMENULOOP**

CWnd::OnFontChange

afx_msg void OnFontChange( );

Remarks

All top-level windows in the system receive an **OnFontChange** call from the framework after the application changes the pool of font resources.

An application that adds or removes fonts from the system (for example, through the **AddFontResource** or **RemoveFontResource** Windows function) should send the **WM_FONTCHANGE** message to all top-level windows.

To send this message, use the **SendMessage** Windows function with the *hWnd* parameter set to **HWND_BROADCAST**.

See Also: **::AddFontResource, ::RemoveFontResource, ::SendMessage, WM_FONTCHANGE**

CWnd::OnGetDlgCode

afx_msg UINT OnGetDlgCode( );

Return Value

One or more of the following values, indicating which type of input the application processes:

- **DLGC_BUTTON**   Button (generic).
- **DLGC_DEFPUSHBUTTON**   Default pushbutton.
- **DLGC_HASSETSEL   EM_SETSEL** messages.
- **DLGC_UNDEFPUSHBUTTON**   No default pushbutton processing. (An application can use this flag with **DLGC_BUTTON** to indicate that it processes button input but relies on the system for default pushbutton processing.)
- **DLGC_RADIOBUTTON**   Radio button.
- **DLGC_STATIC**   Static control.
- **DLGC_WANTALLKEYS**   All keyboard input.
- **DLGC_WANTARROWS**   Arrow keys.
- **DLGC_WANTCHARS   WM_CHAR** messages.
- **DLGC_WANTMESSAGE**   All keyboard input. The application passes this message on to the control.
- **DLGC_WANTTAB**   TAB key.

Remarks

Normally, Windows handles all arrow-key and TAB-key input to a **CWnd** control. By overriding **OnGetDlgCode**, a **CWnd** control can choose a particular type of input to process itself.

The default **OnGetDlgCode** functions for the predefined control classes return a code appropriate for each class.

See Also: WM_GETDLGCODE

CWnd::OnGetMinMaxInfo

afx_msg void OnGetMinMaxInfo(MINMAXINFO FAR* *lpMMI* **);**

Parameters

lpMMI   Points to a **MINMAXINFO** structure that contains information about a window's maximized size and position and its minimum and maximum tracking size. For more about this structure, see the **MINMAXINFO** structure.

Remarks

The framework calls this member function whenever Windows needs to know the maximized position or dimensions, or the minimum or maximum tracking size. The maximized size is the size of the window when its borders are fully extended. The maximum tracking size of the window is the largest window size that can be achieved by using the borders to size the window. The minimum tracking size of the window is the smallest window size that can be achieved by using the borders to size the window.

Windows fills in an array of points specifying default values for the various positions and dimensions. The application may change these values in **OnGetMinMaxInfo**.

Note   This member function is called by the framework to allow your application to handle a Windows message. The parameters passed to your function reflect the parameters received by the framework when the message was received. If you call the base-class implementation of this function, that implementation will use the parameters originally passed with the message and not the parameters you supply to the function.

See Also: WM_GETMINMAXINFO

CWnd::OnHelpInfo

afx_msg BOOL OnHelpInfo(HELPINFO* *lpHelpInfo* **);**

Parameters

lpHelpInfo   Pointer to a **HELPINFO** structure that contains information about the menu item, control, dialog box, or window for which help is requested.

Remarks

Called by the framework when the user presses the F1 key.

If a menu is active when F1 is pressed, **WM_HELP** is sent to the window associated with the menu; otherwise, **WM_HELP** is sent to the window that has the keyboard focus. If no window has the keyboard focus, **WM_HELP** is sent to the currently active window.

See Also: **CWinApp::OnHelp**, **CWinApp::WinHelp**

CWnd::OnHScroll

afx_msg void OnHScroll(UINT $nSBCode$, **UINT** $nPos$, **CScrollBar*** $pScrollBar$ **);**

Parameters

$nSBCode$ Specifies a scroll-bar code that indicates the user's scrolling request. This parameter can be one of the following:

- **SB_LEFT**   Scroll to far left.

- **SB_ENDSCROLL**   End scroll.

- **SB_LINELEFT**   Scroll left.

- **SB_LINERIGHT**   Scroll right.

- **SB_PAGELEFT**   Scroll one page left.

- **SB_PAGERIGHT**   Scroll one page right.

- **SB_RIGHT**   Scroll to far right.

- **SB_THUMBPOSITION**   Scroll to absolute position. The current position is specified by the $nPos$ parameter.

- **SB_THUMBTRACK**   Drag scroll box to specified position. The current position is specified by the $nPos$ parameter.

$nPos$ Specifies the scroll-box position if the scroll-bar code is **SB_THUMBPOSITION** or **SB_THUMBTRACK**; otherwise, not used. Depending on the initial scroll range, $nPos$ may be negative and should be cast to an **int** if necessary.

$pScrollBar$ If the scroll message came from a scroll-bar control, contains a pointer to the control. If the user clicked a window's scroll bar, this parameter is **NULL**. The pointer may be temporary and should not be stored for later use.

Remarks

The framework calls this member function when the user clicks a window's horizontal scroll bar.

The **SB_THUMBTRACK** scroll-bar code typically is used by applications that give some feedback while the scroll box is being dragged.

If an application scrolls the contents controlled by the scroll bar, it must also reset the position of the scroll box with the **SetScrollPos** member function.

Note This member function is called by the framework to allow your application to handle a Windows message. The parameters passed to your function reflect the parameters received by the framework when the message was received. If you call the base-class implementation of this function, that implementation will use the parameters originally passed with the message and not the parameters you supply to the function.

See Also: **CWnd::SetScrollPos**, **WM_VSCROLL**, **WM_HSCROLL**

CWnd::OnHScrollClipboard

afx_msg void OnHScrollClipboard(CWnd* *pClipAppWnd*, **UINT** *nSBCode*, **UINT** *nPos* **);**

Parameters

pClipAppWnd Specifies a pointer to a Clipboard-viewer window. The pointer may be temporary and should not be stored for later use.

nSBCode Specifies one of the following scroll-bar codes in the low-order word:

- **SB_BOTTOM** Scroll to lower right.

- **SB_ENDSCROLL** End scroll.

- **SB_LINEDOWN** Scroll one line down.

- **SB_LINEUP** Scroll one line up.

- **SB_PAGEDOWN** Scroll one page down.

- **SB_PAGEUP** Scroll one page up.

- **SB_THUMBPOSITION** Scroll to the absolute position. The current position is provided in *nPos*.

- **SB_TOP** Scroll to upper left.

nPos Contains the scroll-box position if the scroll-bar code is **SB_THUMBPOSITION**; otherwise not used.

Remarks

The Clipboard owner's **OnHScrollClipboard** member function is called by the Clipboard viewer when the Clipboard data has the **CF_OWNERDISPLAY** format and there is an event in the Clipboard viewer's horizontal scroll bar. The owner should scroll the Clipboard image, invalidate the appropriate section, and update the scroll-bar values.

Note This member function is called by the framework to allow your application to handle a Windows message. The parameters passed to your function reflect the parameters received by the framework when the message was received. If you call the base-class implementation of this function, that implementation will use the parameters originally passed with the message and not the parameters you supply to the function.

See Also: **CWnd::OnVScrollClipboard**, **WM_HSCROLLCLIPBOARD**

CWnd::OnIconEraseBkgnd

afx_msg void OnIconEraseBkgnd(CDC* *pDC* **);**

Parameters

pDC   Specifies the device-context object of the icon. May be temporary and should not be stored for later use.

Remarks

The framework calls this member function for a minimized (iconic) **CWnd** object when the background of the icon must be filled before painting the icon. **CWnd** receives this call only if a class icon is defined for the window default implementation; otherwise **OnEraseBkgnd** is called.

The **DefWindowProc** member function fills the icon background with the background brush of the parent window.

Note This member function is called by the framework to allow your application to handle a Windows message. The parameters passed to your function reflect the parameters received by the framework when the message was received. If you call the base-class implementation of this function, that implementation will use the parameters originally passed with the message and not the parameters you supply to the function.

See Also: **CWnd::OnEraseBkgnd**, **WM_ICONERASEBKGND**

CWnd::OnInitMenu

afx_msg void OnInitMenu(CMenu* *pMenu* **);**

Parameters

pMenu   Specifies the menu to be initialized. May be temporary and should not be stored for later use.

Remarks

The framework calls this member function when a menu is about to become active. The call occurs when the user clicks an item on the menu bar or presses a menu key. Override this member function to modify the menu before it is displayed.

OnInitMenu is only called when a menu is first accessed; **OnInitMenu** is called only once for each access. This means, for example, that moving the mouse across several menu items while holding down the button does not generate new calls. This call does not provide information about menu items.

Note This member function is called by the framework to allow your application to handle a Windows message. The parameters passed to your function reflect the parameters received by the framework when the message was received. If you call the base-class implementation of this function, that implementation will use the parameters originally passed with the message and not the parameters you supply to the function.

See Also: **CWnd::OnInitMenuPopup**, **WM_INITMENU**

CWnd::OnInitMenuPopup

afx_msg void OnInitMenuPopup(CMenu* *pPopupMenu,*
↳ **UINT** *nIndex,* **BOOL** *bSysMenu* **);**

Parameters

pPopupMenu   Specifies the menu object of the pop-up menu. May be temporary and should not be stored for later use.

nIndex   Specifies the index of the pop-up menu in the main menu.

bSysMenu   **TRUE** if the pop-up menu is the Control menu; otherwise **FALSE**.

Remarks

The framework calls this member function when a pop-up menu is about to become active. This allows an application to modify the pop-up menu before it is displayed without changing the entire menu.

Note This member function is called by the framework to allow your application to handle a Windows message. The parameters passed to your function reflect the parameters received by the framework when the message was received. If you call the base-class implementation of this function, that implementation will use the parameters originally passed with the message and not the parameters you supply to the function.

See Also: **CWnd::OnInitMenu**, **WM_INITMENUPOPUP**

CWnd::OnKeyDown

afx_msg void OnKeyDown(UINT *nChar,* **UINT** *nRepCnt,* **UINT** *nFlags* **);**

Parameters

nChar   Specifies the virtual-key code of the given key.

nRepCnt   Repeat count (the number of times the keystroke is repeated as a result of the user holding down the key).

nFlags   Specifies the scan code, key-transition code, previous key state, and context code, as shown in the following list:

Value	Description
0–7	Scan code (OEM-dependent value).
8	Extended key, such as a function key or a key on the numeric keypad (1 if it is an extended key).
9–10	Not used.
11–12	Used internally by Windows.
13	Context code (1 if the ALT key is held down while the key is pressed; otherwise 0).
14	Previous key state (1 if the key is down before the call, 0 if the key is up).
15	Transition state (1 if the key is being released, 0 if the key is being pressed).

For a **WM_KEYDOWN** message, the key-transition bit (bit 15) is 0 and the context-code bit (bit 13) is 0.

Remarks

The framework calls this member function when a nonsystem key is pressed. A nonsystem key is a keyboard key that is pressed when the ALT key is not pressed or a keyboard key that is pressed when **CWnd** has the input focus.

Because of auto-repeat, more than one **OnKeyDown** call may occur before an **OnKeyUp** member function call is made. The bit that indicates the previous key state can be used to determine whether the **OnKeyDown** call is the first down transition or a repeated down transition.

For IBM Enhanced 101- and 102-key keyboards, enhanced keys are the right ALT and the right CTRL keys on the main section of the keyboard; the INS, DEL, HOME, END, PAGE UP, PAGE DOWN, and arrow keys in the clusters to the left of the numeric keypad; and the slash (/) and ENTER keys in the numeric keypad. Some other keyboards may support the extended-key bit in *nFlags*.

Note   This member function is called by the framework to allow your application to handle a Windows message. The parameters passed to your function reflect the parameters received by the framework when the message was received. If you call the base-class implementation of this function, that implementation will use the parameters originally passed with the message and not the parameters you supply to the function.

See Also: **WM_CHAR, WM_KEYUP, WM_KEYDOWN**

CWnd::OnKeyUp

afx_msg void OnKeyUp(UINT *nChar***, UINT** *nRepCnt***, UINT** *nFlags* **);**

Parameters

nChar   Specifies the virtual-key code of the given key.

nRepCnt Repeat count (the number of times the keystroke is repeated as a result of the user holding down the key).

nFlags Specifies the scan code, key-transition code, previous key state, and context code, as shown in the following list:

Value	Description
0–7	Scan code (OEM-dependent value). Low byte of high-order word.
8	Extended key, such as a function key or a key on the numeric keypad (1 if it is an extended key; otherwise 0).
9–10	Not used.
11–12	Used internally by Windows.
13	Context code (1 if the ALT key is held down while the key is pressed; otherwise 0).
14	Previous key state (1 if the key is down before the call, 0 if the key is up).
15	Transition state (1 if the key is being released, 0 if the key is being pressed).

For a **WM_KEYUP** message, the key-transition bit (bit 15) is 1 and the context-code bit (bit 13) is 0.

Remarks

The framework calls this member function when a nonsystem key is released. A nonsystem key is a keyboard key that is pressed when the ALT key is not pressed or a keyboard key that is pressed when the **CWnd** has the input focus.

For IBM Enhanced 101- and 102-key keyboards, enhanced keys are the right ALT and the right CTRL keys on the main section of the keyboard; the INS, DEL, HOME, END, PAGE UP, PAGE DOWN, and arrow keys in the clusters to the left of the numeric keypad; and the slash (/) and ENTER keys in the numeric keypad. Some other keyboards may support the extended-key bit in *nFlags*.

Note This member function is called by the framework to allow your application to handle a Windows message. The parameters passed to your function reflect the parameters received by the framework when the message was received. If you call the base-class implementation of this function, that implementation will use the parameters originally passed with the message and not the parameters you supply to the function.

See Also: WM_CHAR, WM_KEYUP, CWnd::Default, WM_KEYDOWN

CWnd::OnKillFocus

afx_msg void OnKillFocus(CWnd* *pNewWnd* **);**

Parameters

pNewWnd Specifies a pointer to the window that receives the input focus (may be **NULL** or may be temporary).

Remarks

The framework calls this member function immediately before losing the input focus.

If the **CWnd** object is displaying a caret, the caret should be destroyed at this point.

Note This member function is called by the framework to allow your application to handle a Windows message. The parameters passed to your function reflect the parameters received by the framework when the message was received. If you call the base-class implementation of this function, that implementation will use the parameters originally passed with the message and not the parameters you supply to the function.

See Also: **CWnd::SetFocus, WM_KILLFOCUS**

CWnd::OnLButtonDblClk

afx_msg void OnLButtonDblClk(UINT *nFlags*, **CPoint** *point* **);**

Parameters

nFlags Indicates whether various virtual keys are down. This parameter can be any combination of the following values:

- **MK_CONTROL** Set if the CTRL key is down.

- **MK_LBUTTON** Set if the left mouse button is down.

- **MK_MBUTTON** Set if the middle mouse button is down.

- **MK_RBUTTON** Set if the right mouse button is down.

- **MK_SHIFT** Set if the SHIFT key is down.

point Specifies the x- and y-coordinate of the cursor. These coordinates are always relative to the upper-left corner of the window.

Remarks

The framework calls this member function when the user double-clicks the left mouse button.

Only windows that have the **CS_DBLCLKS WNDCLASS** style will receive **OnLButtonDblClk** calls. This is the default for Microsoft Foundation Class windows. Windows calls **OnLButtonDblClk** when the user presses, releases, and then presses the left mouse button again within the system's double-click time limit. Double-clicking the left mouse button actually generates four events: **WM_LBUTTONDOWN, WM_LBUTTONUP** messages, the **WM_LBUTTONDBLCLK** call, and another **WM_LBUTTONUP** message when the button is released.

Note This member function is called by the framework to allow your application to handle a Windows message. The parameters passed to your function reflect the parameters received by the framework when the message was received. If you call the base-class implementation of

this function, that implementation will use the parameters originally passed with the message and not the parameters you supply to the function.

See Also: **CWnd::OnLButtonDown**, **CWnd::OnLButtonUp**, **WM_LBUTTONDBLCLK**

CWnd::OnLButtonDown

afx_msg void OnLButtonDown(UINT *nFlags*, **CPoint** *point* **);**

Parameters

nFlags   Indicates whether various virtual keys are down. This parameter can be any combination of the following values:

- **MK_CONTROL**   Set if the CTRL key is down.

- **MK_LBUTTON**   Set if the left mouse button is down.

- **MK_MBUTTON**   Set if the middle mouse button is down.

- **MK_RBUTTON**   Set if the right mouse button is down.

- **MK_SHIFT**   Set if the SHIFT key is down.

point   Specifies the x- and y-coordinate of the cursor. These coordinates are always relative to the upper-left corner of the window.

Remarks

The framework calls this member function when the user presses the left mouse button.

Note   This member function is called by the framework to allow your application to handle a Windows message. The parameters passed to your function reflect the parameters received by the framework when the message was received. If you call the base-class implementation of this function, that implementation will use the parameters originally passed with the message and not the parameters you supply to the function.

See Also: **CWnd::OnLButtonDblClk**, **CWnd::OnLButtonUp**, **WM_LBUTTONDOWN**

CWnd::OnLButtonUp

afx_msg void OnLButtonUp(UINT *nFlags*, **CPoint** *point* **);**

Parameters

nFlags   Indicates whether various virtual keys are down. This parameter can be any combination of the following values:

- **MK_CONTROL**   Set if the CTRL key is down.

- **MK_MBUTTON** Set if the middle mouse button is down.
- **MK_RBUTTON** Set if the right mouse button is down.
- **MK_SHIFT** Set if the SHIFT key is down.

point Specifies the x- and y-coordinate of the cursor. These coordinates are always relative to the upper-left corner of the window.

Remarks

The framework calls this member function when the user releases the left mouse button.

Note This member function is called by the framework to allow your application to handle a Windows message. The parameters passed to your function reflect the parameters received by the framework when the message was received. If you call the base-class implementation of this function, that implementation will use the parameters originally passed with the message and not the parameters you supply to the function.

See Also: **CWnd::OnLButtonDblClk, CWnd::OnLButtonDown, WM_LBUTTONUP**

CWnd::OnMButtonDblClk

afx_msg void OnMButtonDblClk(UINT *nFlags,* **CPoint** *point* **);**

Parameters

nFlags Indicates whether various virtual keys are down. This parameter can be any combination of the following values:

- **MK_CONTROL** Set if the CTRL key is down.
- **MK_LBUTTON** Set if the left mouse button is down.
- **MK_MBUTTON** Set if the middle mouse button is down.
- **MK_RBUTTON** Set if the right mouse button is down.
- **MK_SHIFT** Set if the SHIFT key is down.

point Specifies the x- and y-coordinate of the cursor. These coordinates are always relative to the upper-left corner of the window.

Remarks

The framework calls this member function when the user double-clicks the middle mouse button.

Only windows that have the **CS_DBLCLKS WNDCLASS** style will receive **OnMButtonDblClk** calls. This is the default for all Microsoft Foundation Class windows. Windows generates an **OnMButtonDblClk** call when the user presses, releases, and then presses the middle mouse button again within the system's double-click time limit. Double-clicking the middle mouse button actually generates four events: **WM_MBUTTONDOWN** and **WM_MBUTTONUP** messages, the **WM_MBUTTONDBLCLK** call, and another **WM_MBUTTONUP** message.

Note This member function is called by the framework to allow your application to handle a Windows message. The parameters passed to your function reflect the parameters received by the framework when the message was received. If you call the base-class implementation of this function, that implementation will use the parameters originally passed with the message and not the parameters you supply to the function.

See Also: **CWnd::OnMButtonDown, CWnd::OnMButtonUp, WM_MBUTTONDBLCLK**

CWnd::OnMButtonDown

afx_msg void OnMButtonDown(UINT *nFlags***, CPoint** *point* **);**

Parameters

nFlags Indicates whether various virtual keys are down. This parameter can be any combination of the following values:

- **MK_CONTROL** Set if the CTRL key is down.
- **MK_LBUTTON** Set if the left mouse button is down.
- **MK_MBUTTON** Set if the middle mouse button is down.
- **MK_RBUTTON** Set if the right mouse button is down.
- **MK_SHIFT** Set if the SHIFT key is down.

point Specifies the x- and y-coordinate of the cursor. These coordinates are always relative to the upper-left corner of the window.

Remarks

The framework calls this member function when the user presses the middle mouse button.

Note This member function is called by the framework to allow your application to handle a Windows message. The parameters passed to your function reflect the parameters received by the framework when the message was received. If you call the base-class implementation of this function, that implementation will use the parameters originally passed with the message and not the parameters you supply to the function.

See Also: **CWnd::OnMButtonDblClk, CWnd::OnMButtonUp, WM_MBUTTONDOWN**

CWnd::OnMButtonUp

afx_msg void OnMButtonUp(UINT *nFlags*, **CPoint** *point* **);**

Parameters

nFlags   Indicates whether various virtual keys are down. This parameter can be any combination of the following values:

- **MK_CONTROL**   Set if the CTRL key is down.

- **MK_LBUTTON**   Set if the left mouse button is down.

- **MK_RBUTTON**   Set if the right mouse button is down.

- **MK_SHIFT**   Set if the SHIFT key is down.

point   Specifies the x- and y-coordinate of the cursor. These coordinates are always relative to the upper-left corner of the window.

Remarks

The framework calls this member function when the user releases the middle mouse button.

Note   This member function is called by the framework to allow your application to handle a Windows message. The parameters passed to your function reflect the parameters received by the framework when the message was received. If you call the base-class implementation of this function, that implementation will use the parameters originally passed with the message and not the parameters you supply to the function.

See Also: CWnd::OnMButtonDblClk, CWnd::OnMButtonDown, WM_MBUTTONUP

CWnd::OnMDIActivate

afx_msg void OnMDIActivate(BOOL *bActivate*, **CWnd*** *pActivateWnd*,
↪ **CWnd*** *pDeactivateWnd* **);**

Parameters

bActivate   **TRUE** if the child is being activated and **FALSE** if it is being deactivated.

pActivateWnd   Contains a pointer to the MDI child window to be activated. When received by an MDI child window, *pActivateWnd* contains a pointer to the child window being activated. This pointer may be temporary and should not be stored for later use.

pDeactivateWnd   Contains a pointer to the MDI child window being deactivated. This pointer may be temporary and should not be stored for later use.

Remarks

The framework calls this member function for the child window being deactivated and the child window being activated.

An MDI child window is activated independently of the MDI frame window. When the frame becomes active, the child window that was last activated with a **OnMDIActivate** call receives an **WM_NCACTIVATE** message to draw an active window frame and caption bar, but it does not receive another **OnMDIActivate** call.

Note This member function is called by the framework to allow your application to handle a Windows message. The parameters passed to your function reflect the parameters received by the framework when the message was received. If you call the base-class implementation of this function, that implementation will use the parameters originally passed with the message and not the parameters you supply to the function.

See Also: **CMDIFrameWnd::MDIActivate**, **WM_MDIACTIVATE**

CWnd::OnMeasureItem

afx_msg void OnMeasureItem(int *nIDCtl,*
↪ **LPMEASUREITEMSTRUCT** *lpMeasureItemStruct* **);**

Parameters

nIDCtl The ID of the control.

lpMeasureItemStruct Points to a **MEASUREITEMSTRUCT** data structure that contains the dimensions of the owner-draw control.

Remarks

The framework calls this member function by the framework for the owner of an owner-draw button, combo box, list box, or menu item when the control is created.

Override this member function and fill in the **MEASUREITEMSTRUCT** data structure pointed to by *lpMeasureItemStruct* and return; this informs Windows of the dimensions of the control and allows Windows to process user interaction with the control correctly.

If a list box or combo box is created with the **LBS_OWNERDRAWVARIABLE** or **CBS_OWNERDRAWVARIABLE** style, the framework calls this function for the owner for each item in the control; otherwise this function is called once.

Windows initiates the call to **OnMeasureItem** for the owner of combo boxes and list boxes created with the **OWNERDRAWFIXED** style before sending the **WM_INITDIALOG** message. As a result, when the owner receives this call, Windows has not yet determined the height and width of the font used in the control; function calls and calculations that require these values should occur in the main function of the application or library.

If the item being measured is a **CMenu**, **CListBox** or **CComboBox** object, then the **MeasureItem** virtual function of the appropriate class is called. Override the **MeasureItem** member function of the appropriate control's class to calculate and set the size of each item.

OnMeasureItem will be called only if the control's class is created at run time, or it is created with the **LBS_OWNERDRAWVARIABLE** or **CBS_OWNERDRAWVARIABLE** style. If the control is created by the dialog editor, **OnMeasureItem** will not be called. This is because the **WM_MEASUREITEM** message is sent early in the creation process of the control. If you subclass by using **DDX_Control**, **SubclassDlgItem**, or **SubclassWindow**, the subclassing usually occurs after the creation process. Therefore, there is no way to handle the **WM_MEASUREITEM** message in the control's **OnChildNotify** function, which is the mechanism MFC uses to implement **ON_WM_MEASUREITEM_REFLECT**.

Note This member function is called by the framework to allow your application to handle a Windows message. The parameters passed to your function reflect the parameters received by the framework when the message was received. If you call the base-class implementation of this function, that implementation will use the parameters originally passed with the message and not the parameters you supply to the function.

See Also: **CMenu::MeasureItem**, **CListBox::MeasureItem**, **CComboBox::MeasureItem**, **WM_MEASUREITEM**

CWnd::OnMenuChar

afx_msg LRESULT OnMenuChar(UINT *nChar*, **UINT** *nFlags*, **CMenu*** *pMenu* **);**

Return Value

The high-order word of the return value should contain one of the following command codes:

Value	Description
0	Tells Windows to discard the character that the user pressed and creates a short beep on the system speaker.
1	Tells Windows to close the current menu.
2	Informs Windows that the low-order word of the return value contains the item number for a specific item. This item is selected by Windows.

The low-order word is ignored if the high-order word contains 0 or 1. Applications should process this message when accelerator (shortcut) keys are used to select bitmaps placed in a menu.

Parameters

nChar Depending on the build settings, specifies the ANSI or Unicode character that the user pressed.

> *nFlags* Contains the **MF_POPUP** flag if the menu is a pop-up menu. It contains the **MF_SYSMENU** flag if the menu is a Control menu.

> *pMenu* Contains a pointer to the selected **CMenu**. The pointer may be temporary and should not be stored.

Remarks

The framework calls this member function when the user presses a menu mnemonic character that doesn't match any of the predefined mnemonics in the current menu. It is sent to the **CWnd** that owns the menu. **OnMenuChar** is also called when the user presses ALT and any other key, even if the key does not correspond to a mnemonic character. In this case, *pMenu* points to the menu owned by the **CWnd**, and *nFlags* is 0.

Note This member function is called by the framework to allow your application to handle a Windows message. The parameters passed to your function reflect the parameters received by the framework when the message was received. If you call the base-class implementation of this function, that implementation will use the parameters originally passed with the message and not the parameters you supply to the function.

See Also: **WM_MENUCHAR**

CWnd::OnMenuSelect

afx_msg void OnMenuSelect(UINT *nItemID*, **UINT** *nFlags* **HMENU** *hSysMenu* **);**

Parameters

> *nItemID* Identifies the item selected. If the selected item is a menu item, *nItemID* contains the menu-item ID. If the selected item contains a pop-up menu, *nItemID* contains the pop-up menu index, and *hSysMenu* contains the handle of the main (clicked-on) menu.

> *nFlags* Contains a combination of the following menu flags:

> - **MF_BITMAP** Item is a bitmap.
> - **MF_CHECKED** Item is checked.
> - **MF_DISABLED** Item is disabled.
> - **MF_GRAYED** Item is dimmed.
> - **MF_MOUSESELECT** Item was selected with a mouse.
> - **MF_OWNERDRAW** Item is an owner-draw item.
> - **MF_POPUP** Item contains a pop-up menu.
> - **MF_SEPARATOR** Item is a menu-item separator.
> - **MF_SYSMENU** Item is contained in the Control menu.

hSysMenu   If *nFlags* contains **MF_SYSMENU**, identifies the menu associated with the message. If *nFlags* contains **MF_POPUP**, identifies the handle of the main menu. If *nFlags* contains neither **MF_SYSMENU** nor **MF_POPUP**, it is unused.

Remarks

If the **CWnd** object is associated with a menu, **OnMenuSelect** is called by the framework when the user selects a menu item.

If *nFlags* contains 0xFFFF and *hSysMenu* contains 0, Windows has closed the menu because the user pressed the ESC key or clicked outside the menu.

Note   This member function is called by the framework to allow your application to handle a Windows message. The parameters passed to your function reflect the parameters received by the framework when the message was received. If you call the base-class implementation of this function, that implementation will use the parameters originally passed with the message and not the parameters you supply to the function.

See Also: **WM_MENUSELECT**

CWnd::OnMouseActivate

afx_msg int OnMouseActivate(CWnd* *pDesktopWnd*, **UINT** *nHitTest*, **UINT** *message* **);**

Return Value

Specifies whether to activate the **CWnd** and whether to discard the mouse event. It must be one of the following values:

- **MA_ACTIVATE**   Activate **CWnd** object.
- **MA_NOACTIVATE**   Do not activate **CWnd** object.
- **MA_ACTIVATEANDEAT**   Activate **CWnd** object and discard the mouse event.
- **MA_NOACTIVATEANDEAT**   Do not activate **CWnd** object and discard the mouse event.

Parameters

pDesktopWnd   Specifies a pointer to the top-level parent window of the window being activated. The pointer may be temporary and should not be stored.

nHitTest   Specifies the hit-test area code. A hit test is a test that determines the location of the cursor.

message   Specifies the mouse message number.

Remarks

The framework calls this member function when the cursor is in an inactive window and the user presses a mouse button.

The default implementation passes this message to the parent window before any processing occurs. If the parent window returns **TRUE**, processing is halted.

For a description of the individual hit-test area codes, see the **OnNcHitTest** member function

Note This member function is called by the framework to allow your application to handle a Windows message. The parameters passed to your function reflect the parameters received by the framework when the message was received. If you call the base-class implementation of this function, that implementation will use the parameters originally passed with the message and not the parameters you supply to the function.

See Also: **CWnd::OnNcHitTest, WM_MOUSEACTIVATE**

CWnd::OnMouseMove

afx_msg void OnMouseMove(UINT *nFlags***, CPoint** *point* **);**

Parameters

nFlags Indicates whether various virtual keys are down. This parameter can be any combination of the following values:

- **MK_CONTROL** Set if the CTRL key is down.

- **MK_LBUTTON** Set if the left mouse button is down.

- **MK_MBUTTON** Set if the middle mouse button is down.

- **MK_RBUTTON** Set if the right mouse button is down.

- **MK_SHIFT** Set if the SHIFT key is down.

point Specifies the x- and y-coordinate of the cursor. These coordinates are always relative to the upper-left corner of the window.

Remarks

The framework calls this member function when the mouse cursor moves. If the mouse is not captured, the **WM_MOUSEMOVE** message is received by the **CWnd** object beneath the mouse cursor; otherwise, the message goes to the window that has captured the mouse.

Note This member function is called by the framework to allow your application to handle a Windows message. The parameters passed to your function reflect the parameters received by the framework when the message was received. If you call the base-class implementation of this function, that implementation will use the parameters originally passed with the message and not the parameters you supply to the function.

See Also: **CWnd::SetCapture, CWnd::OnNCHitTest, WM_MOUSEMOVE**

CWnd::OnMouseWheel

afx_msg BOOL OnMouseWheel(UINT *nFlags***, short** *zDelta***, CPoint** *pt* **);**

Return Value

Nonzero if mouse wheel scrolling is enabled; otherwise 0.

Parameters

nFlags   Indicates whether various virtual keys are down. This parameter can be any combination of the following values:

- **MK_CONTROL**   Set if the CTRL key is down.

- **MK_LBUTTON**   Set if the left mouse button is down.

- **MK_MBUTTON**   Set if the middle mouse button is down.

- **MK_RBUTTON**   Set if the right mouse button is down.

- **MK_SHIFT**   Set if the SHIFT key is down.

zDelta   Indicates distance rotated. The *zDelta* value is expressed in multiples or divisions of **WHEEL_DELTA**, which is 120. A value less than zero indicates rotating back (toward the user) while a value greater than zero indicates rotating forward (away from the user). The user can reverse this response by changing the Wheel setting in the mouse software. See the Remarks for more information about this parameter.

pt   Specifies the x- and y-coordinate of the cursor. These coordinates are always relative to the upper-left corner of the window.

Remarks

The framework calls this member function as a user rotates the mouse wheel and encounters the wheel's next notch. Unless overridden, **OnMouseWheel** calls the default of **WM_MOUSEWHEEL**. Windows automatically routes the message to the control or child window that has the focus. The Win32 function **DefWindowProc** propagates the message up the parent chain to the window that processes it.

The *zDelta* parameter is a multiple of **WHEEL_DELTA**, which is set at 120. This value is the threshold for an action to be taken, and one such action (for example, scrolling forward one notch) should occur for each delta.

The delta was set to 120 to allow for future finer-resolution wheels, such as a freely-rotating wheel with no notches. Such a device might send more messages per rotation, but with a smaller value in each message. To support this possibility, either aggregate the incoming delta values until **WHEEL_DELTA** is reached (so you get the same response for a given delta-rotation), or scroll partial lines in response to the more frequent messages. You could also choose your scroll granularity and accumulate deltas until **WHEEL_DELTA** is reached.

Override this member function to provide your own mouse-wheel scrolling behavior.

Note **OnMouseWheel** handles messages for Windows NT 4.0. For Windows 95 or Windows NT 3.51 message handling, use **OnRegisteredMouseWheel**.

See Also: **mouse_event**

CWnd::OnMove

afx_msg void OnMove(int *x*, int *y*);

Parameters

x   Specifies the new x-coordinate location of the upper-left corner of the client area. This new location is given in screen coordinates for overlapped and pop-up windows, and parent-client coordinates for child windows.

y   Specifies the new y-coordinate location of the upper-left corner of the client area. This new location is given in screen coordinates for overlapped and pop-up windows, and parent-client coordinates for child windows.

Remarks

The framework calls this member function after the **CWnd** object has been moved.

Note This member function is called by the framework to allow your application to handle a Windows message. The parameters passed to your function reflect the parameters received by the framework when the message was received. If you call the base-class implementation of this function, that implementation will use the parameters originally passed with the message and not the parameters you supply to the function.

See Also: **WM_MOVE**

CWnd::OnMoving

afx_msg void OnMoving(UINT *nSide*, LPRECT *lpRect*);

Parameters

nSide   The edge of window to be moved.

lpRect   Address of the **CRect** or **RECT** structure that will contain the item's coordinates.

Remarks

The framework calls this member function while a user is moving a **CWnd** object.

Note This member function is called by the framework to allow your application to handle a Windows message. The parameters passed to your function reflect the parameters received by the framework when the message was received. If you call the base-class implementation of this function, that implementation will use the parameters originally passed with the message and not the parameters you supply to the function.

See Also: **WM_MOVING**

CWnd::OnNcActivate

afx_msg BOOL OnNcActivate(BOOL *bActive* **);**

Return Value

Nonzero if Windows should proceed with default processing; 0 to prevent the caption bar or icon from being deactivated.

Parameters

bActive   Specifies when a caption bar or icon needs to be changed to indicate an active or inactive state. The *bActive* parameter is **TRUE** if an active caption or icon is to be drawn. It is **FALSE** for an inactive caption or icon.

Remarks

The framework calls this member function when the nonclient area needs to be changed to indicate an active or inactive state. The default implementation draws the title bar and title-bar text in their active colors if *bActive* is **TRUE** and in their inactive colors if *bActive* is **FALSE**.

Note   This member function is called by the framework to allow your application to handle a Windows message. The parameters passed to your function reflect the parameters received by the framework when the message was received. If you call the base-class implementation of this function, that implementation will use the parameters originally passed with the message and not the parameters you supply to the function.

See Also: CWnd::Default, **WM_NCACTIVATE**

CWnd::OnNcCalcSize

afx_msg void OnNcCalcSize(BOOL *bCalcValidRects*,
↪ **NCCALCSIZE_PARAMS**** lpncsp* **);**

Parameters

bCalcValidRects   Specifies whether the application should specify which part of the client area contains valid information. Windows will copy the valid information to the specified area within the new client area. If this parameter is **TRUE**, the application should specify which part of the client area is valid.

lpncsp   Points to a **NCCALCSIZE_PARAMS** data structure that contains information an application can use to calculate the new size and position of the **CWnd** rectangle (including client area, borders, caption, scroll bars, and so on).

Remarks

The framework calls this member function when the size and position of the client area needs to be calculated. By processing this message, an application can control the contents of the window's client area when the size or position of the window changes.

Regardless of the value of *bCalcValidRects*, the first rectangle in the array specified by the **rgrc** structure member of the **NCCALCSIZE_PARAMS** structure contains the coordinates of the window. For a child window, the coordinates are relative to the parent window's client area. For top-level windows, the coordinates are screen coordinates. An application should modify the **rgrc[0]** rectangle to reflect the size and position of the client area.

The **rgrc[1]** and **rgrc[2]** rectangles are valid only if *bCalcValidRects* is **TRUE**. In this case, the **rgrc[1]** rectangle contains the coordinates of the window before it was moved or resized. The **rgrc[2]** rectangle contains the coordinates of the window's client area before the window was moved. All coordinates are relative to the parent window or screen.

The default implementation calculates the size of the client area based on the window characteristics (presence of scroll bars, menu, and so on), and places the result in *lpncsp*.

Note This member function is called by the framework to allow your application to handle a Windows message. The parameters passed to your function reflect the parameters received by the framework when the message was received. If you call the base-class implementation of this function, that implementation will use the parameters originally passed with the message and not the parameters you supply to the function.

See Also: **WM_NCCALCSIZE, CWnd::MoveWindow, CWnd::SetWindowPos**

CWnd::OnNcCreate

afx_msg BOOL OnNcCreate(LPCREATESTRUCT *lpCreateStruct* **);**

Return Value

Nonzero if the nonclient area is created. It is 0 if an error occurs; the **Create** function will return **failure** in this case.

Parameters

lpCreateStruct   Points to the **CREATESTRUCT** data structure for **CWnd**.

Remarks

The framework calls this member function prior to the **WM_CREATE** message when the **CWnd** object is first created.

Note This member function is called by the framework to allow your application to handle a Windows message. The parameters passed to your function reflect the parameters received by the framework when the message was received. If you call the base-class implementation of this function, that implementation will use the parameters originally passed with the message and not the parameters you supply to the function.

See Also: **CWnd::Create, CWnd::CreateEx, WM_NCCREATE**

CWnd::OnNcDestroy

afx_msg void OnNcDestroy( );

Remarks

Called by the framework when the nonclient area is being destroyed, and is the last member function called when the Windows window is destroyed. The default implementation performs some cleanup, then calls the virtual member function **PostNcDestroy**.

Override **PostNcDestroy** if you want to perform your own cleanup, such as a **delete this** operation. If you override **OnNcDestroy**, you must call **OnNcDestroy** in your base class to ensure that any memory internally allocated for the window is freed.

See Also: **CWnd::DestroyWindow, CWnd::OnNcCreate, WM_NCDESTROY, CWnd::Default, CWnd::PostNcDestroy**

CWnd::OnNcHitTest

afx_msg UINT OnNcHitTest(CPoint *point* **);**

Return Value

One of the mouse hit-test enumerated values listed below.

Parameters

point   Contains the x- and y-coordinates of the cursor. These coordinates are always screen coordinates.

Remarks

The framework calls this member function for the **CWnd** object that contains the cursor (or the **CWnd** object that used the **SetCapture** member function to capture the mouse input) every time the mouse is moved.

Note   This member function is called by the framework to allow your application to handle a Windows message. The parameters passed to your function reflect the parameters received by the framework when the message was received. If you call the base-class implementation of this function, that implementation will use the parameters originally passed with the message and not the parameters you supply to the function.

See Also: **CWnd::GetCapture, WM_NCHITTEST**

Mouse Enumerated Values

- **HTBORDER**   In the border of a window that does not have a sizing border.
- **HTBOTTOM**   In the lower horizontal border of the window.
- **HTBOTTOMLEFT**   In the lower-left corner of the window border.
- **HTBOTTOMRIGHT**   In the lower-right corner of the window border.

- **HTCAPTION** In a title-bar area.
- **HTCLIENT** In a client area.
- **HTERROR** On the screen background or on a dividing line between windows (same as **HTNOWHERE** except that the **DefWndProc** Windows function produces a system beep to indicate an error).
- **HTGROWBOX** In a size box.
- **HTHSCROLL** In the horizontal scroll bar.
- **HTLEFT** In the left border of the window.
- **HTMAXBUTTON** In a Maximize button.
- **HTMENU** In a menu area.
- **HTMINBUTTON** In a Minimize button.
- **HTNOWHERE** On the screen background or on a dividing line between windows.
- **HTREDUCE** In a Minimize button.
- **HTRIGHT** In the right border of the window.
- **HTSIZE** In a size box (same as **HTGROWBOX**).
- **HTSYSMENU** In a Control menu or in a Close button in a child window.
- **HTTOP** In the upper horizontal border of the window.
- **HTTOPLEFT** In the upper-left corner of the window border.
- **HTTOPRIGHT** In the upper-right corner of the window border.
- **HTTRANSPARENT** In a window currently covered by another window.
- **HTVSCROLL** In the vertical scroll bar.
- **HTZOOM** In a Maximize button.

CWnd::OnNcLButtonDblClk

afx_msg void OnNcLButtonDblClk(UINT *nHitTest*, CPoint *point*);

Parameters

nHitTest Specifies the hit-test code. A hit test is a test that determines the location of the cursor.

point Specifies a **CPoint** object that contains the x and y screen coordinates of the cursor position. These coordinates are always relative to the upper-left corner of the screen.

Remarks

The framework calls this member function when the user double-clicks the left mouse button while the cursor is within a nonclient area of **CWnd**.

If appropriate, the **WM_SYSCOMMAND** message is sent.

Note This member function is called by the framework to allow your application to handle a Windows message. The parameters passed to your function reflect the parameters received by the framework when the message was received. If you call the base-class implementation of this function, that implementation will use the parameters originally passed with the message and not the parameters you supply to the function.

See Also: **WM_NCLBUTTONDBLCLK**, **CWnd::OnNcHitTest**

CWnd::OnNcLButtonDown

afx_msg void OnNcLButtonDown(UINT *nHitTest*, **CPoint** *point* **);**

Parameters

nHitTest Specifies the hit-test code. A hit test is a test that determines the location of the cursor.

point Specifies a **CPoint** object that contains the x and y screen coordinates of the cursor position. These coordinates are always relative to the upper-left corner of the screen.

Remarks

The framework calls this member function when the user presses the left mouse button while the cursor is within a nonclient area of the **CWnd** object.

If appropriate, the **WM_SYSCOMMAND** is sent.

Note This member function is called by the framework to allow your application to handle a Windows message. The parameters passed to your function reflect the parameters received by the framework when the message was received. If you call the base-class implementation of this function, that implementation will use the parameters originally passed with the message and not the parameters you supply to the function.

See Also: **CWnd::OnNcHitTest, CWnd::OnNcLButtonDblClk, CWnd::OnNcLButtonUp, CWnd::OnSysCommand, WM_NCLBUTTONDOWN, CWnd::Default**

CWnd::OnNcLButtonUp

afx_msg void OnNcLButtonUp(UINT *nHitTest*, **CPoint** *point* **);**

Parameters

nHitTest Specifies the hit-test code. A hit test is a test that determines the location of the cursor.

point   Specifies a **CPoint** object that contains the x and y screen coordinates of the cursor position. These coordinates are always relative to the upper-left corner of the screen.

Remarks

The framework calls this member function when the user releases the left mouse button while the cursor is within a nonclient area.

If appropriate, **WM_SYSCOMMAND** is sent.

Note   This member function is called by the framework to allow your application to handle a Windows message. The parameters passed to your function reflect the parameters received by the framework when the message was received. If you call the base-class implementation of this function, that implementation will use the parameters originally passed with the message and not the parameters you supply to the function.

See Also: **CWnd::OnNcHitTest**, **CWnd::OnNcLButtonDown**, **CWnd::OnSysCommand**, **WM_NCLBUTTONUP**

CWnd::OnNcMButtonDblClk

afx_msg void OnNcMButtonDblClk(UINT *nHitTest***, CPoint** *point* **);**

Parameters

nHitTest   Specifies the hit-test code. A hit test is a test that determines the location of the cursor.

point   Specifies a **CPoint** object that contains the x and y screen coordinates of the cursor position. These coordinates are always relative to the upper-left corner of the screen.

Remarks

The framework calls this member function when the user double-clicks the middle mouse button while the cursor is within a nonclient area.

Note   This member function is called by the framework to allow your application to handle a Windows message. The parameters passed to your function reflect the parameters received by the framework when the message was received. If you call the base-class implementation of this function, that implementation will use the parameters originally passed with the message and not the parameters you supply to the function.

See Also: **CWnd::OnNcHitTest**, **CWnd::OnNcMButtonDown**, **CWnd::OnNcMButtonUp**, **WM_NCMBUTTONDBLCLK**

CWnd::OnNcMButtonDown

afx_msg void OnNcMButtonDown(UINT *nHitTest***, CPoint** *point* **);**

Parameters

nHitTest   Specifies the hit-test code. A hit test is a test that determines the location of the cursor.

point   Specifies a **CPoint** object that contains the x and y screen coordinates of the cursor position. These coordinates are always relative to the upper-left corner of the screen.

Remarks

The framework calls this member function when the user presses the middle mouse button while the cursor is within a nonclient area.

Note   This member function is called by the framework to allow your application to handle a Windows message. The parameters passed to your function reflect the parameters received by the framework when the message was received. If you call the base-class implementation of this function, that implementation will use the parameters originally passed with the message and not the parameters you supply to the function.

See Also: CWnd::OnNcHitTest, CWnd::OnNcMButtonDblClk, CWnd::OnNcMButtonUp, WM_NCMBUTTONDOWN

CWnd::OnNcMButtonUp

afx_msg void OnNcMButtonUp(UINT *nHitTest***, CPoint** *point* **);**

Parameters

nHitTest   Specifies the hit-test code. A hit test is a test that determines the location of the cursor.

point   Specifies a **CPoint** object that contains the x and y screen coordinates of the cursor position. These coordinates are always relative to the upper-left corner of the screen.

Remarks

The framework calls this member function when the user releases the middle mouse button while the cursor is within a nonclient area.

Note   This member function is called by the framework to allow your application to handle a Windows message. The parameters passed to your function reflect the parameters received by the framework when the message was received. If you call the base-class implementation of this function, that implementation will use the parameters originally passed with the message and not the parameters you supply to the function.

See Also: **CWnd::OnNcHitTest, CWnd::OnNcMButtonDblClk, CWnd::OnNcMButtonDown, WM_NCMBUTTONUP**

CWnd::OnNcMouseMove

afx_msg void OnNcMouseMove(UINT *nHitTest***, CPoint** *point* **);**

Parameters

nHitTest   Specifies the hit-test code. A hit test is a test that determines the location of the cursor.

point   Specifies a **CPoint** object that contains the x and y screen coordinates of the cursor position. These coordinates are always relative to the upper-left corner of the screen.

Remarks

The framework calls this member function when the cursor is moved within a nonclient area. If appropriate, the **WM_SYSCOMMAND** message is sent.

Note   This member function is called by the framework to allow your application to handle a Windows message. The parameters passed to your function reflect the parameters received by the framework when the message was received. If you call the base-class implementation of this function, that implementation will use the parameters originally passed with the message and not the parameters you supply to the function.

See Also: **CWnd::OnNcHitTest, CWnd::OnSysCommand, WM_NCMOUSEMOVE**

CWnd::OnNcPaint

afx_msg void OnNcPaint( );

Remarks

The framework calls this member function when the nonclient area needs to be painted. The default implementation paints the window frame.

An application can override this call and paint its own custom window frame. The clipping region is always rectangular, even if the shape of the frame is altered.

See Also: **WM_NCPAINT**

CWnd::OnNcRButtonDblClk

afx_msg void OnNcRButtonDblClk(UINT *nHitTest***, CPoint** *point* **);**

Parameters

nHitTest   Specifies the hit-test code. A hit test is a test that determines the location of the cursor.

point   Specifies a **CPoint** object that contains the x and y screen coordinates of the cursor position. These coordinates are always relative to the upper-left corner of the screen.

Remarks

The framework calls this member function when the user double-clicks the right mouse button while the cursor is within a nonclient area of **CWnd**.

Note   This member function is called by the framework to allow your application to handle a Windows message. The parameters passed to your function reflect the parameters received by the framework when the message was received. If you call the base-class implementation of this function, that implementation will use the parameters originally passed with the message and not the parameters you supply to the function.

See Also: **CWnd::OnNcHitTest, CWnd::OnNcRButtonDown, CWnd::OnNcRButtonUp, WM_NCRBUTTONDBLCLK**

CWnd::OnNcRButtonDown

afx_msg void OnNcRButtonDown(UINT *nHitTest***, CPoint** *point* **);**

Parameters

nHitTest   Specifies the hit-test code. A hit test is a test that determines the location of the cursor.

point   Specifies a **CPoint** object that contains the x and y screen coordinates of the cursor position. These coordinates are always relative to the upper-left corner of the screen.

Remarks

The framework calls this member function when the user presses the right mouse button while the cursor is within a nonclient area.

Note   This member function is called by the framework to allow your application to handle a Windows message. The parameters passed to your function reflect the parameters received by the framework when the message was received. If you call the base-class implementation of this function, that implementation will use the parameters originally passed with the message and not the parameters you supply to the function.

See Also: **CWnd::OnNcHitTest, CWnd::OnNcRButtonDblClk, CWnd::OnNcRButtonUp**

CWnd::OnNcRButtonUp

afx_msg void OnNcRButtonUp(UINT *nHitTest*, **CPoint** *point* **);**

Parameters

nHitTest   Specifies the hit-test code. A hit test is a test that determines the location of the cursor.

point   Specifies a **CPoint** object that contains the x and y screen coordinates of the cursor position. These coordinates are always relative to the upper-left corner of the screen.

Remarks

The framework calls this member function when the user releases the right mouse button while the cursor is within a nonclient area.

Note   This member function is called by the framework to allow your application to handle a Windows message. The parameters passed to your function reflect the parameters received by the framework when the message was received. If you call the base-class implementation of this function, that implementation will use the parameters originally passed with the message and not the parameters you supply to the function.

See Also: CWnd::OnNcHitTest, CWnd::OnNcRButtonDblClk, CWnd::OnNcRButtonDown, WM_NCRBUTTONUP

CWnd::OnNotify

virtual BOOL CWnd::OnNotify(WPARAM *wParam*, **LPARAM** *lParam*,
➥ **LRESULT*** *pResult* **);**

Return Value

An application returns nonzero if it processes this message; otherwise 0.

Parameters

wParam   Identifies the control that sends the message if the message is from a control. Otherwise, *wParam* is 0.

lParam   Pointer to a notification message (**NMHDR**) structure that contains the notification code and additional information. For some notification messages, this parameter points to a larger structure that has the **NMHDR** structure as its first member.

pResult   Pointer to an **LRESULT** variable in which to store the result code if the message is handled.

Remarks

The framework calls this member function to inform the parent window of a control that an event has occurred in the control or that the control requires some kind of information.

OnNotify processes the message map for control notification.

Override this member function in your derived class to handle the **WM_NOTIFY** message. An override will not process the message map unless the base class **OnNotify** is called.

For more information on the WM_NOTIFY message, see Technical Note 61 (TN061) online, "ON_NOTIFY and WM_NOTIFY messages." You may also be interested the related topics described in TN060 online, "The New Windows Common Controls," and TN062 online, "Message Reflection for Windows Controls."

CWnd::OnPaint

afx_msg void OnPaint( );

Remarks

The framework calls this member function when Windows or an application makes a request to repaint a portion of an application's window. The **WM_PAINT** message is sent when the **UpdateWindow** or **RedrawWindow** member function is called.

A window may receive internal paint messages as a result of calling the **RedrawWindow** member function with the **RDW_INTERNALPAINT** flag set. In this case, the window may not have an update region. An application should call the **GetUpdateRect** member function to determine whether the window has an update region. If **GetUpdateRect** returns 0, the application should not call the **BeginPaint** and **EndPaint** member functions.

It is an application's responsibility to check for any necessary internal repainting or updating by looking at its internal data structures for each **WM_PAINT** message because a **WM_PAINT** message may have been caused by both an invalid area and a call to the **RedrawWindow** member function with the **RDW_INTERNALPAINT** flag set.

An internal **WM_PAINT** message is sent only once by Windows. After an internal **WM_PAINT** message is sent to a window by the **UpdateWindow** member function, no further **WM_PAINT** messages will be sent or posted until the window is invalidated or until the **RedrawWindow** member function is called again with the **RDW_INTERNALPAINT** flag set.

For information on rendering an image in document/view applications, see **CView::OnDraw**.

For more information about using **WM_Paint**, see the following topics in the *Win32 SDK Programmer's Reference*:

- "The WM_PAINT Message"
- "Using the WM_PAINT Message"

See Also: CWnd::BeginPaint, CWnd::EndPaint, CWnd::RedrawWindow, CPaintDC, CView::OnDraw

CWnd::OnPaintClipboard

afx_msg void OnPaintClipboard(CWnd* *pClipAppWnd***, HGLOBAL** *hPaintStruct* **);**

Parameters

pClipAppWnd   Specifies a pointer to the Clipboard-application window. The pointer may be temporary and should not be stored for later use.

hPaintStruct   Identifies a **PAINTSTRUCT** data structure that defines what part of the client area to paint.

Remarks

A Clipboard owner's **OnPaintClipboard** member function is called by a Clipboard viewer when the Clipboard owner has placed data on the Clipboard in the **CF_OWNERDISPLAY** format and the Clipboard viewer's client area needs repainting.

To determine whether the entire client area or just a portion of it needs repainting, the Clipboard owner must compare the dimensions of the drawing area given in the **rcpaint** member of the **PAINTSTRUCT** structure to the dimensions given in the most recent **OnSizeClipboard** member function call.

OnPaintClipboard should use the **GlobalLock** Windows function to lock the memory that contains the **PAINTSTRUCT** data structure and unlock that memory with the **GlobalUnlock** Windows function before it exits.

Note   This member function is called by the framework to allow your application to handle a Windows message. The parameters passed to your function reflect the parameters received by the framework when the message was received. If you call the base-class implementation of this function, that implementation will use the parameters originally passed with the message and not the parameters you supply to the function.

See Also: ::GlobalLock, ::GlobalUnlock, CWnd::OnSizeClipboard, WM_PAINTCLIPBOARD

CWnd::OnPaletteChanged

afx_msg void OnPaletteChanged(CWnd* *pFocusWnd* **);**

Parameters

pFocusWnd   Specifies a pointer to the window that caused the system palette to change. The pointer may be temporary and should not be stored.

Remarks

The framework calls this member function for all top-level windows after the window with input focus has realized its logical palette, thereby changing the system palette. This call allows a window without the input focus that uses a color palette to realize its logical palettes and update its client area.

The **OnPaletteChanged** member function is called for all top-level and overlapped windows, including the one that changed the system palette and caused the **WM_PALETTECHANGED** message to be sent. If any child window uses a color palette, this message must be passed on to it.

To avoid an infinite loop, the window shouldn't realize its palette unless it determines that *pFocusWnd* does not contain a pointer to itself.

Note This member function is called by the framework to allow your application to handle a Windows message. The parameters passed to your function reflect the parameters received by the framework when the message was received. If you call the base-class implementation of this function, that implementation will use the parameters originally passed with the message and not the parameters you supply to the function.

See Also: **::RealizePalette, WM_PALETTECHANGED, CWnd::OnPaletteIsChanging, CWnd::OnQueryNewPalette**

CWnd::OnPaletteIsChanging

afx_msg void OnPaletteIsChanging(CWnd* *pRealizeWnd* **);**

Parameters

pRealizeWnd   Specifies the window that is about to realize its logical palette.

Remarks

The framework calls this member function to inform applications that an application is going to realize its logical palette.

Note This member function is called by the framework to allow your application to handle a Windows message. The parameters passed to your function reflect the parameters received by the framework when the message was received. If you call the base-class implementation of this function, that implementation will use the parameters originally passed with the message and not the parameters you supply to the function.

See Also: **CWnd::OnPaletteChanged, CWnd::OnQueryNewPalette, WM_PALETTEISCHANGING**

CWnd::OnParentNotify

afx_msg void OnParentNotify(UINT *message*, **LPARAM** *lParam* **);**

Parameters

message   Specifies the event for which the parent is being notified and the identifier of the child window. The event is the low-order word of *message*. If the event is **WM_CREATE** or **WM_DESTROY**, the high-order word of *message* is the identifier of the child window; otherwise, the high-order word is undefined. The event (low-order word of *message*) can be any of these values:

- **WM_CREATE**   The child window is being created.

- **WM_DESTROY**   The child window is being destroyed.

- **WM_LBUTTONDOWN**   The user has placed the mouse cursor over the child window and clicked the left mouse button.

- **WM_MBUTTONDOWN**   The user has placed the mouse cursor over the child window and clicked the middle mouse button.

- **WM_RBUTTONDOWN**   The user has placed the mouse cursor over the child window and clicked the right mouse button.

lParam   If the event (low-order word) of *message* is **WM_CREATE** or **WM_DESTROY**, *lParam* specifies the window handle of the child window; otherwise *lParam* contains the x and y coordinates of the cursor. The x coordinate is in the low-order word and the y coordinate is in the high-order word.

Remarks

A parent's **OnParentNotify** member function is called by the framework when its child window is created or destroyed, or when the user clicks a mouse button while the cursor is over the child window. When the child window is being created, the system calls **OnParentNotify** just before the **Create** member function that creates the window returns. When the child window is being destroyed, the system calls **OnParentNotify** before any processing takes place to destroy the window.

OnParentNotify is called for all ancestor windows of the child window, including the top-level window.

All child windows except those that have the **WS_EX_NOPARENTNOTIFY** style send this message to their parent windows. By default, child windows in a dialog box have the **WS_EX_NOPARENTNOTIFY** style unless the child window was created without this style by calling the **CreateEx** member function.

Note   This member function is called by the framework to allow your application to handle a Windows message. The parameters passed to your function reflect the parameters received by the framework when the message was received. If you call the base-class implementation of this function, that implementation will use the parameters originally passed with the message and not the parameters you supply to the function.

See Also: **CWnd::OnCreate, CWnd::OnDestroy, CWnd::OnLButtonDown, CWnd::OnMButtonDown, CWnd::OnRButtonDown, WM_PARENTNOTIFY**

CWnd::OnQueryDragIcon

afx_msg HCURSOR OnQueryDragIcon( );

Return Value

A doubleword value that contains a cursor or icon handle in the low-order word. The cursor or icon must be compatible with the display driver's resolution. If the application returns **NULL**, the system displays the default cursor. The default return value is **NULL**.

Remarks

The framework calls this member function by a minimized (iconic) window that does not have an icon defined for its class. The system makes this call to obtain the cursor to display while the user drags the minimized window.

If an application returns the handle of an icon or cursor, the system converts it to black-and-white.

If an application returns a handle, the handle must identify a monochrome cursor or icon compatible with the display driver's resolution. The application can call the **CWinApp::LoadCursor** or **CWinApp::LoadIcon** member functions to load a cursor or icon from the resources in its executable file and to obtain this handle.

See Also: **CWinApp::LoadCursor, CWinApp::LoadIcon, WM_QUERYDRAGICON**

CWnd::OnQueryEndSession

afx_msg BOOL OnQueryEndSession( );

Return Value

Nonzero if an application can be conveniently shut down; otherwise 0.

Remarks

The framework calls this member function when the user chooses to end the Windows session or when an application calls the **ExitWindows** Windows function. If any application returns 0, the Windows session is not ended. Windows stops calling **OnQueryEndSession** as soon as one application returns 0 and sends the **WM_ENDSESSION** message with a parameter value of **FALSE** for any application that has already returned nonzero.

See Also: **::ExitWindows, CWnd::OnEndSession, WM_QUERYENDSESSION**

CWnd::OnQueryNewPalette

afx_msg BOOL OnQueryNewPalette( );

Return Value

Nonzero if the **CWnd** realizes its logical palette; otherwise 0.

Remarks

The framework calls this member function when the **CWnd** object is about to receive the input focus, giving the **CWnd** an opportunity to realize its logical palette when it receives the focus.

See Also: **CWnd::Default**, **CWnd::OnPaletteChanged**, **WM_QUERYNEWPALETTE**

CWnd::OnQueryOpen

afx_msg BOOL OnQueryOpen( );

Return Value

Nonzero if the icon can be opened, or 0 to prevent the icon from being opened.

Remarks

The framework calls this member function when the **CWnd** object is minimized and the user requests that the **CWnd** be restored to its preminimized size and position.

While in **OnQueryOpen**, **CWnd** should not perform any action that would cause an activation or focus change (for example, creating a dialog box).

See Also: **WM_QUERYOPEN**

CWnd::OnRButtonDblClk

afx_msg void OnRButtonDblClk(UINT *nFlags*, CPoint *point*);

Parameters

nFlags Indicates whether various virtual keys are down. This parameter can be any combination of the following values:

- **MK_CONTROL** Set if CTRL key is down.

- **MK_LBUTTON** Set if left mouse button is down.

- **MK_MBUTTON** Set if middle mouse button is down.

- **MK_RBUTTON** Set if right mouse button is down.

- **MK_SHIFT** Set if SHIFT key is down.

point   Specifies the x and y coordinates of the cursor. These coordinates are always relative to the upper-left corner of the window.

Remarks

The framework calls this member function when the user double-clicks the right mouse button.

Only windows that have the **CS_DBLCLKS WNDCLASS** style can receive **OnRButtonDblClk** calls. This is the default for windows within the Microsoft Foundation Class Library. Windows calls **OnRButtonDblClk** when the user presses, releases, and then again presses the right mouse button within the system's double-click time limit. Double-clicking the right mouse button actually generates four events: **WM_RBUTTONDOWN** and **WM_RBUTTONUP** messages, the **OnRButtonDblClk** call, and another **WM_RBUTTONUP** message when the button is released.

Note   This member function is called by the framework to allow your application to handle a Windows message. The parameters passed to your function reflect the parameters received by the framework when the message was received. If you call the base-class implementation of this function, that implementation will use the parameters originally passed with the message and not the parameters you supply to the function.

See Also: **CWnd::OnRButtonDown**, **CWnd::OnRButtonUp**, **WM_RBUTTONDBLCLK**

CWnd::OnRButtonDown

afx_msg void OnRButtonDown(UINT *nFlags***, CPoint** *point* **);**

Parameters

nFlags   Indicates whether various virtual keys are down. This parameter can be any combination of the following values:

- **MK_CONTROL**   Set if CTRL key is down.

- **MK_LBUTTON**   Set if left mouse button is down.

- **MK_MBUTTON**   Set if middle mouse button is down.

- **MK_RBUTTON**   Set if right mouse button is down.

- **MK_SHIFT**   Set if SHIFT key is down.

point   Specifies the x and y coordinates of the cursor. These coordinates are always relative to the upper-left corner of the window.

Remarks

The framework calls this member function when the user presses the right mouse button.

Note This member function is called by the framework to allow your application to handle a Windows message. The parameters passed to your function reflect the parameters received by the framework when the message was received. If you call the base-class implementation of this function, that implementation will use the parameters originally passed with the message and not the parameters you supply to the function.

See Also: CWnd::OnRButtonDblClk, CWnd::OnRButtonUp, WM_RBUTTONDOWN

CWnd::OnRButtonUp

afx_msg void OnRButtonUp(UINT *nFlags*, **CPoint** *point* **);**

Parameters

nFlags Indicates whether various virtual keys are down. This parameter can be any combination of the following values:

- **MK_CONTROL** Set if CTRL key is down.

- **MK_LBUTTON** Set if left mouse button is down.

- **MK_MBUTTON** Set if middle mouse button is down.

- **MK_SHIFT** Set if SHIFT key is down.

point Specifies the x and y coordinates of the cursor. These coordinates are always relative to the upper-left corner of the window.

Remarks

The framework calls this member function when the user releases the right mouse button.

Note This member function is called by the framework to allow your application to handle a Windows message. The parameters passed to your function reflect the parameters received by the framework when the message was received. If you call the base-class implementation of this function, that implementation will use the parameters originally passed with the message and not the parameters you supply to the function.

See Also: CWnd::OnRButtonDblClk, CWnd::OnRButtonDown, WM_RBUTTONUP

CWnd::OnRegisteredMouseWheel

afx_msg LRESULT OnRegisteredMouseWheel(WPARAM *wParam*,
↪ **LPARAM** *lParam* **);**

Return Value

Insignificant at this time. Always zero.

Parameters

>   *wParam*   Horizontal position of the pointer.

>   *lParam*   Vertical position of the pointer.

Remarks

>   The framework calls this member function as a user rotates the mouse wheel and encounters the wheel's next notch. Unless overridden, **OnRegisteredMouseWheel** registers the Windows message, routes the message to the appropriate window, and calls the **WM_MOUSEWHEEL** handler for that window.

>   Override this member function to provide your own message routing or to alter the mouse-wheel scrolling behavior.

>   **Note**   **OnRegisteredMouseWheel** handles messages for Windows 95 and Windows NT 3.51. For Windows NT 4.0 message handling, use **OnMouseWheel**.

>   **See Also:**   **RegisterWindowMessage**

CWnd::OnRenderAllFormats

>   **afx_msg void OnRenderAllFormats( );**

Remarks

>   The Clipboard owner's **OnRenderAllFormats** member function is called by the framework when the owner application is being destroyed.

>   The Clipboard owner should render the data in all the formats it is capable of generating and pass a data handle for each format to the Clipboard by calling the **SetClipboardData** Windows function. This ensures that the Clipboard contains valid data even though the application that rendered the data is destroyed. The application should call the **OpenClipboard** member function before calling the **SetClipboardData** Windows function and call the **CloseClipboard** Windows function afterward.

>   **See Also:**   **::CloseClipboard, CWnd::OpenClipboard, ::SetClipboardData, CWnd::OnRenderFormat, WM_RENDERALLFORMATS**

CWnd::OnRenderFormat

>   **afx_msg void OnRenderFormat(UINT *nFormat*);**

Parameters

>   *nFormat*   Specifies the Clipboard format.

Remarks

>   The Clipboard owner's **OnRenderFormat** member function is called by the framework when a particular format with delayed rendering needs to be rendered.

The receiver should render the data in that format and pass it to the Clipboard by calling the **SetClipboardData** Windows function.

Do not call the **OpenClipboard** member function or the **CloseClipboard** Windows function from within **OnRenderFormat**.

Note This member function is called by the framework to allow your application to handle a Windows message. The parameters passed to your function reflect the parameters received by the framework when the message was received. If you call the base-class implementation of this function, that implementation will use the parameters originally passed with the message and not the parameters you supply to the function.

See Also: **::CloseClipboard**, **CWnd::OpenClipboard**, **::SetClipboardData**, **WM_RENDERFORMAT**

CWnd::OnSetCursor

afx_msg BOOL OnSetCursor(CWnd* *pWnd*, **UINT** *nHitTest*, **UINT** *message* **);**

Return Value

Nonzero to halt further processing, or 0 to continue.

Parameters

pWnd   Specifies a pointer to the window that contains the cursor. The pointer may be temporary and should not be stored for later use.

nHitTest   Specifies the hit-test area code. The hit test determines the cursor's location.

message   Specifies the mouse message number.

Remarks

The framework calls this member function if mouse input is not captured and the mouse causes cursor movement within the **CWnd** object.

The default implementation calls the parent window's **OnSetCursor** before processing. If the parent window returns **TRUE**, further processing is halted. Calling the parent window gives the parent window control over the cursor's setting in a child window.

The default implementation sets the cursor to an arrow if it is not in the client area or to the registered-class cursor if it is.

If *nHitTest* is **HTERROR** and *message* is a mouse button-down message, the **MessageBeep** member function is called.

The *message* parameter is 0 when **CWnd** enters menu mode.

Note This member function is called by the framework to allow your application to handle a Windows message. The parameters passed to your function reflect the parameters received by the framework when the message was received. If you call the base-class implementation of

this function, that implementation will use the parameters originally passed with the message and not the parameters you supply to the function.

See Also: **CWnd::OnNcHitTest**, **WM_SETCURSOR**

CWnd::OnSetFocus

afx_msg void OnSetFocus(CWnd* *pOldWnd* **);**

Parameters

pOldWnd   Contains the **CWnd** object that loses the input focus (may be **NULL**). The pointer may be temporary and should not be stored for later use.

Remarks

The framework calls this member function after gaining the input focus. To display a caret, **CWnd** should call the appropriate caret functions at this point.

Note   This member function is called by the framework to allow your application to handle a Windows message. The parameters passed to your function reflect the parameters received by the framework when the message was received. If you call the base-class implementation of this function, that implementation will use the parameters originally passed with the message and not the parameters you supply to the function.

See Also: **WM_SETFOCUS**

CWnd::OnShowWindow

afx_msg void OnShowWindow(BOOL *bShow*, **UINT** *nStatus* **);**

Parameters

bShow   Specifies whether a window is being shown. It is **TRUE** if the window is being shown; it is **FALSE** if the window is being hidden.

nStatus   Specifies the status of the window being shown. It is 0 if the message is sent because of a **ShowWindow** member function call; otherwise *nStatus* is one of the following:

- **SW_PARENTCLOSING**   Parent window is closing (being made iconic) or a pop-up window is being hidden.

- **SW_PARENTOPENING**   Parent window is opening (being displayed) or a pop-up window is being shown.

Remarks

The framework calls this member function when the **CWnd** object is about to be hidden or shown. A window is hidden or shown when the **ShowWindow** member function is called, when an overlapped window is maximized or restored, or when an overlapped or pop-up window is closed (made iconic) or opened (displayed on the screen). When an overlapped window is closed, all pop-up windows associated with that window are hidden.

Note This member function is called by the framework to allow your application to handle a Windows message. The parameters passed to your function reflect the parameters received by the framework when the message was received. If you call the base-class implementation of this function, that implementation will use the parameters originally passed with the message and not the parameters you supply to the function.

See Also: WM_SHOWWINDOW

CWnd::OnSize

afx_msg void OnSize(UINT *nType***, int** *cx***, int** *cy* **);**

Parameters

nType Specifies the type of resizing requested. This parameter can be one of the following values:

- **SIZE_MAXIMIZED** Window has been maximized.

- **SIZE_MINIMIZED** Window has been minimized.

- **SIZE_RESTORED** Window has been resized, but neither **SIZE_MINIMIZED** nor **SIZE_MAXIMIZED** applies.

- **SIZE_MAXHIDE** Message is sent to all pop-up windows when some other window is maximized.

- **SIZE_MAXSHOW** Message is sent to all pop-up windows when some other window has been restored to its former size.

cx Specifies the new width of the client area.

cy Specifies the new height of the client area.

Remarks

The framework calls this member function after the window's size has changed.

If the **SetScrollPos** or **MoveWindow** member function is called for a child window from **OnSize**, the *bRedraw* parameter of **SetScrollPos** or **MoveWindow** should be nonzero to cause the **CWnd** to be repainted.

Note This member function is called by the framework to allow your application to handle a Windows message. The parameters passed to your function reflect the parameters received by the framework when the message was received. If you call the base-class implementation of this function, that implementation will use the parameters originally passed with the message and not the parameters you supply to the function.

See Also: CWnd::MoveWindow, CWnd::SetScrollPos, WM_SIZE

CWnd::OnSizeClipboard

afx_msg void OnSizeClipboard(CWnd* *pClipAppWnd***, HGLOBAL** *hRect* **);**

Parameters

pClipAppWnd   Identifies the Clipboard-application window. The pointer may be temporary and should not be stored.

hRect   Identifies a global memory object. The memory object contains a **RECT** data structure that specifies the area for the Clipboard owner to paint.

Remarks

The Clipboard owner's **OnSizeClipboard** member function is called by the Clipboard viewer when the Clipboard contains data with the **CF_OWNERDISPLAY** attribute and the size of the client area of the Clipboard-viewer window has changed.

The **OnSizeClipboard** member function is called with a null rectangle (0,0,0,0) as the new size when the Clipboard application is about to be destroyed or minimized. This permits the Clipboard owner to free its display resources.

Within **OnSizeClipboard**, an application must use the **GlobalLock** Windows function to lock the memory that contains the **RECT** data structure. Have the application unlock that memory with the **GlobalUnlock** Windows function before it yields or returns control.

Note   This member function is called by the framework to allow your application to handle a Windows message. The parameters passed to your function reflect the parameters received by the framework when the message was received. If you call the base-class implementation of this function, that implementation will use the parameters originally passed with the message and not the parameters you supply to the function.

See Also: **::GlobalLock, ::GlobalUnlock, ::SetClipboardData, CWnd::SetClipboardViewer, WM_SIZECLIPBOARD**

CWnd::OnSizing

afx_msg void OnSizing(UINT *nSide***, LPRECT** *lpRect* **);**

Parameters

nSide   The edge of window to be moved.

lpRect   Address of the **CRect** or **RECT** structure that will contain the item's coordinates.

Remarks

The framework calls this member function to indicate that the user is resizing the rectangle. By processing this message, an application can monitor the size and position of the drag rectangle and, if needed, change its size or position.

Note This member function is called by the framework to allow your application to handle a Windows message. The parameters passed to your function reflect the parameters received by the framework when the message was received. If you call the base-class implementation of this function, that implementation will use the parameters originally passed with the message and not the parameters you supply to the function.

CWnd::OnSpoolerStatus

afx_msg void OnSpoolerStatus(UINT *nStatus***, UINT** *nJobs* **);**

Parameters

nStatus   Specifies the **SP_JOBSTATUS** flag.

nJobs   Specifies the number of jobs remaining in the Print Manager queue.

Remarks

The framework calls this member function from Print Manager whenever a job is added to or removed from the Print Manager queue.

This call is for informational purposes only.

Note This member function is called by the framework to allow your application to handle a Windows message. The parameters passed to your function reflect the parameters received by the framework when the message was received. If you call the base-class implementation of this function, that implementation will use the parameters originally passed with the message and not the parameters you supply to the function.

See Also: **WM_SPOOLERSTATUS**

CWnd::OnStyleChanged

afx_msg void OnStyleChanged(int *nStyleType***, LPSTYLESTRUCT** *lpStyleStruct* **);**

Parameters

nStyleType   Specifies whether the window's extended or nonextended styles have changed. This parameter can be a combination of the following values:

- **GWL_EXSTYLE**   The window's extended styles have changed.

- **GWL_STYLE**   The window's nonextended styles have changed.

lpStyleStruct   Points to a **STYLESTRUCT** structure that contains the new styles for the window. An application can examine the styles, but it can not change them.

Remarks

The framework calls this member function after the **::SetWindowLong** function has changed one or more of the window's styles.

Note This member function is called by the framework to allow your application to handle a Windows message. The parameters passed to your function reflect the parameters received by the framework when the message was received. If you call the base-class implementation of this function, that implementation will use the parameters originally passed with the message and not the parameters you supply to the function.

See Also: WM_STYLECHANGED

CWnd::OnStyleChanging

afx_msg void OnStyleChanging(int *nStyleType***,**
→ **LPSTYLESTRUCT** *lpStyleStruct* **);**

Parameters

nStyleType Specifies whether the window's extended or nonextended styles have changed. This parameter can be a combination of the following values:

- **GWL_EXSTYLE** The window's extended styles have changed.

- **GWL_STYLE** The window's nonextended styles have changed.

lpStyleStruct Points to a **STYLESTRUCT** structure that contains the new styles for the window. An application can examine the styles and change them.

Remarks

The framework calls this member function when the **::SetWindowLong** function is about to change one or more of the window's styles.

Note This member function is called by the framework to allow your application to handle a Windows message. The parameters passed to your function reflect the parameters received by the framework when the message was received. If you call the base-class implementation of this function, that implementation will use the parameters originally passed with the message and not the parameters you supply to the function.

CWnd::OnSysChar

afx_msg void OnSysChar(UINT *nChar***, UINT** *nRepCnt***, UINT** *nFlags* **);**

Parameters

nChar Specifies the ASCII-character key code of a Control-menu key.

nRepCnt Specifies the repeat count (the number of times the keystroke is repeated as a result of the user holding down the key).

nFlags   The *nFlags* parameter can have these values:

Value	Meaning
0-15	Specifies the repeat count. The value is the number of times the keystroke is repeated as a result of the user holding down the key..
16-23	Specifies the scan code. The value depends on the original equipment manufacturer (OEM)
24	Specifies whether the key is an extended key, such as the right-hand ALT and CTRL keys that appear on an enhanced 101- or 102-key keyboard. The value is 1 if it is an extended key; otherwise, it is 0.
25-28	Used internally by Windows.
29	Specifies the context code. The value is 1 if the ALT key is held down while the key is pressed; otherwise, the value is 0.
30	Specifies the previous key state. The value is 1 if the key is down before the message is sent, or it is 0 if the key is up.
31	Specifies the transition state. The value is 1 if the key is being released, or it is 0 if the key is being pressed.

Remarks

The framework calls this member function if **CWnd** has the input focus and the **WM_SYSKEYUP** and **WM_SYSKEYDOWN** messages are translated. It specifies the virtual-key code of the Control-menu key.

When the context code is 0, **WM_SYSCHAR** can pass the **WM_SYSCHAR** message to the **TranslateAccelerator** Windows function, which will handle it as though it were a normal key message instead of a system character-key. This allows accelerator keys to be used with the active window even if the active window does not have the input focus.

For IBM Enhanced 101- and 102-key keyboards, enhanced keys are the right ALT and the right CTRL keys on the main section of the keyboard; the INS, DEL, HOME, END, PAGE UP, PAGE DOWN, and arrow keys in the clusters to the left of the numeric keypad; and the slash (/) and ENTER keys in the numeric keypad. Some other keyboards may support the extended-key bit in *nFlags*.

Note   This member function is called by the framework to allow your application to handle a Windows message. The parameters passed to your function reflect the parameters received by the framework when the message was received. If you call the base-class implementation of this function, that implementation will use the parameters originally passed with the message and not the parameters you supply to the function.

See Also: **::TranslateAccelerator, WM_SYSKEYDOWN, WM_SYSKEYUP, WM_SYSCHAR**

CWnd::OnSysColorChange

afx_msg void OnSysColorChange( );

Remarks

The framework calls this member function for all top-level windows when a change is made in the system color setting.

Windows calls **OnSysColorChange** for any window that is affected by a system color change.

Applications that have brushes that use the existing system colors should delete those brushes and re-create them with the new system colors.

See Also: **::SetSysColors**, **WM_SYSCOLORCHANGE**

CWnd::OnSysCommand

afx_msg void OnSysCommand(UINT *nID*, LPARAM *lParam*);

Parameters

nID   Specifies the type of system command requested. This parameter can be any one of the following values:

- **SC_CLOSE**   Close the **CWnd** object.

- **SC_HOTKEY**   Activate the **CWnd** object associated with the application-specified hot key. The low-order word of *lParam* identifies the **HWND** of the window to activate.

- **SC_HSCROLL**   Scroll horizontally.

- **SC_KEYMENU**   Retrieve a menu through a keystroke.

- **SC_MAXIMIZE** (or **SC_ZOOM**)   Maximize the **CWnd** object.

- **SC_MINIMIZE** (or **SC_ICON**)   Minimize the **CWnd** object.

- **SC_MOUSEMENU**   Retrieve a menu through a mouse click.

- **SC_MOVE**   Move the **CWnd** object.

- **SC_NEXTWINDOW**   Move to the next window.

- **SC_PREVWINDOW**   Move to the previous window.

- **SC_RESTORE**   Restore window to normal position and size.

- **SC_SCREENSAVE**   Executes the screen-saver application specified in the [boot] section of the SYSTEM.INI file.

- **SC_SIZE**   Size the **CWnd** object.

- **SC_TASKLIST** Execute or activate the Windows Task Manager application.

- **SC_VSCROLL** Scroll vertically.

lParam If a Control-menu command is chosen with the mouse, *lParam* contains the cursor coordinates. The low-order word contains the x coordinate, and the high-order word contains the y coordinate. Otherwise this parameter is not used.

- **SC_HOTKEY** Activate the window associated with the application-specified hot key. The low-order word of *lParam* identifies the window to activate.

- **SC_SCREENSAVE** Execute the screen-save application specified in the Desktop section of Control Panel.

Remarks

The framework calls this member function when the user selects a command from the Control menu, or when the user selects the Maximize or the Minimize button.

By default, **OnSysCommand** carries out the Control-menu request for the predefined actions specified in the preceding table.

In **WM_SYSCOMMAND** messages, the four low-order bits of the *nID* parameter are used internally by Windows. When an application tests the value of *nID*, it must combine the value 0xFFF0 with the *nID* value by using the bitwise-AND operator to obtain the correct result.

The menu items in a Control menu can be modified with the **GetSystemMenu**, **AppendMenu**, **InsertMenu**, and **ModifyMenu** member functions. Applications that modify the Control menu must process **WM_SYSCOMMAND** messages, and any **WM_SYSCOMMAND** messages not handled by the application must be passed on to **OnSysCommand**. Any command values added by an application must be processed by the application and cannot be passed to **OnSysCommand**.

An application can carry out any system command at any time by passing a **WM_SYSCOMMAND** message to **OnSysCommand**.

Accelerator (shortcut) keystrokes that are defined to select items from the Control menu are translated into **OnSysCommand** calls; all other accelerator keystrokes are translated into **WM_COMMAND** messages.

Note This member function is called by the framework to allow your application to handle a Windows message. The parameters passed to your function reflect the parameters received by the framework when the message was received. If you call the base-class implementation of this function, that implementation will use the parameters originally passed with the message and not the parameters you supply to the function.

See Also: **WM_SYSCOMMAND**

CWnd::OnSysDeadChar

afx_msg void OnSysDeadChar(UINT *nChar***, UINT** *nRepCnt***, UINT** *nFlags* **);**

Parameters

nChar   Specifies the dead-key character value.

nRepCnt   Specifies the repeat count.

nFlags   Specifies the scan code, key-transition code, previous key state, and context code, as shown in the following list:

Value	Meaning
0–7	Scan code (OEM-dependent value). Low byte of high-order word.
8	Extended key, such as a function key or a key on the numeric keypad (1 if it is an extended key; otherwise 0).
9–10	Not used.
11–12	Used internally by Windows.
13	Context code (1 if the ALT key is held down while the key is pressed; otherwise 0).
14	Previous key state (1 if the key is down before the call, 0 if the key is up).
15	Transition state (1 if the key is being released, 0 if the key is being pressed).

Remarks

The framework calls this member function if the **CWnd** object has the input focus when the **OnSysKeyUp** or **OnSysKeyDown** member function is called. It specifies the character value of a dead key.

Note   This member function is called by the framework to allow your application to handle a Windows message. The parameters passed to your function reflect the parameters received by the framework when the message was received. If you call the base-class implementation of this function, that implementation will use the parameters originally passed with the message and not the parameters you supply to the function.

See Also: **CWnd::OnSysKeyDown**, **CWnd::OnSysKeyUp**, **WM_SYSDEADCHAR**, **CWnd::OnDeadChar**

CWnd::OnSysKeyDown

afx_msg void OnSysKeyDown(UINT *nChar***, UINT** *nRepCnt***, UINT** *nFlags* **);**

Parameters

nChar   Specifies the virtual-key code of the key being pressed.

nRepCnt   Specifies the repeat count.

nFlags   Specifies the scan code, key-transition code, previous key state, and context code, as shown in the following list:

Value	Meaning
0–7	Scan code (OEM-dependent value). Low byte of high-order word.
8	Extended key, such as a function key or a key on the numeric keypad (1 if it is an extended key; otherwise 0).
9–10	Not used.
11–12	Used internally by Windows.
13	Context code (1 if the ALT key is held down while the key is pressed, 0 otherwise).
14	Previous key state (1 if the key is down before the message is sent, 0 if the key is up).
15	Transition state (1 if the key is being released, 0 if the key is being pressed).

For **OnSysKeyDown** calls, the key-transition bit (bit 15) is 0. The context-code bit (bit 13) is 1 if the ALT key is down while the key is pressed; it is 0 if the message is sent to the active window because no window has the input focus.

Remarks

If the **CWnd** object has the input focus, the **OnSysKeyDown** member function is called by the framework when the user holds down the ALT key and then presses another key. If no window currently has the input focus, the active window's **OnSysKeyDown** member function is called. The **CWnd** object that receives the message can distinguish between these two contexts by checking the context code in *nFlags*.

When the context code is 0, the **WM_SYSKEYDOWN** message received by **OnSysKeyDown** can be passed to the **TranslateAccelerator** Windows function, which will handle it as though it were a normal key message instead of a system-key message. This allows accelerator keys to be used with the active window even if the active window does not have the input focus.

Because of auto-repeat, more than one **OnSysKeyDown** call may occur before the **WM_SYSKEYUP** message is received. The previous key state (bit 14) can be used to determine whether the **OnSysKeyDown** call indicates the first down transition or a repeated down transition.

For IBM Enhanced 101- and 102-key keyboards, enhanced keys are the right ALT and the right CTRL keys on the main section of the keyboard; the INS, DEL, HOME, END, PAGE UP, PAGE DOWN, and arrow keys in the clusters to the left of the numeric keypad; and the slash (/) and ENTER keys in the numeric keypad. Some other keyboards may support the extended-key bit in *nFlags*.

Note This member function is called by the framework to allow your application to handle a Windows message. The parameters passed to your function reflect the parameters received by the framework when the message was received. If you call the base-class implementation of this function, that implementation will use the parameters originally passed with the message and not the parameters you supply to the function.

See Also: ::**TranslateAccelerator**, **WM_SYSKEYUP**, **WM_SYSKEYDOWN**

CWnd::OnSysKeyUp

afx_msg void OnSysKeyUp(UINT *nChar*, **UINT** *nRepCnt*, **UINT** *nFlags* **);**

Parameters

nChar   Specifies the virtual-key code of the key being pressed.

nRepCnt   Specifies the repeat count.

nFlags   Specifies the scan code, key-transition code, previous key state, and context code, as shown in the following list:

Value	Meaning
0–7	Scan code (OEM-dependent value). Low byte of high-order word.
8	Extended key, such as a function key or a key on the numeric keypad (1 if it is an extended key; otherwise 0).
9–10	Not used.
11–12	Used internally by Windows.
13	Context code (1 if the ALT key is held down while the key is pressed, 0 otherwise).
14	Previous key state (1 if the key is down before the message is sent, 0 if the key is up).
15	Transition state (1 if the key is being released, 0 if the key is being pressed).

For **OnSysKeyUp** calls, the key-transition bit (bit 15) is 1. The context-code bit (bit 13) is 1 if the ALT key is down while the key is pressed; it is 0 if the message is sent to the active window because no window has the input focus.

Remarks

If the **CWnd** object has the focus, the **OnSysKeyUp** member function is called by the framework when the user releases a key that was pressed while the ALT key was held down. If no window currently has the input focus, the active window's **OnSysKeyUp** member function is called. The **CWnd** object that receives the call can distinguish between these two contexts by checking the context code in *nFlags*.

When the context code is 0, the **WM_SYSKEYUP** message received by **OnSysKeyUp** can be passed to the **TranslateAccelerator** Windows function, which will handle it as though it were a normal key message instead of a system-key message. This allows accelerator (shortcut) keys to be used with the active window even if the active window does not have the input focus.

For IBM Enhanced 101- and 102-key keyboards, enhanced keys are the right ALT and the right CTRL keys on the main section of the keyboard; the INS, DEL, HOME, END, PAGE UP, PAGE DOWN, and arrow keys in the clusters to the left of the numeric keypad; and the slash (/) and ENTER keys in the numeric keypad. Some other keyboards may support the extended-key bit in *nFlags*.

For non-U.S. Enhanced 102-key keyboards, the right ALT key is handled as the CTRL+ALT key combination. The following shows the sequence of messages and calls that result when the user presses and releases this key:

Sequence	Function Accessed	Message Passed
1.	**WM_KEYDOWN**	**VK_CONTROL**
2.	**WM_KEYDOWN**	**VK_MENU**
3.	**WM_KEYUP**	**VK_CONTROL**
4.	**WM_SYSKEYUP**	**VK_MENU**

Note This member function is called by the framework to allow your application to handle a Windows message. The parameters passed to your function reflect the parameters received by the framework when the message was received. If you call the base-class implementation of this function, that implementation will use the parameters originally passed with the message and not the parameters you supply to the function.

See Also: **::TranslateAccelerator**, **WM_SYSKEYDOWN**, **WM_SYSKEYUP**

CWnd::OnTCard

afx_msg void OnTCard(UINT *idAction***, DWORD** *dwActionData* **);**

Parameters

idAction   Indicates the action the user has taken. This parameter can be one of these values:

- **IDABORT**   The user clicked an authorable Abort button.

- **IDCANCEL**   The user clicked an authorable Cancel button.

- **IDCLOSE**   The user closed the training card.

- **IDHELP**   The user clicked an authorable Windows Help button.

- **IDIGNORE**   The user clicked an authorable Ignore button.

- **IDOK**   The user clicked an authorable OK button.

- **IDNO**   The user clicked an authorable No button.

- **IDRETRY**   The user clicked an authorable Retry button.

- **HELP_TCARD_DATA**   The user clicked an authorable button. The *dwActionData* parameter contains a long integer specified by the help author.

- **HELP_TCARD_NEXT**   The user clicked an authorable Next button.

- **HELP_TCARD_OTHER_CALLER** Another application has requested training cards.

- **IDYES** The user clicked an authorable Yes button.

dwActionData If *idAction* specifies **HELP_TCARD_DATA**, this parameter is a long integer specified by the help author. Otherwise, this parameter is zero.

Remarks

The framework calls this member function when the user clicks an authorable button. This function is called only when an application has initiated a training card with Windows Help. An application initiates a training card by specifying the **HELP_TCARD** command in a call to the **WinHelp** function.

See Also: **::WinHelp**, **CWinApp::WinHelp**

CWnd::OnTimeChange

afx_msg void OnTimeChange( );

Remarks

The framework calls this member function after the system time is changed.

Have any application that changes the system time send this message to all top-level windows. To send the **WM_TIMECHANGE** message to all top-level windows, an application can use the **SendMessage** Windows function with its *hwnd* parameter set to **HWND_BROADCAST**.

See Also: **::SendMessage**, **WM_TIMECHANGE**

CWnd::OnTimer

afx_msg void OnTimer(UINT *nIDEvent*);

Parameters

nIDEvent Specifies the identifier of the timer.

Remarks

The framework calls this member function after each interval specified in the **SetTimer** member function used to install a timer.

The **DispatchMessage** Windows function sends a **WM_TIMER** message when no other messages are in the application's message queue.

Note This member function is called by the framework to allow your application to handle a Windows message. The parameters passed to your function reflect the parameters received by the framework when the message was received. If you call the base-class implementation of

this function, that implementation will use the parameters originally passed with the message and not the parameters you supply to the function.

See Also: CWnd::SetTimer, WM_TIMER

CWnd::OnToolHitTest

virtual int CWnd::OnToolHitTest(CPoint *point***, TOOLINFO*** *pTI* **) const;**

Return Value

If 1, the tooltip control was found; If -1, the tooltip control was not found.

Parameters

point   Specifies the x- and y-coordinate of the cursor. These coordinates are always relative to the upper-left corner of the window

pTI   A pointer to a **TOOLINFO** structure. The following structure values are set by default:

- *hwnd* = **m_hWnd**   Handle to a window

- *uId* = **(UINT)hWndChild**   Handle to a child window

- *uFlags* |= **TTF_IDISHWND**   Handle of the tool

- *lpszText* = **LPSTR_TEXTCALLBACK**   Pointer to the string that is to be displayed in the specified window

Remarks

The framework calls this member function to detemine whether a point is in the bounding rectangle of the specified tool. If the point is in the rectangle, it retrieves information about the tool.

If the area with which the tooltip is associated is not a button, **OnToolHitTest** sets the structure flags to **TTF_NOTBUTTON** and **TTF_CENTERTIP**.

Override **OnToolHitTest** to provide different information than the default provides.

See **TOOLINFO**, in the *Win32 SDK Programmer's Reference*, for more information about the structure.

See Also: TOOLINFO, CWnd::FilterTooltipMessage

CWnd::OnVKeyToItem

protafx_msg int OnVKeyToItem(UINT *nKey***, CListBox*** *pListBox***, UINT** *nIndex* **);**

Return Value

Specifies the action that the application performed in response to the message. A return value of –2 indicates that the application handled all aspects of selecting the item and requires no further action by the list box. A return value of –1 indicates that the list box should perform the default action in response to the keystroke. A return value of 0 or greater specifies the zero-based index of an item in the list box and indicates that the list box should perform the default action for the keystroke on the given item.

Parameters

nKey   Specifies the virtual-key code of the key that the user pressed.

pListBox   Specifies a pointer to the list box. The pointer may be temporary and should not be stored for later use.

nIndex   Specifies the current caret position.

Remarks

If the **CWnd** object owns a list box with the **LBS_WANTKEYBOARDINPUT** style, the list box will send the **WM_VKEYTOITEM** message in response to a **WM_KEYDOWN** message.

This member function is called by the framework only for list boxes that have the **LBS_HASSTRINGS** style.

Note   This member function is called by the framework to allow your application to handle a Windows message. The parameters passed to your function reflect the parameters received by the framework when the message was received. If you call the base-class implementation of this function, that implementation will use the parameters originally passed with the message and not the parameters you supply to the function.

See Also: **WM_KEYDOWN, WM_VKEYTOITEM**

CWnd::OnVScroll

afx_msg void OnVScroll(UINT *nSBCode***, UINT** *nPos***, CScrollBar*** *pScrollBar* **);**

Parameters

nSBCode   Specifies a scroll-bar code that indicates the user's scrolling request. This parameter can be one of the following:

- **SB_BOTTOM**   Scroll to bottom.
- **SB_ENDSCROLL**   End scroll.
- **SB_LINEDOWN**   Scroll one line down.
- **SB_LINEUP**   Scroll one line up.
- **SB_PAGEDOWN**   Scroll one page down.
- **SB_PAGEUP**   Scroll one page up.
- **SB_THUMBPOSITION**   Scroll to the absolute position. The current position is provided in *nPos*.

- **SB_THUMBTRACK** Drag scroll box to specified position. The current position is provided in *nPos*.

- **SB_TOP** Scroll to top.

nPos Contains the current scroll-box position if the scroll-bar code is **SB_THUMBPOSITION** or **SB_THUMBTRACK**; otherwise not used. Depending on the initial scroll range, *nPos* may be negative and should be cast to an **int** if necessary.

pScrollBar If the scroll message came from a scroll-bar control, contains a pointer to the control. If the user clicked a window's scroll bar, this parameter is **NULL**. The pointer may be temporary and should not be stored for later use.

Remarks

The framework calls this member function when the user clicks the window's vertical scroll bar.

OnVScroll typically is used by applications that give some feedback while the scroll box is being dragged.

If **OnVScroll** scrolls the contents of the **CWnd** object, it must also reset the position of the scroll box with the **SetScrollPos** member function.

Note This member function is called by the framework to allow your application to handle a Windows message. The parameters passed to your function reflect the parameters received by the framework when the message was received. If you call the base-class implementation of this function, that implementation will use the parameters originally passed with the message and not the parameters you supply to the function.

See Also: **CWnd::SetScrollPos, CWnd::OnHScroll, WM_VSCROLL**

CWnd::OnVScrollClipboard

afx_msg void OnVScrollClipboard(CWnd* *pClipAppWnd*, **UINT** *nSBCode*, **UINT** *nPos* **);**

Parameters

pClipAppWnd Specifies a pointer to a Clipboard-viewer window. The pointer may be temporary and should not be stored for later use.

nSBCode Specifies one of the following scroll-bar values:

- **SB_BOTTOM** Scroll to bottom.

- **SB_ENDSCROLL** End scroll.

- **SB_LINEDOWN** Scroll one line down.

- **SB_LINEUP** Scroll one line up.

- **SB_PAGEDOWN** Scroll one page down.

- **SB_PAGEUP**   Scroll one page up.

- **SB_THUMBPOSITION**   Scroll to the absolute position. The current position is provided in *nPos*.

- **SB_TOP**   Scroll to top.

nPos   Contains the scroll-box position if the scroll-bar code is **SB_THUMBPOSITION**; otherwise *nPos* is not used.

Remarks

The Clipboard owner's **OnVScrollClipboard** member function is called by the Clipboard viewer when the Clipboard data has the **CF_OWNERDISPLAY** format and there is an event in the Clipboard viewer's vertical scroll bar. The owner should scroll the Clipboard image, invalidate the appropriate section, and update the scroll-bar values.

Note   This member function is called by the framework to allow your application to handle a Windows message. The parameters passed to your function reflect the parameters received by the framework when the message was received. If you call the base-class implementation of this function, that implementation will use the parameters originally passed with the message and not the parameters you supply to the function.

See Also: **CWnd::Invalidate**, **CWnd::OnHScrollClipboard**, **CWnd::InvalidateRect**, **WM_VSCROLLCLIPBOARD**, **CWnd::Default**

CWnd::OnWindowPosChanged

afx_msg void OnWindowPosChanged(WINDOWPOS* *lpwndpos* **);**

Parameters

lpwndpos   Points to a **WINDOWPOS** data structure that contains information about the window's new size and position.

Remarks

The framework calls this member function when the size, position, or Z-order has changed as a result of a call to the **SetWindowPos** member function or another window-management function.

The default implementation sends the **WM_SIZE** and **WM_MOVE** messages to the window. These messages are not sent if an application handles the **OnWindowPosChanged** call without calling its base class. It is more efficient to perform any move or size change processing during the call to **OnWindowPosChanged** without calling its base class.

Note   This member function is called by the framework to allow your application to handle a Windows message. The parameters passed to your function reflect the parameters received by the framework when the message was received. If you call the base-class implementation of

this function, that implementation will use the parameters originally passed with the message and not the parameters you supply to the function.

See Also: WM_WINDOWPOSCHANGED

CWnd::OnWindowPosChanging

afx_msg void OnWindowPosChanging(WINDOWPOS* *lpwndpos* **);**

Parameters

lpwndpos   Points to a **WINDOWPOS** data structure that contains information about the window's new size and position.

Remarks

The framework calls this member function when the size, position, or Z-order is about to change as a result of a call to the **SetWindowPos** member function or another window-management function.

An application can prevent changes to the window by setting or clearing the appropriate bits in the **flags** member of the **WINDOWPOS** structure.

For a window with the **WS_OVERLAPPED** or **WS_THICKFRAME** style, the default implementation sends a **WM_GETMINMAXINFO** message to the window. This is done to validate the new size and position of the window and to enforce the **CS_BYTEALIGNCLIENT** and **CS_BYTEALIGN** client styles. An application can override this functionality by not calling its base class.

Note   This member function is called by the framework to allow your application to handle a Windows message. The parameters passed to your function reflect the parameters received by the framework when the message was received. If you call the base-class implementation of this function, that implementation will use the parameters originally passed with the message and not the parameters you supply to the function.

See Also: CWnd::OnWindowPosChanged, WM_WINDOWPOSCHANGING

CWnd::OnWinIniChange

afx_msg void OnWinIniChange(LPCTSTR *lpszSection* **);**

Parameters

lpszSection   Points to a string that specifies the name of the section that has changed. (The string does not include the square brackets that enclose the section name.)

Remarks

The framework calls this member function after a change has been made to the Windows initialization file, WIN.INI.

The **SystemParametersInfo** Windows function calls **OnWinIniChange** after an application uses the function to change a setting in the WIN.INI file.

To send the **WM_WININICHANGE** message to all top-level windows, an application can use the **SendMessage** Windows function with its *hwnd* parameter set to **HWND_BROADCAST**.

If an application changes many different sections in WIN.INI at the same time, the application should send one **WM_WININICHANGE** message with *lpszSection* set to **NULL**. Otherwise, an application should send **WM_WININICHANGE** each time it makes a change to WIN.INI.

If an application receives an **OnWinIniChange** call with *lpszSection* set to **NULL**, the application should check all sections in WIN.INI that affect the application.

Note This member function is called by the framework to allow your application to handle a Windows message. The parameters passed to your function reflect the parameters received by the framework when the message was received. If you call the base-class implementation of this function, that implementation will use the parameters originally passed with the message and not the parameters you supply to the function.

See Also: ::**SendMessage**, ::**SystemParametersInfo**, **WM_WININICHANGE**

CWnd::OnWndMsg

virtual **BOOL OnWndMsg(UINT** *message*, **WPARAM** *wParam*,
↪ **LPARAM** *lParam*, **LRESULT*** *pResult*);

Return Value

Nonzero if message was handled; otherwise 0.

Parameters

message   Specifies the message to be sent.

wParam   Specifies additional message-dependent information.

lParam   Specifies additional message-dependent information.

pResult   The return value of **WindowProc**. Depends on the message; may be **NULL**.

Remarks

This member function is called by **WindowProc**, or is called during message reflection.

For more information about message reflection, see "Handling Reflected Messages" in the *Visual C++ Programmer's Guide* online.

See Also: **CWnd::OnChildNotify**, **CWnd::SendChildNotifyLastMsg**, **CWnd::ReflectChildNotify**, **CCmdTarget::OnCmdMsg**, **CWnd::ReflectLastMsg**

CWnd::OpenClipboard

BOOL OpenClipboard( );

Return Value

Nonzero if the Clipboard is opened via **CWnd,** or 0 if another application or window has the Clipboard open.

Remarks

Opens the Clipboard. Other applications will not be able to modify the Clipboard until the **CloseClipboard** Windows function is called.

The current **CWnd** object will not become the owner of the Clipboard until the **EmptyClipboard** Windows function is called.

See Also: ::CloseClipboard, ::EmptyClipboard, ::OpenClipboard

---

CWnd::PostMessage

BOOL PostMessage(UINT *message,* **WPARAM** *wParam* **= 0, LPARAM** *lParam* **= 0);**

Return Value

Nonzero if the message is posted; otherwise 0.

Parameters

message   Specifies the message to be posted.

wParam   Specifies additional message information. The content of this parameter depends on the message being posted.

lParam   Specifies additional message information. The content of this parameter depends on the message being posted.

Remarks

Places a message in the window's message queue and then returns without waiting for the corresponding window to process the message. Messages in a message queue are retrieved by calls to the **GetMessage** or **PeekMessage** Windows function.

The Windows **PostMessage** function can be used to access another application.

See Also: ::GetMessage, ::PeekMessage, ::PostMessage, ::PostAppMessage, CWnd::SendMessage

CWnd::PostNcDestroy

virtual void PostNcDestroy( );

Remarks

Called by the default **OnNcDestroy** member function after the window has been destroyed. Derived classes can use this function for custom cleanup such as the deletion of the **this** pointer.

See Also: CWnd::OnNcDestroy

CWnd::PreCreateWindow

virtual BOOL PreCreateWindow(CREATESTRUCT& *cs* **);**

Return Value

Nonzero if the window creation should continue; 0 to indicate creation failure.

Parameters

cs   A **CREATESTRUCT** structure.

Remarks

Called by the framework before the creation of the Windows window attached to this **CWnd** object.

Never call this function directly.

The default implementation of this function checks for a **NULL** window class name and substitutes an appropriate default. Override this member function to modify the **CREATESTRUCT** structure before the window is created.

Each class derived from **CWnd** adds its own functionality to its override of **PreCreateWindow**. By design, these derivations of **PreCreateWindow** are not documented. To determine the styles appropriate to each class and the interdependencies between the styles, you can examine the MFC source code for your application's base class. If you choose to override **PreCreateWindow,** you can determine whether the styles used in your application's base class provide the functionality you need by using information gathered from the MFC source code.

For more information on changing window styles, see "Changing the Styles of a Window Created by MFC" in *Visual C++ Programmer's Guide* online.

See Also: CWnd::Create, CWnd::CreateEx, CREATESTRUCT

CWnd::PreSubclassWindow

virtual void PreSubclassWindow( );

Remarks

This member function is called by the framework to allow other necessary subclassing to occur before the window is subclassed. Overriding this member function allows for dynamic subclassing of controls. It is an advanced overridable.

See Also: CWnd::SubclassWindow, CWnd::UnsubclassWindow, CWnd::GetSuperWndProcAddr, CWnd::DefWindowProc, CWnd::SubclassDlgItem, CWnd::Attach, CWnd::PreCreateWindow

---

CWnd::PreTranslateMessage

virtual BOOL PreTranslateMessage(MSG* *pMsg*);

Return Value

Nonzero if the message was translated and should not be dispatched; 0 if the message was not translated and should be dispatched.

Parameters

pMsg   Points to a **MSG** structure that contains the message to process.

Remarks

Used by class **CWinApp** to translate window messages before they are dispatched to the **TranslateMessage** and **DispatchMessage** Windows functions.

See Also: ::TranslateMessage, ::IsDialogMessage, CWinApp::PreTranslateMessage

---

CWnd::Print

void Print(CDC* *pDC*, DWORD *dwFlags*) const;

Parameters

pDC   A pointer to a device context.

dwFlags   Specifies the drawing options. This parameter can be one or more of these flags:

- **PRF_CHECKVISIBLE**   Draw the window only if it is visible.

- **PRF_CHILDREN**   Draw all visible children windows.

- **PRF_CLIENT**   Draw the client area of the window.

- **PRF_ERASEBKGND**   Erase the background before drawing the window.

- **PRF_NONCLIENT** Draw the nonclient area of the window.

- **PRF_OWNED** Draw all owned windows.

Remarks

Call this member function to draw the current window in the specified device context, which is most commonly in a printer device context.

CWnd::DefWindowProc function processes this message based on which drawing option is specified:

- If **PRF_CHECKVISIBLE** is specified and the window is not visible, do nothing.

- If **PRF_NONCLIENT** is specified, draw the nonclient area in the given device context.

- If **PRF_ERASEBKGND** is specified, send the window a **WM_ERASEBKGND** message.

- If **PRF_PRINTCLIENT** is specified, send the window a **WM_PRINTCLIENT** message.

- If **PRF_PRINTCHILDREN** is set, send each visible child window a **WM_PRINT** message.

- If **PRF_OWNED** is set, send each visible owned window a **WM_PRINT** message.

See Also: WM_PRINT, WM_PRINTCLIENT

CWnd::PrintClient

void PrintClient(CDC* *pDC*, **DWORD** *dwFlags* **) const;**

Parameters

pDC A pointer to a device context.

dwFlags Specifies drawing options. This parameter can be one or more of these flags:

- **PRF_CHECKVISIBLE** Draw the window only if it is visible.

- **PRF_CHILDREN** Draw all visible children windows.

- **PRF_CLIENT** Draw the client area of the window.

- **PRF_ERASEBKGND** Erase the background before drawing the window.

- **PRF_NONCLIENT** Draw the nonclient area of the window.

- **PRF_OWNED** Draw all owned windows.

Remarks

Call this member function to draw any window in the specified device context (usually a printer device context).

See Also: **WM_PRINTCLIENT**

CWnd::RedrawWindow

BOOL RedrawWindow(LPCRECT *lpRectUpdate* **= NULL, CRgn*** *prgnUpdate* **= NULL,**
→ **UINT** *flags* **= RDW_INVALIDATE I RDW_UPDATENOW I RDW_ERASE);**

Return Value

Nonzero if the window was redrawn successfully; otherwise 0.

Parameters

lpRectUpdate   Points to a **RECT** structure containing the coordinates of the update rectangle. This parameter is ignored if *prgnUpdate* contains a valid region handle.

prgnUpdate   Identifies the update region. If both *prgnUpdate* and *lpRectUpdate* are **NULL**, the entire client area is added to the update region.

flags   The following flags are used to invalidate the window:

- **RDW_ERASE**   Causes the window to receive a **WM_ERASEBKGND** message when the window is repainted. The **RDW_INVALIDATE** flag must also be specified; otherwise **RDW_ERASE** has no effect.

- **RDW_FRAME**   Causes any part of the nonclient area of the window that intersects the update region to receive a **WM_NCPAINT** message. The **RDW_INVALIDATE** flag must also be specified; otherwise **RDW_FRAME** has no effect.

- **RDW_INTERNALPAINT**   Causes a **WM_PAINT** message to be posted to the window regardless of whether the window contains an invalid region.

- **RDW_INVALIDATE**   Invalidate *lpRectUpdate* or *prgnUpdate* (only one may be not **NULL**). If both are **NULL**, the entire window is invalidated.

The following flags are used to validate the window:

- **RDW_NOERASE**   Suppresses any pending **WM_ERASEBKGND** messages.

- **RDW_NOFRAME**   Suppresses any pending **WM_NCPAINT** messages. This flag must be used with **RDW_VALIDATE** and is typically used with **RDW_NOCHILDREN**. This option should be used with care, as it could prevent parts of a window from painting properly.

- **RDW_NOINTERNALPAINT**   Suppresses any pending internal **WM_PAINT** messages. This flag does not affect **WM_PAINT** messages resulting from invalid areas.

- **RDW_VALIDATE** Validates *lpRectUpdate* or *prgnUpdate* (only one may be not **NULL**). If both are **NULL**, the entire window is validated. This flag does not affect internal **WM_PAINT** messages.

The following flags control when repainting occurs. Painting is not performed by the **RedrawWindow** function unless one of these bits is specified.

- **RDW_ERASENOW** Causes the affected windows (as specified by the **RDW_ALLCHILDREN** and **RDW_NOCHILDREN** flags) to receive **WM_NCPAINT** and **WM_ERASEBKGND** messages, if necessary, before the function returns. **WM_PAINT** messages are deferred.

- **RDW_UPDATENOW** Causes the affected windows (as specified by the **RDW_ALLCHILDREN** and **RDW_NOCHILDREN** flags) to receive **WM_NCPAINT**, **WM_ERASEBKGND**, and **WM_PAINT** messages, if necessary, before the function returns.

By default, the windows affected by the **RedrawWindow** function depend on whether the specified window has the **WS_CLIPCHILDREN** style. The child windows of **WS_CLIPCHILDREN** windows are not affected. However, those windows that are not **WS_CLIPCHILDREN** windows are recursively validated or invalidated until a **WS_CLIPCHILDREN** window is encountered. The following flags control which windows are affected by the **RedrawWindow** function:

- **RDW_ALLCHILDREN** Includes child windows, if any, in the repainting operation.

- **RDW_NOCHILDREN** Excludes child windows, if any, from the repainting operation.

Remarks

Updates the specified rectangle or region in the given window's client area.

When the **RedrawWindow** member function is used to invalidate part of the desktop window, that window does not receive a **WM_PAINT** message. To repaint the desktop, an application should use **CWnd::ValidateRgn**, **CWnd::InvalidateRgn**, **CWnd::UpdateWindow**, or **::RedrawWindow**

CWnd::ReflectChildNotify

BOOL ReflectChildNotify(UINT *message*, **WPARAM** *wParam*, **LPARAM** *lParam*,
↳ **LRESULT*** *pResult* **);**

Return Value

TRUE if message was reflected; otherwise **FALSE**.

Parameters

message Specifies the message to be reflected.

wParam   Specifies additional message-dependent information.

lParam   Specifies additional message-dependent information.

pResult   The result generated by the child window to be returned by the parent window. Can be **NULL**.

Remarks

This message function is called by the framework from **OnChildNotify**. It is a helper function which reflects *message* to its source.

Reflected messages are sent directly to **CWnd::OnWndMsg** or **CCmdTarget::OnCmdMsg**.

For more information about message reflection, see "Handling Reflected Messages" in the *Visual C++ Programmer's Guide* online.

See Also: **CWnd::OnChildNotify, CWnd::SendChildNotifyLastMsg, CWnd::OnWndMsg, CCmdTarget::OnCmdMsg, CWnd::ReflectLastMsg**

CWnd::ReflectLastMsg

static BOOL PASCAL ReflectLastMsg(HWND *hWndChild,*
   ↪ **LRESULT*** *pResult* = **NULL**);

Return Value

Nonzero if the message was handled; otherwise 0.

Parameters

hWndChild   A handle to a child window.

pResult   The result generated by the child window to be returned by the parent window. Can be **NULL**.

Remarks

This member function is called by the framework to reflect the last message to the child window.

This member function calls **SendChildNotifyLastMsg** if the window identified by *hWndChild* is an OLE control or a window in the permanent map.

For more information about message reflection, see "Handling Reflected Messages" in the *Visual C++ Programmer's Guide* online.

See Also: **CWnd::OnChildNotify, CWnd::SendChildNotifyLastMsg, CWnd::ReflectChildNotify, CCmdTarget::OnCmdMsg**

CWnd::ReleaseDC

int ReleaseDC(CDC* *pDC* **);**

Return Value

Nonzero if successful; otherwise 0.

Parameters

pDC   Identifies the device context to be released.

Remarks

Releases a device context, freeing it for use by other applications. The effect of the **ReleaseDC** member function depends on the device-context type.

The application must call the **ReleaseDC** member function for each call to the **GetWindowDC** member function and for each call to the **GetDC** member function.

See Also: **CWnd::GetDC**, **CWnd::GetWindowDC**, **::ReleaseDC**

CWnd::RepositionBars

void RepositionBars(UINT *nIDFirst***, UINT** *nIDLast***, UINT** *nIDLeftOver***,**
    ↪ **UINT** *nFlag* **= CWnd::reposDefault, LPRECT** *lpRectParam* **= NULL,**
    ↪ **LPCRECT** *lpRectClient* **= NULL);**

Parameters

nIDFirst   The ID of the first in a range of control bars to reposition and resize.

nIDLast   The ID of the last in a range of control bars to reposition and resize.

nIDLeftOver   Specifies ID of pane that fills the rest of the client area.

nFlag   Can have one of the following values:

- **CWnd::reposDefault**   Performs the layout of the control bars. *lpRectParam* is not used and can be **NULL**.

- **CWnd::reposQuery**   The layout of the control bars is not done; instead *lpRectParam* is initialized with the size of the client area, as if the layout had actually been done.

- **CWnd::reposExtra**   Adds the values of *lpRectParam* to the client area of *nIDLast* and also performs the layout.

lpRectParam   Points to a **RECT** structure; the usage of which depends on the value of *nFlag*.

lpRectClient   Points to a **RECT** structure containing the available client area. If **NULL**, the window's client area will be used.

Remarks

Called to reposition and resize control bars in the client area of a window. The *nIDFirst* and *nIDLast* parameters define a range of control-bar IDs to be repositioned in the client area. The *nIDLeftOver* parameter specifies the ID of the child window (normally the view) which is repositioned and resized to fill the rest of the client area not filled by control bars.

See Also: CFrameWnd::RecalcLayout

CWnd::RunModalLoop

int RunModalLoop(DWORD *dwFlags* **);**

Return Value

Specifies the value of the *nResult* parameter passed to the **EndModalLoop** member function, which is then used to end the modal loop.

Parameters

dwFlags   Specifies the Windows message to be sent. Can be one of the following values:

- **MLF_NOIDLEMSG** Don't send **WM_ENTERIDLE** messages to the parent.

- **MLF_NOKICKIDLE** Don't send **WM_KICKIDLE** messages to the window.

- **MLF_SHOWONIDLE** Show the window when message queue goes idle.

Remarks

Call this member function to retrieve, translate, or dispatch messages until **ContinueModal** returns **FALSE**. By default, **ContinueModal** returns **FALSE** after **EndModalLoop** is called. Returns the value provided as *nResult* to **EndModalLoop**.

See Also: EndModalLoop, WM_ENTERIDLE

CWnd::ScreenToClient

void ScreenToClient(LPPOINT *lpPoint* **) const;**
void ScreenToClient(LPRECT *lpRect* **) const;**

Parameters

lpPoint   Points to a **CPoint** object or **POINT** structure that contains the screen coordinates to be converted.

lpRect   Points to a **CRect** object or **RECT** structure that contains the screen coordinates to be converted.

Remarks

Converts the screen coordinates of a given point or rectangle on the display to client coordinates.

The **ScreenToClient** member function replaces the screen coordinates given in *lpPoint* or *lpRect* with client coordinates. The new coordinates are relative to the upper-left corner of the **CWnd** client area.

See Also: **CWnd::ClientToScreen**, **::ScreenToClient**

CWnd::ScrollWindow

void ScrollWindow(int *xAmount*, **int** *yAmount*, **LPCRECT** *lpRect* = **NULL**,
↪ **LPCRECT** *lpClipRect* = **NULL**);

Parameters

xAmount Specifies the amount, in device units, of horizontal scrolling. This parameter must be a negative value to scroll to the left.

yAmount Specifies the amount, in device units, of vertical scrolling. This parameter must be a negative value to scroll up.

lpRect Points to a **CRect** object or **RECT** structure that specifies the portion of the client area to be scrolled. If *lpRect* is **NULL**, the entire client area is scrolled. The caret is repositioned if the cursor rectangle intersects the scroll rectangle.

lpClipRect Points to a **CRect** object or **RECT** structure that specifies the clipping rectangle to scroll. Only bits inside this rectangle are scrolled. Bits outside this rectangle are not affected even if they are in the *lpRect* rectangle. If *lpClipRect* is **NULL**, no clipping is performed on the scroll rectangle.

Remarks

Scrolls the contents of the client area of the current **CWnd** object.

If the caret is in the **CWnd** being scrolled, **ScrollWindow** automatically hides the caret to prevent it from being erased and then restores the caret after the scroll is finished. The caret position is adjusted accordingly.

The area uncovered by the **ScrollWindow** member function is not repainted but is combined into the current **CWnd** object's update region. The application will eventually receive a **WM_PAINT** message notifying it that the region needs repainting. To repaint the uncovered area at the same time the scrolling is done, call the **UpdateWindow** member function immediately after calling **ScrollWindow**.

If *lpRect* is **NULL**, the positions of any child windows in the window are offset by the amount specified by *xAmount* and *yAmount*, and any invalid (unpainted) areas in the **CWnd** are also offset. **ScrollWindow** is faster when *lpRect* is **NULL**.

If *lpRect* is not **NULL**, the positions of child windows are not changed, and invalid areas in **CWnd** are not offset. To prevent updating problems when *lpRect* is not

NULL, call the **UpdateWindow** member function to repaint **CWnd** before calling **ScrollWindow**.

See Also: CWnd::UpdateWindow, ::ScrollWindow

CWnd::ScrollWindowEx

int ScrollWindowEx(int *dx*, **int** *dy*, **LPCRECT** *lpRectScroll*, **LPCRECT** *lpRectClip*,
↪ **CRgn*** *prgnUpdate*, **LPRECT** *lpRectUpdate*, **UINT** *flags* **);**

Return Value

The return value is **SIMPLEREGION** (rectangular invalidated region), **COMPLEXREGION** (nonrectangular invalidated region; overlapping rectangles), or **NULLREGION** (no invalidated region), if the function is successful; otherwise the return value is **ERROR**.

Parameters

dx   Specifies the amount, in device units, of horizontal scrolling. This parameter must have a negative value to scroll to the left.

dy   Specifies the amount, in device units, of vertical scrolling. This parameter must have a negative value to scroll up.

lpRectScroll   Points to a **RECT** structure that specifies the portion of the client area to be scrolled. If this parameter is **NULL**, the entire client area is scrolled.

lpRectClip   Points to a **RECT** structure that specifies the clipping rectangle to scroll. This structure takes precedence over the rectangle pointed to by *lpRectScroll*. Only bits inside this rectangle are scrolled. Bits outside this rectangle are not affected even if they are in the *lpRectScroll* rectangle. If this parameter is **NULL**, no clipping is performed on the scroll rectangle.

prgnUpdate   Identifies the region that is modified to hold the region invalidated by scrolling. This parameter may be **NULL**.

lpRectUpdate   Points to a **RECT** structure that will receive the boundaries of the rectangle invalidated by scrolling. This parameter may be **NULL**.

flags   Can have one of the following values:

- **SW_ERASE**   When specified with **SW_INVALIDATE**, erases the newly invalidated region by sending a **WM_ERASEBKGND** message to the window.

- **SW_INVALIDATE**   Invalidates the region identified by *prgnUpdate* after scrolling.

- **SW_SCROLLCHILDREN**   Scrolls all child windows that intersect the rectangle pointed to by *lpRectScroll* by the number of pixels specified in *dx* and *dy*. Windows sends a **WM_MOVE** message to all child windows that intersect *lpRectScroll*, even if they do not move. The caret is repositioned when a child window is scrolled and the cursor rectangle intersects the scroll rectangle.

Remarks

Scrolls the contents of a window's client area. This function is similar to the **ScrollWindow** function, with some additional features.

If **SW_INVALIDATE** and **SW_ERASE** are not specified, the **ScrollWindowEx** member function does not invalidate the area that is scrolled away from. If either of these flags is set, **ScrollWindowEx** invalidates this area. The area is not updated until the application calls the **UpdateWindow** member function, calls the **RedrawWindow** member function (specifying **RDW_UPDATENOW** or **RDW_ERASENOW**), or retrieves the **WM_PAINT** message from the application queue.

If the window has the **WS_CLIPCHILDREN** style, the returned areas specified by *prgnUpdate* and *lpRectUpdate* represent the total area of the scrolled window that must be updated, including any areas in child windows that need updating.

If the **SW_SCROLLCHILDREN** flag is specified, Windows will not properly update the screen if part of a child window is scrolled. The part of the scrolled child window that lies outside the source rectangle will not be erased and will not be redrawn properly in its new destination. Use the **DeferWindowPos** Windows function to move child windows that do not lie completely within the *lpRectScroll* rectangle. The cursor is repositioned if the **SW_SCROLLCHILDREN** flag is set and the caret rectangle intersects the scroll rectangle.

All input and output coordinates (for *lpRectScroll*, *lpRectClip*, *lpRectUpdate*, and *prgnUpdate*) are assumed to be in client coordinates, regardless of whether the window has the **CS_OWNDC** or **CS_CLASSDC** class style. Use the **LPtoDP** and **DPtoLP** Windows functions to convert to and from logical coordinates, if necessary.

See Also: **CWnd::RedrawWindow**, **CDC::ScrollDC**, **CWnd::ScrollWindow**, **CWnd::UpdateWindow**, **::DeferWindowPos**, **::ScrollWindowEx**

CWnd::SendChildNotifyLastMsg

BOOL SendChildNotifyLastMsg(LRESULT* *pResult* **= NULL);**

Return Value

Nonzero if the child window has handled the message sent to its parent; otherwise 0.

Parameters

pResult   The result generated by the child window to be returned by the parent window.

Remarks

This member function is called by the framework to provide a notification message to a child window, from the parent window, so the child window can handle a task.

SendChildNotifyLastMsg send the current message to the source if it is a message that is reflected.

For more information about message reflection, see "Handling Reflected Messages" in the *Visual C++ Programmer's Guide* online.

See Also: **CWnd::OnChildNotify**

CWnd::SendDlgItemMessage

LRESULT SendDlgItemMessage(int *nID***, UINT** *message***, WPARAM** *wParam* **= 0,**
↱ **LPARAM** *lParam* **= 0);**

Return Value

Specifies the value returned by the control's window procedure, or 0 if the control was not found.

Parameters

nID   Specifies the identifier of the dialog control that will receive the message.

message   Specifies the message to be sent.

wParam   Specifies additional message-dependent information.

lParam   Specifies additional message-dependent information.

Remarks

Sends a message to a control.

The **SendDlgItemMessage** member function does not return until the message has been processed.

Using **SendDlgItemMessage** is identical to obtaining a **CWnd*** to the given control and calling the **SendMessage** member function.

See Also: **CWnd::SendMessage**, **::SendDlgItemMessage**

CWnd::SendMessage

LRESULT SendMessage(UINT *message***, WPARAM** *wParam* **= 0,**
↱ **LPARAM** *lParam* **= 0);**

Return Value

The result of the message processing; its value depends on the message sent.

Parameters

message   Specifies the message to be sent.

wParam   Specifies additional message-dependent information.

lParam   Specifies additional message-dependent information.

Remarks

Sends the specified message to this window. The **SendMessage** member function calls the window procedure directly and does not return until that window procedure has processed the message. This is in contrast to the **PostMessage** member function, which places the message into the window's message queue and returns immediately.

See Also: **::InSendMessage**, **CWnd::PostMessage**, **CWnd::SendDlgItemMessage**, **::SendMessage**

CWnd::SendMessageToDescendants

void SendMessageToDescendants(UINT *message*, **WPARAM** *wParam* = **0,**
↪ **LPARAM** *lParam* = **0, BOOL** *bDeep* = **TRUE, BOOL** *bOnlyPerm* = **FALSE);**

Parameters

message   Specifies the message to be sent.

wParam   Specifies additional message-dependent information.

lParam   Specifies additional message-dependent information.

bDeep   Specifies the level to which to search. If **TRUE**, recursively search all children; if **FALSE**, search only immediate children.

bOnlyPerm   Specifies whether the message will be received by temporary windows. If **TRUE**, temporary windows can receive the message; if **FALSE**, only permanent windows receive the message. For more information on temporary windows see Technical Note 3 online.

Remarks

Call this member function to send the specified Windows message to all descendant windows.

If *bDeep* is **FALSE**, the message is sent just to the immediate children of the window; otherwise the message is sent to all descendant windows.

If *bDeep* and *bOnlyPerm* are **TRUE**, the search continues below temporary windows. In this case, only permanent windows encountered during the search receive the message. If *bDeep* is **FALSE**, the message is sent only to the immediate children of the window.

See Also: **CWnd::SendMessage**, **CWnd::FromHandlePermanent**, **CWnd::FromHandle**

CWnd::SendNotifyMessage

BOOL SendNotifyMessage(UINT *message*, **WPARAM** *wParam*,
↪ **LPARAM** *lParam* **);**

Return Value

Nonzero if the function is successful; otherwise 0.

Parameters

message   Specifies the message to be sent.

wParam   Specifies additional message-dependent information.

lParam   Specifies additional message-dependent information.

Remarks

Sends the specified message to the window. If the window was created by the calling
thread, **SendNotifyMessage** calls the window procedure for the window and does
not return until the window procedure has processed the message. If the window was
created by a different thread, **SendNotifyMessage** passes the message to the window
procedure and returns immediately; it does not wait for the window procedure to
finish processing the message.

See Also: CWnd::SendMessage, ::SendNotifyMessage

CWnd::SetActiveWindow

CWnd* SetActiveWindow( );

Return Value

The window that was previously active.

The returned pointer may be temporary and should not be stored for
later use.

Remarks

Makes **CWnd** the active window.

The **SetActiveWindow** member function should be used with care since it allows
an application to arbitrarily take over the active window and input focus. Normally,
Windows takes care of all activation.

See Also: ::SetActiveWindow, CWnd::GetActiveWindow

CWnd::SetCapture

CWnd* SetCapture( );

Return Value

A pointer to the window object that previously received all mouse input. It is **NULL** if there is no such window. The returned pointer may be temporary and should not be stored for later use.

Remarks

Causes all subsequent mouse input to be sent to the current **CWnd** object regardless of the position of the cursor.

When **CWnd** no longer requires all mouse input, the application should call the **ReleaseCapture** function so that other windows can receive mouse input.

See Also: **::ReleaseCapture**, **::SetCapture**, **CWnd::GetCapture**

CWnd::SetCaretPos

static void PASCAL SetCaretPos(POINT *point* **);**

Parameters

point Specifies the new x and y coordinates (in client coordinates) of the caret.

Remarks

Sets the position of the caret.

The **SetCaretPos** member function moves the caret only if it is owned by a window in the current task. **SetCaretPos** moves the caret whether or not the caret is hidden.

The caret is a shared resource. A window should not move the caret if it does not own the caret.

See Also: **CWnd::GetCaretPos**, **::SetCaretPos**

CWnd::SetClipboardViewer

HWND SetClipboardViewer( );

Return Value

A handle to the next window in the Clipboard-viewer chain if successful. Applications should save this handle (it can be stored as a member variable) and use it when responding to Clipboard-viewer chain messages.

Remarks

Adds this window to the chain of windows that are notified (by means of the **WM_DRAWCLIPBOARD** message) whenever the content of the Clipboard is changed.

A window that is part of the Clipboard-viewer chain must respond to **WM_DRAWCLIPBOARD**, **WM_CHANGECBCHAIN**, and **WM_DESTROY** messages and pass the message to the next window in the chain.

This member function sends a **WM_DRAWCLIPBOARD** message to the window. Since the handle to the next window in the Clipboard-viewer chain has not yet been returned, the application should not pass on the **WM_DRAWCLIPBOARD** message that it receives during the call to **SetClipboardViewer**.

To remove itself from the Clipboard-viewer chain, an application must call the **ChangeClipboardChain** member function.

See Also: **CWnd::ChangeClipboardChain, ::SetClipboardViewer**

CWnd::SetDlgCtrlID

int SetDlgCtrlID(int *nID* **);**

Return Value

The previous identifier of the window, if successful; otherwise 0.

Parameters

nID   The new value to set for the control's identifier.

Remarks

Sets the window ID or control ID for the window to a new value. The window can be any child window, not only a control in a dialog box. The window cannot be a top-level window.

See Also: **CWnd::GetDlgCtrlID, CWnd::Create, CWnd::CreateEx, CWnd::GetDlgItem**

CWnd::SetDlgItemInt

void SetDlgItemInt(int *nID,* **UINT** *nValue,* **BOOL** *bSigned* **= TRUE);**

Parameters

nID   Specifies the integer ID of the control to be changed.

nValue   Specifies the integer value used to generate the item text.

bSigned   Specifies whether the integer value is signed or unsigned. If this parameter is **TRUE**, *nValue* is signed. If this parameter is **TRUE** and *nValue* is less than 0, a minus sign is placed before the first digit in the string. If this parameter is **FALSE**, *nValue* is unsigned.

Remarks

Sets the text of a given control in a dialog box to the string representation of a specified integer value.

SetDlgItemInt sends a **WM_SETTEXT** message to the given control.

See Also: **CWnd::GetDlgItemInt**, **::SetDlgItemInt**, **WM_SETTEXT**

CWnd::SetDlgItemText

void SetDlgItemText(int *nID*, **LPCTSTR** *lpszString* **);**

Parameters

nID   Identifies the control whose text is to be set.

lpszString   Points to a **CString** object or null-terminated string that contains the text to be copied to the control.

Remarks

Sets the caption or text of a control owned by a window or dialog box.

SetDlgItemText sends a **WM_SETTEXT** message to the given control.

See Also: **::SetDlgItemText**, **WM_SETTEXT**, **CWnd::GetDlgItemText**

CWnd::SetForegroundWindow

BOOL SetForegroundWindow( );

Return Value

Nonzero if the function is successful; otherwise 0.

Remarks

Puts the thread that created the window into the foreground and activates the window. Keyboard input is directed to the window, and various visual cues are changed for the user. The foreground window is the window with which the user is currently working. The foreground window applies only to top-level windows (frame windows or dialogs boxes).

See Also: **CWnd::GetForegroundWindow**

CWnd::SetFocus

CWnd* SetFocus( );

Return Value

A pointer to the window object that previously had the input focus. It is **NULL** if there is no such window. The returned pointer may be temporary and should not be stored.

Remarks

Claims the input focus. The input focus directs all subsequent keyboard input to this window. Any window that previously had the input focus loses it.

The **SetFocus** member function sends a **WM_KILLFOCUS** message to the window that loses the input focus and a **WM_SETFOCUS** message to the window that receives the input focus. It also activates either the window or its parent.

If the current window is active but does not have the focus (that is, no window has the focus), any key pressed will produce the messages **WM_SYSCHAR**, **WM_SYSKEYDOWN**, or **WM_SYSKEYUP**.

See Also: **::SetFocus, CWnd::GetFocus**

CWnd::SetFont

void SetFont(CFont* *pFont*, **BOOL** *bRedraw* = **TRUE**);

Parameters

pFont   Specifies the new font.

bRedraw   If **TRUE**, redraw the **CWnd** object.

Remarks

Sets the window's current font to the specified font. If *bRedraw* is **TRUE**, the window will also be redrawn.

See Also: **CWnd::GetFont, WM_SETFONT**

CWnd::SetIcon

HICON SetIcon(HICON *hIcon*, **BOOL** *bBigIcon*);

Return Value

A handle to an icon.

Parameters

hIcon   A handle to a previous icon.

bBigIcon   Specifies a 32 pixel by 32 pixel icon if **TRUE**; specifies a 16 pixel by 16 pixel icon if **FALSE**.

Remarks

Call this member function to set the handle to a specific icon, as identified by *hIcon*. When the window class is registered, it selects an icon.

See Also: GetIcon

CWnd::SetMenu

BOOL SetMenu(CMenu* *pMenu* **);**

Return Value

Nonzero if the menu is changed; otherwise 0.

Parameters

pMenu   Identifies the new menu. If this parameter is **NULL**, the current menu is removed.

Remarks

Sets the current menu to the specified menu. Causes the window to be redrawn to reflect the menu change.

SetMenu will not destroy a previous menu. An application should call the **CMenu::DestroyMenu** member function to accomplish this task.

See Also: CMenu::DestroyMenu, CMenu::LoadMenu, ::SetMenu, CWnd::GetMenu

---

CWnd::SetOwner

void SetOwner(CWnd* *pOwnerWnd* **);**

Parameters

pOwnerWnd   Identifies the new owner of the window object. If this parameter is **NULL**, the window object has no owner.

Remarks

Sets the current window's owner to the specified window object. This owner can then receive command messages from the current window object. By default, the parent of the current window is its owner.

It is often useful to establish connections between window objects that are unrelated to the window hierarchy. For example, **CToolBar** sends notifications to its owner instead of to its parent. This allows the toolbar to become the child of one window (such as an OLE container application window) while sending notifications to another window (such as the in-place frame window). Furthermore, when a server window is deactivated or activated during in-place editing, any window owned by the frame window is hidden or shown. This ownership is explicitly set with a call to **SetOwner**.

The ownership concept of this function is different from the ownership concept of **GetWindow**.

See Also: CWnd::GetOwner, CToolBar

CWnd::SetParent

CWnd* SetParent(CWnd* *pWndNewParent* **);**

Return Value

A pointer to the previous parent window object if successful. The returned pointer may be temporary and should not be stored for later use.

Parameters

pWndNewParent   Identifies the new parent window.

Remarks

Changes the parent window of a child window.

If the child window is visible, Windows performs the appropriate redrawing and repainting.

See Also: ::SetParent, CWnd::GetParent

CWnd::SetProperty

void SetProperty(DISPID *dwDispID,* **VARTYPE** *vtProp,* ... **);**

Parameters

dwDispID   Identifies the property to be set. This value is usually supplied by Component Gallery.

vtProp   Specifies the type of the property to be set. For possible values, see the Remarks section for **COleDispatchDriver::InvokeHelper**.

...   A single parameter of the type specified by *vtProp*.

Remarks

Call this member function to set the OLE control property specified by *dwDispID*.

Note   This function should be called only on a **CWnd** object that represents an OLE control.

For more information about using this member function with OLE Control Containers, see the article "ActiveX Control Containers: Programming ActiveX Controls in an ActiveX Control Container" in *Visual C++ Programmer's Guide* online.

See Also: CWnd::InvokeHelper, COleDispatchDriver, CWnd::CreateControl

CWnd::SetRedraw

void SetRedraw(BOOL *bRedraw* = **TRUE**);

Parameters

bRedraw   Specifies the state of the redraw flag. If this parameter is **TRUE**, the redraw flag is set; if **FALSE**, the flag is cleared.

Remarks

An application calls **SetRedraw** to allow changes to be redrawn or to prevent changes from being redrawn.

This member function sets or clears the redraw flag. While the redraw flag is cleared, the contents will not be updated after each change and will not be repainted until the redraw flag is set. For example, an application that needs to add several items to a list box can clear the redraw flag, add the items, and then set the redraw flag. Finally, the application can call the **Invalidate** or **InvalidateRect** member function to cause the list box to be repainted.

See Also: WM_SETREDRAW

CWnd::SetScrollInfo

BOOL SetScrollInfo(int *nBar*, **LPSCROLLINFO** *lpScrollInfo*,
↪ **BOOL** *bRedraw* = **TRUE**);

Return Value

If successful, the return is **TRUE**. Otherwise, it is **FALSE**.

Parameters

nBar   Specifies whether the scroll bar is a control or part of a window's nonclient area. If it is part of the nonclient area, nBar also indicates whether the scroll bar is positioned horizontally, vertically, or both. It must be one of the following:

- **SB_BOTH**   Specifies the horizontal and vertical scroll bars of the window.

- **SB_HORZ**   Specifies that the window is a horizontal scroll bar.

- **SB_VERT**   Specifies that the window is a vertical scroll bar.

lpScrollInfo   A pointer to a **SCROLLINFO** structure. See the *Win32 SDK Programmer's Reference* for more information about this structure.

bRedraw   Specifies whether the scroll bar should be redrawn to reflect the new position. If *bRedraw* is **TRUE**, the scroll bar is redrawn. If it is **FALSE**, it is not redrawn. The scroll bar is redrawn by default.

Remarks

Call this member function to set the information that the **SCROLLINFO** structure maintains about a scroll bar.

The **SCROLLINFO** structure contains information about a scroll bar, including the minimum and maximum scrolling positions, the page size, and the position of the scroll box (the thumb). See the **SCROLLINFO** structure topic in the *Win32 SDK Programmer's Reference* for more information about changing the structure defaults.

The MFC Windows message handlers that indicate scroll-bar position, **CWnd::OnHScroll** and **CWnd::OnVScroll**, provide only 16 bits of position data. **GetScrollInfo** and **SetScrollInfo** provide 32 bits of scroll-bar position data. Thus, an application can call **GetScrollInfo** while processing either **CWnd::OnHScroll** or **CWnd::OnVScroll** to obtain 32-bit scroll-bar position data.

Note CWnd::GetScrollInfo enables applications to use 32-bit scroll-bar positions.

See Also: CWnd::GetScrollInfo, CWnd::SetScrollPos, CWnd::OnVScroll, CWnd::OnHScroll, SCROLLINFO

CWnd::SetScrollPos

int SetScrollPos(int *nBar*, **int** *nPos*, **BOOL** *bRedraw* = **TRUE**);

Return Value

The previous position of the scroll box.

Parameters

nBar   Specifies the scroll bar to be set. This parameter can be either of the following:

- **SB_HORZ**   Sets the position of the scroll box in the horizontal scroll bar of the window.

- **SB_VERT**   Sets the position of the scroll box in the vertical scroll bar of the window.

nPos   Specifies the new position of the scroll box. It must be within the scrolling range.

bRedraw   Specifies whether the scroll bar should be repainted to reflect the new scroll-box position. If this parameter is **TRUE**, the scroll bar is repainted; if **FALSE**, the scroll bar is not repainted.

Remarks

Sets the current position of a scroll box and, if requested, redraws the scroll bar to reflect the new position of the scroll box.

Setting *bRedraw* to **FALSE** is useful whenever the scroll bar will be redrawn by a subsequent call to another function.

See Also: **::SetScrollPos**, **CWnd::GetScrollPos**, **CScrollBar::SetScrollPos**

CWnd::SetScrollRange

void SetScrollRange(int *nBar***, int** *nMinPos***, int** *nMaxPos***, BOOL** *bRedraw* = **TRUE**);

Parameters

nBar   Specifies the scroll bar to be set. This parameter can be either of the following values:

- **SB_HORZ**   Sets the range of the horizontal scroll bar of the window.

- **SB_VERT**   Sets the range of the vertical scroll bar of the window.

nMinPos   Specifies the minimum scrolling position.

nMaxPos   Specifies the maximum scrolling position.

bRedraw   Specifies whether the scroll bar should be redrawn to reflect the change. If *bRedraw* is **TRUE**, the scroll bar is redrawn; if **FALSE**, the scroll bar is not redrawn.

Remarks

Sets minimum and maximum position values for the given scroll bar. It can also be used to hide or show standard scroll bars.

An application should not call this function to hide a scroll bar while processing a scroll-bar notification message.

If the call to **SetScrollRange** immediately follows a call to the **SetScrollPos** member function, the *bRedraw* parameter in the **SetScrollPos** member function should be 0 to prevent the scroll bar from being drawn twice.

The default range for a standard scroll bar is 0 through 100. The default range for a scroll bar control is empty (both the *nMinPos* and *nMaxPos* values are 0). The difference between the values specified by *nMinPos* and *nMaxPos* must not be greater than **INT_MAX**.

See Also: **CWnd::SetScrollPos**, **::SetScrollRange**, **CWnd::GetScrollRange**

CWnd::SetTimer

UINT SetTimer(UINT *nIDEvent***, UINT** *nElapse***,**
    ↪ **void (CALLBACK EXPORT*** *lpfnTimer***)(HWND, UINT, UINT, DWORD));**

Return Value

The timer identifier of the new timer if the function is successful. An application passes this value to the **KillTimer** member function to kill the timer. Nonzero if successful; otherwise 0.

Parameters

nIDEvent   Specifies a nonzero timer identifier.

nElapse   Specifies the time-out value, in milliseconds.

lpfnTimer   Specifies the address of the application-supplied `TimerProc` callback function that processes the **WM_TIMER** messages. If this parameter is **NULL**, the **WM_TIMER** messages are placed in the application's message queue and handled by the **CWnd** object.

Remarks

Installs a system timer. A time-out value is specified, and every time a time-out occurs, the system posts a **WM_TIMER** message to the installing application's message queue or passes the message to an application-defined **TimerProc** callback function.

The *lpfnTimer* callback function need not be named **TimerProc**, but it must be defined as follows:

```
void CALLBACK EXPORT TimerProc(
    HWND hWnd,         // handle of CWnd that called SetTimer
    UINT nMsg,         // WM_TIMER
    UINT nIDEvent      // timer identification
    DWORD dwTime       // system time
);
```

Timers are a limited global resource; therefore it is important that an application check the value returned by the **SetTimer** member function to verify that a timer is actually available.

See Also: **WM_TIMER**, **CWnd::KillTimer**, **::SetTimer**

CWnd::SetWindowContextHelpId

BOOL SetWindowContextHelpId(DWORD *dwContextHelpId* **);**

Return Value

Nonzero if the function is successful; otherwise 0.

Parameters

dwContextHelpId   The help context identifier.

Remarks

Call this member function to associate a help context identifier with the specified window.

If a child window does not have a help context identifier, it inherits the identifier of its parent window. Likewise, if an owned window does not have a help context identifier, it inherits the identifier of its owner window. This inheritance of help context identifiers allows an application to set just one identifier for a dialog box and all of its controls.

See Also: **CWnd::GetWindowContextHelpId**

CWnd::SetWindowPlacement

BOOL SetWindowPlacement(const WINDOWPLACEMENT*lpwndpl **);**

Return Value

Nonzero if the function is successful; otherwise 0.

Parameters

lpwndpl Points to a **WINDOWPLACEMENT** structure that specifies the new show state and positions.

Remarks

Sets the show state and the normal (restored), minimized, and maximized positions for a window.

See Also: **CWnd::GetWindowPlacement, ::SetWindowPlacement**

CWnd::SetWindowPos

BOOL SetWindowPos(const CWnd* *pWndInsertAfter***, int** *x***, int** *y***, int** *cx***, int** *cy***,**
↳ UINT *nFlags* **);**

Return Value

Nonzero if the function is successful; otherwise 0.

Parameters

pWndInsertAfter Identifies the **CWnd** object that will precede this **CWnd** object in the Z-order. This parameter can be a pointer to a **CWnd** or a **Pointer** to one of the following values:

- **wndBottom** Places the window at the bottom of the Z-order. If this **CWnd** is a topmost window, the window loses its topmost status; the system places the window at the bottom of all other windows.

- **wndTop** Places the window at the top of the Z-order.

- **wndTopMost** Places the window above all nontopmost windows. The window maintains its topmost position even when it is deactivated.

- **wndNoTopMost** Repositions the window to the top of all nontopmost windows (that is, behind all topmost windows). This flag has no effect if the window is already a nontopmost window.

See the "Remarks" section for this function for rules about how this parameter is used.

x Specifies the new position of the left side of the window.

y   Specifies the new position of the top of the window.

cx   Specifies the new width of the window.

cy   Specifies the new height of the window.

nFlags   Specifies sizing and positioning options. This parameter can be a combination of the following:

- **SWP_DRAWFRAME**   Draws a frame (defined when the window was created) around the window.

- **SWP_FRAMECHANGED**   Sends a **WM_NCCALCSIZE** message to the window, even if the window's size is not being changed. If this flag is not specified, **WM_NCCALCSIZE** is sent only when the window's size is being changed.

- **SWP_HIDEWINDOW**   Hides the window.

- **SWP_NOACTIVATE**   Does not activate the window. If this flag is not set, the window is activated and moved to the top of either the topmost or the nontopmost group (depending on the setting of the *pWndInsertAfter* parameter).

- **SWP_NOCOPYBITS**   Discards the entire contents of the client area. If this flag is not specified, the valid contents of the client area are saved and copied back into the client area after the window is sized or repositioned.

- **SWP_NOMOVE**   Retains current position (ignores the *x* and *y* parameters).

- **SWP_NOOWNERZORDER**   Does not change the owner window's position in the Z-order.

- **SWP_NOREDRAW**   Does not redraw changes. If this flag is set, no repainting of any kind occurs. This applies to the client area, the nonclient area (including the title and scroll bars), and any part of the parent window uncovered as a result of the moved window. When this flag is set, the application must explicitly invalidate or redraw any parts of the window and parent window that must be redrawn.

- **SWP_NOREPOSITION**   Same as **SWP_NOOWNERZORDER**.

- **SWP_NOSENDCHANGING**   Prevents the window from receiving the **WM_WINDOWPOSCHANGING** message.

- **SWP_NOSIZE**   Retains current size (ignores the *cx* and *cy* parameters).

- **SWP_NOZORDER**   Retains current ordering (ignores *pWndInsertAfter*).

- **SWP_SHOWWINDOW**   Displays the window.

Remarks

Call this member function to change the size, position, and Z-order of child, pop-up, and top-level windows.

Windows are ordered on the screen according to their Z-order; the window at the top of the Z-order appears on top of all other windows in the order.

All coordinates for child windows are client coordinates (relative to the upper-left corner of the parent window's client area).

A window can be moved to the top of the Z-order either by setting the *pWndInsertAfter* parameter to **&wndTopMost** and ensuring that the **SWP_NOZORDER** flag is not set or by setting a window's Z-order so that it is above any existing topmost windows. When a nontopmost window is made topmost, its owned windows are also made topmost. Its owners are not changed.

A topmost window is no longer topmost if it is repositioned to the bottom (**&wndBottom**) of the Z-order or after any nontopmost window. When a topmost window is made nontopmost, all of its owners and its owned windows are also made nontopmost windows.

If neither **SWP_NOACTIVATE** nor **SWP_NOZORDER** is specified (that is, when the application requests that a window be simultaneously activated and placed in the specified Z-order), the value specified in *pWndInsertAfter* is used only in the following circumstances:

- Neither **&wndTopMost** nor **&wndNoTopMost** is specified in the *pWndInsertAfter* parameter.

- This window is not the active window.

An application cannot activate an inactive window without also bringing it to the top of the Z-order. Applications can change the Z-order of an activated window without restrictions.

A nontopmost window may own a topmost window, but not vice versa. Any window (for example, a dialog box) owned by a topmost window is itself made a topmost window to ensure that all owned windows stay above their owner.

With Windows versions 3.1 and later, windows can be moved to the top of the Z-order and locked there by setting their **WS_EX_TOPMOST** styles. Such a topmost window maintains its topmost position even when deactivated. For example, selecting the WinHelp Always On Top command makes the Help window topmost, and it then remains visible when you return to your application.

To create a topmost window, call **SetWindowPos** with the *pWndInsertAfter* parameter equal to **&wndTopMost**, or set the **WS_EX_TOPMOST** style when you create the window.

If the Z-order contains any windows with the **WS_EX_TOPMOST** style, a window moved with the **&wndTopMost** value is placed at the top of all nontopmost windows, but below any topmost windows. When an application activates an inactive window without the **WS_EX_TOPMOST** bit, the window is moved above all nontopmost windows but below any topmost windows.

If **SetWindowPos** is called when the *pWndInsertAfter* parameter is **&wndBottom** and **CWnd** is a topmost window, the window loses its topmost status (**WS_EX_TOPMOST** is cleared), and the system places the window at the bottom of the Z-order.

See Also: ::DeferWindowPos, ::SetWindowPos

CWnd::SetWindowRgn

int SetWindowRgn(HRGN *hRgn*, **BOOL** *bRedraw* **);**

Return Value

If the function succeeds, the return value is nonzero. If the function fails, the return value is zero.

Parameters

hRgn   A handle to a region.

bRedraw   If **TRUE**, the operating system redraws the window after setting the region; otherwise, it does not. Typically, set *bRedraw* to **TRUE** if the window is visible. If set to **TRUE**, the system sends the **WM_WINDOWPOSCHANGING** and **WM_WINDOWPOSCHANGED** messages to the window.

Remarks

Call this member function to set a window's region.

The coordinates of a window's window region are relative to the upper-left corner of the window, not the client area of the window.

After a successful call to **SetWindowRgn**, the operating system owns the region specified by the region handle *hRgn*. The operating system does not make a copy of the region, so do not make any further function calls with this region handle, and do not close this region handle.

See Also: ::SetWindowRgn, CWnd::GetWindowRgn

CWnd::SetWindowText

void SetWindowText(LPCTSTR *lpszString* **);**

Parameters

lpszString   Points to a **CString** object or null-terminated string to be used as the new title or control text.

Remarks

Sets the window's title to the specified text. If the window is a control, the text within the control is set.

This function causes a **WM_SETTEXT** message to be sent to this window.

See Also: **CWnd::GetWindowText, ::SetWindowText**

CWnd::ShowCaret

void ShowCaret( );

Remarks

Shows the caret on the screen at the caret's current position. Once shown, the caret begins flashing automatically.

The **ShowCaret** member function shows the caret only if it has a current shape and has not been hidden two or more times consecutively. If the caret is not owned by this window, the caret is not shown.

Hiding the caret is cumulative. If the **HideCaret** member function has been called five times consecutively, **ShowCaret** must be called five times to show the caret.

The caret is a shared resource. The window should show the caret only when it has the input focus or is active.

See Also: **CWnd::HideCaret, ::ShowCaret**

CWnd::ShowOwnedPopups

void ShowOwnedPopups(BOOL *bShow* **= TRUE);**

Parameters

bShow   Specifies whether pop-up windows are to be shown or hidden. If this parameter is **TRUE**, all hidden pop-up windows are shown. If this parameter is **FALSE**, all visible pop-up windows are hidden.

Remarks

Shows or hides all pop-up windows owned by this window.

See Also: **::ShowOwnedPopups**

CWnd::ShowScrollBar

void ShowScrollBar(UINT *nBar*, **BOOL** *bShow* **= TRUE);**

Parameters

nBar   Specifies whether the scroll bar is a control or part of a window's nonclient area. If it is part of the nonclient area, *nBar* also indicates whether the scroll bar is positioned horizontally, vertically, or both. It must be one of the following:

- **SB_BOTH**   Specifies the horizontal and vertical scroll bars of the window.

- **SB_HORZ**   Specifies that the window is a horizontal scroll bar.

- **SB_VERT**   Specifies that the window is a vertical scroll bar.

bShow   Specifies whether Windows shows or hides the scroll bar. If this parameter is **TRUE**, the scroll bar is shown; otherwise the scroll bar is hidden.

Remarks

Shows or hides a scroll bar.

An application should not call **ShowScrollBar** to hide a scroll bar while processing a scroll-bar notification message.

See Also: ::ShowScrollBar, CScrollBar::ShowScrollBar

CWnd::ShowWindow

BOOL ShowWindow(int *nCmdShow* **);**

Return Value

Nonzero if the window was previously visible; 0 if the **CWnd** was previously hidden.

Parameters

nCmdShow   Specifies how the **CWnd** is to be shown. It must be one of the following values:

- **SW_HIDE**   Hides this window and passes activation to another window.

- **SW_MINIMIZE**   Minimizes the window and activates the top-level window in the system's list.

- **SW_RESTORE**   Activates and displays the window. If the window is minimized or maximized, Windows restores it to its original size and position.

- **SW_SHOW**   Activates the window and displays it in its current size and position.

- **SW_SHOWMAXIMIZED**   Activates the window and displays it as a maximized window.

- **SW_SHOWMINIMIZED**   Activates the window and displays it as an icon.

- **SW_SHOWMINNOACTIVE**   Displays the window as an icon. The window that is currently active remains active.

- **SW_SHOWNA**   Displays the window in its current state. The window that is currently active remains active.

- **SW_SHOWNOACTIVE**   Displays the window in its most recent size and position. The window that is currently active remains active.

- **SW_SHOWNORMAL**   Activates and displays the window. If the window is minimized or maximized, Windows restores it to its original size and position.

Remarks

Sets the visibility state of the window.

ShowWindow must be called only once per application for the main window with **CWinApp::m_nCmdShow**. Subsequent calls to **ShowWindow** must use one of the values listed above instead of the one specified by **CWinApp::m_nCmdShow**.

See Also: **::ShowWindow, CWnd::OnShowWindow, CWnd::ShowOwnedPopups**

CWnd::SubclassDlgItem

BOOL SubclassDlgItem(UINT *nID***, CWnd*** *pParent* **);**

Return Value

Nonzero if the function is successful; otherwise 0.

Parameters

nID   The control's ID.

pParent   The control's parent (usually a dialog box).

Remarks

Call this member function to "dynamically subclass" a control created from a dialog template and attach it to this **CWnd** object. When a control is dynamically subclassed, windows messages will route through the **CWnd**'s message map and call message handlers in the **CWnd**'s class first. Messages that are passed to the base class will be passed to the default message handler in the control.

This member function attaches the Windows control to a **CWnd** object and replaces the control's **WndProc** and **AfxWndProc** functions. The function stores the old **WndProc** in the location returned by the **GetSuperWndProcAddr** member function.

See Also: **CWnd::GetSuperWndProcAddr, CWnd::DefWindowProc, CWnd::SubclassWindow, CWnd::Attach**

CWnd::SubclassWindow

BOOL SubclassWindow(HWND *hWnd* **);**

Return Value

Nonzero if the function is successful; otherwise 0.

Parameters

hWnd   A handle to the window.

Remarks

Call this member function to "dynamically subclass" a window and attach it to this **CWnd** object. When a window is dynamically subclassed, windows messages will route through the **CWnd**'s message map and call message handlers in the **CWnd**'s class first. Messages that are passed to the base class will be passed to the default message handler in the window.

This member function attaches the Windows control to a **CWnd** object and replaces the window's **WndProc** and **AfxWndProc** functions. The function stores the old **WndProc** in the location returned by the **GetSuperWndProcAddr** member function. You must override the **GetSuperWndProcAddr** member function for every unique window class to provide a place to store the old **WndProc**.

See Also: CWnd::GetSuperWndProcAddr, CWnd::DefWindowProc, CWnd::SubclassDlgItem, CWnd::Attach, CWnd::PreSubclassWindow, CWnd::UnsubclassWindow

---

CWnd::UnlockWindowUpdate

> **void CWnd::UnlockWindowUpdate();**

Remarks

Call this member function to unlock a window that was locked with **CWnd::LockWindowUpdate**.

Only one window at a time can be locked using **LockWindowUpdate**. See **CWnd::LockWindowUpdate** or the Win32 function **LockWindowUpdate** for more information on locking windows.

CWnd::UnsubclassWindow

> **HWND UnsubclassWindow( );**

Return Value

A handle to the unsubclassed window.

Remarks

Call this member function to set **WndProc** back to its original value and detach the window identified by **HWND** from the **CWnd** object.

See Also: CWnd::SubclassWindow, CWnd::PreSubclassWindow, CWnd::GetSuperWndProcAddr, CWnd::DefWindowProc, CWnd::SubclassDlgItem, CWnd::Attach

CWnd::UpdateData

BOOL UpdateData(BOOL *bSaveAndValidate* = **TRUE**);

Return Value

Nonzero if the operation is successful; otherwise 0. If *bSaveAndValidate* is **TRUE**, then a return value of nonzero means that the data is successfully validated.

Parameters

bSaveAndValidate   Flag that indicates whether dialog box is being initialized (**FALSE**) or data is being retrieved (**TRUE**).

Remarks

Call this member function to initialize data in a dialog box, or to retrieve and validate dialog data.

The framework automatically calls **UpdateData** with *bSaveAndValidate* set to **FALSE** when a modal dialog box is created in the default implementation of **CDialog::OnInitDialog**. The call occurs before the dialog box is visible. The default implementation of **CDialog::OnOK** calls this member function with *bSaveAndValidate* set to **TRUE** to retrieve the data, and if successful, will close the dialog box. (If the Cancel button is clicked in the dialog box, the dialog box is closed without the data being retrieved.)

See Also: CWnd::DoDataExchange

CWnd::UpdateDialogControls

void UpdateDialogControls(CCmdTarget* *pTarget*, **BOOL** *bDisableIfNoHndler*);

Parameters

pTarget   Points to the main frame window of the application, and is used for routing update messages.

bDisableIfNoHndler   Flag that indicates whether a control that has no update handler should be automatically displayed as disabled.

Remarks

Call this member function to update the state of dialog buttons and other controls in a dialog box or window that uses the **ON_UPDATE_COMMAND_UI** callback mechanism.

If a child control does not have a handler and *bDisableIfNoHndler* is **TRUE**, then the child control will be disabled.

The framework calls this member function for controls in dialog bars or toolbars as part of the application's idle processing.

See Also: CFrameWnd::m_bAutoMenuEnable

CWnd::UpdateWindow

void UpdateWindow( );

Remarks

Updates the client area by sending a **WM_PAINT** message if the update region is not empty. The **UpdateWindow** member function sends a **WM_PAINT** message directly, bypassing the application queue. If the update region is empty, **WM_PAINT** is not sent.

See Also: **::UpdateWindow, CWnd::RedrawWindow**

CWnd::ValidateRect

void ValidateRect(LPCRECT *lpRect* **);**

Parameters

lpRect Points to a **CRect** object or **RECT** structure that contains client coordinates of the rectangle to be removed from the update region. If *lpRect* is **NULL**, the entire window is validated.

Remarks

Validates the client area within the given rectangle by removing the rectangle from the update region of the window. The **BeginPaint** member function automatically validates the entire client area. Neither the **ValidateRect** nor the **ValidateRgn** member function should be called if a portion of the update region needs to be validated before **WM_PAINT** is next generated.

Windows continues to generate **WM_PAINT** messages until the current update region is validated.

See Also: **CWnd::BeginPaint, ::ValidateRect, CWnd::ValidateRgn**

CWnd::ValidateRgn

void ValidateRgn(CRgn* *pRgn* **);**

Parameters

pRgn A pointer to a **CRgn** object that identifies a region that defines the area to be removed from the update region. If this parameter is **NULL**, the entire client area is removed.

Remarks

Validates the client area within the given region by removing the region from the current update region of the window. The given region must have been created previously by a region function. The region coordinates are assumed to be client coordinates.

The **BeginPaint** member function automatically validates the entire client area. Neither the **ValidateRect** nor the **ValidateRgn** member function should be called if a portion of the update region must be validated before the next **WM_PAINT** message is generated.

See Also: **::ValidateRgn**, **CWnd::ValidateRect**

CWnd::WindowFromPoint

static CWnd* PASCAL WindowFromPoint(POINT *point* **);**

Return Value

A pointer to the window object in which the point lies. It is **NULL** if no window exists at the given point. The returned pointer may be temporary and should not be stored for later use.

Parameters

point Specifies a **CPoint** object or **POINT** data structure that defines the point to be checked.

Remarks

Retrieves the window that contains the specified point; *point* must specify the screen coordinates of a point on the screen.

WindowFromPoint does not retrieve a hidden, disabled, or transparent window, even if the point is within the window. An application should use the **ChildWindowFromPoint** member function for a nonrestrictive search.

See Also: **::WindowFromPoint**, **CWnd::ChildWindowFromPoint**

CWnd::WindowProc

virtual LRESULT WindowProc(UINT *message*, **WPARAM** *wParam*,
↪ **LPARAM** *lParam* **);**

Return Value

The return value depends on the message.

Parameters

message Specifies the Windows message to be processed.

wParam Provides additional information used in processing the message. The parameter value depends on the message.

lParam Provides additional information used in processing the message. The parameter value depends on the message.

Remarks

Provides a Windows procedure (**WindowProc**) for a **CWnd** object. It dispatches messages through the window's message map.

Data Members

CWnd::m_hWnd

Remarks

The handle of the Windows window attached to this **CWnd**. The **m_hWnd** data member is a public variable of type **HWND**.

See Also: **CWnd::Attach**, **CWnd::Detach**, **CWnd::FromHandle**

CWordArray

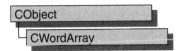

The **CWordArray** class supports arrays of 16-bit words.

The member functions of **CWordArray** are similar to the member functions of class **CObArray**. Because of this similarity, you can use the **CObArray** reference documentation for member function specifics. Wherever you see a **CObject** pointer as a function parameter or return value, substitute a **WORD**.

```
CObject* CObArray::GetAt( int <nIndex> ) const;
```

for example, translates to

```
WORD CWordArray::GetAt( int <nIndex> ) const;
```

CWordArray incorporates the **IMPLEMENT_SERIAL** macro to support serialization and dumping of its elements. If an array of words is stored to an archive, either with an overloaded insertion operator or with the **CObject::Serialize** member function, each element is, in turn, serialized.

Note Before using an array, use **SetSize** to establish its size and allocate memory for it. If you do not use **SetSize**, adding elements to your array causes it to be frequently reallocated and copied. Frequent reallocation and copying are inefficient and can fragment memory.

If you need a dump of individual elements in the array, you must set the depth of the dump context to 1 or greater.

For more information on using **CWordArray**, see the article "Collections" in *Visual C++ Programmer's Guide* online.

#include <afxcoll.h>

CWordArray Class Members

Construction

CWordArray	Constructs an empty array for words.

Bounds

GetSize	Gets number of elements in this array.
GetUpperBound	Returns the largest valid index.
SetSize	Sets the number of elements to be contained in this array.

Operations

FreeExtra	Frees all unused memory above the current upper bound.
RemoveAll	Removes all the elements from this array.

Element Access

GetAt	Returns the value at a given index.
SetAt	Sets the value for a given index; array is not allowed to grow.
ElementAt	Returns a temporary reference to the element pointer within the array.
GetData	Allows access to elements in the array. Can be **NULL**.

Growing the Array

SetAtGrow	Sets the value for a given index; grows the array if necessary.
Add	Adds an element to the end of the array; grows the array if necessary.
Append	Appends another array to the array; grows the array if necessary.
Copy	Copies another array to the array; grows the array if necessary.

Insertion/Removal

InsertAt	Inserts an element (or all the elements in another array) at a specified index.
RemoveAt	Removes an element at a specific index.

Operators

operator []	Sets or gets the element at the specified index.

MFC Macros and Globals

The Microsoft Foundation Class Library can be divided into two major sections:
(1) the MFC classes and (2) macros and globals. If a function or variable is not a
member of a class, it is a global function or variable.

The MFC library and the ActiveX Template library (ATL) share string conversion
macros. See "String Conversion Macros" in the ATL documentation online for a
discussion of these macros.

The MFC macros and globals offer functionality in the following categories:

General MFC

- Data types
- Type Casting of MFC Class Objects
- Run-time object model services
- Diagnostic services
- Exception processing
- CString formatting and message-box display
- Message maps
- Application information and management
- Standard command and window IDs
- Collection class helpers
- ClassWizard comment delimiters

Database

- Record Field Exchange (RFX) functions and Bulk Record Field Exchange
  (Bulk RFX) functions for the MFC ODBC classes
- Record Field Exchange (DFX) functions for the MFC DAO classes
- Dialog Data Exchange (DDX) functions for CRecordView and CDaoRecordView
  (MFC ODBC and DAO classes)
- Dialog Data Exchange (DDX) functions for OLE controls
- Macros to aid in calling Open Database Connectivity (ODBC) API functions
  directly
- DAO Database Engine Initialization and Termination

Internet

- Internet Server API (ISAPI) Parse Maps
- Internet Server API (ISAPI) Diagnostic Macros

OLE

- OLE initialization

- Application control

- Dispatch maps

In addition, MFC provides a function, called **AfxEnableControlContainer**, that enables any OLE container, developed with MFC 4.0, to fully support embedded OLE controls.

OLE Controls

- Variant parameter type constants

- Type library access

- Property pages

- Event maps

- Event sink maps

- Connection maps

- Registering OLE controls

- Class factories and licensing

- Persistence of OLE controls

The first part of this section briefly discusses each of the above categories and lists each global and macro in the category, along with a brief description of what it does. Following this—in alphabetical order—are complete descriptions of the global functions, global variables, and macros in the MFC library.

The main supporting reference for the MFC Macros and Globals section is *Visual C++ Programmer's Guide* online. This is usually the first place you should look to find more information on macros and globals. When necessary, the appropriate article in *Visual C++ Programmer's Guide* online is mentioned with the function or macro description.

Note Many global functions start with the prefix "Afx"—but some, such as the dialog data exchange (DDX) functions and many of the database functions, deviate from this convention. All global variables start with "afx" as a prefix. Macros do not start with any particular prefix, but they are written all in uppercase.

Data Types

This topic lists the data types most commonly used in the Microsoft Foundation Class Library. Most of the data types are exactly the same as those in the Windows Software Development Kit (SDK), while others are unique to MFC.

Commonly used Windows SDK and MFC data types are as follows:

- **BOOL**   A Boolean value.
- **BSTR**   A 32-bit character pointer.
- **BYTE**   An 8-bit integer that is not signed.
- **COLORREF**   A 32-bit value used as a color value.
- **DWORD**   A 32-bit unsigned integer or the address of a segment and its associated offset.
- **LONG**   A 32-bit signed integer.
- **LPARAM**   A 32-bit value passed as a parameter to a window procedure or callback function.
- **LPCSTR**   A 32-bit pointer to a constant character string.
- **LPSTR**   A 32-bit pointer to a character string.
- **LPCTSTR**   A 32-bit pointer to a constant character string that is portable for Unicode and DBCS.
- **LPTSTR**   A 32-bit pointer to a character string that is portable for Unicode and DBCS.
- **LPVOID**   A 32-bit pointer to an unspecified type.
- **LRESULT**   A 32-bit value returned from a window procedure or callback function.
- **UINT**   A 16-bit unsigned integer on Windows versions 3.0 and 3.1; a 32-bit unsigned integer on Win32.
- **WNDPROC**   A 32-bit pointer to a window procedure.
- **WORD**   A 16-bit unsigned integer.
- **WPARAM**   A value passed as a parameter to a window procedure or callback function: 16 bits on Windows versions 3.0 and 3.1; 32 bits on Win32.

Data types unique to the Microsoft Foundation Class Library include the following:

- **POSITION**   A value used to denote the position of an element in a collection; used by MFC collection classes.
- **LPCRECT**   A 32-bit pointer to a constant (nonmodifiable) **RECT** structure.

For a list of the less common data types, see the "Data Types" section of the *Win32 SDK Programmer's Reference*.

Type Casting of MFC Class Objects

Type casting macros provide a way to cast a given pointer to a pointer that points to an object of specific class, with or without checking that the cast is legal.

The following table lists the MFC type casting macros.

Macros that Cast Pointers to MFC Class Objects

DYNAMIC_DOWNCAST	Casts a pointer to a pointer to a class object while checking to see if the cast is legal.
STATIC_DOWNCAST	Casts a pointer to an object from one class to a pointer of a related type. In a debug build, causes an **ASSERT** if the object is not a "kind of" the target type.

Run-Time Object Model Services

The classes **CObject** and **CRuntimeClass** encapsulate several object services, including access to run-time class information, serialization, and dynamic object creation. All classes derived from **CObject** inherit this functionality.

Access to run-time class information enables you to determine information about an object's class at run time. The ability to determine the class of an object at run time is useful when you need extra type-checking of function arguments and when you must write special-purpose code based on the class of an object. Run-time class information is not supported directly by the C++ language.

Serialization is the process of writing or reading an object's contents to or from a file. You can use serialization to store an object's contents even after the application exits. The object can then be read from the file when the application is restarted. Such data objects are said to be "persistent."

Dynamic object creation enables you to create an object of a specified class at run time. For example, document, view, and frame objects must support dynamic creation because the framework needs to create them dynamically.

The following table lists the MFC macros that support run-time class information, serialization, and dynamic creation.

For more information on these run-time object services and serialization, see the article "CObject Class: Accessing Run-Time Class Information" in *Visual C++ Programmer's Guide* online.

Run-Time Object Model Services Macros

DECLARE_DYNAMIC	Enables access to run-time class information (must be used in the class declaration).
DECLARE_DYNCREATE	Enables dynamic creation and access to run-time class information (must be used in the class declaration).
DECLARE_SERIAL	Enables serialization and access to run-time class information (must be used in the class declaration).
IMPLEMENT_DYNAMIC	Enables access to run-time class information (must be used in the class implementation).
IMPLEMENT_DYNCREATE	Enables dynamic creation and access to run-time information (must be used in the class implementation).
IMPLEMENT_SERIAL	Permits serialization and access to run-time class information (must be used in the class implementation).
RUNTIME_CLASS	Returns the **CRuntimeClass** structure that corresponds to the named class.

OLE frequently requires the dynamic creation of objects at run time. For example, an OLE server application must be able to create OLE items dynamically in response to a request from a client. Similarly, an automation server must be able to create items in response to requests from automation clients.

The Microsoft Foundation Class Library provides two macros specific to OLE.

Dynamic Creation of OLE Objects

DECLARE_OLECREATE	Enables objects to be created through OLE automation.
IMPLEMENT_OLECREATE	Enables objects to be created by the OLE system.

Diagnostic Services

The Microsoft Foundation Class Library supplies many diagnostic services that make debugging your programs easier. These diagnostic services include macros and global functions that allow you to track your program's memory allocations, dump the contents of objects during run time, and print debugging messages during run time. The macros and global functions for diagnostic services are grouped into the following categories:

- General diagnostic macros
- General diagnostic functions and variables
- Object diagnostic functions

These macros and functions are available for all classes derived from **CObject** in the Debug and Release versions of MFC. However, all except **DEBUG_NEW** and **VERIFY** do nothing in the Release version.

In the Debug library, all allocated memory blocks are bracketed with a series of "guard bytes." If these bytes are disturbed by an errant memory write, then the diagnostic routines can report a problem. If you include the line

```
#define new DEBUG_NEW
```

in your implementation file, all calls to **new** will store the filename and line number where the memory allocation took place. The function **CMemoryState::DumpAllObjectsSince** will display this extra information, allowing you to identify memory leaks. Refer also to the class **CDumpContext** for additional information on diagnostic output.

In addition, the C run-time library also supports a set of diagnostic functions you can use to debug your applications. For more information, see "Debug Routines" in the *Run-Time Library Reference*.

MFC General Diagnostic Macros

ASSERT	Prints a message and then aborts the program if the specified expression evaluates to **FALSE** in the Debug version of the library.
ASSERT_KINDOF	Tests that an object is an object of the specified class or of a class derived from the specified class.
ASSERT_VALID	Tests the internal validity of an object by calling its **AssertValid** member function; typically overridden from **CObject**.
DEBUG_NEW	Supplies a filename and line number for all object allocations in Debug mode to help find memory leaks.
TRACE	Provides **printf**-like capability in the Debug version of the library.
TRACE0	Similar to **TRACE** but takes a format string with no arguments.
TRACE1	Similar to **TRACE** but takes a format string with a single argument.
TRACE2	Similar to **TRACE** but takes a format string with two arguments.
TRACE3	Similar to **TRACE** but takes a format string with three arguments.
VERIFY	Similar to **ASSERT** but evaluates the expression in the Release version of the library as well as in the Debug version.

MFC General Diagnostic Variables and Functions

afxDump	Global variable that sends **CDumpContext** information to the debugger output window or to the debug terminal.
afxMemDF	Global variable that controls the behavior of the debugging memory allocator.

MFC General Diagnostic Variables and Functions *(continued)*

afxTraceEnabled	Global variable used to enable or disable output from the **TRACE** macro.
afxTraceFlags	Global variable used to turn on the built-in reporting features of MFC.
AfxCheckMemory	Checks the integrity of all currently allocated memory.
AfxDump	If called while in the debugger, dumps the state of an object while debugging.
AfxEnableMemoryTracking	Turns memory tracking on and off.
AfxIsMemoryBlock	Verifies that a memory block has been properly allocated.
AfxIsValidAddress	Verifies that a memory address range is within the program's bounds.
AfxIsValidString	Determines whether a pointer to a string is valid.
AfxSetAllocHook	Enables the calling of a function on each memory allocation.

MFC Object Diagnostic Functions

AfxDoForAllClasses	Performs a specified function on all **CObject**-derived classes that support run-time type checking.
AfxDoForAllObjects	Performs a specified function on all **CObject**-derived objects that were allocated with **new**.

Exception Processing

When a program executes, a number of abnormal conditions and errors called "exceptions" can occur. These may include running out of memory, resource allocation errors, and failure to find files.

The Microsoft Foundation Class Library uses an exception-handling scheme that is modeled closely after the one proposed by the ANSI standards committee for C++. An exception handler must be set up before calling a function that may encounter an abnormal situation. If the function encounters an abnormal condition, it throws an exception and control is passed to the exception handler.

Several macros included with the Microsoft Foundation Class Library will set up exception handlers. A number of other global functions help to throw specialized exceptions and terminate programs, if necessary. These macros and global functions fall into the following categories:

- Exception macros, which structure your exception handler
- Exception-throwing functions, which generate exceptions of specific types
- Termination functions, which cause program termination

For examples and more details, see the article "Exceptions" in *Visual C++ Programmer's Guide* online.

Exception Macros

TRY	Designates a block of code for exception processing.
CATCH	Designates a block of code for catching an exception from the preceding **TRY** block.
CATCH_ALL	Designates a block of code for catching all exceptions from the preceding **TRY** block.
AND_CATCH	Designates a block of code for catching additional exception types from the preceding **TRY** block.
AND_CATCH_ALL	Designates a block of code for catching all other additional exception types thrown in a preceding **TRY** block.
END_CATCH	Ends the last **CATCH** or **AND_CATCH** code block.
END_CATCH_ALL	Ends the last **CATCH_ALL** code block.
THROW	Throws a specified exception.
THROW_LAST	Throws the currently handled exception to the next outer handler.

Exception-Throwing Functions

AfxThrowArchiveException	Throws an archive exception.
AfxThrowFileException	Throws a file exception.
AfxThrowMemoryException	Throws a memory exception.
AfxThrowNotSupportedException	Throws a not-supported exception.
AfxThrowResourceException	Throws a Windows resource-not-found exception.
AfxThrowUserException	Throws an exception in a user-initiated program action.

MFC provides two exception-throwing functions specifically for OLE exceptions:

OLE Exception Functions

AfxThrowOleDispatchException	Throws an exception within an OLE automation function.
AfxThrowOleException	Throws an OLE exception.

To support database exceptions, the database classes provide two exception classes, **CDBException** and **CDaoException**, and global functions to support the exception types:

DAO Exception Functions

AfxThrowDAOException	Throws a **CDaoException** from your own code.
AfxThrowDBException	Throws a **CDBException** from your own code.

MFC provides the following termination function:

Termination Functions

AfxAbort	Called to terminate an application when a fatal error occurs.

See Also: **CException**

CString Formatting and Message-Box Display

A number of functions are provided to format and parse **CString** objects. You can use these functions whenever you have to manipulate **CString** objects, but they are particularly useful for formatting strings that will appear in message-box text.

This group of functions also includes a global routine for displaying a message box.

CString Functions

AfxFormatString1	Substitutes a given string for the format characters "%1" in a string contained in the string table.
AfxFormatString2	Substitutes two strings for the format characters "%1" and "%2" in a string contained in the string table.
AfxMessageBox	Displays a message box.

See Also: **CString**

Application Information and Management

When you write an application, you create a single **CWinApp**-derived object. At times, you may wish to get information about this object from outside the **CWinApp**-derived object.

The Microsoft Foundation Class Library provides the following global functions to help you accomplish these tasks:

Application Information and Management Functions

AfxFreeLibrary	Decrements the reference count of the loaded dynamic-link library (DLL) module; when the reference count reaches zero, the module is unmapped.
AfxGetApp	Returns a pointer to the application's single **CWinApp** object.
AfxGetAppName	Returns a string containing the application's name.

(continued)

Application Information and Management Functions *(continued)*

AfxGetInstanceHandle	Returns an **HINSTANCE** representing this instance of the application.
AfxGetMainWnd	Returns a pointer to the current "main" window of a non-OLE application, or the in-place frame window of a server application.
AfxGetResourceHandle	Returns an **HINSTANCE** to the source of the application's default resources. Use this to access the application's resources directly.
AfxInitRichEdit	Initializes the rich edit control for the application and initializes the common controls library, if the library hasn't already been initialized for the process.
AfxLoadLibrary	Maps a DLL module and returns a handle that can be used to get the address of a DLL function.
AfxRegisterWndClass	Registers a Windows window class to supplement those registered automatically by MFC.
AfxSocketInit	Called in a **CWinApp::InitInstance** override to initialize Windows Sockets.
AfxSetResourceHandle	Sets the **HINSTANCE** handle where the default resources of the application are loaded.
AfxRegisterClass	Registers a window class in a DLL that uses MFC.
AfxBeginThread	Creates a new thread.
AfxEndThread	Terminates the current thread.
AfxGetThread	Retrieves a pointer to the current **CWinThread** object.
AfxWinInit	Called by the MFC-supplied **WinMain** function, as part of the **CWinApp** initialization of a GUI-based application, to initialize MFC. Must be called directly for console applications using MFC.

See Also: **CWinApp**

Standard Command and Window IDs

The Microsoft Foundation Class Library defines a number of standard command and window IDs in AFXRES.H. These IDs are most commonly used within the resource editors and ClassWizard to map messages to your handler functions. All standard commands have an **ID_** prefix. For example, when you use the menu editor, you normally bind the File Open menu item to the standard **ID_FILE_OPEN** command ID.

For most standard commands, application code does not need to refer to the command ID, because the framework itself handles the commands through message maps in its primary framework classes (**CWinThread**, **CWinApp**, **CView**, **CDocument**, and so forth).

In addition to standard command IDs, a number of other standard IDs are defined which have a prefix of **AFX_ID**. These IDs include standard window IDs (prefix **AFX_IDW_**), string IDs (prefix **AFX_IDS_**), and several other types.

IDs that begin with the **AFX_ID** prefix are rarely used by programmers, but you might need to refer to these IDs when overriding framework functions which also refer to the **AFX_ID**s.

IDs are not individually documented in this reference. You can find more information on them in "Technical Notes 20, 21, and 22" online.

Note The header file AFXRES.H is indirectly included in AFXWIN.H. You must explicitly include the statement

```
#include afxres.h
```

in your application's resource script (.RC) file.

Collection Class Helpers

The collection classes **CMap**, **CList**, and **CArray** use templated global helper functions for such purposes as constructing, destroying, and serializing elements. As part of your implementation of classes based on **CMap**, **CList**, and **CArray**, you must override these functions as necessary with versions tailored to the type of data stored in your map, list, or array. For information on overriding **ConstructElements**, **DestructElements**, and **SerializeElements**, see the article "Collections: How to Make a Type-Safe Collection" in *Visual C++ Programmer's Guide* online.

The Microsoft Foundation Class Library provides the following global functions to help you customize your collection classes:

Collection Class Helpers

CompareElements	Indicates whether elements are the same.
ConstructElements	Performs any action necessary when an element is constructed.
CopyElements	Copies elements from one array to another.
DestructElements	Performs any action necessary when an element is destroyed.
DumpElements	Provides stream-oriented diagnostic output.
HashKey	Calculates a hash key.
SerializeElements	Stores or retrieves elements to or from an archive.

See Also: CMap, CList, CArray

Record Field Exchange Functions

This topic lists the Record Field Exchange (RFX, Bulk RFX, and DFX) functions used to automate the transfer of data between a recordset object and its data source and to perform other operations on the data.

If you are using the ODBC-based classes and you have implemented bulk row fetching, you must manually override the **DoBulkFieldExchange** member function of **CRecordset** by calling the Bulk RFX functions for each data member corresponding to a data source column.

If you have not implemented bulk row fetching in the ODBC-based classes, or if you are using the DAO-based classes, then ClassWizard will override the **DoFieldExchange** member function of **CRecordset** or **CDaoRecordset** by calling the RFX functions (for ODBC classes) or the DFX functions (for DAO classes) for each field data member in your recordset.

The record field exchange functions transfer data each time the framework calls **DoFieldExchange** or **DoBulkFieldExchange**. Each function transfers a specific data type.

For more information about how these functions are used, see the articles "Record Field Exchange: How RFX Works (ODBC)" and "DAO Record Field Exchange: How DFX Works." For more information about bulk row fetching, see the article "Recordset: Fetching Records in Bulk (ODBC)." The articles are found in *Visual C++ Programmer's Guide* online.

For columns of data that you bind dynamically, you can also call the RFX or DFX functions yourself, rather than using ClassWizard, as explained in the articles "Recordset: Dynamically Binding Data Columns (ODBC)" and "DAO: Binding Records Dynamically." The articles are found in *Visual C++ Programmer's Guide* online. Note that dynamic binding in DAO is different from dynamic binding in ODBC. Additionally, you can write your own custom RFX or DFX routines, as explained in "Technical Note 43" (for ODBC) online and "Technical Note 53" (for DAO) online.

For an example of RFX and Bulk RFX functions as they appear in the **DoFieldExchange** and **DoBulkFieldExchange** functions, see **RFX_Text** and **RFX_Text_Bulk**. DFX functions are very similar to the RFX functions.

RFX Functions (ODBC)

RFX_Binary	Transfers arrays of bytes of type **CByteArray**.
RFX_Bool	Transfers Boolean data.
RFX_Byte	Transfers a single byte of data.
RFX_Date	Transfers time and date data using **CTime** or **TIMESTAMP_STRUCT**.

RFX Functions (ODBC) *(continued)*

RFX_Double	Transfers double-precision float data.
RFX_Int	Transfers integer data.
RFX_Long	Transfers long integer data.
RFX_LongBinary	Transfers binary large object (BLOB) data via an object of the **CLongBinary** class.
RFX_Single	Transfers float data.
RFX_Text	Transfers string data.

Bulk RFX Functions (ODBC)

RFX_Binary_Bulk	Transfers arrays of byte data.
RFX_Bool_Bulk	Transfers arrays of Boolean data.
RFX_Byte_Bulk	Transfers arrays of single bytes.
RFX_Date_Bulk	Transfers arrays of data of type **TIMESTAMP_STRUCT**.
RFX_Double_Bulk	Transfers arrays of double-precision floating-point data.
RFX_Int_Bulk	Transfers arrays of integer data.
RFX_Long_Bulk	Transfers arrays of long integer data.
RFX_Single_Bulk	Transfers arrays of floating-point data.
RFX_Text_Bulk	Transfers arrays of data of type **LPSTR**.

DFX Functions (DAO)

DFX_Binary	Transfers arrays of bytes of type **CByteArray**.
DFX_Bool	Transfers Boolean data.
DFX_Byte	Transfers a single byte of data.
DFX_Currency	Transfers currency data, of type **COleCurrency**.
DFX_DateTime	Transfers time and date data, of type **COleDateTime**.
DFX_Double	Transfers double-precision float data.
DFX_Long	Transfers long integer data.
DFX_LongBinary	Transfers binary-large object (BLOB) data via an object of the **CLongBinary** class. For DAO, it is recommended that you use **DFX_Binary** instead.
DFX_Short	Transfers short integer data.
DFX_Single	Transfers float data.
DFX_Text	Transfers string data.

See Also: CRecordset::DoFieldExchange, **CRecordset::DoBulkFieldExchange**, **CDaoRecordset::DoFieldExchange**

Dialog Data Exchange Functions for CRecordView and CDaoRecordView

This topic lists the DDX_Field functions used to exchange data between a **CRecordset** and a **CRecordView** form or a **CDaoRecordset** and a **CDaoRecordView** form.

Important DDX_Field functions are like DDX functions in that they exchange data with controls in a form. But unlike DDX, they exchange data with the fields of the view's associated recordset object rather than with fields of the record view itself. For more information, see classes **CRecordView** and **CDaoRecordView** and the article "ClassWizard: Mapping Form Controls to Recordset Fields" in *Visual C++ Programmer's Guide* online.

DDX_Field Functions

DDX_FieldCBIndex	Transfers integer data between a recordset field data member and the index of the current selection in a combo box in a **CRecordView** or **CDaoRecordView**.
DDX_FieldCBString	Transfers **CString** data between a recordset field data member and the edit control of a combo box in a **CRecordView** or **CDaoRecordView**. When moving data from the recordset to the control, this function selects the item in the combo box that begins with the characters in the specified string.
DDX_FieldCBStringExact	Transfers **CString** data between a recordset field data member and the edit control of a combo box in a **CRecordView** or **CDaoRecordView**. When moving data from the recordset to the control, this function selects the item in the combo box that exactly matches the specified string.
DDX_FieldCheck	Transfers Boolean data between a recordset field data member and a check box in a **CRecordView** or **CDaoRecordView**.
DDX_FieldLBIndex	Transfers integer data between a recordset field data member and the index of the current selection in a list box in a **CRecordView** or **CDaoRecordView**.
DDX_FieldLBString	Manages the transfer of **CString** data between a list-box control and the field data members of a recordset. When moving data from the recordset to the control, this function selects the item in the list box that begins with the characters in the specified string.
DDX_FieldLBStringExact	Manages the transfer of **CString** data between a list-box control and the field data members of a recordset. When moving data from the recordset to the control, this function selects the first item that exactly matches the specified string.

DDX_Field Functions *(continued)*

DDX_FieldRadio	Transfers integer data between a recordset field data member and a group of radio buttons in a **CRecordView** or **CDaoRecordView**.
DDX_FieldScroll	Sets or gets the scroll position of a scroll bar control in a **CRecordView** or **CDaoRecordView**. Call from your **DoFieldExchange** function.
DDX_FieldText	Overloaded versions are available for transferring **int**, **UINT**, **long**, **DWORD**, **CString**, **float**, **double**, **short**, **COleDateTime**, and **COleCurrency** data between a recordset field data member and an edit box in a **CRecordView** or **CDaoRecordView**.

Dialog Data Exchange Functions for OLE Controls

This topic lists the DDX_OC functions used to exchange data between a property of an OLE control in a dialog box, form view, or control view object and a data member of the dialog box, form view, or control view object.

DDX_OC Functions

DDX_OCBool	Manages the transfer of **BOOL** data between a property of an OLE control and a **BOOL** data member.
DDX_OCBoolRO	Manages the transfer of **BOOL** data between a read-only property of an OLE control and a **BOOL** data member.
DDX_OCColor	Manages the transfer of **OLE_COLOR** data between a property of an OLE control and an **OLE_COLOR** data member.
DDX_OCColorRO	Manages the transfer of **OLE_COLOR** data between a read-only property of an OLE control and an **OLE_COLOR** data member.
DDX_OCFloat	Manages the transfer of **float** (or **double**) data between a property of an OLE control and a **float** (or **double**) data member.
DDX_OCFloatRO	Manages the transfer of **float** (or **double**) data between a read-only property of an OLE control and a **float** (or **double**) data member.

(continued)

DDX_OC Functions *(continued)*

DDX_OCInt	Manages the transfer of **int** (or **long**) data between a property of an OLE control and an **int** (or **long**) data member.
DDX_OCIntRO	Manages the transfer of **int** (or **long**) data between a read-only property of an OLE control and an **int** (or **long**) data member.
DDX_OCShort	Manages the transfer of **short** data between a property of an OLE control and a **short** data member.
DDX_OCShortRO	Manages the transfer of **short** data between a read-only property of an OLE control and a **short** data member.
DDX_OCText	Manages the transfer of **CString** data between a property of an OLE control and a **CString** data member.
DDX_OCTextRO	Manages the transfer of **CString** data between a read-only property of an OLE control and a **CString** data member.

Database Macros

The macros listed below apply to ODBC-based database applications. They are not used with DAO-based applications.

Prior to MFC 4.2, the macros **AFX_SQL_ASYNC** and **AFX_SQL_SYNC** gave asynchronous operations an opportunity to yield time to other processes. Beginning with MFC 4.2, the implementation of these macros has changed because the MFC ODBC classes now use only synchronous operations. The macro **AFX_ODBC_CALL** is new to MFC 4.2.

Database Macros

AFX_ODBC_CALL	Use this macro to call an ODBC API function that returns **SQL_STILL_EXECUTING**. **AFX_ODBC_CALL** will repeatedly call the function until it no longer returns **SQL_STILL_EXECUTING**.
AFX_SQL_ASYNC	Simply calls **AFX_ODBC_CALL**.
AFX_SQL_SYNC	Use this macro to calls an ODBC API function that does not return **SQL_STILL_EXECUTING**.

DAO Database Engine Initialization and Termination

When using MFC DAO objects, the DAO database engine must first be initialized and then terminated before your application or DLL quits. Two functions, **AfxDaoInit** and **AfxDaoTerm**, perform these tasks.

DAO Database Engine Initialization and Termination

AfxDaoInit	Initializes the DAO database engine.
AfxDaoTerm	Terminates the DAO database engine.

OLE Initialization

Before an application can use OLE system services, it must initialize the OLE system DLLs and verify that the DLLs are the correct version. The **AfxOleInit** function initializes the OLE system DLLs.

OLE Initialization

AfxOleInit	Initializes the OLE libraries.

Application Control

OLE requires substantial control over applications and their objects. The OLE system DLLs must be able to launch and release applications automatically, coordinate their production and modification of objects, and so on. The functions in this topic meet those requirements. In addition to being called by the OLE system DLLs, these functions must sometimes be called by applications as well.

Application Control

AfxOleCanExitApp	Indicates whether the application can terminate.
AfxOleGetMessageFilter	Retrieves the application's current message filter.
AfxOleGetUserCtrl	Retrieves the current user-control flag.
AfxOleSetUserCtrl	Sets or clears the user-control flag.
AfxOleLockApp	Increments the framework's global count of the number of active objects in an application.
AfxOleUnlockApp	Decrements the framework's count of the number of active objects in an application.
AfxOleRegisterServerClass	Registers a server in the OLE system registry.
AfxOleSetEditMenu	Implements the user interface for the *typename* Object command.

Dispatch Maps

OLE Automation provides ways to call methods and to access properties across applications. The mechanism supplied by the Microsoft Foundation Class Library for dispatching these requests is the "dispatch map," which designates the internal and external names of object functions and properties, as well as the data types of the properties themselves and of function arguments.

Dispatch Maps

DECLARE_DISPATCH_MAP	Declares that a dispatch map will be used to expose a class's methods and properties (must be used in the class declaration).
BEGIN_DISPATCH_MAP	Starts the definition of a dispatch map.
END_DISPATCH_MAP	Ends the definition of a dispatch map.
DISP_FUNCTION	Used in a dispatch map to define an OLE automation function.
DISP_PROPERTY	Defines an OLE automation property.
DISP_PROPERTY_EX	Defines an OLE automation property and names the "get" and "set" functions.
DISP_PROPERTY_NOTIFY	Defines an OLE automation property with notification.
DISP_PROPERTY_PARAM	Defines an OLE automation property that takes parameters and names the "get" and "set" functions.
DISP_DEFVALUE	Makes an existing property the default value of an object.

Variant Parameter Type Constants

This topic lists new constants that indicate variant parameter types designed for use with the OLE control classes of the Microsoft Foundation Class Library.

The following is a list of class constants:

Variant Data Constants

- **VTS_COLOR**   A 32-bit integer used to represent a RGB color value.
- **VTS_FONT**   A pointer to the **IFontDisp** interface of an OLE font object.
- **VTS_HANDLE**   A Windows handle value.
- **VTS_PICTURE**   A pointer to the **IPictureDisp** interface of an OLE picture object.
- **VTS_OPTEXCLUSIVE**   A 16-bit value used for a control intended to be used in a group of controls, such as radio buttons. This type tells the container that if one control in a group has a **TRUE** value, all others must be **FALSE**.

- **VTS_TRISTATE** A 16-bit signed integer used for properties that can have one of three possible values (checked, unchecked, gray), for example, a check box.

- **VTS_XPOS_HIMETRIC** A 32-bit unsigned integer used to represent a position along the x-axis in **HIMETRIC** units.

- **VTS_YPOS_HIMETRIC** A 32-bit unsigned integer used to represent a position along the y-axis in **HIMETRIC** units.

- **VTS_XPOS_PIXELS** A 32-bit unsigned integer used to represent a position along the x-axis in pixels.

- **VTS_YPOS_PIXELS** A 32-bit unsigned integer used to represent a position along the y-axis in pixels.

- **VTS_XSIZE_PIXELS** A 32-bit unsigned integer used to represent the width of a screen object in pixels.

- **VTS_YSIZE_PIXELS** A 32-bit unsigned integer used to represent the height of a screen object in pixels.

- **VTS_XSIZE_HIMETRIC** A 32-bit unsigned integer used to represent the width of a screen object in **HIMETRIC** units.

- **VTS_YSIZE_HIMETRIC** A 32-bit unsigned integer used to represent the height of a screen object in **HIMETRIC** units.

Note Additional variant constants have been defined for all variant types, with the exception of **VTS_FONT** and **VTS_PICTURE**, that provide a pointer to the variant data constant. These constants are named using the **VTS_P**_constantname_ convention. For example, **VTS_PCOLOR** is a pointer to a **VTS_COLOR** constant.

Type Library Access

Type libraries expose the interfaces of an OLE control to other OLE-aware applications. Each OLE control must have a type library if one or more interfaces are to be exposed.

The following macros allow an OLE control to provide access to its own type library:

Type Library Access

DECLARE_OLETYPELIB	Declares a **GetTypeLib** member function of an OLE control (must be used in the class declaration).
IMPLEMENT_OLETYPELIB	Implements a **GetTypeLib** member function of an OLE control (must be used in the class implementation).

Property Pages

Property pages display the current values of specific OLE control properties in a customizable, graphical interface for viewing and editing by supporting a data-mapping mechanism based on dialog data exchange (DDX).

This data-mapping mechanism maps property page controls to the individual properties of the OLE control. The value of the control property reflects the status or content of the property page control. The mapping between property page controls and properties is specified by **DDP_** function calls in the property page's DoDataExchange member function. The following is a list of **DDP_** functions that exchange data entered using the property page of your control:

Property Page Data Transfer

DDP_CBIndex	Use this function to link the selected string's index in a combo box with a control's property.
DDP_CBString	Use this function to link the selected string in a combo box with a control's property. The selected string can begin with the same letters as the property's value but need not match it fully.
DDP_CBStringExact	Use this function to link the selected string in a combo box with a control's property. The selected string and the property's string value must match exactly.
DDP_Check	Use this function to link a check box in the control's property page with a control's property.
DDP_LBIndex	Use this function to link the selected string's index in a list box with a control's property.
DDP_LBString	Use this function to link the selected string in a list box with a control's property. The selected string can begin with the same letters as the property's value but need not match it fully.
DDP_LBStringExact	Use this function to link the selected string in a list box with a control's property. The selected string and the property's string value must match exactly.
DDP_PostProcessing	Use this function to finish the transfer of property values from your control.
DDP_Radio	Use this function to link a radio button group in the control's property page with a control's property.
DDP_Text	Use this function to link a control in the control's property page with a control's property. This function handles several different types of properties, such as **double**, **short**, **BSTR**, and **long**.

For more information about the DoDataExchange function and property pages, see the article "ActiveX Controls: Property Pages" in *Visual C++ Programmer's Guide* online.

The following is a list of macros used to create and manage property pages for an OLE control:

Property Pages

BEGIN_PROPPAGEIDS	Begins the list of property page IDs.
END_PROPPAGEIDS	Ends the list of property page IDs.
PROPPAGEID	Declares a property page of the control class.

Event Maps

Whenever a control wishes to notify its container that some action (determined by the control developer) has happened (such as a keystroke, mouse click, or a change to the control's state) it calls an event-firing function. This function notifies the control container that some important action has occurred by firing the related event.

The Microsoft Foundation Class Library offers a programming model optimized for firing events. In this model, "event maps" are used to designate which functions fire which events for a particular control. Event maps contain one macro for each event. For example, an event map that fires a stock Click event might look like this:

```
BEGIN_EVENT_MAP(CSampleCtrl, COleControl)
    //{{AFX_EVENT_MAP(CSampleCtrl)
    EVENT_STOCK_CLICK( )
    //}}AFX_EVENT_MAP
END_EVENT_MAP()
```

The **EVENT_STOCK_CLICK** macro indicates that the control will fire a stock Click event every time it detects a mouse click. For a more detailed listing of other stock events, see the article "ActiveX Controls: Events" in *Visual C++ Programmer's Guide* online. Macros are also available to indicate custom events.

Although event-map macros are important, you generally don't insert them directly. This is because ClassWizard automatically creates event-map entries in your source files when you use it to associate event-firing functions with events. Any time you want to edit or add an event-map entry, you can use ClassWizard.

To support event maps, MFC provides the following macros:

Event Map Declaration and Demarcation

DECLARE_EVENT_MAP	Declares that an event map will be used in a class to map events to event-firing functions (must be used in the class declaration).
BEGIN_EVENT_MAP	Begins the definition of an event map (must be used in the class implementation).
END_EVENT_MAP	Ends the definition of an event map (must be used in the class implementation).

Event Mapping Macros

EVENT_CUSTOM	Indicates which event-firing function will fire the specified event.
EVENT_CUSTOM_ID	Indicates which event-firing function will fire the specified event, with a designated dispatch ID.

Message Mapping Macros

ON_OLEVERB	Indicates a custom verb handled by the OLE control.
ON_STDOLEVERB	Overrides a standard verb mapping of the OLE control.

Event Sink Maps

When an embedded OLE control fires an event, the control's container receives the event using a mechanism, called an "event sink map," supplied by MFC. This event sink map designates handler functions for each specific event, as well as parameters of those events. For more information on event sink maps, see the article "ActiveX Control Containers" in *Visual C++ Programmer's Guide* online.

Event Sink Maps

BEGIN_EVENTSINK_MAP	Starts the definition of an event sink map.
DECLARE_EVENTSINK_MAP	Declares an event sink map.
END_EVENTSINK_MAP	Ends the definition of an event sink map.
ON_EVENT	Defines an event handler for a specific event.
ON_EVENT_RANGE	Defines an event handler for a specific event fired from a set of OLE controls.
ON_EVENT_REFLECT	Receives events fired by the control before they are handled by the control's container.
ON_PROPNOTIFY	Defines a handler for handling property notifications from an OLE control.
ON_PROPNOTIFY_RANGE	Defines a handler for handling property notifications from a set of OLE controls.
ON_PROPNOTIFY_REFLECT	Receives property notifications sent by the control before they are handled by the control's container.

Connection Maps

OLE controls are able to expose interfaces to other applications. These interfaces only allow access from a container into that control. If an OLE control wants to access external interfaces of other OLE objects, a connection point must be established. This connection point allows a control outgoing access to external dispatch maps, such as event maps or notification functions.

The Microsoft Foundation Class Library offers a programming model that supports connection points. In this model, "connection maps" are used to designate interfaces (or connection points) for the OLE control. Connection maps contain one macro for each connection point. For more information on connection maps, see the **CConnectionPoint** class.

Typically, a control will support just two connection points: one for events and one for property notifications. These are implemented by the **COleControl** base class and require no additional work by the control writer. Any additional connection points you wish to implement in your class must be added by hand. To support connection maps and points, MFC provides the following macros:

Connection Map Declaration and Demarcation

BEGIN_CONNECTION_PART	Declares an embedded class that implements an additional connection point (must be used in the class declaration).
END_CONNECTION_PART	Ends the declaration of a connection point (must be used in the class declaration).
CONNECTION_IID	Specifies the interface ID of the control's connection point.
DECLARE_CONNECTION_MAP	Declares that a connection map will be used in a class (must be used in the class declaration).
BEGIN_CONNECTION_MAP	Begins the definition of a connection map (must be used in the class implementation).
END_CONNECTION_MAP	Ends the definition of a connection map (must be used in the class implementation).
CONNECTION_PART	Specifies a connection point in the control's connection map.

The following functions assist a sink in establishing and disconnecting a connection using connection points:

Initialization/Termination of Connection Points

AfxConnectionAdvise	Establishes a connection between a source and a sink.
AfxConnectionUnadvise	Breaks a connection between a source and a sink.

Registering OLE Controls

OLE controls, like other OLE server objects, can be accessed by other OLE-aware applications. This is achieved by registering the control's type library and class.

The following functions allow you to add and remove the control's class, property pages, and type library in the Windows registration database:

Registering OLE Controls

AfxOleRegisterControlClass	Adds the control's class to the registration database.
AfxOleRegisterPropertyPageClass	Adds a control property page to the registration database.
AfxOleRegisterTypeLib	Adds the control's type library to the registration database.
AfxOleUnregisterClass	Removes a control class or a property page class from the registration database.
AfxOleUnregisterTypeLib	Removes the control's type library from the registration database.

AfxOleRegisterTypeLib is typically called in a control DLL's implementation of DllRegisterServer. Similarly, **AfxOleUnregisterTypeLib** is called by DllUnregisterServer. **AfxOleRegisterControlClass**, **AfxOleRegisterPropertyPageClass**, and **AfxOleUnregisterClass** are typically called by the UpdateRegistry member function of a control's class factory or property page.

Class Factories and Licensing

To create an instance of your OLE control, a container application calls a member function of the control's class factory. Because your control is an actual OLE object, the class factory is responsible for creating instances of your control. Every OLE control class must have a class factory.

Another important feature of OLE controls is their ability to enforce a license. ControlWizard allows you to incorporate licensing during the creation of your control project. For more information on control licensing, see the article "ActiveX Controls: Licensing An ActiveX Control" in *Visual C++ Programmer's Guide* online.

The following table lists several macros and functions used to declare and implement your control's class factory and for licensing of your control.

Class Factories and Licensing

DECLARE_OLECREATE_EX	Declares the class factory for an OLE control or property page.
IMPLEMENT_OLECREATE_EX	Implements the control's **GetClassID** function and declares an instance of the class factory.
BEGIN_OLEFACTORY	Begins the declaration of any licensing functions.
END_OLEFACTORY	Ends the declaration of any licensing functions.
AfxVerifyLicFile	Verifies whether a control is licensed for use on a particular computer.

Persistence of OLE Controls

One capability of OLE controls is property persistence (or serialization), which allows the OLE control to read or write property values to and from a file or stream. A container application can use serialization to store a control's property values even after the application has destroyed the control. The property values of the OLE control can then be read from the file or stream when a new instance of the control is created at a later time.

Persistence of OLE Controls

PX_Blob	Exchanges a control property that stores binary-large object (BLOB) data.
PX_Bool	Exchanges a control property of type **BOOL**.
PX_Color	Exchanges a color property of a control.
PX_Currency	Exchanges a control property of type **CY**.
PX_DataPath	Exchanges a control property of type **CDataPathProperty**.
PX_Double	Exchanges a control property of type **double**.
PX_Font	Exchanges a font property of a control.
PX_Float	Exchanges a control property of type **float**.
PX_IUnknown	Exchanges a control property of undefined type.
PX_Long	Exchanges a control property of type **long**.
PX_Picture	Exchanges a picture property of a control.
PX_Short	Exchanges a control property of type **short**.
PX_ULong	Exchanges a control property of type **ULONG**.
PX_UShort	Exchanges a control property of type **USHORT**.
PX_String	Exchanges a character string control property.
PX_VBXFontConvert	Exchanges a VBX control's font-related properties into an OLE control font property.

In addition, the **AfxOleTypeMatchGuid** global function is provided to test for a match between a **TYPEDESC** and a given GUID.

Internet Server API (ISAPI) Parse Maps

The Internet Server API, an extended open API set, provides you with the ability to create add-ons for, and run internet server applications on, your Microsoft Internet Information Server. When a client sends a query to the internet server, the server processes the query by sending it through a series of parsing macros in the "parse map." The parse map maps the client queries to a **CHttpServer**-derived class's functions and parameters.

ISAPI Parse Maps

BEGIN_PARSE_MAP	Starts the definition of a parse map.
ON_PARSE_COMMAND	Parses the client's command
ON_PARSE_COMMAND_PARAMS	Defines a command to an **CHttpServer** object from a client.
DEFAULT_PARSE_COMMAND	Calls the default page that's identified by the *FnName* parameter.
END_PARSE_MAP	Ends the definition of a parse map.

Internet Server API (ISAPI) Diagnostic Macros

The Microsoft Internet Information Server requires the same diagnostic services that MFC programs need; however, the programs written for the Internet Server don't require MFC. The ISAPI macros described below provide the same level of debugging functionality for both MFC programs and programs not written with MFC.

ISAPI Diagnostic Macros

ISAPIASSERT	Provides **ASSERT** functionality.
ISAPITRACE	Provides **TRACE** functionality.
ISAPITRACE0	Provides **TRACE0** functionality.
ISAPITRACE1	Provides **TRACE1** functionality.
ISAPITRACE2	Provides **TRACE2** functionality.
ISAPITRACE3	Provides **TRACE3** functionality.
ISAPIVERIFY	Provides **VERIFY** functionality.

Macros, Global Functions, and Global Variables

The topics in this section provide descriptions of the global functions, global variables, and macros in the MFC library.

Note Many global functions start with the prefix "Afx"—but some, such as the dialog data exchange (DDX) functions and many of the database functions, deviate from this convention. All global variables start with the prefix "afx." Macros do not start with any particular prefix, but they are written all in uppercase.

The MFC library and the Active Template library (ATL) share string conversion macros. See "String Conversion Macros" in the ATL documentation online for a discussion of these macros.

For information on the debug version of the C run-time library and diagnostic functions, see "Debug Routines," in the *Run-Time Library Reference*.

AfxAbort

void AfxAbort( );

Remarks

The default termination function supplied by MFC. **AfxAbort** is called internally by MFC member functions when there is a fatal error, such as an uncaught exception that cannot be handled. You can call **AfxAbort** in the rare case when you encounter a catastrophic error from which you cannot recover.

AfxBeginThread

CWinThread* AfxBeginThread(AFX_THREADPROC *pfnThreadProc***,**
   ↳ **LPVOID** *pParam***, int** *nPriority* **= THREAD_PRIORITY_NORMAL,**
   ↳ **UINT** *nStackSize* **= 0, DWORD** *dwCreateFlags* **= 0,**
   ↳ **LPSECURITY_ATTRIBUTES** *lpSecurityAttrs* **= NULL);**
CWinThread* AfxBeginThread(CRuntimeClass* *pThreadClass***,**
   ↳ **int** *nPriority* **= THREAD_PRIORITY_NORMAL, UINT** *nStackSize* **= 0,**
   ↳ **DWORD** *dwCreateFlags* **= 0,**
   ↳ **LPSECURITY_ATTRIBUTES** *lpSecurityAttrs* **= NULL);**

Return Value

Pointer to the newly created thread object.

Parameters

pfnThreadProc Points to the controlling function for the worker thread. Cannot be **NULL**. This function must be declared as follows:

```
UINT MyControllingFunction( LPVOID pParam );
```

pThreadClass The **RUNTIME_CLASS** of an object derived from

CWinThread.

pParam Parameter to be passed to the controlling function as shown in the parameter to the function declaration in *pfnThreadProc*.

nPriority The desired priority of the thread. If 0, the same priority as the creating thread will be used. For a full list and description of the available priorities, see **SetThreadPriority** in the *Win32 Programmer's Reference*.

nStackSize   Specifies the size in bytes of the stack for the new thread. If 0, the stack size defaults to the same size stack as the creating thread.

dwCreateFlags   Specifies an additional flag that controls the creation of the thread. This flag can contain one of two values:

- **CREATE_SUSPENDED**   Start the thread with a suspend count of one. The thread will not execute until **ResumeThread** is called.

- **0**   Start the thread immediately after creation.

lpSecurityAttrs   Points to a **SECURITY_ATTRIBUTES** structure that specifies the security attributes for the thread. If **NULL**, the same security attributes as the creating thread will be used. For more information on this structure, see the *Win32 Programmer's Reference*.

Remarks

Call this function to create a new thread. The first form of **AfxBeginThread** creates a worker thread. The second form creates a user-interface thread.

AfxBeginThread creates a new **CWinThread** object, calls its **CreateThread** function to start executing the thread, and returns a pointer to the thread. Checks are made throughout the procedure to make sure all objects are deallocated properly should any part of the creation fail. To end the thread, call **AfxEndThread** from within the thread, or return from the controlling function of the worker thread.

For more information on **AfxBeginThread**, see the articles "Multithreading: Creating Worker Threads" and "Multithreading: Creating User-Interface Threads" in *Visual C++ Programmer's Guide* online.

See Also: AfxGetThread

AfxCheckMemory

BOOL AfxCheckMemory( );

Return Value

Nonzero if no memory errors; otherwise 0.

Remarks

This function validates the free memory pool and prints error messages as required. If the function detects no memory corruption, it prints nothing.

All memory blocks currently allocated on the heap are checked, including those allocated by **new** but not those allocated by direct calls to underlying memory allocators, such as the **malloc** function or the **GlobalAlloc** Windows function. If any block is found to be corrupted, a message is printed to the debugger output.

If you include the line

```
#define new DEBUG_NEW
```

in a program module, then subsequent calls to **AfxCheckMemory** show the filename and line number where the memory was allocated.

Note If your module contains one or more implementations of serializable classes, then you must put the #define line after the last **IMPLEMENT_SERIAL** macro call.

This function works only in the Debug version of MFC.

Example

```
// example for AfxCheckMemory
CAge* pcage = new CAge( 21 );   // CAge is derived from CObject.
Age* page = new Age( 22 );      // Age is NOT derived from CObject.
*(((char*) pcage) - 1) = 99;    // Corrupt preceding guard byte
*(((char*) page) - 1) = 99;     // Corrupt preceding guard byte
AfxCheckMemory();
```

The results from the program are as follows:

```
memory check error at $0067495F = $63, should be $FD
DAMAGE: before Non-Object block at $00674960
Non-Object allocated at file test02.cxx(48)
Non-Object located at $00674960 is 2 bytes long
memory check error at $00674905 = $63, should be $FD
DAMAGE: before Object block at $00674906
Object allocated at file test02.cxx(47)
Object located at $00674906 is 6 bytes long
```

AfxConnectionAdvise

BOOL AFXAPI AfxConnectionAdvise(LPUNKNOWN *pUnkSrc*, **REFIID** *iid*,
 ↪ **LPUNKNOWN** *pUnkSink*, **BOOL** *bRefCount*, **DWORD FAR*** *pdwCookie* **);**

Return Value

Nonzero if a connection was established; otherwise 0.

Parameters

pUnkSrc   A pointer to the object that calls the interface.

pUnkSink   A pointer to the object that implements the interface.

iid   The interface ID of the connection.

bRefCount   **TRUE** indicates that creating the connection should cause the reference count of *pUnkSink* to be incremented. **FALSE** indicates that the reference count should not be incremented.

pdwCookie   A pointer to a **DWORD** where a connection identifier is returned. This value should be passed as the *dwCookie* parameter to **AfxConnectionUnadvise** when disconnecting the connection.

Remarks

Call this function to establish a connection between a source, specified by *pUnkSrc*, and a sink, specified by *pUnkSink*.

See Also: **AfxConnectionUnadvise**

AfxConnectionUnadvise

BOOL AFXAPI AfxConnectionUnadvise(LPUNKNOWN *pUnkSrc*, **REFIID** *iid*, ⮑ **LPUNKNOWN** *pUnkSink*, **BOOL** *bRefCount*, **DWORD** *dwCookie* **);**

Return Value

Nonzero if a connection was disconnected; otherwise 0.

Parameters

pUnkSrc   A pointer to the object that calls the interface.

pUnkSink   A pointer to the object that implements the interface.

iid   The interface ID of the connection point interface.

bRefCount   **TRUE** indicates that disconnecting the connection should cause the reference count of *pUnkSink* to be decremented. **FALSE** indicates that the reference count should not be decremented.

dwCookie   The connection identifier returned by **AfxConnectionAdvise**.

Remarks

Call this function to disconnect a connection between a source, specified by *pUnkSrc*, and a sink, specified by *pUnkSink*.

See Also: **AfxConnectionAdvise**

AfxDaoInit

void AfxDaoInit( );

Remarks

This function initializes the DAO database engine. In most cases, you don't need to call **AfxDaoInit** because the application automatically calls it when it is needed.

For related information, and for an example of calling **AfxDaoInit**, see Technical Note 54 online.

See Also: **AfxDaoTerm**

AfxDaoTerm

void AfxDaoTerm( );

Remarks

This function terminates the DAO database engine. Typically, you only need to call this function in a regular DLL; an application will automatically call **AfxDaoTerm** when it is needed.

In regular DLLs, call **AfxDaoTerm** before the **ExitInstance** function, but after all MFC DAO objects have been destroyed.

For more information about calling **AfxDaoTerm**, see the article "DAO: Using DAO in DLLs" in *Visual C++ Programmer's Guide* online. For related information, see Technical Note 54 online.

See Also: AfxDaoInit

AfxDbInitModule

void AFXAPI AfxDbInitModule( );

#include <afxdll.h>

For MFC database (or DAO) support from a regular DLL that is dynamically linked to MFC, add a call to this function in your regular DLL's **CWinApp::InitInstance** function to initialize the MFC database DLL. Make sure this call occurs before any base-class call or any added code which accesses the MFC database DLL.The MFC database DLL is an extension DLL; in order for an extension DLL to get wired into a **CDynLinkLibrary** chain, it must create a **CDynLinkLibrary** object in the context of every module that will be using it. **AfxDbInitModule** creates the **CDynLinkLibrary** object in your regular DLL's context so that it gets wired into the **CDynLinkLibrary** object chain of the regular DLL.

AfxDoForAllClasses

void AFXAPI AfxDoForAllClasses(void (*_pfn_)(const CRuntimeClass* _pClass_,
↪ **void*** _pContext_**), void*** _pContext_ **);**

Parameters

pfn   Points to an iteration function to be called for each class. The function arguments are a pointer to a **CRuntimeClass** object and a void pointer to extra data that the caller supplies to the function.

pContext   Points to optional data that the caller can supply to the iteration function. This pointer can be **NULL**.

Remarks

Calls the specified iteration function for all serializable **CObject**-derived classes in the application's memory space. Serializable **CObject**-derived classes are classes derived using the **DECLARE_SERIAL** macro. The pointer that is passed to **AfxDoForAllClasses** in *pContext* is passed to the specified iteration function each time it is called.

Note   This function works only in the Debug version of MFC.

See Also: DECLARE_SERIAL

AfxDoForAllObjects

void AfxDoForAllObjects(void (*pfn*)(**CObject** *pObject*,
   ↪ **void*** *pContext*), **void*** *pContext*);

Parameters

pfn   Points to an iteration function to execute for each object. The function arguments are a pointer to a **CObject** and a void pointer to extra data that the caller supplies to the function.

pContext   Points to optional data that the caller can supply to the iteration function. This pointer can be **NULL**.

Remarks

Executes the specified iteration function for all objects derived from **CObject** that have been allocated with **new**. Stack, global, or embedded objects are not enumerated. The pointer passed to **AfxDoForAllObjects** in *pContext* is passed to the specified iteration function each time it is called.

Note   This function works only in the Debug version of MFC.

afxDump

CDumpContext afxDump;

Remarks

Use this variable to provide basic object-dumping capability in your application. **afxDump** is a predefined **CDumpContext** object that allows you to send **CDumpContext** information to the debugger output window or to a debug terminal. Typically, you supply **afxDump** as a parameter to **CObject::Dump**.

Under Windows NT and Windows 95 (and earlier versions of Windows), **afxDump** output is sent to the Output-Debug window of Visual C++ when you debug your application. In Console applications, **afxDump** output is sent to **stderr**.

This variable is defined only in the Debug version of MFC. For more information on **afxDump**, see "MFC Debugging Support" in *Visual C++ Programmer's Guide* online. Technical Note 7 online and Technical Note 12 online contain additional information.

Note This function works only in the Debug version of MFC.

Example

```
// example for afxDump
CPerson myPerson = new CPerson;
// set some fields of the CPerson object...
//..
// now dump the contents
#ifdef _DEBUG
afxDump << "Dumping myPerson:\n";
myPerson->Dump( afxDump );
afxDump << "\n";
#endif
```

See Also: **CObject::Dump**, **AfxDump**

AfxDump

   void AfxDump(const CObject* *pOb* **);**

Parameters

pOb   A pointer to an object of a class derived from **CObject**.

Remarks

Call this function while in the debugger to dump the state of an object while debugging. **AfxDump** calls an object's **Dump** member function and sends the information to the location specified by the **afxDump** variable. **AfxDump** is available only in the Debug version of MFC.

Your program code should not call **AfxDump**, but should instead call the **Dump** member function of the appropriate object.

See Also: **CObject::Dump**, **afxDump**

AfxEnableControlContainer

   void AfxEnableControlContainer( );

Remarks

Call this function in your application object's **InitInstance** function to enable support for containment of OLE controls.

For more information about OLE controls (now called ActiveX controls), see "ActiveX Control Topics" in the *Visual C++ Programmer's Guide* online.

AfxEnableMemoryTracking

BOOL AfxEnableMemoryTracking(BOOL *bTrack* **);**

Return Value

The previous setting of the tracking-enable flag.

Parameters

bTrack   Setting this value to **TRUE** turns on memory tracking; **FALSE**
turns it off.

Remarks

Diagnostic memory tracking is normally enabled in the Debug version of MFC. Use
this function to disable tracking on sections of your code that you know are allocating
blocks correctly.

For more information on **AfxEnableMemoryTracking**, see "MFC Debugging
Support" in *Visual C++ Programmer's Guide* online.

Note   This function works only in the Debug version of MFC.

AfxEndThread

void AfxEndThread(UINT *nExitCode* **);**

Parameters

nExitCode   Specifies the exit code of the thread.

Remarks

Call this function to terminate the currently executing thread. Must be called from
within the thread to be terminated.

For more information on **AfxEndThread**, see the article "Multithreading:
Terminating Threads" in *Visual C++ Programmer's Guide* online.

See Also: **AfxBeginThread**

AFX_EXT_CLASS

Remarks

Extension DLLs use the macro **AFX_EXT_CLASS** to export classes; the
executables that link to the extension DLL use the macro to import classes. With the
AFX_EXT_CLASS macro, the same header file(s) used to build the extension DLL
can be used with the executables that link to the DLL.

In the header file for your DLL, add the **AFX_EXT_CLASS** keyword to the
declaration of your class as follows:

```
class AFX_EXT_CLASS CMyClass : public CDocument
{
// <body of class>
};
```

For more information, see "Export and Import Using **AFX_EXT_CLASS**" online.

AfxFormatString1

void AfxFormatString1(CString& *rString*, **UINT** *nIDS*, **LPCTSTR** *lpsz1*);

Parameters

rString A reference to a **CString** object that will contain the resultant string after the substitution is performed.

nIDS The resource ID of the template string on which the substitution will be performed.

lpsz1 A string that will replace the format characters "%1" in the template string.

Remarks

Loads the specified string resource and substitutes the characters "%1" for the string pointed to by *lpsz1*. The newly formed string is stored in *rString*. For example, if the string in the string table is "File %1 not found", and *lpsz1* is equal to "C:\MYFILE.TXT", then *rString* will contain the string "File C:\MYFILE.TXT not found." This function is useful for formatting strings sent to message boxes and other windows.

If the format characters "%1" appear in the string more than once, multiple substitutions will be made.

See Also: AfxFormatString2

AfxFormatString2

void AfxFormatString2(CString& *rString*, **UINT** *nIDS*,
  ↪ **LPCTSTR** *lpsz1*, **LPCTSTR** *lpsz2*);

Parameters

rString A reference to the **CString** that will contain the resultant string after the substitution is performed.

nIDS The string table ID of the template string on which the substitution will be performed.

lpsz1 A string that will replace the format characters "%1" in the template string.

lpsz2 A string that will replace the format characters "%2" in the template string.

Remarks

Loads the specified string resource and substitutes the characters "%1" and "%2" for the strings pointed to by *lpsz1* and *lpsz2*. The newly formed string is stored in *rString*. For example, if the string in the string table is "File %1 not found in directory %2", *lpsz1* points to "MYFILE.TXT," and *lpsz2* points to "C:\MYDIR," then rString will contain the string "File MYFILE.TXT not found in directory C:\MYDIR."

If the format characters "%1" or "%2" appear in the string more than once, multiple substitutions will be made. They do not have to be in numerical order.

See Also: AfxFormatString1

AfxFreeLibrary

BOOL AFXAPI AfxFreeLibrary(HINSTANCE *hInstLib* **);**

Return Value

TRUE if the function succeeds; otherwise, **FALSE**.

Parameters

hInstLib   A handle of the loaded library module. **AfxLoadLibrary** returns this
handle.

Remarks

Both **AfxFreeLibrary** and **AfxLoadLibrary** maintain a reference count for each loaded library module. **AfxFreeLibrary** decrements the reference count of the loaded dynamic-link library (DLL) module. When the reference count reaches zero, the module is unmapped from the address space of the calling process and the handle is no longer valid. This reference count is incremented each time **AfxLoadLibrary** is called.

Before unmapping a library module, the system enables the DLL to detach from the processes using it. Doing so gives the DLL an opportunity to clean up resources allocated on behalf of the current process. After the entry-point function returns, the library module is removed from the address space of the current process.

Use **AfxLoadLibrary** to map a DLL module.

Be sure to use **AfxFreeLibrary** and **AfxLoadLibrary** (instead of the Win32 functions **FreeLibrary** and **LoadLibrary**) if your application uses multiple threads. Using **AfxLoadLibrary** and **AfxFreeLibrary** ensures that the startup and shutdown code that executes when the extension DLL is loaded and unloaded does not corrupt the global MFC state.

See Also: AfxLoadLibrary

AfxGetApp

CWinApp* AfxGetApp( );

Return Value

A pointer to the single **CWinApp** object for the application.

Remarks

The pointer returned by this function can be used to access application information such as the main message-dispatch code or the topmost window.

AfxGetAppName

LPCTSTR AfxGetAppName( );

Return Value

A null-terminated string containing the application's name.

Remarks

The string returned by this function can be used for diagnostic messages or as a root for temporary string names.

AfxGetInstanceHandle

HINSTANCE AfxGetInstanceHandle( );

Return Value

An **HINSTANCE** to the current instance of the application. If called from within a DLL linked with the USRDLL version of MFC, an **HINSTANCE** to the DLL is returned.

Remarks

This function allows you to retrieve the instance handle of the current application. **AfxGetInstanceHandle** always returns the **HINSTANCE** of your executable file (.EXE) unless it is called from within a DLL linked with the USRDLL version of MFC. In this case, it returns an **HINSTANCE** to the DLL.

See Also: AfxGetResourceHandle, AfxSetResourceHandle

AfxGetInternetHandleType

DWORD AFXAPI AfxGetInternetHandleType(HINTERNET *hQuery* **);**

Return Value

Any of the Internet service types defined by WININET.H. See the Remarks section for a list of these Internet services. If the handle is NULL or not recognized, the function returns AFX_INET_SERVICE_UNK.

Parameters

hQuery   A handle to an Internet query.

Remarks

Use this global function to determine the type of an Internet handle.

The following list includes possible Internet types returned by **AfxGetInternetHandleType**.

- INTERNET_HANDLE_TYPE_INTERNET
- INTERNET_HANDLE_TYPE_CONNECT_FTP
- INTERNET_HANDLE_TYPE_CONNECT_GOPHER
- INTERNET_HANDLE_TYPE_CONNECT_HTTP
- INTERNET_HANDLE_TYPE_FTP_FIND
- INTERNET_HANDLE_TYPE_FTP_FIND_HTML
- INTERNET_HANDLE_TYPE_FTP_FILE
- INTERNET_HANDLE_TYPE_FTP_FILE_HTML
- INTERNET_HANDLE_TYPE_GOPHER_FIND
- INTERNET_HANDLE_TYPE_GOPHER_FIND_HTML
- INTERNET_HANDLE_TYPE_GOPHER_FILE
- INTERNET_HANDLE_TYPE_GOPHER_FILE_HTML
- INTERNET_HANDLE_TYPE_HTTP_REQUEST

See Also: AfxParseURL

AfxGetMainWnd

CWnd* AfxGetMainWnd( );

Return Value

If the server has an object that is in-place active inside a container, and this container is active, this function returns a pointer to the frame window object that contains the in-place active document.

If there is no object that is in-place active within a container, or your application is not an OLE server, this function simply returns the **m_pMainWnd** of your application object.

Remarks

If your application is an OLE server, call this function to retrieve a pointer to the active main window of the application instead of directly referring to the **m_pMainWnd** member of the application object.

If your application is not an OLE server, then calling this function is equivalent to directly referring to the **m_pMainWnd** member of your application object.

See Also: **CWinThread::m_pMainWnd**

AfxGetResourceHandle

HINSTANCE AfxGetResourceHandle( );

Return Value

An **HINSTANCE** handle where the default resources of the application are loaded.

Remarks

Use the **HINSTANCE** handle returned by this function to access the application's resources directly, for example, in calls to the Windows function **FindResource**.

See Also: **AfxGetInstanceHandle**, **AfxSetResourceHandle**

AfxGetStaticModuleState

AFX_MODULE_STATE* AFXAPI AfxGetStaticModuleState( );

Return Value

A pointer to an **AFX_MODULE_STATE** structure.

Remarks

Call this function to set the module state before initialization and/or to restore the previous module state after cleanup. The **AFX_MODULE_STATE** structure contains global data for the module, that is, the portion of the module state that is pushed or popped.

By default, MFC uses the resource handle of the main application to load the resource template. If you have an exported function in a DLL, such as one that launches a dialog box in the DLL, this template is actually stored in the DLL module. You need to switch the module state for the correct handle to be used. You can do this by adding the following code to the beginning of the function:

```
AFX_MANAGE_STATE(AfxGetStaticModuleState( ));
```

This swaps the current module state with the state returned from **AfxGetStaticModuleState** until the end of the current scope.

For more information on module states and MFC, see "Managing the State Data of MFC Modules" in "Creating New Documents, Windows, and Views" in *Visual C++ Programmer's Guide* online and Technical Note 58 online.

See Also: **AFX_MANAGE_STATE**

AfxGetThread

CWinThread* AfxGetThread( );

Return Value

Pointer to the currently executing thread.

Remarks

Call this function to get a pointer to the **CWinThread** object representing the currently executing thread. Must be called from within the desired thread.

See Also: **AfxBeginThread**

AfxInitExtensionModule

BOOL AFXAPI AfxInitExtensionModule(AFX_EXTENSION_MODULE& *state*,
↪ **HMODULE** *hModule* **);**

Return Value

TRUE if the extension DLL is successfully initialized; otherwise, **FALSE**.

Parameters

state   A reference to the **AFX_EXTENSION_MODULE** structure that will contain the state of extension DLL module after the initialization. The state includes a copy of the runtime class objects that have been initialized by the extension DLL as part of normal static object construction executed before **DllMain** is entered.

hModule   A handle of the extension DLL module.

Remarks

Call this function in an extension DLL's **DllMain** to initialize the DLL. For example:

```
static AFX_EXTENSION_MODULE extensionDLL;
extern "C" int APIENTRY
DllMain(HINSTANCE hInstance, DWORD dwReason, LPVOID)
{
    if (dwReason == DLL_PROCESS_ATTACH)
    {
```

```
    // Extension DLL one-time initialization
    if (!AfxInitExtensionModule(extensionDLL, hInstance))
        return 0;
...
```

AfxInitExtensionModule makes a copy of the DLL's **HMODULE** and captures the DLL's runtime-classes (**CRuntimeClass** structures) as well as its object factories (**COleObjectFactory** objects) for use later when the **CDynLinkLibrary** object is created.

MFC extension DLLs need to do two things in their **DllMain** function:

- Call **AfxInitExtensionModule** and check the return value.

- Create a **CDynLinkLibrary** object if the DLL will be exporting **CRuntimeClass** objects or has its own custom resources.

You can call **AfxTermExtensionModule** to clean up the extension DLL when each process detaches from the extension DLL (which happens when the process exits, or when the DLL is unloaded as a result of an **AfxFreeLibrary** call).

See Also: AfxTermExtensionModule

AfxInitRichEdit

BOOL AFXAPI AfxInitRichEdit( );

Remarks

Call this function to initialize the rich edit control for the application. It will also initialize the common controls library, if the library hasn't already been initialized for the process. If you use the rich edit control directly from your MFC application, you should call this function to assure that MFC has properly initialized the rich edit control runtime. If you use rich edit via **CRichEditCtrl**, **CRichEditView**, or **CRichEditDoc**, you don't need to call this function.

AfxIsMemoryBlock

BOOL AfxIsMemoryBlock(const void* *p*, UINT *nBytes*,
↳ LONG* *plRequestNumber* = NULL);

Return Value

Nonzero if the memory block is currently allocated and the length is correct; otherwise 0.

Parameters

p   Points to the block of memory to be tested.

nBytes   Contains the length of the memory block in bytes.

plRequestNumber   Points to a **long** integer that will be filled in with the memory
block's allocation sequence number. The variable pointed to by *plRequestNumber*
will only be filled in if **AfxIsMemoryBlock** returns nonzero.

Remarks

Tests a memory address to make sure it represents a currently active memory block
that was allocated by the diagnostic version of **new**. It also checks the specified size
against the original allocated size. If the function returns nonzero, the allocation
sequence number is returned in *plRequestNumber*. This number represents the order in
which the block was allocated relative to all other **new** allocations.

Example

```
// example for AfxIsMemoryBlock
CAge* pcage = new CAge( 21 ); // CAge is derived from CObject.
ASSERT( AfxIsMemoryBlock( pcage, sizeof( CAge ) ) )
```

See Also: AfxIsValidAddress

AfxIsValidAddress

BOOL AfxIsValidAddress(const void* *lp*, **UINT** *nBytes*, **BOOL** *bReadWrite* = **TRUE**);

Return Value

Nonzero if the specified memory block is contained entirely within the program's
memory space; otherwise 0.

Parameters

lp   Points to the memory address to be tested.

nBytes   Contains the number of bytes of memory to be tested.

bReadWrite   Specifies whether the memory is both for reading and writing (**TRUE**)
or just reading (**FALSE**).

Remarks

Tests any memory address to ensure that it is contained entirely within the program's
memory space. The address is not restricted to blocks allocated by **new**.

See Also: AfxIsMemoryBlock, AfxIsValidString

AfxIsValidString

BOOL AfxIsValidString(LPCSTR *lpsz*, **int** *nLength* = –1);

Return Value

Nonzero if the specified pointer points to a string of the specified size; otherwise 0.

Parameters

lpsz   The pointer to test.

nLength   Specifies the length of the string to be tested, in bytes. A value of –1 indicates that the string will be null-terminated.

Remarks

Use this function to determine whether a pointer to a string is valid.

See Also: AfxIsMemoryBlock, AfxIsValidAddress

AfxLoadLibrary

HINSTANCE AFXAPI AfxLoadLibrary(LPCTSTR *lpszModuleName* **);**

Return Value

If the function succeeds, the return value is a handle to the module. If the function fails, the return value is NULL.

Parameters

lpszModuleName   Points to a null-terminated string that contains the name of the module (either a .DLL or .EXE file). The name specified is the filename of the module.

If the string specifies a path but the file does not exist in the specified directory, the function fails.

If a path is not specified and the filename extension is omitted, the default extension .DLL is appended. However, the filename string can include a trailing point character (.) to indicate that the module name has no extension. When no path is specified, the function searches for the file in the following sequence:

- The directory from which the application loaded.

- The current directory.

- **Windows 95:** The Windows system directory. **Windows NT:** The 32-bit Windows system directory. The name of this directory is SYSTEM32.

- **Windows NT only:** The 16-bit Windows system directory. There is no Win32 function that obtains the path of this directory, but it is searched. The name of this directory is SYSTEM.

- The Windows directory.

- The directories that are listed in the PATH environment variable.

Remarks

Use **AfxLoadLibrary** to map a DLL module. It returns a handle that can be used in **GetProcAddress** to get the address of a DLL function. **AfxLoadLibrary** can also be used to map other executable modules.

Each process maintains a reference count for each loaded library module. This reference count is incremented each time **AfxLoadLibrary** is called and is decremented each time **AfxFreeLibrary** is called. When the reference count reaches zero, the module is unmapped from the address space of the calling process and the handle is no longer valid.

Be sure to use **AfxLoadLibrary** and **AfxFreeLibrary** (instead of the Win32 functions **LoadLibrary** and **FreeLibrary**) if your application uses multiple threads. Using **AfxLoadLibrary** and **AfxFreeLibrary** insures that the startup and shutdown code that executes when the extension DLL is loaded and unloaded does not corrupt the global MFC state.

See Also: **AfxFreeLibrary**

AFX_MANAGE_STATE

AFX_MANAGE_STATE(AFX_MODULE_STATE* *pModuleState*)

Parameters

pModuleState   A pointer to an **AFX_MODULE_STATE** structure.

Remarks

Call this macro to protect an exported function in a DLL. When this macro is invoked, *pModuleState* is the effective module state for the remainder of the immediate containing scope. Upon leaving the scope, the previous effective module state will be automatically restored.

The **AFX_MODULE_STATE** structure contains global data for the module, that is, the portion of the module state that is pushed or popped.

By default, MFC uses the resource handle of the main application to load the resource template. If you have an exported function in a DLL, such as one that launches a dialog box in the DLL, this template is actually stored in the DLL module. You need to switch the module state for the correct handle to be used. You can do this by adding the following code to the beginning of the function:

```
AFX_MANAGE_STATE(AfxGetStaticModuleState( ));
```

This swaps the current moudle state with the state returned from **AfxGetStaticModuleState** until the end of the current scope.

For more information on module states and MFC, see "Managing the State Data of MFC Modules" in "Creating New Documents, Windows, and Views" in *Visual C++ Programmer's Guide* online and Technical Note 58 online.

See Also: **AfxGetStaticModuleState**

afxMemDF

int afxMemDF;

Remarks

This variable is accessible from a debugger or your program and allows you to tune allocation diagnostics. It can have the following values as specified by the enumeration **afxMemDF**:

- **allocMemDF**   Turns on debugging allocator (default setting in Debug library).

- **delayFreeMemDF**   Delays freeing memory. While your program frees a memory block, the allocator does not return that memory to the underlying operating system. This will place maximum memory stress on your program.

- **checkAlwaysMemDF**   Calls **AfxCheckMemory** every time memory is allocated or freed. This will significantly slow memory allocations and deallocations.

Example

```
// example for afxMemDF
afxMemDF = allocMemDF | checkAlwaysMemDF;
```

AfxMessageBox

int AfxMessageBox(LPCTSTR *lpszText*, **UINT** *nType* = **MB_OK,**
  ↪ **UINT** *nIDHelp* = **0);**
int AFXAPI AfxMessageBox(UINT *nIDPrompt*, **UINT** *nType* = **MB_OK,**
  ↪ **UINT** *nIDHelp* = **(UINT) –1);**

Return Value

Zero if there is not enough memory to display the message box; otherwise one of the following values is returned:

- **IDABORT**   The Abort button was selected.

- **IDCANCEL**   The Cancel button was selected.

- **IDIGNORE**   The Ignore button was selected.

- **IDNO**   The No button was selected.

- **IDOK**   The OK button was selected.

- **IDRETRY**   The Retry button was selected.

- **IDYES**   The Yes button was selected.

If a message box has a Cancel button, the **IDCANCEL** value will be returned if either the ESC key is pressed or the Cancel button is selected. If the message box has no Cancel button, pressing the ESC key has no effect.

The functions **AfxFormatString1** and **AfxFormatString2** can be useful in formatting text that appears in a message box.

Parameters

lpszText   Points to a **CString** object or null-terminated string containing the message to be displayed in the message box.

nType   The style of the message box. Apply any of the message-box styles to the box.

nIDHelp   The Help-context ID for the message; 0 indicates the application's default Help context will be used.

nIDPrompt   A unique ID used to reference a string in the string table.

Remarks

Displays a message box on the screen. The first form of this overloaded function displays a text string pointed to by *lpszText* in the message box and uses *nIDHelp* to describe a Help context. The Help context is used to jump to an associated Help topic when the user presses the Help key (typically F1).

The second form of the function uses the string resource with the ID *nIDPrompt* to display a message in the message box. The associated Help page is found through the value of *nIDHelp*. If the default value of *nIDHelp* is used (-1), the string resource ID, *nIDPrompt*, is used for the Help context. For more information about defining Help contexts, see the article "Help Topics" in *Visual C++ Programmer's Guide* online and "Technical Note 28" online.

See Also: **CWnd::MessageBox**

AfxNetInitModule

void AFXAPI AfxNetInitModule( );

#include <afxdll.h>

Remarks

For MFC Sockets support from a regular DLL that is dynamically linked to MFC, add a call to this function in your regular DLL's **CWinApp::InitInstance** function to initialize the MFC Sockets DLL. The MFC Sockets DLL is an extension DLL; in order for an extension DLL to get wired into a **CDynLinkLibrary** chain, it must create a **CDynLinkLibrary** object in the context of every module that will be using it. **AfxNetInitModule** creates the **CDynLinkLibrary** object in your regular DLL's context so that it gets wired into the **CDynLinkLibrary** object chain of the regular DLL.

AFX_ODBC_CALL

AFX_ODBC_CALL(*SQLFunc* **)**

Parameters

SQLFunc   An ODBC API function. For more information about ODBC API functions, see the *ODBC SDK Programmer's Reference*.

Remarks

Use this macro to call any ODBC API function that may return **SQL_STILL_EXECUTING**. **AFX_ODBC_CALL** repeatedly calls the function until it no longer returns **SQL_STILL_EXECUTING**.

Before invoking **AFX_ODBC_CALL**, you must declare a variable, nRetCode, of type **RETCODE**. You can use **CRecordset::Check** to check the value of nRetCode after the macro call.

Note that the MFC ODBC classes now use only synchronous processing. In order to perform an asynchronous operation, you must call the ODBC API function **SQLSetConnectOption**. For more information, see the topic "Executing Functions Asynchronously" in the *ODBC SDK Programmer's Reference*.

Example

This example uses **AFX_ODBC_CALL** to call the **SQLColumns** ODBC API function, which returns a list of the columns in the table named by strTableName. Note the declaration of nRetCode and the use of recordset data members to pass parameters to the function. The example also illustrates checking the results of the call with **Check**, a member function of class **CRecordset**. The variable prs is a pointer to a **CRecordset** object, declared elsewhere.

```
// example for AFX_ODBC_CALL

RETCODE nRetCode;

AFX_ODBC_CALL( ::SQLColumns( prs->m_hstmt,
     (UCHAR *)NULL, SQL_NTS, (UCHAR *)NULL,
     SQL_NTS, (UCHAR *)(constchar*)strTableName,
     SQL_NTS, (UCHAR *)NULL, SQL_NTS ) );

if ( !prs->Check( nRetCode ) )
{
   AfxThrowDBException( nRetCode, prs->m_pdb,
               prs->m_hstmt );
   TRACE( "SQLColumns failed\n" );
}
```

See Also: **AFX_SQL_ASYNC, AFX_SQL_SYNC**

AfxOleCanExitApp

BOOL AFXAPI AfxOleCanExitApp( );

#include <afxdisp.h>

Return Value

Nonzero if the application can exit; otherwise 0.

Remarks

Indicates whether the application can terminate. An application should not
terminate if there are outstanding references to its objects. The global functions
AfxOleLockApp and **AfxOleUnlockApp** increment and decrement, respectively,
a counter of references to the application's objects. The application should not
terminate when this counter is nonzero. If the counter is nonzero, the application's
main window is hidden (not destroyed) when the user chooses Close from the
system menu or Exit from the File menu. The framework calls this function in
CFrameWnd::OnClose.

See Also: **AfxOleLockApp**, **AfxOleUnlockApp**

AfxOleGetMessageFilter

COleMessageFilter* AFXAPI AfxOleGetMessageFilter( );

#include <afxwin.h>

Return Value

A pointer to the current message filter.

Remarks

Retrieves the application's current message filter. Call this function to access
the current **COleMessageFilter**-derived object, just as you would call **AfxGetApp**
to access the current application object.

Example

```
COleMessageFilter* pFilter = AfxOleGetMessageFilter();
ASSERT_VALID(pFilter);
pFilter->BeginBusyState();
// do things requiring a busy state
pFilter->EndBusyState();
```

See Also: **COleMessageFilter**, **AfxGetApp**

AfxOleGetUserCtrl

BOOL AFXAPI AfxOleGetUserCtrl( );

#include <afxdisp.h>

Return Value

Nonzero if the user is in control of the application; otherwise 0.

Remarks

Retrieves the current user-control flag. The user is "in control" of the application when the user has explicitly opened or created a new document. The user is also in control if the application was not launched by the OLE system DLLs—in other words, if the user launched the application with the system shell.

See Also: AfxOleSetUserCtrl

AfxOleInit

BOOL AFXAPI AfxOleInit( );

#include <afxdisp.h>

Return Value

Nonzero if successful; 0 if initialization fails, possibly because incorrect versions of the OLE system DLLs are installed.

Remarks

Initializes the OLE DLLs.

AfxOleInitModule

void AFXAPI AfxOleInitModule( );

#include <afxdll.h>

Remarks

For OLE support from a regular DLL that is dynamically linked to MFC, call this function in your regular DLL's **CWinApp::InitInstance** function to initialize the MFC OLE DLL. The MFC OLE DLL is an extension DLL; in order for an extension DLL to get wired into a **CDynLinkLibrary** chain, it must create a **CDynLinkLibrary** object in the context of every module that will be using it. **AfxOleInitModule** creates the **CDynLinkLibrary** object in your regular DLL's context so that it gets wired into the **CDynLinkLibrary** object chain of the regular DLL.

If you are building an OLE control and are using **COleControlModule**, you should not call **AfxOleInitModule** because the **InitInstance** member function for **COleControlModule** calls **AfxOleInitModule**.

AfxOleLockApp

void AFXAPI AfxOleLockApp( );

#include <afxdisp.h>

Remarks

Increments the framework's global count of the number of active objects in the application.

The framework keeps a count of the number of objects active in an application. The **AfxOleLockApp** and **AfxOleUnlockApp** functions, respectively, increment and decrement this count.

When the user attempts to close an application that has active objects—an application for which the count of active objects is nonzero—the framework hides the application from the user's view instead of completely shutting it down. The **AfxOleCanExitApp** function indicates whether the application can terminate.

Call **AfxOleLockApp** from any object that exposes OLE interfaces, if it would be undesirable for that object to be destroyed while still being used by a client application. Also call **AfxOleUnlockApp** in the destructor of any object that calls **AfxOleLockApp** in the constructor. By default, **COleDocument** (and derived classes) automatically lock and unlock the application.

See Also: **AfxOleUnlockApp**, **AfxOleCanExitApp**, **COleDocument**

AfxOleLockControl

BOOL AFXAPI AfxOleLockControl(REFCLSID *clsid* **);**
BOOL AFXAPI AfxOleLockControl(LPCTSTR *lpszProgID* **);**

#include <afxwin.h>

Return Value

Nonzero if the class factory of the control was successfully locked; otherwise 0.

Parameters

clsid   The unique class ID of the control.

lpszProgID   The unique program ID of the control.

Remarks

Locks the class factory of the specified control so that dynamically created data associated with the control remains in memory. This can significantly speed up display of the controls. For example, once you create a control in a dialog box and lock the control with **AfxOleLockControl**, you do not need to create and kill it again every time the dialog is shown or destroyed. If the user opens and closes a dialog box repeatedly, locking your controls can significantly enhance performance. When you are ready to destroy the control, call **AfxOleUnlockControl**.

See Also: **AfxOleUnlockControl**

AfxOleRegisterControlClass

BOOL AFXAPI AfxOleRegisterControlClass(HINSTANCE *hInstance***,**
   ↪ **REFCLSID** *clsid***, LPCTSTR** *pszProgID***, UINT** *idTypeName***,**
   ↪ **UINT** *idBitmap***, int** *nRegFlags***, DWORD** *dwMiscStatus***, REFGUID** *tlid***,**
   ↪ **WORD** *wVerMajor***, WORD** *wVerMinor* **);**

#include <afxctl.h>

Return Value

Nonzero if the control class was registered; otherwise 0.

Parameters

hInstance   The instance handle of the module associated with the control class.

clsid   The unique class ID of the control.

pszProgID   The unique program ID of the control.

idTypeName   The resource ID of the string that contains a user-readable type name for the control.

idBitmap   The resource ID of the bitmap used to represent the OLE control in a toolbar or palette.

nRegFlags   Contains one or more of the following flags:

- **afxRegInsertable**   Allows the control to appear in the Insert Object dialog box for OLE objects.

- **afxRegApartmentThreading**   Sets the threading model in the registry to ThreadingModel=Apartment.

Note   In MFC versions prior to MFC 4.2, the **int** *nRegFlags* parameter was a **BOOL** parameter, *bInsertable*, that allowed or disallowed the control to be inserted from the Insert Object dialog box.

dwMiscStatus   Contains one or more of the following status flags (for a description of the flags, see **OLEMISC** enumeration in the *OLE Programmer's Reference*):

- OLEMISC_RECOMPOSEONRESIZE

- OLEMISC_ONLYICONIC
- OLEMISC_INSERTNOTREPLACE
- OLEMISC_STATIC
- OLEMISC_CANTLINKINSIDE
- OLEMISC_CANLINKBYOLE1
- OLEMISC_ISLINKOBJECT
- OLEMISC_INSIDEOUT
- OLEMISC_ACTIVATEWHENVISIBLE
- OLEMISC_RENDERINGISDEVICEINDEPENDENT
- OLEMISC_INVISIBLEATRUNTIME
- OLEMISC_ALWAYSRUN
- OLEMISC_ACTSLIKEBUTTON
- OLEMISC_ACTSLIKELABEL
- OLEMISC_NOUIACTIVATE
- OLEMISC_ALIGNABLE
- OLEMISC_IMEMODE
- OLEMISC_SIMPLEFRAME
- OLEMISC_SETCLIENTSITEFIRST

tlid The unique ID of the control class.

wVerMajor The major version number of the control class.

wVerMinor The minor version number of the control class.

Remarks

Registers the control class with the Windows registration database. This allows the control to be used by containers that are OLE-control aware. **AfxOleRegisterControlClass** updates the registry with the control's name and location on the system and also sets the threading model that the control supports in the registry. For more information, see "Technical Note 64" online, "Apartment-Model Threading in OLE Controls," and "About Processes and Threads" in the Win32 SDK.

Example

```
// Member function implementation of class COleObjectFactory::UpdateRegistry
//
BOOL CMyApartmentAwareCtrl::CApartmentCtrlFactory::UpdateRegistry(BOOL bRegister)
{
```

```
// TODO: Verify that your control follows
// apartment-model threading rules.
// Refer to MFC TechNote 64 for more information.
// If your control does not conform to the
// apartment-model rules, then you must modify the
// code below, changing the 6th parameter from
// afxRegInsertable | afxRegApartmentThreading to
// afxRegInsertable.

    if (bRegister)
        return AfxOleRegisterControlClass()
        AfxGetInstanceHandle(),
        m_clsid,
        m_lpszProgID,
        IDS_APARTMENT,
        IDB_APARTMENT,
        afxRegInsertable | afxRegApartmentThreading,
        _dwApartmentOleMisc,
        _tlid,
        _wVerMajor,
        _wVerMinor);
    else
        return AfxOleUnregisterClass(m_clsid, m_lpszProgID);
```

The above example demonstrates how **AfxOleRegisterControlClass** is called with the flag for insertable and the flag for apartment model ORed together to create the sixth parameter:

```
afxRegInsertable | afxRegApartmentThreading,
```

The control will show up in the Insert Object dialog box for enabled containers, and it will be apartment model-aware. Apartment model-aware controls must ensure that static class data is protected by locks, so that while a control in one apartment is accessing the static data, it isn't disabled by the scheduler before it is finished, and another instance of the same class starts using the same static data. Any accesses to the static data will be surrounded by critical section code.

See Also: AfxOleRegisterPropertyPageClass, AfxOleRegisterTypeLib, AfxOleUnregisterClass, AfxOleUnregisterTypeLib

---

AfxOleRegisterPropertyPageClass

BOOL AFXAPI AfxOleRegisterPropertyPageClass(HINSTANCE *hInstance*,
→ **REFCLSID** *clsid*, **UINT** *idTypeName*, **int** *nRegFlags*)

#include <afxctl.h>

Return value

Nonzero if the control class was registered; otherwise 0.

Parameters

hInstance   The instance handle of the module associated with the property page class.

clsid   The unique class ID of the property page.

idTypeName   The resource ID of the string that contains a user-readable name for the property page.

nRegFlags   May contain the flag

- **afxRegApartmentThreading** Sets the threading model in the registry to ThreadingModel = Apartment.

Note: In MFC versions prior to MFC 4.2, the **int** *nRegFlags* parameter was not available. Note also that the **afxRegInsertable** flag is not a valid option for property pages and will cause an ASSERT in MFC if it is set

Remarks

Registers the property page class with the Windows registration database. This allows the property page to be used by containers that are OLE-control aware. **AfxOleRegisterPropertyPageClass** updates the registry with the property page name and its location on the system and also sets the threading model that the control supports in the registry. For more information, see "Technical Note 64" online, "Apartment-Model Threading in OLE Controls," and "About Processes and Threads" in the Win32 SDK.

See Also: **AfxOleRegisterControlClass, AfxOleRegisterTypeLib**

AfxOleRegisterServerClass

BOOL AFXAPI AfxOleRegisterServerClass(REFCLSID *clsid*,
↪ **LPCTSTR** *lpszClassName*, **LPCTSTR** *lpszShortTypeName*,
↪ **LPCTSTR** *lpszLongTypeName*, **OLE_APPTYPE** *nAppType* = **OAT_SERVER**,
↪ **LPCTSTR*** *rglpszRegister* = **NULL**, **LPCTSTR*** *rglpszOverwrite* = **NULL**);

#include <afxdisp.h>

Return Value

Nonzero if the server class is successfully registered; otherwise 0.

Parameters

clsid   Reference to the server's OLE class ID.

lpszClassName   Pointer to a string containing the class name of the server's objects.

lpszShortTypeName   Pointer to a string containing the short name of the server's object type, such as "Chart."

lpszLongTypeName   Pointer to a string containing the long name of the server's object type, such as "Microsoft Excel 5.0 Chart."

nAppType   A value, taken from the **OLE_APPTYPE** enumeration, specifying the type of OLE application. Possible values are the following:

- **OAT_INPLACE_SERVER**   Server has full server user-interface.

- **OAT_SERVER**   Server supports only embedding.

- **OAT_CONTAINER**   Container supports links to embeddings.

- **OAT_DISPATCH_OBJECT**   **IDispatch**-capable object.

rglpszRegister   Array of pointers to strings representing the keys and values to be added to the OLE system registry if no existing values for the keys are found.

rglpszOverwrite   Array of pointers to strings representing the keys and values to be added to the OLE system registry if the registry contains existing values for the given keys.

Remarks

This function allows you to register your server in the OLE system registry. Most applications can use **COleTemplateServer::Register** to register the application's document types. If your application's system-registry format does not fit the typical pattern, you can use **AfxOleRegisterServerClass** for more control.

The registry consists of a set of keys and values. The *rglpszRegister* and *rglpszOverwrite* arguments are arrays of pointers to strings, each consisting of a key and a value separated by a **NULL** character ('\0'). Each of these strings can have replaceable parameters whose places are marked by the character sequences %1 through %5.

The symbols are filled in as follows:

Symbol	Value
%1	Class ID, formatted as a string
%2	Class name
%3	Path to executable file
%4	Short type name
%5	Long type name

See Also: COleTemplateServer::UpdateRegistry

AfxOleRegisterTypeLib

BOOL AfxOleRegisterTypeLib(HINSTANCE *hInstance*, **REFGUID** *tlid*,
↪ **LPCTSTR** *pszFileName* = **NULL, LPCTSTR** *pszHelpDir* = **NULL**);

Return Value

Nonzero if the type library was registered; otherwise 0.

Parameters

hInstance The instance handle of the application associated with the type library.

tlid The unique ID of the type library.

pszFileName Points to the optional filename of a localized type library (.TLB) file for the control.

pszHelpDir The name of the directory where the help file for the type library can be found. If **NULL**, the help file is assumed to be in the same directory as the type library itself.

Remarks

Registers the type library with the Windows registration database and allows the type library to be used by other containers that are OLE-control aware. This function updates the registry with the type library name and its location on the system.

See Also: **AfxOleUnregisterTypeLib**, **AfxOleRegisterControlClass**, **AfxOleUnregisterClass**

AfxOleSetEditMenu

void AFXAPI AfxOleSetEditMenu(COleClientItem* *pClient*,
↪ **CMenu*** *pMenu*, **UINT** *iMenuItem*, **UINT** *nIDVerbMin*,
↪ **UINT** *nIDVerbMax* **= 0, UINT** *nIDConvert* **= 0);**

#include <afxole.h>

Parameters

pClient A pointer to the client OLE item.

pMenu A pointer to the menu object to be updated.

iMenuItem The index of the menu item to be updated.

nIDVerbMin The command ID that corresponds to the primary verb.

nIDVerbMax The command ID that corresponds to the last verb.

nIDConvert ID for the Convert menu item.

Remarks

Implements the user interface for the *typename* Object command. If the server recognizes only a primary verb, the menu item becomes "verb *typename* Object" and the *nIDVerbMin* command is sent when the user chooses the command. If the server recognizes several verbs, then the menu item becomes "*typename* Object" and a submenu listing all the verbs appears when the user chooses the command. When the user chooses a verb from the submenu, *nIDVerbMin* is sent if the first verb is chosen, *nIDVerbMin* + 1 is sent if the second verb is chosen, and so forth. The default **COleDocument** implementation automatically handles this feature.

You must have the following statement in your client's application resource script (.RC) file:

#include <afxolecl.rc>

See Also: **COleDocument**

AfxOleSetUserCtrl

void AFXAPI AfxOleSetUserCtrl(BOOL *bUserCtrl* **);**

#include <afxdisp.h>

Parameters

bUserCtrl   Specifies whether the user-control flag is to be set or cleared.

Remarks

Sets or clears the user-control flag, which is explained in the reference for **AfxOleGetUserCtrl**. The framework calls this function when the user creates or loads a document, but not when a document is loaded or created through an indirect action such as loading an embedded object from a container application.

Call this function if other actions in your application should put the user in control of the application.

See Also: **AfxOleGetUserCtrl**

AfxOleTypeMatchGuid

BOOL AfxOleTypeMatchGuid(LPTYPEINFO *pTypeInfo***,**
  ↪ **TYPEDESC FAR*** *pTypeDesc***, REFGUID** *guidType***,**
  ↪ **ULONG** *cIndirectionLevels* **);**

Return Value

Nonzero if the match was successful; otherwise 0.

Parameters

pTypeInfo   Pointer to the type info object from which *pTypeDesc* was obtained.

pTypeDesc   Pointer to a **TYPEDESC** structure.

guidType   The unique ID of the type.

cIndirectionLevels   The number of indirection levels.

Remarks

Call this function to determine whether a type descriptor (obtained from the type info) describes the type indicated by *guidType* with the given number of levels of indirection.

Example

To check whether `typedesc` refers to a pointer to a **IFontDisp**:

```
AfxOleTypeMatchGuid( ptypeinfo, &typedesc, IID_IFontDisp, 1);
```

where `IID_IFontDisp` refers to the type and the number of indirection levels is 1 (because the sample is checking for a simple pointer).

AfxOleUnlockApp

void AFXAPI AfxOleUnlockApp( );

#include <afxdisp.h>

Remarks

Decrements the framework's count of active objects in the application. See **AfxOleLockApp** for further information.

When the number of active objects reaches zero, **AfxOleOnReleaseAllObjects** is called.

See Also: **AfxOleLockApp, CCmdTarget::OnFinalRelease**

AfxOleUnlockControl

BOOL AFXAPI AfxOleUnlockControl(REFCLSID *clsid* **);**
BOOL AFXAPI AfxOleUnlockControl(LPCTSTR *lpszProgID* **);**

#include <afxwin.h>

Return Value

Nonzero if the class factory of the control was successfully unlocked; otherwise 0.

Parameters

clsid   The unique class ID of the control.

lpszProgID   The unique program ID of the control.

Remarks

Unlocks the class factory of the specified control. A control is locked with **AfxOleLockControl**, so that dynamically created data associated with the control remains in memory. This can significantly speed up display of the control because the control need not be created and destroyed every time it is displayed. When you are ready to destroy the control, call **AfxOleUnlockControl**.

See Also: **AfxOleLockControl**

AfxOleUnregisterClass

BOOL AFXAPI AfxOleUnregisterClass(REFCLSID *clsID***, LPCSTR** *pszProgID* **);**

Return Value

Nonzero if the control or property page class was successfully unregistered; otherwise 0.

Parameters

clsID   The unique class ID of the control or property page.

pszProgID   The unique program ID of the control or property page.

Remarks

Removes the control or property page class entry from the Windows registration database.

See Also: **AfxOleRegisterPropertyPageClass**, **AfxOleRegisterControlClass**, **AfxOleRegisterTypeLib**

AfxOleUnregisterTypeLib

BOOL AFXAPI AfxOleUnregisterTypeLib(REFGUID *tlID* **);**

Return Value

Nonzero if the type library was successfully unregistered; otherwise 0.

Parameters

tlID   The unique ID of the type library.

Remarks

Call this function to remove the type library entry from the Windows registration database.

See Also: **AfxOleUnregisterClass**, **AfxOleRegisterTypeLib**

AfxParseURL

BOOL AFXAPI AfxParseURL(LPCTSTR *pstrURL***, DWORD&** *dwServiceType***,**
↪ CString& *strServer***, CString&** *strObject***, INTERNET_PORT&** *nPort* **);**

Return Value

Nonzero if the URL was successfully parsed; otherwise, 0 if it is empty or does not contain a known Internet service type.

Parameters

pstrURL   A pointer to a string containing the URL to be parsed.

dwServiceType Indicates the type of Internet service. Possible values are as follows:

AFX_INET_SERVICE_FTP

AFX_INET_SERVICE_HTTP

AFX_INET_SERVICE_GOPHER

AFX_INET_SERVICE_FILE

AFX_INET_SERVICE_MAILTO

AFX_INET_SERVICE_NEWS

AFX_INET_SERVICE_NNTP

AFX_INET_SERVICE_TELNET

AFX_INET_SERVICE_WAIS

AFX_INET_SERVICE_MID

AFX_INET_SERVICE_CID

AFX_INET_SERVICE_PROSPERO

AFX_INET_SERVICE_AFS

AFX_INET_SERVICE_UNK

strServer The first segment of the URL following the service type.

strObject An object that URL refers to (may be empty).

nPort Ferreted out from either the Server or Object portions of the URL, if either exist.

Remarks

This global is used in **CInternetSession::OpenURL**. It parses a URL string and returns the type of service and its components.

For example, **AfxParseURL** parses URLs of the form **service://server/dir/dir/object.ext:port** and returns its components stored as follows:

strServer   == "server"

strObject   == "/dir/dir/object/object.ext"

nPort   == #port

dwServiceType == #service

See Also: **AfxGetInternetHandleType**

AfxRegisterClass

BOOL AFXAPI AfxRegisterClass(WNDCLASS* *lpWndClass* **);**

Return Value

TRUE if the class is successfully registered; otherwise **FALSE**.

Parameters

lpWndClass Pointer to a **WNDCLASS** structure containing information about the window class to be registered. For more information on this structure, see the Win32 SDK documentation.

Remarks

Use this function to register window classes in a DLL that uses MFC. If you use this function, the class is automatically unregistered when the DLL is unloaded.

In non-DLL builds, the **AfxRegisterClass** identifier is defined as a macro that maps to the Windows function **RegisterClass**, since classes registered in an application are automatically unregistered. If you use **AfxRegisterClass** instead of **RegisterClass**, your code can be used without change both in an application and in a DLL.

AfxRegisterWndClass

LPCTSTR AFXAPI AfxRegisterWndClass(UINT *nClassStyle*,
↳ **HCURSOR** *hCursor* **= 0, HBRUSH** *hbrBackground* **= 0, HICON** *hIcon* **= 0);**

Return Value

A null-terminated string containing the class name. You can pass this class name to the **Create** member function in **CWnd** or other **CWnd**-derived classes to create a window. The name is generated by the Microsoft Foundation Class Library.

Note The return value is a pointer to a static buffer. To save this string, assign it to a **CString** variable.

Parameters

nClassStyle Specifies the Windows class style or combination of styles, created by using the bitwise-OR (|) operator, for the window class. For a list of class styles, see the **WNDCLASS** structure in the Win32 SDK documentation.

hCursor Specifies a handle to the cursor resource to be installed in each window created from the window class.

hbrBackground Specifies a handle to the brush resource to be installed in each window created from the window class.

hIcon Specifies a handle to the icon resource to be installed in each window created from the window class.

Remarks

The Microsoft Foundation Class Library automatically registers several standard window classes for you. Call this function if you want to register your own window classes.

The name registered for a class by **AfxRegisterWndClass** depends solely on the parameters. If you call **AfxRegisterWndClass** multiple times with identical parameters, it only registers a class on the first call. Subsequent calls to **AfxRegisterWndClass** with identical parameters simply return the already-registered classname.

If you call **AfxRegisterWndClass** for multiple CWnd-derived classes with identical parameters, instead of getting a separate window class for each class, each class shares the same window class. This can cause problems if the **CS_CLASSDC** class style is used. Instead of multiple **CS_CLASSDC** window classes, you end up with one **CS_CLASSDC** window class, and all C++ windows that use that class share the same DC. To avoid this problem, call **AfxRegisterClass** to register the class.

See Also: **CWnd::Create, CWnd::PreCreateWindow, WNDCLASS AfxRegisterClass**

AfxSetAllocHook

AFX_ALLOC_HOOK AfxSetAllocHook(AFX_ALLOC_HOOK *pfnAllocHook* **);**

Return Value

Nonzero if you want to permit the allocation; otherwise 0.

Parameters

pfnAllocHook   Specifies the name of the function to call. See the Remarks for the prototype of an allocation function.

Remarks

Sets a hook that enables calling of the specified function before each memory block is allocated. The Microsoft Foundation Class Library debug-memory allocator can call a user-defined hook function to allow the user to monitor a memory allocation and to control whether the allocation is permitted. Allocation hook functions are prototyped as follows:

BOOL AFXAPI AllocHook(size_t *nSize*, **BOOL** *bObject,*
↦ LONG *lRequestNumber* **);**

nSize   The size of the proposed memory allocation.

bObject   **TRUE** if the allocation is for a **CObject**-derived object; otherwise **FALSE**.

lRequestNumber   The memory allocation's sequence number.

Note that the **AFXAPI** calling convention implies that the callee must remove the parameters from the stack.

AfxSetResourceHandle

void AfxSetResourceHandle(HINSTANCE *hInstResource* **);**

Parameters

hInstResource   The instance or module handle to an .EXE or DLL file from which the application's resources are loaded.

Remarks

Use this function to set the **HINSTANCE** handle that determines where the default resources of the application are loaded.

See Also: **AfxGetInstanceHandle**, **AfxGetResourceHandle**

AfxSocketInit

BOOL AfxSocketInit(WSADATA * *lpwsaData* = **NULL);**

Return Value

Nonzero if the function is successful; otherwise 0.

Parameters

lpwsaData   A pointer to a **WSADATA** structure. If *lpwsaData* is not equal to **NULL**, then the address of the **WSADATA** structure is filled by the call to **::WSAStartup**. This function also ensures that **::WSACleanup** is called for you before the application terminates.

Remarks

Call this function in your **CWinApp::InitInstance** override to initialize Windows Sockets.

See Also: **CWinApp::InitInstance**

AFX_SQL_ASYNC

AFX_SQL_ASYNC(*prs*, *SQLFunc* **)**

Parameters

prs   A pointer to a **CRecordset** object or a **CDatabase** object. Beginning with MFC 4.2, this parameter value is ignored.

SQLFunc   An ODBC API function. For more information about ODBC API functions, see the *ODBC SDK Programmer's Reference*.

Remarks

The implementation of this macro has changed in MFC 4.2. **AFX_SQL_ASYNC** now simply calls the macro **AFX_ODBC_CALL** and ignores the *prs* parameter. In previous versions of MFC, **AFX_SQL_ASYNC** was used to call ODBC API functions that might return **SQL_STILL_EXECUTING**. If an ODBC API function did return **SQL_STILL_EXECUTING**, then **AFX_SQL_ASYNC** would call `prs->OnWaitForDataSource`.

Note The MFC ODBC classes now use only synchronous processing. In order to perform an asynchronous operation, you must call the ODBC API function **SQLSetConnectOption**. For more information, see the topic "Executing Functions Asynchronously" in the *ODBC SDK Programmer's Reference*.

See Also: **AFX_ODBC_CALL, AFX_SQL_SYNC**

AFX_SQL_SYNC

AFX_SQL_SYNC(*SQLFunc* **)**

Parameters

SQLFunc   An ODBC API function. For more information about these functions, see the *ODBC SDK Programmer's Reference*.

Remarks

The **AFX_SQL_SYNC** macro simply calls the function *SQLFunc*. Use this macro to call ODBC API functions that will not return **SQL_STILL_EXECUTING**.

Before calling **AFX_SQL_SYNC**, you must declare a variable, `nRetCode`, of type **RETCODE**. You can check the value of `nRetCode` after the macro call.

Note that the implementation of **AFX_SQL_SYNC** has changed in MFC 4.2. Because checking the server status is no longer required, **AFX_SQL_SYNC** simply assigns a value to `nRetCode`. For example, instead of making the call

```
AFX_SQL_SYNC( ::SQLGetInfo( .. ) )
```

you can simply make the assignment

```
nRetCode = ::SQLGetInfo( .. );
```

See Also: **AFX_SQL_ASYNC, AFX_ODBC_CALL**

AfxTermExtensionModule

void AFXAPI AfxTermExtensionModule(AFX_EXTENSION_MODULE& *state*, **↳ BOOL** *bAll* **= FALSE);**

Parameters

state   A reference to the **AFX_EXTENSION_MODULE** structure that contains the state of extension DLL module.

bAll If **TRUE**, cleanup all extension DLL modules. Otherwise, cleanup only the current DLL module.

Remarks

Call this function to allow MFC to cleanup the extension DLL when each process detaches from the DLL (which happens when the process exits, or when the DLL is unloaded as a result of a **AfxFreeLibrary** call). **AfxTermExtensionModule** will delete any local storage attached to the module and remove any entries from the message map cache. For example:

```
static AFX_EXTENSION_MODULE extensionDLL;
extern "C" int APIENTRY
DllMain(HINSTANCE hInstance, DWORD dwReason, LPVOID)
{
   if (dwReason == DLL_PROCESS_ATTACH)
   {
      // Extension DLL one-time initialization
      if (!AfxInitExtensionModule( extensionDLL, hInstance))
      return 0;
      // TODO: perform other initialization tasks here
   }
   else if (dwReason == DLL_PROCESS_DETACH)
   {
      // Extension DLL per-process termination
      AfxTermExtensionModule(extensionDLL);
   // TODO: perform other cleanup tasks here
   }
   return 1;   // ok
}
```

If your application loads and frees extension DLLs dynamically, be sure to call **AfxTermExtensionModule**. Since most extension DLLs are not dynamically loaded (usually, they are linked via their import libraries), the call to **AfxTermExtensionModule** is usually not necessary.

MFC extension DLLs need to call **AfxInitExtensionModule** in their **DllMain**. If the DLL will be exporting **CRuntimeClass** objects or has its own custom resources, you also need to create a **CDynLinkLibrary** object in **DllMain**.

See Also: **AfxInitExtensionModule**

AfxThrowArchiveException

void AfxThrowArchiveException(int *cause*, **LPCTSTR** *lpszArchiveName* **);**

Parameters

cause Specifies an integer that indicates the reason for the exception. For a list of the possible values, see **CArchiveException::m_cause**.

lpszArchiveName Points to a string containing the name of the **CArchive** object that caused the exception (if available).

Remarks

Throws an archive exception.

See Also: CArchiveException, THROW

AfxThrowDaoException

void AFXAPI AfxThrowDaoException(int *nAfxDaoError* =
➞ **NO_AFX_DAO_ERROR, SCODE** *scode* = **S_OK**);

Parameters

nAfxDaoError An integer value representing a DAO extended error code, which can be one of the values listed under **CDaoException::m_nAfxDaoError**.

scode An OLE error code from DAO, of type **SCODE**. For information, see **CDaoException::m_scode**.

Remarks

Call this function to throw an exception of type **CDaoException** from your own code. The framework also calls **AfxThrowDaoException**. In your call, you can pass one of the parameters or both. For example, if you want to raise one of the errors defined in **CDaoException::nAfxDaoError** but you do not care about the *scode* parameter, pass a valid code in the *nAfxDaoError* parameter and accept the default value for *scode*.

For information about exceptions related to the MFC DAO classes, see class **CDaoException** in this book and the article "Exceptions: Database Exceptions" in *Visual C++ Programmer's Guide* online.

See Also: CException

AfxThrowDBException

void AfxThrowDBException(RETCODE *nRetCode*, **CDatabase*** *pdb*,
➞ **HSTMT** *hstmt*);

Parameters

nRetCode A value of type **RETCODE**, defining the type of error that caused the exception to be thrown.

pdb A pointer to the **CDatabase** object that represents the data source connection with which the exception is associated.

hstmt An ODBC **HSTMT** handle that specifies the statement handle with which the exception is associated.

Remarks

Call this function to throw an exception of type **CDBException** from your own code. The framework calls **AfxThrowDBException** when it receives an ODBC

RETCODE from a call to an ODBC API function and interprets the **RETCODE** as an exceptional condition rather than an expectable error. For example, a data access operation might fail because of a disk read error.

For information about the **RETCODE** values defined by ODBC, see Chapter 8, "Retrieving Status and Error Information," in the *ODBC SDK Programmer's Reference*. For information about MFC extensions to these codes, see class **CDBException**.

See Also: CDBException::m_nRetCode

AfxThrowFileException

void **AfxThrowFileException**(int *cause*, **LONG** *lOsError* = –1,
↳ **LPCTSTR** *lpszFileName* = **NULL**);

Parameters

cause   Specifies an integer that indicates the reason for the exception. For a list of the possible values, see **CFileException::m_cause**.

lOsError   Contains the operating-system error number (if available) that states the reason for the exception. See your operating-system manual for a listing of error codes.

lpszFileName   Points to a string containing the name of the file that caused the exception (if available).

Remarks

Throws a file exception. You are responsible for determining the cause based on the operating-system error code.

See Also: CFileException::ThrowOsError, THROW

AfxThrowInternetException

void **AFXAPI AfxThrowInternetException**(**DWORD** *dwContext*,
↳ **DWORD** *dwError* = **0**);

Parameters

dwContext   The context identifier for the operation that caused the error. The default value of *dwContext* is specified originally in **CInternetSession** and is passed to **CInternetConnection**- and **CInternetFile**-derived classes. For specific operations performed on a connection or a file, you usually override the default with a *dwContext* of your own. This value then is returned to **CInternetSession::OnStatusCallback** to identify the specific operation's status. For more information on context identifiers, see the article "Internet First Steps: WinInet" online.

dwError   The error that caused the exception.

Remarks

Throws an Internet exception. You are responsible for determining the cause based on the operating-system error code.

See Also: CInternetException, THROW

AfxThrowMemoryException

void AfxThrowMemoryException( );

Remarks

Throws a memory exception. Call this function if calls to underlying system memory allocators (such as **malloc** and the **GlobalAlloc** Windows function) fail. You do not need to call it for **new** because **new** will throw a memory exception automatically if the memory allocation fails.

See Also: CMemoryException, THROW

AfxThrowNotSupportedException

void AfxThrowNotSupportedException( );

Remarks

Throws an exception that is the result of a request for an unsupported feature.

See Also: CNotSupportedException, THROW

AfxThrowOleDispatchException

void AFXAPI AfxThrowOleDispatchException(WORD *wCode,*
   ↪ **LPCSTR** *lpszDescription,* **UINT** *nHelpID = 0* **);**
void AFXAPI AfxThrowOleDispatchException(WORD *wCode,*
   ↪ **UINT** *nDescriptionID,* **UINT** *nHelpID = –1* **);**

#include <afxdisp.h>

Parameters

wCode   An error code specific to your application.

lpszDescription   Verbal description of the error.

nDescriptionID   Resource ID for the verbal error description.

nHelpID   A help context for your application's help (.HLP) file.

Remarks

Use this function to throw an exception within an OLE automation function. The information provided to this function can be displayed by the driving application (Microsoft Visual Basic or another OLE automation client application).

See Also: COleException

AfxThrowOleException

void AFXAPI AfxThrowOleException(SCODE *sc* **);**
void AFXAPI AfxThrowOleException(HRESULT *hr* **);**

#include <afxdisp.h>

Parameters

sc An OLE status code that indicates the reason for the exception.

hr Handle to a result code that indicates the reason for the exception.

Remarks

Creates an object of type **COleException** and throws an exception. The version that takes an **HRESULT** as an argument converts that result code into the corresponding **SCODE**. For more information on **HRESULT** and **SCODE**, see "Structure of OLE Error Codes" in the OLE documentation.

See Also: COleException, THROW

AfxThrowResourceException

void AfxThrowResourceException( );

Remarks

Throws a resource exception. This function is normally called when a Windows resource cannot be loaded.

See Also: CResourceException, THROW

AfxThrowUserException

void AfxThrowUserException( );

Remarks

Throws an exception to stop an end-user operation. This function is normally called immediately after **AfxMessageBox** has reported an error to the user.

See Also: CUserException, THROW, AfxMessageBox

afxTraceEnabled

BOOL afxTraceEnabled;

Remarks

A global variable used to enable or disable output from the **TRACE** macro.

By default, output from the **TRACE** macro is disabled. Set **afxTraceEnabled** to a nonzero value if you want **TRACE** macros in your program to produce output. Set it to 0 if you don't want **TRACE** macros in your program to produce output.

Usually, the value of **afxTraceEnabled** is set in your AFX.INI file. Alternately, you can set the value of **afxTraceEnabled** with the TRACER.EXE utility. For more information on **afxTraceEnabled**, see Technical Note 7 online.

See Also: **afxTraceFlags**, **TRACE**

---

afxTraceFlags

int afxTraceFlags;

Remarks

Used to turn on the built-in reporting features of the Microsoft Foundation Class Library.

This variable can be set under program control or while using the debugger. Each bit of **afxTraceFlags** selects a trace reporting option. You can turn any one of these bits on or off as desired using TRACER.EXE. There is never a need to set these flags manually.

The following is a list of the bit patterns and the resulting trace report option:

- **0x01** Multiapplication debugging. This will prefix each **TRACE** output with the name of the application and affects both the explicit **TRACE** output of your program as well as the additional report options described below.

- **0x02** Main message pump. Reports each message received in the main **CWinApp** message-handling mechanism. Lists the window handle, the message name or number, **wParam**, and **lParam**.

  The report is made after the Windows **GetMessage** call but before any message translation or dispatch occurs.

  Dynamic data exchange (DDE) messages will display additional data that can be used for some debugging scenarios in OLE.

  This flag displays only messages that are posted, not those that are sent.

- **0x04** Main message dispatch. Like option **0x02** above but applies to messages dispatched in **CWnd::WindowProc**, and therefore handles both posted and sent messages that are about to be dispatched.

- **0x08 WM_COMMAND** dispatch. A special case used for extended **WM_COMMAND/OnCommand** handling to report progress of the command-routing mechanism.

  Also reports which class receives the command (when there is a matching message-map entry), and when classes do not receive a command (when there is no matching message map entry). This report is especially useful to track the flow of command messages in multiple document interface (MDI) applications.

- **0x10** OLE tracing. Reports significant OLE notifications or requests.

  Turn this option on for an OLE client or server to track communication between the OLE DLLs and an OLE application.

- **0x20** Database tracing. Reports warnings for both ODBC and DAO classes, plus additional information for DAO. Turn this option on if you want tracing for either the MFC ODBC classes or the MFC DAO classes. For ODBC, you get only warnings, such as type mismatches in your DFX calls. For DAO, you get information for all exceptions, including the line and function in DAO or in the MFC DAO classes where a failure occurred.

For more information, see Technical Note 7 online.

See Also: afxTraceEnabled, TRACE

AfxVerifyLicFile

BOOL AFXAPI AfxVerifyLicFile(HINSTANCE *hInstance*, **LPCTSTR** ↪ *pszLicFileName*, **LPOLESTR** *pszLicFileContents*, **UINT** *cch* = –1);

Return Value

Nonzero if the license file exists and begins with the character sequence in *pszLicFileContents*; otherwise 0.

Parameters

hInstance The instance handle of the DLL associated with the licensed control.

pszLicFileName Points to a null-terminated character string containing the license filename.

pszLicFileContents Points to a byte sequence that must match the sequence found at the beginning of the license file.

cch Number of characters in *pszLicFileContents*.

Remarks

Call this function to verify that the license file named by *pszLicFileName* is valid for the OLE control. If *cch* is –1, this function uses:

```
_tcslen(pszLicFileContents)
```

See Also: COleObjectFactory::VerifyUserLicense

AfxWinInit

BOOL AFXAPI AfxWinInit(HINSTANCE *hInstance,*
↳ **HINSTANCE** *hPrevInstance,* **LPTSTR** *lpCmdLine,* **int** *nCmdShow* **)**

Parameters

hInstance   The handle of the currently running module.

hPrevInstance   A handle to a previous instance of the application. For a Win32-based application, this parameter is always **NULL**.

lpCmdLine   Points to a null-terminated string specifying the command line for the application.

nCmdShow   Specifies how the main window of a GUI application would be shown.

Remarks

This function is called by the MFC-supplied **WinMain** function, as part of the **CWinApp** initialization of a GUI-based application, to initialize MFC. For a console application, which does not use the MFC-supplied **WinMain** function, you must call **AfxWinInit** directly to initialize MFC.

If you call **AfxWinInit** yourself, you should declare an instance of a **CWinApp** class. For a console application, you might choose not to derive your own class from **CWinApp** and instead use an instance of **CWinApp** directly. This technique is appropriate if you decide to leave all functionality for your application in your implementation of **main**.

The TEAR sample shows how to make a console application using MFC.

Example

```
// this file must be compiled with the /GX and /MT options:
//    cl /GX /MT thisfile.cpp

#include <afx.h>
#include <afxdb.h>
#include <iostream.h>

int main()
{
   // try to initialize MFC

   if (!AfxWinInit(::GetModuleHandle(NULL), NULL, ::GetCommandLine(), 0))
   {
      cerr << "MFC failed to initialize!" << endl;
      return 1;
   }

   // try to connect to an ODBC database that doesn't exist
   // (this wouldn't work at all without initializing MFC)
```

```
CDatabase db;
try
{
    db.Open("This Databsae Doesn't Exist");

    // we shouldn't realistically get here

    cout << "Successful!" << endl;
    cout << "Closing ... ";
    db.Close();
    cout << "Closed!" << endl;
}
catch (CDBException* pEx)
{
    // we got an exception! print an error message
    // (this wouldn't work without initializing MFC)

    char sz[1024];

    cout << "Error: ";
    if (pEx->GetErrorMessage(sz, 1024))
        cout << sz;
    else
        cout << "No error message was available";
    cout << endl;

    pEx->Delete();
    return 1;
}

return 0;
}
```

See Also: **CWinApp**, "CWinApp: The Application Class" online, **main**, **WinMain**

AND_CATCH

AND_CATCH(*exception_class*, *exception_object_pointer_name* **)**

Parameters

exception_class   Specifies the exception type to test for. For a list of standard exception classes, see class **CException**.

exception_object_pointer_name   A name for an exception-object pointer that will be created by the macro. You can use the pointer name to access the exception object within the **AND_CATCH** block. This variable is declared for you.

Remarks

Defines a block of code for catching additional exception types thrown in a preceding **TRY** block. Use the **CATCH** macro to catch one exception type, then the

AND_CATCH macro to catch each subsequent type. End the **TRY** block with an **END_CATCH** macro.

The exception-processing code can interrogate the exception object, if appropriate, to get more information about the specific cause of the exception. Call the **THROW_LAST** macro within the **AND_CATCH** block to shift processing to the next outer exception frame. **AND_CATCH** marks the end of the preceding **CATCH** or **AND_CATCH** block.

Note The **AND_CATCH** block is defined as a C++ scope (delineated by curly braces). If you declare variables in this scope, remember that they are accessible only within that scope. This also applies to the *exception_object_pointer_name* variable.

See Also: TRY, CATCH, END_CATCH, THROW, THROW_LAST, AND_CATCH_ALL, CException

---

AND_CATCH_ALL

AND_CATCH_ALL(*exception_object_pointer_name*)

Parameters

exception_object_pointer_name   A name for an exception-object pointer that will be created by the macro. You can use the pointer name to access the exception object within the **AND_CATCH_ALL** block. This variable is declared for you.

Remarks

Defines a block of code for catching additional exception types thrown in a preceding **TRY** block. Use the **CATCH** macro to catch one exception type, then the **AND_CATCH_ALL** macro to catch all other subsequent types. If you use **AND_CATCH_ALL**, end the **TRY** block with an **END_CATCH_ALL** macro.

The exception-processing code can interrogate the exception object, if appropriate, to get more information about the specific cause of the exception. Call the **THROW_LAST** macro within the **AND_CATCH_ALL** block to shift processing to the next outer exception frame. **AND_CATCH_ALL** marks the end of the preceding **CATCH** or **AND_CATCH_ALL** block.

Note The **AND_CATCH_ALL** block is defined as a C++ scope (delineated by curly braces). If you declare variables in this scope, remember that they are accessible only within that scope.

See Also: TRY, CATCH_ALL, END_CATCH_ALL, THROW, THROW_LAST, AND_CATCH, CException

ASSERT

ASSERT(*booleanExpression*)

Parameters

booleanExpression   Specifies an expression (including pointer values) that evaluates
to nonzero or 0.

Remarks

Evaluates its argument. If the result is 0, the macro prints a diagnostic message and
aborts the program. If the condition is nonzero, it does nothing.

The diagnostic message has the form

```
assertion failed in file <name> in line <num>
```

where *name* is the name of the source file, and *num* is the line number of the assertion
that failed in the source file.

In the Release version of MFC, **ASSERT** does not evaluate the expression and thus
will not interrupt the program. If the expression must be evaluated regardless of
environment, use the **VERIFY** macro in place of **ASSERT**.

Note   This function is available only in the Debug version of MFC.

Example

```
// example for ASSERT
CAge* pcage = new CAge( 21 ); // CAge is derived from CObject.
ASSERT( pcage!= NULL )
ASSERT( pcage->IsKindOf( RUNTIME_CLASS( CAge ) ) )
// Terminates program only if pcage is NOT a CAge*.
```

See Also: VERIFY

ASSERT_KINDOF

ASSERT_KINDOF(*classname*, *pobject*)

Parameters

classname   The name of a **CObject**-derived class.

pobject   A pointer to a class object.

Remarks

This macro asserts that the object pointed to is an object of the specified class, or is an
object of a class derived from the specified class. The *pobject* parameter should be a
pointer to an object and can be **const**. The object pointed to and the class must support
CObject run-time class information. As an example, to ensure that pDocument is a
pointer to an object of the CMyDocument class, or any of its derivatives, you could
code:

```
ASSERT_KINDOF(CMyDocument, pDocument)
```

Using the **ASSERT_KINDOF** macro is exactly the same as coding:

```
ASSERT(pobject->IsKindOf(RUNTIME_CLASS(classname)));
```

This function works only for classes declared with the **DECLARE_DYNAMIC** or **DECLARE_SERIAL** macro.

Note   This function is available only in the Debug version of MFC.

See Also: ASSERT

ASSERT_VALID

ASSERT_VALID(*pObject* **)**

Parameters

pObject   Specifies an object of a class derived from **CObject** that has an overriding version of the **AssertValid** member function.

Remarks

Use to test your assumptions about the validity of an object's internal state. **ASSERT_VALID** calls the **AssertValid** member function of the object passed as its argument.

In the Release version of MFC, **ASSERT_VALID** does nothing. In the Debug version, it validates the pointer, checks against **NULL**, and calls the object's own **AssertValid** member functions. If any of these tests fails, this displays an alert message in the same manner as **ASSERT**.

Note   This function is available only in the Debug version of MFC.

For more information and examples, see "MFC Debugging Support" in *Visual C++ Programmer's Guide* online.

See Also: ASSERT, VERIFY, CObject, CObject::AssertValid

BASED_CODE

Remarks

Under Win32, this macro expands to nothing and is provided for backward compatibility. Under 16-bit MFC, the macro ensures that data will be placed in the code segment rather than in the data segment. The result is less impact on your data segment.

BEGIN_CONNECTION_MAP

BEGIN_CONNECTION_MAP(*theClass*, *theBase*)

Parameters

theClass   Specifies the name of the control class whose connection map this is.

theBase   Specifies the name of the base class of *theClass*.

Remarks

Each **COleControl**-derived class in your program can provide a connection map to specify connection points that your control will support. In the implementation (.CPP) file that defines the member functions for your class, start the connection map with the **BEGIN_CONNECTION_MAP** macro, then add macro entries for each of your connection points using the **CONNECTION_PART** macro. Finally, complete the connection map with the **END_CONNECTION_MAP** macro.

See Also: BEGIN_CONNECTION_PART, DECLARE_CONNECTION_MAP

BEGIN_CONNECTION_PART

BEGIN_CONNECTION_PART(*theClass*, *localClass*)

Parameters

theClass   Specifies the name of the control class whose connection point this is.

localClass   Specifies the name of the local class that implements the connection point.

Remarks

Use the **BEGIN_CONNECTION_PART** macro to begin the definition of additional connection points beyond the event and property notification connection points.

In the declaration (.H) file that defines the member functions for your class, start the connection point with the **BEGIN_CONNECTION_PART** macro, then add the **CONNECTION_IID** macro and any other member functions you wish to implement, and complete the connection point map with the **END_CONNECTION_PART** macro.

See Also: BEGIN_CONNECTION_MAP, END_CONNECTION_PART, DECLARE_CONNECTION_MAP

BEGIN_DISPATCH_MAP

BEGIN_DISPATCH_MAP(*theClass*, *baseClass* **)**

#include <afxdisp.h>

Parameters

theClass   Specifies the name of the class that owns this dispatch map.

baseClass   Specifies the base class name of *theClass*.

Remarks

Use the **BEGIN_DISPATCH_MAP** macro to declare the definition of your dispatch map.

In the implementation (.CPP) file that defines the member functions for your class, start the dispatch map with the **BEGIN_DISPATCH_MAP** macro, add macro entries for each of your dispatch functions and properties, and complete the dispatch map with the **END_DISPATCH_MAP** macro.

See Also: DECLARE_DISPATCH_MAP, END_DISPATCH_MAP, DISP_FUNCTION, DISP_PROPERTY, DISP_PROPERTY_EX, DISP_DEFVALUE

BEGIN_EVENT_MAP

BEGIN_EVENT_MAP(*theClass*, *baseClass* **)**

Parameters

theClass   Specifies the name of the control class whose event map this is.

baseClass   Specifies the name of the base class of *theClass*.

Remarks

Use the **BEGIN_EVENT_MAP** macro to begin the definition of your event map.

In the implementation (.CPP) file that defines the member functions for your class, start the event map with the **BEGIN_EVENT_MAP** macro, then add macro entries for each of your events, and complete the event map with the **END_EVENT_MAP** macro.

For more information on event maps and the **BEGIN_EVENT_MAP** macro, see the article "ActiveX Controls: Events" in *Visual C++ Programmer's Guide* online.

See Also: DECLARE_EVENT_MAP, END_EVENT_MAP

BEGIN_EVENTSINK_MAP

BEGIN_EVENTSINK_MAP(*theClass*, *baseClass* **)**

Parameters

theClass   Specifies the name of the control class whose event sink map this is.

baseClass   Specifies the name of the base class of *theClass*.

Remarks

Use the **BEGIN_EVENTSINK_MAP** macro to begin the definition of your event sink map.

In the implementation (.CPP) file that defines the member functions for your class, start the event sink map with the **BEGIN_EVENTSINK_MAP** macro, then add macro entries for each event to be notified of, and complete the event sink map with the **END_EVENTSINK_MAP** macro.

For more information on event sink maps and OLE control containers, see the article "ActiveX Control Containers" in *Visual C++ Programmer's Guide* online.

See Also: DECLARE_EVENTSINK_MAP, END_EVENTSINK_MAP

BEGIN_MESSAGE_MAP

BEGIN_MESSAGE_MAP(*theClass*, *baseClass* **)**

Parameters

theClass   Specifies the name of the class whose message map this is.

baseClass   Specifies the name of the base class of *theClass*.

Remarks

Use the **BEGIN_MESSAGE_MAP** macro to begin the definition of your message map.

In the implementation (.CPP) file that defines the member functions for your class, start the message map with the **BEGIN_MESSAGE_MAP** macro, then add macro entries for each of your message-handler functions, and complete the message map with the **END_MESSAGE_MAP** macro.

For more information on message maps and the **BEGIN_MESSAGE_MAP** macro, see "Adding a Dialog Box" in *Visual C++ Tutorials* online.

Example

```
// example for BEGIN_MESSAGE_MAP
BEGIN_MESSAGE_MAP( CMyWindow, CFrameWnd )
    //{{AFX_MSG_MAP( CMyWindow )
    ON_WM_PAINT()
    ON_COMMAND( IDM_ABOUT, OnAbout )
    //}}AFX_MSG_MAP
END_MESSAGE_MAP( )
```

See Also: **DECLARE_MESSAGE_MAP, END_MESSAGE_MAP**

BEGIN_OLEFACTORY

BEGIN_OLEFACTORY(*class_name*)

Parameters

class_name   Specifies the name of the control class whose class factory this is.

Remarks

In the header file of your control class, use the **BEGIN_OLEFACTORY** macro to begin the declaration of your class factory. Declarations of class factory licensing functions should begin immediately after **BEGIN_OLEFACTORY**.

See Also: **END_OLEFACTORY, DECLARE_OLECREATE_EX**

BEGIN_PARSE_MAP

BEGIN_PARSE_MAP(*theClass*, *baseClass*)

Parameters

theClass   Specifies the name of the class that owns this parse map.

baseClass   Specifies the base class name of *theClass*. Must be a class derived from **CHttpServer**.

Remarks

Use the **BEGIN_PARSE_MAP** macro to begin the definition of your parse map.

When a client command is received by a **CHttpServer** object, the parse maps associate the command to its class member function and parameters. Only one parse map is created per **CHttpServer** object.

In the implementation (.CPP) file that defines the member functions for your class, start the parse map with the **BEGIN_PARSE_MAP** macro, add macro entries for each of your parse functions and properties, and complete the parse map with the **END_PARSE_MAP** macro.

See **ON_PARSE_COMMAND** for a parse map example.

See Also: **ON_PARSE_COMMAND, ON_PARSE_COMMAND_PARAMS, DEFAULT_PARSE_COMMAND, END_PARSE_MAP, CHttpServer**

BEGIN_PROPPAGEIDS

BEGIN_PROPPAGEIDS(*class_name*, *count* **)**

Parameters

class_name   The name of the control class for which property pages are being specified.

count   The number of property pages used by the control class.

Remarks

Use the **BEGIN_PROPPAGEIDS** macro to begin the definition of your control's list of property page IDs.

In the implementation (.CPP) file that defines the member functions for your class, start the property page list with the **BEGIN_PROPPAGEIDS** macro, then add macro entries for each of your property pages, and complete the property page list with the **END_PROPPAGEIDS** macro.

For more information on property pages, see the article "ActiveX Controls: Property Pages" in *Visual C++ Programmer's Guide* online.

See Also: END_PROPPAGEIDS, DECLARE_PROPPAGEIDS, PROPPAGEID

CATCH

CATCH(*exception_class*, *exception_object_pointer_name* **)**

Parameters

exception_class   Specifies the exception type to test for. For a list of standard exception classes, see class **CException**.

exception_object_pointer_name   Specifies a name for an exception-object pointer that will be created by the macro. You can use the pointer name to access the exception object within the **CATCH** block. This variable is declared for you.

Remarks

Use this macro to define a block of code that catches the first exception type thrown in the preceding **TRY** block. The exception-processing code can interrogate the exception object, if appropriate, to get more information about the specific cause of the exception. Invoke the **THROW_LAST** macro to shift processing to the next outer exception frame. End the **TRY** block with an **END_CATCH** macro.

If *exception_class* is the class **CException**, then all exception types will be caught. You can use the **CObject::IsKindOf** member function to determine which specific exception was thrown. A better way to catch several kinds of exceptions is to use sequential **AND_CATCH** statements, each with a different exception type.

The exception object pointer is created by the macro. You do not need to declare it yourself.

Note The **CATCH** block is defined as a C++ scope (delineated by curly braces). If you declare variables in this scope, remember that they are accessible only within that scope. This also applies to *exception_object_pointer_name*.

For more information on exceptions and the **CATCH** macro, see the article "Exceptions" in *Visual C++ Programmer's Guide* online.

See Also: **TRY, AND_CATCH, END_CATCH, THROW, THROW_LAST, CATCH_ALL, CException**

CATCH_ALL

CATCH_ALL(*exception_object_pointer_name* **)**

Parameters

exception_object_pointer_name   Specifies a name for an exception-object pointer that will be created by the macro. You can use the pointer name to access the exception object within the **CATCH_ALL** block. This variable is declared for you.

Remarks

Use this macro to define a block of code that catches all exception types thrown in the preceding **TRY** block. The exception-processing code can interrogate the exception object, if appropriate, to get more information about the specific cause of the exception. Invoke the **THROW_LAST** macro to shift processing to the next outer exception frame. If you use **CATCH_ALL**, end the **TRY** block with an **END_CATCH_ALL** macro.

Note The **CATCH_ALL** block is defined as a C++ scope (delineated by curly braces). If you declare variables in this scope, remember that they are accessible only within that scope.

For more information on exceptions, see the article "Exceptions" in *Visual C++ Programmer's Guide* online.

See Also: **TRY, AND_CATCH_ALL, END_CATCH_ALL, THROW, THROW_LAST, CATCH, CException**

CompareElements

template< class *TYPE*, **class** *ARG_TYPE* >
  ↪ **BOOL AFXAPI CompareElements(const** *TYPE** *pElement1*,
  ↪ **const** *ARG_TYPE** *pElement2* **);**

Return Value

Nonzero if the object pointed to by *pElement1* is equal to the object pointed to by *pElement2*; otherwise 0.

Parameters

TYPE   The type of the first element to be compared.

pElement1   Pointer to the first element to be compared.

ARG_TYPE   The type of the second element to be compared.

pElement2   Pointer to the second element to be compared.

Remarks

This function is called directly by **CList::Find** and indirectly by **CMap::Lookup** and **CMap::operator []**. The **CMap** calls use the **CMap** template parameters *KEY* and *ARG_KEY*.

The default implementation returns the result of the comparison of **pElement1* and **pElement2*. Override this function so that it compares the elements in a way that is appropriate for your application.

The C++ language defines the comparison operator (**==**) for simple types (**char**, **int**, **float**, and so on) but does not define a comparison operator for classes and structures. If you want to use **CompareElements** or to instantiate one of the collection classes that uses it, you must either define the comparison operator or overload **CompareElements** with a version that returns appropriate values.

See Also: CList, Cmap

ConstructElements

template< class *TYPE* >
  void AFXAPI ConstructElements(*TYPE** *pElements*, **int** *nCount* **);**

Parameters

TYPE   Template parameter specifying the type of the elements to be constructed.

pElements   Pointer to the elements.

nCount   Number of elements to be constructed.

Remarks

This function is called when new array, list, and map elements are constructed. The default version initializes all bits of the new elements to 0.

For information on implementing this and other helper functions, see the article "Collections: How to Make a Type-Safe Collection" in *Visual C++ Programmer's Guide* online.

See Also: **CArray, CList, CMap**

CopyElements

template< class *TYPE* **> void AFXAPI CopyElements (** *TYPE** *pDest*,
↪ **const** *TYPE** *pSrc*, **int** *nCount* **);**

Parameters

TYPE   Template parameter specifying the type of elements to be copied.

pDest   Pointer to the destination where the elements will be copied.

pSrc   Pointer to the source of the elements to be copied.

nCount   Number of elements to be copied.

Remarks

This function is called directly by **CArray::Append** and **CArray::Copy**. The default implementation performs a bit-wise copy.

For information on implementing this and other helper functions, see the article "Collections: How to Make a Type-Safe Collection" in *Visual C++ Programmer's Guide* online.

See Also: **CArray**

CONNECTION_IID

CONNECTION_IID(*iid* **)**

Parameters

iid   The interface ID of the interface called by the connection point.

Remarks

Use the **CONNECTION_IID** macro between the **BEGIN_CONNECTION_PART** and **END_CONNECTION_PART** macros to define an interface ID for a connection point supported by your OLE control.

The *iid* argument is an interface ID used to identify the interface that the connection point will call on its connected sinks. For example:

```
CONNECTION_IID(IID_ISinkInterface)
```

specifies a connection point that calls the ISinkInterface interface.

See Also: **BEGIN_CONNECTION_PART, DECLARE_CONNECTION_MAP, END_CONNECTION_PART**

CONNECTION_PART

CONNECTION_PART(*theClass*, *iid*, *localClass*)

Parameters

theClass   Specifies the name of the control class whose connection point this is.

iid   The interface ID of the interface called by the connection point.

localClass   Specifies the name of the local class that implements the connection point.

Remarks

Use the **CONNECTION_PART** macro to map a connection point for your OLE control to a specific interface ID.

For example:

```
BEGIN_CONNECTION_MAP(CSampleCtrl, COleControl)
    CONNECTION_PART(CSampleCtrl, IID_ISinkInterface, MyConnPt)
END_CONNECTION_MAP()
```

implements a connection map, with a connection point, that calls the IID_ISinkInterface interface .

See Also: BEGIN_CONNECTION_PART, DECLARE_CONNECTION_MAP, BEGIN_CONNECTION_MAP, CONNECTION_IID

DDP_CBIndex

void AFXAPI DDP_CBIndex(CDataExchange* *pDX***, int** *id***,**
  ↪ **int&** *member***, LPCTSTR** *pszPropName* **);**

Parameters

pDX   Pointer to a **CDataExchange** object. The framework supplies this object to establish the context of the data exchange, including its direction.

id   The resource ID of the combo box control associated with the control property specified by *pszPropName*.

member   The member variable associated with the property page control specified by *id* and the property specified by *pszPropName*.

pszPropName   The property name of the control property to be exchanged with the combo box control specified by *id*.

Remarks

Call this function in your property page's DoDataExchange function to synchronize the value of an integer property with the index of the current selection in a combo box on the property page. This function should be called before the corresponding **DDX_CBIndex** function call.

See Also: **DDP_CBString**, **DDP_Text**, **COleControl::DoPropExchange**,
DDX_CBIndex

DDP_CBString

void AFXAPI DDP_CBString(CDataExchange* *pDX***, int** *id***, CString&** *member***,**
↪ **LPCTSTR** *pszPropName* **);**

Parameters

   pDX   Pointer to a **CDataExchange** object. The framework supplies this object to
   establish the context of the data exchange, including its direction.

   id   The resource ID of the combo box control associated with the control property
   specified by *pszPropName*.

   member   The member variable associated with the property page control specified by
   id and the property specified by *pszPropName*.

   pszPropName   The property name of the control property to be exchanged with the
   combo box string specified by *id*.

Remarks

   Call this function in your property page's DoDataExchange function to synchronize the
   value of a string property with the current selection in a combo box on the property
   page. This function should be called before the corresponding **DDX_CBString**
   function call.

   See Also: **DDP_CBStringExact**, **DDP_CBIndex**,
   COleControl::DoPropExchange, **DDX_CBString**

DDP_CBStringExact

void AFXAPI DDP_CBStringExact(CDataExchange* *pDX***, int** *id***,**
↪ **CString&** *member***, LPCTSTR** *pszPropName* **);**

Parameters

   pDX   Pointer to a **CDataExchange** object. The framework supplies this object to
   establish the context of the data exchange, including its direction.

   id   The resource ID of the combo box control associated with the control property
   specified by *pszPropName*.

   member   The member variable associated with the property page control specified by
   id and the property specified by *pszPropName*.

   pszPropName   The property name of the control property to be exchanged with the
   combo box string specified by *id*.

Remarks

Call this function in your property page's `DoDataExchange` function to synchronize the value of a string property that exactly matches the current selection in a combo box on the property page. This function should be called before the corresponding **DDX_CBStringExact** function call.

See Also: **DDP_CBString**, **DDP_CBIndex**, **COleControl::DoPropExchange**, **DDX_CBStringExact**

DDP_Check

void AFXAPI DDP_Check(CDataExchange**pDX***, int** *id***, int &***member***,**
↪ **LPCSTR** *pszPropName* **);**

Parameters

pDX Pointer to a **CDataExchange** object. The framework supplies this object to establish the context of the data exchange, including its direction.

id The resource ID of the check box control associated with the control property specified by *pszPropName*.

member The member variable associated with the property page control specified by *id* and the property specified by *pszPropName*.

pszPropName The property name of the control property to be exchanged with the check box control specified by *id*.

Remarks

Call this function in your property page's `DoDataExchange` function to synchronize the value of the property with the associated property page check box control. This function should be called before the corresponding **DDX_Check** function call.

See Also: **DDP_Radio**, **DDP_Text**, **COleControl::DoPropExchange**, **DDX_Check**

DDP_LBIndex

void AFXAPI DDP_LBIndex(CDataExchange* *pDX***, int** *id***, int&** *member***,**
↪ **LPCTSTR** *pszPropName* **);**

Parameters

pDX Pointer to a **CDataExchange** object. The framework supplies this object to establish the context of the data exchange, including its direction.

id The resource ID of the list box control associated with the control property specified by *pszPropName*.

member The member variable associated with the property page control specified by *id* and the property specified by *pszPropName*.

> *pszPropName*   The property name of the control property to be exchanged with the list box string specified by *id*.

Remarks

Call this function in your property page's `DoDataExchange` function to synchronize the value of an integer property with the index of the current selection in a list box on the property page. This function should be called before the corresponding **DDX_LBIndex** function call.

See Also: **DDP_LBString, DDP_CBIndex, COleControl::DoPropExchange, DDX_LBIndex**

DDP_LBString

> **void AFXAPI DDP_LBString(CDataExchange*** *pDX*, **int** *id*,
> ↪ **CString&** *member*, **LPCTSTR** *pszPropName* **);**

Parameters

> *pDX*   Pointer to a **CDataExchange** object. The framework supplies this object to establish the context of the data exchange, including its direction.

> *id*   The resource ID of the list box control associated with the control property specified by *pszPropName*.

> *member*   The member variable associated with the property page control specified by *id* and the property specified by *pszPropName*.

> *pszPropName*   The property name of the control property to be exchanged with the list box string specified by *id*.

Remarks

Call this function in your property page's `DoDataExchange` function to synchronize the value of a string property with the current selection in a list box on the property page. This function should be called before the corresponding **DDX_LBString** function call.

See Also: **DDP_LBStringExact, DDP_LBIndex, COleControl::DoPropExchange, DDX_LBString**

DDP_LBStringExact

> **void AFXAPI DDP_LBStringExact(CDataExchange*** *pDX*, **int** *id*,
> ↪ **CString&** *member*, **LPCTSTR** *pszPropName* **);**

Parameters

> *pDX*   Pointer to a **CDataExchange** object. The framework supplies this object to establish the context of the data exchange, including its direction.

id   The resource ID of the list box control associated with the control property specified by *pszPropName*.

member   The member variable associated with the property page control specified by *id* and the property specified by *pszPropName*.

pszPropName   The property name of the control property to be exchanged with the list box string specified by *id*.

Remarks

Call this function in your property page's `DoDataExchange` function to synchronize the value of a string property that exactly matches the current selection in a list box on the property page. This function should be called before the corresponding **DDX_LBStringExact** function call.

See Also: **DDP_LBString**, **DDP_LBIndex**, **COleControl::DoPropExchange**, **DDX_LBStringExact**

DDP_PostProcessing

void AFXAPI DDP_PostProcessing(CDataExchange **pDX* **);**

Parameters

pDX   Pointer to a **CDataExchange** object. The framework supplies this object to establish the context of the data exchange, including its direction.

Remarks

Call this function in your property page's **DoDataExchange** function, to finish the transfer of property values from the property page to your control when property values are being saved.

This function should be called after all data exchange functions are completed. For example:

```
void CSamplePage::DoDataExchange(CDataExchange* pDX)
{
    //{{AFX_DATA_MAP(CSpindialPropPage)
    DDP_Text(pDX, IDC_POSITIONEDIT, m_NeedlePosition,
        _T("NeedlePosition"));
    DDX_Text(pDX, IDC_POSITIONEDIT, m_NeedlePosition);
    DDV_MinMaxInt(pDX, m_NeedlePosition, 0, 3);
    //}}AFX_DATA_MAP
    DDP_PostProcessing(pDX);
}
```

See Also: **COleControl::DoPropExchange**

DDP_Radio

> **void AFXAPI DDP_Radio(CDataExchange****pDX*, **int** *id*, **int &***member*,
> ↪ **LPCTSTR** *pszPropName*);

Parameters

pDX   Pointer to a **CDataExchange** object. The framework supplies this object to establish the context of the data exchange, including its direction.

id   The resource ID of the radio button control associated with the control property specified by *pszPropName*.

member   The member variable associated with the property page control specified by *id* and the property specified by *pszPropName*.

pszPropName   The property name of the control property to be exchanged with the radio button control specified by *id*.

Remarks

Call this function in your control's `DoPropExchange` function to synchronize the value of the property with the associated property page radio button control. This function should be called before the corresponding **DDX_Radio** function call.

See Also: DDP_Check, DDP_Text, COleControl::DoPropExchange, DDX_Radio

---

DDP_Text

> **void AFXAPI DDP_Text(CDataExchange****pDX*, **int** *id*, **BYTE &***member*,
> ↪ **LPCTSTR** *pszPropName*);
> **void AFXAPI DDP_Text(CDataExchange****pDX*, **int** *id*, **int &***member*,
> ↪ **LPCTSTR** *pszPropName*);
> **void AFXAPI DDP_Text(CDataExchange****pDX*, **int** *id*, **UINT &***member*,
> ↪ **LPCTSTR** *pszPropName*);
> **void AFXAPI DDP_Text(CDataExchange****pDX*, **int** *id*, **long &***member*,
> ↪ **LPCTSTR** *pszPropName*);
> **void AFXAPI DDP_Text(CDataExchange****pDX*, **int** *id*, **DWORD &***member*,
> ↪ **LPCTSTR** *pszPropName*);
> **void AFXAPI DDP_Text(CDataExchange****pDX*, **int** *id*, **float &***member*,
> ↪ **LPCTSTR** *pszPropName*);
> **void AFXAPI DDP_Text(CDataExchange****pDX*, **int** *id*, **double &***member*,
> ↪ **LPCTSTR** *pszPropName*);
> **void AFXAPI DDP_Text(CDataExchange****pDX*, **int** *id*, **CString &***member*,
> ↪ **LPCTSTR** *pszPropName*);

Parameters

pDX   Pointer to a **CDataExchange** object. The framework supplies this object to establish the context of the data exchange, including its direction.

id   The resource ID of the control associated with the control property specified by *pszPropName*.

member   The member variable associated with the property page control specified by *id* and the property specified by *pszPropName*.

pszPropName   The property name of the control property to be exchanged with the control specified by *id*.

Remarks

Call this function in your control's `DoDataExchange` function to synchronize the value of the property with the associated property page control. This function should be called before the corresponding **DDX_Text** function call.

See Also: **DDP_Check**, **DDP_Radio**, **COleControl::DoPropExchange**, **DDX_Text**

DDV_MaxChars

> **void AFXAPI DDV_MaxChars(CDataExchange*** *pDX*, **CString**
> ↪ **const&** *value*, **int** *nChars* **);**

Parameters

pDX   A pointer to a **CDataExchange** object. The framework supplies this object to establish the context of the data exchange, including its direction.

value   A reference to a member variable of the dialog box, form view, or control view object with which data is validated.

nChars   Maximum number of characters allowed.

Remarks

Call **DDV_MaxChars** to verify that the amount of characters in the control associated with *value* does not exceed *nChars*.

For more information about DDV, see "Adding a Dialog Box" in *Visual C++ Tutorials* online and "Dialog Data Exchange and Validation" in *Visual C++ Programmer's Guide* online.

DDV_MinMaxByte

> **void AFXAPI DDV_MinMaxByte(CDataExchange*** *pDX*, **BYTE** *value*,
> ↪ **BYTE** *minVal*, **BYTE** *maxVal* **);**

Parameters

pDX   A pointer to a **CDataExchange** object. The framework supplies this object to establish the context of the data exchange, including its direction.

value   A reference to a member variable of the dialog box, form view, or control view object with which data is validated.

minVal   Minimum value (of type **BYTE**) allowed.

maxVal   Maximum value (of type **BYTE**) allowed.

Remarks

Call **DDV_MinMaxByte** to verify that the value in the control associated with *value* falls between *minVal* and *maxVal*.

For more information about DDV, see "Adding a Dialog Box" in *Visual C++ Tutorials* online and "Dialog Data Exchange and Validation" in *Visual C++ Programmer's Guide* online.

DDV_MinMaxDouble

void AFXAPI DDV_MinMaxDouble(CDataExchange* *pDX*,
↪ **double const&** *value*, **double** *minVal*, **double** *maxVal* **);**

Parameters

pDX   A pointer to a **CDataExchange** object. The framework supplies this object to establish the context of the data exchange, including its direction.

value   A reference to a member variable of the dialog box, form view, or control view object with which data is validated.

minVal   Minimum value (of type **double**) allowed.

maxVal   Maximum value (of type **double**) allowed.

Remarks

Call **DDV_MinMaxDouble** to verify that the value in the control associated with *value* falls between *minVal* and *maxVal*.

For more information about DDV, see "Adding a Dialog Box" in *Visual C++ Tutorials* online and "Dialog Data Exchange and Validation" in *Visual C++ Programmer's Guide* online.

DDV_MinMaxDWord

void AFXAPI DDV_MinMaxDWord(CDataExchange* *pDX*,
↪ **DWORD const&** *value*, **DWORD** *minVal*, **DWORD** *maxVal* **);**

Parameters

pDX   A pointer to a **CDataExchange** object. The framework supplies this object to establish the context of the data exchange, including its direction.

value   A reference to a member variable of the dialog box, form view, or control view object with which data is validated.

minVal   Minimum value (of type **DWORD**) allowed.

maxVal   Maximum value (of type **DWORD**) allowed.

Remarks

Call **DDV_MinMaxDWord** to verify that the value in the control associated with *value* falls between *minVal* and *maxVal*.

For more information about DDV, see "Adding a Dialog Box" in *Visual C++ Tutorials* online and "Dialog Data Exchange and Validation" in *Visual C++ Programmer's Guide* online.

DDV_MinMaxFloat

void AFXAPI DDV_MinMaxFloat(CDataExchange* *pDX***, float** *value***,**
↳ **float** *minVal***, float** *maxVal* **);**

Parameters

pDX   A pointer to a **CDataExchange** object. The framework supplies this object to establish the context of the data exchange, including its direction.

value   A reference to a member variable of the dialog box, form view, or control view object with which data is validated.

minVal   Minimum value (of type **float**) allowed.

maxVal   Maximum value (of type **float**) allowed.

Remarks

Call **DDV_MinMaxFloat** to verify that the value in the control associated with *value* falls between *minVal* and *maxVal*.

For more information about DDV, see "Adding a Dialog Box" in *Visual C++ Tutorials* online and "Dialog Data Exchange and Validation" in *Visual C++ Programmer's Guide* online.

DDV_MinMaxInt

void AFXAPI DDV_MinMaxInt(CDataExchange* *pDX***, int** *value***,**
↳ **int** *minVal***, int** *maxVal* **);**

Parameters

pDX   A pointer to a **CDataExchange** object. The framework supplies this object to establish the context of the data exchange, including its direction.

value   A reference to a member variable of the dialog box, form view, or control view object with which data is validated.

minVal   Minimum value (of type **int**) allowed.

maxVal   Maximum value (of type **int**) allowed.

Remarks

Call **DDV_MinMaxInt** to verify that the value in the control associated with *value* falls between *minVal* and *maxVal*.

For more information about DDV, see "Adding a Dialog Box" in *Visual C++ Tutorials* online and "Dialog Data Exchange and Validation" in *Visual C++ Programmer's Guide* online.

DDV_MinMaxLong

void AFXAPI DDV_MinMaxLong(CDataExchange* *pDX*, **long** *value*,
↪ **long** *minVal*, **long** *maxVal* **);**

Parameters

pDX   A pointer to a **CDataExchange** object. The framework supplies this object to establish the context of the data exchange, including its direction.

value   A reference to a member variable of the dialog box, form view, or control view object with which data is validated.

minVal   Minimum value (of type **long**) allowed.

maxVal   Maximum value (of type **long**) allowed.

Remarks

Call **DDV_MinMaxLong** to verify that the value in the control associated with *value* falls between *minVal* and *maxVal*.

For more information about DDV, see "Adding a Dialog Box" in *Visual C++ Tutorials* online and "Dialog Data Exchange and Validation" in *Visual C++ Programmer's Guide* online.

DDV_MinMaxUnsigned

void AFXAPI DDV_MinMaxUnsigned(CDataExchange* *pDX*,
↪ **unsigned** *value*, **unsigned** *minVal*, **unsigned** *maxVal* **);**

Parameters

pDX   A pointer to a **CDataExchange** object. The framework supplies this object to establish the context of the data exchange, including its direction.

value   A reference to a member variable of the dialog box, form view, or control view object with which data is validated.

minVal   Minimum value (of type **unsigned**) allowed.

maxVal   Maximum value (of type **unsigned**) allowed.

Remarks

Call **DDV_MinMaxUnsigned** to verify that the value in the control associated with *value* falls between *minVal* and *maxVal*.

For more information about DDV, see "Adding a Dialog Box" in *Visual C++ Tutorials* online and "Dialog Data Exchange and Validation" in *Visual C++ Programmer's Guide* online.

DDX_CBIndex

void AFXAPI DDX_CBIndex(CDataExchange* *pDX***, int** *nIDC***, int&** *index* **);**

Parameters

pDX　A pointer to a **CDataExchange** object. The framework supplies this object to establish the context of the data exchange, including its direction.

nIDC　The resource ID of the combo box control associated with the control property.

index　A reference to a member variable of the dialog box, form view, or control view object with which data is exchanged.

Remarks

The **DDX_CBIndex** function manages the transfer of **int** data between a combo box control in a dialog box, form view, or control view object and a **int** data member of the dialog box, form view, or control view object.

When **DDX_CBIndex** is called, *index* is set to the index of the current combo box selection. If no item is selected, *index* is set to 0.

For more information about DDX, see "Adding a Dialog Box" in *Visual C++ Tutorials* online and "Dialog Data Exchange and Validation" in *Visual C++ Programmer's Guide* online.

See Also:　**DDP_CBIndex**

DDX_CBString

void AFXAPI DDX_CBString(CDataExchange* *pDX***, int** *nIDC***, CString&** *value* **);**

Parameters

pDX　A pointer to a **CDataExchange** object. The framework supplies this object to establish the context of the data exchange, including its direction.

nIDC　The resource ID of the combo box control associated with the control property.

value　A reference to a member variable of the dialog box, form view, or control view object with which data is exchanged.

Remarks

The **DDX_CBString** function manages the transfer of **CString** data between the edit control of a combo box control in a dialog box, form view, or control view object and a **CString** data member of the dialog box, form view, or control view object.

When **DDX_CBString** is called, *value* is set to the current combo box selection. If no item is selected, *value* is set to a string of zero length.

Note If the combo box is a drop-down list box, the value exchanged is limited to 255 characters.

For more information about DDX, see "Adding a Dialog Box" in *Visual C++ Tutorials* online and "Dialog Data Exchange and Validation" in *Visual C++ Programmer's Guide* online.

See Also: DDP_CBString

DDX_CBStringExact

void AFXAPI DDX_CBStringExact(CDataExchange* *pDX*, **int** *nIDC*,
  ↪ **CString&** *value* **);**

Parameters

pDX A pointer to a **CDataExchange** object. The framework supplies this object to establish the context of the data exchange, including its direction.

nIDC The resource ID of the combo box control associated with the control property.

value A reference to a member variable of the dialog box, form view, or control view object with which data is exchanged.

Remarks

The **DDX_CBStringExact** function manages the transfer of **CString** data between the edit control of a combo box control in a dialog box, form view, or control view object and a **CString** data member of the dialog box, form view, or control view object.

When **DDX_CBStringExact** is called, *value* is set to the current combo box selection. If no item is selected, *value* is set to a string of zero length.

Note If the combo box is a drop-down list box, the value exchanged is limited to 255 characters.

For more information about DDX, see "Adding a Dialog Box" in *Visual C++ Tutorials* online and "Dialog Data Exchange and Validation" in *Visual C++ Programmer's Guide* online.

See Also: DDP_CBStringExact

DDX_Check

void AFXAPI DDX_Check(CDataExchange* *pDX***, int** *nIDC***, int&** *value* **);**

Parameters

pDX   A pointer to a **CDataExchange** object. The framework supplies this object to establish the context of the data exchange, including its direction.

nIDC   The resource ID of the check box control associated with the control property.

value   A reference to a member variable of the dialog box, form view, or control view object with which data is exchanged.

Remarks

The **DDX_Check** function manages the transfer of **int** data between a check box control in a dialog box, form view, or control view object and a **int** data member of the dialog box, form view, or control view object.

When **DDX_Check** is called, *value* is set to the current state of the check box control.

For more information about DDX, see "Adding a Dialog Box" in *Visual C++ Tutorials* online and "Dialog Data Exchange and Validation" in *Visual C++ Programmer's Guide* online.

See Also: DDP_Check

DDX_Control

void AFXAPI DDX_Control(CDataExchange* *pDX***, int** *nIDC***, CWnd&** *rControl* **);**

Parameters

pDX   A pointer to a **CDataExchange** object. The framework supplies this object to establish the context of the data exchange, including its direction.

nIDC   The resource ID of the subclassed control associated with the control property.

rControl   A reference to a member variable of the dialog box, form view, or control view object with which data is exchanged.

Remarks

The **DDX_Control** function manages the transfer of data between a subclassed control in a dialog box, form view, or control view object and a **CWnd** data member of the dialog box, form view, or control view object.

For more information about DDX, see "Adding a Dialog Box" in *Visual C++ Tutorials* online and "Dialog Data Exchange and Validation" in *Visual C++ Programmer's Guide* online.

DDX_FieldCBIndex

void AFXAPI DDX_FieldCBIndex(CDataExchange* *pDX*, **int** *nIDC*,
  ↳ **int&** *index*, **CRecordset*** *pRecordset* **);**
void AFXAPI DDX_FieldCBIndex(CDataExchange* *pDX*, **int** *nIDC*,
  ↳ **int&** *index*, **CDaoRecordset*** *pRecordset* **);**

Parameters

pDX A pointer to a **CDataExchange** object. The framework supplies this object to establish the context of the data exchange, including its direction.

nIDC The ID of a control in the **CRecordView** or **CDaoRecordView** object.

index A reference to a field data member in the associated **CRecordset** or **CDaoRecordset** object.

pRecordset A pointer to the **CRecordset** or **CDaoRecordset** object with which data is exchanged.

Remarks

The **DDX_FieldCBIndex** function synchronizes the index of the selected item in the list box control of a combo box control in a record view and an **int** field data member of a recordset associated with the record view. When moving data from the recordset to the control, this function sets the selection in the control based on the value specified in *index*. On a transfer from the recordset to the control, if the recordset field is Null, MFC sets the value of the index to 0. On a transfer from control to recordset, if the control is empty or if no item is selected, the recordset field is set to 0.

Use the first version if you are working with the ODBC-based classes. Use the second version if you are working with the DAO-based classes.

For more information about DDX, see "Adding a Dialog Box" in *Visual C++ Tutorials* online and "Dialog Data Exchange and Validation" in *Visual C++ Programmer's Guide* online. For examples and more information about DDX for **CRecordView** and **CDaoRecordView** fields, see the article "Record Views" in *Visual C++ Programmer's Guide* online.

Example

See **DDX_FieldText** for a general DDX_Field example. The example would be similar for **DDX_FieldCBIndex**.

See Also: DDX_FieldText, DDX_FieldRadio, DDX_FieldLBString, DDX_FieldLBStringExact, DDX_FieldCBStringExact, DDX_FieldLBIndex, DDX_FieldScroll, DDX_CBIndex

DDX_FieldCBString

void AFXAPI DDX_FieldCBString(CDataExchange* *pDX***, int** *nIDC***,**
  ↳ **CString&** *value***, CRecordset*** *pRecordset* **);**
void AFXAPI DDX_FieldCBString(CDataExchange* *pDX***, int** *nIDC***,**
  ↳ **CString&** *value***, CDaoRecordset*** *pRecordset* **);**

Parameters

pDX   A pointer to a **CDataExchange** object. The framework supplies this object to establish the context of the data exchange, including its direction.

nIDC   The ID of a control in the **CRecordView** or **CDaoRecordView** object.

value   A reference to a field data member in the associated **CRecordset** or **CDaoRecordset** object.

pRecordset   A pointer to the **CRecordset** or **CDaoRecordset** object with which data is exchanged.

Remarks

The **DDX_FieldCBString** function manages the transfer of **CString** data between the edit control of a combo box control in a record view and a **CString** field data member of a recordset associated with the record view. When moving data from the recordset to the control, this function sets the current selection in the combo box to the first row that begins with the characters in the string specified in *value*. On a transfer from the recordset to the control, if the recordset field is Null, any selection is removed from the combo box and the edit control of the combo box is set to empty. On a transfer from control to recordset, if the control is empty, the recordset field is set to Null if the field permits.

Use the first version if you are working with the ODBC-based classes. Use the second version if you are working with the DAO-based classes.

For more information about DDX, see "Adding a Dialog Box" in *Visual C++ Tutorials* online and "Dialog Data Exchange and Validation" in *Visual C++ Programmer's Guide* online. For examples and more information about DDX for **CRecordView** and **CDaoRecordView** fields, see the article "Record Views" in *Visual C++ Programmer's Guide* online.

Example

See **DDX_FieldText** for a general DDX_Field example. The example includes a call to **DDX_FieldCBString**.

See Also: DDX_FieldText, DDX_FieldRadio, DDX_FieldLBString, DDX_FieldLBStringExact, DDX_FieldCBStringExact

DDX_FieldCBStringExact

void AFXAPI DDX_FieldCBStringExact(CDataExchange* *pDX,* **int** *nIDC,*
  ↳ **CString&** *value,* **CRecordset*** *pRecordset* **);**
void AFXAPI DDX_FieldCBStringExact(CDataExchange* *pDX,* **int** *nIDC,*
  ↳ **CString&** *value,* **CDaoRecordset*** *pRecordset* **);**

Parameters

pDX A pointer to a **CDataExchange** object. The framework supplies this object to establish the context of the data exchange, including its direction.

nIDC The ID of a control in the **CRecordView** or **CDaoRecordView** object.

value A reference to a field data member in the associated **CRecordset** or **CDaoRecordset** object.

pRecordset A pointer to the **CRecordset** or **CDaoRecordset** object with which data is exchanged.

Remarks

The **DDX_FieldCBStringExact** function manages the transfer of **CString** data between the edit control of a combo box control in a record view and a **CString** field data member of a recordset associated with the record view. When moving data from the recordset to the control, this function sets the current selection in the combo box to the first row that exactly matches the string specified in *value*. On a transfer from the recordset to the control, if the recordset field is Null, any selection is removed from the combo box and the edit box of the combo box is set to empty. On a transfer from control to recordset, if the control is empty, the recordset field is set to Null.

Use the first version if you are working with the ODBC-based classes. Use the second version if you are working with the DAO-based classes.

For more information about DDX, see "Adding a Dialog Box" in *Visual C++ Tutorials* online and "Dialog Data Exchange and Validation" in *Visual C++ Programmer's Guide* online. For examples and more information about DDX for **CRecordView** and **CDaoRecordView** fields, see the article "Record Views" in *Visual C++ Programmer's Guide* online.

Example

See **DDX_FieldText** for a general DDX_Field example. Calls to **DDX_FieldCBStringExact** would be similar.

See Also: **DDX_FieldText, DDX_FieldRadio, DDX_FieldLBString, DDX_FieldLBStringExact, DDX_FieldCBString**

DDX_FieldCheck

void AFXAPI DDX_FieldCheck(CDataExchange* *pDX***, int** *nIDC***, int&** *value***,**
   ↳ **CRecordset*** *pRecordset* **);**
void AFXAPI DDX_FieldCheck(CDataExchange* *pDX***, int** *nIDC***, int&** *value***,**
   ↳ **CDaoRecordset*** *pRecordset* **);**

Parameters

pDX A pointer to a **CDataExchange** object. The framework supplies this object to establish the context of the data exchange, including its direction.

nIDC The resource ID of the check box control associated with the control property.

value A reference to a member variable of the dialog box, form view, or control view object with which data is exchanged.

pRecordset A pointer to the **CRecordset** or **CDaoRecordset** object with which data is exchanged.

Remarks

The **DDX_FieldCheck** function manages the transfer of **int** data between a check box control in a dialog box, form view, or control view object and an **int** data member of the dialog box, form view, or control view object.

When **DDX_FieldCheck** is called, *value* is set to the current state of the check box control, or the control's state is set to *value*, depending on the direction of transfer.

For more information about DDX, see "Adding a Dialog Box" in *Visual C++ Tutorials* online and "Dialog Data Exchange and Validation" in *Visual C++ Programmer's Guide* online.

See Also: **DDX_FieldText**, **DDX_FieldRadio**, **DDX_FieldLBString**, **DDX_FieldLBStringExact**, **DDX_FieldCBString**

DDX_FieldLBIndex

void AFXAPI DDX_FieldLBIndex(CDataExchange* *pDX***, int** *nIDC***, int&** *index***,**
   ↳ **CRecordset*** *pRecordset* **);**
void AFXAPI DDX_FieldLBIndex(CDataExchange* *pDX***, int** *nIDC***, int&** *index***,**
   ↳ **CDaoRecordset*** *pRecordset* **);**

Parameters

pDX A pointer to a **CDataExchange** object. The framework supplies this object to establish the context of the data exchange, including its direction.

nIDC The ID of a control in the **CRecordView** or **CDaoRecordView** object.

index A reference to a field data member in the associated **CRecordset** or **CDaoRecordset** object.

> *pRecordset*   A pointer to the **CRecordset** or **CDaoRecordset** object with which data is exchanged.

Remarks

The **DDX_FieldLBIndex** function synchronizes the index of the selected item in a list box control in a record view and an **int** field data member of a recordset associated with the record view. When moving data from the recordset to the control, this function sets the selection in the control based on the value specified in *index*. On a transfer from the recordset to the control, if the recordset field is Null, MFC sets the value of the index to 0. On a transfer from control to recordset, if the control is empty, the recordset field is set to 0.

Use the first version if you are working with the ODBC-based classes. Use the second version if you are working with the DAO-based classes.

For more information about DDX, see "Adding a Dialog Box" in *Visual C++ Tutorials* online and "Dialog Data Exchange and Validation" in *Visual C++ Programmer's Guide* online. For examples and more information about DDX for **CRecordView** and **CDaoRecordView** fields, see the article "Record Views" in *Visual C++ Programmer's Guide* online.

Example

See **DDX_FieldText** for a general DDX_Field example.

See Also: **DDX_FieldText, DDX_FieldRadio, DDX_FieldLBString, DDX_FieldLBStringExact, DDX_FieldCBStringExact, DDX_FieldCBIndex, DDX_FieldScroll, DDX_LBIndex**

DDX_FieldLBString

    void AFXAPI DDX_FieldLBString(CDataExchange* *pDX*, **int** *nIDC*,
       ↪ **CString&** *value*, **CRecordset*** *pRecordset* **);**
    void AFXAPI DDX_FieldLBString(CDataExchange* *pDX*, **int** *nIDC*,
       ↪ **CString&** *value*, **CDaoRecordset*** *pRecordset* **);**

Parameters

pDX   A pointer to a **CDataExchange** object. The framework supplies this object to establish the context of the data exchange, including its direction.

nIDC   The ID of a control in the **CRecordView** or **CDaoRecordView** object.

value   A reference to a field data member in the associated **CRecordset** or **CDaoRecordset** object.

pRecordset   A pointer to the **CRecordset** or **CDaoRecordset** object with which data is exchanged.

Remarks

The **DDX_FieldLBString** copies the current selection of a list box control in a record view to a **CString** field data member of a recordset associated with the record view. In the reverse direction, this function sets the current selection in the list box to the first row that begins with the characters in the string specified by *value*. On a transfer from the recordset to the control, if the recordset field is Null, any selection is removed from the list box. On a transfer from control to recordset, if the control is empty, the recordset field is set to Null.

Use the first version if you are working with the ODBC-based classes. Use the second version if you are working with the DAO-based classes.

For more information about DDX, see "Adding a Dialog Box" in *Visual C++ Tutorials* online and "Dialog Data Exchange and Validation" in *Visual C++ Programmer's Guide* online. For examples and more information about DDX for **CRecordView** and **CDaoRecordView** fields, see the article "Record Views" in *Visual C++ Programmer's Guide* online.

Example

See **DDX_FieldText** for a general DDX_Field example. Calls to **DDX_FieldLBString** would be similar.

See Also: DDX_FieldText, DDX_FieldRadio, DDX_FieldLBStringExact, DDX_FieldCBString, DDX_FieldCBStringExact, DDX_FieldCBIndex, DDX_FieldLBIndex, DDX_FieldScroll

DDX_FieldLBStringExact

void AFXAPI DDX_FieldLBStringExact(CDataExchange* *pDX***, int** *nIDC***,**
↳ **CString&** *value***, CRecordset*** *pRecordset* **);**
void AFXAPI DDX_FieldLBStringExact(CDataExchange* *pDX***, int** *nIDC***,**
↳ **CString&** *value***, CDaoRecordset*** *pRecordset* **);**

Parameters

pDX   A pointer to a **CDataExchange** object. The framework supplies this object to establish the context of the data exchange, including its direction.

nIDC   The ID of a control in the **CRecordView** or **CDaoRecordView** object.

value   A reference to a field data member in the associated **CRecordset** or **CDaoRecordset** object.

pRecordset   A pointer to the **CRecordset** or **CDaoRecordset** object with which data is exchanged.

Remarks

The **DDX_FieldLBStringExact** function copies the current selection of a list box control in a record view to a **CString** field data member of a recordset associated with the record view. In the reverse direction, this function sets the current selection in the list box to the first row that exactly matches the string specified in *value*. On a transfer from the recordset to the control, if the recordset field is Null, any selection is removed from the list box. On a transfer from control to recordset, if the control is empty, the recordset field is set to Null.

Use the first version if you are working with the ODBC-based classes. Use the second version if you are working with the DAO-based classes.

For more information about DDX, see "Adding a Dialog Box" in *Visual C++ Tutorials* online and "Dialog Data Exchange and Validation" in *Visual C++ Programmer's Guide* online. For examples and more information about DDX for **CRecordView** and **CDaoRecordView** fields, see the article "Record Views" in *Visual C++ Programmer's Guide* online.

Example

See **DDX_FieldText** for a general DDX_Field example. Calls to **DDX_FieldLBStringExact** would be similar.

See Also: DDX_FieldText, DDX_FieldRadio, DDX_FieldLBString, DDX_FieldCBString, DDX_FieldCBStringExact, DDX_FieldCBIndex, DDX_FieldLBIndex, DDX_FieldScroll

---

DDX_FieldRadio

> **void AFXAPI DDX_FieldRadio(CDataExchange*** *pDX,* **int** *nIDC,* **int&** *value,*
> ↪ **CRecordset*** *pRecordset* **);**
> **void AFXAPI DDX_FieldRadio(CDataExchange*** *pDX,* **int** *nIDC,* **int&** *value,*
> ↪ **CDaoRecordset*** *pRecordset* **);**

Parameters

pDX A pointer to a **CDataExchange** object. The framework supplies this object to establish the context of the data exchange, including its direction.

nIDC The ID of the first in a group (with style **WS_GROUP**) of adjacent radio button controls in the **CRecordView** or **CDaoRecordView** object.

value A reference to a field data member in the associated **CRecordset** or **CDaoRecordset** object.

pRecordset A pointer to the **CRecordset** or **CDaoRecordset** object with which data is exchanged.

Remarks

The **DDX_FieldRadio** function associates a zero-based **int** member variable of a record view's recordset with the currently selected radio button in a group of radio buttons in the record view. When transferring from the recordset field to the view, this function turns on the *nth* radio button (zero-based) and turns off the other buttons. In the reverse direction, this function sets the recordset field to the ordinal number of the radio button that is currently on (checked). On a transfer from the recordset to the control, if the recordset field is Null, no button is selected. On a transfer from control to recordset, if no control is selected, the recordset field is set to Null if the field permits that.

Use the first version if you are working with the ODBC-based classes. Use the second version if you are working with the DAO-based classes.

For more information about DDX, see "Adding a Dialog Box" in *Visual C++ Tutorials* online and "Dialog Data Exchange and Validation" in *Visual C++ Programmer's Guide* online. For examples and more information about DDX for **CRecordView** and **CDaoRecordView** fields, see the article "Record Views" in *Visual C++ Programmer's Guide* online.

Example

See **DDX_FieldText** for a general DDX_Field example. Calls to **DDX_FieldRadio** would be similar.

See Also: DDX_FieldText, DDX_FieldLBString, DDX_FieldLBStringExact, DDX_FieldCBString, DDX_FieldCBStringExact, DDX_FieldCBIndex, DDX_FieldLBIndex, DDX_FieldScroll

DDX_FieldScroll

void AFXAPI DDX_FieldScroll(CDataExchange* *pDX***, int** *nIDC***, int&** *value***,**
↪ **CRecordset*** *pRecordset* **);**
void AFXAPI DDX_FieldScroll(CDataExchange* *pDX***, int** *nIDC***, int&** *value***,**
↪ **CDaoRecordset*** *pRecordset* **);**

Parameters

pDX A pointer to a **CDataExchange** object. The framework supplies this object to establish the context of the data exchange, including its direction.

nIDC The ID of the first in a group (with style **WS_GROUP**) of adjacent radio button controls in the **CRecordView** or **CDaoRecordView** object.

value A reference to a field data member in the associated **CRecordset** or **CDaoRecordset** object.

pRecordset A pointer to the **CRecordset** or **CDaoRecordset** object with which data is exchanged.

Remarks

The **DDX_FieldScroll** function synchronizes the scroll position of a scroll bar control in a record view and an **int** field data member of a recordset associated with the record view (or with whatever integer variable you choose to map it to). When moving data from the recordset to the control, this function sets the scroll position of the scroll bar control to the value specified in *value*. On a transfer from the recordset to the control, if the recordset field is Null, the scroll bar control is set to 0. On a transfer from control to recordset, if the control is empty, the value of the recordset field is 0.

Use the first version if you are working with the ODBC-based classes. Use the second version if you are working with the DAO-based classes.

For more information about DDX, see "Adding a Dialog Box" in *Visual C++ Tutorials* online and "Dialog Data Exchange and Validation" in *Visual C++ Programmer's Guide* online. For examples and more information about DDX for **CRecordView** and **CDaoRecordView** fields, see the article "Record Views" in *Visual C++ Programmer's Guide* online.

Example

See **DDX_FieldText** for a general DDX_Field example. Calls to **DDX_FieldScroll** would be similar.

See Also: DDX_FieldText, DDX_FieldLBString, DDX_FieldLBStringExact, DDX_FieldCBString, DDX_FieldCBStringExact, DDX_FieldCBIndex, DDX_FieldLBIndex, DDX_Scroll

DDX_FieldText

void AFXAPI DDX_FieldText(CDataExchange* *pDX*, int *nIDC*, BYTE& *value*,
⮡ CRecordset* *pRecordset*);
void AFXAPI DDX_FieldText(CDataExchange* *pDX*, int *nIDC*, int& *value*,
⮡ CRecordset* *pRecordset*);
void AFXAPI DDX_FieldText(CDataExchange* *pDX*, int *nIDC*, UINT& *value*,
⮡ CRecordset* *pRecordset*);
void AFXAPI DDX_FieldText(CDataExchange* *pDX*, int *nIDC*, long& *value*,
⮡ CRecordset* *pRecordset*);
void AFXAPI DDX_FieldText(CDataExchange* *pDX*, int *nIDC*, DWORD& *value*,
⮡ CRecordset* *pRecordset*);
void AFXAPI DDX_FieldText(CDataExchange* *pDX*, int *nIDC*, CString& *value*,
⮡ CRecordset* *pRecordset*);
void AFXAPI DDX_FieldText(CDataExchange* *pDX*, int *nIDC*, float& *value*,
⮡ CRecordset* *pRecordset*);
void AFXAPI DDX_FieldText(CDataExchange* *pDX*, int *nIDC*, double& *value*,
⮡ CRecordset* *pRecordset*);
void AFXAPI DDX_FieldText(CDataExchange* *pDX*, int *nIDC*, short& *value*,
⮡ CDaoRecordset* *pRecordset*);
void AFXAPI DDX_FieldText(CDataExchange* *pDX*, int *nIDC*, BOOL& *value*,
⮡ CDaoRecordset* *pRecordset*);
void AFXAPI DDX_FieldText(CDataExchange* *pDX*, int *nIDC*, BYTE& *value*,
⮡ CDaoRecordset* *pRecordset*);
void AFXAPI DDX_FieldText(CDataExchange* *pDX*, int *nIDC*, long& *value*,
⮡ CDaoRecordset* *pRecordset*);
void AFXAPI DDX_FieldText(CDataExchange* *pDX*, int *nIDC*, DWORD& *value*,
⮡ CDaoRecordset* *pRecordset*);

void AFXAPI DDX_FieldText(**CDataExchange*** *pDX*, **int** *nIDC*, **CString&** *value*,
↪ **CDaoRecordset*** *pRecordset*);
void AFXAPI DDX_FieldText(**CDataExchange*** *pDX*, **int** *nIDC*, **float&** *value*,
↪ **CDaoRecordset*** *pRecordset*);
void AFXAPI DDX_FieldText(**CDataExchange*** *pDX*, **int** *nIDC*, **double&** *value*,
↪ **CDaoRecordset*** *pRecordset*);
void AFXAPI DDX_FieldText(**CDataExchange*** *pDX*, **int** *nIDC*,
↪ **COleDateTime&** *value*, **CDaoRecordset*** *pRecordset*);
void AFXAPI DDX_FieldText(**CDataExchange*** *pDX*, **int** *nIDC*,
↪ **COleCurrency&** *value*, **CDaoRecordset*** *pRecordset*);

Parameters

pDX   A pointer to a **CDataExchange** object. The framework supplies this object to establish the context of the data exchange, including its direction.

nIDC   The ID of a control in the **CRecordView** or **CDaoRecordView** object.

value   A reference to a field data member in the associated **CRecordset** or **CDaoRecordset** object. The data type of value depends on which of the overloaded versions of **DDX_FieldText** you use.

pRecordset   A pointer to the **CRecordset** or **CDaoRecordset** object with which data is exchanged. This pointer enables **DDX_FieldText** to detect and set Null values.

Remarks

The **DDX_FieldText** function manages the transfer of **int**, **short**, **long**, **DWORD**, **CString**, **float**, **double**, **BOOL**, or **BYTE** data between an edit box control and the field data members of a recordset. For **CDaoRecordset** objects, **DDX_FieldText** also manages transferring **COleDateTime**, and **COleCurrency** values. An empty edit box control indicates a Null value. On a transfer from the recordset to the control, if the recordset field is Null, the edit box is set to empty. On a transfer from control to recordset, if the control is empty, the recordset field is set to Null.

Use the versions with **CRecordset** parameters if you are working with the ODBC-based classes. Use the versions with **CDaoRecordset** parameters if you are working with the DAO-based classes.

For more information about DDX, see "Adding a Dialog Box" in *Visual C++ Tutorials* online and "Dialog Data Exchange and Validation" in *Visual C++ Programmer's Guide* online. For examples and more information about DDX for **CRecordView** and **CDaoRecordView** fields, see the article "Record Views" in *Visual C++ Programmer's Guide* online.

Example

The following **DoDataExchange** function for a **CRecordView** contains **DDX_FieldText** function calls for three data types: IDC_COURSELIST is a combo box; the other two controls are edit boxes. For DAO programming, the *m_pSet* parameter is a pointer to a **CRecordset** or **CDaoRecordset**.

```
//Example for DDX_FieldText
void CSectionForm::DoDataExchange( CDataExchange* pDX )
{
    CRecordView::DoDataExchange( pDX );
    //{{AFX_DATA_MAP(CSectionForm)
    DDX_FieldCBString( pDX, IDC_COURSELIST,
            m_pSet->m_strCourseID, m_pSet);
    DDX_FieldText( pDX, IDC_ROOM, m_pSet->m_nRoomNo,
            m_pSet );
    DDX_FieldText( pDX, IDC_TUITION,
            m_pSet->m_dwTuition, m_pSet );
    //}}AFX_DATA_MAP
}
```

See Also: DDX_FieldRadio, **DDX_FieldLBString**, **DDX_FieldLBStringExact**,
DDX_FieldCBString, **DDX_FieldCBStringExact**, **DDX_FieldCBIndex**,
DDX_FieldLBIndex, **DDX_FieldScroll**

DDX_LBIndex

void AFXAPI DDX_LBIndex(CDataExchange* *pDX*, int *nIDC*, int& *index*);

Parameters

pDX A pointer to a **CDataExchange** object. The framework supplies this
object to establish the context of the data exchange, including its
direction.

nIDC The resource ID of the list box control associated with the control
property.

index A reference to a member variable of the dialog box, form view, or
control view object with which data is exchanged.

Remarks

The **DDX_LBIndex** function manages the transfer of **int** data between a list box
control in a dialog box, form view, or control view object and an **int** data member
of the dialog box, form view, or control view object.

When **DDX_LBIndex** is called, *index* is set to the index of the current list box
selection. If no item is selected, *index* is set to 0.

For more information about DDX, see "Adding a Dialog Box" in *Visual C++
Tutorials* online and "Dialog Data Exchange and Validation" in *Visual C++
Programmer's Guide* online.

See Also: DDP_LBIndex

DDX_LBString

void AFXAPI DDX_LBString(CDataExchange* *pDX*, **int** *nIDC*, **CString&** *value*);

Parameters

pDX A pointer to a **CDataExchange** object. The framework supplies this object to establish the context of the data exchange, including its direction.

nIDC The resource ID of the list box control associated with the control property.

value A reference to a member variable of the dialog box, form view, or control view object with which data is exchanged.

Remarks

The **DDX_LBString** function manages the transfer of **CString** data between the edit control of a list box control in a dialog box, form view, or control view object and a **CString** data member of the dialog box, form view, or control view object.

When **DDX_LBString** is called, *value* is set to the current list box selection. If no item is selected, *value* is set to a string of zero length.

Note If the list box is a drop-down list box, the value exchanged is limited to 255 characters.

For more information about DDX, see "Adding a Dialog Box" in *Visual C++ Tutorials* online and "Dialog Data Exchange and Validation" in *Visual C++ Programmer's Guide* online.

See Also: DDP_LBString

DDX_LBStringExact

void AFXAPI DDX_LBStringExact(CDataExchange* *pDX*, **int** *nIDC*,
⇢ **CString&** *value*);

Parameters

pDX A pointer to a **CDataExchange** object. The framework supplies this object to establish the context of the data exchange, including its direction.

nIDC The resource ID of the list box control associated with the control property.

value A reference to a member variable of the dialog box, form view, or control view object with which data is exchanged.

Remarks

The **DDX_CBStringExact** function manages the transfer of **CString** data between the edit control of a list box control in a dialog box, form view, or control view object and a **CString** data member of the dialog box, form view, or control view object.

When **DDX_CBStringExact** is called, *value* is set to the current list box selection. If no item is selected, *value* is set to a string of zero length.

Note If the list box is a drop-down list box, the value exchanged is limited to 255 characters.

For more information about DDX, see "Adding a Dialog Box" in *Visual C++ Tutorials* online and "Dialog Data Exchange and Validation" in *Visual C++ Programmer's Guide* online.

DDX_OCBool

> **void AFXAPI DDX_OCBool(CDataExchange*** *pDX***, int** *nIDC***, DISPID** *dispid***,
> ↪ BOOL&** *value* **);**

Parameters

pDX A pointer to a **CDataExchange** object. The framework supplies this object to establish the context of the data exchange, including its direction.

nIDC The ID of an OLE control in the dialog box, form view, or control view object.

dispid The dispatch ID of a property of the control.

value A reference to a member variable of the dialog box, form view or control view object with which data is exchanged.

Remarks

The **DDX_OCBool** function manages the transfer of **BOOL** data between a property of an OLE control in a dialog box, form view, or control view object and a **BOOL** data member of the dialog box, form view, or control view object.

For more information about DDX, see "Adding a Dialog Box" in *Visual C++ Tutorials* online and "Dialog Data Exchange and Validation" in *Visual C++ Programmer's Guide* online.

See Also: DDX_OCBoolRO

DDX_OCBoolRO

> **void AFXAPI DDX_OCBoolRO(CDataExchange*** *pDX***, int** *nIDC***, DISPID** *dispid***,
> ↪ BOOL&** *value* **);**

Parameters

pDX A pointer to a **CDataExchange** object. The framework supplies this object to establish the context of the data exchange, including its direction.

nIDC The ID of an OLE control in the dialog box, form view, or control view object.

dispid The dispatch ID of a property of the control.

value A reference to a member variable of the dialog box, form view or control view object with which data is exchanged.

Remarks

The **DDX_OCBoolRO** function manages the transfer of **BOOL** data between a read-only property of an OLE control in a dialog box, form view, or control view object and a **BOOL** data member of the dialog box, form view, or control view object.

For more information about DDX, see "Adding a Dialog Box" in *Visual C++ Tutorials* online and "Dialog Data Exchange and Validation" in *Visual C++ Programmer's Guide* online.

See Also: **DDX_OCBool**

DDX_OCColor

void AFXAPI DDX_OCColor(CDataExchange* *pDX***, int** *nIDC***, DISPID** *dispid***,**
➥ **OLE_COLOR&** *value* **);**

Parameters

pDX   A pointer to a **CDataExchange** object. The framework supplies this object to establish the context of the data exchange, including its direction.

nIDC   The ID of an OLE control in the dialog box, form view, or control view object.

dispid   The dispatch ID of a property of the control.

value   A reference to a member variable of the dialog box, form view or control view object with which data is exchanged.

Remarks

The **DDX_OCColor** function manages the transfer of **OLE_COLOR** data between a property of an OLE control in a dialog box, form view, or control view object and a **OLE_COLOR** data member of the dialog box, form view, or control view object.

For more information about DDX, see "Adding a Dialog Box" in *Visual C++ Tutorials* online and "Dialog Data Exchange and Validation" in *Visual C++ Programmer's Guide* online.

See Also: **DDX_OCColorRO**

DDX_OCColorRO

void AFXAPI DDX_OCColorRO(CDataExchange* *pDX***, int** *nIDC***,**
➥ **DISPID** *dispid***, OLE_COLOR &** *value* **);**

Parameters

pDX   A pointer to a **CDataExchange** object. The framework supplies this object to establish the context of the data exchange, including its direction.

nIDC   The ID of an OLE control in the dialog box, form view, or control view object.

dispid   The dispatch ID of a property of the control.

value A reference to a member variable of the dialog box, form view or control view object with which data is exchanged.

Remarks

The **DDX_OCColorRO** function manages the transfer of **OLE_COLOR** data between a read-only property of an OLE control in a dialog box, form view, or control view object and a **OLE_COLOR** data member of the dialog box, form view, or control view object.

For more information about DDX, see "Adding a Dialog Box" in *Visual C++ Tutorials* online and "Dialog Data Exchange and Validation" in *Visual C++ Programmer's Guide* online.

See Also: DDX_OCColor

DDX_OCFloat

void AFXAPI DDX_OCFloat(CDataExchange* *pDX*, **int** *nIDC*,
  ↳ **DISPID** *dispid*, **float&** *value*);
void AFXAPI DDX_OCFloat(CDataExchange* *pDX*, **int** *nIDC*,
  ↳ **DISPID** *dispid*, **double&** *value*);

Parameters

pDX A pointer to a **CDataExchange** object. The framework supplies this object to establish the context of the data exchange, including its direction.

nIDC The ID of an OLE control in the dialog box, form view, or control view object.

dispid The dispatch ID of a property of the control.

value A reference to a member variable of the dialog box, form view or control view object with which data is exchanged.

Remarks

The **DDX_OCFloat** function manages the transfer of **float** (or **double**) data between a property of an OLE control in a dialog box, form view, or control view object and a **float** (or **double**) data member of the dialog box, form view, or control view object.

For more information about DDX, see "Adding a Dialog Box" in *Visual C++ Tutorials* online and "Dialog Data Exchange and Validation" in *Visual C++ Programmer's Guide* online.

See Also: DDX_OCFloatRO

DDX_OCFloatRO

void AFXAPI DDX_OCFloatRO(CDataExchange* *pDX*, **int** *nIDC*,
↳ **DISPID** *dispid*, **float&** *value* **);**
void AFXAPI DDX_OCFloatRO(CDataExchange* *pDX*, **int** *nIDC*,
↳ **DISPID** *dispid*, **double&** *value* **);**

Parameters

pDX A pointer to a **CDataExchange** object. The framework supplies this object to establish the context of the data exchange, including its direction.

nIDC The ID of an OLE control in the dialog box, form view, or control view object.

dispid The dispatch ID of a property of the control.

value A reference to a member variable of the dialog box, form view or control view object with which data is exchanged.

Remarks

The **DDX_OCFloatRO** function manages the transfer of **float** (or **double**) data between a read-only property of an OLE control in a dialog box, form view, or control view object and a **float** (or **double**) data member of the dialog box, form view, or control view object.

For more information about DDX, see "Adding a Dialog Box" in *Visual C++ Tutorials* online and "Dialog Data Exchange and Validation" in *Visual C++ Programmer's Guide* online.

See Also: DDX_OCFloat

DDX_OCInt

void AFXAPI DDX_OCInt(CDataExchange* *pDX*, **int** *nIDC*, **DISPID** *dispid*,
↳ **int&** *value* **);**
void AFXAPI DDX_OCInt(CDataExchange* *pDX*, **int** *nIDC*, **DISPID** *dispid*,
↳ **long&** *value* **);**

Parameters

pDX A pointer to a **CDataExchange** object. The framework supplies this object to establish the context of the data exchange, including its direction.

nIDC The ID of an OLE control in the dialog box, form view, or control view object.

dispid The dispatch ID of a property of the control.

value A reference to a member variable of the dialog box, form view or control view object with which data is exchanged.

Remarks

The **DDX_OCInt** function manages the transfer of **int** (or **long**) data between a property of an OLE control in a dialog box, form view, or control view object and a **int** (or **long**) data member of the dialog box, form view, or control view object.

For more information about DDX, see "Adding a Dialog Box" in *Visual C++ Tutorials* online and "Dialog Data Exchange and Validation" in *Visual C++ Programmer's Guide* online.

See Also: DDX_OCIntRO

DDX_OCIntRO

void AFXAPI DDX_OCIntRO(CDataExchange* *pDX***, int** *nIDC***,**
   ↪ **DISPID** *dispid***, int&** *value* **);**
void AFXAPI DDX_OCIntRO(CDataExchange* *pDX***, int** *nIDC***,**
   ↪ **DISPID** *dispid***, long&** *value* **);**

Parameters

pDX   A pointer to a **CDataExchange** object. The framework supplies this object to establish the context of the data exchange, including its direction.

nIDC   The ID of an OLE control in the dialog box, form view, or control view object.

dispid   The dispatch ID of a property of the control.

value   A reference to a member variable of the dialog box, form view or control view object with which data is exchanged.

Remarks

The **DDX_OCIntRO** function manages the transfer of **int** (or **long**) data between a read-only property of an OLE control in a dialog box, form view, or control view object and a **int** (or **long**) data member of the dialog box, form view, or control view object.

For more information about DDX, see "Adding a Dialog Box" in *Visual C++ Tutorials* online and "Dialog Data Exchange and Validation" in *Visual C++ Programmer's Guide* online.

See Also: DDX_OCInt

DDX_OCShort

void AFXAPI DDX_OCShort(CDataExchange* *pDX***, int** *nIDC***,**
   ↪ **DISPID** *dispid***, short&** *value* **);**

Parameters

pDX   A pointer to a **CDataExchange** object. The framework supplies this object to establish the context of the data exchange, including its direction.

nIDC   The ID of an OLE control in the dialog box, form view, or control view object.

dispid   The dispatch ID of a property of the control.

value   A reference to a member variable of the dialog box, form view or control view object with which data is exchanged.

Remarks

The **DDX_OCShort** function manages the transfer of short data between a property of an OLE control in a dialog box, form view, or control view object and a short data member of the dialog box, form view, or control view object.

For more information about DDX, see "Adding a Dialog Box" in *Visual C++ Tutorials* online and "Dialog Data Exchange and Validation" in *Visual C++ Programmer's Guide* online.

See Also: DDX_OCShortRO

DDX_OCShortRO

> **void AFXAPI DDX_OCShortRO(CDataExchange*** *pDX***, int** *nIDC***,**
> ↪ **DISPID** *dispid***, short&** *value* **);**

Parameters

pDX   A pointer to a **CDataExchange** object. The framework supplies this object to establish the context of the data exchange, including its direction.

nIDC   The ID of an OLE control in the dialog box, form view, or control view object.

dispid   The dispatch ID of a property of the control.

value   A reference to a member variable of the dialog box, form view or control view object with which data is exchanged.

Remarks

The **DDX_OCShortRO** function manages the transfer of short data between a read-only property of an OLE control in a dialog box, form view, or control view object and a short data member of the dialog box, form view, or control view object.

For more information about DDX, see "Adding a Dialog Box" in *Visual C++ Tutorials* online and "Dialog Data Exchange and Validation" in *Visual C++ Programmer's Guide* online.

See Also: DDX_OCShort

DDX_OCText

void AFXAPI DDX_OCText(CDataExchange* *pDX***, int** *nIDC***,**
↪ **DISPID** *dispid***, CString&** *value* **);**

Parameters

pDX   A pointer to a **CDataExchange** object. The framework supplies this object to establish the context of the data exchange, including its direction.

nIDC   The ID of an OLE control in the dialog box, form view, or control view object.

dispid   The dispatch ID of a property of the control.

value   A reference to a member variable of the dialog box, form view or control view object with which data is exchanged.

Remarks

The **DDX_OCText** function manages the transfer of **CString** data between a property of an OLE control in a dialog box, form view, or control view object and a **CString** data member of the dialog box, form view, or control view object.

For more information about DDX, see "Adding a Dialog Box" in *Visual C++ Tutorials* online and "Dialog Data Exchange and Validation" in *Visual C++ Programmer's Guide* online.

See Also: DDX_OCTextRO

DDX_OCTextRO

void AFXAPI DDX_OCTextRO(CDataExchange* *pDX***, int** *nIDC***,**
↪ **DISPID** *dispid***, CString&** *value* **);**

Parameters

pDX   A pointer to a **CDataExchange** object. The framework supplies this object to establish the context of the data exchange, including its direction.

nIDC   The ID of an OLE control in the dialog box, form view, or control view object.

dispid   The dispatch ID of a property of the control.

value   A reference to a member variable of the dialog box, form view or control view object with which data is exchanged.

Remarks

The **DDX_OCTextRO** function manages the transfer of **CString** data between a read-only property of an OLE control in a dialog box, form view, or control view object and a **CString** data member of the dialog box, form view, or control view object.

For more information about DDX, see "Adding a Dialog Box" in *Visual C++ Tutorials* online and "Dialog Data Exchange and Validation" in *Visual C++ Programmer's Guide* online.

See Also: DDX_OCText

DDX_Radio

void AFXAPI DDX_Radio(CDataExchange* *pDX***, int** *nIDC***, int&** *value* **);**

Parameters

pDX   A pointer to a **CDataExchange** object. The framework supplies this object to establish the context of the data exchange, including its direction.

nIDC   The resource ID of the radio control associated with the control property.

value   A reference to a member variable of the dialog box, form view, or control view object with which data is exchanged.

Remarks

The **DDX_Radio** function manages the transfer of **int** data between a radio control group in a dialog box, form view, or control view object and a **int** data member of the dialog box, form view, or control view object.

When **DDX_Radio** is called, *value* is set to the current state of the radio control group.

For more information about DDX, see "Adding a Dialog Box" in *Visual C++ Tutorials* online and "Dialog Data Exchange and Validation" in *Visual C++ Programmer's Guide* online.

DDX_Scroll

void AFXAPI DDX_Scroll(CDataExchange* *pDX***, int** *nIDC***, int&** *value* **);**

Parameters

pDX   A pointer to a **CDataExchange** object. The framework supplies this object to establish the context of the data exchange, including its direction.

nIDC   The resource ID of the scroll-bar control associated with the control property.

value   A reference to a member variable of the dialog box, form view or control view object with which data is exchanged.

Remarks

The **DDX_Scroll** function manages the transfer of **int** data between a scroll-bar control in a dialog box, form view, or control view object and an **int** data member of the dialog box, form view, or control view object.

When **DDX_Scroll** is called, *value* is set to the current position of the control's thumb.

For more information about DDX, see "Adding a Dialog Box" in *Visual C++ Tutorials* online and "Dialog Data Exchange and Validation" in *Visual C++ Programmer's Guide* online.

DDX_Text

void AFXAPI DDX_Text(CDataExchange* *pDX*, **int** *nIDC*, **BYTE&** *value*);
void AFXAPI DDX_Text(CDataExchange* *pDX*, **int** *nIDC*, **short&** *value*);
void AFXAPI DDX_Text(CDataExchange* *pDX*, **int** *nIDC*, **int&** *value*);
void AFXAPI DDX_Text(CDataExchange* *pDX*, **int** *nIDC*, **UINT&** *value*);
void AFXAPI DDX_Text(CDataExchange* *pDX*, **int** *nIDC*, **long&** *value*);
void AFXAPI DDX_Text(CDataExchange* *pDX*, **int** *nIDC*, **DWORD&** *value*);
void AFXAPI DDX_Text(CDataExchange* *pDX*, **int** *nIDC*, **CString&** *value*);
void AFXAPI DDX_Text(CDataExchange* *pDX*, **int** *nIDC*, **float&** *value*);
void AFXAPI DDX_Text(CDataExchange* *pDX*, **int** *nIDC*, **double&** *value*);
void AFXAPI DDX_Text(CDataExchange* *pDX*, **int** *nIDC*, **COleCurrency&** *value*);
void AFXAPI DDX_Text(CDataExchange* *pDX*, **int** *nIDC*, **COleDateTime&** *value*);

Parameters

pDX   A pointer to a **CDataExchange** object. The framework supplies this object to establish the context of the data exchange, including its direction.

nIDC   The ID of an edit control in the dialog box, form view, or control view object.

value   A reference to a data member in the dialog box, form view, or control view object. The data type of *value* depends on which of the overloaded versions of **DDX_Text** you use.

Remarks

The **DDX_Text** function manages the transfer of **int**, **UINT**, **long**, **DWORD**, **CString**, **float**, or **double** data between an edit control in a dialog box, form view, or control view and a **CString** data member of the dialog box, form view, or control view object.

For more information about DDX, see "Adding a Dialog Box" in *Visual C++ Tutorials* online and "Dialog Data Exchange and Validation" in *Visual C++ Programmer's Guide* online.

DEBUG_NEW

#define new DEBUG_NEW

Remarks

Assists in finding memory leaks. You can use **DEBUG_NEW** everywhere in your program that you would ordinarily use the **new** operator to allocate heap storage.

In debug mode (when the **_DEBUG** symbol is defined), **DEBUG_NEW** keeps track of the filename and line number for each object that it allocates. Then, when you use the **CMemoryState::DumpAllObjectsSince** member function, each object allocated with **DEBUG_NEW** is shown with the filename and line number where it was allocated.

To use **DEBUG_NEW**, insert the following directive into your source files:

```
#define new DEBUG_NEW
```

Once you insert this directive, the preprocessor will insert **DEBUG_NEW** wherever you use **new**, and MFC does the rest. When you compile a release version of your program, **DEBUG_NEW** resolves to a simple **new** operation, and the filename and line number information is not generated.

Note In previous versions of MFC (4.1 and earlier) you needed to put the **#define** statement after all statements that called the **IMPLEMENT_DYNCREATE** or **IMPLEMENT_SERIAL** macros. This is no longer necessary.

For more information on the **DEBUG_NEW** macro, see "MFC Debugging Support" in *Visual C++ Programmer's Guide* online.

DECLARE_CONNECTION_MAP

DECLARE_CONNECTION_MAP( )

Remarks

Each **COleControl**-derived class in your program can provide a connection map to specify additional connection points that your control supports.

If your control supports additional points, use the **DECLARE_CONNECTION_MAP** macro at the end of your class declaration. Then, in the .CPP file that defines the member functions for the class, use the **BEGIN_CONNECTION_MAP** macro, **CONNECTION_PART** macros for each of the control's connection points, and the **END_CONNECTION_MAP** macro to declare the end of the connection map.

See Also: **BEGIN_CONNECTION_PART, BEGIN_CONNECTION_MAP, CONNECTION_IID**

DECLARE_DISPATCH_MAP

DECLARE_DISPATCH_MAP( )

Remarks

If a **CCmdTarget**-derived class in your program supports OLE Automation, that class must provide a dispatch map to expose its methods and properties. Use the **DECLARE_DISPATCH_MAP** macro at the end of your class declaration. Then, in the .CPP file that defines the member functions for the class, use the **BEGIN_DISPATCH_MAP** macro. Then include macro entries for each of your class's exposed methods and properties (**DISP_FUNCTION**, **DISP_PROPERTY**, and so on). Finally, use the **END_DISPATCH_MAP** macro.

Note If you declare any members after **DECLARE_DISPATCH_MAP**, you must specify a new access type (**public**, **private**, or **protected**) for them.

AppWizard and ClassWizard assist in creating Automation classes and in maintaining dispatch maps: see the articles on "AppWizard" and "ClassWizard: Automation Support." For more information on dispatch maps, see "Automation Servers." All of these articles are in *Visual C++ Programmer's Guide* online.

Example

```
// example for DECLARE_DISPATCH_MAP
class CMyDoc : public CDocument
{
    // Member declarations

    DECLARE_DISPATCH_MAP()
};
```

See Also: Dispatch Maps, **BEGIN_DISPATCH_MAP**, **END_DISPATCH_MAP**, **DISP_FUNCTION**, **DISP_PROPERTY**, **DISP_PROPERTY_EX**, **DISP_DEFVALUE**

DECLARE_DYNAMIC

DECLARE_DYNAMIC(*class_name* **)**

Parameters

class_name The actual name of the class (not enclosed in quotation marks).

Remarks

When deriving a class from **CObject**, this macro adds the ability to access run-time information about an object's class.

Add the **DECLARE_DYNAMIC** macro to the header (.H) module for the class, then include that module in all .CPP modules that need access to objects of this class.

If you use the **DECLARE_DYNAMIC** and **IMPLEMENT_DYNAMIC** macros as described, you can then use the **RUNTIME_CLASS** macro and the **CObject::IsKindOf** function to determine the class of your objects at run time.

If **DECLARE_DYNAMIC** is included in the class declaration, then **IMPLEMENT_DYNAMIC** must be included in the class implementation.

For more information on the **DECLARE_DYNAMIC** macro, see "CObject Class Topics" in *Visual C++ Programmer's Guide* online.

See Also: IMPLEMENT_DYNAMIC, DECLARE_DYNCREATE, DECLARE_SERIAL, RUNTIME_CLASS, CObject::IsKindOf

---

DECLARE_DYNCREATE

DECLARE_DYNCREATE(*class_name* **)**

Parameters
class_name   The actual name of the class (not enclosed in quotation marks).

Remarks
Use the **DECLARE_DYNCREATE** macro to enable objects of **CObject**-derived classes to be created dynamically at run time. The framework uses this ability to create new objects dynamically, for example, when it reads an object from disk during serialization. Document, view, and frame classes should support dynamic creation because the framework needs to create them dynamically.

Add the **DECLARE_DYNCREATE** macro in the .H module for the class, then include that module in all .CPP modules that need access to objects of this class.

If **DECLARE_DYNCREATE** is included in the class declaration, then **IMPLEMENT_DYNCREATE** must be included in the class implementation.

For more information on the **DECLARE_DYNCREATE** macro, see "CObject Class Topics" in *Visual C++ Programmer's Guide* online.

See Also: DECLARE_DYNAMIC, IMPLEMENT_DYNAMIC, IMPLEMENT_DYNCREATE, RUNTIME_CLASS, CObject::IsKindOf

---

DECLARE_EVENT_MAP

DECLARE_EVENT_MAP( )

Remarks
Each **COleControl**-derived class in your program can provide an event map to specify the events your control will fire. Use the **DECLARE_EVENT_MAP** macro at the end of your class declaration. Then, in the .CPP file that defines the member functions for the class, use the **BEGIN_EVENT_MAP** macro, macro entries for each

of the control's events, and the **END_EVENT_MAP** macro to declare the end of the event list.

For more information on event maps, see the article "ActiveX Controls: Events" in *Visual C++ Programmer's Guide* online.

See Also: BEGIN_EVENT_MAP, END_EVENT_MAP, EVENT_CUSTOM, EVENT_CUSTOM_ID

DECLARE_EVENTSINK_MAP

DECLARE_EVENTSINK_MAP( )

Remarks

An OLE container can provide an event sink map to specify the events your container will be notified of. Use the **DECLARE_EVENTSINK_MAP** macro at the end of your class declaration. Then, in the .CPP file that defines the member functions for the class, use the **BEGIN_EVENTSINK_MAP** macro, macro entries for each of the events to be notified of, and the **END_EVENTSINK_MAP** macro to declare the end of the event sink list.

For more information on event sink maps, see the article "ActiveX Control Containers" in *Visual C++ Programmer's Guide* online.

See Also: BEGIN_EVENTSINK_MAP, END_EVENTSINK_MAP, ON_EVENT, ON_PROPNOTIFY

DECLARE_MESSAGE_MAP

DECLARE_MESSAGE_MAP( )

Remarks

Each **CCmdTarget**-derived class in your program must provide a message map to handle messages. Use the **DECLARE_MESSAGE_MAP** macro at the end of your class declaration. Then, in the .CPP file that defines the member functions for the class, use the **BEGIN_MESSAGE_MAP** macro, macro entries for each of your message-handler functions, and the **END_MESSAGE_MAP** macro.

Note If you declare any member after **DECLARE_MESSAGE_MAP**, you must specify a new access type (**public**, **private**, or **protected**) for them.

For more information on message maps and the **DECLARE_MESSAGE_MAP** macro, see "Message Handling and Mapping Topics" in *Visual C++ Programmer's Guide* online.

Example

```
// example for DECLARE_MESSAGE_MAP
class CMyWnd : public CFrameWnd
{
    // Member declarations

    DECLARE_MESSAGE_MAP( )
};
```

See Also: **BEGIN_MESSAGE_MAP**, **END_MESSAGE_MAP**

DECLARE_OLECREATE

DECLARE_OLECREATE(*class_name* **)**

#include <afxdisp.h>

Parameters

class_name   The actual name of the class (not enclosed in quotation marks).

Remarks

Use the **DECLARE_OLECREATE** macro to enable objects of **CCmdTarget**-derived classes to be created through OLE automation. This macro enables other OLE-enabled applications to create objects of this type.

Add the **DECLARE_OLECREATE** macro in the .H module for the class, then include that module in all .CPP modules that need access to objects of this class.

If **DECLARE_OLECREATE** is included in the class declaration, then **IMPLEMENT_OLECREATE** must be included in the class implementation. A class declaration using **DECLARE_OLECREATE** must also use **DECLARE_DYNCREATE** or **DECLARE_SERIAL**.

See Also: **IMPLEMENT_OLECREATE**, **DECLARE_DYNCREATE**, **DECLARE_SERIAL**

DECLARE_OLECREATE_EX

DECLARE_OLECREATE_EX(*class_name* **)**

Parameters

class_name   The name of the control class.

Remarks

Declares a class factory and the **GetClassID** member function of your control class. Use this macro in the control class header file for a control that does not support licensing.

Note that this macro serves the same purpose as the following code sample:

```
BEGIN_OLEFACTORY(CSampleCtrl)
END_OLEFACTORY(CSampleCtrl)
```

See Also: BEGIN_OLEFACTORY, END_OLEFACTORY

DECLARE_OLETYPELIB

DECLARE_OLETYPELIB(*class_name* **)**

Parameters

class_name   The name of the control class related to the type library.

Remarks

Declares the **GetTypeLib** member function of your control class. Use this macro in the control class header file.

See Also: IMPLEMENT_OLETYPELIB

DECLARE_PROPPAGEIDS

DECLARE_PROPPAGEIDS(*class_name* **)**

Parameters

class_name   The name of the control class that owns the property pages.

Remarks

An OLE control can provide a list of property pages to display its properties. Use the **DECLARE_PROPPAGEIDS** macro at the end of your class declaration. Then, in the .CPP file that defines the member functions for the class, use the **BEGIN_PROPPAGEIDS** macro, macro entries for each of your control's property pages, and the **END_PROPPAGEIDS** macro to declare the end of the property page list.

For more information on property pages, see the article "ActiveX Controls: Property Pages" in *Visual C++ Programmer's Guide* online.

See Also: BEGIN_PROPPAGEIDS, END_PROPPAGEIDS

DECLARE_SERIAL

DECLARE_SERIAL(*class_name* **)**

Parameters

class_name   The actual name of the class (not enclosed in quotation marks).

Remarks

DECLARE_SERIAL generates the C++ header code necessary for a **CObject**-derived class that can be serialized. Serialization is the process of writing or reading the contents of an object to and from a file.

Use the **DECLARE_SERIAL** macro in a .H module, then include that module in all .CPP modules that need access to objects of this class.

If **DECLARE_SERIAL** is included in the class declaration, then **IMPLEMENT_SERIAL** must be included in the class implementation.

The **DECLARE_SERIAL** macro includes all the functionality of **DECLARE_DYNAMIC** and **DECLARE_DYNCREATE**.

For more information on the **DECLARE_SERIAL** macro, see "CObject Class Topics" in *Visual C++ Programmer's Guide* online.

See Also: **DECLARE_DYNAMIC, IMPLEMENT_SERIAL, RUNTIME_CLASS, CObject::IsKindOf**

DEFAULT_PARSE_COMMAND

DEFAULT_PARSE_COMMAND(*FnName*, *mapClass* **)**

Parameters

FnName   The name of the member function. Also the name of the command.

mapClass   The class name to map the function to.

Remarks

If the request from a client to the **CHttpServer** object does not contain a command, the **DEFAULT_PARSE_COMMAND** macro directs the framework to call the default page that's identified by the *FnName* parameter.

The **DEFAULT_PARSE_COMMAND** macro can appear anywhere in the parse map.

See **ON_PARSE_COMMAND** for a parse map example.

See Also: **BEGIN_PARSE_MAP, ON_PARSE_COMMAND, ON_PARSE_COMMAND_PARAMS, END_PARSE_MAP, CHttpServer**

DestructElements

template< class *TYPE* **>**
↳ **void AFXAPI DestructElements(** *TYPE* pElements*, **int** *nCount* **);**

Parameters

TYPE   Template parameter specifying the type of the elements to be destroyed.

pElements   Pointer to the elements.

nCount   Number of elements to be destroyed.

Remarks

The **CArray**, **CList**, and **CMap** class members call this function when elements are destroyed.

The default implementation does nothing. For information on implementing this and other helper functions, see the article "Collections: How to Make a Type-Safe Collection" in *Visual C++ Programmer's Guide* online.

See Also: **CArray**, **CList**, **CMap**

DFX_Binary

void AFXAPI DFX_Binary(CDaoFieldExchange* *pFX***, LPCTSTR** *szName***,**
   ↪ **CByteArray&** *value***, int** *nPreAllocSize* **= AFX_DAO_BINARY_DEFAULT_SIZE,**
   ↪ **DWORD** *dwBindOptions* **= 0);**

Parameters

pFX   A pointer to an object of class **CDaoFieldExchange**. This object contains information to define the context for each call of the function. For additional information about the operations a **CDaoFieldExchange** object can specify, see the article "DAO Record Field Exchange: How DFX Works" in *Visual C++ Programmer's Guide* online.

szName   The name of a data column.

value   The value stored in the indicated data member—the value to be transferred. For a transfer from recordset to data source, the value, of type **CByteArray**, is taken from the specified data member. For a transfer from data source to recordset, the value is stored in the specified data member.

nPreAllocSize   The framework preallocates this amount of memory. If your data is larger, the framework will allocated more space as needed. For better performance, set this size to a value large enough to prevent reallocations. The default size is defined in the AFXDAO.H file as **AFX_DAO_BINARY_DEFAULT_SIZE**.

dwBindOptions   An option that lets you take advantage of MFC's double buffering mechanism for detecting recordset fields that have changed. The default, **AFX_DAO_DISABLE_FIELD_CACHE**, does not use double buffering and you must call **SetFieldDirty** and **SetFieldNull** yourself. The other possible value, **AFX_DAO_ENABLE_FIELD_CACHE**, uses double buffering, and you do not have to do extra work to mark fields dirty or Null. For performance and memory reasons, avoid this value unless your binary data is relatively small.

These options are explained further in the article "DAO Record Field Exchange: Double Buffering Records" in *Visual C++ Programmer's Guide* online.

Note You can control whether data is double buffered for all fields by default by setting **CDaoRecordset::m_bCheckCacheForDirtyFields**.

Remarks

The **DFX_Binary** function transfers arrays of bytes between the field data members of a **CDaoRecordset** object and the columns of a record on the data source. Data is mapped between type **DAO_BYTES** in DAO and type **CByteArray** in the recordset.

Example

See **DFX_Text**.

See Also: DFX_Text, DFX_Bool, DFX_Currency, DFX_Long, DFX_Short, **DFX_Single, DFX_Double, DFX_DateTime, DFX_Byte, DFX_LongBinary, CDaoFieldExchange::SetFieldType**

DFX_Bool

void AFXAPI DFX_Bool(CDaoFieldExchange* *pFX*, **LPCTSTR** *szName*,
↪ **BOOL&** *value*, **DWORD** *dwBindOptions* =
↪ **AFX_DAO_ENABLE_FIELD_CACHE**);

Parameters

pFX A pointer to an object of class **CDaoFieldExchange**. This object contains information to define the context for each call of the function. For additional information about the operations a **CDaoFieldExchange** object can specify, see the article "DAO Record Field Exchange: How DFX Works" in *Visual C++ Programmer's Guide* online.

szName The name of a data column.

value The value stored in the indicated data member—the value to be transferred. For a transfer from recordset to data source, the value, of type **BOOL**, is taken from the specified data member. For a transfer from data source to recordset, the value is stored in the specified data member.

dwBindOptions An option that lets you take advantage of MFC's double buffering mechanism for detecting recordset fields that have changed. The default, **AFX_DAO_ENABLE_FIELD_CACHE**, uses double buffering. The other possible value is **AFX_DAO_DISABLE_FIELD_CACHE**. If you specify this value, MFC does no checking on this field. You must call **SetFieldDirty** and **SetFieldNull** yourself.

These options are explained further in the article "DAO Recordset: Binding Records Dynamically" in *Visual C++ Programmer's Guide* online.

Note You can control whether data is double buffered by default by setting **CDaoRecordset::m_bCheckCacheForDirtyFields**.

Remarks

The **DFX_BOOL** function transfers Boolean data between the field data members of a **CDaoRecordset** object and the columns of a record on the data source. Data is mapped between type **DAO_BOOL** in DAO and type **BOOL** in the recordset.

Example

See **DFX_Text**.

See Also: **DFX_Text, DFX_Long, DFX_Currency, DFX_Short, DFX_Single, DFX_Double, DFX_DateTime, DFX_Byte, DFX_Binary, DFX_LongBinary, CDaoFieldExchange::SetFieldType**

DFX_Byte

void AFXAPI DFX_Byte(CDaoFieldExchange* *pFX*, **LPCTSTR** *szName*,
↳ **BYTE&** *value*, **DWORD** *dwBindOptions* =
↳ **AFX_DAO_ENABLE_FIELD_CACHE**);

Parameters

pFX   A pointer to an object of class **CDaoFieldExchange**. This object contains information to define the context for each call of the function. For more information about the operations a **CDaoFieldExchange** object can specify, see the article "DAO Record Field Exchange: How DFX Works" in *Visual C++ Programmer's Guide* online.

szName   The name of a data column.

value   The value stored in the indicated data member—the value to be transferred. For a transfer from recordset to data source, the value, of type **BYTE**, is taken from the specified data member. For a transfer from data source to recordset, the value is stored in the specified data member.

dwBindOptions   An option that lets you take advantage of MFC's double buffering mechanism for detecting recordset fields that have changed. The default, **AFX_DAO_ENABLE_FIELD_CACHE**, uses double buffering. The other possible value is **AFX_DAO_DISABLE_FIELD_CACHE**. If you specify this value, MFC does no checking on this field. You must call **SetFieldDirty** and **SetFieldNull** yourself.

These options are explained further in the article "DAO Recordset: Binding Records Dynamically" in *Visual C++ Programmer's Guide* online.

Note   You can control whether data is double buffered by default by setting **CDaoRecordset::m_bCheckCacheForDirtyFields**.

Remarks

The **DFX_Byte** function transfers single bytes between the field data members of a **CDaoRecordset** object and the columns of a record on the data source. Data is mapped between type **DAO_BYTES** in DAO and type **BYTE** in the recordset.

Example

See **DFX_Text**.

See Also: **DFX_Text**, **DFX_Bool**, **DFX_Currency**, **DFX_Long**, **DFX_Short**, **DFX_Single**, **DFX_Double**, **DFX_DateTime**, **DFX_Binary**, **DFX_LongBinary**, **CDaoFieldExchange::SetFieldType**

DFX_Currency

void AFXAPI DFX_Currency(CDaoFieldExchange* *pFX*, **LPCTSTR** *szName*,
↪ **COleCurrency&** *value*, **DWORD** *dwBindOptions* =
↪ **AFX_DAO_ENABLE_FIELD_CACHE**);

Parameters

pFX   A pointer to an object of class **CDaoFieldExchange**. This object contains information to define the context for each call of the function. For more information about the operations a **CDaoFieldExchange** object can specify, see the article "DAO Record Field Exchange: How DFX Works" in *Visual C++ Programmer's Guide* online.

szName   The name of a data column.

value   The value stored in the indicated data member—the value to be transferred. For a transfer from recordset to data source, this value is taken from the specified data member, of type **COleCurrency**. For a transfer from data source to recordset, the value is stored in the specified data member.

dwBindOptions   An option that lets you take advantage of MFC's double buffering mechanism for detecting recordset fields that have changed. The default, **AFX_DAO_ENABLE_FIELD_CACHE**, uses double buffering. The other possible value is **AFX_DAO_DISABLE_FIELD_CACHE**. If you specify this value, MFC does no checking on this field. You must call **SetFieldDirty** and **SetFieldNull** yourself.

These options are explained further in the article "DAO Recordset: Binding Records Dynamically" in *Visual C++ Programmer's Guide* online.

Note   You can control whether data is double buffered by default by setting **CDaoRecordset::m_bCheckCacheForDirtyFields**.

Remarks

The **DFX_Currency** function transfers currency data between the field data members of a **CDaoRecordset** object and the columns of a record on the data source. Data is mapped between type **DAO_CURRENCY** in DAO and type **COleCurrency** in the recordset.

Example

See **DFX_Text**.

See Also: **DFX_Text**, **DFX_Bool**, **DFX_DateTime**, **DFX_Long**, **DFX_Short**, **DFX_Single**, **DFX_Double**, **DFX_Byte**, **DFX_Binary**, **DFX_LongBinary**, **CDaoFieldExchange::SetFieldType**

DFX_DateTime

void AFXAPI DFX_DateTime(CDaoFieldExchange* *pFX*, **LPCTSTR** *szName*,
  ↪ **COleDateTime&** *value*, **DWORD** *dwBindOptions* =
  ↪ **AFX_DAO_ENABLE_FIELD_CACHE**);

Parameters

pFX A pointer to an object of class **CDaoFieldExchange**. This object contains information to define the context for each call of the function. For more information about the operations a **CDaoFieldExchange** object can specify, see the article "DAO Record Field Exchange: How DFX Works" in *Visual C++ Programmer's Guide* online.

szName The name of a data column.

value The value stored in the indicated data member—the value to be transferred. The function takes a reference to a **COleDateTime** object. For a transfer from recordset to data source, this value is taken from the specified data member. For a transfer from data source to recordset, the value is stored in the specified data member.

dwBindOptions An option that lets you take advantage of MFC's double buffering mechanism for detecting recordset fields that have changed. The default, **AFX_DAO_ENABLE_FIELD_CACHE**, uses double buffering. The other possible value is **AFX_DAO_DISABLE_FIELD_CACHE**. If you specify this value, MFC does no checking on this field. You must call **SetFieldDirty** and **SetFieldNull** yourself.

These options are explained further in the article "DAO Recordset: Binding Records Dynamically" in *Visual C++ Programmer's Guide* online.

Note You can control whether data is double buffered by default by setting **CDaoRecordset::m_bCheckCacheForDirtyFields**.

Remarks

The **DFX_DateTime** function transfers time and date data between the field data members of a **CDaoRecordset** object and the columns of a record on the data source. Data is mapped between type **DAO_DATE** in DAO and type **COleDateTime** in the recordset.

Note **COleDateTime** replaces **CTime** and **TIMESTAMP_STRUCT** for this purpose in the DAO classes. **CTime** and **TIMESTAMP_STRUCT** are still used for the ODBC-based data access classes.

Example

See **DFX_Text**.

See Also: **DFX_Text**, **DFX_Bool**, **DFX_Currency**, **DFX_Long**, **DFX_Short**, **DFX_Single**, **DFX_Double**, **DFX_Byte**, **DFX_Binary**, **DFX_LongBinary**, **CDaoFieldExchange::SetFieldType**

DFX_Double

void AFXAPI DFX_Double(CDaoFieldExchange* *pFX*, **LPCTSTR** *szName*,
↳ **double&** *value*, **DWORD** *dwBindOptions* = **AFX_DAO_ENABLE_FIELD_CACHE**);

Parameters

pFX   A pointer to an object of class **CDaoFieldExchange**. This object contains information to define the context for each call of the function. For more information about the operations a **CDaoFieldExchange** object can specify, see the article "DAO Record Field Exchange: How DFX Works" in *Visual C++ Programmer's Guide* online.

szName   The name of a data column.

value   The value stored in the indicated data member—the value to be transferred. For a transfer from recordset to data source, the value, of type **double**, is taken from the specified data member. For a transfer from data source to recordset, the value is stored in the specified data member.

dwBindOptions   An option that lets you take advantage of MFC's double buffering mechanism for detecting recordset fields that have changed. The default, **AFX_DAO_ENABLE_FIELD_CACHE**, uses double buffering. The other possible value is **AFX_DAO_DISABLE_FIELD_CACHE**. If you specify this value, MFC does no checking on this field. You must call **SetFieldDirty** and **SetFieldNull** yourself.

These options are explained further in the article "DAO Recordset: Binding Records Dynamically" in *Visual C++ Programmer's Guide* online.

Note   You can control whether data is double buffered by default by setting **CDaoRecordset::m_bCheckCacheForDirtyFields**.

Remarks

The **DFX_Double** function transfers **double float** data between the field data members of a **CDaoRecordset** object and the columns of a record on the data source. Data is mapped between type **DAO_R8** in DAO and type **double float** in the recordset.

Example

See **DFX_Text**.

See Also: **DFX_Text, DFX_Bool, DFX_Currency, DFX_Long, DFX_Short, DFX_Single, DFX_DateTime, DFX_Byte, DFX_Binary, DFX_LongBinary, CDaoFieldExchange::SetFieldType**

DFX_Long

> **void AFXAPI DFX_Long(CDaoFieldExchange*** *pFX*, **LPCTSTR** *szName*,
> ↪ **long&** *value*, **DWORD** *dwBindOptions* = **AFX_DAO_ENABLE_FIELD_CACHE**);

Parameters

    pFX A pointer to an object of class **CDaoFieldExchange**. This object contains information to define the context for each call of the function. For more information about the operations a **CDaoFieldExchange** object can specify, see the article "DAO Record Field Exchange: How DFX Works" in *Visual C++ Programmer's Guide* online.

    szName The name of a data column.

    value The value stored in the indicated data member —the value to be transferred. For a transfer from recordset to data source, the value, of type **long**, is taken from the specified data member. For a transfer from data source to recordset, the value is stored in the specified data member.

    dwBindOptions An option that lets you take advantage of MFC's double buffering mechanism for detecting recordset fields that have changed. The default, **AFX_DAO_ENABLE_FIELD_CACHE**, uses double buffering. The other possible value is **AFX_DAO_DISABLE_FIELD_CACHE**. If you specify this value, MFC does no checking on this field. You must call **SetFieldDirty** and **SetFieldNull** yourself.

    These options are explained further in the article "DAO Recordset: Binding Records Dynamically" in *Visual C++ Programmer's Guide* online.

    Note You can control whether data is double buffered by default by setting **CDaoRecordset::m_bCheckCacheForDirtyFields**.

Remarks

The **DFX_Long** function transfers long integer data between the field data members of a **CDaoRecordset** object and the columns of a record on the data source. Data is mapped between type **DAO_I4** in DAO and type **long** in the recordset.

Example

See **DFX_Text**.

See Also: **DFX_Text, DFX_Bool, DFX_Currency, DFX_Short, DFX_Single, DFX_Double, DFX_DateTime, DFX_Byte, DFX_Binary, DFX_LongBinary, CDaoFieldExchange::SetFieldType**

DFX_LongBinary

void AFXAPI DFX_LongBinary(CDaoFieldExchange* *pFX***, LPCTSTR** *szName***,**
> ↪ **CLongBinary&** *value***, DWORD** *dwPreAllocLength* **=**
> ↪ **AFX_DAO_LONGBINARY_DEFAULT_SIZE, DWORD** *dwBindOptions* **= 0);**

Parameters

pFX   A pointer to an object of class **CDaoFieldExchange**. This object contains information to define the context for each call of the function. For more information about the operations a **CDaoFieldExchange** object can specify, see the article "DAO Record Field Exchange: How DFX Works" in *Visual C++ Programmer's Guide* online.

szName   The name of a data column.

value   The value stored in the indicated data member —the value to be transferred. For a transfer from recordset to data source, the value, of type **CLongBinary**, is taken from the specified data member. For a transfer from data source to recordset, the value is stored in the specified data member.

nPreAllocSize   The framework preallocates this amount of memory. If your data is larger, the framework will allocated more space as needed. For better performance, set this size to a value large enough to prevent reallocations.

dwBindOptions   An option that lets you take advantage of MFC's double buffering mechanism for detecting recordset fields that have changed. The default, **AFX_DISABLE_FIELD_CACHE**, does not use double buffering. The other possible value is **AFX_DAO_ENABLE_FIELD_CACHE**. Uses double buffering, and you do not have to do extra work to mark fields dirty or Null. For performance and memory reasons, avoid this value unless your binary data is relatively small.

These options are explained further in the article "DAO Recordset: Binding Records Dynamically" in *Visual C++ Programmer's Guide* online.

Note   You can control whether data is double buffered by default by setting **CDaoRecordset::m_bCheckCacheForDirtyFields**.

Remarks

Important   It is recommended that you use **DFX_Binary** instead of this function. **DFX_LongBinary** is provided for compatibility with the MFC ODBC classes.

The **DFX_LongBinary** function transfers binary large object (BLOB) data using class **CLongBinary** between the field data members of a **CDaoRecordset** object and the columns of a record on the data source. Data is mapped between type **DAO_BYTES** in DAO and type **CLongBinary** in the recordset.

Example

See **DFX_Text**.

See Also: **DFX_Text**, **DFX_Bool**, **DFX_Currency**, **DFX_Long**, **DFX_Short**, **DFX_Single**, **DFX_Double**, **DFX_DateTime**, **DFX_Byte**, **CDaoFieldExchange::SetFieldType**, **CLongBinary**

DFX_Short

void AFXAPI DFX_Short(CDaoFieldExchange* *pFX***, LPCTSTR** *szName***,**
↪ **short&** *value***, DWORD** *dwBindOptions* **= AFX_DAO_ENABLE_FIELD_CACHE);**

Parameters

pFX A pointer to an object of class **CDaoFieldExchange**. This object contains information to define the context for each call of the function. For more information about the operations a **CDaoFieldExchange** object can specify, see the article "DAO Record Field Exchange: How DFX Works" in *Visual C++ Programmer's Guide* online.

szName The name of a data column.

value The value stored in the indicated data member—the value to be transferred. For a transfer from recordset to data source, the value, of type **short**, is taken from the specified data member. For a transfer from data source to recordset, the value is stored in the specified data member.

dwBindOptions An option that lets you take advantage of MFC's double buffering mechanism for detecting recordset fields that have changed. The default, **AFX_DAO_ENABLE_FIELD_CACHE**, uses double buffering. The other possible value is **AFX_DAO_DISABLE_FIELD_CACHE**. If you specify this value, MFC does no checking on this field. You must call **SetFieldDirty** and **SetFieldNull** yourself.

These options are explained further in the article "DAO Recordset: Binding Records Dynamically" in *Visual C++ Programmer's Guide* online.

Note You can control whether data is double buffered by default by setting **CDaoRecordset::m_bCheckCacheForDirtyFields**.

Remarks

The **DFX_Short** function transfers short integer data between the field data members of a **CDaoRecordset** object and the columns of a record on the data source. Data is mapped between type **DAO_I2** in DAO and type **short** in the recordset.

Note DFX_Short is equivalent to **RFX_Int** for the ODBC-based classes.

Example

See **DFX_Text**.

See Also: **DFX_Text**, **DFX_Bool**, **DFX_Currency**, **DFX_Long**, **DFX_Single**, **DFX_Double**, **DFX_DateTime**, **DFX_Byte**, **DFX_Binary**, **DFX_LongBinary**, **CDaoFieldExchange::SetFieldType**

DFX_Single

void AFXAPI DFX_Single(CDaoFieldExchange* *pFX*, **LPCTSTR** *szName*,
↪ **float&** *value*, **DWORD** *dwBindOptions* =
↪ **AFX_DAO_ENABLE_FIELD_CACHE**);

Parameters

pFX   A pointer to an object of class **CDaoFieldExchange**. This object contains information to define the context for each call of the function. For more information about the operations a **CDaoFieldExchange** object can specify, see the article "DAO Record Field Exchange: How DFX Works" in *Visual C++ Programmer's Guide* online.

szName   The name of a data column.

value   The value stored in the indicated data member—the value to be transferred. For a transfer from recordset to data source, the value, of type **float**, is taken from the specified data member. For a transfer from data source to recordset, the value is stored in the specified data member.

dwBindOptions   An option that lets you take advantage of MFC's double buffering mechanism for detecting recordset fields that have changed. The default, **AFX_DAO_ENABLE_FIELD_CACHE**, uses double buffering. The other possible value is **AFX_DAO_DISABLE_FIELD_CACHE**. If you specify this value, MFC does no checking on this field. You must call **SetFieldDirty** and **SetFieldNull** yourself.

These options are explained further in the article "DAO Recordset: Binding Records Dynamically" in *Visual C++ Programmer's Guide* online.

Note   You can control whether data is double buffered by default by setting **CDaoRecordset::m_bCheckCacheForDirtyFields**.

Remarks

The **DFX_Single** function transfers floating point data between the field data members of a **CDaoRecordset** object and the columns of a record on the data source. Data is mapped between type **DAO_R4** in DAO and type **float** in the recordset.

Example

See **DFX_Text**.

See Also: **DFX_Text, DFX_Bool, DFX_Currency, DFX_Long, DFX_Short, DFX_Double, DFX_DateTime, DFX_Byte, DFX_Binary, DFX_LongBinary, CDaoFieldExchange::SetFieldType**

DFX_Text

> **void AFXAPI DFX_Text(CDaoFieldExchange*** *pFX*, **LPCTSTR** *szName*,
> ↪ **CString&** *value*, **int** *nPreAllocLength* = **AFX_DAO_TEXT_DEFAULT_SIZE**,
> ↪ **DWORD** *dwBindOptions* = **AFX_DAO_ENABLE_FIELD_CACHE**);

Parameters

pFX   A pointer to an object of class **CDaoFieldExchange**. This object contains information to define the context for each call of the function. For more information about the operations a **CDaoFieldExchange** object can specify, see the article "DAO Record Field Exchange: How DFX Works" in *Visual C++ Programmer's Guide* online.

szName   The name of a data column.

value   The value stored in the indicated data member—the value to be transferred. For a transfer from recordset to data source, the value, of type **CString**, is taken from the specified data member. For a transfer from data source to recordset, the value is stored in the specified data member.

nPreAllocSize   The framework preallocates this amount of memory. If your data is larger, the framework will allocated more space as needed. For better performance, set this size to a value large enough to prevent reallocations.

dwBindOptions   An option that lets you take advantage of MFC's double buffering mechanism for detecting recordset fields that have changed. The default, **AFX_DAO_ENABLE_FIELD_CACHE**, uses double buffering. The other possible value is **AFX_DAO_DISABLE_FIELD_CACHE**. If you specify this value, MFC does no checking on this field. You must call **SetFieldDirty** and **SetFieldNull** yourself.

These options are explained further in the article "DAO Record Field Exchange: Double Buffering Records" in *Visual C++ Programmer's Guide* online.

Note   You can control whether data is double buffered by default by setting **CDaoRecordset::m_bCheckCacheForDirtyFields**.

Remarks

The **DFX_Text** function transfers **CString** data between the field data members of a **CDaoRecordset** object and columns of a record on the data source. Data is mapped between type **DAO_CHAR** in DAO (or, if the symbol **_UNICODE** is defined, **DAO_WCHAR**) and type **CString** in the recordset.

Example

This example shows several calls to **DFX_Text**. Notice also the two calls to **CDaoFieldExchange::SetFieldType**. ClassWizard normally writes the second call to **SetFieldType** and its associated **DFX** calls. You must write the first call and its **DFX** call. It is recommended that you put any parameter items before the "//{{AFX_FIELD_MAP" comment. You must put parameters outside the comments.

```
//Example for DFX_Text
void CSections::DoFieldExchange(CDaoFieldExchange* pFX)
{
    pFX->SetFieldType(CDaoFieldExchange::param);
    DFX_Text(pFX, "Name", m_strNameParam);
    //{{AFX_FIELD_MAP(CSections)
    pFX->SetFieldType(CDaoFieldExchange::outputColumn);
    DFX_Text(pFX, "CourseID", m_strCourseID);
    DFX_Text(pFX, "InstructorID", m_strInstructorID);
    DFX_Short(pFX, "LabFee", m_nRoomNo);
    DFX_Text(pFX, "LabFee", m_strSchedule);
    DFX_Short(pFX, "SectionNo", m_nSectionNo);
    DFX_Currency(pFX, "LabFee", m_currLabFee);
    //}}AFX_FIELD_MAP
}
```

See Also: **DFX_Bool, DFX_Long, DFX_Currency, DFX_Short, DFX_Single, DFX_Double, DFX_DateTime, DFX_Byte, DFX_Binary, DFX_LongBinary, CDaoFieldExchange::SetFieldType**

DISP_DEFVALUE

DISP_DEFVALUE(*theClass*, *pszName* **)**

#include <afxdisp.h>

Parameters

theClass   Name of the class.

pszName   External name of the property that represents the "value" of the object.

Remarks

This macro makes an existing property the default value of an object. Using a default value can make programming your automation object simpler for Visual Basic applications.

The "default value" of your object is the property that is retrieved or set when a reference to an object does not specify a property or member function.

See Also: "Dispatch Maps," **DECLARE_DISPATCH_MAP, DISP_PROPERTY_EX, DISP_FUNCTION, BEGIN_DISPATCH_MAP, END_DISPATCH_MAP**

DISP_FUNCTION

DISP_FUNCTION(*theClass*, *pszName*, *pfnMember*, *vtRetVal*, *vtsParams*)

#include <afxdisp.h>

Parameters

theClass   Name of the class.

pszName   External name of the function.

pfnMember   Name of the member function.

vtRetVal   A value specifying the function's return type.

vtsParams   A space-separated list of one or more constants specifying the function's parameter list.

Remarks

The **DISP_FUNCTION** macro is used in a dispatch map to define an OLE automation function.

The *vtRetVal* argument is of type **VARTYPE**. Possible values for this argument are taken from the **VARENUM** enumeration. They are as follows:

Symbol	Return Type
VT_EMPTY	**void**
VT_I2	**short**
VT_I4	**long**
VT_R4	**float**
VT_R8	**double**
VT_CY	**CY**
VT_DATE	**DATE**
VT_BSTR	**BSTR**
VT_DISPATCH	**LPDISPATCH**
VT_ERROR	**SCODE**
VT_BOOL	**BOOL**
VT_VARIANT	**VARIANT**
VT_UNKNOWN	**LPUNKNOWN**

The *vtsParams* argument is a space-separated list of values from the **VTS_** constants. One or more of these values separated by spaces (not commas) specifies the function's parameter list. For example,

```
VTS_I2 VTS_PI2
```

specifies a list containing a short integer followed by a pointer to a short integer.

The **VTS_** constants and their meanings are as follows:

Symbol	Parameter Type
VTS_I2	short
VTS_I4	long
VTS_R4	float
VTS_R8	double
VTS_CY	const CY or CY*
VTS_DATE	DATE
VTS_BSTR	LPCSTR
VTS_DISPATCH	LPDISPATCH
VTS_SCODE	SCODE
VTS_BOOL	BOOL
VTS_VARIANT	const VARIANT* or VARIANT&
VTS_UNKNOWN	LPUNKNOWN
VTS_PI2	short*
VTS_PI4	long*
VTS_PR4	float*
VTS_PR8	double*
VTS_PCY	CY*
VTS_PDATE	DATE*
VTS_PBSTR	BSTR*
VTS_PDISPATCH	LPDISPATCH*
VTS_PSCODE	SCODE*
VTS_PBOOL	BOOL*
VTS_PVARIANT	VARIANT*
VTS_PUNKNOWN	LPUNKNOWN*

See Also: "Dispatch Maps," **DECLARE_DISPATCH_MAP, DISP_PROPERTY, DISP_PROPERTY_EX, BEGIN_DISPATCH_MAP, END_DISPATCH_MAP**

DISP_PROPERTY

DISP_PROPERTY(*theClass*, *pszName*, *memberName*, *vtPropType* **)**

#include <afxdisp.h>

Parameters

theClass   Name of the class.

pszName   External name of the property.

memberName   Name of the member variable in which the property is stored.

vtPropType   A value specifying the property's type.

Remarks

The **DISP_PROPERTY** macro is used in a dispatch map to define an OLE automation property.

The *vtPropType* argument is of type **VARTYPE**. Possible values for this argument are taken from the **VARENUM** enumeration:

Symbol	Property Type
VT_I2	**short**
VT_I4	**long**
VT_R4	**float**
VT_R8	**double**
VT_CY	**CY**
VT_DATE	**DATE**
VT_BSTR	**CString**
VT_DISPATCH	**LPDISPATCH**
VT_ERROR	**SCODE**
VT_BOOL	**BOOL**
VT_VARIANT	**VARIANT**
VT_UNKNOWN	**LPUNKNOWN**

When an external client changes the property, the value of the member variable specified by *memberName* changes; there is no notification of the change.

See Also: "Dispatch Maps," **DECLARE_DISPATCH_MAP, DISP_PROPERTY_EX, DISP_FUNCTION, BEGIN_DISPATCH_MAP, END_DISPATCH_MAP**

DISP_PROPERTY_EX

DISP_PROPERTY_EX(*theClass, pszName, memberGet, memberSet, vtPropType* **)**

#include <afxdisp.h>

Parameters

theClass   Name of the class.

pszName   External name of the property.

memberGet   Name of the member function used to get the property.

memberSet   Name of the member function used to set the property.

vtPropType   A value specifying the property's type.

Remarks

The **DISP_PROPERTY_EX** macro is used in a dispatch map to define an OLE automation property and name the functions used to get and set the property's value.

The *memberGet* and *memberSet* functions have signatures determined by the *vtPropType* argument. The *memberGet* function takes no arguments and returns a value of the type specified by *vtPropType*. The *memberSet* function takes an argument of the type specified by *vtPropType* and returns nothing.

The *vtPropType* argument is of type **VARTYPE**. Possible values for this argument are taken from the the **VARENUM** enumeration. For a list of these values, see the Remarks for the *vtRetVal* parameter in **DISP_FUNCTION**. Note that **VT_EMPTY**, listed in the **DISP_FUNCTION** remarks, is not permitted as a property data type.

See Also: "Dispatch Maps," **DECLARE_DISPATCH_MAP**, **DISP_PROPERTY**, **DISP_FUNCTION**, **BEGIN_DISPATCH_MAP**, **END_DISPATCH_MAP**

DISP_PROPERTY_NOTIFY

DISP_PROPERTY_NOTIFY(*theClass*, *szExternalName*, *memberName*, *pfnAfterSet*,
↪ *vtPropType*)

#include <afxdisp.h>

Parameters

theClass   Name of the class.

szExternalName   External name of the property.

memberName   Name of the member variable in which the property is stored.

pfnAfterSet   Name of the notification function for *szExternalName*.

vtPropType   A value specifying the property's type.

Remarks

The **DISP_PROPERTY_NOTIFY** macro is used in a dispatch map to define an OLE automation property with notification. Unlike properties defined with **DISP_PROPERTY**, a property defined with **DISP_PROPERTY_NOTIFY** will automatically call the function specified by *pfnAfterSet* when the property is changed.

The *vtPropType* argument is of type **VARTYPE**. Possible values for this argument are taken from the **VARENUM** enumeration:

Symbol	Property Type
VT_I2	**short**
VT_I4	**long**
VT_R4	**float**
VT_R8	**double**
VT_CY	**CY**
VT_DATE	**DATE**

(continued)

(continued)

Symbol	Property Type
VT_BSTR	**CString**
VT_DISPATCH	**LPDISPATCH**
VT_ERROR	**SCODE**
VT_BOOL	**BOOL**
VT_VARIANT	**VARIANT**
VT_UNKNOWN	**LPUNKNOWN**

See Also: "Dispatch Maps," **DISP_PROPERTY**, **DISP_FUNCTION**

DISP_PROPERTY_PARAM

DISP_PROPERTY_NOTIFY(*theClass*, *pszExternalName*, *pfnGet*, *pfnSet*,
↪ *vtPropType*, *vtsParams* **)**

#include <afxdisp.h>

Parameters

theClass   Name of the class.

pszExternalName   External name of the property.

pfnGet   Name of the member function used to get the property.

pfnSet   Name of the member function used to set the property.

vtPropType   A value specifying the property's type.

vtsParams   A string of space-separated **VTS_** variant parameter types, one for each
parameter.

Remarks

This macro defines a property accessed with separate **Get** and **Set** member functions.
Unlike the **DISP_PROPERTY_EX** macro, this macro allows you to specify a
parameter list for the property. This is useful for implementing properties which are
indexed or parameterized.

For example, consider the following declaration of get and set member functions that
allow the user to request a specific row and column when accessing the property:

```
afx_msg short GetArray(short row, short column);
afx_msg short SetArray(short row, short column, short nNewValue);
```

These correspond to the following **DISP_PROPERTY_PARAM** macro in the
control dispatch map:

```
DISP_PROPERTY_PARAM(CMyCtrl, "Array", GetArray, SetArray, VT-I2, VTS_I2 VTS_I2)
```

As another example, consider the following get and set member functions:

```
LPDISPATCH CMyObject::GetItem(short index1, short index2, short index3);
void CMyObject::SetItem(short index1, short index2, short index3,
↳ LPDISPATCH newValue);
```

These correspond to the following **DISP_PROPERTY_PARAM** macro in the control dispatch map:

```
DISP_PROPERTY_PARAM(CMyObject, "item", GetItem, SetItem, VT_DISPATCH,
↳     VTS_I2 VTS_I2 VTS_I2)
```

See Also: "Dispatch Maps," **DISP_PROPERTY_EX**

DumpElements

template< class *TYPE* **>void AFXAPI DumpElements(CDumpContext&** *dc*,
↳ **const** *TYPE** *pElements*, **int** *nCount* **);**

Parameters

dc   Dump context for dumping elements.

TYPE   Template parameter specifying the type of the elements.

pElements   Pointer to the elements to be dumped.

nCount   Number of elements to be dumped.

Remarks

Override this function to provide stream-oriented diagnostic output in text form for the elements of your collection. The **CArray::Dump**, **CList::Dump**, and **CMap::Dump** functions call this if the depth of the dump is greater than 0.

The default implementation does nothing. If the elements of your collection are derived from **CObject**, your override will typically iterate through the collection's elements, calling **Dump** for each element in turn.

For information on diagnostics and on the **Dump** function, see "MFC Debugging Support" in *Visual C++ Programmer's Guide* online.

See Also: **CDumpContext::SetDepth**, **CObject::Dump**, **CArray**, **CList**, **CMap**

DYNAMIC_DOWNCAST

DYNAMIC_DOWNCAST(*class*, *pointer* **)**

Parameters

class   The name of a class.

pointer   A pointer to be cast to a pointer to a object of type *class*.

Remarks

The **DYNAMIC_DOWNCAST** macro provides a handy way to cast a pointer to a pointer to a class object while checking to see if the cast is legal. The macro will cast the *pointer* parameter to a pointer to an object of the *class* parameter's type.

If the object referenced by the pointer is a "kind of" the identified class, the macro returns the appropriate pointer. If it isn't a legal cast the macro returns **NULL**.

See Also: STATIC_DOWNCAST

END_CATCH

END_CATCH

Remarks

Marks the end of the last **CATCH** or **AND_CATCH** block.

For more information on the **END_CATCH** macro, see the article "Exceptions" in *Visual C++ Programmer's Guide* online.

See Also: TRY, CATCH, AND_CATCH, THROW, THROW_LAST

END_CATCH_ALL

END_CATCH_ALL

Remarks

Marks the end of the last **CATCH_ALL** or **AND_CATCH_ALL** block.

See Also: TRY, CATCH_ALL, AND_CATCH_ALL, THROW, THROW_LAST

END_CONNECTION_MAP

END_CONNECTION_MAP( )

Remarks

Use the **END_CONNECTION_MAP** macro to end the definition of your connection map.

See Also: BEGIN_CONNECTION_MAP, DECLARE_CONNECTION_MAP

END_CONNECTION_PART

END_CONNECTION_PART(*localClass* **)**

Parameters

localClass   Specifies the name of the local class that implements the connection point.

Remarks

Use the **END_CONNECTION_PART** macro to end the declaration of your connection point.

See Also: **BEGIN_CONNECTION_PART, DECLARE_CONNECTION_MAP**

END_DISPATCH_MAP

END_DISPATCH_MAP( )

#include <afxdisp.h>

Remarks

Use the **END_DISPATCH_MAP** macro to end definition of your dispatch map. It must be used in conjunction with **BEGIN_DISPATCH_MAP**.

See Also: "Dispatch Maps," **DECLARE_DISPATCH_MAP, BEGIN_DISPATCH_MAP, DISP_FUNCTION, DISP_PROPERTY, DISP_PROPERTY_EX, DISP_DEFVALUE**

END_EVENT_MAP

END_EVENT_MAP( )

Remarks

Use the **END_EVENT_MAP** macro to end the definition of your event map.

See Also: **DECLARE_EVENT_MAP, BEGIN_EVENT_MAP**

END_EVENTSINK_MAP

END_EVENTSINK_MAP( )

Remarks

Use the **END_EVENTSINK_MAP** macro to end the definition of your event sink map.

See Also: **DECLARE_EVENTSINK_MAP, BEGIN_EVENTSINK_MAP**

END_MESSAGE_MAP

END_MESSAGE_MAP( )

Remarks

Use the **END_MESSAGE_MAP** macro to end the definition of your message map.

For more information on message maps and the **END_MESSAGE_MAP** macro, see "Message Handling and Mapping Topics" in *Visual C++ Programmer's Guide* online.

See Also: DECLARE_MESSAGE_MAP, BEGIN_MESSAGE_MAP, Message Map Function Categories

---

END_OLEFACTORY

END_OLEFACTORY(*class_name* **)**

Parameters

class_name   The name of the control class whose class factory this is.

Remarks

Use the **END_OLEFACTORY** macro to end the declaration of your control's class factory.

See Also: BEGIN_OLEFACTORY, DECLARE_OLECREATE_EX

END_PARSE_MAP

END_PARSE_MAP(*theClass* **)**

Parameters

theClass   Specifies the name of the class that owns this parse map.

Remarks

Use the **END_PARSE_MAP** macro to end the definition of your parse map. It must be used in conjunction with **BEGIN_PARSE_MAP**.

See **ON_PARSE_COMMAND** for a parse map example.

See Also: BEGIN_PARSE_MAP, ON_PARSE_COMMAND, ON_PARSE_COMMAND_PARAMS, DEFAULT_PARSE_COMMAND, CHttpServer

END_PROPPAGEIDS

END_PROPPAGEIDS(*class_name* **)**

Parameters

class_name   The name of the control class that owns the property page.

Remarks

Use the **END_PROPPAGEIDS** macro to end the definition of your property page ID list.

See Also: DECLARE_PROPPAGEIDS, **BEGIN_PROPPAGEIDS**

EVENT_CUSTOM

EVENT_CUSTOM(*pszName*, *pfnFire*, *vtsParams* **)**

Parameters

pszName   The name of the event.

pfnFire   The name of the event firing function.

vtsParams   A space-separated list of one or more constants specifying the function's parameter list.

Remarks

Use the **EVENT_CUSTOM** macro to define an event-map entry for a custom event.

The *vtsParams* parameter is a space-separated list of values from the **VTS_** constants. One or more of these values separated by spaces (not commas) specifies the function's parameter list. For example:

```
VTS_COLOR VTS_FONT
```

specifies a list containing a short integer followed by a **BOOL**.

The **VTS_** constants and their meanings are as follows:

Symbol	Parameter Type
VTS_I2	**short**
VTS_I4	**long**
VTS_R4	**float**
VTS_R8	**double**
VTS_COLOR	**OLE_COLOR**
VTS_CY	**CURRENCY**
VTS_DATE	**DATE**
VTS_BSTR	**const char***

(continued)

(continued)

Symbol	Parameter Type
VTS_DISPATCH	LPDISPATCH
VTS_FONT	IFontDispatch*
VTS_HANDLE	HANDLE
VTS_SCODE	SCODE
VTS_BOOL	BOOL
VTS_VARIANT	const VARIANT*
VTS_PVARIANT	VARIANT*
VTS_UNKNOWN	LPUNKNOWN
VTS_OPTEXCLUSIVE	OLE_OPTEXCLUSIVE
VTS_PICTURE	IPictureDisp*
VTS_TRISTATE	OLE_TRISTATE
VTS_XPOS_PIXELS	OLE_XPOS_PIXELS
VTS_YPOS_PIXELS	OLE_YPOS_PIXELS
VTS_XSIZE_PIXELS	OLE_XSIZE_PIXELS
VTS_YSIZE_PIXELS	OLE_YSIZE_PIXELS
VTS_XPOS_HIMETRIC	OLE_XPOS_HIMETRIC
VTS_YPOS_HIMETRIC	OLE_YPOS_HIMETRIC
VTS_XSIZE_HIMETRIC	OLE_XSIZE_HIMETRIC
VTS_YSIZE_HIMETRIC	OLE_YSIZE_HIMETRIC

Note Additional variant constants have been defined for all variant types, with the exception of **VTS_FONT** and **VTS_PICTURE**, that provide a pointer to the variant data constant. These constants are named using the **VTS_P***constantname* convention. For example, **VTS_PCOLOR** is a pointer to a **VTS_COLOR** constant.

See Also: EVENT_CUSTOM_ID, DECLARE_EVENT_MAP

EVENT_CUSTOM_ID

EVENT_CUSTOM_ID(*pszName*, *dispid*, *pfnFire*, *vtsParams*)

Parameters

pszName   The name of the event.

dispid   The dispatch ID used by the control when firing the event.

pfnFire   The name of the event firing function.

vtsParams   A variable list of parameters passed to the control container when the event is fired.

Remarks

Use the **EVENT_CUSTOM_ID** macro to define an event firing function for a custom event belonging to the dispatch ID specified by *dispid*.

The *vtsParams* argument is a space-separated list of values from the **VTS_** constants. One or more of these values separated by spaces (not commas) specifies the function's parameter list. For example:

```
VTS_COLOR VTS_FONT
```

specifies a list containing a short integer followed by a **BOOL**.

For a list of the **VTS_** constants, see **EVENT_CUSTOM**.

See Also: EVENT_CUSTOM

HashKey

template< class *ARG_KEY* **> UINT AFXAPI HashKey(** *ARG_KEY key* **);**

Return Value

The key's hash value.

Parameters

ARG_KEY   Template parameter specifying the data type used to access map keys.

key   The key whose hash value is to be calculated.

Remarks

Calculates a hash value for the given key.

This function is called directly by **CMap::RemoveKey** and indirectly by **CMap::Lookup** and **CMap::Operator []**.

The default implementation creates a hash value by shifting *key* rightward by four positions. Override this function so that it returns hash values appropriate for your application.

See Also: CMap

IMPLEMENT_DYNAMIC

IMPLEMENT_DYNAMIC(*class_name*, *base_class_name* **)**

Parameters

class_name   The actual name of the class (not enclosed in quotation marks).

base_class_name   The name of the base class (not enclosed in quotation marks).

Remarks

Generates the C++ code necessary for a dynamic **CObject**-derived class with run-time access to the class name and position within the hierarchy. Use the **IMPLEMENT_DYNAMIC** macro in a .CPP module, then link the resulting object code only once.

For more information, see "CObject Class Topics" in *Visual C++ Programmer's Guide* online.

See Also: **DECLARE_DYNAMIC, RUNTIME_CLASS, CObject::IsKindOf**

IMPLEMENT_DYNCREATE

IMPLEMENT_DYNCREATE(*class_name, base_class_name*)

Parameters

class_name   The actual name of the class (not enclosed in quotation marks).

base_class_name   The actual name of the base class (not enclosed in quotation marks).

Remarks

Use the **IMPLEMENT_DYNCREATE** macro with the **DECLARE_DYNCREATE** macro to enable objects of **CObject**-derived classes to be created dynamically at run time. The framework uses this ability to create new objects dynamically, for example, when it reads an object from disk during serialization. Add the **IMPLEMENT_DYNCREATE** macro in the class implementation file. For more information, see "CObject Class Topics" in *Visual C++ Programmer's Guide* online.

If you use the **DECLARE_DYNCREATE** and **IMPLEMENT_DYNCREATE** macros, you can then use the **RUNTIME_CLASS** macro and the **CObject::IsKindOf** member function to determine the class of your objects at run time.

If **DECLARE_DYNCREATE** is included in the class declaration, then **IMPLEMENT_DYNCREATE** must be included in the class implementation.

See Also: **DECLARE_DYNCREATE, RUNTIME_CLASS, CObject::IsKindOf**

IMPLEMENT_OLECREATE

IMPLEMENT_OLECREATE(*class_name, external_name, l, w1, w2, b1, b2, b3,* ↪ *b4, b5, b6, b7, b8*)

#include <afxdisp.h>

Parameters

class_name   The actual name of the class (not enclosed in quotation marks).

external_name   The object name exposed to other applications (enclosed in quotation marks).

l, w1, w2, b1, b2, b3, b4, b5, b6, b7, b8   Components of the class's **CLSID**.

Remarks

This macro must appear in the implementation file for any class that uses **DECLARE_OLECREATE**.

The external name is the identifier exposed to other applications. Client applications use the external name to request an object of this class from an automation server.

The OLE class ID is a unique 128-bit identifier for the object. It consists of one **long**, two **WORD**s, and eight **BYTE**s, as represented by *l*, *w1*, *w2*, and *b1* through *b8* in the syntax description. ClassWizard and AppWizard create unique OLE class IDs for you as required.

See Also: **DECLARE_OLECREATE**, **CLSID Key**.

IMPLEMENT_OLECREATE_EX

IMPLEMENT_OLECREATE_EX(*class_name, external_name, l, w1, w2, b1, b2,* ↪ *b3, b4, b5, b6, b7, b8* **)**

Parameters

class_name   The name of the control property page class.

external_name   The object name exposed to applications.

l, w1, w2, b1, b2, b3, b4, b5, b6, b7, b8   Components of the class's **CLSID**. For more information on these parameters, see the Remarks for **IMPLEMENT_OLECREATE**.

Remarks

Implements your control's class factory and the **GetClassID** member function of your control class. This macro must appear in the implementation file for any control class that uses the **DECLARE_OLECREATE_EX** macro or the **BEGIN_OLEFACTORY** and **END_OLEFACTORY** macros. The external name is the identifier of the OLE control that is exposed to other applications. Containers use this name to request an object of this control class.

See Also: **DECLARE_OLECREATE_EX**, **BEGIN_OLEFACTORY**, **END_OLEFACTORY**, **IMPLEMENT_OLECREATE**

IMPLEMENT_OLETYPELIB

IMPLEMENT_OLETYPELIB(*class_name, tlid, wVerMajor, wVerMinor* **)**

Parameters

class_name   The name of the control class related to the type library.

tlid   The ID number of the type library.

wVerMajor   The type library major version number.

wVerMinor   The type library minor version number.

Remarks

Implements the control's **GetTypeLib** member function. This macro must appear in the implementation file for any control class that uses the **DECLARE_OLETYPELIB** macro.

See Also: DECLARE_OLETYPELIB

IMPLEMENT_SERIAL

IMPLEMENT_SERIAL(*class_name, base_class_name, wSchema* **)**

Parameters

class_name   The actual name of the class (not enclosed in quotation marks).

base_class_name   The name of the base class (not enclosed in quotation marks).

wSchema   A **UINT** "version number" that will be encoded in the archive to enable a deserializing program to identify and handle data created by earlier program versions. The class schema number must not be –1.

Remarks

Generates the C++ code necessary for a dynamic **CObject**-derived class with run-time access to the class name and position within the hierarchy. Use the **IMPLEMENT_SERIAL** macro in a .CPP module; then link the resulting object code only once.

For more information, see the "CObject Class Topics" in *Visual C++ Programmer's Guide* online.

See Also: DECLARE_SERIAL, RUNTIME_CLASS, CObject::IsKindOf

ISAPIASSERT

ISAPIASSERT(*booleanExpression*)

Parameters

booleanExpression   Specifies an expression (including pointer values) that evaluates to nonzero or 0.

Remarks

Works exactly like the MFC macro **ASSERT**. Evaluates its argument. If the result is 0, the macro prints a diagnostic message and aborts the program. If the condition is nonzero, it does nothing.

The diagnostic message has the form

```
assertion failed in file <name> in line <num>
```

where *name* is the name of the source file, and *num* is the line number of the assertion that failed in the source file.

In the release version of your application, **ISAPIASSERT** does not evaluate the expression and thus will not interrupt the program. If the expression must be evaluated regardless of environment, use the **ISAPIVERIFY** macro in place of **ISAPIASSERT**. **ISAPIASSERT** is available only in the debug version of your application.

ISAPI applications do not have to use MFC. If MFC is not linked to your application, **ISAPIASSERT** provides the same **ASSERT** functionality. If your application is linked to the MFC, **ISAPIASSERT** simply calls MFC's **ASSERT**.

See Also: ISAPITRACE, ISAPITRACE0, ISAPITRACE1, ISAPITRACE2, ISAPITRACE3, ISAPIVERIFY

ISAPITRACE

ISAPITRACE(*exp*)

Parameters

exp   Specifies a variable number of arguments that are used in exactly the same way that a variable number of arguments are used in the run-time function **printf.**

Remarks

Works exactly like the MFC macro **TRACE**, which itself provides functionality similar to the **printf** function by sending a formatted string to a dump device such as debug monitor. Like **printf** for C programs under MS-DOS, the **ISAPITRACE** macro is a convenient way to track the value of variables as your program executes. In the Debug environment, the **ISAPITRACE** macro output goes to the Debug window of Visual C++. In the Release environment, it does nothing.

ISAPI applications do not have to use MFC. If MFC is not linked to your application, **ISAPITRACE** provides the same **TRACE** functionality. If your application is linked to the MFC, **ISAPITRACE** simply calls MFC's **TRACE**.

See Also: **ISAPIASSERT, ISAPITRACE0, ISAPITRACE1, ISAPITRACE2, ISAPITRACE3, ISAPIVERIFY**

ISAPITRACE0

ISAPITRACE0(*exp* **)**

Parameters

exp   A format string as used in the run-time function **printf**.

Remarks

ISAPITRACE0 is one variant of a group of trace macros that you can use for debug output. This group includes **ISAPITRACE0, ISAPITRACE1, ISAPITRACE2**, and **ISAPITRACE3**. The difference between these macros is the number of parameters taken. **ISAPITRACE0** only takes a format string and can be used for simple text messages. **ISAPITRACE1** takes a format string plus one argument—a variable to be dumped. Likewise, **ISAPITRACE2** and **ISAPITRACE3** take two and three parameters after the format string, respectively.

ISAPITRACE0 does nothing if you have compiled a release version of your application. As with **ISAPITRACE**, it only dumps data to the debug output device if you have compiled a debug version of your application.

ISAPITRACE0 works exactly like the MFC macro **TRACE0**. ISAPI applications do not have to use MFC. If MFC is not linked to your application, **ISAPITRACE0** provides the same **TRACE0** functionality. If your application is linked to the MFC, **ISAPITRACE0** simply calls MFC's **TRACE0**.

See Also: **ISAPIASSERT, ISAPITRACE, ISAPITRACE1, ISAPITRACE2, ISAPITRACE3, ISAPIVERIFY**

ISAPITRACE1

ISAPITRACE1(*exp*, *param1* **)**

Parameters

exp   A format string as used in the run-time function **printf**.

param1   The name of the variable whose value should be dumped.

Remarks

Works exactly like the MFC macro **TRACE1**. See **ISAPITRACE0** for a description of **ISAPITRACE1**.

ISAPI applications do not have to use MFC. If MFC is not linked to your application, **ISAPITRACE1** provides the same **TRACE1** functionality. If your application is linked to the MFC, **ISAPITRACE1** simply calls MFC's **TRACE1**.

See Also: **ISAPIASSERT**, **ISAPITRACE**, **ISAPITRACE0**, **ISAPITRACE2**, **ISAPITRACE3**, **ISAPIVERIFY**

ISAPITRACE2

ISAPITRACE2(*exp*, *param1*, *param2*)

Parameters

exp   A format string as used in the run-time function **printf**.

param1, *param2*   The name of the variable whose value should be dumped.

Remarks

Works exactly like the MFC macro **TRACE2**. See **ISAPITRACE0** for a description of **ISAPITRACE2**.

ISAPI applications do not have to use MFC. If MFC is not linked to your application, **ISAPITRACE2** provides the same **TRACE2** functionality. If your application is linked to the MFC, **ISAPITRACE2** simply calls MFC's **TRACE2**.

See Also: **ISAPIASSERT**, **ISAPITRACE**, **ISAPITRACE0**, **ISAPITRACE1**, **ISAPITRACE3**, **ISAPIVERIFY**

ISAPITRACE3

ISAPITRACE3(*exp*, *param1*, *param2*, *param3*)

Parameters

exp   A format string as used in the run-time function **printf**.

param1, *param2*, *param3*   The name of the variable whose value should be dumped.

Remarks

Works exactly like the MFC macro **TRACE3**. See **ISAPITRACE0** for a description of **ISAPITRACE3**.

ISAPI applications do not have to use MFC. If MFC is not linked to your application, **ISAPITRACE3** provides the same **TRACE3** functionality. If your application is linked to the MFC, **ISAPITRACE3** simply calls MFC's **TRACE3**.

See Also: **ISAPIASSERT**, **ISAPITRACE**, **ISAPITRACE0**, **ISAPITRACE1**, **ISAPITRACE2**, **ISAPIVERIFY**

ISAPIVERIFY

ISAPIVERIFY(*booleanExpression* **)**

Parameters

booleanExpression   Specifies an expression (including pointer values) that evaluates to nonzero or 0.

Remarks

Works exactly like the MFC macro **VERIFY**. In the debug version of your application, the **ISAPIVERIFY** macro evaluates its argument. If the result is 0, the macro prints a diagnostic message and halts the program. If the condition is nonzero, it does nothing.

The diagnostic message has the form

```
assertion failed in file <name> in line <num>
```

where *name* is the name of the source file and *num* is the line number of the assertion that failed in the source file.

In the release version of your application, **ISAPIVERIFY** evaluates the expression but does not print or interrupt the program. For example, if the expression is a function call, the call will be made.

ISAPI applications do not have to use MFC. If MFC is not linked to your application, **ISAPIVERIFY** provides the same **VERIFY** functionality. If your application is linked to the MFC, **ISAPIVERIFY** simply calls MFC's **VERIFY**.

See Also: ISAPIASSERT, ISAPITRACE, ISAPITRACE0, ISAPITRACE1, ISAPITRACE2, ISAPITRACE3

METHOD_PROLOGUE

METHOD_PROLOGUE(*theClass*, *localClass* **)**

Parameters

theClass   Specifies the name of the class whose interface map is being implemented.

localClass   Specifies the name of the local class that implements the interface map.

Remarks

Use the **METHOD_PROLOGUE** macro to maintain the proper global state when calling methods of an exported interface.

Typically, member functions of interfaces implemented by **CCmdTarget**-derived objects already use this macro to provide automatic initialization of the *pThis* pointer. For example:

```
class CInnerUnknown : public IUnknown
    ...
    CInnerUnknown InnerUnknown;
    ...
// Inner IUnknown implementation

    STDMETHODIMP_(ULONG) CInnerUnknown::AddRef()
    {
    METHOD_PROLOGUE(CCmdTarget, InnerUnknown)
    return pThis->InternalAddRef();
    }
```

For additional information, see Technical Note 38 online and "Managing the State Data of MFC Modules" in "Creating New Documents, Windows, and Views," which is in *Visual C++ Programmer's Guide* online.

ON_COMMAND

ON_COMMAND(*id,* *memberFxn* **)**

Parameters

id   The command ID.

memberFxn   The name of the message-handler function to which the command is mapped.

Remarks

This macro is usually inserted in a message map by ClassWizard or manually. It indicates which function will handle a command message from a command user-interface object such as a menu item or toolbar button.

When a command-target object receives a Windows **WM_COMMAND** message with the specified ID, **ON_COMMAND** will call the member function *memberFxn* to handle the message.

Use **ON_COMMAND** to map a single command to a member function. Use **ON_COMMAND_RANGE** to map a range of command ids to one member function. Only one message-map entry can match a given command id. That is, you can't map a command to more than one handler. For more information and examples, see "Message Handling and Mapping Topics" in *Visual C++ Programmer's Guide* online.

Example

```
// example for ON_COMMAND
BEGIN_MESSAGE_MAP( CMyDoc, CDocument )
    //{{AFX_MSG_MAP( CMyDoc )
    ON_COMMAND( ID_MYCMD, OnMyCommand )
    // ... More entries to handle additional commands
    //}}AFX_MSG_MAP
END_MESSAGE_MAP( )
```

See Also: **ON_UPDATE_COMMAND_UI**

ON_COMMAND_RANGE

ON_COMMAND_RANGE(*id1*, *id2*, *memberFxn* **)**

Parameters

id1   Command ID at the beginning of a contiguous range of command IDs.

id2   Command ID at the end of a contiguous range of command IDs.

memberFxn   The name of the message-handler function to which the commands are mapped.

Remarks

Use this macro to map a contiguous range of command IDs to a single message handler function. The range of IDs starts with *id1* and ends with *id2*.

Use **ON_COMMAND_RANGE** to map a range of command IDs to one member function. Use **ON_COMMAND** to map a single command to a member function. Only one message-map entry can match a given command ID. That is, you can't map a command to more than one handler. For more information on mapping message ranges, see "Handlers for Message-Map Ranges" in *Visual C++ Programmer's Guide* online.

ClassWizard does not support message map ranges, so you must place the macro yourself. Be sure to put it outside the message map `//{{AFX_MSG_MAP` delimiters.

See Also: ON_UPDATE_COMMAND_UI_RANGE, ON_CONTROL_RANGE, ON_COMMAND

ON_CONTROL

ON_CONTROL(*wNotifyCode*, *id*, *memberFxn* **)**

Parameters

wNotifyCode   The notification code of the control.

id   The command ID.

memberFxn   The name of the message-handler function to which the command is mapped.

Remarks

Indicates which function will handle a custom-control notification message. Control notification messages are those sent from a control to its parent window.

There should be exactly one **ON_CONTROL** macro statement in your message map for every control notification message that must be mapped to a message-handler function.

For more information and examples, see "Message Handling and Mapping Topics" in *Visual C++ Programmer's Guide* online.

See Also: **ON_MESSAGE**, **ON_REGISTERED_MESSAGE**

ON_CONTROL_RANGE

ON_CONTROL_RANGE(*wNotifyCode*, *id1*, *id2*, *memberFxn* **)**

Parameters

wNotifyCode   The notification code to which your handler is responding.

id1   Command ID at the beginning of a contiguous range of control IDs.

id2   Command ID at the end of a contiguous range of control IDs.

memberFxn   The name of the message-handler function to which the controls are mapped.

Remarks

Use this macro to map a contiguous range of control IDs to a single message handler function for a specified Windows notification message, such as **BN_CLICKED**. The range of IDs starts with *id1* and ends with *id2*. The handler is called for the specified notification coming from any of the mapped controls.

ClassWizard does not support message map ranges, so you must place the macro yourself. Be sure to put it outside the message map //{{AFX_MSG_MAP delimiters.

See Also: **ON_UPDATE_COMMAND_UI_RANGE**, **ON_COMMAND_RANGE**

ON_EVENT

ON_EVENT(*theClass*, *id*, *dispid*, *pfnHandler*, *vtsParams* **)**

Parameters

theClass   The class to which this event sink map belongs.

id   The control ID of the OLE control.

dispid   The dispatch ID of the event fired by the control.

pfnHandler   Pointer to a member function that handles the event. This function should have a **BOOL** return type, and parameter types that match the event's parameters (see *vtsParams*). The function should return **TRUE** to indicate the event was handled; otherwise **FALSE**.

vtsParams   A sequence of **VTS_** constants that specifies the types of the parameters for the event. These are the same constants that are used in dispatch map entries such as **DISP_FUNCTION**.

Remarks

Use the **ON_EVENT** macro to define an event handler function for an event fired by an OLE control.

The *vtsParams* argument is a space-separated list of values from the **VTS_** constants. One or more of these values separated by spaces (not commas) specifies the function's parameter list. For example:

```
VTS_I2 VTS_BOOL
```

specifies a list containing a short integer followed by a **BOOL**.

For a list of the **VTS_** constants, see **EVENT_CUSTOM**.

See Also: **ON_EVENT_RANGE**, **ON_PROPNOTIFY**, **ON_PROPNOTIFY_RANGE**

ON_EVENT_RANGE

ON_EVENT_RANGE(*theClass*, *idFirst*, *idLast*, *dispid*, *pfnHandler*, *vtsParams* **)**

Parameters

theClass The class to which this event sink map belongs.

idFirst The control ID of the first OLE control in the range.

idLast The control ID of the last OLE control in the range.

dispid The dispatch ID of the event fired by the control.

pfnHandler Pointer to a member function that handles the event. This function should have a **BOOL** return type, a first parameter of type **UINT** (for the control ID), and additional parameter types that match the event's parameters (see *vtsParams*). The function should return **TRUE** to indicate the event was handled; otherwise **FALSE**.

vtsParams A sequence of **VTS_** constants that specifies the types of the parameters for the event. The first constant should be of type **VTS_I4**, for the control ID. These are the same constants that are used in dispatch map entries such as **DISP_FUNCTION**.

Remarks

Use the **ON_EVENT_RANGE** macro to define an event handler function for an event fired by any OLE control having a control ID within a contiguous range of IDs.

The *vtsParams* argument is a space-separated list of values from the **VTS_** constants. One or more of these values separated by spaces (not commas) specifies the function's parameter list. For example:

```
VTS_I2 VTS_BOOL
```

specifies a list containing a short integer followed by a **BOOL**.

For a list of the **VTS_** constants, see **EVENT_CUSTOM**.

See Also: **ON_EVENT**, **ON_PROPNOTIFY**, **ON_PROPNOTIFY_RANGE**

ON_EVENT_REFLECT

ON_EVENT_REFLECT(*theClass*, *dispid*, *pfnHandler*, *vtsParams* **)**

Parameters

theClass   The class to which this event sink map belongs.

dispid   The dispatch ID of the event fired by the control.

pfnHandler   Pointer to a member function that handles the event. This function should have a **BOOL** return type and parameter types that match the event's parameters (see *vtsParams*). The function should return **TRUE** to indicate the event was handled; otherwise **FALSE**.

vtsParams   A sequence of **VTS_** constants that specifies the types of the parameters for the event. These are the same constants that are used in dispatch map entries such as **DISP_FUNCTION**.

Remarks

The **ON_EVENT_REFLECT** macro, when used in the event sink map of an OLE control's wrapper class, receives events fired by the control before they are handled by the control's container.

The *vtsParams* argument is a space-separated list of values from the **VTS_** constants.

One or more of these values separated by spaces (not commas) specifies the function's parameter list. For example:

```
VTS_I2 VTS_BOOL
```

specifies a list containing a short integer followed by a **BOOL**.

For a list of the **VTS_** constants, see **EVENT_CUSTOM**.

See Also: **ON_EVENT**, **ON_PROPNOTIFY**, **ON_PROPNOTIFY_REFLECT**

ON_MESSAGE

ON_MESSAGE(*message*, *memberFxn* **)**

Parameters

message   The message ID.

memberFxn   The name of the message-handler function to which the message is mapped.

Remarks

Indicates which function will handle a user-defined message. User-defined messages are usually defined in the range **WM_USER** to 0x7FFF. User-defined messages are any messages that are not standard Windows **WM_MESSAGE** messages. There should be exactly one **ON_MESSAGE** macro statement in your message map for every user-defined message that must be mapped to a message-handler function.

For more information and examples, see "Message Handling and Mapping Topics" in *Visual C++ Programmer's Guide* online.

Example

```
// example for ON_MESSAGE
#define WM_MYMESSAGE (WM_USER + 1)
BEGIN_MESSAGE_MAP( CMyWnd, CMyParentWndClass )
   //{{AFX_MSG_MAP( CMyWnd
   ON_MESSAGE( WM_MYMESSAGE, OnMyMessage )
   // ... Possibly more entries to handle additional messages
   //}}AFX_MSG_MAP
END_MESSAGE_MAP( )
```

See Also: ON_UPDATE_COMMAND_UI, **ON_CONTROL**, **ON_REGISTERED_MESSAGE**, **ON_COMMAND**, "User-Defined Handlers"

ON_OLECMD

ON_OLECMD(*pguid*, *olecmdid*, *id*)

Parameters

pguid   Identifier of the command group to which the command belongs. Use **NULL** for the standard group.

olecmdid   The identifier of the OLE command.

id   The menu ID, toolbar ID, button ID, or other ID of the resource or object issuing the command.

Remarks

Routes commands through the command dispatch interface **IOleCommandTarget**. **IOleCommandTarget** allows a container to receive commands that originate in a DocObject's user interface, and allows the container to send the same commands (such as New, Open, SaveAs, and Print on the File menu; and Copy, Paste, Undo, and so forth on the Edit menu) to a DocObject.

IOleCommandTarget is simpler than OLE Automation's **IDispatch**. **IOleCommandTarget** relies entirely on a standard set of commands that rarely have arguments, and no type information is involved (type safety is diminished for command arguments as well). If you do need to dispatch commands with arguments, use **COleServerDoc::OnExecOleCmd**.

The **IOleCommandTarget** standard menu commands have been implemented by MFC in the following macros:

ON_OLECMD_CLEARSELECTION( )
Dispatches the Edit Clear command. Implemented as:
```
ON_OLECMD(NULL, OLECMDID_CLEARSELECTION, ID_EDIT_CLEAR)
```

ON_OLECMD_COPY( )
Dispatches the Edit Copy command. Implemented as:
```
ON_OLECMD(NULL, OLECMDID_COPY, ID_EDIT_COPY)
```

ON_OLECMD_CUT( )
Dispatches the Edit Cut command. Implemented as:
```
ON_OLECMD(NULL, OLECMDID_CUT, ID_EDIT_CUT)
```

ON_OLECMD_NEW( )
Dispatches the File New command. Implemented as:
```
ON_OLECMD(NULL, OLECMDID_NEW, ID_FILE_NEW)
```

ON_OLECMD_OPEN( )
Dispatches the File Open command. Implemented as:
```
ON_OLECMD(NULL, OLECMDID_OPEN, ID_FILE_OPEN)
```

ON_OLECMD_PAGESETUP( )
Dispatches the File Page Setup command. Implemented as:
```
ON_OLECMD(NULL, OLECMDID_PAGESETUP, ID_FILE_PAGE_SETUP)
```

ON_OLECMD_PASTE( )
Dispatches the Edit Paste command. Implemented as:
```
ON_OLECMD(NULL, OLECMDID_PASTE, ID_EDIT_PASTE)
```

ON_OLECMD_PASTESPECIAL( )
Dispatches the Edit Paste Special command. Implemented as:
```
ON_OLECMD(NULL, OLECMDID_PASTESPECIAL, ID_EDIT_PASTE_SPECIAL)
```

ON_OLECMD_PRINT( )
Dispatches the File Print command. Implemented as:
```
ON_OLECMD(NULL, OLECMDID_PRINT, ID_FILE_PRINT)
```

ON_OLECMD_PRINTPREVIEW( )
Dispatches the File Print Preview command. Implemented as:
```
ON_OLECMD(NULL, OLECMDID_PRINTPREVIEW, ID_FILE_PRINT_PREVIEW)
```

ON_OLECMD_REDO( )
Dispatches the Edit Redo command. Implemented as:
```
ON_OLECMD(NULL, OLECMDID_REDO, ID_EDIT_REDO)
```

ON_OLECMD_SAVE( )
Dispatches the File Save command. Implemented as:
```
ON_OLECMD(NULL, OLECMDID_SAVE, ID_FILE_SAVE)
```

ON_OLECMD_SAVE_AS( )

Dispatches the File Save As command. Implemented as:

`ON_OLECMD(NULL, OLECMDID_SAVEAS, ID_FILE_SAVE_AS)`

ON_OLECMD_SAVE_COPY_AS( )

Dispatches the File Save Copy As command. Implemented as:

`ON_OLECMD(NULL, OLECMDID_SAVECOPYAS, ID_FILE_SAVE_COPY_AS)`

ON_OLECMD_SELECTALL( )

Dispatches the Edit Select All command. Implemented as:

`ON_OLECMD(NULL, OLECMDID_SELECTALL, ID_EDIT_SELECT_ALL)`

ON_OLECMD_UNDO( )

Dispatches the Edit Undo command. Implemented as:

`ON_OLECMD(NULL, OLECMDID_UNDO, ID_EDIT_UNDO)`

See Also: COleCmdUI, COleServerDoc::OnExecOleCmd

ON_OLEVERB

ON_OLEVERB(*idsVerbName*, *memberFxn* **)**

Parameters

idsVerbName　The string resource ID of the verb's name.

memberFxn　The function called by the framework when the verb is invoked.

Remarks

This macro defines a message map entry that maps a custom verb to a specific member function of your control.

The resource editor can be used to create custom verb names that are added to your string table.

The function prototype for *memberFxn* is:

BOOL memberFxn(LPMSG *lpMsg*, **HWND** *hWndParent*, **LPCRECT** *lpRect* **);**

The values of the *lpMsg*, *hWndParent*, and *lpRect* parameters are taken from the corresponding parameters of the **IOleObject::DoVerb** member function.

See Also: ON_STDOLEVERB

ON_PARSE_COMMAND

ON_PARSE_COMMAND(*FnName*, *mapClass*, *Args* **)**

Parameters

FnName　The name of the member function. Also the name of the command.

mapClass   The class name to map the function to.

Args   The arguments that map to the parameter's *FnName*. See Remarks for a list of symbols.

Remarks

The **ON_PARSE_COMMAND** macro is used in a parse map to define a command to a **CHttpServer** object from a client.

The member function identified by *FnName* must take a pointer to the **CHttpServerContext** as its first parameter. *FnName* is of the type **LPSTR**, and is identified by the symbol **ITS_LPSTR** in the parse map; that is, *FnName* points to a string containing the member function in class *mapClass*.

The parameter *Args* can take one of the following values:

Symbol	Type or Comment
ITS_EMPTY	*Args* cannot be blank. Use **ITS_EMPTY** if you have no arguments.
ITS_PSTR	A pointer to a string.
ITS_I2	a short
ITS_I4	a long
ITS_R4	a float
ITS_R8	a double

Example

```
BEGIN_PARSE_MAP(CDerivedClass, CHttpServer)
   DEFAULT_PARSE_COMMAND(Myfunc, CDerivedClass)
   ON_PARSE_COMMAND(Myfunc, CDerivedClass, ITS_PSTR
      ITS_I2)
   ON_PARSE_COMMAND_PARAMS("string integer=42")
   ON_PARSE_COMMAND(Myfunc2, CDerivedClass, ITS_PSTR
      ITS_I2 ITS_PSTR)
   ON_PARSE_COMMAND_PARAMS("string integer
      string2='Default value'")
END_PARSE_MAP(CDerivedClass)
```

Note   Use single quotes if you incorporate spaces into the default values for optional ITS_PSTRs.

```
void Myfunc(CHttpServerContext* pCtxt, LPTSTR pszName, int nNumber);
void Myfunc2(CHttpServerContext* pCtxt, LPTSTR pszName, int nNumber,
   pszTitle);
```

Note   The handlers for a parse map command must take a pointer to a **CHttpServerContext** as the first parameter, and the parameters must be declared in the same order in which they're defined in **ON_PARSE_COMMAND**.

See Also: BEGIN_PARSE_MAP, END_PARSE_MAP, ON_PARSE_COMMAND_PARAMS, DEFAULT_PARSE_COMMAND, CHttpServer

ON_PARSE_COMMAND_PARAMS

> **ON_PARSE_COMMAND_PARAMS(** *Params* **)**

Parameters

Params The parameters, mapped to the *Args* parameter and associated with the function identified by *FnName*, in the macro **ON_PARSE_COMMAND** immediately preceding **ON_PARSE_COMMAND_PARAMS**.

Remarks

The macro **ON_PARSE_COMMAND_PARAMS** identifies and specifies defaults for the parameters associated with the function that is mapped to a command to a **CHttpServer** object by a client. The macro **ON_PARSE_COMMAND_PARAMS** must immediately follow the **ON_PARSE_COMMAND** macro with which it is associated.

If a parameter is named, the client must supply the parameter name in the query. For example, if your parameters are as follows:

```
ON_PARSE_COMMAND_PARAMS("string int=42")
```

then the parameter *string* must be supplied by the client, or the query will fail.

If the parameter is optional, the client need not supply it, and the parse map will supply the default value. For example, if your parameters are as follows:

```
ON_PARSE_COMMAND_PARAMS("string=default int=42")
```

then neither parameter must be defined in the client's query, and the parameter *string* is by default an empty string.

See **ON_PARSE_COMMAND** for a parse map example.

See Also: BEGIN_PARSE_MAP, END_PARSE_MAP, ON_PARSE_COMMAND, DEFAULT_PARSE_COMMAND, CHttpServer

---

ON_PROPNOTIFY

> **ON_PROPNOTIFY(** *theClass*, *id*, *dispid*, *pfnRequest*, *pfnChanged* **)**

Parameters

theClass The class to which this event sink map belongs.

id The control ID of the OLE control.

dispid The dispatch ID of the property involved in the notification.

pfnRequest Pointer to a member function that handles the **OnRequestEdit** notification for this property. This function should have a **BOOL** return type and a

BOOL* parameter. This function should set the parameter to **TRUE** to allow the property to change and **FALSE** to disallow. The function should return **TRUE** to indicate the notification was handled; otherwise **FALSE**.

pfnChanged   Pointer to a member function that handles the **OnChanged** notification for this property. The function should have a **BOOL** return type and a **UINT** parameter. The function should return **TRUE** to indicate that notification was handled; otherwise **FALSE**.

Remarks

Use the **ON_PROPNOTIFY** macro to define an event sink map entry for handling property notifications from an OLE control.

The *vtsParams* argument is a space-separated list of values from the **VTS_** constants. One or more of these values separated by spaces (not commas) specifies the function's parameter list. For example:

```
VTS_I2 VTS_BOOL
```

specifies a list containing a short integer followed by a **BOOL**.

For a list of the **VTS_** constants, see **EVENT_CUSTOM**.

See Also: **ON_EVENT_RANGE**, **ON_PROPNOTIFY_RANGE**

ON_PROPNOTIFY_RANGE

ON_PROPNOTIFY_RANGE(*theClass*, *idFirst*, *idLast*, *dispid*, *pfnRequest*, *pfnChanged* **)**

Parameters

theClass   The class to which this event sink map belongs.

idFirst   The control ID of the first OLE control in the range.

idLast   The control ID of the last OLE control in the range.

dispid   The dispatch ID of the property involved in the notification.

pfnRequest   Pointer to a member function that handles the **OnRequestEdit** notification for this property. This function should have a **BOOL** return type and **UINT** and **BOOL*** parameters. The function should set the parameter to **TRUE** to allow the property to change and **FALSE** to disallow. The function should return **TRUE** to indicate that notification was handled; otherwise **FALSE**.

pfnChanged   Pointer to a member function that handles the **OnChanged** notification for this property. The function should have a **BOOL** return type and a **UINT** parameter. The function should return **TRUE** to indicate that notification was handled; otherwise **FALSE**.

Remarks

Use the **ON_PROPNOTIFY_RANGE** macro to define an event sink map entry for handling property notifications from any OLE control having a control ID within a contiguous range of IDs.

See Also: ON_EVENT_RANGE, ON_PROPNOTIFY, ON_EVENT

ON_PROPNOTIFY_REFLECT

ON_PROPNOTIFY_REFLECT(*theClass, dispid, pfnRequest, pfnChanged* **)**

Parameters

theClass   The class to which this event sink map belongs.

dispid   The dispatch ID of the property involved in the notification.

pfnRequest   Pointer to a member function that handles the **OnRequestEdit** notification for this property. This function should have a **BOOL** return type and a **BOOL*** parameter. This function should set the parameter to **TRUE** to allow the property to change and **FALSE** to disallow. The function should return **TRUE** to indicate the notification was handled; otherwise **FALSE**.

pfnChanged   Pointer to a member function that handles the **OnChanged** notification for this property. The function should have a **BOOL** return type and no parameters. The function should return **TRUE** to indicate the notification was handled; otherwise **FALSE**.

Remarks

The **ON_PROPNOTIFY_REFLECT** macro, when used in the event sink map of an OLE control's wrapper class, receives property notifications sent by the control before they are handled by the control's container.

See Also: ON_EVENT_REFLECT, ON_PROPNOTIFY

ON_REGISTERED_MESSAGE

ON_REGISTERED_MESSAGE(*nMessageVariable, memberFxn* **)**

Parameters

nMessageVariable   The registered window-message ID variable.

memberFxn   The name of the message-handler function to which the message is mapped.

Remarks

The Windows **RegisterWindowMessage** function is used to define a new window message that is guaranteed to be unique throughout the system. This macro indicates which function will handle the registered message.

For more information and examples, see "Message Handling and Mapping Topics" in *Visual C++ Programmer's Guide* online.

Example

```
// example for ON_REGISTERED_MESSAGE
const UINT   wm_Find = RegisterWindowMessage( FINDMSGSTRING )
BEGIN_MESSAGE_MAP( CMyWnd, CMyParentWndClass )
   //{{AFX_MSG_MAP( CMyWnd )
   ON_REGISTERED_MESSAGE( wm_Find, OnFind )
   // ... Possibly more entries to handle additional messages
   //}}AFX_MSG_MAP
END_MESSAGE_MAP( )
```

See Also: ON_MESSAGE, ON_UPDATE_COMMAND_UI, ON_CONTROL, ON_COMMAND, ::RegisterWindowMessage, "User-Defined Handlers"

ON_REGISTERED_THREAD_MESSAGE

ON_REGISTERED_THREAD_MESSAGE(*nMessageVariable***,** *memberFxn* **)**

Parameters

nMessageVariable   The registered window-message ID variable.

memberFxn   The name of the **CWinThread**-message-handler function to which the message is mapped.

Remarks

Indicates which function will handle the message registered by the Windows **RegisterWindowMessage** function. **RegisterWindowMessage** is used to define a new window message that is guaranteed to be unique throughout the system. **ON_REGISTERED_THREAD_MESSAGE** must be used instead of **ON_REGISTERED_MESSAGE** when you have a **CWinThread** class.

See Also: ON_REGISTERED_MESSAGE, ON_THREAD_MESSAGE, ::RegisterWindowMessage, CWinThread

---

ON_STDOLEVERB

ON_STDOLEVERB(*iVerb***,** *memberFxn* **)**

Parameters

iVerb   The standard verb index for the verb being overridden.

memberFxn   The function called by the framework when the verb is invoked.

Remarks

Use this macro to override the default behavior of a standard verb.

The standard verb index is of the form **OLEIVERB_**, followed by an action. **OLEIVERB_SHOW**, **OLEIVERB_HIDE**, and **OLEIVERB_UIACTIVATE** are some examples of standard verbs.

See **ON_OLEVERB** for a description of the function prototype to be used as the *memberFxn* parameter.

See Also: ON_OLEVERB

ON_THREAD_MESSAGE

ON_THREAD_MESSAGE(*message*, *memberFxn* **)**

Parameters

message   The message ID.

memberFxn   The name of the **CWinThread**-message-handler function to which the message is mapped.

Remarks

Indicates which function will handle a user-defined message. **ON_THREAD_MESSAGE** must be used instead of **ON_MESSAGE** when you have a **CWinThread** class. User-defined messages are any messages that are not standard Windows **WM_MESSAGE** messages. There should be exactly one **ON_THREAD_MESSAGE** macro statement in your message map for every user-defined message that must be mapped to a message-handler function.

See Also: ON_MESSAGE, ON_REGISTERED_THREAD_MESSAGE, CWinThread

ON_UPDATE_COMMAND_UI

ON_UPDATE_COMMAND_UI(*id*, *memberFxn* **)**

Parameters

id   The message ID.

memberFxn   The name of the message-handler function to which the message is mapped.

Remarks

This macro is usually inserted in a message map by ClassWizard to indicate which function will handle a user-interface update command message.

There should be exactly one **ON_UPDATE_COMMAND_UI** macro statement in your message map for every user-interface update command that must be mapped to a message-handler function.

For more information and examples, see "Message Handling and Mapping Topics" in *Visual C++ Programmer's Guide* online.

See Also: **ON_MESSAGE, ON_REGISTERED_MESSAGE, ON_CONTROL, ON_COMMAND, CCmdUI**

ON_UPDATE_COMMAND_UI_RANGE

ON_UPDATE_COMMAND_UI_RANGE(*id1*, *id2*, *memberFxn* **)**

Parameters

id1   Command ID at the beginning of a contiguous range of command IDs.

id2   Command ID at the end of a contiguous range of command IDs.

memberFxn   The name of the update message-handler function to which the commands are mapped.

Remarks

Use this macro to map a contiguous range of command IDs to a single update message handler function. Update message handlers update the state of menu items and toolbar buttons associated with the command. The range of IDs starts with *id1* and ends with *id2*.

ClassWizard does not support message map ranges, so you must place the macro yourself. Be sure to put it outside the message map //{{AFX_MSG_MAP delimiters.

See Also: **ON_COMMAND_RANGE, ON_CONTROL_RANGE**

PROPPAGEID

PROPPAGEID(*clsid* **)**

Parameters

clsid   The unique class ID of a property page.

Remarks

Use this macro to add a property page for use by your OLE control.
All **PROPPAGEID** macros must be placed between the
BEGIN_PROPPAGEIDS and **END_PROPPAGEIDS** macros in your
control's implementation file.

See Also: **BEGIN_PROPPAGEIDS, END_PROPPAGEIDS**

PX_Blob

BOOL PX_Blob(CPropExchange* *pPX*, **LPCTSTR** *pszPropName*,
↪ **HGLOBAL&** *hBlob*, **HGLOBAL** *hBlobDefault* = **NULL**);

Return Value

Nonzero if the exchange was successful; 0 if unsuccessful.

Parameters

pPX   Pointer to the **CPropExchange** object (typically passed as a parameter to **DoPropExchange**).

pszPropName   The name of the property being exchanged.

hBlob   Reference to the variable where the property is stored (typically a member variable of your class).

hBlobDefault   Default value for the property.

Remarks

Call this function within your control's DoPropExchange member function to serialize or initialize a property that stores binary large object (BLOB) data. The property's value will be read from or written to the variable referenced by *hBlob*, as appropriate. This variable should be initialized to **NULL** before initially calling **PX_Blob** for the first time (typically, this can be done in the control's constructor). If *hBlobDefault* is specified, it will be used as the property's default value. This value is used if, for any reason, the control's initialization or serialization process fails.

The handles *hBlob* and *hBlobDefault* refer to a block of memory which contains the following:

- A **DWORD** which contains the length, in bytes, of the binary data that follows, followed immediately by

- A block of memory containing the actual binary data.

Note that **PX_Blob** will allocate memory, using the Windows **GlobalAlloc** API, when loading BLOB-type properties. You are responsible for freeing this memory. Therefore, the destructor of your control should call **GlobalFree** on any BLOB-type property handles to free up any memory allocated to your control.

See Also: COleControl::DoPropExchange

PX_Bool

> **BOOL PX_Bool(CPropExchange*** *pPX*, **LPCTSTR** *pszPropName*,
> ↪ **BOOL&** *bValue* **);**
> **BOOL PX_Bool(CPropExchange*** *pPX*, **LPCTSTR** *pszPropName*,
> ↪ **BOOL&** *bValue*, **BOOL** *bDefault* **);**

Return Value

Nonzero if the exchange was successful; 0 if unsuccessful.

Parameters

pPX   Pointer to the **CPropExchange** object (typically passed as a parameter to **DoPropExchange**).

pszPropName   The name of the property being exchanged.

bValue   Reference to the variable where the property is stored (typically a member variable of your class).

bDefault   Default value for the property.

Remarks

Call this function within your control's DoPropExchange member function to serialize or initialize a property of type **BOOL**. The property's value will be read from or written to the variable referenced by *bValue*, as appropriate. If *bDefault* is specified, it will be used as the property's default value. This value is used if, for any reason, the control's serialization process fails.

> **See Also:**   **COleControl::DoPropExchange**

PX_Color

> **BOOL PX_Color(CPropExchange*** *pPX*, **LPCTSTR** *pszPropName*,
> ↪ **OLE_COLOR&** *clrValue* **);**
> **BOOL PX_Color(CPropExchange*** *pPX*, **LPCTSTR** *pszPropName*,
> ↪ **OLE_COLOR&** *clrValue*, **OLE_COLOR** *clrDefault* **);**

Return Value

Nonzero if the exchange was successful; 0 if unsuccessful.

Parameters

pPX   Pointer to the **CPropExchange** object (typically passed as a parameter to **DoPropExchange**).

pszPropName   The name of the property being exchanged.

clrValue   Reference to the variable where the property is stored (typically a member variable of your class).

clrDefault   Default value for the property, as defined by the control developer.

Remarks

Call this function within your control's `DoPropExchange` member function to serialize or initialize a property of type **OLE_COLOR**. The property's value will be read from or written to the variable referenced by *clrValue*, as appropriate. If *clrDefault* is specified, it will be used as the property's default value. This value is used if, for any reason, the control's serialization process fails.

See Also: **COleControl::DoPropExchange**

PX_Currency

> **BOOL PX_Currency(CPropExchange*** *pPX*, **LPCTSTR** *pszPropName*,
> ↳ **CY&** *cyValue* **);**
> **BOOL PX_Currency(CPropExchange*** *pPX*, **LPCTSTR** *pszPropName*,
> ↳ **CY&** *cyValue*, **CY** *cyDefault* **);**

Return Value

Nonzero if the exchange was successful; 0 if unsuccessful.

Parameters

pPX   Pointer to the **CPropExchange** object (typically passed as a parameter to **DoPropExchange**).

pszPropName   The name of the property being exchanged.

cyValue   Reference to the variable where the property is stored (typically a member variable of your class).

cyDefault   Default value for the property.

Remarks

Call this function within your control's `DoPropExchange` member function to serialize or initialize a property of type **currency**. The property's value will be read from or written to the variable referenced by *cyValue*, as appropriate. If *cyDefault* is specified, it will be used as the property's default value. This value is used if, for any reason, the control's serialization process fails.

See Also: **COleControl::DoPropExchange**

PX_DataPath

> **BOOL PX_DataPath(CPropExchange*** *pPX*, **LPCTSTR** *pszPropName*,
> ↳ **CDataPathProperty&** *dataPathProperty* **);**
> **BOOL PX_DataPath(CPropExchange*** *pPXe*,
> ↳ **CDataPathProperty&** *dataPathProperty* **);**

Return Value

Nonzero if the exchange was successful; 0 if unsuccessful.

Parameters

pPX Pointer to the **CPropExchange** object (typically passed as a parameter to **DoPropExchange**).

pszPropName The name of the property being exchanged.

dataPathProperty Reference to the variable where the property is stored (typically a member variable of your class).

Remarks

Call this function within your control's DoPropExchange member function to serialize or initialize a data path property of type **CDataPathProperty**. Data path properties implement asynchronous control properties. The property's value will be read from or written to the variable referenced by *dataPathProperty*, as appropriate.

See Also: **COleControl::DoPropExchange**, **CDataPathProperty**

PX_Double

BOOL PX_Double(CPropExchange* *pPX*, **LPCTSTR** *pszPropName*,
↪ **double&** *doubleValue*);
BOOL PX_Double(CPropExchange* *pPX*, **LPCTSTR** *pszPropName*,
↪ **double&** *doubleValue*, **double** *doubleDefault*);

Return Value

Nonzero if the exchange was successful; 0 if unsuccessful.

Parameters

pPX Pointer to the **CPropExchange** object (typically passed as a parameter to **DoPropExchange**).

pszPropName The name of the property being exchanged.

doubleValue Reference to the variable where the property is stored (typically a member variable of your class).

doubleDefault Default value for the property.

Remarks

Call this function within your control's DoPropExchange member function to serialize or initialize a property of type **double**. The property's value is read from or written to the variable referenced by *doubleValue*, as appropriate. If *doubleDefault* is specified, it will be used as the property's default value. This value is used if, for any reason, the control's serialization process fails.

See Also: **COleControl::DoPropExchange**, **PX_Float**, **PX_Short**

PX_Float

BOOL PX_Float(CPropExchange* *pPX*, **LPCTSTR** *pszPropName*, **float&** *floatValue* **);**
BOOL PX_Float(CPropExchange* *pPX*, **LPCTSTR** *pszPropName*, **float&** *floatValue*,
↪ **float** *floatDefault* **);**

Return Value

Nonzero if the exchange was successful; 0 if unsuccessful.

Parameters

pPX   Pointer to the **CPropExchange** object (typically passed as a parameter to **DoPropExchange**).

pszPropName   The name of the property being exchanged.

floatValue   Reference to the variable where the property is stored (typically a member variable of your class).

floatDefault   Default value for the property.

Remarks

Call this function within your control's DoPropExchange member function to serialize or initialize a property of type **float**. The property's value is read from or written to the variable referenced by *floatValue*, as appropriate. If *floatDefault* is specified, it will be used as the property's default value. This value is used if, for any reason, the control's serialization process fails.

See Also: COleControl::DoPropExchange, PX_Double, PX_String

PX_Font

BOOL PX_Font(CPropExchange* *pPX*, **LPCTSTR** *pszPropName*,
↪ **CFontHolder&** *font*, **const FONTDESC FAR*** *pFontDesc* = **NULL**,
↪ **LPFONTDISP** *pFontDispAmbient* = **NULL** **);**

Return Value

Nonzero if the exchange was successful; 0 if unsuccessful.

Parameters

pPX   Pointer to the **CPropExchange** object (typically passed as a parameter to **DoPropExchange**).

pszPropName   The name of the property being exchanged.

font   A reference to a **CFontHolder** object that contains the font property.

pFontDesc   A pointer to a **FONTDESC** structure containing the values to use in initializing the default state of the font property, in the case where *pFontDispAmbient* is **NULL**.

pFontDispAmbient   A pointer to the **IFontDisp** interface of a font to use in initializing the default state of the font property.

Remarks

Call this function within your control's `DoPropExchange` member function to serialize or initialize a property of type font. The property's value is read from or written to *font*, a **CFontHolder** reference, when appropriate. If *pFontDesc* and *pFontDispAmbient* are specified, they are used for initializing the property's default value, when needed. These values are used if, for any reason, the control's serialization process fails. Typically, you pass **NULL** for *pFontDesc* and the ambient value returned by **COleControl::AmbientFont** for *pFontDispAmbient*. Note that the font object returned by **COleControl::AmbientFont** must be released by a call to the **IFontDisp::Release** member function.

See Also: **COleControl::DoPropExchange**, **COleControl::AmbientFont**

PX_IUnknown

BOOL PX_IUnknown(CPropExchange* *pPX*, **LPCTSTR** *pszPropName*,
↪ **LPUNKNOWN&** *pUnk*, **REFIID** *iid*, **LPUNKNOWN** *pUnkDefault* = **NULL**);

Return Value

Nonzero if the exchange was successful; 0 if unsuccessful.

Parameters

pPX   Pointer to the **CPropExchange** object (typically passed as a parameter to **DoPropExchange**).

pszPropName   The name of the property being exchanged.

pUnk   Reference to a variable containing the interface of the object that represents the value of the property.

iid   An interface ID indicating which interface of the property object is used by the control.

pUnkDefault   Default value for the property.

Remarks

Call this function within your control's `DoPropExchange` member function to serialize or initialize a property represented by an object having an **IUnknown**-derived interface. The property's value is read from or written to the variable referenced by *pUnk*, as appropriate. If *pUnkDefault* is specified, it will be used as the property's default value. This value is used if, for any reason, the control's serialization process fails.

See Also: **COleControl::DoPropExchange**

PX_Long

BOOL PX_Long(CPropExchange* *pPX*, **LPCTSTR** *pszPropName*, **long&** *lValue* **);**
BOOL PX_Long(CPropExchange* *pPX*, **LPCTSTR** *pszPropName*, **long&** *lValue*,
↳ **long** *lDefault* **);**

Return Value

Nonzero if the exchange was successful; 0 if unsuccessful.

Parameters

pPX   Pointer to the **CPropExchange** object (typically passed as a parameter to **DoPropExchange**).

pszPropName   The name of the property being exchanged.

lValue   Reference to the variable where the property is stored (typically a member variable of your class).

lDefault   Default value for the property.

Remarks

Call this function within your control's DoPropExchange member function to serialize or initialize a property of type **long**. The property's value is read from or written to the variable referenced by *lValue*, as appropriate. If *lDefault* is specified, it will be used as the property's default value. This value is used if, for any reason, the control's serialization process fails.

See Also: COleControl::DoPropExchange

PX_Picture

BOOL PX_Picture(CPropExchange* *pPX*, **LPCTSTR** *pszPropName*,
↳ **CPictureHolder&** *pict* **);**
BOOL PX_Picture(CPropExchange* *pPX*, **LPCTSTR** *pszPropName*,
↳ **CPictureHolder&** *pict*, **CPictureHolder&** *pictDefault* **);**

Return Value

Nonzero if the exchange was successful; 0 if unsuccessful.

Parameters

pPX   Pointer to the **CPropExchange** object (typically passed as a parameter to **DoPropExchange**).

pszPropName   The name of the property being exchanged.

pict   Reference to a **CPictureHolder** object where the property is stored (typically a member variable of your class).

pictDefault   Default value for the property.

Remarks

Call this function within your control's `DoPropExchange` member function to serialize or initialize a picture property of your control. The property's value is read from or written to the variable referenced by *pict*, as appropriate. If *pictDefault* is specified, it will be used as the property's default value. This value is used if, for any reason, the control's serialization process fails.

See Also: COleControl::DoPropExchange

PX_Short

BOOL PX_Short(CPropExchange* *pPX*, **LPCTSTR** *pszPropName*, **short&** *sValue*);
BOOL PX_Short(CPropExchange* *pPX*, **LPCTSTR** *pszPropName*, **short&** *sValue*,
↳ **short** *sDefault*);

Return Value

Nonzero if the exchange was successful; 0 if unsuccessful.

Parameters

pPX   Pointer to the **CPropExchange** object (typically passed as a parameter to **DoPropExchange**).

pszPropName   The name of the property being exchanged.

sValue   Reference to the variable where the property is stored (typically a member variable of your class).

sDefault   Default value for the property.

Remarks

Call this function within your control's `DoPropExchange` member function to serialize or initialize a property of type **short**. The property's value is read from or written to the variable referenced by *sValue*, as appropriate. If *sDefault* is specified, it will be used as the property's default value. This value is used if, for any reason, the control's serialization process fails.

See Also: COleControl::DoPropExchange

PX_String

BOOL PX_String(CPropExchange* *pPX*, **LPCTSTR** *pszPropName*,
↳ **CString&** *strValue*);
BOOL PX_String(CPropExchange* *pPX*, **LPCTSTR** *pszPropName*,
↳ **CString&** *strValue*, **CString** *strDefault*);

Return Value

Nonzero if the exchange was successful; 0 if unsuccessful.

Parameters

pPX   Pointer to the **CPropExchange** object (typically passed as a parameter to
DoPropExchange).

pszPropName   The name of the property being exchanged.

strValue   Reference to the variable where the property is stored (typically a member
variable of your class).

strDefault   Default value for the property.

Remarks

Call this function within your control's DoPropExchange member function to serialize
or initialize a character string property. The property's value is read from or written to
the variable referenced by *strValue*, as appropriate. If *strDefault* is specified, it will be
used as the property's default value. This value is used if, for any reason, the control's
serialization process fails.

See Also: COleControl::DoPropExchange, CString

PX_ULong

BOOL PX_ULong(CPropExchange* *pPX*, **LPCTSTR** *pszPropName*,
↳ **ULONG&** *ulValue*);
BOOL PX_ULong(CPropExchange* *pPX*, **LPCTSTR** *pszPropName*,
↳ **ULONG&** *ulValue*, **long** *ulDefault*);

Return Value

Nonzero if the exchange was successful; 0 if unsuccessful.

Parameters

pPX   Pointer to the **CPropExchange** object (typically passed as a parameter to
DoPropExchange).

pszPropName   Name of the property being exchanged.

ulValue   Reference to the variable where the property is stored (typically a member
variable of your class).

ulDefault   Default value for the property.

Remarks

Call this function within your control's DoPropExchange member function to serialize
or initialize a property of type **ULONG**. The property's value is read from or written
to the variable referenced by *ulValue*, as appropriate. If *ulDefault* is specified, it will
be used as the property's default value. This value is used if, for any reason, the
control's serialization process fails.

See Also: COleControl::DoPropExchange

PX_UShort

BOOL PX_UShort(CPropExchange* *pPX*, **LPCTSTR** *pszPropName*,
↳ **USHORT&** *usValue*);
BOOL PX_UShort(CPropExchange* *pPX*, **LPCTSTR** *pszPropName*,
↳ **USHORT&** *usValue*, **USHORT** *usDefault*);

Return Value

Nonzero if the exchange was successful; 0 if unsuccessful.

Parameters

pPX   Pointer to the **CPropExchange** object (typically passed as a parameter to **DoPropExchange**).

pszPropName   Name of the property being exchanged.

usValue   Reference to the variable where the property is stored (typically a member variable of your class).

usDefault   Default value for the property.

Remarks

Call this function within your control's DoPropExchange member function to serialize or initialize a property of type **unsigned short**. The property's value is read from or written to the variable referenced by *usValue*, as appropriate. If *usDefault* is specified, it will be used as the property's default value. This value is used if, for any reason, the control's serialization process fails.

See Also: COleControl::DoPropExchange

PX_VBXFontConvert

BOOL PX_VBXFontConvert(CPropExchange* *pPX*, **CFontHolder&** *font*);

Return Value

Nonzero if the exchange was successful; 0 if unsuccessful.

Parameters

pPX   Pointer to the **CPropExchange** object (typically passed as a parameter to **DoPropExchange**).

font   The font property of the OLE control that will contain the converted VBX font-related properties.

Remarks

Call this function within your control's DoPropExchange member function to initialize a font property by converting a VBX control's font-related properties.

This function should be used only by an OLE control that is designed as a direct replacement for a VBX control. When the Visual Basic development environment converts a form containing a VBX control to use the corresponding replacement OLE control, it will call the control's **IDataObject::SetData** function, passing in a property set that contains the VBX control's property data. This operation, in turn, causes the control's **DoPropExchange** function to be invoked. **DoPropExchange** can call **PX_VBXFontConvert** to convert the VBX control's font-related properties (for example, "FontName," "FontSize," and so on) into the corresponding components of the OLE control's font property.

PX_VBXFontConvert should only be called when the control is actually being converted from a VBX form application. For example:

```
void CSampleCtrl::DoPropExchange(CPropExchange* pPX)
{
    ExchangeVersion(pPX, MAKELONG(_wVerMinor, _wVerMajor));
    COleControl::DoPropExchange(pPX);

    if (IsConvertingVBX())
        PX_VBXFontConvert(pPX, InternalGetFont());
}
```

See Also: **COleControl::DoPropExchange, COleControl::AmbientFont, PX_Font**

RFX_Binary

void RFX_Binary(CFieldExchange* *pFX*, **const char*** *szName*,
    ↪ **CByteArray&** *value*, **int** *nMaxLength* = **255**);

Parameters

pFX   A pointer to an object of class **CFieldExchange**. This object contains information to define the context for each call of the function. For more information about the operations a **CFieldExchange** object can specify, see the article "Record Field Exchange: How RFX Works" in *Visual C++ Programmer's Guide* online.

szName   The name of a data column.

value   The value stored in the indicated data member —the value to be transferred. For a transfer from recordset to data source, the value, of type **CByteArray**, is taken from the specified data member. For a transfer from data source to recordset, the value is stored in the specified data member.

nMaxLength   The maximum allowed length of the string or array being transferred. The default value of *nMaxLength* is 255. Legal values are 1 to **INT_MAX**. The framework allocates this amount of space for the data. For best performance, pass a value large enough to accommodate the largest data item you expect.

Remarks

The **RFX_Binary** function transfers arrays of bytes between the field data members of a **CRecordset** object and the columns of a record on the data source of ODBC type **SQL_BINARY**, **SQL_VARBINARY**, or **SQL_LONGVARBINARY**. Data in the data source of these types is mapped to and from type **CByteArray** in the recordset.

Example

See **RFX_Text**.

See Also: **RFX_Text**, **RFX_Bool**, **RFX_Long**, **RFX_Int**, **RFX_Single**, **RFX_Double**, **RFX_Date**, **RFX_Byte**, **RFX_LongBinary**, **CFieldExchange::SetFieldType**

RFX_Binary_Bulk

void RFX_Binary_Bulk(CFieldExchange* *pFX,* **LPCTSTR** *szName,*
↪ **BYTE**** *prgByteVals,* **long**** *prgLengths,* **int** *nMaxLength* **);**

Parameters

pFX   A pointer to a **CFieldExchange** object. This object contains information to define the context for each call of the function. For more information, see the article "Record Field Exchange: How RFX Works" in *Visual C++ Programmer's Guide* online.

szName   The name of a data column.

prgByteVals   A pointer to an array of **BYTE** values. This array will store the data to be transferred from the data source to the recordset.

prgLengths   A pointer to an array of long integers. This array will store the length in bytes of each value in the array pointed to by *prgByteVals*. Note that the value **SQL_NULL_DATA** will be stored if the corresponding data item contains a Null value. For more details, see the ODBC API function **SQLBindCol** in the *ODBC SDK Programmer's Reference*.

nMaxLength   The maximum allowed length of the values stored in the array pointed to by *prgByteVals*. To ensure that data will not be truncated, pass a value large enough to accommodate the largest data item you expect.

Remarks

The **RFX_Binary_Bulk** function transfers multiple rows of byte data from a column of an ODBC data source to a corresponding array in a **CRecordset**-derived object. The data source column can have an ODBC type of **SQL_BINARY**, **SQL_VARBINARY**, or **SQL_LONGVARBINARY**. The recordset must define a field data member of type pointer to **BYTE**.

If you initialize *prgByteVals* and *prgLengths* to **NULL**, then the arrays they point to will be allocated automatically, with sizes equal to the rowset size.

Note Bulk record field exchange only transfers data from the data source to the recordset object. In order to make your recordset updatable, you must use the ODBC API function **SQLSetPos**. For an example of how to do this, see the sample DBFETCH.

For more information, see the articles "Recordset: Fetching Records in Bulk (ODBC)" and "Record Field Exchange (RFX)" in *Visual C++ Programmer's Guide* online.

Example

See **RFX_Text_Bulk**.

See Also: **RFX_Bool_Bulk**, **RFX_Byte_Bulk**, **RFX_Date_Bulk**, **RFX_Double_Bulk**, **RFX_Int_Bulk**, **RFX_Long_Bulk**, **RFX_Single_Bulk**, **RFX_Text_Bulk**, **CFieldExchange::SetFieldType**

RFX_Bool

void RFX_Bool(CFieldExchange* *pFX*, **const char*** *szName*, **BOOL&** *value* **);**

Parameters

pFX   A pointer to an object of class **CFieldExchange**. This object contains information to define the context for each call of the function. For more information about the operations a **CFieldExchange** object can specify, see the article "Record Field Exchange: How RFX Works" in *Visual C++ Programmer's Guide* online.

szName   The name of a data column.

value   The value stored in the indicated data member —the value to be transferred. For a transfer from recordset to data source, the value, of type **BOOL**, is taken from the specified data member. For a transfer from data source to recordset, the value is stored in the specified data member.

Remarks

The **RFX_BOOL** function transfers Boolean data between the field data members of a **CRecordset** object and the columns of a record on the data source of ODBC type **SQL_BIT**.

Example

See **RFX_Text**.

See Also: **RFX_Text**, **RFX_Long**, **RFX_Int**, **RFX_Single**, **RFX_Double**, **RFX_Date**, **RFX_Byte**, **RFX_Binary**, **RFX_LongBinary**, **CFieldExchange::SetFieldType**

RFX_Bool_Bulk

void RFX_Bool_Bulk(CFieldExchange* *pFX*, **LPCTSTR** *szName*,
↳ **BOOL**** *prgBoolVals*, **long**** *prgLengths*);

Parameters

pFX   A pointer to a **CFieldExchange** object. This object contains information to define the context for each call of the function. For more information, see the article "Record Field Exchange: How RFX Works" in *Visual C++ Programmer's Guide* online.

szName   The name of a data column.

prgBoolVals   A pointer to an array of **BOOL** values. This array will store the data to be transferred from the data source to the recordset.

prgLengths   A pointer to an array of long integers. This array will store the length in bytes of each value in the array pointed to by *prgBoolVals*. Note that the value **SQL_NULL_DATA** will be stored if the corresponding data item contains a Null value. For more details, see the ODBC API function **SQLBindCol** in the *ODBC SDK Programmer's Reference*.

Remarks

The **RFX_Bool_Bulk** function transfers multiple rows of Boolean data from a column of an ODBC data source to a corresponding array in a **CRecordset**-derived object. The data source column must have an ODBC type of **SQL_BIT**. The recordset must define a field data member of type pointer to **BOOL**.

If you initialize *prgBoolVals* and *prgLengths* to **NULL**, then the arrays they point to will be allocated automatically, with sizes equal to the rowset size.

Note   Bulk record field exchange only transfers data from the data source to the recordset object. In order to make your recordset updatable, you must use the ODBC API function **SQLSetPos**. For an example of how to do this, see the sample DBFETCH online.

For more information, see the articles "Recordset: Fetching Records in Bulk (ODBC)" and "Record Field Exchange (RFX)" in *Visual C++ Programmer's Guide* online.

Example

See **RFX_Text_Bulk**.

See Also: **RFX_Binary_Bulk**, **RFX_Byte_Bulk**, **RFX_Date_Bulk**, **RFX_Double_Bulk**, **RFX_Int_Bulk**, **RFX_Long_Bulk**, **RFX_Single_Bulk**, **RFX_Text_Bulk**, **CFieldExchange::SetFieldType**

RFX_Byte

> **void RFX_Byte(CFieldExchange*** *pFX***, const char*** *szName***, BYTE&** *value* **);**

Parameters

pFX   A pointer to an object of class **CFieldExchange**. This object contains information to define the context for each call of the function. For more information about the operations a **CFieldExchange** object can specify, see the article "Record Field Exchange: How RFX Works" in *Visual C++ Programmer's Guide* online.

szName   The name of a data column.

value   The value stored in the indicated data member —the value to be transferred. For a transfer from recordset to data source, the value, of type **BYTE**, is taken from the specified data member. For a transfer from data source to recordset, the value is stored in the specified data member.

Remarks

The **RFX_Byte** function transfers single bytes between the field data members of a **CRecordset** object and the columns of a record on the data source of ODBC type **SQL_TINYINT**.

Example

See **RFX_Text**.

See Also: **RFX_Text**, **RFX_Bool**, **RFX_Long**, **RFX_Int**, **RFX_Single**, **RFX_Double**, **RFX_Date**, **RFX_Binary**, **RFX_LongBinary**, **CFieldExchange::SetFieldType**

RFX_Byte_Bulk

> **void RFX_Byte_Bulk(CFieldExchange*** *pFX***, LPCTSTR** *szName***,**
> **↳ BYTE**** *prgByteVals***, long**** *prgLengths* **);**

Parameters

pFX   A pointer to a **CFieldExchange** object. This object contains information to define the context for each call of the function. For more information, see the article "Record Field Exchange: How RFX Works" in *Visual C++ Programmer's Guide* online.

szName   The name of a data column.

prgByteVals   A pointer to an array of **BYTE** values. This array will store the data to be transferred from the data source to the recordset.

prgLengths   A pointer to an array of long integers. This array will store the length in bytes of each value in the array pointed to by *prgByteVals*. Note that the value **SQL_NULL_DATA** will be stored if the corresponding data item contains a Null value. For more details, see the ODBC API function **SQLBindCol** in the *ODBC SDK Programmer's Reference*.

Remarks

The **RFX_Byte_Bulk** function transfers multiple rows of single bytes from a column of an ODBC data source to a corresponding array in a **CRecordset**-derived object. The data source column must have an ODBC type of **SQL_TINYINT**. The recordset must define a field data member of type pointer to **BYTE**.

If you initialize *prgByteVals* and *prgLengths* to **NULL**, then the arrays they point to will be allocated automatically, with sizes equal to the rowset size.

Note Bulk record field exchange only transfers data from the data source to the recordset object. In order to make your recordset updatable, you must use the ODBC API function **SQLSetPos**. For an example of how to do this, see the sample DBFETCH online.

For more information, see the articles "Recordset: Fetching Records in Bulk (ODBC)" and "Record Field Exchange (RFX)" in *Visual C++ Programmer's Guide* online.

Example

See **RFX_Text_Bulk**.

See Also: RFX_Binary_Bulk, RFX_Bool_Bulk, RFX_Date_Bulk, RFX_Double_Bulk, RFX_Int_Bulk, RFX_Long_Bulk, RFX_Single_Bulk, RFX_Text_Bulk, CFieldExchange::SetFieldType

---

RFX_Date

void RFX_Date(CFieldExchange* *pFX*, **const char*** *szName*, **CTime&** *value*);
void RFX_Date(CFieldExchange* pFX, **const char*** *szName*,
  ↪ **TIMESTAMP_STRUCT&** *value*);

Parameters

pFX   A pointer to an object of class **CFieldExchange**. This object contains information to define the context for each call of the function. For more information about the operations a **CFieldExchange** object can specify, see the article "Record Field Exchange: How RFX Works" in *Visual C++ Programmer's Guide* online.

szName   The name of a data column.

value   The value stored in the indicated data member —the value to be transferred. The two versions of the function take different data types for value. The first version of the function takes a reference to a **CTime** object. For a transfer from recordset to data source, this value is taken from the specified data member. For a transfer from data source to recordset, the value is stored in the specified data member. The second version of the function takes a reference to a **TIMESTAMP_STRUCT**. You must set up this structure yourself prior to the call.

Neither dialog data exchange (DDX) support nor ClassWizard support is available for this version. In your field map, place your call to the second version of **RFX_Date** outside the ClassWizard comment delimiters.

Remarks

The **RFX_Date** function transfers **CTime** or **TIMESTAMP_STRUCT** data between the field data members of a **CRecordset** object and the columns of a record on the data source of ODBC type **SQL_DATE**, **SQL_TIME**, or **SQL_TIMESTAMP**.

The **CTime** version of the function imposes the overhead of some intermediate processing and has a somewhat limited range. If you find either of these factors too limiting, use the second version of the function. But note its lack of ClassWizard and DDX support and the requirement that you set up the structure yourself.

Example

See **RFX_Text**.

See Also: **RFX_Text**, **RFX_Bool**, **RFX_Long**, **RFX_Int**, **RFX_Single**, **RFX_Double**, **RFX_Byte**, **RFX_Binary**, **RFX_LongBinary**, **CFieldExchange::SetFieldType**

RFX_Date_Bulk

void **RFX_Date_Bulk**(CFieldExchange* *pFX*, LPCTSTR *szName*,
➥ **TIMESTAMP_STRUCT**** *prgTSVals*, **long**** *prgLengths*);

Parameters

pFX   A pointer to a **CFieldExchange** object. This object contains information to define the context for each call of the function. For more information, see the article "Record Field Exchange: How RFX Works" in *Visual C++ Programmer's Guide* online.

szName   The name of a data column.

prgTSVals   A pointer to an array of **TIMESTAMP_STRUCT** values. This array will store the data to be transferred from the data source to the recordset. For more information about the **TIMESTAMP_STRUCT** data type, see the topic "C Data Types" in Appendix D of the *ODBC SDK Programmer's Reference*.

prgLengths   A pointer to an array of long integers. This array will store the length in bytes of each value in the array pointed to by *prgTSVals*. Note that the value **SQL_NULL_DATA** will be stored if the corresponding data item contains a Null value. For more details, see the ODBC API function **SQLBindCol** in the *ODBC SDK Programmer's Reference*.

Remarks

The **RFX_Date_Bulk** function transfers multiple rows of **TIMESTAMP_STRUCT** data from a column of an ODBC data source to a corresponding array in a **CRecordset**-derived object. The data source column can have an ODBC type of

SQL_DATE, **SQL_TIME**, or **SQL_TIMESTAMP**. The recordset must define a field data member of type pointer to **TIMESTAMP_STRUCT**.

If you initialize *prgTSVals* and *prgLengths* to **NULL**, then the arrays they point to will be allocated automatically, with sizes equal to the rowset size.

Note Bulk record field exchange only transfers data from the data source to the recordset object. In order to make your recordset updatable, you must use the ODBC API function **SQLSetPos**. For an example of how to do this, see the sample DBFETCH online.

For more information, see the articles "Recordset: Fetching Records in Bulk (ODBC)" and "Record Field Exchange (RFX)" in *Visual C++ Programmer's Guide* online.

Example

See **RFX_Text_Bulk**.

See Also: RFX_Binary_Bulk, RFX_Bool_Bulk, RFX_Byte_Bulk, RFX_Double_Bulk, RFX_Int_Bulk, RFX_Long_Bulk, RFX_Single_Bulk, RFX_Text_Bulk, CFieldExchange::SetFieldType

RFX_Double

void RFX_Double(CFieldExchange* *pFX***, const char*** *szName***, double&** *value* **);**

Parameters

pFX   A pointer to an object of class **CFieldExchange**. This object contains information to define the context for each call of the function. For more information about the operations a **CFieldExchange** object can specify, see the article "Record Field Exchange: How RFX Works" in *Visual C++ Programmer's Guide* online.

szName   The name of a data column.

value   The value stored in the indicated data member—the value to be transferred. For a transfer from recordset to data source, the value, of type **double**, is taken from the specified data member. For a transfer from data source to recordset, the value is stored in the specified data member.

Remarks

The **RFX_Double** function transfers **double float** data between the field data members of a **CRecordset** object and the columns of a record on the data source of ODBC type **SQL_DOUBLE**.

Example

See **RFX_Text**.

See Also: RFX_Text, RFX_Bool, RFX_Long, RFX_Int, RFX_Single, RFX_Date, RFX_Byte, RFX_Binary, RFX_LongBinary, CFieldExchange::SetFieldType

RFX_Double_Bulk

> **void RFX_Double_Bulk(CFieldExchange*** *pFX*, **LPCTSTR** *szName*,
> ⟶ **double**** *prgDblVals*, **long**** *prgLengths* **);**

Parameters

pFX   A pointer to a **CFieldExchange** object. This object contains information to define the context for each call of the function. For more information, see the article "Record Field Exchange: How RFX Works" in *Visual C++ Programmer's Guide* online.

szName   The name of a data column.

prgDblVals   A pointer to an array of **double** values. This array will store the data to be transferred from the data source to the recordset.

prgLengths   A pointer to an array of long integers. This array will store the length in bytes of each value in the array pointed to by *prgDblVals*. Note that the value **SQL_NULL_DATA** will be stored if the corresponding data item contains a Null value. For more details, see the ODBC API function **SQLBindCol** in the *ODBC SDK Programmer's Reference*.

Remarks

The **RFX_Double_Bulk** function transfers multiple rows of double-precision floating-point data from a column of an ODBC data source to a corresponding array in a **CRecordset**-derived object. The data source column must have an ODBC type of **SQL_DOUBLE**. The recordset must define a field data member of type pointer to **double**.

If you initialize *prgDblVals* and *prgLengths* to **NULL**, then the arrays they point to will be allocated automatically, with sizes equal to the rowset size.

Note   Bulk record field exchange only transfers data from the data source to the recordset object. In order to make your recordset updatable, you must use the ODBC API function **SQLSetPos**. For an example of how to do this, see the sample DBFETCH online.

For more information, see the articles "Recordset: Fetching Records in Bulk (ODBC)" and "Record Field Exchange (RFX)" in *Visual C++ Programmer's Guide* online.

Example

See **RFX_Text_Bulk**.

See Also: **RFX_Binary_Bulk**, **RFX_Bool_Bulk**, **RFX_Byte_Bulk**, **RFX_Date_Bulk**, **RFX_Int_Bulk**, **RFX_Long_Bulk**, **RFX_Single_Bulk**, **RFX_Text_Bulk**, **CFieldExchange::SetFieldType**

RFX_Int

>   void **RFX_Int**(**CFieldExchange*** *pFX*, **const char*** *szName*, **int&** *value*);

Parameters

>   *pFX*   A pointer to an object of class **CFieldExchange**. This object contains
>   information to define the context for each call of the function. For more
>   information about the operations a **CFieldExchange** object can specify, see the
>   article "Record Field Exchange: How RFX Works" in *Visual C++ Programmer's
>   Guide* online.
>
>   *szName*   The name of a data column.
>
>   *value*   The value stored in the indicated data member —the value to be transferred.
>   For a transfer from recordset to data source, the value, of type **int**, is taken from the
>   specified data member. For a transfer from data source to recordset, the value is
>   stored in the specified data member.

Remarks

>   The **RFX_Int** function transfers integer data between the field data members of a
>   **CRecordset** object and the columns of a record on the data source of ODBC type
>   **SQL_SMALLINT**.

Example

>   See **RFX_Text**.
>
>   **See Also: RFX_Text**, **RFX_Bool**, **RFX_Long**, **RFX_Single**, **RFX_Double**,
>   **RFX_Date**, **RFX_Byte**, **RFX_Binary**, **RFX_LongBinary**,
>   **CFieldExchange::SetFieldType**

RFX_Int_Bulk

>   void **RFX_Int_Bulk**(**CFieldExchange*** *pFX*, **LPCTSTR** *szName*, **int*** *prgIntVals*,
>   ↪ **long**** *prgLengths*);

Parameters

>   *pFX*   A pointer to a **CFieldExchange** object. This object contains information to
>   define the context for each call of the function. For more information, see the
>   article "Record Field Exchange: How RFX Works" in *Visual C++ Programmer's
>   Guide* online.
>
>   *szName*   The name of a data column.
>
>   *prgIntVals*   A pointer to an array of integers. This array will store the data to be
>   transferred from the data source to the recordset.
>
>   *prgLengths*   A pointer to an array of long integers. This array will store the length in
>   bytes of each value in the array pointed to by *prgIntVals*. Note that the value
>   **SQL_NULL_DATA** will be stored if the corresponding data item contains a Null

value. For more details, see the ODBC API function **SQLBindCol** in the *ODBC SDK Programmer's Reference*.

Remarks

The **RFX_Int_Bulk** function transfers multiple rows of integer data from a column of an ODBC data source to a corresponding array in a **CRecordset**-derived object. The data source column must have an ODBC type of **SQL_SMALLINT**. The recordset must define a field data member of type pointer to **int**.

If you initialize *prgIntVals* and *prgLengths* to **NULL**, then the arrays they point to will be allocated automatically, with sizes equal to the rowset size.

Note Bulk record field exchange only transfers data from the data source to the recordset object. In order to make your recordset updatable, you must use the ODBC API function **SQLSetPos**. For an example of how to do this, see the sample DBFETCH online.

For more information, see the articles "Recordset: Fetching Records in Bulk (ODBC)" and "Record Field Exchange (RFX)" in *Visual C++ Programmer's Guide* online.

Example

See **RFX_Text_Bulk**.

See Also: **RFX_Binary_Bulk, RFX_Bool_Bulk, RFX_Byte_Bulk, RFX_Date_Bulk, RFX_Double_Bulk, RFX_Long_Bulk, RFX_Single_Bulk, RFX_Text_Bulk, CFieldExchange::SetFieldType**

RFX_Long

void RFX_Long(CFieldExchange* *pFX*, **const char*** *szName*,
  ↳ **LONG&** *value* **);**

Parameters

pFX   A pointer to an object of class **CFieldExchange**. This object contains information to define the context for each call of the function. For more information about the operations a **CFieldExchange** object can specify, see the article "Record Field Exchange: How RFX Works" in *Visual C++ Programmer's Guide* online.

szName   The name of a data column.

value   The value stored in the indicated data member—the value to be transferred. For a transfer from recordset to data source, the value, of type **long**, is taken from the specified data member. For a transfer from data source to recordset, the value is stored in the specified data member.

Remarks

The **RFX_Long** function transfers long integer data between the field data members of a **CRecordset** object and the columns of a record on the data source of ODBC type **SQL_INTEGER**.

Example

See **RFX_Text**.

See Also: **RFX_Text**, **RFX_Bool**, **RFX_Int**, **RFX_Single**, **RFX_Double**, **RFX_Date**, **RFX_Byte**, **RFX_Binary**, **RFX_LongBinary**, **CFieldExchange::SetFieldType**

RFX_Long_Bulk

void RFX_Long_Bulk(CFieldExchange* *pFX,* **LPCTSTR** *szName,*
↪ **long**** *prgLongVals,* **long**** *prgLengths* **);**

Parameters

pFX   A pointer to a **CFieldExchange** object. This object contains information to define the context for each call of the function. For more information, see the article "Record Field Exchange: How RFX Works" in *Visual C++ Programmer's Guide* online.

szName   The name of a data column.

prgLongVals   A pointer to an array of long integers. This array will store the data to be transferred from the data source to the recordset.

prgLengths   A pointer to an array of long integers. This array will store the length in bytes of each value in the array pointed to by *prgLongVals*. Note that the value **SQL_NULL_DATA** will be stored if the corresponding data item contains a Null value. For more details, see the ODBC API function **SQLBindCol** in the *ODBC SDK Programmer's Reference*.

Remarks

The **RFX_Long_Bulk** function transfers multiple rows of long integer data from a column of an ODBC data source to a corresponding array in a **CRecordset**-derived object. The data source column must have an ODBC type of **SQL_INTEGER**. The recordset must define a field data member of type pointer to **long**.

If you initialize *prgLongVals* and *prgLengths* to **NULL**, then the arrays they point to will be allocated automatically, with sizes equal to the rowset size.

Note   Bulk record field exchange only transfers data from the data source to the recordset object. In order to make your recordset updatable, you must use the ODBC API function **SQLSetPos**. For an example of how to do this, see the sample DBFETCH online.

For more information, see the articles "Recordset: Fetching Records in Bulk (ODBC)" and "Record Field Exchange (RFX)" in *Visual C++ Programmer's Guide* online.

Example

See **RFX_Text_Bulk**.

See Also: **RFX_Binary_Bulk, RFX_Bool_Bulk, RFX_Byte_Bulk, RFX_Date_Bulk, RFX_Double_Bulk, RFX_Int_Bulk, RFX_Single_Bulk, RFX_Text_Bulk, CFieldExchange::SetFieldType**

RFX_LongBinary

void RFX_LongBinary(CFieldExchange* *pFX*, **const char*** *szName*,
↳ **CLongBinary&** *value*);

Parameters

pFX   A pointer to an object of class **CFieldExchange**. This object contains information to define the context for each call of the function. For more information about the operations a **CFieldExchange** object can specify, see the article "Record Field Exchange: How RFX Works" in *Visual C++ Programmer's Guide* online.

szName   The name of a data column.

value   The value stored in the indicated data member—the value to be transferred. For a transfer from recordset to data source, the value, of type **CLongBinary**, is taken from the specified data member. For a transfer from data source to recordset, the value is stored in the specified data member.

Remarks

The **RFX_LongBinary** function transfers binary large object (BLOB) data using class **CLongBinary** between the field data members of a **CRecordset** object and the columns of a record on the data source of ODBC type **SQL_LONGVARBINARY** or **SQL_LONGVARCHAR**.

Example

See **RFX_Text**.

See Also: **RFX_Text, RFX_Bool, RFX_Long, RFX_Int, RFX_Single, RFX_Double, RFX_Date, RFX_Byte, RFX_Binary, CFieldExchange::SetFieldType, CLongBinary**

RFX_Single

void RFX_Single(CFieldExchange* *pFX*, **const char*** *szName*, **float&** *value*);

Parameters

pFX   A pointer to an object of class **CFieldExchange**. This object contains information to define the context for each call of the function. For more information about the operations a **CFieldExchange** object can specify, see the article "Record Field Exchange: How RFX Works" in *Visual C++ Programmer's Guide* online.

szName   The name of a data column.

value   The value stored in the indicated data member—the value to be transferred. For a transfer from recordset to data source, the value, of type **float**, is taken from the specified data member. For a transfer from data source to recordset, the value is stored in the specified data member.

Remarks

The **RFX_Single** function transfers floating-point data between the field data members of a **CRecordset** object and the columns of a record on the data source of ODBC type **SQL_REAL**.

Example

See **RFX_Text**.

See Also: **RFX_Text**, **RFX_Bool**, **RFX_Long**, **RFX_Int**, **RFX_Double**, **RFX_Date**, **RFX_Byte**, **RFX_Binary**, **RFX_LongBinary**, **CFieldExchange::SetFieldType**

RFX_Single_Bulk

void RFX_Single_Bulk(CFieldExchange* *pFX*, **LPCTSTR** *szName*,
↳ **float**** *prgFltVals*, **long**** *prgLengths* **);**

Parameters

pFX   A pointer to a **CFieldExchange** object. This object contains information to define the context for each call of the function. For more information, see the article "Record Field Exchange: How RFX Works" in *Visual C++ Programmer's Guide* online.

szName   The name of a data column.

prgFltVals   A pointer to an array of **float** values. This array will store the data to be transferred from the data source to the recordset.

prgLengths   A pointer to an array of long integers. This array will store the length in bytes of each value in the array pointed to by *prgFltVals*. Note that the value **SQL_NULL_DATA** will be stored if the corresponding data item contains a Null value. For more details, see the ODBC API function **SQLBindCol** in the *ODBC SDK Programmer's Reference*.

Remarks

The **RFX_Single_Bulk** function transfers multiple rows of floating-point data from a column of an ODBC data source to a corresponding array in a **CRecordset**-derived object. The data source column must have an ODBC type of **SQL_REAL**. The recordset must define a field data member of type pointer to **float**.

If you initialize *prgFltVals* and *prgLengths* to **NULL**, then the arrays they point to will be allocated automatically, with sizes equal to the rowset size.

Note Bulk record field exchange only transfers data from the data source to the recordset object. In order to make your recordset updatable, you must use the ODBC API function **SQLSetPos**. For an example of how to do this, see the sample DBFETCH online.

For more information, see the articles "Recordset: Fetching Records in Bulk (ODBC)" and "Record Field Exchange (RFX)" in *Visual C++ Programmer's Guide* online.

Example

See **RFX_Text_Bulk**.

See Also: **RFX_Binary_Bulk**, **RFX_Bool_Bulk**, **RFX_Byte_Bulk**, **RFX_Date_Bulk**, **RFX_Double_Bulk**, **RFX_Int_Bulk**, **RFX_Long_Bulk**, **RFX_Text_Bulk**, **CFieldExchange::SetFieldType**

RFX_Text

void RFX_Text(CFieldExchange* *pFX*, **const char*** *szName*, **CString&** *value*,
↳ **int** *nMaxLength* = **255**, **int** *nColumnType* = **SQL_VARCHAR**, **short** *nScale* = **0**);

Parameters

pFX A pointer to an object of class **CFieldExchange**. This object contains information to define the context for each call of the function. For more information about the operations a **CFieldExchange** object can specify, see the article "Record Field Exchange: How RFX Works" in *Visual C++ Programmer's Guide* online.

szName The name of a data column.

value The value stored in the indicated data member—the value to be transferred. For a transfer from recordset to data source, the value, of type **CString**, is taken from the specified data member. For a transfer from data source to recordset, the value is stored in the specified data member.

nMaxLength The maximum allowed length of the string or array being transferred. The default value of *nMaxLength* is 255. Legal values are 1 to **INT_MAX**. The framework allocates this amount of space for the data. For best performance, pass a value large enough to accommodate the largest data item you expect.

nColumnType Used mainly for parameters. An integer indicating the data type of the parameter. The type is an ODBC data type of the form **SQL_XXX**.

nScale Specifies the scale for values of ODBC type **SQL_DECIMAL** or **SQL_NUMERIC**. *nScale* is only useful when setting parameter values. For more information, see the topic "Precision, Scale, Length, and Display Size" in Appendix D of the *ODBC SDK Programmer's Reference*.

Remarks

The **RFX_Text** function transfers **CString** data between the field data members of a **CRecordset** object and columns of a record on the data source of ODBC type

SQL_LONGVARCHAR, **SQL_CHAR**, **SQL_VARCHAR**, **SQL_DECIMAL**, or **SQL_NUMERIC**. Data in the data source of all of these types is mapped to and from **CString** in the recordset.

Example

This example shows several calls to **RFX_Text**. Notice also the two calls to **CFieldExchange::SetFieldType**. ClassWizard normally writes the second call to **SetFieldType** and its associated RFX calls. You must write the first call and its RFX call. It is recommended that you put any parameter items before the "//{{AFX_FIELD_MAP" comment. You must put parameters outside the comments.

```
//Example for RFX_Text
void CSections::DoFieldExchange(CFieldExchange* pFX)
{
    pFX->SetFieldType(CFieldExchange::inputParam);
    RFX_Text(pFX, "Name", m_strNameParam);

    //{{AFX_FIELD_MAP(CSections)
    pFX->SetFieldType(CFieldExchange::outputColumn);
    RFX_Text(pFX, "CourseID", m_strCourseID);
    RFX_Text(pFX, "InstructorID", m_strInstructorID);
    RFX_Int(pFX, "RoomNo", m_nRoomNo);
    RFX_Text(pFX, "Schedule", m_strSchedule);
    RFX_Int(pFX, "SectionNo", m_nSectionNo);
    RFX_Single(pFX, "LabFee", m_flLabFee);
    //}}AFX_FIELD_MAP
}
```

See Also: **RFX_Bool**, **RFX_Long**, **RFX_Int**, **RFX_Single**, **RFX_Double**, **RFX_Date**, **RFX_Byte**, **RFX_Binary**, **RFX_LongBinary**, **CFieldExchange::SetFieldType**

RFX_Text_Bulk

> **void RFX_Text_Bulk(CFieldExchange*** *pFX*, **LPCTSTR** *szName*,
> ↳ **LPSTR*** *prgStrVals*, **long**** *prgLengths*, **int** *nMaxLength*);

Parameters

pFX A pointer to a **CFieldExchange** object. This object contains information to define the context for each call of the function. For more information, see the article "Record Field Exchange: How RFX Works" in *Visual C++ Programmer's Guide* online.

szName The name of a data column.

prgStrVals A pointer to an array of **LPSTR** values. This array will store the data to be transferred from the data source to the recordset. Note that with the current version of ODBC, these values cannot be Unicode.

prgLengths A pointer to an array of long integers. This array will store the length in bytes of each value in the array pointed to by *prgStrVals*. This length excludes the null termination character. Note that the value **SQL_NULL_DATA** will be stored if the corresponding data item contains a Null value. For more details, see the ODBC API function **SQLBindCol** in the *ODBC SDK Programmer's Reference.*

nMaxLength   The maximum allowed length of the values stored in the array pointed to by *prgStrVals*, including the null termination character. To ensure that data will not be truncated, pass a value large enough to accommodate the largest data item you expect.

Remarks

The **RFX_Text_Bulk** function transfers multiple rows of character data from a column of an ODBC data source to a corresponding array in a **CRecordset**-derived object. The data source column can have an ODBC type of **SQL_LONGVARCHAR**, **SQL_CHAR**, **SQL_VARCHAR**, **SQL_DECIMAL**, or **SQL_NUMERIC**. The recordset must define a field data member of type **LPSTR**.

If you initialize *prgStrVals* and *prgLengths* to **NULL**, then the arrays they point to will be allocated automatically, with sizes equal to the rowset size.

Note   Bulk record field exchange only transfers data from the data source to the recordset object. In order to make your recordset updatable, you must use the ODBC API function **SQLSetPos**. For an example of how to do this, see the sample DBFETCH online.

For more information, see the articles "Recordset: Fetching Records in Bulk (ODBC)" and "Record Field Exchange (RFX)" in *Visual C++ Programmer's Guide* online.

Example

ClassWizard does not support the Bulk RFX functions, so you must manually write calls in your **DoBulkFieldExchange** override. This example shows a call to **RFX_Text_Bulk**, as well as a call to **RFX_Long_Bulk**, for data transfer. These calls are preceded by a call to **CFieldExchange::SetFieldType**. Note that for parameters, you must call the RFX functions instead of the Bulk RFX functions.

```
void MultiRowSet::DoBulkFieldExchange( CFieldExchange* pFX )
{
    pFX->SetFieldType( CFieldExchange::outputColumn );
    RFX_Long_Bulk( pFX, _T( "[colRecID]" ),
                   &m_rgID, &m_rgIDLenghts );
    RFX_Text_Bulk( pFX, _T( "[colName]" ),
                   &m_rgName, &m_rgNameLengths, 30 );

    pFX->SetFieldType( CFieldExchange::inputParam );
    RFX_Text( pFX, "NameParam", m_strNameParam );
}
```

See Also: RFX_Binary_Bulk, RFX_Bool_Bulk, RFX_Byte_Bulk, RFX_Date_Bulk, RFX_Double_Bulk, RFX_Int_Bulk, RFX_Long_Bulk, RFX_Single_Bulk, CFieldExchange::SetFieldType

RUNTIME_CLASS

RUNTIME_CLASS(*class_name*)

Parameters

class_name   The actual name of the class (not enclosed in quotation marks).

Remarks

Use this macro to get the run-time class structure from the name of a C++ class.

RUNTIME_CLASS returns a pointer to a **CRuntimeClass** structure for the class specified by *class_name*. Only **CObject**-derived classes declared with **DECLARE_DYNAMIC**, **DECLARE_DYNCREATE**, or **DECLARE_SERIAL** will return pointers to a **CRuntimeClass** structure.

For more information, see "CObject Class Topics" in *Visual C++ Programmer's Guide* online.

Example

```
// example for RUNTIME_CLASS
CRuntimeClass* prt = RUNTIME_CLASS( CAge );
ASSERT( lstrcmp( prt->m_lpszClassName, "CAge" )  == 0 );
```

See Also: DECLARE_DYNAMIC, DECLARE_DYNCREATE, DECLARE_SERIAL, CObject::GetRuntimeClass, CRuntimeClass

---

SerializeElements

template< class *TYPE* **> void AFXAPI SerializeElements**
↪ **(CArchive&** *ar*, *TYPE** *pElements*, **int** *nCount* **);**

Parameters

TYPE   Template parameter specifying the type of the elements.

ar   An archive object to archive to or from.

pElements   Pointer to the elements being archived.

nCount   Number of elements being archived

Remarks

CArray, **CList**, and **CMap** call this function to serialize elements. The default implementation does a bit-wise read or write.

For information on implementing this and other helper functions, see the article "Collections: How to Make a Type-Safe Collection" in *Visual C++ Programmer's Guide* online.

See Also: CArchive

STATIC_DOWNCAST

STATIC_DOWNCAST(*class_name*, *pobject*)

Parameters

class_name   The name of a class.

pobject   A pointer to be cast to a pointer to a object of type *class_name*.

Remarks

In builds of your application with the **_DEBUG** preprocessor symbol defined, this macro will cast a pointer to an object from one class to a pointer of a related type. The macro will **ASSERT** if the pointer is not **NULL** and points to an object that is not a "kind of" the target type.

In non-**_DEBUG** builds, the macro performs the cast without any checking.

The target type is specified by the *class_name* parameter, while the *pobject* parameter identifies the pointer. You might, for example, cast a pointer to CYourDocument called pYourDoc to a pointer to **CDocument** using this expression:

```
CDocument* pDoc = STATIC_DOWNCAST(CDocument, pYourDoc);
```

If pYourDoc does not point to a **CDocument** object, the macro will **ASSERT**.

See Also: DYNAMIC_DOWNCAST

THIS_FILE

Remarks

This macro expands to the name of the file that is being compiled. The information is used by the **ASSERT** and **VERIFY** macros. AppWizard and ClassWizard place the macro in source code files they create.

See Also: ASSERT, VERIFY

THROW

THROW(*exception_object_pointer*)

Parameters

exception_object_pointer   Points to an exception object derived from **CException**.

Remarks

Throws the specified exception. **THROW** interrupts program execution, passing control to the associated **CATCH** block in your program. If you have not provided the **CATCH** block, then control is passed to a Microsoft Foundation Class Library module that prints an error message and exits.

For more information, see the article "Exceptions" in *Visual C++ Programmer's Guide* online.

See Also: **THROW_LAST, TRY, CATCH, AND_CATCH, END_CATCH, CATCH_ALL, AND_CATCH_ALL, END_CATCH_ALL, AfxThrowArchiveException, AfxThrowFileException, AfxThrowMemoryException, AfxThrowNotSupportedException, AfxThrowResourceException, AfxThrowUserException**

THROW_LAST

THROW_LAST( )

Remarks

Throws the exception back to the next outer **CATCH** block.

This macro allows you to throw a locally created exception. If you try to throw an exception that you have just caught, it will normally go out of scope and be deleted. With **THROW_LAST**, the exception is passed correctly to the next **CATCH** handler.

For more information, see the article "Exceptions" in *Visual C++ Programmer's Guide* online.

See Also: **THROW, TRY, CATCH, AND_CATCH, END_CATCH, CATCH_ALL, AND_CATCH_ALL, END_CATCH_ALL**

TRACE

TRACE(*exp* **)**

Parameters

exp   Specifies a variable number of arguments that are used in exactly the same way that a variable number of arguments are used in the run-time function **printf.**

Remarks

Provides similar functionality to the **printf** function by sending a formatted string to a dump device such as a file or debug monitor. Like **printf** for C programs under MS-DOS, the **TRACE** macro is a convenient way to track the value of variables as your program executes. In the Debug environment, the **TRACE** macro output goes to **afxDump**. In the Release environment, it does nothing.

TRACE is limited to sending a total of 512 characters at a time. If you call **TRACE** with formatting commands, the total string length after the formatting commands have been expanded cannot be more than 512 characters, including the terminating NULL. Exceeding this limit causes an **ASSERT**.

Note   This macro is available only in the debug version of MFC.

For more information, see "MFC Debugging Support" in *Visual C++ Programmer's Guide* online.

Example

```
// example for TRACE
int i = 1;
char sz[] = "one";
TRACE( "Integer = %d, String = %s\n", i, sz );
// Output: 'Integer = 1, String = one'
```

See Also: **TRACE0, TRACE1, TRACE2, TRACE3, AfxDump, afxTraceEnabled**

TRACE0

TRACE0(*exp* **)**

Parameters

exp   A format string as used in the run-time function **printf**.

Remarks

TRACE0 is similar to **TRACE,** and is one variant of a group of trace macros that you can use for debug output. The group includes:

- **TRACE0** - Takes a format string **(Only)** and can be used for simple text messages which are dumped to afxDump

- **TRACE1** - Takes a format string plus one argument (one variable which is dumped to afxDump)

- **TRACE2** - Takes a format string plus two arguments (two variables which are dumped to afxDump)

- **TRACE3** - Takes a format string plus three arguments (three variables which are dumped to afxDump)

TRACE0 does nothing if you have compiled a release version of your application. As with **TRACE**, it only dumps data to **afxDump** if you have compiled a debug version of your application.

Note   This macro is available only in the debug version of MFC.

Example

```
// example for TRACE0
TRACE0( "Start Dump of MyClass members:" );
```

See Also: **TRACE, TRACE1, TRACE2, TRACE3**

TRACE1

TRACE1(*exp*, *param1*)

Parameters

exp A format string as used in the run-time function **printf**.

param1 The name of the variable whose value should be dumped.

Remarks

See **TRACE0** for a description of the **TRACE1** macro.

Example

```
// example for TRACE1
int i = 1;
TRACE1( "Integer = %d\n", i );
// Output: 'Integer = 1'
```

TRACE2

TRACE2(*exp*, *param1*, *param2*)

Parameters

exp A format string as used in the run-time function **printf**.

param1 The name of the variable whose value should be dumped.

param2 The name of the variable whose value should be dumped.

Remarks

See **TRACE0** for a description of the **TRACE2** macro.

Example

```
// example for TRACE2
int i = 1;
char sz[] = "one";
TRACE2( "Integer = %d, String = %s\n", i, sz );
// Output: 'Integer = 1, String = one'
```

TRACE3

TRACE3(*exp*, *param1*, *param2*, *param3*)

Parameters

exp A format string as used in the run-time function **printf**.

param1 The name of the variable whose value should be dumped.

param2 The name of the variable whose value should be dumped.

param3 The name of the variable whose value should be dumped.

Remarks

See **TRACE0** for a description of the **TRACE3** macro.

TRY

TRY

Remarks

Use this macro to set up a **TRY** block. A **TRY** block identifies a block of code that might throw exceptions. Those exceptions are handled in the following **CATCH** and **AND_CATCH** blocks. Recursion is allowed: exceptions may be passed to an outer **TRY** block, either by ignoring them or by using the **THROW_LAST** macro. End the **TRY** block with an **END_CATCH** or **END_CATCH_ALL** macro.

For more information, see the article "Exceptions" in *Visual C++ Programmer's Guide* online.

See Also: CATCH, AND_CATCH, END_CATCH, CATCH_ALL, AND_CATCH_ALL, END_CATCH_ALL, THROW, THROW_LAST

VERIFY

VERIFY(*booleanExpression*)

Parameters

booleanExpression   Specifies an expression (including pointer values) that evaluates to nonzero or 0.

Remarks

In the debug version of MFC, the **VERIFY** macro evaluates its argument. If the result is 0, the macro prints a diagnostic message and halts the program. If the condition is nonzero, it does nothing.

The diagnostic message has the form

```
assertion failed in file <name> in line <num>
```

where *name* is the name of the source file and *num* is the line number of the assertion that failed in the source file.

In the release version of MFC, **VERIFY** evaluates the expression but does not print or interrupt the program. For example, if the expression is a function call, the call will be made.

See Also: ASSERT

ClassWizard Comment Delimiters

In order for ClassWizard to distinguish between code entered by the user and code created by ClassWizard, several types of special delimiters are used. These delimiters are formatted to appear as comments in the code. Therefore they are never compiled or modified by anything except ClassWizard.

The following is a list of the ClassWizard comment delimiters. For more information, see the topics in this section.

Comment Delimiters

AFX_DATA Marks the beginning and end of member variable declarations in a header file (.H) used for dialog data exchange (DDX).

AFX_DATA_INIT Marks the beginning and end of dialog data exchange (DDX) member variable initializations in a dialog class's constructor.

AFX_DATA_MAP Marks the beginning and end of dialog data exchange (DDX) function calls in a dialog class's **DoDataExchange** member function.

AFX_DISP Marks the beginning and end of OLE Automation declarations in a class's header (.H) file.

AFX_DISP_MAP Marks the beginning and end of OLE Automation mapping in a class's implementation (.CPP) file.

AFX_EVENT Marks the beginning and end of OLE event declarations in a class's header (.H) file.

AFX_EVENT_MAP Marks the beginning and end of OLE events in a class's implementation (.CPP) file.

AFX_FIELD Marks the beginning and end of member variable declarations in a header file (.H) used for database record field exchange (RFX).

AFX_FIELD_INIT Marks the beginning and end of record field exchange (RFX) member variable initializations in a recordset class's constructor.

AFX_FIELD_MAP Marks the beginning and end of record field exchange function calls in a recordset class's **DoFieldExchange** member function.

AFX_MSG Marks the beginning and end of ClassWizard entries in a header file (.H) related to message maps.

AFX_MSG_MAP Marks the beginning and end of message map entries in a class's message map (in the .CPP file).

AFX_VIRTUAL Marks the beginning and end of virtual function override declarations in a class's header (.H) file.

AFX_DATA

Remarks

ClassWizard and AppWizard insert specially formatted comment delimiters in your source code files to mark the places in your files that ClassWizard can write to. **AFX_DATA** is used to mark the beginning and end of member variable declarations in your header file (.H) used for dialog data exchange (DDX):

```
//{{AFX_DATA(classname)
...
//}}AFX_DATA
```

For more information, see **AFX_DATA_MAP** and **AFX_DATA_INIT**.

AFX_DATA_INIT

Remarks

ClassWizard and AppWizard insert specially formatted comment delimiters in your source code files to mark the places in your files that ClassWizard can write to. **AFX_DATA_INIT** is used to mark the beginning and end of dialog data exchange (DDX) member variable initializations in a dialog class's constructor:

```
//{{AFX_DATA_INIT(classname)
...
//}}AFX_DATA_INIT
```

For more information, see **AFX_DATA_MAP** and **AFX_DATA**.

AFX_DATA_MAP

Remarks

ClassWizard and AppWizard insert specially formatted comment delimiters in your source code files to mark the places in your files that ClassWizard can write to. **AFX_DATA_MAP** is used to mark the beginning and end of dialog data exchange (DDX) function calls in a dialog class's **DoDataExchange** member function:

```
//{{AFX_DATA_MAP(classname)
...
//}}AFX_DATA_MAP
```

For more information, see **AFX_DATA_INIT** and **AFX_DATA**.

AFX_DISP

Remarks

ClassWizard and AppWizard insert specially formatted comment delimiters in your source code files to mark the places in your files that ClassWizard can write to. **AFX_DISP** is used to mark the beginning and end of OLE Automation declarations in a class's header (.H) file:

```
//{{AFX_DISP(classname)
...
//}}AFX_DISP
```

For more information, see **AFX_DISP_MAP**.

AFX_DISP_MAP

Remarks

ClassWizard and AppWizard insert specially formatted comment delimiters in your source code files to mark the places in your files that ClassWizard can write to. **AFX_DISP_MAP** is used to mark the beginning and end of OLE Automation mapping in a class's implementation (.CPP) file:

```
//{{AFX_DISP_MAP(classname)
...
//}}AFX_DISP_MAP
```

For more information, see **AFX_DISP**.

AFX_EVENT

Remarks

ClassWizard and AppWizard insert specially formatted comment delimiters in your source code files to mark the places in your files that ClassWizard can write to. **AFX_EVENT** is used to mark the beginning and end of OLE event declarations in a class's header (.H) file:

```
//{{AFX_EVENT(classname)
...
//}}AFX_EVENT
```

For more information, see **AFX_EVENT_MAP**.

AFX_EVENT_MAP

Remarks

ClassWizard and AppWizard insert specially formatted comment delimiters in your source code files to mark the places in your files that ClassWizard can write to. **AFX_EVENT_MAP** is used to mark the beginning and end of OLE events in a class's implementation (.CPP) file:

```
//{{AFX_EVENT_MAP(classname)
...
//}}AFX_EVENT_MAP
```

For more information, see **AFX_EVENT**.

AFX_FIELD

Remarks

ClassWizard and AppWizard insert specially formatted comment delimiters in your source code files to mark the places in your files that ClassWizard can write to. **AFX_FIELD** is used to mark the beginning and end of member variable declarations in your header file (.H) used for database record field exchange (RFX):

```
//{{AFX_FIELD(classname)
...
//}}AFX_FIELD
```

For more information, see **AFX_FIELD_MAP** and **AFX_FIELD_INIT**.

AFX_FIELD_INIT

Remarks

ClassWizard and AppWizard insert specially formatted comment delimiters in your source code files to mark the places in your files that ClassWizard can write to. **AFX_FIELD_INIT** is used in MFC database applications to mark the beginning and end of record field exchange (RFX) member variable initializations in a recordset class's constructor:

```
//{{AFX_DATA_FIELD(classname)
...
//}}AFX_DATA_FIELD
```

For more information, see **AFX_FIELD_MAP** and **AFX_FIELD**.

AFX_FIELD_MAP

Remarks

ClassWizard and AppWizard insert specially formatted comment delimiters in your source code files to mark the places in your files that ClassWizard can write to. **AFX_FIELD_MAP** is used in MFC database applications to mark the beginning and end of record field exchange function calls in a recordset class's **DoFieldExchange** member function:

```
//{{AFX_FIELD_MAP(classname)
...
//}}AFX_FIELD_MAP
```

For more information, see **AFX_FIELD_INIT** and **AFX_FIELD**.

AFX_MSG

Remarks

ClassWizard and AppWizard insert specially formatted comment delimiters in your source code files to mark the places in your files that ClassWizard can write to. **AFX_MSG** is used to mark the beginning and end of ClassWizard entries in your header file (.H) related to message maps:

```
//{{AFX_MSG(classname)
...
//}}AFX_MSG
```

For more information, see **AFX_MSG_MAP**.

AFX_MSG_MAP

Remarks

ClassWizard and AppWizard insert specially formatted comment delimiters in your source code files to mark the places in your files that ClassWizard can write to. **AFX_MSG_MAP** is used to mark the beginning and end of message map entries in a class's message map (in the .CPP file):

```
//{{AFX_MSG_MAP(classname)
...
//}}AFX_MSG_MAP
```

For more information, see **AFX_MSG**.

AFX_VIRTUAL

Remarks

ClassWizard and AppWizard insert specially formatted comment delimiters in your source code files to mark the places in your files that ClassWizard can write to. **AFX_VIRTUAL** is used to mark the beginning and end of virtual function override declarations in a class's header (.H) file:

```
//{{AFX_VIRTUAL(classname)
...
//}}AFX_VIRTUAL
```

There is no corresponding ClassWizard section in the .CPP file.

Structures, Styles, and Callback Functions

This section documents the structures, styles, and callback functions used by the Microsoft Foundation Class Library.

Structures Used by MFC

A description of structures that are called from various member functions follows this topic. For further information on individual structure usage, refer to the classes and member functions noted in the See Also list for each structure.

ABC Structure

The **ABC** structure has the following form:

```
typedef struct _ABC { /* abc */
    int     abcA;
    UINT    abcB;
    int     abcC;
} ABC;
```

The ABC structure contains the width of a character in a TrueType® font.

Members

abcA   Specifies the A spacing of the character. The A spacing is the distance to add to the current position before drawing the character glyph.

abcB   Specifies the B spacing of the character. The B spacing is the width of the drawn portion of the character glyph.

abcC   Specifies the C spacing of the character. The C spacing is the distance to add to the current position to provide white space to the right of the character glyph.

Comments

The total width of a character is the summation of the A, B, and C spaces. Either the A or the C space can be negative to indicate underhangs or overhangs.

See Also: **CDC::GetCharABCWidths**

ABCFLOAT Structure

The **ABCFLOAT** structure has the following form:

```
typedef struct _ABCFLOAT { /* abcf */
    FLOAT    abcfA;
    FLOAT    abcfB;
    FLOAT    abcfC;
} ABCFLOAT;
```

The **ABCFLOAT** structure contains the A, B, and C widths of a font character.

Members

abcfA Specifies the A spacing of the character. The A spacing is the distance to add to the current position before drawing the character glyph.

abcfB Specifies the B spacing of the character. The B spacing is the width of the drawn portion of the character glyph.

abcfC Specifies the C spacing of the character. The C spacing is the distance to add to the current position to provide white space to the right of the character glyph.

Comments

The A, B, and C widths are measured along the base line of the font. The character increment (total width) of a character is the sum of the A, B, and C spaces. Either the A or the C space can be negative to indicate underhangs or overhangs.

See Also: CDC::Get CharABCWidths

AFX_EXTENSION_MODULE Structure

The **AFX_EXTENSION_MODULE** structure has the following form:

```
struct AFX_EXTENSION_MODULE
{
    BOOL bInitialized;
    HMODULE hModule;
    HMODULE hResource;
    CRuntimeClass* pFirstSharedClass;
    COleObjectFactory* pFirstSharedFactory;
};
```

The **AFX_EXTENSION_MODULE** is used during initialization of MFC extension DLLs to hold the state of extension DLL module.

Members

bInitialized   **TRUE** if the DLL module has been initialized with **AfxInitExtensionModule**.

hModule Specifies the handle of the DLL module.

hResource Specifies the handle of the DLL custom resource module.

pFirstSharedClass A pointer to information (the **CRuntimeClass** structure) about the DLL module's first runtime class. Used to provide the start of the runtime class list.

pFirstSharedFactory A pointer to the DLL module's first object factory (a **COleObjectFactory** object). Used to provide the start of the class factory list.

Comments

MFC extension DLLs need to do two things in their **DllMain** function:

- Call **AfxInitExtensionModule** and check the return value.

- Create a **CDynLinkLibrary** object if the DLL will be exporting **CRuntimeClass** objects or has its own custom resources.

The **AFX_EXTENSION_MODULE** structure is used to hold a copy of the extension DLL module state, including a copy of the runtime class objects that have been initialized by the extension DLL as part of normal static object construction executed before **DllMain** is entered.
For example:

```
static AFX_EXTENSION_MODULE extensionDLL;
extern "C" int APIENTRY
DllMain(HINSTANCE hInstance, DWORD dwReason, LPVOID)
{
   // initialize this DLL's extension module
   VERIFY(AfxInitExtensionModule(extensionDLL, hInstance));
```

The module information stored in the **AFX_EXTENSION_MODULE** structure can be copied into the **CDynLinkLibrary** object.
For example:

```
// CDynLinkLibrary class
IMPLEMENT_DYNAMIC(CDynLinkLibrary, CCmdTarget)
// Constructor
CDynLinkLibrary::CDynLinkLibrary(AFX_EXTENSION_MODULE& state, BOOL bSystem)
{
#ifndef _AFX_NO_OLE_SUPPORT
   m_factoryList.Construct(offsetof(COleObjectFactory, m_pNextFactory));
#endif
   m_classList.Construct(offsetof(CRuntimeClass, m_pNextClass));

   // copy info from AFX_EXTENSION_MODULE struct
   ASSERT(state.hModule != NULL);
   m_hModule = state.hModule;
   m_hResource = state.hResource;
   m_classList.m_pHead = state.pFirstSharedClass;
#ifndef _AFX_NO_OLE_SUPPORT
   m_factoryList.m_pHead = state.pFirstSharedFactory;
#endif
   m_bSystem = bSystem;
```

See Also: **AfxInitExtensionModule, AfxTermExtensionModule**

BITMAP Structure

The **BITMAP** structure has the following form:

```
typedef struct tagBITMAP {   /* bm */
    int     bmType;
    int     bmWidth;
    int     bmHeight;
    int     bmWidthBytes;
    BYTE    bmPlanes;
    BYTE    bmBitsPixel;
    LPVOID  bmBits;
} BITMAP;
```

The **BITMAP** structure defines the height, width, color format, and bit values of a logical bitmap.

Members

bmType   Specifies the bitmap type. For logical bitmaps, this member must be 0.

bmWidth   Specifies the width of the bitmap in pixels. The width must be greater than 0.

bmHeight   Specifies the height of the bitmap in raster lines. The height must be greater than 0.

bmWidthBytes   Specifies the number of bytes in each raster line. This value must be an even number since the graphics device interface (GDI) assumes that the bit values of a bitmap form an array of integer (2-byte) values. In other words, **bmWidthBytes** * 8 must be the next multiple of 16 greater than or equal to the value obtained when the **bmWidth** member is multiplied by the **bmBitsPixel** member.

bmPlanes   Specifies the number of color planes in the bitmap.

bmBitsPixel   Specifies the number of adjacent color bits on each plane needed to define a pixel.

bmBits   Points to the location of the bit values for the bitmap. The **bmBits** member must be a long pointer to an array of 1-byte values.

Comments

The currently used bitmap formats are monochrome and color. The monochrome bitmap uses a 1-bit, 1-plane format. Each scan is a multiple of 16 bits.

Scans are organized as follows for a monochrome bitmap of height *n*:

```
Scan 0
Scan 1
 .
 .
 .
Scan n-2
Scan n-1
```

The pixels on a monochrome device are either black or white. If the corresponding bit in the bitmap is 1, the pixel is turned on (white). If the corresponding bit in the bitmap is 0, the pixel is turned off (black).

All devices support bitmaps that have the **RC_BITBLT** bit set in the **RASTERCAPS** index of the **CDC::GetDeviceCaps** member function.

Each device has its own unique color format. In order to transfer a bitmap from one device to another, use the **GetDIBits** and **SetDIBits** Windows functions.

See Also: **CBitmap::CreateBitmapIndirect**

BITMAPINFO Structure

The **BITMAPINFO** structure has the following form:

```
typedef struct tagBITMAPINFO {
    BITMAPINFOHEADER    bmiHeader;
    RGBQUAD             bmiColors[1];
} BITMAPINFO;
```

The **BITMAPINFO** structure defines the dimensions and color information for a Windows device-independent bitmap (DIB).

Members

bmiHeader   Specifies a **BITMAPINFOHEADER** structure that contains information about the dimensions and color format of a device-independent bitmap.

bmiColors   Specifies an array of **RGBQUAD** or **DWORD** data types that define the colors in the bitmap.

Comments

A device-independent bitmap consists of two distinct parts: a **BITMAPINFO** structure describing the dimensions and colors of the bitmap, and an array of bytes defining the pixels of the bitmap. The bits in the array are packed together, but each scan line must be padded with zeroes to end on a **LONG** boundary. If the height is positive, the origin of the bitmap is the lower-left corner. If the height is negative, the origin is the upper-left corner.

The **biBitCount** member of the **BITMAPINFOHEADER** structure determines the number of bits that define each pixel and the maximum number of colors in the bitmap. This member can be one of the following values:

- The bitmap is monochrome, and the **bmiColors** member contains two entries. Each bit in the bitmap array represents a pixel. If the bit is clear, the pixel is displayed with the color of the first entry in the **bmiColors** table; if the bit is set, the pixel has the color of the second entry in the table.

- The bitmap has a maximum of 16 colors, and the **bmiColors** member contains up to 16 entries. Each pixel in the bitmap is represented by a 4-bit index into the color table. For example, if the first byte in the bitmap is 0x1F, the byte represents two pixels. The first pixel contains the color in the second table entry, and the second pixel contains the color in the sixteenth table entry.

- The bitmap has a maximum of 256 colors, and the **bmiColors** member contains up to 256 entries. In this case, each byte in the array represents a single pixel.

- The bitmap has a maximum of 216 colors. The **biCompression** member of the **BITMAPINFOHEADER** must be **BI_BITFIELDS**. The **bmiColors** member contains 3 **DWORD** color masks which specify the red, green, and blue components, respectively, of each pixel. Bits set in the **DWORD** mask must be contiguous and should not overlap the bits of another mask. All the bits in the pixel do not have to be used. Each **WORD** in the array represents a single pixel.

- The bitmap has a maximum of 224 colors, and the **bmiColors** member is **NULL**. Each 3-byte triplet in the bitmap array represents the relative intensities of blue, green, and red, respectively, of a pixel.

- The bitmap has a maximum of 232 colors. The **biCompression** member of the **BITMAPINFOHEADER** must be **BI_BITFIELDS**. The **bmiColors** member contains three **DWORD** color masks which specify the red, green, and blue components, respectively, of each pixel. Bits set in the **DWORD** mask must be contiguous and should not overlap the bits of another mask. All the bits in the pixel do not have to be used. Each **DWORD** in the array represents a single pixel.

The **biClrUsed** member of the **BITMAPINFOHEADER** structure specifies the number of color indices in the color table that are actually used by the bitmap. If the **biClrUsed** member is set to zero, the bitmap uses the maximum number of colors corresponding to the value of the **biBitCount** member.

The colors in the **bmiColors** table should appear in order of importance. Alternatively, for functions that use DIBs, the **bmiColors** member can be an array of 16-bit unsigned integers that specify indices into the currently realized logical palette, instead of explicit RGB values. In this case, an application using the bitmap must call the Windows DIB functions (**CreateDIBitmap**, **CreateDIBPatternBrush**, and **CreateDIBSection**) with the **iUsage** parameter set to **DIB_PAL_COLORS**.

If the bitmap is a packed bitmap (that is, a bitmap in which the bitmap array immediately follows the **BITMAPINFO** header and which is referenced by a single pointer), the **biClrUsed** member must be set to an even number when using the **DIB_PAL_COLORS** mode so the DIB bitmap array starts on a **DWORD** boundary.

Note The **bmiColors** member should not contain palette indices if the bitmap is to be stored in a file or transferred to another application. Unless the application has exclusive use and control of the bitmap, the bitmap color table should contain explicit RGB values.

See Also: **CBrush::CreateDIBPatternBrush**

CDaoDatabaseInfo Structure

The **CDaoDatabaseInfo** structure has the following form:

```
struct CDaoDatabaseInfo
{
    CString m_strName;        // Primary
    BOOL m_bUpdatable;        // Primary
    BOOL m_bTransactions;     // Primary
    CString m_strVersion;     // Secondary
    long m_lCollatingOrder;   // Secondary
    short m_nQueryTimeout;    // Secondary
    CString m_strConnect;     // All
};
```

The **CDaoDatabaseInfo** structure contains information about a database object defined for data access objects (DAO). The database is a DAO object underlying an MFC object of class **CDaoDatabase**. The references to Primary, Secondary, and All above indicate how the information is returned by the **CDaoWorkspace::GetDatabaseInfo** member function.

Members

m_strName   Uniquely names the database object. To directly retrieve this property, call **CDaoDatabase::GetName**. For details, see the topic "Name Property" in DAO Help.

m_bUpdatable   Indicates whether changes can be made to the database. To directly retrieve this property, call **CDaoDatabase::CanUpdate**. For details, see the topic "Updatable Property" in DAO Help.

m_bTransactions   Indicates whether a data source supports transactions—the recording of a series of changes that can later be rolled back (canceled) or committed (saved). If a database is based on the Microsoft Jet database engine, the Transactions property is nonzero and you can use transactions. Other database engines may not support transactions. To directly retrieve this property, call **CDaoDatabase::CanTransact**. For details, see the topic "Transactions Property" in DAO Help.

m_strVersion   Indicates the version of the Microsoft Jet database engine. To retrieve the value of this property directly, call the database object's **GetVersion** member function. For details, see the topic "Version Property" in DAO Help.

m_lCollatingOrder   Specifies the sequence of the sort order in text for string comparison or sorting. Possible values include:

- **dbSortGeneral**   Use the General (English, French, German, Portuguese, Italian, and Modern Spanish) sort order.

- **dbSortArabic**   Use the Arabic sort order.

- **dbSortCyrillic**   Use the Russian sort order.

- **dbSortCzech**   Use the Czech sort order.

- **dbSortDutch**   Use the Dutch sort order.

- **dbSortGreek**   Use the Greek sort order.

- **dbSortHebrew**   Use the Hebrew sort order.

- **dbSortHungarian**   Use the Hungarian sort order.

- **dbSortIcelandic**   Use the Icelandic sort order.

- **dbSortNorwdan**   Use the Norwegian or Danish sort order.

- **dbSortPDXIntl**   Use the Paradox International sort order.

- **dbSortPDXNor**   Use the Paradox Norwegian or Danish sort order.

- **dbSortPDXSwe**   Use the Paradox Swedish or Finnish sort order.

- **dbSortPolish**   Use the Polish sort order.

- **dbSortSpanish**   Use the Spanish sort order.

- **dbSortSwedFin**   Use the Swedish or Finnish sort order.

- **dbSortTurkish**   Use the Turkish sort order.

- **dbSortUndefined**   The sort order is undefined or unknown.

For more information, see the topic "Customizing Windows Registry Settings for Data Access" in DAO Help.

m_nQueryTimeout   The number of seconds the Microsoft Jet database engine waits before a timeout error occurs when a query is run on an ODBC database. The default timeout value is 60 seconds. When QueryTimeout is set to 0, no timeout occurs; this can cause the program to hang. To retrieve the value of this property directly, call the database object's **GetQueryTimeout** member function. For details, see the topic "QueryTimeout Property" in DAO Help.

m_strConnect   Provides information about the source of an open database. For information about connect strings, and for information about retrieving the value of this property directly, see the **CDaoDatabase::GetConnect** member function. For more information, see the topic "Connect Property" in DAO Help.

Comments

Information retrieved by the **CDaoWorkspace::GetDatabaseInfo** member function is stored in a **CDaoDatabaseInfo** structure. Call **GetDatabaseInfo** for the **CDaoWorkspace** object in whose Databases collection the database object is stored. **CDaoDatabaseInfo** also defines a **Dump** member function in debug builds. You can use **Dump** to dump the contents of a **CDaoDatabaseInfo** object.

For information on using this and other MFC DAO Info structures, see the article "DAO Collections: Obtaining Information About DAO Objects" in *Visual C++ Programmer's Guide* online.

See Also: **CDaoWorkspace**, **CDaoDatabase**, **CDaoWorkspace::GetDatabaseCount**

CDaoErrorInfo Structure

The **CDaoErrorInfo** structure has the following form:

```
struct CDaoErrorInfo
{
    long m_lErrorCode;
    CString m_strSource;
    CString m_strDescription;
    CString m_strHelpFile;
    long m_lHelpContext;
};
```

The **CDaoErrorInfo** structure contains information about an error object defined for data access objects (DAO). MFC does not encapsulate DAO error objects in a class. Instead, the **CDaoException** class supplies an interface for accessing the Errors collection contained in the DAO **DBEngine** object, the object that also contains all workspaces. When an MFC DAO operation throws a **CDaoException** object that you catch, MFC fills a **CDaoErrorInfo** structure and stores it in the exception object's **m_pErrorInfo** member. (If you choose to call DAO directly, you must call the exception object's **GetErrorInfo** member function yourself to fill **m_pErrorInfo**.)

For more information about handling DAO errors, see the article "Exceptions: Database Exceptions" in *Visual C++ Programmer's Guide* online. For related information, see the topic "Error Object" in DAO Help.

Members

m_lErrorCode   A numeric DAO error code. See the topic "Trappable Data Access Errors" in DAO Help.

m_strSource   The name of the object or application that originally generated the error. The Source property specifies a string expression representing the object that originally generated the error; the expression is usually the object's class name. For details, see the topic "Source Property" in DAO Help.

m_strDescription   A descriptive string associated with an error. For details, see the topic "Description Property" in DAO Help.

m_strHelpFile   A fully qualified path to a Microsoft Windows Help file. For details, see the topic "HelpContext, HelpFile Properties" in DAO Help.

m_lHelpContext   A context ID for a topic in a Microsoft Windows Help file. For details, see the topic "HelpContext, HelpFile Properties" in DAO Help.

Comments

Information retrieved by the **CDaoException::GetErrorInfo** member function is stored in a **CDaoErrorInfo** structure. Examine the **m_pErrorInfo** data member from a **CDaoException** object that you catch in an exception handler, or call **GetErrorInfo** from a **CDaoException** object that you create explicitly in order to check errors that might have occurred during a direct call to the DAO interfaces. **CDaoErrorInfo** also defines a **Dump** member function in debug builds. You can use **Dump** to dump the contents of a **CDaoErrorInfo** object.

For information on using this and other MFC DAO Info structures, see the article "DAO Collections: Obtaining Information About DAO Objects" in *Visual C++ Programmer's Guide* online.

See Also: **CDaoException**

CDaoFieldInfo Structure

The **CDaoFieldInfo** structure has the following form:

```
struct CDaoFieldInfo
{
    CString m_strName;              // Primary
    short m_nType;                  // Primary
    long m_lSize;                   // Primary
    long m_lAttributes;             // Primary
    short m_nOrdinalPosition;       // Secondary
    BOOL m_bRequired;               // Secondary
    BOOL m_bAllowZeroLength;        // Secondary
    long m_lCollatingOrder;         // Secondary
    CString m_strForeignName;       // Secondary
    CString m_strSourceField;       // Secondary
    CString m_strSourceTable;       // Secondary
    CString m_strValidationRule;    // All
    CString m_strValidationText;    // All
    CString m_strDefaultValue;      // All
};
```

The **CDaoFieldInfo** structure contains information about a field object defined for data access objects (DAO). The references to Primary, Secondary, and All above indicate how the information is returned by the **GetFieldInfo** member function in classes **CDaoTableDef**, **CDaoQueryDef**, and **CDaoRecordset**.

Field objects are not represented by an MFC class. Instead, the DAO objects underlying MFC objects of the following classes contain collections of field objects: **CDaoTableDef**, **CDaoRecordset**, and **CDaoQueryDef**. These classes supply member functions to access some individual items of field information, or you can access them all at once with a **CDaoFieldInfo** object by calling the **GetFieldInfo** member function of the containing object.

Besides its use for examining object properties, you can also use **CDaoFieldInfo** to construct an input parameter for creating new fields in a tabledef. Simpler options are available for this task, but if you want finer control, you can use the version of **CDaoTableDef::CreateField** that takes a **CDaoFieldInfo** parameter.

Members

m_strName   Uniquely names the field object. For details, see the topic "Name Property" in DAO Help.

m_nType   A value that indicates the data type of the field. For details, see the topic "Type Property" in DAO Help. The value of this property can be one of the following:

- **dbBoolean**   Yes/No, same as **TRUE/FALSE**
- **dbByte**   Byte
- **dbInteger**   Short
- **dbLong**   Long
- **dbCurrency**   Currency; see MFC class **COleCurrency**
- **dbSingle**   Single
- **dbDouble**   Double
- **dbDate**   Date/Time; see MFC class **COleDateTime**
- **dbText**   Text; see MFC class **CString**
- **dbLongBinary**   Long Binary (OLE Object); you might want to use MFC class **CByteArray** instead of class **CLongBinary** as **CByteArray** is richer and easier to use.
- **dbMemo**   Memo; see MFC class **CString**
- **dbGUID**   A Globally Unique Identifier/Universally Unique Identifier used with remote procedure calls. For more information, see the topic "Type Property" in DAO Help.

Note   Do not use string data types for binary data. This causes your data to pass through the Unicode/ANSI translation layer, resulting in increased overhead and possibly unexpected translation.

m_lSize   A value that indicates the maximum size, in bytes, of a DAO field object that contains text or the fixed size of a field object that contains text or numeric values. For details, see the topic "Size Property" in DAO Help. Sizes can be one of the following values:

Type	Size (Bytes)	Description
dbBoolean	1 byte	Yes/No (same as True/False)
dbByte	1	Byte
dbInteger	2	Integer
dbLong	4	Long
dbCurrency	8	Currency (**COleCurrency**)

(continued)

(continued)

Type	Size (Bytes)	Description
dbSingle	4	Single
dbDouble	8	Double
dbDate	8	Date/Time (**COleDateTime**)
dbText	1-255	Text (**CString**)
dbLongBinary	0	Long Binary (OLE Object; **CByteArray**; use instead of **CLongBinary**)
dbMemo	0	Memo (**CString**)
dbGUID	16	A Globally Unique Identifier/Universally Unique Identifier used with remote procedure calls.

m_lAttributes   Specifies characteristics of a field object contained by a tabledef, recordset, querydef, or index object. The value returned can be a sum of these constants, created with the C++ bitwise-OR (l) operator:

- **dbFixedField**   The field size is fixed (default for Numeric fields).

- **dbVariableField**   The field size is variable (Text fields only).

- **dbAutoIncrField**   The field value for new records is automatically incremented to a unique long integer that cannot be changed. Only supported for Microsoft Jet database tables.

- **dbUpdatableField**   The field value can be changed.

- **dbDescending**   The field is sorted in descending (Z-A or 100-0) order (applies only to a field object in a Fields collection of an index object; in MFC, index objects are themselves contained in tabledef objects). If you omit this constant, the field is sorted in ascending (A-Z or 0-100) order (default).

When checking the setting of this property, you can use the C++ bitwise-AND operator (**&**) to test for a specific attribute. When setting multiple attributes, you can combine them by combining the appropriate constants with the bitwise-OR (l) operator. For details, see the topic "Attributes Property" in DAO Help.

m_nOrdinalPosition   A value that specifies the numeric order in which you want a field represented by a DAO field object to be displayed relative to other fields. You can set this property with **CDaoTableDef::CreateField**. For details, see the topic "OrdinalPosition Property" in DAO Help.

m_bRequired   Indicates whether a DAO field object requires a non-Null value. If this property is **TRUE**, the field does not allow a Null value. If Required is set to **FALSE**, the field can contain Null values as well as values that meet the conditions specified by the AllowZeroLength and ValidationRule property settings. For details, see the topic "Required Property" in DAO Help. You can set this property for a tabledef with **CDaoTableDef::CreateField**.

m_bAllowZeroLength   Indicates whether an empty string ("") is a valid value of a DAO field object with a Text or Memo data type. If this property is **TRUE**, an empty string is a valid value. You can set this property to **FALSE** to ensure that you cannot use an empty string to set the value of a field. For details, see the topic "AllowZeroLength Property" in DAO Help. You can set this property for a tabledef with **CDaoTableDef::CreateField**.

m_lCollatingOrder   Specifies the sequence of the sort order in text for string comparison or sorting. For details, see the topic "Customizing Windows Registry Settings for Data Access" in DAO Help. For a list of the possible values returned, see the **m_lCollatingOrder** member of the **CDaoDatabaseInfo** structure. You can set this property for a tabledef with **CDaoTableDef::CreateField**.

m_strForeignName   A value that, in a relation, specifies the name of the DAO field object in a foreign table that corresponds to a field in a primary table. For details, see the topic "ForeignName Property" in DAO Help.

m_strSourceField   Indicates the name of the field that is the original source of the data for a DAO field object contained by a tabledef, recordset, or querydef object. This property indicates the original field name associated with a field object. For example, you could use this property to determine the original source of the data in a query field whose name is unrelated to the name of the field in the underlying table. For details, see the topic "SourceField, SourceTable Properties" in DAO Help. You can set this property for a tabledef with **CDaoTableDef::CreateField**.

m_strSourceTable   Indicates the name of the table that is the original source of the data for a DAO field object contained by a tabledef, recordset, or querydef object. This property indicates the original table name associated with a field object. For example, you could use this property to determine the original source of the data in a query field whose name is unrelated to the name of the field in the underlying table. For details, see the topic "SourceField, SourceTable Properties" in DAO Help. You can set this property for a tabledef with **CDaoTableDef::CreateField**.

m_strValidationRule   A value that validates the data in a field as it is changed or added to a table. For details, see the topic "ValidationRule Property" in DAO Help. You can set this property for a tabledef with **CDaoTableDef::CreateField**.

For related information about tabledefs, see the **m_strValidationRule** member of the **CDaoTableDefInfo** structure.

m_strValidationText   A value that specifies the text of the message that your application displays if the value of a DAO field object does not satisfy the validation rule specified by the ValidationRule property setting. For details, see the topic "ValidationText Property" in DAO Help. You can set this property for a tabledef with **CDaoTableDef::CreateField**.

m_strDefaultValue   The default value of a DAO field object. When a new record is created, the DefaultValue property setting is automatically entered as the value for the field. For details, see the topic "DefaultValue Property" in DAO Help. You can set this property for a tabledef with **CDaoTableDef::CreateField**.

Comments

Information retrieved by the **GetFieldInfo** member function (of the class that contains the field) is stored in a **CDaoFieldInfo** structure. Call the **GetFieldInfo** member function of the containing object in whose Fields collection the field object is stored. **CDaoFieldInfo** also defines a **Dump** member function in debug builds. You can use **Dump** to dump the contents of a **CDaoFieldInfo** object.

For information on using this and other MFC DAO Info structures, see the article "DAO Collections: Obtaining Information About DAO Objects" in *Visual C++ Programmer's Guide* online.

See Also: **CDaoTableDef::GetFieldInfo**, **CDaoRecordset::GetFieldInfo**, **CDaoQueryDef::GetFieldInfo**

CDaoIndexInfo Structure

The **CDaoIndexInfo** structure has the following form:

```
struct CDaoIndexInfo {
    CDaoIndexInfo( );                        // Constructor

    CString m_strName;                       // Primary
    CDaoIndexFieldInfo* m_pFieldInfos;       // Primary
    short m_nFields;                         // Primary
    BOOL m_bPrimary;                         // Secondary
    BOOL m_bUnique;                          // Secondary
    BOOL m_bClustered;                       // Secondary
    BOOL m_bIgnoreNulls;                     // Secondary
    BOOL m_bRequired;                        // Secondary
    BOOL m_bForeign;                         // Secondary
    long m_lDistinctCount;                   // All

    // Below the // Implementation comment:
    // Destructor, not otherwise documented
};
```

The **CDaoIndexInfo** structure contains information about an index object defined for data access objects (DAO). The references to Primary, Secondary, and All above indicate how the information is returned by the **GetIndexInfo** member function in classes **CDaoTableDef** and **CDaoRecordset**.

Index objects are not represented by an MFC class. Instead, DAO objects underlying MFC objects of class **CDaoTableDef** or **CDaoRecordset** contain a collection of index objects, called the Indexes collection. These classes supply member functions to access individual items of index information, or you can access them all at once with a **CDaoIndexInfo** object by calling the **GetIndexInfo** member function of the containing object.

CDaoIndexInfo has a constructor and a destructor in order to properly allocate and deallocate the index field information in **m_pFieldInfos**.

Members

m_strName   Uniquely names the field object. For details, see the topic "Name Property" in DAO Help.

m_pFieldInfos   A pointer to an array of **CDaoIndexFieldInfo** objects indicating which tabledef or recordset fields are key fields in an index. Each object identifies one field in the index. The default index ordering is ascending. An index object can have one or more fields representing index keys for each record. These can be ascending, descending, or a combination.

m_nFields   The number of fields stored in **m_pFieldInfos**.

m_bPrimary   If the Primary property is **TRUE**, the index object represents a primary index. A primary index consists of one or more fields that uniquely identify all records in a table in a predefined order. Because the index field must be unique, the Unique property of the Index object is also set to **TRUE** in DAO. If the primary index consists of more than one field, each field can contain duplicate values, but each combination of values from all the indexed fields must be unique. A primary index consists of a key for the table and usually contains the same fields as the primary key.

When you set a primary key for a table, the primary key is automatically defined as the primary index for the table. For more information, see the topics "Primary Property" and "Unique Property" in DAO Help.

Note There can be, at most, one primary index on a table.

m_bUnique   Indicates whether an index object represents a unique index for a table. If this property is **TRUE**, the index object represents an index that is unique. A unique index consists of one or more fields that logically arrange all records in a table in a unique, predefined order. If the index consists of one field, values in that field must be unique for the entire table. If the index consists of more than one field, each field can contain duplicate values, but each combination of values from all the indexed fields must be unique.

If both the Unique and Primary properties of an index object are set to **TRUE**, the index is unique and primary: It uniquely identifies all records in the table in a predefined, logical order. If the Primary property is set to **FALSE**, the index is a secondary index. Secondary indexes (both key and nonkey) logically arrange records in a predefined order without serving as an identifier for records in the table.

For more information, see the topics "Primary Property" and "Unique Property" in DAO Help.

m_bClustered   Indicates whether an index object represents a clustered index for a table. If this property is **TRUE**, the index object represents a clustered index; otherwise, it does not. A clustered index consists of one or more nonkey fields that, taken together, arrange all records in a table in a predefined order. With a clustered index, the data in the table is literally stored in the order specified by the clustered index. A clustered index provides efficient access to records in a table. For more information, see the topic "Clustered Property" in DAO Help.

Note The Clustered property is ignored for databases that use the Microsoft Jet database engine because the Jet database engine does not support clustered indexes.

m_bIgnoreNulls Indicates whether there are index entries for records that have Null values in their index fields. If this property is **TRUE**, fields with Null values do not have an index entry. To make searching for records using a field faster, you can define an index for the field. If you allow Null entries in an indexed field and expect many of the entries to be Null, you can set the IgnoreNulls property for the index object to **TRUE** to reduce the amount of storage space that the index uses. The IgnoreNulls property setting and the Required property setting together determine whether a record with a Null index value has an index entry, as the following table shows.

IgnoreNulls	Required	Null in index field
True	False	Null value allowed; no index entry added.
False	False	Null value allowed; index entry added.
True or False	True	Null value not allowed; no index entry added.

For more information, see the topic "IgnoreNulls Property" in DAO Help.

m_bRequired Indicates whether a DAO index object requires a non-Null value. If this property is **TRUE**, the index object does not allow a Null value. For more information, see the topic "Required Property" in DAO Help.

Tip When you can set this property for either a DAO index object or a field object (contained by a tabledef, recordset, or querydef object), set it for the field object. The validity of the property setting for a field object is checked before that of an index object.

m_bForeign Indicates whether an index object represents a foreign key in a table. If this property is **TRUE**, the index represents a foreign key in a table. A foreign key consists of one or more fields in a foreign table that uniquely identify a row in a primary table. The Microsoft Jet database engine creates an index object for the foreign table and sets the Foreign property when you create a relationship that enforces referential integrity. For more information, see the topic "Foreign Property" in DAO Help.

m_lDistinctCount Indicates the number of unique values for the index object that are included in the associated table. Check the DistinctCount property to determine the number of unique values, or keys, in an index. Any key is counted only once, even though there may be multiple occurrences of that value if the index permits duplicate values. This information is useful in applications that attempt to optimize data access by evaluating index information. The number of unique values is also known as the cardinality of an index object. The DistinctCount property will not always reflect the actual number of keys at a particular time. For example, a change caused by a transaction rollback will not be reflected immediately in the

DistinctCount property. For more information, see the topic "DistinctCount Property" in DAO Help.

Important Obtaining this information can be time-consuming.

Comments

Information retrieved by the **GetIndexInfo** member function of a tabledef object is stored in a **CDaoIndexInfo** structure. Call the **GetIndexInfo** member function of the containing tabledef object in whose Indexes collection the index object is stored. **CDaoIndexInfo** also defines a **Dump** member function in debug builds. You can use **Dump** to dump the contents of a **CDaoIndexInfo** object.

For information on using this and other MFC DAO Info structures, see the article "DAO Collections: Obtaining Information About DAO Objects" in *Visual C++ Programmer's Guide* online.

See Also: **CDaoTableDef::GetIndexInfo**

CDaoIndexFieldInfo Structure

The **CDaoIndexFieldInfo** structure has the following form:

```
struct CDaoIndexFieldInfo
{
    CString m_strName;          // Primary
    BOOL m_bDescending;         // Primary
};
```

The **CDaoIndexFieldInfo** structure contains information about an index field object defined for data access objects (DAO). An index object can have a number of fields, indicating which fields a tabledef (or a recordset based on a table) is indexed on. The references to Primary above indicate how the information is returned in the **m_pFieldInfos** member of a **CDaoIndexInfo** object obtained by calling the **GetIndexInfo** member function of class **CDaoTableDef** or **CDaoRecordset**.

Index objects and index field objects are not represented by an MFC class. Instead, the DAO objects underlying MFC objects of class **CDaoTableDef** or **CDaoRecordset** contain a collection of index objects, called the Indexes collection. Each index object, in turn, contains a collection of field objects. These classes supply member functions to access individual items of index information, or you can access them all at once with a **CDaoIndexInfo** object by calling the **GetIndexInfo** member function of the containing object. The **CDaoIndexInfo** object, then, has a data member, **m_pFieldInfos**, that points to an array of **CDaoIndexFieldInfo** objects.

Members

m_strName Uniquely names the index field object. For details, see the topic "Name Property" in DAO Help.

m_bDescending Indicates the index ordering defined by the index object. **TRUE** if the order is descending.

Comments

Call the **GetIndexInfo** member function of the containing tabledef or recordset object in whose Indexes collection is stored the index object you are interested in. Then access the **m_pFieldInfos** member of the **CDaoIndexInfo** object. The length of the **m_pFieldInfos** array is stored in **m_nFields**. **CDaoIndexFieldInfo** also defines a **Dump** member function in debug builds. You can use **Dump** to dump the contents of a **CDaoIndexFieldInfo** object.

For information on using this and other MFC DAO Info structures, see the article "DAO Collections: Obtaining Information About DAO Objects" in *Visual C++ Programmer's Guide* online.

See Also: **CDaoTableDef::GetIndexInfo**, **CDaoRecordset::GetIndexInfo**

CDaoParameterInfo Structure

The **CDaoParameterInfo** structure has the following form:

```
struct CDaoParameterInfo
{
    CString m_strName;        // Primary
    short m_nType;            // Primary
    ColeVariant m_varValue;   // Secondary
};
```

The **CDaoParameterInfo** structure contains information about a parameter object defined for data access objects (DAO). The references to Primary and Secondary above indicate how the information is returned by the **GetParameterInfo** member function in class **CDaoQueryDef**.

MFC does not encapsulate DAO parameter objects in a class. DAO querydef objects underlying MFC **CDaoQueryDef** objects store parameters in their Parameters collections. To access the parameter objects in a **CDaoQueryDef** object, call the querydef object's **GetParameterInfo** member function for a particular parameter name or an index into the Parameters collection. You can use the **CDaoQueryDef::GetParameterCount** member function in conjunction with **GetParameterInfo** to loop through the Parameters collection.

Members

m_strName Uniquely names the parameter object. For more information, see the topic "Name Property" in DAO Help.

m_nType A value that indicates the data type of a parameter object. For a list of the possible values, see the **m_nType** member of the **CDaoFieldInfo** structure. For more information, see the topic "Type Property" in DAO Help.

m_varValue The value of the parameter, stored in a **COleVariant** object.

Comments

Information retrieved by the **CDaoQueryDef::GetParameterInfo** member function is stored in a **CDaoParameterInfo** structure. Call **GetParameterInfo** for the querydef object in whose Parameters collection the parameter object is stored.

Note If you want to get or set only the value of a parameter, use the **GetParamValue** and **SetParamValue** member functions of class **CDaoRecordset**.

CDaoParameterInfo also defines a **Dump** member function in debug builds. You can use **Dump** to dump the contents of a **CDaoParameterInfo** object. For information on using this and other MFC DAO Info structures, see the article "DAO Collections: Obtaining Information About DAO Objects" in *Visual C++ Programmer's Guide* online.

See Also: CDaoQueryDef

CDaoQueryDefInfo Structure

The **CDaoQueryDefInfo** structure has the following form:

```
struct CDaoQueryDefInfo
{
    CString m_strName;              // Primary
    short m_nType;                  // Primary
    COleDateTime m_dateCreated;     // Secondary
    COleDateTime m_dateLastUpdated; // Secondary
    BOOL m_bUpdatable;              // Secondary
    BOOL m_bReturnsRecords;         // Secondary
    CString m_strSQL;               // All
    CString m_strConnect;           // All
    short m_nODBCTimeout;           // All
};
```

The **CDaoQueryDefInfo** structure contains information about a querydef object defined for data access objects (DAO). The querydef is an object of class **CDaoQueryDef**. The references to Primary, Secondary, and All above indicate how the information is returned by the **GetQueryDefInfo** member function in class **CDaoDatabase**.

Members

m_strName Uniquely names the querydef object. For more information, see the topic "Name Property" in DAO Help. Call **CDaoQueryDef::GetName** to retrieve this property directly.

m_nType A value that indicates the operational type of a querydef object. The value can be one of the following:

- **dbQSelect** Select—the query selects records.

- **dbQAction** Action—the query moves or changes data but does not return records.

- **dbQCrosstab** Crosstab—the query returns data in a spreadsheet-like format.

- **dbQDelete** Delete—the query deletes a set of specified rows.

- **dbQUpdate** Update—the query changes a set of records.

- **dbQAppend** Append—the query adds new records to the end of a table or query.

- **dbQMakeTable** Make-table—the query creates a new table from a recordset.

- **dbQDDL** Data-definition—the query affects the structure of tables or their parts.

- **dbQSQLPassThrough** Pass-through—the SQL statement is passed directly to the database backend, without intermediate processing.

- **dbQSetOperation** Union—the query creates a snapshot-type recordset object containing data from all specified records in two or more tables with any duplicate records removed. To include the duplicates, add the keyword **ALL** in the querydef's SQL statement.

- **dbQSPTBulk** Used with **dbQSQLPassThrough** to specify a query that does not return records.

Note To create an SQL pass-through query, you do not set the **dbQSQLPassThrough** constant. This is set automatically by the Microsoft Jet database engine when you create a querydef object and set the Connect property.

For more information, see the topic "Type Property" in DAO Help.

m_dateCreated The date and time the querydef was created. To directly retrieve the date the querydef was created, call the **GetDateCreated** member function of the **CDaoTableDef** object associated with the table. See Comments below for more information. Also see the topic "DateCreated, LastUpdated Properties" in DAO Help.

m_dateLastUpdated The date and time of the most recent change made to the querydef. To directly retrieve the date the table was last updated, call the **GetDateLastUpdated** member function of the querydef. See Comments below for more information. And see the topic "DateCreated, LastUpdated Properties" in DAO Help.

m_bUpdatable Indicates whether changes can be made to a querydef object. If this property is **TRUE**, the querydef is updatable; otherwise, it is not. Updatable means the querydef object's query definition can be changed. The Updatable property of a querydef object is set to **TRUE** if the query definition can be updated, even if the resulting recordset is not updatable. To retrieve this property directly, call the querydef's **CanUpdate** member function. For more information, see the topic "Updatable Property" in DAO Help.

m_bReturnsRecords   Indicates whether an SQL pass-through query to an external database returns records. If this property is **TRUE**, the query returns records. To directly retrieve this property, call **CDaoQueryDef::GetReturnsRecords**. Not all SQL pass-through queries to external databases return records. For example, an SQL **UPDATE** statement updates records without returning records, while an SQL **SELECT** statement does return records. For more information, see the topic "ReturnsRecords Property" in DAO Help.

m_strSQL   The SQL statement that defines the query executed by a querydef object. The SQL property contains the SQL statement that determines how records are selected, grouped, and ordered when you execute the query. You can use the query to select records to include in a dynaset- or snapshot-type recordset object. You can also define bulk queries to modify data without returning records. You can retrieve the value of this property directly by calling the querydef's **GetSQL** member function. For more information, see the article "DAO Queries" in *Visual C++ Programmer's Guide* online and the topic "SQL Property" in DAO Help.

m_strConnect   Provides information about the source of a database used in a pass-through query. This information takes the form of a connect string. For more information about connect strings, and for information about retrieving the value of this property directly, see the **CDaoDatabase::GetConnect** member function.

m_nODBCTimeout   The number of seconds the Microsoft Jet database engine waits before a timeout error occurs when a query is run on an ODBC database. When you're using an ODBC database, such as Microsoft SQL Server, there may be delays because of network traffic or heavy use of the ODBC server. Rather than waiting indefinitely, you can specify how long the Microsoft Jet engine waits before it produces an error. The default timeout value is 60 seconds. You can retrieve the value of this property directly by calling the querydef's **GetODBCTimeout** member function. For more information, see the topic "ODBCTimeout Property" in DAO Help.

Comments

Information retrieved by the **CDaoDatabase::GetQueryDefInfo** member function is stored in a **CDaoQueryDefInfo** structure. Call **GetQueryDefInfo** for the database object in whose QueryDefs collection the querydef object is stored. **CDaoQueryDefInfo** also defines a **Dump** member function in debug builds. You can use **Dump** to dump the contents of a **CDaoQueryDefInfo** object. Class **CDaoDatabase** also supplies member functions for directly accessing all of the properties returned in a **CDaoQueryDefInfo** object, so you will probably seldom need to call **GetQueryDefInfo**.

When you append a new field or parameter object to the Fields or Parameters collection of a querydef object, an exception is thrown if the underlying database does not support the data type specified for the new object.

The date and time settings are derived from the computer on which the querydef was created or last updated. In a multiuser environment, users should get these settings directly from the file server using the **net time** command to avoid discrepancies in the DateCreated and LastUpdated property settings. For information on using this and other MFC DAO Info structures, see the article "DAO Collections: Obtaining Information About DAO Objects" in *Visual C++ Programmer's Guide* online.

See Also: **CDaoQueryDef**, **CDaoDatabase**

CDaoRelationInfo Structure

The **CDaoRelationInfo** structure has the following form:

```
struct CDaoRelationInfo
{
    CDaoRelationInfo( );                        // Constructor

    CString m_strName;                          // Primary
    CString m_strTable;                         // Primary
    CString m_strForeignTable;                  // Primary
    long m_lAttributes;                         // Secondary
    CDaoRelationFieldInfo* m_pFieldInfos;       // Secondary
    short m_nFields;                            // Secondary

    // Below the // Implementation comment:
    // Destructor, not otherwise documented
};
```

The **CDaoRelationInfo** structure contains information about a relation defined between fields of two tables in a **CDaoDatabase** object. The references to Primary and Secondary above indicate how the information is returned by the **GetRelationInfo** member function in class **CDaoDatabase**.

Relation objects are not represented by an MFC class. Instead, the DAO object underlying an MFC object of the **CDaoDatabase** class maintains a collection of relation objects: **CDaoDatabase** supplies member functions to access some individual items of relation information, or you can access them all at once with a **CDaoRelationInfo** object by calling the **GetRelationInfo** member function of the containing database object.

Members

m_strName   Uniquely names the relation object. For more information, see the topic "Name Property" in DAO Help.

m_strTable   Names the primary table in the relation.

m_strForeignTable   Names the foreign table in the relation. A foreign table is a table used to contain foreign keys. Generally, you use a foreign table to establish or enforce referential integrity. The foreign table is usually on the many side of a one-to-many relationship. Examples of foreign tables include tables containing codes for the American states or Canadian provinces or customer orders.

m_lAttributes   Contains information about the relation type. The value of this member can be any of the following:

- **dbRelationUnique**   Relationship is one-to-one.

- **dbRelationDontEnforce**   Relationship is not enforced (no referential integrity).

- **dbRelationInherited**   Relationship exists in a noncurrent database that contains the two attached tables.

- **dbRelationLeft**   The relationship is a left join. A left outer join includes all of the records from the first (left-hand) of two tables, even if there are no matching values for records in the second (right-hand) table.

- **dbRelationRight**   The relationship is a right join. A right outer join includes all of the records from the second (right-hand) of two tables, even if there are no matching values for records in the first (left-hand) table.

- **dbRelationUpdateCascade**   Updates will cascade.

- **dbRelationDeleteCascade**   Deletions will cascade.

m_pFieldInfos   A pointer to an array of **CDaoRelationFieldInfo** structures. The array contains one object for each field in the relation. The **m_nFields** data member gives a count of the array elements.

m_nFields   The number of **CDaoRelationFieldInfo** objects in the **m_pFieldInfos** data member.

Comments

Information retrieved by the **CDaoDatabase::GetRelationInfo** member function is stored in a **CDaoRelationInfo** structure. **CDaoRelationInfo** also defines a **Dump** member function in debug builds. You can use **Dump** to dump the contents of a **CDaoRelationInfo** object. For information on using this and other MFC DAO Info structures, see the article "DAO Collections: Obtaining Information About DAO Objects" in *Visual C++ Programmer's Guide* online.

See Also: CDaoRelationFieldInfo

CDaoRelationFieldInfo Structure

The **CDaoRelationFieldInfo** structure has the following form:

```
struct CDaoRelationFieldInfo
{
    CString m_strName;          // Primary
    CString m_strForeignName;   // Primary
};
```

The **CDaoRelationFieldInfo** structure contains information about a field in a relation defined for data access objects (DAO). A DAO relation object specifies the fields in a primary table and the fields in a foreign table that define the relation. The references to Primary in the structure definition above indicate how the information is returned in the **m_pFieldInfos** member of a **CDaoRelationInfo** object obtained by calling the **GetRelationInfo** member function of class **CDaoDatabase**.

Relation objects and relation field objects are not represented by an MFC class. Instead, the DAO objects underlying MFC objects of class **CDaoDatabase** contain a collection of relation objects, called the Relations collection. Each relation object, in turn, contains a collection of relation field objects. Each relation field object correlates a field in the primary table with a field in the foreign table. Taken together, the relation field objects define a group of fields in each table, which together define the relation. **CDaoDatabase** lets you access relation objects with a **CDaoRelationInfo** object by calling the **GetRelationInfo** member function. The **CDaoRelationInfo** object, then, has a data member, **m_pFieldInfos**, that points to an array of **CDaoRelationFieldInfo** objects.

Members

m_strName The name of the field in the primary table of the relation.

m_strForeignName The name of the field in the foreign table of the relation.

Comments

Call the **GetRelationInfo** member function of the containing **CDaoDatabase** object in whose Relations collection is stored the relation object you are interested in. Then access the **m_pFieldInfos** member of the **CDaoRelationInfo** object. **CDaoRelationFieldInfo** also defines a **Dump** member function in debug builds. You can use **Dump** to dump the contents of a **CDaoRelationFieldInfo** object.

For information on using this and other MFC DAO Info structures, see the article "DAO Collections: Obtaining Information About DAO Objects" in *Visual C++ Programmer's Guide* online.

See Also: CDaoRelationInfo

CDaoTableDefInfo Structure

The **CDaoTableDefInfo** structure has the following form:

```
struct CDaoTableDefInfo
{
    CString m_strName;              // Primary
    BOOL m_bUpdatable;             // Primary
    long m_lAttributes;            // Primary
    COleDateTime m_dateCreated;    // Secondary
    COleDateTime m_dateLastUpdated; // Secondary
    CString m_strSrcTableName;     // Secondary
    CString m_strConnect;          // Secondary
```

```
CString m_strValidationRule;      // All
CString m_strValidationText;      // All
long m_lRecordCount;              // All
};
```

The **CDaoTableDefInfo** structure contains information about a tabledef object
defined for data access objects (DAO). The tabledef is an object of class
CDaoTableDef. The references to Primary, Secondary, and All above indicate
how the information is returned by the **GetTableDefInfo** member function in class
CDaoDatabase.

Members

m_strName   Uniquely names the tabledef object. To retrieve the value of this
property directly, call the tabledef object's **GetName** member function. For more
information, see the topic "Name Property" in DAO Help.

m_bUpdatable   Indicates whether changes can be made to the table. The quick way
to determine whether a table is updatable is to open a **CDaoTableDef** object for
the table and call the object's **CanUpdate** member function. **CanUpdate** always
returns nonzero (**TRUE**) for a newly created tabledef object and 0 (**FALSE**) for an
attached tabledef object. A new tabledef object can be appended only to a database
for which the current user has write permission. If the table contains only
nonupdatable fields, **CanUpdate** returns 0. When one or more fields are updatable,
CanUpdate returns nonzero. You can edit only the updatable fields. For more
information, see the topic "Updatable Property" in DAO Help.

m_lAttributes   Specifies characteristics of the table represented by the tabledef
object. To retrieve the current attributes of a tabledef, call its **GetAttributes**
member function. The value returned can be a combination of these long constants
(using the bitwise-OR (|) operator):

- **dbAttachExclusive**   For databases that use the Microsoft Jet database engine,
  indicates the table is an attached table opened for exclusive use.

- **dbAttachSavePWD**   For databases that use the Microsoft Jet database engine,
  indicates that the user ID and password for the attached table are saved with the
  connection information.

- **dbSystemObject**   Indicates the table is a system table provided by the
  Microsoft Jet database engine. (Read-only.)

- **dbHiddenObject**   Indicates the table is a hidden table provided by the
  Microsoft Jet database engine (for temporary use). (Read-only.)

- **dbAttachedTable**   Indicates the table is an attached table from a non-ODBC
  database, such as a Paradox database.

- **dbAttachedODBC**   Indicates the table is an attached table from an ODBC
  database, such as Microsoft SQL Server.

m_dateCreated The date and time the table was created. To directly retrieve the date the table was created, call the **GetDateCreated** member function of the **CDaoTableDef** object associated with the table. See Comments below for more information. For related information, see the topic "DateCreated, LastUpdated Properties" in DAO Help.

m_dateLastUpdated The date and time of the most recent change made to the design of the table. To directly retrieve the date the table was last updated, call the **GetDateLastUpdated** member function of the **CDaoTableDef** object associated with the table. See Comments below for more information. For related information, see the topic "DateCreated, LastUpdated Properties" in DAO Help.

m_strSrcTableName Specifies the name of an attached table if any. To directly retrieve the source table name, call the **GetSourceTableName** member function of the **CDaoTableDef** object associated with the table.

m_strConnect Provides information about the source of an open database. You can check this property by calling the **GetConnect** member function of your **CDaoTableDef** object. For more information about connect strings, see **GetConnect**.

m_strValidationRule A value that validates the data in tabledef fields as they are changed or added to a table. Validation is supported only for databases that use the Microsoft Jet database engine. To directly retrieve the validation rule, call the **GetValidationRule** member function of the **CDaoTableDef** object associated with the table. For related information, see the topic "ValidationRule Property" in DAO Help.

m_strValidationText A value that specifies the text of the message that your application should display if the validation rule specified by the ValidationRule property is not satisfied. For related information, see the topic "ValidationText Property" in DAO Help.

m_lRecordCount The number of records accessed in a tabledef object. This property setting is read-only. To directly retrieve the record count, call the **GetRecordCount** member function of the **CDaoTableDef** object. The documentation for **GetRecordCount** describes the record count further. Note that retrieving this count can be a time-consuming operation if the table contains many records.

Comments

Information retrieved by the **CDaoDatabase::GetTableDefInfo** member function is stored in a **CDaoTableDefInfo** structure. Call the **GetTableDefInfo** member function of the **CDaoDatabase** object in whose TableDefs collection the tabledef object is stored. **CDaoTableDefInfo** also defines a **Dump** member function in debug builds. You can use **Dump** to dump the contents of a **CDaoTableDefInfo** object.

The date and time settings are derived from the computer on which the base table was created or last updated. In a multiuser environment, users should get these settings directly from the file server to avoid discrepancies in the DateCreated and LastUpdated property settings.

For information on using this and other MFC DAO Info structures, see the article "DAO Collections: Obtaining Information About DAO Objects" in *Visual C++ Programmer's Guide* online.

See Also: **CDaoTableDef**, **CDaoDatabase**, **CDaoTableDef::CanUpdate**, **CDaoTableDef::GetAttributes**, **CDaoTableDef::GetDateCreated**, **CDaoTableDef::GetDateLastUpdated**, **CDaoTableDef::GetRecordCount**, **CDaoTableDef::GetSourceTableName**, **CDaoTableDef::GetValidationRule**, **CDaoTableDef::GetValidationText**

CDaoWorkspaceInfo Structure

The **CDaoWorkspaceInfo** structure has the following form:

```
struct CDaoWorkspaceInfo
{
    CString m_strName;              // Primary
    CString m_strUserName;         // Secondary
    BOOL m_bIsolateODBCTrans;      // All
};
```

The **CDaoWorkspaceInfo** structure contains information about a workspace defined for data access objects (DAO) database access. The workspace is an object of class **CDaoWorkspace**. The references to Primary, Secondary, and All above indicate how the information is returned by the **GetWorkspaceInfo** member function in class **CDaoWorkspace**.

Members

m_strName   Uniquely names the workspace object. To retrieve the value of this property directly, call the querydef object's **GetName** member function. For more information, see the topic "Name Property" in DAO Help.

m_strUserName   A value that represents the owner of a workspace object. For related information, see the topic "UserName Property" in DAO Help.

m_bIsolateODBCTrans   A value that indicates whether multiple transactions that involve the same ODBC database are isolated. For more information, see **CDaoWorkspace::SetIsolateODBCTrans**. For related information, see the topic "IsolateODBCTrans Property" in DAO Help.

Comments

Information retrieved by the **CDaoWorkspace::GetWorkspaceInfo** member function is stored in a **CDaoWorkspaceInfo** structure. **CDaoWorkspaceInfo** also defines a **Dump** member function in debug builds. You can use **Dump** to dump the contents of a **CDaoWorkspaceInfo** object. For information on using this and other MFC DAO Info structures, see the article "DAO Collections: Obtaining Information About DAO Objects" in *Visual C++ Programmer's Guide* online.

See Also: CDaoWorkspace

CODBCFieldInfo Structure

The **CODBCFieldInfo** structure has the following form:

```
struct CODBCFieldInfo
{
    CString m_strName;
    SWORD m_nSQLType;
    UDWORD m_nPrecision;
    SWORD m_nScale;
    SWORD m_nNullability;
};
```

The **CODBCFieldInfo** structure contains information about the fields in an ODBC data source. To retrieve this information, call **CRecordset::GetODBCFieldInfo**.

Members

m_strName   The name of the field.

m_nSQLType   The SQL data type of the field. This can be an ODBC SQL data type or a driver-specific SQL data type. For a list of valid ODBC SQL data types, see "SQL Data Types" in Appendix D of the *ODBC SDK Programmer's Reference*. For information about driver-specific SQL data types, see the driver's documentation.

m_nPrecision   The maximum precision of the field. For details, see "Precision, Scale, Length, and Display Size" in Appendix D of the *ODBC SDK Programmer's Reference*.

m_nScale   The scale of the field. For details, see "Precision, Scale, Length, and Display Size" in Appendix D of the *ODBC SDK Programmer's Reference*.

m_nNullability   Whether the field accepts a Null value. This can be one of two values: **SQL_NULLABLE** if the field accepts Null values, or **SQL_NO_NULLS** if the field does not accept Null values.

See Also: CRecordset::GetODBCFieldInfo, CRecordset::GetFieldValue

COLORADJUSTMENT Structure

The **COLORADJUSTMENT** structure has the following form:

```
typedef struct  tagCOLORADJUSTMENT {     /* ca */
    WORD  caSize;
    WORD  caFlags;
    WORD  caIlluminantIndex;
    WORD  caRedGamma;
    WORD  caGreenGamma;
    WORD  caBlueGamma;
    WORD  caReferenceBlack;
    WORD  caReferenceWhite;
    SHORT caContrast;
    SHORT caBrightness;
    SHORT caColorfulness;
    SHORT caRedGreenTint;
} COLORADJUSTMENT;
```

The **COLORADJUSTMENT** structure defines the color adjustment values used by the Windows **StretchBlt** and **StretchDIBits** functions when the **StretchBlt** mode is **HALFTONE**.

Members

caSize   Specifies the size of the structure in bytes.

caFlags   Specifies how the output image should be prepared. This member can be set to **NULL** or any combination of the following values:

- **CA_NEGATIVE**   Specifies that the negative of the original image should be displayed.

- **CA_LOG_FILTER**   Specifies that a logarithmic function should be applied to the final density of the output colors. This will increase the color contrast when the luminance is low.

caIlluminantIndex   Specifies the luminance of the light source under which the image object is viewed. This member can be set to one of the following values:

- **ILLUMINANT_EQUAL_ENERGY**

- **ILLUMINANT_A**

- **ILLUMINANT_B**

- **ILLUMINANT_C**

- **ILLUMINANT_D50**

- **ILLUMINANT_D55**

- **ILLUMINANT_D65**

- **ILLUMINANT_D75**

- **ILLUMINANT_F2**

- **ILLUMINANT_TURNGSTEN**

- **ILLUMINANT_DAYLIGHT**

- **ILLUMINANT_FLUORESCENT**

- **ILLUMINANT_NTSC**

caRedGamma   Specifies the n-th power gamma-correction value for the red primary of the source colors. The value must be in the range from 2,500 to 65,000. A value of 10,000 means no gamma-correction.

caGreenGamma   Specifies the n-th power gamma-correction value for the green primary of the source colors. The value must be in the range from 2,500 to 65,000. A value of 10,000 means no gamma-correction.

caBlueGamma   Specifies the n-th power gamma-correction value for the blue primary of the source colors. The value must be in the range from 2,500 to 65,000. A value of 10,000 means no gamma-correction.

caReferenceBlack   Specifies the black reference for the source colors. Any colors that are darker than this are treated as black. The value must be in the range from 0 to 4,000.

caReferenceWhite   Specifies the white reference for the source colors. Any colors that are lighter than this are treated as white. The value must be in the range from 6,000 to 10,000.

caContrast   Specifies the amount of contrast to be applied to the source object. The value must be in the range from -100 to 100. A value of 0 means no contrast adjustment.

caBrightness   Specifies the amount of brightness to be applied to the source object. The value must be in the range from -100 to 100. A value of 0 means no brightness adjustment.

caColorfulness   Specifies the amount of colorfulness to be applied to the source object. The value must be in the range from -100 to 100. A value of 0 means no colorfulness adjustment.

caRedGreenTint   Specifies the amount of red or green tint adjustment to be applied to the source object. The value must be in the range from -100 to 100. Positive numbers would adjust towards red and negative numbers adjust towards green. A 0 means no tint adjustment.

See Also: CDC::GetColorAdjustment

COMPAREITEMSTRUCT Structure

The **COMPAREITEMSTRUCT** data structure has this form:

```
typedef struct tagCOMPAREITEMSTRUCT {
    UINT    CtlType;
    UINT    CtlID;
    HWND    hwndItem;
    UINT    itemID1;
    DWORD   itemData1;
    UINT    itemID2;
    DWORD   itemData2;
} COMPAREITEMSTRUCT;
```

The **COMPAREITEMSTRUCT** structure supplies the identifiers and application-supplied data for two items in a sorted, owner-drawn list box or combo box. Whenever an application adds a new item to an owner-drawn list box or combo box created with the **CBS_SORT** or **LBS_SORT** style, Windows sends the owner a **WM_COMPAREITEM** message. The *lParam* parameter of the message contains a long pointer to a **COMPAREITEMSTRUCT** structure. Upon receiving the message, the owner compares the two items and returns a value indicating which item sorts before the other.

Members

CtlType   **ODT_LISTBOX** (which specifies an owner-draw list box) or **ODT_COMBOBOX** (which specifies an owner-draw combo box).

CtlID   The control ID for the list box or combo box.

hwndItem   The window handle of the control.

itemID1   The index of the first item in the list box or combo box being compared.

itemData1   Application-supplied data for the first item being compared. This value was passed in the call that added the item to the combo or list box.

itemID2   Index of the second item in the list box or combo box being compared.

itemData2   Application-supplied data for the second item being compared. This value was passed in the call that added the item to the combo or list box.

See Also: **CWnd::OnCompareItem**

CREATESTRUCT Structure

The **CREATESTRUCT** structure has the following form:

```
typedef struct tagCREATESTRUCT {
    LPVOID    lpCreateParams;
    HANDLE    hInstance;
    HMENU     hMenu;
    HWND      hwndParent;
    int       cy;
    int       cx;
    int       y;
    int       x;
    LONG      style;
    LPCSTR    lpszName;
    LPCSTR    lpszClass;
    DWORD     dwExStyle;
} CREATESTRUCT;
```

The **CREATESTRUCT** structure defines the initialization parameters passed to the window procedure of an application.

Members

lpCreateParams   Points to data to be used to create the window.

hInstance   Identifies the module-instance handle of the module that owns the new window.

hMenu   Identifies the menu to be used by the new window. If a child window, contains the integer ID.

hwndParent   Identifies the window that owns the new window. This member is **NULL** if the new window is a top-level window.

cy   Specifies the height of the new window.

cx   Specifies the width of the new window.

y   Specifies the y-coordinate of the upper-left corner of the new window. Coordinates are relative to the parent window if the new window is a child window; otherwise coordinates are relative to the screen origin.

x   Specifies the x-coordinate of the upper-left corner of the new window. Coordinates are relative to the parent window if the new window is a child window; otherwise coordinates are relative to the screen origin.

style   Specifies the new window's style.

lpszName   Points to a null-terminated string that specifies the new window's name.

lpszClass   Points to a null-terminated string that specifies the new window's Windows class name (a **WNDCLASS** structure; for more information, see the Win32 SDK documentation).

dwExStyle   Specifies the extended style for the new window.

See Also: CWnd::OnCreate

DELETEITEMSTRUCT Structure

The **DELETEITEMSTRUCT** structure has the following form:

```
typedef struct tagDELETEITEMSTRUCT { /* ditms */
    UINT CtlType;
    UINT CtlID;
    UINT itemID;
    HWND hwndItem;
    UINT itemData;
} DELETEITEMSTRUCT;
```

The **DELETEITEMSTRUCT** structure describes a deleted owner-drawn list-box or combo-box item. When an item is removed from the list box or combo box or when the list box or combo box is destroyed, Windows sends the **WM_DELETEITEM** message to the owner for each deleted item. The **lParam** parameter of the message contains a pointer to this structure.

Members

CtlType Specifies **ODT_LISTBOX** (an owner-drawn list box) or **ODT_COMBOBOX** (an owner-drawn combo box).

CtlID Specifies the identifier of the list box or combo box.

itemID Specifies index of the item in the list box or combo box being removed.

hwndItem Identifies the control.

itemData Specifies application-defined data for the item. This value is passed to the control in the **lParam** parameter of the message that adds the item to the list box or combo box.

See Also: **CWnd::OnDeleteItem**

DEVMODE Structure

The **DEVMODE** structure has the following form:

```
typedef struct _devicemode {     /* dvmd */
    TCHAR   dmDeviceName[32];
    WORD    dmSpecVersion;
    WORD    dmDriverVersion;
    WORD    dmSize;
    WORD    dmDriverExtra;
    DWORD   dmFields;
    short   dmOrientation;
    short   dmPaperSize;
    short   dmPaperLength;
    short   dmPaperWidth;
    short   dmScale;
    short   dmCopies;
    short   dmDefaultSource;
```

```
        short   dmPrintQuality;
        short   dmColor;
        short   dmDuplex;
        short   dmYResolution;
        short   dmTTOption;
        short   dmCollate;
        TCHAR   dmFormName[32];
        WORD    dmUnusedPadding;
        USHORT  dmBitsPerPel;
        DWORD   dmPelsWidth;
        DWORD   dmPelsHeight;
        DWORD   dmDisplayFlags;
        DWORD   dmDisplayFrequency;
} DEVMODE;
```

The **DEVMODE** data structure contains information about the device initialization and environment of a printer.

Members

dmDeviceName   Specifies the name of the device the driver supports; for example, PCL/HP LaserJet in the case of PCL/HP LaserJet®. This string is unique among device drivers.

dmSpecVersion   Specifies the version number of the initialization data specification on which the structure is based.

dmDriverVersion   Specifies the printer driver version number assigned by the printer driver developer.

dmSize   Specifies the size, in bytes, of the **DEVMODE** structure except the **dmDriverData** (device-specific) member. If an application manipulates only the driver-independent portion of the data, it can use this member to determine the length of the structure without having to account for different versions.

dmDriverExtra   Contains the number of bytes of private driver-data that follow this structure. If a device driver does not use device-specific information, set this member to zero.

dmFields   Specifies which of the remaining members in the **DEVMODE** structure have been initialized. Bit 0 (defined as **DM_ORIENTATION**) corresponds to **dmOrientation**; bit 1 (defined as **DM_PAPERSIZE**) specifies **dmPaperSize**, and so on. A printer driver supports only those members that are appropriate for the printer technology.

dmOrientation   Selects the orientation of the paper. This member can be either **DMORIENT_PORTRAIT** (1) or **DMORIENT_LANDSCAPE** (2).

dmPaperSize   Selects the size of the paper to print on. This member can be set to zero if the length and width of the paper are both set by the **dmPaperLength** and **dmPaperWidth** members. Otherwise, the **dmPaperSize** member can be set to one of the following predefined values:

- **DMPAPER_LETTER**   Letter, 8 1/2 by 11 inches
- **MPAPER_LEGAL**   Legal, 8 1/2 by 14 inches
- **DMPAPER_A4**   A4 Sheet, 210 by 297 millimeters
- **DMPAPER_CSHEET**   C Sheet, 17 by 22 inches
- **DMPAPER_DSHEET**   D Sheet, 22 by 34 inches
- **DMPAPER_ESHEET**   E Sheet, 34 by 44 inches
- **DMPAPER_LETTERSMALL**   Letter Small, 8 1/2 by 11 inches
- **DMPAPER_TABLOID**   Tabloid, 11 by 17 inches
- **DMPAPER_LEDGER**   Ledger, 17 by 11 inches
- **DMPAPER_STATEMENT**   Statement, 5 1/2 by 8 1/2 inches
- **DMPAPER_EXECUTIVE**   Executive, 7 1/4 by 10 1/2 inches
- **DMPAPER_A3**   A3 sheet, 297 by 420 millimeters
- **DMPAPER_A4SMALL**   A4 small sheet, 210 by 297 millimeters
- **DMPAPER_A5**   A5 sheet, 148 by 210 millimeters
- **DMPAPER_B4**   B4 sheet, 250 by 354 millimeters
- **DMPAPER_B5**   B5 sheet, 182-by-257-millimeter paper
- **DMPAPER_FOLIO**   Folio, 8-1/2-by-13-inch paper
- **DMPAPER_QUARTO**   Quarto, 215-by-275-millimeter paper
- **DMPAPER_10X14**   10-by-14-inch sheet
- **DMPAPER_11X17**   11-by-17-inch sheet
- **DMPAPER_NOTE**   Note, 8 1/2 by 11 inches
- **DMPAPER_ENV_9**   #9 Envelope, 3 7/8 by 8 7/8 inches
- **DMPAPER_ENV_10**   #10 Envelope, 4 1/8 by 9 1/2 inches
- **DMPAPER_ENV_11**   #11 Envelope, 4 1/2 by 10 3/8 inches
- **DMPAPER_ENV_12**   #12 Envelope, 4 3/4 by 11 inches
- **DMPAPER_ENV_14**   #14 Envelope, 5 by 11 1/2 inches
- **DMPAPER_ENV_DL**   DL Envelope, 110 by 220 millimeters
- **DMPAPER_ENV_C5**   C5 Envelope, 162 by 229 millimeters
- **DMPAPER_ENV_C3**   C3 Envelope, 324 by 458 millimeters
- **DMPAPER_ENV_C4**   C4 Envelope, 229 by 324 millimeters

- **DMPAPER_ENV_C6** C6 Envelope, 114 by 162 millimeters
- **DMPAPER_ENV_C65** C65 Envelope, 114 by 229 millimeters
- **DMPAPER_ENV_B4** B4 Envelope, 250 by 353 millimeters
- **DMPAPER_ENV_B5** B5 Envelope, 176 by 250 millimeters
- **DMPAPER_ENV_B6** B6 Envelope, 176 by 125 millimeters
- **DMPAPER_ENV_ITALY** Italy Envelope, 110 by 230 millimeters
- **DMPAPER_ENV_MONARCH** Monarch Envelope, 3 7/8 by 7 1/2 inches
- **DMPAPER_ENV_PERSONAL** 6 3/4 Envelope, 3 5/8 by 6 1/2 inches
- **DMPAPER_FANFOLD_US** US Std Fanfold, 14 7/8 by 11 inches
- **DMPAPER_FANFOLD_STD_GERMAN** German Std Fanfold, 8 1/2 by 12 inches
- **DMPA PER_FANFOLD_LGL_GERMAN** German Legal Fanfold, 8 1/2 by 13 inches

dmPaperLength Overrides the length of the paper specified by the **dmPaperSize** member, either for custom paper sizes or for devices such as dot-matrix printers, which can print on a page of arbitrary length. These values, along with all other values in this structure that specify a physical length, are in tenths of a millimeter.

dmPaperWidth Overrides the width of the paper specified by the **dmPaperSize** member.

dmScale Specifies the factor by which the printed output is to be scaled. The apparent page size is scaled from the physical page size by a factor of **dmScale**/100. For example, a letter-sized page with a **dmScale** value of 50 would contain as much data as a page of 17 by 22 inches because the output text and graphics would be half their original height and width.

dmCopies Selects the number of copies printed if the device supports multiple-page copies.

dmDefaultSource Reserved; must be zero.

dmPrintQuality Specifies the printer resolution. There are four predefined device-independent values:

- **DMRES_HIGH**
- **DMRES_MEDIUM**
- **DMRES_LOW**
- **DMRES_DRAFT**

If a positive value is given, it specifies the number of dots per inch (DPI) and is therefore device dependent.

dmColor Switches between color and monochrome on color printers. Following are the possible values:

- **DMCOLOR_COLOR**

- **DMCOLOR_MONOCHROME**

dmDuplex Selects duplex or double-sided printing for printers capable of duplex printing. Following are the possible values:

- **DMDUP_SIMPLEX**

- **DMDUP_HORIZONTAL**

- **DMDUP_VERTICAL**

dmYResolution Specifies the y-resolution, in dots per inch, of the printer. If the printer initializes this member, the **dmPrintQuality** member specifies the x-resolution, in dots per inch, of the printer.

dmTTOption Specifies how TrueType® fonts should be printed. This member can be one of the following values:

- **DMTT_BITMAP** Prints TrueType fonts as graphics. This is the default action for dot-matrix printers.

- **DMTT_DOWNLOAD** Downloads TrueType fonts as soft fonts. This is the default action for Hewlett-Packard printers that use Printer Control Language (PCL).

- **DMTT_SUBDEV** Substitute device fonts for TrueType fonts. This is the default action for PostScript® printers.

dmCollate Specifies whether collation should be used when printing multiple copies. Using **DMCOLLATE_FALSE** provides faster, more efficient output, since the data is sent to a page printer just once, no matter how many copies are required. The printer is told to simply print the page again. This member can be one of the following values:

- **DMCOLLATE_TRUE** Collate when printing multiple copies.

- **DMCOLLATE_FALSE** Do NOT collate when printing multiple copies.

dmFormName Specifies the name of the form to use; for example, Letter or Legal. A complete set of names can be retrieved through the Windows **EnumForms** function.

dmUnusedPadding Used to align the structure to a **DWORD** boundary. This should not be used or referenced. Its name and usage is reserved, and can change in future releases.

dmBitsPerPel Specifies in bits per pixel the color resolution of the display device. For example: 4 bits for 16 colors, 8 bits for 256 colors, or 16 bits for 65,536 colors.

dmPelsWidth Specifies the width, in pixels, of the visible device surface.

dmPelsHeight   Specifies the height, in pixels, of the visible device surface.

dmDisplayFlags   Specifies the device's display mode. The following are valid flags:

- **DM_GRAYSCALE**   Specifies that the display is a non-color device. If this flag is not set, color is assumed.

- **DM_INTERLACED**   Specifies that the display mode is interlaced. If the flag is not set, non-interlaced is assumed.

dmDisplayFrequency   Specifies the frequency, in hertz (cycles per second), of the display device in a particular mode.

Comments

A device driver's private data will follow the **dmDisplayMode** member. The number of bytes of private data is specified by the **dmDriverExtra** member.

See Also: **CDC::ResetDC**, **CPrintDialog::GetDevMode**

DEVNAMES Structure

The **DEVNAMES** structure has the following form:

```
typedef struct tagDEVNAMES { /* dvnm */
    WORD wDriverOffset;
    WORD wDeviceOffset;
    WORD wOutputOffset;
    WORD wDefault;
    /* driver, device, and port-name strings follow wDefault */
} DEVNAMES;
```

The **DEVNAMES** structure contains strings that identify the driver, device, and output-port names for a printer. The **PrintDlg** function uses these strings to initialize members in the system-defined Print dialog box. When the user closes the dialog box, information about the selected printer is returned in this structure.

Members

wDriverOffset   (Input/Output) Specifies the offset to a null-terminated string that contains the filename (without the extension) of the device driver. On input, this string is used to determine the printer to display initially in the dialog box.

wDeviceOffset   (Input/Output) Specifies the offset to the null-terminated string (maximum of 32 bytes including the null) that contains the name of the device. This string must be identical to the **dmDeviceName** member of the **DEVMODE** structure.

wOutputOffset   (Input/Output) Specifies the offset to the null-terminated string that contains the DOS device name for the physical output medium (output port).

wDefault   Specifies whether the strings contained in the **DEVNAMES** structure identify the default printer. This string is used to verify that the default printer has not changed since the last print operation. On input, if the **DN_DEFAULTPRN**

flag is set, the other values in the **DEVNAMES** structure are checked against the current default printer. If any of the strings do not match, a warning message is displayed informing the user that the document may need to be reformatted. On output, the **wDefault** member is changed only if the Print Setup dialog box was displayed and the user chose the OK button. The **DN_DEFAULTPRN** flag is set if the default printer was selected. If a specific printer is selected, the flag is not set. All other bits in this member are reserved for internal use by the Print Dialog box procedure.

See Also: CPrintDialog::CreatePrinterDC

DOCINFO Structure

The **DOCINFO** structure has the following form:

```
typedef struct {    /* di */
    int     cbSize;
    LPCSTR  lpszDocName;
    LPCSTR  lpszOutput;
} DOCINFO;
```

The **DOCINFO** structure contains the input and output filenames used by the **CDC::StartDoc** function.

Members

cbSize   Specifies the size of the structure, in bytes.

lpszDocName   Points to a null-terminated string specifying the name of the document. This string must not be longer than 32 characters, including the null terminating character.

lpszOutput   Points to a null-terminated string specifying the name of an output file. This allows a print job to be redirected to a file. If this value is **NULL**, output goes to the device for the specified device context.

See Also: CDC::StartDoc

DRAWITEMSTRUCT Structure

The **DRAWITEMSTRUCT** structure has the following form:

```
typedef struct tagDRAWITEMSTRUCT {
    UINT    CtlType;
    UINT    CtlID;
    UINT    itemID;
    UINT    itemAction;
    UINT    itemState;
    HWND    hwndItem;
    HDC     hDC;
    RECT    rcItem;
    DWORD   itemData;
} DRAWITEMSTRUCT;
```

The **DRAWITEMSTRUCT** structure provides information the owner window must have to determine how to paint an owner-drawn control or menu item. The owner window of the owner-drawn control or menu item receives a pointer to this structure as the *lParam* parameter of the **WM_DRAWITEM** message.

Members

CtlType   The control type. The values for control types are as follows:

- **ODT_BUTTON**   Owner-drawn button
- **ODT_COMBOBOX**   Owner-drawn combo box
- **ODT_LISTBOX**   Owner-drawn list box
- **ODT_MENU**   Owner-drawn menu
- **ODT_LISTVIEW**   List view control
- **ODT_STATIC**   Owner-drawn static control
- **ODT_TAB**   Tab control

CtlID   The control ID for a combo box, list box, or button. This member is not used for a menu.

itemID   The menu-item ID for a menu or the index of the item in a list box or combo box. For an empty list box or combo box, this member is a negative value, which allows the application to draw only the focus rectangle at the coordinates specified by the **rcItem** member even though there are no items in the control. The user can thus be shown whether the list box or combo box has the input focus. The setting of the bits in the **itemAction** member determines whether the rectangle is to be drawn as though the list box or combo box has input focus.

itemAction   Defines the drawing action required. This will be one or more of the following bits:

- **ODA_DRAWENTIRE**   This bit is set when the entire control needs to be drawn.
- **ODA_FOCUS**   This bit is set when the control gains or loses input focus. The **itemState** member should be checked to determine whether the control has focus.
- **ODA_SELECT**   This bit is set when only the selection status has changed. The **itemState** member should be checked to determine the new selection state.

itemState   Specifies the visual state of the item after the current drawing action takes place. That is, if a menu item is to be dimmed, the state flag **ODS_GRAYED** will be set. The state flags are as follows:

- **ODS_CHECKED**   This bit is set if the menu item is to be checked. This bit is used only in a menu.
- **ODS_DISABLED**   This bit is set if the item is to be drawn as disabled.

- **ODS_FOCUS**   This bit is set if the item has input focus.

- **ODS_GRAYED**   This bit is set if the item is to be dimmed. This bit is used only in a menu.

- **ODS_SELECTED**   This bit is set if the item's status is selected.

- **ODS_COMBOBOXEDIT**   The drawing takes place in the selection field (edit control) of an ownerdrawn combo box.

- **ODS_DEFAULT**   The item is the default item.

hwndItem   Specifies the window handle of the control for combo boxes, list boxes, and buttons. Specifies the handle of the menu (**HMENU**) that contains the item for menus.

hDC   Identifies a device context. This device context must be used when performing drawing operations on the control.

rcItem   A rectangle in the device context specified by the **hDC** member that defines the boundaries of the control to be drawn. Windows automatically clips anything the owner draws in the device context for combo boxes, list boxes, and buttons, but it does not clip menu items. When drawing menu items, the owner must not draw outside the boundaries of the rectangle defined by the **rcItem** member.

itemData   For a combo box or list box, this member contains the value that was passed to the list box by one of the following:

- **CComboBox::AddString**

- **CComboBox::InsertString**

- **CListBox::AddString**

- **CListBox::InsertString**

For a menu, this member contains the value that was passed to the menu by one of the following:

- **CMenu::AppendMenu**

- **CMenu::InsertMenu**

- **CMenu::ModifyMenu**

See Also: **CWnd::OnDrawItem**

EXTENSION_CONTROL_BLOCK Structure

The **EXTENSION_CONTROL_BLOCK** structure has the following form:

```
typedef struct _EXTENSION_CONTROL_BLOCK {

    DWORD       cbSize;                             //IN
    DWORD       dwVersion                           //IN
    HCONN       ConnID;                             //IN
    DWORD       dwHttpStatusCode;                   //OUT
    CHAR        lpszLogData[HSE_LOG_BUFFER_LEN];    //OUT
    LPSTR       lpszMethod;                         //IN
    LPSTR       lpszQueryString;                    //IN
    LPSTR       lpszPathInfo;                       //IN
    LPSTR       lpszPathTranslated;                 //IN
    DWORD       cbTotalBytes;                       //IN
    DWORD       cbAvailable;                        //IN
    LPBYTE      lpbData;                            //IN
    LPSTR       lpszContentType;                    //IN

    BOOL ( WINAPI * GetServerVariable )
        ( HCONN         hConn,
        LPSTR           lpszVariableName,
        LPVOID          lpvBuffer,
        LPDWORD         lpdwSize );

    BOOL ( WINAPI * WriteClient )
        ( HCONN         ConnID,
        LPVOID          Buffer,
        LPDWORD         lpdwBytes,
        DWORD           dwReserved );

    BOOL ( WINAPI * ReadClient )
        ( HCONN         ConnID,
        LPVOID          lpvBuffer,
        LPDWORD         lpdwSize );

    BOOL ( WINAPI * ServerSupportFunction )
        ( HCONN         hConn,
        DWORD           dwHSERRequest,
        LPVOID          lpvBuffer,
        LPDWORD         lpdwSize,
        LPDWORD         lpdwDataType );

} EXTENSION_CONTROL_BLOCK, *LPEXTENSION_CONTROL_BLOCK;
```

The server communicates with the ISA via the **EXTENSION_CONTROL_BLOCK**.

The references to IN and OUT above indicates whether the member applies to messages to the extension (IN) or from the extension (OUT).

Members

The **EXTENSION_CONTROL_BLOCK** structure contains the following fields:

cbSize   The size of this structure.

dwVersion   The version information of **HTTP_FILTER_REVISION**. The **HIWORD** has the major version number and the **LOWORD** has the minor version number.

ConnID   A unique number assigned by the HTTP server. It must not be modified.

dwHttpStatusCode   The status of the current transaction when the request is completed. Can be one of the following:

- **HTTP_STATUS_BAD_REQUEST**

- **HTTP_STATUS_AUTH_REQUIRED**

- **HTTP_STATUS_FORBIDDEN**

- **HTTP_STATUS_NOT_FOUND**

- **HTTP_STATUS_SERVER_ERROR**

- **HTTP_STATUS_NOT_IMPLEMENTED**

lpszLogData   Buffer of size **HSE_LOG_BUFFER_LEN**. Contains a null-terminated log information string, specific to the ISA, of the current transaction. This log information will be entered in the HTTP server log. Maintaining a single log file with both HTTP server and ISA transactions is very useful for administration purposes.

lpszMethod   The method with which the request was made. This is equivalent to the CGI variable **REQUEST_METHOD**.

lpszQueryString   Null-terminated string containing the query information. This is equivalent to the CGI variable **QUERY_STRING**.

lpszPathInfo   Null-terminated string containing extra path information given by the client. This is equivalent to the CGI variable **PATH_INFO**.

lpszPathTranslated   Null-terminated string containing the translated path. This is equivalent to the CGI variable **PATH_TRANSLATED**.

cbTotalBytes   The total number of bytes to be received from the client. This is equivalent to the CGI variable **CONTENT_LENGTH**. If this value is 0xffffffff, then there are four gigabytes or more of available data. In this case, **CHttpServerContext::ReadClient** should be called until no more data is returned.

cbAvailable   The available number of bytes (out of a total of **cbTotalBytes**) in the buffer pointed to by **lpbData**. If **cbTotalBytes** is the same as **cbAvailable** the variable **lpbData** will point to a buffer which contains all the data sent by the client. Otherwise **cbTotalBytes** will contain the total number of bytes of data received. The ISA will then need to use the callback function

CHttpServerContext::ReadClient to read the rest of the data (starting from an offset of **cbAvailable**).

lpbData   Points to a buffer of size **cbAvailable** that has the data sent by the client.

lpszContentType   Null-terminated string containing the content type of the data sent by the client. This is equivalent to the CGI variable **CONTENT_TYPE**.

GetServerVariable   This function copies information (including CGI variables) relating to an HTTP connection, or to the server itself, into a buffer. **GetServerVariable** takes the following parameters:

- *hConn*   A handle to a connection.

- *lpszVariableName*   Null-terminated string indicating which variable is being requested. Variable names are:

Variable Name	Description
ALL_HTTP	All HTTP headers that were not already parsed into one of the above variables. These variables are of the form HTTP_<header field name>.
AUTH_PASS	This will retrieve the password corresponding to **REMOTE_USER** as supplied by the client. It will be a null-terminated string.
AUTH_TYPE	Contains the type of authentication used. For example, if Basic authentication is used, the string will be "Basic". For Windows NT Challenge-response, it will be "NTLM". Other authentication schemes will have other strings. Because new authentication types can be added to Internet Server, it is not possible to list all possible strings. If the string is empty then no authentication is used.
CONTENT_LENGTH	The number of bytes which the script can expect to receive from the client.
CONTENT_TYPE	The content type of the information supplied in the body of a POST request.
GATEWAY_INTERFACE	The revision of the CGI specification to which this server complies. The current version is CGI/1.1.
HTTP_ACCEPT	Special case HTTP header. Values of the Accept: fields are concatenated, separated by ",". For example, if the following lines are part of the HTTP header:

```
accept: */*; q=0.1
accept: text/html
accept: image/jpeg
```
then the **HTTP_ACCEPT** variable will have a value of:

/; q=0.1, text/html, image/jpeg

(continued)

Variable Name	Description
PATH_INFO	Additional path information, as given by the client. This comprises the trailing part of the URL after the script name but before the query string (if any).
PATH_TRANSLATED	This is the value of PATH_INFO, but with any virtual path name expanded into a directory specification.
QUERY_STRING	The information which follows the **?** in the URL that referenced this script.
REMOTE_ADDR	The IP address of the client.
REMOTE_HOST	The hostname of the client.
REMOTE_USER	This contains the username supplied by the client and authenticated by the server.
REQUEST_METHOD	The HTTP request method.
SCRIPT_NAME	The name of the script program being executed.
SERVER_NAME	The server's hostname (or IP address) as it should appear in self-referencing URLs.
SERVER_PORT	The TCP/IP port on which the request was received.
SERVER_PROTOCOL	The name and version of the information retrieval protocol relating to this request. Normally HTTP/1.0.
SERVER_SOFTWARE	The name and version of the web server under which the CGI program is running.

- *lpvBuffer* Pointer to buffer to receive the requested information.

- *lpdwSize* Pointer to **DWORD** indicating the number of bytes available in the buffer. On successful completion the **DWORD** contains the number of bytes transferred into the buffer (including the null terminating byte).

WriteClient Sends information to the client from the indicated buffer. **WriteClient** takes the following parameters:

- *ConnID* A unique connection number assigned by the HTTP server.

- *Buffer* Pointer to the buffer where the data is to be written.

- *lpdwBytes* Pointer to the data to be written.

- *dwReserved* Reserved for future use.

ReadClient Reads information from the body of the Web client's HTTP request into the buffer supplied by the caller. **ReadClient** takes the following parameters:

- *ConnID* A unique connection number assigned by the HTTP server.

- *lpvBuffer* Pointer to the buffer area to receive the requested information.

- *lpdwSize* Pointer to **DWORD** indicating the number of bytes available in the buffer. On return *lpdwSize* will contain the number of bytes actually transferred into the buffer.

ServerSupportFunction Provide the ISAs with some general-purpose functions as well as functions that are specific to HTTP server implementation. **ServerSupportFunction** takes the following parameters:

- *hConn* A handle to a connection.

- *dwHSERRequest* An HTTP Server Extension value. See **CHttpServerContext::ServerSupportFunction** for a list of possible values and related parameters.

- *lpvBuffer* When used with **HSE_REQ_SEND_RESPONSE_HEADER**, it points to a null-terminated optional status string (i.e., "401 Access Denied"). If this buffer is null, a default response of "200 Ok" will be sent by this function. When used with **HSE_REQ_DONE_WITH_SESSION**, it points to a **DWORD** indicating the status code of the request.

- *lpdwSize* When used with **HSE_REQ_SEND_RESPONSE_HEADER**, it points to the size of the buffer *lpdwDataType*.

- *lpdwDataType* A null-terminated string pointing to optional headers or data to be appended and sent with the header. If **NULL**, the header will be terminated by a "\r\n" pair.

Comments

A server identifies files with the extensions .EXE and .BAT as CGI (Common Gateway Interface) executables. In addition, a server will identify a file with a DLL extension as a script to execute.

When the server loads the DLL, it calls the DLL at the entry point **CHttpServer::GetExtensionVersion** to get the version number of the **HTTP_FILTER_REVISION** the ISA is based on and a short text description for server administrators. For every client request, the **CHttpServer::HttpExtensionProc** entry point is called. The extension receives the commonly-needed information such as the query string, path info, method name, and the translated path.

See Also: CHttpServerContext::ReadClient,
CHttpServer::GetExtensionVersion, CHttpServer::HttpExtensionProc

FILETIME Structure

The **FILETIME** structure has the following form:

```
typedef struct _FILETIME {
    DWORD dwLowDateTime;   /* low 32 bits */
    DWORD dwHighDateTime;  /* high 32 bits */
} FILETIME, *PFILETIME, *LPFILETIME;
```

The **FILETIME** structure is a 64-bit value representing the number of 100-nanosecond intervals since January 1, 1601.

Members

dwLowDateTime   Specifies the low 32 bits of the file time.

dwHighDateTime   Specifies the high 32 bits of the file time.

See Also: CTime::CTime

HSE_VERSION_INFO Structure

The **HSE_VERSION_INFO** structure has the following form:

```
typedef struct   _HSE_VERSION_INFO {

    DWORD   dwExtensionVersion;
    CHAR    lpszExtensionDesc[HSE_MAX_EXT_DLL_NAME_LEN];

} HSE_VERSION_INFO, *LPHSE_VERSION_INFO;
```

This structure is pointed to by the *pVer* parameter in the **CHttpServer::GetExtensionVersion** member function. It provides the ISA version number and a text description of the ISA.

Members

dwExtensionVersion   The version number of the ISA.

lpszExtensionDesc   The text description of the ISA. The default implementation provides placeholder text; override **CHttpServer::GetExtensionVersion** to provide your own description.

See Also: CHttpServer::GetExtensionVersion

HTTP_FILTER_AUTHENT Structure

The **HTTP_FILTER_AUTHENT** structure has the following form:

```
typedef struct _HTTP_FILTER_AUTHENT{

CHAR*    pszUser;                    //IN/OUT
DWORD    cbUserBuff;                 //IN
CHAR*    pszPassword;                //IN/OUT
DWORD    cbPasswordBuff;             //IN
} HTTP_FILTER_AUTHENT, *PHTTP_FILTER_AUTHENT;
```

This structure is pointed to by the *pvNotification* in the **CHttpFilter::HttpFilterProc** when *NotificationType* is **SF_NOTIFY_AUTHENTICATION**, which indicates when the server is about to authenticate the client. This structure can be used to implement a different authentication scheme by overriding **CHttpFilter::OnAuthentication**.

The references to IN or IN/OUT above indicate whether the member applies to messages to the filter (IN) or both to and from the filter (IN/OUT).

Members

pszUser   Pointer to a string containing the username for this request. An empty string indicates an anonymous user.

cbUserBuff   Size of the buffer pointed to by **pszUser**. This is guaranteed to be at least **SF_MAX_USERNAME**.

pszPassword   Pointer to a string containing the password for this request.

cbPasswordBuff   Size of the buffer pointed to by **pszPassword**. This is guaranteed to be at least **SF_MAX_PASSWORD**.

See Also: CHttpFilter::HttpFilterProc, CHttpFilter::OnAuthentication

---

HTTP_FILTER_CONTEXT Structure

The **HTTP_FILTER_CONTEXT** structure has the following form:

```
typedef struct _HTTP_FILTER_CONTEXT
{

DWORD    cbSize;                     //IN
DWORD    Revision;                   //IN
PVOID    ServerContext;              //IN
DWORD    ulReserved;                 //IN
BOOL     fIsSecurePort;              //IN
PVOID    pFilterContext;             //IN/OUT

BOOL    (WINAPI * GetServerVariable) (
   struct _HTTP_FILTER_CONTEXT *    pfc,
   LPSTR        lpszVariableName,
```

```
LPVOID      lpvBuffer,
LPDWORD     lpdwSize
);

BOOL    (WINAPI * AddResponseHeaders) (
    struct _HTTP_FILTER_CONTEXT *    pfc,
    LPSTR     lpszHeaders,
    DWORD     dwReserved
    );

BOOL    (WINAPI * WriteClient)  (
    struct _HTTP_FILTER_CONTEXT *    pfc,
    LPVOID      Buffer,
    LPDWORD     lpdwBytes,
    DWORD       dwReserved
    );

VOID *      (WINAPI * AllocMem) (
    struct _HTTP_FILTER_CONTEXT *    pfc,
    DWORD       cbSize,
    DWORD       dwReserved
    );

BOOL    (WINAPI * ServerSupportFunction) (
    struct _HTTP_FILTER_CONTEXT *    pfc,
    enum SF_REQ_TYPE    sfReq,
    PVOID       pData,
    DWORD       ul1,
    DWORD       ul2
    );

} HTTP_FILTER_CONTEXT, *PHTTP_FILTER_CONTEXT;
```

The references to IN or IN/OUT above indicate whether the member applies to messages to the filter (IN) or both to and from the filter (IN/OUT).

Members

cbSize   Size of this structure, in bytes.

Revision   Revision level of this structure. Less than or equal to the version of the **HTTP_FILTER_REVISION**.

ServerContext   Reserved for server use.

ulReserved   Reserved for server use.

fIsSecurePort   **TRUE** indicates that this event is occurring over a secure port.

pFilterContext   A pointer to be used by the filter for any context information that the filter wants to associate with this request. Any memory associated with this request can be safely freed during the **SF_NOTIFY_END_OF_NET_SESSION** notification.

GetServerVariable   Pointer to a function to retrieve information about the server and this connection. See **CHttpServerContext::GetServerVariable** for details. **GetServerVariable** takes the following parameters:

- *pfc*   Pointer to a filter context passed to **CHttpFilter::HttpFilterProc**.

- *lpszVariableName*   Server variable to retrieve.

- *lpvBuffer*   Buffer to store value of variable.

- *lpdwSize*   Size of buffer *lpvBuffer*.

AddResponseHeaders   Pointer to a function that adds a header to the HTTP response. See the description of **HSE_REQ_SEND_RESPONSE_HEADER** at **CHttpServerContext::ServerSupportFunction** for details. **AddResponseHeaders** takes the following parameters:

- *pfc*   Pointer to a filter context passed to **CHttpFilter::HttpFilterProc**.

- *lpszHeaders*   Pointer string containing headers to add.

- *dwReserved*   Reserved for future use. Must be 0.

WriteClient   Pointer to a function that sends raw data back to the client. See **CHttpFilterContext::WriteClient** for details. **WriteClient** takes the following parameters:

- *pfc*   Pointer passed to **CHttpFilter::HttpFilterProc**.

- *Buffer*   Buffer containing data to send to the client.

- *lpdwBytes*   Size of the buffer pointed to by *Buffer*.

- *dwReserved*   Reserved for future use.

AllocMem   Pointer to a function used to allocate memory. Any memory allocated with this function will automatically be freed when the request is completed. **AllocMem** takes the following parameters:

- *pfc*   Pointer passed to **CHttpFilter::HttpFilterProc**.

- *cbSize*   Size of the buffer to allocate.

- *dwReserved*   Reserved for future use.

ServerSupportFunction   Pointer to a function used to extend the ISAPI filter APIs. Parameters, listed below, are specific to the ISA used.

- *pfc*   Pointer to a function used to extend the ISAPI filter APIs.

- *sfReq*   Server function notification. Possible values:

  SF_REQ_SEND_RESPONSE_HEADER   Sends a complete HTTP server response header including the status, server version, message time and MIME version. Server extensions should append other information at the end, such as Content-type, Content-length, and so forth, followed by an extra '\r\n'.

SF_REQ_ADD_HEADERS_ON_DENIAL   If the server denies the HTTP request, add the specified headers to the server error response. This allows an authentication filter to advertise its services without filtering every request. Generally the headers will be WWW-Authenticate headers with custom authentication schemes, but no restriction is placed on what headers may be specified.

SF_REQ_SET_NEXT_READ_SIZE   Only used by raw data filters that return **SF_STATUS_READ_NEXT**.

- *pData*   Pointer to a string. Specific to the ISA. See the table under the **Comments** section for the appropriate values for each **sfReq** value.

- *ul1, ul2*   Specific to the ISA. See the table under the **Comments** section for the appropriate values for each **sfReq** value.

Comments

Below are the corresponding possible values for the **ServerSupportFunction** parameters:

sfReq	*pData*	*ul1, ul2*
SF_REQ_SEND_RESPONSE_HEADER	Zero-terminated string pointing to optional status string (i.e., "401 Access Denied") or NULL for the default response of "200 OK".	Zero-terminated string pointing to optional data to be appended and set with the header. If NULL, the header will be terminated with an empty line.
SF_REQ_ADD_HEADERS_ON_DENIAL	Zero-terminated string pointing to one or more header lines with terminating '\r\n'.	
SF_REQ_SET_NEXT_READ_SIZE		Size in bytes for the next read.

See Also: CHttpFilter::HttpFilterProc, CHttpFilter::OnLog, CHttpServerContext, CHttpServerContext::GetServerVariable, CHttpServerContext::ServerSupportFunction, CHttpServerContext::WriteClient

HTTP_FILTER_LOG Structure

The **HTTP_FILTER_LOG** structure has the following form:

```
typedef struct _HTTP_FILTER_LOG

{

const CHAR *    pszClientHostName;          //IN/OUT
const CHAR *    pszClientUserName;          //IN/OUT
const CHAR *    pszServerName;              //IN/OUT
const CHAR *    pszOperation;               //IN/OUT
const CHAR *    pszTarget;                  //IN/OUT
const CHAR *    pszParameters;              //IN/OUT
DWORD           dwHttpStatus;               //IN/OUT
DWORD           dwWin32Status;              //IN/OUT

} HTTP_FILTER_LOG, *PHTTP_FILTER_LOG;
```

This structure is pointed to by the *pvNotification* in the
CHttpFilter::HttpFilterProc when *NotificationType* is **SF_NOTIFY_LOG**,
which indicates that the server is about to log information to the server log file.
The strings cannot be changed but pointers can be replaced. If the string
pointers are changed, the memory they point to must remain valid until the
next notification.

The references to IN/OUT above indicate that the member applies to messages
to (IN) and from (OUT) the filter.

Members

pszClientHostName   Client's host name.

pszClientUserName   Client's user name.

pszServerName   Name of the server the client connected to.

pszOperation   HTTP command.

pszTarget   Target of the HTTP command.

pszParameters   Parameters passed to the HTTP command.

dwHttpStatus   HTTP return status.

dwWin32Status   Win32 error code.

See Also: CHttpFilter::HttpFilterProc, CHttpFilter::OnLog

HTTP_FILTER_PREPROC_HEADERS Structure

The **HTTP_FILTER_PREPROC_HEADERS** structure has the following form:

```
typedef struct _HTTP_FILTER_PREPROC_HEADERS

{
BOOL    (WINAPI * GetHeader) (
   struct _HTTP_FILTER_CONTEXT *    pfc,
   LPSTR    lpszName,
   LPVOID   lpvBuffer,
   LPDWORD  lpdwSize
   );
BOOL    (WINAPI * SetHeader) (
   struct _HTTP_FILTER_CONTEXT *    pfc,
   LPSTR    lpszName,
   LPSTR    lpszValue
   );
BOOL    (WINAPI * AddHeader) (
   struct _HTTP_FILTER_CONTEXT *    pfc,
   LPSTR    lpszName,
   LPSTR    lpszValue
   );
DWORD    dwReserved;

} HTTP_FILTER_PREPROC_HEADERS, *PHTTP_FILTER_PREPROC_HEADERS;
```

This structure is pointed to by the *pvNotification* in **CHttpFilter::HttpFilterProc** when *NotificationType* is **SF_NOTIFY_PREPROC_HEADERS**, which indicates when the server is about to process the client headers.

Members

GetHeader   Pointer to a function that retrieves the specified header value. Header names should include the trailing colon (":"). The special values "method", "url" and "version" can be used to retrieve the individual portions of the request line. **GetHeader** takes the following parameters:

- *pfc*   Filter context for this request from the pointer to the filter context passed to the **CHttpFilter::HttpFilterProc**.

- *lpszName*   The name of the header to retrieve.

- *lpvBuffer*   Pointer to a buffer of size *lpdwSize* where the value of the header will be stored.

- *lpdwSize*   Size of the buffer pointed to by *lpvBuffer*.

SetHeader   Pointer to a function used to change or delete the value of a header. **SetHeader** takes the following parameters:

- *pfc*   Filter context for this request from the pointer to the filter context passed to the **CHttpFilter::HttpFilterProc**.

- *lpszName*   Pointer to the name of the header to change or delete.

- *lpszValue*   Pointer to the string to change the header to, or a pointer to "\0" to delete the header.

AddHeader   Pointer to a function to add a header. **AddHeader** takes the following parameters:

- *pfc*   Filter context for this request from the pointer to the filter context passed to the **CHttpFilter::HttpFilterProc**.

- *lpszName*   Pointer to the name of the header to change or delete.

- *lpszValue*   Pointer to the string to change the header to, or a pointer to "\0" to delete the header.

See Also: CHttpFilter::HttpFilterProc, **CHttpFilter::OnPreprocHeaders**

HTTP_FILTER_RAW_DATA Structure

The **HTTP_FILTER_RAW_DATA** structure has the following form:

```
typedef struct _HTTP_FILTER_RAW_DATA
{
PVOID       pvInData;                        //IN
DWORD       cbInData;                        //IN
DWORD       cbInBuffer;                      //IN
DWORD       dwReserved;                      //IN
} HTTP_FILTER_RAW_DATA, *PHTTP_FILTER_RAW_DATA;
```

This structure is passed to the **SF_NOTIFY_READ_RAW_DATA** and **SF_NOTIFY_SEND_RAW_DATA** notification types for **CHttpFilter::HttpFilterProc**.

The references to IN above indicate that the message being processed is going to the filter.

Members

pvInData   Pointer to the data buffer (input or output).

cbInData   Amount of data in the buffer pointed to by **pvInData**.

cbInBuffer   Size of the buffer pointed to by **pvInData**.

dwReserved   Reserved for future use.

See Also: CHttpFilter::HttpFilterProc, **CHttpFilter::OnReadRawData**, **CHttpFilter::OnSendRawData**

HTTP_FILTER_URL_MAP Structure

The **HTTP_FILTER_URL_MAP** structure has the following form:

```
typedef struct _HTTP_FILTER_URL_MAP

{
const CHAR *    pszURL;                    //IN
CHAR *          pszPhysicalPath;           //IN/OUT
DWORD           cbPathBuff;                //IN
} HTTP_FILTER_URL_MAP, *PHTTP_FILTER_URL_MAP;
```

This structure is pointed to by the *pvNotification* in the **CHttpFilter::HttpFilterProc** when the *NotificationType* is **SF_NOTIFY_URL_MAP**, which indicates when the server is about to map the specified URL to a physical path. Filters can modify the physical path in place.

The references to IN or IN/OUT above indicate whether the member applies to messages to the filter (IN) or to and from the filter (IN/OUT).

Members

pszURL   Pointer to the URL that is being mapped to a physical path.

pszPhysicalPath   Pointer to the buffer where the physical path is stored.

cbPathBuff   Size of the buffer pointed to by **pszPhysicalPath**.

See Also: CHttpFilter::HttpFilterProc, CHttpFilter::OnUrlMap

HTTP_FILTER_VERSION Structure

The **HTTP_FILTER_VERSION** structure has the following form:

```
typedef struct _HTTP_FILTER_VERSION

{
DWORD   dwServerFilterVersion;                      //IN
DWORD   dwFilterVersion;                            //OUT
CHAR    lpszFilterDesc[SF_MAX_FILTER_DESC_LEN+1];   //OUT
DWORD   dwFlags;                                    //OUT
} HTTP_FILTER_VERSION, *PHTTP_FILTER_VERSION;
```

This structure is passed to the application's **CHttpFilter::HttpFilterProc** entrypoint by the server to associate any context information with the HTTP request.

The references to IN or OUT above indicate whether the member applies to messages to the filter (IN) or from the filter (OUT).

Members

> **dwServerFilterVersion** Version of the header used by the filter. The version of the current header file is **HTTP_FILTER_REVISION**.
>
> **dwFilterVersion** Version of **HTTP_FILTER_REVISION**.
>
> **lpszFilterDesc** Location to store a short string description of the ISAPI filter application.
>
> **dwFlags** Combination of **SF_NOTIFY_*** flags to specify what events this application needs, and at what priority the filter is loaded. See **CHttpFilter::GetFilterVersion** and **CHttpFilter::HttpFilterProc** for lists of valid flags.
>
> **See Also:** **CHttpFilter::HttpFilterProc, CHttpFilter::GetFilterVersion**

LINGER Structure

> The **LINGER** structure has the following form:

```
struct linger {
    u_short l_onoff;        // option on/off
    u_short l_linger;       // linger time
};
```

> The **LINGER** structure is used for manipulating the **SO_LINGER** and **SO_DONTLINGER** options of **CAsyncSocket::GetSockOpt**.

Comments

> Setting the **SO_DONTLINGER** option prevents blocking on member function **Close** while waiting for unsent data to be sent. Setting this option is equivalent to setting **SO_LINGER** with **l_onoff** set to 0.
>
> **See Also:** **CAsyncSocket::GetSockOpt, CAsyncSocket::SetSockOpt**

LOGBRUSH Structure

> The **LOGBRUSH** structure has the following form:

```
typedef struct tag LOGBRUSH { /* lb */
    UINT     lbStyle;
    COLORREF lbColor;
    LONG     lbHatch;
} LOGBRUSH;
```

> The **LOGBRUSH** structure defines the style, color, and pattern of a physical brush. It is used by the Windows **CreateBrushIndirect** and **ExtCreatePen** functions.

Members

> **lbStyle** Specifies the brush style. The **lbStyle** member must be one of the following styles:

- **BS_DIBPATTERN**   A pattern brush defined by a device-independent bitmap (DIB) specification. If **lbStyle** is **BS_DIBPATTERN**, the **lbHatch** member contains a handle to a packed DIB.

- **BS_DIBPATTERNPT**   A pattern brush defined by a device-independent bitmap (DIB) specification. If **lbStyle** is **BS_DIBPATTERNPT**, the **lbHatch** member contains a pointer to a packed DIB.

- **BS_HATCHED**   Hatched brush.

- **BS_HOLLOW**   Hollow brush.

- **BS_NULL**   Same as **BS_HOLLOW**.

- **BS_PATTERN**   Pattern brush defined by a memory bitmap.

- **BS_SOLID**   Solid brush.

lbColor   Specifies the color in which the brush is to be drawn. If **lbStyle** is the **BS_HOLLOW** or **BS_PATTERN** style, **lbColor** is ignored. If **lbStyle** is **BS_DIBPATTERN** or **BS_DIBPATTERNBT**, the low-order word of **lbColor** specifies whether the **bmiColors** members of the **BITMAPINFO** structure contain explicit red, green, blue (RGB) values or indices into the currently realized logical palette. The **lbColor** member must be one of the following values:

- **DIB_PAL_COLORS**   The color table consists of an array of 16-bit indices into the currently realized logical palette.

- **DIB_RGB_COLORS**   The color table contains literal RGB values.

lbHatch   Specifies a hatch style. The meaning depends on the brush style defined by **lbStyle**. If **lbStyle** is **BS_DIBPATTERN**, the **lbHatch** member contains a handle to a packed DIB. If **lbStyle** is **BS_DIBPATTERNPT**, the **lbHatch** member contains a pointer to a packed DIB. If **lbStyle** is **BS_HATCHED**, the **lbHatch** member specifies the orientation of the lines used to create the hatch. It can be one of the following values:

- **HS_BDIAGONAL**   A 45-degree upward, left-to-right hatch

- **HS_CROSS**   Horizontal and vertical crosshatch

- **HS_DIAGCROSS**   45-degree crosshatch

- **HS_FDIAGONAL**   A 45-degree downward, left-to-right hatch

- **HS_HORIZONTAL**   Horizontal hatch

- **HS_VERTICAL**   Vertical hatch

If **lbStyle** is **BS_PATTERN**, **lbHatch** is a handle to the bitmap that defines the pattern. If **lbStyle** is **BS_SOLID** or **BS_HOLLOW**, **lbHatch** is ignored.

Comments

Although **lbColor** controls the foreground color of a hatch brush, the **CDC::SetBkMode** and **CDC::SetBkColor** functions control the background color.

See Also: **CDC::GetCharABCWidths**

LOGFONT Structure

The **LOGFONT** structure has the following form:

```
typedef struct tagLOGFONT { /* lf */
    LONG lfHeight;
    LONG lfWidth;
    LONG lfEscapement;
    LONG lfOrientation;
    LONG lfWeight;
    BYTE lfItalic;
    BYTE lfUnderline;
    BYTE lfStrikeOut;
    BYTE lfCharSet;
    BYTE lfOutPrecision;
    BYTE lfClipPrecision;
    BYTE lfQuality;
    BYTE lfPitchAndFamily;
    CHAR lfFaceName[LF_FACESIZE];
} LOGFONT;
```

The **LOGFONT** structure defines the attributes of a font.

Members

lfHeight   Specifies the height, in logical units, of the font. The font height can be specified in one of three ways. If **lfHeight** is greater than zero, it is transformed into device units and matched against the cell height of the available fonts. If it is zero, a reasonable default size is used. If it is less than zero, it is transformed into device units and the absolute value is matched against the character height of the available fonts. For all height comparisons, the font mapper looks for the largest font that does not exceed the requested size; if there is no such font, it looks for the smallest font available. This mapping occurs when the font is actually used for the first time.

lfWidth   Specifies the average width, in logical units, of characters in the font. If **lfWidth** is zero, the aspect ratio of the device is matched against the digitization aspect ratio of the available fonts to find the closest match, determined by the absolute value of the difference.

lfEscapement   Specifies the angle, in tenths of degrees, of each line of text written in the font (relative to the bottom of the page).

lfOrientation   Specifies the angle, in tenths of degrees, of each character's base line (relative to the bottom of the page).

lfWeight   Specifies the weight of the font, in the range 0 through 1000 (for example, 400 is normal and 700 is bold). If **lfWeight** is zero, a default weight is used.

lfItalic   Specifies an italic font if set to **TRUE**.

lfUnderline   Specifies an underlined font if set to **TRUE**.

lfStrikeOut   Specifies a strikeout font if set to **TRUE**.

lfCharSet   Specifies the character set. The following values are predefined:

- **ANSI_CHARSET**
- **OEM_CHARSET**
- **SYMBOL_CHARSET**
- **UNICODE_CHARSET**

The OEM character set is system dependent.

Fonts with other character sets may exist in the system. If an application uses a font with an unknown character set, it should not attempt to translate or interpret strings that are to be rendered with that font.

lfOutPrecision   Specifies the output precision. The output precision defines how closely the output must match the requested font's height, width, character orientation, escapement, and pitch. It can be one of the following values:

- **OUT_CHARACTER_PRECIS**
- **OUT_DEFAULT_PRECIS**
- **OUT_STRING_PRECIS**
- **OUT_STROKE_PRECIS**

lfClipPrecision   Specifies the clipping precision. The clipping precision defines how to clip characters that are partially outside the clipping region. It can be one of the following values:

- **CLIP_CHARACTER_PRECIS**
- **CLIP_DEFAULT_PRECIS**
- **CLIP_STROKE_PRECIS**

lfQuality   Specifies the output quality. The output quality defines how carefully the graphics device interface (GDI) must attempt to match the logical-font attributes to those of an actual physical font. It can be one of the following values:

- **DEFAULT_QUALITY**   Appearance of the font does not matter.
- **DRAFT_QUALITY**   Appearance of the font is less important than when **PROOF_QUALITY** is used. For GDI fonts, scaling is enabled, which means that more font sizes are available, but the quality may be lower. Bold, italic, underline, and strikeout fonts are synthesized if necessary.

- **PROOF_QUALITY** Character quality of the font is more important than exact matching of the logical-font attributes. For GDI fonts, scaling is disabled and the font closest in size is chosen. Although the chosen font size may not be mapped exactly when **PROOF_QUALITY** is used, the quality of the font is high and there is no distortion of appearance. Bold, italic, underline, and strikeout fonts are synthesized if necessary.

lfPitchAndFamily Specifies the pitch and family of the font. The two low-order bits specify the pitch of the font and can be one of the following values:

- **DEFAULT_PITCH**

- **FIXED_PITCH**

- **VARIABLE_PITCH**

Bits 4 through 7 of the member specify the font family and can be one of the following values:

- **FF_DECORATIVE**

- **FF_DONTCARE**

- **FF_MODERN**

- **FF_ROMAN**

- **FF_SCRIPT**

- **FF_SWISS**

The proper value can be obtained by using the Boolean OR operator to join one pitch constant with one family constant. Font families describe the look of a font in a general way. They are intended for specifying fonts when the exact typeface desired is not available. The values for font families are as follows:

- **FF_DECORATIVE** Novelty fonts. Old English is an example.

- **FF_DONTCARE** Don't care or don't know.

- **FF_MODERN** Fonts with constant stroke width (fixed-pitch), with or without serifs. Fixed-pitch fonts are usually modern. Pica, Elite, and CourierNew® are examples.

- **FF_ROMAN** Fonts with variable stroke width (proportionally spaced) and with serifs. MS Serif® is an example.

- **FF_SCRIPT** Fonts designed to look like handwriting. Script and Cursive are examples.

- **FF_SWISS** Fonts with variable stroke width (proportionally spaced) and without serifs. MS® Sans Serif is an example.

lfFaceName   Points to a null-terminated string that specifies the typeface name of the font. The length of this string must not exceed 32 characters. The Windows **EnumFonts** function can be used to enumerate the typeface names of all currently available fonts. If **lfFaceName** is **NULL**, GDI uses a default typeface.

See Also: CDC::GetCharABCWidths, CFontDialog::CFontDialog, CGdiObject::GetObject

LOGPEN Structure

The **LOGPEN** structure has the following form:

```
typedef struct tagLOGPEN {  /* lgpn */
    UINT     lopnStyle;
    POINT    lopnWidth;
    COLORREF lopnColor;
} LOGPEN;
```

The **LOGPEN** structure defines the style, width, and color of a pen a drawing object used to draw lines and borders. The **CPen::CreatePenIndirect** function uses the **LOGPEN** structure.

Members

lopnStyle   Specifies the pen type. This member can be one of the following values:

- **PS_SOLID**   Creates a solid pen.

- **PS_DASH**   Creates a dashed pen. (Valid only when the pen width is 1.)

- **PS_DOT**   Creates a dotted pen. (Valid only when the pen width is 1.)

- **PS_DASHDOT**   Creates a pen with alternating dashes and dots. (Valid only when the pen width is 1.)

- **PS_DASHDOTDOT**   Creates a pen with alternating dashes and double dots. (Valid only when the pen width is 1.)

- **PS_NULL**   Creates a null pen.

- **PS_INSIDEFRAME**   Creates a pen that draws a line inside the frame of closed shapes produced by GDI output functions that specify a bounding rectangle (for example, the **Ellipse Rectangle**, **RoundRect Pie**, and **Chord** member functions). When this style is used with GDI output functions that do not specify a bounding rectangle (for example the **LineTo** member function), the drawing area of the pen is not limited by a frame.

  If a pen has the **PS_INSIDEFRAME** style and a color that does not match a color in the logical color table, the pen is drawn with a dithered color. The **PS_SOLID** pen style cannot be used to create a pen with a dithered color. The **PS_INSIDEFRAME** style is identical to **PS_SOLID** if the pen width is less than or equal to 1.

When the **PS_INSIDEFRAME** style is used with GDI objects produced by functions other than **Ellipse Rectangle** and **RoundRect**, the line may not be completely inside the specified frame.

lopnWidth   Specifies the pen width in logical units. If the **lopnWidth** member is 0, the pen is 1 pixel wide on raster devices regardless of the current mapping mode.

lopnColor   Specifies the pen color.

Comments

The **y** value in the **POINT** structure for the **lopnWidth** member is not used.

See Also: **CPen::CreatePenIndirect**

MEASUREITEMSTRUCT Structure

The **MEASUREITEMSTRUCT** data structure has the following form:

```
typedef struct tagMEASUREITEMSTRUCT {
    UINT    CtlType;
    UINT    CtlID;
    UINT    itemID;
    UINT    itemWidth;
    UINT    itemHeight;
    DWORD   itemData
} MEASUREITEMSTRUCT;
```

The **MEASUREITEMSTRUCT** structure informs Windows of the dimensions of an owner-drawn control or menu item. This allows Windows to process user interaction with the control correctly. Failure to fill out the proper members in the **MEASUREITEMSTRUCT** structure will cause improper operation of the control.

Members

CtlType   Contains the control type. The values for control types are as follows:

- **ODT_COMBOBOX**   Owner-draw combo box

- **ODT_LISTBOX**   Owner-draw list box

- **ODT_MENU**   Owner-draw menu

CtlID   Contains the control ID for a combo box, list box, or button. This member is not used for a menu.

itemID   Contains the menu-item ID for a menu or the list-box-item ID for a variable-height combo box or list box. This member is not used for a fixed-height combo box or list box, or for a button.

itemWidth   Specifies the width of a menu item. The owner of the owner-draw menu item must fill this member before it returns from the message.

itemHeight Specifies the height of an individual item in a list box or a menu. Before it returns from the message, the owner of the owner-draw combo box, list box, or menu item must fill out this member. The maximum height of a list box item is 255.

itemData For a combo box or list box, this member contains the value that was passed to the list box by one of the following:

- **CComboBox::AddString**
- **CComboBox::InsertString**
- **CListBox::AddString**
- **CListBox::InsertString**

For a menu, this member contains the value that was passed to the menu by one of the following:

- **CMenu::AppendMenu**
- **CMenu::InsertMenu**
- **CMenu::ModifyMenu**

See Also: **CWnd::OnMeasureItem**

MINMAXINFO Structure

The **MINMAXINFO** structure has the following form:

```
typedef struct tagMINMAXINFO {
    POINT ptReserved;
    POINT ptMaxSize;
    POINT ptMaxPosition;
    POINT ptMinTrackSize;
    POINT ptMaxTrackSize;
} MINMAXINFO;
```

The **MINMAXINFO** structure contains information about a window's maximized size and position and its minimum and maximum tracking size.

Members

ptReserved Reserved for internal use.

ptMaxSize Specifies the maximized width (point.x) and the maximized height (point.y) of the window.

ptMaxPosition Specifies the position of the left side of the maximized window (point.x) and the position of the top of the maximized window (point.y).

ptMinTrackSize Specifies the minimum tracking width (point.x) and the minimum tracking height (point.y) of the window.

ptMaxTrackSize Specifies the maximum tracking width (point.x) and the maximum tracking height (point.y) of the window.

See Also: CWnd::OnGetMinMaxInfo

MSG Structure

The **MSG** structure has the following form:

```
typedef struct tagMSG {       // msg
   HWND    hwnd;
   UINT    message;
   WPARAM  wParam;
   LPARAM  lParam;
   DWORD   time;
   POINT   pt;
} MSG;
```

The **MSG** structure contains message information from a thread's message queue.

Members

hwnd   Identifies the window whose window procedure receives the message.

message   Specifies the message number.

wParam   Specifies additional information about the message. The exact meaning depends on the value of the **message** member.

lParam   Specifies additional information about the message. The exact meaning depends on the value of the **message** member.

time   Specifies the time at which the message was posted.

pt   Specifies the cursor position, in screen coordinates, when the message was posted.

NCCALCSIZE_PARAMS Structure

The **NCCALCSIZE_PARAMS** structure has the following form:

```
typedef struct tagNCCALCSIZE_PARAMS {
   RECT            rgrc[3];
   PWINDOWPOS      lppos;
} NCCALCSIZE_PARAMS;
```

The **NCCALCSIZE_PARAMS** structure contains information that an application can use while processing the **WM_NCCALCSIZE** message to calculate the size, position, and valid contents of the client area of a window.

Members

rgrc   Specifies an array of rectangles. The first contains the new coordinates of a window that has been moved or resized. The second contains the coordinates of the window before it was moved or resized. The third contains the coordinates of the client area of a window before it was moved or resized. If the window is a child window, the coordinates are relative to the client area of the parent window. If the window is a top-level window, the coordinates are relative to the screen.

lppos Points to a **WINDOWPOS** structure that contains the size and position values specified in the operation that caused the window to be moved or resized.

See Also: **CWnd::OnNcCalcSize**

PAINTSTRUCT Structure

The **PAINTSTRUCT** structure has the following form:

```
typedef struct tagPAINTSTRUCT {
    HDC  hdc;
    BOOL fErase;
    RECT rcPaint;
    BOOL fRestore;
    BOOL fIncUpdate;
    BYTE rgbReserved[16];
} PAINTSTRUCT;
```

The **PAINTSTRUCT** structure contains information that can be used to paint the client area of a window.

Members

hdc Identifies the display context to be used for painting.

fErase Specifies whether the background needs to be redrawn. It is not 0 if the application should redraw the background. The application is responsible for drawing the background if a Windows window-class is created without a background brush (see the description of the **hbrBackground** member of the **WNDCLASS** structure in the Win32 SDK documentation).

rcPaint Specifies the upper-left and lower-right corners of the rectangle in which the painting is requested.

fRestore Reserved member. It is used internally by Windows.

fIncUpdate Reserved member. It is used internally by Windows.

rgbReserved[16] Reserved member. A reserved block of memory used internally by Windows.

See Also: **CPaintDC::m_ps**

POINT Structure

The **POINT** data structure has the following form:

```
typedef struct tagPOINT {
    LONG x;
    LONG y;
} POINT;
```

The **POINT** structure defines the x- and y-coordinates of a point.

Members

x   Specifies the x-coordinate of a point.

y   Specifies the y-coordinate of a point.

See Also: CPoint

RECT Structure

The **RECT** data structure has the following form:

```
typedef struct tagRECT {
    LONG left;
    LONG top;
    LONG right;
    LONG bottom;
} RECT;
```

The **RECT** structure defines the coordinates of the upper-left and lower-right corners of a rectangle.

Members

left   Specifies the x-coordinate of the upper-left corner of a rectangle.

top   Specifies the y-coordinate of the upper-left corner of a rectangle.

right   Specifies the x-coordinate of the lower-right corner of a rectangle.

bottom   Specifies the y-coordinate of the lower-right corner of a rectangle.

See Also: CRect

RGNDATA Structure

The **RGNDATA** structure has the following form:

```
typedef struct _RGNDATA { /* rgnd */
    RGNDATAHEADER rdh;
    char          Buffer[1];
} RGNDATA;
```

The **RGNDATA** structure contains a header and an array of rectangles that compose a region. These rectangles, sorted top to bottom left to right, do not overlap.

Members

rdh   Specifies a **RGNDATAHEADER** structure. (For more information on this structure, see the Win32 SDK documentation.) The members of this structure specify the type of region (whether it is rectangular or trapezoidal), the number of rectangles that make up the region, the size of the buffer that contains the rectangle structures, and so on.

Buffer   Specifies an arbitrary-size buffer that contains the **RECT** structures that make up the region.

See Also: **CRgn::CreateFromData**, **CRgn::GetRegionData**

SIZE Structure

The **SIZE** structure has the following form:

```
typedef struct tagSIZE {
    int cx;
    int cy;
} SIZE;
```

The **SIZE** structure specifies the width and height of a rectangle.

Members

cx   Specifies the x-extent when a function returns.

cy   Specifies the y-extent when a function returns.

Comments

The rectangle dimensions stored in this structure can correspond to viewport extents, window extents, text extents, bitmap dimensions, or the aspect-ratio filter for some extended functions.

See Also: **CSize**

SOCKADDR Structure

The **SOCKADDR** structure has the following form:

```
struct sockaddr {
    unsigned short sa_family;
    char           sa_data[14];
};
```

The **SOCKADDR** structure is used to store an Internet Protocol (IP) address for a machine participating in a Windows Sockets communication.

Members

sa_family Socket address family.

sa_data Maximum size of all of the different socket address structures.

Comments

The Microsoft TCP/IP Sockets Developer's Kit only supports the Internet address domains. To actually fill in values for each part of an address, you use the **SOCKADDR_IN** data structure, which is specifically for this address format. The **SOCKADDR** and the **SOCKADDR_IN** data structures are the same size. You simply cast to switch between the two structure types. For more information, see "Windows Sockets Programming Considerations" in the Win32 SDK documentation.

See Also: **SOCKADDR_IN, CAsyncSocket::Create, CSocket::Create**

SOCKADDR_IN Structure

The **SOCKADDR_IN** structure has the following form:

```
struct sockaddr_in{
    short           sin_family;
    unsigned short  sin_port;
    struct  in_addr sin_addr;
    char            sin_zero[8];
};
```

In the Internet address family, the **SOCKADDR_IN** structure is used by Windows Sockets to specify a local or remote endpoint address to which to connect a socket. This is the form of the **SOCKADDR** structure specific to the Internet address family and can be cast to **SOCKADDR**.

Members

sin_family Address family (must be **AF_INET**).

sin_port IP port.

sin_addr IP address.

sin_zero Padding to make structure the same size as **SOCKADDR**.

Comments

The IP address component of this structure is of type **IN_ADDR**. The **IN_ADDR** structure is defined in Windows Sockets header file WINSOCK.H as follows:

```
struct  in_addr {
    union   {
        struct{
            unsigned  char   s_b1,
                             s_b2,
                             s_b3,
                             s_b4;
        } S_un_b;
```

```
     struct  {
     unsigned  short  s_w1,
                      s_w2;
       }  S_un_w;
        unsigned long  S_addr;
   }  S_un;
};
```

For more information, see "Windows Sockets Programming Considerations" in the Win32 SDK documentation.

See Also: SOCKADDR

SYSTEMTIME Structure

The **SYSTEMTIME** structure has the following form:

```
typedef struct _SYSTEMTIME {
   WORD wYear;
   WORD wMonth;
   WORD wDayOfWeek;
   WORD wDay;
   WORD wHour;
   WORD wMinute;
   WORD wSecond;
   WORD wMilliseconds;
} SYSTEMTIME;
```

The **SYSTEMTIME** structure represents a date and time using individual members for the month, day, year, weekday, hour, minute, second, and millisecond.

Members

wYear   The current year.

wMonth   The current month; January is 1.

wDayOfWeek   The current day of the week; Sunday is 0, Monday is 1, and so on.

wDay   The current day of the month.

wHour   The current hour.

wMinute   The current minute.

wSecond   The current second.

wMilliseconds   The current millisecond.

See Also: CTime::CTime

TEXTMETRIC Structure

The **TEXTMETRIC** structure has the following form:

```
typedef struct tagTEXTMETRIC {   /* tm */
    int  tmHeight;
    int  tmAscent;
    int  tmDescent;
    int  tmInternalLeading;
    int  tmExternalLeading;
    int  tmAveCharWidth;
    int  tmMaxCharWidth;
    int  tmWeight;
    BYTE tmItalic;
    BYTE tmUnderlined;
    BYTE tmStruckOut;
    BYTE tmFirstChar;
    BYTE tmLastChar;
    BYTE tmDefaultChar;
    BYTE tmBreakChar;
    BYTE tmPitchAndFamily;
    BYTE tmCharSet;
    int  tmOverhang;
    int  tmDigitizedAspectX;
    int  tmDigitizedAspectY;
} TEXTMETRIC;
```

The **TEXTMETRIC** structure contains basic information about a physical font. All sizes are given in logical units; that is, they depend on the current mapping mode of the display context.

For more complete information about this structure, see **TEXTMETRIC** in the Win32 SDK documentation.

See Also: **CDC::GetTextMetrics**, **TEXTMETRIC**

WINDOWPLACEMENT Structure

The **WINDOWPLACEMENT** data structure has the following form:

```
typedef struct tagWINDOWPLACEMENT {    /* wndpl */
    UINT  length;
    UINT  flags;
    UINT  showCmd;
    POINT ptMinPosition;
    POINT ptMaxPosition;
    RECT  rcNormalPosition;
} WINDOWPLACEMENT;
```

The **WINDOWPLACEMENT** structure contains information about the placement of a window on the screen.

Members

length   Specifies the length, in bytes, of the structure.

flags   Specifies flags that control the position of the minimized window and the method by which the window is restored. This member can be one or both of the following flags:

- **WPF_SETMINPOSITION**   Specifies that the x- and y-positions of the minimized window can be specified. This flag must be specified if the coordinates are set in the **ptMinPosition** member.

- **WPF_RESTORETOMAXIMIZED**   Specifies that the restored window will be maximized, regardless of whether it was maximized before it was minimized. This setting is valid only the next time the window is restored. It does not change the default restoration behavior. This flag is valid only when the **SW_SHOWMINIMIZED** value is specified for the **showCmd** member.

showCmd   Specifies the current show state of the window. This member can be one of the following values:

- **SW_HIDE**   Hides the window and passes activation to another window.

- **SW_MINIMIZE**   Minimizes the specified window and activates the top-level window in the system's list.

- **SW_RESTORE**   Activates and displays a window. If the window is minimized or maximized, Windows restores it to its original size and position (same as **SW_SHOWNORMAL**).

- **SW_SHOW**   Activates a window and displays it in its current size and position.

- **SW_SHOWMAXIMIZED**   Activates a window and displays it as a maximized window.

- **SW_SHOWMINIMIZED**   Activates a window and displays it as an icon.

- **SW_SHOWMINNOACTIVE**   Displays a window as an icon. The window that is currently active remains active.

- **SW_SHOWNA**   Displays a window in its current state. The window that is currently active remains active.

- **SW_SHOWNOACTIVATE**   Displays a window in its most recent size and position. The window that is currently active remains active.

- **SW_SHOWNORMAL**   Activates and displays a window. If the window is minimized or maximized, Windows restores it to its original size and position (same as **SW_RESTORE**).

ptMinPosition   Specifies the position of the window's top-left corner when the window is minimized.

ptMaxPosition Specifies the position of the window's top-left corner when the window is maximized.

rcNormalPosition Specifies the window's coordinates when the window is in the normal (restored) position.

See Also: **CWnd::SetWindowPlacement**

WINDOWPOS Structure

The **WINDOWPOS** data structure has the following form:

```
typedef struct tagWINDOWPOS { /* wp */
    HWND    hwnd;
    HWND    hwndInsertAfter;
    int     x;
    int     y;
    int     cx;
    int     cy;
    UINT    flags;
} WINDOWPOS;
```

The **WINDOWPOS** structure contains information about the size and position of a window.

Members

hwnd Identifies the window.

hwndInsertAfter Identifies the window behind which this window is placed.

x Specifies the position of the left edge of the window.

y Specifies the position of the right edge of the window.

cx Specifies the window width, in pixels.

cy Specifies the window height, in pixels.

flags Specifies window-positioning options. This member can be one of the following values:

- **SWP_DRAWFRAME** Draws a frame (defined in the class description for the window) around the window. The window receives a **WM_NCCALCSIZE** message.

- **SWP_FRAMECHANGED** Sends a **WM_NCCALCSIZE** message to the window, even if the window's size is not being changed. If this flag is not specified, **WM_NCCALCSIZE** is sent only when the window's size is being changed.

- **SWP_HIDEWINDOW** Hides the window.

- **SWP_NOACTIVATE** Does not activate the window.

- **SWP_NOCOPYBITS** Discards the entire contents of the client area. If this flag is not specified, the valid contents of the client area are saved and copied back into the client area after the window is sized or repositioned.

- **SWP_NOMOVE** Retains current position (ignores the **x** and **y** members).

- **SWP_NOOWNERZORDER** Does not change the owner window's position in the Z-order.

- **SWP_NOSIZE** Retains current size (ignores the **cx** and **cy** members).

- **SWP_NOREDRAW** Does not redraw changes.

- **SWP_NOREPOSITION** Same as **SWP_NOOWNERZORDER**.

- **SWP_NOSENDCHANGING** Prevents the window from receiving the **WM_WINDOWPOSCHANGING** message.

- **SWP_NOZORDER** Retains current ordering (ignores the **hwndInsertAfter** member).

- **SWP_SHOWWINDOW** Displays the window.

See Also: **CWnd::OnWindowPosChanging**

WSADATA Structure

The **WSADATA** structure has the following form:

```
struct WSAData {
    WORD            wVersion;
    WORD            wHighVersion;
    char            szDescription[WSADESCRIPTION_LEN+1];
    char            szSystemStatus[WSASYSSTATUS_LEN+1];
    unsigned short  iMaxSockets;
    unsigned short  iMaxUdpDg;
    char FAR *      lpVendorInfo;
};
```

The **WSADATA** structure is used to store Windows Sockets initialization information returned by a call to the **AfxSocketInit** global function.

Members

wVersion The version of the Windows Sockets specification that the Windows Sockets DLL expects the caller to use.

wHighVersion The highest version of the Windows Sockets specification that this DLL can support (also encoded as above). Normally this is the same as **wVersion**.

szDescription A null-terminated ASCII string into which the Windows Sockets DLL copies a description of the Windows Sockets implementation, including vendor identification. The text (up to 256 characters in length) can contain any characters, but vendors are cautioned against including control and formatting characters: the most likely use that an application will put this to is to display it (possibly truncated) in a status message.

szSystemStatus A null-terminated ASCII string into which the Windows Sockets DLL copies relevant status or configuration information. The Windows Sockets DLL should use this field only if the information might be useful to the user or support staff; it should not be considered as an extension of the **szDescription** field.

iMaxSockets The maximum number of sockets which a single process can potentially open. A Windows Sockets implementation can provide a global pool of sockets for allocation to any process; alternatively it can allocate per-process resources for sockets. The number can well reflect the way in which the Windows Sockets DLL or the networking software was configured. Application writers can use this number as a crude indication of whether the Windows Sockets implementation is usable by the application. For example, an X Windows server might check **iMaxSockets** when first started: if it is less than 8, the application would display an error message instructing the user to reconfigure the networking software. (This is a situation in which the **szSystemStatus** text might be used.) Obviously there is no guarantee that a particular application can actually allocate **iMaxSockets** sockets, since there can be other Windows Sockets applications in use.

iMaxUdpDg The size in bytes of the largest User Datagram Protocol (UDP) datagram that can be sent or received by a Windows Sockets application. If the implementation imposes no limit, **iMaxUdpDg** is zero. In many implementations of Berkeley sockets, there is an implicit limit of 8192 bytes on UDP datagrams (which are fragmented if necessary). A Windows Sockets implementation can impose a limit based, for instance, on the allocation of fragment reassembly buffers. The minimum value of **iMaxUdpDg** for a compliant Windows Sockets implementation is 512. Note that regardless of the value of **iMaxUdpDg**, it is inadvisable to attempt to send a broadcast datagram which is larger than the Maximum Transmission Unit (MTU) for the network. (The Windows Sockets API does not provide a mechanism to discover the MTU, but it must be no less than 512 bytes.)

lpVendorInfo A far pointer to a vendor-specific data structure. The definition of this structure (if supplied) is beyond the scope of the Windows Sockets specification. For more information, see "Windows Sockets Programming Considerations" in the Win32 SDK documentation.

Note In MFC, the **WSADATA** structure is returned by the **AfxSocketInit** function, which you call in your `InitInstance` function. You can retrieve the structure and store it in your program if you need to use information from it later.

See Also: AfxSocketInit

XFORM Structure

The **XFORM** structure has the following form:

```
typedef struct  tagXFORM {   /* xfrm */
    FLOAT eM11;
    FLOAT eM12;
    FLOAT eM21;
    FLOAT eM22;
    FLOAT eDx;
    FLOAT eDy;
} XFORM;
```

Comments

The **XFORM** structure specifies a world-space to page-space transformation. The **eDx** and **eDy** members specify the horizontal and vertical translation components, respectively. The following table shows how the other members are used, depending on the operation:

Operation	eM11	eM12	eM21	eM22
Rotation	Cosine of rotation angle	Sine of rotation angle	Negative sine of rotation angle	Cosine of rotation angle
Scaling	Horizontal scaling component	Nothing	Nothing	Vertical scaling component
Shear	Nothing	Horizontal proportionality constant	Vertical proportionality constant	Nothing
Reflection	Horizontal reflection component	Nothing	Nothing	Vertical reflection component

See Also: CRgn::CreateFromData

Styles Used by MFC

The styles described in the following topics are, in most cases, specified with the *dwstyle* parameter. For further information, refer to the member functions listed in the See Also list for each style.

Button Styles

- **BS_AUTOCHECKBOX**   Same as a check box, except that a check mark appears in the check box when the user selects the box; the check mark disappears the next time the user selects the box.

- **BS_AUTORADIOBUTTON**   Same as a radio button, except that when the user selects it, the button automatically highlights itself and removes the selection from any other radio buttons with the same style in the same group.

- **BS_AUTO3STATE**   Same as a three-state check box, except that the box changes its state when the user selects it.

- **BS_CHECKBOX**   Creates a small square that has text displayed to its right (unless this style is combined with the **BS_LEFTTEXT** style).

- **BS_DEFPUSHBUTTON**   Creates a button that has a heavy black border. The user can select this button by pressing the ENTER key. This style enables the user to quickly select the most likely option (the default option).

- **BS_GROUPBOX**   Creates a rectangle in which other buttons can be grouped. Any text associated with this style is displayed in the rectangle's upper-left corner.

- **BS_LEFTTEXT**   When combined with a radio-button or check-box style, the text appears on the left side of the radio button or check box.

- **BS_OWNERDRAW**   Creates an owner-drawn button. The framework calls the **DrawItem** member function when a visual aspect of the button has changed. This style must be set when using the **CBitmapButton** class.

- **BS_PUSHBUTTON**   Creates a pushbutton that posts a **WM_COMMAND** message to the owner window when the user selects the button.

- **BS_RADIOBUTTON**   Creates a small circle that has text displayed to its right (unless this style is combined with the **BS_LEFTTEXT** style). Radio buttons are usually used in groups of related but mutually exclusive choices.

- **BS_3STATE**   Same as a check box, except that the box can be dimmed as well as checked. The dimmed state typically is used to show that a check box has been disabled.

See Also: **CButton::Create**

Combo-Box Styles

- **CBS_AUTOHSCROLL** Automatically scrolls the text in the edit control to the right when the user types a character at the end of the line. If this style is not set, only text that fits within the rectangular boundary is allowed.

- **CBS_DROPDOWN** Similar to **CBS_SIMPLE**, except that the list box is not displayed unless the user selects an icon next to the edit control.

- **CBS_DROPDOWNLIST** Similar to **CBS_DROPDOWN**, except that the edit control is replaced by a static-text item that displays the current selection in the list box.

- **CBS_HASSTRINGS** An owner-draw combo box contains items consisting of strings. The combo box maintains the memory and pointers for the strings so the application can use the **GetText** member function to retrieve the text for a particular item.

- **CBS_OEMCONVERT** Text entered in the combo-box edit control is converted from the ANSI character set to the OEM character set and then back to ANSI. This ensures proper character conversion when the application calls the **AnsiToOem** Windows function to convert an ANSI string in the combo box to OEM characters. This style is most useful for combo boxes that contain filenames and applies only to combo boxes created with the **CBS_SIMPLE** or **CBS_DROPDOWN** styles.

- **CBS_OWNERDRAWFIXED** The owner of the list box is responsible for drawing its contents; the items in the list box are all the same height.

- **CBS_OWNERDRAWVARIABLE** The owner of the list box is responsible for drawing its contents; the items in the list box are variable in height.

- **CBS_SIMPLE** The list box is displayed at all times. The current selection in the list box is displayed in the edit control.

- **CBS_SORT** Automatically sorts strings entered into the list box.

- **CBS_DISABLENOSCROLL** The list box shows a disabled vertical scroll bar when the list box does not contain enough items to scroll. Without this style, the scroll bar is hidden when the list box does not contain enough items.

- **CBS_NOINTEGRALHEIGHT** Specifies that the size of the combo box is exactly the size specified by the application when it created the combo box. Normally, Windows sizes a combo box so that the combo box does not display partial items.

See Also: **CComboBox::Create**

Edit Styles

- **ES_AUTOHSCROLL** Automatically scrolls text to the right by 10 characters when the user types a character at the end of the line. When the user presses the ENTER key, the control scrolls all text back to position 0.

- **ES_AUTOVSCROLL** Automatically scrolls text up one page when the user presses ENTER on the last line.

- **ES_CENTER** Centers text in a multiline edit control.

- **ES_LEFT** Aligns text flush left.

- **ES_LOWERCASE** Converts all characters to lowercase as they are typed into the edit control.

- **ES_MULTILINE** Designates a multiple-line edit control. (The default is single line.) If the **ES_AUTOVSCROLL** style is specified, the edit control shows as many lines as possible and scrolls vertically when the user presses the ENTER key. If **ES_AUTOVSCROLL** is not given, the edit control shows as many lines as possible and beeps if ENTER is pressed when no more lines can be displayed. If the **ES_AUTOHSCROLL** style is specified, the multiple-line edit control automatically scrolls horizontally when the caret goes past the right edge of the control. To start a new line, the user must press ENTER. If **ES_AUTOHSCROLL** is not given, the control automatically wraps words to the beginning of the next line when necessary; a new line is also started if ENTER is pressed. The position of the wordwrap is determined by the window size. If the window size changes, the wordwrap position changes and the text is redisplayed. Multiple-line edit controls can have scroll bars. An edit control with scroll bars processes its own scroll-bar messages. Edit controls without scroll bars scroll as described above and process any scroll messages sent by the parent window.

- **ES_NOHIDESEL** Normally, an edit control hides the selection when the control loses the input focus and inverts the selection when the control receives the input focus. Specifying **ES_NOHIDESEL** deletes this default action.

- **ES_OEMCONVERT** Text entered in the edit control is converted from the ANSI character set to the OEM character set and then back to ANSI. This ensures proper character conversion when the application calls the **AnsiToOem** Windows function to convert an ANSI string in the edit control to OEM characters. This style is most useful for edit controls that contain filenames.

- **ES_PASSWORD** Displays all characters as an asterisk (*) as they are typed into the edit control. An application can use the **SetPasswordChar** member function to change the character that is displayed.

- **ES_RIGHT** Aligns text flush right in a multiline edit control.

- **ES_UPPERCASE** Converts all characters to uppercase as they are typed into the edit control.

- **ES_READONLY**   Prevents the user from entering or editing text in the edit control.
- **ES_WANTRETURN**   Specifies that a carriage return be inserted when the user presses the ENTER key while entering text into a multiple-line edit control in a dialog box. Without this style, pressing the ENTER key has the same effect as pressing the dialog box's default pushbutton. This style has no effect on a single-line edit control.

See Also: CEdit::Create

Frame-Window Styles

- **FWS_ADDTOTITLE**   Specifies information to append to the end of a frame window title. For example, "Microsoft Draw—Drawing in Document1." You can specify the strings displayed in the Advanced Options dialog box in AppWizard. If you need to turn this option off, override the **CWnd::PreCreateWindow** member function.
- **FWS_PREFIXTITLE**   Shows the document name before the application name in a frame window title. For example, "Document—WordPad." You can specify the strings displayed in the Advanced Options dialog box in AppWizard. If you need to turn this option off, override the **CWnd::PreCreateWindow** member function.
- **FWS_SNAPTOBARS**   Controls sizing of the frame window that encloses a control bar when it is in a floating window rather than docked to a frame window. This style sizes the window to fit the control bar.

List-Box Styles

- **LBS_EXTENDEDSEL**   The user can select multiple items using the SHIFT key and the mouse or special key combinations.
- **LBS_HASSTRINGS**   Specifies an owner-draw list box that contains items consisting of strings. The list box maintains the memory and pointers for the strings so the application can use the **GetText** member function to retrieve the text for a particular item.
- **LBS_MULTICOLUMN**   Specifies a multicolumn list box that is scrolled horizontally. The **SetColumnWidth** member function sets the width of the columns.
- **LBS_MULTIPLESEL**   String selection is toggled each time the user clicks or double-clicks the string. Any number of strings can be selected.
- **LBS_NOINTEGRALHEIGHT**   The size of the list box is exactly the size specified by the application when it created the list box. Usually, Windows sizes a list box so that the list box does not display partial items.

- **LBS_NOREDRAW** List-box display is not updated when changes are made. This style can be changed at any time by sending a **WM_SETREDRAW** message.
- **LBS_NOTIFY** Parent window receives an input message whenever the user clicks or double-clicks a string.
- **LBS_OWNERDRAWFIXED** The owner of the list box is responsible for drawing its contents; the items in the list box are the same height.
- **LBS_OWNERDRAWVARIABLE** The owner of the list box is responsible for drawing its contents; the items in the list box are variable in height.
- **LBS_SORT** Strings in the list box are sorted alphabetically.
- **LBS_STANDARD** Strings in the list box are sorted alphabetically, and the parent window receives an input message whenever the user clicks or double-clicks a string. The list box contains borders on all sides.
- **LBS_USETABSTOPS** Allows a list box to recognize and expand tab characters when drawing its strings. The default tab positions are 32 dialog units. (A dialog unit is a horizontal or vertical distance. One horizontal dialog unit is equal to one-fourth of the current dialog base width unit. The dialog base units are computed based on the height and width of the current system font. The **GetDialogBaseUnits** Windows function returns the current dialog base units in pixels.)
- **LBS_WANTKEYBOARDINPUT** The owner of the list box receives **WM_VKEYTOITEM** or **WM_CHARTOITEM** messages whenever the user presses a key while the list box has input focus. This allows an application to perform special processing on the keyboard input.
- **LBS_DISABLENOSCROLL** The list box shows a disabled vertical scroll bar when the list box does not contain enough items to scroll. Without this style, the scroll bar is hidden when the list box does not contain enough items.

See Also: CListBox::Create

Message-Box Styles

Message_Box Types
- **MB_ABORTRETRYIGNORE** The message box contains three pushbuttons: Abort, Retry, and Ignore.
- **MB_OK** The message box contains one pushbutton: OK.
- **MB_OKCANCEL** The message box contains two pushbuttons: OK and Cancel.
- **MB_RETRYCANCEL** The message box contains two pushbuttons: Retry and Cancel.
- **MB_YESNO** The message box contains two pushbuttons: Yes and No.
- **MB_YESNOCANCEL** The message box contains three pushbuttons: Yes, No, and Cancel.

Message-Box Modality

- **MB_APPLMODAL** The user must respond to the message box before continuing work in the current window. However, the user can move to the windows of other applications and work in those windows. The default is **MB_APPLMODAL** if neither **MB_SYSTEMMODAL** nor **MB_TASKMODAL** is specified.

- **MB_SYSTEMMODAL** All applications are suspended until the user responds to the message box. System-modal message boxes are used to notify the user of serious, potentially damaging errors that require immediate attention and should be used sparingly.

- **MB_TASKMODAL** Similar to **MB_APPLMODAL**, but not useful within a Microsoft Foundation class application. This flag is reserved for a calling application or library that does not have a window handle available.

Message-Box Icons

- **MB_ICONEXCLAMATION** An exclamation-point icon appears in the message box.

- **MB_ICONINFORMATION** An icon consisting of an "i" in a circle appears in the message box.

- **MB_ICONQUESTION** A question-mark icon appears in the message box.

- **MB_ICONSTOP** A stop-sign icon appears in the message box.

Message-Box Default Buttons

- **MB_DEFBUTTON1** The first button is the default. Note that the first button is always the default unless **MB_DEFBUTTON2** or **MB_DEFBUTTON3** is specified.

- **MB_DEFBUTTON2** The second button is the default.

- **MB_DEFBUTTON3** The third button is the default.

  See Also: AfxMessageBox

Scroll-Bar Styles

- **SBS_BOTTOMALIGN** Used with the **SBS_HORZ** style. The bottom edge of the scroll bar is aligned with the bottom edge of the rectangle specified in the **Create** member function. The scroll bar has the default height for system scroll bars.

- **SBS_HORZ** Designates a horizontal scroll bar. If neither the **SBS_BOTTOMALIGN** nor **SBS_TOPALIGN** style is specified, the scroll bar has the height, width, and position given in the **Create** member function.

- **SBS_LEFTALIGN** Used with the **SBS_VERT** style. The left edge of the scroll bar is aligned with the left edge of the rectangle specified in the **Create** member function. The scroll bar has the default width for system scroll bars.

- **SBS_RIGHTALIGN** Used with the **SBS_VERT** style. The right edge of the scroll bar is aligned with the right edge of the rectangle specified in the **Create** member function. The scroll bar has the default width for system scroll bars.

- **SBS_SIZEBOX** Designates a size box. If neither the **SBS_SIZEBOXBOTTOMRIGHTALIGN** nor **SBS_SIZEBOXTOPLEFTALIGN** style is specified, the size box has the height, width, and position given in the **Create** member function.

- **SBS_SIZEBOXBOTTOMRIGHTALIGN** Used with the **SBS_SIZEBOX** style. The lower-right corner of the size box is aligned with the lower-right corner of the rectangle specified in the **Create** member function. The size box has the default size for system size boxes.

- **SBS_SIZEBOXTOPLEFTALIGN** Used with the **SBS_SIZEBOX** style. The upper-left corner of the size box is aligned with the upper-left corner of the rectangle specified in the **Create** member function. The size box has the default size for system size boxes.

- **SBS_TOPALIGN** Used with the **SBS_HORZ** style. The top edge of the scroll bar is aligned with the top edge of the rectangle specified in the **Create** member function. The scroll bar has the default height for system scroll bars.

- **SBS_VERT** Designates a vertical scroll bar. If neither the **SBS_RIGHTALIGN** nor **SBS_LEFTALIGN** style is specified, the scroll bar has the height, width, and position given in the **Create** member function.

See Also: CScrollBar::Create

Static Styles

- **SS_BLACKFRAME** Specifies a box with a frame drawn with the same color as window frames. The default is black.

- **SS_BLACKRECT** Specifies a rectangle filled with the color used to draw window frames. The default is black.

- **SS_CENTER** Designates a simple rectangle and displays the given text centered in the rectangle. The text is formatted before it is displayed. Words that would extend past the end of a line are automatically wrapped to the beginning of the next centered line.

- **SS_GRAYFRAME** Specifies a box with a frame drawn with the same color as the screen background (desktop). The default is gray.

- **SS_GRAYRECT** Specifies a rectangle filled with the color used to fill the screen background. The default is gray.

- **SS_ICON** Designates an icon displayed in the dialog box. The given text is the name of an icon (not a filename) defined elsewhere in the resource file. The *nWidth* and *nHeight* parameters are ignored; the icon automatically sizes itself.

- **SS_LEFT** Designates a simple rectangle and displays the given text flush-left in the rectangle. The text is formatted before it is displayed. Words that would extend past the end of a line are automatically wrapped to the beginning of the next flush-left line.

- **SS_LEFTNOWORDWRAP** Designates a simple rectangle and displays the given text flush-left in the rectangle. Tabs are expanded, but words are not wrapped. Text that extends past the end of a line is clipped.

- **SS_NOPREFIX** Unless this style is specified, Windows will interpret any ampersand (&) characters in the control's text to be accelerator prefix characters. In this case, the ampersand (&) is removed and the next character in the string is underlined. If a static control is to contain text where this feature is not wanted, **SS_NOPREFIX** may be added. This static-control style may be included with any of the defined static controls. You can combine **SS_NOPREFIX** with other styles by using the bitwise OR operator. This is most often used when filenames or other strings that may contain an ampersand (&) need to be displayed in a static control in a dialog box.

- **SS_RIGHT** Designates a simple rectangle and displays the given text flush-right in the rectangle. The text is formatted before it is displayed. Words that would extend past the end of a line are automatically wrapped to the beginning of the next flush-right line.

- **SS_SIMPLE** Designates a simple rectangle and displays a single line of text flush-left in the rectangle. The line of text cannot be shortened or altered in any way. (The control's parent window or dialog box must not process the **WM_CTLCOLOR** message.)

- **SS_USERITEM** Specifies a user-defined item.

- **SS_WHITEFRAME** Specifies a box with a frame drawn with the same color as the window background. The default is white.

- **SS_WHITERECT** Specifies a rectangle filled with the color used to fill the window background. The default is white.

See Also: CStatic::Create

Window Styles

- **WS_BORDER** Creates a window that has a border.
- **WS_CAPTION** Creates a window that has a title bar (implies the **WS_BORDER** style). Cannot be used with the **WS_DLGFRAME** style.
- **WS_CHILD** Creates a child window. Cannot be used with the **WS_POPUP** style.
- **WS_CLIPCHILDREN** Excludes the area occupied by child windows when you draw within the parent window. Used when you create the parent window.

- **WS_CLIPSIBLINGS** Clips child windows relative to each other; that is, when a particular child window receives a paint message, the **WS_CLIPSIBLINGS** style clips all other overlapped child windows out of the region of the child window to be updated. (If **WS_CLIPSIBLINGS** is not given and child windows overlap, when you draw within the client area of a child window, it is possible to draw within the client area of a neighboring child window.) For use with the **WS_CHILD** style only.

- **WS_DISABLED** Creates a window that is initially disabled.

- **WS_DLGFRAME** Creates a window with a double border but no title.

- **WS_GROUP** Specifies the first control of a group of controls in which the user can move from one control to the next with the arrow keys. All controls defined with the **WS_GROUP** style **FALSE** after the first control belong to the same group. The next control with the **WS_GROUP** style starts the next group (that is, one group ends where the next begins).

- **WS_HSCROLL** Creates a window that has a horizontal scroll bar.

- **WS_MAXIMIZE** Creates a window of maximum size.

- **WS_MAXIMIZEBOX** Creates a window that has a Maximize button.

- **WS_MINIMIZE** Creates a window that is initially minimized. For use with the **WS_OVERLAPPED** style only.

- **WS_MINIMIZEBOX** Creates a window that has a Minimize button.

- **WS_OVERLAPPED** Creates an overlapped window. An overlapped window usually has a caption and a border.

- **WS_OVERLAPPEDWINDOW** Creates an overlapped window with the **WS_OVERLAPPED, WS_CAPTION, WS_SYSMENU, WS_THICKFRAME, WS_MINIMIZEBOX,** and **WS_MAXIMIZEBOX** styles.

- **WS_POPUP** Creates a pop-up window. Cannot be used with the **WS_CHILD** style.

- **WS_POPUPWINDOW** Creates a pop-up window with the **WS_BORDER, WS_POPUP,** and **WS_SYSMENU** styles. The **WS_CAPTION** style must be combined with the **WS_POPUPWINDOW** style to make the Control menu visible.

- **WS_SYSMENU** Creates a window that has a Control-menu box in its title bar. Used only for windows with title bars.

- **WS_TABSTOP** Specifies one of any number of controls through which the user can move by using the TAB key. The TAB key moves the user to the next control specified by the **WS_TABSTOP** style.

- **WS_THICKFRAME** Creates a window with a thick frame that can be used to size the window.

- **WS_VISIBLE**   Creates a window that is initially visible.

- **WS_VSCROLL**   Creates a window that has a vertical scroll bar.

See Also: CWnd::Create, **CWnd::CreateEx**

Extended Window Styles

- **WS_EX_ACCEPTFILES**   Specifies that a window created with this style accepts drag-and-drop files.

- **WS_EX_CLIENTEDGE**   Specifies that a window has a 3D look¾that is, a border with a sunken edge.

- **WS_EX_CONTEXTHELP**   Includes a question mark in the title bar of the window. When the user clicks the question mark, the cursor changes to a question mark with a pointer. If the user then clicks a child window, the child receives a **WM_HELP** message.

- **WS_EX_CONTROLPARENT**   Allows the user to navigate among the child windows of the window by using the TAB key.

- **WS_EX_DLGMODALFRAME**   Designates a window with a double border that may (optionally) be created with a title bar when you specify the **WS_CAPTION** style flag in the *dwStyle* parameter.

- **WS_EX_LEFT**   Gives window generic left-aligned properties. This is the default.

- **WS_EX_LEFTSCROLLBAR**   Places a vertical scroll bar to the left of the client area.

- **WS_EX_LTRREADING**   Displays the window text using left-to-right reading order properties. This is the default.

- **WS_EX_MDICHILD**   Creates an MDI child window.

- **WS_EX_NOPARENTNOTIFY**   Specifies that a child window created with this style will not send the **WM_PARENTNOTIFY** message to its parent window when the child window is created or destroyed.

- **WS_EX_OVERLAPPEDWINDOW**   Combines the **WS_EX_CLIENTEDGE** and **WS_EX_WINDOWEDGE** styles.

- **WS_EX_PALETTEWINDOW**   Combines the **WS_EX_WINDOWEDGE** and **WS_EX_TOPMOST** styles.

- **WS_EX_RIGHT**   Gives a window generic right-aligned properties. This depends on the window class.

- **WS_EX_RIGHTSCROLLBAR**   Places a vertical scroll bar (if present) to the right of the client area. This is the default.

- **WS_EX_RTLREADING**   Displays the window text using right-to-left reading order properties.

- **WS_EX_STATICEDGE**   Creates a window with a three-dimensional border style intended to be used for items that do not accept user input.

- **WS_EX_TOOLWINDOW**   Creates a tool window, which is a window intended to be used as a floating toolbar. A tool window has a title bar that is shorter than a normal title bar, and the window title is drawn using a smaller font. A tool window does not appear in the task bar or in the window that appears when the user presses ALT+TAB.

- **WS_EX_TOPMOST**   Specifies that a window created with this style should be placed above all nontopmost windows and stay above them even when the window is deactivated. An application can use the **SetWindowPos** member function to add or remove this attribute.

- **WS_EX_TRANSPARENT**   Specifies that a window created with this style is to be transparent. That is, any windows that are beneath the window are not obscured by the window. A window created with this style receives **WM_PAINT** messages only after all sibling windows beneath it have been updated.

- **WS_EX_WINDOWEDGE**   Specifies that a window has a border with a raised edge.

See Also: **CWnd::CreateEx**

Callback Functions Used by MFC

Three callback functions appear in the Microsoft Foundation Class Library. A description of callback functions that are passed to **CDC::EnumObjects**, **CDC::GrayString**, and **CDC::SetAbortProc** follows this topic. For the general usage of the callback functions, see the Remarks section of these member functions. Note that all callback functions must trap MFC exceptions before returning to Windows, since exceptions cannot be thrown across callback boundaries. For more information about exceptions, see the article "Exceptions" in *Visual C++ Programmer's Guide* online.

Callback Function for CDC::EnumObjects

int **CALLBACK EXPORT** *ObjectFunc*(**LPSTR** *lpszLogObject*, **LPSTR*** *lpData*);

Parameters

lpszLogObject   Points to a **LOGPEN** or **LOGBRUSH** data structure that contains information about the logical attributes of the object.

lpData   Points to the application-supplied data passed to the **EnumObjects** function.

Return Value

The callback function returns an **int**. The value of this return is user-defined. If the callback function returns 0, **EnumObjects** stops enumeration early.

Remarks

The *ObjectFunc* name is a placeholder for the application-supplied function name. The actual name must be exported.

See Also: CDC::EnumObjects

Callback Function for CDC::GrayString

BOOL CALLBACK EXPORT *OutputFunc*(**HDC** *hDC*, **LPARAM** *lpData*, **int** *nCount*);

Return Value

The callback function's return value must be **TRUE** to indicate success; otherwise it is **FALSE**.

Parameters

hDC   Identifies a memory device context with a bitmap of at least the width and height specified by *nWidth* and *nHeight* to **GrayString**.

lpData   Points to the character string to be drawn.

nCount   Specifies the number of characters to output.

Remarks

OutputFunc is a placeholder for the application-supplied callback function name. The callback function (*OutputFunc*) must draw an image relative to the coordinates (0,0) rather than (*x*, *y*).

See Also: CDC::GrayString

Callback Function for CDC::SetAbortProc

BOOL CALLBACK EXPORT *AbortFunc*(**HDC** *hPr*, **int** *code*);

Return Value

The return value of the abort-handler function is nonzero if the print job is to continue, and 0 if it is canceled.

Parameters

hPr Identifies the device context.

code Specifies whether an error has occurred. It is 0 if no error has occurred. It is **SP_OUTOFDISK** if the Print Manager is currently out of disk space and more disk space will become available if the application waits. If *code* is **SP_OUTOFDISK**, the application does not have to abort the print job. If it does not, it must yield to the Print Manager by calling the **PeekMessage** or **GetMessage** Windows function.

Remarks

The name *AbortFunc* is a placeholder for the application-supplied function name. The actual name must be exported as described in the Remarks section of **CDC::SetAbortProc**.

See Also: CDC::SetAbortProc

Index

Index

M

P

Q

X

Contributors to *MFC Reference*

Nancy Avinger, Writer

Walden Barcus, Writer

David Adam Edelstein, Art Director

Roger Haight, Editor

Lisa Hedley, Writer

Dan Jinguji, Writer

Nancy Rager, Writer

Robert Reynolds, Illustrator

Arlene Roth, Copy Editor

Kathleen Thompson, Writer

Qian Wen, Writer

Rod Wilkinson, Editor

WASSER*Studios*, Production

Grasp
the power of
Microsoft
Visual C++
in both hands.

This four-volume collection is the complete printed product documentation for Microsoft Visual C++ version 5.0, *the* development system for Win32®. In book form, this information is portable, easy to access and browse, and a comprehensive alternative to the substantial online help system in Visual C++. The volumes are numbered as a set—but you can buy any or all of the volumes, any time you need them. So take hold of all the power. Get the MICROSOFT VISUAL C++ 5.0 PROGRAMMER'S REFERENCE SET.

Microsoft® Visual C++® MFC Library Reference, Part 1
U.S.A.	**$39.99**
U.K.	£36.99
Canada	$53.99
ISBN 1-57231-518-0	

Microsoft® Visual C++® MFC Library Reference, Part 2
U.S.A.	**$39.99**
U.K.	£36.99
Canada	$53.99
ISBN 1-57231-519-9	

Microsoft® Visual C++® Run-Time Library Reference
U.S.A.	**$39.99**
U.K.	£36.99
Canada	$53.99
ISBN 1-57231-520-2	

Microsoft® Visual C++® Language Reference
U.S.A.	**$29.99**
U.K.	£27.49
Canada	$39.99
ISBN 1-57231-521-0	

Microsoft Press® products are available worldwide wherever quality computer books are sold. For more information, contact your book retailer, computer reseller, or local Microsoft Sales Office.

To locate your nearest source for Microsoft Press products, reach us at www.microsoft.com/mspress/, or call 1-800-MSPRESS in the U.S. (in Canada: 1-800-667-1115 or 416-293-8464).

To order Microsoft Press products, call 1-800-MSPRESS in the U.S. (in Canada: 1-800-667-1115 or 416-293-8464).

Prices and availability dates are subject to change.

Microsoft Press

Register Today!

Return this
Microsoft® Visual C++®
MFC Library Reference Part 2
registration card for
a Microsoft Press® catalog

U.S. and Canada addresses only. Fill in information below and mail postage-free. Please mail only the bottom half of this page.

1-57231-519-9A **MICROSOFT® VISUAL C++®** *Owner Registration Card*
MFC LIBRARY REFERENCE PART 2

_____

NAME

_____

INSTITUTION OR COMPANY NAME

_____

ADDRESS

_____

CITY   STATE   ZIP

Microsoft *Press*
Quality Computer Books

For a free catalog of
Microsoft Press® products, call
1-800-MSPRESS